Christian Counseling

GARY R. COLLINS

Christian Counseling

A COMPREHENSIVE GUIDE

Third Edition

THOMAS NELSON
Since 1798

NASHVILLE DALLAS MEXICO CITY RIO DE JANEIRO BEIJING

Christian Counseling: A Comprehensive Guide, third edition

Book design and composition by Mark McGarry, Texas Type & Book Works
Set in Meridien

Library of Congress Cataloging-in-Publication Data
Collins, Gary R.
Christian counseling : a comprehensive guide / Gary R. Collins. — 3rd ed.
p. cm.
Includes bibliographical references and index.

ISBN-13 9-781-4185-0329-1
1. Pastoral counseling. I. Title.
BV4012.2.C56 2006
253.5--dc22
2006021285

Printed in the United States of America
    10—12 11 10

Counseling is all about stories; stories about people's lives.

*Life stories include early experiences, beliefs, triumphs, tragedies,
decisions, disappointments, crises, and times of great joy.*

And life stories are about people.

*Much of my life story is about doing life together with Julie.
It's about her presence, love, support, understanding, encouragement,
and persistent walk with me as my closest friend.*

*I am proud to dedicated this book to her even though no book dedication fully
expresses my gratitude for the walk that we have had together over the years.
That walk includes her encouragement alongside me as I have written this manuscript.*

*I am profoundly grateful to God and to Julie for the ways in which she
has shaped and continues to impact my ongoing life story.*

Contents

1-4
5-8
9-12

Key Pts
Personal Insights
Your Counseling Style

Preface

Twenty-five years have passed between the publication of this book's first edition and the third edition that you now are reading. It is no secret that a lot has changed during the past quarter century. The world into which this book was first introduced bears little resemblance to the world today. There have been quantum leaps of technology, communication capabilities, biomedical advances, and global-political restructuring. Many long-held values have changed, and we've shifted our views of spirituality, religion, education, the family, business ethics, politics, multicultural diversity, and what we accept as entertainment. Some of the old problems still persist: there always will be people who are depressed, anxious, in conflict with others, struggling with transitions, and spiritually confused. But like everything else, counseling has changed, research has pushed forward our knowledge of human behavior, and fears of an East-West conflict have been replaced with fears of terrorism and new uncertainties about the future.

Many years ago I learned that it can be easier to write a new book than to update and revise one that is older and in some ways out of date. For well over a year, I have plugged away at my computer day after day, deleting outdated ideas, revising sentences, reevaluating hundreds of research articles, adding a lot of new material, and stating ideas in new ways that better connect with readers today, including international readers and those with diverse cultural perspectives. I have completely revised and rewritten the earlier editions of this book, included new case histories, added several new chapters, and inserted discussions of topics that are significant issues now but were of little concern even a few years ago. Working with the editors and publisher, I have tried to produce a book that is more reader friendly but that will continue to be seen as clearly written, easy to read, and relatively free of technological, psychological, or theological jargon.

One thing has not changed since this book first appeared. It still has a yellow cover, at least in the North American edition, and it continues to be known around the world as the *big yellow book*. If you have seen earlier editions, you know that the big yellow book (some call it the BYB) has now become even bigger. I hope you will find that it also has become even better, more complete, and more useful.

Once again, I write these introductory words after my work on the following pages has been completed. As in the past, I am amazed at how many people have been involved in the production of this book. Many of them I have never met, but I am very grateful to:

- The people in the publishing industry who worked on earlier editions of this book and those who have done behind-the-scenes work in editing, designing, producing, and marketing this third edition.
- The professors in colleges, seminaries, universities, and graduate schools who have assigned this book for their courses and who I hope will assign it again. Thanks especially to those of you who have written to me during the past ten years urging me to do whatever was necessary to get a third edition into print. Your words helped sustain me on a long journey.
- The students who will read through this book. For some of you, this book is required reading for a course. I know you wish that I had written something shorter, cheaper, and less comprehensive, so I ask your forgiveness for the size of this tome! I hope the book will have a significant impact in your lives and careers and in your work as counselors. I hope as well that you will refer to this book repeatedly in the coming years, using it as a practical and trusted reference guide.
- The pastors and church leaders who have used earlier editions of this book in your ministries. You still are on the front lines of counseling and, more than for any other group, I have written this book for you. Thanks to those who have urged people in your congregations to use this book to learn about themselves and as part of lay counselor training courses.
- The translators who have spent hundreds of hours turning earlier editions of this book into Korean, Chinese, Portuguese, Russian, and several other languages, including the recent Polish edition, which also is big and with a bright yellow cover. Thanks, as well, to those of you who have produced English-language editions of this book for use in countries other than the United States. I apologize to those of you who wish I had forsaken the American spelling and written words like *counselling, counsellor,* and *counsellee* with two ells.
- The booksellers who will make this book available to buyers and who continue to work diligently in a difficult business that is so needed but undergoing so much change.
- The people from Buffalo Grove Fitness Center who work out with me before dawn every morning and who have been very supportive, even

though most of them will never see or read this book. They have been consistent encouragers and great workout colleagues.

- The friends from around the world who have encouraged me, prayed for me, asked how the revision was coming, and helped me in numerous ways. There is no way that I can express my deep gratitude to all of you who have stood alongside me while I worked on this book and who prayed for me when an unexpected surgery knocked me off my feet for a few weeks when I should have been working on the BYB. I apologize in advance for anybody that I have forgotten. Thanks so much to:

Jean-Christophe Bieselaar	Lynwood Morris
Keith Bjorge	Jacob Mung
Brian Boone	David and Barbara Olsson
Joshua Scott Chang	Miriam Stark Parent
Jon S. Ebert	Bruce Rifkind
Sam George	Issam Smeir
Robson Gomes	Mervin van der Spuy
Wei-Jen Huang	Brett Waliczek
Stephen Kemp	Robert D. Wolgemuth
Baris Konur	Erik Wolgemuth
Christopher McCluskey	Rick Wager
Terry L. McDowell	John Warlow
Tom McKeown	Christopher Watson
Sergio Mijingos	Mark Yarhouse
Darren Young	

- I've saved the best for the last. Thanks to Lynn, Robin, Jan, and especially Julie, who has walked alongside me for more than forty years. Only my family knows what really was entailed in this project. Because of your love for me and because you knew what would be involved, each of you struggled at first about giving your full support to this endeavor. But from the beginning each of you saw the value of a third edition, and it was not long before each of you came on board and supported me all the way through, in ways that nobody outside of our family could understand or appreciate fully. There are no words to express my love and gratitude to each of you. This sounds like a cliché, but it is true that without your encouragement, understanding and support this book never would have been completed.
- Above all is my gratitude to God, who has led in so many ways, guided me, strengthened me, empowered me, and helped me, even though he knew that the end product would be imperfect. I pray that this book will be used to impact the lives of innumerable people and ultimately to bring honor to Jesus Christ, who alone holds the secrets of competent Christian counseling.

GARY R. COLLINS

Suggestions for Using This Book

Like its predecessors, this third edition of *Christian Counseling: A Comprehensive Guide* is written to assist Christian leaders and future leaders in their counseling work. The book is divided into nine sections. The first section, consisting of seven chapters, gives an overview of counseling principles that can apply to most of the problem issues that counselors are likely to encounter in their work. The final chapter of the book is a look into the possible future of counseling, built on what is happening in the present. In between, each section of the book has five chapters. These chapters stand alone and can be read in any order. Most of these middle section chapters (8–42) begin with a case history and introduction, followed by a look at the biblical teaching about the problem issue being considered. Then comes a survey of causes, effects, counseling recommendations, and suggestions for preventing each problem. All of this is intended to give relevant, up-to-date information that can be practical, useful, and easy to find.

Experience has shown that the book is used as a resource guide for individual counselors, a manual for Christian leaders (including pastors), a textbook for students and their professors, a training tool for lay counselors, a source of information for those who want a greater understanding of human behavior, a guide to the biblical basis of counseling, and a sourcebook that gives greater awareness of people-helping skills.

The present edition includes more case histories than earlier editions, and concise summaries at the end of each chapter. The book is being published in the United States, and it is likely that most readers will be in the United States and Canada. I have kept this North American audience in mind as I have written, but I also have been aware of international readers. During my career I have been honored to visit many countries where cultures are different and American methods often do not work. I have worked hard to make the book understandable to non-American readers and applicable in countries where counselor training, counseling methods, cultural expectations, and legal limitations are different from those in the community where I live and the country where I was born and grew up (Canada). Within most of the countries where this book will be read, adapted, or translated, there will be people of different ethnic and cultural backgrounds. I have tried to keep these uniquenesses in mind as I have written.

In addition to reading this book, please consider the following as additional ways to learn and to use this book.

1. *Mark Up the Book.* Unless the book is borrowed, you may want to underline parts of the text, make comments in the margins, or find other ways to make key ideas easy to spot and use.

2. *Log On to the Web Site That Accompanies This Book.* The web site is a free source of information that accompanies this book and can be accessed at *www.garyrcollins.com.* This is not intended to be an ongoing source of information that is updated consistently and filled with the latest research and new trends in counseling. Instead, this is the author's informal effort to keep in contact with readers. The Gary Collins weekly newsletter on coaching and counseling will be posted on the site (you also can have a copy come to your computer at no cost if you go to the web site, click on the *newsletter* icon and then on *subscribe*). The web site will give you opportunity to respond to the book, connect with other readers, read occasional postings about recent research or new books, find links to other helpful sites, learn about adjunct materials that will accompany this book, and sometimes keep abreast of what Gary Collins is up to next.

3. *Use the Adjunct Materials That Accompany This Book.* These materials include a case history manual to accompany the big yellow book and other resources that will be announced on the web site as they become available.

4. *Share and Use the Book.* Every teacher knows that the best way to learn is to teach others. As you read the following chapters, ask how you can share what you are learning. Some people have used material from this book in speeches, teaching, sermons, and newsletters. Friends who struggle with one or more of the problems listed in this book may be helped if you share informally what the book says about their struggles. When you use the book to help others, even apart from counseling, you can help them and strengthen your own learning. A book like this is meant to be used; it is not intended to be tucked into a bookcase and forgotten.

5. *Do Role Plays Based on the Book.* This often happens in teaching situations where instructors encourage students to divide into groups of three. One person plays the role of the counselor, one is the counselee, one observes. After each of these role play sessions, discuss what you learned and how you could improve. Then shift roles and repeat the process.

6. *Build on the Book.* This volume contains the basics of counseling. Most of the material is likely to persist and not change with the times. But we live

and work in changing environments, and even the basics need to be applied to new situations. Use this book as a trigger to get more information to build on what is here. The Internet is a good starting place, especially if you limit your searches to the web sites of professional groups (like the Alzheimer's Association or the American Psychological Association), government web sites, or university sites. The web site that accompanies this book will give links as information is increasingly posted.

7. *Connect with Others Who Have Read the Book.* The accompanying web site will make it possible for you to do this.

8. *Answer and Discuss Questions Based on the Book.* It can be helpful to ponder and discuss questions, such as the following. Answers can be written to test your understanding of the chapter, or these can be discussion questions for student classes or groups. They also could be the basis of tests on the book. Some of these questions may not apply to all of the chapters, but these are a beginning for you to develop additional questions that might be stimulating and helpful.

- What questions do you have about this chapter?
- Can you summarize the biblical teaching on the problem discussed in this chapter? Summarize the causes and effects of the problem.
- Can you think of other causes or effects that the author may have missed?
- What have you learned about counseling people with this problem?
- Can you give examples of people who have had this problem? (Be sure not to reveal names of people involved; change any details that might reveal the person's identity.) How could this person have been counseled?
- Outline a program for preventing the development of this problem.
- How might you share information from this chapter? With whom would you share it? How?
- What questions do you have that have not been answered? Where could you get information that would answer your questions?

9. *Start Reading the Book.* As you turn to the first chapter, I hope your journey through this book is rewarding. As you go, you can contact me through the web site. I can't guarantee that I will answer because the volume of messages prevents this. I usually do read my own e-mail messages, however, so I would be glad to hear from you. Please note that I am not able to give e-mail counseling guidance to those who might want help or advice to those of you who are counseling others and have questions. If you need help, please try to find a Christian counselor who can be consulted personally.

Thanks for moving with me through this introduction. Now I wish you God's special guidance and happy reading as you move through the remaining portions of this book.

PART ONE

Introductory Issues

The Changes in Counseling

RW[1] grew up in the city, in a poor neighborhood gripped by poverty, violence, gang activity, substance abuse, and young drug dealers. He never knew the identity of his father and lived with his mother, who was usually drunk. There never were any Christmas presents for RW. He never had a birthday party and never knew what it was like to live in a stable family. The closest he ever had to a family were the other kids in his neighborhood who had similar backgrounds. RW learned to use his fists to survive, and long before his teen years, he was experimenting with drugs. He was a drug dealer before he got to high school, and he first went to jail when he was seventeen.

One day he met a Christian counselor, a single woman from the suburbs who had moved to his neighborhood to work with kids like RW. She was the first person who ever believed in him, affirmed him, and tried to help him. She encouraged him, told him about Christ, and helped him grow in his Christian walk after he became a believer. Her influence was that of a counselor and confidante, but she knew how to challenge him and resist his attempts to manipulate her. Once, she helped him enter a rehabilitation program, but he quit after three days and returned to the streets, to the drugs, to the violence. "I can't handle the structure and rules," he told his rehabilitation counselor before he left. "Now there are only two possibilities for my future. Within a month I'll either be dead or in jail." And he was right.[2]

Most of you who read this book won't be counseling people like RW, but you'll meet others whose lives are equally twisted and confused. Like that counselor who lives in that drug-infested neighborhood and works every day with people like RW, at times you will be disappointed, frustrated, and not sure what to say or do. Some of the people you counsel will get better; then they'll relapse and get worse. Some will drain your energy and stretch your creativity, leaving you depleted and wondering why you became so involved with the lives of hurting people. But like that inner-city counselor—who happens to be my daughter—you will know the joy of pouring your life into people and seeing them change. You'll see lives touched by God, and you will watch in amazement as your counseling efforts are used to teach people how to live differently, overcome past abuses, change their perspectives on life, get free of debilitating inner conflicts, and move in healthy new directions.

As you read the following pages, you will be reminded of this one basic fact: *counseling is all about change.* It's about people who want to change, people who don't know how to change, people who need help to change, people who resist change, and people like RW, who seem unable to leave their current circumstances and accept the help of others to change. Counselors work with those who are overwhelmed by the circumstances or changes in their lives, people who have no idea how to cope or what they can do to bring about change. Adding to the complexity and uncertainty, the people we counsel live in a world engulfed in galloping change that impacts all of our lives, workplaces, ministries, and communities.

The Nature of Change

Death and taxes are the only things in life that are certain. Probably you have heard that old adage. In the twenty-first century, maybe we should add that in addition to death and taxes, change will be a certainty for almost everybody, at least in the foreseeable future. When I did a quick Internet search for articles, books, and other references to change, my computer quickly identified 122 million hits and offered to group these into 19 million categories. The numbers changed upward even as I was writing this paragraph.

With all this emphasis on change, it is surprising that we don't know more about how to help our counselees cope with unexpected change, how to help them change, and how to make that change last. While change is common and familiar, it also can be very difficult and painful. Novelist James Baldwin wrote that "most of us are about as eager to be changed as we are to be born, and we go through our changes in a similar state of shock."[3] RW wanted to change his life. He went to a Christian rehabilitation center that has an outstanding record for bringing about change in the lives of its residents, but he was unwilling to let the staff introduce any changes in his life. The temptation to go back to his drug-addicted familiar life on the streets was too strong to resist, despite the earnest efforts of his counselors to dissuade him.

Change can be expected or unanticipated, sudden or gradual, highly disruptive or of minimal impact, easily controlled or out of our control. How a person responds will depend in part on his or her personality, life circumstances, or past experiences in handling change. When a marriage disintegrates or a progressive disease affects our bodies, there may be panic or an overreaction that leads to behavior or words that might be regretted later. Alternatively, changes like these might be denied as the person avoids facing the changing circumstances for as long as possible. More abrupt changes, like the sudden death of a loved one or a job termination, are crises that can't be ignored. Less dramatic changes, such as a decline in the quality of one's neighborhood or new approaches to worship in one's traditional church, may be resisted, ignored, or accepted reluctantly, but only after a long period of reflection and getting used to the new realities. At other times we accept change enthusiastically, enjoy it, and even seek it out, like trying a new sport or going off to school to prepare for a new career. Then there are those creative people who enjoy making change, stirring things up, and cutting new pathways through our world of uncertainty. In all of this much depends on who controls the change. We are more inclined to resist and fear change when things are beyond our control. Maybe that is why we fear violent weather or resist going to the dentist.

As a counselor, you are a change specialist. Your job is to help people deal with the changes that come into their lives and make changes that will improve their lives. If you want to counsel effectively, it is essential that you understand the change process. You must have knowledge of how people try to change themselves, why change is difficult, and what makes change last.

Understanding Self-Change

Have you ever made a New Year's resolution and given up a few weeks—or maybe a few hours—into the new year? You are not alone. Researchers have discovered that 25 percent of New Year's resolutions are abandoned within the first week; 60 percent are gone within six months. Of those who fail, the majority will make the same resolution year after year for as long as ten years before they either give up or finally succeed in making a change that lasts for a least six months. This isn't very encouraging for those of us who, for example, determine to stop some harmful or sinful habit, set out to add spiritual disciplines into our lives, or are involved in urging others to make changes in their lives. Unlike the psychological researchers, Christians understand the role of the Holy Spirit in bringing lasting change, but is the effectiveness of self-change in Christians really any different from that of nonbelievers? Regardless of one's beliefs, it is true that self-change is difficult, and relapse is common among all of us.[4]

This may be one reason why many people give up trying to change themselves and turn to friends and family seeking help. When this doesn't work, they turn to pastors and other religious leaders or to professional mental-health professionals and other counselors.

In an effort to understand why self-change often fails, two Canadian psychologists did long-term research and proposed what they termed the False-Hope Syndrome (FHS).[5] Figure 1–1 is a summary.[6]

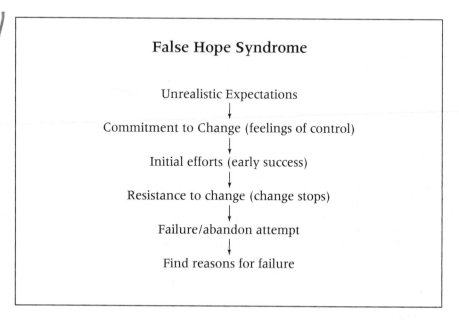

False Hope Syndrome

Unrealistic Expectations
↓
Commitment to Change (feelings of control)
↓
Initial efforts (early success)
↓
Resistance to change (change stops)
↓
Failure/abandon attempt
↓
Find reasons for failure

Figure 1–1. The False Hope Syndrome. Adapted from Janet Polivy and C. Peter Herman, "If at First You Don't Succeed: False Hopes of Self-Change," *American Psychologist* 57 (September 2002): 684.

According to this research-based theory, self-change often fails because we set *unrealistic expectations*. Suppose a person approaches a new year resolving to lose fifty pounds in the first ten weeks, to go to the fitness club every morning before work, or to pray and study the Bible for an hour each day. Each of these is likely to fail because these resolutions are too ambitious and unrealistic. Initially, there is a strong *commitment to change*, and the person feels in control of the process. Often, *initial efforts* lead to early success. The dieter, for example, notices a quick weight loss as the body sheds fluids and the scale shows a weight drop. Very soon, however, this *change stops*. The body adjusts to the reduced food input. The spiritual hour every morning gets missed when the person does not hear the alarm and sleeps in. People don't realize that relapse and periodic *failures* are common, so they blame themselves when these happen, sometimes try again once or twice, but eventually give up and determine to try again later.

At this point, it is common to find reasons why the effort failed. Consider that diet again. Thinking may go something like this, much of which is irrational: "I guess I shouldn't have had that little piece of cake yesterday. Probably that is what caused the weight loss to stop. Now I have failed and have to start all over. But that may not be wise right now because I'll be going to a birthday party next week. I think I'll wait until after the party and then start again. Maybe I'll also wait until after the wedding that I'll be attending at the end of the month. Then there will be less temptation, and probably I will be able to succeed." By using rationalizations like these, people avoid blaming themselves, conclude that external circumstances are the biggest problem—like that birthday party and wedding—assume that they will do better next time, and determine to try again later. Hope for change dies slowly, usually only after repeated failures, when it becomes clearer that the self-change is not going to work.

There are ways to prevent the operation of the False-Hope Syndrome and to make self-changes that last. These include the following, all of which counselors can teach to the people they counsel:

- Set realistic expectations in terms of how much time will be involved (usually things take longer than expected).
- Set goals that are realistic and attainable.
- Be realistic about the ease with which the change will occur (since it usually is harder than expected).
- Focus on success rather than on failures. This may involve keeping a record of successes and setting up rewards when goals are reached.
- Expect relapses. These are going to occur. When they are expected, they are less disappointing and disrupting, especially if there is a commitment to start again immediately after the relapse occurs.
- Be aware of tempting situations and avoid these.
- Get social support, encouragement, and accountability from a counselor or trusted friend so the change process is not attempted alone. When we try to change without social accountability, it is easier to abandon the process. And without another person, it is easier to justify cheating and find excuses for failure.
- Challenge the reasons for failure. This is easier when another person is involved and can challenge your reasons for quitting or for a relapse.

Is God a part of this whole process? What about spiritual warfare in which Satan and his forces may try to prevent change, especially if there is determination to abandon a sinful habit or develop a more godly lifestyle? Changes like these go beyond psychological analysis. Prayer is important in the self-change process and so is a regular commitment to the guidance and influence of the Holy Spirit. Often, however, spiritual changes come in the context of relationships when others give the practical advice and prayer support that help the self-changer succeed.

The Difficulty of Change

There are two broad categories of change that concern counselors and will be woven throughout the following chapters. _Reactive changes_ are those that come into our lives from the outside and require a response. Sudden crises are the most dramatic examples, but the people we counsel more often come for help in responding to issues such as disappointments, financial setbacks, interpersonal conflicts, loneliness, or the need to make important decisions. These are called reactive changes because they all come as a reaction to some event or situation in life.

Proactive changes, in contrast, are the changes we are trying to make happen. Losing weight, building a better marriage, parenting more effectively, building spiritual disciplines into our life, or acting on the suggestions of counselors are all examples of proactive changes. These two types of change can and often do overlap.

GA is a professional athlete who was stopped for drunk driving and charged with possession of illegal drugs when the police searched his car. GA had a good income, a stable marriage, and two great kids, but his life was under constant stress from his career. Every day he faced overwhelming change. He was away from home often, traveling with his team from city to city. The fans and sportswriters expected him to perform and were verbal in their criticism when he didn't meet their expectations. The drinking and occasional drug use had started to help relieve his stress when he went out after the games with his teammates. Sometimes he had sexual relations with strangers that he met in the bars. He felt guilty for being unfaithful to his wife and afraid, lest he pick up some kind of sexual disease and pass that on when he got home. When he talked to a counselor following his arrest, GA said that he was overwhelmed by the pressures that were part of his life and frustrated by his inability to make the changes in his lifestyle that he needed to make. His counselor helped him cope better with the external changes and guided him as he made important reactive choices to get better control over his "out of control" behavior when he was away from home. The arrest had been a serious wake-up call that led him to change.

Why is change so difficult? And why do people resist change, even when they say they want it? There are many reasons, but the following are among the most common. You probably will see some of these in your counseling work. At times, you might even see them in yourself. People resist change because:

- They are unwilling to give up what is safe, predictable, and familiar.
- They have no real conviction that change is better than the status quo.
- They have a fear of what life might be like if the change takes place. Often it feels safer to stay where they are, even though they are miserable, than

to risk making changes and facing what could be unpredictable, unfamiliar, and potentially threatening.

- They lack the skills, knowledge, abilities, experience, or resources that would make change possible and likely to last.
- The proposed changes are not realistic or practical.
- Other people want the change, but the person does not. For example, change will be less likely in the adolescent who has no desire to change but is sent for counseling because her parents want her to change.
- They may hold a conviction that change is not possible—so they are less motivated to try.
- There is no trusted person available to give support, understanding, encouragement, and guidance during the change process.
- They have unrealistic beliefs about what they can do. Often these beliefs come from others (sometimes even from counselors) who say things like "All things are possible, so just do it," "Take control and you can reach your goals," "Imagine success and you will get it," "Try harder and it will work out," or "Pray about it and have enough faith, and the change will come easily." Often these motivational slogans give unrealistic expectations about the difficulty of change and put pressure on the person who wants to change.

Closely related to the above, people have been told by parents, teachers, coaches, or others that they are incompetent and unlikely to ever be different. This negative input drains away any motivation to work at change.

Bringing Change That Lasts

When we consider these difficulties, it might be easy to conclude that change, especially lasting change, is next to impossible. But there is abundant evidence that lasting change *is* possible, given the right conditions. Jeffrey Kottler is a counselor, researcher, and prolific author who has spent over twenty years talking to counselors and change specialists, reviewing scientific research relating to change, working with the people who have come for counseling, encouraging his graduate students to write papers about change, and collecting stories of people who have made significant changes that last. Armed with all this information, Kottler moved to Iceland for several months, where he pulled all his conclusions together into an information-packed book that he titled *Making Changes Last*.[7]

When he arrived in Iceland, ready to begin writing, Kottler encountered significant change himself. He was "perfectly miserable"—lonely, depressed, disoriented, anxious, and sick. "It was dark all the time," he wrote. "I couldn't understand the language or the customs. . . . I thought about nothing but going home."[8] But he adjusted to the changes and wrote later that his days had become so filled with excitement and stimulation that he could barely sleep at night. Many of Kottler's research conclusions about change were experienced in his own life.

1. *Commitment.* This is what Kottler calls "the single most important ingredient" in bringing lasting change. Commitment concerns how badly the person wants to change and, more important, how motivated he or she is to maintain the changes

once they occur. Often people want very much to change, and they work at doing whatever is necessary until they reach their goals. Then they relax. They assume they have arrived and fail to realize how easily they could fall back into the old patterns. For them, overconfidence becomes the greatest enemy to lasting change.

We see this frequently in diet programs. After months of hard work and the slow decrease in weight, people get to the place where they want to be. Then they let down their guard, slide back into the old eating habits, and watch their weight soar back to what it was prior to the diet. For weight loss to last, however, the post-diet maintenance stage is even more important than the dieting. Weight-loss counselors know this and often discourage their clients from using the words *diet* or *dieting* because these terms imply a change in eating habits that can end when the goal is reached. Instead, there needs to be commitment to a permanent change in eating habits if the weight loss is to be maintained.

Kottler adds that the best predictor of lasting change is what he calls "self-efficacy," which means that the person expects to change, is confident that he or she will change, is willing to do whatever is necessary to bring about lasting change, and is in this for the long run, not just for a short term.

2. *Attainable Goals.* This was mentioned earlier, but nothing "dooms change efforts more than setting goals that are unrealistic and impossible to reach."[9]

Attainable goals are specific rather than vague. They are more likely to bring lasting change if these goals can become part of one's lifestyle. Goals also persist longer if the person receives consistent and accurate feedback on his or her progress. For example, weighing in at the fitness center on a weekly basis gives specific and regular indications about how the weight loss is progressing.

3. *Relapse Prevention.* Earlier I stated that relapses will occur in any change process. That is almost guaranteed. But there are ways to reduce these to a minimum and to help a person quickly recover and keep going when the temporary failures do occur. The counselee can be helped to evaluate past failures so he or she can determine what went wrong and consider how similar mistakes can be avoided in the future. Counselees need to know that relapse is not unusual so they are not devastated when they do fail. Make sure, however, that they know as well that the best way to recover and to keep going is to resume the desired new behaviors as quickly as possible. When a dieter succumbs to a high-calorie dessert, the temptation is to think "as long as I blew it I might as well eat other things that are not good for my diet. Then I'll start again." This is a big step toward failure. It is much better is to return to the diet immediately after a failure.

Overall, there are three ways to identify and prevent relapse.[10]

First, identify the high-risk situations. It is best if the counselee can be specific in listing the highly tempting situations that are likely to arise in the future. One example would be the chronically shy person who is learning to be more self-assured and assertive but who knows that she is intimidated by aggressive domineering people. It is worse when she is alone with these people. Knowing this, she can try to avoid contact with these threatening people and never be with them alone. A more obvious example is the former problem drinker who knows the danger of meeting friends in a bar, even if the plan is only to get together for coffee or a soft drink. Similarly, the teenager who has trouble controlling his sexuality may conclude that there are certain places and people that he needs to avoid.

Second, learn the coping skills that enable a person to avoid the problems. It is fine to tell teenagers to "just say no" when they are tempted to take drugs, but when they are with their friends, they often do not know how to resist the temptation and to say *no*. The counselor can teach "refusal skills" and practice these with the counselee in counseling situations. These skills will help to equip the person to resist the temptation more effectively.

Third, help people develop a lifestyle that reduces the possibility of temptation. A man who was becoming addicted to Internet pornography might have been encouraged to get rid of his computer, but this was not realistic because he needed computers for his work. Instead, at work and at home he moved his desk so the computer screen was obvious to anyone who entered the room. By doing this, he learned to avoid any patterns of behavior that would allow him to hide his computer screen from his wife and others.

4. *Support Systems*. It will come as no surprise that the maintenance of change depends, in large part, on whether there is a partner and/or support system to give encouragement and accountability. The most effective support systems are available when needed. Members of Alcoholics Anonymous know this principle and commit to making themselves available immediately to anybody who is facing temptation to drink. Ideally, there should be more than one supporter so someone is always available. That way, there is less likelihood of unhealthy dependency on one person. The supporters should be good role models and be willing to provide honest, sensitive, and constructive feedback even when the person does not want to hear it.[11]

In addition to these four established guidelines for bringing lasting change, a number of others have been suggested, some more controversial and less strongly supported by research. These include introducing your counselees to solid self-help programs (e.g., Alcoholics Anonymous), helping people identify the warning signs that signal a pending relapse so evasive action can be taken, encouraging people to keep track of their behavior in systematic ways so they can monitor their experiences, and teaching your counselees how to recognize and counter the self-talk "lies we tell ourselves."

In a book I read many years ago, Jeffrey Kottler suggested "transformative travel" as another tool for making change last.[12] There are dangers in travel, of course. We are away from our support networks and sometimes more subject to temptation. However, travel often pulls people away from the pressures, lets them get a fresh perspective on their lives, forces them to face and surmount fears or discomforts, and enables them to experience the rejuvenation that comes from times of relaxation.

No matter what we face, it is the awesome power of God that brings lasting change which might never come otherwise. In his Ephesian letter, Paul gave glory to God because "by his mighty power at work within us, he is able to accomplish infinitely more than we would ever dare to ask or hope."[13] The apostle prayed that "from his glorious, unlimited resources he [God] will give you mighty inner strength through his Holy Spirit."[14] The radical and lasting change in Paul's own life direction was an example of his belief that human effort was of limited value but that he could do everything with the help of Christ who continually gave him the strength he needed.[15] It does not take long for Christian counselors to see what God can and does do—usually in his own ways and his own timing.

The Changing World of Christian Counseling

The counselor's work is to stimulate lasting change in the people we counsel. This work can be influenced by the constant changes that take place in the world around us. Periodically, I am invited to give a talk on these cultural changes, but I have never given the same speech more than once because things change quickly and new developments keep emerging that were not issues previously. Before September 11, 2001, for example, I never included the threats of worldwide terrorism in my talks, but now and for the foreseeable future this is likely to be a concern for many counselees and for their counselors.

By the time you read these words, the world will have changed in ways that I cannot predict. What follows, then, are only a few examples of how the changing world is changing counselors. Perhaps you will want to add to the list.

The pace of life is changing, and many people are overwhelmed with busyness. This fast-paced life probably is more common in urban areas than in rural settings where life tends to be slower. When the pace of life is too fast, or when we are too busy or overwhelmed by work, there is limited time and energy for spiritual growth, marriage and family building, or even counseling. One result has been the growth of short-term therapies that seek to speed along the process and let counselees get back to their busy lifestyles as quickly as possible.[16]

Ever-advancing technology has changed the ways in which we live and do our work. I write this book on a computer, access the Internet from any time or place if I want more research data, and can keep the entire manuscript along with various other files in a two-inch long storage unit that I carry on my key ring. Technology enables us to be in close easy touch with counselees in other parts of the neighborhood or world, keep and access records when we need them, consult specialists, get specialized information when we encounter questions, and urge our counselees to get their own information from the Internet or join virtual support groups. My teaching as well as my public speeches are different now because of technology. All of this can overwhelm the non-technical counselor, but we are surrounded with technical experts, some as young as six or seven, who can solve the computer problem that we "non-techies" might encounter.[17]

Closely connected is the *ever-escalating flood of information* that can be both useful and overwhelming. When I wrote the first edition of this book in the late 1970s, I had to rely mostly on printed materials that were in my files, in my books, or in my local library. Not anymore. All of us, including our counselees, can access a wealth of information efficiently. Increasingly, counselees come to us with detailed and sophisticated understanding of their problems and know more about possible treatment plans than we do. As a result, the counselors become the learners.

Another significant part of the technology revolution is the *ever-increasing impact of biotechnology* that is advancing our understanding of human behavior. "The nascent understanding of genetics is beginning to rattle our world in much the same way as Galileo did 500 years ago when he argued that the earth revolved around the sun," wrote John Naisbitt and his co-authors.[18] "Genetic technology will overwhelm all other technology, including information technologies . . . presenting perhaps the greatest challenge ever to traditional religious faiths."[19] Perhaps nothing will have a greater impact on counseling as we move further into the twenty-first century. We're even seeing unlikely partnerships such as the alliances of artists and scientists. Naisbitt and his colleagues wrote that artists and scientists are "the canaries in the mine. They pick up the first signals, map new territories, invite risk, and all the while are inspired by each other's work. They are the fringe voices and harbingers of things to come."[20] Like most books about the future, Naisbitt's work was outdated before it was published, but it gave fascinating insights into how the world is changing in ways that are high-tech and in danger of losing the high-touch caring that humans need.

Is it surprising that all this change has created an environment where *spiritualities* and a search for foundational beliefs and values have exploded? Only a few years ago, counselors avoided anything spiritual. Many still do. But the widespread spiritual quest has given Christian counselors and others a new freedom to raise spiritual issues and to bring these into counseling relationships. No longer is spirituality rejected as evidence of neurosis, as Freud proclaimed a century ago. But for most people spirituality no longer is equated with Jesus, religion, or anything Christian.[21]

The list of changes that impact counselors can go on. We could consider the increasing role of non-Western alternative medicine, changing values (including changing views about gender and family issues), or the huge problems associated with worldwide poverty, famine, political unrest, and children at risk (including the alarming growth of an industry that buys and sells women and children for sexual exploitation). In later chapters we will give more detailed discussion to the psychological impact of globalization and the increase of terrorism.

The Changing Face of Christian Counseling

Perhaps none of this has made a greater impact on our world than the rise and general acceptance of the postmodern worldview. This loosely defined and ever-changing philosophy cannot be described in a few paragraphs here, but there are many books available for those who want to deepen their knowledge further.[22]

Several years ago, the congregation of our local church agreed that we needed clearer vision and a fresh direction. For several months I was part of a future development team that looked carefully at our church, our community, and biblical roots. At the time we knew that *postmodernism* was a vague and somewhat threatening word for some Christians, so we developed the summary that comprises Table 1–1. Like all summaries of anything complex, this is simplified, but it enabled our congregation to see how the world is changing and how churches need to change as well, even as they hold firm to their biblical values and foundations.

What does this mean for Christian counselors? Probably people have always received guidance from one another or from the older and more experienced members of their families and communities. The concept of counseling was known at least as early as Bible times, but we have refined the word and given it more specific meaning in the past 150 years, especially in Western cultures. We have developed mental-health professions who are anchored to the logical and scientific thinking of modernity and who specialize in helping those with psychological problems. Older counselors and other mental-health professionals, along with perhaps the majority of churches, have clung to the traditional ways of caring, communicating, and bringing change. Yet with the explosive growth of postmodernism, the foundations of our work have begun to shift.

Most of the world population is young, and even in underdeveloped countries,

Table 1-1 Modernism and Postmodernism	
Traditional "Modern" Culture	Contemporary "Postmodern" Culture
Prominent in 19th and 20th centuries	*Prominent in the non-Christian world of the late 20th and 21st centuries*
Science based	Experience based
Values facts, logic	Values stories, parables
Leaders are experts	Leaders are authentic
Leaders "have it together"	Leaders are "wounded" and growing
Leaders get respect because of their roles and position	Leaders earn respect: this is more important than roles or position
Top-down leadership	Leadership is in teams
Audiences listen passively (both in education and worship)	Audiences participate in learning (both in education and worship)
People aspire to get ahead	People are inspired to move forward
Non-believers respect what the Bible says	Non-believers respect what they see working in believers' lives
This type of thinking tends to be declining	*This type of thinking permeates the culture, including the media, and is likely to increase*

postmodern values and influences have infiltrated most of the culture by means of the media, the Internet, interactive technologies, innovative ways of learning, and even politics, business, and the entertainment industries. Some people, including a declining number of theologians and academicians, cling to the fading idea that postmodernism reflects generational differences or is an evil force that must be resisted at all costs. But there is broader consensus that postmodernism, in its ever-emerging forms, is the basis of a significant paradigm shift that will continue to shape every aspect of our world at least for the next century or two. In the next chapter we will consider how this shift is shaping the church, but it also is shaping the changing face of Christian counseling. Table 1–2 summarizes some of these changes.

The picture is never static and may be different by the time you read these words. Most of us have begun to see that postmodernism is neither all good nor all bad. Its influence on the people we counsel means that we must adjust our methods and maybe forsake some of the theories and techniques that were more appropriate and effective in previous decades. In the pages that follow, we will seek to give the clearest and best perspectives on the ways in which Christian counselors can help people with the problems and issues they bring to our attention. Postmodernism or the cultural trends that are summarized in this chapter may not be discussed in detail, but they will never be far from our thinking as we make our journey through the fascinating and ever-changing world of Christian counseling.

Table 1–2	
Traditional and Newer Approaches to Christian Counseling	
Traditional Christian Counseling	*The New Christian Counseling*
Modernist and scientific	Postmodern
Focus on the past	Focus on the present and future
Long-term strategies	Brief strategic counseling
Hierarchical—the counselor is the expert, superior in knowledge and training	The counselor is a "wounded healer" who may be trained but is not superior
Goal is healing	Goal is empowerment
Focus on facts and data	Focus on telling and creating one's story (narrative therapy)
Counselor guides	Counselor and counselee participate and interact
Counselor's degrees and credentials important	Counselor's authenticity is more important
Cultural issues minimized	Cultural issues important
Minimal emphasis on art	Art may be very significant, such as music therapy, art therapy including "expressive therapies," or dance therapy.[23]
Technology minimized or ignored	Technology viewed as valuable and important
Holy Spirit largely ignored	Holy Spirit empowers
Counselors aloof from the church	Counselors partner with the church
Biblical foundation	Biblical foundation

KEY POINTS FOR BUSY COUNSELORS

➤ Counseling is all about change.

➤ The best counselors are change specialists.

➤ Self-change often fails.

➤ To prevent this failure, encourage people to:
  ■ Set expectations that are realistic in terms of what can be accomplished, and the time and effort that will be needed.
  ■ Avoid situations and people that might create temptations to relapse.

- Expect occasional relapse but determine to resume the changed behavior immediately afterward.
- After relapse, discuss what happened and take steps to prevent a recurrence.
- Provide support and accountability from others.

➤ Change that lasts is characterized by:
- Commitment from the person who wants to change.
- The setting of attainable goals.
- Active efforts to prevent relapse.
- Support from other people.

➤ Counseling today is complicated by trends that impact our work, including:
- A faster pace of life and busyness.
- Galloping technology, including biotechnology.
- An overload of information.
- Greater interest in spirituality, including non-Christian spirituality.

➤ Counselors must have some understanding of postmodernism and know the ways in which it is changing counseling methodology.

2

The Counselor and Counseling

Anne is a middle-aged wife and mother who lives in a big city and works in a downtown office. She is liked by her fellow workers, has received several promotions from her employer, and has a good relationship with her husband and children. At her church and elsewhere, people see her as a friendly, capable, cheerful person who is pleasant to be with and well liked. Few would suspect that the one person who does not like Anne is Anne herself. Raised in a home where she was criticized constantly and reminded of all her short-comings, Anne lacks confidence in her own God-given capabilities and can't believe that people really like her.

At the urging of her husband, Anne went to see a counselor. She talked about her insecurities, but the counselor didn't seem inclined to listen. He told her that Christians have no reason to feel good about themselves. He talked about human depravity, stated that people are like worms that have no self-worth, quoted Bible verses that he told Anne to memorize, and described her desire to gain self-confidence as evidence of sin for which she should repent. As she left the counselor's office, Anne thought of the criticisms from her family in the past. Instead of helping, the counselor had only reinforced Anne's self-condemnation and made her feel guilty for wanting to change.

A s you may have detected, Anne's story is fictional, but her problem is common and will be discussed in a later chapter on inferiority and self-esteem. Sadly, the description of her counselor also is common, especially among some well-intentioned church leaders who view counseling as telling people what to do, quoting the Bible, and giving direction. These are people who talk instead of listening, who try to find a Bible verse to fit every problem, who tend to be condemning, and who lack the compassion that marked the ministry of Jesus.

There is something innately attractive about being a counselor. Apparently, many people see counseling as a glamorous activity that involves giving advice, healing broken relationships, and helping people solve their problems. Certainly, counseling can be gratifying work, but it doesn't take long for most of us to discover that this also can be difficult, emotionally draining work. It is work that involves intensive concentration and wisdom, regardless of one's age, training, or amount of experience. Counselors who are inexperienced or insecure in the counseling role sometimes make hasty judgments and dispense advice like the fictional counselor who met with Anne. A greater number are more sensitive to the people who come for counseling, but for all of us, it can be difficult to see so much pain and to feel so inadequate in bringing help. When our counselees fail to improve, as often happens, it is easy to blame ourselves. We try harder and wonder what went wrong. As more and more needy people come for help, the tendency is to keep increasing our counseling loads—pushing ourselves closer to the limits of our endurance. Sometimes, counselees are reminded of their own insecurities or conflicts and this can threaten counselor stability or feelings of self-worth. Little wonder that counseling can be both fulfilling and hazardous as an occupation. In this chapter we will discuss some of these hazards and consider ways to make the counselor's work more fulfilling and successful.

The Counselor's Characteristics

In all counseling situations, helpers must try to answer four questions: (1) What is the real problem? (This may be different from the problem that the counselee presents.) (2) Should I try to help? (3) What could I do to help? (4) Would someone else be better qualified to help?[1] It is important for Christian counselors to have an understanding of problems (how they arise and how they might be resolved), a knowledge of biblical teaching about the problems that people bring to counselors, and both experience and familiarity with counseling skills.

There is evidence that the counselor's personal characteristics are of even greater significance in helping. Forty years ago, researchers began studying the qualities of effective counselors. The first studies found that patients in psychiatric hospitals were most likely to improve when their counselors showed high levels of warmth, empathy, and genuineness, regardless of the counselors' techniques or theoretical perspectives. When these traits were not present, the patients grew worse, regardless of what methods their counselors used.[2]

Christian psychologist Les Parrott did an in-depth review of numerous research studies and concluded that there are several important qualities for counselor effectiveness.[3] None of us has all of these in abundance, but the following list allows counselors to be aware of what may be making them effective as well as what may be lacking in their lives and in need of further development.

- *Psychological health* does not mean that the counselor always will be free of problems. Effective counselors should have a sense of meaning and purpose that gives them inner strength to adjust to circumstances beyond their control. People with psychological health, including counselors, are willing to take responsibility for themselves without blaming others or acting like passive victims. Instead of dwelling on the past or constantly dreaming of the future, these people are at peace with the present and at peace with themselves.
- *A genuine interest in people* describes less what these effective counselors do and more who they are. Concern for others is part of their nature. It is not some role they take on. It is a personal authenticity that lets people see they are genuine—"the real thing."
- *Empathy* is the ability to "feel with" the counselee and to see the world as he or she sees it. Robert Carkhuff, who did much of the earliest research in counselor characteristics, has written that "without an empathic understanding of the helpee's world and his difficulties as he sees them, there is no basis for helping."[4]
- *Personal warmth* describes counselors who are caring, attentive, accepting, and genuinely interested in their counselees without being possessive or

controlling. Most of us know and respond positively to people like this. They tend to be open, relaxed, and nonjudgmental. Many of them are friendly people who smile a lot.

- *Self-awareness* means that counselors are aware of their true motives, limitations, personal issues, and strengths as well as their weaknesses. Self-aware counselors are committed to ongoing introspection, personal growth, and a willingness to change. They are able to put aside their own desires to be liked or admired in favor of doing what is best for the people they are tying to help.

- *Awareness of values* is at the core of personal stability. Business leaders, politicians, or anyone else who lacks clearly defined values is at risk of being swayed by the latest trends or by persuasive people. Values are the convictions or beliefs that are at the core of our being and that shape our behavior. The counselor who values success at any cost, riches, acclaim, personal freedom, or selfish ambition is likely to let these values impact the counseling unless he or she is aware of their potential impact. Effective counselors have thought through their values, live in accordance with these values, and understand how their values can impact others. These counselors also are sensitive to the values of other people, including the values in their counselees.

- *Tolerance of ambiguity* is a psychological term that means an ability to live with uncertainty. The people who come for counseling often are vague about their symptoms or desires. The good counselor can accept this uncertainly even as he or she tries to bring greater clarity and understanding to the problem. Since every counselee and every problem are unique, there is no one approach that applies to every case. The best counselors are able to be flexible and to work with uncertainty without becoming anxious or without needing to be in control. Counselors tend to be less effective when they are impatient and need a structured approach they can apply to everybody. Good counselors know there is no recipe book to guide their treatment.

This list, adapted from a secular textbook, makes no mention of the spiritual characteristics of the counselor. However, Christian counselors know that they are most likely to be effective when they seek to be like Jesus, reflecting the spiritual and God-given traits of love, joy, peace, patience, kindness, goodness, faithfulness, gentleness and self-control.[5] A detailed study of mentoring by two Christian psychologists reported three additional characteristics that appear to be critical for counselors. Good Christian counselors, like good mentors, need to demonstrate *integrity* (having a clear sense of what is right and consistently living in accordance with this conviction), *courage* both to accept one's shortcomings and to challenge or empower others, and *care* that expresses a sincere concern for one's counselees.[6]

The Christian Counselor's Uniqueness

Like specialists in medicine, education, preaching, and other fields of work, Christian counselors use techniques that have been developed by nonbelievers. Our understanding of counseling issues and effective ways to give help have many roots in the massive body of research that has been produced in the secular communities. In addition, Christian counseling has at least four distinctives.

1. *Unique Assumptions.* No counselor is completely free of values or neutral in terms of assumptions. We each bring our own beliefs and viewpoints into the counseling situation. These assumptions influence our judgments and comments whether we recognize it or not.

Despite widespread interest in spirituality, many secular counselors would agree with the view of psychoanalyst Erich Fromm, who stated that we all live "in a universe indifferent to our fate." Such a viewpoint leaves no place for belief in a compassionate, sovereign God. There is no room for prayer, meditating on "the Word of God," experiencing divine forgiveness, or looking toward life after death. Fromm's assumptions influenced his writing and shaped his methods of counseling.

Although they have different views of theology, most counselors who call themselves Christian have (or should have) beliefs about the attributes of God, the nature of human beings, the authority of the Bible, the reality of sin, the forgiveness of God, and hope for the future.[7] Read, for example, the first four verses of the New Testament book of Hebrews. Won't our lives and our counseling be different from our secular colleagues if we believe that God has spoken to the human race and still communicates, created the universe through his Son, provided for the forgiveness of sins, and now holds together and *sustains the universe by the mighty power of his command?*

2. *Unique Goals.* All counselors seek to help people change their behavior, attitudes, values, and/or perspectives. We teach skills, including social and problem-solving skills; encourage the recognition and expression of emotion; give support in times of need; teach responsibility; instill insight; guide as decisions are made; help counselees mobilize inner and environmental resources in times of crisis; and work to increase counselee competence and self-confidence.

The Christian goes further. Without ignoring the counselee's concerns and problems and without manipulating in any way, the Christian care-giver hopes to stimulate spiritual growth in those who come for help. At times, we may encourage the confession of sin and the experience of divine forgiveness. We may encourage counselees to commit themselves to Jesus Christ and to live lives that are consistent with biblical teaching instead of living in accordance with the relativistic human standards that have permeated our society. Because of who we are, we model and disseminate Christian standards, values, attitudes, and lifestyles, even when we work in settings where proselytizing or any talk about religion is prohibited.

Some will criticize this as "bringing religion into counseling." To ignore theological and spiritual issues, however, is to build our counseling on the humanistic religion of modernity, to stifle our own beliefs, and to compartmentalize our lives into sacred and secular segments. In addition, the prohibition of religion from the counseling room ignores the increasing evidence that while some people view spirituality and religion as a source of their distress, a much larger number find their spiritual beliefs to be a source of strength and coping.[8] Scientific studies have demonstrated that "religiosity keeps kids from smoking, drinking and using" drugs by "buffering the impact of stress" and stressful situations such as illness or an unemployed parent. Adults involved in regular church attendance are more likely to have harmonious marital relationships and better parenting skills.[9] In turn, this promotes a teenager's competence, self-regulation, psychological adjustment, and school performance.[10] Other evidence suggests that discussion of religious beliefs and spiritual resources helps counselees gain hope, meaning, and support so they can cope with their problems better.[11] No good counselor, Christian or non-Christian, forces beliefs on counselees. We have an obligation to treat people with respect and to give them freedom to make their own decisions.[12] But honest and authentic people-helpers do not stifle their beliefs and pretend to be something they are not.

3. *Unique Methods.* All counseling techniques have at least four characteristics: (a) They seek to instill hope by arousing the belief that help is possible; (b) they correct the counselee's erroneous beliefs; (c) they help people develop skills so they can live more competently; (d) and they help people accept themselves as persons of worth. To accomplish these goals, counselors consistently use such basic techniques as listening, showing interest, attempting to understand, and at least occasionally giving direction. Christians and non-Christian counselors use many of the same helping methods.

All competent counselors avoid techniques that would be considered immoral, but the Christian also avoids any method that would be inconsistent with biblical teaching. For example, encouraging people to engage in extramarital or premarital sexual intercourse, using offensive language, urging counselees to develop antibiblical values, or helping people develop behaviors that are inconsistent with biblical teaching would all be avoided, regardless of their use by secular therapists.

Other techniques are distinctively Christian and are used in Christian counseling with some frequency. Examples include prayer in the counseling session, reading from the Bible, gentle confrontation with Christian truths, or encouraging counselees to become involved in a local church or with other groups of believers.

4. *Unique Giftedness.* Especially in the beginning, counselors often discover a gap between their formal academic learning and the actual experience of helping somebody with a real problem. Once we discover the difficulty of counseling, it is common to wonder if we really can do this work effectively. Even experienced counselors sometimes find themselves facing doubts and feelings of inadequacy about the effectiveness of their counseling.

It is well known that some people are better counselors than others. This raises an important, basic question. Is it possible for every Christian to be an effective counselor, or is counseling a gift, reserved for selected members of the body of Christ? According to the Bible, all believers should have compassionate concern for their fellow human beings, but from that it does not follow that all believers can or should become effective counselors.

It is not difficult to know if you are one of those people who is specially gifted as a counselor. Ask the people who know you best if caring for others is one of your strengths. Look over your life and ask yourself if people seem to gravitate to you naturally to talk about their problems. Do you get personal satisfaction in helping, supporting, encouraging, challenging, or guiding other people? Does it appear that people are being helped when they talk with you? If so, you may be especially equipped by God to do counseling work. Thank God for this and learn to do counseling better.

In contrast, if your counseling seems ineffective, perhaps God has gifted you in some other way. This does not excuse anyone from being a people-helper, but it may encourage you to put your major efforts elsewhere and leave the art of counseling to those who are more gifted in that area.

What if you are a pastor, youth worker, or some other person whose role includes counseling but you don't sense a special gifting in that area? This does not mean that you should avoid counseling or that nobody will improve as a result of your counseling work. A lack of giftedness in some area means that you will have to work a little harder than the person who is more gifted. A similar conclusion applies to speaking, teaching, or being an administrator if these are part of your role but you know they are not your strengths. Work hard to do as well as you can and try to focus on your strengths and let others cover the areas where you are weaker.

Clearly, we who are a part of the church need one another, and counseling is a part—but only a part—of the functioning church. Inside or outside of the church, people are helped by counseling, but we also help by evangelism, teaching, social action, leading worship, and other aspects of ministry.

The Counselor's Motivation

Why do you want to counsel?[13] It always is difficult to evaluate our own motives. Perhaps this is especially true when we examine our reasons for choosing counseling as a profession. A sincere desire to help people is a valid reason for becoming a counselor. Also valid is the objective evidence that your counseling really has a positive influence on others, that people seek you out spontaneously to talk about their problems, or that you find helping people to be personally fulfilling. But there are other issues, sometimes unrecognized, that may be pulling you toward counseling. Some of these might hinder your counseling effectiveness rather than help you counsel better.

When you counsel primarily to meet your own needs, you are less likely to be of help to your counselees. Consider the following:

1. *The Need for Relationships.* Everybody needs closeness and intimate contact with at least two or three other people. For some counselees, the counselor will be their closest friend, at least temporarily. But suppose the counselor has no close friends apart from his or her counselees. In such cases the counselor's need for a relationship clouds objectivity and can hinder the attempt to help. If you notice that you are looking for opportunities to prolong the counseling, to call the counselee between sessions, or to get together socially, it may be that the relationship is meeting your needs for companionship as much as (or more than) it is helping the counselee. At this point the counselor-counselee involvement has ceased to be an effective helping relationship. If you are a professional counselor, crossing this kind of boundary is unethical, and the formal counseling needs to stop. It is often in the best interest of both parties to refer the person to another counselor. Helping your friends isn't necessarily bad, but friends are not always the best counselors, and friendships that grow out of counseling are best avoided, at least until after the counseling ends.

2. *The Need for Control.* The authoritarian counselor likes to "straighten out" others, give advice (even when it is not requested), and play the "problem-solver"

role. Some dependent counselees may want this, but eventually most people resist or resent controller-type counselors because they can be demeaning and don't really help.

When counselees are told what to do, they might confuse the Christian counselor's opinion with the will of God. Some feel guilty and incompetent if they don't follow the advice they've received. Counselees are not likely to mature spiritually or emotionally if they can't make decisions without the help of a counselor. The counselor and counselee must work together as a team in which the counselor serves as a teacher-coach whose eventual goal is to withdraw from the playing field.

3. *The Need to Rescue.* The rescuer often has a sincere desire to help, but this type of counselor takes responsibility away from the counselee by displaying an attitude that says, "You can't handle this; let me do it for you." This may satisfy the counselee for a while, but it rarely helps permanently. When the rescue technique fails (as often happens), the counselor may feel rejected, unappreciated, inadequate, sometimes guilty, hurt, and deeply frustrated.

4. *The Need for Information.* In describing their problems, counselees often give interesting tidbits of information that might not be shared otherwise. When a counselor is overly curious, especially about sexual or other personal behavior, he or she has slipped into meeting counselor needs over the needs of the counselee. Sometimes, these pieces of information become subject for gossip that rarely stays confidential. Overly curious counselors take the risk of engaging in unethical behavior. They rarely are helpful, and eventually people stop asking them for help.

5. *The Need for Affirmation and Acceptance.* Counselees often speak positively about their counselors, especially if the counseling is going well. Some counselors, including those who feel insecure or incompetent, are starved for affirmation and expressions of appreciation or praise. This "need to be liked" influences everything the counselor says or does, often preventing any counseling interventions that could help the counselee but might bring disapproval or resistance.

6. *The Need for Personal Healing.* Most of us carry hidden needs and insecurities that could interfere with our people-helping work. This is one reason why graduate schools of counseling usually require students to get counseling for themselves before they start helping others. Counseling sessions are not likely to be effective if the counselor is using the counselee to fulfill his or her personal needs. These include a counselor's need to manipulate others, atone for guilt, please some authority figure, deal with sexual conflicts, express hostility, or prove that he or she is intellectually capable, spiritually mature, and psychologically stable. It is unethical and unfair to use counselees to meet your needs or to help heal issues in your own life.

Probably every counselor (including some who are experienced) will sense these tendencies at times, but it is important that personal needs be dealt with apart from our work with counselees. When people come for counseling, they take the risk of sharing personal information and committing themselves to the counselor's care. The counselor violates this trust and undermines counseling effectiveness if the helping relationship is used primarily to satisfy the helper's own needs.

The Counselor's Mistakes

Few things in life are guaranteed, but here is one: as a counselor you will make mistakes. It won't take long for you to compile your own list of mistakes, but what follows are a few areas where counselors fail, especially at the beginning.

- *The counselor visits instead of counseling.* Visiting is a friendly activity that involves mutual sharing. Counseling is a problem-centered, goal-directed conversation that focuses primarily on the needs of one person—the counselee. All counseling involves periodic visiting, but when visiting is prolonged and primary, counseling effectiveness is reduced. If you are too inclined to chat informally, ask if you are trying to avoid dealing with the counselee's issues. Then ask yourself why.
- *The counselor starts problem-solving too early.* Busy, goal-directed people can be impatient. As counselees, they want immediate answers and quick relief from their symptoms. In turn, counselors may be eager to help, so they start giving advice and answers too quickly. As a result, there is insufficient time for listening, clarifying the issues, and reflecting on what the counselee is trying to say.

  Sometimes, counselors approach counseling with a more relaxed pace, but they can become discouraged and anxious when they don't see immediate progress. It is true that counselors should not waste time, but it also is true that counseling cannot be rushed. Problems frequently take a long time to develop, and it is unrealistic to assume that they will disappear quickly and solely in response to the counselor's interventions. Instant changes do happen, but these are rare. When the pace is deliberate and relaxed, the counselor is less inclined to make hasty judgments, and the counselee is more likely to feel the support, understanding, and serious interest of the counselor. In most cases it takes time for counselees to give up their old ways of thinking or behaving and to replace them with something new and better.
- *The counselor becomes an interrogator.* When they are asked too many questions too quickly, counselees often feel misunderstood. They also might assume that when the questioning is over, the counselor will come up with a diagnosis and solution like a mechanic who asks a series of questions about your ailing car. It is more helpful to ask fewer questions, using questions that will encourage the counselee to talk. Allow time for silence while the counselee collects his or her thoughts in order to give a more complete picture of the issues.
- *The counselor is disrespectful or judgmental.* Some counselors (not the better ones) quickly categorize people. It may be assumed, for example, that a counselee is a "carnal Christian," a "carefree bachelor," or a "phlegmatic type." Then people are pigeon-holed into categories and dismissed with hurried evaluations, quick confrontation, judgmental statements, or insensitive and rigid advice. No person likes to be treated with such disrespect, and nobody likes to be dumped into categories and made the object of prejudice. Rarely is anyone helped by counselors who judge or fail to listen sympathetically and respectfully.

  Jesus understood people perfectly. Even today he is in touch with the feelings of our infirmities. He never downplayed problems or overlooked sin, but he understood sinners and always showed kindness and respect for those, like the woman at the well, who were willing to learn, repent, and change their behavior.

- *The counselor becomes overly involved emotionally.* There is a fine line between caring and becoming too involved to be helpful. This is especially true when a counselee is deeply disturbed, confused, or facing a problem that is similar to the counselor's own struggles.

  Emotional overinvolvement can cause the counselor to lose objectivity, and this in turn reduces counseling effectiveness. To some extent, compassionate people are not able to avoid emotional involvement, but the Christian counselor can resist this tendency by viewing the counseling as a professional helping relationship that clearly must be limited in terms of length or number of appointments. These boundary limitations are intended to keep the counselor objective enough to be helpful.

- *The counselor appears distant and artificial.* This may not be true of you, but counselors sometimes burden themselves with the belief that everything must be done right. They work on the assumption that good counselors always say the appropriate words, avoid mistakes, or demonstrate that they have the knowledge and skills to handle any kind of counseling situation. Often such counselors are reluctant to admit their own weaknesses or knowledge gaps. They are so anxious to be professional and successful that they appear artificial and aloof. It is difficult, perhaps impossible, for a counselee to relax and share honestly with a counselor who gives the impression of being distant or of "having it all together."

  In the history of this world, only one counselor ever reached perfection, never made mistakes, and always said the right things. We who are his followers need to relax, admit that we all make mistakes, quit hiding behind the professional role, and trust him to give us the words and the wisdom to counsel people effectively.

- *The counselor is defensive.* At times most counselors feel threatened in counseling. The ability to listen empathetically is hindered when we are being criticized unfairly, aware that we aren't helping, bothered by guilt, or afraid of being harmed by a counselee.

  When threats like these arise, it is helpful to ask yourself why. If you don't know the answer, consider discussing the situation with a friend or fellow counselor. The more we know and accept about ourselves, the less likely we are to be threatened by counselees.

The counselor must maintain a vigilant attitude if he or she is to avoid the mistakes we have been discussing. As Christian helpers we honor God by doing the best job possible. Apologize when you make mistakes, and use your mistakes as learning situations and stepping stones to improvement.

Mistakes and role confusions are not irreversible tragedies. Good rapport with counselees can cover a multitude of counseling mistakes, but you should not use this as an excuse for sloppy and incompetent counseling. When you make mistakes or slip into unhealthy counseling roles, apologize and, if necessary, restructure the relationship. You may tell the counselee how you intend to change (by setting firmer counseling hours, for example; refusing to drop everything else when a counselee calls; becoming more patient; or being less directive). This restructuring is always difficult because it involves admitting a failure or taking back something that has been given. The alternative may be further role confusion and ineffective counseling.

The Counselor's Vulnerability

Counseling would be much easier if we could assume that every counselee wanted help, was honest and trustworthy, and would participate fully in the counseling process. Of course, this does not always happen. Some counselees have a conscious or unconscious desire to manipulate, frustrate, distort facts, or not cooperate. This is a difficult discovery for the counselor who wants to help and who finds fulfillment and pleasure when people change. It always is difficult to work with resistant and uncooperative people. By agreeing to help, we are opening ourselves to the possibility of power struggles, exploitation, and failure.

There are several ways people frustrate the counselor and increase his or her vulnerability.

1. *Manipulation.* Some people are masters at getting what they want by controlling others. The story is told of an insecure young counselor who wanted to be helpful. Not wishing to be labeled like the "previous counselor who didn't care," the new counselor was determined to please. The counseling sessions lengthened and became more frequent. Before long the counselor was making phone calls, running errands, giving small loans, and even shopping for the counselee, who constantly expressed gratitude but mournfully kept asking for more.

This inexperienced counselor quickly learned that *manipulated counselors are rarely helpful counselors.* People who attempt to manipulate their counselors often do this subtly and well; for them, manipulation has become a way of life. The counselor must challenge these tactics, refuse to be controlled by them, and teach more satisfying ways of relating to others.

Since manipulation can be so smooth and subtle, the wise counselor continually asks: "Am I being manipulated?" "Am I going beyond my responsibilities as a counselor?" "Is there evidence that I am losing my objectivity or being pushed into saying or doing things that might not be wise?" Even experienced counselors can fail to see that they are being manipulated, so it is common for counselors to have professional partners or friends who can help them see what they don't see in themselves.

It also can be helpful to ask yourself what the counselee really wants. Sometimes, people ask for help with a problem, but what they really want is your attention and time, your sanctioning of sinful or otherwise harmful behavior, or your support as an ally in some family or other conflict. At times people come because they hope concerned spouses, family members, or employers will stop complaining about their behavior if it appears they are in counseling. When you suspect this type of false motivation or sense that you are being manipulated, gently raise your concern with the counselee, expect that the idea will be rejected, but then structure the counseling in a way that will prevent manipulation or exploitation in the future. Don't assume that all counselees are manipulators. Probably the people who genuinely want help are less likely to be manipulative, secretive, dishonest, or demanding.

2. *Emotional Entanglements. Countertransference* is a technical word that Freud

first suggested. This occurs when a counselee reminds you of a person who has had an influence in your life. If a counselee reminds you of your son, your father, or a former employer, for example, you can lose your objectivity and treat the counselee in a way that would not happen if this resemblance were not present. If you disliked your former boss, unconsciously you might transfer this dislike onto the client who looks like that boss.

Emotional entanglements come when the counselor's own needs or perceptions interfere with the therapeutic relationship. It is then that the counseling sessions can become a place for solving the counselor's problems. When this happens, counselees do not receive the help they need. In fact, you could be tempted to make statements or act in ways you would regret later. Suppose, for example, that you begin to have romantic or sexual feelings toward a counselee, that you are tempted to hover over and protect one or more of your counselees, that you fantasize about a counselee between sessions, that you have a constant need for acceptance and approval from your counselees, or that you feel so close to a counselee that you cannot separate your own feelings from those of your client. Maybe you find ways to avoid counselees you dislike but spend extra time and longer sessions with others you like more. These can all be indications that your own needs and problems are intruding on your work as a counselor.

If they have been trained effectively, counselors are less likely to be influenced by countertransference and other emotional entanglements, but at times they surface in all of us. A first step toward avoiding entanglement and vulnerability is to recognize the dangers and possibility of unhealthy emotional involvement with some counselees. It can also be helpful to discuss this with a perceptive friend or other counselor. This person can help you keep things in perspective and help you see issues in your own life that may be interfering with some of your people-helping activities.

3. *Resistance.* People often come for help because they want relief from their symptoms or painful circumstances. When they discover that lasting change and relief might require time, effort, and greater pain, they resist counseling. Surprisingly, perhaps, there are times when people are distressed by their problems, but they are reluctant to change because their problems provide benefits that they do not really want to give up. These benefits could include attention and sympathy from others, disability compensation, decreased responsibility, or more subtle gratifications such as self-punishment for wrongdoing or the opportunity to make life difficult for others. Since successful counseling would take away these benefits, the counselee does not cooperate. Then there are people who get a sense of power and accomplishment by frustrating the efforts of others, including their counselors. At a subconscious level, these people may convince themselves, "I'm beyond help—but then that counselor who couldn't succeed with me isn't much good either." So the counselor continues to counsel, the counselee pretends to cooperate, and nothing changes.

Counseling is likely to be disruptive to a person's life, so when the process begins, the counselee's psychological defenses may be threatened. This could lead to anxiety, anger, and resistance to facing facts about oneself that may be painful and unflattering. If the resistance and noncooperation persist, more in-depth counseling may be needed. When counselees are relatively well-adjusted, however, resistance can be discussed gently and openly. Let the counselee know that nobody can be forced to change. Ultimately, he or she (not the counselor) is responsible for improvement or lack of improvement. The counselor provides a safe and structured relationship, avoids getting on the defensive, and realizes eventually that one's effectiveness as a counselor (and as a person) is not necessarily correlated with the improvement rate of counselees. Recognize, too, that while resistance most often comes from the counselee, there are times when the problem rests with insensitive or excessively directive counselors whose words or actions undercut the trusting relationship that is needed for successful counseling.

Counselors can remain alert to potential problems when they ask themselves (and each other) questions such as the following:[14]

- Why do I say this is the worst (or best) person I have ever counseled?
- Is there a reason why I or the counselee is always late?
- Is there a reason why I or the counselee wants more (or less) time than we had agreed previously?
- Do I overreact to statements this counselee makes?
- What are the reasons that I feel bored when I am with this person?
- Is this boredom because of the counselee, me, or both of us?
- Why do I always disagree (or agree) with this counselee?
- Do I find myself wanting to end this relationship or to hold on to it, even though it should end?
- Am I beginning to feel too much emotional involvement or sympathy for the counselee?
- Do I think about the counselee frequently between sessions, daydream about him or her, or show an unusual interest in the person or the problem? If so, what might this say about me?

4. *Sexuality.* Whenever two people work closely together on a common goal, feelings of camaraderie and warmth often arise between them. When these people have similar backgrounds and especially when they are of the opposite sex, the feelings of warmth frequently have a sexual component. This can include sexual attraction and sometimes inappropriate sexual comments or behavior involving the counselor and counselee. This inappropriate sexuality also can appear in the form of sexual harassment and abuse arising from the counselor's power in the counseling relationship and influence over more vulnerable counselees. The counselor's sexuality and sexual behavior will be discussed in greater detail in a later chapter.

The Counselor's Burnout

Counseling students sometimes assume that the act of helping people will provide a lifetime of satisfaction and vocational fulfillment. In time, however, most of us discover that counseling can be hard work. Many counselees do not get better, and constant involvement with the problems and miseries of others is psychologically, physically, and sometimes spiritually draining. All of this contributes to the progressive loss of idealism, energy, and purpose, which has come to be known as *burnout.* Originally, burnout was a term that applied only to people in the helping professions, where the demands are great and the rewards can be few. Today, burnout is applied more broadly to include people in any vocation who began with high expectations and enthusiasm only to experience the "physical, emotional, and mental exhaustion caused by unrealistically high aspirations and illusory and impossible goals."[15] These people include athletes, performers, business executives, professional people, and others (including book writers) whose work is pressure filled, threatening to their self-esteem, and/or no longer psychologically rewarding.[16] Most often, burnout occurs in perfectionist people who are idealistic, deeply committed to their work, reluctant to say "no," and inclined to be workaholics, even though they might resist that label.

Sometimes, burnout occurs in whole groups of people, such as a pastoral staff, group of counselors, or hospital work team where demands are so high that performance suffers and the team members lack the energy or ability to focus on doing their work competently. Like burned-out individuals, the whole team shows the three most common characteristics of burnout: (1) *emotional exhaustion,* with its feelings of being overwhelmed by the work load; (2) *depersonalization,* which is a big psychological word meaning that the burned-out people withdraw emotionally from their work and the people who want to be served; and (3) *reduced feelings of accomplishment,* which causes individuals or teams to feel they no longer are making a positive contribution to others. Counselees or the other people we serve don't always notice that the counselor is burned out, although many eventually sense the emotional distance.[17]

Burnout tends to be accompanied by feelings of futility, powerlessness, fatigue, cynicism, apathy, irritability, and frustration. Counselors who believe in the importance of warmth, genuineness, and empathy instead become cold, aloof, unsympathetic, detached, worn-out helpers. In a subtle and sometimes unconscious effort at self-protection, the professional dons such thick armor that no one can get through. These symptoms are not limited to counselors or medical practitioners, and burnout is not limited to any one part of the world. For example, overburdened relief workers experience burnout wherever they work.[18]

To prevent burnout, we first need the spiritual strength that comes through regular periods of prayer, worship, meditation on the Scriptures, and other spiritual disciplines. Second, we need support from others who accept us for who we are rather than for what we do. Each of us needs at least one loving and understanding person with whom we can cry, one person who knows our weaknesses but can be trusted not to use this knowledge against us. Third, each of us must constantly evaluate the underlying drive to achieve. We need to remind ourselves, or have somebody else remind us, that personal worth comes from God and not from our ability to succeed, produce, and help others consistently. We must honestly admit to ourselves that "We can't do everything, so we will do what we can with the time we've got."

Fourth, we need to take time off—regular periods away from demanding people, work schedules, cell phones, and e-mail messages. Jesus took time away, and so must his followers if we are to remain efficient and capable helpers. Fifth, it helps to improve our ministry skills, learn to manage conflict, or counsel better to be able to say "no" even when we might feel more like saying "yes." Finally, we can share the load by encouraging and training others to be sensitive lay counselors, burden-bearers, and people-helpers. The church leader or other Christian counselor who tries to help everyone is heading for ineffectiveness if not eventual burnout. It helps as well if you can keep a sense of humor about life and not take yourself too seriously.

If you are a helper who already senses burnout, try to get away as soon as you can for at least a brief period of reevaluation. Before God, consider how you can apply the suggestions listed in the preceding paragraphs. How can these lighten your load and add self-fulfillment and relaxation back into your life? If you are married, get your spouse's perspective, the one who lives with your burnout and might be feeling a sense of burnout as well. People who work with others or have demanding jobs need to find balance in their activities. They need time to rest, play, interact with others informally, and laugh. Otherwise life becomes boring, routine, and lackluster. This isn't pleasant for the counselor or for the people around. And certainly it does nothing to improve one's ability to help counselees cope with all the stresses of modern-day life.

The Counselor's Counselors

It is not always possible, especially in smaller schools, but the best counselor training programs require students to have personal therapy, supervision as they counsel with real clients, and other experiences designed to increase self-aware-ness and to remove those emotional and psychological spiritual blocks that hinder counseling effectiveness. These exercises are helpful and highly recommended, but frequently they overlook the greatest available source of strength and wisdom for Christian counselors—the Holy Spirit who guides and dwells in the life of each believer. Christians can become so involved in the theories and technicalities of counseling that they forget the source from which all lasting help comes—the Lord himself.

Throughout the Bible we see that God also works through human beings. In the early church, believers devoted themselves to one another, ate together, and shared what they had "with great joy and generosity."[19] God often helps his children, counselors included, through other people with whom we can share, maintain per-spective, relax, pray, and sometimes cry. Without the support, encouragement, and the perspectives of people we trust, the counselor's work is likely to be more diffi-cult and less effective. Often two or more counselors can meet regularly to read the Bible, encourage, and pray for each other. If you lack such a relationship, ask God to help you find a colleague or two with whom you can share.

Many years ago a group of counselors was asked how they would spend the rest of their lives if they had the financial means to do anything they wanted. Of more than one hundred counselors surveyed, only three said they would spend their lives doing counseling work, and of these, one person preferred to do coun-seling as a spare-time activity.[20] There is no reason to believe that counselors today are more likely to persist. Counseling is not easy, even though at times it can be fulfilling. If you keep this in mind, your people-helping ministry will be more satisfying, and you likely will be more effective as a Christian counselor.

Jesus as Counselor

Jesus Christ is the best model we have of an effective "wonderful counselor" whose personality, knowledge, and skills enabled him to assist anyone who needed help. In attempting to analyze the counseling of Jesus, we must be aware that each of us could have a tendency, unconscious or deliberate, to view Christ's ministry in a way that reinforces our own views about how people are helped.

For example, the directive-confrontational counselor recognizes that Jesus was confrontational at times. The nondirective "client-centered" counselor finds support for this approach in other examples of Christ's helping ministry. Surely, it is more accurate to state that Jesus used a variety of counseling techniques, depending on the situation, the nature of the counselee, and the specific problem. At times he listened to people carefully but without giving much overt direction; on other occasions he taught decisively. He gave encouragement and support, but he also confronted and challenged. He accepted people who were sinful and needy, but he also demanded repentance, obedience, and action. Then there were times when he gave help by telling a story with a moral.

Basic to Jesus' style of helping, however, was his personality. In his teaching, caring, and counseling, he demonstrated those traits, attitudes, and values that made him effective as a people-helper and that serve as a model for us. Jesus was absolutely honest, deeply compassionate, highly sensitive, and spiritually mature in all his dealings with people. He was committed to serving his heavenly Father and his fellow human beings (in that order), prepared for his work through frequent periods of prayer and meditation, was deeply familiar with Scripture, and sought to help needy persons turn to him, in whom they could find ultimate peace, hope, and security.[21]

Often Jesus helped people through sermons, but he also debated skeptics, challenged individuals, healed the sick, talked with the needy, encouraged the downhearted, and modeled a godly lifestyle. In his contacts with people, he shared examples taken from real-life situations, and he constantly sought to stimulate others to think and act in accordance with divine principles. Apparently, he believed that some people need an understanding helper to listen, comfort, and discuss before they can learn from confrontation, challenge, advice-giving, or public preaching.

According to the Bible, Christians are to teach *all* that Christ commanded and taught.[22] Surely, this includes his teaching about God, authority, salvation, spiritual growth, prayer, the church, the future, angels, demons, and human nature. But Jesus also taught about marriage, parent-child relationships, obedience, race relations, care for the poor, and freedom for both women and men. He taught about personal issues such as sex, anxiety, fear, loneliness, doubt, pride, sin, and discouragement.

All these are issues that people bring to counselors today. When Jesus dealt with people, he frequently listened to the inquirers and accepted them before encouraging them to think or act differently. At times he told people what to do, but he also used skillful and divinely guided questioning to help individuals resolve their problems. Thomas was helped with his problem of doubting when Jesus showed the evidence; Peter learned from reflecting (with Jesus) about past mistakes; Mary of Bethany learned by listening; and Judas learned by painful experience.

Teaching all that Christ taught includes instruction in doctrine, but it also involves helping people get along better with God, with others, and with themselves. These are issues that concern almost everyone. Some learn from lectures, sermons, or books; others learn from personal Bible study or from discussion; many learn from hearing or telling stories; most of us learn from experiences; often people learn from formal or informal counseling; and perhaps all of us have learned from some combination of these approaches.

At the core of true Christian helping, private or public, is the influence of the Holy Spirit, the one whom Jesus identified as "the counselor."[23] His presence and influence make Christian counseling truly unique. It is he who gives the most effective counselor characteristics: love, joy, peace, patience, kindness, goodness, faithfulness, gentleness, and self-control.[24] He is the comforter or helper who teaches "all things," reminds us of Christ's sayings, convicts people of sin, and guides us into all truth.[25] When the counselor's work brings anxieties and confusion, these can be cast on God himself, who has promised to sustain and help.[26] Through prayer, meditation on the Scriptures, regular confessions of sin, and daily deliberate commitment to Christ, the counselor-teacher becomes an instrument through whom the Holy Spirit may work to comfort, help, teach, convict, or guide another human being. This should be the goal of every believer (pastor or lay person, professional counselor or nonprofessional): to be used by the Holy Spirit to touch lives, to change them, and to bring others toward both spiritual and psychological maturity.[27]

KEY POINTS FOR BUSY COUNSELORS

➤ Counseling can be both fulfilling and difficult work.

➤ The most effective counselors show characteristics, all of which can be developed. These counselor traits include:
- Psychological health and stability.
- A genuine interest in people.
- Empathy, which is the ability to "feel with" counselees.
- Personal warmth.
- Self-awareness.
- Tolerance for ambiguity, which means the ability to live with uncertainty.
- Awareness of one's values.
- Integrity, courage, and the genuine ability to care.

➤ Christian counselors have:
- Unique assumptions.
- Unique goals.
- Unique methods.
- Unique giftedness.

➤ There are many valid reasons to counsel, but beware of personal needs that satisfy the counselor but have potential to harm the counseling. These counselor needs include:
- The need for relationships.
- The need to control.
- The need to rescue.
- The need for information, built mostly on curiosity.

- The need for affirmation, acceptance or approval.
- The need for help with one's own problems.

➤ **All counselors make mistakes at times. These mistakes include:**
- Visiting instead of counseling.
- Trying to solve problems too quickly.
- Asking too many questions, too rapidly.
- Being disrespectful or judgmental.
- Getting too involved emotionally.
- Being artificial or distant.
- Being defensive when one feels threatened.

➤ **Counselors can be vulnerable if they are not alert. Be especially aware of:**
- Counselees who manipulate.
- Emotional entanglements with counselees, including countertransference.
- Counselee resistance.
- Feelings of sexual attraction involving the counselor and counselee.

➤ **Counselors can burn out easily. Be aware of the symptoms of burnout, including exhaustion, feelings of detachment from your counselees, and tendencies to withdraw.**

➤ **To prevent or recover from burnout, we need:**
- Spiritual strength.
- Support from others.
- Freedom from the drive to achieve.
- A realization that no one person can do everything.
- Regular times away from other people.
- Constant growth in our helping skills.
- Other people with whom we can share the load.

➤ **Every counselor should have counselor friends who can give perspective and remind us of the perfect counselor—Jesus Christ. He gives hope, strength, and guidance through his Holy Spirit. He is the ultimate counselor, often working through us.**

3

The Church and Counseling*

Rod had been out of seminary for only a few months, but he already had learned that ministry could be exciting and overwhelming at the same time. His little church was growing, and the people were enthusiastic. They were responding positively to Rod's leadership, and there were signs that the people were growing spiritually. Even so, the young pastor's days, and many of his nights, seemed to be filled with an unending stream of hurting people. Each was looking to him for encouragement, guidance, and counseling.

The only preparation Rod had received in seminary were two counseling courses. No professor had warned him that a pastor might have to deal with mate beating, father-daughter incest, fear, confusion, threats of suicide, homosexuality, alcoholism, drug abuse, depression, anxiety, guilt, family problems, eating disorders, chronic stress, and a host of other serious problems. Some appeared in the lives and families of the most respected leaders of the congregation, almost all of whom kept their problems hidden. Many of these were dedicated Christians who smiled and talked so confidently on the outside while they struggled on the inside. When he arrived to pastor his new flock, how could Rod have suspected the depth and variety of heart-breaking problems that he would encounter?

W ayne Oates was one of the early leaders in the field of pastoral counseling. Many years ago he wrote that no pastor, regardless of training, can choose whether or not to counsel with people. They *will* bring their problems to the pastor, whose choice "is not between counseling or not counseling, but between counseling in a disciplined and skilled way or counseling in an undisciplined and unskilled way."[1]

When Oates wrote these words, almost a half-century ago, it was not easy to counsel in a disciplined and skilled way. It still can be difficult. The problems we encounter appear to be more diverse, the culture is changing quickly, the needs are unending, and the available counseling techniques can be confusing and contradictory, even after all these years. But books and articles on therapy and people-helping roll off the presses with great regularity, supplemented by counseling courses, seminars, and hundreds of thousands of Internet resources.[2] While some of these resources, theories, and counselor training aids may be of questionable

* I am deeply grateful to Stephen Kemp of BILD International, a leading church-based theological education ministry, for his helpful insights in the preparation of this chapter.

validity, many can be very effective in helping pastors and other counselors to be more effective people-helpers.

Today counseling is widely accepted among Christians, but in some churches and in some parts of the world counseling is criticized and condemned as being unnecessary and even satanic. Some outspoken critics, including influential pastors, have attacked counselors and the counseling professions in emotional sermons, and have misled many believers into thinking that counseling is never needed, especially if it has any basis in psychology. Some well-meaning but naive Christian leaders have proposed simplistic "new methods" that are claimed to be uniquely Christian but are of debatable effectiveness.

Jesus, who is the Christian's example, spent many hours talking to needy people in groups and in face-to-face contact. The apostle Paul, who was very sensitive to the needs of hurting individuals, wrote that we who are strong must bear the weaknesses and help carry the burdens of those who are weaker.[3] Paul probably was writing about those who had doubts, fears, and sinful lifestyles, but his compassionate concern extended to many of the problems that counselors encounter today.

The biblical writers do not present people-helping as an option. It is a responsibility for every believer, including church leaders.[4] At times, counseling may seem too difficult or a waste of time, but it can be an effective, important, and necessary part of any ministry. And as most counselors quickly learn, there are times when counseling appears to be unsuccessful but eventually proves to be amazingly effective.

We have seen that some pastors and other Christian leaders are not gifted in this area nor called to counsel. Because of their temperaments, interests, skills, training, or calling, some Christian leaders avoid counseling, preferring instead to devote their time and gifts to other ministries. This is a legitimate decision, especially if it is made in consultation with fellow believers.

Each of us must be careful, however, not to turn away from counseling. This can be a personally enriching, potentially powerful, and biblically based way of ministering to others. Despite its difficulty, people from a variety of backgrounds can learn effective counseling skills. That could include you.

Congregations and Counseling

When I was a young professor, my wife and I were invited to accompany one of the college choirs on its spring concert tour. Every night for three weeks, the choir sang in a different church, and afterward the students dispersed to spend the night in the homes of various church members. My wife, Julie, and I almost always stayed with the pastor's family. Usually, we would end our days sitting around the table, drinking coffee and talking about ministry. Because I taught psychology and counseling, the conversations invariably went to the challenge of counseling.

During those late-night conversations, we met a number of pastors like Rod, people who were doing a great job in their churches but who felt swamped by all the counseling needs in their congregations and communities. Looking back, I think God used those pastors and their spouses to open my mind to the tremendous potential of counseling in and through the church. These conversations also stimulated my thinking about the church, its purpose, and some of its challenges. After the choir tour, I started reading about counseling in congregations, spending more time with pastors, writing about how people are helped in the church, and eventually moving to spend most of my teaching career on seminary faculties.

I used to think of churches as buildings, as gathering places where Christians and others go at least once a week to do religious things. For many years I assumed that the best churches had bigger buildings, numerous programs, well-planned and polished church meetings (with high-quality music and powerful pastor-speakers), a missions program that supported missionaries overseas, and large numbers of people who came every week to attend church meetings. I knew what I believed as a Christian and tended to evaluate churches and their members in terms of how closely their beliefs aligned with mine. I am not proud of this perspective, but I think it was shared by most of the church people I knew.

I don't think in these ways anymore.[5] I no longer think of the church in terms of buildings or denominations or places where people gather. I see churches as different-sized communities of people, at different places in their spiritual journeys, joining with others to worship, to learn, to grow, to serve, to give. I've come to view church communities as caring groups of developing people who sometimes come together for crucially important corporate worship but who also seek to live every day in ways that show their dedication to Christ and their love for others. No church is perfect, and none of us fully reaches our ideals, but ideally, church communities are safe environments where people can struggle, grow, care, share, and learn how to be like Jesus. How does this apply to counseling and the church?

> While every Christian has a responsibility to help and counsel others, it is probable that counseling is one of the spiritual gifts that is given for building up the church and strengthening individual believers. As described in Romans 12, 1 Corinthians 12, and Ephesians 4, these gifts are more than natural abilities. They are something extra, given to believers by the Holy Spirit. Although all believers have been given one or more spiritual gifts, none of us has them all. Some Christians are especially gifted teachers, pastors, evangelists, or administrators; others are gifted as people-helpers or counselors.
>
> In Romans 12:8 we read about the gift of exhortation. The Greek word is *paraklesis*, which means "coming alongside to help." The word implies admonishing, confronting, supporting, and encouraging people to face the future. All of this sounds much like counseling, and it all refers to a gift given by God to a select group of believers.
>
> From this it should not be concluded that only the specially gifted are to be involved in counseling. In this respect, people-helping is similar to evangelism or teaching. Although some believers have a special gift of evangelism (Ephesians 4:11), every Christian is to be a witness, seeking to win men and women to Christ. Some Christians are specially gifted teachers (Romans 12:7; Ephesians 4:11), but all of us have the responsibility of teaching our children and others. In the same way, we must all be burden-bearers and people-helpers, even though some may have a special gift of counseling.[6]

The counseling gift appears in many who are church leaders, but care-givers are not limited to the people we know as pastors or elders. In your church, the best counselor or other care-giver might be you. Or the best care-giver may be some other person who can be encouraged, mentored, and trained in care-giving/counseling skills.

Care and Counseling

Counseling attempts to provide encouragement and guidance for those who are facing losses, decisions, or disappointments. Counseling can stimulate personality growth and development. It helps people cope more effectively with the problems of living, with inner conflict, and with crippling emotions. Counseling is able to assist individuals, family members, and married couples to resolve interpersonal tensions or relate effectively to one another. And counseling can help those whose life patterns are self-defeating and causing unhappiness. The Christian counselor seeks to bring people into a personal relationship with Jesus Christ and to help them find forgiveness and relief from the crippling effects of sin and guilt. Ultimately, the Christian care-giver hopes to help others become disciples of Christ and disciplers of others.

Pastoral Care. Some people may find it useful to make a distinction between pastoral care, pastoral counseling, and pastoral psychotherapy. Of the three terms, pastoral care is the broadest in scope. It refers to the church's overall ministries of healing, sustaining, guiding, and reconciling people to God and to one another. Sometimes called "the care of souls," this can include preaching and teaching, but more often it refers to shepherding people, to nurturing, caring in times of need, sometimes disciplining and administering the sacraments. Since the time of Christ, the church has been committed to pastoral care. Despite the term "pastoral," this care is given by all believers. It appears to be an expectation of elders, and certainly it is not limited to ordained clergy.

Pastoral Counseling. This is a more specialized part of pastoral care that involves helping individuals, families, or groups as they cope with the pressures and crises of life. Usually, it is done by pastors with theological education and often with specialized training in pastoral counseling. It uses a wide variety of healing methods to help people deal with problems in ways that are consistent with sound biblical and theological teaching. The ultimate goal is to help counselees experience healing, learn coping and relational skills, and grow both personally and spiritually.

The Bible teaches that all believers are to bear the burdens of one another[7] and that all believers are priests.[8] From this we could conclude that pastoral types of counseling can and should be a ministry of sensitive and caring Christians, whether or not they are ordained as clergy. In the pages that follow, pastoral counseling and Christian counseling will be used interchangeably.

Pastoral Psychotherapy. This term appears to be used with less frequency than it was a few years ago. It refers to a long-term, in-depth helping process that attempts to bring fundamental changes in the counselee's personality, spiritual values, and ways of thinking. It is a form of help-giving that seeks to remove blocks, often from the past, that inhibit personal and spiritual growth. It is the work of a trained specialist and rarely will be mentioned in this book.

Christian Counseling and Spiritual Direction

The world in which we live has taught us to value autonomy and individualism. Even within the church, we tend to see spirituality as something that is personal and private, but this view is changing. A growing movement of forward-looking Christians is reminding us what the church has known for centuries but has forgotten during the past few decades, especially among Protestants: *Isolation generally leads to spiritual barrenness. Spiritual formation and transformation must be nurtured through community.* We need companions on the spiritual journey.[9] About a century ago, when counseling and psychotherapy began to emerge as separate areas of expertise, the fascination with science was strong and getting stronger. Materialism, hedonism, and secularism were prevailing philosophies, at least in the West, and within the helping professions there was little place for religion and spirituality, both of which were considered to be outdated and nonscientific. When Freud wrote that religion was a narcotic and an illusion, most psychologists and professional mental-health experts agreed. But as the twentieth century progressed, the worship of science, consumerism, and individualism began to fade. Many people realized that their lives were bankrupt and spiritually empty. Even faithful Christians started to see that despite the benefits and impact of church programs and busy activities, there was an emptiness in their lives and a longing for deeper encounters with God.

All of this has led to a worldwide revival of interest in spirituality. For most outside the church, it is a spirituality based on human initiative and creativity or rooted in ancient spiritual traditions that know nothing of the biblical God.[10] Some secular counselors still cling to their past training and traditional therapies, failing to see or acknowledge the roles of religion or spirituality in the lives of their counselees.[11] Others—their numbers are increasing—are beginning to acknowledge that spirituality plays a significant role in many lives and cannot be ignored in counseling.[12] For Christians, including Christian counselors, there has been a remarkable interest in the practice of *spiritual direction.*

The descriptions of this practice differ, but one of the best definitions appeared in a book written more than twenty years ago.[13] The authors define spiritual direction as help given by one Christian to another, which enables the recipient to:

- More effectively pay attention to God's personal communication.
- Respond to this God who communicates personally.
- Grow in intimacy with this God.
- Live out the consequences of this relationship.[14]

The focus of spiritual direction is on experience, not ideas. The emphasis is not on advice giving, discipling, authoritarian direction, teaching, or dealing with personal problems. Instead, spiritual direction is a process in which "a person seeking help in cultivating a deeper personal relationship with God meets with another for prayer and conversation that is focused on" two major issues: "increasing awareness of God in the midst of life experiences and facilitating surrender to God's will."[15] The goal is to develop a deeper relationship with God that goes beyond the programs and hyperactivity that characterize many churches.[16] As it has grown in popularity, spiritual direction has emerged as an area of expertise that is the work of trained specialists. Now, however, Christians are beginning to recognize that spiritual direction is a church-wide function that is the responsibility of all believers, even those who are not specially trained.

David Benner and Gary Moon are both Christian clinical psychologists and spiritual directors. In their teaching and writing they acknowledge that the lines of distinction between spiritual direction and counseling are not always clear, especially in people who seek spiritual direction but who also experience depression, anxiety, and other types of psychological distress. Counseling tends to be more problem-centered, while spiritual direction is Spirit-centered. Counseling seeks to resolve problems, but spiritual direction focuses more on helping the person grow in his or her relationship with God. Despite these differences, Christian counselors often seek the spiritual growth of their counselees. Whereas the focus is on problem resolution and a relief of symptoms, the Christian counselor does not hesitate to use spiritual practices and other religious resources, especially if the counselee has given permission for this.[17]

Counseling and the Emergent Church

When they hear the word *church*, most people probably think of buildings, denominations, or groups of people. The church, however, is undergoing some radical changes as a new generation assumes leadership and begins to shape the church in ways that their parents or grandparents might not recognize. Erwin Raphael McManus, for example, is a nontraditional pastor who believes that the church of Jesus Christ is "an unstoppable force," even though most churches have lost touch with the contemporary culture and are widely viewed as irrelevant and outdated, especially by people who have been raised in a media-saturated, high-tech, postmodern society.[18] McManus is lead pastor (not "senior" pastor—that term is rarely used in these newer churches) of Mosaic, an innovative and international congregation that began by meeting in a nightclub that was unoccupied on Sunday mornings.

Brian McLaren is a writer, speaker, and pastor who travels internationally, proclaiming a "revolution that will affect, to one degree or another, every church in the world."[19] Reggie McNeal would agree. He writes that at least in North America the church is "on life support. It is living off the work, money, and energy of previous generations from a previous world order" that fails to connect with the majority of people today. "The church of Jesus is moving into a postmodern world," McNeal writes in a deeply insightful book. "The world is profoundly different than it was at the middle of the last century . . . [but] the church largely has responded with heavy infusions of denial, believing that culture will come to its senses and come back around to the church" the way it has been in the past.[20]

These books are not written by disgruntled former traditional church members who enjoy shooting at the churches and denominations where they grew up. These are a host of writers with a similar passion, men and women who are dedicated followers of Jesus Christ who have committed their lives to various types of ministry and are respected church leaders. They believe that the message of the Gospel never changes and must not be diluted, but the ways in which we present the message must always be sensitive to the worldviews of the people we are called to lead. These contemporary church leaders and their congregations believe with all their hearts that the Great Commission of Jesus will not be fulfilled so long as we lose touch with the culture and build churches that are unaware of what God is doing in the world today.

It is true that some of those who build these new and more culturally attuned churches have a weak biblical literacy, a tendency to capitulate to popular culture, and a materialistic self-centeredness despite their social outreach. While the most influential leaders often have formal theological training and mature spiritual perspectives, many of the newer churches are led by enthusiastic but sometimes undisciplined leaders who resist accountability and are biblically shallow.

Seminary professor Robert Webber has written one of the most in-depth analyses of the contemporary church, at least in North America.[21] His discussions about the Evangelical Protestant church could apply equally well to churches and to denominations that have different theological persuasions. The three broad church groups that Webber identifies consist of sincere Christ followers who are united in their desire to serve God, bring others to Christ, and live in accordance with biblical principles. But they build their churches and do ministry in significantly different ways.

According to Webber, the *traditional Evangelicals* emerged with their greatest strength after the Second World War. Their churches and seminaries are built on a modern worldview with the emphasis on verbal communication and rational thinking, local churches headed by a pastor-leader, information-centered Sunday Schools, traditional worship that includes older hymns (perhaps interspersed with a few more contemporary music styles), and rules that guide behavior and spiritual life.

The second group, *pragmatic Evangelicals,* dominated the last quarter of the twentieth century and still thrive with their contemporary seeker-sensitive services, innovative worship, awareness of meeting needs, up-beat music, and use of technology. Many of these have become huge mega-churches, often headed by pastors who operate as CEOs and run the church like a business. Many of these pastors and their congregations are very supportive of Christian counseling. Despite the worldwide growth and current dominance of pragmatic churches, Webber believes that these churches are transitional and will fade after perhaps a one-hundred-year life, eventually giving way to the *younger Evangelicals.*

More often these are known as emergent churches (or sometimes as missional churches) that have special appeal to a younger generation, although most have a growing cadre of older believers, many over sixty-five, who believe that these churches are the wave of the future.[22] The emergent churches have a more postmodern worldview. They emphasize relationships and prefer interaction and experiential worship in place of the pulpit-based sermons that characterize their grandparents' churches or the polished presentations and big seeker-sensitive gatherings of the pragmatic mega-churches. Return to Table 1–1 on page 13 and read the characteristics of the contemporary postmodern culture. These same traits are seen clearly in the emergent churches. And their views of counseling more closely fit the new Christian counseling of Table 1–2 than traditional counseling approaches.[23]

These three church types do not represent distinct groups separated by firm boundaries. Many of us who are older grew up in the traditionalist churches where we were nurtured and taught about Christ. These churches continue strong, although their congregations tend to be aging and many are losing their younger people, who either forsake the church completely or go to another church that suits their preferences. The pragmatic seeker-sensitive churches have their roots in the traditional congregations. Probably more than any other person, Bill Hybels has been used by God to launch and grow the pragmatic church movement. Willow Creek Community Church, which he pastors, is a huge and highly influential church that continues to be instrumental in bringing many "unchurched" people to Christ and then guiding them into subsequent spiritual growth. The resulting Willow Creek Association continues to grow as thousands of churches around the world seek to emulate many of the approaches that Willow Creek has developed. Saddleback Community Church in California has had an equally huge impact, especially through the books and messages of its "purpose-driven" pastor Rick Warren. With their creative programs and relevant ministries, these churches continue to attract people of all ages, including thousands who are younger. As they grow older, many will remain in these churches, but there appears to be a dissatisfaction with what many consider to be the slick, performance-dominated worship meetings built around high-profile preachers who often appear on huge video screens. Many Christians apparently prefer the smaller, more interactive and people-friendly emergent churches.

These emergent churches are less visible, but there are many who believe that their numbers and impact will increase as the postmodern generation swells, the Baby Boomer generation gets older, and Baby Boomer values begin to fade. As the emergent church movement spreads, both in North America and around the world, there will be changes in the ways churches communicate, educate, do youth ministry, worship, develop people spiritually, evangelize, reach out through missions, utilize art, speak to social issues, train leaders, and develop pastors. It is likely, as well, that counseling and pastoral care will be done in ways that are different from what we do today.

These changes will not be limited to emergent churches, whatever their future. A perceptive and theologically astute friend reminded me that there are many parts of the North American and worldwide church that are untouched by the emergent church. Roman Catholic, Orthodox, mainline Protestant, and especially the rapidly growing Pentecostal churches are changing, but in their own new directions. In the United States, African American churches continue to make an impact, but many are unaware of the emergent conversations. "I love what newer churches are doing in terms of being relevant, understanding, and engaging with culture, being authentic, and worshiping well," my friend wrote. But he suggests that the younger believers who make up many emergent churches are far too transient to have the kind of authenticity that they claim and that only can develop over time. Further, some still lack the intergenerational dimension that characterized biblical community in the Old and New Testaments, both for the short-term benefit of everyone in the fellowship and the long-term benefit of being an institution that endures for generations. Although these churches are engaged with culture, they are only going to experience lasting impact if that engagement can be sustained over time.

Whatever your view of the church today, perhaps you will agree that the culture is undergoing a major paradigm shift from a modernist to a postmodern era. Living through dramatic change can be challenging, exciting, and scary, all at the same time. But that is where God has placed us to minister and to do the work of counseling.

The Church as a Caring Community

We all know that Jesus often talked with individuals about their personal needs, and he met frequently with small groups. Chief among these was the little band of disciples that he prepared to "take over" after his ascension into heaven. It was during one of these times with the disciples that Jesus first mentioned the church.[24]

In the years that followed, it was this church of Jesus Christ that continued his ministry of teaching, evangelizing, ministering, and care-giving. These activities were not seen as the special responsibility of pastors and other church leaders; they were done by ordinary believers working, sharing, and caring both for one another and for the nonbelievers outside the body. If we read Acts[25] and the Epistles, it becomes clear that the church was not only a worshiping, evangelizing, teaching, discipling community. It was also an extremely caring community.

Caring communities are groups of people who have a strong commitment to the group and a common interest in giving encouragement, guidance, and healing when there are psychological, spiritual, relational, or other needs. For many years, mental-health professionals have known the value of therapeutic groups in which the participants care for one another by giving and receiving support, accountability, guidance, and encouragement that might not be possible otherwise. Of course such groups can be harmful, especially when they become uncontrolled encounters that criticize and embarrass the participants instead of building them up or challenging them to openness and more effective behavior. If conducted by a sensitive leader, however, group sessions can be very effective therapeutic experiences for all the people involved.

Of course, caring groups need not be limited to counselees meeting with one another and with a trained counselor. Families, church cell groups, study groups, trusted friends, professional colleagues, employee groups, and other small bands of people often provide the help that is needed both in times of crisis and as individuals face the daily challenges of living. Most often this is done naturally, without any formal group organization and without the help of a counselor. In all of society, the church has the greatest potential for being a caring and healing community. Local bodies of believers can bring a sense of belonging to the members, opportunities to develop skills, support to those who feel weak, healing to troubled individuals, and guidance as people make decisions and move toward maturity. It is sad that many churches are not caring communities. They are more like social clubs where everybody smiles, nobody ever admits to having problems, and congregations are far from the dynamic growth-producing fellowship that Christ intended them to be.[26]

In his final words before going back to heaven, Jesus told his followers to go and make disciples of all nations, baptizing them in the name of the Father and the Son and the Holy Spirit, and teaching the new believers to obey all the commands that Jesus had given.[27] The church was created to fulfill the Great Commission of making disciples (this includes evangelism) and teaching. The early believers came together in a fellowship, or *koinonia*, that involved a community relationship with one another, a partnership that actively promoted the Gospel and built up believers, and a mutual sharing of insights, experiences, worship, needs, and material possessions. The true church always has been headed by Jesus Christ, who showed us how to evangelize, teach, and live. By his life and instruction, he pointed us to the practical as well as to the theoretical aspects of Christianity. He summarized his teaching in two laws: to love God and to love others. As a result, the early believers "turned the world upside down" and made a significant impact on their culture.

All of this is meant to take place within the confines of a group of believers, each of whom has been given the gifts and abilities needed to build up the church. As a group, guided by a pastor leading a team of other chosen leaders, the believers direct their attention and activities upward through worship of God, outward through evangelism and community care-giving, and inward through teaching, camaraderie, and mutual burden-bearing. When any of these is missing, the group is unbalanced, the believers are incomplete, and the church is not able to be a completely caring community.

Does Psychology Help?

To increase their counseling effectiveness, many church leaders have turned to the insights of psychologists and other social-service or mental-health professionals. Thousands of books, seminars, sermons, radio programs, and magazine articles have drawn on psychology to help people understand themselves better and learn how to live more effectively. Some church leaders and individual Christians have so enthusiastically embraced psychology that they have elevated various Christian psychologists to near-prophetic roles.[28]

Historically, however, there have been tension, mistrust, and bias on both sides of what became a strong psychology-religion divide. In some places the mistrust and antagonism persist, but the adversarial mentality has been changing as both psychologists and Christian leaders are beginning to appreciate the expertise of one another and as initial efforts at collaboration are producing useful results.[29]

In the pages of this book you will find frequent references to the Bible. God's Word *is* a healing balm for mental-emotional disorders. It speaks to people today about contemporary issues because its message is timeless and applicable cross-culturally. It has profound and lasting relevance to the counselor's work and to the needs of his or her counselees.

But the Bible never claims to be a textbook on counseling. It deals with anxiety, loneliness, discouragement, relationships, marriage problems, grief, anger, fear, parent-child relations, and a host of other situations related to counseling, but it never was meant to be God's sole revelation about people-helping. Even many of psychology's critics acknowledge that biological and chemical influences can have a great impact on the causes and treatment of problems that people bring to counselors. In medicine, teaching, and other "people-centered" helping fields, we have been permitted to learn much about God's creation through science and academic study. Psychology should also be used according to what it contributes to the work of the counselor or to the ministries of the church.

During the past century or more, psychological investigators have developed careful research tools for studying human behavior and have disseminated this information in printed form and over the Internet. As they have worked with their counselees, professional care-givers have learned about the causes of behavior and how they can help people experience lasting change. In recent years the long-term emphasis on pathology has been supplemented by the new field of positive psychology with its growing understanding of human strengths, optimism, and the nature of forgiveness, hope, courage, well-being, wisdom, and emotional intelligence.[30]

Psychological knowledge is far from complete, and neither is it error free. Many of the critics' complaints are valid, and many have been raised by psychologists themselves. But careful psychological research, observation, and data analysis have led to a vast reservoir of conclusions that are known to help counselees and people who want to be effective people-helpers. Even those who would dismiss the field of psychology frequently use psychological terms in their writings or sermons and psychologically derived techniques in their counseling.

The following chapters assume that all truth comes from God, including truth about the people that he created. He has revealed this truth through the Bible, God's written Word to human beings, but he also has permitted us to discover truth through experience, through research investigation, and through the insights that come through reflection, observation, and the words of books and sermons. Discovered truth must always be consistent with, and tested against, the norm of revealed biblical truth. But we limit our counseling effectiveness when we pretend that the discoveries of psychology, neuropsychology, psychobiology, human genetics, and related fields have nothing to contribute to the understanding and solution of problems. We compromise our integrity when we overtly reject psychology but then smuggle its concepts into our counseling—sometimes naively and without even realizing what we are doing.

But how do we wade through the overload of psychological techniques, theories, technical terms, and Internet information to find insights that truly are helpful? The answer involves finding a guide—some person or persons who are committed followers of Jesus Christ, familiar with the psychological and counseling literature, trained in counseling and in research methods (so the accuracy of psychologists' conclusions can be evaluated), and effective as counselors. It is crucial that the guides be committed to the inspiration and authority of the Bible, both as the standard against which all psychology must be tested and as the written Word of God with which all valid counseling must agree.

The author of this book and others who have critiqued portions of the manuscript together have the preparation and experience to assist Christian counselors in the joyful but demanding task of helping others. None of us claims to be perfect and error-free, but we're committed to doing our best to distill accurate and useful information that can provide a comprehensive guide for counselors. We have many competent colleagues around the world who have a similar commitment, many of whom are mentioned in the pages of this book. As you read, you will discover that this is not meant to be a cookbook volume of never-fail recipes designed for producing master counselors. Human beings are far too complicated to always be helped in the same ways. At times, even the most skilled and knowledgeable counselors have failures, sometimes because of the counselor's misperceptions or errors but also because some counselees cannot or will not change. Even so, improvements are more likely when the counselor has both an understanding of the problems that people bring to counseling and an awareness of how to intervene. The following chapters have been written to help with this understanding and to provide some of the needed knowledge.

Church–Psychology Collaboration

Dr. Mark McMinn is a professional psychologist, researcher, and professor who has a passion for stimulating collaboration between psychologists and churches. While committed to "the burgeoning professions of counseling, clinical psychology, and psychiatry," McMinn has grieved what he calls "the loss of the historic role of the Church in promoting emotional and spiritual health and caring for troubled souls." The result was the creation of a Center for Church-Psychology Collaboration, which existed "to help reclaim the connection between spirituality, mental health, and community that formed the basis of soul care prior to modernity." In its short history,[31] the Center trained students and pastors, conducted church evaluations and consultations, did surveys, led seminars, and stimulated an increasing number of research articles on pastor-psychology cooperation.[32]

It is well documented that psychologists are less interested in religious beliefs and activities than the general public.[33] The growing interest in spirituality has attracted the attention of many psychologists,[34] but it is still common to find counselors who dismiss religion as harmful or superficial, who lack respect for clergy, and who have personal animosity toward religion. It is understandable, then, that pastors are reluctant to refer their parishioners to professional counselors who may not be spiritually sensitive. Deeply religious counselees, in turn, prefer to consult counselors (including professional counselors) who have similar spiritual beliefs. If a theological disparity arises between the counselor and counselee, the religious counselees are more guarded and less willing to disclose intimate topics openly.[35]

Most often, psychologist-pastor collaboration has involved pastors referring their parishioners to psychologists or other mental-health professionals who can give more intensive, specialized treatment. Also common is the practice of pastors seeking consultation from psychologists to get helpful information about specific issues and counseling cases. Referral or consultation almost never goes the other way; psychologists rarely refer clients to pastors or seek information from church leaders.

But all of this is beginning to change. Psychologists and church leaders are coming to see the values of collaboration and are working together on projects such as establishing crisis hot lines and support groups, providing and evaluating community services, doing seminars together, producing information brochures and other publications, meeting together to pool their perspectives on given counselees, working with chaplaincy programs, and developing supportive recovery groups.[36] The most effective collaboration occurs when the pastor and psychologist:

- Trust and respect each other as equals.
- View each other as professionals.
- Value the expertise that the other brings.
- Share similar values and, in ideal situations, have similar faith commitments.
- Have similar goals for their clients.
- Are creative enough to think of ways in which psychology and theology can be applied within each other's setting.
- Are willing to find innovative ways for working together beyond the pastor referring parishioners for treatment.

Trusting relationships like this take time to build, and there are skeptics on both sides who are reluctant to get involved. Whoever initiates the collaboration may be rebuffed and disappointed, but genuine partnerships can develop and continue to develop in ways that help the people we counsel and that bring glory to God.

KEY POINTS FOR BUSY COUNSELORS

➤ Unlike counseling, spiritual direction
  - Does not focus on problem-solving or advice-giving.
  - Involves at least two people praying and meeting together to cultivate greater supernatural awareness and deeper relationships with God.

➤ Counselors need to be aware of changes taking place in churches today:
  - *Traditional churches* tend to worship using older hymns, have strong pastoral leaders, emphasize preaching and rational thinking, often have rules to guide behavior, and utilize traditional counseling approaches.
  - *Pragmatic, "seeker-sensitive" churches* have innovative worship, try to meet needs, emphasize reaching out, often have CEO-type leaders and high-quality, technologically sophisticated programs.
  - *Emergent churches* tend to have younger congregations that are sensitive to postmodernism, value relationships, and prefer worship that involves all members of the congregation and uses art, stories, and the different senses. These church members prefer more informal counseling and coaching to traditional therapy and counseling approaches.

➤ In all of society the church has the greatest potential for being a caring and healing community. It also has a divine mandate to care and to heal.

➤ Increasing numbers of church leaders now see that the insights of psychology can be extremely valuable in understanding and helping people who come for counseling.

➤ All counselors have failures, sometimes because of the counselor's inability, misperceptions, or error, but also because the counselee cannot or will not change.

➤ When church-psychology relationships are characterized by mutual trust and respect, the collaboration between pastors and mental-health professionals can have a significantly positive impact on ministry and on the people we seek to help through counseling.

4

The Community and Counseling

The message was crisp and to the point. It came a few minutes before this chapter was started:

"Please pray for us. We have to depend on the Lord's protection. There are no police officers, no judge, no mayor, no school, and no major activities going on except church. Nobody knows what is going on now and what is going to happen next.

"The problem started with political parties and people being unhappy with the government. They asked the president to resign, but he refuses. So his adversaries have organized themselves and are going from city to city to take over. Everywhere they go, they try to take control by oppressing police officers. If the officers fight back, they have major conflicts. In many areas they are being killed. This morning they were only a few miles from our city. Roads are blocked, and robberies are taking place everywhere. Local police who feel so vulnerable have left their posts vacant. If there is a problem, there is no one to go to but God.

"Everybody is running out of goods. I have to go now." This e-mail is not completed . . .

The writer of these words is a friend, a pastor, a counselor, a community leader overseas. He knows about counseling, counsels a lot of people, and even has translated a counseling book into the language of his country. But in times like this, nobody will come to his office for a counseling session. If he wants to help people during these perilous days of intense stress, he has to leave his office and go into the community. Even in less traumatic settings, Christian counselors are learning that going into the community often is the best way to counsel.

When he created human beings, the Lord God declared that it was not good for a man to be alone. So God created woman and the human race began.

It wasn't long before people were in conflict with one another. It started with Adam and Eve. Then the sibling rivalry between Cain and Abel led to murder, and soon the whole earth was filled with violence.[1] After the Great Flood, the conflicts resumed,[2] and they have continued until this day, as my friend who wrote the e-mail message knows. Throughout the centuries, a few hermits have sought to live solitary lives, far from the maddening crowd, but most of us can appreciate John Donne's oft-quoted statement that "no man is an island, entire of itself." Human beings may compete with one another and live in conflict, but we also need each other. It isn't good or healthy to exist in isolation. And it isn't always possible.

Despite these conclusions, there are parts of the world where individuals, companies, churches, and governments still place high value on independence and rugged individualism. In much of the Western world, for example, there is talk about cooperation and mutual support, but we admire and reward "self-made" people who "make it on their own." We compete with groups that could work with us as partners and often assume that personal problems are best handled alone. At least until recently, counseling was usually a one-to-one relationship with one counselor, one counselee, one hour in duration, one session per week. This way of thinking is changing.

Counseling between two individuals can be helpful, but the benefits are likely to be greater when the counselee is part of one or more supportive caring groups. Often the family gives this encouragement, or the help comes from friends or from colleagues at work. Ideally, the local body of believers should also be giving much of the fellowship, guidance, feedback, accountability, acceptance, and support that individuals, couples, and others need. Surely, something is lacking when Christian counseling ignores the fellowship of believers and attempts to help people completely apart from the community of faith.

Community Counseling

Most counselors would agree that behavior, including problem behavior, is influenced by the social and physical environment of the counselee. Instead of the traditional views that look only inside the counselee to find the cause of problems, now it is more common to assume that human problems occur as an interaction between what is inside our brains and our bodies, the people around us, and our environments.

None of this is meant to imply that individuals are not responsible for their actions. If a young person in your church or neighborhood attempts suicide or becomes addicted to drugs, ultimately that person is responsible for his or her own behavior. The causes of this behavior may be found within the individual, perhaps the result of confused thinking, a low self-concept, an unwillingness to avoid sin, or an inability to change because of chemical imbalances or other physical influences. But the counselor also looks outside of the counselee for the influence of family tension, peer pressure, or stresses coming from school, work, and dating relationships. Some counselors still insist that any problem or harmful behavior can be stopped willfully by confessing and forsaking personal sin, but such a view builds on a simplistic and limited view of the complexity of human behavior. Despite their best intentions, human beings cannot defeat sin or addictions with their own power. Paul openly struggled with his own temptations when he wrote to the Romans. He noted that "it seems to be a fact of life that when I want to do what is right, I inevitably do what is wrong." But he could thank God that the answer to this human struggle is in Jesus Christ.

Because of this diversity, there is no one way to do effective counseling. Approaches differ depending on the particular situation and all its unique components. Often the counselor and counselee still talk together in private, discussing inner struggles and insecurities, but sometimes family members or people from the community join in the problem-solving process. There is growing recognition that the community which sometimes creates problems also can be a strong source of support, a place for learning, and a safe environment for healing.

Community counseling is an approach to helping that may involve:

- *Building social support* by promoting more cooperation, better communication, and unity in a family or community organization (including the church) so there is greater support and less isolation among the members.
- *Getting help from others*, including people in the community who have specialized expertise and are able to contribute to the counselor's understanding or to the counselee's problem-solving efforts.
- *Teaching social skills* so people are more competent in coping with stress, relating to others, and managing their lives.
- *Equipping lay people,* giving them training and encouragement so they can provide counseling, education, tangible assistance, self-help group support, and other aid to needy people in their communities.
- *Preventing problems* by anticipating the future and helping both individuals and groups of people develop the skills and make the life changes that will prevent future problems from developing.
- *Changing the community,* sometimes by taking social, political, or other action to reduce poverty, stress, unemployment, pornography, violence, ignorance, sinful behavior, or other environmental problem-causing influences.

Community counseling is an approach that seeks to improve the environment instead of concentrating solely on helping the victims of a community's shortcomings.[3] The community counselor may deal with groups as well as with individuals. At times, he or she may be an educator or a social activist as well as a counselor. The community counselor must be aware of the social forces affecting individuals, be willing to use new techniques and skills, recognize that the counselor is only one positive resource among many, and work alongside others to stimulate caring, support, and competence within the community. Community counselors do not resist individual counseling given in a private office. They know that the counselor's office often provides a safe, quiet place for people to talk in confidence with a caring person, away from the turmoil and stresses of their homes, neighborhoods, or workplaces. But this is not the only way to help people, and it is not always the best. Sometimes counselors, including Christian counselors, have to reach out to include and intervene in the community.

Of course, pastors and other Christians have been doing this for centuries. Sadly, many congregations still retreat to their church buildings and isolate themselves from "the world" in which they live. There are counselors who work within the confines of their offices and seem oblivious to the growing needs of their own communities or to the ways in which counselees are influenced by their communities. But effective counselors do not ignore the community. Christian counselors do not overlook the body of believers who can exist to care for the needy, welcome strangers, do good to all people, heal the broken-hearted, bring forgiveness to the repentant, comfort the sorrowing, hold up the weak, and point all people to Christ. It may be difficult for one church to fulfill all these responsibilities, but surely it is the Christian counselor's duty to work with others to make the local body of believers more caring and compassionate—in conformity to biblical teaching.

The Environment and Counseling

Have you ever tried to counsel in a place that is noisy, cluttered, too hot, or filled with distractions? Have you considered the stress that could come from living in such an environment? The places where we live and work can contribute to personal problems and can interfere with counseling effectiveness, but these places also can contribute to improvement. An effective way to help people or to prevent further problems is to change existing conditions or find ways to remove counselees from stressful environments. When this is not possible, the role of the counselor is to help the counselees understand the role of their environments and learn to adapt to their difficult circumstances.

The influence of environments and surrounding circumstances is illustrated in the experience of Rachael Kaplan, a professor at University of Michigan. When she moved from an office overlooking a plain wall and barren courtyard to an office that gave her a treetop view, she noticed that her whole attitude became brighter. She felt invigorated, more focused, and less fatigued when she could sit at her computer or talk on the phone and watch birds and squirrels in the trees outside. Her move illustrated the concept of *restorative environments*, the research-backed idea that mental clarity and physical healing both come from exposure to brighter environments, especially those that involve nature. One study found that office workers with a view of nature liked their jobs more, enjoyed better health, and reported greater life satisfaction. Other researchers investigated the improvement rates of patients recovering from abdominal surgery. The patients whose rooms overlooked trees recovered faster and were released from the hospital sooner than patients whose rooms overlooked brick walls. Even a small exposure to nature makes a difference. Children living in high-rise apartments had better test scores and greater capacity for paying attention in school when their windows overlooked something as minor as a tiny spot of green grass and one tree.[4]

Nature is not the only environmental influence on behavior. Four other environmental influences are of special importance to counseling.[5]

Noise. In urban areas especially, people are constantly bombarded by noise from traffic, airplanes, radios, construction, barking dogs, people talking, telephones, background television, and other sources of "noise pollution." While some sounds (such as desired music) can be soothing and relaxing, other noises can increase tension and irritability, prevent sleep, and interfere with job performance.[6] People who live in noisy environments often find the perpetual sound to be annoying, disruptive, and stress-producing. In addition, it is well known that noise can hinder work productivity.

Crowding. Most people enjoy a little—but not too much—distance between themselves and other human beings. We like stimulation from others, but too much or too little can be distracting or harmful to our feelings of well-being. We like to be near people, but we don't like to be crowded. At times we need a quiet place where we can withdraw for a time of solitude. When such withdrawal is impossible (as often is true in crowded cities, campus dormitories, ships at sea, and many work settings), tensions develop, tempers often flare, and people can feel trapped.

Architecture. Architects and interior decorators have long recognized that room shape, colors, type and arrangement of furniture, decorations (such as pictures, plants, or books), temperature, and lighting can all affect people psychologically. These architectural and design effects have a subtle bearing on work productivity, interpersonal relations, attitudes, emotions, and the extent to which people feel comfortable and relaxed. Think of the implications of these findings on the way in which you decorate your office. Ponder, as well, how the design of church buildings and meeting places can impact worship. And what do these buildings communicate to the newcomers who attend church gatherings?

Weather. It is well known that weather can have a great influence on human behavior. Everyone knows that people feel sluggish and tired when the heat and humidity are high. Investigations of Seasonal Affective Disorders (SAD) have confirmed that long dark winters with lack of sunshine can lead to depression, increased alcoholism, and suicide rates.[7] Weather also can influence accident rates, crime, academic performance, productivity, degree of participation in social activities, mood, subjective feelings, and attitudes. When weather conditions are extreme—as in heat waves, blizzards, or intense storms—an additional stress is applied to everyone. People who are under stress already may see these weather pressures as "the last straw," which then produce dramatic changes in behavior. Following a major snowstorm in one large city, for example, travel was restricted, people were forced to stay home, frustration and domestic quarrels increased, and the number of family murders rose sharply.

These environmental influences affect counseling in two important ways. First, as we have seen, they can create stress and complicate counseling. In the midst of his busy life, Jesus moved away from the noise, crowds, and other environmental pressures to get alone with his Father.[8] Counselees and counselors at times need to do the same. The sensitive counselor keeps alert to environmental stresses that may intensify both the counselor's and the counselee's pressures and thus hinder counseling effectiveness.

The second major environmental influence on counseling concerns the places where we counsel. We have seen that is not necessary or always desirable to counsel in a formal office. When you do use an office, however, recognize that comfortable chairs, pleasant surroundings, neatness, healthy plants, warm colors (like beige, brown, yellow, orange, or even pale blue—never white), soft floor coverings, comfortable temperatures, soothing music, or silence can all reduce tension—providing the counselee feels comfortable in this kind of environment. If you are counseling in a restaurant or other public place, counselees may feel more relaxed, but be alert to the potentially adverse influences of background music, commotion, overly attentive servers, architectural design, and other environmental influences.

Systems and Social Networks

Harry is a sixty-eight-year-old man who lives in a high-rise apartment building on the outskirts of a large city. He and his wife have been married for over forty years and have three grown children, all of whom live in other parts of the country. The family keeps in telephone contact, and periodically there are visits, but since his retirement, Harry and his wife have spent most of their time watching television, visiting with friends, or attending church activities.

Late one night, Harry had a heart attack. His wife called a neighbor, who, in turn, called the paramedics and accompanied the stricken couple to the hospital. For almost three months, Harry remained hospitalized, receiving treatment not only for his heart condition but also for a form of can-

cer that the doctors discovered as part of their examinations. When he came home, Harry was weak, barely able to walk, and sustained by an oxygen supply that constantly stayed by his side. Each of his children came for a visit during the crisis, but their family and work responsibilities kept the visits brief. Harry and his wife were forced to cope largely on their own. Their experiences illustrate what counselors mean by systems and social networks.

Systems are the social groups to which we belong. Each of us may be part of a family, a group of residents who live in the same apartment complex, a college community, a neighborhood, a church, a group of co-workers in a work setting, a Bible-study group, or some other band of people. You or your counselee may be part of an organization (like the company where you work or the school where you study), a vocation (like the ministry or psychology), or an interest group (like a basketball team or investors' club). Most of us are involved in a number of these groups, and often they overlap to form a *social network* of groups. Each of these systems and social networks can be the cause of stress and personal tension, but each can also give help in times of need.

Following the devastating tsunami that impacted so much of southeast Asia on the day after Christmas in 2004, people from around the world sprang into action, giving emotional support, practical assistance, money, and whatever else appeared to be needed. Governments, corporations and companies, communities, churches, mosques, Hindu temples, and hundreds of thousands of individuals did what they could to meet the needs of people who had lost everything, including family members and other loved ones. Three years earlier, the terrorist attacks in the United States had evoked a similar response. Both in North America and around the world, every part of the social system was impacted by the events of that traumatic day. A recent computer search uncovered literally thousands of reports and articles documenting the effectiveness of the social support that followed these events.

Two days after the terrorist attack in New York, the staff of one professional counseling center decided to give whatever help they could. The Institute for Contemporary Psychotherapy is a secular, "not-for-profit training and treatment center" that serves thousands of low- to moderate-income people across the city of New York. The counselors who work there had no experience in public health emergencies, disaster counseling, or working with large corporations, but people from the institute decided to contact an official of a corporation with several hundred employees, many of whom had worked in the World Trade Center and escaped moments before the first tower collapsed. The counselors offered to give free counseling to any of the employees who wanted it. At first there was skepticism and even resistance, but then people started coming forward, including other counselors who had heard what was happening. The employees who normally would never mention their anxieties or vulnerabilities became much more open and willing to participate in groups.

"Did we help?" asked one of the counselors several months later. "I think we did," he wrote as an answer to his own question, "in thousands of sometimes small, often critical and usually unpredictable ways." They did emergency counseling with hundreds of people who broke down under the strain, helped people understand their feelings, and encouraged others to take time for rest and reflection. Key to the whole process was the willingness of these counselors to set aside their familiar and comfortable ways of working and, instead, give the people what they wanted and were asking for.[9]

In countries all over the world, many others have studied and described the role of social support and intervention in times of terrorist attacks, natural disaster, and political upheaval, such as the situation described in the opening words of this chapter. The same is true with more personal crises, like the one that Harry and his wife faced with the onset of his physical illness. They were able to cope because they had emotional support from each other, from their children (even though these children were far away), from the neighbors in their apartment, from extended family members (brothers and in-laws who lived nearby), from caring medical personnel at the local hospital, from former work associates, from acquaintances who sent cards and called occasionally, and from the pastor and members of their church. At different times during the crisis, these people provided the seven forms of help that everybody needs on occasion:[10]

- Tangible help in the form of money, food, clothing, or other provisions.
- Physical assistance that might include the provision of transportation, lawn care, grocery shopping, house cleaning, or similar tasks.
- Guidance, including offerings of advice or practical suggestions.
- Listening while feelings, personal concerns, frustrations, and fears are expressed.
- Feedback, which involves giving people information about themselves or their actions.
- Social participation that could involve informal conversation, relaxation opportunities, and temporary diversion from demanding and difficult conditions.
- Spiritual support that comes when people are encouraged and helped to participate in worship, spiritual disciplines, and other activities that can stimulate hope, a sense of peace, and an awareness of God's presence and help.[11]

Following a community-wide trauma or personal crisis, healing often comes in part because caring people step forward to help. Harry and his wife found these helpers among their wide circle of friends, but in every community there are people who do not have these contacts and social relationships. Individuals who are elderly or living alone may have few social contacts. Others, like drug and alcohol abusers or some former prisoners, may have many social contacts, but all are part of pathological and problem-creating social networks. These people who lack community support often struggle on their own unless others, including church people and counselors, can be encouraged and shown how to reach out and become helpers to those in need.

Resiliency

Resiliency is the ability of people to come back from adverse experiences and to move on with life. Resiliency is not a new idea. Most counselors have seen it in their counselees. Researchers have been studying it for several decades, and there now is abundant evidence of this widespread ability of people to experience life upheavals, re-adapt to life, maintain their stability, and then move on to new challenges and fulfillment.[12] Studies of resiliency often have focused on families or younger people, but with the rise of worldwide terrorism, there has come a greater interest in resiliency in general.[13] There also is a growing awareness that resiliency operates best when people have resiliency-building conditions in their lives.

After working as a counselor for over thirty years and spending a lot of time with refugees, psychologist Mary Pipher concluded that several influences bring healing and stimulate resilience. These include a calm place to retreat on occasion, a connection with somebody who can be trusted, opportunities to reflect on one's experiences, and the discovery of meaning and purpose in life and a reason to go on.[14] Researchers would agree. In addition to trust, it appears that with younger people, resiliency is more likely when there are stable, caring adults who can be trusted and who bring availability, empathy, affirmation, respect, and clear values.[15] Positive emotions like love, gratitude, or hope also reduce stress levels and stimulate resiliency because they offset the negative feelings of hopelessness and despair.[16] It will come as no surprise, as well, that continued contact and support from important people in one's life can be of great importance. Counselors have to deal with the problems and crises of life, but perhaps we have underestimated the human capacity to thrive under extremely aversive events.

The Other Helpers

In many parts of the world we appear to be in the midst of a counseling boom with increasing numbers of counseling centers, numerous training programs, and an expanding list of counseling books and journals. Despite all this activity (and perhaps because of it), we still hear about a continuing shortage of trained counselors, especially in smaller communities and in countries where counseling is a new concept. To meet the growing demands for counseling and to fill in when professionals and other trained counselors are not available, a large network of "other helpers" has appeared. Most of these nonprofessional care-givers have been around for decades or for centuries, but now they are seen as important adjuncts to any counseling ministry.

The other helpers vary in the extent of their training, psychological knowledge, sensitivity, therapeutic skills, and ability to help. Despite good intentions, some may do more harm than good,[17] but undoubtedly the vast majority are people-helpers who genuinely want to be of assistance. There is considerable evidence that these nonprofessional counselors can be very effective, sometimes even more effective than professionals.[18] Some people with needs feel less threatened and more at ease when they can talk to a nonprofessional. Others prefer to get their help from a magazine article or from a radio talk show, but that too can be helpful. Many would rather talk with a pastor or with the members of a self-help group.

As a counselor, you may choose to ignore these community sources of help, but it is unlikely that your counselees will ignore them. Whether or not you think about this, most of your counseling is likely to be supplemented by the less formal and sometimes unsolicited help-giving that comes from friends, relatives, and other people in the community. Instead of ignoring or resisting these other helpers, the counselor should be aware of their existence. Don't be reluctant to enlist the assistance of these other helpers, even as you work with your counselees. Who are these helpers?

Medical Professionals. The counselor would be foolish and irresponsible to ignore the help that can come to counselees from doctors, nurses, clinics, and other community medical resources. Most of these professional care-givers have at least some training in psychiatry, and their work often puts them in contact with patients who have severe emotional problems in addition to physical illnesses. In addition, people with medical training can help nonmedical counselors determine if the cause or best treatment of some problem may be biological or chemical. Because they don't know each other, nonmedical and medical care-givers often need to work at building rapport and mutual respect before they are able to cooperate in helping those who need counseling.

Community Agents. These are the lawyers, school teachers, policemen, paramedics, union leaders, clergy, chaplains, athletic coaches, taxicab drivers, shopkeepers, funeral directors, youth workers, beauticians, bartenders, and others in the community who may have limited or no training in counseling but who often are the first to see people in times of psychological crises. Probably, it is unrealistic to think that many cab drivers or bartenders would be willing to take courses in lay counseling, but in many segments of the community such training is being offered.[19] Police officers now get trained in crisis management and mental-health intervention because they are often the first and only outsiders present when there is domestic violence or the threat of suicide.[20] Teachers, school officials, attorneys, and, of course, seminary students, among others, routinely get training in counseling and mental-health management as part of their educational background.

Mutual Aid Groups. Nobody knows how many self-help groups meet on a regular basis to help members deal with their stresses. Alcoholics Anonymous (AA) and various national weight reduction programs are best known, but groups exist to deal with almost every common problem. There are widows groups, groups of former mental patients, people impacted by national disasters, parents without partners, cancer survivor groups, compulsive gamblers, parents of mentally handicapped children, pregnant teenagers, disabled war veterans, people who care for relatives with Alzheimer's Disease, and hundreds of others. Christian leaders might be most familiar with church small groups (sometimes called cell groups) that may exist for prayer or Bible study, but these groups often provide mutual encouragement and help as well. Sometimes working through churches or with professional counselors, but more often on their own, all these groups have members who give mutual support, tangible assistance, pertinent information, opportunities to help others, social interaction, encouragement, protection, acceptance, and special help in times of crisis. All these groups vary in their effectiveness, depending in part on the people involved and their leadership. But overall, their effectiveness is such that even people who have stable families and caring churches still join these mutual aid groups because of the closeness that comes from contact with others who share similar problems or concerns. In addition, one of the greatest benefits of these groups is the help the members give to others and, indirectly, to themselves as they reach out.[21]

Family Members and Friends. Most people probably talk about problems with friends or family members long before they seek help from a counselor. Parents, for example, are major sources of encouragement, behavior change, and guidance, even though we rarely view them as mental-health providers. Numerous books have been written to help parents with these challenges, and countless seminars teach parents how to do a better job. With the aging of the population, middle-aged people are also learning how to meet the needs of their aging parents. Alcoholics can be helped by their spouses and children, terminally ill patients get support from their families, and relatives frequently rally to help and give advice during times of need.

This input from friends and family may not always be helpful. At some time, every counselor has the experience of working with a counselee and then having this work undermined by parents, other relatives or friends, most of whom sincerely want to be helpful. By listening carefully, the counselor can detect these outside influences and help counselees evaluate the advice and learn how to cope with the potentially harmful input from others.

Since they so often are genuinely concerned about your counselee's problems, don't overlook the possibility of getting family members and friends involved in the counseling process. Enlist them as your allies if your counselees agree. You can show friends and relatives how to be genuinely helpful. Often they will support, reinforce, and supplement what you are doing in the counseling room. In contrast, if you ignore the counselee's friends and family members, your work as a counselor may be much more difficult, and you may end up cutting off a valuable additional resource for helping your counselee overcome his or her problem.

Media Help. Several years ago, a series of teenage suicides rocked our community and became headline news across the country. The method of death was always the same, and many denounced the media for reporting the suicides, drawing attention to the victims, and subtly teaching other distressed young people how to kill themselves. Reporters replied that publicity can alert communities to serious problems that are being ignored.

This debate reminds us that movies, television, radio, newspapers, books, and magazines may stimulate violence or arouse stress, but these same media influences can provide valuable information, give guidance, and show people how and where to get the help they need. The American Psychological Association even has a division of its members devoted to media psychology. The purpose, stated in somewhat academic terms, is to focus on the roles that psychologists, counselors, mental-health providers, and others can play "in various aspects of the media, including, but not limited to, radio, television, film, video, newsprint, magazines, and newer technologies." The group seeks "to promote research into the impact of media on human behavior; to facilitate interaction between psychology and media representatives; to enrich the teaching, training, and practice of media psychology; and to prepare psychologists to interpret psychological research to the lay public and to other professionals."[22] These professionals see the value of the media and are committed to working with media people to bring about good. Certainly that would include the use of media to supplement what counselors do in their offices.

Exotic Helpers. Almost every community has palm readers, fortune-tellers, psychics, exorcists, faith-healers, spiritists, and other exotic "helpers." Often these are sincere people who strongly believe in their powers, but trained counselors, including pastors, tend to see these individuals as charlatans or deceivers who prey on the fears, hopes, and superstitions of troubled people. Some counselors have suggested that these community healers should be enlisted to practice their healing arts alongside more traditional counselors. Since the exotic helpers often are revered by uneducated and poorer people, some believe that these needy individuals will be more open to healing if their helper-heroes are part of the treatment process.

Christian counselors should be very cautious about encouraging counselees to talk with exotic helpers. Many people appear to be involved with occult practices, and counselors should take extreme care to keep these influences well away from their counseling and their counselees.

Coaches. This word most often refers to men and women who guide athletes and sports teams toward improved performance and winning games. Not all coaches are athletic coaches, however. There are voice coaches to help singers, fitness coaches at health clubs to help people get in shape, financial coaches to help people with financial planning, and coaches for actors, public speakers, musicians, and writers. Some coaches help politicians or other leaders handle their public appearances. Executive or corporate coaches work with people in business to help them accomplish their goals.

Within recent years the field of life coaching has attracted the attention of many people, including counselors who get training to become skilled life coaches themselves. Coaching can be a significant adjunct to the counselor's work, or, as is more often true, coaching can be completely separate from counseling. Like counselors, life coaches work with people who are dissatisfied with their lives and want to change; however, the goals of coaching and counseling are different, as are many of the techniques. Whether or not you do coaching or recommend it, it is important to be aware of coaching basics, including the fast-growing field of Christian coaching.[23]

Christian Coaching

The word *coach* originally referred to a horse-drawn vehicle that would take people from where they were to where they wanted to be. Contemporary coaching has a similar purpose. At its core, *coaching is the art and practice of guiding a person or group from where they are toward the greater competence and fulfillment they desire.* Coaching helps people expand their visions, build their confidence, unlock their potential, increase their skills, and take practical steps toward their goals. Unlike counseling or therapy, coaching is less threatening, less concerned about problem solving, more inclined to help people reach their potentials. Coaching is not for those who need therapy to overcome disruptive painful influences from the past. Instead, coaches help people build vision and move forward toward the future. Coaching is not reactive looking back; it's pro-active looking ahead. It is not about healing; it's about growing. It focuses less on overcoming weaknesses and more on building skills and strengths. Usually, coaching is less formal than the therapist-patient relationship and more of a partnership between two equals, one of whom has experiences, perspectives, or knowledge that can be useful to the other.

Most often, life coaches work with individuals and help them find focus and direction for their lives and careers. Coaches also work with couples, small groups, church boards, management teams, and almost anybody who wants to move from where they are to where they want to be. Coaching can be a tool for counselors, but it also can be a source of guidance for all of us. "No matter how long you've been in ministry or where your church is presently, outside coaching is a must," wrote one experienced pastor.[24]

1. *How does coaching differ from counseling?* The emerging popularity of coaching may come, in part, because it appears to be less threatening than counseling. Counseling still has a negative image that implies weakness and sometimes the false idea that "only crazy people go for counseling." Coaching suggests something more positive. Counselors and coaches use many of the same methods and similar skills, such as concentrated listening, careful questioning, and focus on helping people improve their lives and relationships. But there are significant differences that can be illustrated in the following diagram.

−10	0	+10
Counseling		Coaching

Assume that your counselees could be put on a scale from -10 to 0. A person with serious depression or a major conflict might be given a -8 or -9. The counselor's goal is to help this person get closer to the zero point, which is the point of stability.

Coaching works on the other side of this arrow line. The people who come for coaching do not need or want counseling. They are not struggling with problems but are frustrated because their lives, careers, or churches are not very fulfilling or successful. The want help in moving from where they begin, perhaps at a +2 or +3, to a much higher place on the scale.

Of course, counseling and coaching overlap. Much of what counselors do could more accurately be described as coaching, and sometimes coaches find themselves in the role of counselors. As a counselor or as a coach, your goal is to help people move more to the right side of the arrow.

- Counseling helps people deal with pain, problems, and symptoms; coaching guides people as they work to attain specific goals.
- Counseling often focuses on the past; coaching emphasizes the present and the future.
- Counseling is about healing and recovery; coaching is more about growth and learning how to move forward.
- Counseling assumes that something is wrong and needs to be made better; coaching assumes that new visions need to be clarified and that people need to be empowered to reach new accomplishments.
- Counseling often is about pathology; coaching is about possibilities.
- Counseling seeks to help people overcome weaknesses; coaching focuses on helping people develop strengths and build on these to take action.
- Counseling looks at feelings and often focuses on what the person is experiencing inside; coaching focuses more on results and developing strategies for reaching goals.
- Counseling usually occurs in a face-to-face relationship; coaching often is done over the telephone.

2. *What happens in coaching?* Like counseling, every coaching situation is unique. Some find it helpful to have a road map for coaching similar to the one shown in Figure 4–1. Usually, coaches will begin by exploring the *issues* the person wants to change. In what areas does he or she want to grow? Before there can be movement forward, we need to have a better *awareness* of where the person is at the present moment. What are his or her strengths, abilities, interests, spiritual gifts, values, and hopes? Often the coach will use tests to help people learn more about themselves.

This brings us to *vision*. What does the person being coached have as a vision for the future? Coaches might guide people, organizations, or churches to formulate life-vision or life-mission statements. A coach could ask this question, for example: "Considering your gifts, abilities, driving passions, and unique God-given personality, what is your life mission?" It takes time to answer that question. Without a clear answer, without a clear vision, people, churches, organizations, even governments tend to drift with no direction. Coaches help people clarify their vision.

Once we have a vision we need a *strategy* for getting there. That might include setting goals, making decisions about education, changing attitudes, managing life differently, or building new relationships. Even with a strategy plan, it takes courage and encouragement from someone like a friend or a coach to help the person *take action* and not quit when things get difficult. During this process of moving forward, the person is certain to face *obstacles*, including discouragement, temporary failure, or even self-defeating activities that prevent the person from getting to where he or she wants to be. Coaches are present to help people get past the obstacles.

Most important is that all of this revolves around the person of Jesus Christ. He is like the axle at the center, keeping the wheel from spinning off in a variety of directions. In practical terms, what does it mean to have our coaching revolve around Jesus? It means that we commit all of our coaching (and our lives) to his

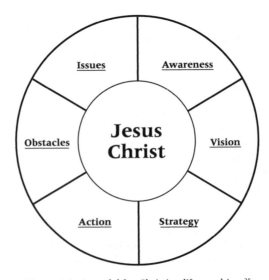

Figure 4–1. A model for Christian life coaching.[25]

Lordship and direction. It means that through Scripture reading, prayer, and worship we seek to be men and women who know him and are more sensitive to the leading of his Holy Spirit. It means that we seek to be clear on our values, politely declining to coach anybody who wants our services for the purpose of developing behaviors or lifestyles that clearly are inconsistent with Christian principles and thus self-defeating. Having Jesus Christ at the center means, as well, that we commit to praying for the people we coach, asking God to change their lives as we work with them through our gifts and training.

Some of the people we coach may not have Christ at the center of their lives. Their lives revolve around attaining success, power, money, position, or some other value they deem important. At some time the coach will focus on the core that is at the center of the person's life.

3. *What makes coaching Christian?* Apart from the above references to Jesus Christ, much of what happens in Christian coaching is similar to coaching that makes no claim to be Christian. Unlike secular approaches, however, Christian coaching is not focused primarily on helping people get from where they are to where they want to be. *Christian coaching is about helping people get from where they are to where they believe God wants them to be.* This involves helping people hear God's voice, sense his direction for their lives, and seek his Spirit's guidance to reach God-given goals rather than the more human goals that shape most of our lives. Jesus came to point people to the Father, to show how we could have life everlasting and lives that are more full and abundant.[26] The Christian coach helps people imagine ways in which their lives can be better and more consistent with the will of God. The coach walks with people as they make the changes that will improve their careers, their families, their walks with God, their churches and businesses, and their world.

4. *Are there dangers in coaching?* The growing field of coaching tends to be an optimistic, hope-filled venture that sees possibilities in people and looks for ways to help clients reach their goals and attain success. But professional counselors argue that coaches who are not trained as counselors sometimes overlook serious problems that need to be addressed before coaching can be successful. One coach, for example, praised a business executive for making clear decisions and delegating responsibility to others. The coach did not see that this executive was controlling, power hungry, and so afraid of failure that he never completed anything. Instead, he turned all his responsibilities over to others and then complained and berated these employees when they failed.

When coaches fail to notice the unhealthy tendencies in the people they coach, the whole coaching process can do more harm than good.[27] Even so, coaching continues to grow and be a significant way to help people. Many of the issues that people bring to Christian counselors are really coaching issues. Because of this many Christian counselors now get training in coaching and make it a part of their work.

Community Counseling and the Christian

One theme has been woven throughout the pages of this chapter: we cannot help people without, at the same time, dealing with and being aware of the community. Even as other issues are discussed in the counseling room, counselors need to keep aware of several basic questions:[28]

1. To what extent can the problem be solved apart from the environment and largely through inner change in the counselee?
2. To what extent does the solution really rest in the environment instead of in the individual?
3. What resources are available in the community and environment that could help the counselee change or grow?
4. What could or should the counselor, coach, and/or the counselee do to bring changes in the environment?

In addition to personal counseling, community counselors are involved in activities such as finding or providing educational programs; developing self-help programs and giving training in self-help skills; assisting governments and social service agencies in planning social programs; identifying community support groups; working to establish community resources such as telephone hot lines, rehabilitation centers, or crisis-pregnancy centers; and at times participating in political or other movements in an effort to improve the community.

Community counselors recognize that they are not alone in trying to improve the community and should not try to do it alone. For this reason they work with a variety of professional, political, and other resource people whose values or beliefs may differ from those of the counselor but who all share common goals for bringing about change. By improving the community, it is assumed that community residents will be enabled to better cope with life and its problems.

How does this relate to Christian counseling? In many ways, Jesus was a community counselor. He tenderly and sensitively helped individuals with their doubts and struggles, but he also spoke against hypocrisy and poverty in the community. He drove moneychangers out of the temple, criticized the government, spoke out against pious and self-centered religious leaders, and talked about a day when his kingdom would come and eliminate injustice.

As individuals who live in communities and seek to obey biblical teachings, Christians—including counselors—must have an active concern about hunger, poverty, injustice, crime, pornography, family violence, government incompetence, ecological irresponsibility, declining moral standards, and other social ills that give rise to many of the issues discussed in the following chapters. The church, as a community within a community, must ask how it can stay focused on its mission but still have an impact both on the unchurched and on church members. Following his instructions to share each other's troubles and problems, Paul wrote that we should not "get tired of doing what is good. Don't get discouraged and give up, for we will reap a harvest of blessing at the appropriate time. Whenever we have opportunity, we should do good to everyone, especially to our Christian brothers and sisters."[29]

Christian community counseling may be a new territory for some counselors, but it is clearly consistent with the teachings of the Bible.

KEY POINTS FOR BUSY COUNSELORS

➤ Counseling between two individuals can be helpful, but the benefits are likely to be greater when the counselee is part of one or more supportive caring groups.

➤ Community counseling is an approach to helping that means getting involved with the community to build social support networks so people feel less isolated. Community counselors show people how to give and get help from the community. These counselors teach social skills, equip lay people, work to prevent problems within the community, and sometimes get involved in political or social action.

➤ Community counseling also seeks to improve the environment instead of concentrating solely on helping individuals.

➤ Community counselors deal with groups as well as with individuals.

➤ The counselee's environment—including the presence of noise, crowding, architectural influences, unpleasant weather, and degree of exposure to nature—can all impact behavior and counseling.

➤ Effective ways to help people or to prevent further problems include changing existing conditions, finding ways to remove counselees from stressful environments, or teaching them how to cope.

➤ We all live within systems of other people who impact us or are impacted by us. Counselors must never forget the power of systems to create problems or to facilitate healing.

➤ Resiliency is the ability of some people to bounce back after adversities, even without counseling.

➤ There are other helpers in every community. Some of these can be enlisted to work with you in bringing help and recovery. These helpers include:
  - Medical professionals.
  - Community agencies.
  - Mutual aid groups.
  - Family members and friends.
  - Media.
  - Exotic helpers.
  - Coaches.

➤ Life coaching is a new concept that focuses on people who do not need or want counseling but who want help in getting from where they are to where they want to be. It involves guiding a person or group from where they are toward the greater competence and fulfillment that they desire.

Christian coaching is a Spirit-guided enterprise that helps people get from where they are to where they sense God wants them to be.

➤ There are different approaches to coaching, but in general the coach:
  ▪ Helps people identify the relevant issues.
  ▪ Builds self-awareness by looking at the individual's or group's strengths. abilities, interests, spiritual gifts, values, and hopes.
  ▪ Helps in the formulation of a vision.
  ▪ Works to develop a strategy for reaching goals.
  ▪ Stimulates action and holds people accountable for their actions.
  ▪ Identifies and helps people deal with the obstacles that prevent progress.

➤ Every individual, like every group, builds around a central life core of beliefs or values. For the sincere Christian, life is built around a committed devotion to Jesus Christ.

➤ Community counselors recognize that they are not alone in trying to improve individuals or the community and should not try to do it alone.

➤ In many ways, Jesus was a community counselor.

5

The Core of Counseling

The Old Testament book of Job describes a man who was godly, famous, wealthy, and highly respected by his contemporaries until the time when everything fell apart. Without warning, Job lost his wealth and his health. His children all died in a tornado, plunging him into intense grief and despair. Instead of giving support, his wife preferred to nag and complain. Three friends came to help, but they spent most of their time telling Job what he had done wrong to bring all this disaster upon himself. In the midst of all this suffering, God must have seemed far away.

Then came Elihu, a young man who listened to Job and tried to understand his struggles and frustrations. Elihu was critical of those well-meaning but insensitive counselors who had lectured Job and given him their empty advice. In contrast, Elihu showed acceptance and concern, a humble willingness to be on the same level as Job (without any holier-than-thou attitude), a courage to confront, and an unswerving desire to point this counselee to God, who alone is sovereign and able to help in times of need. Elihu was the one counselor who succeeded where others had failed.[1]

Job's story is unique, but the Bible is filled with many examples of human need. Its authors write honestly about anxiety, loneliness, discouragement, doubt, grief, violence, abnormal sex, bitterness, sickness, tensions between people, inner turmoil, and a variety of other problems. Sometimes, struggles and needs like these are seen in the lives of the Bible's greatest heroes.

Does counseling really help people deal with problems? The answer is yes, according to a growing body of research.[2] Of course some counselors are ineffective and perhaps even harmful.[3] Most pastors feel under-prepared for their counseling responsibilities, and there is evidence that some are not very competent as counselors.[4] However, many do succeed, and they counsel very effectively. These care-givers are characterized by personalities that radiate sincerity, understanding, compassion, and the ability to confront in a genuine and constructive manner. These counselors are skilled in techniques that help counselees move toward specific goals.[5] These techniques of effective counseling will be the focus of this chapter.

Before we turn to specifics, there is one caution to keep in mind. Nobody learns skills from reading a book. No pianist, painter, athlete, carpenter, or cook becomes skilled in his or her craft solely by learning what should be done. Skills are learned by practice. For this reason counselor training programs usually require many hours of practical counseling experience under the supervision of counselors who are experienced and competent. Knowledge is important, but the real learning comes in the doing.

The Goals of Counseling

Why do people come for counseling? What do they want to accomplish? What are your goals in trying to help people through counseling? These are difficult questions. Each can have a variety of answers, depending on both the counselee and the counselor. Contrary to what you might think, relatively few people come to Christian counselors with problems concerning prayer, doubt, doctrine, spiritual growth, or guilt over sinful behavior.[6] More often, people come with marriage problems, crises, depression, interpersonal conflicts, and other problems, including anxiety in these times of instability and fear of terrorism that has gripped our world.

Jesus was concerned about these kinds of problems. He came to make it possible for us to have eternal life in heaven and abundant life on earth.[7] The counselor who follows Jesus Christ has the same ultimate goals. He or she points individuals to the eternal life that comes to those who believe in him and shows believers how to have abundant lives on earth. If we take the words of Jesus seriously, we are likely to reach the conclusion that a fully abundant life only comes to those who seek to live in accordance with his teachings.

It is well known that there are many sincere Christians who will have eternal life in heaven but who are not experiencing a very abundant life on earth. These people need counseling that involves something other than evangelism, one-to-one preaching, or traditional Christian education. They need sensitive, competent counselors who are guided by the Holy Spirit and able to help their counselees recognize hidden harmful attitudes, learn better social and conflict-management skills, make wise decisions, change their lifestyles, or learn how to mobilize their inner resources to cope with a crisis. Such counseling can free counselees from persisting hang-ups, past memories, or present attitudes that prevent them from growing toward maturity. For nonbelievers, Christian counseling can serve as a kind of "pre-evangelism" that allows people to experience genuine Christian love and, in time, clear away some of the obstacles to conversion. Evangelism, spiritual growth, and helping people experience a more abundant life on earth are at the core of the Christian counselor's efforts, even though these are not the only goals.[8]

Many counselees have only vague notions about what they want from counseling—except, perhaps, to understand themselves or to feel better. If their counselors are equally vague, the counseling process is likely to be aimless and ineffective. However, any list of goals is likely to include at least the following.

1. *Symptom Relief.* The people who come for counseling know there is something wrong with their lives. Their top priority may be relief from the despair, anxiety, inner turmoil, debilitating insecurity, personal conflicts, or other tension that is making their lives miserable. Often the counselor helps simply by listening and showing compassion. It can be helpful, as well, to make one or two suggestions that might reduce the immediate stresses and arouse a sense of hope. Ultimately, relieving symptoms brings only temporary relief, like taking an aspirin to dull the pain of a toothache without treating the real cause of the problem.

2. *Self-Understanding.* To understand oneself often is a first step in healing.

Many problems are self-created, but the counselee may fail to recognize that he or she has biased perspectives, harmful attitudes, or self-destructive ways of behaving. For example, consider the person who complains that "Nobody likes me," but fails to see that the complaining annoys others, drives people away, and becomes one reason for the rejection. One counseling goal is for an objective, perceptually alert helper to assist those being helped to get a true picture of what is going on within themselves and within the world that surrounds them.

3. *Learning New Skills and Changing Behavior.* Most of our behavior is learned. Counseling, therefore, involves helping counselees unlearn ineffective behavior and learn more effective ways of doing things. This learning may come from instruction, but it is more likely to last when the counselee can imitate the counselor, or some other model, and experience the change through trial and error. At times it also will be necessary to analyze what went wrong when failure has occurred. Then the counselee must be encouraged to try again.

Assume, for example, that you are counseling a young man who feels insecure about relating to women, especially in dating. Dating is learned behavior, but if you reread the previous paragraph, you will be able to think of ways to help your date-fearing counselee.

Counselors often find themselves teaching new skills for living. One of the areas where this is most needed is in the area of communication skills. Some people have constant problems because they never have learned to communicate effectively. It is well known that many marriage breakdowns involve failures in husband-wife communication, but the lack of communication skill goes far beyond marriage. Many people are unable or unwilling to communicate. Frequently, counselees must be encouraged to communicate feelings, thoughts, and attitudes both accurately and effectively. Effective communication involves clearly expressing oneself and accurately receiving messages from others.

4. *Conflict Resolution.* Many people come for counseling because they are having conflict with some other person or persons. This appears to have been so common in the early church that many portions of the epistles focus on giving direction for restoring peace to troubled relationships. Gentiles and Jews should get along, Paul writes in Ephesians, because Christ himself has broken down the wall of hostility that used to separate them.[9] Loving one another is crucially important, we read in several places, but sometimes, instead of showing love among themselves, the early believers were "biting and devouring one another," even destroying one another,[10] presumably within the confines of the church. The biblical writers wrote about building better marriages, having better parent-child relationships, developing smooth employer-employee rapport, and even going to Christians who were in conflict and helping them reconcile.[11]

None of this has changed in our modern world. At some time every counselor will be involved in helping people reconcile. It is hard work, and often it is stressful work. For most of us it is not work that we enjoy. Nonetheless, it has plenty of support in the Bible and is a key goal for Christian counseling.

5. *Support.* Often people are able to meet their goals, solve their problems, and work effectively, except for temporary periods of unusual stress or crisis. During these times we all can benefit from the support, encouragement, and "burden bearing" that comes from compassionate others, including counselors. Support better enables people to remobilize their personal and spiritual resources to effectively meet the problems of living.

6. *Spiritual Growth and Wholeness*. Even with the current widespread interest in spirituality, many counseling professionals fail to see or admit that there is a spiritual dimension to all human problems. In contrast, the famous psychiatrist Carl Jung concluded that among his patients who were over thirty-five: "There has not been one whose problem in the last resort was not that of finding a religious outlook on life."[12]

The Christian counselor becomes a spiritual leader who guides spiritual growth, helps counselees deal with spiritual struggles, and enables them to find meaningful beliefs and values. Instead of dialogue between counselor and counselee, the Christian strives for a "trialogue" that acknowledges the presence of God at the heart of effective people-helping. Helping people deal with spiritual needs and bringing spiritual wholeness are basic to much of Christian counseling.

7. *Self-Development*. Not everybody who comes for counseling is struggling with a major problem. Sometimes, people come because they want help in becoming more fulfilled or better able to reach their potential. Some counselors have proposed that a goal for all humans should be *self-actualization*, the process of learning to achieve and maintain one's optimal potential. This can be a valid goal for counseling, although it appears to fit better with what we now know as coaching.

The concept of self-actualization is very humanistic because it focuses exclusively on human abilities and potential. The Christian values each person developing his or her God-given strengths, gifts, and abilities to their greatest capability to fulfill God's purpose for their lives. But we believe, as well, that ultimately our goal in life is to be complete in Christ, developing one's greatest potential through the power of the Holy Spirit, who brings us to spiritual maturity.

Whatever goals we might have for counseling, the process rarely is effective if counselors impose their own goals on counselees. It is better if the counselor and counselee work together in setting goals. This is not always possible, but the best goals are specific rather than vague, realistic, and (if there are several) organized into some logical sequence that identifies the goals to be worked on first and, perhaps, for how long. None of this should be allowed to stifle the counseling. There will be times throughout the counseling when one of the goals will emerge as something that needs immediate attention regardless of what might have been planned.

The Relationship in Counseling

It is not easy for people to come for counseling. Few of us want to admit that we need help. There are those who are in awe of counselors or afraid of what they might think, ask, or see. Some problems are embarrassing or so personal that any talk about them is sure to be unsettling and arouse discomfort in the counselee— and sometimes in the counselor. Christians may feel, or have been told, that believers shouldn't have overwhelming problems that persist even after there has been prayer and a pleading with God to take them away. People like these often view the need for counseling as an indication of personal and spiritual failure.

A good counselor is aware of these insecurities and, from the beginning, actively tries to help counselees relax. This can be done long before anybody arrives for counseling by developing a "therapeutic climate" where the counselee feels comfortable and where there are few distractions or interruptions. This may be in an office or counseling center, but effective helping can take place almost anywhere, providing confidentiality is assured within the confines of the law.[13] For some people, meeting in the quiet corner of some restaurant can be less threatening than the more formal setting of a counseling office.[14]

More important than location is the relationship between the helper and the person who gets the help. This is so widely accepted that counselors speak routinely of the counseling relationship. It is at the core of the helping process.[15]

How is this therapeutic relationship built and maintained? Psychologist Carl Rogers was one of the first to study and develop this question in depth. Many years ago he reported a four-year study conducted with hospital patients and a variety of counselors. It was found that relationships grew and patients improved when the therapists showed high levels of warmth, genuineness, and accurate empathic understanding.[16] When these counselor qualities were lacking, the hospital patients grew worse. Of course, it is important to be sensitive and to use whatever techniques you can to set counselees at ease. But years of subsequent research supports the idea that the heart of the helping relationship centers on the counselor characteristics that Rogers identified.

We discussed these in more detail in chapter 2. *Warmth* implies caring, respecting, or possessing a sincere, nonsmothering concern for the counselee—regardless of his or her actions or attitudes. *Genuineness* in a counselor indicates that he or she is "for real"—an open, sincere person who avoids phoniness or playing some superior role. *Empathy* involves counselor sensitivity and the ability to "feel with" the counselee and understand the person's struggles. The counselor who can empathize (especially near the beginning of counseling) is most likely to connect with people and be effective as a helper.

Although warmth, genuineness, and empathy are among the most frequently mentioned attributes of a good counselor, there are other important characteristics, including those we considered earlier. In addition, the Christian counselor's life must show evidence of the Holy Spirit's fruit: joy, peace, patience, kindness, goodness, faithfulness, gentleness, self-control, and what probably is the most important—love.[17]

More than half a century ago, this was emphasized by a former president of the American Psychological Association who called love "incomparably the greatest psychotherapeutic agent . . . something that professional psychiatry cannot of itself create, focus, nor release."[18] Might it be, the writer suggested, that Christianity offers an approach to life that is based wholly upon love and thus is able to help where secular counseling fails? This presents a challenge to Christian counselors, especially those with secular training who keep their Christian values tucked away whenever they enter the counseling room. A basic way to help is to show love and to ask God to make us more loving and to love needy people through us. For some people the sense that they are experiencing love is all they need to get better.

Every experienced counselor knows that most people also need discipline, structure, challenge, and other therapeutic interventions. For many counselees, perhaps most, love alone is not enough. With this awareness, the effective Christian helper seeks to develop counseling relationships based on love, but he or she also strives to become proficient in the knowledge and use of basic counseling skills.[19]

Skills in Counseling

Unlike more casual discussions between friends, the helping relationship is characterized by a clear purpose—that of helping the counselee. The helper's needs are mostly met elsewhere, and he or she does not depend on the counselee for love, affirmation, or help. In the helping relationship, counselors lay aside their own struggles or conflicts, seek to become aware of counselee needs, and communicate both understanding and a willingness to help.

There is no simple formula to summarize how this help is given. The help-giving process can be complicated, and it is impossible to summarize in a few paragraphs. Every counseling situation is unique, but all effective counselors use a variety of skills, the most basic of which include the following.[20]

1. *Attending Skills.* Counselors must try to give undivided attention to each counselee, even though this can be difficult to sustain. Attending is done through (a) eye contact—looking without staring as a way to convey concern and understanding; (b) posture, which should be relaxed rather than tense (nobody feels comfortable with an up-tight counselor) and may involve at least occasional leaning toward the counselee; and (c) gestures, including head nods, that are natural but not excessive or distracting.[21] The counselor communicates attention when he or she is courteous, kind, and strongly motivated to understand.

Recognize that your own fatigue, impatience, preoccupation with other matters, daydreaming, or restlessness can all prevent you from giving careful attention to the counselee. I would emphasize again that people-helping is demanding work that involves sensitivity, genuine expressions of care, and alertness to what the counselee may be trying to communicate.

2. *Listening Skills.* These involve more than giving passive or half-hearted attention to the words that come from another person. Effective listening is an active process. It involves:

- Being able to set aside your own conflicts, biases, and preoccupations so you can concentrate on what the counselee is communicating.
- Avoiding subtle verbal or nonverbal expressions of disapproval or judgment about what is being said, even when the content is offensive or shocking.
- Using both your eyes and your ears to detect messages that come from the tone of voice, pace of talking, ideas that are repeated, posture, gestures, facial expressions, and other clues apart from what the person is saying.
- Hearing not only what the counselee says, but noticing what gets left out.
- Noticing the counselee's physical characteristics and general appearance such as grooming and dress.
- Waiting patiently through periods of silence or tears as the counselee summons enough courage to share something painful or pauses to collect his or her thoughts and regain composure.
- Looking at the counselee as he or she speaks, but without either staring or letting our eyes wander around the room.
- Realizing that you can accept the counselee, even though you may not condone his or her actions, values, or beliefs. Sometimes, it can be helpful to imagine yourself in the counselee's situation and attempt to see things from his or her point of view.

It is easy to ignore all of this, to let your mind wander (especially if the counselee's story is boring or repetitive), or to slip into excessive talking and advice-giving. Sometimes, we find ourselves evaluating what the person is saying, trying to think of solutions to the problem, interrupting, or wondering what we will say next. When this happens, the counselee often detects that you are not listening and becomes reluctant to express hurts honestly or to share details. In such situations counselees often feel that they have not been understood. In contrast, active listening is a way to tell counselees "I'm really interested, I sincerely care, and I want to understand."

When we don't listen but try instead to counsel by talking, this often expresses the counselor's own insecurity or inability to deal with threatening, vague, or emotional topics. Something similar may be true with advice-giving. What you say may be worthwhile, but even good advice is seldom heard and even less likely to be followed, especially if the counselee feels you have not listened carefully.

3. *Responding Skills.* There was a time when counselors were taught to pay attention and listen, but to make only occasional specific comments. These comments were intended to spur the counselee on to more evaluation until he or she came up with solutions to the problem. That approach (which is oversimplified in the previous sentence) left people frustrated because the counselor appeared to be listening and not doing much more. But in addition to their listening, good counselors are good responders. Jesus is an example. He listened carefully to the perplexed men as they walked along the road to Emmaus, but his helping also was marked by action and specific verbal responses. How do we respond in helpful ways?

- *Leading* is a skill that lets the counselor gently direct the conversation. "What happened next?" "Tell me what you mean by . . . ? "Then what?" are brief questions that can steer the discussion in directions that will give useful information. Occasionally, you also will need to remind counselees that they are off track and gently suggest that they "come back to the thing you were telling me before. . . ."
- *Reflecting* is a way of letting counselees know that we are "with them" and able to understand how they feel or think. Examples include statements like, "You must feel . . . ," "I bet that was frustrating," "That must have been fun." All of these reflect what is going on in counseling. Be careful not to reflect after every statement, but, instead, do it periodically. Try not to repeat what the counselee says word for word because this can seem artificial and be annoying to the listener. Resist the urge to start almost every sentence with stereotyped phrases such as "You must think . . ." or "I hear you saying . . ."
- *Summarizing* what has been going on also can be a way of reflecting and stimulating more counselee exploration. It also lets you check the accuracy of what you have been hearing. The counselor may summarize feelings ("that must have hurt") and/or general themes of what has been said ("from all of this it sounds as though you have had a whole string of failures"). Of course, summaries should not come too often. Whenever you summarize or make any other comment, give the counselee time and opportunity to respond to what you have said.

- *Supporting and encouraging* are important parts of any counseling situation, especially at the beginning. When people are burdened by needs and conflicts, they can benefit from the stability and care of an empathic person who shows acceptance and gives reassurance. Support includes guiding the counselee to take stock of his or her spiritual and psychological resources, encouraging action, and helping with any problems or failures that may come as a result of this action.

- *Interpreting* involves explaining to the counselee what his or her behavior or other events mean. As you do this, be careful. Interpreting is a highly technical skill with great potential for enabling counselees to see themselves and their situations more clearly. But interpretations also can be harmful, especially if they are introduced before the counselee can handle the material emotionally, or if the interpretations are wrong. If you begin to see possible explanations for the counselee's problems or actions, ask yourself if he or she is intellectually and emotionally ready to handle such an insight. Keep the terms simple as you interpret, present your interpretations in a tentative way (e.g., "Could it be that . . . ?"), and allow time for the counselee to respond. As you discuss the interpretation, the counselee often develops greater insights and is able to explore future courses of action with the counselor.

4. *Questioning Skills*, if done carefully, can bring forth a great deal of useful information. The best questions are those that require at least a few sentences to answer (e.g., "Tell me about your marriage." "What sorts of things are making you unhappy?") rather than those that can be answered in one word ("Are you married?" "Are you unhappy?" "What is your age?"). It is easy to feel uncomfortable when we are stuck and not sure what to say next. As a result, beginning counselors tend to ask a series of the short-answer questions to give themselves time to think about what to do next. But the counselee assumes you are asking questions for a reason and concludes that this is like a doctor's office, where the patient expects a diagnosis and proposal for treatment at the end of the appointment time after responding to all the questions. Good questions can be invaluable in obtaining information for the counselor and clarifying issues for the counselee, but too much questioning can stifle communication. Also, it is best to avoid questions that begin with *Why*. These tend to sound judgmental, or they stimulate long intellectual discussions and analyses that keep the counselee from coming to grips with real feelings or hurts.

Even when counselees want to be honest and cooperative, there are issues or pieces of information they never think to mention. Prompting and probing are special forms of questioning that help people talk in more detail about themselves. These prompts and probes may not always sound like questions; sometimes they are more like interjections. Examples are "Tell me more about that?" "What happened then?" "So . . . ?" "Then . . . ?" "What do you mean by 'the things that' . . . ?" "This means that . . . ?" Often these give you pertinent information, but they also help counselees better clarify the issues they are presenting.

5. *Challenging Skills*. Sometimes, it is not enough for a counselor to show empathy, to express understanding, or to give encouragement. Instead, counselees need to be challenged to face problems they would rather avoid, develop

new perspectives about themselves or their environments, take actions to resolve conflict with others, or stop bitterness, whining, or other self-defeating behaviors and attitudes. Every counselor meets with people who enjoy complaining and feeling like victims but who are reluctant to take any action to change. Despite their complaints many of these people are afraid to change, don't know how to change, perhaps have something biochemical that is preventing the change, or in some cases feel more comfortable staying with their problems rather than taking responsibility and the risk to do something different.

For many years, counselors talked about confronting people to get moving and do something about their situations. *Confrontation*, however, is a biting word that implies condemnation and criticism. Some Christians work on the assumption that counseling and confrontation are synonymous terms. For them, to counsel is to confront. This has neither biblical nor psychological support. Sometimes, Jesus confronted people, but more often he used a gentler approach.

In contrast to the more negative and condemnatory concept of condemnation, *challenge* is a more positive term that implies respect and a prod for counselees to do whatever it takes to change. Counselees can be challenged to face and do something about sin in their lives, failures, inconsistencies, excuses, harmful attitudes, or other self-defeating behavior and ways of thinking. At times, counselees need to be challenged to admit that they are behaving in ways that are irresponsible, harmful to others, or making things worse rather than better. Sometimes, people need to be challenged about their perceptions of themselves or others. For example, parents might perceive their teenage son as being rebellious and intent on making life miserable for them. This may not at all be an accurate portrayal of the son or of the struggles that might be going on inside of him. Whatever the situation, challenging is most effective when it is done in a loving, gentle, nonjudgmental but firm manner. If there are several issues about which you want to challenge your counselee, don't raise them all at once, since this can overwhelm the person. Focus on one issue at a time.

As you might expect, people respond differently to being challenged. Sometimes, there is agreement with the counselor, a determination to make changes, or a confession of sin with a significant experience of forgiveness. Often challenges bring resistance, guilt, hurt, or anger. It is important to let counselees respond verbally to your challenge. Give them time to discuss alternative ways of behaving and then guide them as they make changes.

6. *Teaching Skills*. In many ways, all counseling techniques are specialized forms of spiritual and psychological education. The counselor is an educator who uses different ways to teach: instruction, modeling, telling brief stories, pointing to movies or video recordings that can be helpful, and guiding counselees as they learn by experience to deal with the problems of life. Like other less personal forms of education, counseling is more effective when the counselee's different senses are involved. It helps, too, when discussions are specific rather than vague, and focused on concrete situations ("How can I control my temper when I am criticized by my wife?") rather than on nebulous goals ("I want life to be happier").

One powerful learning tool is the *immediacy* response. This involves the ability of a counselor and counselee to discuss openly and directly what is happening in the "immediate" here-and-now of the relationship. "I think our conversation has stalled," a counselor might say, for example, or "I feel that you are resisting every thing that I say." Such honest, on-the-spot statements let individuals express and deal with feelings and other issues before they grow and then break down the counseling process. Immediacy responses help both counselees and counselors to better understand how the counselee's actions or attitudes affect or may be seen by others. This understanding is an important educational aspect of counseling.

Usually, immediacy responses are initiated by the counselor but not always. At times, counselees learn to use immediacy responses to challenge their counselors. This, too, gives opportunity to discuss what is happening within the counseling relationship that may have a bearing on the counseling process and issues. These responses from counselees can also challenge counselors to consider how they are doing (or failing to do) their work. If the counselor is failing, consider this primarily as an issue that is considered by the counselor outside the counseling room and not with the counselee.

Informing is another teaching tool that involves giving facts to people who need information. Try to avoid giving too much information at any one time. Be clear in what you say, as brief as possible (nobody remembers long lectures), and always aware that when people are hurting they respond best to information that is relevant to their immediate needs or concerns. This kind of informing is a common and widely accepted part of counseling.

Informing is not the same as the advice-giving that we raised cautions about earlier. Advice-givers often lack enough accurate knowledge of a situation to give competent advice. Their advice-giving can encourage counselees to be dependent, but if the advice proves to be invalid, it is the counselor who later is blamed and made to feel responsible for giving bad direction. Frequently, the counselee listens to the advice, accepts it with thanks, but then does nothing to apply it to life.

Whenever you are asked for advice or inclined to give advice, be sure that you are well informed about the situation. Ask yourself, "Do I have enough information and expertise to give this person competent advice?" "What might be the end results of this advice-giving?" "Is it likely to make the counselee more dependent?" "Does the person know how to follow up on the advice?" "Can I handle the reactions that might come if the advice is rejected or proven wrong?" If you do give advice, offer it in the form of a tentative suggestion, then give the counselee time to react or talk through your advice, and follow up later to see the extent to which the advice was helpful and is being followed.

7. *Filtering.* Counselors are not innately skeptical people who disbelieve every thing a counselee says, but it is wise to remember that counselees don't always tell the whole story and don't always say what they really want, need, or intend. Sometimes, a counselee deliberately presents a distorted picture, leaving out embarrassing or potentially incriminating details. Often counselees fail to see their problems in broader perspective, and sometimes they come for help with one problem but fail to see or are reluctant to raise other, deeper problems.

As you counsel, therefore, mentally try to sort through the counselee's words. What is he or she really asking? What does this person really want from a counselor? Does it seem as though there may be problems or issues other than the ones that are being presented? At times people talk about one issue, but they really have little desire to change. Instead, they are looking for sympathy, attention, catharsis, another person's viewpoint, a way to escape from some unpleasant situation, or words from you that they can use as ammunition to attack somebody they strongly dislike. As you listen, you begin to suspect these underlying motives and you realize that often these aren't even recognized by the counselee.

In time you will want to raise these issues and talk about them in counseling. The counselor does not try to invent new issues or force counselees to consider topics they don't want to discuss. Even so, your work will be more effective if you learn to listen with sensitivity and try not to accept everything at face value. It helps, as well, if you are aware that no person, not even counselors, can listen with complete objectivity.

We all have personal, family, cultural, theological, and other filters that help us sort out and make sense of the information that comes into our brains. These filters help us make sense of the world, but they also can add bias to the ways counselors listen.

All of this points again to the counselor's need for wisdom and discernment. Some of this comes with experience, but Christians know that sensitivity more often comes when we pray, asking for the insights, guidance, clarity, and accurate perception that comes from the Holy Spirit.

The Process of Counseling

Counseling is not a step-by-step process like baking a cake or changing a tire. Each counselee is unique—with problems, attitudes, values, strengths, weaknesses, expectations, and experiences that are unlike any other. Each situation is a unique combination of influences from the counselee, other people, and the environment. The counselor (whose own unique problems, attitudes, values, expectations, and experiences are brought into the counseling situation) must approach each individual a little differently from others. The course of counseling also will vary from person to person and often from each session and the one that came before.

Even though counseling cannot be reduced to a series of steps or stages, in all counseling there appears to be several overlapping phases, some of which may be repeated several times as issues are considered and then reconsidered.

1. *Connecting.* Often termed *rapport building*, this involves initiating, building, and maintaining a relationship between the counselor and counselee. As we have seen, the warmth of an office setting contributes to this, but, more important, the counselor builds rapport by listening attentively and showing sincere concern and caring as the counselee begins, sometimes tentatively, to share feelings, concerns, or problems.

2. *Exploring.* Counselees need to "tell their stories," revealing details of problem situations, missed opportunities, and frustrating experiences. This is a time when counselees are encouraged to share their feelings, talk about their thoughts, and describe their actions and symptoms. The counselor listens attentively, asks good questions, and responds with respect, empathy, and sensitivity. This thorough exploration of issues lets the counselor and counselee build rapport and get a clearer understanding of the problem situation that needs to be addressed.

3. *Planning.* In time, the counselee begins to see the problem in a different light, and discussion moves toward goals and actions that can be taken to find

solutions. How could the counselee change? Are there things that can be done to make matters better? Must some things be accepted because they can't be changed? Are there sins to be confessed, actions to be taken, attitudes to be changed, goals to be reached, relationships to be mended, skills to be learned? Together, the counselor and counselee develop some plans for bringing about the desired change.

Some counselors try to skip this and the previous two phases so they can move directly into the process of giving advice and challenging people to take action. Occasionally this works, but more often it is ineffective, like surgery done by an insensitive physician who didn't take the time to make a diagnosis or build a relationship with the patient.

4. *Progressing*. Planning is not very useful unless it is followed by action. After people decide what needs to be done, they must be encouraged to start moving toward their goals. The counselor gives support, direction, encouragement, and often gentle prodding. Sometimes, counselees take action and experience failure. The counselor then helps the counselee evaluate what went wrong, and together they make plans to try again.

At this point it should be emphasized that this and the preceding phase of planning are highly oversimplified, built on the assumption that all problems can be handled intellectually and resolved by an act of will. This rarely happens because of physical, spiritual, psychological, relational, situational, personality, and other obstacles that get in the way and need to be dealt with before the person can move forward.

One exception is the *brief strategic therapy* (sometimes called brief solution-focused therapy) that has gained popularity over the past few decades. After half a century of accepting the assumption that counseling always must be long term, researchers began to discover that for some issues the brief strategic approaches are equally effective and sometimes superior to the long-term approaches.[22] Counselees often prefer more direct intervention, and some Christian counselors have used it very effectively.[23] The approaches vary from person to person but usually include a partnership approach where the counselor and counselee decide together on the issues that need to be dealt with, there is agreement to focus on one specific issue, the counselee is helped to articulate specific ways in which he or she would like to change, a plan is developed, and the counselor-counselee team works to accomplish the plan and reach the goals.[24]

While they acknowledge that brief strategic therapy often works well, critics point out that many problems do not yield to this approach. A woman who has been sexually abused for many years, for example, and who carries these wounds in the form of deep insecurity, feelings of worthlessness, and fear of men is unlikely to be changed in a few sessions of strategic planning.

5. *Stopping*. Counseling does not last forever. In time, both the counselor and counselee back away from their more intense problem-solving relationship. Often there is a summarizing of what has been learned or accomplished. There may be discussion of ways in which the counselee can cope more effectively in the future. Often the time between sessions is increased, and eventually the counseling terminates, although the door remains open for future counseling contacts if they are ever needed.

On paper all of this looks straightforward and simple, but as we have seen, the phases rarely are identified as clearly or as easily as the previous paragraphs imply. For example, the first step of connecting with counselees and building a relationship is extremely important at the beginning when people might be nervous and apprehensive. Once a relationship has begun, it must be maintained. This means that the counselor must never lose sight of step one. As counseling progresses, there is continual vacillation back and forth between these phases as problem issues become clearer, solutions are found and tried, and counseling moves toward termination.

Theories of Counseling

Sigmund Freud's famous system of psychoanalysis was one man's theory of counseling. It summarized Freud's views about human nature, the causes of personal problems, and the best methods for helping people change. Like every theorist since, Freud sought to build his theory on facts, objective information, good logic, and his own knowledge about human beings based on his years of working with patients. Unlike some other theorists, however, Freud did not seem to understand that every theory is also a reflection of its creator's personality, interests, biases, values, beliefs, goals, past experiences, culture, training, and even the country or historical era in which one lives.

It is impossible to give an accurate estimate of the number of counseling theories that currently exist. Adlerian theory, Jungian analysis, existential therapy, Rogers' person-centered therapy, Gestalt therapy, transactional analysis (TA), Glasser's reality therapy, existential therapy, the rational-emotive therapy (RET) of Albert Ellis, the various behavior therapies, social-learning theory, and family systems therapy are among those that are best known. In addition, a number of Christians have proposed Christian approaches to counseling. These include Jay Adams' nouthetic counseling, various theories of "biblical counseling," Charles Solomon's spirituotherapy, Ed Smith's theophostic approach, and the growth counseling of Howard Clinebell. Most of these theories were developed in the early or middle years of the twentieth century.[25] More recent theories tend to focus on specific issues and are less inclined to give broad overviews of human nature or ways to bring major change.

Some counseling theories are highly developed and presented in formal language; others are more speculative and informal. Some theorists emphasize feelings, while others stress behavior change or counselee thinking. Some assume that counselees must take primary responsibility for helping themselves; others put more emphasis on the counselor's role. Many Christian approaches are built on the theorist's views of biblical teaching; other theories place greater emphasis on the findings of psychological insights and theory. Some theories are complicated and difficult to summarize; others are brief and much simpler. Although a summary of these various positions is beyond the scope of this book, good overviews and critiques are available for those who want further information.[26]

Why Bother with Theory? Some have argued that theories are of little importance, that they exist primarily to boost the egos of the theory builders, that they don't have much influence on the actual experience of counseling, and that they are increasingly irrelevant in a postmodern era. To some extent these arguments are true, but theories can serve a useful purpose.

Theories are like systems of theology. They summarize what we know and believe, what we are seeking to accomplish, and how we go about reaching our goals. As the size of this book would indicate, there is a massive amount of information about the complexities of human behavior, the causes of human problems, and the ways that counselors can help. Theories help us to incorporate all of these facts into some kind of an integrated, understandable, and useful framework. Theoretical approaches guide counselors as we seek to help people cope with their problems.

Which Theory Is Right? The answer is "none." Theories are human inventions, created by fallible human beings, and likely to be revised as our knowledge and understanding increase. Many professionals have their favorite theories (and theorists), but almost half of those who responded to one survey identified themselves as "eclectic."[27] This word describes those who prefer to draw concepts and techniques from a variety of approaches instead of being restricted to a single theory. Eclecticism is not a haphazard, intellectually lazy collecting of ideas. Instead, this is an approach that draws from the various sources in a thoughtful manner and enables counselors, in time, to arrive at their own counseling styles.

There is no one way to do this, just as there is no "single" right way to counsel. Jesus used a variety of approaches, depending on the needs of the counselee. Christian counselors, even those who seek most diligently to be biblical, utilize a variety of approaches and sometimes disagree with the theoretical viewpoints of their Christian brothers and sisters. It can be helpful to understand the different theories, but ultimately each of us must trust the Holy Spirit to work through our own personalities and perspectives to enable us to help others most effectively.

Taking Counseling Home

How do you learn best? Each of us has a unique way in which we learn most effectively. Some people learn best through *hearing*—listening to the words of others. Some are best able to learn through *seeing*—reading books, watching movies, and looking at diagrams. Others learn by *doing*—completing projects, doing role plays, or acting out their feelings. Experienced speakers and teachers know that learning is more likely to be retained if more than one of these learning channels is stimulated. Most counseling appears to still use the traditional "talking cure" approach that involves primarily verbal one-hour sessions separated by a week or more in between.

With the growth of generations steeped in postmodernism and raised with so many media and technical influences, many counselors are using forms of helping that go beyond the traditional counseling room. For example, it is common for counselors to recommend homework assignments that enable people to extend their learning beyond the counseling sessions and incorporate both seeing and doing in addition to hearing.

The idea of homework sometimes raises thoughts of dull busywork imposed upon unwilling recipients. It is better if the counselor and counselee drop the word *homework* and agree on useful and specific *follow-up* activities that can be done between sessions. These activities can help counselees keep aware of counseling goals, gain additional information (often through reading, listening to tapes, or going to the Internet), develop and practice new skills, eliminate harmful behavior, test what is being learned in counseling, and try out new ways of thinking and acting.

When possible, involve counselees in this follow-up process. At the end of each session, for example, you might ask, "After our meeting today, how can you put into practice what we have been talking about?" Try to help the counselee think of creative answers and useful activities that are specific and realistic enough to get completed. Here are suggestions:

1. *Written Activities.* These include the use of questionnaires, standardized tests, or completing sentence completion forms or other paper and pencil inventories. Also helpful are between-session writing projects, such as preparing an autobiography, determining life goals, listing one's strengths and weaknesses, keeping a diary, or making a list of what might be good or bad about a contemplated change. These written responses are then taken back to the counselor, where they are discussed. The Internet allows counselees to access online fill-in-the-blank questionnaires or to take tests and get immediate results that can be discussed in counseling later.

2. *Discussion and Study Guides.* Some study guides appear in the back of books, but there are many volumes exclusively devoted to guide home study or to promote small-group discussion. These books may be read by individuals who answer the author's questions and fill in the blanks but never discuss any of this with another person. Others work on the books or Internet guides between counseling sessions and subsequently discuss these resources with a counselor.

The quality of these programs and workbooks varies. And despite many years of research, there still is no clear evidence of the extent to which these programs are effective.[28] Most often these "do-it-yourself treatment books" are of greatest value with motivated people whose problems are not severe and who have regular contact with counselors.[29]

3. *Behavior Assignments.* Sometimes, counselees are encouraged to change their actions in some small but important ways between counseling sessions. Saying "thank you" once every day, giving periodic compliments, not complaining about some annoying practice in one's mate, getting to work on time, practicing a communication skill learned in the counseling session, attending a church service, reading the Bible for ten minutes daily, spending fifteen minutes playing with one's children—these are the kinds of specific behavior change suggestions that counselors give and discuss later with counselees. In addition, it may be helpful to have counselees record how much time is spent in specific situations, such as talking on the phone or watching television, or counselees might keep a record of their spending or eating behaviors. These activities can reveal helpful information both to the counselor and the counselee.

4. *Reading.* Books and articles often contain helpful information that supplements the counseling session. There is danger, however, that counselees will misinterpret what has been written or that something will be pulled out of context. No counselor has time to screen all potentially relevant books, and it will be difficult to find a variety of written materials with which the counselor agrees totally. In spite of these limitations, articles and books can be a helpful adjunct to counseling, especially if the reading is discussed subsequently within the counseling session.[30]

5. *Internet Resources.* The Internet has had a major impact in counseling. It is not unusual to have counselees search the Internet for information following their counseling sessions and return the following week with articles they have downloaded and printed. This can be a helpful adjunct to the counseling because excellent factual information can be obtained easily, including helpful resources for treatment. Many organizations have web sites that provide updated information and allow counselees to interact with others who have similar concerns. One side benefit for counselors is that our counselees often uncover helpful ideas and resources that can supplement our knowledge, understanding, and therapeutic interventions. Many counselors also provide their own sources of information through their web sites and can keep in contact with counselees through brief e-mail exchanges.[31]

Of course, it must be recognized that Internet sources vary in their quality and accuracy. It is easy to access Internet articles and web sites that have personal opinion presented as fact and conclusions that are of dubious validity. Encourage counselees to treat Internet information cautiously, to look at the source of the information, and to discuss the Internet materials with the counselor or some other knowledgeable person.

The Internet is more than a source of useful information. For example, some counselors do testing through the Internet, and others counsel or supplement their counseling with online resources. According to one survey of the published research, "studies have shown that people receiving computer interventions have as good, or better, outcomes as people in comparison or control groups."[32] Many professionals still question the effectiveness of Internet counseling, and questions have been raised about the accuracy and confidentiality of Internet testing.[33] Less controversial are the numbers of virtual support groups and chat rooms that allow counselees to be in contact with others who have similar concerns and problems.[34] These can be a significant source of support for many people.

6. *Audiotape, Videotape, and DVD Recordings.* Music therapy—the use of music to help people with their problems—is at least as old as the soothing melodies that David played to calm the troubled King Saul. Many people today relax by turning on the stereo after a busy day of work.

We live in a high-tech world with sophisticated stereo systems in our cars and multichannel entertainment systems in our homes that were undreamed of when the previous editions of this book were written. Audio and video tapes are available on almost every subject. Interactive video, Internet programs, and other new resources that can benefit counselees and their counselors appear constantly. When we work with technically knowledgeable younger counselees, both the counselor and the counselee can benefit from resources that greatly enhance our work as counselors.

One commonly used tool is the taping of counseling sessions with the counselees' permission. Consider the impact, for example, of a couple viewing a video tape of an argument that occurred in a prior session, seeing how each of them reacted and must have appeared to the other, and then reviewing all of the exchange with the counselor. Video taping is almost standard practice in counselor education as beginning counselors are taped and then able to evaluate their counseling while a supervisor watches and comments. Experienced counselors can benefit from similar taping and evaluation experiences.

7. *Other Computer Resources.* It will come as no surprise that as this book is being written, I move back and forth between my writing and an Internet database that includes thousands of relevant professional articles and web sites. Increasingly, counselors are using the Internet not only to counsel but also to give and evaluate home assignments, although there continues to be widespread concern about ethical dangers inherent in these practices.[35] Computers are used with children, adolescents, and others who may lack verbal skills or the courage to express their concerns in face-to-face discussions but who feel more secure writing their feelings into a computer. Computerized testing is now common, educational and behavior modification programs are available by computer, and increasingly sophisticated therapy programs have been designed for computer users. One group of counselors is using computer images to treat people with fear of heights, claustrophobia, or fear of flying. People who have difficulty relaxing are being helped with vivid and realistic images and sounds on their computers.[36] There are books to describe these and other procedures, although some appear to be outdated even before they are published.[37] Research in these fascinating areas is continuing to unlock new and previously unimagined opportunities that can be genuinely helpful to counselees and their counselors. All of this presents exciting possibilities for creative counselors who are not afraid of innovation.

Groups and Counseling

The early Christians probably did not meet under ideal environmental conditions, but they came together in small groups for the teaching, fellowship, breaking of bread, and prayer described in Acts 2:42. Undoubtedly, there was mutual support, encouragement, sharing, and burden-bearing. For Christians, this was the beginning of group helping.

Modern group therapy has been traced to the beginning of the twentieth century when a Boston internist set up "classes" for his tuberculosis patients. Soon it became apparent that these gatherings were providing opportunity for the patients to share their struggles, encourage one another, and develop feelings of closeness and solidarity. The value of this mutual interaction became known to psychiatrists, and group counseling developed as a unique and specialized form of treatment. Today, of course, groups are common both outside the church and within. They are at the core of many mega-churches and hold special attraction for postmodern people with the high value they place on being authentic, interactive, and inclusive.

Among their many benefits are the abilities of groups to:

- Instill hope and optimism.
- Decrease each participant's sense of feeling alone with his or her problem.
- Impart information about mental health, illness, spiritual growth, and specific counselee problems.
- Create a climate where participants can give and receive help, support, encouragement, and love.
- Provide feedback so members can learn how they are perceived by others, including people outside the group.
- Teach new learning so people can change their behavior and learn to function more effectively.

- Help people acquire and practice social skills so they can learn to relate to others in more positive and mature ways.
- Give positive models as the participants observe effective and mature behavior in the leader or other group members.
- Provide opportunity for the expression of feelings in a safe environment.
- Give a sense of belonging, acceptance, and cohesiveness.
- Help people deal with significant issues such as personal responsibility, basic values, planning for the future, the meaning of life, or one's sense of self-worth.
- Provide opportunity for believers to pray, study Scripture, and seek divine guidance together.

It is beyond the scope of this book to discuss issues such as how to select group participants, how to train leaders, how to maintain confidentiality, what to do with uncooperative or domineering group members, the stages through which developing groups evolve, how to terminate groups, what techniques to use, or the possible dangers of groups.[38] Many of these issues will differ depending on the purpose of the group. A group of carefully selected counselees, for example, may not function the same as a church cell group that exists for spiritual edification or as a way of involving people from the community who want to investigate Christian spirituality.

If groups with a counseling focus are led by inexperienced or untrained leaders, the group interaction can create more problems than are solved. For example, the relaxed group atmosphere may encourage individuals to discuss their problems openly, but later they may feel betrayed and hurt because they "told everything" but experienced no immediate healing. Frustration can be intense if group members are insensitive to one another, fail to keep confidences, are inclined to explode in criticism or verbal abuse, are unwilling to show respect or patience for other group members, or gossip after they leave the group meeting. Christian counselors should be aware of both the unique benefits and the potential harm in small-group counseling. If you want to work in this area, it is important to you and to your counselees that you get supervised training in the process of group counseling.

The contents of this long chapter may seem overwhelming at first, but we learn by focusing on one technique at a time. Keep reviewing your counseling and ask some counselees for permission to videotape occasional sessions so you can evaluate your techniques. Like any new skill, what you are learning will seem awkward at times, but eventually it will become automatic. With your hard work and the goodness and guidance of God, you can become an effective counselor. This chapter gives you the blueprint.

KEY POINTS FOR BUSY COUNSELORS

➤ Counseling is a skill. You learn it by doing.

➤ Counseling goals depend, in part, on the counselee. Goals include:
  - Relief from symptoms.
  - Self-understanding.
  - Learning new skills.
  - Help in changing behavior.
  - Resolving conflict.
  - Support and encouragement.
  - Spiritual growth.
  - Self-development.

➤ At the core of effective counseling is a relationship marked by warmth, genuineness, and empathy.

➤ Counseling skills that need to be learned and utilized frequently include:
  - Attending to what the counselee is communicating.
  - Listening carefully and actively.
  - Responding carefully with responses that involve:
    - ◆ leading the conversation,
    - ◆ reflecting on what is being said,
    - ◆ giving periodic summaries,
    - ◆ giving support and encouragement, and
    - ◆ offering careful interpretations.
  - Asking good questions so the conversation moves forward.
  - Challenging people.
  - Teaching how to change.
  - Filtering what is being said.

➤ The process of counseling includes:
  - Connecting with the counselee and keeping good rapport.
  - Exploring issues.
  - Helping people plan.
  - Guiding progress forward.
  - Terminating the counseling.

➤ Theories can guide counselors in their work, but there is no one theory that has been shown to be better than all others. In general, depending on the problem, the theories that help people learn new behaviors tend to be somewhat better.

➤ Counselors often give homework assignments to help people keep moving forward between counseling sessions. Homework could include:
  - Written assignments.

- Discussions and study guides.
- Assignments to monitor or change specific behaviors.
- Reading.
- Referral to Internet resources.
- Use of audio and video recordings.
- Other computer resources.

➤ Sometimes, counselees improve best when they can meet with other counselees in groups.

➤ You can grow as a counselor.

6

The Legal, Ethical, and Moral Issues in Christian Counseling*

It must have been an overwhelming time. Moses had led the whole nation of Israel out of Egypt and through the desert for forty years. There had been victories and times for rejoicing, but there also had been grumbling, failures, and revolts against their leader. From the beginning, Joshua had seen it all. He took over when Moses died, but it soon became clear that as the new leader he would be expected to do more than follow the example set by his mentor. Joshua had been chosen as God's man to lead the whole nation across a raging river and on to conquer a land of muscular, well-armed people who were determined to fight.

God's first words to the new leader are recorded in the Old Testament. They are words of encouragement and reassurance spoken to a man who must have felt insecure in taking up his new duties. "Be strong and courageous!" God said more than once. "Do not be afraid or discouraged. For the LORD your God is with you wherever you go."[1]

As a counselor, do you ever feel scared, incompetent, unsure what to say, and not very courageous or knowledgeable about what you are called to do? If you don't feel this way at times, you are in a minority, and maybe you don't fully appreciate the gravity of the counseling challenge. Like Joshua, counselors are called to lead people into new territory where there can be dangers and resistance. As we go forward, God's word to Joshua applies to us. "Be strong and very courageous. Obey all the laws Moses gave you. Do not turn away from them, and you will be successful in everything you do. Study this Book of the Law continually. Meditate on it day and night so you may be sure to obey all that is written in it. Only then will you succeed."[2]

There was a time, not many years ago, when people in the industrialized countries showed respect for authority in general and for the Bible's teachings, including the Ten Commandments. Christian counselors could quote the Bible even to nonbelievers, and the message was taken seriously. For those of us who are followers of Jesus, the biblical message is still authoritative, but this is not true for many of the people who enter our counseling rooms. Even church leaders

* I am deeply grateful to Dr. Miriam Stark Parent for her helpful insights in the preparation of this chapter.

and many Christian counselors have replaced biblical and church authority with more humanistic ways of thinking. Where, then, is the place of biblical teaching in Christian counseling as we move further into the twenty-first century?

Paul, the apostle, does not address this in Acts 17, but he gives us a model for interacting with people who have spiritual interests and a love for debating but who lack a firm philosophical foundation for their lives. In the first half of the chapter, Paul was interacting with Jewish listeners who respected and were knowledgeable about the Scriptures. The people who heard the message in Berea were described as being open minded, eager listeners, and active in searching the Scriptures day after day to see if Paul and his associate were teaching the truth.[3]

It was different when Paul got to Athens. This was a secular city, filled with idols and inhabited by people who "seemed to spend all their time discussing the latest ideas."[4] Paul got to know their city, saw what they worshiped, read their poetry, and was not afraid to debate the Gentiles or to interact with people in the public square. When he was invited to speak to their council of philosophers, the apostle respected them as people and showed that he was familiar with their culture. He didn't quote the Scriptures because they had no knowledge of the Scriptures and no reason to view these writings as a source of authority for their lives. But Paul did not compromise his beliefs or water down his message. He talked about God in whom we all live and move and exist.[5] He discussed repentance, judgment, and the resurrection, all in terms that they understood so clearly that some believed even as others laughed.

We who counsel in the midst of a world like Athens can use our theological terminology and refer to the Bible when we work with believers. When we counsel those outside of the Christian faith we show understanding, talk about biblical teaching without necessarily quoting Scripture, and seek to guide people in ways that are consistent with God's Word. We express ourselves and interact in different ways, depending on the counselee, the setting where we work, our own personalities, and our Christian worldviews.

Counselor Worldviews

One of our neighbors loves politics and has strong views about the superiority of the political party that he embraces. Whenever the neighbors get together, somebody raises the issue of politics, probably because it always brings a lot of humorous debate, especially between people who have differing political views. In our neighborhood the debates are friendly and good-natured, but we all know that political differences can lead to angry confrontation and occasionally violence. People can differ strongly in their views of politics, but also in their opinions about abortion, homosexuality, child rearing, ways of conducting business, the quality of different sports teams, and a variety of other issues, including religion and theology. Due largely to our past experiences and upbringing, each of us has a set of lenses through which we view the world. Most often these lenses are known as *worldviews*.[6]

A worldview is a set of assumptions and beliefs that we hold (consciously or subconsciously) that guide our behavior. These assumptions about the world and about life are rarely questioned, hardly ever mentioned to friends, and usually ignored unless somebody disrupts what we believe by showing a different perspective. A worldview helps us make sense of life, decide what is right or wrong, make decisions, choose values, settle on a lifestyle, and plan for the future. A counselor's worldview determines what he or she thinks about human nature, the causes of emotional problems, the extent to which problems come from sin, the best treatment strategies, and how to evaluate the counseling progress. Each counselee brings a worldview as well, and these impact our work, especially if counselor and counselee worldviews collide in the counseling room.

Consider, for example, how worldviews could impact the counseling of a woman with depression. Some counselors see emotional problems as basically biological, so the person is given antidepression medication and encouraged to have a complete physical examination. Counselors who see problems as the result of stress and the inability to cope might work to help the counselee understand her pressures and learn new stress-management techniques, different ways of thinking (including self-talk), or new forms of behavior. Others take a systems approach and look for the ways in which one's system of friends, family, work colleagues, environmental influences, or church leaders both create problems and can become the means through which healing comes. More common has been the view that problems come from within, from past experiences and buried conflicts that need to be uncovered and handled through insight. A large group of Christians believe that if anyone has a problem, it is because that person has sinned, so recovery depends on confession and going one's way without sinning further. Some of the depressed woman's friends might think that the problems would be gone if she would just "cheer up." Christian friends might assume that everything would be fine if she would pray about her problem and trust God. Some might think she should attend a healing service or see somebody who believes that a "power encounter" is needed in which there is confrontation with demonic forces that are dragging her down physically, psychologically, and spiritually. Many counselors use a number of these approaches, but even these are built on the worldviews that we have developed and accepted as we have grown up or gone through our training.

Every book writer (including the writer of this book) brings his or her values to a book, including beliefs, worldview, and theological perspectives. Because my worldview colors the pages of this book and influences my perspectives on Christian counseling, it is only fair that you know where I am coming from, do not have to guess, and can keep this in mind as you read. My worldview is summarized further in the footnotes.[8]

More important than my worldview, however, is yours. There is no doubt that your worldview will impact your counseling, so before getting further involved with people and their problems, it can be helpful to jot down your basic beliefs about the world. Then share these with one or two people who know you well and who have seen how your worldview is lived out in your life.

A well-rounded and useful worldview deals with at least five major topics, each of which can impact your counseling.

- What we believe about *God* is our theology. This includes whether or not we believe God exists, what this divine being is like, and the extent to which God influences our daily lives. For example, there are vast differences between the views of Christians (with their various doctrinal or denominational perspectives), atheists, different groups of Muslims, and pantheists who believe that God is in everything and/or that every human being is a god.

- What we believe about the *universe* includes our answers to questions like these: How did the universe come into existence? To what extent does it operate in accordance with natural laws? Is everything orderly or chaotic? Is there a purpose for the universe and its inhabitants? Do supernatural interventions occur and if so, when and how?

- *How we get knowledge* and accurate information is known as *epistemology*. Can we know anything with certainty? Can we trust our senses, intuition, or research methods? Will logic get us to the truth? Is there objective truth? What, if any, is the role of divine revelation? Is the Bible trustworthy? What about the Qur'an? How do we know if we are getting accurate information from the Internet, television news programs, or the pronouncements of politicians or preachers?

- What do we believe about *human beings*? Are we really different from animals and, if so, what sets us apart? Can we make free choices or are we controlled by deterministic forces? What are our beliefs about life after death, human limitations and potential, the ability to change, or whether we have souls? Each of these has big implications for counselors as we seek to help people change.

- How do we determine what is *right and wrong*? What are our views about war, vengeance in response to terrorist attacks, homosexual marriage, abortion rights, euthanasia, forgiveness, the ethical behavior of business leaders, or clergy sexual abuse? These topics all deal with morality issues. What we think about these issues can indicate whether we believe there are absolute standards of right and wrong or whether some or all morality depends on the situation or the culture. If there are moral standards that are greater than individuals, then who or what sets these standards, and how do we respond to those who have different standards? Do moral standards ever change? And how does the counselor respond if his or her moral standards differ from those of a counselee?

Theological systems and theories of counseling are built on worldviews that often differ. Debates about which position is superior or correct usually can be reduced to differences in basic worldview assumptions. Since our worldviews shape much of what we do in counseling, none of us should seek to help others if our worldviews are not clear, at least in our own minds. Table 6–1 gives guidelines for choosing and testing your worldview.[9]

Legal Issues in Counseling

If you read and apply the principles of this book, are you qualified to counsel? In the place where you live, is it legal for you to identify yourself as a counselor and charge a fee for your counseling services? If you counsel a person who later commits suicide or harms another person, could you be sued, fined, or even imprisoned for malpractice because you failed to anticipate and prevent the violence?

The answer to these questions depends on where you live. In the United States, Canada, and other countries, there are very specific laws about who is legally qualified to counsel, what training that person needs, and what the coun-

Table 6–1

Choosing and Testing a Worldview

Worldviews influence how counselors think about people, evaluate their problems, and make interventions for change. Unclear or inadequate worldviews, like faulty eyeglasses, can cloud our vision and hinder our efforts to see clearly. Without a clear worldview, the counselor has more potential for confusion, fumbling, and misunderstanding. The best worldviews are clear, plausible, coherent, able to make sense of life, and useful in helping us make decisions. How do we choose a good worldview or clarify and test the one we have?

Use reason. The best worldviews hold together logically and make sense without contradictions and inconsistencies.

Look at the evidence. Is there factual evidence to support your worldview? Assume, for example, that someone believes that all people have the best interests of others at heart. Is there evidence to support this optimistic assumption? Empirical evidence does not tell us everything (according to the author's worldview), but a worldview is suspect if it goes against strong evidence.

Check it out with others. It is not true that "if most people believe it, it must be true," but since our worldviews are subject to bias and distortion, it can be helpful to ask others to challenge or evaluate your worldviews. Recognize, of course, that the evaluations will depend, in part, on the worldviews of the people you ask. For this reason it can be helpful to ask different kinds of people.

Test it against experience. Experience is volatile and often influenced by emotions, but be suspicious of worldviews that claim to give explanations that are opposite to our experiences. For example, it is contrary to most of our experiences to believe that pain is an illusion, that we can go through life without every being discouraged, or that all problems will disappear if we become committed Christians. Look back over your life and see if some worldview beliefs have served you well or if others have proven to be worthless and unfounded.

Consider whether it feels right. This is subjective and cannot be the sole determinant of a worldview, but some worldview conclusions do not feel right and are not worth being the foundation for our lives.

Test it out. Does the worldview work consistently? Can you live, counsel, or build relationships, careers, or lifestyles on the worldview you hold?

Change cautiously. Since worldviews are deeply ingrained beliefs about life and the world, they often define who we are and resist change. But worldviews are not rigid or inerrant. Sometimes, we must or want to make changes in our basic assumptions. Usually, this occurs slowly and without our conscious awareness of the changes.

selor is allowed to do. My professional license as a clinical psychologist was issued only after I completed doctoral level training, completed a certain number of counseling sessions that were supervised, and took a licensing examination. To maintain a license, professionals must abide by state counseling laws and often are required to take continuing education courses every year to keep their knowledge and skills updated. If I moved only a few miles to another state, I would need to get a new license under the laws of that state before I could practice my profession. The issue becomes more complicated if somebody from another state or country calls to talk about a counseling issue. Is it a violation of my license to counsel by telephone or give recommendations to a person in another part of the country or the world? And if subsequent legal problems arose, like a lawsuit against me, under which set of state laws would I be judged?

In many parts of the world there are no laws to govern counselors, but with increasing frequency they are being created, often following heated debate between psychiatrists, nonmedical practitioners, clergy, and others who fear that their freedom to counsel will be disrupted or curtailed. Frequently, these debates swirl around the requirements and standards for counselors, often reducing to arguments about who is qualified to counsel and who is not. The goal of all this is to prevent harm to innocent people, but in many cases the debates often are about protecting one's turf.[10]

Laws that cover counseling issues vary from place to place and frequently are updated and changed. Here are some examples:

- *Who Is Competent to Counsel?* In Canada, the United States, and other countries, the law determines who is legally qualified to counsel, what titles the counselor may use, which counselors are exempt from revealing details about counseling in a court of law, the educational requirements for professional counselors, who can legally accept fees in return for counseling services, what constitutes counseling malpractice, and the conditions under which a counselor can be sued for professional negligence. You may be exempt from these laws if you counsel informally, do not call yourself a counselor, and do not charge for your services. Also, the laws may not all apply if you counsel within the confines of a church or educational institution, providing that you do not charge for your services and providing that the institution where you work is legally designated as a nonprofit entity. Wherever you counsel, however, there are laws that determine the civil liberties of counselees and the conditions under which individuals can be hospitalized involuntarily because of mental problems. Clearly, it would be wise to check with a lawyer to determine how local laws could influence or limit your counseling, or what you can do to prevent malpractice law suits even if you are a country pastor in an isolated community.
- *Should You Keep Records?* Absolutely. Records must be kept confidential and in a safe place. If you don't keep records, however, you can have difficulty in proving what you did as a counselor should your counselee sue you or develop more serious problems later and blame you.
- *Should You Record Counseling Sessions?* Never record a session without the counselee's written permission. State clearly why you are making the recording and what you will do with the tape. In general, it is not wise to tape sessions because this opens your work to intense scrutiny should there be legal or other problems later.

This discussion is a reminder that no counseling takes place in a vacuum.[11] Counselors and counselees live as members of a society and community. Sometimes, the community creates problems and restricts counseling effectiveness, but the opposite is also true. The community (including the Christian community) can facilitate your work as a helper, protecting both counselor and counselee against incompetence, legal challenges, unfair treatment, misrepresentation, and long-term emotional damage.

Counseling Ethics

Government laws are not the only regulations that impact and guide counselors.

Most professional counseling organizations, including Christian counseling associations, have developed ethical codes to protect the public from unethical practices, to guide counselors in ethical decisions, and to set standards. These ethical codes set the standards for counseling care. In courts of law and in professional organizations, counselors are evaluated against these guidelines. Sometimes, counselors are disciplined or dismissed from professional organizations if the standards are violated. Christian counselors usually attempt to honor and comply with these ethical codes, but since we view the Bible as God's Word, we accept the Scriptures as the ultimate standard against which all ethical decisions are tested.

The Christian counselor respects each individual as a person of worth, created by God in the divine image, marred by the human fall into sin, but loved by God and the object of divine redemption. Each person has feelings, thoughts, a will, and freedom to behave as he or she chooses.

Counselors sincerely seek what is best for each counselee's welfare. We do not attempt to manipulate, meddle in the counselee's life, ask questions to satisfy our own curiosity, or use counselees to meet our own needs. As servants of God, each counselor has a responsibility to live, act, and counsel in accordance with scriptural principles. As employees, counselors attempt to fulfill their responsibilities and perform duties faithfully and competently. As citizens and members of society, counselors obey the laws, submit to governmental authorities and contribute to the good of the culture.[12]

When everyone has similar assumptions and values, the counselor's work can proceed smoothly. Ethical problems arise when values conflict or when difficult decisions have to be made. Many (but not all) of these decisions involve issues of confidentiality. Consider the following as examples:

- The unmarried teenage daughter of your church chairman reveals that she is pregnant and planning to have an abortion. What do you do with this information?
- After getting your promise to keep all issues confidential, a young man reveals that he is planning to leave home and run away with his girlfriend.
- A young man requests help in gaining self-confidence around women so he can more comfortably encourage his female friends to have sexual intercourse with him. What is your responsibility as a counselor if you believe that premarital sex is wrong? Assume that you work in a church counseling center where it is assumed that you would not violate the church's ethical standards. Would your answer be different if you were employed in a secular setting?
- A seminary graduate currently seeking pastoral placement reveals in counseling that he is a practicing homosexual but seeking placement in a denomination that is opposed to overt homosexuality. Do you reveal this or say nothing when you are asked by a prospective church to complete a recommendation form on the candidate?
- In confidence, a counselee reveals that he has broken the law or that he intends to harm another person. Do you remain silent or tell the police and warn the intended victim?

Questions like these have no easy answers. The counselor is committed to keeping information confidential, but not when the welfare of the counselee or some other person is at stake. At times like these, the counselee should be encouraged to share information directly with the people involved (police, employers, family members, intended victims, or others). As a general rule, information should not be shared by a counselor without the counselee's knowledge, but sometimes information must be shared. In most of North America, including every U.S. state and Canadian province, it is a violation of the law to withhold information from authorities if a counselee reports elder or child abuse, including the sexual exploitation of children. Currently, the law does not always require the reporting of a counselee's involvement in criminal actions, or intended behavior that will harm the counselee or another person. However, the counselor is open to subsequent law suits or perhaps other legal difficulties if he or she withholds such information and fails to warn the intended victims.

In addition to these issues, the ethical counselor does not give medical, legal, or financial advice or offer other services for which he or she is neither trained nor qualified. At the beginning of their work with new counselees, most experienced counselors explain the limits of confidentiality and indicate when confidentiality must be broken. Often counselees are given a printed statement outlining the counselor's commitments. This might include a statement that sessions will not be tape recorded without the counselee's permission and whether the counseling will be discussed with a supervisor. The counseling services agreement is signed by both parties, outlining the guidelines of the relationship. This may seem like unnecessary precaution, but the existence of such documents can prevent potential problems later. In Canada and the United States, among other countries, these informed consent documents are mandatory. Since they are legal documents, a lawyer should be consulted when you design these statements. The person who counsels frequently also would be wise to consult a lawyer or some other knowledgeable person concerning the prospects of being sued for counseling malpractice and the wisdom of getting malpractice insurance.

In every ethical decision the Christian counselor seeks to act in ways that will honor God, conform with biblical teaching, and respect the welfare of the counselee and others. When difficult decisions must be made, counselors have an obligation to discuss the situation in confidence with one or two other Christian counselors and/or with a lawyer, physician, or pastor who can help in making ethical decisions. Ethical guidelines stipulate that these consultations can be done without your having to reveal the counselee's name or details that would reveal his or her identity. When difficult ethical decisions must be made, the Christian counselor gets as much factual data as possible (including biblical data), sincerely trusts that God will lead, and then makes as wise a decision as possible based on the best evidence available.[13]

Making Referrals

There are times when even the most experienced counselors refer their counselees to someone else whose training, expertise, and availability can be of special assistance. Referral does not mean that the original counselor is incompetent or trying to get rid of a difficult counselee. Instead, referral is an acknowledgment that no one person has the time, stamina, emotional stability, knowledge, skill, or experience to help everyone. In general, we should refer whenever a counselee does not appear to be improving or when we are stuck and not sure what to do next. More specifically, counselees should be referred when they:

- Have severe financial problems and need financial guidance.
- Need legal advice.
- Would appear to require a medical evaluation or treatment from a physician.
- Show bizarre or extremely aggressive behavior.
- Are extremely anxious, paranoid, or appear to be severely disturbed emotionally.
- Stir up strong feelings of dislike or sexual arousal in the counselor.
- Want to move to another counselor.
- Have a problem that appears to be getting worse in spite of your help.
- Have other problems that are beyond the counselor's area of expertise.

Counselors should become familiar with community resources and persons to whom counselees can be referred. These include private practitioners such as physicians, lawyers, psychiatrists, psychologists, and other counselors; pastoral counselors and other church leaders; private and public clinics or hospitals; service agencies such as crisis pregnancy centers or the Society for the Blind; government agencies in your community, career counselors, or the unemployment bureau; school guidance counselors and local educational institutions; private employment agencies; suicide or drug prevention centers; volunteer organizations like the Red Cross or those who deliver "meals on wheels"; and self-help groups such as Alcoholics Anonymous. Many of these are listed in the telephone book, or you can talk to other counselors who might know what is available. In time you will build your own file of referral resources. As you consider referral, do not overlook church or community groups that often can give support and practical help in times of need. Recognize that some counselees don't need counseling at all but could profit from a good coach.[14]

Whenever possible, it is best to refer your counselees to helpers who are both competent and Christian. Regretfully, many communities do not have professional Christian counselors, and some Christians in the helping professions are not very competent. Many problems (medical issues, for example, or learning disorders) do not need to be treated by a Christian. Even when the counselee is struggling with deep personal issues, non-Christians often are sympathetic to religious values and not inclined to undermine a counselee's faith. If Christian help is not available in your community, you must decide—for each individual— whether to make a referral or whether to continue seeing the counselee yourself, even though you would prefer to make a referral. If you do not refer, it can be helpful to consult with experts in your community, providing that you do not violate the counselee's confidentiality.

Before suggesting referral to a counselee, it is best to know what sources of help are available. Check first with the possible referral group or individual to see if they really are able to give the needed assistance. (It can be devastating to counselees if they approach a source of help based on your recommendation and then get turned away.) In suggesting referral to the counselee, be sure to indicate your reasons for making this recommendation. Present this as a way to get the best possible help. Some will resist the idea of referral and may conclude that you think they are too disturbed or too much of a problem for you to treat. Take time to discuss these fears and try to involve the counselee in the decision to move to a different source of help.

Most often it is best to let counselees make their own appointments with the new counselor. Sometimes, these new counselors will request information from you, but this should only be given if the counselee has granted his or her consent in written form. When the referral has been made, keep an interest in the counselee, but remember that somebody else is now responsible for the counseling.

The Counselor's Sexuality

Whenever two people work closely together on a common goal, feelings of camaraderie and warmth often arise between them. Frequently, these feelings of warmth have a sexual component, including a sexual attraction between counselor and counselee. Almost all counselors experience this at least periodically. The sexual attractions can be of different types, including counselees who are attracted to their counselors, counselors who are attracted to their counselees, same-gender attractions, and counselors who are attracted sexually to younger people, including children. Each of these is evidence of the sinful nature within us all.

Counseling often involves the discussion of intimate details that would never be discussed elsewhere. This can be sexually arousing to both the counselor and counselee, even to those who hold the highest standards of sexual purity. Many years ago, Freud wrote that subtle sexual influences within the counseling relationship "bring with them the danger of making a man forget his technique and medical task for the sake of a fine experience." Perhaps almost every reader of this book knows of counselors, including pastoral counselors, who have compromised their standards "for the sake of a fine experience." Their ministries, reputations, counseling effectiveness, and sometimes their marriages have been destroyed as a result—to say nothing of the adverse effects this can have on counselees. Sexual feelings toward counselees are common, and the wise counselor makes a special effort to maintain self-control.

1. *Spiritual Protection.* Meditation on the Word of God, prayer (including the intercession of others), and reliance on the Holy Spirit to protect us are all crucially important. In addition, counselors should watch what they do with their minds.

Fantasy often precedes action, and the alert counselor makes a practice of not dwelling on lustful thoughts. Focus instead on that which is true, honorable, right, pure, lovely and good.[15] When fantasies come to mind, bring them to God, draw near to him, and consciously resist the devil, who is their source.[16] Avoid pornographic materials, sexually explicit magazines or books, and sexually arousing movies because these stimulate fantasy, lower resistance, and slowly increase a person's vulnerability.

There also is value in finding another believer who will hold you accountable for your actions and fantasies. This can have a powerful impact on your own behavior. Finally, be careful not to fall into the dangerous trap of thinking, "It happens to others but would never happen to me." This kind of pride can increase the dangers of falling into temptation. It is thinking that ignores the biblical warning that "if you think you are standing strong, be careful, for you, too, may fall into . . . sin."[17]

And what if you do fall? We serve a God who forgives,[18] even though the scars—in the form of guilt feelings, a ruined reputation, or a marriage break-down—may remain for a lifetime. If we confess any sin we are forgiven, but then we have the obligation to change our subsequent thinking and behavior, making them more consistent with scriptural teaching.

2. *Knowing One's Vulnerabilities.* What would increase the likelihood that you would engage in sexual misconduct with a counselee? The list of influences might differ from one person to another, but the more of the following that are present, the greater the vulnerability:

- Emotional and sexual needs are not being met elsewhere.
- Marital intimacy is poor.
- Sexual fantasies are common (perhaps stimulated by pornographic images).
- The counselor has rigid moral attitudes and a denial that he or she could fall.
- There are no outside activities or interests apart from helping others.
- Workaholic tendencies are present.
- The counselor tends to be a loner, isolated from friends and colleagues.
- Peer accountability is disregarded or assumed to be unimportant.
- The counselor has secret struggles and conflicts about his or her own sexuality.[19]

3. *Awareness of Danger Signals.* The counseling setting itself can stimulate vulnerability, including the privacy and openness to discuss intimate issues. Before any misconduct, however, signs of danger usually appear. These might be divided into external signs that come from others and internal danger signals that rise within the counselor.

External danger signs include:

- A growing dependence—the counselee increasingly requests more time and attention.
- Affirmation and praise—the counselee frequently expresses appreciation, praise, and admiration for the counselor, often indicating how much the counselor is needed.
- Complaints about loneliness—sometimes the counselee accompanies these with statements about the counselor's compassion and ability to be helpful.
- The giving of gifts—which can indicate the counselee's increasing emotional involvement and sometimes create a subtle sense of obligation or manipulation. (To avoid this, counselors often state at the beginning of counseling that they will not accept gifts.)
- Increasing physical contact—which may start with harmless touch but move to more physical involvement.
- A frequent desire to discuss sexual issues—which can be arousing to the counselor.
- Evidence of seductive behavior—including how the counselee dresses, sexually explicit comments, or comments about the counselor's attractiveness.

- Power struggles—these may be passively aggressive techniques used by counselees to entrap counselors, bring them down, discredit them, or demonstrate the counselee's superiority.

Every counselor should be alert to the following *internal signs* that could indicate growing danger for sexual misconduct:

- You think about the counselee between sessions and let your mind dwell on his or her personality traits.
- You compare the counselee with your spouse, forgetting that the counselee is new, always attractive when you meet, different, and possibly very impressed with you.
- You begin to believe that the counselee is special and different from the others, so that ordinary rules and boundaries do not apply.
- You find excuses to prolong contact with the counselee, perhaps by frequent telephone calls, attendance at the same church meetings or social gatherings, or by prolonged counseling or more frequent counseling sessions.
- You allow your mind to dwell on fantasies about the counselee, including sexual fantasies or fantasies of you being the person's rescuer or hero.
- You want to share your own problems with this person who appears to be so sensitive and caring.

All of this is more dangerous if the counselor lacks fulfilling social contact elsewhere or if his or her own marriage has grown cold or unstable.

4. *Setting Limits.* By setting and maintaining clear limits, we can avoid some of the sexual dangers in counseling.

- Even before counseling begins, clearly decide on the frequency and length of counseling sessions, communicate these in writing, then stay within these limits.
- Refuse to engage in long telephone conversation.
- Meet in a place and seat yourself in a way that discourages wandering eyes or an opportunity for personal intimacies.
- Discourage lengthy detailed discussions of sexual topics.
- Avoid every appearance of evil.[20]
- Never let down your guard so that you risk falling into temptation.[21]

Table 6–2 gives further guidelines to protect yourself against sexual involvement with counselees.

5. *Telling Yourself the Truth.* There is nothing to be gained by denying your sexual feelings. These are common, sometimes embarrassing, often arousing, but clearly controllable. Try to remember that yielding to sexual temptation can have:

(a) Social Consequences. Yielding to temptation can ruin one's reputation, marriage, ministry, and counseling effectiveness.

(b) Professional Implications. Sexual intimacies with counselees never help the person with problems and invariably damage a counselor's career, effectiveness, and professional image.

Table 6–2

Prevention Guidelines

Protecting Yourself Against Sexual Involvement with Counselees

1. Be aware of your own needs and well-being.
2. Develop and maintain fulfilling relationships apart from your counseling work.
3. Maintain quality supervision and consultation.
4. Be conservative in terms of touch.
5. To the extent that this is possible, limit contact with counselees in social settings and other relationships apart from the counseling room.
6. Keep a professional manner in counseling by adhering to time limits, meeting in appropriate places, or keeping guidelines for emergency contact.
7. Before counseling begins, set the guidelines in writing, sign an agreement, and review this on a regular basis.
8. Be careful about self-disclosure. If you do talk about yourself, consider how this is helping the counselee rather than meeting your own needs. Usually, another counselor can help you keep this in perspective.[22]

(c) Theological Effects. Sexual involvement outside of marriage is sin and must be avoided. We may complain that "the devil made me do it," but the devil only tempts. He never makes us do anything. We choose to sin by thinking and acting contrary to what we know is right. We sin because we ignore or are insensitive to the promptings of the Holy Spirit, who resides within every believer and is greater than Satan.[23] Present circumstances or past influences may make us more vulnerable to temptation, but each of us is responsible for our own choices and behavior.

6. *Support-Group Protection.* Most counselors would agree that sexual involvement with counselees is wrong or at least very unwise. In the midst of temptation, however, emotions often take over and our most reasonable and determined resistance begins to melt. A close walk with God can inoculate us against this descent into sin, but it also helps to honestly admit one's vulnerability and to discuss this openly with one or two trusted confidants.

First on the list is one's spouse. A good marriage does not prevent one's being sexually attracted to a counselee, but marriage has a significant influence on the counselor's ability to cope. Sometimes because of fear, embarrassment, or a desire not to hurt, the counselor never discusses this issue with his or her mate. As a result we miss a good opportunity for in-depth marital communication, support, and reassurance. If a counselee becomes a serious threat to the counselor's marriage, there is a good possibility that there were underlying problems in the marriage before the counselee came along.[24]

There also is value in discussing one's feelings with another trusted counselor or close friend. In this way the problem can be kept in perspective, the Christian friend can pray for protection, and the counselor has someone to whom he or she can be accountable.

Should the sexual attraction be discussed with the counselee? Perhaps on rare occasions this could contribute to the counselee's self-understanding and growth. But the risks involved in such discussions are so high that most counselors make it a practice to never discuss their sexual feelings with a counselee. Some counselees could misinterpret such discussions as an invitation to greater intimacy. Others, especially immature or flattered counselees, may talk to others about your discussion. This in turn could have disastrous consequences for you and your counseling work or reputation. Rather than mentioning one's sexual feelings to a counselee, it is wiser to discuss this with another friend or professional consultant.

We have devoted an unusual amount of space to this discussion of counselor sexuality, but perhaps no topic is more important for protection of both the counselor and the counselee. We all are vulnerable. But the vulnerabilities are greater in the counseling relationship because of unequal power. The counselee comes because he or she is needy and wanting help. Often there is a desire to please the counselor and comply with his or her suggestions. The counselor, in turn, has a position of power in the relationship and can exert more influence than would exist in more casual relationships. The counselee's desire to please and the counselor's ability to influence can combine to make a volatile relationship that is more open to sexual misconduct unless the counselor sets clear boundaries from the beginning.

Usually, it is best for everyone if you refer your counselee to another counselor if you sense any of the following:

- A tendency to flirt with your counselee.
- Continuing anxiety in yourself during the counseling sessions.
- An excessive desire to please the counselee.
- Preoccupation with thoughts and fantasies (including sexual fantasies) about the counselee between sessions.
- Obvious anticipation of the next session coupled with fears that the session may be canceled or the counseling will be terminated.

Avoiding Extremes

The field of counseling can be controversial. Advocates of different counseling techniques or theories sometimes disagree strongly, criticize those who think differently, and proclaim the superiority of their favorite counseling theories or theorists. These debates are not limited to secular counselors; often they appear in the Christian circles where the debaters try to justify their different approaches using Bible verses.

Most counselors recognize that problems can have a variety of causes, but probably most of us have favorite theories, many of which have been studied scientifically. Some counselors work on the assumption that problems most often arise from inner psychic conflicts or past trauma, some of which may no longer be remembered. Others place the cause of their problems in the environment on their family system. Another prevalent view maintains that the majority of problems come from faulty human learning. These views are also held by Christian counselors, but for many believers the different views about the causes and cures of personal problems most often appear to center around physiology, theology, and demonology.

Physiology. There is increasing research evidence that most if not all personality problems and psychological disorders have a biological component, including chemical imbalances, glandular malfunctioning, genetic influences, disease, or other physical influences. Often these physiological influences cause problems, but they also can arrive as a result of the problems' existence. For many years medical practitioners have argued that emotional problems have a physical cause that only can be diagnosed accurately or treated effectively by someone with medical training. This book recognizes that all behavior has a biological element, but we don't assume that all or even most personal problems are physiologically caused, and neither do we maintain that problems are always treated best by medication or other biological interventions.

Theology. Are most problems the result of individual sin in the counselee's life? Many counselors and theologians still hold this viewpoint. They argue that counseling must consist primarily of confronting people with sin, urging them to confess their sin and repent, then teaching them how to live in accordance with biblical teachings.

Counseling is not likely to be effective, long term, if it ignores the pungent reality of sin, the need for forgiveness, and the crucial importance of Christ-honoring behavior. The following chapters mention sin frequently and consider it seriously. But we do not assume that all or even most problems come primarily because of specific sinful behavior or thinking in the counselee.

Demonology. Within the church there always have been those who assume that problems most often arise from demonic influences and must be treated by different forms of spiritual warfare, including exorcism. Some Christians gather regularly to pray for deliverance and command that demons of depression, lust, anxiety, anger, bitterness, or confusion depart when they are commanded to do so.

In Ephesians 6 the Bible clearly teaches that Christians are engaged in a spiritual battle. Satan is described in Scripture as a schemer who masquerades as an angel of light but who prowls the earth like a roaring lion looking for someone to devour.[25] Satan's demonic forces are mentioned often in the Bible, and there is no reason to think that the devil's agents are inactive today. Christians disagree about the extent to which demons are involved in personal problems; in this book we will assume that demonic forces at times create or complicate the lives of counselees and the work of their counselors.

Counselors might ponder the conclusion of C. S. Lewis, who wrote that "There are two equal and opposite errors into which our race can fall about the devils. One is to disbelieve in their existence. The other is to believe and to feel an excessive and unhealthy interest in them. They themselves are equally pleased with both errors."[26] There are Christian counselors who fall into both of these extremes, undoubtedly to the detriment of their counselees. The following pages accept the reality of the demonic but assume that exorcism should be used rarely and only in a context of prayer and with the full support of spiritually mature and biblically astute church leaders.

KEY POINTS FOR BUSY COUNSELORS

➤ Be cautious of the terminology you use. The theological or psychological terms that counselors use may not be understood in the same ways by counselees.

➤ Everybody has a worldview. Worldviews are basic assumptions and beliefs that we hold (consciously or subconsciously) and that guide our behavior. Every counselor should take the time to clearly articulate his or her worldview.

➤ A well-rounded and useful worldview deals with at least five major topics, each of which can impact your counseling.
- What is your view of *God*?
- What is your view of *the universe*? How did it come into existence? Why does it exist? Where is God in this?
- How do we get *knowledge* and how do we know if it is accurate?
- What is your view of *human beings*? Why do we exist? How do we relate to God?
- How do we determine what is *right and wrong*?

➤ In many parts of the world there are laws that determine who is qualified and permitted to counsel. Be sure you know the laws of your government.

➤ Ethics are standards of right and wrong that govern counselors. Here are examples:
- Every counselee should be respected as a person of worth.
- The counselor seeks the welfare of the counselee.
- The counselor does not use the counselee or the counseling relationship to meet the counselor's own needs.
- The counselor keeps information confidential except when sharing information could prevent harm to some person or when sharing information may be required by law (as, for example, when the counselor discovers child abuse).
- Many ethical decisions are difficult and best decided in consultation with another counselor (but without revealing unnecessary information).
- The Christian counselor seeks to honor God, be in conformity with biblical teaching, and respect the welfare of the counselee.

➤ At times, every counselor makes referrals to another counselor who is better able to help the counselee. This should be viewed as evidence of getting what is best for the counselee, not as an admission of failure or incompetence.

➤ No one counselor can work effectively with every kind of person or problem.

➤ There are times when every counselor feels a sexual attraction toward a counselee or when the counselee feels sexually attracted to the counselor.

➤ Great care must be taken to protect oneself from increasing vulnerability that leads to a fall.

Counselor self-control comes through:
- Spiritual protection.
- Knowing one's vulnerabilities.
- Being aware of danger signals.
- Setting limits.
- Telling oneself the truth.
- Finding support and accountability with others.

➤ Christian counselors should be cautious of extremes that include:
- A failure to recognize the biological basis of behavior including problems,
- Both an overemphasis and an underemphasis on the role of sin and forgiveness in counseling,
- Both an overemphasis and an underemphasis on the role of demons in the causes and treatment of emotional problems.

The Multicultural Issues in Christian Counseling*

After arriving in an Eastern European country to be the speaker at a conference on counseling, I learned that the program also included workshop presentations from a group that had come from a prominent American church. These speakers brought special expertise to the conference and were warmly received—except for one person. In her home church she was known as an effective seminar leader with excellent speaking abilities. Her announced topic was of great interest to the European audience, and many people came to the first session. But the numbers were down for the second session, and almost nobody came after that, apparently because the speaker had made a major mistake. Before leaving home, she had made no effort to learn about the country where she would be speaking. She assumed that her overseas audience would respond like American audiences to her speaking style, jokes, figures of speech, stories, recommended counseling methods, and suggestions for audience participation. Her cultural insensitivity alienated the audience and left many unable to understand what was so clear to people at the speaker's church back home in Texas.

Salim is a trained Christian counselor from the Middle East who works with refugees at a counseling center in Canada. Many of his counselees are Muslims who appreciate Salim's Middle Eastern upbringing, cultural understanding, and ability to counsel in the Arabic language. Although he was trained in North America, he discovered quickly that the counseling methods he learned in graduate school often are not appropriate with his counselees from other countries. For example, many of the people he sees have no understanding of counseling, of counselor boundaries, or of time limits for counseling. Trust and rapport only come when Salim meets these counselees in their homes, at least in the beginning, drinking strong coffee and building friendships in a relaxed setting—as they would do in Ankara, Amman, or Cairo. Once, Salim was asked to counsel people who had been farmers in their native African country but had been resettled in an American city. Most were frustrated because they no longer could do farming, so their counselor approached the pastor of a large church to ask if these people could "farm" an adjacent lot that the church owned. When Salim worked with them to plant vegetable gardens, he built a bridge of trust that transferred later to the counseling room. As a side benefit Salim learned how to plant a garden and grow vegetables, something he had never done when he was growing up in Beirut.

T he early church was planted in a diverse cultural setting. Before returning to heaven, Jesus instructed his followers to tell people about him everywhere, in Jerusalem, throughout Judea, in Samaria, and to the ends of the earth.[1] On the day of Pentecost, people from a variety of nations were amazed to hear the Gospel message in their own languages.[2] The first missionary journeys went throughout the eastern Mediterranean. The early believers spoke different lan-

* I am deeply grateful to Issam Smeir and to Lynwood Morris for their helpful insights in the preparation of this chapter.

guages, came from different countries, represented different social classes, and sometimes had tensions between them. In this environment, Paul wrote that in Christ we are all one. "There is no longer Jew or Gentile, slave or free, male or female. For you are all Christians—you are one in Christ Jesus."[3] We have the same God, the same Scriptures, the same Holy Spirit to guide us. Could it be that we have the same biblically based counseling principles that can be applied cross-culturally without any adaptation? There are committed counselors and teachers of counseling who believe that Christian counseling is above culture and can be applied in the same way to anybody.

In contrast are those who believe that every counselor and counselee comes with a unique set of experiences, worldviews, theological perspectives, and cultural expectations. Jesus approached people in different ways, depending on the place where they met, their backgrounds, and their cultures. When he talked with the woman in Samaria, for example, he recognized her cultural expectations and spoke to her differently than he spoke to Roman officials like Pilate or Herod, Jewish leaders in Jerusalem, or fishermen from Galilee. His message was the same wherever he spoke, but his counseling, preaching, and one-on-one contacts showed an awareness of cultural differences.

It is common for counselors to assume that cross-cultural issues are of relevance only to overseas speakers or to people like Salim who work with counselees from other countries. Surely cross-cultural sensitivity would be of minimal importance for people who counsel in communities or churches where everyone has a similar cultural background. This chapter assumes, however, that *all counseling is cross-cultural*. You may not counsel people of a different race or ethnic background, and you may never go overseas to counsel or speak at a conference. But you cannot assume that every counselee will be like you. You are counseling cross-culturally if you work with someone of an age, background, gender, level of education, set of values, socioeconomic status, belief system, or sexual orientation that differs from yours. And you are likely to be doing more explicit cross-cultural counseling as communities become increasingly diverse due to the arrival of people from various ethnic, racial, and multicultural backgrounds—including international students, immigrants and temporary workers, missionaries and others who have lived in another culture for many years, or visitors who experience crises or the need to make decisions while they are in your community.

Compared to other people in their communities, many members of minority groups have a greater need for counseling and other mental health services. In part, this is because of the greater number of stressors in their lives. Even with these needs, however, ethnic minorities are not inclined to use the counseling opportunities that are available. Often people from minority groups do not know that help is available, are not accustomed to thinking that emotional problems can be treated, are dissuaded by language barriers, or are afraid about what might happen in counseling. Some lack transportation to appointments or lack trust in counselors. Others have the belief that only crazy people go to counselors, so they are reluctant to admit to themselves or to others that they need help. As a result, people who could benefit from counseling fail to get it. Even counselors who normally are very effective can fail if they do not appreciate these multicultural issues.

Describing the Territory

When psychologist Mary Pipher wrote a book titled *Another Country*, her work was described as "a field guide to a foreign landscape."[4] It was a book intended to help counselors and other readers who were "entering a new territory, with very different family structures, work options," values, worldviews, anxieties, communication styles, and interests. It may surprise you to know that Pipher was not writing about the people of some foreign land far from her own. She was writing about old age as a "foreign country with an unknown language to the young and even to the middle aged."[5]

Pipher's decision to describe the world of the elderly as another country points to the diverse meanings that might be attached to words like *multicultural, multiracial,* or *ethnicity.* Most often, these words refer to different minorities, nationalities, or racial-ethnic groups.

Minorities. As the word implies, these are people in age, cultural, religious, or racial groups that are not part of the majority. Examples include Asian Americans in the United States, Jews in Saudi Arabia, Christians in Malaysia, or elderly people in almost any country. Minority groups, like Americans with black skin, may be very visible, highly diversified, and large in numbers. Other minorities, including many religious groups, may be small, and are sometimes careful to keep their presence and activities quiet. Groups like the poor (who, in many countries are majorities rather than minorities) often strive to change their status; others, like the wealthy and privileged, usually enjoy their minority position and have no desire to be different.

Nationalities. This term refers to people identified with different countries. Every country is different from all others, and each has great diversity within its own borders. The diversity increases when people emigrate from these countries and take their national identities with them to their new places of residence. Chicago, for example, is an American city, but a large group of Chinese people live there, many in a neighborhood known as Chinatown. The city has a Polish population second only to Warsaw, and the Greek population is second only to Athens. Many of these Chicago residents retain their native languages, food preferences, and customs. Others have assimilated into the culture where they live and become American citizens. Many have been born into immigrant families but consider themselves to be Americans whose Chinese, Polish, Greek, or other backgrounds are of secondary importance.

Racial-Ethnic Groups. In Canada, where I grew up, French-Canadians were perceived as being very different from English-speaking Canadians, and both differed from the "first-nation peoples" that we used to refer to as Eskimos. In the United States the major racial-ethnic groups are Asian Americans, African Americans, Latino/Hispanic Americans, and Native Americans. Each has unique features as a group, but within each of the groups there is great diversity.

You will recognize that some people can be considered part of all three groups. A person from India who lives in Great Britain or Australia would be an example. All of this is complicated further by the existence of prejudices that often have little or no basis in fact but shape behaviors and attitudes as people from one group counsel or interact with the others.

Because of this diversity, Christian counseling cannot be defined or applied in the same way to all of the groups, nationalities, and cultures that make up this world which God created. Christian counseling had many of its origins in Caucasian, middle- to upper-class, Western (mostly American), largely Protestant cultures that value individualism, verbal communication, openness, a willingness to express emotions, adherence to time restrictions, a cause-effect perspective, the importance of being successful, and a commitment to reaching long-range goals. Much Christian counseling seeks to build on the Bible, but there are denominational and other differences in biblical interpretation that influence what the counselor does. Hopefully, you can learn a great deal about Christian counseling from the pages of this book, but how you apply the principles will depend, in large measure, on your own cultural perspective and on the people with whom you work. The most effective Christian counselors never lose sight of cultural differences but seek to be guided by the Holy Spirit, who is not culture bound and who can lead you and your counselees into all truth and growth, regardless of different cultural perspectives.

Building Multicultural Competence

Several years ago, The American Psychological Association noted that counselors and other "providers of psychological services" should be aware of ten groups that could be discriminated against unless they were diagnosed and treated in unique ways. Care-givers were alerted to the danger of unfairly treating people on the basis of their gender, age, race, ethnicity, national origin, religion, sexual orientation, disability, language, or socioeconomic status.[6] Soon there were detailed guidelines and training programs to help professional counselors be more competent in dealing with multicultural issues.[7]

This may be fine for professional therapists, but what about the Christian counselor who wants to have cultural sensitivity without enrolling in long diversity training programs? How do we develop what has been called *multicultural competence*—the ability to understand and help others effectively while we keep aware of the cultural influences that shape how each person sees the world? One research project found fifty-one multicultural competencies that counselors need to learn and practice, but we will reduce these to five.[8]

1. *The counselor should develop awareness of his or her own cultural values and biases.* Freud has been criticized because he proposed universal laws of behavior based on his work with affluent patients in Vienna. He failed to realize that his own perspectives, culture, experiences, and biases shaped the conclusions that he thought would apply to everybody.

What may be true of Freud is a danger for all of us. The counselor who was hurt by an abusive parent or a rigid religious upbringing could begin to assume that all counselees have been abused and need to be freed from past trauma.[9] The pastor who has seen the power of small groups in bringing healing could conclude that participation in small group settings is the best approach for everybody. Your biases and attitudes toward people of a different gender, religion, race, or sexual orientation can impact how you counsel members of these groups, even though you might not recognize that this is happening. Probably most of us have "a strong belief in the superiority of our own group's cultural heritage, history, values, language, beliefs, religion, traditions, and arts and crafts." Often this is accompanied with a belief in the inferiority of other groups.[10]

Most people seem to be unaware of their biases and how these may be influencing their counseling. To reduce bias in your counseling, review your own worldviews. What is your perspective on issues such as the basis of right and wrong, how people change, or the role of sin or biology in the development and treatment of counselee problems? Take a few minutes to write down your core values. Get the perspective of a supervisor, good friend, or some other person who knows you well and who would be willing to share what he or she sees as your biases, values, or deeply held beliefs. Get the perspective of a good friend from another culture or ethnic group. What does this person see as your cultural values and biases?[11] Whenever I teach or speak to a group of people from another culture, often I encourage the people to tell me about attitudes or cultural perceptions that they see in me that may not be appropriate for them. Your counselees can teach you as well. This gives you greater self-insight and prevents culturally hampered counseling.

Early in my teaching career, I taught a course on pastoral counseling to a group of mostly African American pastors. I was not far into my first lecture when a hand went up, and a class member had a comment. "I'm sure this is fine for white people," he said, "but this won't work in the black community." This happened repeatedly during my course, and I always responded the same way: "Okay. What will work in the black community?" Looking back, I think the discussions with these experienced pastors taught me more about counseling than I taught them. For me it was a powerful learning experience.

With all of us there will be times when the cultural barriers are too big to cross. For example, despite your best efforts you may have limited effectiveness if you are a male counselor working with a female counselee who has been abused by male authorities. If you have never left your own country, you may have difficulty trying to counsel refugees who are victims of trauma and relocation. And you may have difficulties if you are an English-speaking suburbanite who has no understanding of the difficulties faced by a counselee who is Spanish speaking, poor, and living in difficult circumstances.[12] In situations like these, everybody benefits if your counselee can be helped to find a more compatible counselor.

2. *The counselor should try to become aware of the cultural background of each counselee.* Often this is not a big issue, especially if you counsel people from your own community who have backgrounds similar to yours. Even then, however, there can be differences in attitudes, values, expectations, and worldviews. Counsel a teenager or a grandparent from the same family, and you are likely to find differences, all of which will be brought into the counseling room. If you are not sure of a counselee's perspective, do not hesitate to ask. Table 7–1 summarizes areas where the counselee and counselor may differ because of different cultural perspectives.

Christian counselors often face a dilemma when they consider the topics of this chapter. We are told to recognize and acknowledge cultural differences. But we also are told to avoid relying on stereotypes because there are so many differences within each cultural group. As an example, consider the challenge that a white counselor may face when counseling with a young African American male.[13] It is well documented that many of these young men are angry, both because of discrimination that they face currently, but also because of their knowledge of how racism and discrimination have shaped African American history for decades. In their influential book, *Black Rage*, two writers introduced the term "healthy cultural paranoia" to argue that black Americans have had to be

Table 7–1

Potentially Significant Multicultural Issues

This table illustrates some of the major areas where counselors and counselees may differ. These questions are not listed in any order of priority, and neither is this intended to be a complete list. Counselors might consider their own honest responses to questions like these before counseling others. Then recognize that your counselees may bring different answers. For example, consider the first question. You may not think the extended family is very relevant to the counselee's problem, but the counselee may believe that there will never be healing unless the extended family is involved in the counseling process.

1. Marriage, Family, and Gender
   - What is the role or importance of extended family members such as grandparents, aunts, uncles, cousins, and others?
   - Is the nuclear family (mother, father, children) always the ideal family unit?
   - Is marriage viewed as a permanent life-long relationship?
   - Under what circumstances is divorce permitted?
   - How are major family-related decisions made?
   - What are the mother's role and the father's role in child rearing?
   - Are the partners equal, or is one spouse considered to be superior to the other?
   - Are the genders equal, or is one superior to the other?
2. Self-Perception
   - Is the person self-deprecating?
   - Is the person self-promoting?
   - Does the person have a positive self-image and a strong sense of self-worth?
   - Is a positive self-image viewed favorably in the counselee's home or cultural group?
   - Is a self-critical or demeaning attitude culturally expected?
3. Cultural Identity
   - Does the person struggle with confusion about cultural identity (e.g., a young person raised on the mission field may feel torn, with roots in two cultures but not fitting completely into either)?
   - What are the person's attitudes and beliefs about his or her own culture? (Some people are proud of their cultural and ethnic background, but others are not.)
   - What are the person's attitudes and beliefs about your culture—and toward you as a member of your culture?
   - What are the person's attitudes and beliefs about other cultures, including minorities?
   - Does the person feel cultural bound, having to act like others in his or her cultural group but unable or afraid to find and express his or her uniqueness or identity?

4. God and Religion
   - What are the person's beliefs about God?
   - To what extent are the religious beliefs a significant part of the person's daily life?
   - What, if any, is God's role in causing or allowing problems?
   - What is God's role in resolving the problems?
   - Is there tolerance for people with other religions or with no religious faith?
   - What is the role of the church or other religious institution in helping people live and cope with problems?
   - What is the role of the religious leader?
   - How does the person respond to the counselor's attitudes and beliefs about God and religion?

5. Values
   - To what extent are independence, autonomy, and originality valued?
   - How important are commitment to family unity or commitment to cultural identity? (Is it more important to succeed as an individual or to bring honor to one's family or cultural group?)
   - Is mental illness the same as any other problem, or is it shameful and dishonoring to the individual or to one's family or nationality?
   - How important is success?
   - What are the implications of personal failure?
   - How important is materialism? (Is it important to have property, space, or possessions that are highly visible to others?)
   - How important are power, position, titles, or credentials such as academic degrees?

6. Control-Responsibility
   - Does the person believe that individuals are in control of their futures, or is the future viewed as being mostly in the hands of some other person or force?
   - Does the person assume that he or she can and should take personal responsibility for change?
   - Is there a sense of powerlessness, and a belief that events are under the control of another?
   - Does the person feel like a victim?
   - In what areas does the person feel that he or she is in control?
   - When is the person not in control?
   - Is there a belief in the value of harmony and inner peace, without resisting or trying to overcome circumstances?

7. Time
   - Does the person view time as a precious commodity that we can waste, control, or spend wisely?
   - Is there greater emphasis on the future, the present, or the past?
   - How important is punctuality and keeping tight schedules?
   - Does the person want immediate results, or can he or she wait?
   - Is the person impatient with delays and driven by the clock?
   - In terms of behavior, what does it mean to arrange a meeting for, say, one o'clock? Does that mean 1:00 p.m. sharp, around 1:00 p.m., or after lunch sometime?

- How does the counselee or the counselor respond when an appointment does not start at the previously arranged time?
8. Communication Styles
   - Is it culturally appropriate to speak loudly and fast?
   - Is it appropriate to make eye contact (as in Western cultures) or to not make eye contact (as is common in some Asian cultures)?
   - What is the meaning of different gestures, including head nods, leaning forward in a chair, or hugs?
   - Is saving face more important than telling the truth?
   - When, if ever, is it appropriate to use confrontation or bluntness?
   - What is the meaning of silence? In some cultures it means respect. In others it may reflect withdrawal, anger, or a fear of responding.
9. Emotional Expression
   - Is the expression of emotion a sign of weakness?
   - Is it culturally appropriate to restrain feelings?
   - Are some emotions (such as anger in the face of injustice) more appropriate than others (such as fear which might indicate weakness)?
   - When, if ever, is it culturally appropriate to talk about emotions openly?
10. Attitudes toward Counseling
    - Is it culturally appropriate to seek counseling?
    - Is going to a counselor perceived as a sign of weakness?
    - Is it culturally appropriate for the individual to talk one-on-one about his or her personal problems without the family or other social group being involved?
    - Is the counselor expected to be directive, or expected to guide the counselee to his or her own conclusions?
    - Are there subjects that are inappropriate to discuss with counselors?
    - What can be done to build trust?

paranoid and angry in order to survive.[14] Some even have been mistreated by counselors and other mental-health professionals whose prejudices have led them to conclusions and counseling interventions that are invalid and unfair. Is it surprising that many of these young men feel misunderstood, helpless, defeated, and inclined to give up? Is it surprising that many turn to competitive athletics as a way to express aggression, to build self-esteem, and to find hope? Is it surprising that many African Americans of all ages mistrust counselors, especially counselors who are not black?[15]

An African American counselor who read this chapter commented that many of his older counselees still remember the controversy surrounding the Tuskegee experiments where several hundred black men, diagnosed with syphilis, were allowed to think they were being treated by their white doctors, while in reality they were observed to see the effects of advanced stages of syphilis. This is part of a racial history that has influenced many of my friend's counselees to avoid anything like counseling if it is connected to a white person or institution.[16]

What, then, does the culturally sensitive counselor do? First, don't assume that your counselee automatically thinks of you in a negative way because the two of you are different. You might ask a casual question like this: "I'm curious about how you feel about counseling with someone who is white?" (Or you might end the sentence with a different word like black, Asian, Catholic, blind, younger than you, female, or whatever identifies you as being different from your counselee.) Let the person answer without making any assumptions. This lets counselees know that ethnic differences can be freely discussed in counseling. At some time you might acknowledge that anger, paranoia, and mistrust are legitimate methods for coping with racism and discrimination in some communities. According to one experienced counselor, we increase distrust if we ignore or dismiss these behaviors, attitudes, complaints, or beliefs. Instead, counselors must "be open to learning from their clients, and they must be nonjudgmental about the client's cultural perspectives, including their level of cultural mistrust."[17]

3. *The counselor should seek to understand the ways in which culturally diverse counselees see the world.* This involves seeking to understand the other person's worldviews. One way to accomplish this is to become involved with minority individuals outside of counseling settings. Make an effort to become friends with people who are culturally different. Earlier we mentioned one counselor's involvement with the Hmong people from Southeast Asia. The counselor has visited Hmong churches, been involved with Hmong social gatherings. and interacted with Hmong leaders, including a Hmong-American who is a state senator in Minnesota. This involvement builds both understanding of the culture and trust among Hmong counselees.

To understand cultural differences more clearly, it can be helpful to think of an iceberg.[18] Only a small part of the iceberg is visible above water; most of the ice is below the surface where it can't be seen. If we look only at the visible and ignore the invisible, there could be disastrous consequences, as the captain of the Titanic and his passengers discovered.

The visible parts of the culture can be seen and respected by a sensitive

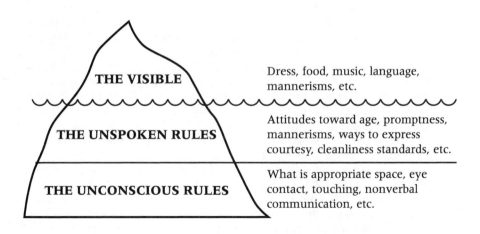

THE VISIBLE	Dress, food, music, language, mannerisms, etc.
THE UNSPOKEN RULES	Attitudes toward age, promptness, mannerisms, ways to express courtesy, cleanliness standards, etc.
THE UNCONSCIOUS RULES	What is appropriate space, eye contact, touching, nonverbal communication, etc.

Figure 7–1. The Cultural Iceberg

observer. The ways in which people dress, greet one another, or relate to each other are examples. If the people of another culture speak a different language, it can be important for the outsider to learn the language and to eat the same food as the people of the host culture. American tourists who run to McDonald's for their meals may be perceived as being insensitive and not willing to try the local food, but this is not usually viewed as a major cultural blunder. Tourists who eat the local food, at least on occasion, connect better with people in the host culture and often benefit from some pleasant eating experiences. Barriers can be created when missionaries, foreign students, or other permanent residents from abroad refuse to eat the local food or learn the local ways of behaving.

The level of unspoken rules is not visible at first, but these are behaviors that can be discovered and learned. They include the cultural expectations for how people are greeted, what is appropriate tipping in a restaurant, how loudly one speaks, how close you get to others when you talk, and various forms of etiquette. In some countries it is expected that the person who receives a gift will open it immediately. In other countries the gift is accepted graciously but not opened until later. Some cultures value punctuality whereas others do not. In American culture it is common and acceptable to use first names, but in many cultures the use of first names is restricted to very close friends, and younger people would never use an older person's first name. In some cultures, men and women who are not married to each other never sit next to each other, whereas that is no problem elsewhere. On a recent international flight, my wife and I were seated in a row with three seats. In accordance with his cultural expectations, the man next to the window asked if I could sit in that middle seat rather than my wife. These unspoken rules can be learned by asking about them, but more often we learn by making observations and by trial and error.

The deepest level of the cultural iceberg involves mostly unconscious standards, attitudes, and ways of behaving that are learned by children in the culture as they grow up. These are things that visitors may never notice, but they are behaviors that can be deeply offensive if violated. When, if ever, is it appropriate to hug? Is it polite to make direct eye contact with a stranger or older person? Is it appropriate to share personal problems with a stranger, even if that person is a professional counselor? When one sits in a chair is it appropriate to cross one's legs? In some cultures this can be highly offensive. One Chinese web site helps visitors by pointing out that in China and other Asian cultures it is important for people to save face, to consistently respect elders, to preserve the family name, and to abide by the principles of Confucianism. As this chapter was being written, a young man was kicked off the Chinese Olympic diving team for being too self-centered. A previous gold medalist, he was criticized for hiring an agent, lining up endorsements, and not showing "proper modesty and team spirit." His dismissal was because he failed to promote "traditional Chinese values." This is a clear example of how cultural values in one country differ from those in another, and can lead to cross-cultural misunderstandings.

More than forty years ago psychologists began describing people as having an internal or external *locus of control*. This refers to people's expectations about what controls their lives and destinies. Those who have an internal locus of control believe that people shape their own destinies. The future depends on the choices we make and the actions we take. When problems arise, it is the individual's responsibility to make decisions and take control. When businesses or other groups need to move forward, the people with an internal control mentality conclude that the group needs to take action. According to this view, outcomes depend mostly on us.

People who work from an internal control perspective often show superior coping strategies, greater success in mastering their circumstances, lower anxiety, greater involvement in social issues, higher motivation to succeed, and a greater belief in the value of determined activity. All these reflect Western values and Euro-American views of good mental health.

In contrast, people with an external locus of control assume that the events in life are more dependent on some external force or forces, including God, spiritual entities, fate, luck, the political system, the economy, or the universe. This can lead to a sense of hopelessness, powerlessness, or being a victim. But the external control perspective also can lead a group to take actions, including protests, efforts to change the system, or attempts to gain God's favor and intervention. Members of minorities, the poor, immigrants, and others who feel powerless most often embrace the external-locus-of-control perspective. This view is more likely to lead people to pass responsibility on to somebody else and to work at getting that other person or system to take action.[19]

It should not be assumed that the external control perspective always leads to feelings of hopelessness. Asian Confucian philosophy, for example, does not value the internal take-control mentality that characterizes many Westerners. Instead, there is a respect for family togetherness, harmony between people, submission to circumstances, and belief in the value of inner peace and freedom from striving. Tragic events are accepted as acts of God, and attempts by therapists to change circumstances may be resisted because change could bring disharmony and lack of balance.

Usually, there is overlap between the internal and external positions. Even though we believe in a God who is alive, at work, responsive to our prayers, and able to intervene (external control), Christian counseling most often reflects an internal-control, "let's take responsibility and make it happen," perspective. This can create conflict if we bring the internal perspective to a counselee who has grown up in a culture that values more of an external-locus-of-control viewpoint.

4. *The counselor could benefit from an understanding of cultural adaptation.* What is common among international students, missionaries, diplomats, and people working for companies overseas? To have maximum effectiveness and happiness in their new surroundings, they all need to make cultural adjustments. As we have seen, every culture has a set of shared assumptions, accepted ways of behaving, values, social expectations, and common experiences. Learning and adapting to these unique features of a culture involves time, energy, and determination. This is true for counselors who move to another culture (even to live within a subculture in their own country) and for immigrants, internationals, and others who come to live in our culture. Very often, this adaptation involves culture shock. It has the following stages that are important for counselors to understand:

- The *enthusiasm* stage involves a love of the new environment. Often it is embraced wholeheartedly, and the newcomer enjoys the new experiences, opportunities, food, and people.
- Sooner or later there often is a *critical* stage that can involve discouragement,

feelings of dissatisfaction, and a longing for home. Often at this stage the newcomer struggles with the language, feels out of place, is impatient and negative. This can be a time when critical comments or annoying attitudes can be shown both in the newcomer and among people in the host culture.

- Eventually there is an *adjustment and adaptation* stage. A more balanced outlook appears. The person from a different culture begins to realize that things are not all bad in the new place, and that many things are good. The person begins to pick up some of the habits, values, and customs of the new culture and may even prefer these to what was left at home.

- The stage of *reentry* into one's original culture is a reverse type of culture shock. When the long-term visitor goes home, there is a jolt as he or she begins to realize how the old culture has changed, and how the new culture has shaped one's thinking and preferences. Some people face an inner confusion about which culture they prefer and where they fit best. Students who have lived abroad for several years or children of missionaries, diplomats, or military families are among those known as third-culture kids. They do not fit completely in either culture, but they often connect with others who have the same struggles with their cultural identities.

As a counselor you may notice that some people never make the cultural adjustment. They remain steeped in their culture of origin, even though they are living someplace else. Others embrace the new culture so completely that they abandon their cultural roots. Another group rejects both cultures. As you might expect, the first and third of these tend to have the poorest mental health.[20] The people who work through the acculturation process are mentally the healthiest.

5. *The counselor should develop and use appropriate counseling strategies and techniques.* This can be difficult. Most psychological tests and many counseling interventions have been developed within one cultural group. You risk being unfair, arriving at incorrect conclusions, and sometimes getting resistance if you fail to adapt these methods if they are used with people of other cultures. As an example, consider the client-centered approach to counseling developed many years ago by psychologist Carl Rogers. This can work well with American college students who are accustomed to solving their own problems with minimal intervention from the counselor, but the approach is much less effective in Asian and African settings, where counselors are expected to be older, wiser advisors who give direction often within the context of families. Most Americans have no difficulty meeting with a stranger to talk about personal problems, but in other cultures intimate details might never be shared and certainly not with a stranger.

Of special significance are language differences. Counselors should be able to send and receive both verbal and nonverbal messages. This is difficult if there is not a common language. Sometimes, there is no person to whom you can make a referral, so you will need to work as best you can with the cultural differences. Being aware of these differences, however, is a part of making sure that your counseling is as effective as possible.[21]

Indigenous Methods

As a Christian counselor, how would you respond if a counselee stated that his depression was caused by evil spirits, that a shaman with special powers would be needed to deal with the problem, and that the only effective cure would be the ritual chanting and burning of incense by the healer? Assume that your counselee had spent many hours with a counselor trained in the West and that no symptom relief had come until the shaman worked his magic and brought healing.

Stories like these are not limited to counselors who work with tribal people in primitive cultures. There may be people in your neighborhood who hold similar beliefs—people who look very much like you but who have been impressed with the indigenous healing methods of other cultures or with the alternative therapies that have become increasingly popular at home.[22] In the United States, for example, evidence suggests that far more people seek treatment from practitioners of alternative medicine and therapy than from traditional Western physicians.[23] Over half of U.S. medical schools teach courses in alternative medicine, and professional counselors are taking these approaches more seriously than they did even a few years ago. Nontraditional approaches to healing (including acupuncture, aromatherapy, homeopathy, reflexology, therapeutic massage, Indian Ayurveda, naturopathy, and many others) have been shown to be effective in treating anxiety, depression, headaches, pain management, stress, and other psychological problems.

These approaches, along with shamanism, voodoo, and demon exorcisms, no longer are as ridiculed as they once were. Brad Keeney, for example, was a respected psychology professor who left the academic world to study with the most powerful shamans, witch doctors, medicine men, and healers in the world. According to the publisher of a book about his journey "through the world of spiritual healers and doctors of the oldest cultures on earth," Keeney's work "challenges the foundation of everything we think we know and understand about helping and healing."[24]

Nontraditional treatment methods are not limited to the secular world or to the beliefs of immigrants who bring healing approaches from their various cultures. The exorcism of demons is an approach used by some Christians and based on biblical precedent. Prayer therapy, theo-therapy, healing of memories, and Theophostic Ministry[25] are other examples of methods that Christian counselors use and sometimes advocate enthusiastically. This is not because the nontraditional methods have been studied scientifically,[26] but because they have been found to work, at least with some people, and because they are proposed as being consistent with biblical teaching.

How do Christian counselors respond to indigenous and alternative approaches to healing psychological and spiritual problems? There can be several guidelines including the following:

- Try to determine the assumptions or theories on which the methods are built. Are these foundations consistent with biblical teaching? If not, be very cautious about using any of the methods. It seems probable that most Christian counselors would not use these at all.
- Recognize that although God heals through nontraditional means, Satan is able to do this as well. Using satanic methods can "give the devil a foothold" that can create serious problems later.
- Do not assume that a method is acceptable for use by Christian counselors simply because the methods bring change in some situations. Pragmatism is not a basis for deciding truth or selecting techniques. For example,

excessive drinking can be effective in relieving stress temporarily, but alcohol is not the best way to cope with stress, in part because the "cure" often brings additional problems of its own.

- Try to determine if there is research to support a method's long-term effectiveness. This is not the only basis for deciding which nontraditional methods to use because supernatural forces cannot be confined to scientific research methods. But if there is no basis other than the enthusiastic reports of a few people, be cautious until somebody carefully investigates to determine if the method is as good as it claims.
- Remember the placebo effect. It is well known that many people improve because they believe a drug or nontraditional method will work, even though the method has no power apart from the beliefs of people desperately wanting to get better.
- Discuss the method with other Christians who are qualified to judge its effectiveness and consistency with Christian beliefs.
- If in doubt, or if you feel uncomfortable using some method, avoid it.

Looking Ahead

Earlier in its development, counseling was divided into three categories: remedial, preventive, and educational. Remedial counseling involved helping people deal with existing problems, preventive counseling sought to stop problems from getting worse or from occurring at all, and educational counseling involved the counselor in teaching principles of mental health to groups, book readers, or listeners to audio cassette tapes. Currently, as in the past, remedial counseling appears to take the vast majority of counselor time and energy. Graduate training programs contribute to this lopsided emphasis, and professionals know that it is easier to make a living by offering remedial counseling than with preventive or educational activities. Many people will pay to get help with an existing problem, but few will spend money or time to have a problem prevented.

Over the years there have been efforts to put more emphasis on prevention and education.[27] In addition, the growing field of positive psychology has taken some of the focus away from strictly remedial efforts and focused more on building strengths, virtues, and sense of purpose.[28] Counselors continue to work with people who come to our offices, but counseling also takes place in the communities where we live, work, worship, and interact. Alongside the more traditional emphases on counseling theories and techniques, now there is a strong focus on the use of books, manuals, distance learning, Internet resources, and other technology-based materials. None of this assumes that remedial counseling will fade or disappear. It always will be important and needed. But the field of counseling is changing and broadening. Christian counselors often experience or benefit from these changes, and creative counselors are leading some of the change.

When the pastoral counseling movement arose at the beginning of the previous century, the church increased its emphasis on individual helping, but the larger role of educating people and helping them find spiritual and mental health has never been abandoned. Pastoral counselors have always taken a more proactive approach, going to hospital rooms, homes, schools, accident scenes, and other places that professional counselors usually avoid. Christian outreach as well as educative and preventive efforts have not always been effective, and neither have our goals been clear. Within the church there already exists a way of thinking that gives education a place of prominence, often surpassing the emphasis on remedial counseling.

In writing the following chapters, I have attempted to reflect both the traditional remedial-rehabilitative approach to counseling and the educative-preventive perspective. The chapters are written (1) to give an understanding of each problem area, (2) to present guidelines for helping those who are experiencing problems, and (3) to suggest ways to educate Christians and others so problems can be prevented in the future.

Each of the following chapters is designed to stand alone. They do not need to be read in any special order. This allows the volume to be a handbook with chapters that can be used for general information and used for reference when specific counseling issues arise. Hopefully, the book and accompanying casebook also will be used in training programs for counselors and as a basis for the education of nonprofessionals.

Christian counseling is a difficult but challenging venture. It involves developing therapeutic personality traits, being sensitive to people, learning skills, understanding the counseling process, becoming familiar with the basics of common problems, being alert to the dangers involved in counseling, having a growing familiarity with the Scriptures, and being sensitive to the guidance of the Holy Spirit. All of this can be discussed in a book or presented in lectures, but counseling cannot be learned completely from reading or from passively taking notes as a student. We become good Christian counselors through commitment to Christ, through training under the supervision and guidance of more experienced counselor-teachers, and through the practical experience of helping people with their problems. These problems are discussed in the pages that follow.

KEY POINTS FOR BUSY COUNSELORS

➤ All counseling is cross-cultural.

➤ Every counselor and counselee comes with a unique set of experiences, worldviews, theological perspectives, and cultural expectations. Jesus approached people in different ways, depending on the place where they met, their backgrounds, and their cultures.

➤ You are counseling cross-culturally if you work with someone of an age, background, gender, level of education, set of values, socioeconomic status, belief system, or sexual orientation that differs from yours.

➤ Multicultural counseling refers to care-giving to people of different minorities, nationalities, or membership in racial-ethnic groups.

➤ Counselors are sensitive to the dangers of treating people unfairly on the basis of their gender, age, race, ethnicity, national origin, religion, sexual orientation, disability, language, or socioeconomic status.

➤ Christian counseling cannot be defined or applied in the same way to all groups, nationalities, and cultures.

➤ Christian counselors should have "multicultural competencies" in at least five areas:

1. The counselor should develop awareness of his or her own cultural values and biases.
2. The counselor should try to become aware of the cultural perspective of each counselee.
3. The counselor should seek to understand the ways in which culturally diverse counselees see the world.
4. The counselor could benefit from an understanding of cultural adaptation.
5. The counselor should develop and use culturally appropriate counseling strategies and techniques.

➤ Leaders, teachers, and counselors who ignore culture often appear arrogant, insensitive, disrespectful, and incompetent.

➤ Indigenous (culture specific) and alternative methods are increasing in popularity. How does the Christian counselor respond?

 ▪ Try to determine the assumptions on which the methods are built and be cautious of any that are not consistent with biblical teaching.
 ▪ Recognize that although God heals through nontraditional means, Satan is able to do this as well.
 ▪ Do not assume that a method is acceptable for use by Christian counselors simply because the methods bring change and seem to work.
 ▪ Try to determine if there is research to support a method's long-term effectiveness.
 ▪ Remember the placebo effect. Some people get better simply because they believe an approach will work whether or not it has any impact on its own.

➤ The remainder of this book will deal with specific issues both from a remedial and from a preventive-educational perspective.

PART TWO

Prominent Issues

8

Depression

It was June, 2001. A young mother sat with a blank expression on her face and confessed to police that she had just drowned her five children, one by one. The oldest was seven, the youngest only six months. Next morning the front page of every newspaper in the country told the story.[1]

Andrea and her husband, Russell Yates, are Christians, but today they are separated for life. Andrea is in prison for the drowning deaths of her children. Russell, known to his friends as Rusty, lives alone, trying to rebuilt his life and make sense of the tragedy that took away his family.

At her trial, Andrea pleaded not guilty by reason of insanity, but the jury found her guilty, and she was sent to prison instead of to a psychiatric treatment facility. There had been mental illness in Andrea's family for years. Three of her four siblings had been diagnosed with psychological problems, including depression. There is some evidence that her father suffered at times from depression, and her mother was very negative, critical about everything, and never happy. All of her life Andrea tried to please and be good. When she thought she had failed, she was overcome with shame, guilt, and a determination to do better.

Her marriage was good, and the couple decided to have a big family. But the postpartum depression appeared after the birth of their fourth child, and it became stronger after the next pregnancy. The death of Andrea's father appeared to trigger a deeper depression, but the doctors were not able to pull her out despite massive doses of antidepressant medication. The situation appeared to have been aggravated by the family's contact with a legalistic, "fire and brimstone" preacher whose teaching showed no grace or mercy. Despite every evidence that she was a sensitive and caring mother, Andrea convinced herself that she was a horrible mother, and twice she attempted suicide. But prior to the drownings, there had been no evidence that Andrea was so severely depressed and psychotic that she would harm her own kids.

The sad story of Andrea Yates is an extreme example of the impact of depression. Symptoms of depression following the birth of a child are not unusual.[2] They can last from a few days to a few months. In addition to feeling depressed, the woman can feel lethargic, anxious, and worthlessness, especially over her ability to be a good mother. Suicide thoughts may appear, but with help, most mothers recover and go on to raise and enjoy their children.

Someone has suggested that most of our days are of three kinds.[3] On mountaintop days everything is going well and the world looks bright. These experiences are temporary: they don't go on forever. It is unrealistic to expect, as some people do, that we can spend life leaping from one mountain peak to another as if there were no plains or valleys in between. Instead, most of life consists of ordinary days when we work at our usual tasks, neither elated nor depressed. Then there are the dark days when we trudge on through confusion, doubt, discouragement, and sometimes despair. These days may be occasional, or they may string together into months or even years before there is a brighter outlook and a sense of relief. When the dark days persist, they are days of depression.

For more than three thousand years, depression has been recognized as a common problem. It is a worldwide phenomenon that affects individuals of all ages, including infants. In the United States alone, an estimated seventeen million people suffer from clinical depression. One web site suggests that depression has an impact on nearly everybody if we consider both the depressed people and their family members, friends, work colleagues, and others.[4] Depression disrupts lives, interferes with normal functioning, often causes problems at work, reduces efficiency, hinders spiritual growth, and can destroy family and social life. It has a major impact on the economy as billions of dollars are lost annually because of depression in the workforce. Some of history's greatest military leaders, statesmen, musicians, scientists, and theologians have been its victims, including Winston Churchill, George Frederick Handel, Edgar Allen Poe, Napoleon Bonaparte, Vincent van Gogh, and Charles Haddon Spurgeon. But depression is no respecter of persons. It is known as the common cold of mental disorders. On occasion probably all of us experience depression, sometimes when we least expect it. In its milder forms depression may come as a passing period of sadness that follows a loss or personal disappointment. More severe depression overwhelms its victims with feelings of despair, fear, exhaustion, immobilizing apathy, hopelessness, inner desperation, and thoughts of suicide. On rare occasions, when it is a part of severe mental illness, it can lead to actions like the murder of Andrea Yates' children. In one form or another, depression probably brings more people to counselors than any other issue.

Depression covers a wide variety of symptoms that differ in severity, frequency, duration, and origin. The signs of depression might be grouped into four categories: feelings, thinking, behavior, and physical health. Each of these is a change from what the person experiences and shows when depression is absent.

- *Feelings.* Depression can bring sadness, sometimes for no apparent reason; low self-esteem often accompanied by self-criticism and feelings of guilt, shame, worthlessness, and helplessness; pessimism and hopelessness; and sometimes irritability, so the person is more prone to impatience and loss of temper.
- *Thinking.* Depressed people frequently have negative thoughts. In their minds they ruminate on their own incompetence and lack of worth. Many experience difficulties in concentration, problems with memory, pessimism, guilt, self-criticism, self-condemnation, and sometimes thoughts of self-destruction.
- *Behavior.* Apathy and a sense of inertia are common, so the person lacks motivation and finds it difficult to get motivated or to face decisions. Also common are loss of spontaneity, social withdrawal, and constant complaining. In more extreme cases, there may be a neglect of personal appearance and hygiene. Work productivity goes down and household responsibilities are neglected.
- *Physical Health.* General fatigue is common, despite more time spent sleeping. Depression also brings a loss of energy; a lack of interest in work, sex, religion, hobbies, or other activities; insomnia; an inability to concentrate; loss of appetite; and sometimes frequent complaining about aches and pains.

In what has become known as masked depression, a person may have many of the above symptoms but denies that he or she feels sad. The alert counselor may suspect that depression is present even behind a smiling countenance. In many cases the symptoms of depression hide anger that has not been expressed, sometimes isn't recognized, and may be directed inward against oneself. Whether the symptoms are masked or more obvious to others, a large majority of depressed people do not get treated. Perhaps some are embarrassed by their symptoms, too depressed to go for treatment, or convinced that they can handle the problems without help. Of those that do get help, an estimated 80 percent improve and see changes in their feelings, energy levels, and ability to adjust to life.

Depressive reactions have been classified in a number or ways. *Reactive* depression, for example, usually comes as a reaction to some real or imagined loss or trauma, is accompanied with high levels of anxiety, is of short duration, and often is self-correcting. *Endogenous* depression (sometimes called psychotic depression) is more likely to arise spontaneously from within, involves intense despair sometimes accompanied by self-destructive tendencies, persists for a longer period of time, is more resistant to treatment, and has a high recurrence rate. *Primary* depression occurs by itself, while *secondary* depression comes as the side effect of some medication, the influence of one's diet, or the result of an illness like cancer, diabetes, or even influenza. Other types of depression include the following:

- *Dysthemic disorders* are characterized with chronic daily depression that is not severe enough to prevent normal functioning, although the person has low energy, little enthusiasm, and not much creativity or ability to enjoy life. Technically, this is defined as a low-grade depression that has lasted for more than two years and without a break longer than two months, but many report that they never can remember a time when the depression was absent. Frequently, these symptoms come from physical conditions that can be treated medically, although sometimes the depression causes the physical illness. Counseling can be effective in most cases.
- *Seasonal affective disorders* are periods of depression, apathy, and withdrawal that most often appear in the winter months in places where the days are shorter and the periods of darkness are longer. There is some speculation that sunlight, entering through the retina, stimulates chemicals that have an antidepressant effect. Most often the symptoms disappear as days get longer in the spring. There is evidence that light therapy in the winter months can be helpful. Counseling also is effective.
- *Bipolar disorders* (which used to be called manic-depressive disorders) involve periods of mania interspersed with depressive behavior. Generally assumed to be of genetic origin, the condition usually appears in young adulthood and persists throughout life. Each individual has a unique manic-depressive cycle in terms of severity and frequency. Some people have mostly manic or mostly depressive symptoms. In the mania phase there is boundless energy, uncontrolled behavior, and a willingness to take great risks. The depressive stages reflect the more common symptoms of depression. These mood swings can be controlled through medication, but counseling also helps, both with individuals and with the family. Sadly, many see no need for counseling during the manic phase, and there is little energy for counseling when the person is depressed.[5]

- *Postpartum disorders* differ from what has been called "postpartum blues," a relatively brief period of depressive symptoms that disappear once hormone levels stabilize. Postpartum disorders are more serious and last longer, but they can be treated with counseling and medication. They only degenerate into extreme behavior, as we saw with Andrea Yates, when there are other severe psychological issues that complicate the postpartum condition or that are triggered by it.
- *Major depressive disorders* are the most severe, and probably the most complex and most studied of the depressive disorders. Usually, the major depressions come in episodes and are very disruptive to everyone involved. The causes can be psychological and/or physical, although like all depression the major disorders reflect changes in the brain chemistry. This more severe depression does respond to intensive counseling, but most professionals use antidepressant medications as well. This more serious form of depression is best treated by an expert.
- *Mood disorders* are a group of emotional states that include depression and other emotions. Sometimes, the term *mood disorders* is used as an umbrella term that includes each of the depressive types described above.[6]

All of the above should be distinguished from discouragement, which is a mild, usually temporary and almost universal mood swing that comes in response to disappointments, failures, and losses.

The Bible and Depression

Our discussion thus far shows that depression is a common, complicated condition, difficult to define, hard to describe with accuracy, and not easy to treat. Since depression is a clinical term, it is not discussed in the Bible, even though the condition appears to have been common. Psalms 69, 88, and 102, for example, are songs of despair, but notice that these are set in the context of hope. In Psalm 43 King David expresses both depression and rejoicing when he writes:

> Why am I so discouraged?
> Why so sad?
> I will put my hope in God!
> I will praise him again—
> My Savior and my God.

Elsewhere in the Bible it appears that Job, Moses, Jonah, Peter, and the whole nation of Israel experienced depression.[7] Jeremiah the prophet wrote a whole book of lamentations. Elijah saw God's mighty power at work on Mount Carmel, but when Jezebel threatened murder, Elijah fled into the wilderness, where he plunged into despondency. He wanted to die and might have done so except for the "treatment" that came from an angel sent by God.[8]

Then there was Jesus in Gethsemane, where he was greatly distressed, an observation that is poignantly described in the words of the Amplified Bible: "He began to show grief and distress of mind and was deeply depressed. Then He said to them, My soul is very sad and deeply grieved, so that I am almost dying of sorrow."[9]

These examples, accompanied by numerous references to the pain of grieving, show the realism that characterizes the Bible. It is a realistic despair contrasted with a certain hope. Each of the believers who plunged into depression eventually came through and experienced a new and lasting joy, even when their circumstances did not change. The biblical emphasis is less on human despair and more on belief in God and the assurance of abundant life in heaven, if not on earth.[10] Paul wrote, "We are pressed on every side by troubles, but we are not crushed and broken. We are perplexed, but we don't give up and quit. We are hunted down, but God never abandons us. We get knocked down, but we get up again and keep going. . . . For our present troubles are quite small and won't last very long. . . . So we don't look at the troubles we can see right now; rather, we look forward to what we have not yet seen. For the troubles we see will soon be over, but the joys to come will last forever."[11] Paul's confident prayer for the Romans someday will be answered for all Christians: "I pray that God, who gives you hope, will keep you happy and full of peace as you believe in him. May you overflow with hope through the power of the Holy Spirit.[12]

The Causes of Depression

A number of myths about the causes of depression continue to be accepted and sometimes preached from church pulpits. It is *not* true, however, that depression always results from sin or a lack of faith in God, that all depression is caused by self-pity, that it is wrong for a Christian to be depressed, that depressed feelings always can be removed permanently by spiritual exercises, that antidepressive medication is the best form of treatment, that happiness is a choice, or that a "depressed Christian is a contradiction of terms."[13] Like everyone else, Christians get depressed. There can be a variety of causes that often work together, so one of the counselor's first tasks is to uncover, understand, and eventually help counselees deal with these causes.[14] Although there are numerous theories and explanations for depression, it probably is most common for mental-health professionals to take what has been termed a bio-psycho-social approach. This groups the causes into three categories that work in combination: the biological causes, the psychological causes, and the social influences.

1. *The Biological-Genetic Causes.* Like most psychological problems, depression has physical implications, including chemical imbalances in the brain. Sometimes, the physical changes result from the depression; at other times physical influences are the cause. At the simplest level, we know that lack of sleep, insufficient exercise, the side effects of drugs, physical illnesses, or improper diet can all create depression. Thousands of women experience depression at part of a monthly premenstrual syndrome (PMS), and, as we have seen, some develop postpartum depression following childbirth. Less recognized is a testosterone-induced depression that comes to men during periods of reduced sexual activity.[15] Other physical influences, like neurochemical malfunctioning, brain tumors, or glandular disorders, are more complicated creators of depression. Simpler, perhaps, is seasonal affective disorder (SAD) that, at least in part, reflects the body's response to a lack of light.

There is considerable evidence that depression runs in families, but it can be difficult to distinguish the genetic from the possible environmental reasons.[16]

Highly sophisticated genetic research continues around the world, and there is wide agreement that genes influence the body in many ways, including biochemical activity in the brain. For the nonmedical counselor, perhaps it is enough to be aware of the genetic influences and to recognize that some of this research has a bearing on the development of new and more effective antidepressant medications. Over twenty years ago one former president of the American Psychiatric Association predicted that research in the genetics and biochemistry of depression is where a Nobel Prize will be won some day in the future.[17]

2. *Psychological-Cognitive Causes.* Depression is a significant mental-health problem for as much as 10 percent of the general population, but these figures differ from country to country, rise during times of political upheaval and economic uncertainty, and differ depending on one's age. Depression in the elderly is well recognized, especially among older people with health problems. Among younger people, about one in eight American teenagers suffers from depression or anxiety. Sometimes, this leads to physical self-mutilation that could be interpreted as a cry for help.[18] Depression impacts an estimated 25 percent of college students, is experienced by about one-third of college dropouts before they leave school, and is high among international students who feel intense pressure to get good grades.[19] All of this suggests that developmental, psychological, interpersonal, spiritual, and other nonphysical influences are at the basis of much depression.[20]

(a) Background and Family Causes. Many years ago a researcher named Rene Spitz published a study of children who had been separated from their parents and raised in an institution.[21] Deprived of ongoing, warm human contact with adults, these children showed apathy, poor health, and sadness—all indicative of depression that could continue into later life. Depression can occur when parents ignore or reject their children or when status-seeking families set unrealistically high or rigid standards that family members feel pressured to meet. It is a common experience for young people to strive to meet parental expectations and to feel the parents' disappointment and rejection when the standards are not met. This can have devastating and life-long impact on the young person's self-esteem and feelings of worth. Depression often follows and persists into their adult years.

Teenagers who are in conflict with their parents, young adults who are having trouble becoming independent of their families, people who come from unstable homes, and college students who have negative opinions about their families—all are more inclined to be depressed.[22]

(b) Stress and Significant Losses. It is well known that the stresses of life stimulate depression, especially when these stresses make us feel threatened or involve a loss. Losses of people through death, divorce, or prolonged separations are painful and known to be among the most powerful depression-producing events of life. Also influential can be the loss of an opportunity, job, career, status, health, freedom, a contest, possessions, or other valued object. One study of young adults found that members of racial and ethnic minorities experience higher than average rates of depression because of the increased stresses they encounter through prejudice, denied opportunities, or the extra effort and disappointments associated with succeeding and feeling acceptance in the majority population.[23]

Research by psychologist Sidney J. Blatt expands on the stress explanation for depression by describing two types of depression, each having distinct roots. One type of depression comes from feelings of loneliness and abandonment. The other arises from feelings of failure and worthlessness.[24]

(c) Learned Helplessness. One well-established theory has demonstrated that depression often comes when we encounter situations over which we have little or no control. It is easy to get depressed when we learn that our actions are futile no matter how hard we try, or that nothing can be done to relieve suffering, reach a goal, or bring about change. These are times when we feel helpless and give up trying. This could explain some of the previously mentioned depression in minority groups, in grieving people who can do nothing to bring back a loved one, or in the older person who is powerless to turn back the clock and restore lost physical capacities. Depression may subside or even disappear when people who feel helpless are able to control at least a portion of their environments.[25]

(d) Cognitive Causes. How a person thinks often determines how he or she feels. This is a basic assumption of the cognitive views of depression. If we think negatively, for example, see only the dark side of life, maintain a pessimistic mind-set, and overlook the positive, then depression is almost inevitable. Not surprisingly, the most effective counseling for these people is to help them change their thinking.

According to psychiatrist Aaron Beck, depressed people show negative thinking in three areas.[26]

- First, the world is viewed negatively. Life is seen as a succession of burdens, obstacles, and defeats in a world that is falling apart or "going down the drain."
- Second, many depressed people view themselves negatively. They perceive themselves to be inadequate, unworthy, incapable of performing adequately, and lacking the skills, traits, or physical features that they value. This attitude can lead to self-blame and self-pity.
- Third, some people view the future in a negative way. Looking ahead they see continuing hardship, frustration, and hopelessness.

It is not surprising that when people think like this they protect themselves from being hurt or disappointed should their thinking come true. Often the negative attitudes take away motivation, the person stops trying, and the failure that was feared becomes reality. In addition, negative thinking can be used in an attempt to control others (including counselors) and influence how they respond. A comment like, "I'm no good," often is an unconscious way of getting others to disagree and make affirming positive comments. In this way, self-condemnation becomes a way of manipulating others to give compliments. Such compliments rarely satisfy, however, so the depression and negative thinking continue.

(e) Anger. A widely accepted viewpoint suggests that depression comes when anger is held within and turned against oneself. Many children are raised in homes, sent to schools, or raised in countries where the expression of anger is not approved. Some people attend churches where all anger is condemned as sin. Whatever their backgrounds, many people reach adulthood convinced that they shouldn't even feel angry, so they deny hostile feelings when these do arise. A widow, for example, may be angry at her husband who died, leaving her to raise the children alone, but anger like that seems irrational and is sure to arouse guilt. As a result, the anger is denied and kept buried within.

What happens then? If the anger is pushed out of our minds, it festers "under cover" and eventually affects us in some other way. The following diagram illustrates this process.[27]

This shows the close association between depression and anger. The anger often begins when the person feels hurt as the result of a disappointment or because of the actions of some other person. Instead of admitting the hurt, the individual mulls it over mentally, ponders what happened, and begins to get angry. The anger then builds and becomes so strong that it hides the hurt. If the anger is not admitted and expressed or dealt with in some other way, it often leads to thoughts of revenge. This may involve thoughts about hurting another person, either the one who caused the original hurt or someone else who is nearby and might have had nothing to do with the original cause of pain.

Thoughts of revenge sometime leads to destructive violent actions, but this can

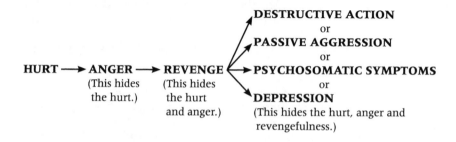

get us into trouble, and violence is not socially acceptable, especially for a Christian. As a result, many people try to hide their feelings. Sometimes, the anger then is expressed in a passive kind of aggression. Consider the example of a woman who has been hurt by her husband, feels the anger, which is a common response to having been hurt, and begins to think how she can get even. Violence may not be a viable alternative, so she smiles and maintains a happy countenance while she expresses her anger in more subtle ways, such as finding excuses to resist his sexual advances or consistently failing to follow through on things that she agreed to do. Work colleagues or team members, including people on church committees, often function in this way. Everybody smiles and is pleasant on the outside, but they undercut each other behind the scenes.

It takes energy to deny one's hurt or anger, express overt violence, or engage in more passive forms of aggression, including noncooperation. Eventually, then, the energy may wear down the body so that emotions appear in the form of psychosomatic symptoms. Others, consciously or unconsciously, condemn themselves for their attitudes, dwell on the hopelessness, and become depressed as a result. This depression may be a form of emotional self-punishment that may even lead to suicide.

Sometimes, people use depression as a subtle and socially acceptable way both to express anger and to get revenge. By his or her actions, the depressed person seems to be saying, "I'm depressed and miserable, it isn't my fault, and if I don't get attention and sympathy, I may get more even depressed or do something desperate." This is a form of manipulation and psychological blackmail that most often is unconscious.

The diagram explains some of the complexities of depression, even though it does not claim to account for all the psychological explanations.

(f) Sin and Guilt. It is easy to understand why sin and guilt can lead to depression. When a person feels that he or she has failed or done something wrong, guilt usually follows along with self-condemnation, frustration, hopelessness, and other depressive symptoms. Guilt and depression so often occur together that it is difficult to determine which comes first and leads to the other. Often a vicious cycle emerges in which guilt causes depression, which causes more guilt, and the cycle continues.

Could any of this explain the depression that Elijah the prophet experienced?[28] Elijah was under stress when he ran from Jezebel, who was determined to use all the king's armies to kill him. There must have been a lot of adrenaline pumping in Elijah's body as he fled. God had used him to discredit and cause the destruction of Baal's prophets. This in itself must have been an adrenaline-producing experience. Then he outran the king's chariot back to Jezreel and ran again as he fled from Jezebel. He must have been having a major post-adrenaline letdown when he found a secure hiding place and his fatigue and hunger pulled him down further. Complicating all of this was the stress of being a fugitive, so great in fact that he asked God to take his life. There is no evidence that he felt angry, filled with revenge, or inclined to fight back. The diagram in this chapter shows how he might have slipped into depression after the pain of experiencing a great victory that immediately put his life in danger. Of course there were no news reports to let him know how Jezebel's search was progressing, so there may have been more than a little anxiety. Elijah's tired body forced him to take time to rejuvenate physically. In those days there was no alternative, and probably he wanted no alternative, but to rely on God for the protection and guidance for the next steps he would take.

3. *Social-Environmental Influences.* Not long after the fall of Communism, I was invited to visit an Eastern European country to give a seminar on counseling. Never have I had an audience so lacking in emotional expression. The participants, many of whom were pastors, never laughed, rarely smiled, and gave very little indication that they understood or were interested in what I was saying. During a break, I discussed this with my translator. "Don't worry," he replied. "These people are very much listening to what you are saying. They are soaking up every word. This is all new to them." He then explained how they had learned to suppress all emotional expression during the former regime. Many, he said, had become severely depressed during the Communist era, and it was difficult for them to change now that they had freedom.

Repressive political regimes create fear, rob people of hope, drain their joy, and stimulate depression. Of course, these are not the only environmental causes of depression. Being trapped in a demanding job with an unreasonable boss can lead to depression, and so can abusive marriages, the demands of caring for a chronically ill family member, or the financial difficulties that come when no jobs are available. Increasingly, there is evidence that young people develop depressive symptoms following the divorce of their parents, the threat of parental breakups, the departure of a parent, or the acrimony that can follow a separation.[29] Some evidence suggests that the high prevalence of depression in women—about twice that of men—can arise because of female gender roles. This can include depression that comes as women are expected to give consistent support to family members in times of difficulty, often have multiple roles, have fewer career opportunities than men, and sometimes are socialized to think of themselves as inferior or helpless.[30]

Too often, perhaps, counselors listen to their counselees in office settings, draw conclusions about the causes of depression or other problems, and devise treatment plans. If they could step out of their offices and follow their counselees around for a couple of days, these same counselors might have a broader perspective and clearer understanding of the environmental influences that create much of the depression that we see and are told about in the counseling room.

Effects of Depression

The problems that lead to depression are not always bad. Sometimes, problems serve a useful purpose. When we are physically sick, for example, we are excused from work, people may show us attention or sympathy, others take over our responsibilities temporarily, and sometimes we can enjoy a period of rest and relaxation. The same thing can be true when we are emotionally down or distraught. Depression can give people a reason to avoid responsibilities, save face, attract attention, and have an excuse for inactivity. Every experienced counselor has seen people who complain about their depression but, at the same time, seem to enjoy it and resist efforts to change. For some it is more secure being depressed, even though they dislike it, than facing the stresses and uncertainties of getting help and making changes. Eventually, however, most emotionally hurting people realize that the benefits of depression are not really satisfying. Such people begin to hate what they are experiencing, and, in time, they may end up hating themselves. This, as we have seen, can create more depression.

Depression leads to any or all of the following effects. In general, the deeper the depression, the more intense the effects.

1. *Unhappiness and Inefficiency*. Depressed people feel down emotionally. They feel sad, hopeless, self-critical, and miserable, although they can be very effective in hiding these feelings when they are with others. It is harder for them to hide their lack of enthusiasm, indecisiveness, and loss of energy for doing even simple things, like getting out of bed in the morning. Life for them is characterized by discouragement, inefficiency, underachievement, and an increased dependence on others.

2. *Physical Illness*. Depression, including the sadness that comes with grief or loneliness, tends to suppress the body's immune system. As a result, the person is more susceptible to illness, and the body is less able to fight viruses and other diseases. Depressed people, therefore, are more likely than others to get sick. And the reverse is true as well: whenever any of us has a prolonged physical illness, depression often follows as a result.

Most counselors realize that depressed people may show a broad range of physical symptoms. However, it is not widely known that coronary heart disease is one of the major health consequences of depression.[31] This is true in women as well as in men. Depression also is a predictor of how well a person recovers after the onset of cardiovascular disease. This suggests that helping people deal with depression both prevents cardiovascular disease and can play a major role in helping people recover from heart attacks and other physical illness.

3. *Decreased Sexual Interest.* Depression often leads to a loss of sexual interest and an inability to perform sexually. In men, for example, one report states that impotence occurs in 90 percent of severely depressed men. When depression is mild, impotence appears in one man out of every four.[32] This declining sexual interest can lead to marital tensions and further feelings of incompetence, frustration, and despair.

4. *Low Self-Esteem and Withdrawal.* When a person is discouraged, unmotivated, and bored with life, there often is low self-esteem, self-pity, a lack of self-confidence, and the strong desire to get away from other people. Church members who previously were active in their congregations prefer to stay at home and may lack the energy or motivation to pray, read the Bible, or be in contact with God. Social contacts may be too demanding, especially if the person is trying to hide the depression. Instead, the depressed person tries to avoid communicating. Often there is daydreaming and escape into the fantasy worlds of television or novels. Sometimes, regular duties are abandoned. The depressed homemaker may fail to fix dinner for the family, for example, or the house may never get cleaned. Some people dream of running away or finding a simpler job. A few do this, but more often the depressed person lacks the energy or the courage to take the risk.

4. *Suicide.* There is no more complete way to escape than to take one's own life. Suicide and suicide attempts are often seen among teenagers, people who live alone, the unmarried (especially the divorced), adults who were abused as children, and persons who are depressed.[33] Many depressed people never even consider suicide, at least seriously, but others do, often in a sincere attempt to escape. Sometimes, suicide attempts may be an unconscious cry for help, an opportunity for revenge, or a manipulative gesture designed to influence some person who is close emotionally. While some suicide attempts are blatantly clear (as when a man leaves a note and shoots himself), others are more subtle and made to look like accidents. Some depressed people plan their self-destructive actions carefully. Others drive recklessly, drink excessively, or find other ways to flirt with death. All of this illustrates the pervasive and potentially destructive influence of depression.

We have seen that some people try to hide depression from others, but depression also may be hidden from themselves. In times like these, the depression comes out in other ways, including physical symptoms and complaints; aggressive actions and angry temper outbursts; impulsive behavior, including gambling, drinking, violence, destructiveness, or impulsive sex; compulsive work; and sexual problems, to name the most common. These are symptoms of *masked depression*. It occurs in children and adolescents as well as in adults. The person may be hurting emotionally but expressing this pain in ways that hide the real inner despair. It is not unusual for this hiding to be so effective that even close friends or counselors fail to recognize the depression.

More often, the depression has a strong impact on others. People who live with a depressed person often feel burdened by the patient's worrying, fatigue, feelings of hopelessness, and lack of interest in social activities. According to one study, the burden of living with a chronically depressed person is so great that 40 percent of relatives need counseling themselves.[34]

Counseling and Depression

Depressed people often are passive, nonverbal, poorly motivated, pessimistic, and characterized by a resigned "what's the use?" attitude. Because of this, the counselor must show a high degree of sensitivity. He or she must reach out verbally, taking a more active role than what might be shown with other counselees. As a counselor, your goal is to pull the person into dialogue with you. It can help to give optimistic reassurance, providing you are not unrealistic, insincere, and too sentimental. Also helpful can be the sharing of facts about how depression affects people, patiently encouraging counselees to talk (but not pushing them to talk), asking questions, giving periodic compliments, and gently sharing Scripture but without preaching. Try to avoid confrontation, persistent probing questions or demands for action, especially in the beginning. These techniques often increase anxiety, which can create more discouragement and pessimism.

As the counselee talks about the depression, you should listen attentively. Watch for evidence of anger, hurt, negative thinking, poor self-esteem, and guilt—all of which you might want to discuss later. Encourage counselees to talk about those life situations that are bothersome. Avoid "taking sides," but try to be understanding and accepting of feelings. Watch for talk about losses, failures, rejection, and other incidents that may have stimulated the current depression.

As you work with depressed people, be aware of your own feelings. Are you impatient when you have a negative, complaining counselee? Are you inclined to let your mind wander or be pulled into despondent negative thinking yourself? Counseling the depressed can be a demanding test for your helping skills. These counselees are not easy to work with, and many need special effort and attention.

For example, many depressed people have a strong need to be dependent. As you counsel, ask yourself if you are encouraging dependence in an already depressed person. If so, might you be trying to build your own feelings of power or importance? Might you be encouraging anger or negative thinking? Could you be making so many demands that the counselee feels overwhelmed and thus inclined to cling to you? In all of your counseling, it is good to be aware of what is happening in yourself. When counselors are not aware of these tendencies, sometimes they increase depression instead of contributing to its relief.

In counseling the depressed, some combination of the following approaches can be helpful.

1. *Dealing with the Physiology.* In their enthusiasm to help the depressed, nonmedical counselors sometimes forget that many depressive reactions have a physical basis. Often depression results from physical illness, some of which may not even be diagnosed. Other depression may come from the counselee's poor eating habits, insufficient sleep, or lack of exercise. Few counselors would recommend that a depressed person begin an exercise program as the only form of treatment. However, given the mounting evidence for the impact of exercise on the reduction of depression, it is not surprising that many counselors strongly urge their counselees to exercise consistently as part of their counseling.[35]

If there are persisting physical symptoms or if the depression does not yield to your initial counseling, it is important to refer your counselee to a competent and psychologically astute physician. The nonmedical counselor is not qualified to decide whether a counselee's symptoms are biologically induced, and neither can the nonphysician make valid evaluations about whether the depression has physical causes. Often the depression lessens or disappears when the underlying physical condition is treated.

Nonmedical counselors also may want to contact a psychiatrist, general physician, or other specialist who is qualified and licensed to prescribe antidepressant drugs.[36] If the depression has a biological cause, treatment with medications may remove the problem. Often, however, drugs bring symptom relief that changes the counselee's mood and makes him or her more amenable to therapy. It is then that the counseling is able to focus on the nonphysical sources of depression.

Professionals continue to debate the relative effectiveness of counseling versus the administration of antidepressant medications. Increasing research evidence supports the conclusion that in many cases, one of these is as effective as the other. Two Australian researchers studied the effectiveness of treatment with women suffering from postpartum depression. They concluded that "psychological and pharmacological interventions produced similar clinical benefit in the treatment of psychological symptoms. . . . Receiving both treatments in combination was of no added clinical benefit in the immediate or longer term." Even though postpartum depression has a biological cause, the report "strongly advocated" the use of psychological counseling with these women, whether or not medication was used.[37]

The treatment of seasonal affective disorder (SAD) uses a different physical treatment. Instead of taking drugs, these people are exposed to artificial light during the dark winter months. Researchers are discovering, however, that prolonged periods of darkness may not be the only sources of seasonal depression. Research from the United Kingdom discovered that SAD is more common in people who have had negative life experiences, have low levels of social support, are women, and are immigrants.[38] Once again a combination of psychical and psychological treatments appears to be the most effective.

The most controversial treatment in psychiatry [39] is the use of electroconvulsive therapy (sometimes called ECT, or shock treatment) in which a pulse of electrical energy is passed through the brain. This leads to convulsions and a period of confusion, followed by a brightening mood. Widely given in the 1940s and 1950s, this treatment has been criticized because of its risks and possible adverse side effects. It still is used in some places, especially with severely depressed or actively suicidal people who cannot take drugs or who fail to respond to pharmacological or other medical treatment.

2. *Dealing with the Causes.* Counseling will be easier if you can find the psychological and spiritual causes that produce the symptoms. Review the causes of depression listed earlier in this chapter and then try to discover—through questioning and careful listening—what might be producing the depression.

(a) Background. Are there past influences or current family pressures creating depression? If so, it may be helpful to discuss these to help counselees see them in a different perspective and, if possible, to take remedial action. Counselees may need help in learning how to relate to their families in more effective ways. Family members can be urged to accept the counselee, to challenge negative thinking, to encourage action in place of inactivity, and to include the depressed person in family activities. When communication is good and when the family is caring, accepting, and involved, counselees often improve more quickly.

(b) Stress. Is the counselee experiencing stress, especially the stress that comes from a loss? Encourage the person to share his or her feelings about this, discuss practical approaches to stress management, and help the counselee find ways to continue with life in spite of the loss.[40]

(c) Learned Helplessness. In the hectic days in which we live it is not unusual for counselees (and sometimes their counselors) to feel that life is out of control. If your counselee feels this way, talk about what might be done to get life back into more order, starting with the small tasks and moving on to the more difficult. You can discuss the inevitability of uncontrollable events, and can help counselees see that God is always in control, even when we are not.[41]

If depression comes because people have learned to feel helpless, is there an antidote to helplessness? Leaders in the fast growing field of positive psychology think the answer is found in learned optimism.[42] This is more than the power of positive thinking. Optimism grows (and depression declines) when people are helped to persevere in their tasks, when they begin to see that goals can be reached, and when they rediscover hope. It is not likely that most people can be talked into being optimistic, but if they can be helped to take steps that lead to positive experiences, often their thinking begins to change.

(d) Anger. Is there evidence of anger, bitterness, or thoughts of revenge in the counselee? These emotions must be discussed and expressed—even if they seem irrational. Hurt can be deeply embedded and sometimes uncovered only after considerable probing and a lot of careful listening. Perhaps you will want to draw the diagram from a few pages back and show counselees how hurt can lead so easily to depression.

(e) Guilt. Has the person sinned or done something else to arouse guilt? Has there been confession to God and perhaps to others? Does the counselee know about divine forgiveness and about the importance, and the difficulty, of forgiving oneself? Issues like this will be discussed in more detail in chapter 11.

In discussing these possible causes of depression, the counselee often gains insights into the problem and can think of ways to deal with the depression-producing influences. At times the counselor may want to give his or her own insights and observations, but allow time for the counselee to respond to these interpretations. All of this contributes to better understanding, and often that leads to change and improvement.

3. *Dealing with Thinking.* Most people do not "snap out" of depression. The road to recovery may be long, difficult, and marked by mood fluctuations that come with special intensity when there are disappointments, failures, or separations. Depressed people want to *feel* better, but feelings by themselves are difficult, if not impossible, to change. Telling a person "You shouldn't feel depressed" does nothing to relieve the depression and often adds guilt, since most of us cannot change our feelings at will.

The way we think invariably influences the way we feel. To change feelings, therefore, we must change our thinking. Since depressed people often think negatively, the counselor can help to change this thinking. When problems or disappointments come, it is helpful to ask what the counselee thinks. Often he or she decides "this is terrible," "this proves I'm no good," "nobody wants me now," or "I never do anything right." These self-criticisms rarely are based on solid fact. If a person fails, for example, it does not follow that he or she is "no good" or unwanted. Failure means, instead, that we are not perfect (nobody is), that we have made a mistake and should try to act differently in the future.

Effective counseling must encourage counselees to reevaluate depression-producing thoughts and attitudes toward life. In a way that does not arouse defensiveness and resistance, ask, "Is your conclusion about your life or yourself valid? Could there be another way of viewing the situation? In their minds, everybody talks to themselves. In your self-talk, are you telling yourself things about the world, yourself, and the future that are not really true? Do you think there is solid evidence for what you are telling yourself?"

All of this is designed to challenge the counselee's thinking and to teach ways of evaluating conclusions so he or she can learn to think more positively and more realistically. Without denying the depression-producing situation, the counselor and counselee both must be guided by the truth of Philippians 4:8: "Fix your thoughts on what is true and honorable and right. Think about things that are pure and lovely and admirable. Think about things that are excellent and worthy of praise."

Sometimes, Christians convince themselves that they always must be spiritually alive and enthusiastic but never angry, lethargic, or discouraged. When failure or disappointment come, as they do inevitably, these believers feel crushed because their unrealistic expectations have not been met. The counselor tries to help these Christians and other counselees to evaluate their expectations, attitudes, values, assumptions, and sometimes their spiritual beliefs. Help counselees see which of these are unrealistic, nonbiblical, and harmful. Since these kinds of negative thoughts often are well entrenched, often coming from a lifetime of wrong thinking, it may take repeated efforts to help people reevaluate and change their attitudes toward life and themselves.

4. *Dealing with Inactivity.* Many counselors aim to help their counselees develop insight into their problems and actions. But often insight is not enough. Even when they have some understanding of their own depression, counselees often have difficulty in doing something about it. Lack of action is common in all of us, but especially in depressed people, who lack the energy or the motivation to take steps to deal with the problem. For many, it is easier to stay in bed or to sit alone brooding and thinking about the miseries of life.

Gently, but firmly, the counselor may need to push the depressed person to take actions, even if these are small actions like getting involved in daily routines, family activities, and recreation. Start by encouraging activities in which the counselee is likely to succeed. This increases optimism and interrupts the tendency to ruminate on negative ideas. When the counselee does take action, try to give encouragement and compliments.

5. *Dealing with the Environment.* Sometimes, the best way to help a depressed person is to help change the environment that is contributing to the depression. Realistically, counselors may not be able to do much to change the depression-producing circumstances in a person's life, but it is possible to encourage counselees to modify routines, reduce work loads if possible, find ways to avoid stress-inducing situations, or take periodic vacations. Counselees also can be encouraged to find groups of people who can help to create a supportive environment. Chief among these can be fellow believers in a church, although some churches have little understanding or tolerance for people who are honest about their inner struggles and looking to experience support and the love of Christ from others.

6. *Dealing with the Potential for Self-Harm.* People can harm themselves in many

ways—by changing jobs, for example, by quitting school, or by making unwise marriage decisions. The counselor must be alert to a tendency for people to make major long-lasting decisions when they are in the grips of depression. Helping counselees decide if they "really want to do" what they are proposing, helping them see the possible consequences of the decisions, and urging them to "wait a while" can all prevent actions that could be harmful.

Suicide is one action that is contemplated by many depressed people. Since most people give prior clues about their intentions, the counselor should be alert to indications that suicide is being considered. Be sensitive, for example, to any of the following:[43]

- Talk of suicide.
- Evidence of a realistic plan of action for killing oneself.
- Knowledge regarding the most effective methods of suicide (guns and carbon monoxide work best; wrist slashing is least successful; drug overdose depends on how much is taken and the type of drug).
- Feelings of hopelessness and/or meaninglessness.
- Indications of guilt feelings and worthlessness.
- Recent environmental stresses (such as job loss, divorce, or death in the family).
- An inability to cope with stress.
- Excessive concern about physical illness.
- Preoccupation with insomnia.
- Evidence of depression, disorientation, and/or defiance.
- A tendency to be dependent and dissatisfied at the same time.
- A sudden and unexplainable shift to a happy, cheerful mood (which often means that the decision to attempt suicide has been made).
- A history of prior suicide attempts (those who have tried before often try suicide again).

Counselors should not hesitate to ask the counselee if he or she has been thinking of suicide. This questioning gets the issue out into the open and lets the counselee consider it rationally and with an insightful counselor. Rather than encouraging suicide (as is commonly assumed), open discussion more often reduces its likelihood.

If a person really is determined to commit suicide, the counselor may delay this action, but in time the counselee is likely to try and try again. Even the most competent and dedicated helper may not be able to prevent suicide forever. It is well to remember this when a suicide does occur. Otherwise, as a counselor, you may berate yourself and wallow in guilt because you have not been able to prevent the counselee's death. Often this can be a good time for you to get some counseling for yourself.

Preventing Depression

It is unrealistic to assume that all depression can be prevented. There is no evidence that we can prevent many of the biologically produced attacks of depression, and neither is it always possible to prevent the depression that comes from an illness. To learn that one has a terminal illness or a diagnosis of cancer, for example, is not likely to be followed with rejoicing. Yet even in situations like these, it can help to give people an indication of what to expect. When surgical patients and their families learn in advance what to expect after the operation, there is less shock and depression when these symptoms actually do appear, especially if these have been presented as a normal part of the treatment and recovery.

There will be times when the pressures of life are certain to plunge each of us into deep sadness, if not depression. Disappointments, losses, rejections, and failures come to everyone and lead to periods of unhappiness and discouragement. Even so, there are ways by which we can prevent or soften the blows of depression.

1. *Trust in God.* Writing from prison, the apostle Paul once stated that he had learned to be content in all circumstances. Knowing that God gives strength to his children and is able to supply all our needs, Paul had learned how to live joyfully, both in poverty and in prosperity.[44] Through his experiences, and undoubtedly through a study of the Scriptures, Paul had learned to trust in God, which helped to prevent depression.

The same can be true today. A conviction that God is alive and in control can give hope and encouragement, even when we are inclined to be discouraged and without hope. If modern people can learn this lesson, and if church leaders and Christian counselors can teach it, then discouragement and feelings of hopelessness need not hit as hard as they might hit otherwise.

It is regrettable that the teaching of some well-intentioned Christians can make the depression worse, instead of relieving and preventing it. When people are told to "trust in God and the depression will go away," there can be guilt and deeper discouragement if the depression persists. When teachers or writers show little understanding of biological depression, or when they present their lists of "Christian" rules for getting rid of depression, depressed people sometimes feel deeper despair and frustration when they can't make the formulas work. It is much more helpful to give support and assurance of our prayers even when we fail to understand what is causing the depression.

2. *Teach About Depression.* In recent years researchers have studied practical ways through which depression can be prevented.[45] Almost all of these reports mention the value of teaching about depression. This teaching can be done personally with individuals, with families, or with groups. It can involve giving people information to read or presenting material in sermons or classrooms. What should be taught?

(a) Teach people to expect discouragement and depression. The second verse of a famous hymn[46] proclaims that "we should never be discouraged" if we take things to the Lord in prayer. This is a popular view for which there is no scriptural support. Jesus warned that we would have problems, and the apostle James wrote that trials and temptations would come to test our faith and teach us patience.[47] It is unrealistic to smile and laugh in depressing circumstances, pretending that we are never going to be discouraged.

Consider Jesus at the time of the crucifixion. He was "filled with anguish and deep distress," openly acknowledging that his soul was crushed.[48] We can't imagine him smiling in Gethsemane or on the cross, trying to convince everyone that he was "bubbling over" with happiness. Jesus trusted in his Father, but he expected pain and was not surprised when it came. In a similar way, when we are realistic enough to expect pain and informed enough to know that God is sovereign, then we can handle discouragement better and often keep from slipping into deep depression.

(b) Teach people to be alert to depression-prone situations. Everyone expects the recent widow to be depressed and in need of special support during the months following her husband's death. We know that she may be especially "down" on the first Father's Day, Christmas, or anniversary following the death. By helping people anticipate these sad times, and by providing special social support, the predictable depression can be prevented from being worse.

Most counselors are aware that holidays or other celebrations can be depression-producing times even for people who are not grieving. Christmas, for example, may not be a time of joy and happiness for people who are separated from loved ones, without friends, have no money to buy presents, worried about relatives who drink too much at holiday celebrations, pressured by the demands of the season, or reminded of deaths or other traumatic experiences that took place in a previous December. People who are prone to "holiday-blues" may need special understanding and encouragement if they are to keep from slipping into deeper depression at times when most other people are celebrating joyfully.

(c) Teach skills. These can include skills in handling anger, stress-management skills, and skills in thinking more clearly.

- Handling Anger. Some people slide into depression because their minds dwell on past injustices or past failures. This may sound obvious or simplistic, but these people must ask God to help them overlook and stop dwelling on the past, forgive those who have sinned against them, and forgive themselves. When people continue to dwell on past events and wallow in anger, guilt, and the misery of discouragement, this would suggest that the thinking has some purpose. Is it an excuse for avoiding responsibility or seeking forgiveness? Are they finding satisfaction in thinking about revenge or in their fantasies about the fate of the people who caused the hurt? Counselors and churches can teach people to admit their anger or guilt and show how these can be overcome (see chapters 10 and 11). If individuals can learn to let go of anger and guilt, depression can be reduced or prevented.
- Managing Stress. When people can learn how to master and cope with the stresses of life, they feel more in control of their circumstances and less likely to be overwhelmed by the helplessness that often leads to depression.[49] Instead of helping people cope, some family members and counselors tend to be overprotective. This interferes with the their ability to learn how to cope with or to master the stresses of life. In contrast, if people can see how others cope, and can learn how to cope themselves, despair and depression are less likely. This learning of stress-management and coping skills can come in more formal ways like classroom instruction, but it is likely to be more beneficial if the stressful situations are discussed one at a time and stress-management suggestions are tried out and found to be effective.
- Thinking Differently. If it is true that we each talk silently to ourselves all day, then all of us, including our counselees, should notice what is being said internally. This self-talk often can be like a cassette tape that plays

over and over in the brain, implanting ideas that may be harmful and wrong. If, for example, the idea that "I am incompetent" is repeated often enough, this can undermine self-confidence and lead to depression. To challenge this thinking the person needs to ask, "What is the evidence for the view that I am incompetent?" "In what areas am I incompetent (and where am I more competent)?" "Is it okay to be incompetent in some things?" "How can I become more competent in the areas that matter?" When people learn to challenge their own thinking, and that of others, this can prevent or reduce the severity of depression.

Also helpful can be meditation on the Word of God[50] and on things that are good, positive, and just.[51] Meditation is a form of self-talk that directs our minds to God and away from thinking that is negative and inclined to produce depression.

3. *Encourage Support.* As we have seen, withdrawal from others is common in people who feel depressed, but at such times they need the support of others. A concerned group of people who have learned to be caring can soften the trauma of crises and provide strength and help in times of need. This support can come from counselors, but even more helpful can be the influence of caring friends and sensitive church members. In stimulating support, be careful not to overlook the role of families. Depression often arises in family settings, but families also can be taught how to give consistent understanding and encouragement. Wherever the support originates, people in crises or other stressful situations are able to cope better and thus avoid severe depression when they know that they are not alone. [52]

4. *Urge People to Reach Out.* Alcoholics Anonymous has shown conclusively that needy people help themselves when they reach out to assist others. This is an example of what has come to be known as the "helper therapy" principle. It states that those who reach out to help others are the ones who benefit and are helped the most.

This principle doesn't always work; sometimes depressed people pull one another down. Healing also is unlikely if the depressed helper selfishly concludes, "I don't care about others, but I'll help grudgingly if this is what I have to do to feel better myself." In contrast, when there is a willingness to help others, including other depressed people, then everybody benefits and further depression may be prevented. Once again we see evidence that the creation of a caring community is an indirect but effective way to prevent depression.

5. *Stimulate Physical Fitness.* Since poor diet and lack of exercise can make people depression-prone, individuals can be encouraged—by word and by the counselor's example—to take care of their bodies. Earlier we noted that it would be simplistic to assume that exercise could completely prevent more serious physically based depression, but it is well known that a healthy body is less susceptible to mental as well as physical illness.

Conclusions About Depression

Vance Havner was a Southern Baptist preacher whose wife lay dying. He prayed that she would be healed through a miracle, but she died and her husband plunged into grief. The old man did not understand why this had happened when it did. "Whoever thinks he has the ways of God conveniently tabulated, analyzed, and correlated with convenient, glib answers to ease every question from aching hearts has not been far in this maze of mystery we call life and death," Havner wrote later. God has "no stereotyped way of doing what He does. He delivered Peter from prison but left John the Baptist in a dungeon to die. . . . I accept whatever He does, however He does it."[53]

This man was deeply saddened when his wife died, but I suspect he never became deeply depressed. He had a realistic perspective on life and death and on his God. This is a perspective that can do much to help both counselors and counselees to deal more effectively with the problem of depression.

KEY POINTS FOR BUSY COUNSELORS

➤ Depression is a common, universal condition that varies in terms of symptoms, severity, origins, and duration, and that affects large segments of the population.

➤ Depression is characterized by:
- Feelings of sadness, low self-esteem, worthlessness, helplessness, and lack of hope.
- Thinking characterized by negative thoughts, self-criticism, pessimism, and sometimes self-destruction (suicide).
- Behavior marked by apathy, a sense of inertia, social withdrawal, and sometimes a neglect of normal duties or personal hygiene.
- Physical symptoms including fatigue, loss of energy, lack of interest in normal activities, loss of appetite, and complaining about aches and pains.

➤ The Bible does not use the term *depression* but describes the experience of being down, sad, downcast, or discouraged. In most places this experience is linked to hope in God.

➤ *Biological-genetic causes* of depression reflect the impact of brain chemistry, hormone imbalance, disease, genetic influences, and even the impact of poor sleep, eating, and exercise habits.

➤ *Psychological-cognitive causes* include:
- Background and family influences such as conflict or lack of closeness with parents or other significant family members.
- Stress and significant losses.
- Learned helplessness.
- The impact of negative thinking.
- Anger.
- Sin and Guilt.

➤ *Social-environmental causes* arise from stressful environments.

➤ Effects of depression include unhappiness, inefficiency, physical illness, decreased sexual interest, low self-esteem, withdrawal and—in its more serious forms—suicide.

➤ Effective counseling for depression includes:
- Dealing with the physical causes and symptoms, often through use of anti-depressant medications.
- Working to resolve the impact of the psychological causes.
- Helping people change their thinking.
- Guiding in behavior changes.
- Assisting counselees in coping with environmental influences.
- Developing social support.
- Identifying and taking action to prevent suicide. This involves knowing the signs that indicate a possible suicide attempt.

➤ To prevent depression, help people:
- Trust in God.
- Understand the nature of depression.
- Learn skills for dealing with depression. These include: (a) learning to handle anger, (b) stress-management skills, and (c) learning to control and change self-defeating thoughts.
- Find networks of support.
- Reach out to others.
- Keep physically fit.

➤ King David asked, "Why am I so discouraged? Why so sad?" and then wrote, "I will put my hope in God!" (Psalm 43:5).

9

Anxiety

Wanda is thirty-nine, married, a stay-at-home mom who left her career as a teacher to be with her three children. Her husband is a successful businessman whose work is demanding and who sometimes is gone on business trips. To those who know her, Wanda appears to be unruffled by the long periods without adult companionship or by the challenges of handling and home-schooling her young and active children.

But appearances can be deceptive. Internally, Wanda struggles to keep control of her growing anxiety. She worries constantly about the safety of her family, struggles with insecurity, and has trouble sleeping despite the fact that her days are exhausting. Every night, after the children are in bed, she watches the evening news and hears about violence in her city and the ever-present danger from terrorist attacks. Sometimes, she has difficulty concentrating, and she tends to be irritable with herself as well as with her husband and children.

"What's wrong with me?" she asked a neighbor who dropped in for coffee. "I feel tense and worried all the time, and I never relax." Wanda has memorized the Bible verses that tell us to not worry about anything, to pray about our needs, and to thank God for all he has done. But she never has experienced the promised "peace which is far more wonderful than the human mind can understand."[1] And when she is alone, she wonders if she can go on or if she might "snap" because of the anxiety, and hurt herself or her children.

A*nxiety, stress, fear, phobia, panic,* and *tension* are words that have different technical meanings but often are used interchangeably to describe a common condition that may have reached epidemic proportions. It appears in all age groups, including the elderly, children, and teenagers. "I've talked to, literally, thousands of parents, kids, and professionals all over the country and across practically all socioeconomic groups," one counselor wrote in an article on teenage anxiety. "I've gotten the same message in a crescendo: kids everywhere are overwhelmed by a tidal wave of culturally induced anxiety."[2] Chaotic overscheduling, worry over tests, the disappearance of family routines or stability, endless exposure to disturbing information, lack of close connections, constant change, insecurity, information overload, pressures from peers, and the fading of clear moral guidelines all combine to raise anxiety levels in young people. Outwardly, they appear vivacious, carefree, and filled with potential. Inside, they are scared. Constant reminders about the ongoing activity of terrorists around the world have heightened our insecurities and led to what has been called "the new anxiety."[3] The 1950s and 1960s used to be called the age of anxiety, but that generation could not have imagined the anxiety-producing stresses of the early twenty-first century.

Anxiety is an inner feeling of apprehension, uneasiness, worry, and/or dread that is accompanied by a heightened physical arousal. In times of anxiety, the body appears to be on alert, ready to flee or fight. The heart beats faster, blood pressure and muscle tensions increase, neurological and chemical changes occur within, and the person may feel faint, jumpy, and unable to relax or sleep. Anxiety can arise in response to some specific danger (many writers would call this "fear" rather than anxiety), or it may come in reaction to an imaginary or unknown threat. This latter kind of anxiety has been termed "free-floating." The anxious person senses that something terrible is going to happen, but he or she does not know what it is or why.

A search of the Internet suggests that anxiety continues to be studied by thousands of researchers. Some have proposed detailed categories to help us define anxiety more clearly, but we will consider only six: normal and neurotic, moderate and intense, state and trait. *Normal anxiety* comes to all of us at times, usually when there is some threat or situational danger. Most often, this anxiety is proportional to the danger: the greater the threat, the greater the anxiety, although sometimes we can't know how serious a threat may be. This is anxiety that can be recognized, managed, and reduced, especially when circumstances change and the danger is reduced. *Neurotic anxiety* involves intense exaggerated feelings of helplessness and dread even when the danger is mild or nonexistent. Many counselors believe this anxiety cannot be faced directly or dealt with rationally because it may arise from inner conflicts that are not conscious.

Anxiety also varies in its intensity, duration, and influence. *Moderate anxiety* can be healthy and serve a useful purpose. Often it is motivating, helps people avoid dangerous situations, and leads to increased efficiency. *Intense anxiety*, in contrast, is more stressful. It can shorten one's attention span, make concentration difficult, cause forgetting, hinder performance, interfere with problem solving, block effective communication, arouse panic, and sometimes cause unpleasant physical symptoms such as paralysis, rapid heartbeat, or intense headaches.

Anxiety also could be described as a state or a trait.[4] *State anxiety* comes quickly, may or may not be of high intensity, and has a short duration. This is an acute, relatively brief apprehensive reaction that comes to all of us from time to time. Usually, it is a response to some real or imagined threat, like the inner surge of adrenaline you feel before making a speech or taking an important exam. Sometimes, the anxiety is accompanied by excitement, in part because anxiety and excitement release the same hormones and turn on the same parts of the nervous system.[5] *Trait anxiety* is different. It is a persistent, ever-present, ingrained emotional tension seen in people who appear to worry all the time. Often this causes physical illness because the body cannot function effectively when it remains in a perpetual state of tension and arousal.

Panic attacks and post-traumatic stress disorder are more serious anxiety. Often this is the anxiety that brings people to counselors. *Panic attacks* involve sudden, often unexpected, rushes of intense fear accompanied by rapid heartbeat, trembling, shortness of breath, dizziness, chest pain, or feelings of losing control. These attacks reach peak intensity within a few minutes and fade quickly after that. Many times they become associated with specific places or situations, such as being in a crowd, going to a dentist, riding in a car, or feeling trapped in a room. Because these attacks can be so scary and unpredictable, victims avoid the situations or places where the anxiety occurred in the past, lest they occur again.

In more extreme cases, the person is afraid to leave home or go to certain parts of the house. Many times panic attacks result in trips to the emergency room because of the physical symptoms, such as heart pounding or difficulties in breathing. When the doctors find nothing wrong physically, some kind of calming medication is given and the patient is sent home.[6]

Post-traumatic stress disorder (PTSD) first appeared as a psychiatric diagnosis in 1980, but the condition has been known for many years. It has become more visible since the increase in terrorist attacks and ongoing violence in different parts of the world. PTSD arises following intense stress, such as observing or experiencing events that involved death or great danger. These could include military conflict, rape, involvement in a serious accident, kidnapping, a violent crime, prisoner abuse, or natural disasters, such as a tornado or earthquake. Any of these can leave a lifelong legacy of anxiety. For years after the trauma, some people have nightmares, irrational fears, depression, and loss of interest in activities that once were pleasant. For these people, anxiety has become a way of life that follows in the wake of an earlier stress experience. This form of anxiety will be discussed in more detail later in this book.[7]

The Bible and Anxiety

The Bible views anxiety in two ways, as a healthy concern and as fret or worry.

Anxiety in the form of realistic concern is neither condemned nor forbidden. Paul wrote that he was not anxious (that is, worried) about the possibility of being beaten, cold, hungry, or in danger, but he did experience anxiety (that is, concern) about the welfare of the churches. This sincere care for others put a daily burden on the apostle[8] and made Timothy "genuinely anxious" (concerned and interested) as well.[9]

Anxiety as fret and worry appears to be what Jesus had in mind in the Sermon on the Mount. He taught that we should not worry (be anxious) about the future or about life's basic needs, such as food and clothing. We have a heavenly Father, Jesus said, who knows what we need and will provide.[10] In the New Testament Epistles, both Peter and Paul echoed this conclusion. "Give all your worries [anxieties] and cares to God, for he cares about what happens to you," Peter wrote.[11] "Don't worry about anything," we read in Philippians. Instead, Christians are to bring their requests to God, with an attitude of thanksgiving, expecting to experience "God's peace, which is far more wonderful than the human mind can understand."[12]

Anxiety as fret and worry comes when we turn from God, shift the burdens of life on to ourselves, and show by our attitudes and actions that we alone are taking responsibility for handling problems. Instead of acknowledging God's sovereignty and power, or determining to live for him and make his kingdom our primary concern,[13] many of us—both counselors and counselees—slip into sinful self-reliance and preoccupation with our own life pressures.

None of this suggests that we should ignore danger and blithely wait for a miracle from heaven. The Bible does not say there is anything wrong with facing anxious situations honestly or with using our God-given brains to find ways for dealing with the identifiable problems of life. To ignore danger is foolish and wrong. Christians can move forward with confidence, especially if they commit their actions to God and seek his guidance. But it is wrong, and unhealthy, to be immobilized by excessive worry. Our persisting concerns must be committed in prayer to God, who, sometimes working through Christian counselors, can release us from paralyzing fear or anxiety and can free us to deal realistically with the needs and welfare both of others and of ourselves.

Everyone knows that it is difficult to never worry about anything.[14] It is not easy to cast our burdens on the Lord and to trust that God will meet our needs. We don't always know when to wait for his help and when we should take responsibility for meeting a difficult, anxiety-producing situation. Impatience often accompanies anxiety, and anxious people want help in handling their pressures quickly. It can be very hard to wait for God's perfect time schedule.

The Christian counselor can be an example of one who is calm and trusting in God to meet needs. The counselor also can help counselees see God's promises, recognize his power and influence in our daily lives, and take action when appropriate. For many counselees it also is helpful if they can understand the causes and effects of their persisting anxiety.

The Causes of Anxiety

Counseling textbooks have proposed several theories about the causes of anxiety. Psychoanalytic theory arose from the work of Sigmund Freud and led to a variety of explanations, most based on the idea that anxiety reflects various forms of unresolved inner conflict. More common today are cognitive-behavior theories that view anxiety as a response to perceived danger and the individual's belief that he or she has lost control and lacks the resources to deal with the threat. In recent years biological and genetic theories have built evidence that anxiety has a significant biological component. Perhaps no one person has been able to shift through all the viewpoints, but today it is generally recognized that anxiety is more than a purely psychological or purely physiological condition. It has elements of both, and both must be considered when anxiety is treated. In this section we will consider how anxiety arises from threat, conflict, fear, unmet needs, biological influences, and individual differences.

1. *Threat.* Anxiety often is caused by a threat to something that an individual considers important. Sometimes, anxiety arises because one's life or well-being is threatened. Following the terrorist attacks on the United States in September 2001, counselors across the country reported significant increases in the numbers of people seeking help to control their anxiety. These people felt threatened by a danger that they could not see or predict. Other anxiety-producing threats include unstable environments, fear of losing self-esteem, separation from others, the undermining of our values, or the impact of unconscious influences. All of these contain a strong element of uncertainty.

(a) Unstable Environments. Most people feel threatened and anxious when they live with high crime in their neighborhoods, war, political instability, violent weather, unexplained and unexpected illness, or even visits to the doctor. When we move into a new situation, take a new job, go into the examination room, or step on to the stage in front of an audience, we can feel threatened lest we make a mistake or do something foolish in a situation where we feel trapped. In almost all of these situations, the individual feels out of control, uncertain about what to expect, and largely helpless to prevent or reduce the threat.

(b) Self-esteem. Most people like to look good and perform appropriately. We feel threatened by anything that might harm the self-image or imply (to others or to ourselves) that we are not competent. Many self-conscious people sense a mild anxiety in new social situations because they aren't sure how to act or are threatened by the possible reaction of others. On a more serious level, some people avoid taking exams, accepting a promotion, or risking failure because the possibility of not succeeding is too threatening to their self-esteem.

(c) Separation. It never is easy to be separated from significant other people. Being on your own can be confusing, and the pain is especially intense when we have been left or rejected by an important person. The death of a loved one, moving, divorce, the breakup of an engagement—these and other separations can leave us feeling uncertain about the future, saddened by a gaping inner emotional void, and threatened as we wonder what to do next.

(d) Values. As they grow up, children learn values from their parents, peers, teachers, religions, and media. In earlier times and in some parts of the world, core values have remained the same for centuries, but all of this appears to be changing. Nowhere has this been more evident than in the influential worlds of media, politics, and business. Following several highly visible scandals involving top business leaders, one executive wrote, "The velocity of change in today's economy requires a steady commitment to your fundamental values. If you don't have something that you can hold on to, everything is up for grabs and people lose their way."[15] It also can be threatening and anxiety-producing when the things we value are in danger of being undermined or taken away. The employee who fails to get a valued promotion feels threatened by his or her inability to succeed, be affirmed, and advance economically or professionally. The child who turns from the family religion or rejects traditional sexual standards is likely to create anxiety (and often both discouragement and anger) in parents whose values are being challenged and perhaps threatened. The politician who gets elected on a political platform that contrasts with our values can make any of us feel threatened and anxious.

(e) Unconscious Influences. Even counselors who reject many of Freud's theories often agree that unconscious influences may be at the basis of some anxiety. There are so many (real and imagined) dangers in this world that most people ignore some potential stresses and push these out of their minds. This may not be bad if it is done deliberately and temporarily, but according to Freud, threats and concerns that are pushed into the unconscious can fester while they remain out of sight. Later these unconscious ideas might move toward becoming conscious. That can be threatening because we then are forced to face difficult issues that we don't understand or know how to resolve.

The story is told about a young man who was seized with intense anxiety one evening as he watched a ballet. He felt better as soon as he left the theater. When he described this later, his counselor began to suspect that the man had strong unconscious homosexual tendencies that he was struggling to keep from becoming conscious. During the performance, he was attracted unconsciously to the male ballet dancers with their tight clothing. The anxiety that followed was thought to be in reaction to the threat that his defenses might break down, allowing the homosexual tendencies to become apparent to himself and to others.

Interpretations like this are difficult for the counselors to see at first, and we can't always be sure that the interpretations are correct. There even is disagreement among counselors—both Christian and non-Christian—about whether the unconscious even exists.[16] Nevertheless, the young man's panic at the ballet is a good example of anxiety that arises in response to a specific threatening situation. By considering the times and places when anxiety has been aroused, the counselor often is able to obtain a clue about the specific issue or issues that might be threatening the counselee.

2. *Conflict.* Whenever a person is influenced by two or more pressures, there is a sense of uncertainty that often leads to anxiety. Most introductory psychology books suggest that conflicts come from two tendencies: approach and avoidance. Approach involves doing or moving in a direction that will be pleasurable and satisfying. Avoidance involves resisting something, most often because it is unlikely to be pleasurable or satisfying. There are three basic kinds of conflicts: approach-approach, approach-avoidance, and avoidance-avoidance.

(a) Approach-Approach Conflict. Here is a conflict because of two desirable but incompatible goals. For example, we may be faced with two dinner invitations on the same night, either of which would be pleasant. Often making such a decision is difficult, and sometimes it arouses anxiety. You will understand if you ever have had two attractive job opportunities or been accepted by two graduate schools and, as a result, have been forced to make a decision.

(b) Approach-Avoidance Conflict. Here is a desire both to do something and not to do it. For example, a person may grapple with the offer of a new job. To accept might bring more pay and opportunity (approach), but it also may bring the necessity of a move and the inconvenience of a training program (avoidance). Making such decisions can involve considerable anxiety.

(c) Avoidance-Avoidance Conflict. Here there are two alternatives, both of which may be unpleasant: like living with a painful illness that may or may not get better versus having an operation that also could be painful and that may or may not fix the problem.

Most conflicts involve a struggle between two or more alternatives, each of which may have several approach and avoidance characteristics. A couple may wonder, for example, whether to stay in their present home, which is too small and crowded, add an addition to their house, or move elsewhere. Each of these alternatives has several positive and negative aspects, and anxiety persists until the choice is made. Often it continues to persist after the choice is made as the buyers wonder if they have made the right decision. Realtors often refer to this anxiety as "buyer's remorse." The buyer is anxious about whether this was the best choice, whether there will be sufficient money to move, or whether another house might have been a better choice. Do you think there could also be buyer's remorse after the decision to purchase a car, return to school, or get married?

3. *Fear.* Even though most counselors distinguish fear from anxiety, a similar inner apprehension characterizes both. We may not think much about our fears, but each of us has our own list. These lists might include fear of failure, the future, rejection, intimacy, success, taking responsibility, conflict, meaninglessness in life (this is sometimes called existential anxiety), sickness, death, loneliness, change, or a host of other real or imagined possibilities. Sometimes, these fears can build up in one's mind and create extreme anxiety—even in the absence of any real danger.

Anxiety often comes because people have irrational beliefs that create fear. Examples include counselees who conclude that "everything about my situation is sure to get worse," "nothing can be done to change my circumstances," or "I'll never be able to give a public speech." Beliefs like these tend to be repeated in our minds as self-talk. They are irrational beliefs that create persisting fear and further anxiety. Ultimately, beliefs like these need to be challenged.

4. *Unmet Needs*. What are the basic human needs? Each of us might have different answers, perhaps depending on where we live. The need for survival would be on most lists, and in more developed societies we might add needs for security, fulfillment, a sense of identity, intimacy, and significance (which is the need to amount to something worthwhile). If we fail to meet these and other needs, we can feel anxious, uncertain, "up-in-the-air," afraid, and frustrated.

But what if all of these needs are met? What if we had all the money, success, influence, or relationships that we think we need? Would our lives then be complete, satisfying, and anxiety-free? Probably not! There still would be questions that transcend life on earth: Where will I go after death? Does existence consist of only a few short years on earth and nothing after that? What is my purpose for living? These are "existential questions" that often lead to considerable anxiety. We can have no lasting freedom from this kind of anxiety until we are at peace with God, resting in his promises for eternity and knowing the stability that comes when our sins have been confessed and we are completely forgiven.[17] When I was in graduate school, I had a professor who was an existentialist. One day she invited me into her office and asked about my faith. We had never discussed this previously, but she had seen the evidence of it in my life. After my explanation she replied "I wish I could believe like that." She could have, but she chose to stay with her existential uncertainties.

5. *Physiology*. Neuropsychology, neurophysiology, neurobiology, and neuroscience all refer to one of the most exciting and fast-paced fields of research relating to human behavior. Most counselors "regard the subject with blank incomprehension, if not downright terror" because of the complexity of the subject, the never-ending flood of cutting-edge research, and the difficulty in learning about the brain and how it impacts behavior.[18] But every problem discussed in this book has a physiological component, and even an elementary understanding can improve our effectiveness as counselors.

In his book *The Anxiety Cure*, Christian psychologist Archibald Hart gives a lay person's guide to the physical causes of anxiety.[19] The human brain comprises billions of nerve cells, each connecting electrochemically with an average of ten thousand others. Not surprisingly, this has been called "the most complex biological entity known on earth,"[20] and each reader of this book carries one in his or her head.

Neurotransmitters are chemicals in the brain that transport information between the nerve cells, but neurotransmitters also spur some nerve cells to be more activated and responsive while forcing others to calm down and remain quiet. According to Hart, two kinds of neurotransmitters are of special importance to the understanding of anxiety. *GABA* (gamma-aminobutyric acid) transmitters are the most important calming neurotransmitters in the brain. They exist in abundance and serve as natural tranquilizers that control over-excitability, calm overzealous nerves, and help us feel at peace. Hart calls GABA the "happy messengers" because they contribute to our peace of mind. He notes that "the brain has its own system of natural tranquilizers. Artificial tranquilizers only mimic what the brain is already doing for itself.... When there is an adequate supply of these natural tranquilizers, we remain calm and happy. But when they are depleted, we become anxious and sad."[21]

The second kind of transmitter that impacts anxiety is *cortisol*, a close partner to adrenaline. Cortisol is activated by stress. It gives us energy for survival and helps people cope. We need cortisol and can't live without it. But when there is excessive and prolonged stress, the GABA is depleted. "The stress-activated cortisol disrupts the happy messengers and prevents them from communicating their message to your brain. The result? Severe anxiety."[22] When there is too much stress, the level of cortisol is raised, the natural GABA tranquilizers are prevented from reaching their receptor sites, and anxiety goes up. Lowering stress reduces cortisol and restores the natural tranquilizers, "putting the happy messengers back in control." When stress is prolonged, so is anxiety. When stress is reduced and the brain's natural tranquilizers take over, anxiety goes down.

The medications that we know as tranquilizers replace the natural tranquilizers in the brain and relieve anxiety so that the person is better able to focus and deal with the anxiety-producing stress. Almost every day new discoveries are being made that enable us to understand how the brain functions and how its balance can be restored to the way God intended it to be. Although there is opposition to tranquilizers in some Christian circles, there is abundant evidence that treatment can be very effective when medications are used in partnership with counseling.

6. *Individual Differences*. It is well known that people react differently to anxiety-producing situations. Some people are almost never anxious, some seem anxious most of the time, and the majority are in between. Some people get anxious in a variety of situations; others find that only one or two issues create apprehension. Free-floating anxiety—the kind with no clear cause—characterizes some; others only become anxious when there are clearly identified dangers. Then there are those with claustrophobia, fear of heights (acrophobia), fear of animals (zoophobia), and other phobias. These include irrational fears of water, open spaces, social gatherings, or other situations, most of which are not in themselves dangerous.

Why are there individual differences in anxiety? The answers lie in issues such as each person's learning and past experiences, personality, social environment, physiology, and theological beliefs.

(a) Learning. Most behavior is learned—from personal experience, from watching people, and from the teaching of parents and others. These learning experiences can build anxiety into each of us. For example, if a mother is anxious during a thunderstorm, her young child will learn to be anxious. If a child is taught that speaking to strangers can be dangerous, then he or she may feel anxious in situations where no familiar people are present. If a teacher or parent demands more than you can give, you feel anxious when you are with that person. The individual who has failed important examinations in the past is likely to be anxious about trying again. Since we all have different experiences, we view the world differently and differ in the frequency and intensity of our anxieties.

(b) Personality. Most of us know people who are more fearful and "high strung" than others. Some are more sensitive, insecure, hostile, self-centered, or worrisome than others. These personality differences arise from a combination of inherited and learning influences that, in turn, create individual differences in anxiety.

(c) *Social Environment.* A lot of anxiety comes from the society where we live. The anxiety-arousing influences include political instability, economic uncertainty, media images, information overload, mobility that disturbs our sense of rootedness, changing moral standards, or spiritual confusion. These and other influences in the world where we live can stimulate anxiety. Other influences can help create a more secure environment where anxiety is reduced.

(d) *Physiology.* The threat or presence of disease can stimulate or contribute to increased anxiety, and so can pain, dietary imbalance, glandular disorders, vitamin deficiencies, genetic influences, and neurological disorders. Lack of sleep or exercise also can contribute to anxiety, and, in some people, so does caffeine or caffeine withdrawal. Even as physiological imbalance or changes can trigger anxiety, anxiety in turn can create various kinds of sickness and physical reactions, including substance abuse or addiction.[23]

(e) *Theology.* Beliefs have a great bearing on anxiety level. If God is seen as all-powerful, loving, good, and in ultimate control of the universe (which is the biblical teaching), then there can be security and a sense of peace, even in the midst of turmoil. If we believe that God forgives when we confess our sins, that he promises eternal life, and that he meets our needs on earth, then there is less cause for anxiety. In contrast, anxiety is not lessened if God is seen as angry and looking for vengeance. There also are implications for anxiety in the person who does not believe in God and assumes that when problems come, all people are on our own.

In his farewell address to the people of Israel, Moses listed anxiety and trembling as one of the consequences of disobedience to God. "The LORD will give you an anxious mind, eyes weary with longing, and a despairing heart. You will live in constant suspense, filled with dread both night and day, never sure of your life."[24]

From this we must not conclude that anxiety always indicates disobedience or a lack of faith, and neither can we assume that believers will be less anxious than nonbelievers. The causes of anxiety are too complex for such simplistic explanations. Even so, if you want to understand why people differ in the ways they experience and handle anxiety, try to discover what they believe about God and his universe.

The Effects of Anxiety

Anxiety is not always bad. When there is no anxiety, life can be boring, inefficient, and not much fun. A moderate amount of anxiety (not too little, not too much) motivates people and adds zest to life. When we are able to control the situations that create anxiety, it can even be a welcome experience. Perhaps this is one reason why some people get a thrill from bungee jumping and others line up for hours waiting to be "scared to death" by a horror movie or a ride on the "screaming eagle" roller coaster.

When it is intense, prolonged, or uncontrollable, however, anxiety can lead to crippling physical, psychological, defensive, and spiritual reactions.

1. *Physical Reactions.* It is common knowledge that anxiety can lead to ulcers, headaches, skin rashes, back pain, and a variety of other physical problems. During times of anxiety, almost everyone has experienced stomach discomfort ("butterflies"), shortness of breath, an inability to sleep, increased fatigue, loss of appetite,

and a frequent desire to urinate. Less conscious are changes in blood pressure, increased muscle tension, a slowing of digestion, and chemical changes in the blood. If these are temporary they cause little, if any, harm. Instead, they prepare the body to deal with stress and become physiological messengers signaling that the body is under stress even when this is not yet recognized consciously. When the physical reactions persist over time, however, the body begins to break under the pressure. This is the origin of psychosomatic (psychologically caused) illnesses.

Research on the effects of stress shows how busy people often wear out their own bodies by the overproduction of adrenaline. These are people who are driven to accomplish a lot but feel pressured by limited time. Suffering from what has been termed the "stress disease," these people push themselves to the point of collapse, and then wonder why their busy and anxious lifestyles lead them to feel worn-out, unable to sleep, and prone to sickness.[25]

2. *Psychological Reactions*. Everyone who has taken an examination or gone for a job interview knows how anxiety can influence psychological functioning. Anxiety can reduce productivity (so we don't get much done even when we work harder), harm relationships (so we have difficulties getting along with others), cause irritability and impatience, stifle creativity and originality, dull the personality, and interfere with the ability to think or remember. The student whose "mind goes blank" during a test and the actor who forgets his lines on stage both show evidence of anxiety-produced memory failure. In extreme cases, anxiety so immobilizes an individual that he or she is unable to function independently as an adult.

3. *Defensive Reactions*. When anxiety builds, most people unconsciously rely on behavior and thinking that dull the pain of anxiety and make coping easier. Often seen in counseling, these defensive reactions include ignoring the feelings of anxiety, pretending that the anxiety-producing situation does not exist, convincing oneself that there is "nothing to worry about," rationally explaining away the symptoms, blaming someone else for the problems, developing physical illnesses that distract from the anxiety, or slipping back into childish ways of thinking and responding. These are mind games that we use to deny the problem so that we do not have to face the anxiety-producing situation squarely and deal with it. Sometimes, people escape through alcohol, drugs, hyperactivity, television, or withdrawal into various kinds of mental illness. All of these are ways of trying to cope.

4. *Spiritual Reactions*. In times of anxiety many people turn to God and seek divine help. This is true even in people who had no prior interest in anything spiritual or religious. It is widely known, for example, that intense anxiety and fear often lead military people in combat zones to pray and rely on God for help and protection. Sadly, this aroused spiritual interest often fades when the war is over.

But anxiety also can drive people away from God at a time when they need him most. Fraught with worry and distracted by pressures, even religious people find there is little time for prayer, decreased desire or ability to concentrate on Bible reading, reduced interest in church worship services, bitterness about heaven's seeming silence in the face of crisis, and anger because God seems to let bad things happen to good people. The Christian counselor may be welcomed as a spiritual guide or rejected because he or she represents a God who has permitted the stresses and left the impression that he doesn't care.

In all of this discussion, it is important to remember that there are large individual differences in the effects of anxiety. Even mild amounts of anxiety can immobilize some people, but others seem to thrive even under intense pressure.

Counseling and Anxiety

Anxiety can be psychologically contagious. When anxious people begin to describe their anxieties, others can become anxious as well, including the counselor who wants to help. In counseling anxious people, therefore, the counselor must first be alert to his or her own feelings.

1. *Recognizing Your Own Anxieties.* As a counselor, when you feel anxiety in the presence of an anxious counselee, ask yourself questions like these: What about this situation is making me anxious? Is the counselee anxious about something that makes me anxious too? What does my anxiety tell me about the counselee—and about myself? By considering one's own anxiety, it sometimes is possible to gain insight into the counselee's anxiety. These questions also enable the counselor to keep from confusing his or her own anxieties with those of the counselee.

2. *Calming the Tension.* Counseling is not likely to be effective if the counselee is too tense to concentrate. In contrast, if the counselor is calm, sensitive, caring, and reassuring, this can reduce anxiety considerably. Dr. Robert Allen is a psychologist who works with cardiac patients before they leave the hospital following a heart attack. He teaches people about the disease, explains how they can lessen the risk for further heart problems, and gives suggestions about managing stress and anger. Anxiety is a major concern for many of these patients and their families, but they relax and find encouragement in the presence of someone who reflects calmness and gives hope.[26]

Although some Christians criticize this approach, many counselors use relaxation methods to help their anxious counselees learn how to be calmer.[27] Encourage the counselee to sit quietly, breathe deeply, and try to relax the muscles. Sometimes, it helps to tighten different groups of muscles, such as the fist or the shoulders, and then let the muscles relax as freely as possible. Some counselees find it helpful to close their eyes and imagine that they are relaxing on a beach or sitting in some other nonthreatening situation. Away from the counseling session, many counselees will find that music can have a calming effect, and so can reading, reciting Scripture, or simply getting away for a time to a quiet place indoors or outside. Before you see your counselee, try to have a waiting room that is free of clutter or music that is loud or fast paced. Reduce clutter or other distracting influences in your office so the counseling environment is more calming.

Of course, none of this removes the underlying causes of anxiety, but by showing calmness and helping people feel more relaxed and in control, you temporarily direct attention away from the symptoms. With a calm counseling environment and a counselor who is relaxed, counselees are better able to focus attention on the sources of their anxiety.

3. *Showing Love.* Love has been called the greatest therapeutic force of all,[28] but nowhere is this truer than in the reduction of fear and anxiety. The Bible states "perfect love expels all fear."[29] The Christian counselor can help to drive out fear and anxiety when he or she shows love mixed with patient understanding. Counselees can be enabled to see the love and help that come from Christ.[30] Show them, as well, that allowing others to love them and reaching out to love others can both contribute to reduced anxiety.[31]

4. *Identifying the Anxiety's Sources.* Anxiety and fear are God-created emotions. They warn of danger or internal conflict, and they rarely disappear solely in response to the counselor's reassurances or expressions of Christian love. The sensitive helper does not tell the counselee to "cheer up" or "stop being anxious." Most of us get no help from the well-meaning but naive Christian who proclaims that worry is a sin that can be stopped at will. Instead, the effective counselor seeks to assist the counselee in the difficult task of uncovering the sources of anxiety. Where is it coming from? What purpose is it serving? What is causing it to persist? Answers to questions like these can be found in several ways.

(a) Counselor Anxiety. Since anxiety tends to be contagious, be aware of your own feelings. If you begin to sense anxiety in yourself, silently ask what is being discussed at the time. The anxiety in you may be a clue to anxiety that the counselee is experiencing and communicating.

(b) Observation. In counseling sessions, when does the counselee show evidence of anxiety, including shifting position, shortness of breath, perspiration, or change in voice pitch and speed? What topics are being discussed when these evidences appear?

(c) Reflection. Can the counselee suggest circumstances that have raised or currently raise anxiety? It might be helpful to ask, "When are you most anxious?" "When are you not anxious?" "When was the last time you felt really anxious?" "What was happening in your life at that time?" Never underestimate the counselee's insights into the reasons for his or her own anxiety.

(d) Contemplation. Remind yourself of the causes of anxiety listed a few pages back. Ask yourself if any of these might be creating the counselee's anxiety. Raise some of these issues and watch for signs of anxiety as the counselee responds to your questions. Tell the counselee about your hunches and ask for the person's reaction. For example, you might comment that the person looked uncomfortable when he or she was talking about school. Then ask, "I wonder if something there may have happened that still arouses anxiety in you today. What do you think?"

In all of this, remember the need for patience and understanding. By its very nature, anxiety often arises in response to threats that are vague and difficult to identify. By pushing the counselee to "snap out of it" or to "hurry and tell me what is wrong," we increase the anxiety, create more confusion, and risk losing or alienating the anxious person.

5. *Making Interventions.* Anxiety differs from person to person—each has a unique set of symptoms, so there will need to be different forms of treatment. Specialists in the treatment of anxiety have developed hundreds of techniques.[32] There are different approaches to dealing with occasional anxiety, severe and debilitating anxiety, panic attacks, phobias, or post-traumatic stress. Despite these differences there are some interventions that can be adapted for all individuals.

(a) Cognitive-Behavioral Interventions. A massive body of evidence demonstrates the effectiveness of cognitive-behavioral approaches, where the focus is on helping people change the way they think and/or change their behavior. For example, one approach exposes people (beginning in small amounts) to the situations that make them anxious. This is followed with relaxation, which they have learned to do, homework assignments so they can practice at home, and teaching them how to monitor their own behaviors. A number of controlled studies have proven the value of this approach for various anxiety conditions, including generalized anxiety, phobias, medical conditions associated with high anxiety, and performance anxiety.[33]

It is not surprising that people with deep anxieties often resist cognitive-behavioral treatment. For them it is easier to talk endlessly about their anxieties, take medications, pray, and to wait for a miracle. According to one experienced counselor, many anxious people have learned to value certainty, comfort, and worry more than they value a release from their anxieties.[34] Accompanying the goal of certainty is a determination to have physical and emotional *comfort*. These people strive to avoid anything that would create tension. They arrange their lives in ways that keep their minds off distressing thoughts, even if these life changes severely limit the person's activities or relationships. In addition, *worrying* becomes a way of life. Most don't realize that instead of protecting them from anxiety, worry creates more anxiety by stimulating the brain and adrenal glands to secrete tension-producing, heart-racing hormones into the blood stream. The counselor's goal, then, is to encourage people to risk facing their anxiety and to move away from the concern for certainty, comfort, and worry that can dominate and restrict their lives. This kind of change is very uncomfortable, and many people rush back to their old ways. Those who improve are often the people who can find the courage to face their anxieties and move forward to deal with the sources.

The various cognitive-behavioral therapies are based on the assumption that anxiety responses usually are learned, so counselors attempt to teach people how to relax in anxiety-producing situations. This can involve visualizing calm situations, reciting Scripture, and breathing more slowly and deeply when the anxiety situations or symptoms appear. Teaching counselees to relax physically and then exposing them slowly to the feared objects helps them learn that they do not need to be anxious because the dangers are less than they feared. At other times, counselees can be encouraged to act (pretend) as if they were in an anxious situation, then the counselor teaches effective ways to cope. Techniques like these are most effective when the anxieties are known to be in response to a specific situation or object that can be identified.

(b) Biological Interventions. When anxiety has a physical cause, such as an illness, genetic malfunction, or nutritional imbalance,[35] there needs to be medical treatment. Often a physician will work in cooperation with a nonmedical counselor.

Should this cooperation include the giving of anxiety-reducing medications?[36] For some psychiatrists and other physicians, use of anti-anxiety medications is the first and sometimes the only method of treatment. While this deals directly with the anxiety-related chemical changes in the brain, medications rarely deal with the root causes of anxiety. In contrast, some pastors and other Christian counselors too quickly criticize the use of medications, even though these substances can calm the counselee and facilitate counseling. Counselors who recognize the value of anti-anxiety medications may have difficulties convincing counselees who have a strong bias against medication. The suggestion that they take a medication increases anxiety in some counselees who only relent if the anxiety becomes unbearable.[37] Try to work with a physician who is cautious about the overuse of tranquilizers but who is willing to prescribe and monitor the use of such medication when anxiety seems high.

Over the years numerous studies have compared the effectiveness of medication in contrast to more psychological and other therapeutic approaches. Both have been shown to reduce anxiety, but is one better than the other? Much depends on the person and the situation. In one published report the author evaluated a variety of articles on the treatment of anxiety disorders and compared the effectiveness of psychosocial treatments, pharmacotherapy, and psychosurgery. The research concluded that "while some medications look clearly beneficial or potentially effective in the treatment of anxiety disorders . . . a combination of proven pharmacotherapies and psychotherapies may be the most clinically prudent approach to the treatment of anxiety disorders."[38] This conclusion appears frequently in the scientific articles. Medication can be helpful, but often it is not better, and sometimes it is not as effective as counseling alone. Cognitive-behavioral counseling methods, often used in conjunction with medication, frequently produce the best results.[39]

(c) Environmental Intervention. Sometimes, the best and most direct way to deal with anxiety is to change one's lifestyle, relationships, place of residence, or career direction. These changes may sound easy when we read about them in a book, but they can be overwhelming and hard to bring about without help. On one's own, it is extremely difficult and often impossible to break off anxiety-producing relationships, for example, to move to a new residence, or to change careers. Changes like these need the encouragement and guidance that come from others, including caring counselors.

Writing about his experiences in counseling anxious young people, one insightful counselor concluded that "living in their parallel universe of endless exposure to disturbing information and constant change, teens need an ongoing relationship with a grown-up. Therapy is a chance to create exactly those experiences and support those values that are missing in the rudderless, anxiety-driven world that surrounds them."[40] In this environment, these young people need to experience the rules, rituals, reasons, and regard that many never got at home.

Establishing *rules* in counseling can create some of the security that is needed in times of anxiety. Holding people accountable for keeping commitments, setting priorities, or meeting obligations can bring structure and some evidence of stability. *Rituals* can be simple, like eating meals together, going to church on a regular basis, or doing things together once or twice a week. In times of anxiety, rituals tend to disappear along with the security these bring. The best rituals are those that the counselee can suggest and then seek to follow. *Reason* concerns giving advice or guidelines to help people make wise decisions or keep out of trouble. Counselors are taught to avoid giving advice, but on occasion, especially in times of anxiety, giving advice can be very helpful, even if the advice is not heeded. *Regard* is similar to showing respect and helping people feel that they are valuable. In a poor neighborhood, a twenty-one-year-old told a Christian social worker, "You are the only person in the whole world who really believes in me." That social worker was showing an attitude of respect and regard that the young man clung to through difficult times of anxiety and personal turmoil in his life.

6. *Encouraging Action.* The purpose of counseling is not to eliminate all anxiety. Instead, the goal is to assist counselees in discovering the sources of their anxiety. Then they must learn how to cope and be encouraged to take action. Help coun-

selees see that they can gain more by facing and trying to overcome the anxiety—even though this can be risky and uncomfortable—than by persisting in a state of inner tension that may be familiar but painful. Try to avoid intellectual talk that may sound reassuring but does nothing to help people plan and take direct specific action in dealing with anxiety.

Here the counselor serves as a guide and a coach, helping people set goals and decide on some steps to reach their objectives. There may be skills they need to develop, information they need to get, relationships they need to reestablish if there is to be movement forward. Even when your counselees know what to do, there still is resistance because of apprehensions and fears about taking risks. It is then that the counselor becomes an encourager who walks alongside the person as he or she takes the first steps. At some time, you may want to suggest that it is an act of courage to step out and take action even when one is fearful and anxious.[41]

7. *Giving Support.* It is easy to be impatient in the presence of an anxious counselee, but instead, the helper must be supportive and patient as he or she watches progress that may be very slow and interrupted by setbacks. Sometimes, there seems to be nothing counselees can do to take action against the source of their anxieties. For example, people living in war zones or other potentially dangerous circumstances feel like helpless victims. At such times they need to feel the presence and caring support of an understanding counselor. And they need to be helped to realize that whatever the outward circumstances each of us can still control our attitudes and personal values.

8. *Encouraging a Christian Response.* The Bible gives unusually specific and clear directions for overcoming anxiety. In Philippians 4:6 we are instructed to stop being anxious and worried about anything. As we have seen, it is practically impossible to stop worrying by an act of the will. Such deliberate effort directs our attention to the problem and can increase anxiety instead of decreasing it. A better approach is to focus on activities and thoughts that reduce anxiety indirectly. The Bible shows how this can be done, and in so doing it gives a formula to be shared with counselees:

(a) Rejoice. This is a command in Philippians 4:4. It means to be "full of joy in the Lord." When the world is dark and dreary, the Christian still can be filled with joy. This is because Jesus promised he would never leave us, that he would give us peace, that he would come again to take believers to a place prepared for them in heaven, and that in the meantime he would send his Holy Spirit (whom Jesus called the Counselor) to stay with us and to remind us of truths we need to remember. With this knowledge we can believe in God and not let our minds be troubled or fearful.[42]

(b) Be Considerate. The Greek word means to let everybody see your kind, gentle, caring, gracious attitude.[43] These qualities do not come naturally. They come with the help of God as we work to control our tendencies to condemn others or to demand our rights. A negative condemning outlook on life builds anxiety; a gracious forbearing attitude reduces it.

(c) Pray. Philippians 4:6 gives instructions about prayer in times of anxiety. This kind of prayer is to be about everything (even small details), should include definite and precise petitions—telling God what we need, and should involve thanksgiving for all that God has done. "If you do this," the Bible promises, "you will experience God's peace, which is far more wonderful than the human mind can understand." Clearly prayer is a major antidote to anxiety.

(d) Think on the Positive. Anxiety often increases when we continually think about human weaknesses, evil influences in the world, and things that might go wrong. Philippians 4:8 instructs us, instead, to let our minds dwell on positive ideas including that which is true, honorable, right, pure, lovely, admirable, excellent, and worthy of praise. This is not suggesting that we deny problems or ignore dangers. In contrast, the Scriptures are giving evidence for the power and calming influence of positive, biblically based thinking.

(e) Take Action. In Philippians 4:9, the apostle Paul sets himself up as a model for action. "Keep putting into practice all you learned from me and heard from me and saw me doing, and the God of peace will be with you." The Christian's task is to *do* what the Bible teaches and not simply to sit listening.[44] Anxiety reduction involves obedience and godly behavior even in the midst of anxiety.

Preventing Anxiety

Philippians 4 gives more than guidelines for counseling. It also is a formula for preventing anxiety. When people can be helped to rejoice, be considerate, pray, think, and act in accordance with Scriptural teachings, there is progress toward anxiety prevention and control. Within recent years there has been increased research into the ways in which anxiety can be prevented,[45] but at the core, prevention begins with God.

1. *Trust in God.* The person who learns to walk in daily contact with God comes to agree with the hymn writer who wrote, "I know not what the future holds, but I know who holds the future." This conviction that God is in control can bring great security even when others are inclined to be anxious.

Sometimes, such trust leads to a blind denial of reality, a refusal to accept responsibilities, or a rigidity of thinking that ultimately prevents the person from adapting to changing circumstances. In contrast, the Bible encourages realistic confrontation with problems and flexible decision making. This lets people grow and adapt to change or danger, even as they maintain an underlying confidence in the sovereignty and wisdom of an all-powerful God.

2. *Learn to Cope.* Coping with the causes of anxiety, when and before they arise, can prevent the development of anxiety. Such coping includes the following, each of which can become part of a person's lifestyle:

- Admitting fears, insecurities, conflicts, and anxieties when they arise.
- Talking these over with someone else, like a friend, prayer partner, spouse, or accountability partner, on a regular basis if necessary.
- Building self-esteem and self-confidence, which involves belief in one's abilities to meet the challenges and dangers of life.
- Acknowledging that separations hurt, attempting to maintain contact with separated friends, restoring broken relationships and building new relationships with others, all of which give us a support network.
- Being involved in work and other meaningful activities that give fulfillment, thereby expending nervous energy and distracting one from dwelling on anxiety-producing situations.
- Learning effective communication skills.
- Learning to relax, and doing it.
- Developing good time-management principles.

- Evaluating and periodically restructuring one's priorities and life goals.
- Committing to competent leaders who are able to instill confidence and hope.
- Getting into the habit of seeking help from God and from others who can help in times of need.

3. *Keep Things in Perspective.* In threatening, challenging, or potentially danger-ous situations, it is easy to panic, but it is better to ponder the circumstances and try to determine the best ways to cope. This process of "cognitive appraisal" helps to explain why two people may look at the same situation but respond in very different ways. How one evaluates a situation depends largely on one's perspec-tive or point of view.

Past experiences and personality characteristics influence these perceptions. Some people see the bad in everything; others are more optimistic and inclined to look on the bright side of life. To help prevent anxiety, we can encourage people (especially those who tend to be negative) to keep a realistic perspective that does not always make immediate assumptions that the worst is likely to happen.

4. *Reach Out to Others.* Caring about others and reaching out to help may be among the most effective ways to deal with the cares and anxieties in one's own life. People-helping and bearing one another's burdens can be effective ways to prevent anxiety.

Conclusions About Anxiety

Some counselors believe that anxiety is a basic part of all psychological problems; it goes along with most of the issues discussed in the following chapters. Anxiety warns people of danger and motivates them to take action. When it creates panic or immobilizes individuals, the anxiety is harmful. When it challenges us to deal more effectively with the challenges of life, it can be helpful.

Jesus put all of this in perspective when he spoke about worry in the Sermon on the Mount. God knows about our needs and anxieties, Jesus said. If we give him first priority in our lives, we can rest assured that our needs will be sup-plied,[46] and there will be no need to worry. This is a message that makes Christian counseling unique.

KEY POINTS FOR BUSY COUNSELORS

➤ Anxiety is an inner feeling of apprehension, uneasiness, worry, and/or dread that is accompanied by a heightened physical arousal. In times of anxiety, the body appears to be on alert, ready to flee or fight.

➤ The Bible uses the term *anxiety* in two ways. Both are common. Anxiety that is realistic concern is neither condemned nor forbidden. Anxiety that is fret and worry is more distressing and, at its core, reflects a lack of confidence in

God and a tendency to take burdens on to ourselves. The second type of anxiety is what counselors most often deal with in their counseling.

➤ The causes of anxiety include:
- Threat from (a) unstable environments, (b) low self-esteem, (c) separation from others, (d) changing moral values and/or (e) unconscious influences.
- Conflict.
- Fear.
- Unmet needs.
- Physiological reactions.
- Individual differences in terms of a person's learning, past experiences, social environment, physiology, and theological beliefs.

➤ Anxiety is not always bad. It can alert us to dangerous or threatening situations and can protect us from danger.

➤ When anxiety is intense, prolonged, or uncontrollable, it can lead to
- Physiological reactions.
- Psychological reactions.
- Defensive reactions.
- Spiritual reactions.

➤ Effective counseling for anxiety includes:
- Recognizing and dealing with the counselor's own anxieties.
- Calming the anxious person's tension.
- Showing a spirit of love.
- Identifying the anxiety's sources.
- Making anxiety-reducing interventions. The most effective are:
  ◆ Cognitive-behavioral interventions.
  ◆ Biological interventions including medications.
  ◆ Making environmental changes.
- Encouraging action.
- Giving support.
- Encouraging a Christian response (based on Philippians 4).

➤ To prevent anxiety, help people:
- Trust in God.
- Learn to cope with anxiety.
- Keep things in perspective.
- Reach out to others.

➤ Anxiety is so basic and so common that it is a part of all the problems that are discussed in subsequent chapters of this book.

10

Anger

Pastor Frank recently celebrated his thirtieth year in ministry.[1] *Now fifty-six, he has served in several churches, where he has been respected by parishioners and denominational leaders alike.*

Few of them know about Frank's anger. Most of the time he keeps it under control, although sometimes he gets red-faced in his sermons and pounds the pulpit with a vehemence that looks more like an angry outburst than a preacher's indignation over sin. In church business meetings, Frank often feels on the verge of exploding with tension, but to this point he has hidden his real feelings behind a pious facade and a sense of humor that sometimes barely conceals his cynicism and sarcasm.

His anger isn't hidden at home, however. Once inside the parsonage, Frank often shouts, pounds the furniture, complains about the weaknesses of the church leaders, and sometimes swears. He has never harmed his wife or children physically, but they all have been stung by his verbal abuse, and their father's outbursts have convinced at least two of his children that they want nothing to do with his church or his religion.

Frank is bothered by his anger. He knows it isn't right, and after his outbursts he often apologizes to his family and asks God for forgiveness. Despite his years in ministry, Frank has begun to wonder if he is really a hypocrite, acclaimed by others but unable to control himself.

After a lot of deliberation and with considerable hesitation, he decided to talk about his anger with an older pastor. As he shared his concerns, Frank was surprised how angry and frustrated he sounded. He had never talked about his feelings with anyone, but as the angry words poured from his mouth, he began to see how he had passively accepted unfair criticism and harbored resentment because of the unreasonable demands of others. Sometimes, even innocent and well-intended requests had triggered hostile feelings that were taken out on his innocent family.

Throughout his ministry, Frank had spent many hours helping others. Now, at last, somebody was helping him. He was learning to cope with his frustrations and to handle his anger more effectively. The counselor did not condemn Frank for his anger—he already had condemned himself repeatedly over the years. Instead, he was getting help from a caring pastor-counselor who knew first-hand about the pressures of the pastorate.

How different is the tragic story of a quiet seventeen-year-old high school student who never complained about his parents, never got into trouble at school, and never showed anger—until the night of the murder! While most of the neighbors slept, he returned to the tree-lined suburban street where he lived, quietly entered the house, and brutally murdered his parents and brother in what police called an angry and "frenzied killing of bullets and multiple stab wounds."

Why would a likable small-town boy suddenly explode in an angry outburst of violence? His teachers couldn't answer and neither could the police, the neighbors, or anybody else who had known the teenager before news of his aggressive actions spread over the pages of newspapers nationwide.

Anger is an emotional state, experienced by everyone, but difficult to define. It occurs in varying forms and degrees of intensity—from mild annoyance or feelings of aggravation to violent rage. There is debate about whether it begins in infancy,[2] but it appears early in life and continues to the later years. It may be hidden and held inside or expressed openly and freely. It can be of short duration, coming and going quickly, or it may persist for decades in the form of bitterness, resentment, or hatred. Anger often is destructive, especially when it persists in the form of aggression or revenge, but it also can be constructive if it motivates us to correct injustice or to think creatively.[3] Anger is aroused when we feel threatened, demeaned, or blocked in our progress toward some desired goal. Usually, we know when we are angry, and others know as well. But sometimes anger is hidden behind a calm and smiling facade, or buried in the recesses of our brains. Anger, openly displayed, deliberately hidden from others, or unconsciously expressed, is at the root of many psychological, interpersonal, physical, and spiritual problems.

Anger is a leading cause of depression, accidents, road rage, sickness, inefficiency, anxiety, grief, marital conflict, and other interpersonal tension. It can lead to wars, terrorist attacks, church splits, and disruption in the workplace. Anger can interfere with our ministries, as it did with Pastor Frank, but it also can hinder our counseling, especially when counselees trigger anger in their counselors. An understanding of anger, including the counselor's own anger, is basic for effective Christian counseling.

The Bible and Anger

Divine wrath and human anger are mentioned repeatedly in the Bible. In the Old Testament alone, there are almost six hundred references to wrath or anger, and this theme continues in the New Testament. In the Bible, God's anger, fury, and wrath are mentioned more frequently than his love and tenderness. Since anger is an attribute of God and a part of his nature, we cannot conclude that anger, in itself, is bad. God is completely good and holy, so we must conclude that divine wrath also is good. According to James I. Packer, "God's wrath in the Bible is never the capricious, self-indulgent, irritable, morally ignoble thing that human anger so often is. It is, instead, a right and necessary reaction to objective moral evil."[4] Divine anger is intense, controlled, and consistent with God's love and mercy. It is anger directed both at sin and at people who are sinners. Repeatedly, God was angry with the unfaithful Israelites. Jesus, whose wrath clearly is seen in Mark 3, was angry at the "hard hearts" of the religious leaders in his day.[5]

Because all human beings are sinners,[6] we deserve to receive the full outpouring of God's wrath against sin. But God, who is just, also is merciful and forgiving. For this reason, "many a time he held back his anger and did not unleash his fury!"[7] He gives human beings the time and opportunity to repent,[8] although at times "God shows his anger against all sinful, wicked people who push the truth away from themselves.[9] This is not popular theology in the twenty-first century, but according to the Bible at some time in the future God's full anger against sin will be unleashed.[10]

An understanding of the divine wrath of God is important if we are to comprehend the biblical teachings about human anger and how all of this applies to our counseling. The Bible never criticizes the anger of God, but it warns against human anger repeatedly.[11] This is not inconsistency. Anger against injustice is right and good in both God and human beings. Because God is wise, sovereign, powerful, perfect, and all-knowing, he never misinterprets a situation, never feels threatened, never loses control, and always shows anger because of sin and injustice. In contrast, we humans misinterpret circumstances, make mistakes in judgment, react quickly when we feel threatened or hurt, and sometimes respond with vengeance and vindictiveness. As a result, human anger can be harmful and dangerous. The Bible cautions us about this because human anger can provide an opportunity for Satan to get a foothold that creates further problems.[12] "Don't sin by letting anger gain control over you," we read in Ephesians 4:26. "Don't let the sun go down while you are still angry."

From these and similar Bible passages, we can reach several helpful conclusions about human anger.

1. *Human Anger Is Normal and Not Necessarily Sinful.* Human beings were created in the image of God and given emotions, including anger. This anger is a necessary and useful emotion. It was seen in Jesus and is not sinful in and of itself.

2. *Human Anger May Result from Faulty Perception.* God is perfect, omniscient, and always completely accurate in the way he sees things. Because of this, divine anger always is a reaction of righteous indignation against some form of unrighteousness. Human beings, in contrast, are imperfect, and we see each situation from our own perspectives. We are not always able to judge accurately between real injustice (as perceived accurately by an omniscient God) and apparent injustice. As a result, we sometimes become angry over issues that we think are wrong but which, in fact, would not be considered wrong if we had all the facts. Sinful self-interest often causes our perceptions to be distorted. Because we feel vulnerable, threatened, or inclined to be critical, we can misinterpret the actions of others and jump to angry, perhaps unjustified conclusions.

3. *Human Anger Often Leads to Sin.* Like other emotions, anger can be constructive (serving a useful purpose) or destructive. It can be Christ-honoring, or it can be sinful.

Because it so easily leads to sinful, harmful behavior, anger often is condemned in the Bible, and we are urged to turn away from anger and rage.[13] For this reason we should stop our anger, rage, and envy because these lead to harm. Although it isn't wrong in itself, anger clearly can get out of control and cause a variety of problems, including vengeance, verbal and physical abuse, and passive aggression. Each of these appears frequently in our counselees and at times in counselors themselves.

(a) Vengeance. Bitterness, hatred, revenge, and an attitude of judgment all result from anger, and all are condemned in Scripture.[14] Vengeance is God's responsibility, not ours.[15] There can be no scriptural justification for human revenge or hostile attempts to get even.[16]

(b) Abuse. Christians are responsible for controlling their words, but this is especially difficult when we are angry. In the Old Testament the person who ventilates verbally and loses his or her temper is described as a fool.[17] In the Letter of James, the dangers of verbal abuse are clearly outlined, and in the same sentence readers are urged to be "quick to listen, slow to speak, and slow to get angry."[18]

Verbal abuse can be a powerful form of mistreatment arising from anger. Often it occurs behind closed doors, where it is hidden from outsiders, including neighbors, teachers, or fellow church members. Sexual abuse also remains hidden, often because the victims are too afraid or embarrassed to reveal it. Evidences of physical abuse are more apparent to others. All three forms of abuse—verbal, sexual, and physical—arise because of the abuser's uncontrolled anger.[19] Angry people do foolish things.[20] We are warned to stay away from them lest we pick up their anger and become like them.[21] We see this in terrorists and militants but also in families or groups (including church groups or groups of associates at work), where the anger of one or two people gets passed to others, who become angry and sometimes abusive as well.

(c) Subtle Aggression. Anger and hostility can be expressed in subtle ways. Previously, we have mentioned the examples of people who express their anger in passive ways, including noncooperation. Gossip also can be an expression of anger, even when a gossiper claims to have admirable reasons for sharing the information, including the sharing of prayer requests. Often the details of gossip are not completely true. The gossiper's words can be a sinful form of vengeance that ignores the Bible's words condemning and warning against gossip.[22]

(d) Withdrawal. It is not easy to express anger in a way that lets others know that we feel hurt. As a result, some people refuse to admit their anger, even to their counselors. These people gloss over their feelings of anger in a well-intentioned attempt to maintain peace or to protect themselves from admitting their own anger. Sometimes, the motivation for this silence may be commendable, but the effects can be harmful. The other person never realizes that he or she has made someone angry or never knows why a subtle tension has been developing. As a result, there is no opportunity to resolve the issue or to bring change for the better. In turn, the person who represses anger sometimes harbors a bitterness that can lead to depression.[23] The Bible condemns this hiding of anger or hostility and even calls it a form of lying.[24]

4. *Human Anger Can Be Used for Good.* With all of this discussion of the harmful effects of anger, it is important to recognize the Bible's teaching that there is value in expressing anger if this will lead another person to repent and change for the better.[25] This is a proper and healthy use of anger. Since we are instructed to express anger when it is for the good of another, then it is wrong to always deny, ignore, distort, or refuse to share our feelings.

5. *Human Anger Can Be Controlled.* It is unlikely that God would have instructed us to control anger if human anger control is impossible. Several Bible passages imply that control *is* possible and indicate how this can be done.

(a) Anger Must Be Acknowledged. Before we can "put away" our bitterness, wrath, anger, and malice, we must admit, at least to ourselves, that these feelings exist.

(b) Outbursts Must Be Restrained. The man or woman of God thinks before acting. There must be a quiet weighing of issues instead of a gushing forth of sinful verbal explosions.[26]

Sometimes, it is helpful to share one's burden of anger with a friend; it is always good to pour out one's feelings to God. This verbal activity often leads to new perspectives that reduce or dissipate anger before it is expressed inappropriately and allowed to harm others or damage relationships.

This is seen clearly in Psalm 73. The writer was angry and "embittered" because the wicked seemed to be so happy and successful while the godly were having trouble. Instead of exploding in anger, the psalmist came into the presence of God and began to get a fresh new perspective on the apparent injustice in the world. His anger, as a result, subsided and was replaced by praise.

(c) Confession and Forgiveness Must Be Given Freely. This involves confession to God, confession to others, and a willingness both to forgive and to receive forgiveness—repeatedly if necessary.[27]

(d) Ruminating and Revenge Must be Resisted. It would seem that when Jesus was persecuted he had every right to get angry and to respond with revenge. Nevertheless, "he did not retaliate when he was insulted. When he suffered, he did not threaten to get even. He left his case in the hands of God, who always judges fairly."[28] Angry people often enjoy ruminating on their difficulties, thinking vengeful thoughts and pondering ways to get even. Ultimately, this tendency harms the angry person. It is a tendency that must be resisted and replaced with an attitude of entrusting oneself and one's circumstances to God.

(e) Love Must Be Cultivated. Everybody knows that we can get angry with the people we love, but long-term love and anger do not mix very well. When we are motivated by love, often we can overlook some of the causes of anger or deal with them in an honest, controlled, and respectful manner.[29]

The Bible says more about anger than about most of the topics discussed in this book. In summary, the Scriptures present anger as a universal emotion that is good when expressed against real injustice, harmful when expressed for self-centered motives, and clearly an emotion that needs to be controlled. "It is better to have self-control than to conquer a city," wrote Solomon.[30] This self-control is difficult on our own, but others can help, and the greatest force for self-control is the Holy Spirit.[31]

The Causes of Anger

Several years ago, a group of forty-one counselors at a large university were asked to describe their own feelings of anger. One counselor replied, "We get angry when counselees are resistant to counseling despite our best efforts or when people impose upon us by making demands on our time and calling our homes when that isn't necessary." Most felt anger when they were attacked verbally or physically, and some said they got angry when people tried to manipulate them by demanding special attention or trying to make them feel guilty.[32]

For many people, anger seems to come more often because of the actions of others than because of circumstances or events. The Bible gives several illustrations of this. Jonah became upset and very angry when God spared the people of Nineveh after they had repented, largely as a result of Jonah's reluctant preaching.[33] King Herod was furious and responded with violence when the wise men tricked him and failed to report where Jesus had been born.[34] The ten disciples were indignant when they learned that James and John had asked for special prominence in the kingdom.[35] Jesus, himself, got angry at the self-righteous attitudes of the religious leaders and at the disciples' impatience with the little children who wanted to see the Lord.[36]

Counselors have different viewpoints about the origins of anger. Some take an *instinct approach* and assume, with Freud, that anger is an innate biological drive that can be aroused by a hostile environment, the actions of other people, or the restrictions that come from living in a society. The instinct view assumes that anger boils within and is likely to explode if it isn't released.[37] The *frustration-aggression approach* assumes that anger and aggression always come in response to frustration. Since frustration is a universal experience, all of us get angry at times. Building on this is the *social learning approach*, which sees anger as an emotional state of arousal that comes because of frustration but can be expressed in a variety of ways, depending on the person's perceptions and past learning.

Perhaps there are as many causes of anger as there are situations and human actions that make people angry. Nevertheless, most of these causes can be summarized under a few headings.

1. *Biology.* The story is told about a boy who got along with everyone, except during a temper tantrum. Periodically, without apparent provocation, he would fly into a furious rage that looked like a seizure. After it was over, the boy would cry and apologize, saying he couldn't stop himself.

The cause for these outbursts was found to be in bananas. Whenever the boy ate a banana, his brain chemistry reacted in a way that produced rage and aggression. When bananas were eliminated from his diet, the angry outbursts stopped.[38]

This is an unusual case; anger rarely can be understood and treated so simply. There is evidence, however, that allergies, brain disease, disorders of the body's chemistry, and perhaps genetic abnormalities can cause anger or at least make some people more prone than others to become angry.

Whatever the cause, anger (like every other emotion) has a biological component. This includes the adrenaline reaction that we discussed earlier—rapid heartbeat, rising blood pressure, pupil dilation, and aroused muscle tension that prepare the body to flee or fight. There really is a biological basis for the popular idea that when people get angry their blood pressure goes up and they get red in the face.

2. *Injustice.* We have seen that injustice is a reason for divine wrath, and this can arouse anger in people as well. Consider, for example, the actions of Jesus when he drove the money changers out of the temple. The Bible does not state that he was angry, but his overturning their tables and his strong criticisms of their disrespect for God's house all imply that he was extremely angry. When the pompous religious leaders criticized him for healing a man on the Sabbath, Jesus was angry and deeply disturbed about their hard hearts.[39] Anger in response to injustice is one of the most valid reasons for anger (perhaps the only valid reason), but it probably is one of the least to be mentioned.

This kind of anger is not rare. We see it in the child who defends his brother against unfair treatment or in children who defend their mother against abuse. We see it as well in the dedicated people around the world who work without much encouragement to fight the abuse of children, women, and others who are being exploited sexually or used as "cheap labor."

3. *Frustration.* A frustration is an obstacle (an event, person, or physical barrier) that hinders our progress toward some goal. Frustration may come (a) because of what someone else has done or failed to do, (b) because of unwanted events or circumstances, or (c) because of our own failures or inabilities to reach some desired goal. The extent to which we feel frustrated will depend on the importance of the goal, the size of the obstacles, and the duration of the frustration. It is mildly frustrating to be late in arriving at work because you encountered a string of red stoplights. It may be more frustrating to be only partway through reading a long chapter on anger in a fat book on counseling that is required reading for some course. It is much more frustrating and serious if you fail an important exam, are denied a promotion, or have an illness that does not get better. It does not follow that anger increases automatically as one's frustration level goes up, but the potential for anger probably increases as the severity, frequency, and length of the frustrations increase.

4. *Threat and Hurt.* Anger is often aroused when a person perceives that he or she is rejected, "put down," ignored, humiliated, unjustly criticized, or otherwise threatened. Sometimes, we feel that others demand too much from us, have unrealistic expectations or treat us unfairly. Threats like these challenge our self-esteem, remind us of our imperfections or limitations, and make us feel so vulnerable that anger and aggression become ways to fight back.[40] Sometimes, the anger hides the fact that we are hurt or threatened, and lets us feel better at someone else's expense. Because hurt and anger so often occur together, the first leading to the second, it is easy to focus on the anger and fail to see the threat or hurt that came first.

5. *Learning.* People from different cultures get angry over different issues and express their anger in different ways. The same is true of people in differing ethnic or socioeconomic groups and different neighborhoods. There also can be differences in anger expression between males and females. Most of this comes from learning. For example, boys often learn that aggression is masculine, while girls are socialized to be less overt in their anger expressions.[41] By watching or listening to others (including what is seen in the home or in movies or televisions), we learn how to act when we are angry and we learn what to be angry about.

6. *Personality and Perception.* Have you ever noticed that the same situation can make one person respond with strong anger, but another person is barely ruffled? In part, these differences can arise from differences in personality, maturity level, and the ways in which a situation is perceived. It is probable that stressful events in the environment are less likely to arouse anger than the ways in which we see and interpret a situation.[42] If we can persuade others to change their interpretations of an event or situation, we often can change their emotions.

Road rage—the anger that some drivers express behind the wheel of a car—illustrates the impact of personality differences and the ways in which a situation is perceived. How do you respond, for example, when another driver "cuts you off" in traffic or races to get the parking space that you were approaching? Some drivers would respond with anger and a determination to get even because they view this as a challenge to their driving skills, as a threat to their masculinity, or as a stealing of their rights to the parking space. Others might be annoyed but conclude "If that's the only way the other driver can boost his or her self-esteem and assert superiority, then that person's got the problem; not me." There are studies to determine whether road rage is a psychiatric disability,[43] but in most cases it seems better to assume that whether or not one gets angry on the road will depend on the drivers' personalities or on how they view the situation.

The Effects of Anger

"I see many clients who have problems with anger," one counselor wrote. "They have such varying concerns and differences that no single treatment fits them all."[44] Table 10–1 summarizes some of the different types of anger that have been identified.

At different times counselors are likely to see each of these. Sometimes, more than one of these anger styles appears in the same person, and each benefits from a different counseling approach.

Anger influences people in at least five basic ways: the angry person can (1) hold back and withdraw from an anger-producing situation; (2) turn his or

Table 10–1

Anger Styles

Anger can appear in various forms, including violence, abuse, passive resistance, and criticisms of the counselor. But there are different anger styles, according to counselor Ronald T. Potter-Efron. Each is a predictable, repeated, unique way of handling anger. Counselors can learn to identify the different anger styles. Each responds to an approach to counseling that fits the style. Counselors can help best by focusing on the styles or combination of styles that each counselee uses most frequently. The most common styles are these:

- *Anger Avoidance* is seen in people who avoid both conflict and anger. They need to learn how to recognize and express their anger in healthy ways.
- *Passive Aggression* involves the expression of anger in subtle ways that include non-cooperation, stalling, and other actions that are sabotaging. These counselees benefit from help in handling disagreements and expressing their anger openly.
- *Distrust-Based Anger* often is paranoid. People project their anger onto others, expect to be hurt, and then justify their own outrage and aggression as self-defense. Here we help people recognize their own anger, evaluate the accuracy of their perceptions of others, and learn to be more trusting.
- *Sudden Anger* is seen in people with a "short fuse," who blow up at others but need help in self-control, including learning to take time-outs before exploding.
- *Shame-Based Anger* appears in people who handle their shame by getting angry at their accusers, or people who are assumed to be accusers. This anger style needs counseling that helps people separate anger from shame and helps counselees deal with their own guilt and shame.
- *Deliberate Anger* is a display of anger intended to be intimidating. The person may look angrier than he or she feels. This won't stop until it is made clear that intimidation and bullying do more harm than good.
- *Habitual Anger (similar to what others have called toxic anger)*[45] involves a critical, hostile worldview and the perception that nothing is right. Counselors can challenge the automatic anger-producing thinking patterns, but it also may be necessary to uncover and deal with its origins.
- *Depressive Anger* looks more like depression rather than anger; the anger is suppressed and reappears in depression. Treat the depression and help people cope with the source of the anger.
- *Moral Anger* is the righteous indignation that appears when people are fighting for a cause. Sometimes, this leads to violence and insensitivity. Help people channel this anger into more useful directions. Teach empathy, which leads to caring and reduces the sense of moral superiority.
- *Resentment and Hatred* are long lasting, often emerging from persisting bitterness that has the person entrapped. Resenters need to learn forgiveness and how to let go.

Adapted from Ronald T. Potter-Efron, "One Size Does Not Fit All: Learning to Recognize the Many Faces of Anger," *Psychotherapy Networker* 28 (May-June 2004): 27–28.

her feelings inward where others don't see them; (3) act out by attacking the source of anger or some substitute; (4) face and deal directly with the causes of the anger; (5) or channel the anger into something positive. These approaches overlap, and each of us may shift from one to another, depending on the individual, on one's perceptions, and on the situation.

1. *Holding Back.* This may be the easiest but least effective way to deal with anger. When we withdraw from a situation, it is easier to ignore our anger and hold back from facing and expressing our frustrations. Withdrawal can take several forms:

- Leaving the room, taking a vacation, dropping out of a church, or otherwise removing oneself physically from the situation that stimulates anger.
- Avoiding the problem by plunging into work or other activities, thinking about other things, or escaping into a world of television, video games, or novels.
- Hiding from the problem by drinking, taking drugs, or other behavior that, in some cases, might be a way to "get back" at the person who makes us angry.

Holding back anger can be healthy for a while. It gives the person time to reevaluate the situation and can prevent angry outbursts and the possible harm and guilt that the outbursts might produce. When anger is ignored, however, it begins to affect us in other ways.

2. *Turning Inward.* Sometimes, people force anger out of awareness and deny, consciously or unconsciously, that it even exists. This can be an unhealthy way to cope with the problem. At best, the relief is only temporary, and in time the pressure builds until it bursts out to create more difficulties.

When anger is kept within and not expressed, there may be calmness and smiling on the outside but boiling rage inside. This internal anger is a powerful force that may express itself in:

- Physical symptoms ranging from a mild headache to ulcers, high blood pressure, or heart attacks.
- Psychological reactions such as anxiety, fear, or feelings of tension and depression.[46]
- Unconscious attempts to harm oneself (seen, for example, in accident proneness or a tendency to make mistakes).
- Thinking characterized by self-pity, thoughts of revenge, or ruminations on the injustices that one is experiencing.
- Spiritual struggles that come because we wallow in bitterness, wrath, anger, and thoughts of revenge. This grieves the Holy Spirit because we are ignoring his spiritual guidance and direction.[47]

3. *Acting Out.* It can be helpful to remember that anger is not the same as aggression, even though the two frequently go together. Anger is an emotional response that includes both physical and mental arousal. Aggression is a type of behavior that inflicts pain or pressure onto others. It is possible to be angry and not aggressive; we also can be aggressive without being angry. One study found,

for example, that anger is followed by aggression only about 10 percent of the time.[48]

When anger leads to aggression, the person is said to be acting out. This can be done in three ways: direct aggression, passive aggression, and redirected aggression.

(a) Direct Aggression. The most natural and immediate response to anger is to lash out, verbally or physically, against the person or situation that has made us angry. When an individual explodes in anger, he or she may feel better for a short period of time, but people almost always are hurt in the process. Often the person who exploded feels later embarrassment and guilt, relationships are damaged, friendships or jobs sometimes are terminated, and property may be destroyed. There is a widespread belief that the direct expression of anger releases the rage and helps people calm down. This theory has led counselors to use punching bags so angry counselees can punch out their anger and hopefully release the pent-up emotion. But the research suggests a different conclusion. These outward anger expressions are likely to lead to more anger rather than less.[49]

(b) Passive Aggression. Some people are pleasant and apparently cooperative in face-to-face situations, but they give vent to their anger in subtle ways. "My wife is a wonderful cook," a preacher said in his sermon. "She makes wonderful burnt sacrifices." Everybody laughed, including the wife, but beneath the humor she felt her husband's barb.

Passive-aggressive people may gossip and spread damaging stories, "forget" to do what they promised, refuse to cooperate, make "put-down" or embarrassing comments when others can't respond, or leave another person's property where it is likely to be damaged or stolen. Drinking, failing in school, or having an extramarital affair are examples of subtle ways that people use to attack or get even with parents, a mate, or some other person who has made them angry. The passive-aggressive person seems to have an unusual talent for doing what hurts the most, but often these actions can be explained away, excused, or justified so that their real motivation is hidden. This is an indirect form of acting out aggression aimed at the source of the anger.

(c) Redirected Aggression. Sometimes, aggressive anger is aimed at somebody who is innocent. The man who is angry with his boss may stifle his anger at work (lest he be fired), but he "takes it out" on his wife or children at home in the evening because this is a safer place to ventilate. The family may not have caused the anger, but they bear the brunt of the angry person's feelings. It is difficult to imagine how many innocent spouses and children live with this kind of redirected anger until they can't take it anymore. Children, for example, reach adulthood hating their perpetually angry fathers who may have succeeded in building their careers but who have destroyed their families in the process.

Anger is especially difficult to handle when we cannot identify who is to be blamed or when we cannot reach the person who created the situation that made us angry. If inflation causes prices to raise, who do we blame? The supermarket may be charging more for groceries, but the store manager is not responsible for inflation. If we decide that the real source of the problem rests with some government leader, this may be some aloof, distant politician who is difficult to contact and never available to hear our complaints or criticisms. As a result, we may verbally, physically, or cognitively attack some largely innocent but accessible person. Angry mobs that burn and loot stores in an attempt to bring down a political leader often do nothing to change the leader, but in giving vent to their anger, they destroy the property of innocent store owners who might be their neighbors.

All these acting-out approaches ultimately are destructive. They can be forms of the "eye-for-an-eye, tooth-for-a-tooth," get-even philosophy that Jesus so clearly condemned.[50]

4. *Facing the Anger's Sources.* Here the effect of anger is to arouse the person to deal directly with the threatening, incapacitating, or fear-producing situation that is causing the anger. The individual admits the anger, tries to see its causes, sometimes looks at the situation in a fresh way, and then does whatever seems best to accept or to change the anger-producing situation. This is a constructive approach to anger that often takes courage and maturity. It can be a difficult approach that some people only learn with the help of a respected mentor or counselor.

5. *Bringing Improvements.* We have seen the evasive and destructive effects of anger, but there is also a constructive type of anger. In one community study, 40 percent of the people concluded that angry episodes led to positive long-term outcomes.

Thirty-six percent concluded the anger had a neutral effect, and only one person in four felt the anger had created lasting problems.[51] Expressions of anger help people feel they are doing something about a situation. This takes away the sense of being out of control. According to one report, "anger can help clarify relationship problems, clinch business deals, fuel political agendas, and give people a sense of control during uncertain times. More globally . . . it can spur an entire culture to change for the better, as witnessed by the civil rights movement of the 1960s."[52] Of course anger can also spur terrorism or lead to war. Anger is most likely to be constructive when people view it as a way of solving problems rather than as a venting of feelings.

Counseling and Anger

Still angry? Get over it! These five words appeared at the top of a magazine advertisement for a new book on forgiveness. Apparently, the publisher wanted to imply that we could get over anger by an act of will or by reading a book.

It's not that simple. Some people have grown up in homes or neighborhoods surrounded by anger. These are environments where differences are settled by angry outbursts and flying fists. These people reach the teenage years or adulthood with no awareness that there can be other ways to deal with anger. They have learned that without anger they can't relate to others, protect themselves, or survive.[53] Others are victims of childhood abuse or other forms of violence, racial injustice, discrimination, or equally disturbing experiences that implant and fuel anger that may remain hidden but can lead to a variety of problems.[54] Some people may have listened to teachers or religious leaders who urged them to bring change through political means or through working with the police or welfare agencies. But when their efforts have been rebuffed and frustrated consistently, they give up and go back to handling things on their own.

Unlike most of the topics in this book, anger does not have its own listing in most categorizations of psychiatric and emotional disorders. Perhaps this is because anger is so pervasive that it is part of almost all personal problems. It doesn't yield to glib admonitions to "get over it."

Since anger can cause so much harm to others and to themselves, why do so many people persist in being aggressive, hostile, or bitter and harboring grudges? It appears that anger makes some people feel powerful, superior, and right. Trying to handle the anger maturely or "turning the other cheek" seems to imply that they are weak, inclined to back down, or easily "pushed around." In the guise of maintaining self-esteem or standing up for their rights, these people refuse to take actions that could change the anger-producing situations and eliminate misunderstanding.

All of this suggests that some of our counselees might enjoy being angry or find that they need anger to survive or relate to others. Counseling doesn't help much because there is little desire for change. When you encounter such an attitude, there can be value in stating your suspicion that the counselee really doesn't want to be different. Be prepared for the counselee to disagree, but remember that this can lead to further discussion about one's desires and motives for changing. When there is a desire for change, counseling can take several forms.

1. *Help Counselees Admit Anger.* Anger that is denied will never be eliminated, but sometimes the most difficult challenge in counseling is to help people see and admit that they are angry. Such an admission can be threatening, especially for people who are angry at a loved one or who think that all anger is wrong. It may help to point out that anger is a common, God-given emotion that, for most people, gets out of control periodically. Point out some of the signs of hidden anger (depression, physical symptoms, criticism, a tendency to gossip or not cooperate, impatience, or similar behaviors). If the counselee persists in denying the anger even after hearing the evidence, perhaps he or she will admit the *possibility* that anger is present.

2. *Help Counselees Express Anger.* One of the greatest and most destructive myths about anger is the view that we need to "get it out of our systems," "let off steam," swear, holler, scream, pound a pillow, or find some other way to vent hostility—all in an effort to decrease feelings of anger. This idea is never suggested in Scripture, and, as we have seen, it is not supported by psychological research. In contrast, there is plenty of evidence that ventilation, expressions of rage, tantrums, and continual talking about our anger all tend to increase anger instead of reducing it.[55]

How, then, can anger be expressed in more healthy ways? Sports and hobbies can sometimes be harmless ways to redirect energies. Specialists in sports psychology are using basketball and other sports to teach people how to deal with the anger that competition uncovers.[56] More realistic for most counselors is helping people talk honestly about the anger and its sources. Try to keep the discussion focused on specific instances of anger or hurt. Help counselees recognize that anger is a normal reaction to pain or frustration, not something they should be ashamed of or deny. Whenever possible, encourage and guide counselees to talk about their anger with the person who caused it. Of course, this needs to be done in a calm and non-accusatory way. This talking keeps the anger from being denied, but it clears the air and often leads to apology, forgiveness, and reconciliation. Often this is best done in the presence of the counselor, who can keep things calm and in perspective. If the other person is unavailable, unwilling to talk, or defensive and angry in return, the counselee's honest feelings can then be discussed with the counselor, along with ways to keep the anger under control or redirected into healthy channels without denying its existence. All of this can be of special help to counselees who have a tendency to explode first and talk later.

3. *Help Counselees Consider the Sources of Anger.* Even if the anger is denied, there can be value in asking, "What kinds of things do make you angry?" From this general beginning, move to the specifics: "I'd like you to think of a time when you were really mad. Tell me about it." In discussing specific examples, the counselee and counselor can begin to see what caused the angry feelings, when they occurred, and how they were expressed and handled. In considering the sources of anger, watch for excuses. Comments like "I've got red hair, so how can I help being angry?" or "My father had ulcers from being angry, so I guess it runs in the family" can be attempts to avoid facing the real source of the anger. When statements like these aren't challenged, the anger is more likely to persist.

Counselees can be taught to ask themselves questions like the following whenever they feel angry.

- What is making me feel angry?
- Have I been hurt—disregarded, blamed, devalued, rejected, made to feel inadequate or stupid?[57]
- Is there something about this situation that threatens me and makes me feel afraid or inferior?
- Am I jumping to conclusions about the situation or person who is making me feel angry?
- Has my anger come because I've had some unrealistic expectations?
- How might others, including the person who is angering me, view this situation?
- Is there another way to look at the situation?
- What could I do to change the situation in order to reduce my anger?

All of this is easy to read in a book, but when a person gets angry, he or she rarely thinks about questions like these. The questions can guide discussions of specific anger situations. The more the counselee learns to think like this, the more it becomes automatic, sometimes even in the midst of the anger-producing setting.

4. *Focus on Humility, Confession, and Forgiveness.* Teaching people to admit and evaluate their anger may be good first steps in dealing with the issue, but these are not permanent solutions. As we have seen, anger can lead to sinful thoughts, desires, words, and actions. Counselees must be helped to deal with these issues if they want to learn to control their anger.

(a) Humility. It can be a humbling experience to admit that we are angry or have lost self-control and acted inappropriately. Some people apparently prefer to remain angry rather than risk admitting their weaknesses or failure. Others, however, are willing to acknowledge the reality of their anger along with any accompanying sinful side effects. This attitude must come before confession.

(b) Confession. The Bible emphasizes the importance and value of confessing to God and to others.[58] When we confess to God, telling him honestly that we are angry and admitting that we are sorry for our acts of aggression,[59] then we can know for certain that we are forgiven.[60] If we confess to one or more fellow believers, they can support, forgive, encourage, and pray for us.

(c) Forgiveness. Some people know intellectually that they are forgiven, but since they don't "feel" forgiven, they continue in their guilt. Perhaps one way to feel forgiven is to remind ourselves repeatedly of 1 John 1:9. An additional technique is to be sure that we forgive others.

When Jesus was asked about this one day, he said that we should forgive repeatedly. He told a story about forgiveness and anger, concluding that people who refuse to forgive others will not be forgiven.[61] This has great relevance for those who hold grudges. Their anger is certain to continue, with all the accompanying misery and tension that stay with them.

Forgiveness can be very difficult, especially in situations that are unjust. Both counselees and counselors need to ask God for the ability to forgive. We need help in giving up feelings of revenge, in casting off all feelings of hatred, and in being open to the possibility of a restored relationship. When we can accept forgiveness and learn to forgive others, then we are freed from many of the hurts and frustrations from the past. Memories of past injustices may not disappear—to forgive does not mean that we automatically forget. But giving and receiving forgiveness leaves us less bogged down by anger, and better able to focus our energies on other, more wholesome activities. Forgiveness is an act of choice that can help people let go of their bitterness. Forgiveness may be the most crucial step in dealing with anger.

5. *Teach Anger Management.* Some counselors were dismayed when a movie appeared about a man who was court-ordered to get anger-management counseling. Movie critics noted that the stars of the movie, *Anger Management*, are known for being angry men in real life, so they were able to depict the emotion convincingly on the screen. The movie was a comedy that, in the opinion of some counselors, tended to make a joke about a serious problem: difficulty in controlling chronic anger.[62]

Three strategies for managing anger have significant scientific support for their effectiveness.[63]

(a) Relaxation Techniques. This begins by teaching people how to relax by deep slow breathing, imagining a peaceful scene, or thinking about some person or object that helps them relax. One lady learned to visualize a cross. After they have learned how to relax, counselees are asked to think of themselves being in a situation that creates anger. If being in a traffic jam or meeting with a difficult boss stimulates anger, the counselee imagines he or she is there and then immediately uses the relaxation methods. This is done over and over again. After several sessions, the relaxation response takes over immediately whenever there is an anger-arousing situation. Anger is always handled better when the person is relaxed and can keep calm.

(b) Cognitive Therapy. This therapy involves helping people avoid or get rid of an angry mind-set. It involves teaching people to think differently about their anger-producing situations, including the people involved. It may include seeing the situation from the other person's point of view. Often it involves developing healthier self-talk to replace the bitter and revenge-laden ideas that often ruminate in our minds when we are angry.

Some people look for the worst in almost every situation. They are perpetually critical, always negative, and invariably hostile. Sometimes, these people are in positions of Christian leadership, and too often they are counselors. Almost always they are basically unhappy.

Most people find themselves slipping periodically into a negative mind-set, and unless they resist it, they can get caught in what has been called a "hostility trap."[64] The Scriptures instruct us to think about things that are right, pure, good, and praiseworthy.[65] It is impossible to think such thoughts repeatedly while, at the same time, we wallow in anger, bitterness, and hostility. Perhaps it is even harder to hold on to angry thoughts if we sincerely pray for those who cause our frustration and anger. The apostle Paul had a positive mind-set and an attitude of thanksgiving and praise to God. As a result, he avoided ruminating in anger, even when circumstances were unjust and difficult.[66]

(c) Skill Development. Sometimes, anger arises because people have poor parenting skills, conflict management skills, communication skills, or even driving skills. Learning new skills helps people deal with anger and prevent its arousal in the future.

6. *Teach Principles of Self-Control.* When a person gets angry, clear thinking often gives way to feelings, and something is said or done that often is regretted later. At least three principles can help counselees gain greater self-control over anger.

(a) Growing Spiritually. This, of course, is an ongoing process that doesn't suddenly start when something makes us mad. Self-control is listed in Galatians 5 as one of the fruits of the Spirit. Believers who sincerely want to be led by the Holy Spirit will discover a slow decline in strife, jealousy, outbursts of anger, and other "deeds of the flesh." With God's help we can learn love, patience, gentleness, and self-control.[67] Only counselors who are Christians can share such teaching and model it in their own lives. Self-control is not something that we each do alone and without divine help.

(b) Slowing Reactions. The old idea of counting to ten before speaking sometimes helps one gain control before reacting.[68] Others have suggested the value of speaking slowly, not raising one's voice, pausing periodically (if possible), tensing the muscles and then letting them relax, and mentally telling oneself to calm down.

(c) Using "I-statements." Some counselees may need help in distinguishing between anger and aggression. Point out that we can be angry without hurting others or thinking hostile thoughts. Stress the importance of using "I-statements." "I was hurt by what you did," "I feel frustrated," or "I felt angry and put down by what you said" are all clear, non-blaming statements that express feelings without aggression or loss of self-control.

7. *Build a Healthy Self-Concept.* Hostility and anger, including prolonged hostility, often indicate that a person feels inferior, insecure, and lacking in self-esteem or self-confidence. Individuals who are made to feel inferior often react with anger and attempts to assert superiority. This can lead to arguments in which two people try to bolster themselves and each tries to make the other feel inferior.

Counselees are better able to control their anger when we as counselors help them develop a healthy self-esteem, based on their value as God's special creatures. Christians recognize that we are sinners, subject to pride and the dangers of exalted self-importance. Nevertheless, we recognize that God has redeemed us, made us his children, and given us the worth that we didn't deserve. God's perspective of our value is the basis for a healthy self-image and self-confidence. Some counselors would agree that people with strong self-concepts are better able to manage their anger than people with low self-esteem.

All these counseling suggestions are designed to help people deal with anger in healthy ways without venting it in a vain attempt to "clear the air."

Preventing Anger

Since anger is a God-given emotion, it cannot and should not be eliminated or prevented. However, there are several ways in which the unhealthy, destructive, and nonbiblical aspects of anger can be prevented.

1. *Biblical Teaching.* As we have seen, the Bible says a great deal about anger and self-control, but some of our counselees may have little awareness of this. Clear biblical teaching can help Christians understand practical issues such as the seeming contradictions between the wrath of God and the biblical instruction to control anger. Effective teaching also can help individuals distinguish between righteous anger and personal reactions, and can help people avoid the long-lasting destructive effects of anger and hostility.

2. *Avoiding Anger-Arousing Situations and People.* Problems are never solved if we avoid them in an attempt to maintain peace. Sometimes, duty or wisdom demand that we face frustrating situations squarely or deal directly with difficult people. Even so, there are times when one can stay away from situations, events, or people who are likely to arouse unnecessary anger.[69]

3. *Learning to Reevaluate Situations.* Athletic coaches sometimes encourage players to be angry, hoping that this will stimulate adrenaline and improve performance. Regretfully, some athletes find it difficult to control physical aggression outside the sports arena,[70] and others find that anger destroys their concentration and interferes with athletic skill. Studies have found that the best athletes remain calm, undistracted, and not angry even when they are provoked by opposition players. These self-controlled athletes have learned to expect setbacks. In preparing mentally for the game, they have anticipated the potentially upsetting events and have rehearsed ways to handle them. As a result, the distractions have produced increased concentration instead of disruptive rage.[71]

It is difficult to control emotions, but we can control the thoughts that give rise to feelings.[72] In the home, but also in the church and school, people can be taught—by words and by example—to evaluate each anger-arousing situation. They can learn to see that anger often comes from hurt, frustration, and disappointment. They can learn to respond calmly, perhaps by using "I-statements," and without blaming, overreacting, or saying things that might be regretted later. Instruction about these issues is helpful, but lasting learning is not likely to come from a lecture or book. Most people will learn slowly, by watching others and by having experiences—sometimes including failure experiences—that in time can teach more about anger control.

4. *Redirecting Anger to Good Purposes.* Mahatma Gandhi and Martin Luther King, Jr., were leaders who led legitimately angry people to direct their frustrations into nonviolent and constructive directions. History is filled with such courageous leaders. They understand and have shown that anger, redirected to admirable purposes, can change the world.

5. *Building Self-Esteem.* It has been said that we can no more insulate ourselves from irritating remarks, attitudes, and actions than we can hide from germs. But we can protect ourselves by maintaining the resistance that comes from a healthy

self-respect.[73] Anger is less destructive and more easily controlled when a person is secure as an individual and not plagued by excessive feelings of inferiority and self-doubt. Chapter 23 discusses inferiority and self-esteem, including ways to prevent a poor self-concept. When Christians have realistic pictures of themselves as persons of value, there is less need or inclination to get angry.

6. *Avoiding Ruminations.* Anger often arouses ongoing reflections on the causes of the anger. As this ruminating continues, the original causes often grow to false proportions. This can cause the anger to increase, especially when critical people associate with other critical people and share their dissatisfactions and critical thoughts. In this way some people develop a whole mind-set of negativism and bitterness that grows worse as they get older.

This kind of thinking may be fun, at first, because it lets the thinker fantasize about his or her own superiority. But since this type of thinking is destructive, the person must resist it and replace these ruminations with thinking that is positive and less critical. I once had a job where a group of employees met for coffee every morning and criticized our leaders. We made up jokes about them and laughed heartily, but I began to realize what was happening to me. I was becoming hypercritical and cynical like everybody else in the group. This did not change in me until I quit meeting with the group. As individuals, we should teach and model this message in the church and at home. When we avoid ruminating on angry thoughts and associating with hypercritical people, we see things more realistically and can prevent the harmful buildup of anger.

7. *Learning to Confront.* Conflict and disagreement are a part of life that cannot be avoided. It can be valuable, therefore, to teach people how they can express their feelings, say what they want, and what they think. This need not be done in a critical and confrontational manner that stimulates anger. Instead, the truth can be spoken gently and in love. When we learn to communicate honestly and effectively, anger often is reduced and further anger is prevented.

8. *Spirit Control.* Uncontrolled anger, as we have seen, is listed in the Bible as one of the deeds of the flesh, but self-control is one of the fruits of the Spirit. As believers in Jesus Christ who seek to avoid sin and sincerely desire to be led by his Holy Spirit, we can experience a slow but predictable growth in self-control and a steady decline in chronic anger and hostility. Committing one's life to the Spirit's control on a daily basis can be an effective approach to the prevention of destructive anger.

Conclusions About Anger

All of this chapter has focused on the people we counsel, but it is worth reminding ourselves that counselors get anger too, especially when our counselees are angry at us, critical, or resisting our efforts in what might appear to be passive aggression. Counselors need to acknowledge this reality, talk about it with a trusted friend, and learn to apply to ourselves what we have been applying to others.

There can be no easy answers to explain completely why a young high school student would kill his family in a late-night fit of rage. Severe anger, like angry feelings that are less intense, can have a variety of causes and ways to be treated. As this chapter has shown, the Bible and psychology can combine to increase our understanding of anger, and can help counselors be more effective in working with people who struggle with anger and self-control.

KEY POINTS FOR BUSY COUNSELORS

➤ Anger is an emotional state, experienced by everyone but difficult to define. It occurs in varying forms and degrees of intensity—from mild annoyance or feelings of aggravation to violent rage. Anger is a leading cause of depression, accidents, sickness, and interpersonal tension.

➤ Since anger is an attribute of God and a part of his nature, we cannot conclude that anger, in itself, is bad. But uncontrolled, vindictive anger is wrong and sinful. This includes vengeance, abuse, subtle aggression, and angry withdrawal.

➤ With determination, the help of others, and the power of the Holy Spirit, human anger can be controlled, and even used for good.

➤ The most commonly encountered causes of anger are:
  - Biological or chemical influences that either arouse anger or make the person more prone to get angry.
  - Injustice that arouses a righteous indignation.
  - Frustration.
  - Threat or a physical or psychological hurt.
  - Learning that teaches us when to be angry and how to express anger.
  - Ways in which we perceive a situation rising, in part, from personality differences.

➤ There are different anger styles, but in essence anger influences people in at least five basic ways:
  - The anger is held back and hidden from others.
  - The anger is denied or pushed from conscious awareness, but it makes its appearance in other ways, such as physical symptoms or psychological reactions including anxiety, tension, depression, or spiritual struggles.
  - The anger is expressed in direct or passive ways. Sometimes, it is redirected from the source of the anger to some innocent person.
  - The sources of the anger are faced and dealt with.
  - The anger is channeled into actions that are positive and beneficial.

➤ Counseling people with anger issues can take several forms:
  - Helping people admit their anger. This can be an important first step for further counseling.
  - Helping counselees express their anger in appropriate and healthy ways.
  - Helping counselees face and admit the sources of their anger.
  - Encouraging a humble attitude along with confession and forgiveness.
  - Teaching anger management using relaxation techniques, cognitive therapy, or skill development.
  - Teaching principles of self-control.
  - Helping counselees build a healthy self-concept.

➤ Anger or its unhealthy expression can be prevented through any combination of:

- Biblical teaching.
- Encouraging people to avoid anger-arousing situations or people.
- Helping people learn to reevaluate situations that could lead to anger.
- Redirecting anger to more constructive purposes.
- Building self-esteem.
- Learning to avoid mental ruminations or reflections that can stimulate further anger.
- Teaching people how to confront in healthy ways.
- Spirit control.

➤ A focus on anger in counselees should not distract counselors from the fact that often they have anger in themselves, even anger caused by counselees. This needs to be acknowledged and handled in productive ways.

11

Guilt and Forgiveness

It started innocently. Late one evening JD was at his desk answering email when he opened a message that included pornographic photographs. Alone in the room, he clicked on the icon that invited him to see more. He continued looking, all the while becoming increasingly aroused sexually.

"Why am I looking at this?" JD asked himself as he abruptly stopped what he was doing and deleted the message. He knew about Internet pornography and had urged the kids in his youth group to steer away from it, but here he was, a Christian, the youth leader in a thriving church, letting himself be aroused by pornography. JD confessed his guilt to God and asked for forgiveness, but the feelings of guilt about what he had done stayed with him for weeks.

Then it happened again. And again. Soon the Christian youth leader was looking forward to those late-night opportunities to look at pornographic materials, which, by this time, he knew how to find with ease. He felt guilty about his behavior and confessed his sin to God after every incident, but he kept repeating the pattern. His computer screen was turned away from the door of his home office, so he could always change the image on the screen if anybody appeared, but sometimes he thought of how his wife would react if she discovered his secret. He wondered if one of the computer-literate kids from his youth group might someday skim the hard drive and learn about his pornographic viewing habits.

One afternoon, a teenager from JD's youth group confessed that he had a similar problem. After the teenager left, JD realized that he was a hypocrite, trying to help somebody else get over a problem in which he himself had become trapped. It was then that he called me—his former professor. He cried as we talked, clearly overwhelmed by guilt, but relieved that his secret was finally being shared with somebody who could be trusted to keep his secret confidential.[1]

The struggle with sexual temptation and self-control has been called "every man's problem," especially in this era when there is blatant sexuality in the culture, frequent sexual language and behavior in the movies or other media, and easy access to pornography on the Internet. It's a struggle that creates feelings of persisting guilt, despair, and self-condemnation, as it did in JD and the young man who came to his office.

At the counselor's suggestion, JD rearranged his office so the computer screen was visible from the door, making the pornographic viewing too risky to continue. Then he found an accountability partner, a friend to whom he would confess his failures (James 5:16). More important, this was a friend who held JD accountable, prayed with him, asked him for weekly reports about his sexual behavior, including his viewing and reading habits, was available and "on call" whenever JD felt increasing temptation, and had the freedom to call when JD was up late at night to be sure he was not viewing anything pornographic. Almost immediately the problem lessened and so did the guilt. JD began to accept God's forgiveness, and in time he learned to forgive himself and keep away from sexually explicit Internet sites.

Guilt can be an emotionally painful experience, and it comes up repeatedly in counseling. "I'll never get used to it," one counselor said. "As Christians involved in counseling, we encounter guilt-ridden problems daily."[2] Talk with people who are depressed, lonely, grieving, members of violent families, homosexual, alcoholic, terminally ill, or facing almost any other problem, and you will find people who experience guilt as part of their difficulties. Guilt has been described as the place where religion and psychology most often meet.[3] According to psychologist Bruce Narramore, an understanding of guilt feelings is central to any understanding of psychological maladjustment.[4]

Several types of guilt have been identified.[5] These can be grouped into two broad categories: objective guilt and subjective guilt. Objective guilt occurs when a law has been broken and the lawbreaker *is* guilty, even though he or she may not *feel* guilty. Subjective guilt refers to the inner feelings of remorse and self-condemnation that come because of our actions. Your counseling is likely to be more difficult if you fail to distinguish between the different types of guilt.

1. *Objective Guilt.* This can be divided into four types: legal, theological, personal, and social guilt. These overlap, merge with one another, and often are less distinctive than the following paragraphs might imply.

First, there is *legal guilt*—the violation of society's laws. A person who steals from a department store is legally guilty of theft, even if he or she is never caught and regardless of whether or not the person feels any remorse.

Theological guilt involves a failure to obey the laws of God. The Bible describes divine standards for human behavior—standards that we all violate at times by our actions or thoughts. According to the Scriptures, we are all sinners.[6] We are all guilty before God whether or not we feel remorse.

Many psychiatrists and psychologists do not admit the existence of theological guilt. To do so would be to admit that there are absolute moral standards. If absolute standards exist, there must be a standard-setter, that is, a God. For many, it is easier to believe that right and wrong are relative—dependent on one's own experiences, training, and subjective values. As we will see, this has great practical implications for counseling.

A third type of objective guilt is *personal guilt*. Here the individual violates his or her own personal standards or resists the urgings of conscience. No laws have been broken, and neither has the guilty person disobeyed God. If a father determines to spend each Sunday with the family, for example, he experiences personal guilt when business keeps him away from home over a weekend. His overweight wife may feel this kind of guilt when she indulges in a tempting dessert. This is not illegal, immoral, or unbiblical, but the person feels guilt nevertheless.

Social guilt comes when we break an unwritten but socially accepted rule. If a person is rude, talks loudly in a quiet library, pushes into the front of a queue, or fails to bring a wedding gift when this is expected, no law has been broken, and the offender may not feel any remorse. Nevertheless, the person is guilty of violating the social expectations of other people in the neighborhood, church, workplace, or society.

Probably most people feel uncomfortable when they break a civil law (legal guilt), deliberately resist or ignore God (theological guilt), violate a personal standard (personal guilt), and/or act contrary to social expectations (social guilt). It is possible to do all of these, however, and never feel guilty. The hardened criminal may act violently but feel no sadness or remorse. Millions of people, including professed Christians, forget God every day, sin against him, and think nothing about it. These people *are* guilty before God, but they do not *feel* guilty about their failures or actions.

2. *Subjective Guilt.* This is the uncomfortable feeling of regret, remorse, shame, and self-condemnation that often comes when we have done or thought something that we feel is wrong, or failed to do something that should have been done. Often there is discouragement, anxiety, fear of punishment or rejection, self-condemnation, and a sense of isolation, all tied together as part of the guilt feeling. In some Asian cultures, or with Asian counselees, this is described as a "loss of face," which includes shame, embarrassment, guilt, and self-criticism.[7] These subjective feelings may be strong or weak. Usually, they are unpleasant but they are not always bad. They can stimulate us to change our behavior and seek forgiveness from God or from other human beings. But guilt feelings also can be destructive, inhibitory influences that make life miserable.

Subjective guilt feelings can be appropriate or inappropriate.[8] *Appropriate guilt feelings* are present when we have broken a law, disobeyed biblical teachings, or violated the dictates of our conscience and feel remorse in proportion to the seriousness of our actions. *Inappropriate guilt feelings* are out of proportion to the seriousness of the act. For example, suppose somebody feels guilty for days about having made a joking comment that he later regrets because of how it might have been misinterpreted. Often these inappropriate guilt feelings come from within ourselves, but at times other people make statements or judgments that make us feel guilty. Sometimes, these comments are made with no harm intended, but at other times they are designed to create guilt that persists.

All of this shows that guilt is a pervasive and complex subject. In counseling it is important to distinguish between objective and subjective guilt, although most counselees will be concerned about the latter. It also is important to understand the biblical teaching about guilt.

The Bible and Guilt

When people talk about guilt, usually they are referring to subjective guilt feelings, but the Bible never describes guilt in this way. The three Greek words translated "guilt" or "guilty" refer to the theological guilt that was described earlier. A person is guilty, in the biblical sense, when he or she has broken God's law. In the Bible, there appears to be little difference between guilt and sin.

Even though the biblical writers never mention subjective guilt, we see this type of guilt scattered throughout the pages of Scripture. The Psalms are filled with deep expressions of remorse over sin, especially in what have been called the penitential psalms.[9] In Psalm 32, for example, David writes about how his sin left him feeling "weak and miserable," without strength, until he had the courage to seek God's forgiveness. In Romans 7:18–25, Paul never mentions guilt, but he describes his inner anguish as he tries but fails to avoid wrong and to do good. It is true that the believer has no reason to have guilt feelings because Christ has paid for and forgiven our sins. Even so, we continue with mental self-punishment, dwelling on the guilt we feel over our sins or other actions.

Since the Bible never talks about subjective guilt feelings, in no place does it imply that we should try to arouse guilt feelings in others. In spite of this, many well-intentioned parents, teachers, preachers, and athletic coaches attempt to stir up guilt on the assumption that this will motivate others, change behavior, stimulate Christian growth, punish wrongdoers, prevent pride, protect people from future sin, or stimulate financial contributions. These tactics may work temporarily, but they tend to be manipulative, they can arouse unhealthy guilt feelings, and they rarely bring lasting changes. More often they bring resistance, anger, and resentment.

Is it possible to help people deal with their sin or objective guilt without creating unhealthy guilt feelings? To answer, it is useful to consider the concepts of constructive sorrow and divine forgiveness.

Constructive sorrow, sometimes called godly sorrow, is a term used by Bruce Narramore[10] and based on 2 Corinthians 7:8–10. In this passage, Paul contrasts worldly sorrow (this seems to be equivalent to guilt feelings) and godly sorrow, which helps us turn away from sin and seek salvation. We never regret that kind of sorrow. Godly sorrow is "constructive sorrow" because it leads to constructive change.

Narramore illustrates this by describing a situation in which two people are in a café and one accidentally spills coffee on the other person's lap. A guilt feeling reaction would be, "How stupid I am. Look at the mess I've made because I'm so clumsy. I'm sorry." The coffee spiller feels embarrassed and self-critical. Constructive sorrow is different. The individual might say, "I'm very sorry. Let me try to help you wipe it up," and later there is an offer to pay the cleaning bill. The first response, psychological guilt, is self-condemning and not biblical; the latter, constructive sorrow, is scriptural and healthy.

Many Christians appear to be like JD who was described earlier in this chapter. They go through repeated cycles of sin, guilt feelings, confession, temporary relief, and then more sin. For some, 1 John 1:9 "has come to be used as a kind of psychological spot remover for emotional guilt,"[11] but there is no change. This is because the confession is based on a selfish motive that may not even be conscious—to get relief from guilt feelings. As soon as this relief is experienced, the person feels free to sin again and the cycle is repeated.

In contrast, Peter followed his denial of Christ by weeping bitterly.[12] He experienced deep remorse, sincere repentance, and a genuine desire to change. He confessed his sin, was freed from any feelings of guilt, did not repeat his behavior, and knew he was forgiven.

Divine forgiveness is a major biblical theme, especially in the New Testament. Jesus Christ came to die so sinful human beings could be forgiven and restored to complete fellowship with God.[13]

Some passages of Scripture mention forgiveness without discussing repentance, but other passages imply that at least two conditions must be met before God forgives. First, we must confess our sins and repent. Repentance involves the admission of what we have done. But repentance involves more. It implies that we acknowledge that our actions are wrong, that we are genuinely sorry, and that we want to change. When we confess in this way, God freely forgives and cleanses us.[14]

Second, we must be willing to forgive others. Jesus stated this clearly: "If you forgive those who sin against you, your heavenly Father will forgive you. But if you refuse to forgive others, your Father will not forgive your sins."[15] The person who seeks forgiveness must be genuinely repentant and willing to forgive others.

Most of the biblical discussion of forgiveness concerns confession to God and forgiveness from God, but there also are instructions for people to forgive one another, even as God forgives us.[16] The parable of the unforgiving debtor is a good example in which a man is forgiven a huge debt but in turn refuses to forgive a small debt that was owed to him. The results were disastrous. Jesus concluded the story with a comment about the need to forgive brothers and sisters "in your heart."[17] Christian counselors must help people find forgiveness from God, help them forgive others (and accept forgiveness from others), and help them forgive themselves. Many people can get through the first two of these, but they have problems with self-forgiveness. When subjective guilt feelings persist, an inability to forgive oneself often is a problem.

The Causes of Guilt

As we have seen, objective guilt comes when we have violated legal, theological, personal, and/or social laws and moral standards. It is rare for someone to come for counseling solely because of objective guilt, although sometimes lawbreakers come because they are afraid of being caught. More often, the guilty person has been caught and is afraid of punishment, or the person is experiencing subjective feelings of guilt. Why do people feel guilty? There can be several reasons.

1. *Past Experience and Unrealistic Expectations.* In childhood, most of us develop standards of what is right and wrong, or good and bad. As thinking and reasoning develop, children learn the standards of their parents and others. Each child comes to understand the difference between right and wrong, and soon there is an awareness of the punishments or other reactions that come when one disobeys.

In some homes the standards are so rigid and so high that the child almost never succeeds. There is little if any praise or encouragement because the parents are never satisfied. Instead, the child is blamed, condemned, criticized, and punished so frequently that he or she is made to feel like a constant failure. As a result, there is self-blame, self-criticism, a feeling of inferiority, and ongoing guilt feelings, all because the child has learned a set of standards that seem impossible to reach. Often these children strive desperately to please their parents, but they never reach the standards and always feel guilty for their failures. While parents most often express these demanding standards, sometimes they come from teachers, or they may come from church leaders who believe individuals can and should live completely free of sin.[18] If the young person decides to rebel against his or her moral upbringing, there may be additional feelings of guilt, some of which may come from the words of parents or other significant people who disapprove and condemn but make no effort to understand and give realistic guidance.

As they grow older, children usually come to accept the standards of their parents and other adults. When these standards are unrealistically rigid, the young people come to expect perfection in themselves, set up standards that never can be reached, and slide into feelings of guilt and self-blame following the inevitable failures. Guilt feelings are one of the ways by which we both punish ourselves and push ourselves to keep trying to do better. Some workaholics, for example, seem to be influenced strongly by feelings of guilt. Because of their past learning and experiences, these people fear they are not producing enough or not "redeeming the time." As a result, they keep working in an attempt to accomplish more. Some of them produce remarkable works and reach great heights of achievement, but they're never satisfied. Sometimes, they take no pleasure in their work because the result is not perfect, not good enough. For many there even is guilt over their lack of perceived success despite the acclaim of others. Perhaps unconsciously there is hope that more activity will keep them from feeling guilty. In contrast, others don't even try to achieve. They may feel guilty about their lack of success, especially in a success-worshiping world, but they resign themselves to staying where they are and never do much with their lives.

The best response to unrealistic standards is the adoption of realistic standards. God expects us to keep pressing on toward the goal of Christian maturity.[19] He disapproves of sin and disobedience, but he sent his Son so we could find forgiveness and life in abundance. Surely, he does not want us to wallow in self-condemnation and guilt feelings. Such an attitude has no biblical basis.

2. *Inferiority and Social Pressure.* It is difficult to know whether a feeling of inferiority creates guilt feelings, or whether guilt feelings produce inferiority. In his widely influential book, *Guilt and Grace*, Swiss counselor Paul Tournier titled the first chapter "Inferiority and Guilt." He argued that there can be no clear distinction between guilt and inferiority, since "all inferiority is experienced as guilt."[20] Narramore agrees that guilt feelings include "feelings of self-rejection, self-punishment, and a loss of self-esteem."[21]

Why do people feel inferior? This is discussed more fully in chapter 23, but it appears that our self-perceptions are greatly influenced by the opinions and criticisms of others. Tournier writes that in "everyday life we are continually soaked in this unhealthy atmosphere of mutual criticism, so much so that we are not always aware of it and we find ourselves drawn unwittingly into an implacable vicious circle: every reproach evokes a feeling of guilt in the critic as much as in the one criticized." In turn, this can lead to self-justification and criticisms of others. This cycle shows how social pressure and social suggestion can be the source of innumerable feelings of guilt.[22]

3. *Faulty Development of the Conscience.* The word "conscience" does not appear in the Old Testament, and although it is used 31 times by New Testament writers, the word is never clearly defined.[23] Paul wrote that consciences are built on universal, divinely given moral principles that are "written within" us,[24] and probably placed in us by God before we are able to even think about right and wrong. But the conscience can become dead, even in religious people, dulled into insensitivity by persistent involvement with sin, by abandoning biblical teachings, and by dabbling in demonic ideas.[25] Consciences can be weak, and they can be strengthened.[26] Clearly, the conscience can be altered by the teachings and actions of others.[27]

Beginning with Freud, psychologists and psychiatrists have maintained that the conscience is molded early in life by the prohibitions and expectations of parents. The child learns how to act in ways that will bring praise and avoid punishment.

At this early stage in life, the child also learns about guilt. When parents are good models of what they want to teach, when the home is warm, predictable, and secure, and when there is more emphasis on approval and giving encouragement than on punishment and criticism, then the child knows what it means to experience acceptance and forgiveness. In contrast, when moral training is punitive, critical, fear-ridden, and unrealistically demanding, then the child becomes angry, rigid, critical, and burdened by a continuing sense of guilt. In time there may be rebellion against parental teachings and acceptance of the alternate views that come from one's peers.

Peers have a special influence in children who get little or no moral training from their parents. Around the world hundreds of thousands of children are raising themselves. These include the street kids in many countries, children who are conscripted into armies or prostitution, children who live in families with parents who provide poor parental models or who are uninvolved in the moral development of the children. These young people learn the often vague and ill-defined standards of their peers.

Regardless of their backgrounds, most children eventually shift away from the belief that something is right or wrong simply because of what parents, teachers, religious leaders, or even one's peers say. As they mature, children move toward a personal commitment to ideals they believe "in their hearts" to be right. This may not involve ridding themselves of parental or other instruction, much of which reflects the generally accepted moral values of the society. Instead, the maturing young person reflects on what has been taught, ponders the competing values of peers, and eventually comes to accept his or her own standards. This is not always done deliberately, but over time there is a general acknowledgment of what is right or wrong.

In addition to all of this, the Christian's conscience is furthered by sound instruction from the Bible, good adult models, and opportunities to express doubts and raise questions about authority. The maturing believer begins to understand the impact of sin, the reality and availability of forgiveness, and the importance of confession and restitution. Of course, many people do not reach this ideal. Trained to think rigidly about right and wrong, convinced of their own imperfections and incompetencies, fearful of failures or punishment, and lacking in the awareness of God's complete forgiveness, these people constantly are plagued with guilt feelings. These guilt feelings come not because of sorrow for sin or regret over lawbreaking. They are signs that the person is preoccupied with a fear of punishment, isolation, or lowered self-esteem. To bolster themselves, such people often are rigid, critical of others, unforgiving, afraid of making moral decisions, domineering, and inclined to show an attitude of moral superiority. They are difficult to have at home or in the church, but because they so often are angry and unhappy, these are people who need understanding and help.

4. *Supernatural Influences.* Before the Fall, Adam and Eve apparently had no conscience, no knowledge of good or evil, and no sense of guilt.[28] Immediately after their disobedience, however, they realized that they had done wrong, and they tried to hide from God.[29] Objective theological guilt and subjective guilt feelings had entered God's perfect creation.

As the rest of the Bible demonstrates, God's standards are high, and people fool themselves if they pretend to be without sin.[30] An awareness of objective guilt, therefore, can come from the promptings of the Holy Spirit, who convicts men and women of sin.[31] This supernaturally produced awareness is for our own cleansing and growth.

Satan also attempts to intervene in our lives both before and after sin. We know that he tempts us and tries to make us stumble, and the Bible states that he accuses believers, at least before God.[32] Adam and Eve would not have known guilt if Satan had left them alone. It seems likely that he creates many of our guilt feelings. Perhaps he also stimulates believers to continue feeling guilty and unforgiven, even when we have done nothing wrong or when we have confessed a sin and then been forgiven by God.

5. *A Lack of Forgiveness*. Technically, this is not a cause of guilt, but when people cannot find forgiveness, the guilt persists and sometimes becomes stronger. Forgiveness is discussed in more detail later in this chapter.

The Effects of Guilt

In the year following South Africa's first democratic elections, President Nelson Mandela appointed Archbishop Desmond Tutu as chairman of a Truth and Reconciliation Commission (known as the TRC), whose duties were to investigate human rights abuses that had been committed during the apartheid regime and recommend amnesty and reparations. For two years, while the world watched, South Africans were exposed to public testimony from victims and their oppressors. The commission learned with dramatic clarity how people had suffered under extreme forms of torture, abuse, and violence sanctioned by the state. Many of the people involved with the proceedings experienced intense stress, including mental breakdown, poor health, broken relationships, and overwhelming sadness. Archbishop Tutu, himself, did not try to hide his tears, and neither did a prominent poet and journalist named Antjie Krog, who heard all the testimony as she led the South African Broadcasting Corporation team that gave daily reports of the hearings and who later wrote a moving book.[33] Krog's powerful account of the horrors presented before the TRC was also an expression of her own mental anguish and struggles to reconcile herself with a dark period of time in her country's history.

The public testimony before the Truth and Reconciliation Commission demonstrated repeatedly how people can be impacted by guilt and by their role as victims. The very existence of the TRC was a model of national confession and expression of guilt. Very few countries ever have had the courage to express their guilt so openly and to make restitution so honestly.

The TRC showed what many counselors discover in their counseling. Objective guilt can have a variety of consequences. Breaking the law can lead to arrest and conviction, even in people who do not feel guilty. Social guilt may bring criticism from other people. Personal guilt often leads to self-criticism and condemnation. Theological guilt has consequences that are even more serious. God, who is just and holy, does not wink at sin, and neither does he fail to notice our acts of disobedience. According to the Bible, the ultimate punishment for sin is death—although God pardons and gives forgiveness and eternal life when we confess our sin and put our faith in Jesus Christ who died to pay for our sins.[34] Sometimes, it appears that lawbreakers are avoiding their punishment and never experiencing guilt over their actions, but God will bring justice in the end.[35]

Earlier I indicated that counselors do not always see the effects of objective guilt. Instead, people come for counseling because of subjective guilt feelings, or these guilt feelings arise as people discuss other problems such as marital tensions or past experiences. Guilt feelings can influence us in several ways.

1. *Defensive Thinking*. Introductory psychology textbooks usually describe these as defense mechanisms, ways of thinking that most people use to avoid or reduce feelings of anxiety, frustration, and stress. These thoughts tend to distort reality in

some way, and usually we are not consciously aware that we are using them.[36] To some extent all defensive mechanisms protect us from feelings of guilt. Repression is one of the most common. It simply excludes troubling thoughts from conscious awareness. If we look for ways to blame others for what we might have done (that is the defense mechanism known as projection), deny wrongdoing, withdraw from people, or rationalize and find excuses in an attempt to justify our actions—these are all ways by which we can avoid anxiety and keep from facing responsibility for our guilt-arousing thoughts or actions. Sometimes, when guilt feelings begin to arise, we get angry at others, try to justify our behavior, deny any personal responsibility for what has happened, or even apologize profusely.

One Christian counselor has identified another way of thinking that appears to be used by Christians, especially when they feel guilty about sexual lusts. Convinced that mental or behavioral lapses in moral purity are part of the sinful nature, people may continue to sin with their minds (and sometimes with their bodies), admit that this is wrong, ask God to forgive, and freely rely on his grace to take away the guilt. Then, as we have seen earlier in the chapter, the cycle tends to be repeated. This kind of thinking "minimizes the severity of sin, cheapens grace and fails to comprehend the meaning of a life lived under the lordship of Jesus Christ."[37]

2. *Self-Condemnation*. Guilt feelings almost always arouse anxiety and self-condemning feelings of inferiority, inadequacy, weakness, low esteem, pessimism, and insecurity. Sometimes, there is self-punishment: the person acts like a martyr who is pushed around by others. At times there may be a "poor-little-me-I-don't-deserve-to-be-treated-well" attitude. For others there is an inability to relax, a refusal to accept compliments, sexual inhibition, an unwillingness to say "no" to the demands of others, or an avoidance of leisure activities—all because the person feels guilty and unable to accept forgiveness. Often there is anger that is held within and unexpressed. This can lead the person into depression, sometimes with thoughts of suicide. Some people continually "put themselves down" and then wonder why this alienates and drives away their friends, who don't enjoy being with someone who wallows in self-condemnation.

Some of this self-condemnation may have roots in childhood. For example, there is a difference between parenting that uses guilt to mold a child's behavior and parenting that uses shame. Guilt-inducing parenting points out disobedience, weaknesses, or failures and then shows children how to behave differently. Shame-inducing parenting focuses on telling children how bad, clumsy, stupid, or worthless they are. As they grow older, the shame-taught children are more likely to carry self-images that are negative and defeatist. As adults, failures often lead to strong feelings of self-condemnation, anger, helplessness, and more shame.[38]

3. *Physical Reactions*. Guilt feelings, like any other psychological reaction, can produce physical tension. This is seen clearly in Psalm 38 and the other penitential psalms. Whenever tensions build in a person and are not released, the body weakens and eventually starts to break down. Some psychiatrists view this as an unconscious form of self-punishment. It may be more accurate to assume that the physical symptoms are the body's way of distracting us from the emotional pain of our guilt. Psychologically and emotionally it may be easier to tolerate physical pain than to bear the burden of guilt that would otherwise attract our attention.

4. *Moral Pain.* What is the impact when young people, many not even out of their teens, go to war and witness excessive acts of brutality, cruelty, and violence—some of which they may have committed themselves? It is not surprising that many veterans are severely affected by the stress. Because they are so distressing and painful, the memories of these events often are pushed from awareness, but they fester below the surface and eventually surface as the post-traumatic stress reactions that we will consider in more detail in later chapters.

Because of their experiences with intense violence, many veterans feel an ongoing guilt that doesn't go away but is accompanied by shame, confusion, depression, anger, inner emptiness, a fear of intimacy, and an inability to trust others. This is a deep moral pain that arises from the realization that one has committed acts with horrible and lasting consequences. Because of what they have done, sometimes even under orders from their superiors, these people struggle with the realization that they may have ended lives, torn apart families, brought incredible suffering, or inflicted debilitating physical conditions and maiming that can never be atoned for or undone. These realizations persist as moral pain in veterans, incarcerated prisoners, law enforcement people, or others who might seek counseling. They try, often in vain, to get help from counselors who know about stress management and may even understand guilt but who have no idea how to help guilt-burdened people find forgiveness.

5. *Repentance and Forgiveness.* The effects of guilt feelings are not all negative. Some people learn to accept mistakes, to grow from them, to confess to God and to others, and to rest content in the assurance that "if we confess our sins to him [Christ], he is faithful and just to forgive us and to cleanse us from every wrong."[39]

Counseling and Guilt

The Mission is a movie about a slave trader in South America named Rodrigo Mendoza who was involved in capturing Indians and selling them as slaves.[40] One day, Rodrigo got into a fight, killed his brother with a knife, and was put into prison, where he was visited by Father Gabriel, who headed a mission to Indians. Rodrigo sat dejected in his cell, overwhelmed by guilt, refusing to eat, and disdainful of the visiting priest. "Nothing can be done to redeem me," he insisted, but eventually he agreed to follow the priest's guidance with the hope of finding relief.

In a very poignant part of the movie, Father Gabriel and others are climbing a steep hill toward an Indian village. Trailing behind is Rodrigo, laboriously straining to pull up a heavy bag of Spanish armor. The ground is rough, with boulders, streams, and other obstacles. Near the top of the hill a group of Indian children is watching. When they see Rodrigo they race to tell the elders of the tribe, who gather with spears, watching the man struggle to the top of the hill. When he arrives, he collapses to the ground exhausted, apparently convinced that all his efforts could not redeem his sin and free him from the guilt. When the chief nodded, a warrior ran to Rodrigo and held a knife to his throat. The former slave trader must have assumed that his life was about to be ended by some of the Indians that he had tried earlier to capture. But the chief motioned again, and instead of cutting Rodrigo's throat, the warrior cut through the rope, freeing the quivering man from his burden and kicking it over the cliff. The heavy load fell to the water below, hit with a mighty splash, and sank. Rodrigo began to sob as Father Gabriel ran to hug him, the chief came forward, and the Indians gathered around. At that moment, Rodrigo learned that he could not earn forgiveness by his own efforts no matter how hard he tried. Forgiveness and freedom from the burden of guilt are a gift from God without condition. In Rodrigo's life, the forgiveness of the Indians must also have added to his sense of liberation.[41]

In counseling people with guilt, the Christian counselor has an advantage over the nonbeliever. Guilt is a moral issue, and guilt feelings arise from moral failures. Few secular counselor training programs discuss morals, and the counselor who does not believe in God must somehow deal with values, forgiveness, atonement, and related theological issues about which there may be little understanding and no formal training. Psychological approaches have been based on helping people to express anger, make restitution, lower their standards or expectations, improve performance, and get insight into their own behavior. At best, these are stopgap efforts that rarely seem to bring permanent change.

In a controversial book published several decades ago, psychologist O. Hobart Mowrer argued that individuals sicken "in mind, soul, and perhaps even body because of unconfessed and unatoned real guilt."[42] Mowrer proposed that mental illness most often is a moral sickness that only can be cured by confession to significant other people and by making restitution. Although Mowrer's book attacked some basic Christian doctrines (such as the subsitutionary atonement and the concept of original sin), his work challenged both counselors and pastors, urging them to acknowledge the central place of sin and forgiveness in counseling. A decade later, psychiatrist Karl Menninger expressed similar ideas in a book with the intriguing title *Whatever Became of Sin?*[43] Apparently, he once suggested that if he could convince the patients in his psychiatric hospital that their sins were forgiven, three-fourths of them could leave the next day. Menninger and Mowrer both wrote from a humanistic perspective. Even though they used theological language, they failed to acknowledge or maybe understand biblical truths about confession, forgiveness, and justification—concepts that must be in the thinking of every Christian counselor who attempts to help those with guilt feelings.

More recently, beginning in the late 1980s or early 1990s, a "small quiet movement" has been taking place in psychology. Prior to that time, forgiveness was rarely mentioned in psychological circles, but today an increasing number of research studies are investigating the positive impact that follows when people experience forgiveness, forgive others, and learn to forgive themselves.[44] Helping people find forgiveness and handle guilt begins by helping counselees face their guilt and its causes.

1. *Understanding and Acceptance.* People with guilt feelings frequently condemn themselves and expect to be condemned by others. As a result, they may come to counseling with a self-defensive or a self-blaming attitude.

The attitude of Jesus must have surprised the woman caught in the act of adultery.[45] She was objectively guilty, probably she felt ashamed, and perhaps she felt a deep sense of guilt, but Jesus was not like the others who wanted to condemn her. He did not condone her sin—it clearly was wrong—but he talked kindly to her and told her to sin no more. The way he reacted in this situation is a model for counselors.

As a counselor, what is your attitude toward people who have fallen into sin? How do you feel when these people are repentant and determined to change? What is your response if there seems to be no awareness of wrongdoing and no sense of shame or sorrow? Christian counselors must not try to minimize the reality of sin, and neither do they take an attitude of moral superiority. All of us are tempted, and any of us could fall into the sin or experience the moral pain that we see in our counselees.[46] Our task is not to condemn[47] or to expect that the counselee's guilt feelings can be stopped at will. Instead, we approach others with an attitude of love and a willingness to understand. To restate an old cliché, we accept the sinner, even though we do not accept the sin.

2. *Instilling Insight.* When the prophet Nathan confronted King David with his sin, the issues were clear: gross immorality, murder, and deception.[48] The king immediately admitted his sin, confessed his wrongdoing, and found forgiveness. For the rest of his life, David lived with the consequences of his actions, but he was free of moral pain because he had repented and changed in response to Nathan's challenge.

Counseling the guilty is not always that easy. Some people don't know why they feel guilty. Others freely admit their wrong actions or attitudes, but the guilt feelings still persist. At times you will encounter those who have broken the law or hurt another person, but there are no feelings of sorrow or remorse.

These people can be helped if they have some understanding of the forces that influence them from within. You might discuss issues such as the following. Try to focus on specific examples rather than on theoretical ideas or thoughts of what they might do.

- Are there things in your life that are making you feel guilty? What are they?
- How have you dealt with your guilt feelings in the past?
- What have you done that has been helpful? What has not helped?
- What expectations did your parents have about right and wrong?
- Were your parents' standards so high that you could never succeed in meeting them? Give an example.
- What happened when you failed?
- Were blame, criticism, and punishment frequent? How did this influence you?
- What did your church teach about right and wrong? Focus especially on the issue that is concerning the counselee.
- What are some things that seem to make others feel guilty but don't seem to bother you?
- What do you know about God's forgiveness? What about forgiveness from others?
- Were there times when you were able to forgive other people? How did you do this? Be specific by giving examples.
- Were there times when you were able to forgive yourself? How did you do this?
- How does this talk about forgiveness relate to the guilt you feel now?

Questions like these can help you understand why counselees feel guilty and can let you look for defensive reactions, self-condemnation, fear of punishment, physical reactions, and other responses to guilt. Counselees can be helped to recognize how their guilt feelings may have arisen from past moral training. Is the person striving to act in ways or accomplish goals that are impossible to reach? How would the person react, and what might happen if the goals are not accomplished? Are the person's standards consistent with biblical teaching? Does the counselee understand what the Bible says about forgiveness? It is here that insight may merge into spiritual teaching.

3. *Moral Education.* In many ways, counseling is a process of education in which the counselee and counselor work together and often learn together. In helping people deal with guilt, they must be helped to reexamine their standards of right and wrong. This may take a long time. Some people feel guilty about things the Bible doesn't call sin; others have moral values that clearly violate biblical standards.

In helping others deal with their guilt, it is important that counselors are in touch with their own standards, and with God's. He knows us perfectly. He understands that we are merely dust, and he recognizes that we will sin so long as we are on earth.[49] He does not expect perfection, but he wants a sincere attempt to do God's will as we understand it and as best we can. God is compassionate. He loves unconditionally and will forgive our sins without demanding personal atonement and penance. Human atonement and repentance are no longer necessary because Christ has already paid for human sins "once for all, the righteous for the unrighteous, to bring you to God."[50]

This is basic theology, so relevant and practical that it can revolutionize and completely free human thinking. The ultimate solution to guilt and guilt feelings is to honestly admit our pain, suffering, failures, and guilt; to confess sin to Christ and at times to other human beings;[51] to pray for forgiveness and a sincere desire to repent and change behavior; and then to believe with divine help that we are forgiven and accepted by the God of the universe. It is he who in turn helps us to accept, love, and forgive both ourselves and others.

4. *Repentance and Forgiveness.* Experiencing forgiveness and extending forgiveness to others can have a major positive impact on people who experience guilt. Forgiveness brings greater physical and mental health, heals racial and cultural divisions, restores marital stability, and builds relationships.[52] Forgiveness "calms turbulence, dampens the need to lash out at others, keeps families together and maintains harmony in relationships," according to one research team.[53] Such "forgiveness is often sought but less often found."[54]

There are numerous approaches to forgiveness, and this list will have grown by the time you read these words.[55] The recent flood of articles on forgiveness most often refer to the benefits of forgiving others and sometimes to the need for guilt-ridden people to forgive themselves. Equally significant, however, is the importance of accepting forgiveness from others and from God. Until we accept forgiveness, especially the forgiveness that comes from God, it is unlikely that we can fully forgive others and forgive ourselves.

It is possible for a counselee to understand what the Bible says about guilt and forgiveness, but obstacles like the following still may persist. In their minds people think:

(a) I can't ask for forgiveness. It is not the counselor's task to push people to pray, to confess, and to ask God to forgive. For some counselees it may take a while to reach that point, The counselor must be content to pray for the counselee and continue to work at accepting and helping the guilt-ridden person to understand the principles of forgiveness more clearly. The view that we earn divine favor by good works and that we pay for our sins by undergoing punishment is so widespread that it dies slowly. But the Bible teaches that repentance and confession are all we need to obtain forgiveness. Failure to understand this basic tenet of Christianity has caused countless people, including Christians, to experience unhealthy guilt feelings that lead to worry, depression, loss of inner peace, fear, low self-esteem, loneliness, and a sense of alienation from God. Often these are the people who feel unable to ask for forgiveness.

(b) I don't feel forgiven. When we ask others to forgive us, sometimes we don't feel forgiven because we haven't really been forgiven. According to the Bible, if we confess our sins and pain to him, he forgives—in every case.[56] Guilt feelings may not disappear overnight, but our counselees can rest in the assurance that they *are* forgiven, even if they don't feel like it. This may have to be restated frequently and accompanied with prayer that the feelings of liberation will come.

(c) I know God has forgiven me, but I can't forgive others. Lewis Smedes wrote that forgiving is hard work that seems almost unnatural. Most of us have to keep working at it, and often we forgive only with God's help. Perhaps your counselee will agree that "if you are *trying* to forgive, even if you manage forgiving in fits and starts, if you forgive today, hate again tomorrow, and have to forgive again the day after, you are (nevertheless) a forgiver."[57] Most of us are amateurs and bunglers when we try to forgive. All of us need God to help us forgive—especially when we don't feel like it.

(d) How can I forgive when I can't seem to forget? God alone is able to forgive and forget. We humans tend to remember past sins and injustices even when they have been completely forgiven. Sometimes, it may not be wise to forget. By trying to ignore some past evils, we run the risk of their happening again. In most situations, old memories are best abandoned. When there has been forgiveness, these memories may linger, but if we refuse to dwell on them, they will begin to fade. When an individual has sincerely forgiven others and has genuinely been willing to accept God's forgiveness, then there is no reason to mull over life's injustices. The memories will return, sometimes when they are least expected, but these memories will have decreasing power. Forgiving must come first. Then complete or partial forgetting will follow.

(e) I know I'm forgiven, but I still feel guilt because I can't forgive myself. The previous paragraph applies equally to the inability to forgive oneself. When the guilt and self-condemnation still persist, even after the person has experienced forgiveness, it is good to explore some of the reasons for this. Perhaps the person really doubts whether he or she has been forgiven. This person will need reassurance that the forgiveness from God really is valid. Unconsciously, the counselee also may be gaining some personal benefits from hanging on to the guilt. When we wallow in guilt and self-criticism, we are spared the responsibility of moving forward with our lives. Sometimes, it is enough to talk to people about how God has forgiven them and point out to them gently that they are refusing to follow his lead and to forgive themselves even as God has forgiven. Several New Testament passages show that God expects us to forgive. By not forgiving ourselves, is that disobedience?

Confession and forgiveness from God often occur in the privacy of one's room. Sometimes, we forgive others privately, especially when it is not possible to go to the person and extend forgiveness face-to-face. More often, confession and forgiveness are best accomplished in the context of a group. Sometimes, the act of confession and forgiveness occurs between two people. This was demonstrated in a remarkable way when Pope John II went to a prison cell and offered his forgiveness to the man who had tried to assassinate the church leader in Saint Peter's Square. At times, the confession and forgiveness will occur between two or more people in the presence of a counselor or mediator. Then there are times when this process occurs in a more public setting. When the process involves more than one person, the healing may be stronger and sooner.[58]

5. *Making Restitution.* True forgiveness almost always is followed by a change in behavior and in thinking. For example, assume that a businessman feels guilty because he mistreated a former employee and withheld some of the wages that should have been paid. Confessing the sin to a counselor might help the businessman feel better, and he knows that if he confesses to God, he will be forgiven. If there is to be true freedom from guilt, however, the businessman needs to seek out his former employee, apologize for the mistreatment, and pay the wages that are owed. Let us assume that the two men meet and the former employee tells the boss that he is forgiven. After the meeting, the employee continues to think about the prior mistreatment, ruminate on the former employer's faults, and frequently complain to his friends about the previous injustice. Despite what he said, the employee has not really forgiven if he continues in his bitterness and criticisms. When there is true forgiveness, there is a genuine attempt to bring reconciliation, to make restitution, and to abandon bitter and complaining attitudes.[59] Counseling can help with these behavior and attitude changes that must accompany forgiveness if there is to be true freedom from guilt.

Preventing Guilt

The old adage "Let your conscience be your guide" is not always a wise principle for living. We have seen that individual standards of morality differ from person to person, and sometimes from country to country or from one religion to another. In part, this is because early moral teaching and parental expectations can have such profound influences on an individual's later thinking about right and wrong. The place to start the prevention of unhealthy guilt feelings, therefore, is with children and with their parents.

1. *Help Parents Teach Values.* Children (like adults) learn both from what they hear and from what they observe. Parents who are hypercritical and excessively demanding teach their children to feel like constant failures. When they cannot meet parental standards, these young people feel guilty and believe they are failures. In time, they begin to accept the parental attitudes, and the children grow up to also become critical, demanding, and able to instill guilt in others. To break this cycle, the counselor can encourage the parents to model healthier values. They can be guided as they teach standards to their children but learn, as well, to point out failure in the context of abundant love, encouragement, and forgiveness. Since guilt feelings are tied so intimately with self-esteem, it also can be helpful to follow the prevention guidelines listed in chapter 23.

2. Help People Find Values. The early years of the twenty-first century witnessed some highly publicized examples of business and church leaders who claimed to hold traditional values but whose actions demonstrated that their real values were more consistent with greed and lust. We live in an era where, with their words or their actions, many reject or ignore traditional values, but have difficulty in finding alternative values. Movies, television, and the lifestyles of high-profile people in various professions all reinforce the confusion and uncertainty about values.

The culture may do most to create the moral confusion and ethical uncertainty that so many of our counselees face, but is it possible that the church sometimes shares this value confusion and even makes it worse? Some well-intentioned religious groups may try, mostly in vain, to reimpose the old ethical certainties that worked in the past but may have little relevance for the postmodern world in which we live. Sometimes, this rigid push for older values involves the condemnation and rejection of nonconformists. As a result, there is both resistance and guilt in people who fail to meet the imposed standards. A more constructive approach would let people express their confusion but seek—with the help of sensitive counselors and other Christian leaders—to find ethical standards that are relevant to our changing society but derived from and consistent with biblical teaching.

In the church, Christians must be helped to understand God's high standards of morality. Each believer should realize, too, that God understands our weaknesses and is willing to forgive freely when we fall. Try to show the difference between guilt feelings and constructive sorrow.

Encourage people to examine their own self-expectations and standards of right and wrong. Are any of these unrealistic and unbiblical? Remind others that two good ways to learn about forgiveness are to experience it and to practice it. If church people can seek God's help in forgiving one another,[60] there can be a reduction in bitterness, decreased guilt, and less resistance to understanding and accepting forgiveness from God. Of course, strong values and their importance can and often are taught from pulpits and in small groups.

Finally, there is the issue of obedience. When we attempt to obey the law, meet social expectations, and do what God wants, we are less likely to experience objective guilt. This in turn prevents the development of many subjective guilt feelings.

In themselves, guilt feelings are not all bad. Sometimes, they stimulate us to confess sin and to act more effectively. When these feelings persist as paralyzing influences, they are harmful. It is such harmful guilt feelings that we seek to prevent and eliminate.

Conclusions About Guilt

Jesus never relaxed his standards when he talked with the woman caught in the act of adultery. God's standards are perfect, and he never winks at sin or settles for anything less than conformity to his divine principles. The woman was told to sin no more, and hopefully her lifestyle changed radically.

It is certain that she never reached perfection. None of us does. Nevertheless, we are accepted by God, forgiven unconditionally when we confess our sins, and assured that some day we will reach and live in accordance with divine standards because of what Christ has done and is doing.

Most of the problems discussed in this book will involve people with guilt. Counselors can work to help people let go of their guilt, but as this chapter has shown, the ultimate answer to guilt is not found in psychology. It is found in the biblical teachings about forgiveness. Because God forgives, we can be forgiven, our guilt can be removed, and a way is provided to deal with feelings of shame and guilt.

KEY POINTS FOR BUSY COUNSELORS

➤ Guilt appears in a majority of the problems that are brought to counselors.

➤ There are two major types of guilt.

1. *Objective guilt* occurs when a law has been violated and the lawbreaker is guilty even though he or she may have no feelings of guilt. This includes the following:
   - ◆Legal guilt when one has broken the laws of the state.
   - ◆Theological guilt when God's standards are not met.
   - ◆Personal guilt when one's personal standards of right and wrong are violated.
   - ◆Social guilt when one breaks an unwritten but socially expected rule
2. *Subjective guilt* refers to inner feelings of remorse and self-condemnation because of one's actions or failures.

➤ When the Bible uses the word *guilt*, it refers to the violation of God's laws. Subjective guilt feelings are not mentioned, but they are described, especially in the Psalms where David expresses anguish over his sin.

➤ Forgiveness is a major biblical theme. Confession and repentance are necessary if one is to receive divine forgiveness. A willingness to forgive others is also crucial if one is to receive God's forgiveness.

➤ Most counselees who talk about guilt are referring to subjective guilt feelings.

➤ Issues with guilt can arise when:

- ■ A person is unable to meet unrealistic standards that he or she has learned from demanding parents or other significant adults.
- ■ There is social pressure, or an individual feels inferior and never able to meet his or her standards.
- ■ A person has never developed clear standards of right and wrong or has a conscience that is undeveloped. Mostly this is due to past experiences or lack of direction.
- ■ Supernatural influences alert us to our sin and guilt.
- ■ A person cannot find forgiveness, so the guilt feelings remain and often grow stronger.

➤ Guilt can lead to:
  ▪ Defensive thinking—using the well-known defense mechanisms.
  ▪ Self-condemnation.
  ▪ Physical symptoms.
  ▪ An inner sense of anguish or moral pain.
  ▪ Repentance and forgiveness.

➤ Counseling people with guilt issues includes:
  ▪ Showing understanding and acceptance.
  ▪ Helping people get insight into their actions and the sources of their guilt feelings.
  ▪ Teaching moral issues; helping people find healthy standards of right and wrong.
  ▪ Helping people experience forgiveness and/or forgive others.

➤ Forgiving is hard work. Most people have to keep working at it, and often they forgive only with God's help and then only after a long period of time.

➤ When people seem unable to forgive themselves, take some time to explore the reasons for this. Are there some benefits that come from not forgiving oneself?

➤ To prevent unhealthy guilt feelings,
  ▪ Help parents teach values.
  ▪ Help people find clear values—ethical standards that are relevant to our changing society but derived from and consistent with biblical teaching.

➤ The ultimate solution to guilt and guilt feelings is to honestly admit our pain, suffering, failures, and guilt; to confess sin to Christ and at times to other human beings; to pray for forgiveness and a sincere desire to repent and change behavior; and then to believe with divine help that we are forgiven and accepted by the God of the universe.

12

Loneliness

Dr. N. is a bright young professor at a university in Canada. She is well liked by her teaching col-leagues, popular with her students, and competent as a researcher. Early in her career she received the outstanding teacher of the year award, and she appears to be well on her way to building a suc-cessful career as a scholar and a researcher.

Few people know that intense feelings of loneliness are hidden behind Dr. N.'s vivacious personal-ity and intellectually competent manner. In a magazine article, she read that one person in six doesn't even have a single friend with whom she or he can talk about personal issues and that 40 percent of the population feels shy and isolated. Dr. N. feels that this is a description of her life. Every hour of her busy days she is surrounded by people, but she doesn't know any of them personally, and most of them don't even call her by her first name. Her family lives miles away, so at the end of each day she goes back to her apartment, talks to the cat, and reads by herself. There is not much else to do.

Dr. N. lives in a large metropolitan area where there are concerts and plays, but she has no desire to attend these by herself. She doesn't feel comfortable looking for friends in bars, and she feels like a misfit in church. The people there all seem to have their own friends, and nobody knows how to relate to a single person—especially when they find that she is a university professor with a Ph.D. Once she went on a cruise and met some nice people, but they are scattered around the country and too far away to be friends.

Despite her professional competence, Dr. N. feels like a personal failure. She is an attractive person with good social skills and a bright mind. She knows that God accepts and cares for her, but she also knows of her need for human companionship—people with whom she can relax and be herself. Her loneliness makes her feel depressed, and recently she has been wondering if she should resign from her position and move someplace else. She knows, however, that the loneliness would move with her.

Recently, Dr. N. decided to talk with a counselor. "I've been wondering if something is wrong with me when I am surrounded by so many people but still feel lonely," she said. Dr. N. does not appear to have any deep-seated emotional problems, but she needs another person's perspective and help in finding ways to overcome the feelings of loneliness that now appear to be interfering with her ability to concentrate at work.

Loneliness is a painful inner emptiness that everybody experiences at times. It may last for a short time or persist throughout life. It impacts people of all ages, including early childhood, but it appears to grow during the teenage years and may reach its highest peak in young adults in their early twenties. Although it appears in all cultures, it is most prevalent in societies that emphasize individu-alism. It occurs frequently in single adults living alone, elderly people who have lost a spouse, parents without partners, or people away from home, including students. It can characterize people who live apart from other human beings, but it is possible to be lonely surrounded by other people. Many married people live with their spouses but feel lonely and alienated, especially when there is marital tension.[1]

There is some evidence that highly ambitious, "fast-track," upwardly mobile people have an especially high incidence of loneliness.[2] The same is true of leaders who feel alone at the top, workaholics consumed by activities that interfere with personal intimacy, and counselors who spend their lives giving to others but failing to bring closeness into their own lives. Once called "the world's most common mental-health problem," loneliness has been studied by hundreds of researchers, but the massive *Comprehensive Textbook of Psychiatry* doesn't even mention loneliness in its index. It's a popular topic on the Internet, however. Type "loneliness" into one popular search engine, and you will find over a million web-site hits.

Loneliness is the painful awareness that we lack close and meaningful contact with others. It involves a painful feeling of isolation, and sadness and a deep desire to connect with others. Even when they are surrounded by others, lonely people may feel left out, unwanted, rejected, or misunderstood. Frequently there is depression, self-criticism, restlessness, and anxiety, accompanied by a longing to be wanted and needed by at least one other human being. Despite this desire, lonely people often feel uncertain about how to reach out or unable to initiate and continue close relationships.

It is not surprising that many lonely people tend to look down on themselves. Weighted down with feelings of isolation, the lonely person may think "nobody wants me, so I guess I'm not worth anything or not needed by others." Sometimes, there is a sense of hopelessness and a strong desire for almost any kind of relationship that might end the powerful pain of involuntary aloneness. This can lead to a vulnerability to unethical people who prey on the chronically lonely and lure them into unhealthy relationships or unwise financial decisions. Many people try to find relief in bars, encounter groups, church meetings, or involvement with the billion-dollar "loneliness industry" that provides seminars, dating services, singles vacation trips, self-help books, and a variety of other promised, often valuable, antidotes to loneliness. Even when they do have human contact, many lonely people still are unable to build significant relationships or gain emotional satisfaction from others.

Loneliness can be transient and situational or chronic and long-lasting. Transient-situational loneliness lasts from a few minutes to a few months. Usually, it occurs because of some event, like moving away from close friends, separation from family members, a misunderstanding or disagreement, divorce or death, a young person's move to college, or graduation and the subsequent scattering of one's classmates. Chronic-persisting loneliness more often comes because of an individual's shyness, a poor self-image, or self-condemnation. Sometimes, poor social skills or socially insensitive behavior drives people away, and so do self-defeating efforts to barge into another's social group or to draw attention to oneself.

Whereas some people feel lonely even when they are surrounded by groups or crowds, other people may be by themselves and not feel lonely at all. This has led some psychologists to conclude that loneliness is primarily an inner feeling that doesn't always depend on whether others are present. The inner feeling of loneliness comes when we perceive ourselves to be isolated from others, fail in our efforts to find friends, or lack the social skills needed to relate to others. This sense of isolation is felt when the person is separated from God and feels that life has no meaning or purpose. People like this need a committed and growing relationship with God, preferably within a caring community of believers.

It is important for counselors to recognize that loneliness is not the same as solitude. Loneliness comes when a person is forced to be alone. It is a negative experience. Solitude is a voluntary withdrawal from others that most often is positive. Loneliness can sweep over us and hang on in spite of our best efforts to cast it off; solitude can be started and ended at will. Loneliness is painful, draining, and unpleasant; solitude can be refreshing, rejuvenating, and enjoyable. People talk to counselors about the problem of loneliness; solitude rarely is mentioned in the counseling room.

Solitude often takes the form of a voluntary retreat from daily habits, demanding relationships, schedules, cell-phones, and email. Solitude can be a time for self-reflection, communication with God, and contact with one's inner being. It can be a nourishing experience that cultivates a deeper relationship with God, new energy, and greater creativity. Spiritual directors often recommend solitude as one of the disciplines that contribute to spiritual growth and greater maturity. Depending on the situation, counselors may recommend periods of solitude for their counselees, but in general, this is not the best approach for people struggling with loneliness.[3]

The Bible and Loneliness

Shortly after Adam's creation, God said, "It is not good for the man to be alone. I will make a companion who will help him."[4] Adam and God had talked together in the garden, but the Creator knew that human beings need other humans if they are to function effectively. So God created Eve, and God blessed the couple, telling them to "multiply and fill the earth and subdue it."[5] In fellowship with God and with each other, Adam and Eve were neither alone nor lonely.

When they fell into sin, the first married couple broke their communication with God, and a wedge was driven between the husband and wife. Selfishness and interpersonal tension came into their relationship, and feelings of loneliness must have entered the human race at that point.

Loneliness is rarely discussed in the Scriptures, but it is seen repeatedly, even in the lives of Bible heroes such as Moses, Job, Nehemiah, Elijah, and Jeremiah. David once wrote about being "alone and in deep distress."[6] Jesus, who knows all our infirmities, surely felt lonely in Gethsemane and later on the cross when he called to God and asked, "Why have you forsaken me?[7] John must have been lonely in those years of exile on the Isle of Patmos. In prison, at the end of his life, Paul wrote that his friends had left, that some had forsaken him, and that he needed his younger colleague to "please come as soon as you can."[8]

The Bible also refers to solitude. Jesus was led by the Holy Spirit into the wilderness for a period of spiritual testing where he had nothing to eat.[9] At other times he voluntarily retreated to isolated places where he could have time for solitude, prayer, and meditation.[10] Sometimes, in his retreats, he was accompanied by the disciples.[11] This voluntary decision to pull away from others for times of quietness and retreat in solitude is far different from the helpless feelings of being alone that characterize loneliness.

The entire Bible focuses on our need for communion with God and for people, especially Christians, to love, help, encourage, forgive, and care for one another. A growing relationship with God and with others becomes the basis for any solution to the problem of loneliness. But how do individuals build relationships with God and with others? To answer, it is helpful to consider the causes of loneliness.

The Causes of Loneliness

The many causes of loneliness could be grouped into five categories: social, developmental, psychological, situational, and spiritual.

1. *Social Causes.* Loneliness increases during times of change and turmoil. This may account for the higher reports of loneliness among teenagers and young people following high school. It also suggests that rapid social changes may be creating loneliness by isolating people from close contact with one another. Social issues that increase loneliness include:

(a) Technology. As government, business, educational institutions, and churches have grown in size and become more impersonal, it is easy for people to feel smaller, less noticed, and less needed. As efficiency, productivity, and convenience have become more important, there is less time for developing deep, satisfying relationships. Complex technology increases the need for specialists, and these people sometimes have neither the time nor the ability to communicate with nonspecialists. As a result, relationships are shallow, understanding decreases, and loneliness becomes more prevalent, even among those who are surrounded every day by other hard-driving, technology-driven people.[12]

More than any other technological invention, the Internet may have had the greatest relationship to loneliness. Frequent Internet use may pull people away from face-to-face contact and relationship building. As a result, they become more alienated from normal social contacts and may even cut these off as the Internet becomes the predominant way of relating to others.[13] This, in turn, could create feelings of loneliness. Some research evidence has shown that the Internet not only creates loneliness, but it also attracts lonely people. They go online for companionship, but they are able to remain anonymous, feel less social anxiety, retreat quickly when they feel uncomfortable, and control what personal information they share. One study of students found that the highest Internet users scored highest on a loneliness test and used the Internet to find social support. A few of these students even gained more confidence from the experience and were able to build friendships that helped them feel less lonely.[14]

(b) Television. There are relatively few homes in the developed world that do not have at least one television set. Television enhances separation both by program content that can promote superficiality and arouse fear, and by the viewing habits of people who sit in front of the screen for long periods of time, seldom communicating directly or in depth with each other. Caught in the unreality of television (and video tape or DVD) productions, it is easy to live one's life through the people on the screen instead of interacting with neighbors and relatives. Swayed by the attractive presentations of some television religious programs, it is more convenient to stay home and avoid the local church with the supportive relationships that come from the body of believers.

(c) Mobility. Modern and cheaper transportation that makes moving easier, the development of large corporations that move people around, and sometimes the lure of education or a better life elsewhere all contribute to widespread mobility. This disrupts friendships, separates families, eliminates neighborhood and community spirit, and causes people to avoid close friendships that could end later in painful separations.

(d) Changing Demographics and Lifestyles. As people have moved closer together, especially in cities, there has been a tendency to withdraw from others. Sometimes, there is a fear of strangers or of inner-city crime, which leads to suspicion and withdrawal. Living in the midst of crowds, noise, and commotion, some city people prefer to avoid additional close proximity to others, but this can lead to intense isolation and loneliness.

The withdrawal from others is not limited to cities, however. Depending on where you live, people in suburban and some rural communities don't know their neighbors and make no effort to get acquainted. This is because of the hectic lifestyles that have come to characterize so many of our lives. When everybody is busy and in a hurry, there is no time to connect with others, so people go their own ways but often feel lonely as a result.

Along with its many benefits, our changing, dehumanizing, technological society has disrupted people, shattered traditional sources of security, and created the potential for greater isolation and greater loneliness.

2. *Developmental Causes.* In an early study of the causes of loneliness, psychologist Craig Ellison concluded that three needs must be met, especially in the early years, if long-term loneliness is to be avoided.[15] These are the needs for attachment, acceptance, and adequate social skills.

(a) Attachment. All human beings, but especially children, need to feel close bonds with other human beings. This is the core of what has become known as attachment theory.[16] When children are separated from their parents, for example, there is anxiety and often emotional aloofness. If one parent remains, or if the departed parents return, the child clings to the father or mother, apparently afraid that separation will occur again. It is easy to recognize why many young people feel alienated and unattached when we consider the increasing divorce rate, the alarming prevalence of abuse, the large numbers of abandoned or neglected children, or the many young people who come home to empty houses every day because their parents are at work. Often these children grow up feeling lonely.

(b) Acceptance. Parents communicate acceptance in a variety of ways: by touching, by spending time with their children, by listening, by discipline, by showing affection. When these clues are missing, or when children are ignored or excessively criticized, they begin to feel worthless. According to one research review, loneliness in children also is influenced by how well they are accepted by peers, whether they are overtly victimized or bullied, whether they have friends, and the durability and quality of their best friendships.[17] Each of these experiences can lead some kids to conclude that they don't belong, so they either withdraw from others or force themselves on others in a way that brings more rejection. These experiences contribute to loneliness.

We who are older respond in similar ways when we feel unaccepted. Sometimes, people feel lonely because they believe they are different from others, or they conclude that people are indifferent to them. Parents who feel that they are no longer accepted or wanted by their children, spouses who feel rejected by their mates, pastors who feel unappreciated by their congregations, or employees who feel shunned by their employers and co-workers—all are examples of people who feel unaccepted, not needed, and often lonely.

(c) Social Skills. All of us know people who are misfits. They are insensitive to the needs or attitudes of others, and they do not know how to build smooth interpersonal relationships. They may try to manipulate or force themselves onto others, but their attempts only bring rejection, frustrations, lowered self-esteem, and increased loneliness. These are people who have never learned how to relate to others in socially appropriate ways. They keep trying, fail continually, and remain in their loneliness.

These lonely feelings are accentuated if we grow up surrounded by social values that undermine closeness. In many societies people tend to value material things more than they value other people. We judge a person's worth by his or her achievements or outward appearance. People who aren't affluent or outwardly successful tend to be ignored, and this can increase their loneliness.

3. *Psychological Causes.* To some extent loneliness depends on perceptions—the way we look at the world. One person may live alone and not feel lonely because she knows she has many friends. Another may be surrounded by people but still feel lonely because "others have more friends than I do." People with power, influence, fame, and money often feel lonely because they know they are valued not for themselves but for what they possess. Have you ever wondered if somebody like Queen Elizabeth feels lonely? She is surrounded by people who come when she calls, but how many people does she have who value her for who she is, who would stick with her if she lost all she had, people with whom she can share honestly without fear of having her words leak to the press? Chronically lonely people sometimes conclude that nothing can be done to improve the condition, so they sink further into their loneliness. In addition, loneliness appears often in people who have low self-esteem, self-defeating attitudes, depression, inability to communicate, lack of control, hostility, or fear.

(a) Low Self-Esteem. When we have low opinions of ourselves, we underestimate our worth and either withdraw from others or overexaggerate our qualities so that we appear conceited and push people away. Both reactions interfere with our closeness to others. It is difficult to build friendships when we have little self-confidence. It is not easy to develop intimacy when we feel unattractive or afraid of being rejected.

Self-esteem gives us the confidence to build close relationships, which, in turn, decreases loneliness. In contrast, low self-esteem makes the person feel weak or shy. This results in a tendency to withdraw, accompanied sometimes by an excessive need to depend on others. When others are not available, there can be intense insecurity and deep loneliness.

(b) Self-Defeating Attitudes. To some extent loneliness may be the person's own fault. People increase the potential for loneliness when they are intensely competitive, struggling for self-sufficiency, preoccupied with themselves and their successes, inclined to be critical or intolerant, holding grudges, or demanding attention from others. When attitudes like these persist, people are driven away, and the loneliness intensifies.

It is well known that leaders often are lonely. Sometimes, this loneliness comes because of the leader's self-defeating behaviors, like withdrawing from confidants, having no social relationships apart from work, ignoring the family, showing critical and authoritarian attitudes that push others away, or never taking the time to relax or reflect through retreat times or journaling. Increasingly isolated, these lonely leaders undercut their ability to lead and sometimes destroy their organizations as a result.[18]

(c) Depression. Depressed people also can feel lonely. When they withdraw from others because of the depression, loneliness often results. This, in turn, fuels the depression and leads to a downward spiral.

(d) Inability to Communicate. Communication breakdowns are at the root of many interpersonal problems. When people are unwilling to communicate, or when they don't know how to communicate effectively, there can be a persisting isolation and loneliness even when these individuals are surrounded by others.

(e) Lack of Control. A voluntary walk by yourself in the countryside can be a pleasant and relaxing interlude, but to be abandoned in the same location at dusk can be a terrifying anxiety-producing experience. The difference depends on the person's ability to be in control of the situation. Hermits, some artists, or people on personal religious retreats can be productive and motivated, even though they may be miles from other people. In contrast, individuals who are widowed, divorced, abandoned, or confined to prison cells can feel intensely lonely because of their forced isolation. Having control over the situation sometimes is the difference between experiencing solitude as opposed to feeling lonely.

(f) Hostility. Have you ever noticed that some people appear to be angry all the time? These people constantly criticize others, complain, or let others know about their unhappiness. Nobody likes to be around negative people like this, so the hostile attitudes drive others away. This, in turn, leads to both loneliness and more anger and unhappiness.

(g) Fear. I once had a plaque that read "People are lonely because they build walls instead of bridges." This is not the only cause of loneliness, but sometimes people erect barriers to keep others out. Most of us know people who hide behind facades, pretending to be competent, always unruffled or in control, and never appearing to be bothered by criticism or emotion. Behind these masks can lie deep feelings of loneliness and fear: fear of intimacy, fear or being known, fear of rejection, fear of acting inappropriately in social situations, fear of losing control emotionally, fear of having one's work and plans disrupted, or fear of being hurt. This kind of loneliness is painful, but for these people it seems less painful to be lonely than to face the fear and insecurity of contact with others.

4. *Situational Causes*. Ronald Reagan, former President of the United States, spent his last years increasingly incapacitated by the growing impact of Alzheimer's disease (AD). It is well known that some of the loneliest people in this world are the relatives and others who care for loved ones with AD. As the years pass and the condition worsens, loneliness in the care-givers often increases, depression appears and gets worse, and other relationships suffer. The greater the loneliness, the greater the accompanying depression.[19]

These care-givers are lonely because of the special circumstances in with they find themselves. The same can be true of young people away from home for the first time, affluent people who seem to be in a financial class all by themselves, leaders who have moved ahead of or away from their peers, extremely talented people, those who are intensely dedicated to a sport or artistic venture, foreigners and newcomers to an area, older people who live alone, individuals who have been widowed or divorced, and compulsive workaholics. All have been identified as especially prone to loneliness, although it cannot be assumed that all of these people are lonely.

People with diseases or deformed bodies also can be prone to loneliness. In our society these individuals tend to be rejected by healthy people who say, by their actions if not by their words, "You are different," or "I don't know how to react around you." Sadly, as a result of this rejection, handicapped people tend to withdraw. Their physical conditions often prevent easy access to others, and further loneliness can result.

5. *Spiritual Causes.* In a famous prayer, Augustine once expressed our need for God: "Thou has formed us for Thyself and our hearts are restless till they find rest in Thee." God created human beings for himself, but he respected us enough to let us decide whether to rebel. This, or course, is what we have done, and human hearts have been restless ever since because we have been cut off from our Creator.

At the time of creation, Adam and Eve enjoyed intimacy with God and with each other, but when sin entered the human race, true intimacy disappeared. In its place came deception, defensiveness, blaming, self-interest, and power struggles. Loneliness often comes because sin has alienated us from God and from one another. Instead of turning to God in repentance and seeking restitution with fellow human beings, thousands of lonely people seek to escape from their loneliness through involvement with drugs, sex, work, sports, therapy, Eastern spiritualities, or a host of other activities that fail to remove the inner restlessness. When God is ignored or sin is unconfessed, loneliness and a deep inner sense of alienation often persist.

The Effects of Loneliness

What does loneliness do to people? What are the symptoms? How can it be spotted by a counselor? Because of human uniqueness, each person will show loneliness in a different way.

Surely, the most obvious indication of loneliness is *isolation* from people, often accompanied by periodic but futile attempts to reach out to others. Once again, however, it should be stated that many "loners," older people, singles, and others who live by themselves, are not lonely even though they appear to have little contact with others.

Low self-esteem and feelings of worthlessness can be symptoms as well as causes of loneliness. Failure in relationships or in activities can lower self-esteem and lead to greater loneliness. Unable to relate to others as they would like, lonely people sometimes withdraw into self-centered thinking, a poor-little-me attitude, the belief that nobody understands, and a conviction that things will never get better.

As we have seen, *depression* is also common. Some chronically lonely people are not depressed even as many depressed people are not lonely, but many are both. Lonely people sometimes have a hopelessness that can lead to despair and even thoughts of suicide. When loneliness is too great, suicide becomes a way out that might also be intended to give a clear message to the people who didn't seem to care.

In contrast, some people resort to *exhibitionist behavior*, like becoming the class or office clown, wearing outlandish clothing that is likely to be noticed, or acting in attention-getting ways. A few cover their loneliness by workaholic behavior, frequent travel, or accumulated possessions.

Substance abuse, including alcoholism, also comes from loneliness and provides a way to escape. People turn to these in an attempt to find friends among other abusers or to dull the pain of being alone.

Escaping into the worlds of *pornography* also provides temporary relief. Henri Nouwen wrote that pornography "is intimacy for sale." "In the many 'porno shops' [or online pornographic experiences] hundreds of lonely young and old men . . . gaze silently at the pictures of nude girls drawing their minds into intimate close rooms where some stranger will melt away their loneliness." Then they leave the world of virtual intimacy to return to "the contagious disease of loneliness in a world in which a competitive individualism tries to reconcile itself with a culture that speaks about togetherness, unity and community as the ideals to strive for."[20]

Others express their frustration through *violence*. Apparently, teenagers are well aware of this. Following shootings at Columbine High School that left several people dead, a survey of students in several high schools asked why the two young shooters had reacted as they did. The top causes listed were loneliness, family problems, and a desire for attention. Another listed cause was inattention from other students and teachers, both of which could contribute to loneliness.[21] Long before the Columbine tragedy, one writer reviewed the literature and concluded that "very lonely people, who get angry rather than depressed, will be prone to express their lonely frustration in destructive ways."[22] When loneliness is expressed with violence or delinquency, this may become a release from pain and a cry for attention.

Sometimes, loneliness is expressed in the form of *physical problems*, such as heart disease or high blood pressure. Like most of the problems discussed in this book, loneliness can be hidden from the casual observer, but it can have a profound effect on the body and sometimes shows itself through physical symptoms.

Counseling and Loneliness

There have been many suggestions for dealing with loneliness: get involved in church or community activities, join a volunteer organization, reach out to people in need, ask others about themselves to show your interest in them, learn to be assertive, join a fitness club, find fulfillment in Christ, and others. Many of these suggested remedies can dull the pain of loneliness for a while, but they fail to deal with the problem at the deepest level and rarely produce lasting solutions.

How, then, can the problem of loneliness be handled more effectively?

1. *Admitting the Problem*. Loneliness has a negative connotation in our society. For many people, admitting that they are lonely is like admitting that they are social misfits, unattractive, or unable to relate to others. Remind counselees that everyone is lonely at times. When people feel lonely, the first steps toward recovery are to admit the loneliness, to acknowledge that it is painful, and to decide to do something about its causes.

2. *Considering the Causes*. As we have seen, loneliness can arise from a variety of causes. If these causes can be identified—through discussions with the counselee

and through probing questions and careful listening—then it is possible to work on the sources of the loneliness rather than trying to eliminate the symptoms or urging more social involvement.

Is the counselee caught in social turmoil, driven workplaces, or the pursuit of success that brings alienation from others? Is the counselee afraid of intimacy, highly insecure in the presence of others, angry and inclined to alienate others, afraid of reaching out, or caught in some situation like a controlling or needy family, so there is no opportunity or motivation to change? These are all issues that could be dealt with in counseling, ultimately releasing your counselee to move from the cage of loneliness.

3. *Changing Thinking.* In considering the causes, try to remember that some things can be changed (such as a poor self-concept or inappropriate social skills), but others are unchangeable. The lonely widow, for example, cannot bring back her husband, and neither can we stop the modern tendency of people to move frequently—with the alienation and loneliness that this produces.

Even when circumstances cannot be altered, counselees still can be helped to change their attitudes toward loneliness. Often there is self-pity, pessimistic thinking, and ruminations about the unfairness of life. All of this needs to be gently but firmly challenged. Loneliness is unlikely to persist if people can be helped to see the bright side of life, even in the midst of disturbing personal and social change.

Sometimes, in our determination to uncover the deeper causes of loneliness, we miss what is simple and obvious. Some people need no more than to be guided into social activities, including contacts at work, with neighbors, or at churches. This contact can often pull people out of loneliness or a tendency to withdraw into self-pity and brooding. Reminders about the power, sovereignty, and compassion of God also can help people change their perspectives and see life in a more realistic perspective even when surrounding circumstances seem to be unchangeable and defeating. Sometimes, it helps to remind your counselee that loneliness does not always last forever.

Most of the people who come for counseling, however, have tried these more simple solutions, and yet the loneliness persists. They need something more.

4. *Developing Self-Esteem.* Lonely people must be helped to see and acknowledge their strengths, abilities, and spiritual gifts as well as their weaknesses. Most of us go through life silently talking to ourselves, and often we convince ourselves that we are unattractive, incompetent, or disliked by others. At times we compare ourselves to people who are more popular or successful, and in so doing we become convinced of our own inferiorities. As a result, individuals develop low self-esteem and possess little confidence to tackle new problems.

Counselees need to be reminded that in God's sight every human being is valuable and loved,[23] every sin can be forgiven,[24] each of us has abilities and gifts that can be developed, and all people have weaknesses that can be lived with and for which we can make adjustments. As a counselor, you can help counselees see that no person ever attains perfection in what he or she does, so we should quit striving for the impossible. Instead, we must learn to do the best we can with God's supernatural help, with the encouragement of a counselor or friend, and with the abilities and circumstances that we have been given.

Self-esteem is considered more fully in chapter 23. If this is a problem for the lonely counselee, it might be good to work on the self-esteem problem as an important step in conquering loneliness.

5. *Teaching New Behavior and Social Skills*. Sometimes, loneliness can be reduced when situations or ways of behaving are altered, corrected, or removed. For example, people can watch less television, spend more time in family activities, reevaluate their workaholic and self-centered lifestyles, or move into useful church activities.

All this reaching out may be difficult for some people because they lack the necessary communication and social skills needed to handle themselves appropriately in social situations. Counselors can point out social errors, teach individuals how to relate to others, and help counselees evaluate the effectiveness of their attempts to interact. Chapter 18 discusses relationships and may be of further help to counselors working with lonely people who lack basic communication skills and social finesse.

6. *Encouraging and Guiding Risk-Taking*. Even when someone does have a positive self-image, it sometimes takes great courage to reach out to others. What if people criticize or reject us? What if they fail to respond? That can be embarrassing and threatening. It is here that the counselor can provide the encouragement and support that the counselee needs as he or she risks making contact with others. To encourage social contact, ask the counselee, "To whom can you reach out?" "In what special ways can you reach out to make contact with others?" "What have you done or failed to do in the past that prevents contact with others and creates more loneliness?" "How can you avoid making these same mistakes again?" "If you take the risk of reaching out, what is the worst thing that can happen?" As counselees risk getting involved, the counselor can give encouragement and provide opportunities to discuss how this social outreach is working, where it might be failing, and how failure can be prevented.

7. *Meeting Spiritual Needs*. A once-popular Christian song began with the words: "Why should I be lonely? I have Jesus only." These lyrics implied that true believers have no need of human companionship. There is no doubt that many Christians find comfort and companionship in their walk with the Savior, but even while Adam was in the Garden of Eden, God declared that it was not good for human beings to be alone. People need each other if they are to avoid loneliness.[25]

From this we should not conclude that human contact is the only solution to loneliness. Loneliness never disappears completely until an individual is introduced to Jesus Christ. He loves each of us unconditionally,[26] died for us, makes it possible for us to come to him by confession of our sins, welcomes us as adopted children,[27] and becomes a friend who sticks closer than a brother.[28] His Holy Spirit lives inside of every believer,[29] helps us, prays for us, and makes us more Christlike.[30]

God is real and his presence can be sensed. He communicates through his Word and often through other people, even though we cannot hear him with our ears. God also is intangible; he cannot be touched or seen. This is where his tangible body, the church, enters the picture. The church should be a healing, helping community that radiates love, acceptance, and support. As a member of this community and a follower of Jesus Christ, the counselor should radiate this loving acceptance and point the counselee both to Christ himself and to the local church—which the Bible calls "the body of Christ" here on earth.

It is sad that many churches do not seem to show the love and acceptance that lonely people need. Self-focused and functioning more like an elite social club than an other-centered community, there are churches that rarely see visitors and almost never see them return for a second visit because they feel isolated and alone rather than accepted warmly. Outside of the counseling room, counselors have a responsibility for helping their churches become genuinely caring communities. After having dealt with hurting people all week, however, even counselors find it more comfortable to be a part of the social club that rarely reaches out.[31]

It would be wrong to assume that religious people are never lonely. On the contrary, one research study found no difference in reported loneliness between religious and nonreligious people.[32] The groups did differ, however, in the way they coped. Believers, especially theologically conservative Christians, were more likely to see God's hand in their loneliness and to seek divine help in facing the problem. For some, this became a reason to do nothing about their loneliness apart from prayer and waiting for God to act. For most of the believers, however, faith in God, prayer, and Bible study all helped make the loneliness more tolerable and open to additional ways of coping.

Some spiritual counselors would add that solitude can also be a way out of loneliness. Half a century ago, Thomas Merton the Trappist monk wrote, "It is in deep solitude that I find the gentleness with which I can truly love my brother. The more solitary I am, the more affection I have for them." Solitude "did not separate him from his contemporaries but instead brought him into a deep communion with them," according to Nouwen.[33] Also writing almost a half century ago, Paul Tournier concluded that solitude was one way to escape from loneliness.[34] Solitude does not put lonely people into face-to-face contact with others, but it does help many get free from the deep pain of feeling alone.

Preventing Loneliness

There are several ways by which the causes of loneliness can be attacked and the experiences of loneliness can be reduced.

1. *Strengthening the Local Church.* The local congregation can and should be the best antidote to loneliness. To prevent loneliness, people should be encouraged to worship in the church, to participate in church activities, and to accept the friendship of church members. Small Bible study or growth groups, informal social gatherings, church-sponsored workdays or community projects, group attendance at local concerts, participation in the choir or worship team—these are among the church ministries that provide community for lonely people to build meaningful contact with others.

As we have seen, not all church members are open to receiving new people, especially those who are different or appear to be social misfits. Some churches are cold, indifferent, and cliquish. Visitors may be ignored or greeted only superficially. In many parts of the world, the church is viewed with suspicion, especially by younger people who have grown up in a postmodern culture. They may be lonely, but they would consider aligning only with believers who are genuine, without pretense, and sincerely accepting.

In preventing loneliness, therefore, the church leader can encourage individuals to become involved with the church. In addition, he or she must model to church members how to accept, support, care for, love, forgive, and welcome individuals into the fellowship. For most of us, this is not easy. It can help to remind church members of how they felt when they were alone in a community. This is an era when many people are separated by distance from their natural families, so the church can provide a network of substitute families. Some churches attempt to provide meaningful activities on the weekends, when lonely people so often drift into bars and engage in casual sexual encounters and intimate experiences with strangers, all in an effort to find human contact, love, and companionship.

2. *Helping People Cope with Change.* Most of us want the experience of community with others, but we have full schedules and incessant demands on our time, so we also value freedom, convenience, and privacy. How, then, can people experience intimacy and closeness in an age that values mobility, computer technology, urbanization, television, VCRs, cocooning,[35] and other dehumanizing influences? Relationship building takes time, energy, and commitment. To develop a meaningful friendship, each person involved must commit to giving the time and effort needed to build the relationship, even though superficiality may be more convenient. Pulpit messages, seminars, and counseling sessions can all be used to help people manage their time or their relationships in ways that prevent loneliness.

3. *Building Self-Esteem and Competence.* We have seen that loneliness can occur because people are self-defeating in their attitudes or actions, immobilized by a poor self-concept, or lacking in effective social skills. By reducing or eliminating these problems, loneliness can be prevented. When children and adults learn social skills, communication ability, and healthy realistic attitudes toward life, they are better able to relate to others and avoid loneliness.

These skills can be taught in counselors' offices but also in schools, churches, or through seminars, books, articles, and tapes. Probably this teaching is most effective if it can be started and practiced in the home. Teaching family members to communicate openly; to respect and care for one another; to accept individual differences; to work, relax, and worship together are among the ways that counselors and church members can reduce loneliness and prevent its increase or recurrence.

4. *Stimulating Spiritual Growth.* Loneliness is reduced or prevented when individuals are shown how to build intimate relationships with God as well as with other human beings. People begin to experience more meaning in life when they learn the value of solitude, understand their gifts, build a closer intimacy with God, and discover his deep purposes for them. Helping people grow spiritually is one of the most significant ways of preventing loneliness.

Conclusions About Loneliness

Loneliness is a universal experience. It occurs in people of most cultures and in all parts of the word. Nevertheless, there are cultural differences in some of the causes, effects, and treatment of loneliness that we have considered in this chapter. Loneliness may be expressed, experienced, or handled differently among people who live in small rural communities as opposed to those who live in Jakarta, Athens, or Mexico City.[36]

Regardless of where we live, most of us reside in what might be called loneliness-producing societies where rapid change and modern technology discourage intimacy and stimulate loneliness. Even in homes and churches, people avoid one another. In an attempt to find closeness and escape inner feelings of isolation, many individuals throw themselves blindly into open sharing with strangers (like fellow drinkers, or seatmates on airplanes).

Caring relationships with others will help remove loneliness, especially when individuals can be free of hostility, poor self-esteem, social incompetence, and personal insecurity. But inner self-confidence and human togetherness, in themselves, will not give a permanent solution to the loneliness problem. We need to help people develop intimate relationships with God and learn the benefits of solitude. We need to help them build strong involvements with at least a few people, including family members, where there can be mutual openness, acceptance, and respect for each other's uniqueness as created by God.

KEY POINTS FOR BUSY COUNSELORS

➤ Loneliness is a painful inner emptiness that everybody experiences at times.

➤ Loneliness doesn't always depend on whether others are present. Some people feel lonely even when they are surrounded by groups or crowds; others can be by themselves and not feel lonely at all.

➤ Loneliness is not the same as solitude. Loneliness is a negative experience that comes when a person is forced to be alone. Solitude is a voluntary withdrawal from others that most often is positive.

➤ In the Bible, loneliness is not often discussed, but it is often seen in the lives of leaders, including Moses, Daniel, Jeremiah, and Jesus.

➤ The causes of loneliness can be divided into five categories.
  ■ Social causes include the impact of technology, the Internet, television, mobility, changing demographics, and busy lifestyles.
  ■ Developmental causes include unmet needs for attachment, acceptance, and the development of competent social skills.
  ■ Psychological causes depend in part on the person's perceptions and may include low self-esteem, self-defeating attitudes, depression, inability to communicate, lack of control, hostility, and fear.
  ■ Situational causes may involve illness in the family that pulls a person into the lonely role of care-giver, leadership that separates leaders from followers, the loss of a spouse, or moving to a new and unfamiliar community.
  ■ Spiritual causes center on a person feeling cut off from God.

➤ There can be many effects of loneliness, including feelings of isolation, low self-esteem, depression, exhibitionist behavior that attracts attention, substance abuse, use of pornography, violence, and physical symptoms.

➤ Counseling lonely people can involve helping them:
  ▪ Admit the problem.
  ▪ Consider the causes.
  ▪ Change thinking
  ▪ Develop self-esteem.
  ▪ Teach new behavior and social skills.
  ▪ Encourage and guide risk-taking.
  ▪ Meet spiritual needs.

➤ To prevent loneliness:
  ▪ Encourage the local church to be more caring and inclusive.
  ▪ Help people cope with change.
  ▪ Encourage the development of healthy self-esteem and greater competence.
  ▪ Stimulate spiritual growth, including the value of solitude.

➤ Loneliness is universal but it can be expressed and dealt with in different ways, depending on one's culture. Cultural differences should not be overlooked.

PART THREE

Developmental Issues

13

Childhood

The teachers called him a troubled child. His parents called him unmanageable. The other kids called him a variety of derogatory names. The neighbors called him a spoiled brat, and sometimes they called the police.

Kevin was only thirteen and still with a boy-sized body, but he could swear like a trooper, and he already had created more havoc than all the other kids in the neighborhood combined.

He was constantly at odds with his parents, in conflict with his teachers, and unable to get along with his peers. His three sisters hated him, and his presence in Sunday School always disrupted the class.

Kevin's mischief in the neighborhood was well known. Using a can of spray paint, he had left graffiti on the side of the local supermarket. Twice he had been caught shoplifting, and once he was suspected of starting a fire in a neighbor's garage, even though his guilt was never proven.

In an effort to reform their son, the parents sent him to boarding school one year. The discipline was strict, and Kevin seemed to respond well to the routine, but his behavior was even more out of control when he came home.

The school scheduled conferences. The juvenile authorities discussed his case. The family doctor prescribed tranquilizers. The parents went for counseling. Kevin went to a different counselor, and eventually the whole family was involved.

The problem was accentuated by the prominence of the parents. Kevin's father was a successful gynecologist, and his mother was involved in local politics. Both were active in their church. The counselor wondered if the parents were neglecting their son—if Kevin's attention-seeking behavior was an attempt to be loved and to get noticed by his busy parents. But Kevin's behavior didn't seem to change regardless of the amount of attention that came his way. The boy seemed to be sincerely sorry for his behavior and often vowed to change, but he seemed powerless to do so. Some men in the church concluded that Kevin must be demon-possessed, and they met with the pastor to discuss the possibility of exorcism.

One day Kevin's grandmother read an article about a chemical imbalance that sometimes leads to hyperactive, out-of-control childhood behavior. The parents were desperate and not much interested in some new theory about their son's behavior. Secretly, the father had concluded that Kevin would become a juvenile delinquent and probably spend the rest of his life in jail.

Nevertheless, at the grandmother's urging, Kevin was taken to a well-known clinic, where he was seen by a specialist in chemical disorders. The physician prescribed a treatment program consisting of a changed diet and the use of medication that would correct the imbalance in Kevin's system.

The change in this young man's behavior was radical. He and his family continued in counseling for a while, but before long Kevin was back in school trying to catch up on the things he hadn't learned. His behavior problems have largely disappeared and everybody is grateful—including the neighbors and the police.

In his infinite wisdom, God chose to entrust tender young lives to the guidance of adults (including some very immature adults) who have little or no experience in child-rearing, but who face a variety of challenges and perhaps an even greater variety of child-rearing articles and books. Some parents devour these books and even write to the authors, all in an attempt to become better mothers and fathers. Others ignore the advice-givers and try to do "what comes naturally." Better, perhaps, is the approach that gathers information and encouragement from books and more experienced parents, but then tries, *with divine help*, to do the best we can in the task of training up children in the ways they should go.

At times the Christian counselor will be involved in counseling with children directly, but more often the emphasis will be on parental guidance. This is the task of offering parents encouragement, information, advice, clarification, support, or other counsel that will help the child indirectly. Parental guidance recognizes that parents can influence children more profoundly than any counselor. It assumes a cooperative working alliance between the parents and counselor, sometimes in partnership with the school or community resources, all together interested in the welfare and maturing of the child. Literally, thousands of books have been written about children, childhood problems, and child-rearing.[1] In addition, thousands of research studies have investigated the abilities and psychological maturation of developing children, while other research has studied physical malfunctioning, psychological retardation, and childhood pathology. Pediatrics, the well-known medical specialty, has been paralleled by child psychiatry, child psychology and related specialties. Clearly, it is not possible to summarize in one chapter the massive literature that has built up in this field, but some general principles are identifiable and useful for the Christian counselor.

In all of this, the influence of cultural differences cannot be far from our minds. Every family is different—every community, every religious community, every country, every ethnic group. Generations differ as well. Significant moments in history change the ways in which parents look at their children and the environments in which children grow up.[2] Children born and raised during World War II or in Communist countries in the years that followed now look at the world and at child-rearing differently than the baby boomer parents or the younger parents raised in an era of emerging postmodernism. Every parent and every counselor brings a perspective, shaped in part by his or her generation, and sometimes this will impact the counseling. Despite these differences, there are biblical guidelines that are universal and basic to counseling children and their parents.

The Bible and Child-Rearing

Shortly after the creation, God instructed Adam and Eve to "multiply and fill the earth." Unlike most divine commands, this one was obeyed, and the world quickly filled with people. In Old Testament times a large family was considered a source of special blessing from God, and childlessness was regarded with reproach.[3] Today many people have chosen to limit the size of their families, but infertility is of deep concern to many couples, and children are still very important. Jesus showed them special attention and spoke of them highly.[4]

Biblical teaching on children and parental guidance can be divided into two categories: comments about children and comments about parents and parenting.

1. *Children.* In the Bible, children are seen as gifts from God that can bring both joy and sorrow. Young people are to be loved, honored, and respected as persons; they are important in God's kingdom, and they are not to be harmed.[5] Children also are given responsibilities: to honor and respect parents, care for them, listen to them, and be obedient.[6] "Children, obey your parents because you belong to the Lord, for this is the right thing to do," we read in Ephesians 6:1–3. "Honor your father and mother. . . . And this is the promise: If you honor your father and mother, 'you will live a long life, full of blessing.'"

Elsewhere in his writings, Paul strongly criticizes childhood disobedience,[7] but it seems unlikely that children are expected to obey forever. If parents expect compliance with something unbiblical, it should be remembered that God's laws always take a higher priority than human instruction.[8] It would seem, further, that adults who leave their parents and cleave to a spouse have moved to establish new families, although these families are never freed from the responsibility of honoring older parents.

2. *Parents.* Mothers and fathers have a responsibility to model mature Christian behavior, to love their children, to care for their needs, to teach the young, and to discipline fairly.[9] "Don't make your children angry by the way you treat them," Ephesians 6:4 states. "Rather, bring them up with the discipline and instruction approved by the Lord."

According to one commentator,[10] we anger and exasperate children when we abuse them physically, abuse them psychologically (by humiliating them and failing to treat them with respect), neglect them, don't try to understand them, expect too much from them, withhold love unless they perform, force them to accept our goals or ideas, and refuse to admit our mistakes. In contrast, we "bring them up" by being examples to our children and by giving instruction and encouragement. All of this is more easily discussed than accomplished. Children, like parents, have different personalities, and the biblical directives for child-rearing are not as specific as many people might like.

In the Old Testament, however, there is one section that puts all the principles together and summarizes the biblical teachings about child-rearing. Although this was written for the Israelites prior to their entrance into the Promised Land, these paragraphs have great practical relevance for modern child-rearing and parental guidance.

> These are all the commands, laws, and regulations that the LORD your God told me to teach you so you may obey them . . . and so you and your children and grandchildren might fear the LORD you God as long as you live. If you obey all his laws and commands, you will enjoy a long life. Listen closely, Israel, to everything I say. Be careful to obey. Then all will go well with you, and you will have many children in the land flowing with mild and honey, just as the LORD, the God of your ancestors, promised you.
>
> Hear, O Israel! The LORD is our God, the LORD alone. And you must love the LORD your God with all your heart, all your soul, and all your strength. And you must commit yourselves wholeheartedly to these commands I am giving you today. Repeat them again and again to your children. Talk about them when you are at home and when you are away on a journey, when you are lying down and when you are getting up.[11]

Christian parenting involves the following:

(a) Listening. The good parent wants to hear God's commandments and to understand them so well that these become an integral part of one's being. This learning comes through regular study of God's Word, the Bible, made clear to us by the Holy Spirit.

(b) Obeying. Knowledge is not enough. In addition to hearing, parents must be intent on keeping God's decrees and commands. It is possible that when parents show no apparent desire to obey God, their children, in turn, are less inclined to obey parents.

(c) Loving. We are to love the Lord and give ourselves to him wholeheartedly—heart, soul, and strength. Notice that the emphasis here is for the parents. In spite of their importance, children are not prominent in the Bible. Although we read that Jesus grew psychologically (in wisdom), physically (in stature), spiritually (in favor with God), and socially (in favor with others),[12] we know very little about his childhood. The early years are important, but children are with their parents temporarily and then they leave—as God intended. Parents, therefore, do not exist primarily for their children. Parents exist first as individuals who love and serve God. If we are given children, then raising them is part of our life purpose, but this is not our only purpose.

(d) Teaching. There are four ways by which teaching is to be done:

- Diligently. Even though child-rearing is not a parent's sole task in life, it is an important responsibility that is not to be taken lightly.
- Repeatedly. The Scriptures indicate that teaching is not a one-time effort. It is to concern parents repeatedly, continually, through the day and night.
- Naturally. When we sit, walk, lie down, and rise up, we are to look for teaching opportunities. Daily family devotions are valuable, but parents are to teach whenever the opportunity arises.
- Personally. What one says is rarely as influential as what one does. This returns us to the first part of the Deuteronomy passage. When parents listen, obey, and love, they provide a model for children that reinforces what is being said in the home.

Notice the words "in the home." Peers and teachers are important, but the most significant teaching and child-rearing occurs at home.

Causes of Problems in Children

In 1799 a young boy was found running naked in the woods near Aveyron, France. The child was unable to communicate, behaved like an animal, and apparently had not had human contact for a number of years. The young boy, known to generations of psychology students as the wild boy of Aveyron, was sent to Paris, where, with patience and determination, a physician named Jean-Marc Gaspard Itard undertook the task of trying (largely in vain) to rehabilitate the boy.

If he were living today, Dr. Itard might not be any more successful in his rehabilitation efforts, but he would have considerably more evidence to help him understand why children and their parents have problems during the child-rearing years. Complex theories of childhood development and psychopathology have described how young people mature and why problems develop. Specialists have analyzed the causal roots of diverse issues such as mental retardation, childhood depression, a variety of learning disorders, speech pathology, excessive rebellion, violence, childhood schizophrenia, and the difficulties many young people have in adjusting to frequent moves, parental divorce, periods of hospitalization, adoption, the threat of terrorism, and other childhood stresses.[13] As the books and articles continue to appear, it becomes apparent that the more we learn, the more complicated the problems seem to become.

At times, children and their parents do not even agree on what constitutes a problem. A parent may view disobedience as a source of family stress, but the child may not see this as a problem at all. An issue that might not be a problem at one age (bed-wetting, for example) only becomes a major issue if it persists into later childhood or adolescence. Sometimes, the neighbors or school officials may think some child has a problem, but the parents may disagree. Despite these differences, several themes appear repeatedly in discussions about the causes of problems in children and in child-rearing.

1. *Spiritual Neglect or Abuse*. Psychology textbooks almost never recognize the spiritual bases of child development, but this is important to biblical writers.[14] Psalm 78:1–8, for example, emphasizes that children should receive spiritual instruction so they will put their faith in God, remember his faithfulness, and not become unruly, stubborn, or rebellious. The Scriptures clearly teach that biblical education is beneficial to children; its absence surely is harmful. Equally harmful, no doubt, is a rigid indoctrination that crams religion into young minds, pictures God as a boring and stern disciplinarian, and leaves no room to let young people ask questions and grow into spiritual maturity.

2. *Instability in the Home*. When parents cannot cope with their stresses or when they do not get along with each other, children can feel anxious, guilty, and angry. They are anxious because the stability of the home is threatened, guilty because they suspect that they may have caused the strife, and angry because they often feel left out, forgotten, and sometimes manipulated into taking sides, which is not what they want to do. They may fear being abandoned physically or psychologically. To escape the pressures and often to express their anger, thousands of young people run away from home in an effort to find security elsewhere. Sometimes, these runaway kids are victims of parental instability, but other issues may be the cause. These include parent-child conflict over school performance, inability of parents to cope with their children's mental-health concerns, cultural differences, marital strife between the parents, inappropriate family boundaries, and harsh discipline.[15]

Instability in the home can lead to a variety of behavioral problems in children. Falling grades, conflict with other children, including bullying, or petty crimes, can all indicate problems at home and a cry for help. Even so, many children from unstable homes do survive family stress and grow into normal, successful, and well-adjusted adulthood. These are the resilient children that we discussed earlier. Efforts continue to determine why some children from unstable homes are resilient but their brothers and sisters are not. Even so, it remains true that unstable homes tend to produce unstable children.

3. *Psychological Abuse*. The physical abuse of children (an issue that we discuss with more detail in a later chapter) has attracted a lot of popular and professional attention within recent years. Less noticed are the actions of parents who never hurt their children physically but abuse them psychologically. When they are

rejected subtly or overtly, nagged and criticized excessively, punished unrealistically (or not at all), disciplined inconsistently, humiliated persistently, shown love spasmodically (or never), or threatened periodically with abandonment, children often experience personal problems or show disruptive behaviors that, in turn, are annoying to parents. Child development experts have alerted us to the harmful effects of parental overprotection, overpermissiveness, overstrictness and overmeticulousness—all of which can arouse anxiety and create insecurity in children.

It should not be assumed that psychological mistreatment is always deliberate. Many parents are confused or overwhelmed by child behavior, insensitive to their children's needs, and unsure how to respond. Think, for example, of the problems faced by immigrant parents who must deal with unfamiliar circumstances, food, language, and expectations. Their children go to schools where they learn the ways of the new culture even as the parents try to raise their offspring according to what they learned in their culture of origin.[16]

Other parents are tense and have a low tolerance for the essentially normal behavior of active children. Anxious parents, for example, often disengage from their children, praise the children less, and ignore them more. Eventually, the parents' anxiety gets passed on to the children, but when the children show signs of anxiety, the parents do not give much support. They try to squelch the anxiety instead of teaching their children how it can be handled in better ways.[17]

All of these parents need understanding, encouragement, and guidance so that psychological abuse and its harmful consequences can be reduced, eliminated, or prevented.

4. *Poverty.* Jesus spoke often about poverty, but the topic rarely makes its way into counseling books, even though the majority of the world's population is poor, including the majority of children. Of course, many poor homes have loving parents and relatively stable environments, but a disproportionate number of poor kids are exposed to harmful conditions.[18] These include family turmoil, chaotic households, anxiety, limited educational opportunities, environments that do nothing to stimulate young minds, unhealthy living conditions, overcrowding, noise, and parents who tend to be uninvolved in their children's activities. In addition, there probably are hundreds of thousands of children who grow up in homes where parents struggle with alcohol, drugs, the effects of sexually transmitted diseases, and the inability to control their anger, handle stress, or deal with conflict and frustration. Sometimes, these people live in neighborhoods that are dangerous, and where violence is a daily experience, along with the fear of having nothing to eat. There are no simple counseling tools to help children from these environments.[19] More often they need outside intervention from caring individuals and groups who can help them get free of the effects of their poor environments.[20]

5. *Overscheduled Lifestyles.* Periodically, counselors and social observers awaken to see a problem that was previously unnoticed or ignored. This is the opinion of William Doherty, a perceptive American psychologist who believes that the major problem of the early twenty-first century is hyperactive, overscheduled lifestyles. "For many kids, childhood is becoming a rat race of hyperscheduling, overbusyness, and loss of family time."[21] Sometimes, children have no time to play, and they go to school tired because of their busy schedules. When parents and children have busy lifestyles, family time is sacrificed. Doherty cites a University of

Michigan research finding that more meal times at home, together as a family, was the strongest single predictor of better achievement scores, fewer behavioral problems, and better psychological adjustment.[22] When asked to list their major concerns, one poll of teenagers found that "not having enough time with my parents" was at the top of the list.

This problem of being overly busy may not be an issue to all the readers of this book, but in many parts of the world it is a huge concern. And it does appear to have a serious impact on children and on how they are raised.

6. *Unmet Needs.* Psychologists do not always agree on what to include in any listing of basic human needs. The needs for security, acceptance, discipline, or encouragement are included in most lists, and some counselors have noted that gifted children or those with disabilities have special needs that differ from those of their peers. Most important, however, is the need for love. Even if other needs are met, when children are deprived of love, maturation can be hindered, and problems frequently develop.

7. *Physical Influences.* Generations of parents and pediatricians have known that prolonged illness, hospitalization, and surgery can all be confusing and disruptive to children. The amount of disruption will depend on the nature of the illness, the organ systems affected, the types of treatment required, the reactions of parents or other significant adults, and the child's ability to cope with it all. The stress of serious illness often leads to intense anxiety, negativism, withdrawal, resentment of parents, fear, and other psychological reactions.[23] Illness is difficult for any of us to handle; it is especially hard for children and for their parents.

To illustrate how physical influences can lead to child-related problems, let us consider two examples.

(a) Mental Retardation. This might be defined as a condition of below average intellectual functioning—an Intelligence Quotient (IQ) of 70 or below, when the average is 100. Depending on the severity, mentally retarded people (mentally disabled people is a more commonly used term) can have difficulty with school work, communication, self-care, decision making, and getting along with others. The people who are mildly disabled may show no obvious signs of their intellectual defects. They can learn and are able to hold simple jobs. Of the more severe forms of retardation, Down's syndrome is probably best known, largely because of the distinctive facial features.

Mental disabilities can come from a variety of causes. Many children fail to develop normally because they live in impoverished environments where there is so little stimulation that brain development is slowed and intellectual functioning is hindered. The wild boy of Aveyon (whom Dr. Itard named Victor) was assumed to be retarded, probably in part because of his lack of intellectual and social stimulation. However, he had enough intellectual capabilities to survive alone in the woods for what was assumed to be several years. More severely disabled children, including those with Down's syndrome, are victims of physical malfunctioning. Genetic abnormalities, prenatal disease, head injuries, or other complications at the time of birth, infant infections, nervous system damage, and a variety of acquired childhood diseases have all been listed as causes of retardation.[24]

These physical influences often create irreversible mental conditions that counselors cannot eliminate. Nevertheless, you can help parents, family members, and retarded people adjust. Sometimes, parents need help in facing the reality of the child's disabilities and in answering questions about rearing a retarded child. In addition, counselors can give support, encouragement, accurate information, and guidance as parents struggle with their feelings of guilt and disappointment.

(b) Attention Deficit Disorder. This has been called "the best studied yet the most controversial" of all disorders arising in children, accounting for "more child mental-health referrals than any other single disorder.[25] The symptoms often persist throughout life, but they tend to be spotted first in grade school children or in those who are younger. Characteristics include an inability to concentrate or pay attention, distractibility, impulsivity, impatience, inability to relax, hyperactivity, disorganization, mood swings, feelings of low self-confidence, difficulty in getting along with peers, sleep disorders, and anxiety. Children often have difficulty playing quietly, don't seem to listen, have problems in following instructions, and talk excessively (parents might say "incessantly"). Many of these people are "always on the go" and feel as if they are "driven by an internal motor." This has led to the term Attention Deficit Hyperactivity Disorder (ADHD), although some people with ADD do not have the hyperactivity.

Frustrated teachers and parents often urge these children to "settle down" and to stop squirming and fidgeting. For many this is physiologically impossible, but sometimes adults don't realize this and try to calm the behavior with punishment and criticism. Too often, when there is little adult understanding or supervision, the disruptive behavior at age four turns into more serious behavior problems by age eight and leads to adolescent aggression, defiance, substance abuse, and sometimes depression and suicide.

ADD is a genetic condition that appears in families and almost certainly arises from a chemical deficiency in the brain. In many cases there is a startling change in behavior and a reduction of the symptoms, including the hyperactivity, when the chemical dopamine is replaced through the use of medications. The condition was first diagnosed in the nineteenth century, but it came into more prominence in the later decades of the twentieth century. In some countries it still is not recognized; in others, ADD is assumed to be the cause of almost all behavior problems. As a result, the condition is too often misdiagnosed, and children are sometimes given medication when it is not needed.

Christian counselors can help parents and teachers understand the facts about ADD, get an accurate diagnosis, and arrange for medical treatment from a competent physician who understands the condition. Many counselors, learning specialists, nutritionists, and ADD coaches also have developed measures to help both children and adults with ADD manage their lives more efficiently.[26]

8. *Child Victimization.* Is the victimization of children more prevalent in these times when we live, or has it always been present but not noticed? Regardless of the answer, there is evidence that millions of children are victims of harm that comes from both insensitive peers and exploitive adults.

(a) Peer Victimization. Every morning, thousands of children are afraid to go to school because they know they will be taunted, teased, or physically harmed by other children. Bullying is nothing new, but for a long time it was ignored or seen as a normal part of human development. Within recent years, however, bullying and other forms of peer harassment have become a major concern among educators, parents, and counselors. Books and research articles from all over the world have documented the harmful effects of bullying, both on the victims and on the perpetrators.[27] Bullying is not restricted by age (for example, bullying of adults in the workplace is common), and neither is it limited by gender, although some evidence suggests that males are more inclined to be bullies than females.[28] Bullying can impact children by creating anxiety, lowered self-worth, academic problems, feelings of loneliness, and poorer overall adjustment in schools. In contrast, school bullies sometimes have prestige, power, good grades, and respect from their peers, but we might wonder what kind of adults these bullying children become in later life.[29]

(b) Victimization from Adults. The exploitation of children by adults is a major international social problem. In addition to children who are exploited by their parents or their governments to work or to serve in military conflicts, the trafficking of children for sexual exploitation has become the third largest illegal industry in the world after trafficking in drugs and firearms. This is not limited to parts of Southeast Asia. It is an international problem that exists in the United States as well as elsewhere.[30] Closer to your counseling center or church, an unknown number of children are exploited by parents, teachers, clergy, coaches, youth leaders, and others. Often these children suffer in silence because they are afraid to report the abuse, or they don't know whom to tell.

9. *Other Influences.* Traumatic early experiences (such as accidents, a serious fire in the home, severe weather, or a near drowning), peer rejection, the serious illness or death of a close friend or relative, and the frustration of failure can each lead to problems in later life. As a result of these and similar experiences, children can develop unhealthy self-concepts, preoccupation with danger, a fear of failure or rejection, continuing insecurity, or an attitude of bitterness and rebellion. Reading this could be discouraging to counselors and parents, who might wonder if it ever is possible to raise a child successfully and without the development of severe problems.

Undoubtedly, it is true that all of us are wounded on the way to adulthood, but two facts need to be remembered when we consider these issues. First, it appears that most children grow up normally in spite of parental mistakes and failures. Even when the home has abusive, psychotic, or desperately poor parents, many resilient children respond by developing extraordinary competence.[31] Poor home situations or traumatic childhoods do not always produce problem children.

Second, there are times when problems arise through no fault of the parents. When their children rebel or go wrong, many parents blame themselves, but the problems may arise from other sources. Peers can be very influential in leading each other astray, and sometimes the child's failures or rebellion are really attempts to assert independence. Even if parents could be perfect, the possibility of rebellion and problems still exists because children have minds and free wills of their own.

Of course, no one could be more perfect than God, and yet Isaiah's prophecy shows that even God had problems with his kids. The book of Isaiah begins with these words: "This is what the LORD says: 'The children I raised and cared for have turned against me.'"[32] Child problems are not always caused by parental failures. This realization can be a source of encouragement to the parents of problem children.

The Effects of Problems in Children

When he was a boy, the Old Testament prophet Samuel received a message from God about Eli the priest. "I am going to carry out all my threats against Eli and his family. I have warned him continually that judgment is coming for his family, because his sons are blaspheming God and he hasn't disciplined them."[33] It is not surprising that the young Samuel was reluctant to pass on the message that he had received, but soon Eli and his rebellious sons died. When Samuel grew up and became a leader, his own sons were a source of embarrassment. They did not walk in the ways of God but became dishonest, greedy, and willing to accept bribes, even though they were judges. The Bible does not say if Samuel had neglected his parental duties, but the children still turned from God and behaved dishonestly. When parent-child problems occur, this can influence the society, parents, and the children.

1. *Society Effects.* Counselors most often work with individuals, couples, or small groups. We see the impact of trauma or other problems in the lives of our counselees, and this is where we focus our work. Too often, perhaps, we forget how entire communities are impacted by the events that can disrupt the lives of children. Our eyes are opened whenever a local child disappears, a distraught parent murders his or her own children, or a pedophile begins to operate in the neighborhood. These are reminders that the whole church or community is impacted, sometimes intensely, when a child or family among them is hurt. At times, counselors or spiritual leaders will be called upon to bring healing to these communities in response to the traumatic events.

2. *Parental Effects.* It is difficult for parents to have their children "turn out" differently than parents had hoped. Fathers and mothers often feel—with or without good evidence—that childhood problems have come because the parents are incompetent. This can lead to frustration, discouragement, conflict between the husband and wife, anger expressed toward the children or toward innocent other people, guilt, fear of what might happen next, and sometimes frantic attempts to assert authority and get back in control. On occasion there may be attempts to defend or protect the child, but often this is mixed with anger because of a belief that the young person should not need defending or protection. Then, there are parents who appear to be like Eli—unwilling or perhaps powerless to do anything about a deteriorating situation, so they watch as things get worse.

3. *Child Effects.* When there are parent-child problems, the children sometimes act in ways similar to parents. Anger, hostility directed toward parents and other family members, guilt, frustration, and fear can all occur. Unlike parents who can express themselves verbally, children often resort to nonverbal means of expression. Temper tantrums, rebellion, underachievement (especially in school), delinquency, fighting, silliness, excessive crying, dawdling, and other attention-getting behavior are ways of saying nonverbally, "Notice me. I'm hurting too!" Of course, this rarely is conscious or deliberate, and we cannot always assume that these behaviors mean that the child senses something is wrong. Neither does the absence of such behavior mean that the child is oblivious to the problem. Sometimes, children are afraid to express themselves, or they may not know how. Adults use words to communicate, but children, especially young children, lack the verbal abilities and the abstract thinking abilities to express themselves in

words. As a result, they express themselves through their actions or through their play. If there has been trauma or if there is fear, children may try to deny reality, or they may quietly conclude that they are incompetent failures. The seeds of inferiority and low self-esteem are being planted, even though they may not bloom into prominence until much later in life.

4. *Pathological Effects*. Sometimes, more severe disturbances develop, all of which indicate the existence of problems in the children, and some (but not all) imply that there are problems in the home. Even when parent-child relationships are good, these conditions put a strain on the family and often indicate a need for counseling.

(a) Psychophysiological Disorders. These physical reactions include asthma, ulcers, bed-wetting, and headaches. Each may have physical causes or may come as a psychological reaction to severe stress, strict discipline, disappointments, loss of family members, or a smothering mother-child relationship. Children with these disorders should be seen by a physician, but often counseling can help both parents and children handle stress better.

(b) Developmental Disorders. Sometimes, speech, motor, social, thinking, or other abilities are slowed down by family pressures, frequent moves, or other stresses. Eventually, most children catch up, but even temporary developmental slowdowns can be difficult for everybody in the family.

(c) Personality Disorders. As is true in adults, children sometimes are not aware of conflict or anxiety, but they develop personalities that are high-strung, overly inhibited, isolated, excessively independent, or distrustful. Sometimes, anxiety is seen when children experience extreme discomfort in separating from parents or other secure figures (separation anxiety disorders), or have school phobia, the fear of what might be encountered in school.[34] All of this can reflect inner tension.

(d) Disruptive Behavior Disorders. When a child is frustrated by the environment, he or she may express the frustration and anger in the form of frequent temper tantrums, delinquency, disregard for the rights and feelings of others, and sometimes aggressive or sexually impulsive behavior. Sometimes, known as conduct disorders, these behaviors are a reaction to frustration that involves "lashing out" at others but without any feelings of remorse or desire to change. Society, including parents, is burdened with the effects of aggression and with the challenge of attempting to rehabilitate the aggressor.[35]

(e) Mood Disorders. All of us, including children, get depressed at times. In addition to feelings of sadness and deep disappointment, depressed children often withdraw, refuse to eat, are apathetic, have physical complaints, and sometimes run away or show sullenness, aggression, or immobility. None of this is serious if it comes periodically and is short lived, but the prolonged appearance of these symptoms indicates more troublesome underlying problems. Some of these depressed children try to escape from their tensions by attempting to kill themselves.[36]

(f) Adjustment Disorders. Psychological functioning is likely to be hindered when conflicts are held within or when aggressive and sexual impulses are denied or suppressed. Anxiety, irrational fears, excessive guilt reactions, sleeping disturbances, poor self-images, eating disorders, and compulsive behavior all may be clues that something is bothering the young person within.

In more severe cases, emotionally disturbed children show bizarre behavior, severe fears, extreme withdrawal, lack of self-control, and irrational thinking, to list a few symptoms. Childhood schizophrenia is a more severe form of pathology characterized by hallucinations, delusions, disorganized speech, and a deterioration in functioning.[37] A different condition is the infantile autism seen in very young children. This condition is characterized by withdrawal, emotional blandness, repetitive behavior, and fascination with inanimate things (such as a chair) rather than with people. All of these are examples of disorders that will require intervention from a mental-health professional.

(g) Attachment Disorders. Early in life, children bond with trusted adults who provide nurture, stability, and emotional security. Usually, the first of these attachments is with the mother or other primary care-giver, but later others are taken into the circle of people who can be trusted. When attachments are lacking, it is difficult for children to form and maintain intimate relationships. When the attachments are broken—by events such as the death or disappearance of a primary care-giver, abuse or neglect by a trusted adult, frequent hospitalizations that remove the child from home, placement in foster homes, or traumatic events such as sexual abuse or injury—the child is robbed of the ability or courage to trust the world as a safe place. As a result, children can become fearful, emotionally demanding, disruptive, and lacking in social skills.

(h) Learning and Communication Disorders. These are widespread and relatively common.[38] They include reading disorders, problems with speech, poor learning skills, difficulties in listening and comprehending, writing difficulties, or impairment in mathematical skills. These are not necessarily the result of low intelligence or poor schooling. They can occur in very bright children and in children from homes with highly intellectual parents. Sometimes, these disabilities occur because the child has hearing or visual problems, but they also happen because of the ways in which the brain is developing. Apart from correcting hearing or visual difficulties, most of these problems can be corrected by special education given by specialists trained in helping children with learning difficulties.

Sometimes, these disabilities reflect childhood stress and anxiety, often arising from unstable or disruptive home situations. Whatever the cause, when children learn slowly or have difficulty expressing themselves, they may be ridiculed by peers, criticized by parents, or pressured by teachers. All these factors can damage the child's self-concept and make the learning disabilities worse. If these children grow older without improvement, there can be school failures, truancy, self-condemnation, delinquency, and subsequent adult irresponsibility and employment difficulties.

Each of these conditions will concern parents and can affect the child's development adversely. Usually, these conditions are treated by physicians, psychologists, educators, and others who are specially trained in children's problems. Unless the Christian counselor is a specialist in these areas, he or she should seek professional consultation if it is available, or should refer the child and parents to some person who specializes in the disorders of childhood.

Counseling and Problems in Children

Christian counselors have three responsibilities in working with the problems of children: counseling the children, counseling the parents, and making referrals. In each case you may do one, two, or all three.

1. *Counseling Children*. Unlike adults, children (especially very young children) often lack the verbal skills or self-awareness to discuss their feelings and frustrations verbally. Because of this, child counselors often observe children at home, ask them to make up stories, or watch as the young people play with doll families, draw pictures, model with clay, or play house. These and other play-therapy techniques,[39] along with the use of psychological tests, are used by child specialists to build rapport, elicit information, uncover childhood problems, and provide opportunity for giving help.

Even though children differ from adults psychologically, cognitively, and developmentally, it should not be assumed that talking is never helpful. Children are spontaneous and sometimes share their worries and concerns openly, often when they are drawing or playing. During these times, you can ask questions about what makes the child happy or unhappy, what is scary, what is the funniest or saddest thing he or she can think of, what the child would ask for if he or she had three wishes, or similar questions that have potentially revealing answers. In addition, counseling may involve instruction, skills training, the demonstration of kindness and respect, and the giving or withholding of reinforcement.[40]

Child counselors should remember the obvious but easily forgotten fact that children are people. They have feelings, needs, and insecurities. At times they try to manipulate adults, but children respond to love and firmness. They need to be treated with sensitivity, empathy, warmth, consideration, and a respect that does not treat them with disdain or convey a smug adult superiority.

Although the goals of child counseling largely depend on the stated and identified problems, counselors also seek to reduce irrational fears and disturbing behavior, resolve conflicts, increase the child's ability to express feelings, improve interpersonal relationships at home or school, and teach skills. In working with children, most counselors use a variety of approaches in reaching their counseling goals. It is not surprising that some counselors have developed special expertise in working with children.

Whatever methods are used or goals are established, it is important for the counselor to work in partnership with parents. Some counselors prefer to have the parents in the room when they work with children, but this depends, in part, on the age of the child, the child's level of comfort with the counselor, and the counselor's preferences. Whether or not the parents are in the room, it is important to include the father as well as the mother as part of the counseling process. Mothers most often bring the children for counseling, but increasing evidence shows that fathers also need to have active involvement.[41] While some parents may feel uncomfortable or threatened when they have a child in counseling, most are cooperative and supportive, especially when the counselor shows that he or she can express hope, understands the parents, and welcomes their involvement in the treatment.[42]

Of course, some childhood problems develop because of problems in the home or between the parents. Often, then, the counseling of children occurs in conjunction with the separate counseling of the parents.

2. *Counseling Parents*. Sometimes, the Christian counselor will first come into contact with the "problem child" and then make contact with the parents. More often, it is the parents who come seeking help, and the child is seen later, with or without the parents being present. The ongoing involvement of parents in the overall counseling process is important both because parents give additional per-

spectives and because they have the ability to undermine your counseling work if they are uncooperative, threatened, or uninformed about what you are trying to accomplish. Sometimes, helping the entire family to function better may be the best way to help the child.[43]

(a) General Issues. There are several general guidelines for working with parents regardless of the specific problem. These include the following.

Appreciate the parents' position. Child-rearing can be frustrating, and in spite of their failures and mistakes, it can be assumed that most parents really want to succeed in this task. It doesn't help, therefore, to blame, criticize, or demean the parents with whom you counsel. Try to discourage parents from condemning each other for the child's problems. Attempt to understand their perspectives and express your desire to work together in helping them help their children.

Use various approaches. Some parents need nothing more than simple information or a clearer understanding of their situation. Others may need advice, cautioning, support, encouragement, and/or suggestions for dealing with problems. Some parents have a good idea about what to do, but they need a counselor to give a little push and offer "backup" support once they take action. At times you will have to gently challenge parental myths (for example, "children should be seen and not heard," "all teenagers are rebellious," or "boys are harder to raise than girls"). Frequently, you may decide to break down a problem into smaller issues that can be dealt with more easily one at a time. It is only after listening and observing for a while that counselors can decide on suitable guidance techniques.

Be sensitive to parental needs. In raising their children, many parents feel self-doubt, a sense of being overwhelmed, competition (perhaps with the child or with a spouse over the child's affections), jealousy, a fear of losing one's children, or a need to exercise authoritarian control over the family. When these needs are intense or when they are unmet, tensions often result. In your counseling, you should identify, discuss, and reevaluate these needs.

Be aware of family dynamics. Family systems therapies treat entire families rather than focusing on individual family members. Whenever a child (or adult) has a problem, it is assumed that the whole family is dysfunctional in some way, and the whole family comes for treatment. As a simple example, consider the child who develops behavior problems and falling grades when his mother goes to work. Counseling the child alone could be helpful, but it would be better to involve the whole family in discussions about ways of adapting to the mother's dual career. Whenever you counsel with children, try to learn about family issues that might be creating or complicating the child's problems.[44]

Model the parental role. Even when we are not aware, counselors model parenting traits such as good communication skills, a willingness to understand, and sometimes a kind firmness. If the counselor talks to the children in the parents' presence, this can be an example of adult-child respect and interaction.

Recognize that you are expendable. One goal in counseling is to promote maturing, Christ-centered relationships between family members. The counselor is a facilitator of this process. His or her ultimate plan is to withdraw from the situation when the counselor's services are no longer needed. To help you reach this goal, one psychiatrist has recommended two valuable approaches.[45] When advising parents to do something the child won't like, such as being stricter or less inclined to give in to the child's demands, state this to the parents with the child present. This lets the counselor take the blame, helps the parents feel less guilty, and motivates them to carry out the recommendation. In contrast, when encouraging the parents to do something the child will like, such as relaxing restrictions or spending more time together, tell the parents privately, without the children present. This lets the parents take full credit for the pleasant changes and does not put them in a position where their children can criticize them when the counselor's recommendations are forgotten or rejected.

Someone has said that an effective parent is the child's most important counselor. If this is true, then one important way to help children is to teach parents how to be effective in helping their sons and daughters.[46] Sometimes, known as *filial therapy*, this is an approach in which the counselor meets regularly with the parents and serves as a coach, helping them apply principles described in this chapter. This works best when at least one parent is relatively well adjusted and when the children are free of severe internal conflict.

(b) Theological Issues. The Bible says relatively little about the family, compared to what it teaches about the church. According to Gene Getz, this is because "the Christian home in the New Testament world was almost synonymous with the Church. . . . What was written to the Church was also written to individual families . . . the family is really the *Church in miniature*."[47] Issues that concern the church—evangelism, Christian education, the teaching of moral standards and compassion, helping young people learn about the meaning of life and death—are issues that parents also must face in raising their children. Parents who are failing in these areas should be challenged and helped to make their homes more alert to the presence of Jesus Christ and the guiding power of the Holy Spirit. The Christian counselor must be willing to raise and discuss these and other theological or moral issues. This is a crucial aspect of effective Christian counseling with parents and children.

(c) Psychological Issues. Several psychological issues commonly arise as parents are counseled.

First, there often is a need for *understanding*. One way to help parents understand is to encourage them to think of the world and the family from the child's perspective. Remind parents that children have feelings and the need for significance, security, acceptance, love, praise, discipline, and faith in God. It can help to discuss specific examples of conflict or misunderstanding. What happened? Why? How could the situation have been handled better? Be careful to acknowledge that parents need understanding too.

Second, families should be helped with *communication*. The principles of good interpersonal relations that we discuss in chapter 18 can apply within the family and can be shared, modeled, and practiced in counseling sessions. If they want to communicate with their children, parents should model good husband-wife communication. The family should establish a time for communication, perhaps over dinner. Children need to know that their opinions, gripes, and experiences are of interest to their parents, and the parents should show a willingness to listen. Parents also can share their ideas, experiences, frustrations, and dreams. Although there should be no limits on the subject matter to be discussed, these open times of family discussion should be free of disrespectful language or long nagging. Each family member should be encouraged to talk, but in addition each should have a right to privacy and personal opinions. Sometimes, the family must agree on rules such as "no interruptions until the person who is talking has time to finish." When questions are raised, they should be answered honestly and fully. All of this takes time to learn and is difficult to put into practice. Teaching these communication skills can be an important part of counseling.

Third, *behavior management* is of concern to many parents. Most know that punishment can be a way to curb undesired behavior, and it may instill some respect for authority. But punishment tends to lose its effectiveness if it is repeated too often, and it rarely brings permanent change. More efficient is rewarding desired behavior and not rewarding undesired behavior. If the child's whining and temper tantrums are ignored, for example, they usually disappear if the parents persist in their refusal to yield. In contrast, little things like words of approval, stars stuck on a chart (for younger children), the reading of a story, or other reinforcers can help mold a child toward more positive behavior. Parents can be taught how to give such reinforcements immediately after desirable behavior. With the counselor's help, parents can decide what behavior they want to instill. Then, they decide on the steps necessary to bring this about, and reinforce each specific behavior that helps move the child toward the desired goal. This type of program sometimes can be taught by counselors who have only a small knowledge of reinforcement principles, but for more extreme cases it is better to refer to a specialist.

Behavioral principles like these appear to work best when there is general stability in the family and a high level of involvement between the father and the children. One research study on "taming tyrants" in the home found that traditional individual counseling did not work well. More effective were programs that educated parents in how to interact with their children, how and when to give positive reinforcement (like praise and hugs), how to deal with undesirable behavior, and how to instruct children effectively.[48]

As we stated earlier, much of your counseling will involve teaching parents how to be more skillful and effective in their child-rearing. Parents often get discouraged because their children are not learning social skills such as politeness, good grammar, athletic capabilities, effective study habits, or remembering to pick up clothes that most often get "hung" on the floor. Sometimes, parents need encouragement, mixed perhaps with a little humor.[49] You can help parents understand that many of these childhood actions are common and will disappear in time. Point out that parents can help best when they give gentle reminders to their children, try to avoid nagging, praise desirable behavior, and lower their parental expectations—at least a little.

(d) Special Problem Issues. Parents often express concern about special problems such as autism, bed-wetting, stuttering, school phobia, aggressive behavior, excessive nightmares, intense fears, or reactions to traumas such as accidents, deaths, or hospitalization. Many of these problems are transitory, and often they are evidences of anxiety. For example, nightmares or other expressions of terror during the night can arise from fears that occur during the day: overstimulation from books, interactive computer programs, video or television programs that are seen especially at bedtime. Fears of hospitalization or worry over death often surface when a grandparent or other significant person dies. These fears reflect anxiety about the unknown fear of being harmed, abandoned, or rejected.

Bed-wetting and stuttering may indicate that the child feels pressure from parents and others, pressure that sometimes increases as the bed-wetting and stuttering persist.

As a counselor, you can teach parents how to give reassurance, approval, acceptance, and support. Fears are best discussed openly in the home, and over-stimulation with anxiety-arousing technology or stories should be avoided. It often helps if parents are encouraged to discuss their concerns with teachers or with other parents who have dealt successfully with the offending problem. If none of these simple tactics relieves the symptoms, counselors may want to consult some of the books that deal more in depth with these special problems faced by children.

(e) The Issue of Disturbed Parents. Sometimes, children are brought to counseling by parents who want help for themselves but are too embarrassed to ask. More often, parents are less aware of their own problems, but it becomes clear to the counselor that the child's symptoms result from parental problems. When these parents are helped to deal with their own problems and insecurities, children often improve spontaneously as a result. The counselor must not impose counseling on parents who do not want it, but whenever children are brought for help, it is important to be alert to parental problems, many of which can be handled in the context of discussing the child. For example, a parent might be asked, "What could you do differently to help solve this problem?" This could open the opportunity to talk about parental frustrations, fears, and actions.

It is not unusual for parents, especially younger parents in poorer neighborhoods, to lose patience with their young children and respond with beatings that are intended to silence the child but do severe harm instead and sometimes even cause death. At times parents are severely disturbed or so overwhelmed by their own problems that they are unable to meet their children's needs effectively. Child abusers, socially incompetent people, or substance-abusing parents are examples. The counselor has the challenge of providing stability and strength for these parents and their children, while helping them deal with conflicts in themselves and in their homes. This is a difficult task that requires experience, resilience, and the capacity for endless patience to deal with constant complaining, trivial resentments, endless blaming, breaking appointments without warning, telephone calls at all hours of the day or night, unexpected withdrawals from the counseling process, and sudden reappearance with loud demands for immediate help. Often these parents are threatened by counseling, afraid of change, or concerned that government agencies will take their children elsewhere for their own protection. All of this reduces to a denial of problems and an unwillingness or an inability to cooperate in counseling. To work with parents and children of these families, counselors must be flexible and at times willing to make referrals or seek guidance from more specialized professionals.

3. *Counseling Referrals.* Child counseling is a specialty within the helping professions. The Christian counselor who works mostly with adults may wish to refer children and their parents, especially disturbed parents, to counselors who are more skilled or experienced in the treatment of children, families, or adult psychopathology.

Preventing Child-Rearing Problems

Not long ago, *American Psychologist*, the journal of the American Psychological Association, published a special issue titled "Prevention That Works for Children and Youth." A variety of articles cited research to document the extent to which preventive programs can work effectively to prevent childhood, adolescent, and child-rearing problems. According to the editors, "the widespread implementation of effective prevention programs for children and youth is a sound investment in society's future."[50]

The professional research has focused on prevention in several areas: the family, the school, the community, and health-care centers.

- Family: Abundant evidence shows that a positive family environment (with positive parent-child relationships, parental supervision, consistent discipline, and family values that are communicated clearly) is the major reason that young people do not engage in delinquent or other unhealthy activities. Counselors can help by reducing family conflict, ineffective parenting, parental stress, parental depression, and inappropriate parenting methods.[51]
- School: The primary function of schools is to concentrate on teaching and learning. But problems often breed in schools, so teachers and others have the opportunity for taking action to prevent problems from escalating or even from starting in the first place. Programs to help troubled students, special learning opportunities, systematic monitoring and accountability, and partnerships with parents all help to prevent problems.[52]
- Communities: Delinquency, substance abuse, bullying, health problems, and family violence are among the behaviors that can be reduced significantly when people in communities work together through their government, the media, community agencies, athletic leagues, parenting classes, and community-wide recreation programs for children and family, among others.[53] To this might be added the growing importance of keeping child molesters from children. For many years pedophiles and other sex offenders were assumed to be harmless and easily spotted by their mannerisms around children. It is now known that most molesters befriend their future victims, build trust with the parents or local church leaders, and even work in local schools or volunteer in community projects or church programs. Pastors, parents, and counselors can join together with communities to prevent life-long harm to children from predators in their midst.[54]
- Health-Care Settings: Doctors, nurses, and other health-care professionals have always been interested in preventing physical problems. Within recent years, psychologists and other counselors have been partnering with hospitals, clinics, dental offices, and other treatment facilities to help people change behavior and prevent psychological as well as physical problems.[55]

All of this may be of mild interest to Christian counselors. Nevertheless, it illustrates partnerships that can be developed to prevent childhood and child-rearing problems, especially if you are a counselor who has a special interest in this subject.

Perhaps you have noticed one significant omission in all of these professional writings. They fail to recognize that in all of society there is no institution that can match the church in its potential influence on childhood, parenting, and family development. Although this is less common than it was a few years ago, entire families still come to church. They bring their infant children for dedication or christening, and often they return consistently for church services, Sunday School classes, relationship building with other worshipers, and spiritual help in times of need. In a variety of ways the church can prevent family problems through its influence on child-rearing.

1. *Spiritual Training.* Earlier in this chapter we discussed biblical teachings about the home and child-rearing. Sermons, Christian education classes, seminars, retreats, and small study groups can all teach families how to build Christian homes. Parents can be guided into becoming exemplary believers. They can learn to teach their children in accordance with the approach outlined in Deuteronomy 6, making spiritual issues a normal part of family discussions.

The home is the backbone of society, and stable Christian homes are built on the guidance that comes from the Bible, often through the church.[56]

2. *Marital Enrichment.* When marriages are good and growing, this influences the children positively by creating stability and security at home. Problems with children can put a strain on the parents' marriage, just as marital problems can adversely influence the children. Stimulating good marriages, therefore, is one way to prevent child-rearing problems.

3. *Parental Training.* Parenting can be a difficult and sometimes overwhelming responsibility. On occasion almost all parents feel that they have failed, and most have periods of discouragement and confusion. At such times parents need understanding, encouragement, and guidance concerning the needs and characteristics of children. Christian leaders can provide this help. Suggest books or other helpful resources on child-rearing. Alert parents to the child's need for security, love, discipline, self-esteem, acceptance, and an awareness of God's presence. Point out the dangers of overprotection, overpermissiveness, overrestrictiveness, and overmeticulousness. Emphasize that both parents need to be actively involved in child-rearing; abundant evidence shows that the presence of fathers leads to children who grow up with fewer emotional problems. Then, as part of parent training, it may be helpful to consider the principles of effective parent-child communication, teach ways to discipline, talk about behavior management, and discuss how children's needs can be met. All of these may be discussed in church settings where parents can share with one another.

Be careful to emphasize that while child-rearing is a serious responsibility, everyone makes mistakes, and parents who are too rigid or "uptight" probably create problems because of their anxiety and inflexibility. Child-rearing can be difficult and challenging, but it also can be fun—especially when parents can discuss their mutual concerns informally with other parents, including Christian counselors.

4. *Encouragement.* A man was invited to speak to a group of teenagers and asked his daughter what to say. "Tell them," the daughter replied, "that they should be patient because their parents are just learning how to raise kids."

This is a simple message that should be proclaimed to both parents and children. It is biblical to encourage one another,[57] and there are times when family members should be encouraged, prayed for, given verbal emotional support, and reminded that all of us are "just learning."

Conclusions About Counseling Children and Their Parents

The statistics keep changing, but the vast majority of the world's population consists of children and young people. Millions of these kids are growing up in poverty. Millions are exploited sexually or by governments and rebel groups that conscript them into child labor or military activities. Millions are trying to make their way in a troubled world without caring parents. Some of these young people roam the big cities, street kids surviving as best they can. Missing, exploited, and runaway children have become a major social problem in many Western countries. Perhaps millions of kids around the world live in homes with parents who don't care about their children, who abuse them, or who are absent for prolonged periods of time.

In the midst of the needs, it is easy to feel helpless and sad. Relief agencies and sympathetic governments do what they can, but too many children grow up without love and without social skills to function successfully in this complex world. Far too many never hear about the love of Christ. Individual counselors can give to relief agencies, and maybe we can take short-term trips to places where there are children at risk. Mostly, however, the Christian counselor does what he or she does best. We work with families and children in our own communities to help them deal with problems, prevent problems, and grow into mature Christ-following adults who can, in turn, impact future generations of children. The Christian counselor who works with children and parents has a high calling.

KEY POINTS FOR BUSY COUNSELORS

➤ When children have problems, almost always this means counselors must work both with the children and with their parents.

➤ The Bible views children as a gift from God. Parents have a responsibility to model mature Christian behavior, to love their children, to care for their needs, to teach the young, and to discipline fairly.

➤ Even as there can be a variety of problems in children, these problems can arise from a variety of causes, including:

- Spiritual neglect or abuse.
- Instability in the home.
- Psychological abuse.
- Poverty.
- Overscheduled lifestyles.
- Unmet needs.

- Physical influences, including mental disabilities and attention deficit disorder.
- Victimization from adults or from other children.

➤ More severe pathological problems in children include the following, any of which might appear when you counsel children:
  - Psychophysiological disorders.
  - Developmental disorders.
  - Personality disorders.
  - Disruptive behavior disorders.
  - Mood disorders.
  - Adjustment disorders.
  - Attachment disorders.
  - Learning and communication disorders.

➤ Christian counselors have three responsibilities in working with the problems of children: counseling the children, counseling the parents, and making referrals.

➤ All of this should be done with an attitude of sensitivity, respect, and understanding.

➤ In working with parents, try to:
  - See and respect the parents' position.
  - Use various approaches.
  - Be sensitive to the parents' needs.
  - Be aware of family dynamics.
  - Model the parental role.
  - Recognize that you are expendable—and try to work yourself out of your work with the family, so that they can function without your help.

➤ Parents may need help with understanding, communication, and practical skills in managing behavior.

➤ Counselors should be aware of the issues of:
  - Special childhood problems that may require you to get more specific information.
  - Disturbed parents who may need help more than their children.
  - The importance of making referrals.

➤ The family, the school, the community, health-care facilities, and the church can all play a role in preventing childhood problems.

➤ Problems relating to children can be overwhelming because they are so complex and prevalent around the world. The Christian counselor who works with children and parents has a high calling.

Adolescence

His parents named him Patrick Charles. His family calls him PC. His friends call him cool and fun to have around. His teachers call him a troubled child. His basketball coach calls him a great player. His parents call him surly and disrespectful. His youth leader at church calls him disruptive. He calls himself a free spirit, not willing to be bound by rules and traditions.

PC is a teenager, making his way through the time of life when he is no longer a child but not yet an adult. During the childhood years, things went smoothly at home and at school, but he always chafed under his parents' discipline. He didn't like the rules and boredom at church, and sometimes he got into trouble at school. When PC became a teenager, his rebellious streak became more apparent.

He started dressing in ways that his teenage friends liked, but his parents did not. He stopped going to church, started experimenting with drugs and sex, got a tattoo on his neck where others would notice, spent hours playing video games and getting involved with Internet pornography, began hanging out with other teens whose values and language disgusted his conservative parents, had some minor run-ins with the police, and did not even try to do homework or cooperate with teachers. One day he got into a fight at school and was suspended for a week. His overwhelmed parents decided he needed to be straightened out by a counselor, so they made an appointment and marched their son into the counselor's office.

PC slouched in the chair and showed his defiance by the way he sat, crossed his arms, and glared. He saw the counselor as a part of the system, an ally of his parents, and PC was in no mood to cooperate. With everyone together in the same room, the counselor asked the parents to describe the problem, and then they were excused. Alone with the counselor, PC refused to talk.

Weeks passed before he began to trust this man with all the psychology training. The counselor was patient, understanding, and not inclined to push PC into changing his behavior. As trust built, PC began to describe his frustrations, to talk about his boredom at school and church, to express his frustration with his controlling parents. Eventually, the counselor began to see PC as a confused child in a man's body, struggling to make sense of life, overwhelmed by his fears and his hormones, chaffing for independence, but longing for acceptance, stability, relationships, and answers to some of life's ultimate spiritual questions. Working with his young counselee and with the parents, sometimes together and sometimes separate, the family slowly began to change. It's a change that is ongoing and will continue, probably as long at PC is in the home. It's a change that is coming because a compassionate Christian counselor took the time to understand the family of a teenager, to pray for the family, to share insights and observations, to engage PC and his family in serious conversation, and to show acceptance, firmness, and Christian love.

If you are age eighteen or older, you have been through adolescence. Perhaps that period of your life was both stressful and exciting. For you it may have been what psychiatrist Armand Nicholi called "the most confusing, challenging, frustrating, and fascinating phase of human development."[1] Wherever you were during those teenage years, it is probable that your adolescence was different from that of everyone else. It depended on your family, community, country of residence, physiological makeup, personality, peer groups, and religious beliefs. Each of us was shaped, as well, by events in the world when we were adolescents. Teenagers today live in a teenage culture that is radically different from the teen cultures during World War II, during the sixties, or in other decades when the Internet, cell phones, or video games were nonexistent.

The word *adolescence* means a "period of growth to maturity." It begins at puberty (the beginning of the growth spurt and sexual maturation) and extends to the late teens or early twenties when the person largely is able to manage his or her own life. This is a time of physical, sexual, emotional, intellectual, and social change when the young person moves away from dependence on parents and protective confines of the family and toward relative independence and social productivity. Depending on the environment where one grows up, adolescence can be a time filled with friends, television, video games, iPods, music, sports, study, jobs, hobbies, and other activity, frequently accompanied by a lot of sexual activity and a variety of stresses. Adolescence also can be a time of reflective thinking about spirituality, values, relationships, and life purpose. The teenager's world can be confusing and changing so quickly that immature young people aren't always able to keep up and often don't adjust efficiently.

This has led some to describe adolescence as a highly disruptive period characterized by rebellion, perpetual turmoil, conflict, and stormy periods of stress.[2] This popular view does not find much support in professional psychological publications or in the experiences of adults who work with young people. Research studies confirm that adolescence is a period of rapid growth and frequent change, but it probably is true that "taken as a whole, adolescents are *not* in turmoil, *not* deeply disturbed, *not* at the mercy of their impulses, *not* resistant to parental values . . . and *not* rebellious."[3] It has been estimated that between 10 percent and 20 percent of adolescents experience serious turmoil during the teenage years, but this figure is about the same as that of children and adults. All of this suggests that adolescence is not a particularly stressful period of life and that the vast majority are free of trouble and special stress during the teenage years.[4]

Nevertheless, people in this age group do go through a significant change period, which includes adjusting to great social pressures, a variety of physical changes, and the challenge of making life-determining decisions about values, beliefs, identity, careers, lifestyles, and relationships with others, including those with the opposite sex.

Adolescence can be divided into three overlapping periods: *preadolescence* (sometimes called "pubescence" or "early adolescence"), beginning around age ten or eleven and continuing for at least a couple of years; *middle adolescence*, the period from ages fourteen to eighteen when the young person is in high school; and *postadolescence* (sometimes called "late adolescence" or "young adulthood"), which includes the late teenage years and extends into the early twenties.[5]

Preadolescence. This period begins with a bursting of biological changes that can evoke simultaneous feelings of anxiety, bewilderment, and delight. In both sexes there is a spurt of growth, especially in the limbs (this creates clumsiness and a gangly appearance), a change in body proportions (boys widen in the shoulders and develop thicker muscles; girls expand in the hips and develop breasts), a lowering of the voice in males, an enlargement of the sexual organs, an increase in sex hormones, the growth of pubic hair, an increase in the size of skin pores with more active glandular activity (this often leads to acne), and the appearance of hair on the face and body, which, of course, generally is heavier in boys. A need for new emotional adjustments comes with the beginning of female menstruation and the occurrence in young males of both ejaculations and a sharp increase in the frequency of erections. During the past hundred or more years, there has been a steady decline in the age of first menstruation and first ejaculation of semen. This means that the onset of adolescence has been occurring earlier in life.

These physical changes have social and psychological implications. Most adolescents have times when they feel awkward, self-conscious, and dissatisfied with their physical appearance. Often there is difficulty in controlling emerging sexual urges, and people who develop quickly or slowly often feel embarrassed, especially in the locker room, where their peers easily observe and sometimes comment freely about the differences. Girls who feel awkward about using sanitary pads or young males who have erections at the most unexpected and potentially embarrassing times are bothered by these preadolescent influences.

Peer influences and pressures, the insecurities of shifting into middle school or high school, the development of close friendships, hero worship and "crushes" on people of the opposite (or same) sex—including adult "idols" in the entertainment world—all indicate social adjustments during this period. There is, in addition, a new spirit of independence from parents, sometimes accompanied by increased conflict in the home. The development of more abstract, self-critical, and reflective thinking leads to an initial questioning of parental values and an increased ability to worry and be anxious. All of this is accompanied by increased peer friendships and influences.

Middle Adolescence. This period has fewer physical changes, but the adolescent must adapt to his or her new identity as a person with an adult body. Sexual urges become more intense, especially in boys, and control is difficult in view of peer pressures, strong needs for intimacy, and the temptations from a sexually permissive society that no longer considers self-control to be important or even possible. The result has been an upsurge in the number of sexually active teenagers (including those associated with the church), and a staggering increase in the number of teenage pregnancies[6] and sexually transmitted diseases (STDs).

Peers become increasingly significant as adolescents seek to break away from parental influences, values, and controls. The family still provides money, transportation, and a place to live and get the laundry done, but teenagers often criticize parental standards and may have decreased desire to accompany parents to church, on vacations, or on shopping trips. Depending on the family, communication at home may be minimal, but daydreaming is common, and long hours are spent talking with friends on the telephone, playing Internet games, or surfing the web. There is a great desire to be accepted and to identify with current teenage language, heroes, music, styles of dress, and forms of entertainment. But teenagers often like to maintain their unique identity, so they strive for individuality within the cultural expectations. Dating or other relationships with the opposite sex also become very important, and "breakups" are extremely painful.

During this period several issues become important, including sex, drugs, motor vehicles, and technology. Each of these relates to the peer pressures, physical changes, insecurities, and adolescent struggles for identity. The need for love and acceptance, the influence of sexual hormones, the sexual openness in society, the values portrayed in movies and television, and the relative ease of finding privacy (such as in a car) make sexual intercourse and other forms of sexual behavior a common experience for adolescents, even though this often causes guilt, self-criticism, and sometimes pregnancy. The use of drugs, including alcohol, has always characterized adolescence, especially those who are seeking an unusual experience, escape from anxiety and boredom, or acceptance with drug-using friends. Cars and motorcycles also lead to greater acceptance from peers and provide a way to express power or bolster feelings of security. Technology, especially the Internet, creates easy access to pornography, potentially addictive video games, communication with a variety of strangers, and other potentially harmful influences.

Hidden behind all these influences is the pressure to face some serious challenges about the future. According to the Barna Research Group, nine out of ten teenagers think about the future every week, even though most feel poorly prepared for that future.[7] Future issues include thoughts about choosing a college or finding a job, leaving home, shifting responsibility onto themselves, and coping with the subtle but often unconscious attempts of parents to keep their growing children dependent and close to home.

Postadolescence. This is the period that begins in the late teenage years. The young person in this period usually has a good ability to think abstractly and make plans for the future. He or she is faced with the tasks of moving into adult society, assuming adult responsibilities, shifting to a more independent status, and formulating a distinct lifestyle. Planning for the future, focusing on further education, and moving into a career are all tasks that take time and energy. There is less concern about how one looks. Dating tends to be more serious, and going steady

---

Table 14-1

Teenage Personalities

According to the Barna Research Group, teenagers can be divided into four overlapping personality niches.

- **Interactives**, which include almost half the teenage population, are highly personable, focused on relationships, and sensitive to others. They live with a relaxed approach to problem solving and tend to be hospitable and minimally influenced by stress.
- **Dynamos** represent one-quarter of the teen world. They are aggressive, focused, driven, above average in productivity, and effective problem solvers. They also can irritate others with their high energy, competitiveness, and self-assurance.
- **Stabilizers** describe about one-fifth of adolescents. They are marked by consistency, loyalty, thoroughness, and predictability, but they also can be rigid and lacking in creativity.
- **Evaluators** are the smallest group. They like details and insist on accuracy and completeness. They tend to be perfectionists who put high demands on themselves and others.[8]

becomes more common as they anticipate marriage, even though most will not marry until later.

During this period of life, at least four important questions need to be answered. Each of these has been considered during the previous years, but each can become more focused in late adolescence.

1. The Question of Identity: "Who am I?" Early in life, children imitate and identify with their parents and family members. Later they model their behavior after admired adults, develop relationships with peers, and then struggle, at least in Western societies, to develop their own self-concepts, uniqueness, values, and identities.[9] For many, adolescence can be a time of self-searching, anxiety, confusion, experimentation with lifestyles, and drifting goal-less behavior.

2. The Question of Relationships: "How do I get along with others?" In addition to developing relationships with both sexes, adolescents must learn how to build intimacy with selected peers, how to set boundaries, how to fit into society, and how to shift the nature of the parent-child bond so there is less dependency on parents. During the adolescent years, attempts to learn social skills and build meaningful relationships can be seen in activities that include teenage "crushes," conflicts with authority, gang behavior, sexual involvements, hero worship, "best-friend" relationships, petty squabbles, resistance to adult suggestions, and yielding to peer pressure. More mature relationship building takes over as the high school years end.

3. The Question of the Future: "Where will I fit?" The answer to this question depends in part on one's strengths, values, personality traits, capabilities, socioeconomic level, and family expectations. Choosing a career can be a difficult decision, and adolescents, like people in their twenties and thirties, often make a number of vocational "false starts." Because they are idealistic and sometimes overly optimistic, young people may move in unrealistic career directions. This can lead to frustration, pessimism, and the need to reevaluate vocational choices.

4. The Question of Ideology: "What do I believe?" This includes but goes beyond questions about religion. Spirituality is a popular topic among this generation, but many adolescents have a widespread distrust of religion, especially highly organized, denominational religion that appears to be rigid and controlling. Adults may not be willing or able to give answers, but young people need to struggle with these issues on their own. Many wonder about a number of troubling issues that the older people in their lives rarely seem to discuss. These issues change from year to year and from place to place, but they can include questions about why so many people in this world go hungry; why some people live in poverty while others freely flaunt their affluence; why terrorism seems to have such a powerful foothold; why governments continue to go to war when centuries of history have shown that wars rarely solve anything; whether certain religious or political views are really "right"; what is wrong with free experiences of sexuality; why it is useful to attend worship services; or why the Bible, religious leaders, or the government should be sources of authority. In their attempts to find what they believe and why, young people have always asked hard questions of their generation. In the process of finding answers, adolescents develop their own values, religious beliefs, and life philosophies. In the end, often these are not as far removed from parental values as the parents might have feared.

What Are Mosaics?

People currently in the teenage years and early twenties are sometimes known as the mosaics—a term that may stick with them as they get older. Unlike some who are older, the mosaics are nonlinear in their thinking style and comfortable with contradictions in their spirituality, values, politics, and morality. They are less constrained by relationships, traditional sexual standards, religious and spiritual beliefs, or lifestyle choices. This is a group that has grown up with postmodern influences. They are heavily impacted by the Internet and are the most information-overloaded generation ever. They value diverse experiences and are constantly bombarded by advances in technology. Put all of this together, and we have a mosaic of ideas, lifestyles, choices, spiritualities, possibilities, and creative alternatives all seen in a "mosaic" group of young people.

Perhaps overwhelmed by the generations that are now reaching adulthood, or unwilling to face their questions, many people who are older cannot or do not want to respect or to take the mosaic generation seriously. Potential mentors tend to pull away and fail to help younger people define their values or mark out their paths in life. Perhaps it is not surprising that many adolescents struggle with feelings of inner emptiness, confusion, interpersonal tension, and anxiety.

The Bible and Adolescence

The concept of adolescence, as we know it, did not appear in the literature on child-rearing until late in the nineteenth century. The word *adolescent* does not appear anywhere in the Bible, and it may be that the biblical writers did not think of adolescence as a separate period of development. As we saw in chapter 13, childhood and youth are mentioned frequently in Scripture, but we have no suggestion that these are separate periods and no indication of when this period ends. The Bible's teachings on children, therefore, undoubtedly apply to "children" of adolescent age.

Scripture also speaks of "young men" and "young women." For example, the writer of Ecclesiastes, writes, "Young man, it's wonderful to be young! Enjoy every minute of it. Do everything you want to do; take it all in. But remember that you must give an account to God for everything you do. So banish grief and pain, but remember that youth, with a whole life before it, still faces the threat of meaninglessness."[10]

It is unlikely that Jesus ever faced meaninglessness in his younger years. In what appears to be a summary of his early life, the book of Luke tells us that Jesus "grew both in height and in wisdom, and he was loved by God and by all who knew him."[11] A more detailed glimpse into his early life is given in Luke 2:41–52, where we read about the family trip to Jerusalem when Jesus was twelve. Clearly not a typical adolescent,[12] Jesus pulled away from his peers and family members to have in-depth discussions of deep questions with the religious teachers. The discussion must have been so engaging that he missed the family caravan going home. His disappearance caused a lot of anxiety for Mary and Joseph as they rushed back to Jerusalem and looked everywhere for three days in "frantic searching" for him. "Why have you done this to us?" Mary asked. Apparently, the only sinless adolescent who every lived still caused his parents anxiety and inner reflection as he grew toward adulthood.

Overall, young people growing into adulthood are portrayed in Scripture as visionaries who are strong, able to incorporate the Word of God into their lives, capable of overcoming Satan, expected to be submissive to elders, and instructed to humble themselves "under the mighty power of God, and in his good time he will honor you. Give all your worries and cares to God, for he cares about what happens to you."[13] These few phrases, like the teachings of the entire Bible, can be helpful to counselors who work with young people struggling with adolescence.

The Causes of Adolescent Problems

Adolescent society changes quickly, and it is easy for adults to be out of touch with contemporary teenagers. In spite of the changes, several issues persist and create problems for adolescents regardless of the countries or times in which they live. When counselors are aware of these issues, they can be more perceptive in giving useful help.

1. *Physical Changes*. Adolescents can be influenced psychologically by uneven physical growth, skin problems, excess fat, periodic decreases in energy, changes in body proportions, development of body hair, lowering of voice pitch, and other physical changes. At a time when it is important to look attractive, a teenager's physical development can bring embarrassment and dissatisfaction, especially if biological changes are obvious to others or if maturation is slow in coming. Late maturers tend to be treated as children by both peers and adults. This can lead to problems in social adjustment and feelings of rejection. Although these effects of late maturation usually can be overcome, some young people carry their insecurities and adjustment problems into adulthood. All of this is complicated by the widespread awareness that at least in the United States, teenagers, as a group, are not in good health. Many are out of shape, overweight, physically unfit, and not inclined to exercise or to eat nutritionally.[14]

2. *Sexual Changes*. Even when they are expecting the sexual changes of adolescence, most young people experience anxiety over the physical changes in their bodies, the increasing erotic impulses within, and the confusion about sexual behavior. Sexual fantasies, masturbation, heavy petting, and adolescent intercourse can all produce guilt, at least in some teenagers. Crushes on people of the same sex can lead to concerns about homosexuality. Intimate contact with others can increase the fear of AIDS or sexually transmitted diseases. Sudden physical growth can create confusion over one's identity and uncertainty about how to act appropriately as an adult male or female. Dating may be feared and desired at the same time. Sexual struggles in teenagers are enhanced by the sexual freedom in contemporary society, a parental reluctance to give clear sex education, and frequent opportunities to engage in sexual experimentation.

In addition, declining moral standards leave many adolescents confused. One study of American adolescents found, for example, that sex outside of marriage was considered morally acceptable by 54 percent of the mosaic generation as opposed to 40 percent of their baby boomer parents. Other findings showed that cohabitation was considered morally accepted by 75 percent of mosaics compared to 60 percent of boomers. Looking at sexually explicit pictures was acceptable to 50 percent of mosaics and 38 percent of boomers. The comparable figures for the acceptability of having a sexual relationship with someone of the same sex were

40 percent and 32 percent.[15] All of this can lead to confusion about what is right or wrong, along with greater concerns about self-control, guilt, unwanted pregnancies, and the emotional trauma that follows.

3. *Interpersonal Changes*. As we have seen, adolescence is a time when there are changes in relationships with parents, peers, and others. It is important to be liked and accepted by other adolescents, especially those of the opposite sex, but even as they move away from parental control, young people need to feel that their environments have stability. Adolescents often feel confused, anxious, and angry when there is a lack of parental guidance, conflict in the home, instability at school, or nothing in the world that seems to be stable.

4. *Changing Values, Morals, and Religious Beliefs*. Prior to adolescence, the young person may accept parental standards with little question or challenge. As they get older, however, adolescents begin to question parental viewpoints, and peers have a greater impact on the molding of core beliefs and values. Often, young people get no help with the process of values clarification except from other equally confused and struggling teenagers.

It is generally accepted that the commonly accepted values and beliefs of one generation may differ greatly from the values of those who were adolescents a few years earlier. Within the past several years, for example, attitudes toward sex have been changing, and there have been changes in beliefs about the roles of women, the acceptability of homosexuality, or the importance of career success. Many of these and other value changes appear to reflect changes in adult thinking and behavior.

Concerning spiritual values, it is common for adolescents to conclude that religion is boring, outdated, and irrelevant. Much to the distress of parents and church leaders, many teenagers drop out of church-related activities but turn to other forms of spirituality. In addition to explorations of alternative religious groups, teenagers now have the ability to explore spirituality topics on the Internet. Often, however, they lack the critical skills to differentiate between valid information and that which can be harmful and manipulative.[16]

One writer interviewed 250 teenagers and their families to discover what they really believed.[17] She concluded that many young people between ages 11 and 21 value personal experience over traditional religious authority. They consider themselves to be spiritual but not religious. Often they gravitate to a spirituality that blends elements from the Judeo-Christian-Islamic tradition with new interests in mysticism, Eastern religions, and the occult. Many are fascinated with what author Lynn Schofield Clark calls "the dark side of evangelicalism" with its focus on demons, hell, the apocalypse, and frightening stories about the end times. This is supplemented by movies, television programs, and popular books about vampires, angels, aliens, supernatural forces, and the end times. Perhaps it is not surprising that many teenagers are confused and turned off by anything religious that seems irrelevant to their lives.

None of this should overlook the phenomenal work of many churches and parachurch groups that are effectively reaching teenagers with empathy, respect, compassion, patience, and clear values. As we will note in the next chapter, after periods of exploring, young people often long for beliefs that are time tested and shown to work in authentic communities of believers. These young people are drawn to vibrant spiritual groups that show faith in action rather than to churches and groups that focus on words, rules, criticism, or lackadaisical attitudes toward religion. All of this can alert older Christians, including Christian leaders and counselors, to the fact that we in the church may be ignoring pressing adolescent issues while we seek to answer questions that nobody is asking or provide programs that most teenagers do not want.

5. *The Move to Independence.* Aware that they are no longer children, adolescents want freedom in large doses, but they handle it better in small and slowly increasing amounts. What young people want and think they can handle often differs from what parents are willing or think it wise to give. This can create tension, frustration, rebellion, and persisting power struggles. An old cliché says that parents often find it easier to give their children roots than to give them wings.

6. *Acquiring Skills and Building Self-Esteem.* Often, teenagers do not feel good about their physical attractiveness, intelligence, athletic abilities, relationships, or finances. Frequently, there are feelings of self-criticism, social incompetence, academic and athletic ineptness, and spiritual failure. These feelings are emphasized whenever there is criticism, social rejection, or the inability to succeed in some important area of life.

Sometimes, self-esteem problems come because adolescents lack social skills. Each of us must learn how to cope with stress, deal with disappointment, study effectively, manage time, interact smoothly with others, resist temptation, hold a job, mature spiritually, relate to the opposite sex, or handle money. These are some of the survival skills that individuals must learn if they are to get along smoothly in life. When adolescents have limited opportunities to learn these skills, adjustments to life can be much more difficult.

7. *Concerns About the Future.* Late adolescence has been called a period when young people are free to regroup psychologically and socially while they seek to find their niches in society.[18] Yet even during this time, many older adolescents feel pressure to make decisions about careers, college majors, values, lifestyles, and what to do with their lives. No decision is permanent at this age, and it is possible to change later, at least in our society. Nevertheless, some adolescent decisions can have lifelong implications. An awareness of this creates pressure and anxiety for people who want to make wise choices about their futures.

Drawing on his many years of working with teenagers, Bill Beausay writes that these are complicated years, both for young people and their parents. But even as teenagers respond in individual ways to all the radical changes in their thinking, hormones, and physical development, there are at least four conclusions that apply universally:[19]

- Every teenager is in transition. Each is dealing with changes in his or her mental abilities, hormones, physical development, and social skills. These changes create the need for adjustments, experimenting with new ways of thinking, acting, and relating to others. Stability in the home and church is important to give a firm anchorage during changing times.
- Almost every teenager will rebel through words, attitudes, ideas, or actions. Even when there is no open rebellion, teenagers balk at authority. Like caged animals, they want freedom, but it takes time for them to mature to the place where they can handle the freedoms they want.
- Almost every teenager has a secret life. This is a period of intense privacy when teenagers often pull away from parents, share less than they did before, reflect on where they are, and talk less often with parents and

more with peers and perhaps a trusted adult who is not part of the family.

- Almost every teenager wants to connect and have a good relationship with his or her parents. This can be true even when adolescents criticize and argue with their parents or are embarrassed to be seen with their parents in public. Even as they form their own identities and ways of thinking, young people want love, affirmation, and both emotional and financial support from their parents. Most hope that sooner or later they will have good relationships with their parents.

The Effects of Problems in Adolescence

Even though the majority of teenagers grow up into a relatively normal adulthood (sometimes to the amazement of their beleaguered parents), the pressures of adolescence do take their toll. Teenage insecurities, feelings of guilt, inferiority, loneliness, and rejection can persist far into the adult years. This long-term persistence of problems may depend, in part, on how problems were handled during the teenage years.

1. *Holding In the Problems.* Some adolescents struggle with their problems alone. There may be daydreaming, alienation or withdrawal from friends, apathy, a forsaking of usual interests and activities, or perpetual inner turmoil. Sometimes, this appears in the form of psychosomatic illness, anxiety, loneliness, scholastic failure, or more serious emotional and behavioral disorders. Depression, anxiety, and unexplainable changes in mood or behavior tend to be common in adolescence, but these are not pathological unless they are prolonged and intense. More common are the adjustment reactions of adolescence. These come in response to stress and are characterized by irritability, persisting depression, brooding, and temper outbursts.[20]

2. *Acting Out the Problems.* Adolescents often act out their problems in socially disapproved ways that resist parents or other authorities and assert independence. Excessive drinking, substance abuse, lying, stealing, crime, gang violence, self-mutilation, or other forms of rebellion or delinquency give the adolescent a sense of power, a feeling of independence, a way of challenging authority, and a means for gaining and retaining the attention and acceptance of one's friends—most of whom also may be acting out. More recently, school violence, including the shooting of teachers and peers, has come to worldwide attention and is an especially aggressive form of acting out.[21]

Sometimes acting out takes other forms, such as failing in school subjects or rejecting parental religious beliefs and moral standards. Suicide, murder, and automobile accidents (often the result of speeding or intoxicated teenage drivers) have become the major causes of death among adolescents and young adults. All of these actions can be ways of resisting authority and expressing uniqueness. With some young people, impulsive acting out is a way to create distance from other teens and thus avoid difficult social situations or the fear of revealing secrets (like "I'm gay") that they want to keep hidden. In addition, sexual experimentation of all types can become a way for adolescents to act like adults and gain peer acceptance.

Teenagers often feel intense social pressures to experiment sexually. Their views of sexuality appear to be influenced by sexual talk among peers, sexually explicit messages in prime-time television and on daytime talk shows, the articles about sexuality and sexual health issues in teens' magazine, and sexual references in music, music videos, and in movies favored by teens.[22] Sometimes sexual behavior is not an acting out; instead, it is an attempt to overcome inhibitions, find meaningful relationships, prove one's virility, bolster self-esteem, or escape loneliness. Depending on the individual and his or her peer group, this sexual permissiveness can lead to pervasive feelings of guilt, self-contempt, empty relationships, fears of AIDS or sexually transmitted diseases (STDs), and persisting concerns that they are using others or being used as sex objects. The result can be an epidemic of STDs and continuing high rates of teenage pregnancies. In some cases, these pregnancies are ways for insecure and immature young men and women to prove that they are adults, at least in their own minds.

The prevalence of teenage pregnancies leads to a concern for the care and welfare of the babies, but there is evidence that, compared to their classmates, teenage parents get less education, earn less money in life, hold lower prestige jobs, experience less vocational satisfaction, and have a higher than average rate of divorce and remarriage.[23] When compared to their peers, the children of teenage parents have poorer outcomes in cognitive development, school achievement, emotional development, and social skills.[24] Of course, these findings may not be due to teenage pregnancy alone, but the contrasts between adolescent child-bearers and those who do not bear children strongly suggest that teenage childbearing can radically change a young person's whole educational, occupational, social, and marital future. This clearly is a long-term effect of adolescent "acting-out" in response to sexual impulses.

3. *Running from the Problems.* Every year large numbers of adolescents run away from home. Many of these young people are frustrated at school, unable to communicate or get along with parents, lacking in self-esteem, victimized by abusive family members, and sometimes impulsive or having problems with peers.[25] Many come from poorly functioning families, and it appears that some of these runaway people have been kicked out of their homes. It is not difficult for counselors to imagine the long-term impact of such traumatic childhood experiences.

Leaving home is not the only way to escape. Some withdraw from the world psychologically with or without the help of drugs and alcohol. Others attempt to withdraw by gambling. This is an activity that is increasing among teenagers, perhaps because it can be exciting as well as distracting from other problems. But the cost can be high and long lasting.[26] Still other young people withdraw from their troubles by taking their own lives. According to the American Association of Suicidology, suicide is the third leading cause of deaths among adolescents, after accidents and homicides. It is even more common in college students.[27]

The causes are varied.[28] Social pressures, the example of peers who have attempted suicide, adolescent depression, sadness, disappointments, problems with self-esteem, and sometimes even the pressures of being gifted can all lead to suicide. For many young people, suicide is attempted after an interpersonal conflict and appears to be motivated by the desire to impact the behavior, emotions, or attitudes of the people who later will learn about the death. Often suicide is attempted because the young person is unable to cope effectively with the problems of life. While these suicide attempts may indicate a real desire to die, probably it is more common for the suicidal young person to be crying for help with his or her struggles and ultimate life issues.

Self-destruction and other forms of running from problems can be subtle. Young athletes, for example, might build their entire identities and feelings of self-worth around their athletic skills and performances. If one of these players is dropped from the team, or if an injury prevents further participation in sports, the effects can be devastating. Depression, anger, confusion over one's identity, feelings of failure, plummeting self-esteem, a sense of rejection, and withdrawal from other people can all follow. Sometimes, the individual lashes out in anger or slips into self-destructive behaviors that include excessive drinking, substance abuse, or other forms of irresponsible running away.

4. *Staying with the Problems.* Not all adolescents hold in, act out, or run away from their problems. Even those who show unhealthy responses temporarily join with the majority who tackle their problems squarely, talk them over with friends or trusted adults, react to failures by trying harder next time, learn from their mistakes, and move through the era of adolescence in a relatively smooth fashion. These young people and their parents could benefit from preventive, educative, and supportive counseling, but they rarely come for help. Instead, Christian counselors tend to see people whose adjustment problems are more disruptive to the teenagers, their families, and society.

Counseling and the Problems of Adolescents

There are two primary ways to approach adolescent problems: by counseling the young person and by helping parents. In both cases, the counselor must show that he or she has a broad understanding of the struggles of adolescents and a knowledge of the kinds of tensions that build up both inside teenagers and within their homes. If you counsel young people with some frequency, it is important to know their worlds, their music, their video games, their language, their values. Expect to be surprised and maybe abhorred, but learn with an attitude of curiosity and open-mindedness, without judging or condemnation. Your willingness to know the teenage world often gives you more influence to change that world and the people who live there.

One experienced therapist wrote that counselors can help parents and adolescent children reconnect, but counselors "won't be able to re-create the families many of us idealistically (and often falsely) recall from our own teen years—a time before sex, drugs, alcohol and violent media were easily and routinely available to every 12–year old . . . a time before the Internet gave kids the kind of magic invisibility on the Web that no parent has the X-ray vision to penetrate."[29]

Frequently, parents and teenagers are confused, disappointed, and hurt over the interpersonal tensions and adolescent pressures that have developed. There may be anger, a loss of self-esteem, anxiety about the future, and feelings of guilt over the past. The counselor who understands and accepts such problems without taking sides can have a significant impact on both teenagers and the significant adults in their lives. The impact can be greater if the counselor is sensitive, calm, compassionate, and secure enough to tolerate criticism and adulation— sometimes in the same counseling session. Adolescents and their parents need a steady, caring, wise, self-confident helper who provides a haven of calm guidance in times of strong upheaval.

1. *Counseling Parents.* In the previous chapter we considered ways for helping parents cope with the problems of their children. Most of these principles also

apply when you are counseling the parents of adolescents, but you might want to ponder several additional guidelines.

(a) Support and Encouragement. When adolescent problems arise, parents often conclude that they are to blame, that they are not good parents, or that their children are headed for certain disaster. Counselors do not help if they ignore or explain away such feelings, but there is value in reassuring and encouraging parents. Almost all children, even the children of effective parents, go through periods of anger, rebellion, withdrawal, discouragement, and self-criticism. Earlier we noted that God, the only perfect parent, had children that rebelled against him.[30] It can be comforting for parents to know that he understands their struggles. It also is helpful to remind parents that they are not the only people who struggle with difficult teenagers, most of whom will turn out well when they get older. At home, parents need to relax, listen, try to understand their teenagers, and show love even when they disapprove of teenage attitudes or behavior.[31] Most important is the seeking of continual daily help and divine guidance from a God who guides and knows the best way to handle problems, even adolescent problems.

Counselors sometimes discover that growing independence in teenagers can lead to an identity crisis in their parents. It is difficult for many parents to accept their changing roles or to let their children go. Rarely does this get mentioned when teenage problems are discussed, but the development of adolescent children can remind parents of their own aging, their declining attractiveness, or their lifestyles that may not be satisfying. Without seeing or admitting this, even to themselves, some parents are jealous of their teenage children, with their exuberance, sexual attractiveness, freedom, endless opportunities, bright futures, and willingness to try new experiences and take risks. In contrast, parents can feel discouraged, trapped in nonfulfilling lives, lacking in hope for the future, powerless, and anxious about how their children will turn out. Counselors who are aware of parents struggling in this area can help teenagers by helping their parents deal with their own identity crises. [32]

(b) Family Counseling. Parents should not be blamed for all teenage stresses, but this does not mean that parents are never at fault. When an adolescent or some other member of the family is having problems, the real root of the trouble often lies with a malfunctioning family. When parents have serious marriage problems, for example, children may act out, run away, or develop other noticeable behavior that may signify something wrong at home. These problems in the child or adolescent distract the parents from their marriage difficulties, bring them together while they focus on the young person's problem, and sometimes give the teenager a way to escape from an intolerable home situation.

Some counselors ask the whole family to come for counseling, at least at the beginning, even though an adolescent son or daughter is identified as the one with the problem. The problem person may really be reflecting deeper issues in the home. If the family can be helped to function better, the adolescent's problems frequently improve dramatically.

From this it should not be assumed that all teenage problems come from dysfunctional families. Some insensitive counselors have assumed that families are usually at fault and have put pressure on families to change, even when the teenager's problems come from sources other than the home. Family counseling is most effective when the teenager's problems relate to family conflict, including the parent's difficulty in readjusting to the adolescent's increasing need for greater independence.[33]

(c) Setting Limits. Some of the home conflicts in adolescence come because young people push for more freedom than the parents are willing to give, at least initially. When adolescents react adversely to the setting of limits, parents may begin to wonder if they are being rigid and unreasonable. Some feel threatened and overwhelmed. Others respond by tightening the rules and refusing to negotiate or yield. Many question their competence as parents.

Instead of giving in to adolescent demands (an action that usually leads to more demands), parents can be helped to recognize that all family members have rights in the household. To ensure these rights, some limits must be set and maintained, regardless of adolescent or other pressures, although there also must be flexibility, communication, and discussion. By their own words and actions, parents can show love, acceptance, and respect for each other and for all other members of the family. This modeling is much more effective than nagging, criticizing, or advice giving. As the teenagers get older, parents should give them greater freedom; however, at all times there must be an emphasis on the rights and interests of others. Counselors can help parents set limits that are practical, sensitive to the young person's needs, and conforming to biblical standards. At times, the parent already knows what to do, but he or she needs an outsider to give support, especially in times of family stress.[34]

(d) Spiritual Guidance. Parents and church leaders have long been concerned about teenagers who forsake the family religion and either dismiss spiritual matters completely or begin to explore other religions or forms of spirituality. This kind of exploration is not necessarily unhealthy, since most young people need to find their own beliefs rather than riding on the faith of their parents. The journey away from early religious training is likely to come sooner and lead to more stress in the home if the family religion is based on rigid rules rather than on the Christian virtues of compassion, understanding, acceptance, and forgiveness. Rebellion is more likely if the parents are inflexible and legalistic, or if the family is greatly concerned about social status, acceptance in the neighborhood, or power and position in the congregation. At times, these family attitudes are really a cover for the parents' underlying insecurity and anxiety. Counseling in these areas may prove helpful, but it is more effective to help parents grow spiritually, develop biblical values, and live a consistent Christian lifestyle. This kind of counseling benefits both the parents and the family members, who are helped indirectly.

2. *Counseling Adolescents.*[35] Perhaps the most difficult task involved in counseling adolescents is to establish trusting relationships and to help the young counselees recognize the need for help. Some counselees come voluntarily for help, but often the adolescent sees no need for counseling and is sent by a parent, teacher, or judge. When this happens, the counselor is seen as the parent's ally, and resistance often is present from the beginning. Every person is unique, however. Don't expect resistance from everybody, especially from teenagers who know they need help and are willing to receive it.

(a) Building Rapport. Honesty and respect, mixed with compassion and gentle firmness, are all important, especially as counseling begins. If there is resistance, deal with it directly and give the counselee opportunity to respond. "Could you tell me what brought you here?" you might ask. If the counselee doesn't respond, ask, "Well, somebody else must have wanted you to come. I'm sure you must have some ideas why." Show respect for the counselee and avoid asking questions in ways that imply judgment or criticism. This only serves to stir up resistance and increase the adolescent's defensiveness. Attempt to focus the discussion on specific concrete issues, listen carefully to what the counselee is saying, permit the expressing of feelings, and periodically point out what is happening emotionally during the interview. "You look like you're really mad," or "I sense that you feel pretty confused right now," are examples of comments that stimulate discussion of feelings. Try to keep all of this on a relaxed, informal, conversational level.

(b) Setting Limits. Counseling with teens often involves a power struggle in which the teenager can be manipulative, coercing, and dominating. Two experienced counselors have suggested that power struggles are reduced when counselors avoid four common mistakes of counseling teenagers.[36]

- **Mistake One: Courting the Teenage Counselee.** Often teens refuse to come for counseling. When counselors try to persuade the teenager or make promises that lure the teenager into the counseling room, the young person is given power to control or negotiate. Instead, explain to the adolescent (or suggest that the parents explain) that there will a meeting between the counselor and the parents, that the teenager will be discussed, and that decisions will be made without the teen's input unless he or she is present. Most teens come for the first session, and the majority return for subsequent sessions.
- **Mistake Two: Telling Parents to Back Off.** It is easy to assume that teenagers have a right to privacy and that parents should be more lenient and less controlling. But demands for privacy can be ways for troubled teens to conceal their self-destructive and sometimes illegal behavior. Parents who have little information tend to be angry, reactive, and inconsistent. This makes the home problems worse. In most cases, parents (and sometimes other significant adults such as selected teachers or youth workers) need to be involved with the counseling or at least be aware of what is happening in the counseling room.
- **Mistake Three: Putting No Limits on Family Criticism.** When adolescents are angry and explosive, it is not always helpful to let them express themselves and their feelings freely because this behavior can inflame the conflicts, damage communication, and make matters worse. Feelings are significant, but they need to be tempered with respect.
- **Mistake Four: Giving In to Tunnel Vision.** Don't get so focused on what you hear from parents or teens that you miss the bigger picture. What does the school say, for example? How is the teenager perceived in the community? Relying on the teenager and/or the parents alone can give you a distorted picture of the problem situation.

(c) Transference. As we noted earlier, this word refers to the tendency of some individuals to transfer feelings about a person in the past to a person in the present. For example, a young counselee who hates his father may transfer this hatred to the male counselor. The counselor must recognize that he or she often will be treated with hostility, suspicion, fear, or praise primarily because the counselor resembles some other adult. Counselors may want to discuss these transference feelings with their counselees. This may lead to helpful insights and behaviors that the counselees can take away from the counseling session.

Counselors should try not to respond like the counselee's parent, hero, or other individual with whom they are being compared. In addition, be alert to countertransference. This refers to the counselor's tendency to see similarities between the counselee and some other person. If the counselee reminds you of your own daughter, for example, or if you are reminded of the neighborhood troublemaker, your feelings toward these other people may transfer onto the counselee and interfere with your objectivity as a helper. It is best not to disclose this to the counselee, but it can be helpful for you to discuss it with another counselor.

(d) Problem Identification. It is difficult to help if you cannot identify the problem. Since adolescent counselees tend to deny that they have problems, counseling becomes a challenge. Instead of trying to classify or diagnose problems, it is more effective to encourage adolescents to talk about issues such as school, leisure activities, interests, likes and dislikes, parents, friends, plans for the future, religion, dating, sex, worries, and similar issues. Start with relatively nonthreatening items (for example, "Tell me about your school or family," "What has happened recently that interested you?"). Move to more sensitive areas later. In all of this you should show that you really want to listen, but try not to be an interrogator. Some general questioning may be necessary to get the process started, but once the counselee starts talking and you show a willingness to understand, the adolescent counselee may begin to reveal his or her fears, feelings, attitudes, complaints, worries, impulses, interpersonal tensions, personal defenses, and other significant issues.

(e) Goal Setting. After you have built rapport, begun to identify the problems, and gained some insight into why earlier plans of action have not been working, it is good to set some goals. In chapter 5 we considered the goals of self-understanding, building better communication with others, helping people acquire skills or change behavior, giving support, and stimulating spiritual growth. These apply to adolescents as well as to adults.

In any counseling situation, goals should be as specific as possible. If you and your counselee have differing goals, this discrepancy should be resolved. The problem is complicated if parents have a third set of goals or if the teenager is uncooperative and refuses to agree to goals. These discrepancies must be discussed, and some compromise must be reached before you can move forward. When clear and mutually acceptable goals are established, try to help the counselee to take action that will move toward reaching these goals. This is a very important stage in counseling. It can be easy to agree on goals, but it is much harder to make the changes that will move one toward attaining these ends.

(f) What About Confidentiality? People who go for counseling assume that whatever they tell a counselor will be kept confidential and not shared with anyone outside of the counseling room. There are times, however, when confidentiality cannot be maintained. For example, what does the Christian counselor do when he or she learns that a teenager is suicidal, intending to harm another person, or engaging in risky sexual behavior, drug use, or excessive drinking? Should parents, school leaders, or governmental authorities be told?

New Rules for Working with Adolescents[37]

Find Out About Interests First, "Issues" Later. Without engaging the teen there can be no counseling. Instead of asking, "What is your problem?" or "Why are you here?" consider starting with a question about the teenager's interests, heroes, or friends.

Find Out What Is Annoying About Their Home Life. You can open conversation with questions such as, "What are your gripes (or concerns, or struggles) right now?" Ask about their expectations with questions such as, "What would you like to change about your family (or other parts of life)?" "What would you like to happen in your life?"

Open the Borders of Counseling. Some counselors will disagree with this—but suggest that kids bring a friend or two with them to the counseling sessions. And do not exclude the parents. They are a vital part of the helping process.

Hold Kids to Expectations. Let them know that you expect them to be on time, to be respectful, to not be rude, silly, or inattentive. Model this behavior in yourself.

Be Emotionally Honest and Willing to Give Feedback. Many teenagers complain that counselors never reveal what they are thinking. Tell the adolescents what you think and do not be afraid to answer their questions or to give advice.

Be Flexible About Time and What You Mean by a Session. Teenagers don't always want to talk in fifty-minute sessions that are scheduled at specific times. Sometimes the time needs to expand or shrink depending on the teenager's need or desire to talk. Some counselors are flexible and can be available to talk at unscheduled times.

Insist That Parents Get to Know Their Kids' World. Encourage parents to open their homes to the friends of their teenagers. Know their music and interests, but at the same time set expectations that need to be respected.

Don't Promise Confidentiality. At least in Western societies teenagers have a lot of privacy and independence. Tell kids that while you respect their privacy, you realize that sometimes it is best for them if you talk to others, including parents. Point out that one goal is to protect the young person. Another is to help parents or teachers be the best they can be.

Counselors face at least four issues in making decisions about breaking confidentiality with their adolescent counselees.[38]

- First, what does the law require? In all the states in the U.S., in all Canadian provinces, and in many other countries, counselors are required by law to report child abuse, including the abuse of younger adolescents.
- Second, what are the issues that the counselor might consider reporting? Most counselors agree that if a person is in danger of committing suicide, harming another person, or committing a crime, this cannot be kept confidential. It is in everyone's best interests to report these intentions. Unless the police need to be involved immediately, reporting suicide threats or the intent to harm someone else usually means talking to the parents. Unlike abuse, there is no central agency to report intent to harm oneself or others.

Counselors are less united in their conclusions about reporting sexual behavior, drinking or drug use. Parents are legally responsible for their underage children so they have a right to know about these behaviors, but most counselors keep quiet if the behaviors are infrequent or one-time events.

- Third, what will breaking confidences do to the counseling relationship? Will this violate trust and destroy the counseling process? Professional counselors who work with teenagers usually have an initial meeting with the parents and the adolescent to describe what will and what may not be kept confidential. This agreement is then signed by all people involved. When counselors tell their young clients at the beginning that some things will not be kept confidential, there are no surprises later. During counseling, if the counselor decides to reveal confidential information, it can be helpful to tell the counselee beforehand that this is going to happen and to spend time in the counseling room considering the implications of this decision and the young person's reaction. Sometimes breaking confidences is more beneficial to the counselee than keeping quiet so the counseling relationship is protected.
- Fourth, what are the counselor's values? Some counselors do not share information about behavior that they consider to be typical of adolescents. This includes active sexual activity or drinking. But the Christian counselor surely is held to a higher standard and needs to work in partnership with the parents so that even common teenage behaviors are reported if they are harmful to the adolescent personally, psychologically, and/or spiritually.

(g) Group Counseling. Ultimately, the Christian counselor seeks to help young people grow into maturity and become adults who honor Christ with their lifestyles, beliefs, inner serenity, and interpersonal relationships. To help counselees reach this goal we focus on present, more immediate problems and guide counselees as they change their thinking, perceptions, and behavior. At times you may want to encourage group counseling. This can be of special help to adolescents who have interpersonal problems, tendencies to withdraw, or problems that others share—such as family abuse, an alcoholic parent, or a terminally ill relative. The relationships and mutual sharing that come in group counseling can give support and teach adolescents important lessons about how to relate to others effectively. Often this frees them to move on to the spiritual growth that brings ultimate answers to the problems of life.

Preventing the Problems of Adolescence

It is well known that baby chicks struggle to peck their way through the shell of the egg. If a sympathetic observer tries to help by breaking the shell, the chick gets out faster and with less effort, but it fails to develop in a healthy, normal way because it did not experience the struggles and build the strength that would have prepared it for the stresses of life.

In some ways, adolescents are similar to those baby chicks. It can be painful and difficult to break out from the restraints of childhood, but with each challenge the adolescent can gain in confidence, competence, and knowledge, even though there may be failures along the way. Parents and other sympathetic adults sometimes try to prevent the problems and protect teenagers from the stresses of life, but this is both impossible and poor child-rearing. Instead, we should seek to help young people mature but without the painful and unnecessary consequences that come when there is a breaking of the law, sexual immorality, severe emotional disturbance, inability to succeed academically, interpersonal conflict, or loss of faith. There are several ways by which counselors and other Christian leaders can help parents prepare for adolescence, and can help young people mature without falling into many of the painful pitfalls of the teenage years.

1. *Building a Spiritual Foundation.* Someone has said that the best time to begin preparing for adolescence is at least ten years before it begins. By building communication skills, mutual respect, concern for others, and an open attitude about problems, parents help children learn how to deal honestly and immediately with issues when they arise.

This training is of special importance in the spiritual realm. Adolescents are not impressed by theological legalism or religion that has a lot of talk but little action. They are much more impressed when their parents *show* that theirs is a live faith, characterized by a sincere commitment to Jesus Christ and a daily willingness to worship and serve him. When parents can be taught to grow spiritually, there is greater love, stability, acceptance, and forgiveness in the home. This creates a firm foundation on which adolescents can build lives, formulate values, solve problems, and plan for the future.

2. *Working to Develop Family Examples and Stability.* The example of parents is one of the most effective preventive influences in the adolescent's life. How do parents cope with stress in their own lives, resolve differences, or respond to temptation? Is their marriage stable and the family able to provide a haven in times of stress or a place of certainty when the world around seems to be in turmoil?

Stimulating better marriages is one crucial way by which the church can prevent teenage problems. Encourage parents to love their kids (despite how they act or think), to accept them as they are, to try to understand, to point out their good points, and to avoid constant nagging. Counselors can help parents realize that if they can overlook minor irritations, they will have a better chance of being heard when they have to draw the line on issues that are of greater importance.

Abundant research supports the importance of the family in the prevention of youth problems.[39] Studies give "considerable empirical support" to the conclusion that effective parenting can prevent a variety of adolescent problems, including conduct disorders, violent and aggressive behaviors, delinquency, substance abuse, depression, suicide, teen pregnancy, HIV disease, school failure, and eating disorders.[40] Two family-based approaches to prevention have proven to be especially effective: teaching parents to be better parents and teaching family skills, including better communication, decision making, and problem solving. Seminars on these issues, given by a speaker on a public platform, are of less benefit than teaching and guiding small groups in how-to-do-it activities that they can practice and apply to their families. In some cases, family counseling also helps families function better to the benefit of every family member.

3. *Education.* A variety of school programs have been developed to educate teenagers about the dangers of teenage drinking, drug use, unrestrained sex, and related issues. This information can be helpful, but adolescents often know (or think they know) more about drugs and sex than their teachers, and frequently

factual knowledge fades in the face of peer pressure or the excitement of "taking a chance." Urging teenagers to "say no to drugs" is an admirable goal, but slogans are of little help if the person hasn't learned skills that teach *how* to say no when the pressures arise. Educational efforts to prevent teenage suicide can be constructive, but only if suicide is not made to sound glamorous. Students must be given factual information about suicide and then shown how to cope with their pressures in less destructive ways.

Sometimes drug, sex, and health education programs are more credible and effective if this comes from people who have experienced the pain of chemical abuse or sexual promiscuity. Even more important is the consideration of moral standards, values, and biblical teachings about right and wrong. These issues must be discussed openly and honestly, preferably at home, and before they arise unexpectedly in the young person's experience. In addition, adolescents must be helped to find love and acceptance in life so they feel less need to escape into chemical euphoria, immoral sex, or suicide attempts.

Christian parents and church leaders often assume that God will protect our children if we pray for them regularly. This is a valid conclusion, but sometimes it becomes an excuse that we use to ignore developing problems and do nothing about the pressures that teenagers face daily. God intervenes directly in lives, but surely there are times when he answers our prayers and protects our adolescents through the moral teaching and forewarning that come from parents, youth leaders, and Christian teachers. This learning does not occur if issues such as sexual intercourse, birth control, drinking, teenage pregnancies, and drug abuse are never mentioned. When these are discussed openly before they arise, they can be discussed again and with greater freedom when the temptations come.[41]

4. *Stimulating Interpersonal Support.* Peer support and encouragement are crucial at all stages of life but especially during adolescence. Of course, teenage rebellion, drug abuse, drinking, and sexual immorality occur in church and parachurch groups, but when friends and sensitive, concerned leaders are available to provide a place for discussion of real problems, give emotional and social support, help young people have fun, build self-esteem, and give both direction and spiritual teaching, then the church can have a powerful positive and preventive impact. Modeling, as we have noted, is one of the most important means of teaching adolescents. If older believers can be godly models or mentors who get to know the adolescents and gain their respect, this can have a significant influence on teenage development.[42] No counselor or parent should underestimate the importance of youth leaders and effective youth organizations.

5. *Giving Guidance.* Choosing a career, finding one's place in life, learning to date, developing an identity, formulating values, deciding what to believe—these are among the decisions that adolescents must face. No one else can make these decisions for them, although parents, school guidance counselors, leaders in the church, and Christian counselors can give guidance and encouragement as the decisions are being made. Youth groups and retreats can stimulate discussion and thinking about these issues—and so can parents.

Conclusions About Adolescence

It is not easy to be an adolescent or to help young people through their adolescent years, but surely the crisis nature of this period in life has been overrated.

Considering the changes that occur and the adjustments that are required, most young people reach adulthood in remarkably good shape. Immediately before his ascension into heaven, Jesus told his followers that they had one basic responsibility to complete in his absence: to make disciples.[43] Where could this be done more effectively than in the home? As children become teenagers, parental discipline should move into parental discipleship, teaching by word and example how to be a follower of Jesus Christ. Teenagers are old enough to respond to logic, persuasion, fairness, interest, positive reinforcement, love, parental example, and the power of prayer. Rather than trying to force or manipulate adolescents into some parental mold or religious dogma, our task as counselors and parents is to help them grow into Christian personal maturity. Few tasks could be more challenging, fulfilling, or important.

KEY POINTS FOR BUSY COUNSELORS

➤ Adolescence has been called the most confusing, challenging, frustrating, and fascinating phase of human development, but the stresses and disruptions of adolescence are not nearly as bad as many counselors assume and as parents fear. An estimated 10 percent to 20 percent experience serious turmoil during this period.

➤ Adolescence is a period of growth from childhood to maturity, and most of the struggles faced by teenagers and their families reflect this significant change and growth.

➤ Adolescence can be divided into three overlapping periods:
  ▪ *Preadolescence* begins around age ten or eleven, lasts about two years and is marked by a growth spurt, sexual maturation, greater peer influences, and a new desire for independence from parents.
  ▪ *Adolescence* is between ages fourteen and eighteen, when there is adjustment to having an adult body, increasing disengagement from parents, increasing sexual drive and experiences, frequent dating, and sometimes increased involvement with drugs, alcohol, technology (including the Internet), and spirituality.
  ▪ *Postadolescence* extends into the early twenties and involves consideration of questions concerning one's identity, relationships, future, values, and core beliefs.

➤ The Bible says nothing about adolescence, probably because this was not considered to be a period separate from childhood in biblical times. Instructions to children and young adults, however, can apply to this period.

➤ There can be numerous causes of adolescent problems, including:
  ▪ Physical changes.
  ▪ Sexual changes.

- Interpersonal changes.
- Changing values, morals, and religious beliefs.
- The move to independence.
- The need to acquire skills and build self-esteem.
- Concerns about the future.

➤ Problems tend to be dealt with in one or more of the following ways:
- The problems are *held in* while adolescents struggle alone and sometimes become depressed or withdrawn.
- The problems are *acted out,* often in ways that are socially disapproved.
- The problems are *run away* from, including leaving home; withdrawal into drugs, alcohol, fantasy games, pornography, and excessive Internet use; pulling away from friends and family or, in more extreme cases, suicide.
- The problems are not avoided when the adolescent *stays with* the challenges of this period of life and makes efforts to solve problems and move forward.

➤ Counseling adolescence includes counseling parents and counseling the teenagers.

➤ Counseling the parents includes:
- Giving support and encouragement.
- Family counseling.
- Help with setting limits.
- Spiritual guidance.

➤ Counseling teenagers includes:
- Building trust and rapport.
- Setting limits.
- Being aware of transference.
- Identifying the problems.
- Setting goals and working toward these.
- Establishing clear guidelines regarding confidentiality.
- Sometimes doing group counseling.

➤ Problem prevention involves building a spiritual foundation in the young person prior to adolescence.

➤ Prevention also includes building family stability, educating parents and teens, and giving personal support and guidance.

➤ Helping adolescents mature into adulthood can be challenging at times, but it also can be rewarding and very fulfilling.

15

Twenties and Thirties

Nels is the twenty-nine-year-old pastor of a small church in a community where the people are not very religious and where congregations consist mostly of older people without any desire to change. Nels and his wife are well liked by the people in their church, most of whom dote like loving grandparents over the pastor's two-year-old daughter. Since arriving at the church shortly after his graduation from seminary, Nels and his wife have never doubted their call to the ministry, but they have increasing frustrations with what appears to be a dead-end situation in their no-grow church.

Not far away is a thriving congregation of mostly twenty- and thirty-years-olds, with creative leaders, and an active presence in the community. Although his people are critical of this new upstart, Nels and his wife look longingly at what is happening down the street from his church. They know many of the people involved and wonder if they should leave their church and join them. But this would mean leaving the ministry, at least temporarily, and forsaking his older parishioners as others had done before. Late at night the young pastor and his wife talk about what might happen if the two churches could connect in some way. What if the younger believers could see the value of learning from older and more mature believers? What might happen if these older people could put aside their rigidities, their prejudices, and their fears, and the two groups could learn from each other? One day Nels shared his frustrations and his dreams with an older pastor in his denomination, but the response was firm and decisive. To leave the church would be to forsake God, Nels was told. To think about connecting with a younger congregation would be like aligning with a group of immature kids who probably were not even Christians. Such a move would kill the faithful church that had been around for so long. Clearly, the older pastor was more prejudiced, rigid, and maybe threatened by this new group than the people Nels was trying to lead.

How would you counsel this young pastor? He is bright, creative, committed to Christ, and excited about the impact of dynamic churches even in this age of religious skepticism. He also is frustrated, lonely, discouraged, struggling financially, and trapped. He wants to be faithful to where God has called him, but he has no supporters, nobody to give him encouragement. Even his friends in the church down the street have difficulty understanding his aching feelings of frustrations.

They may be in different work situations, but Nels knows that a lot of people his age are frustrated as well. Unlike Nels, some are unemployed, entangled in miserable marriages, struggling with large debts or the results of wasted years. Nels wants to reach these people and to be used by God to make a difference in their lives and in this world. Even so, he stays where he is. Trapped.

In 1991 a Canadian novelist named Douglas Coupland published a book titled *Generation X: Tales for an Accelerated Generation*.[1] Not everyone agrees, but generally it is assumed that Coupland was the first person to apply the term *generation X* to group of young people, born in the 1960s and 1970s, the children of post-World War II baby boomers. The generation X term stuck, but as the original generation entered middle age, generation X came to describe anybody in their twenties or early thirties, regardless of when they were born. Other terms came before and after Coupland's book. *Baby boomers* described those born between 1946 and 1964. *Baby busters* described those who came between the mid 1960s and 1970s, although, in time, they became know as generation X instead. *Generation Y* came later, but they have tended to be confused with the mosaics and, more recently the millennials, born between 1977 and 1994.[2]

A different way of defining the period between late teens and mid-thirties is to abandon the catchy titles and to think of *emerging adulthood* and *young adulthood* as two overlapping stages in the life span.[3] Emerging adults no longer consider themselves as teenagers, but they do not yet feel comfortable calling themselves adults. Many still live at home or at college, at least in the industrialized cultures, and most are finding careers, getting training, and exploring relationship issues that eventually will lead to marriage and family. This has been called a novice phase of life that gives way to young adulthood, when people settle into more stable patterns and pursue future dreams and hopes.

Many of these terms have been used to describe stereotyped characteristics of a limited age cohort. Gen Xers, for example, are supposed to be pessimistic, alienated, lazy, and angst-ridden. Gen Y people are described as more relaxed, footloose, hang-loose, and idealistic. Ask people in any of these groups if the descriptions fit, and they are likely to protest that "I'm an individual. I don't fit into any of these descriptions."

By the time you read this book, there will be new terms to label people in their twenties and thirties. Whatever their label, these young men and women are breaking away from their families of origin, finding their place in the adult world and getting established. Most are married, at least by the time they enter their thirties, and parents of young children. They compose a large proportion of the workforce and have massive buying power and political clout.[4] Sandwiched between middle-aged or elderly parents and the adolescents who attract so much media attention, these younger adults have unique needs and problems of their own, but this is the age group that is most overlooked by writers of psychiatric or counseling psychology textbooks.

The period of life that extends from the late teens to the late thirties has been called a time of rich satisfaction in terms of love, sexuality, family life, occupational advancement, creativity, and realization of one's major life goals. It also can be a time of intense stress. Two young authors in their twenties described this time of life as a *Quarterlife Crisis*,[5] similar in many ways to the later midlife crisis. The chapter titles of their book give an insightful overview of the challenges: How am I supposed to figure out who I really am? What if I'm scared to stop being a kid? What if I fail? What do all these doubts mean? How do I know if the decisions I'm making are the right ones? How do I work out the right balance among my career, friends, family, and romance? Can I carry any part of my college experience into the real world?

Over thirty years ago, Daniel Levinson and a team of Yale University researchers began a study of adulthood. They divided early adulthood into four overlapping periods, each of which lasts for about five to seven years.[6] First is the period between ages seventeen and twenty-two. The Yale researchers describe this as the *early adult transition*. This overlaps with what we termed postadolescence in the previous chapter. It is a time in life when people are making decisions about the future. Often the choices are difficult, and the separations from parents may be painful, but for most, this is a time in life that is challenging, exciting, difficult, and frightening—all at the same time.

When they reach age twenty-two or twenty-three, young adults move to the stage that Levinson's researchers call *entering the adult world*. This is a time when there is increasing need to make practical decisions. These years of the mid-twenties are when people decide more seriously about careers or occupations, and many are moving into marriage, parenthood, and more permanent living arrangements. As with all attempts to summarize stages, this era has many individual differences. Some decide to continue their education, to travel before settling down, or to delay decisions about marriage. A group known as "boomerang kids" finishes college and returns home where living is cheaper, responsibilities may be less, and there is more time to decide what is next. At this time in life, often there are a variety of alternatives to explore. Sometimes decisions are made too quickly, or based on immediate circumstances, only to be regretted later.

The *age thirty transition* begins in the late twenties and extends into the early thirties. For many, this is a time of reappraisal when past choices are examined and sometimes modified. By this time, most people have discovered talents, abilities, and interests that may have been missed earlier. Some people conclude that their idealistic youthful values and dreams are unrealistic or unattainable. Those who have made unwise decisions or few commitments during their twenties now may feel fragmented, rootless, and inclined to think that their lives are drifting or wasted. Often this leads to efforts to change this pattern so the future can have greater stability. This can also be a time of such upheaval that young men and women wonder if they are encountering a midlife crisis ten years early.[7] When they turn thirty, some are struck with the realization that they are well into adulthood and have already begun to set the path that the rest of their lives might take. Having spent many years of my adult life as a professor, I have concluded that most young people do not really settle on a career and life direction until they are thirty. If they are still struggling five years later, they may continue to drift, somewhat unfulfilled, throughout life.

Between ages thirty-three and forty, most individuals go through a period of *settling down*. Demands from one's family, community, and occupation are at a peak. In many societies there is competition for professional and economic advancement during this period, and many people have increasing concerns about achieving greater autonomy, independence, and self-sufficiency.

Summaries like this can be helpful for counselors, but any discussion of young adulthood must be set in the context of the times and places where these people live. We have already seen the confusion of labels for this group, and it is clear that twenty-year-olds today are different from twenty-year-olds of ten years ago. In ten years the twenty-year-olds will be different again. And even now, twenty- or thirty-year-olds in the community where you live probably are different in some ways from those who live in the community where this book has been written.

Perhaps it can help our understanding if we look at what came to be known as the baby boom. Following the Second World War, in 1946, the worldwide birth rate experienced a sudden and expected upsurge as military personnel returned home and settled back into peacetime living. In most countries, the increase in pregnancies and childbirth soon dropped back to pre-war levels, but in four countries—Australia, New Zealand, Canada, and the United States—the birth rate stayed high for almost twenty years.[8] This created a great population bulge that has been moving through life, radically changing society at each stage, and greatly affecting the generations that are behind.[9] In the Western world, this is the first generation raised on television, free of infectious diseases like diphtheria or polio, knowledgeable about AIDS, sophisticated in the use of computers, familiar with space travel, and experienced in limitless educational opportunities. It is a generation that has sought to reform society, liberate women, pursue affluence, change sexual values, tolerate diversity, and challenge established tradition. It is a generation that is proud of being open-minded but is criticized for being intellectually impoverished and culturally closed-minded. It also is a generation with intense competition for the jobs, promotions, and affluence that many grew up learning to expect. Within Christian circles, this is the generation that turned away from the more traditional church that had not changed in decades, replacing it with more lively seeker-sensitive churches, many of which have grown into mega-churches that reach fellow baby boomers effectively but are less successful in connecting with younger or older generations.[10]

The oldest baby boomers are now moving into retirement. Several generations have followed them, each with its unique characteristics, values, expectations, and perspectives on life and spirituality. Even so, there are characteristics of twenty- and thirty-year-olds that apply across the years, and often across cultures. These are issues that concern emergent churches, alert political leaders, marketers, educators, and Christian counselors.

The Bible and the Twenties and Thirties

In the Bible, no person is mentioned more frequently than David. His life history is cited in four Old Testament books, and throughout Scripture his name is recorded even more than the name of Jesus.[11] David's mobile lifestyle, his struggles with King Saul, his friendship with Jonathan, his spiritual growth, and perhaps his marriage difficulties[12] all appear to have taken place before he was thirty.[13] Many of the Psalms must have been written while David was in the early years of young adulthood.

Is it possible that most biblical leaders made their mark on history when they were young adults like David? Joseph was thirty when he became the ruler or Egypt, second only to Pharaoh.[14] Jesus was in his early thirties when he carried out his whole ministry and changed the course of history, aided by a group of disciples that may have been barely out of their teens. Many of the early church leaders appear to have been young people. They all had struggles, but many were used by God in mighty ways. "Don't let anyone think less of you because you are young," the apostle Paul wrote to Timothy, probably when he was a young adult. "Be an example to all believers in what you teach, in the way you live, in your live, your faith, and your purity."[15] Elsewhere, Titus was instructed to "encourage the young men to live wisely in all they do. And you yourself must be an example to them by doing good deeds of every kind. Let everything you do reflect the integrity and seriousness of your teaching.[16] In the pages of the Bible, young adults were mentioned often as well as many of the concerns and problems of this age group. Anxiety, discouragement, marriage, sex, lust, money management, careers, relationships with parents and children, temptation, and spiritual growth are among the issues mentioned in the Bible and of special concern to people in their twenties and thirties.

The Causes of Problems in Twenty- and Thirty-Year-Olds

Like every stage of life, young adulthood can have an up side and a down side. It can be exciting moving fully into adulthood, experiencing long-desired freedoms, able to pursue one's dreams, young enough to take risks, but flexible enough to back off and change course when things do not work out as planned. One young man described his life and his generation as being at the beginning of a road trip. "I don't go on a road trip to solve problems," he said. "I go to have fun, freedom to explore, new experiences, and great times with my friends." As they journey through this period, however, many people discover that is it not easy taking charge of one's life, handling both money and relationships, making decisions about the future, and facing realities that might have been ignored earlier. Even though cultural trends and conditions change, young adults of every generation can feel alone in the world. They may be surrounded by friends and immersed in activities, but it is easy for them to feel like solitary sailors in leaking boats, so concerned about their own safety, survival, and future direction that there is little energy left to worry about much else.

The challenges of these young adult years could be grouped into five major categories: competency, independence, intimacy, spirituality, and direction. Each can challenge young adults, but each also gives rise to problems.

1. *Competency*. Most of childhood is spent learning the skills we need to survive and get along with others. As we get older, we learn how to study, to solve problems, to handle stress and frustrations, to deal with emotions like anger or anxiety, and to relate to parents and peers. Along the way, personal failures come because we have not learned the skills needed to function well in this complex culture. If individuals are to live successfully as adults, they must continue to develop competence in several skill areas.[17]

(a) Physical Skills. By the time we reach adulthood, almost everybody has learned the importance of good grooming, regular exercise, and a balanced diet. But some young people—even those who might be reading this book—punish their bodies with unhealthy eating, crash diets, lack of sleep, laziness, or excessive use of alcohol and other drugs. Chip is a twenty-four-year-old graduate student in Chicago who goes to school but spends extra hours playing video games. He started when he was seven and sometimes plays until he cannot keep his eyes open. "All I have every wanted is cyberspace," Chip told a reporter in his crowded apartment, playing games alongside his two equally enthralled roommates.[18] Young bodies rejuvenate quickly, so people like Chip may forget that tired, overweight, sluggish, poorly nourished, self-abused bodies do not function optimally or cope with stress efficiently. At times, complicated problems arise or worsen because people fail to take care of themselves physically. This applies to counselors as well as to the twenty- and thirty-year-olds we counsel.

(b) Intellectual, Problem-Solving Skills. Individuals must be able to learn efficiently, communicate effectively, and think clearly if they are to have success in handling stress, solving problems, and adapting to change. Regrettably, many young people go through the educational system and graduate without the ability to think clearly. Some schools may have put so much emphasis on creativity, tolerance, and "fun learning" that students don't know how to learn or think.

Basic problem solving involves clarifying the issues, setting goals, exploring possible solutions, trying out one or more of these alternatives, evaluating what happened, and sometimes repeating the process. On occasion problems arise or worsen because people fail to think clearly, don't know where to get helpful information, or have no concept about how to solve problems. It is then that the counselor becomes an educator, teaching intellectual and problem-solving skills.

(c) Emotional Intelligence Skills. There was a time when intelligence was viewed solely as an intellectual, cognitive ability. Today, however, there is abundant research to show that each of us has multiple intelligences, including musical intelligence, interpersonal intelligence, and existential intelligence.[19] Psychologist Daniel Goleman took this further with his concept of emotional intelligence.[20] All leaders, he found, have high degrees of emotional intelligence. This involves the following skills that people can learn, even though not all succeed in doing so.

- Self-awareness, the ability to recognize and understand your moods and emotions, and to know how these influence others.
- Self-control, the ability to control impulses and think before acting.
- Goal commitment, the ability to pursue goals with energy and persistence, and to work for reasons that go beyond money or status.
- Sensitivity to the emotional makeup of others, along with skill in treating people according to their abilities and emotional makeup.
- Relationship proficiency, which includes managing relationships, building rapport, and building networks.[21]

As everyone knows, emotion is a part of human nature that sometimes appears when it is least expected. Disappointment, anxiety, anger, excitement, guilt, lust, enthusiasm, compassion, and a host of others can affect our thinking and influence behavior. Sometimes people squelch their emotions, ignore them, express them inappropriately, or even fail to recognize that they exist. All of this can lead to serious psychological and social difficulties.

As the concept of emotional intelligence shows, each person must learn to be sensitive to his or her own feelings and to the feelings of others. Some counselees must be taught where to express their feelings and how to express them in ways that are socially appropriate. Some young men, for example, still do not realize that crying is normal and healthy, although this seems to be less characteristic of current generations than of those who came before. Much depends on where one cries, with whom, and when.

(d) Self-Management Skills. Some overly compulsive people live lives that are so disciplined that they become rigid and lack any form of fun or spontaneity. More often, I suspect, counselors hear about wasted time, squandered money, missed opportunities, lack of self-control, and lazy lifestyles. Because they lack self-discipline and self-management skills, young adults may fritter away some of their best years. Only later do they awaken to discover that their lives are drifting without direction or purpose, and that other more disciplined people have passed them by. Others may have motivation and discipline, but they lack the skills needed to turn their dreams into reality, so they, too, miss opportunities and reach middle age steeped in frustration. Still others have lifestyles that are so busy and out of control that there is no room for reflection and balance.

The counselor may be faced with the challenge of teaching money-management skills, self-discipline, handling relationships, career planning, or ways to manage time. Without these skills, young adult problems are likely to persist throughout life.[22]

(e) Interpersonal Skills. Getting along with people is one of the most difficult challenges of life.[23] This is a task that requires determination, tact, hard work, sensitivity, and sometimes a lot of patience. The Bible tells us to live in peace with each other but implies that this isn't always possible, and that sometimes the peacemaking effort is one-sided.[24]

Many of the challenges of young adulthood require interpersonal skills. Getting launched in a career, finding a mate, building a marriage, starting a family, getting along in the community, becoming involved in a church—all involve such "people skills" as learning to listen, being able to communicate clearly, resolving disagreements, and acting appropriately in social situations. Each of these skills involves knowledge (knowing how to respond) and action (doing what is appropriate). Each takes time and effort to learn. When the learning has not occurred, problems are likely to develop.

(f) Spiritual Skills. Within recent years the Western world has seen an upsurge of interest in Eastern religions, altered states of consciousness, and new spiritualities.[25] Much of this interest has been among young adults, many of whom are looking for greater meaning and purpose in life. Along with the interest in alternative forms of spirituality, young people have shown an encouraging interest in spiritual disciplines and in the writings of early church fathers or of more contemporary spirituality writers.[26] Many of these twenty- and thirty-year-olds have turned from the traditional churches or big mega-churches, and become involved in emergent churches that are led by younger leaders or by older pastoral leaders who understand younger people and think in ways that connect with people between their late teens and into their thirties.[27] Among many there also has been a discovery of spiritual direction that has long been familiar to Roman Catholics and Orthodox believers, but only recently has it grown in popularity among Evangelicals and other non-Catholic believers.[28]

For many young adults, these are years of searching for a spirituality that is meaningful and fulfilling. Many fail to realize that rather than acquiring another form of spirituality, they need to relate to a person, Jesus Christ. We learn about him in the Bible, a book that is filled with examples and instructions of ways by which we grow in a relationship with God. It takes a lifetime to learn how to pray, how to study Scripture, how to practice spiritual disciplines, how to select and benefit from devotional literature, how to worship, how to have true connectivity and community with other believers, or how to grow spiritually. Young believers (like those who are older) often encounter frustrations in their spiritual and personal lives if they lack a basic knowledge of these spiritual skills or never discipline themselves to put the skills into practice.

2. *Independence.* During their twenties and sometimes later, people need to break away from home and develop a sense of autonomy. Often this takes time and effort; sometimes it involves frustration, tension, feelings of insecurity, periods of uncertainty, and struggles with a number of questions. Can I make it on my own? Can I find workable living and roommate arrangements? Where do I get a good job, and how do I succeed? How can I get financially free from my parents without going into debt? Is there a way to stay connected with my family without having to remain a child? How do I make the right decisions? How do I deal with the guilt and loneliness associated with my separation from the family? How do I move into marriage, and what do we do to develop good relationships with in-laws? Some face the problem of how to fit back into the family temporarily after tasting the independence of living away at college or elsewhere.

The challenge of becoming independent involves at least four overlapping and ongoing tasks: developing self-sufficiency, building an identity, finding values, and coping effectively.

(a) Developing Self-Sufficiency. Self-sufficiency has been defined as "a sometimes complicated balance between self-direction and sensitivity to the needs of others."[29] To be self-sufficient does not mean that we are stubborn about doing things "my way," totally independent or insensitive to the feelings and opinions of others. For the Christian, self-sufficiency does not mean that we pull away from God and try to live solely on the basis of human strength. Instead, the self-sufficient Christian trusts God to give direction and recognizes that other people, including parents, counselors, and mature Christian leaders can give helpful guidance and valuable counsel. The move to greater independence involves self-initiated planning, a willingness to tackle problems and make decisions, taking responsibility for one's own choices and finances, admitting and learning from mistakes, and listening to the advice of others—even if this guidance subsequently is rejected.

One university senior described how he faced the issue of self-sufficiency shortly after his arrival on campus: "It occurred to me not long after I arrived here that, with 15,000 students around, no one was going to be watching over me to see how I was doing. I'd really have to have a huge problem before anyone would notice. I made it a point to seek out my advisor, get to know her, and stay in touch. Last week, she wrote me a great letter of recommendation for a job."[30]

(b) Building an Identity. Identity is a fairly stable mental picture of who you are, a picture that seems to be shared by others who know you and whom you consider to be significant.[31] Identity development is a continuing process of seeking to answer such questions as "Who am I?" "What is unique about me?" or "Where do I fit in this world?" These questions come with special urgency in late adolescence and early adulthood. How we relate to others and to the world around us is a reflection of our identity. If there are not at least tentative answers to the questions, young people often experience confusion, inner turmoil, a lack of direction, and sometimes a sense of quiet desperation while they go through a young adult identity crisis.[32]

As they reflect on their goals, interests, beliefs, hopes, personality traits, strengths, aptitudes, and abilities, most people begin to get a clearer picture of who they are. Sometimes there will be clarity in one area (a recognition of one's abilities, for example) while there is fluctuation in other areas (such as what one believes or what would be a good career). As their identities slowly become clearer—sometimes with the help of a counselor—young people are able to move more confidently into the future. Identity issues are likely to surface again, but that may not happen until middle age.

(c) Finding Values. Values are foundational beliefs that anchor our lives. They are at the core of who we are, how we live and make decisions, what we consider to be most important in lives. Values are at the basis of one's character, actions, attitudes, ethics, choices, and religious beliefs.[33] They govern how we think and the way we act.

As they move into adulthood and are forced to make decisions about lifestyles, vocations, spending priorities, and time management, people have to decide what they really believe—and why. They must determine to what extent they will keep the values that came from parents and other significant adults. Often the young adult is idealistic and accepts standards of right and wrong that may be unrealistic and impossible to follow. Some throw out traditional standards and try to live a value-free life, but in addition to being an impossibility, the decision to be value free still reflects a value. Others fail to give much thought to their values until they are presented with the opportunity to act in a way that might violate the values of one's family or of the larger society. At such times, one is forced to make value decisions, often without much time for reflection.

Values are reflected in how we spend our time and money, what we claim to believe, the people we spend time with, the things we read, or what we think about when our minds wander. Young people often struggle over finding their values. This can create confusion and indecision about moral choices, about social behavior, and about plans for the future.

As we have noted, young adults differ from generation to generation and from place to place. Unlike some previous generations that may have been more self-focused, many people in their twenties and thirties today value compassion and empathy for others, especially the homeless, oppressed, or needy. When young adults are in the twenties and before they have marriage and family responsibilities, it is common for them to be passionately involved in feeding people who are hungry, visiting the lonely, caring for orphans both at home and overseas, helping people who are powerless, and ministering evangelistically. For some, this social awareness leads to political activism or active efforts to protect and preserve the environment. These social values can persist throughout life.

(d) Coping Effectively. Independent people can accomplish the tasks of day-to-day living and handle the hassles and stresses of life without seeking to be rescued or to get continual assistance from others. These people are willing to seek or accept help when necessary, and they are willing to help others. But in the routine tasks of living, they function by themselves, with little or no assistance from others. In contrast, when people can't cope, they are more likely to have problems.

3. *Intimacy.* According to psychiatrist Erik Erikson, the greatest need in young adulthood is the need for intimacy. This is the capacity to commit oneself to relationships and partnerships and to develop the strength to abide by such commitments, even though at times this may call for significant sacrifices.[34]

The people in our lives might be divided into three groups. Acquaintances are people whom we know only casually. Friends are closer. They are people who care for one another, spend time together, and have similar interests and viewpoints. Intimates have all the characteristics of friends, but, in addition, they share mutual concerns and personal struggles. Intimate friends understand each other and experience closeness, acceptance, loyalty, vulnerability, accountability, caring, empathy, and love that are not present in mere friendship. In marriage, intimacy includes sexuality, but it should not be assumed that all intimacy involves sex. David and Jonathan, Ruth and Naomi, Paul and Timothy—each of these biblical friends had nonsexual intimate relationships.

Relationships like these are rare, perhaps in part because they require a degree of commitment to others that is not common in our society. More often, it seems, there is competition, selfishness, personal status seeking, avoidance of friendships, and a resulting loneliness and sense of isolation. According to Erikson, when young adults fail to develop intimacy, the future is more difficult because people feel isolated and distant from other human beings.

4. *Direction.* In their studies of young adults, the Yale researchers found that many young people have a "Dream" of the kind of life they want to lead.[35] This Dream is an imaginary picture of what life could be like. At first the Dream is vague and unrealistic, but as one moves into the twenties the Dream gets clearer. Life circumstances, parents, or friends may encourage or interfere with the Dream, but regardless of what others may think, this Dream can generate excitement, vitality, and life purpose. The Yale research team demonstrated that people who build their lives around a Dream in early adulthood have a better chance for personal fulfillment, even though there may be times of struggle in maintaining the commitment and working toward the Dream's fulfillment. When there is no Dream, people drift.

In a book that became very popular among adults of all ages, David Wilkinson wrote that Dreams for life come from the Dream Giver, who is God. Many people fail to see their life Dream or to fulfill it, so Wilkinson took on the role of a Dream Coach and gave practical guidelines for helping readers find their dreams and turn them into reality.[36]

Often, Dreams are formed, clarified, and strengthened through a relationship with a mentor. A mentor is a teacher, model, advisor, guide, sponsor, or discipler who usually is at least several years older than the young adult and experienced in the world into which the young person is entering. Some young adults have mentors whom they admire, respect, and seek to emulate, even though they have never met. More effective is a mutual caring relationship between two adults in which the older person guides the younger, at least until he or she is able to stand alone. Sometimes, the closeness of this relationship makes it difficult to terminate, especially when the mentor's help is no longer needed. When the mentor and protégé are close, and when the mentor is not threatened by the younger person's independence or success, the two can become long-time friends who support and challenge each other as they journey together through life.

Mentoring has become a popular concept in recent years, but as one young leader has written, "Everybody seems to be talking about mentoring. But where's the hard evidence that it exists?"[37] Maybe we talk about mentoring more than we do it. Even though they may never use the word, counselors often take on the role of mentors to their counselees and give a lot of help as a result.[38]

Two major choices must be made if young adults are to move smoothly through this period of time. They must choose an occupation and make a decision about marriage. Of course, these may occur simultaneously or separately, and each may take several years. When a young person wants to choose carefully and wisely, he or she may go through a period of exploring alternatives before making a serious choice. In some societies or parts of the country, young people rarely are viewed as fully adults until they are established in a career and marriage. Children may or may not follow. Unlike previous generations, many young adults now appear to be marrying later and postponing the decision to have children until they are into their thirties or their careers are successfully in place.

5. *Spirituality.* "A new spirituality is engulfing the world and invading our lives with lightning speed," I wrote in a book on spirituality. "It is strong and growing stronger, grabbing the attention of thousands with its recognition of individual needs, its focus on personal experiences, and its willingness to let people go on their own spiritual journeys without having to worry about religious rituals, rules, or creeds."[39] With a growing rejection of the "unworkable philosophies of hedonism, narcissism, and materialism,"[40] especially among the young, there has been a new search for spiritual moorings. Entering adulthood in times of great change, uncertainty, information overload, and fluctuating values, younger people are longing for something solid on which to build their lives. For many this search means spirituality without traditional religion. It also means pursuing God in the company of friends.[41]

A surprising number of younger adults, at least in Western societies, are finding new hope and spiritual fulfillment in the emergent or somewhat similar missional churches that tend to express their beliefs uniquely but build on centuries of theology, biblical study, and spiritual formation.[42] These are religious communities that show acceptance, offer hope, reach out unselfishly, are not afraid of pop culture, embrace experiential worship, but avoid forcing anybody to join. These are communities of fellow journeyers who go about their lives and their work but who have a desire to follow Jesus whatever this may mean and wherever it leads.

Regardless of their conclusions about religion or spirituality, finding a workable faith is a quest for many adults in their twenties and thirties. Without this anchor they can flounder, lacking the spiritual attachments that help give meaning and purpose to their lives.

These challenges of this age group—competence, independence, intimacy, direction, and spirituality—can be exciting and, at the same time, the cause of personal concerns and problems. When counselors understand the challenges this age group faces, it is easier to give the guidance and the help that people need during the third and fourth decades of life.

The Effects of Problems in Twenty- and Thirty-Year-Olds

People in their twenties and thirties are known as young adults, but vast differences exist within this broad age group. In their twenties, young adults are breaking away from their families, exploring careers and dreams, clarifying values, and building relationships. The three greatest challenges facing twenty-somethings are achieving an adult identity, sustaining intimate relationships with others, and developing a distinct career or work identity.[43] A lack of one of these can lead to intense loneliness. As they approach thirty, young adults should have established independence, made many of the significant decisions of adult life, corrected the course of their lives at different times, and moved to the place where they are ready to prove themselves. Some feel an urgency about reaching their goals, especially those who still have confusion about where their lives are going. For many, life becomes a whirlwind of work, child-rearing, and balancing demands and responsibilities. Intimacy begins to slip, and sex is often forgotten in the midst of other activities. It is common to find those who have started down the long road of young adulthood but have stumbled. Most people pick themselves up and keep going, but by the time they reach midlife many are struggling with past failures, trying to recover from broken relationships, facing disillusions about life, and passing into a painful tumultuous time of life reevaluation. Why do so many people seem to pass through young adulthood with these kinds of scars and disappointments?

Part of the answer lies in the life patterns that young people develop in their twenties and early thirties. Popular writer Gail Sheehy suggested these more than a quarter century ago, but they still apply.[44]

- Transients are unwilling or unable to make any firm commitments in their twenties. These are people who try to prolong the period of youth, and some seem tied to their families in unhealthy ways. Around age thirty many feel an urgent push to establish some long-term goals and attachments, but they realize that they have been passed by their peers who have moved forward.

- Locked-in people made solid commitments in their twenties without giving their decisions much thought. This might include people who went into the family business, entered a profession to please some family member, or took a job without much thought and now are trapped because they lack the skills or training to move on. Some of these people may feel secure financially, but they're also trapped in a rut and angry with themselves because they never took the time earlier to decide what they really wanted. Couples trapped in dull- or tension-filled marriages may have similar feelings.

- Workaholics are hard-driving people, goal-dominated, ambitious, and seemingly filled with energy. They also may be insecure, unwilling to let others get close, insensitive, afraid of failure, and vaguely hoping that all insecurities will vanish when they reach the top of their professions.

- Early peakers are an elite group who reached their goals early, perhaps because of exceptional musical or acting talent, athletic success, inherited money, or unusual opportunities. These people have built their identities around their careers or fame, but many burn out when they reach the thirties and feel alienated, without goals, and living in their pasts.

- Integrators are a healthier group that has learned to balance their ambitions, work, family, and personal lives. This may mean balancing careers, marriage, parenting, and spiritual lives. This rarely comes before one is thirty and usually only happens to those who work for it.

- Care-givers include young parents who find fulfillment in building their families, but also teachers, missionaries, pastors, or medical practitioners who are committed to serving others rather than building their careers.

The dedication and achievements of these people often are admired, but problems arise if they are not realistic enough to take care of their own needs, as well as the needs of others.

Is it possible for young adults to fit into more than one of these groups, such as being nurturers and achievers without running themselves ragged? As they move through young adulthood, perhaps individuals need to keep several options open, focus attention primarily on one or two roles, and leave the others for the future. Otherwise, the young person may be overwhelmed by the pressures and conflicts that seem to come with special intensity during this time in life.

Counseling Twenty- and Thirty-Year-Olds

Professional journals often include articles on counseling college students (perhaps because most journal articles are written by college professors), but far fewer publications discuss counseling young adults who are not in school or who are beyond college age. Often these counselees come with problems of depression, career uncertainty, anxiety, interpersonal conflicts, or other issues that are not limited to any one age group. When compared with older people, counselees in their twenties or thirties often are more flexible, enthusiastic, willing to change, and less threatened by the idea of counseling.

Like counselees of all ages, young adults often show most improvement when they work with a counselor who is willing to build a caring relationship, who understands the unique needs and struggles of this age group, and who is willing to serve at least temporarily as a mentor. Counselors of young adults might keep the following goals in mind as they work.

1. *Problem Awareness.* Counselees are not likely to change until they have a clear awareness of the problem. Together, the counselor and counselee first attempt to clarify the problems, to better understand what counselee behaviors might be creating the problems, and then to set a temporary goal or goals for change.

2. *Support.* Young counselees often need reassurance that their problems are common and not evidence of mental illness. When they are taking steps to change or learning life skills, counselees often slip and fail. This can lead to self-castigation and increased frustration, even though failures are common. The existence of a helping, reassuring relationship enables the counselor to show acceptance, empathy, understanding, encouragement, and the support that counselees need as they try new behaviors, take action, make decisions, learn new skills, and work to bring about change. It is especially important that counselors provide encouragement during times of turmoil or uncertainty. Counselors can bring understanding and help when young adults deal with intimacy and sexual issues, including struggles and fears about homosexuality, difficulties with self-control, or support in resolving interpersonal conflicts and building intimacy. In addition to practical guidance, there also is a need for compassionate assistance in coping with stress, anger, feelings of failure, depression, or thoughts of suicide.[45]

3. *Taking Action.* This is the process of helping counselees answer questions about what can be done to bring change or to solve problems. Depending on the counselee, you may want to spend time brainstorming about ideas, alternative

solutions, or actions that might be taken. Consider writing these down without stopping to evaluate any of them. Then go back over the list. Ask what has been tried before and found to work. Would something similar work again? What is new that might work, realistically? Eventually, perhaps after a time of prayer, select one or two strategies to try and then evaluate carefully later.

4. *Skill Development.* One of the greatest counseling challenges of this age group is to teach life skills that will help people reach their goals and make changes. Many need help in building relationship skills, decision-making skills, time-management skills, or skills in selecting and building a career. Few people are likely to work at learning new life skills, however, until they see the need for skill development. Counselees can be helped to determine the skills that need to be learned if the desired change is to come about. Then consider how to acquire, practice, and apply these skills.

5. *Getting Unstuck.* Much of counseling involves helping people who feel stuck in an undesirable job, living situation, geographical area, relationship, obligation, or other situation. The older we get, the harder it is to change; the risks may be greater, and the consequences that come with failure could be harder to accept or overcome. In the younger years, however, change may be easier. When I was an unmarried university student, for example, I felt stuck in my hometown where I had been attending college classes. So I went to study in England without enough money to live or to get back across the Atlantic. Overall, living in London was a wonderful experience, but if I did that today, especially if I tried to do it without enough money, my family could suffer, my mortgage wouldn't get paid, and people might be more critical and less tolerant of a jaunt overseas than they were when I was twenty-three.

Once a person becomes aware that he or she is stuck in a situation that needs to be changed, it helps to consider what behavior may be making the problem intolerable and what needs to be changed. With the counselor's help, the individual can consider the alternatives. What skills are needed to get unstuck? What actions can be taken? What is a viable plan for solving the problem? If a big change may be involved—like moving to a new location or going back to school—plan the change carefully and consider the risks, making a note of all that needs to be done and when.[46]

These counseling suggestions present a more cognitive-behavioral approach that often works well with twenty- and thirty-year-olds but may not work with everyone. Sometimes there needs to be opportunity to experience and talk about feelings, to deal with painful past experiences such as failure or abuse, to get helpful insights into the causes of problems, or to build the courage to take difficult steps toward change. You may have to deal with resistance to change or with fears about doing things differently. You may need to help some counselees deal with moral failure, guilt, and the need to forgive themselves as well as others. With counselees who respect or believe the Bible—and often with others—it can be helpful to look at Bible passages that encourage, challenge, or give insights into young adult behaviors.

The counselor can give acceptance, encouragement, prayer support, and guidance as these changes are being considered and implemented. Remember, however, that some people may choose not to change but to stay as they are. Sometimes, even young people have gone through so many life changes that they lack the energy, motivation, or courage to attempt another change. Point out that it is acceptable to wait until later. The longer they wait and avoid making decisions or taking action, the less likely they will be to attempt change or the less successful in reaching their goals or fulfilling the Dream.

Preventing Problems in Twenty- and Thirty-Year-Olds

After completing their in-depth studies of young men, the Yale researchers concluded that "the twenties and thirties are perhaps the most abundant and the most stressful decades in the life cycle. Given the tremendously difficult tasks of adaptation and development a young man [or woman] must deal with, this era cannot be made easy or simple to traverse. Still, much can be done to reduce the excessive stress and facilitate work on the developmental tasks."[47] To begin, the researchers suggest that it helps to assist young people in finding work and living environments where their personal and career development will be stimulated and not hindered.

Early in my counseling career, when I was working in a university counseling center, one of my counselees took ill. Since he didn't have a car, I offered to drive him home. When I saw the psychologically unhealthy family in which he lived, I had a new appreciation of the reasons why he was having problems and why the counseling was not working as well as I had hoped. Everything we had tried to accomplish in counseling was being undercut by his family. Regardless of age, if any counselee lives in a disorganized, fragmented, hypercritical environment, it will be difficult to prevent problems from developing or becoming worse. At times, the best preventive therapy may be helping the young adult to move. But there are other preventive approaches.

1. *Education and Encouragement.* As they move into adulthood and settle in, many people are surprised and overwhelmed by the pressures. College orientation courses often give warnings and practical coping suggestions to incoming students, but nothing can prepare us for the decisions and challenges that come in the early adult years. Church discussion groups, clubs for young mothers or for junior executives, suggestions for reading, cell groups, or an occasional sermon might alert young adults to the stresses, make recommendations for handling pressure, provide opportunity for discussion, and give participants an opportunity to encourage one another. When church or other preventive programs speak to real needs, sometimes the people come and participate.

But not always. A postmodern generation has grown skeptical of organized religion no matter how attractive or sophisticated the church's programs. In an era when everybody is busy, seminars and discussion groups do not attract many participants. People in their twenties and thirties are more likely to turn to their friends for guidance, to the Internet, or to chat rooms. In the context of counseling, people-helpers can give information or suggest reading or web sites that educate and help prevent future problems. These same counselors often educate through talks or articles that could reach younger audiences. But churches wanting to give education and encouragement may have a larger challenge. They must think of new and creative ways to reach out to a massive group of people who see no relevance in religion but who are starved for guidance. Start by getting to know people in their twenties and thirties and asking them how they can be reached. You might discover that even in their thirties and older, many people are less interested in preventive programs and more inclined to look for models and mentors who can point the way.

2. *Models.* Recently, I was invited to speak to a large group of people in their twenties. Before the meeting the chairman of the group asked if he could introduce me as a "grandfather type." He explained that "these people don't care a lot about your credentials or about the books you have written. They are looking for models, for people who have been on the road for a long time, for people who have lives and experiences that can be helpful to others." This group wanted me to "tell my story" and to give them hope and guidance for their life journeys. My friend added that many of these young adults do not respect parents, but they are more open to people who remind them of their grandparents.

If you are a counselor, you are a model to the people you counsel, even if this is never mentioned or if it never enters your mind. If you are a speaker, teacher, pastor, musician, businessperson, or even a neighbor or participant in a church, you also are a model. Looking back over my career as a professor, I have concluded that more important than my classroom teaching has been the example that my wife and I set for the students of my classes.

3. *Mentors.* It is a myth to conclude that people must have mentors to succeed, but there is abundant evidence, including evidence from the Yale researchers, to show that mentoring can be very helpful both to the mentors and to their young adult protégés. This may be true especially in cultures where family closeness tends to be rare. It also is true for people entering new vocations. One large company discovered, for example, that the organization and individuals both benefited when there was voluntary mentoring, with genuine bonds between mentors and protégés, and maximum freedom for people to spend time together discussing whatever they found to be helpful.[48] Formally organized mentoring programs for young adults do not always succeed. More often, people in their twenties and thirties respond to informal mentoring that is consistent but unstructured and more focused on topics as they arise. For counselors or church leaders who are interested in mentoring, it is a valid approach to pray about a mentoring relationship and then to be alert to finding some person who can mentor you, or to whom you can be a mentor. In that previously mentioned meeting where I spoke to people in their twenties, one participant said, "This is a room of people all of whom are starved for mentors and almost none of whom know how to find them."

4. *Dream Development.* The young adult's Dream—that imagined possibility that generates excitement and vitality—will be vague and ill-defined at first, but with time the idea becomes clearer. To translate that Dream into reality, a person must ponder, plan, and take step-by-step action to reach one's goal. The process begins when one asks "What would I like to be doing in ten years?" "Is this what God wants me to do?" "What steps would I have to take to reach my Dream?" When they work toward fulfilling a Dream, people of any age are less likely to develop self-defeating or frustrating life patterns.

5. *Parental Patience and Prayer.* It isn't easy for parents to watch their grown children flounder as they struggle with the emerging issues of adulthood. Sometimes, parents make matters worse because of their intolerance, frequent criticisms, and well-intentioned advice-giving. It is better if parents give encouragement, support, and a clear indication that they are available and willing

to talk. Parents should be reluctant to rescue their adult children with offers of money or other provisions that can give short-term help but that also enable the young adult to avoid responsibility. It is better to give gentle guidance when the needs arise. Sometimes, the best help for young adults is the guidance that Christian counselors or other church leaders give to the parents.

6. *Spiritual Support.* A friend once described how she was kept from a potentially disastrous and impulsive marriage. "My parents didn't lecture me," she said. "I knew they didn't care for my fiancé, but I also knew they were praying. They had a tremendous faith that their God was powerful enough to guide their grown kids in making important life decisions. Shortly before the wedding, I realized what a mistake I was making. I am convinced that a tremendous problem was prevented by the deep faith and consistent prayers of my parents." This could be a slogan for all Christian counselors, including parents, who counsel their children: Prayer often prevents potential problems.

Conclusions About Twenty- and Thirty-Year-Olds

If you have any interest in leadership, you may have heard the name of Warren Bennis. A former university president and founder of the Leadership Institute at University of Southern California, Bennis has written a number of books, including one titled *Geeks and Geezers*.[49] When Bennis was well into his seventies, he and his co-author set out to contrast people over seventy who are creative and filled with energy (those are the geezers) with potential-filled younger people in their twenties (the geeks) who, despite their youth, already had demonstrated leadership ability. At a conference one day, I sat fascinated as Bennis talked about his research, and afterward I rushed out to buy and read the book.

Books can get outdated quickly, and the Bennis conclusions will fade in accuracy as the years pass and as his observations are extended to other cultures, but consider what the researchers concluded about American twenty-year-olds around the turn of the century. They were described as people who:

- Grew up in an era of almost limitless options.
- Were "smothered with possibilities."
- Were very sophisticated in terms of media, computers, and other technology.
- Had few heroes.
- Were fascinated with spirituality, New Age philosophy and holistic living. even as organized religion faded in importance.
- Had "grander and more ambitious aspirations than geezers did at the same age."
- Were very impatient to achieve their goals.
- Were interested in technology, globalization, and growth, but not much concerned about financial or career security.
- Expected to have a number of careers over their lifetimes.
- Valued balance in life so that they would not be engulfed in work like older generations.
- Above all else revered the lessons learned from "just going out and doing it."

- Are in a hurry. According to most geeks, a central feature of their era, if not the central feature, is "speed."

Is it surprising to you that the people over seventy, who are most alive and vibrant, tend to be people who mentor, connect with, and learn from twenty- and thirty-year-olds like the people that Bennis and his co-author describe? These younger people may be overlooked in many counseling books, but this is a crucially important stage in human development. There can be problems at this time in life, and there often is a need for counseling, but helping twenty- and thirty-years-olds can be among the Christian counselor's most rewarding experiences.

KEY POINTS FOR BUSY COUNSELORS

➤ People between ages eighteen and thirty-nine have been given a number of labels, including *baby busters, generations X* and *Y, mosaics,* and even *young adults,* but these labels change in meaning as the years pass and as new labels emerge. Probably it is more accurate to refer to this group as people in their twenties and thirties, knowing that despite the many changes in this age stage, there also are common challenges and problems.

➤ Whatever their label, these young men and women are breaking away from their families of origin, finding their place in the adult world, and getting established.

➤ The Bible says very little about this era specifically, although many problems of the twenties and thirties are common in people at all ages, and many of the leaders in biblical history were younger people. Their numbers include Jesus, his mother Mary, Joseph, the young King David, and possibly Daniel, Esther, Nehemiah, and all of the disciples.

➤ The major challenges of the twenties and thirties are developing:
  - *Competency,* including
    - physical skills,
    - intellectual problem-solving skills,
    - emotional intelligence,
    - self-management skills,
    - interpersonal skills, and
    - spiritual skills.
  - *Independence,* which includes
    - developing self-sufficiency,
    - building an identity,
    - finding values, and
    - coping effectively.

- *Intimacy.*
- *Direction.*
- *Spirituality.*

➤ People in their twenties and thirties often get locked into life patterns that set their direction.

➤ The process of counseling includes:
  - Clarifying the problems that they are facing, bringing them to greater awareness.
  - Giving support.
  - Helping people take action.
  - Developing skills.
  - Helping counselees get unstuck.

➤ Problem prevention involves:
  - Education and encouragement.
  - Pointing to models.
  - Helping people find mentors.
  - Dream development.
  - Encouraging parental patience and prayer.
  - Giving spiritual support.

➤ Counseling twenty- and thirty-year-olds can be among the Christian counselor's most rewarding experiences.

16

Forties and Fifties

There was a big birthday celebration when Brad turned forty. His friends planned it carefully, and Brad was completely surprised when he entered a room where over fifty friends, relatives, and work associates were waiting. There was a pile of cards and presents on a table in the corner of the room, and Brad's wife had arranged for a great birthday dinner and a big cake. There were toasts to Brad, touching comments about his influence in the lives of his friends, jokes about his old age, and prayers for his future. Everybody agreed: It has been a wonderful celebration.

In the days that followed, Brad thought often about the party. He appreciated the efforts of his wife and his friends to make everything so special, but deep within his soul he felt an aching emptiness. The accolades had been sincere and affirming, but Brad's insecurities kept reminding him of his failures, lost opportunities, missed promotions, and unfulfilled dreams. He had laughed at the jokes, along with everybody else, but he often thought about the coming of old age and looked back at the party as a reminder that he was getting older. Brad had a good marriage and three great children, but nothing excited him much anymore. Work was boring, and so were his church, time with the kids, and sex with his wife. He knew he was more critical and irritable than he used to be; he struggled to pay the bills, rarely said anything positive, and hated the conflicts with his teenage son.

Brad never gave the appearance of being depressed, but his wife knew about his struggles and so did his best friend, who was having similar difficulties of his own. Brad understood why people his age might get involved with younger women, abandon their families, or quit their jobs in search of something better. He had been tempted to do both and recognized his own vulnerabilities. But Brad kept plugging away, living a routine life, and wondering if things would ever get better.

When I was growing up, my parents used to remind each other that life begins at forty. The people of my parents' generation had never heard of a midlife crisis, and if they experienced problems like Brad's, they kept them well hidden. People believed—or maybe tried to convince themselves—that forty was the midpoint in life (even though few people at the time lived to be eighty) and that the best years were still ahead. It's a belief that still persists. The years between forty and sixty often are the best time in life, according to one psychiatrist. This is the golden age of adulthood when physical health, emotional maturity, work satisfaction, and gratifying relationships can all be at their best.[1] Carl Jung, the famous Swiss psychiatrist, described these years as the time in life when people are free to move on to other things because they pretty much have completed tasks such as the "begetting of children . . . protecting the brood" and the "gaining of money and social position."[2]

For many people, however, moving into the forties can be a reminder that life is rushing by, that youthful opportunities are fading, and that there are fewer options for the future. "By your late thirties you may feel misguided by your earlier dreams, exhausted by your frenetic activities, and trapped in your career and intimate relationships," wrote Frederic Hudson.[3] Even if you have reached your dream and been successful, "you may feel disappointed that so much of your life has been consumed in that pursuit, at the expense of other activities that now seem important to you." The forties usher in a time of growing realization that all goals will not be reached, that time is running out, and that one must decide whether to keep moving in the same direction, or to make changes before it is too late.

Earlier editions of this book referred to the years between forty and sixty as middle age. Today, *middle age* is like the words *youth, young adulthood,* or *old age.* These are vague terms, defined differently depending on your age and on the life expectancies of the country where you live. When I was ten, living in Canada, I did not think that people in their forties were middle aged. I thought they were old. Today, I look at forty-year-olds and see them as being relatively young and in the prime of life. Regardless of our perceptions, the forties and fifties are decades of life characterized by self-examination, reevaluation of beliefs and values, readjustment to physical change, and reconsideration of one's lifestyle, career direction, and priorities.

All of this has relevance for Christian counseling. In churches, as in business, politics, and other parts of the society, people in their forties and fifties make most of the decisions, fulfill most top leadership positions, appear to have most of the power, and, despite some notable younger exceptions, earn and disperse most of the money. But these also are years when people struggle with boredom, declining vitality, marriage disintegration, shifting values, and sometimes the sense that they are stuck in demanding or dead-end careers and monotonous lives.[4] Clearly the concerns of this age group are basic to a lot of Christian counseling.

The Bible and the Forties and Fifties

Scripture says little about this age period, perhaps because relatively few people lived that long in Bible times, despite the famous individuals who lived to be very old. It is estimated that the life expectancy for people in the Bronze Age was eighteen years. In Greece it wasn't much longer, and by medieval times the average life span had risen only to thirty-seven years. Even in 1900, life expectancy was a relatively low fifty years, so there has been little historical precedent, age-related biblical instruction, or theological insight to guide modern people through their forties and fifties.[5]

Of greater help for Christian counselors are those biblical passages that speak to the major problems that are faced by people in this age group—problems relating to marriage, self-esteem, life purpose, work and careers, grief, interactions with children and older parents, spiritual issues, impatience, physical illness, disappointment, and similar issues. When these are discussed in Scripture, there is rarely reference to age. The biblical teachings and principles for living that apply universally must be adapted to each counselee's unique personal needs regardless of age.

The Causes of Problems in Forty- and Fifty-Year-Olds

According to Jung, most people are wholly unprepared to embark on the second half of life. Often we reach middle age without realizing that we now face new problems, but we cannot rely on the same solutions that were effective earlier.[6] Yale psychologist Daniel Levinson, whose work was discussed in the previous chapter, concluded that about the time they reach forty, most people go through a midlife transition. Eighty percent of the men in Levinson's study experienced the transition into middle age as a time of crisis as they began to realize that time was getting short and that important life goals were not likely to be reached. Search the Internet, and you will find a plethora of popular articles about midlife crises, even though some experts now believe that midlife crises are mostly confined to men, much rarer than previously thought, and "experienced by only a few."[7]

Whether or not there is crisis, turning forty brings a change in perspective. Most people stay in their jobs and carry on with their regular activities, at least for a while, but many begin to feel unsettled and sense that something is different. They begin to wonder about their purposes in life, their contributions, their values. They know that youth is fading, opportunities will be fewer, vitality is declining, and that life goals are not being reached. In their more reflective moments, some begin to wonder if marriage, occupation, religion, family, leisure, or other areas of life really satisfy or if they are becoming more frustrating and inhibiting. As they move into their early forties, many people feel pressure to take greater charge of their lives and to make changes before it is too late. Whenever we deal with transitions, including the changes that appear with the move into the forties, it is helpful to have people around us who are supportive and can guide in decision making. Too often, however, the comments, jokes about being "over the hill," and actions of others make the problems worse.

The twenty years between turning forty and reaching sixty is a large part of life. There are huge differences between what a man or woman faces at forty and what he or she deals with one or two decades later. Despite these differences, there are several issues that can cause problems throughout this period. We will look at four of these: physical, psychological, vocational, and marriage-family changes.

1. *Physical Changes*. The body already has begun to decline before midlife, but in the forties it is more difficult to ignore or to hide the changes. Gray hair, baldness, coarser skin, bags under the eyes, less flexibility in movements, decreased physical strength and stamina, the loss of a youthful appearance, and changes in body build all occur in midlife, and all are visible reminders that we are aging. The cessation of menstruation, declining sex drive, and increasing urinary frequency are more private reminders, as is the slowly emerging awareness that death is not as far away as we might like to think. Few people take physical changes as lightly as the middle-aged movie actress who remarked that her bust and hip measurements were the same as ever, except that within recent years "everything has slipped down about six inches." More often, people over forty begin to monitor their bodies, making comparisons to the shape of their bodies a decade earlier or comparing themselves with the youthful and more attractive bodies of others. Whereas body fat is only 10 percent of body weight in adolescence (more in people who habitually eat a lot of unhealthy foods), it is at least 20 percent by middle age, and most of that settles around or below the waist. As the bust or chest gets smaller, the abdomen and hips get larger. All of this can lead appearance-conscious people to go on diets, start exercise programs, and give more attention to clothing and cosmetics.

Many people move into the fourth decade aware that they need to take better care their bodies. Most mornings around 5 a.m., I work out at a fitness club along with a few younger people and a stalwart group of older men and women who have been exercising for years. But the majority of my fellow early morning exercisers appear to be in their forties or early fifties. Some people at this age are discouraged about the perceived loss of youthfulness and attractiveness. Many begin to realize that weight gains, feelings of stagnation, increasing lethargy, weakened bodies, and unattractive paunches can all be one's own fault. All can be made worse by drug and alcohol use, by work-driven lifestyles, and by overeating and too much sedentary living.

With both sexes, the middle years bring a decline in vigor. For twenty or more years, most people are involved in building a career, working at their jobs, developing a family, and a variety of activities. Eventually, most reach a time in life when they feel tired and unenthusiastic about the fact that at least twenty or thirty more years must pass before retirement. Men and women who have not succeeded in reaching their youthful goals may push themselves at this point in a concerted effort to be successful and to prove their worth. Others work harder to keep ahead of their demanding schedules. All of this can cause some people to collapse physically or emotionally, while others begin to think of ways to change, withdraw, or slow down and reduce stress.

2. *Psychological Changes.* In 2004 the last of the baby boomers (the post-World War II generation) moved into the forties, and the oldest of the group were close to retirement. Although there are many exceptions, this is a generation that came into adulthood with high expectations. They became men and women who were well educated, driven to succeed, filled with optimism, steeped in rock music, committed to self-gratification, and enamored by affluence and possessions. Many abandoned organized religion and looked for nontraditional spiritual experiences, but those who stayed connected with the church often wanted high-quality worship productions and state-of-the-art facilities. Many of the baby boomers are active, take-charge people who are unlikely to accept aging without resisting. Their high expectations for life probably will stay with many until they die.

For many people in their forties and fifties, this is the prime of life when they are at the height of their influence, creativity, personal accomplishments, and earning capacity. This also can be a time when people feel overwhelmed by too many obligations, duties, and seemingly insignificant demands for their time. People in this age group have many friends, work acquaintances, relatives, fitness club colleagues, and religious associates, most of whom are active, in good health, and still feeling far removed from worries about retirement or terminal illness. Even so, middle age can be a time of boredom, fear, and reappraisal.

(a) Boredom. In the middle years, the excitement and challenge of establishing a career and launching a marriage can give way to what has been called "middle-age blahs." Everyday routines at work or home, dull and uninspiring church services, marriages that have lost their luster, and duty-motivated visits with uninteresting relatives can all merge into a routine of boredom. This boredom can be made worse by ongoing daily frustrations, such as a house that always needs work, monthly bills that must be paid, bosses that make continual demands, and children with perpetual needs. The boredom problem is greater in what have been called "constrained people" and "excitement addicts."[8] Constrained people are fearful, never-take-a-chance personalities who always abide by the rules and rarely allow themselves to have pleasurable or intellectually stimulating experiences. It is not surprising that their lives are boring. In contrast, the excitement addicts thrive on taking risks, but they get bored when they run out of exciting things to do or when declining physical strength or increasing responsibilities force them to slow down. For some, boredom leads to depression, inertia, excessive worry, or mindless addiction to television. Others try to escape their boredom through extramarital affairs, radical lifestyle or job changes, the pursuit of more exciting activities such as gambling, or unconventional and outlandish dress.

(b) Fear. It is common for people to feel afraid as they see physical changes within themselves, watch their aging parents, and observe the struggles of their middle-aged friends. For many this time in life brings the first major health problems or thoughts about death. Many are concerned about the empty nest that will come when the children leave home. Some fear that younger people will replace them at work or that physical limitations will force them to accept unwanted lifestyle changes. They may not talk about it, but others are afraid that they may lose the desire or ability to be sexually active and attractive. Plenty of evidence indicates sexual drive and fulfillment persist in people whose sexual activity has been pleasurable and consistent during earlier years, but fear of impotence, lack of privacy, a lifestyle that is too busy or rushed, marital tensions, and worry about decreased sex drive can all create tension in bed. It is then that the feared inability to perform becomes a reality.

(c) Reappraisal. All of this can stimulate middle-age reflection, reevaluation, dissatisfaction, and search for new purpose and self-esteem. Bob Buford was a successful businessman whose life was driven by the pursuit of success. When he entered his forties, Buford realized that he was now at the halftime point in life and concluded that he wanted to move from the pursuit of success into activities that would make a difference and lead to significance. Buford wrote a best-selling book titled *Halftime*, followed by seminars and other books designed to help people deal with the halftime issues and move from success to significance as they entered the second half of life.[9] Many people are addicted to the drive for success by the time they reach the forties and fifties according to Buford. Some try to disengage from this, but they lack the resources to make the shift, are afraid to try something new, or are too tied to their comfortable lives. Others jump too quickly into new careers or take early retirement only to discover that the long anticipated changes or a life of relaxation quickly leads to frustration, boredom, and a sense of meaninglessness. All of this stimulates further reappraisal of one's ambitions, life direction, and priorities. This reappraisal is both a common characteristic of the middle years and a basis for much of the counseling that is done with people in this age group.

3. *Vocational Changes.* As people mature, they appear to develop a greater inclination to silently talk to themselves about life experiences. When work is not satisfying, this inner dialogue may involve anger directed toward the job or toward the people at work, and self-criticism for being in such an undesirable vocation. Every line of work has its less attractive features, which become more obvious the longer we work at a job. If we feel bored, no longer challenged, taken for granted, pressured, or afraid of failure, it is easy to get disappointed and disillusioned. If career goals are not being met, we feel restless, frustrated, and sometimes trapped. Often we struggle intellectually about whether to hold on to a secure but unfulfilling job, or to let go and risk finding something better.

Even people who have been successful in their careers can reach a point when they feel inadequate and self-critical. Several years ago, *Fortune* magazine devoted a cover story to the problem of guilt among successful executives. According to a survey of the magazine's readers, the number one cause of executives' guilt concerned their children: Who was taking care of the kids and how would they turn out?[10] As one moves up the ladder of success, responsibilities become greater, time with families may become scarcer, and competition at work may become stronger—all at a time when physical energies are declining. Some people are asked to train new and younger workers who, in time, could take their jobs. Others lose their jobs at midlife, including executives with major responsibilities or long-time employees who are let go in times of downsizing or mergers. These people face the lowered self-esteem and the psychological trauma of being unemployed and unable to find work that is consistent with their capabilities, experience, or previous earning capacity. Homemakers, whose lives may have been busy and productive, reach the middle-age years and discover that the nest is emptying and there is less need for their services at home. These changes can lead to frustration and self-pity, but it also leads some to step out and find a vocation that is new, different, and potentially more fulfilling. Taking a new job can lead to conflict at home if the spouse or family is not supportive of this move.

4. *Marriage-Family Changes.* Freud once said that the need of every person is *leben und arbeiten*—to love and to work. If we don't find fulfillment in these areas, our lives are incomplete. We have already discussed work, but what about middle-aged love? We will consider four aspects of this issue: love as it relates to children, parents, spouse, and sex.

(a) Children. When they are in their forties and fifties, parents watch their children grow into adulthood and leave to build their own lives. This can create tensions, especially if parents are unsuccessful in the three tasks of letting their children go, achieving equality with their adult children, and integrating new members into the family.

It can be difficult *letting go.* When children leave home, it is common for parents to grieve, to hang on, and to feel depressed, empty, and lonely. Some parents struggle with guilt over past failures and feel they no longer are needed or useful. Interspersed with these feelings may be parental envy over the freedom their children now experience, family competition, or feelings of being excluded from the lives and activities of their maturing offspring. Some parents experience an identity crisis as the last child leaves. They begin to reexamine their roles in the home and wonder, "What is my purpose in life now?" It is not surprising that this sense of loss is most acute when children move far away or emigrate to other countries.[11] This letting go and watching adult children leave tends to be less painful when one or both parents work or find other satisfaction outside the home. Instead of a depressed mood, these parents experience relief, freedom, and renewed vigor when the children leave. There also are fewer hassles.[12] But with the children gone, both parents must face each other and more realistically evaluate the status of their marriage.

As part of letting children go, parents need to accept autonomy and independence in their offspring, working with their offspring at *achieving equality* in place of the unequal relationship that has existed previously. This shift in attitudes and behavior will be difficult until the parents accept the reality that their adult child or children have lives of their own and are involved in close, sometimes intimate, relationships with others, apart from the original family.

After the parents and their adult children have achieved some measure of equality, there arises the challenge of *integrating new members into the family*. Weddings can be joyful occasions, but even as the young couple learns to be a part of at least three families (their own and each of the families where they grew up), parents must learn to be in-laws. This involves accepting the new family member, cultivating the relationship, and adjusting to the idea that one's own son or daughter has a new primary family identity. The birth of children can smooth this process, although more problems can develop if the grandparents are critical or overcontrolling. When all of this integration is not smooth, tensions appear that can last for years.

(b) Older Parents. Caught up with the challenges of raising a family and growing in their careers, adults often fail to notice that their own parents are growing older. Sometimes, a major health problem comes as a wake-up call to grown children who are confronted with the fact that their parents are not as healthy as they once were, and perhaps not as independent or financially stable. In time, the parents become more dependent on their middle-aged children, some of whom find themselves in what has been called the "sandwich generation." This is a time of life when adults feel caught and sometimes torn between two generations, one older and one younger, both of whom have needs for help and guidance. Eventually, roles become reversed, and the parents become dependent on the adult children. This can create added pressure in middle age, along with the constant reminders that everybody is growing older.[13]

(c) Marriage. It is widely agreed that individuals go through a series of stages as they progress through life, but parenting and marriages also go through stages. For example, at some time in the years between forty and sixty, marriages often move into a stage of increased stress. Many people begin to reappraise their marriages, and some struggle with the question of whether to settle for what they have or to search for a new partner who might be better. Bored with family routines, well aware of the weaknesses of one's mate, no longer held together by dependent children, and tired of routine sex, many couples conclude that their marriages are in a state of instability or crisis. The husband and wife each get further involved in their own activities, and their intimacy and ability to communicate often decline. The couple may live in the same house and sleep in the same bed, but emotionally they go in different directions, resign themselves to the reality of marital boredom, decide on divorce, or find that one (or both) of the partners has slipped into a midlife affair.[14] Affairs may give temporary excitement, the experience of being cared for, a new sense of closeness, and reassurance of one's sexual prowess or continuing attractiveness to the opposite sex. But long-term affairs, like short-term unfaithfulness, can create a lot of tension, arouse guilt, and put so much strain on a marriage that divorce often follows.

(d) Sexual Changes. Aware of their reduced vigor, loss in attractiveness, and declining sexual urges, people often lose interest in sex and conclude that satisfying intercourse is rare after forty or fifty. Counselor Jim Conway has described the problem concisely. He wrote that at midlife,

a man's sexual capacity is his single greatest concern. Often he is afraid of losing his sexual ability. The drama goes something like this: a man is overextended at work. He is running out of energy. Younger men seem eager to take his place. He is on innumerable boards and committees for the community and the church. His family has giant financial needs, and there never seems to be enough money to go around. With that as a background, he crawls into bed at night. His wife is experiencing a new sexual awakening. Instead of being passive, she begins aggressive sexual moves on him. To his amazement, he finds he is extremely slow in being ready for the sex act. Partway through intercourse, he may lose his erection, and at that moment, he suddenly believes life is all over. He no longer is a man. It's exactly as he had heard— the middle years mean the end of sex.[15]

This attitude can lead people to "give up" on sex or to plunge into an affair in order to prove one's attractiveness and virility. The prevalence of such affairs shows that sex after forty or after menopause is not only possible—it can be better and more satisfying than it was in the earlier years.

This emphasis on marriage and family must not ignore the fact that single people reach their forties and fifties too. One Christian counselor has suggested that there cannot be a successful resolution of midlife problems unless the twin issues of vocation and marriage can be faced and worked through.[16] This presents unique challenges to unmarried people, including the divorced and single parents. Many are forced to accept the reality that many single people in their forties remain alone for the rest of their lives. This possibility can intensify midlife struggles and push many singles either to withdraw or to find ways to live full and meaningful lives as unmarried adults. The forty to fifty age period, therefore, affects each person, married or single, in unique ways.

The Effects of Problems in Forty- and Fifty-Year-Olds

Counseling books tend to focus on what is wrong with life without mentioning what is good. While some people struggle with the problems of making it from forty to fifty, others are like a friend of our family who described her philosophy of living. "I'm forty-seven and this is the best age to be," she exclaimed enthusiastically. "I don't want to be younger or older." She had kept that attitude even when some intense stresses—including middle-age stresses—had invaded her life. Today, she lives in another country, and we have lost contact. Probably, she is in her seventies, but I suspect she has the same positive attitude and still believes that whatever her age, "this is the best age to be."

Even when our attitudes are positive, however, almost everyone is affected in some way by middle age and its pressures. These effects can be hidden within and experienced internally, shown in outward behavior, seen at work, or reflected in all our relationships, including our marriages and families.

1. *Hidden Emotional Effects.* General Douglas McArthur once said that age is a mind-set. Regardless of how their bodies change, some people accept the fact that they are growing older and determine that the second half of life will be even better than the first half. Others resist the aging process, at least in their minds, and sometimes experience anger, bitterness, frustration, a sense of failure, boredom, self-pity, and discouragement. These inner feelings may be ignored for a while but then come and go, one or two at a time. Each swells up with brief intensity but then recedes into the background until they rise up again in response to some reminder that the aging process is making progress. There may be disenchant-

ment with life, periods of sadness, the fears that were mentioned earlier, a sense of futility, and some envy of the freedom, exuberance, and potential in young people. This turmoil or emotional conflict may have been present for years, but the long hidden problems don't come into focus until a person encounters the pressures and realities of middle life.

2. *Outward Behavioral Effects.* Whenever a person tries to keep feelings hidden, they appear in other ways. People become irritable, impatient, complaining, preoccupied with things other than their work or family, less efficient, restless, and sometimes prone to overactivity. Some people try to escape by working harder, getting more involved in more social activities, heavier drinking, excessive involvement with television and spectator sports, or by preoccupation with hypochondriacal physical symptoms. Undoubtedly, many members of fitness clubs work out intensely, in part to convince themselves that they can still keep up with the younger club members. In addition, there may be the frequently noticed middle-age attempts to break out of one's routine by changing jobs or residence, altering lifestyles, or dressing in styles that are designed to create a new and more youthful image.

3. *Vocational Effects.* There are three ways in which a man or woman can react to the midlife disillusionment with work.[17] First, there can be a harder push in an effort toward greater success. Since many people measure their worth in terms of work, it becomes critically important to succeed at the job even if this means becoming a workaholic.

A second reaction is to give up in discouragement. Sometimes there is anger, resistance in the form of lowered productivity, or an attitude of resignation that says, "It makes no sense to work so hard since I'll never be appreciated or get anywhere here." This dissatisfaction may come because the person's interests, values, goals, strengths, and abilities do not match what the job requires. This can be true of the frustrated employee as well as the frustrated housewife who is tired of her work as a homemaker. Both may feel trapped in their unsatisfying jobs.

A third reaction is to use one's dissatisfaction as a springboard for change. This may involve risk and often it takes courage. Some people change their jobs in an attempt to find new work that better fits their interests, abilities, and personality characteristics. Others choose to stay in the same unfulfilling vocations, but they reorganize other parts of their lives so there is more overall satisfaction in living.[18]

In addition, there are those who lose their jobs. This is especially devastating at midlife or later when financial or family responsibilities are great, and when few good-paying, challenging positions are available for people in their forties or older.

4. *Marriage-Family Effects.* It can be difficult to live with a family member who is struggling through issues relating to midlife and beyond. People in the home can be greatly affected by the vacillating emotions, changing attitudes, and on-again-off-again planning that sometimes occurs in middle age. The family suffers most when there is an affair, an abrupt change in lifestyle, or the loss of work with its resulting influence on family finances and on the unemployed family member's self-esteem.

All of these changes can lead to inner reflection about one's relationships, achievements, failures, appearance, and future plans. Sometimes, this reflection and reappraisal of life are painful and self-critical. Often people in their forties and older decide to live differently in the future, even if this means changing careers, making major moves, or ending a marriage. Most often these are thoughtful decisions, often made after talking them over with friends or family. In the United States and many other countries, this kind of thinking is a very common part of midlife transitions whether we talk about it or not.

At some time during these middle years, many people do experience the midlife crisis that we mentioned earlier. This crisis can be "an upheaval of major proportions," a revolutionary turning point that involves significant life changes and emotional turmoil. Often the internal agitation is followed by a flurry of impulsive activity, such as leaving one's family, becoming involved with new sexual partners, or abandoning a career, all within a short period of time. The people who are left behind often are shocked by the abruptness of the change, wondering what happened and struggling to readjust.[19]

Counseling Forty- and Fifty-Year-Olds

It is easy for people in this age group to reach conclusions about themselves that are unrealistic and often negative. Counselors can help these people reach more realistic perceptions about their place in life, their past successes and failures, and their prospects for the future. Many counselees find great value in talking through their fears and uncertainties about the second half of life. They can be helped to reorder their priorities and values, see new potential for growth and fulfillment, set new goals, and be educated about both the pressures and the opportunities of the coming years. Sometimes, people need to acknowledge the positive features of their lives and relationships. There may be a need to change how one relates to parents or children. Often forty- and fifty-year-olds need help in admitting that they are getting older and that time is getting shorter.

Magazine articles and popular self-help books offer common sense, but often-forgotten or neglected suggestions about middle life that might be shared, at times, with a counselee:

- Get periodic and regular physical checkups.
- Make regular exercise and sufficient rest a part of your routine.
- Work to control your diet and keep your weight down.
- Try to find and take the time for reading and reflection.
- Get into the habit of saying no to the outside demands that so frequently crowd the schedules of people in this time of life.
- Even as you say no to some things, consider taking on new challenges or activities that could add variety to life and change from regular routines—providing these activities do not add significant additional stress.
- Listen to music or make time for other activities that can be relaxing.
- Postpone major decisions, especially about your job, residence, or marriage, until you have taken sufficient time for reflection and discussion with insightful friends or a counselor.
- Make prayer a priority, and cultivate your spiritual life and relationship with God.

Building a good counselor-counselee relationship is basic to all counseling, but it is especially important when working with someone who feels inadequate, discouraged about the future, or trapped by an unfulfilling career or relationships. A good counseling relationship provides the emotional support that frees the middle-aged person to express frustrations and to slowly regain self-esteem and the courage to move more freely into the second half of life. At times, a strong dependency on the counselor may develop. This may be needed for a while, but the counselee can be helped to make decisions and take responsibilities that eventually will lead to greater self-reliance. This is more likely if the counselor can build a collaborative let's-work-together-on-this attitude into the counseling.

Counselors need to model tolerance, patience, interest, understanding, and acceptance mixed with a strong dose of realistic thinking that helps the counselee keep things in perspective. Periodically remind counselees that problems in the fifties and fifties often are temporary. Most people have no crisis at this time in life, and it can be reassuring for counselees to know that prognosis for improvement is usually excellent. There are several issues to remember in working with people in their forties and fifties

1. *Focus on Specific Problem Issues.* By careful listening and periodic questioning, seek to determine exactly what is bothering the middle-aged counselee. What are his or her feelings? How much clear evidence is there to support the complaints? In practical ways, what can be done about the inner turmoil and its causes?

As people move into the forties, most problems develop because individuals fail to admit that they are changing and growing older, or feel confused and uncertain about what to do with their lives from this point forward. The counselor's task is to stimulate discussion of specific midlife concerns and to help counselees reach realistic solutions. At times, counselees will need guidance as they make important decisions about life, values, vocation, marriage, and family issues. The counselee may need encouragement to slow down, to modify life goals, or to talk about physical changes or the inevitability of death. Some may need help in letting grown children develop their own independent lives. Often people need help with stress or time management, and some may need encouragement to play, to find activities that they can enjoy apart from work, or to learn how to move from a life driven by success to a life that has greater significance for oneself, for others, and for God's kingdom.

As they deal with specific issues, some people need help in making a distinction between courage and foolhardiness.[20] It can be courageous and exciting to move into a new career, to launch an innovative project, or to build new relationships. But it is foolhardy to plunge into something new without taking the time to consider and reduce the risks involved. Most of us know of men who became buoyed by the passion and excitement of a sexual affair, so they decided to divorce their wives and launch a new marriage—only to conclude later that they made a terrible and foolhardy mistake.

When they are about to make foolhardy decisions, people aren't always willing to listen to reason—especially that which comes from a spouse, pastor, or other counselor. If you condemn or ridicule an idea that seems foolish, the counselee is likely to resist or become defensive. In times like these, rational thinking gives way to emotions. When he decided to leave his family, move away from the church, and give up his practice, a counselor friend was urged to reconsider by a number of his Christian counseling colleagues. "I understand your arguments, and I know why you are telling me this," he responded. "But I know in my heart that I this is what I have to do, so I am going to do it whatever you say." Urge these people to think about the long-term consequences and implications of their plans before they take action. Try to convince them to get the perspective and guidance of others whom they respect. If the counselee is considering a residential, career, or job change, suggest that no action be taken until they reflect further and get additional information. If they think it through thoroughly and get all the facts, the planned change may then seem less desirable than it appeared at first.

In all things, encourage counselees to pray and seek God's divine guidance before making a change. Often there is an inner sense of peace when one is moving in the right direction. Realistically, of course, people who make impulsive decisions at any time in life are less inclined to listen to the voice of God, who might nudge them in a direction that is not where they want to go.[21] As you might expect, people who are on the verge of making foolish decisions often will do anything possible to avoid friends or others who would caution them to reconsider or to examine their emotions and motivations. These are people whose minds often are already made up, and they are not interested in getting alternative perspectives from other people or from God.

2. *Work with Families.* When a person does leave the family or take impulsive or other actions, the counselor's task is to help the family pick up the pieces and go on with life. This is an extremely challenging task. The people left behind often feel hurt, rejected, angry, sad, self-critical because of their own assumed failures, and confused about what to do next.

Of course, not all families experience such difficult circumstances. Often an understanding, supportive, and interested family can do much to help an individual deal with the transition into middle life and move successfully through the forties and fifties. The Christian counselor can help the family, especially the spouse, understand the problems of this time of life, give support and encouragement in the home, participate in and sometimes guide decisions, and help in dealing with boredom, fatigue, changing self-image, fears, vocational frustrations, and marital tensions. The spouses can help each other work at maintaining and building better sexual relationships. This, in turn, can prevent some of the frustrations that make one or both of the spouses susceptible to affairs.

Do not assume that family members will have an easy task as they try to help someone face the second half of life. Since husbands and wives often face this time together, it can be difficult for one to help the other. Spouses and other family members will need patience, a willingness to understand, and the courage to challenge the middle-aged person's thinking when this seems wise. Since the counselee may be moody and not easy to live with, family members may need periodic encouragement and coaching from an understanding counselor.

Counseling books focus on problems, so the previous paragraphs may have painted a picture of the forties and fifties that is too negative. It needs to be emphasized that people find this to be a good time in life, maybe the best time. Often this is a time of greater independence, freedom from the heavier expenses and demands of growing children, greater security in work, and a time to let up on some of the push to get ahead and drive for success. This is the time when some people start to think about legacy and begin making life changes that will make the second half of life better than the first half.

3. *Stimulate Mentoring and Generativity.* Erik Erikson was one of the most respected psychiatric writers of the twentieth century. After a distinguished and sometimes politically controversial career as a professor and psychoanalyst, Erikson turned his attention to in-depth studies of human development and the life

cycle. He wrote about youth in *Young Man Luther*, and when he was going through his own midlife transition and then moving into his sixties, Erikson wrote an in-depth study of Mohandas Gandhi.[22]

According to Erikson, people between the ages of forty and sixty move toward either generativity or stagnation. Generativity is a concern for establishing and guiding the next generation. This is more than caring for one's own children. Generativity involves passing on one's knowledge and skills to younger people and organizations. People who do this experience great satisfaction as they draw on their experiences and give from what they have learned in life. In contrast, if people in their forties and fifties avoid this giving generativity role, they stagnate. Stagnation involves a self-focus, sometimes accompanied by depression or an escape into alcohol or other forms of substance abuse, marital infidelities, or other irresponsibility. If these persons head companies or organizations, the stagnation spreads, and the organizations decline just like their leaders.

Probably most people have not heard of generativity, but they do know about mentoring. The Yale research on adult development stressed the value of mentors in guiding younger men and women as they entered their careers. For decades businesses, universities, and professions have seen the value of mentors and tried to stimulate mentoring programs. Many churches have done the same. Even though it is easier to talk about mentoring than to do it, there is evidence that when young people have mentors, they often benefit from the relationship. Erikson was one of the first to show that in this process the mentor can benefit as much as (or more than) the protégé. Counselors, therefore, can encourage people in their forties and older to be mentors, but there is one warning. When protégés begin to grow beyond their mentors or have more success, tension can develop between mentor and protégé, especially if the mentor feels threatened.[23]

4. *Encourage Spiritual Awareness*. The Bible was written to teach us about God and ourselves. Its pages bring comfort and direction to any person who takes the time to read carefully. The comfort and direction do not always come quickly, and neither are they usually experienced as emotional highs. Instead, consistent communion with God helps us remember that he is present with us and ministering through his Holy Spirit, regardless of the circumstances in our lives.

As they reevaluate the direction of their lives, people in their forties and fifties can benefit greatly from a walk with God that gives them supernatural support. They benefit, too, from the close friendship of others with whom they can pray, share thoughts and feelings, get fresh perspectives, find accountability, laugh when they feel like it, and feel free to cry when they feel depressed. The Christian counselor can fill this role, but so can family and friends.

Preventing Problems in Forty- and Fifty-Year-Olds

Many years ago Carl Jung noted that we have schools and colleges to help people prepare for early adulthood, but there are no colleges for forty-year-olds who need to be educated in the intricacies of living as older adults.[24] If we did have such colleges, most people in their forties or fifties would be too busy to attend. Even so, community institutions, especially churches, can offer the preparation and help to prevent serious midlife problems. This can be done in several ways.

1. *Anticipation*. While the forties and fifties can be a time for problems, these years also can be filled with rewards and challenges. For many in this age group,

these are the years when there is a sense of being settled, of having found one's place in life, and of being freed from the demands and responsibilities of raising small children. When compared with younger adults, middle-aged people often have more financial security, positions of prestige and leadership in the community, more opportunity to travel, and increased wisdom. This is not true for everybody, of course, but for many people the striving to get established and the financial struggles of the twenties and thirties have passed and the forties or fifties present a greater opportunity for fulfilling activities and for significant Christian service. It should not be assumed or implied that there is nothing to live for after thirty-nine—or after one turns fifty. People can be helped to anticipate both the positive and negative aspects of this period in life. Magazine or newspaper articles, occasional sermons or seminars, and even birthday celebrations can all help people anticipate the midlife transition and the years that follow. The best people to give these anticipatory signals are counselors, pastors, and others who are over forty and thriving.

2. *Education*. Family conferences, couples' retreats, discussion groups, Sunday School classes, seminars, and periodic sermons can and should deal with the major issues of adult living. In many churches the seats are filled with people in their forties or fifties who fail to understand and never may mention the turmoil that simmers within. These people may have heard about midlife crises and may have joked about them, but there is little recognition that the struggles of this stage of life are common and best handled when they are accepted and discussed. Perhaps many of these people feel like moral, spiritual, or personal failures. The sermons they hear every week talk about needs or about issues like forgiveness, love, and acceptance, but everybody around seems to radiate success or stability, and there is little evidence of struggles about careers or families' problems at midlife. When they can share some of their own issues in appropriate and sensitive ways, church leaders often break this image and free people to face their own issues.

Within the church or without, each of us can deal more realistically with the problems of this age when they are anticipated, accepted, and faced in sensitive and caring ways with others who can give us the support we need.

3. *Outreach*. Shortly after his fiftieth birthday, a respected pastor gave wise advice to his fellow church members who had passed the half-century mark. "Don't huddle around with people your own age all the time," he suggested. If you do, then "when you die, everything you know will die too—because they'll be dying about the same time you do! Pour your knowledge into people twenty or thirty years younger than you. And when you're gone, everything you've taught them will be walking around this earth for another twenty or thirty years teaching others. Extend your life!"[25] Bob Buford gives a similar message in his books and seminars about facing halftime and then moving on to a second half of life filled with significance.

Erik Erikson said the same thing when he concluded that to avoid stagnation in the forties and fifties, we need to be involved in working to establish and guide the next generation. As we have seen, Erikson called this generativity. It is a one-to-one reaching out to people who are younger, needy, and/or eager to learn. Teachers and professors have unusual opportunities to reach out in this way, but so do counselors, parents, business leaders, and any person who has contact with younger people. Mentors of any age experience the satisfaction of knowing that their lives and observations can be meaningful and useful to others.

Employers, book writers, magazine editors, government leaders, counselors, teachers, and broadcasters can all contribute to the prevention of middle-age problems. But the church can be most helpful of all. Its members know the healing power of love and can demonstrate the burden-bearing that should characterize Christians. This caring can bring crucial support and guidance to people in middle age.

Conclusions About Forty- and Fifty-Year-Olds

Readers of this book are likely to see themselves in its pages at times, but so does the writer. In preparing this chapter, for example, I have reflected on my own struggles and victories in passing through the forties and fifties. I have thought, too, about several of my closest friends who are in their early forties, facing some of the struggles described in the previous pages, but moving into the second half of their lives. It has been encouraging for me to realize afresh that the emotions and struggles of middle age are common, temporary, and ultimately able to contribute to spiritual growth and personal maturity. With God's help, we can guide ourselves or our counselees through this or any other stage of life, helping people grow and live lives that honor God and fulfill his purposes. Regardless of age, that should be a goal or all of us—the writer of this book, the readers, and the people to whom we minister and offer counsel.

KEY POINTS FOR BUSY COUNSELORS

➤ The definition of middle age depends on one's perspective. Around forty people reach the midpoint of life—depending on the life expectancy of where one lives—but often we refer to the twenty-year period between forty and sixty as middle age.

➤ The Bible speaks about children, young men and women, and old age, but it does not speak specifically about the period between the late thirties and late fifties. Most of the problems of this age period (depression, anxiety, or loneliness, for example) are dealt with in passages that are not age specific.

➤ When people enter their forties, they begin to view life differently from before. This is a period of reevaluation, taking stock of life, setting new goals, and facing the reality of the coming old age.

➤ At least four issues remind people that they are growing older and often become the basis of problems.
- Physical changes are reminders that the body is aging. Sometimes, these are followed by efforts to hide the aging process and keep a youthful appearance.

- Psychological changes include the reexamination of lifestyles and priorities, boredom, fear, reappraisal of where one is and where one wants to go.
- Vocational changes come as people in their forties and fifties look again at their careers and sometimes make changes.
- Marriage and family changes include adjusting as children reach adulthood, developing new relationships with parents who are aging, evaluating the state of one's marriage and sometimes making changes, and dealing with the reality of changing sexuality.

➤ The reality of being at the midpoint of life or later can lead to inner struggles, changes in behavior, alterations in a person's attitudes toward work, and sometimes marital struggles.

➤ The well-known midlife crisis is a period of turmoil that has a major impact in the lives and families of some people, especially men, at times leading to impulsive and irresponsible actions and lifestyle changes. This is common enough for most of us to have observed, but the midlife crisis is much less prominent than is popularly assumed. Most people go through the struggles of midlife with little or no major life disruption.

➤ As is true of all counseling, counselors who work with people in the forty to sixty age group need to model tolerance, patience, interest, understanding, and acceptance mixed with a strong dose of realistic thinking that helps the counselee keep things in perspective.

➤ Counseling involves:
- Focusing on specific problem issues.
- Working with families who may need help but who also can assist the counseling.
- Stimulating people in their forties and fifties to mentor others or to engage in what Erikson calls generativity, guiding and sharing with the next generation.
- Encouraging spiritual awareness.

➤ Prevention includes:
- Helping people anticipate what is coming.
- Education for people in this age period.
- Encouraging outreach, including generativity. Without generativity, people in their forties and fifties often experience stagnation.

➤ Even though there can be major readjustments and problems at midlife and in the twenty years between forty and sixty, this can be the best time of life. Counselors can help make this a reality.

17

The Later Years

Cara was a gracious, neatly dressed, seventy-three-year old accountant whose voice expressed anxiety and despair when she called a counselor to request an appointment to talk about some bad news from her doctor. A lady with numerous friends, boundless energy, a bright outlook on life, Cara went for a routine physical examination and learned that she had cancer and would need to have surgery and chemotherapy beginning immediately. Until she got the news, Cara had taken pride in her independence, her good health, her active lifestyle, and her consistent involvement with a local fitness club. She had never thought much about retirement but assumed that she would go on working and living life fully, well into her eighties and maybe longer.

Widowed in her fifties, Cara had struggled back from her grief and picked up life with the encouragement of her friends and the long-distance support from her two grown sons who lived in other parts of the country. As she shared her worries with the counselor, Cara enumerated one concern after another: How would she handle being in the hospital with no family nearby? How would she get along living alone while she went through her chemotherapy? Would she still be able to drive, do the grocery shopping, and see a few of her clients? What would happen to her business? What would she look like if her hair fell out and her appearance changed? Would she still be accepted by her friends? Would she ever be able to return to her exercise routine and the camaraderie she enjoyed with her friends at the fitness club? Would the doctors discover other physical problems that were still unsuspected? During her hospitalization, who would take care of her poodle? Was this the end of her life? If not, would she have to retire? If so, what would she do then? Cara's mind had gone into overdrive. She was overwhelmed with worries, some about possible problems that probably would never arise.

The counselor listened compassionately, but then he interrupted Cara's string of fears. He reassured her that the fears were normal, that others had come through similar experiences successfully, that God cared about her and would not abandon her. Cara acknowledged that her friends probably would stick with her as well and agreed that she and the counselor should talk about her worries one at a time. He helped her prepare a list of questions to ask her doctor, who, in turn, could set her mind at ease. Even before the end of her first counseling session, Cara had begin to relax. In the weeks that followed, the counselor helped her face and think through the issues of aging that she had denied to this point in her life. There were times when Cara appeared to be overly dependent on the counselor, but he helped her make wise decisions about her future, take things at a realistic pace, and eventually get past her medical crisis.

Until the time of her illness, Cara had lived an active and independent life with few thoughts about her own aging process. The medical crisis was a wake-up that brought her face-to-face with the reality of growing older and led Cara to review her life, to assess her current situation with fresh honesty, and to plan for the future in ways that she had never done before.

A few days after the presidential inauguration that ushered him into one of the world's most strenuous jobs, Ronald Reagan celebrated his seventieth birthday. The former radio announcer and movie actor was starting a new career— joining the ranks of those who have made significant contributions to this world, long after most of their peers have retired. Architect Frank Lloyd Wright created some of his best works when he was in his eighties and finished the impressive Guggenheim Museum when he was ninety-one. Douglas MacArthur became commander of United Nations forces in Korea when he was seventy. Later, after telling Congress that "old soldiers never die, they just fade away," the general refused to fade but went on to become a successful businessman. Guitarist Andrés Segovia was still giving classical concerts at age ninety-two. Comedians Bob Hope and George Burns failed to let old age slow down their entertainment schedules, and Sir Georg Solti led his world-renowned Chicago Symphony Orchestra in a gala concert to celebrate his own birthday when the maestro turned seventy-five. Colonel Harland Sanders was sixty-two when he launched the Kentucky Fried Chicken business that he grew to extend around the world. Grandma Moses attained fame as an artist when she was in her eighties. Winston Churchill, Konrad Adenauer, and Golda Meir were among those who continued to influence their countries and the world as elder statesmen. After turning eighty, psychologist B. F. Skinner and psychoanalyst Erik Erikson each wrote books about the experience of growing old.[1]

It could be argued that these are exceptions. Men and women with unusual vision and abilities are always exceptions, regardless of age, but these famous people—and thousands like them who never have fame—show that the later years need not be times of misery, rigidity, and inactivity. French writer André Maurois once observed that "growing old is no more than a bad habit which a busy man has no time to form." Robert Browning might have agreed when he invited readers to "Grow old with me! The best is yet to be. "

This optimism is not shared by everyone. Egyptian philosopher Ptah-hotep wrote in 2500 B.C. that "old age is the worst of misfortunes that can afflict a man." Emerson described the elderly as "rags and relics," while Shakespeare wrote that the later years usher in a "second childishness and mere oblivion, sans [without] teeth, sans eyes, sans taste, sans everything." Media images of the elderly tend to agree. In the popular television series, *The Simpsons,* Bart Simpson's grandfather lived in a nursing home surrounded by pathetic figures who often were confused, lonely, depressed, and mistreated. Award-winning actress Doris Roberts, who starred on the television show *Everybody Loves Raymond,* gave testimony before a U.S. Senate Committee. "My peers and I are portrayed as dependent, helpless, unproductive and demanding rather than deserving," Roberts said. "In reality, the majority of seniors are self-sufficient, middle-class consumers with more assets than most young people, and the time and talent to offer society."[2]

The negative image of older people is known as *ageism.* It appears in jokes that poke fun at old people assuming that most are set in their ways, out of date, socially isolated, negative, with poor memories and physically decrepit bodies. Sadly, many older people view themselves in the same way, and apparently many counselors have similar attitudes. Perhaps this explains, in part, why there is a great shortage of professional counselors who are willing to focus on working with the elderly.[3]

Regardless of how we view aging, the numbers and percentages of older people in the population have been increasing at a phenomenal rate. This is a worldwide trend that results from better medical care, improved diet, and increasing interest in physical fitness. In the United States, the number of people over 65 increases by 1,600 every day, and by 2030 it is estimated that people over 65 will constitute 20 percent of the population. The American Association of Retired Persons (AARP) has become one of the largest and most powerful political forces in the country.[4] According to the research of gerontologist Ken Dychtwald, the twenty-first century will be ruled by what he terms "the new old."[5] These are active people, many of whom live into their eighties and nineties and have no intention of retiring, especially at the relatively young age of 65.[6]

For many years it has been widely agreed (at least by younger people) that old age begins between sixty and sixty-five. But people age at different rates, both physically and psychologically. Among sixty-five-year-olds, for example, there are wide differences in health, attitudes, abilities, beliefs, physical appearance, intellectual alertness, spiritual maturity, and capability for handling stress or managing one's life. Some people seem to be old at forty, while others seem youthful and vigorous even when they get into their eighties and beyond. For everyone, however, growing old and adjusting to the realities of old age can be the source of new problems and challenges. These challenges often can be met more efficiently with the help of a Christian counselor.

The Bible and Old Age

The Bible describes people who lived to a very old age. Methuselah's 969-year age was unusual, but many of the Old Testament patriarchs lived until they were well past 100. It was recognized that wisdom often increases with age,[7] but the people in Bible times apparently faced rejection and frustration like many older people today. The psalmist even prayed that God would not abandon him when he was old.[8]

Perhaps Ecclesiastes 12 gives the clearest biblical picture of the later years. Over a century ago, pioneer psychologist G. Stanley Hall called this Bible description the most pessimistic—albeit realistic—description of old age ever written. People in the later years face a variety of physical problems and "no longer enjoy living," we read.[9] Days can be cloudy, strength fails, often there is noting to do, sight and hearing decline, fears increase, we find ourselves "dragging along without any sexual desire," and there is a new realization of the nearness of death.

Even among the elderly, however, life does not need to be "utterly meaningless." Every person, regardless of age, can find meaning in life when one fears God and keeps his commandments.[10] While young people have strength, the elderly should be respected for their wisdom and experience.[11] In turn, the elderly are to be temperate, dignified, sensible, sound in faith, loving and willing to persevere. They should be people who teach what is good, avoid malicious gossips, and are not excessive drinkers.[12] This is a picture of hope. Nowhere should this be more apparent than in the community of believers. We read that "if you honor your father and mother, you will live a long life, full of blessing."[13] This is a promise that clearly is positive.

The Bible, therefore, is realistic in its portrayal of old age, positive in its attitude toward the value of old age, and specific in its commands concerning how older people should live and how the elderly should be treated. Older persons are to be respected, cared for, and loved as human beings. Christians have no other options.

Causes of Problems in the Later Years

Pat Moore was a twenty-six-year-old industrial designer who wanted to know what it was like to cope with the physical limitations of advanced age or to experience the attitudes that older people encounter. To find out, she enlisted the help of a professional makeup artist who provided a gray wig and showed Moore how to apply makeup that would make her look old. To blur her vision, the young woman applied baby oil to her eyes. She wore splints and bandages under her clothes to stiffen her joints and put plugs in her ears to dull her hearing. Then, looking like a woman in her eighties, Pat Moore ventured out into the city streets. For three years, in sixteen cities, fourteen states, and two Canadian provinces, whenever she went on one of her many business trips, the young woman rarely missed a chance to add a few hours when she would dress like an old woman and observe how people reacted.

These experiences put Pat Moore into contact with many caring people who are sensitive to the needs of the elderly. Despite the problems that many older people face, she concluded that "they generally whine and complain less, despite more valid reasons to do so, than any other group of people I have ever been around."[14] As she continued to play the role of an old woman, however, Moore became intimidated by the impatience and critical attitudes that many people show toward older people. On several occasions she went into the same stores and made identical purchases, once disguised as an old person and once as herself. Invariably, the clerks showed different attitudes. They were more impatient and negative with the "old" Pat Moore.

I debated about including Pat Moore's story in these pages. I reasoned that attitudes toward older people surely are different now when Moore did her experiments. But then I pondered some of my own attitudes and wondered if I have some of the same prejudices that Moore encountered, even though I now have entered the later years. How we respond to old age and to the elderly probably depends on our attitudes and experiences. This is true of older people as well as those who are younger. Undoubtedly, older people encounter less prejudice when they have positive attitudes toward aging and when they are able to be friendly, socially at ease, and interested in others.

Despite the prevalence of ageism and the onset of late-life problems, do not assume that life is difficult for all people in the later years. For many, the later years are a fulfilling and happy time of life. Not all persons over sixty-five are lonely, failing in health, bored, poverty stricken, depressed, intellectually dull, or exploited. Even when money is short and health is poor, many older people have good memories of the past, positive outlooks, hope for the future, and lives that are as active as they can make them. One long-term research study found that older people who viewed aging positively lived an average of 7.5 years longer than those who had a negative perception.[15] While some people become old in their attitudes and actions long before they reach the later years, others maintain enthusiasm and a positive outlook to the end. A previous chapter made reference to the Warren Bennis book on *Geeks and Geezers*.[16] He and his co-author focused on older people who thrive and who never become "old geezers." These people are always learning (many are avid readers), have a positive outlook, purposely make the effort to spend time with younger people, and constantly anticipate the future rather than dwelling on the past.

When problems do arise, their causes can be grouped into several categories.

1. *Attitudinal Causes.* As the numbers of older people increase, there has been a growing number of research reports and self-help books or articles from professionals who are interested in gerontology, the study of aging. Even a casual reading of these publications is likely to lead you to this conclusion: *The problems of aging are real, but more than anything else, the older person's attitudes determine how he or she will deal with the problems and overcome them.*

Several years ago a science museum featured a "Facing Aging" exhibit for children. Access to the open booth was forbidden to anybody over fifteen, so parents and others watched from the outside as these youngsters sat down, one at a time, and had a portrait taken by an automatic camera. Once this image appeared on the TV monitor, the kids could tap a button on a remote control device and bring up a computer simulation of what they would look like at one-year intervals until age sixty-nine. "In seconds the computer added grotesque pouches, reddish skin, and blotches to their familiar features; the faces became elongated and then wider and then saggy; lines became more heavily rutted. Boys lost hair. Hair turned gray. The heads on both boys and girls grew and then shrank. The children were almost uniformly shaken."[17] Nobody stayed in the booth very long. Nobody left with a positive attitude toward aging.

After watching children go through this experience, writer Margaret Morgantroth Gullette concluded that the exhibit was modeled on the dominant cultural assumption that aging equals decline and that we will all decline in the same way regardless of how we treat our bodies. Gullette called this a spectacle that "offers a prophecy about your own appearance that makes human aging entirely bodily, predictable, and inescapably awful."[18] It also is a prophecy that is blatantly wrong.

Human beings are aged by their experiences, their cultures, their expectations, their character, their religious beliefs, and their views about aging. We don't all age in the same ways that can be predicted by computers. As I write, three men come to mind, all about the same age in their seventies. One is enthusiastic about the future, actively involved with other people—including those who are younger, dynamic, and not afraid to try new things. The second keeps busy playing golf and enjoying his grandchildren, but he looks old, dresses like an old man, and likes to reminisce about the past. The third has given up on life. He talks about the difficulties of being old, sits in a chair all day watching television, and expects to die soon. All three have had serious health problems, but each one responded differently. The first two men followed doctors' orders and have regained a good measure of health and strength. The third has refused to exercise, quit smoking, or get involved in physical rehabilitation following his illness. Instead, he is critical of the medical profession and complains because he is not getting better. Here are three men with three different perspectives. If the men walked into a room, it would be easy to see the differences. They all were born about the same time, but they have not all aged in a way that could have been predicted by a computer simulation.

In the later years there are legitimate problems that impact lives, limit activities, and change our relationships with others. However, since successful aging largely depends on the attitudes of the older person, a crucial part of counseling is helping people with their attitudes in the later years.

2. *Physical Causes.* As we get older, all of our bodies run down, and visits to the

doctor become more frequent. Even so, the vast majority of older people are able to move about independently, and only 5 or 6 percent are confined to institutions for physical or mental care. Physical decline tends to come sooner and hit harder when bodies have been weakened by earlier disease or by breakdowns in the immune system. Other bodies wear out more quickly because they have been deprived of exercise or sufficient rest, permanently harmed by pollution or unhealthy work conditions, or abused by too much smoking, unhealthy eating, or alcohol consumption. Sometimes, stress is the villain that hinders normal physical functioning, and as we have seen, an individual's mental attitude can have an important impact on the types and speed of physical decline. There are at least five types of physical changes that can occur.

(a) Cosmetic Changes. Graying and thinning hair, loss of teeth, decreasing weight, wrinkling skin, including "bags under the eyes," and dark spots on the hands and wrists are changes that begin long before a person turns sixty-five. They are much harder to ignore or hide in the later years. In a world that values youth and physical attractiveness, these evidences of aging can influence one's self-esteem and sense of security. The problem is accentuated when older people stop taking care of their physical appearance and allow themselves to look disheveled.

(b) Sensory Changes. It is well known that older people cannot see or hear as well as they once could. In addition, there often is a degeneration in the senses of taste and smell, a stiffness of joints so that movement is hindered, a decline in strength and energy level, a slower reaction time, changes in kinesthetic sensitivity so that balance is more difficult, and greater problems with memory. These changes come slowly and rarely appear as a "jolt," but as Pat Moore demonstrated so effectively, they can greatly interfere with one's ability to get along and to get around. Since the changes do not appear suddenly or all at the same time, most people are able to adapt and compensate for the losses, one at a time. Consider, for example, the man who loses part of his hearing in one ear. His friends might not even know about the hearing problem because the man gets into the habit of holding the telephone to his good ear, paying more attention to nonverbal messages, or sitting in ways that expose his good ear to the conversation with his friends.

(c) System Changes. Physiological degeneration and changes often are seen in the body's organs and systems. In the skeletal system, for example, bones become more brittle, less able to resist stress, and much slower to heal. Rheumatoid arthritis often restricts movement and creates pain. Osteoporosis influences millions of women and men, bringing pain,[19] restricted movement, and shriveling of the spine.

Other changes occur in the muscular, reproductive, gastrointestinal, cardiovascular, respiratory, and central nervous systems. As they grow older people learn to adapt to these changes. They avoid foods that upset the gastrointestinal system, for example, or they take precautions to prevent heart attacks and other cardiovascular illnesses. These adaptations to physical changes are harder when there is a major body breakdown that interferes with normal functioning. Physical disabilities or chronic diseases can influence the overall health of older people, depleting their energy and limiting their abilities to engage in more productive or fulfilling activities.

Sometimes, the physical changes lead to elderly hypochondriacs. Most of these people complained about their health when they were younger as well, but in the later years they worry more about their bodies and the costs of health care. Prone to anxiety or neuroticism, these people talk a lot about their symptoms and go to doctors even when treatment isn't necessary.[20]

(d) Sexual Changes. Reproductive capacities diminish as one grows older, but it is not true that sexual interest and activity automatically diminish as well. Older people need physical closeness and human contact, just like the young. Pleasurable sexual experiences are possible for both sexes well into the later years.[21]

It is true that older couples take longer to achieve orgasm, and the intensity may be reduced, but for many older people, sexual activity and satisfaction increase as they grow older. Jokes about old age as "a time when a man flirts with girls but can't remember why," or about sex in adulthood as a progression from "tri-weekly, to try-weekly, to try-weakly" are all a mixture of humor with an attitude that dismisses sex in the elderly as something wrong or lecherous. When older people believe these attitudes, there is less sexual involvement, physical closeness, or physical expressions of love with one's mate.[22]

(e) Changes Due to Disease and Illness. It is not correct to assume that old age is a time of inevitable physical decline, incapacitating illness, and immobility. In developed countries, at least half of all people between seventy-five and eighty-four are free of health problems that require special care or curb their activities. Even in the oldest group, those above eighty-five, more than one-third report no limitations due to health. Eventually, however, more than four out of five older persons have one or more chronic health problems as internal organs begin to break down. These illnesses arouse anxiety, diminish mobility, and create discouragement. When a person is healthy, the later years can be interesting and fulfilling, but when one is sick, this can be a terrifying and depressing time of life.

3. *Intellectual Causes.* Thousands of research projects have attempted to determine the extent to which older people change in terms of creativity, memory, intellectual ability, or capacity to learn new things.[23] It is well known that older persons may think more slowly, take longer to respond, be less able to understand new ideas or develop new skills, and have difficulty with short-term memory. Yet, how old people respond to these cognitive activities depends less on chronological age and more on issues such as their education, verbal skills, involvement with people, and intellectual activities. Unless there are interfering physical illnesses, many older people maintain strong mental abilities, especially if they have stimulating lifestyles. It also helps to be married to an intelligent spouse.[24] In addition, older people often draw on their wisdom and experience to remain mentally acute, creative, and able to learn in their later years. In speaking to an overflow crowd at a professional convention, psychologist B. F. Skinner once shared his own methods for adapting to old age, and then he paraphrased the wise Samuel Johnson, who said, "An aging lecturer is like a dog walking on his hinder legs. It is not done well; but you are all surprised to find it done at all."

The decline in mental ability is most apparent when one has to make a quick decision—like stepping on the brakes or jumping out of danger. Aware of their slower reaction time, many people learn to act cautiously—as many younger drivers have discovered when they get behind an older person who is behind the wheel of a car crawling along a freeway.

It isn't always possible to compensate for declining mental abilities, and some people give up trying. Bored by the inactivity of retirement, saddened by the death of friends, and frustrated by the inability to move about, it is easy for an older person (and his or her family) to accept a number of persisting myths (see table 17–1) about the assumed mental declines in the elderly. When these myths are believed, they become self-fulfilling prophecies; people begin to act in accordance with their false beliefs, whether or not they are valid.

Others spend great amounts of time daydreaming about the "good old days." The present is uncomfortable for many people in the later years, and the future offers little hope, so many escape into past memories that become distorted both by the passage of time and by the human tendency to forget that which was painful or unpleasant. These mental retreats into the past can contribute to confusion and evidences of senility that sometimes may be more psychological than physiological.

4. *Emotional Causes.* Emotional problems in the later years often come because of losses, many of which occur at the same time. These losses include death of one's marital partner and other friends, loss of health and physical agility, or loss of sensory abilities, such as declines in hearing or vision. Retirement or leaving a

---

Table 17–1

Myths About Aging and Mental Abilities[25]

1. **Mental Abilities Keep Getting Worse.** In tests of mathematical and reasoning abilities, comprehension, concentration, and other mental skills, a quarter to a third of people in their eighties performed as well as their younger counterparts; many did better. Very few old people had mental declines that interfered with their daily living.
2. **Memory Is the First to Go.** Brain studies show that the mind's storehouses of knowledge remain largely intact, although it may take longer to tap into the stored information. Memory is not the first to go mentally. The first to go is special relationships, such as the ability to read a map or to remember where we put things. (But that happens as well to people in their forties.)
3. **Use It or Lose It.** There is no doubt that idle minds decay faster than active minds, but there is no guarantee that people who use their mental abilities will retain them. Treating the brain to novel experiences and stimuli, including reading, seems to keep the mind agile and flexible.
4. **Sound Bodies and Sound Minds Go Together.** A sick body can sap one's mental powers, and some diseases do lead to mental decay, but in many cases illness does not lead to mental decline. At every age, exercise benefits the brainpower of the healthy and the sick.
5. **You Can't Teach an Old Dog New Tricks.** An old brain has an astonishing ability to rejuvenate itself. Learning and relearning may be slower in the later years, but older people have a good ability to learn.
6. **Older Is Wiser.** This is true sometimes but not always. Research shows that while older people may take longer to make decisions, the decisions usually are better.

career for other reasons can lead to a loss of one's purpose for living. Without work, many people feel that they have lost their usefulness, status, or close friendships from work. With reduced incomes and greater difficulty in getting around, older people lose the ability to participate in social activities, attend religious services, or see their friends. In addition, many older people face physical illnesses that require them to cope, often when they are alone, without the support of old friends. They now lack the resources or strength to be flexible as they adapt to their health losses. These losses can demand enormous amounts of physical and emotional energy as the older person adjusts to the changes and tries to recover. It is not surprising that depression, anxiety, anger, grieving, and withdrawal are common. All of this, combined with physical decline, can lead to the various geriatric psychiatric conditions that are unique to the later years.[26]

5. *Economic Causes*. Retirement brings a departure from work, but for many it also brings a lower income, a reduced standard of living, and adjustment to a pay scale that often fails to keep pace with the rate of inflation. Less income can create problems, such as finding an affordable place to live, meeting medical expenses, maintaining a balanced diet, being able to afford transportation costs to continue contact with friends, or facing the self-esteem problems that come when one has declining resources and may have to apply for public welfare or other charitable assistance. Of course, there are variations from country to country. The elderly are better cared for in some countries and some cultures than in others. Differences also depend on the nearness of family members, as well as their willingness and/or ability to help.[27]

6. *Interpersonal Causes*. To function adequately as human beings, each of us needs human beings with whom we can socialize and exchange ideas. Other people challenge us, encourage us, keep us in contact with reality, and enable us to feel useful.

As we have seen, many older people experience a devastating loss of social contact. Retirement can bring isolation from the occupational world that gives many people their main reason for living. Friends and relatives, including one's spouse, often die and leave surviving older people without companionship and peers to bolster morale. Declining health limits one's ability to get away from home, friends may change residence or move away, and adult children sometimes are too busy, too far away, or too critical to provide contact. This can contribute to the older person's loneliness, to a withdrawal from social contact, to the feeling that he or she is not longer useful or needed, and sometimes to a self-centered mentality that can lead to premature death. Even in retirement communities, where people are surrounded by other senior citizens, there can be a tendency to withdraw from others. In contrast, older persons who have one or more close, intimate relationships seem to be happier, better adjusted, and in better mental health than those without such confidants.[28]

It is a sad fact that many people in the later years are mentally, financially, and physically abused, often by their own children and other family members. Many of these victims are too weak to defend themselves, unable or unwilling to report the abuse, and often in a position of dependency on the same people who inflict the pain and abuse. These older people feel ashamed or embarrassed about what is happening and are afraid of the consequences that might follow if they report the abuse. Perhaps there are few issues more likely to arouse the compassion and anger of sensitive counselors.

7. *Self-Esteem Causes.* Based on her experiences dressed as an old person, Pat Moore concluded that perhaps the worst thing about aging is the "overwhelming sense that everything around you is letting you know that you are not terribly important anymore." People constantly seemed exasperated by the slow-moving "old" woman, and in time it was easy for her to conclude, "You're right. I'm just a lot of trouble. I'm really not as valuable as all these other people, so I'll just get out of your way as soon as possible so you won't be angry with me."[29] Even people who are healthy and active pick up clues that their input and opinions no longer count as they once did. Retirement can add to the lowering of self-esteem. Eagerly anticipated and enjoyed by many people, retirement also can be a stark reminder that society considers us too old to work and make a useful contribution to society. Often one's income and sense of self-worth both drop substantially.

The self-confidence and self-esteem of older people are undermined frequently by the misconceptions and prejudices of those who think the elderly are too old to make decisions, do useful work, make valuable contributions, create new things, accept responsibilities, or even go out alone. These attitudes are evidences of the ageism that we mentioned earlier. This is a form of prejudice that demeans old age, discriminates against the elderly, and assumes that younger is better. Like sexism and racism, ageism creates problems for its victims and contributes further to the older person's decline in self-esteem. When they are assumed to be incompetent or best treated like children, it is easy for the elderly to feel useless and unimportant. It is not surprising that many have a poor opinion of themselves and of their value as persons.

Once again, however, we find individual differences in the way people adjust to the later years. It is true that a person's health, financial security, and attitudes all contribute to how one adapts, but there is more. The people who adapt best to old age appear to be those who were well adjusted when they were younger, who have a realistic view of their strengths and weaknesses, who thought about and made some preparations for retirement before it occurred, and who had a positive self-concept during the younger years. Those who have less success in coping are people who are unable or unwilling to face the realities of age, react with anger, condemn themselves, and blame others for life's miseries and failure to achieve goals. A person's adjustment, attitudes, and self-concept at forty or earlier may be the best predictor of what one will be like decades later. Angry and bitter old people probably were angry and bitter when they were younger.

8. *Spiritual and Existential Causes.* Physical changes, declining health, and the passing of friends all bring us face-to-face with the reality and inevitability of death. For some there is worry about prolonged terminal illness, fear of death itself, and uncertainty about the existence or nonexistence of life after death. Some people reach the later years with a burden of guilt and a sense of failure that they don't know how to handle. Others conclude that they are of no value to anyone, that nobody depends on them any more, or that their lives have not made much of a difference. "I have spent all of my life in business," one man told his counselor. "I have all this experience, but then along come the young college graduates who understand the latest about computers and technology, so they are more valuable to the company." All these issues can lead to a lot of reflection, a new search for meaning, increasing depression, a sense of futility, and sometimes even to suicide.

This is a time when the church can make a big difference, but many older people are unable to attend worship services. When they do attend, sometimes they feel unwanted and unwelcome in congregations that emphasize unfamiliar forms of worship, youth programs, family ministries, and activities designed for couples. Even the design of church buildings, many with high stairs and hard-to-reach washrooms, can leave the subtle message that older people—especially those with problems—are not welcome. It is a challenge for churches to minister to the spiritual and other needs of older people, without adding to their burdens.

9. *Other Causes.* How does rapid social change influence people who are slowing down but want to keep up to date? How does an older person handle postmodernism, the emergent church, immorality on television, or morally disturbing activities and social values in one's own children or grandchildren? And what is the impact of technology on older people—complex communication devices, ever-increasing computer sophistication, new gadgets that quickly go from being the wave of the future to devices that most people posses and can't live without? For many people the later years are complicated further by alcoholism, neighborhood decline, crime, political corruption or incompetence that adversely impacts the elderly, cut-backs in government funding, the deterioration of one's home, or local prejudices against older citizens. Often these issues can be overlooked by busy counselors, but they have a profound effect on many older people.

The Effects of the Later Years

"I was just fifty-six years old when I was involuntarily retired from my position in the White House. What made losing the job even worse was that it was a highly publicized event, with maybe half the people in the world knowing about my embarrassing defeat." With these words Jimmy Carter, thirty-ninth president of the United States, began an insightful little book about his experiences with involuntary retirement. "Moving from Washington back to our home in Plains was not a pleasant experience," he wrote. "It was not easy to forget about the past, overcome our fear of the future, and concentrate on the present. In this small and tranquil place, it was natural to assume . . . that our productive lives were about over. Like many other involuntary retirees, we had to overcome our distress and make the best of the situation."[30]

Regardless of how they might view the political career and accomplishments of President Carter and his wife, Rosalynn, there appear to be millions of people in the United States and around the world who have profound admiration for the Carters today. They overcame a variety of genuine setbacks, refused to sit and do nothing, and even though it was not easy, eventually they "gathered enough courage to assess our talents, experience, and potential influence in affecting some of the social and political issues in which we still were interested." Then they made the decision to move forward and to "try to explore completely new commitments."[31]

One effective way for a counselor to understand aging people is to imagine life from an old person's perspective. Ask yourself how you would feel having to face a forced retirement like the Carters. How would you feel if you had failing health, no useful work, limited income, a loss of friends, and a declining ability to think or act quickly? Ponder how it would feel to be lonely, rejected by a society that has little respect for the elderly, and living in a neighborhood where the crime rate is high, but you have neither the strength nor the agility to escape or to defend yourself. What would it be like to wonder if you might run out of money before you die, or if you live with the realization that you might have to move from your current home because you couldn't afford to stay there? When we imagine how an older person might think or feel, we can better understand the effects of aging. This should enable us to be more sympathetic and effective counselors.

Books and articles on aging often focus on the difficulties of growing old. We read about the effects of aging on one's self-concept, emotions, interpersonal relations, lifestyle, and intellectual capabilities. We know that with aging there also may be a new anxiety over the future, self-pity, loneliness, worries about finances, depression, and sometimes attempted suicide. It can be difficult to grow old and to be old. But none of this should hide what Carter calls "the virtues of aging." While many people are defeated by aging or need help in overcoming the adverse effects of the later years, others are able to surmount the problems, rise to new heights, and live the last years of life with purpose and genuine fulfillment.

This is the message of Richard Leider and David Shapiro, two authors who challenged the "decline mentality" that is so much a part of our culture and that was demonstrated in the science museum exhibit. Leider and Shapiro urge, instead, that people over fifty become *new elders*. These are people who do not deny their age (they know they look sixty or seventy or older). If they are inclined to forget, their bodies remind them that they are changing and slowing down. Despite their age, they can communicate effectively with twenty-one-year-olds and they "are people who use the second half of life as an empty canvas, a blank page, a hunk of clay to be crafted on purpose. These are people who never stop reinventing themselves."[32] They "have committed themselves to continual reinvention through giving and growing."[33] New elders "have an opportunity to rewrite the second chapter by drawing upon what we've learned during the first."[34] New elders look back over their lives, review what they have learned, and deliberately seek to answer four basic questions (questions that also are important for younger people):

- The question of identity: *Who am I?* This involves thinking about one's life stories, pondering how one has been shaped, and using that knowledge and those stories to impact the next generation.
- The question of community: *Where do I belong?* This involves "refinding our place" in life. It lets people clarify where they belong in the world as they live out the rest of life.
- The question of passion: *What do I care about?* "New elders care passionately about those who follow in their footsteps . . . no challenge is greater for people in the second half of life than to find something meaningful and valuable to do with their gifts."[35] Their concern is all about giving.
- The question of meaning: *What is my legacy?* This is what empowers new elders to forge ahead and become people in their eighties and nineties who still look to the future.

Helping older people answer these questions and become new elders can be at the basis of effective counseling with people in the later years.

Counseling and the Later Years

Even though older people can benefit from counseling, many do not get this help. Some people in this age group are suspicious of counselors, have the view that counseling is only for crazy people, or assume that getting help is a sign of weakness. Others are resistant to change or afraid of losing their independence. Even when they don't have these and other myths about counseling, older people may not know where to get help, or they are unable to afford the costs. This suggests that counselors need to continue their efforts to educate older people about the nature and value of counseling.

More often, the lack of help comes because of ageism in professionals who hold prejudiced and pessimistic views about older people. These include the false assumptions that most older people can't change, are unpleasant to work with, are frail and ill, tend to be inflexible and stubborn, have no interest in sex, or think mostly about the past and have little interest in the future. These attitudes can cloud the counselor's ability to see older counselees accurately. This can lead to decreased expectations about the person's ability to improve and can cause some counselors to invest less energy in their older counselors, since "they probably won't change much anyway." Some of these attitudes come because working with older people reminds counselors of their own insecurities about aging or their experiences with aging parents.[36] Clearly, then, the best place to start our consideration of counseling with older people is with an honest appraisal of the counselor's own attitudes.

1. *Counselor Self-Examination.* What is your attitude toward the elderly? Try to answer honestly. Do you hold some of the common stereotypes about old people being incompetent, rigid, cranky, childish, focused on the past, and preoccupied with physical aches and pains? Do you resent old people, look down on them, or try to avoid them? In your heart do you believe that counseling the elderly probably will be a waste of your time?

These perspectives must disappear before a counselor can be helpful. All counselors know that to admit a bias is the first step in removing a bias. Ask God to make you more compassionate and loving toward the elderly. Get more training and accurate information about working with older people.[37] Ask a friend or another counselor to help you sort through the origin of these negative attitudes so you can deal with them. Most important of all, spend time talking with a few older people about their lives, problems, hopes, challenges, and needs. Nothing removes prejudice like face-to-face discussion with the people against whom we hold negative opinions. As you talk, your attitudes probably will change and you will see the elderly for what they really are—valuable human beings who are loved by God and often optimistic about the future. It is then that you will be able to counsel more successfully with those who are old.

2. *Physical Examination and Counseling.* Since many problems in the elderly have a physical cause or influence, older people should be encouraged to have regular physical checkups by a competent physician. In addition to treatment, medical personnel can reassure and answer the questions of older people like Cara, who was described at the beginning of the chapter. When medical treatment helps people feel better, some of their psychological problems disappear and others can be dealt with more efficiently.

Among the elderly, Alzheimer's disease (AD) is the most well-known and dis-

turbing example of physical deterioration that can influence psychological functioning. A progressive and incurable disease, AD is the leading cause of dementia
among older people. About 10 percent of Americans over age sixty-five have the
disease, but almost half of those over eighty-five have AD. From the time it starts
until death, the disease lasts from two to fifteen years, although some people survive as long as twenty years or more. Beginning with mild memory loss, impaired
judgment, and decreasing ability to handle routine tasks, the disease eventually
destroys large areas of the brain so that AD patients become progressively disoriented and confused, unable to comprehend or communicate, inclined to wander,
agitated, and in time completely incontinent, bed ridden, and dependent.
Although AD still has no clearly identifiable cause and no known cure, extensive
research is continuing.[38] Initially, family members care lovingly for their older relatives with AD. Even when this care continues, however, eventually the entire
family can be disrupted, hindered in functioning, financially drained, and filled at
times with anger, frustration, and guilt. It has been suggested that caring for an
AD patient is like living a thirty-six-hour day, with no breaks or time for rest.[39]
The counselor's help may begin with the patient, but in time the spouse and
whole family are more likely to be the focus of counseling help.

3. *Individual Counseling*. Older people can benefit from the opportunity to talk
about their problems. Probably most would prefer to talk with their pastors,
physicians, social workers, or other helpers rather than making appointments to
meet with professional counselors. Whoever does the counseling, older counselees can benefit from several helpful approaches.

(a) Supportive Counseling. Older people often feel encouragement and a
greater ability to face the realities of advanced age when a counselor listens sensitively and gives reassurance. The goal is not to encourage complaining and self-
pity. Instead, supportive counseling helps people cope with their concerns and
fears. Many are dealing with losses, fears about losing control of their freedom or
independence, worries about the future, or concerns about whether their lives
have made a difference. Counselors can help people talk through these issues and
find reassurance. The elderly can be helped to forgive others and themselves and
to know that God forgives and cares. When the love of God is mentioned, the
counselor also can discuss God's plan of salvation, his justice, and his provisions for
believers after death. At times, the counselor will need to help the older person
face the difficulties of sickness, deal with the pain of grief, and find the courage
and ability to carry on when faced with the realities of permanent changes. While
trying not to foster unhealthy dependency, the counselor can become a strong figure who gives reassurance and encouragement when the older person feels weak.
This type of counseling can be done through visits to a counselor's office, but often
it is more effective if a group of friends or fellow believers, including the pastor or
counselor, consistently shows care, support, and acceptance, having face-to-face
contacts supplemented with telephone calls and cheerful notes.

(b) Educative Counseling. Old people, like those who are younger, have many
misconceptions about the later years. These can be discussed, and true facts about
aging can be taught. Discussions like these can give reassurance, reduce anxiety,
and in turn prevent defeatist attitudes and maladaptive behavior. Cognitive-
behavioral approaches can help people learn to think or act differently and more
effectively.

Consider, for example, the issue of sex after sixty. It is helpful for older people to recognize that this is not wrong, that physical satisfaction is both possible and common, that problems like impotence can be temporary, and that sexual satisfaction need not stop at the time of retirement. Conversations like this can answer questions, give reassurance, and help people put aside fears. A very different subject is that of living accommodations in the later years. These might include practical discussions such as the costs, advantages, and other relevant issues involved in living alone, moving to a retirement community, or moving in with one's children. The counselor may have to consult with experts and community leaders to get accurate information to share with counselees.

(c) Retirement Counseling. People approach retirement with a variety of attitudes. Some look forward to it. Others dread it, resist it, and hate it when retirement is forced upon them. For increasing numbers of people, retirement means a career change, leaving something that has been one's primary involvement and source of income and moving on to something else.[40] Many people want to do something that is meaningful and productive, but they aren't sure which way to go. Others view retirement as an opportunity to enter a lifestyle of tension-free pleasurable activities, but they soon get bored and begin looking for something useful to do. Most discover that the transition into retirement can be a major adjustment both for the retiring person and for his or her spouse and family. Counselors can assist people as they manage change, reexamine their priorities, find ways to grow and to give, develop new skills, find new activities, rekindle relationships, and learn to be mentors and coaches to organizations and younger workers.

(d) Life Review Counseling. In the past, counselors tended to ignore or dismiss the older person's seemingly endless supply of dull and oft-repeated stories about the past. More recently, gerontologists and others have concluded that reminiscences, especially those that are discussed and shared, can help older people reexamine the past, reflect on their failures and accomplishments, deal with prior frustrations, and get a more balanced perspective on both the past and the future.

A life review is more than telling stories and talking about the good old days of the past. Ideally, life review counseling involves preparing a biography. Sometimes, people can be encouraged to write or tape an autobiography. You might ask the older person to show you photographs, diaries, and other memorabilia. It also can be helpful to talk to family members. These activities are intended to help the person think through memories, come to understand them in new ways, express and resolve tensions from the past, discuss and accept failures, get rid of guilt feelings, solve conflicts that continue to give difficulty, and learn new ways to cope with problems. As people begin to look at the past in light of the present, they come to understand past events in new ways and begin to see more meaning in their lives. Often, they are able to look at life more realistically, find fresh ways to cope with challenges, and prepare realistically for a smooth transition to the coming years.[41] Older members of minority groups often can be helped to talk about their experiences with discrimination and enabled to find greater pride in their cultural heritages and worldviews.[42] Life reviews also must include discussions about the older person's spiritual life, relationship with Jesus Christ, and expectations about life after death. In addition, consider the person's marital and family history, earliest memories, education and work history, happiest and saddest memories, and plans for the future. Among other benefits, life reviews reduce the effects of depression, improve self-esteem, and lead to greater effectiveness in maintaining and improving quality of life in the later years.[43]

(e) In-depth Counseling. Freud believed that psychoanalysis with people over fifty was doomed to failure because of the amount of material to be dealt with, the time required, the inflexibility of the mental processes, and the inability of older people to learn. Over the years this view has proven to be wrong. People who are depressed, withdrawn, or otherwise inclined to show severe or persisting personal problems can often benefit from in-depth involvement with a counselor. This is especially true with people at the beginning of their later years, but even the most elderly can benefit from counseling, especially if the approach is more structured, supportive, and accompanied by helpful changes in the environment.[44] Prognosis is especially good in counselees who are actively involved in the process and who want to get better.[45]

In counseling with the elderly, the counselor often is younger that the counselee. This can create awkwardness, since young people usually are not thought of as counselors to the elderly. Sometimes, the younger counselor views or treats the older person like a father or mother, and the older counselee in turn might view the counselor like a son or daughter. These transference-countertransference issues can interfere with counseling, especially if they are not recognized by counselors.

4. *Family Counseling.* Unlike some other age groups, when problems surface in the elderly, they almost always involve or affect family members. We have seen how the family is disrupted by advancing Alzheimer's disease in an older relative, but families also are influenced by depression, financial problems, health decline, increased stress, interpersonal conflict, and almost every other problem in the aged.

Counseling with the elderly, therefore, is likely to be most effective if other family members are involved. At times, the counselor may serve as a mediator, helping resolve intergenerational conflicts. Sometimes, the counselor gives information to family members, including practical and tangible suggestions for managing unusual behavior, getting medical treatment, deciding on appropriate living accommodations, and handling finances. With the counselor's help, the family can make plans for the future, support and encourage one another, and cope with their own grief or guilt. When an older person is resistant to counseling or unable to benefit from counseling, the only way to give help may be through family members.[46]

5. *Spiritual Counseling.* When compared to those who are younger, people in their later years tend to be more religious and interested in spiritual issues. There is abundant research to support the conclusion that religious beliefs and activities in older people are related to lower depression and anxiety, greater happiness and life satisfaction, better self-rated health, fewer stressful life events, more social activity, and fewer interpersonal problems.[47] When they experience illness, older people often turn to religion to find reasons for their suffering and to help them cope. Even older people who do not consider themselves to be religious nevertheless are more inclined to turn to spiritual things when they encounter the problems of later life. The elderly often tend to prefer counselors and other helpers who are men and women of faith who can discuss spiritual issues with ease and who can help older counselees find hope and comfort. The spiritual needs of older people offer unique opportunities to Christian counselors who have an understanding and familiarity with spiritual counseling.

6. *Group Counseling.* People in the later years tend to be reluctant to discuss their problems in groups, but group counseling with older people has been used

since 1950.[48] Many elderly people are eager to participate once they get over their initial distrust and suspicion. Social contact, emotional catharsis, and sometimes insight are among the main objectives of group counseling, but groups also are used to help people deal with retirement issues, personal growth, loneliness, discouragement, family and life crises, prejudice against the elderly, and most other issues.[49] For some, the experience of meeting together can help people adjust to their problems, find acceptance, and obtain assurance that their problems are not unique or abnormal. Groups might be organized by churches or community agencies, but they are common in senior citizen centers, retirement communities, and almost anyplace else where older people congregate.

7. *Environmental Counseling.* One effective way to change an individual is to change his or her environment. Attractive accommodations, adequate meals, recreational opportunities, the acceptance of even minor responsibilities, and contact with cheerful, encouraging people—especially younger people—can all help to alter the older person's outlook and adjustment to later life. Technically, this is not counseling, but some helpers mobilize community resources, stimulate self-help and self-care in the elderly, assist older people in getting legal and medical services, or guide in money management. Within the church, youth groups and others can serve useful roles in brightening the lives of older people who are part of the congregation or community.

Preventing Problems in the Later Years

Recently I was having coffee with a group of friends in their forties and early fifties and mentioned that I was working on this chapter. This led to a discussion about how older people would be different when the baby boomers reach retirement age. Even though their bodies would break down as they aged, my friends predicted that their generation will be in better shape, more active, more positive, more determined to keep a good outlook on life, more focused on the future, and less inclined to dwell on the past or talk about their aches and pains. When compared to their parents and grandparents, it also seems likely that the twenty-first-century elderly will be more politically active and what gerontologist Ken Dychtwald has called "wielders of power."[50] Time will tell if these predictions are correct, but I suspect my friends are right. Within the next decade or two, we will see people entering the retirement years with a more positive perspective on aging. It is a perspective that will prevent some of the problems that we have discussed in this chapter. As in the past, however, there are things counselors can do to motivate older people toward a more positive old age.

1. *Stimulate Realistic Planning.* On her sixtieth birthday, the friends of feminist writer Betty Friedan held a big party. "I was depressed for weeks after that birthday party," Friedan wrote later. "I could not face being sixty." Most adults appear to move through life without giving much thought to aging until they are confronted with a startling reminder or two that they are getting old. For Friedan it was a surprise party at age sixty with lots of jokes about her age. For others it is a health crisis or the death of a peer. We all know we are getting older, of course, but the realities of age can come like a jolt when there has been little prior preparation or thought about aging.

Counselors and church leaders can encourage people in their forties, fifties, and early sixties to evaluate their attitudes toward aging, discuss how to use leisure time in the future, reevaluate their relationships with aging parents and with grown children, talk about death, and help with plans for retirement. These discussions can be positive, upbeat, and presented as a healthy, useful exercise. While this planning for the future could take place in a one-to-one counseling situation, it probably is more realistic to do this in groups, such as workshops, retreats, or Sunday School class discussions. Discussions like these can encourage people to think about their own aging, serve as inoculation against the psychological traumas of aging, and encourage planning.

As an example of realistic planning, consider how people might be helped to prepare for retirement. Try to clear up misunderstandings about retirement and encourage people to think about the future, even when they are physically healthy and hardly aware of even gradual changes that come with advancing age. Encourage a consideration of questions such as these:

- When will I (we) retire?
- What does God want me (or us) to do after retirement?
- Where will I retire?
- Where will I live?
- How will I spend my time after retirement?
- How will I keep fit and healthy after retirement?
- What will I do to keep my mind alert and active?
- What financial needs will I have in retirement?
- What are my financial resources?
- How will I pay for my health needs in retirement?
- Do I have sufficient insurance?
- Will I have the resources to live in an assisted-living facility if I ever need this?
- Is my will complete and up to date?
- Specifically, what can I do now to prepare for the later years?
- What kind of an old person will I be?
- What can I do now to increase the likelihood that I will be the kind of person I want to be in my later years?

Discussion of questions like these can prevent future problems and help deal with present concerns about the later years. Some of these issues need to be discussed with experts, especially physicians or financial planners who can give more technical assistance. Financial advisors often state that it never is too early to plan for retirement, but neither is it ever too late. In addition, as the numbers of older people continue to increase, it is likely that there will be an increase in useful self-help books and articles designed to prepare people for post-retirement years.

2. *Stimulate Realistic Attitudes.* An important way to prevent problems in the later years is to help people identify and correct some of the widely held myths about aging and biases against the elderly. The Bible clearly respects the elderly, and followers of Christ are expected to do likewise. Counselors can help develop both community and church programs that enable people to plan for their later years and to have more positive attitudes. If a whole church can care for older people compassionately and develop positive attitudes toward old age, the older person will be encouraged to do the same.

One way to develop good attitudes toward aging is to get the congregation in contact with the elderly and involved in helping. This could include any of the following:[51]

- Plan specific programs for senior citizens, but keep these attractive and not something that looks patronizing. In general, people of any age are more likely to get involved if they have ownership in the planning and leading of programs and seminars.
- Speak to the spiritual needs of the later years, including feelings of insecurity, insignificance, alienation from God, regret over past failures, and fear of death.
- Educate people to help them cope better with the problems of life. In this process perhaps nothing works better than the sensitive and upbeat example of people who have overcome obstacles and are doing fine.
- Expose the church to older people whose lives radiate healthy and positive attitudes.
- Involve older people in leadership and decision making. This does not mean that younger and more vigorous people are excluded, but a lot is communicated if the opinions and experiences of older people are valued, especially if these are the perspectives of forward-looking elders.
- Stimulate social, spiritual, and recreational contact between older people and others who are of the same age or younger.
- Help people cope with the problems of life and experience success in solving their problems so they have more hope for the future.
- Create opportunities for older people to be involved in useful (not busy work) service, such as teaching, visiting, praying, or doing clerical, maintenance, or other needed service activities.
- Be sure that physical facilities are such that older people can come to church and move about without hardship.
- Initiate or influence civic affairs or government programs for the elderly.
- Involve youth groups in ministering to older members of the congregation. This benefits both groups.
- Encourage the involvement of older people in mentoring those who are younger.

Activities like these show everyone that the elderly are important and that old people can have positive contributions. This can reduce fears, encourage more positive attitudes, and facilitate smoother adjustment to the later years.

3. *Stimulate Education and Activity*. People can avoid some of the problems of aging if they can be encouraged to use their minds, exercise their bodies, plan their diets and eat in healthy ways, make good use of their leisure time, and find creative ways of serving others. The evidence is overwhelming that mental and physical activity will do much to keep one from becoming apathetic, lethargic, and senile. Try to find ways to discourage the idea that the later years should be spent focused on television screens or on endless leisure activity. Eventually, both of these can lead to boredom and intellectual or physical stagnation.

4. *Stimulate Spiritual Growth*. No person is ever too old to come to Christ or to mature spiritually. A growing relationship with Jesus Christ does not prevent life's problems, but the committed believer should be able to deal with stress more effectively because he or she has confidence in an all-powerful, sovereign

God. Throughout life, even long-time Christians can learn more about the one with whom we will spend eternity. People of all ages need encouragement to pray, read the Scriptures, worship regularly, have time and relationships with other believers, and become involved—in so far as this is possible—in active service. All of this can start early. With God's help, the believer who has been positive, involved, and rejoiced in the earlier years likely will carry the same joyful attitude into late adulthood.

Conclusions About the Later Years

Liz Carpenter served as press secretary to Lady Bird Johnson when her husband, Lyndon, was President of the United States. The press secretary's role was fulfilling and exciting, but one day, when she was in her fifties, Ms. Carpenter was jarred with the news that her husband had died. "Old age came early," she wrote later. "I was instantly plunged into shock, abandonment, sadness, anger, loneliness, isolation—and then came the inevitable restlessness." The president's wife became her first counselor, and soon Liz Carpenter was involved in facing her later years.

In thinking about her anxieties during this time, five fears appeared to be basic: the fears of not feeling needed, losing a sense of purpose, losing control over her own destiny, not feeling loved, and not being touched physically. Instead of withdrawing into herself, she determined to keep as active as possible and to never stop learning. "The lessons learned in maturity aren't simple," she concluded. They "go beyond the acquisition of information and skills. You learn to avoid self-destructive behavior. You learn not to burn up energy in anxiety. You learn to manage tension. You learn that self-pity and resentment are among the most toxic of drugs. You learn to bear the things you can't change. . . . You learn that no matter what you do, some people aren't going to love you—a lesson that is at first troubling, then relaxing."[52]

Some people never learn these kinds of lessons. It is generally accepted that one-fifth or more of the American population experiences *gerontophobia*, the fear of growing old. The figure may be different in other parts of the world, but it is clear that many people recoil from thoughts of their own old aging. The development, marketing, and use of products that help us look younger point to the widespread attempts of people trying to deny aging. These same people often avoid those who are older and persist in believing common but unfounded myths about the disadvantages of the later years.

Preparations for the later years begin with the attitudes, lifestyle, activities, and spiritual maturing that come when we are younger. Inactive, critical, bitter, nervous, self-centered young people usually carry these characteristics into their later years. Perhaps Plato recognized this centuries ago. He wrote, "He who is of calm and happy nature will hardly feel the pressure of age, but to him who is of opposite disposition youth and age are equally a burden."[53] Counselors and other Christian leaders can help people face and adapt to the process of aging—beginning with themselves.

KEY POINTS FOR BUSY COUNSELORS

➤ The numbers of older people are increasing at a rapid rate, especially as the baby boomers reach retirement age.

➤ There are many examples of people who have aged positively and lived useful and productive lives well into their eighties, nineties, and later.

➤ Despite the positive examples of aging, the elderly still are viewed negatively by many people. *Ageism* is a bias against aging and the holding of negative myths and stereotypes about older people. Even counselors sometimes demonstrate ageism.

➤ The Bible gives detailed descriptions of people who lived to advanced age, realistically describes the weaknesses and strengths of aging, and encourages respect for the elderly.

➤ The causes of problems in the later years include:
  - Attitude causes: many older people view old age negatively and this, in turn, can contribute to greater problems.
  - Physical causes, including the following:
    - ◆ decline in physical appearance so that aging is emphasized;
    - ◆ sensory changes;
    - ◆ emotional intelligence;
    - ◆ system changes, including changes in digestive, cardiovascular, and gastrointestinal systems;
    - ◆ sexual changes; and
    - ◆ changes due to disease and illness.
  - Intellectual causes, including changes in cognitive abilities.
  - Emotional causes that can lead to depression, anxiety, fears, and other concerns, often about losses.
  - Economic causes, including reduced income and related worries.
  - Interpersonal causes, including changing relationships.
  - Self-esteem causes: many people have a loss in self-esteem as they age. This can contribute to declining self-confidence.
  - Spiritual causes.
  - Other causes, including life circumstances.

➤ The process of aging can influence people both positively and negatively. Some writers suggest that older people should seek to become new elders who understand who they are, where they fit, what they care about, and what they hope to leave as their legacy.

➤ Counseling may include:
  - The counselor being in touch with his or her own attitudes toward older counselees.

- Encouraging physical examinations and counseling concerning the counselee's physical conditions.
- Individual counseling. This can include:
  - giving support and encouragement,
  - educating people about the later years,
  - retirement counseling, helping people prepare,
  - life reviews, and
  - in-depth therapy.
- Family counseling.
- Spiritual counseling.
- Group counseling.
- Environmental counseling, helping people cope and make changes.

➤ It is probable that as the current generation of middle-aged people reaches the later years, the whole cultural outlook on aging will change.

➤ To prevent problems of the later years:
- Stimulate realistic planning, including retirement planning.
- Stimulate realistic attitudes.
- Stimulate education and activity.
- Stimulate spiritual growth.

➤ Counselors and other Christian leaders can help people face and adapt to the process of aging—beginning with themselves.

PART FOUR

Interpersonal Issues

18

Conflict and Relationships

Kate and Maria have been close friends for most of their lives. They lived in the same neighborhood, attended the same schools when they were growing up, and were roommates at college. After they married and went their separate ways, they kept in close contact and sometimes joked that they had always been best friends.

Nobody was surprised when the two friends opened a small decorating business and worked together as business partners. A lawyer suggested that they should have a legal agreement outlining their business relationship and setting guidelines for the time when they might separate in the future, but Kate and Maria agreed that they would always be able to resolve any future differences because they were such close friends.

They were wrong. As the business grew, they hired a few employees, divided some of their responsibilities, and took on new challenges. No longer were they able to make all their decisions together, and at times there were irritations between them when one made a decision that the other did not completely approve. A major disagreement arose over one of their employees. Kate thought he should be fired, but Maria disagreed. Slowly, the business partners drifted further and further apart even as they tried to run their business together. They began to distrust each other, to avoid one another, and to disagree more often.

Eventually, they decided to separate. Maria would keep the business; Kate would resign. To facilitate their separation and keep everything legal, they each hired lawyers, but endless debates followed concerning the value of the business, how they would divide the assets, and whether Kate could start a competing business in another location. The lack of legal guidelines at the beginning of their partnership made their separation much more difficult.

Kate and Maria still attend the same church. There is no overt hostility between them, but each feels deeply hurt by the other and wounded about their soured relationship. They no longer get together socially, and apart from an occasional "hello" after church, they never talk. The two former best friends have gone in different directions, and each realizes, sadly, that their old closeness as friends will never return.

Human beings are social creatures. At the time of creation, God declared that it was not good for us to be alone, so he gave Adam a companion, instructed the human race to multiply, and has permitted us to expand into the billions of people who now occupy planet Earth.

Whenever two or more of these people get together, there are interpersonal relations. Often these relationships are compatible, mutually supportive, respectful, and characterized by clear, concise, and efficient communication. At other times, interpersonal relations are strained and marked by conflict. There are cultural differences around the world, but at least in Western countries most twenty-first-century people value individualism, independence, self-determination, and personal freedom. These values can be motivating, but they also cut us off from other people and make us more insensitive, lonely, and unable to get along with one another. Beginning early in childhood, we chafe at authority, rules, regulations, and cultural traditions, but when we get free of these constraints, we can become more isolated and uncertain about our actions and future directions.[1] Populations that are liberated from oppressive dictators sometimes disintegrate into chaos and paralysis because the people confuse their new freedom with the license to do whatever they want to satisfy their own desires. In this information age, with its many technical devices to aid communication and interaction, we still misunderstand each other, fail to resolve conflict or get along, and often feel alone. All counseling, and almost all of the issues discussed in this book, deal directly or indirectly with interpersonal relations. How people get along with each other, or how and why they don't get along, are issues that concern all Christian counselors.

The Bible, Conflict, and Interpersonal Relations

The Bible records a long human history of interpersonal problems and communication breakdowns. Adam and Eve, the first married couple, had a disagreement about the reasons for their sin in the Garden of Eden. Their first two sons had a conflict that led one to murder the other. Then as its population multiplied, the earth filled with violence.[2] The Bible reports the arguments between the herdsmen of Abram and Lot, the conflicts between Joseph and his brothers, the jealousy that led Saul to be at odds with David, the disagreement between Job and his three friends, numerous examples of family disputes, and a whole succession of wars that continued throughout Old Testament history.

Things were not much better in New Testament times. The disciples of Jesus argued among themselves about who would be greatest in heaven.[3] Ananias and Sapphira lied to their fellow believers, the Jews and Greeks were at odds with each other, and there were disputes over doctrine.[4] Many times in his letters, the apostle Paul commented on the disunity of the church and appealed for peace and reconciliation. In his own missionary activities there was conflict,[5] and on one occasion he wrote to the Corinthians expressing fear that if he came to visit he might find "quarreling, jealousy, outbursts of anger, selfishness, backstabbing, gossip, conceit," disorder, and other evidences of interpersonal tension and sin.[6]

Although the Bible records many examples of interpersonal conflict, this is never condoned. On the contrary, dissension and interpersonal strife are dealt with honestly, and principles for building or maintaining good relationships are mentioned frequently. The book of Proverbs, for example, instructs us to hold our tongues and avoid slander, tell the truth, speak gently, think before we talk, listen carefully, resist the temptation to gossip, avoid flattery, and trust in God.[7] Unrestrained anger, hasty words, personal pride, dishonesty, envy, the struggle for riches, and a host of other harmful attributes are mentioned as sources of tension. There is no book in the Bible that equals Proverbs in clear, consistent teaching about good relationships between people.

Teaching about relationships does occur elsewhere, however. Much of the Sermon on the Mount concerns interpersonal relations.[8] Throughout his later ministry Jesus taught about conflict resolution, and he intervened in several disputes.[9] Paul warned Timothy not to be quarrelsome, especially over unimportant things; and in other Bible passages there are instructions to live in harmony, demonstrate love, and replace bitterness and wrath with kindness, forgiveness, and tender-hearted actions.[10] After a warning against those who cause trouble because they do not control their tongues, James notes that quarrels and conflicts come because of personal lust and envy.[11] In listing practical guidelines for living, Paul instructs his readers to "never pay back evil for evil to anyone," to live in harmony with each other, and to "do your part to live at peace with everyone, as much as possible."[12] Jesus and the biblical writers were peacemakers who dealt with conflict in a straightforward way but who taught by their example and words. They expected believers to be peacemakers as well.[13]

As we ponder the many biblical statements about conflict and interpersonal relations, several themes are apparent. Good relationships begin with Jesus Christ, depend on people, face the issues honestly, and involve determination and skill. Relationship issues also can build maturity.

1. *Good Relationships and Conflict Resolution Begin with Jesus Christ.* Isaiah called him the Prince of Peace, and at his birth, hosts of angels sang glory to God in the highest and proclaimed "peace on earth to all whom God favors."[14] During his ministry he predicted that tension would arise between his followers and their nonbelieving relatives and friends,[15] but he was described as a maker of peace who is able to break down interpersonal barriers and the walls of hostility that divide people.[16]

Further, the followers of Jesus have been promised a supernaturally produced inner peace of mind[17] that gives internal stability, even in times of turmoil and interpersonal tension. Peace with God comes to people who pray about everything, put their trust in God, ask him to take control of their lives, and expect that he will give the peace that the Word of God promises. This peace, in turn, can bring calm in times of interpersonal dissension.

Despite these biblical promises, all of us still worry at times, and Christians have conflicts with each other and with nonbelievers. This leads to other biblical statements about interpersonal relations.

2. *Good Interpersonal Relations Depend on People.* Relationships can be maintained and conflicts can be managed when people are willing to work together to resolve their differences. Counselors are among those who serve as mediators, sometimes helping with negotiations between individuals in conflict, including married couples, political factions, church members who disagree with others, or protagonists in labor disagreements. Some people are specialists in guiding negotiations between people in legal disputes or even helping to resolve conflict between nations. Although these efforts at peacemaking often can be helpful, the Bible often puts greater emphasis on the attitudes and characteristics of the persons involved in the disagreements.

In his first letter to the Corinthians, Paul appears to divide people into three categories.[18] The first of these are people who aren't Christians.[19] There are individual differences, of course, and many are morally upright people, but as a group they are more prone to sexual immorality, impure thoughts, eagerness for lustful pleasure, idolatry, participation in demonic activity, hostility, quarreling, jealousy, outbursts of anger, selfish ambition, and other sinful activities.[20] These people may desire and strive for peace, but their basic alienation from God makes both inner peace and interpersonal peace more difficult to attain. The second group are people who have committed their lives to Christ, but they have never grown spiritually. They act like nonbelievers who are controlled by their own sinful natures and act like people who do not belong to the Lord. They are jealous of one another and quarrel with each other.[21] Sadly, many church members appear to be in this group, so we often see the sad spectacle of believers in conflict, sometimes in violent conflict, with their neighbors and with each other. Some of these immature Christians read the Bible regularly and have good understanding of theology, but their beliefs mostly are intellectual and seem to have had little influence in their daily lives and interpersonal relationships. In contrast, the third group, described in the Bible as mature Christians, consists of believers who are yielded to divine control and are seeking to think and live like Christ. At times most of these people slip back into their former worldly ways and actions, at least temporarily, but more often their lives show increasing evidence of the "fruit of the Spirit" that involves love, joy, peace, patience, kindness, goodness, faithfulness, gentleness, and self-control.[22]

When people are transformed within, a slow process of change begins in their outward behavior. In time this enables them to build better interpersonal relationships. Christian counselors can remember this important principle: *For real peace to be felt within or to occur between individuals, there first must be a peace with God.* This comes when individuals commit their lives to Christ and have regular times of worship, prayer, and meditation on God's Word. Changed thoughts and actions often follow.

3. *Good Interpersonal Relations Focus on Issues.* Interpersonal tensions can arise because people have different attitudes, personalities, prejudices, values, or styles. Unlike his brother Esau, Jacob was a schemer who took advantage of his more passive sibling. King Saul was threatened and jealous when he pursued David, intent on taking his life. Sometimes the focus on counseling is to help people accept each other and learn to get along despite their different personalities, traditions, or working styles.

Often, however, tensions come from differences concerning more specific issues. The herdsmen of Lot and Abram argued over use of the limited pastureland. When the two men sat down to discuss this, their focus specifically was on the disputes between the two groups of herdsmen.[23] In the early church there were "rumblings of discontent" over the issue of whether the Hebrew-speaking people and the Greek speakers were each being treated fairly.[24] As a basic principle, counseling is most effective when there can be a focus on specific issues of disagreement. This principle works in any area of difference between people, including marriage.

4. *Good Interpersonal Relations Involve Determination, Effort, and Skill.* People don't always get along automatically even when they are committed Christians. The Bible and psychology agree that good relationships depend on the consistent development and application of skills, such as listening carefully, watching, understanding oneself and others, trying hard to communicate accurately, and refraining from unkind comments or emotional outbursts. All of this is learned. All can be forgotten in the heat of a disagreement. All can be taught by a perceptive Christian counselor who also can remind counselees to exercise determination, effort, and social skills if relationships are to be good.

5. *Interpersonal Conflicts Can Build Maturity.* This is true even when the conflicts are not resolved. In his book on the life of Abraham, Henry Blackaby wrote that with God there are no shortcuts to maturity. There also is "no possibility of avoid-

ing real-life situations. And life always brings some measure of conflict, even real battles. But God is always with those He chooses to (1) bring them through the battles, (2) bring them to new understanding of Himself, and (3) shape their character in new and fresh ways. Conflicts are God's means of developing character, especially faith in Him."[25] This is a positive side of interpersonal tension that can point individuals and groups to God and better enable them to grow.

The Causes of Conflict and Problems in Interpersonal Relations

Why do people have difficulty getting along with each other? The major causes can be summarized into several categories.

1. *Satan's Influence.* The Bible describes Satan as a deceiver and the father of lies, who disguises himself as an angel of light and goes around the earth tempting individuals and looking for people to devour.[26] Although many people deny or laugh away his existence, the devil and his legions are powerful, evil schemers whom Christians are instructed to resist in the name of Jesus Christ.[27] According to counselor Joyce Huggett, Satan "takes an informed interest in all Christian relationships and schemes either to bring about their downfall or to pollute them."[28] At the core of interpersonal conflict always lies the subtle and manipulative hand of Satan.

But Satan is not all-powerful. Believers know that God is greater than the forces of the devil. They have limited power and ultimately will be defeated,[29] but at present they are permitted to afflict God's people and to bring interpersonal tension and conflict throughout the world.

2. *Personal Attributes, Attitudes, and Actions.* Interpersonal tension often begins and escalates with people whose personality traits, attitudes, perceptions, feelings, mannerisms, and behavior create conflict and distrust. Have you ever known critical people who seem to stir up conflict wherever they go? Others will do anything to avoid conflict, even if this means overlooking disagreements and pretending that they don't exist. Jesus once was approached by a man who called from the crowd, "Teacher, please tell my brother to divide our father's estate with me." This sounds like a legitimate request, but instead of arbitration, Jesus gave a warning against greed.[30] Apparently, the family conflict came because of the man's selfish attitude. At another time, Jesus warned us against finding fault in others when there are even worse faults in ourselves.[31]

The faults that hinder good interpersonal relations include:

- A self-centered need to be noticed, to be in control, to have one's own way, or to have money, prestige, and status.
- A nonforgiving, bitter attitude.
- A tendency to be hypercritical, judgmental, and angry.
- An insecurity that involves feelings of threat, fear of rejection, and a reluctance to trust others.
- Prejudice, often unrecognized or denied.
- An unwillingness or inability to "open up" and share one's feelings and thoughts.
- A failure or unwillingness to recognize and accept individual differences. This is the erroneous idea that everybody thinks, feels, and sees situations in a similar way.

- Rigid expectations about what others should be like, how they should act or lead, or what values they should hold. When two people hold different expectations, conflict can result, especially if both parties hold their expectations rigidly.

It would be incorrect to assume that all of these are deliberate attempts to hinder smooth relationships. For example, fear of getting close, innate shyness, or a reluctance to trust others may be ingrained attitudes that are difficult to change without help from a friend or counselor. In contrast, people can change more easily when they have not been holding grudges, demanding their own ways, or refusing to forgive.

Sometimes, however, people behave in ways that are intended to control others and create tension.[32] Interpersonal problems are more prevalent when these difficult people are involved even when their motives are not selfish. Some people have the erroneous belief, for example, that the best way to motivate others is to put people under pressure. I have worked with colleagues who believe that aggressive confrontation is the best way to motivate students, engage in counseling, or defend the faith. Regardless of their motives, these people cause disruption in organizations or churches and create frustration in others. Difficult people include *abrasive personalities,* who are arrogant, frequently cynical, insensitive, intimidating, and inclined to explode in anger when they don't get their way. Different are the *complainers,* who find fault with everything and can be very verbal, but who never do anything about their complaints, either because they feel powerless or because they lack the courage to take responsibility. Some difficult people are *silent-unresponsive individuals,* who are difficult because they say very little and rarely reveal what they are thinking or doing behind the scenes. Other people may be always agreeable and unwilling to offend, but they are difficult to work with because they are *overcommitted* and not able to follow through on their promises. *Negative personalities,* in contrast, are those who take the pessimistic attitude that whatever someone proposes won't work, so the negative people criticize and refuse to cooperate or try. The *know-it-all "experts"* tend to be pompous, condescending, verbose, and unwilling to cooperate. Different from these are the *indecisive people,* who never act or make decisions until they can be absolutely sure that a decision is correct. As a result they almost never take action. Some of these people might be called *"control freaks,"* who will do whatever they can to control others or control their organizations. Almost all of the controllers are difficult to handle and require what Christian psychologist Les Parrott calls "high-maintenance relationships."[33] Please stop reading for a minute, look over this paragraph again, and then ask yourself who you know that fits any of the above categories. Most counselors have seen people with these traits among their counselees, colleagues, fellow Christians, or family members. Too often, we see ourselves on this list.

3. *Group Attitudes and Beliefs.* Counselors most often work with individuals or couples, so we tend to forget that large groups also have attitudes and beliefs. These group beliefs impact individuals within the group, influencing how they think and act toward people who are in a different group. Two psychologists who studied group beliefs concluded that group beliefs can be "dangerous ideas . . . that propel groups to conflict."[34] We see these differences in nations that engage in ideological and sometimes violent struggles with people of other countries. We

see the differences, as well, in divided political parties, churches, or other organizations. Five of these group beliefs are especially lethal.

- Superiority. This core belief revolves around the firm conviction within an individual or group that I (or we) am better than another. In a superior or self-righteous manner, the people in each group see themselves as being morally better than the other, chosen by God, having a special destiny, entitled to certain rights or privileges, defenders of certain values or principles. Think of the views of terrorist groups as opposed to the perspectives of established Western nations. Each carries the attitude of being superior to the other. Often, each believes as well that their side is invincible and destined to win.
- Injustice. This is a mind-set that sees injustice either in groups (such as sexually exploited children) or individuals (including oneself) who have been victimized. Mobilized by often legitimate grievances against the perpetrators of this mistreatment, the individual or group determines to fight the injustice, to defend the victims, and to bring change. Often the motivation of these people is honorable, but their determination can create conflict.
- Vulnerability. This is the core conviction that an individual or group is in harm's way. The belief that an individual, family, group, or nation is in danger can bring high levels of anxiety, exaggerated conclusions about the threat, concerted efforts at self-defense, and determination to weaken or annihilate those who are threatening. Examples include the animosity between Catholics and Protestants in Northern Ireland or between Israelis and Palestinians, in which each group sees itself as being vulnerable to attacks from the other. Militants within these groups disrupt any movement toward reconciliation because they feel threatened and especially vulnerable.
- Distrust. This involves an assumption that others are hostile and not to be trusted despite what might be said. This produces a defensive attitude and sometimes fosters a collective paranoia that refuses to trust because it is assumed that the trust will be violated.
- Helplessness. This leads to a mind-set of feeling powerless and dependent. When people feel helpless, they can become depressed, demoralized, and less likely to mobilize for combat. This has been seen in racial or ethnic groups who perceive their conditions as being hopeless, so they fail to rise up to throw off the restraints.

Undoubtedly, there are other beliefs that need to be faced when larger groups disagree (churches, denominations, church factions, or nations). Helping to gain resolution of differences like these is a major challenge because often the beliefs are firmly held and resistant to change.

4. *Conflict Patterns.* Conflict involves a struggle that occurs when two or more people have goals that appear to be incompatible, or when they want something that is scarce. Although conflicts can be threatening and potentially destructive power struggles, conflicts also can serve a useful purpose. They can clarify goals, unify groups, and sometimes bring previously ignored disagreements to a point of discussion and resolution.

Just as they have unique perspectives and worldviews, it appears that individuals and groups also have unique conflict styles that may be very rigid. This, in turn, can further escalate the conflict. Some people throw adult temper tantrums, pouting and stomping away when they don't get their way. Others resort to such diverse approaches as shouting, interrupting frequently, attempting to intimidate or attack the opposition, ignoring the other side, trying to manipulate either subtly or openly, attempting to bribe with money or other favors, or pretending to be disinterested in the issue being debated. Think of couples who are at odds or parents in conflict with their teenage children, and you will see some of these behaviors at work, often in our own counseling rooms. More helpful are those who approach conflict by using the gentle answer that calms anger,[35] and by facing issues both openly and honestly.

When there is conflict, the counselor should attempt to discover the real issues involved (these may be different from the issues that are stated). Watch for the personality traits and conflict styles that may be making matters worse.

5. *Lack of Commitment.* Many people, including those influenced by postmodernism, appear to be afraid of making commitments.[36] Loyalty to friends, family, church, business associates, and one's country is given only lip service and then discarded when it gets in the way of self-fulfillment or personal advancement. Perhaps because they are too hedonistic, too cautious, or too threatened by commitment, many people refuse to pledge themselves to another person or to some cause. They display an unwillingness to make any promises, or easily abandon verbal agreements when something or someone more attractive comes along. Many would feel uncomfortable with the words of an anonymous writer who urged us to consider the postage stamp. "Its usefulness consists in its ability to stick to one thing until it gets there."

Even when people try to avoid commitments, they often pledge themselves to something else by default. When we fail to commit ourselves to another person, to God, to some cause such as finishing school, or when we freely abandon our verbal commitments, then we really are committing ourselves to loneliness, a lack of intimacy, personal failure, and a variety of interpersonal tensions or frustrations.

This lack of commitment is not always due to laziness or self-centered values. Sometimes, people forget their earlier commitments, get busy with other things, or later question the wisdom of an earlier commitment. At times, commitment is severely shaken when we trust a mate or business partner but discover later that our trust has been violated. It has been said that a relationship in which partners have difficulty trusting each other is a relationship in trouble. In working with people having interpersonal difficulties, counselors often need to help their counselees make, keep, and sometimes reestablish commitments.

6. *Communication Failure.* The essence of good interpersonal relations is good communication. Interpersonal tensions often arise when communication is inefficient or in danger of breaking down. Even when two people want to communicate, however, there can be reasons for failure. At the simplest level, a *sender* tries to communicate a message to a *receiver*. This process is hindered if:

- The sender is unclear in his or her own mind about the message. (If the sender doesn't think clearly, communication cannot be clear.)
- The sender is afraid, ashamed, deceptive, unsure, or otherwise reluctant to send a clear message.

- The sender does not put the message into clearly understandable words or gestures.
- The sender says one thing but communicates a different message by his or her behavior. (For example, if the sender says, "I'm sad," but at the same time is laughing and joking, the message is confused.) When we say one thing with our lips but show something else with our actions, we are sending what are known as *double messages*. These can be powerful hindrances to good communication.
- The sender mumbles, yells, or in other ways distorts the message so it is not sent clearly.
- The receiver is unable to understand the message.
- The receiver is distracted from listening, or does not want to listen, perhaps because of disinterest, mistrust, distracting influences, fear of being persuaded, or some other reason.
- The receiver adds his or her interpretation to the message, or misses ideas that are too threatening to hear.

Next time you meet with two people who are in conflict, listen carefully to how they talk with each other and watch for some of these hindrances to effective communication.

Even when the communication process begins clearly, the receiver responds with facial features, gestures, and verbalizations, often before the whole message is sent. This can interrupt the sender and, usually without conscious awareness, can cause the sender to change the words or tone of the message, even in midsentence.

When communicators do not know each other well, communication will depend largely on words and widely understood gestures. When the communicators are in intimate contact (like two close friends or a married couple), they know each other so well that much is communicated by facial expression, tone of voice, a half sentence, or even a grunt. These shortcuts speed up communication, but they also create potential for misunderstanding. This is because intimates often are inclined to interpret what is being said, based on past experience, instead of concentrating on the message or the messenger.

7. *Social Irritants*. Events or conditions in society can prevent or hinder good interpersonal relations. It appears, for example, that tensions are more likely to erupt in crowded, uncomfortable urban areas than in the more spacious suburbs or rural communities. Prolonged heat waves or bad weather that forces people to stay indoors can wear down patience and contribute to strife (as any mother of squabbling, house-bound young children knows). Economic problems in the community, shortages of essential supplies, strikes or layoffs, crime waves, political corruption or unpopular decisions by government officials, disagreements between neighbors or supporters of rival football teams—all are social situations that can create a climate for further disagreements, racial or labor violence, student unrest, church splits, political disruption, or even military uprisings and sometimes war.

On a more personal level, daily hassles, those annoying and frustrating demands that plague us every day, can wear us down and stir up anger, fear, anxiety, jealousy, or other emotions. Abundant evidence shows that marital conflict can create a variety of problems in the children, including behavior problems, health problems, and interpersonal conflicts with siblings and peers.[37] When there is no opportunity to get away from noise, from the demands of a difficult work setting, or from other people (including demanding or disrupting family members), tension frequently builds and interpersonal conflict follows.

The Effects of Conflict and Poor Interpersonal Relations

Tim Ursiny is a psychologist and executive coach who hates conflict but wrote a book about it. "I hate conflict! I really do," he wrote on the first page of his book.[38] "I hated it growing up, I hated it when I got married, and I hate it now that I'm a psychologist and executive coach and corporate trainer. To me, there never was a need for conflict. . . . However, I have grown to be very capable of dealing with it. I've also grown to believe that conflict is actually (gasp) good at times. While I don't love it, I can appreciate the need for it and the actual benefits that can come from healthy disagreements." When Dr. Ursiny handed me a copy of his book, he autographed it to "Gary, From one coward to another." I laughed because I'm a coward when it comes to handling conflict and interpersonal tension too.

Not everybody feels the same way. People react differently to interpersonal tension. While some hate it and resist it, others avoid it, many feel deeply distressed by it, some are overwhelmed by it, and there are those who appear to thrive on it. Interpersonal tension is potentially threatening, both to the counselee and to the counselor, so we tend to act in ways that protect ourselves from the discomfort. We may hide our true feelings and insecurities, subtly try to manipulate others, or pretend to be something that we are not. These tactics take a toll and can influence us physically, psychologically, socially, and spiritually.

The *physical* effects of interpersonal tension are well known. Fatigue, tense muscles, headaches, stomach upsets, ulcers—these and a variety of other biological reactions come, especially when tensions are denied or kept hidden. When we try to hide our emotions or interpersonal tensions, our stomachs keep score and eventually break down.

Psychologically, poor interpersonal relations can trigger almost every human emotion, and the actions of people in conflict can range from a mild inclination to not cooperate all the way to murder. While I was writing this chapter, a taxi driver and passenger got into a disagreement about the cab fare. Suddenly, the disgruntled passenger jumped into the taxi, drove toward the amazed taxi driver, and ran over him. Arrested the next day and charged with murder, the man expressed both remorse and amazement that his conflict with the driver over a few dollars had led to such a violent reaction. This is an extreme reaction, of course, but when there is tension, individuals can feel angry, put down, depressed, guilty, lacking in self-confidence, or anxious. At times there may be bitterness, cynicism, and attempts to get revenge. When they feel threatened or frustrated in their attempts to get along, people don't always think clearly. As a result, things sometimes are said or done that are regretted later.

This leads to the *social* effects of interpersonal stress, including verbal outbursts, violence, withdrawal from others, and the breaking of previous relationships. This may be seen, for example, when two business associates abruptly terminate their partnership, a family stomps out of church because they are unhappy with the church leadership, an employee quits "on the spot," a couple decides to separate, or two nations go to war over a minor issue. Actions like these often escalate and maintain the conflict, but they rarely solve anything. They may bring temporary feelings of superiority, control, power, or revenge, but they are destructive and immature reactions that often lead to suffering, negative attitudes, increased anger, loneliness, and later feelings of regret.

None of this helps people *spiritually*. In the Garden of Eden, the devil succeeded in creating interpersonal tension between the Creator and his creatures. When they ate the fruit, Adam and Even were alienated from God and soon were in conflict, blaming each other. In a broad sense, therefore, all interpersonal tension is a result and reflection of sin. When people are separated from God or from each other, they cannot mature emotionally and spiritually.

When conflict exists because of the immaturity or self-centered attitudes of individuals, then conflict is wrong and potentially harmful. In contrast, when conflict is faced and dealt with in healthy ways, it also may lead to better relationships, greater respect for others, mutual understanding, increased self-confidence, less fear, reduced anger and anxiety, and personal growth. Counselors can help turn interpersonal tension into positive interpersonal relationships.

Counseling, Conflicts and Interpersonal Relations

In this life, you will have interpersonal tension, unless you are a hermit, reading this book by yourself in an isolated cave or cabin. Conflict is inevitable in a world filled with sinful people who have selfish needs, limited resources, the freedom to make choices, and the need to be mutually dependent. Most of us get along fine with some people, but others present more of a challenge. Getting along with difficult people involves determination, effort, and the development of personal characteristics, such as self-awareness, kindness, sensitivity, and patience. Good relationships also involve skills, including the ability to listen, understand, and communicate effectively. These skills do not appear magically. They are learned and applied, often with the help of a counselor. This help may be given in several areas.

1. *Starting with the Basics.* Love is rarely mentioned in the counseling literature, but it dominates the New Testament. It was love that motivated God to send his Son into the world to die for lost human beings. It is love that has been called the greatest of all attributes and a characteristic so crucial to Christianity that it becomes the distinguishing mark of believers.[39]

One goal in counseling is to help people become more loving. In any counseling situation we begin by listening and trying to understand the problem, but the counselor also demonstrates love and sometimes talks about this with the counselee. In some cases you might point out that complete yielding to Christ can change our attitudes and our relationships with others. It would be wrong to imply that interpersonal problems disappear automatically when one is yielding to Christ and trying to see a situation from God's perspective. Skill acquisition also is important, but interpersonal skills are more effective when the skill-user is characterized by a spirit of love, patience, self-control, and the other fruits of the Spirit.

The sensitive Christian counselor also recognizes that satanic involvement is at the basis of interpersonal tension. The devil's power does not yield to humanly created counseling techniques unless the helper is strengthened and guided daily by the Holy Spirit, familiar with the Word of God, and trusting God to intervene both in the counseling and in the lives of his or her clients. In addition, the counselor keeps alert to supernatural influences and prays persistently for others, including counselees.[40] Paul prayed for the right words to proclaim the good news about Christ.[41] Surely, we can pray as well for the right words to help counselees deal with their struggles and be able to get along better with one another.

2. *Evaluating Yourself.* Laura is a counselor and coach who thrives on helping people deal with conflict. When there is conflict between people in a corporate office, board of directors, or church group, Laura has an outstanding ability to go into the situation, calm the tension, and get the people working toward a solution. We might guess that most counselors would not want her job. The people we counsel often avoid conflict rather than face it, and counselors may prefer to do the same.

Conflict can be highly emotional, disruptive, and threatening. It is easier to avoid or ignore conflict than to deal with the inner discomfort that it arouses. Ursiny suggests that people most often avoid conflict because of fears, many of which are unconscious.[42] There are fears of being rejected or harmed. Sometimes, there is fear of losing emotional control, saying the wrong thing, destroying a relationship, hurting somebody, or being seen as selfish. In addition, counselors may fear losing control of the counseling situation, be afraid of not knowing what to say, or fear abandoning their objectivity and getting caught up emotionally in the tensions.

Counselors need to face the fears in themselves, recognize that most are irrational, and accept the fact that admitting them and moving forward is better than being immobilized by inactivity. Recognize, too, that facing and resolving conflict can be a good thing. The counselor may not have all the answers, but if he or she can get the people working together in finding solutions, relationships can be much better. Often an outside observer can see the situation differently from the way the combatants see it and can offer helpful insights about what is going on and what needs to change. If counselors are afraid of conflict, keep avoiding it, or pretend that it does not exist, they are unlikely to be very helpful to counselees who have the same fears.

3. *Understanding Conflict Stages.* Every relationship problem is unique, but most conflicts go through stages. These may be long or short, but they often proceed in the same order. Conflict can be resolved at any stage, but the earlier the intervention, the easier it is to solve the problem. Five stages have been identified.[43]

- Tension Development Stage. All conflict begins at this level. People sense that tension is developing, that something is not right, but they aren't sure what is causing the inner sense of discomfort. Often a person may feel embarrassed or afraid to mention the tensions, perhaps hoping they will fade on their own. This is the best time to talk about the discomforts because there still is a measure of trust and communication, and talking is not likely to do any harm to the participants. Talking may clear up misunderstandings and prevent greater conflict from developing.
- Role Confusion Stage. Here participants are confused about what is happening, what is causing the problem, and how they should relate to the person or people with whom they sense conflict. At this stage, people begin to wonder if they have done something to cause the problem. They

experience increasing discomfort and often feelings of threat. As a result, the two parties pull away from each other and stop communicating. Here the conflict manager must help the two sides clarify their roles in starting and maintaining the conflict and help each of them take whatever responsibility is necessary for finding a mutually acceptable resolution.

- Injustice Collecting Stage. Next the participants begin to collect evidence to support their positions. Couples in conflict often begin to collect examples of what the other person has done to create the problem. Next time there is an argument, they bring out the collected stories and throw them at the spouse. This is a stage when participants have pulled away from each other, begun name calling, and started attacking each other rather than attacking the issues. The counselor needs the courage to take control of the situation and focus on the facts and the issues, giving each side freedom to express their views and concerns without being interrupted. The more mature and skilled the mediator is at this and the following stages, the better.

- Confrontation Stage. This is a potentially volatile stage. It can turn into an opportunity for each side to justify its own positions and to blame the other. Permanent harm can follow if there are emotionally charged criticisms and damaging statements that cannot be withdrawn later. The counselor can permit the expression of the different positions, but he or she needs to keep the confrontation from getting out of control. Try to get people to the point of agreeing that "we can't keep going on this way. We need to do something about this." When they stop defending themselves and hurling charges, they can settle down to the business of finding a resolution.

- Adjustments State. Here the parties look for ways to adjust to the situation. They could sever the relationship and split up; one party could determine to dominate the other; they may decide to return to the way things were before, even though this rarely works after a conflict; or they could negotiate a new set of mutual agreements and commitments. The counselor's role is to get all parties involved in the resolution process and to help stimulate creative solutions that can be applied.

4. *Working to Change the Individual.* Since interpersonal conflicts often result from the attributes, attitudes, and abrasive actions of people, there can be value in working to change individuals. Often counselees are unaware of the ways in which their mannerisms, words, tone of voice, and actions can create or escalate interpersonal tension. Sometimes, a counselee is quick to see fault in others, but much slower to see his or her own weaknesses or ways of contributing to the problem.[44] It can be helpful, therefore, to gently point out these personal flaws and self-defeating behaviors. Try to give specific examples to support your observations and then invite the counselee to respond.

Change often is stimulated by sharing and making oneself known to at least one significant other person to whom we are accountable. We don't encourage counselees to reveal intimate details of their lives indiscriminately or with a variety of people, but when counselees share with one or two others, sometimes in an accountability group, individuals can find acceptance and greater self-understanding from people who are not afraid to give support and occasional confrontation.[45] Being vulnerable and open can lead to behavior changes that contribute to smoother relationships with others. Counselors or accountability partners also can help individuals face and learn to deal with their fears of conflict so they can be freed to focus on the issues that are causing the tensions.

The Christian counselor knows that the most basic and lasting changes in individuals come from God. For counselees and counselors, a consistent and growing relationship with Jesus Christ can help to break down walls between people, can help them get rid of the bitterness and insensitivity that divide individuals, and can contribute to interpersonal peace and unity.[46]

5. *Teaching Conflict Resolution.* Counselors can help individuals change in ways that will reduce conflict and build better relationships. Counselors also can meet with two or more people who are at odds with one another and serve as a mediator while they work out their differences. In either role, the counselor is a teacher who guides conflict resolution.

In doing this work, try to find a meeting place that is pleasant, private, and neutral. If an employer and employee had a conflict, for example, it would not be good to meet in the office of the boss. The room might be intimidating for the employee, and it could give the employer an image of power. Keep in mind that timing also is important. The best time for a mutual talk is when everyone is relaxed and rested, not after a major argument when tempers are high and emotions are volatile. It helps if the counselor/mediator is optimistic, respectful of both parties, relaxed and not afraid to make an occasional humorous comment to reduce the tension. Encourage mutual trust and acceptance, and set the tone for the meeting with prayer.

As you work, either with an individual or group, consider each of the following.

(a) Clarify the Issues and Relationships. Most conflicts involve both issues and relationships. A father and teenage daughter, for example, may disagree about the merits of the girl's new boyfriend. That is the issue being debated, but underneath there may be the more significant relationship question of who has more power in the family, the father or the daughter. The concerns of these people may be seen in terms of the stated issue, which is to reach some conclusion about the boyfriend. Of equal or greater importance may be the relationship as each tries to assert and maintain control over the other person. These relationship differences will not always be recognized or stated, so the counselor must observe the interaction and attitudes in an attempt to determine if the stated issues of disagreement are the real or most pressing issues. Even when relationship problems are complex—as they usually are—it usually is good to deal with specific rather than general topics. For example, it is easier to deal with the question of whether the boyfriend shows respect for the daughter rather than whether he is a nice guy.

Conflicts usually involve feelings, so let people express their frustrations and emotions before you move to the issues that divide. Near the beginning try to get both parties to agree about the issue that really is dividing them. Are the father and daughter at odds over this particular boyfriend, or about some other issue such as the girl's overall dating standards? Often you will discover that neither side has an accurate picture of what the other side is thinking, how the other person or group perceives the situation, or what the other side wants. At other times everybody is surprised to discover that both parties have similar desires and hope for the future.

(b) Clarify the Goals. When people are in conflict, they often share many of the same goals in spite of their differences. A college faculty, for example, may want quality education but be in conflict over how to best attain their goal in a curriculum. A husband and wife may both want a good marriage but be in conflict over details of lifestyle, money management, or child-rearing. Both sides may want to see the conflict resolved in a way that will be mutually agreeable, beneficial to both, and inclined to enhance the relationship so that future communication will be better.

In working with these people, try to discourage bargaining over positions. In theory, position bargaining occurs when each side takes a position, argues for it, and tries to reach a mutually agreeable solution. In practice, each side tends to adopt a rigid position, stubbornly hold to it, and argue. As a result, tempers often flare, compromise is interpreted as weakness or losing face, both sides dig in and refuse to budge, agreement is slow in coming, and when a solution is reached, a residue of persisting anger and dissatisfaction still exists.[47] To avoid this, ask disputants to consider what they each really want and whether they have similar goals. When goals are similar, conflict resolution is easier.

Often, however, the two sides have different goals. If a wife wants the marital discord to be mended but the husband wants a divorce so he can marry his new girlfriend, then conflict resolution is more difficult. Talking to this couple about issues such as finances, lifestyle, or contrasting views of religion doesn't help to bring peace because the ultimate goals of the husband and wife are about something else, and each has a position that is unacceptable to the other. Sometimes, in counseling, two people first can be reminded of the goals they do share. Then there can be a discussion of differences.

(c) Identify and Respect Conflict-Management Styles. We rarely think about this, but as we have seen, each of us has unique ways of relating to other people. These differences reflect our personalities, backgrounds, past experiences, training, beliefs, and values. Often known as our *styles*, these are patterns of behavior that appear in different situations. Composers and performers have musical styles; authors have writing styles; others have unique speaking, teaching, counseling parenting, selling, management, or leadership styles. It should come as no surprise, therefore, that each person has a particular style of dealing with conflict. When two people are at odds, they sometimes show different behavior styles, which can make reconciliation harder and increase the tension.

Church consultant Norman Shawchuck has identified five common conflict-management styles. Counselees tend to use one of these preferred styles, depending in part on how serious an issue is at stake, and counselors may do the same. An understanding of the styles lets us understand our counselees better. This also lets us communicate better because we can respond in ways that reflect the styles.

(d) Reconciling Differences. In talking to his disciples, Jesus outlined a procedure for restoring relationships between Christians who are at odds with each other.[48] They are guidelines that the Christian counselor should encourage counselees to follow.

Step one: The person who has been wronged or has a disagreement with another person should take the initiative and go to that other person in a sincere effort to deal with the conflict and to settle the dispute. The New Testament implies that this should be done in person, if possible, and done in private. By making this move, it is best if the person goes with a spirit of humility, with a

Table 18-1
Conflict Styles*

STYLE	MOTTO	GOAL	BEHAVIOR	RESULTS	EXAMPLE
Avoiding	"I will stay out of this."	To avoid getting involved.	The avoider says little, is passive and unassertive.	The conflict continues with no resolution. It often gets worse.	When people are insecure or when they feel powerless to take action.
Accommodating	"I will give in."	To avoid risk and preserve relationships.	Tries to keep everyone at peace even if own interests are sacrificed.	The person always gives in so is not heard or taken seriously.	Good if the issue is not significant or one's position is weak.
Collaborating	"Let's get together for everyone's good."	To respect everyone and to reach a mutually acceptable compromise.	The person is assertive but flexible, wants win-win results that are fair.	Everyone benefits, participates, and shares decision making.	For most conflict this is the best style, leading to group consensus.
Compromising	"I will meet you halfway."	To give at least something to all parties.	Bargaining and trading: each party gets some of what he or she wants and gives up other parts.	Both win some and lose some. Parties continue to compete in subtle ways. Commitments may be halfhearted.	When collaboration fails, both parties are stubborn but of equal strength.
Competing	"I will get my way."	The goal is to win, regardless of the costs.	Be assertive, domineering, some-times manipulative. "My way is the only way."	A "we versus them" mentality prevails, and conflict persists.	When things are paralyzed and a leader has to take even unpopular action.

*Adapted from Norman Sawchuck, *How to Manage Conflict in the Church*, Conflict Intervention and Resources (Schaumburg, IL: Spiritual Growth Resources, 1983).

willingness to listen, with a determination to be nondefensive, and with a willingness to forgive.[49]

Step two: Call some witnesses. If a one-to-one meeting fails to resolve the conflict or the other person will not listen or change, there should be another meeting with one or two witnesses present. These people are to listen, evaluate, determine facts, and presumably try to arbitrate and bring a resolution to the dispute.

Step three: Tell it to the church. If the person who has been visited still refuses to listen, change, or cooperate in resolving the dispute, or if he or she won't even agree to a meeting, then the church leaders or the whole church should be brought in. If the person who has been contacted still refuses to cooperate, then he or she may be asked to leave the church or group.

Does all of this sound old-fashioned? Interpersonal tensions are difficult to face, and we can understand why church leaders would prefer to avoid involvement. Sadly, there are some churches where the sins of individual members are overlooked or where there even is joking about the infighting in the church. Perhaps fewer people today would be distressed if they were threatened with excommunication. One woman sued her church when the leaders tried to follow these biblical principles by bringing the woman's actions to the attention of the church. The woman's suit charged that the church leaders had exposed the woman's lifestyle and invaded her privacy by telling the church about her immorality.

It can be difficult to follow biblical guidelines for interpersonal living. To forgive seventy times seven, to turn the other cheek, to repay evil with good, to pray for those who persecute us—these and other guidelines in Table 18–2 are all difficult to implement in our modern culture.[50] Nevertheless, the believer and the Christian counselor seek to follow biblical principles, even when they are difficult. Often, counselees and counselors must ponder together what Jesus would do today if he were in the situation facing the counselee.

(e) Resolving Conflicts. When individuals, groups, or nations are in conflict, they have four major choices about the direction they will take. They may seek to avoid the conflict, maintain it at its present level, escalate it, or reduce it. As we have seen, people don't always want conflict reduction, and sometimes the participants may decide to deal with disagreements in different ways. When a husband and wife have tensions, for example, one of them may want to avoid facing the conflict in hopes that it might go away or clear up by itself if it is ignored for a while. The other may want to escalate the conflict, perhaps in an attempt to gain power, to get the differences out in the open, or to find an excuse for separation.

Conflict resolution often means that the counselor takes on the role of a mediator. This role can demand a lot of skill, wisdom, and emotional restraint. The intervener will feel pressure to take sides, will be required to make quick analytical decisions, and will be responsible for keeping communication smooth. It may not always be wise for the counselor to get involved in some other person's conflict even when he or she is asked to do so. Sometimes, the disputing parties are better helped by a professional mediator.[51] If you do choose to be involved as a mediator/counselor try to:

- Explain at the beginning that all parties will be respected and that each will be given opportunity to express his or her positions.
- Show your respect for all parties.

Table 18–2

Some Biblical Guidelines for Interpersonal Relations

DO:

- Be sympathetic, kind, and loving. (Gal. 5:22; Eph. 4:32; Col. 3:12, 14; 1 Pet. 3:8; 4:8; 1 John 3:11)
- Be gentle, mild, and tactful. (Gal. 5:23; Eph. 4:2; Col.3:12, 4:6; 1 Tim. 3:3; Titus 1:8; 3:2; 1 Pet. 3:4)
- Be humble, meek, deferring to others. (Matt. 5:3–5; John 13:34; Eph 4:2; Col. 3:12; 1 Pet. 3:8; 5:5)
- Be generous and willing to give. (Matt. 5:42; 10:42; 25:35–36, 42–43; Mark 12:41–44; Rom. 12:8, 13; 1 Pet. 4:9; 1 John 3:17)
- Be hospitable without grumbling. (Rom. 12:13; Heb. 13:2; 1 Pet. 4:9; 1 Tim. 3:2)
- Be self-controlled and temperate. (Gal. 5:23; 1 Tim. 3:2; Titus 1:8; 2:1, 5, 6; 1 Pet. 5:8; 2 Pet. 1:6)
- Be willing to show mercy, even when it is undeserved. (Matt. 5:7; 18:33; Luke 6:36; Rom. 12:8; James 2:13; 3:17)
- Be a peacemaker, seeking to live in peace with everyone. (Matt. 5:4; Rom. 12:18; Gal. 5:22; 1 Thess. 5:13; 1 Pet. 3:8; 2 Pet. 3:14; James 3:17)
- Be patient, even when provoked. (1 Cor. 13:4, 5, 7; Gal. 5:22; Eph. 4:2; Col. 3:12; 1 Thess. 5:14; 2 Tim. 2:24)
- Be content, not longing for what we don't have in terms of possessions, happiness, or relationships. (2 Cor. 12:10; Phil. 4:11; 1 Tim. 6:6–8; Heb. 13:5)
- Be strong, immovable, not wavering in faith. (Matt. 14:29–31; 1 Cor. 15:58; James 1:6–8)
- Be subject to one another. (Eph. 5:21; 1 Pet. 2:13, 18; 3:1; 5:5)
- Be forgiving, repeatedly. (Matt. 6:14; 18:21–22; Col. 3:13)
- Be consistently encouraging and inclined to build up others. (Eph. 4:29; 6:22; 1 Thess. 4:18; 5:11, 14; Heb. 3:13; 10:25)
- Be truthful, speaking the truth in love. (2 Tim. 2:15; 1 Pet. 2:15; 3:15–16; Eph. 4:15; 2 Cor. 6:7)
- Be praying, even for those who create problems for us. (Matt. 5:44; Luke 6:28)

DON'T

- Be proud or arrogant. (Rom. 12:16; 1 Cor. 13:4; 2 Tim. 3:1, 2, 4; Jude 16)
- Be angry or quick-tempered. (Matt. 5:22; Gal. 5:20, 23; Col. 3:8; 1 Tim. 3:2; Titus 1:7; James 1:19, 20)
- Be selfish, insisting on your own way, self-indulgent. (John 3:14, 16; Rom. 12:10; 15:1–3; 1 Cor. 10:33; Phil. 2:3; 2 Pet. 2:3; Jude 12)
- Give offense. (1 Cor. 10:32; 2 Cor. 6:3)
- Swear, call other people names, or use abusive language. (Matt. 5:22; 12:36; Col. 3:8; James 5:12)
- Judge or point out faults in others. (Matt. 7:1–5; Luke 6:37; Phil. 4:8; Jude 16)
- Try to get even, repaying evil for evil. (Rom. 12:17–20; 1 Thess. 5:15; 1 Pet. 3:9)
- Gossip. (2 Cor. 12:20; 1 Tim. 6:20; 2 Tim. 2:16, 23; Titus 3:9)
- Complain or grumble. (John 6:43; 1 Cor. 10:10; 1 Pet. 4:9; James 5:9; Jude 16)
- Argue; be contentious, belligerent, or strong-willed. (2 Tim. 2:24; Titus 3:2; 1 Tim. 3:3)
- Slander or malign. (2 Cor. 12:20; Eph. 4:31; Col. 3:8; 2 Tim. 3:3; Titus 3:2; 2 Pet. 3:3; Jude)

- Acknowledge the tension and pain that the conflict probably is creating in both parties.
- Understand both positions without openly taking sides.
- Ask questions to get additional information or to clarify positions.
- Maintain a positive tone, reassure people, and give them hope if you feel there is reason to do so.
- Encourage open communication, and mutual listening.
- Determine if there are issues that are relevant but are not being discussed (for example, is the present problem being influenced by a long-standing grudge from the past or by jealousy?)
- Focus on things that can be changed.
- Guide as the parties analyze their problem, narrow the issues, and work toward finding realistic solutions.
- Prevent conflict from escalating (since this can break down communication).
- Summarize the situation and positions frequently.
- Help the counselees find additional help if your mediation does not seem to be effective.

According to one team of experienced negotiators, conflict resolution is most likely to be successful if a four-step method is used.[52]

Step One: Separate the people from the problem. This means that the disagreeing parties treat one another with respect, give attention to the issues, and avoid all defensive statements, name calling, or character judgments. Even though they disagree, each side should attempt to understand the other side's perceptions, fears, insecurities, and desires. Parties should think of themselves as partners in a hard, side-by-side search for an agreement that is fair to each.

Step Two: Focus on the issues, not the positions. When one of our daughters was about nineteen, she announced that she was planning to buy a motorcycle. Her mother and I disagreed with our daughter immediately. Here were two conflicting positions that had potential for considerable family conflict: she said she would get the motorcycle; we said she would not. Some reflection revealed that although our daughter liked the idea of having a motorcycle, the real issue was her desire to have reliable and inexpensive transportation. When we identified the common issue, and when we all agreed to work on this problem with open minds, we explored various options and reached a compromise (a small used car that the father helped finance) without a war in our home. The conflict was resolved because the parents and daughter focused on the real issue, transportation, and avoided defending rigid positions about motorcycles.

Step Three: Think of various options that might solve the problem. In the beginning there is no attempt to evaluate the options or to arrive at a single solution. Each side makes suggestions in a brainstorming session or two. After a number of creative and perhaps new alternatives have been proposed, then each of the options can be evaluated.

Step Four: Insist on objective criteria. Conflict is less likely to occur if both sides agree beforehand on an objective way to reach a solution. If both sides agree to abide by the results of a coin toss, a judge's ruling, or a mediator's evaluation, the end results may not be equally satisfying to both parties, but everybody agrees on the solution because it was determined beforehand by objective, fair, mutually accepted methods.

Sometimes, it will be necessary to break larger issues into smaller parts and deal with them one at a time. The counselor will attempt to understand both sides, and although he or she will try to stay objective, the Christian counselor must challenge decisions that are nonbiblical—even if both parties agree to a solution that is not consistent with the Bible's teachings.[53]

6. *Teaching Communication Skills.* The ability to communicate effectively and nonabrasively is a skill. Like all skills, effective communication is learned slowly. It comes as a result of watching how others do it and then practicing. Sadly, many people never learn good communication principles, rarely see them, never practice them, ignore them, or forget them in the heat of argument. Often these are people who have grown up in families and communities where shouting, criticism, and verbal attacks are the norm. These people have learned to use emotionally charged words to hurt others and get their own way. They have experienced few or no examples of how to communicate effectively, speak the truth in love, or discuss issues honestly and with an attitude of respect. Unfamiliar with good communication skills, these people take their unhealthy ways of interacting into the workplace, into their marriages, and later into their parenting. As we will see in a later chapter, marriage counselors repeatedly point to faulty communication as the most common cause of marital discord.

There is good news in the midst of this picture. There are principles for effective communication. Some of these are summarized in Table 18–3. When these guidelines are followed consistently, communication and interpersonal relations tend to be smooth, differences are more likely to be discussed honestly, destructive criticism is avoided, and conflicts are more often resolved satisfactorily. The counselor has the responsibility to: (a) learn these and similar principles, (b) practice them in his or her own life, (c) model them in talking with counselees, (d) share them with counselees, and (e) discuss how they could be applied to the counselees' interpersonal relationships.

For example, look at the first guideline stating that we communicate by our actions, gestures, facial expressions, and tone of voice as much as we communicate by our words. Ask your counselee to think of a recent specific conflict situation. Did anyone give a contradictory message in which what was said was contradicted by nonverbal signals? How could this have been avoided? How could something similar be avoided in the future? As a counselor working with people who are at odds with each other, look for examples of double messages and point these out to the counselees. Perhaps as an assignment outside of counseling, the counselee could concentrate on avoiding double messages. Discuss this at an appropriate time in a later counseling session.

Real communication, the kind that eases interpersonal tension and builds good relationships, only occurs when there is a genuine willingness to respect, accept, understand, and care for others. Important as they are, communication skills, by themselves, are of limited value without good-will and sincerity in the communicators.

7. *Changing the Environment.* Since the environment contributes to interpersonal tension, counselors and counselees should attempt to change stress-producing conditions. Whenever possible, discuss conflict resolution in a quiet, comfortable place, where crowding is minimal and noise is reduced. Some people like to discuss their conflicts in a restaurant while drinking coffee. This can be a nonthreatening, relaxing place except where there is loud music, distracting cus-

Table 18–3

Principles for Effective Communication

1. Recognize that we communicate by our actions, gestures, facial expressions, and tone of voice as much as we communicate by words. Avoid communicating one message in words and contradicting this with your gestures. This is known as a double message. These are always confusing, but the nonverbal usually is what people notice.

2. Deal with conflict as soon as it appears. The longer it remains under cover, the worse it can get.

3. In communicating cross-culturally, be aware that people from different cultures may attach different meanings to the same actions or gestures.

4. Always communicate in ways that show respect for the other person's value as a human being.

5. Recognize that every issue can be seen from a unique point of view. Even if you feel strongly, do not assume that your perspective is the only valid perspective. Others may see things differently.

6. Decide what is important and focus on that issue. Communication is clouded when too many issues are being discussed at the same time or when either person brings in unrelated grievances or complaints.

7. Avoid fault finding, exaggerated statements, sarcasm, bullying, put-downs, ridicule, name calling, insults, blaming, or sentences that start with "You always . . ." or "You never . . ." All of these escalate arguing and take the focus away from the issue that is causing the strife. In most cases it also is wise to avoid sentences that start "You should . . ." or "You shouldn't . . . "

8. Try to be clear, concise, and specific in your statements.

9. Be honest about your feelings without assigning blame. Instead of "You make me feel worthless" (which sounds like an accusation and can lead to defensive or hostile responses), say "I feel worthless when you speak to me in this way" (which puts the emphasis on you and not on the other person). "I" statements are more difficult to argue against.

10. Do not hold back statements that might disturb the other person. These can be stated in ways that are honest but with sensitivity to the other person's feelings.

11. Acknowledge or explain your actions but avoid making excuses or too quickly accepting the excuses of others.

12. Listen carefully, courteously, and respectfully to the other person's viewpoints, without interrupting or criticizing.

13. Ask questions to clarify, listen to the answers, and willingly answer the other person's questions about your position.

14. Speak kindly, softly, and politely. Shouting stimulates arguments instead of calming them. Remember that every disagreement has strong emotions on both sides. These should be communicated, when possible, in ways that do not make things worse. Remember that a gentle answer turns away wrath, but harsh words stir up anger (Proverbs 15:1).

15. Realize that humor and positive comments can keep the conversation going.

16. In all of this, remember that communication is more than conflict resolution. Get in the practice of complimenting others, showing acts of kindness, always listening carefully, looking for the positive, and making time to communicate.

tomers, eavesdroppers at a nearby table, or gaudy decorations. Environment makes a difference, even when we are counseling.

The place where conflicts are discussed can be less important than the environment in which people live. It is not easy to reduce neighborhood noise, eliminate poverty and violence in the street, improve working conditions, create more pleasant home atmospheres, or decrease crowding and other physical discomforts. The counselor must have a concern for more than the counseling process. He or she must be committed to the elimination of the social and environment conditions that stimulate and escalate interpersonal tensions. Each counselor must decide on the extent of this involvement.

Preventing Conflict and Poor Interpersonal Relationships

A lot of Christianity is about relationships. Its founder is the God of love, and love is its most distinguishing characteristic. This is not a sentimental, wishy-washy affection. It is a powerful, sacrificial, giving love that involves the characteristics described in 1 Corinthians 13 and reflects the love of God, who sent his Son to die for individuals in a sinful world. The church does its duty when it preaches and practices this love, which is so central to the Christian message. Whenever such a message is proclaimed and practiced, interpersonal tensions tend to diminish.

But God also has given more specific guidelines for showing this love.[54] A lot of advice about relationships is given in the Bible. In addition, God has allowed us to discover other principles for getting along and communicating effectively. Interpersonal relationships can improve, and many interpersonal tensions can be prevented when people of all ages are taught and encouraged to practice:

- The biblical teachings about good relationships (see Table 18–2).
- A daily walk with Jesus Christ; a walk characterized by prayer, meditation on Scripture, confession of sin, practicing the other spiritual disciplines, and a willingness to seek and obey divine leading.
- A self-examination that leads to the removal, with God's help, of bitterness, cynicism, and other personal attitudes or actions that could stimulate dissention.
- An understanding of conflict and a practice of those tactics that reduce conflict.
- The guidelines for effective communication as listed in Table 18–3.
- The reduction, avoidance, or elimination of conflict-producing environmental stress.

This is a major task, but one that should be emphasized, especially in the church. When Christian leaders, including counselors, are involved in preventing interpersonal tension, they are helping individuals to live in peace and harmony with one another, to avoid destructive conflict, and to experience something of the peace that comes from God. [55]

Conclusions About Conflict and Interpersonal Relations

Human beings are complex creatures with individual personalities and strong wills. We are crowded on a planet overpopulated with individuals whose sinful natures put them at odds with God and with each other. Many of us want to get along with others, but this isn't always easy.

Perhaps the apostle Paul was thinking like this when he instructed his readers to "do your part to live in peace with everyone, as much as possible."[56] These divinely inspired words come near the end of a few paragraphs dealing with practical rules for getting along. Don't just pretend that you love others, but really love them with genuine affection. Take delight in honoring each other. When God's children are in need, be the one to help them out. Live in harmony with others. Enjoy the company of ordinary people. Never pay back evil to anyone.

Surely, it is interesting that the instruction to live in peace is linked to the words, "as much as possible." This implies that sometimes it isn't possible to live in harmony with others. Even so, each person is told to "do your part," in getting along with others. With the help of the Holy Spirit, Christian counselors try to establish such peace and prevent the strain that is characteristic of so many interpersonal relationships.

KEY POINTS FOR BUSY COUNSELORS

➤ Human beings are social creatures. Whenever two or three people get together, there are interpersonal relationships. Often there also can be interpersonal tensions and conflicts.

➤ The Bible records many examples of interpersonal conflict, but this is never condoned. On the contrary, dissension and interpersonal strife are dealt with honestly, and principles for building or maintaining good relationships are mentioned frequently.

➤ The Bible shows that:
- Good relationships and conflict resolution begin with Jesus Christ.
- Good relationships depend on the efforts of people.
- Good relationships focus on issues.
- Good relationships involve determination, efforts, and interpersonal skills.
- Conflicts can contribute to maturity even when the tensions between people persist.

➤ Conflicts and interpersonal tensions are caused by:
- The influence of Satan.
- The attitudes, attributes, and actions of people.
- Group attitudes and beliefs, including superiority, a concern about injustice, fear of being harmed, distrust, and feelings of helplessness.
- Conflict patterns that escalate the tensions.
- Fear of making commitments.
- Communication failures.
- Social irritants.

- ➤ Conflict can impact people physically, psychologically, socially, and spiritually.

- ➤ To help people deal with conflict and build better relationships:
  - Start with the basics, recognizing the overarching importance of love.
  - Be in touch with one's own attitude toward dealing with conflict.
  - Understand the stages of conflict:
    - ◆ The tension development stage.
    - ◆ The role confusion stage.
    - ◆ The injustice collecting stage.
    - ◆ The confrontation stage.
    - ◆ The adjustments state.
  - Work to help the individual change.
  - Teach principles of conflict resolution:
    - ◆ Clarify the issues and relationships.
    - ◆ Help people reach mutually acceptable goals.
    - ◆ Identify and respect individual conflict management styles.
    - ◆ Work to reconcile difference (Matthew 18).
    - ◆ Work to resolve conflicts.
  - Teach effective communication skills.
  - Try to change the environment.

- ➤ There are four steps to resolving conflicts:
  - Step one: Separate the people from the problem.
  - Step two: Focus on the issues, not the positions.
  - Step three: Think of various options that might solve the problem.
  - Step four: Insist on an objective, mutually accepted way to agree on how the problem will be solved.

- ➤ The Bible instructs us to "do your part to live in peace with everyone, as much as possible." Counselors help people reach this goal, guided by the Holy Spirit.

19

Sex Apart from Marriage

"Psychiatrist Charged with Molesting Boys."

The newspaper headline caught my attention because I knew the doctor. He lives in my community and was working in a children's treatment facility at the time of his arrest. The news aroused a mixture of emotions and questions when I read the report on the morning I started work on this chapter.

What would motivate a Christian mental-health professional to sexually molest young boys and think he could avoid getting caught? How is his wife reacting? What about his children, his patients, his grandchildren who may be too young to understand their grandfather's disappearance while he sits in jail? Was he accountable to anybody about his sexuality? Did his family know about his sexual attraction to young males? When the doctor molested these boys, should these be considered acts of sex apart from marriage, or are they really acts of abuse, violence, or lack of self-control? Were there other victims who now might step forward? What is the impact on young people when a trusted adult takes sexual advantage of them? What does all this mean for the doctor's future?

Sexual temptation and lust have been described as "every man's battle,"[1] and clearly women can be tempted as well.[2] Ours is a world where pornography is readily available and sex portrayed in the media is taken for granted. Different surveys show that sex apart from marriage is common and that Christians often are as sexually active outside of marriage as their non-Christian neighbors. At some time every counselor will see people wanting to talk about their addictions to pornography, compulsive masturbation, sex with minors, premarital or extramarital sexual intercourse, homosexual acts by men or women, including those who are married but whose mates never suspect the unfaithfulness. How much of this sexuality is kept hidden? How much causes inner strife, guilt, and turmoil in people who live with their secrets for decades?

"Sexuality, like everything else created, has fallen into trouble. We are more vulnerable than ever, living in a society that crowds sexual innuendoes into every available space, whether billboards or office conversations." This conclusion, written about twenty years ago, gets to the core of an issue that may be of greater concern as we move through these first decades of the twenty-first century. The whole society is reeling, according to Christian journalist Tim Stafford.[3] We are burdened by "ruined families, staggered by millions of abortions, and terrified by a sexual epidemic." Sex apart from marriage is widely accepted in Western society and frequently tolerated within the church. Cohabitation, an unmarried male and female living together with full sexual relationships, is so widespread that hardly anyone criticizes the practice today. Unquestioned acceptance of both premarital and extramarital sex has become a part of the culture's values, reinforced by television, practiced by millions, and criticized by almost no one. For many, sex no longer is something that may be right or wrong; it is little more than a pleasurable way for two people to interact with each other.

Sexual intercourse apart from marriage is not the only issue that is widely accepted. Homosexual sex has been practiced for centuries and probably was more common in Greek and Roman cultures than it is at present. As gay and lesbian liberation groups have become more visible and more active, overt homosexuality has become more accepted. Masturbation, probably the most common sexual behavior apart from intercourse, is so prevalent that it rarely concerns sexual researchers and even has been promoted as a "means for achieving sexual health,"[4] despite the fact that this practice arouses a lot of guilt and anxiety, especially among boys and young men. A controversial government commission report on pornography drew attention not only to the dangers but also to the widespread consumption of pornographic literature and films.[5] The availability of Internet pornography has made sexually explicit materials more available, often targeted to adolescent boys. Then there are the rarer and more pathological forms of nonmarital sexual behavior, including the erotic exploitation of children, exhibitionism, rape, transvestism, bestiality (sex with animals), and voyeurism, each of which continues to attract the periodic attention of the media and mental-health professionals.

Have we become obsessed with sex? It is a central issue in much of television, magazines, advertising, music, literature, the theatre, movies, art, and popular conversation. It often appears in business, education, politics, and the church. One would have to be a hermit to avoid the sexually arousing stimuli of contemporary culture. That which God created for our enjoyment and intimacy has become perverted. Sexual perversion has become *the* major example of the sin and moral sickness that characterize modern human beings.

This chapter will limit our discussion to three of the four most common examples of sex outside of marriage: masturbation, premarital sex, and extramarital sex. Homosexuality is considered in chapter 21. Abuse, including sexual abuse, and other examples of unhealthy sexuality will be discussed elsewhere throughout this book.

The Bible and Sex Apart from Marriage

Most people realize that sex is more than a physical instinct or biological attraction. Sexuality pervades all of life and ranges from mild feelings of pleasure about human relationships to sensual lovemaking and stimulating orgasms. Sex involves intimacy and intense communication even in the absence of physical contact. "Sexuality throbs within us as movement toward relationship, intimacy, companionship," wrote Lewis Smedes. It is "an exciting desire, sometimes a melancholy longing, to give ourselves in trust to another." It is an urge toward closeness and the expression of a deep personal relationship with someone else.[6]

When he wrote to the Corinthians, the apostle Paul was unmarried and inclined to favor singleness,[7] but this does not mean that he was unfulfilled or nonsexual. He understood lust and the passions of sensuality,[8] but surely he also appreciated his maleness and experienced both intimacy and personal wholeness without physical sex. Within the Scriptures, sexual intercourse is intended to be confined to marriage. It is true that the Bible does little to define marriage, but sex apart from the marital commitment was condemned.[9] The well-known one-night stand of David with Bathsheba is only one illustration of the destructive nature of sex apart from marriage.

When it deviates from God's perfect plans for human beings, sex may bring temporary pleasure, but ultimately it is destructive. It destroys intimacy and communication, is self-centered, and often expresses a desire to manipulate, control, or hurt another person. It is true that the sexual experience can dull one's sense of loneliness, temporarily reduce anxiety, and give a feeling of intimacy, but all of its allures are fleeting, dehumanizing, and ultimately unfulfilling.

Perhaps this is why the Bible writers so soundly condemn fornication (which usually refers to premarital sex), adultery (sexual relations with a person other than one's spouse), and other forms of sex outside of marriage.[10] These pleasures are enjoyable, but the pleasure is "fleeting"[11] because sex outside of marriage deviates from God's plan for what ultimately is good for human beings. Consider, for example, what the Bible says about fornication and adultery. In the New Testament alone, the word "fornication" (*porneia*) occurs thirty-nine times, and often refers to general immorality.[12] Although it sometimes is used as a synonym for adultery,[13] fornication more often means voluntary sexual intercourse by an unmarried person with someone of the opposite sex (i.e., premarital sex).[14] The word would include what today is known as casual sex, including sex with a prostitute.[15] In every case, fornication is presented as behavior opposed to the plan and will of God.

"Adultery" is used two ways in the Bible. One meaning refers to idol worship and unfaithfulness to God;[16] the other concerns sexual intercourse by a married person with someone other than his or her mate (i.e., extramarital sex). In both cases, adultery is forbidden and strongly condemned.[17]

Several times in the writings of Paul, lists of sinful behavior are given—lists that include adultery and fornication, along with "immorality," "impurity," "sensuality," and "homosexuality."[18] It is significant that the wrath of God will come upon those who engage in such behaviors. Clearly, God does not take a light view of physical sexual intimacies apart from marriage.

What, then, can we conclude from our discussion thus far?

1. *Sex Is Created by God and Is Good.* This is the place to begin all considerations of sexuality. God created the human race with male and female bodies capable of sexual intimacy, including genital orgasm. As with other parts of his creation, God called sexual human beings "very good," and instructed us to "multiply."[19] When the human race fell into sin, God's creation was marred and the potential for unhealthy sexuality came into being. Adam and Eve, who previously did not feel any shame about their nakedness, suddenly became self-conscious about their bodies.[20]

2. *Sex Apart from Marriage Is Sinful.* This is stated most firmly in 1 Corinthians 6 where sexual sin is described as something that affects the body, the place where the Holy Spirit lives. "Our bodies were not made for sexual immorality," we read in Scripture. Our bodies were "made for the Lord. . . . No other sin so clearly affects the body as this one does. For sexual immorality is a sin against your own body." We are implored, therefore to "run away from sexual sin."[21]

Repeatedly, the Bible warns against the enslaving influence of sexual behavior apart from marriage.[22] There is nothing to even hint that sexually aroused persons are free to engage in sexual intercourse, even if they intend to marry. If you cannot restrain yourself, the apostle Paul wrote, then get married because it is better to marry than to burn with lust.[23]

This kind of thinking is widely rejected today, even by many within the church. Committed Christians appear to have higher rates of sexual abstinence when compared with believers who are less committed.[24] Overall, however, research studies have shown repeatedly that evangelical young people are almost as active sexually as their non-Christian classmates. Many people violate God's laws of sexual behavior and appear to suffer little for their indiscretions, so there seem to be no logical reasons to abstain—especially when everyone else is "doing it" and seems to be getting along fine.[25] It would appear that this philosophy contributes to major social problems, including the breakdown of the family, the increase in AIDS and other sexually transmitted diseases (STDs), the increase in one-parent families, the upsurge in teenage pregnancies, and the huge number of abortions—to cite the most apparent. Psalm 73 describes the personal end results of ignoring God's laws, and 1 Corinthians 6 implies that immoral sex hinders the potential oneness that can come within marriage.

3. *Sex Apart from Marriage Includes Sinful Thinking.* Some have maintained that no adultery occurs as long as the male does not let his penis enter the female's vagina. This legalistic view was challenged by Jesus in the Sermon on the Mount. Anyone who "even looks at a woman with lust in his eye has already committed adultery with her in his heart," Christ stated.[26] Clearly adultery, lust, and fornication can all take place in the mind without genital contact at all.

Lust is difficult to define accurately. Surely, it does *not* refer to normal God-given sexual desires or feelings of attraction toward sexually stimulating people. It seems unlikely that God would give us sexual needs and interests and then condemn these as lust. The Greek word for *lust* is sometimes translated "strong desire," and the word is used in a positive and nonsexual sense elsewhere in the Bible.[27] In commenting on mental adultery, perhaps Jesus was referring not to fantasies, but to mental desire. According to one writer[28] the Lord might have phrased his words in this way: "To want what is wrong sexually is just as evil as to do what is wrong sexually."

Even when they do not lead to subsequent genital contact, obsessive sexual fantasies can be harmful, especially when the thinking involves fantasies about forbidden acts with specific people. Sometimes, these fantasies can become a substitute for intimacy, especially when the fantasizing person is unable or unwilling to engage in sexual communication with a real person.

Engaging in sex before marriage harms at least two people. Mental lusting primarily influences the one who lusts. According to Jesus, both are wrong.

4. *Sex Apart from Marriage Includes Sinful Talk.* The Bible condemns loose sexual talk. Among Christians there should be "no sexual immorality, impurity, or greed among you. Such sins have no place among God's people. Obscene stories, foolish talk, and course jokes . . . are not for you."[29] Dirty language, humor with sexual connotations, impropriety in terms of one's talk and behavior—all can undermine the Christian's reputation and raise questions about the believer's purity, even when there is no improper behavior. The believer must avoid even the appearance of evil and seek to maintain his or her good reputation.[30] This can quickly be undermined by sinful sexual talk.

5. *Sex Apart from Marriage Restricts Freedom.* Many things in this world are possible, but this does not mean that everything is wise. This conclusion is stated at the beginning of one important New Testament discussion of immorality.[31] In this world, everything has a design and function, and we get along best when we stay within these guidelines. A fish, for example, is designed to swim in water, and

although it is free to jump onto the shore, the results would be tragic. In the same way, the Bible states that the human body is created for sex within marriage. We are most fulfilled when we stay within that divine guideline. Of course, we are free to engage in immorality, but ultimately such actions will have harmful after-effects. The person who cannot resist sexual temptation is not free or sexually liberated. He or she is caught in the strangling hold of uncontrolled impulses,[32] and often that person has trouble getting free without the help of a counselor or friend.

The Causes of Sex Apart from Marriage

There can be a variety of overlapping reasons for sexual behavior apart from marriage, but they could be grouped into two categories: environmental stimulation and internal pressure.[33]

1. *Environmental Stimulation.* It is no secret that our sex-saturated culture stimulates people to think about sex and encourages us to seek hedonistic physical sexual gratification. "We have become . . . so used to daily portrayals of live-action sexuality that we fail to appreciate how desensitized we have become," write Christopher and Rachel McCluskey. Many Christians "simply slide, rather than suddenly fall, into sexual sin. They have been moving in that direction for much of their lives without even realizing it."[34]

(a) Social Atmosphere. Especially in the West, modern society emphasizes the value of immediate, physical sexual pleasure. Many popular magazines—some at the checkout counters of the supermarket, movie ads on television, daytime soap operas, perhaps most Hollywood films, numerous commercial advertisements, explicit music lyrics, easy Internet access to pornography, blatant sexual references and portrayals on television, and literally thousands of novels seem designed to arouse our sexual urges and stimulate our desires. Citizen or government attempts to "clean up" the media or reduce pornography often are met with resistance in the form of compelling arguments: "We shouldn't restrict the rights of others to view what they want." "What people see and do in private is their own business." "Although media stimulate sexual (and violent) urges, the media also reflect what most people really want—and are willing to pay for."

This sexually supercharged atmosphere is soaked up by all of us, even against our wills. In addition to their enticement to sin, these influences hide the dangers of irresponsible sex and cause us to develop unrealistic expectations about what sex should be like.[35] The cultural influences also can merge into a powerful form of peer pressure, especially among the young. At a time when sexual urges are most intense, and the need for peer approval is most pressing, adolescents often succumb to social pressures and enter into sexual encounters in an attempt to find acceptance and status.

The social atmosphere and social pressures also can influence adults, including traveling businesspeople, entertainers, public speakers, and others whose work draws them away from home and repeatedly puts them into secluded motel rooms where pornographic movies and other materials may be available to stimulate the mind and bring sexual arousal. These materials may appear harmless and "entertaining," but they distort sexuality, stimulate fantasy, and portray sex as no more than ecstatic physical activity that dehumanizes and uses other human beings.

(b) Sexual Convenience. A newspaper report once described the difficulties faced by couples who want privacy in countries where cars are scarce, motel rooms are difficult to rent, and apartments are crowded with relatives. This is not the case in countries where people with cars (including teenagers) can get to private locations easily. Independent people who have less social and parental surveillance can be less anxious about sexual experimentation. College dormitory rooms that once were strictly segregated now can be used as places for sexual activities, including on-campus brothels that increasingly are accepted without question both by students and by the university officials who ignore what is happening.[36] The easy availability of contraceptive devices and abortions leaves people less worried about STDs or unwanted pregnancies. Convenient adultery is becoming more and more accessible to teenagers and adults.

(c) Liberal Values. Sex apart from marriage is no longer a taboo subject. Our generation probably knows more about birth control, sexual intercourse, sexual experimentation, and masturbation than any previous generation. Cohabitation, mate swapping, unfaithfulness, and similar behaviors are openly discussed and widely tolerated, if not accepted. The sexual immorality of American movie stars, British royalty, and politicians around the world are detailed on the front pages of newspapers, and none of us are surprised or shocked. Sexual restrictions have lessened, sexual standards have loosened, and sexual expectations have become more liberal. Marriage vows are taken less seriously, and when the sexual thrill is gone or when more attractive potential partners appear, then adultery or divorce are accepted as easy alternatives. For many, loyalty is discarded when it stands in the way of self-advancement or self-satisfaction.

In itself, openness about sex is not necessarily bad. Some Victorian inhibitions probably are best discarded. But the changes in our sexual values have become a stampede to license and licentiousness. These values make it more difficult for sexually vulnerable people to resist temptation.

(d) Inappropriate Education. Many people, especially young people, enter sexual relationships with inaccurate or inadequate knowledge of the emotional and physical consequences. Novels and films often give a distorted picture of sexual love, and sex education classes teach the facts of biology without principles of morality or facts about the results of uncontrolled sexual behavior. For many people the basis of their behavior is the still-prevalent ethic "if it feels good, do it!"

(e) Globalization. Historically, different cultures have maintained fairly strict control over the ways in which human sexuality is viewed and practiced.[37] Within recent years, however, television, movies, other media, and a greater ease of travel have made it more possible for the sexual values and behaviors of one culture to cross borders into other cultures. As people in these cultures are exposed to the outside world, their citizens are introduced to sexual standards and practices that are new and can be socially disruptive. In many Western countries, for example, women are viewed much differently and have greater sexual freedom than their female counterparts in some Muslim or other countries. When new and/or nonbiblical sexual mores are introduced to traditional cultures, new justifications and possibilities for sexual immorality are introduced.

2. *Internal Pressure.* The environment makes it easier to yield to sexual temptation, but an equally potent source of trouble rests inside the individual's mind. Jesus indicated this clearly during one of his talks with the pious Pharisees. Evil thoughts, adultery, and other forms of defilement and sexual immorality come

from an evil heart, he said.[38] Additional internal "heart" pressures might include the following.

(a) Curiosity. With the present emphasis on sex, it is easy for anyone, married or single, to conclude "I must be missing something good that I'd like to try." Bored or dissatisfied with one's current sexual behavior (or lack of behavior), there is a temptation to try something new and different. This increases the likelihood that a person might take advantage of sexual opportunities when they become available—especially if there is little likelihood that one will be caught.

(b) Uncontrolled Fantasy. Many people (one report says about 95 percent of males and 50 percent of females) engage in sexual fantasies.[39] This mental activity is sexually arousing and often occurs before and during intercourse to enrich the sexual experience. Some people fantasize to reduce anxiety about sex, to mentally explore taboo acts they would not consider trying in real life, or to add sensual stimulation to a life that has little sexual excitement otherwise. In some people fantasies are aroused by viewing erotic movies or reading pornographic materials, but others can be equally aroused by their own imaginations. Since nobody else can see what we fantasize or even know if or when we have sexual fantasies, this mental sexuality often continues unchecked in the mind. When fantasy is frequent and lustful, it is more likely that overt sexual acts will occur if and when the opportunity presents itself.

(c) The Search for Identity and Self-Esteem. Many people feel inferior, insignificant, insecure, and lacking in any real life purpose. On a partially unconscious level, some view sex apart from marriage as a way to be accepted or loved (even for a few minutes), to prove oneself, to feel needed, and to bolster self-esteem. Middle-aged and older people, fearing a loss of virility and attractiveness, may have an affair in an attempt to convince themselves that they still are desirable sexually. Masturbation, accompanied by fantasies of sexual exploits, can give a passing feeling of self-acceptance and sexual capability, without the risks of real intimacy with another person. Regrettably, the transitory nature of sexual behaviors like these often leaves the participants feeling more rejected and self-condemned than before. As a result, some run from relationship to relationship in a never satisfying attempt to fill the emptiness and find a more stable self-identity.

(d) The Search for Intimacy and Closeness. As we have seen, sexuality involves more than genital contact. It involves deep communication, acceptance, and sincere love. When people feel lonely, unwanted, unloved, and emotionally deprived, they often seek intimacy, tenderness, excitement, and fulfillment in sexual relationships apart from marriage.

(e) Escape or Rebellion. Sexual behavior, including masturbation, sometimes can be a way to relieve tension, escape boredom, and temporarily avoid the pressures of life. At other times, sexual behavior is an indication of rebellion against parental or church authority, a declaration of independence from one's past, or an expression of anger and defiance against one's mate or some other person, including God.

(f) Distorted Thinking. It is easier to document the prevalence of sexual deviation than to uncover its causes. People may involve themselves in perverse sexual activities because of distorted views about sex, negative sexual experiences in the past, failure to anticipate the consequences of one's actions, an unconscious desire to be caught and punished, excessive daring and risk-taking, or a desire to punish one's spouse or former sex partner. Unhealthy thinking about sex usually is detected as the counselor listens carefully to a counselee's views about sex.

(g) Satanic Influence. The Bible makes it clear that Christians are in a spiritual battle against "all the strategies and tricks of the Devil . . . against the evil rulers and authorities of the unseen world, against those mighty powers of darkness who rule the world, and against wicked spirits in the heavenly realms."[40] Satan is alert to this battle and very wise. He is a "great enemy" who disguises himself as an angel of light and prowls around like a roaring lion, looking for some victim to devour.[41] Since many people appear to be vulnerable in the area of sexual temptation, it is here that the attack often comes, and it is here that many fall. In a desire to be sexually liberated and free of "hang-ups," many people allow themselves to enter potentially disastrous, compromising situations. Even Christians fail, at times, to rely on the protective power of the Holy Spirit. Satan is successful because believers try to fight the battle alone, failing to appreciate the truth of 1 John 4:4: "the Spirit who lives in you is greater than the spirit who lives in the world." It is the Holy Spirit within believers who alone can give us power to resist satanic influences.

The Effects of Sex Apart from Marriage

It is not possible to understand or adequately describe the effects of sex apart from marriage. Much of this sexual activity is sin, and according to the Bible, all sin that is not forgiven will be punished in a time of future judgment. But the effects of sin often come much sooner. For a while there is pleasure, but the harmful influences of nonmarital sex eventually become apparent to many people.

It would be inaccurate to imply, however, that sex outside of marriage always (or even frequently) leads to immediate guilt and remorse. Many people report little or no guilt following nonmarital sex, especially if the participants feel a genuine affection for each other. And as sex apart from marriage continues, initial qualms and insecurities often disappear.

But a lack of remorse does not make such sexual activity morally right. Sometimes, people develop an attitude that is "hardened" to biblical teaching and unable to sense inner promptings from the Holy Spirit.[42] In time, these people, some of whom may be highly respected and educated members of the church and society, deliberately choose to believe things that are not true, so God lets them "go ahead and do whatever shameful things their hearts desired," degrading each other's bodies. Even worse, they encourage others to engage in these indulgent sexual practices as well.[43]

The Christian counselor cannot ignore these biblical statements. The contemporary world, having rejected biblical standards, largely is insensitive to the ultimate dangers and harms of the debauchery which surrounds us and which we take for granted. Like the proverbial frog in the water pot whose temperature rises slowly as the surrounding water approaches the boiling point, many people are blithely unaware of the consequences of their attitudes or behaviors until it is too late to jump.

Sex apart from marriage has the potential to cause harm in several areas.

1. *Emotional Effects.* It is true that many people engage in sexual acts apart from marriage and feel no immediate remorse or ill effects. Even so, emotional turmoil,

guilt, jealousy, fear, anxiety, insecurity, self-condemnation, anger, and depression are among the common reactions that may follow sexual behavior apart from marriage.

2. *Interpersonal Effects.* How does nonmarital sex (including masturbation and heavy petting) influence one's dating, family, marriage, and other relationships? To some extent, the answer may depend on one's gender, educational level, attitudes, and ethnic group. The so-called double standard that tolerates sexual looseness in men, but not in women, seems to be disappearing, but it still is strong in some countries and in some levels and segments of society. Probably, it is true that premarital and extramarital sex do not have an adverse influence on all marriages, but there are many examples of people whose marriages have disintegrated, careers and ministries have been wrecked, families have broken up, and personal relationships have been destroyed because of the affairs of one or both partners or other nonmarital sexual actions.

3. *Spiritual Effects.* As we have seen, fornication, adultery, lust, and other forms of nonmarital sex are condemned in Scripture and described as sin. The Christian is obligated to forsake sin and follow the teachings of Christ. Attempting to maintain a Christian witness while engaging in sinful sexual practices is a contradiction. If the sexual immorality continues, one's spiritual vitality and influence are certain to decline. Sin must be confessed and forsaken if one is to expect spiritual growth and avoid spiritual stagnation.

4. *Physical Effects.* It is well known that sex apart from marriage increases the prospects of illegitimate pregnancies and sexually transmitted diseases, including HIV infections—all of which are increasing, especially AIDS. There also is evidence that sexual intercourse within marriage is influenced by nonmarital sex. Some popular viewpoints maintain that the influence usually is good, others say the effects are neutral, many say the influence is harmful—and each view has research evidence to support its claim. The Christian counselor accepts the biblical teaching about the ultimate harmfulness of nonmarital sex. This harmfulness is most apparent when guilt, mistrust, emotional involvements in other relationships, comparisons with other partners, anger, anxiety, or insecurity is brought to the marriage bed. In these circumstances, or when at least one partner finds major sexual fulfillment apart from marriage, it is difficult for a married couple to attain maximum physical satisfaction and sexual fulfillment.

As sexual standards continue to change, debate is likely to continue about the effects of sex apart from marriage. It is difficult for any researcher, writer, or counselor to maintain complete neutrality in evaluating this sensitive and important issue of nonmarital sex. The Christian counselor should recognize that our ultimate authority is not scientific data, cultural mores, or the opinions of some respected leader or communicator. The Christian's ultimate authority is the Bible, God's Word. The Scriptures affirm what our own experiences show us: the real world of sexuality is far different from the glitzy photos of sensual magazines or Internet pornography. Unrestrained sexuality includes tragedy, loss, aloneness, regret, and disease, along with the ecstasy and triumph.[44]

Counseling and Sex Apart from Marriage

Sexual problems can have a variety of causes, including a lack of accurate information, unconscious avoidance of healthy sexuality, anxiety about sex, past traumatic experiences, or interpersonal tension between partners. Understanding the cause of one's problems or reading about healthy sexuality may bring some relief, but problems often remain unsolved until attitude and behavioral changes take place. Sometimes, these only come with the help of a counselor who is willing to face difficult issues with a counselee.[45] The counseling might include any of the following.

1. *Look at Your Own Attitudes and Actions.* Someone has defined counseling as a relationship between two anxious people. Perhaps this is never more true than with sexual counseling. When counselors are embarrassed, ill at ease, and uncertain how to proceed, they tend to express shock, discomfort, or a tendency to provide pat answers that may do nothing to help anxious, searching counselees. Some clinical evidence suggests that counselors tend to be more harsh and condemning when they are guilty of the same thoughts and behavior that bring their counselees for help.

Like everyone else, the Christian counselor is open to temptation and sexual arousal, especially when counselees talk in detail about their own sexual experiences and struggles. It can be very difficult to help another person with a temptation, struggle, or behavior that the counselor may be facing in his or her own life.[46] Each of us must seek to maintain a close personal walk with God, an honest accountability relationship with some other Christian, and sexual purity in our own lives. This enables us to show an understanding and compassionate attitude that acknowledges the reality of sin, the lure of temptation, and the healing power of forgiveness. Your help is not likely to be effective if you are outraged, embarrassed, vindictive, condemning, ill-informed, or sexually aroused by your own counselee. All these feelings and attitudes can alienate the counselee when what he or she needs most is help. A nonunderstanding or threatened counselor might withdraw unconsciously from the counselee, batter his or her self-esteem, and communicate hopelessness. This can create despair and sometimes pushes the counselee back into further immorality.

When we hear about sexual involvement apart from marriage, it can be difficult to show a caring and understanding attitude, especially if we know the individuals involved. The counselor needs divine help to show love without compromising biblical standards, compassion without denying reality, and directness without becoming insensitive, critical, or vindictive. If sexual counseling is too threatening for you or too difficult, it is wise to evaluate your attitudes (perhaps with the help of another counselor) and probably avoid this kind of counseling, at least until your feelings or attitudes change.

2. *Listen with Sensitivity.* This is the basic starting point for all counseling, but it sometimes is forgotten when we hear about sexual issues. If we excessively exalt or trivialize sexuality, we convey the impression that sexual difficulties, including sexual sins, somehow are in a class by themselves and fundamentally different from other human problems. In contrast, when we listen, we show a willingness to understand another human being's distress, and we convey a desire to help with the counselee's real problem. It is appropriate to ask clarifying questions, providing that these increase understanding and do not satisfy our own curiosity. Try to avoid giving advice, preaching, expressing opinions, or even quoting Scripture, at least until you have a clear perspective on the problem.

One sex counselor suggests that you should not expect to be surprised at anything.[47] At times, for example, you may hear about sexual exploits in your counselee or in some person who is respected in the community or even in the church. Initially this may come as a shock, but instead of reacting with anger or gossip, try to determine whether this information is important for helping your counselee and whether you need to verify if the information is correct. Sometimes, you will hear allegations that are partially or totally untrue, told to you by counselees who are misinformed, deliberately spreading gossip and error, or trying to deflect attention from their own behavior. Try to explore why the counselee may be passing on the information and how it will impact your counseling.

3. *Learn What the Counselee Thinks About Sex.* As we listen, we will begin to understand the counselee's sexual values and attitudes. These greatly influence sexual behavior and often have to be changed before behavior can be altered. In addition, be alert to the counselee's knowledge about sex. Misinformation and misunderstanding frequently contribute to attitudes and sexual behavior that the counselee later regrets.

4. *Consider Counseling Goals.* My first counseling job was in a university counseling center. A few days after I began work, a female student came to my office, talked about breaking up with her boyfriend, and asked for help in "finding somebody to go to bed with." The counselee's goals were clear—and clearly in conflict with my values. When you counsel in the area of human sexuality, try to determine what the counselee wants to accomplish. If you do not establish at the beginning what the counselee expects to accomplish, counseling may falter because you have one set of goals (helping the counselee avoid immoral sexual behavior apart from marriage, for example), but the counselee may have another (such as reducing guilt over sexual behavior that he or she plans to continue). When counselor and counselee goals are different, this *must* be discussed because the Christian counselor, in conscience, cannot work to help others pursue goals that are antibiblical, and thus ultimately harmful to the counselee.

5. *Help with Practical Issues.* Counseling is most effective when it deals with specifics. Sometimes, counselees need support and practical suggestions for resisting sexual approaches, fleeing temptation, terminating sexual relationships, or informing a mate or parents about illicit sex or an illegitimate pregnancy. Depending on the situation, it also may be helpful for counselees to discuss their feelings about masturbation, premarital or extramarital intercourse, homosexuality, abortion, or related issues. Once again, it is not helpful to give advice too quickly, but neither is it helpful to maintain a consistent "nondirective" approach that gives little practical guidance and ignores the clear teachings of the Bible.

In dealing with practical issues, remember that people always respond best when the desire and motivation to change come from within. Instead of telling counselees what to do, encourage them to think of different courses of action that might work. Point out dangers or problems that they might not see, and encourage them to commit to one of the alternatives that does not violate biblical teaching. If such action fails to resolve or reduce the problem, help the counselee find another biblically appropriate alternative and keep giving guidance, support, and encouragement until the situation improves.

6. *Help Counselees Find Forgiveness.* This is at the heart of the Christian message. Because God forgives, we can have freedom from guilt, abundant life on earth, and eternal life in heaven.[48] It is inconsistent and confusing to talk about forgive

ness but never to show it. As believers, we experience God's forgiveness, but we, in turn, are expected to forgive others.[49] When Christian counselors model forgiveness, we help others forgive people who have participated in sexual acts apart from marriage, and we encourage counselees to forgive themselves, just as God and the counselor forgive.

In past decades, church members tended to be too condemning and not much inclined to forgive. Now, when the value of forgiveness is widely affirmed, even among nonbelievers and secular mental-health professionals, have we gone in the direction of forgiving so freely and with such ease that there is no spirit of repentance and no motivation to change? When Jesus talked with the woman who had been caught in the act of adultery, the theologians of his day were inclined to condemn. Jesus, in contrast, forgave the woman, but he followed this with a concise directive: "Go and sin no more."[50] Forgiveness doesn't mean much if the forgiven person has no desire to follow this with obedience and changed behavior.

7. *Give Accurate Information*. Christian counseling often is a specialized form of Christian education. At times the counselor must give accurate information or know where to find such information.[51] Many counselees also need help in learning self-control, evaluating current sexual standards, forming a personal set of values that is consistent with biblical truth, determining appropriate dating behavior, evaluating the moral issues surrounding masturbation, and understanding biblical teachings on sex. These and other sexual issues can be discussed openly, especially if counselees are encouraged to ask questions that are answered candidly and without shock or condemnation. Often, too, the counselor's behavior and general comments will model an accurate, consistent, and unashamed picture of sex as God intended.

8. *Consider the Need for Referral*. At times, every counselor faces situations in which referral to another counselor would be most helpful for the counselee. Referral is appropriate when counselees appear to have more complicated sexual problems than the counselor can handle, when sexual problems are accompanied by intense anxiety or depression, when there is strong guilt or self-condemnation, when sexual perversions are involved, when counselees need detailed sexual information that the counselor is unable to provide, when you suspect physiological disease or malfunctioning, or when the counselor feels a strong and/or persisting sexual attraction to the counselee. In situations like these, the counselor must decide whether to continue counseling, to terminate the relationship, or to make a referral. Whatever you decide, remember that referral can be threatening to many people, especially if they have shared intimate details of their lives and then discover that the counselor wants to make a referral. These people need to know that referral is common, is not rejection by the present counselor, and ultimately can be for the greatest benefit of the counselee.

Preventing Sex Apart from Marriage

Spirituality and sexuality are two fundamental forces in life that cannot be ignored. Both can bring wonder and amazement, euphoria, physical and emotional arousal, a closeness to others, and a sense of God's presence. Both can be horribly distorted and a source of misery. Both can be used to manipulate others or to bring great fulfillment in life. How can counselors help others prevent attitudes and behaviors that destroy rather than edify? The prevention of immoral, unfulfilling, and unhealthy sexual behavior can focus on three overlapping goals: providing accurate sex education, helping people decide about practical issues that deal with self-control, and helping people find realistic alternatives to uncontrolled sexuality.[52]

1. *Providing Accurate Sex Education.* Most educators and parents would agree that sex education should occur at home, and many agree that sex education can be taught in the schools. But what about the role of the church in sex education?

The church can influence sex education in two ways: *indirectly*, by encouraging and instructing parents about what to teach at home,[53] and *directly* through sermons, classes, discussion groups, and retreats. This teaching must involve giving factual information, but of equal importance is teaching biblically based principles of morality. The teaching must be honest, practical, and in good taste. To be sure it is accurate, do not hesitate to bring in resource persons, such as a physician or psychologist who can give specialized information. To ensure the relevance of the information, encourage honest questioning and try to avoid pat answers. Written questions submitted anonymously can be one way to uncover real issues. For some, there is value in recommending books that connect with younger people and provide accurate information.

Whatever one might feel about sex education in the school, church, or home, it is important to recognize that young people hear, talk, and think a lot about sex. They learn from their peers, from pornography, from magazines and the media, and from adults, including school officials who distribute contraceptives on the dubious assumption that young people are not capable of controlling their own sexual appetites. This view is challenged by many unmarried people themselves who are embracing abstinence. The church should be actively involved in helping young people say no to immoral sex.

2. *Helping People Decide About Practical Issues That deal with Self-Control.* Although premarital and extramarital sex are discussed in the Bible, other practical sexual issues are not even mentioned. Two of these are the physical activities that accompany dating and the act of masturbation.

(a) Dating and Petting. Dating, the relationship between two people of the opposite sex, provides mutual human companionship, better understanding of the opposite sex, greater self-understanding, sexual stimulation, and some sexual fulfillment. The rules and practices of dating vary from place to place, and they change frequently. Dating may involve little physical contact except for periodic touching that communicates interest, compassion, empathy, and affection. However, in many cases touch is much more sensual in nature and intended to bring sexual arousal. The term *petting* may not be used as much as it was previously, but it refers to sexual touching that does not involve intercourse. Petting may involve little more than hugging and kissing, but often it refers to conscious mutual physical stimulation and exploration designed to bring erotic arousal through the fondling of sexually excitable areas of the body. For those who see no harm in nonmarital sex, petting is no problem. If it becomes a form of foreplay that leads to sexual intercourse—as it often does—this is acceptable to the parties involved.

But what should be the attitude and behavior of couples who believe that intercourse should be confined to marriage? Can there be "responsible petting" that expresses intimacy and exists for mutual discovery and sexual gratification apart from intercourse?[54] Some Christians say no and argue for minimal physical contact, but most single Christians seem to show by their actions that their answer is yes. The church often gives no guidance in this significant area. Perhaps this is because there are no easy answers to questions about dating and petting, but several counseling and prevention conclusions can be helpful:[55]

- Sexual attractiveness and sexual feelings have been created by God and should be considered good, not sinful.
- All persons, male and female, are created in God's image, and each should be respected. To use another person to satisfy one's own sexual desires is to violate that person's personhood, making him or her an object.
- God wants his people to live holy lives. Whatever they do should be done to the glory of God.[56]
- Christians must respect God's directions for expressing sexuality. The Bible warns against the misuse of sex,[57] which includes anything that is done contrary to the revealed Word of God.
- From God's perspective, the only proper place for sexual intercourse is within the context of a mutual, lifelong commitment of a man and woman, in the form of marriage. God has our best interests in view when he commands us to wait for intercourse until we are married.
- Petting is a common activity among people who are not married to each other. Unlike foreplay, which is a tender preparation for sexual intercourse, petting is a tender exploration of one another by two people who do not intend to have intercourse.
- Petting has many risks, spiritual and psychological. One adverse effect of heavy petting is illustrated by the law of diminishing returns: with constant repetition over a period of time, the effect of a stimulus on an individual tends to decrease. To keep the original effect, the stimulation must be increased. Petting is a physical stimulation that conforms to this law. After reaching a certain point of intimacy, a couple almost always finds that retreat to less intimate involvement proves very difficult. In contrast, petting creates the desire for more intimate sexual union. In advanced stages, petting is especially difficult to stop and may result in frustration, tenseness, irritability, and decreasing self-control.
- God, through his Holy Spirit, is the source of personal, practical power to help us guide and control our sexuality. Sex need not be a drive that enslaves, but it is an appetite we can feed, sometimes illicitly. For those who seek his help, God will cleanse us on a moment-by-moment basis to keep us from wrong attitudes and actions.[58]

These are preventive principles that counselors and church leaders can communicate, sometimes in public presentations, followed by discussion.

(b) Masturbation. The stimulation of one's own genitals (usually but not necessarily to the point of orgasm) is a very common form of sexual arousal apart from marriage—especially in males. The frequency of masturbation declines following adolescence and marriage, but it does not disappear. Many married men and some married women continue to masturbate at times throughout their lives, and it does not appear that religious people or church attenders masturbate less frequently than others.[59]

There is no medical evidence to indicate that the practice is harmful to the body or that it interferes with subsequent sexual intercourse. Unlike fornication and adultery, masturbation is never mentioned in the Bible,[60] so opinions differ about whether the practice is wrong. While some condemn masturbation, others argue that it is not much of an issue with God, since he never mentioned it. There are others who suggest that it even is a gift from God that enables unmarried people to find sexual relief apart from premarital sexual intercourse. Probably, most would agree that masturbation is not wrong when, for example, a married man masturbates when his wife is ill or recovering from a pregnancy, when a couple cannot have sexual intercourse because the husband is away on a business trip, or when a couple agrees to refrain temporarily from intercourse but agrees that masturbation is acceptable as an alternative to more intimate sex. Is masturbation wrong when practiced by a single high-school, college, or seminary student whose sex drive is intense and who seeks to keep from engaging in nonmarital sexual intercourse?

It is widely agreed that masturbation most often is accompanied by lustful thoughts, which in themselves are wrong, whether or not they are accompanied by genital stimulation. Many men stimulate their minds with mental fantasies or pornographic imagery to accompany their masturbation, and these are practices that violate the biblical principle that we should focus our minds on what is good, doing all to the glory of God.[61] Since masturbation has a way of growing in frequency and intensity, it can become a compulsive habit that violates biblical principles[62] and is very difficult to forsake even within the bonds of a subsequent marriage. It is not surprising that masturbation often is accompanied by feelings of guilt, frustration, or self-condemnation. Many feel angry and discouraged because of its compulsive grip. Some may be like the members of a Christian college group who described themselves as "a group of guys in an accountability group, trying to eliminate pornography, lust, and masturbation from our lives," and wondering if there was "any special way to masturbate without sinning." There are no clear answers to this question, but there are numerous arguments against and some in favor of masturbation, many of which give little direction to those who struggle with the problem.[63]

How, then, do counselors or churches speak to what surely is the most universally practiced form of sexual behavior apart from sexual intercourse? It is difficult for Christian counselors to prevent the start, continuance, or increase of masturbation, but the following observations could be helpful if shared, perhaps in small same-sex groups.

- Masturbation is very common and of no harm physically, except in instances where it is compulsive so that genital tissues are injured.
- Masturbation is never mentioned in the Bible. This does not make it right; theological arguments from silence are weak. Nevertheless, when we consider the range of sexual behavior that is discussed in Scripture—homosexuality, bestiality, adultery, prostitution, rape, sexual abuse, incest, and others—it is difficult to conclude that masturbation is left out by accident. Masturbation does not seem to be one of God's great concerns; his Word

says more about the mistreatment of animals.[64] We must be careful not to harshly condemn something that the Bible does not condemn.

- Masturbation can be helpful in relieving sexual or other tensions, and it is a substitute for sexual intercourse apart from marriage. Many singles and married people away from their spouses masturbate as a sexual release.

- Christian counselors differ in their views of masturbation. It has been called "sin," "a gift from God," and an issue that is minor on God's list of priorities.

- Most often, masturbation is practiced in conjunction with visual stimulation (especially pornography or other images) or with mental fantasies that often involve images of other people involved in sexual acts. These forms of arousal appear to be the "lusting in one's heart" that Jesus condemned.[65] The more often this lusting is linked with genital arousal, the firmer is the bond between the two and the harder the bond is to break later, even within marriage. Breaking the link between fantasy and masturbation requires considerable self-discipline. According to one Christian counselor, "if using masturbation without viewing pornography or fantasizing can provide a release of sexual tension and help you avoid engaging in lustful thoughts, and if you can give God thanks for this means of helping yourself gain mastery" over sexual problems that you are trying to control, then limited masturbation may be acceptable.[66]

- Those who masturbate should understand the biblical perspective on sex and marriage. Masturbation clearly is a substitute activity.

- Although it causes no known physical harm, masturbation can be harmful in other ways, especially if it becomes compulsive, excessive, or a way to retreat from close contacts with others. It can increase self-centeredness, lower self-esteem, produce guilt, and both stimulate and be stimulated by sinful lust.

- Masturbation rarely is stopped solely by a determination to quit. Trying hard to quit can focus attention on the issue, sometimes increase anxiety, and even make failure more incriminating.

- Masturbation can be reduced by prayer and a sincere willingness to let the Holy Spirit be in control. Understanding the biblical perspective on sex and marriage may also help to control masturbation

- Masturbation is more likely to be controlled when there are deliberate efforts to avoid pornographic and other sexually arousing materials.

- Especially valuable is having an accountability relationship with some other Christian or group where there is prayer together and regular accountability reports about one's masturbation temptations and activity. Like many addictions, this is a problem that often is handled best by people coming together to pray and to give support and mutual accountability.

Any person who teaches (or writes) about masturbation is likely to be criticized. Since there is no clear biblical guidance on this issue, we are left with a variety of conflicting opinions, often given by sincere, compassionate counselors whose views we should understand and try to respect even if we don't agree. Surely masturbation is a sin when it is accompanied by a lusting for sexual relationships that God forbids, when it masters us, when it interferes with sexual intercourse and thereby denies sexual fulfillment to the spouse, and when it hinders one's relationship with God. People who struggle with masturbation need to know that God helps and forgives, and that open communication about masturbation helps to diffuse its destructive impact. For most people, it will be replaced, in time, by more fulfilling sexuality within marriage.[67]

3. *Helping People Find Realistic Alternatives.* Human sexuality is a topic that concerns far more than genital stimulation. It includes issues of intimacy, communication, self-control, self-concept, interpersonal relationships, and gender identity. It involves people struggling with what it means to be male or female, how one relates appropriately to the opposite sex, or how to deal with sexual feelings toward people of one's own gender. Often these become struggles that individuals face alone, too embarrassed or afraid to discuss them with a friend or counselor, unaware that others have similar concerns. Like all topics in this book, sex is best considered in the context of a caring, supportive Christian community where people can feel accepted and loved. The church should be a place where people can discuss problems and questions in private with a counselor or accountability partner, where values and sexual ethics can be formulated through counseling or group interaction, and where meaningful activities can be provided, especially for young people and adults who otherwise might find themselves bored, lonely, or tempted by sexually attractive but morally dangerous situations. Churches, youth groups, and individual counselors may not want to have discussions about sex, but significant misery and disappointment can be avoided when sexual issues are confronted honestly, compassionately, and realistically.

Conclusions About Sex Apart from Marriage

As this chapter was being written, the chief executive officer of a large American corporation was dismissed from his position because he had been having an affair with a female employee of his company. The news made headlines in the business world and pointed to a company policy that the board of directors courageously chose to follow. At times, perhaps all of us are tempted to put aside our values and engage in some action that would bring sexual pleasure outside of God's standards but which risks censure, embarrassment, and personal consequences like those the chief executive officer faced.

How do Christian counselors respond when they want to be compassionate and forgiving, but they also want to please God and abide by his standards? How do we deal with apparent conflict between social pressure and the Bible or between scientific data and Scripture?

It is helpful, first, to examine the scientific, social, and scriptural data to see if the conflict can be resolved. Perhaps most of us would agree that the wisdom of this world, if it *really* is true, cannot be in conflict with the truth that comes through written revelation. If conflict persists, many Christians, including the author of this book, would agree that the Word of God, understood as accurately as possible, must be accepted as the final authority to which other findings must be submitted. In time, as more clear information becomes available, the conflict may be resolved, but at present we live with the discrepancy.

This is not a popular view, and neither is it comfortable. Nevertheless, it raises questions that must be considered whenever sex outside of marriage is discussed.

Society's values and some scientific data can be in conflict with biblical teachings, so the counselor must choose whether the Bible is the ultimate guide for our own counseling and moral behavior. We all know that the Bible does not always address specific issues that counselors and their counselees face. In these instances, we must seek as best we can to determine the overall moral teachings of Scripture and conform to these. The inferred principles must then be our guide in all counseling, not just in our dealing with issues of sex apart from marriage.

KEY POINTS FOR BUSY COUNSELORS

➤ Sex is more than a physical instinct or biological attraction. Sexuality pervades all of life and ranges from mild feelings of pleasure about human relationships to sensual lovemaking and stimulating orgasms. Sex involves intimacy, communication, companionship, and self-identity.

➤ Sexual experiences can dull one's sense of loneliness, temporarily reduce anxiety, and give feelings of intimacy, but when sexual behavior is outside of God's guidelines, the positive feelings can be fleeting, dehumanizing, and ultimately unfulfilling.

➤ The Bible condemns fornication (which usually refers to premarital sex), adultery (sexual relations with a person other than one's spouse), and other forms of sex outside of marriage because these deviate from God's plan and commands. Within marriage sexual intercourse is good—created by God for reproduction, intimacy, and pleasure.

➤ The Bible teaches that:
  - Sex is created by God and is good.
  - Sex apart from marriage is sinful.
  - Sex apart from marriage involves sinful thinking.
  - Sex apart from marriage includes sinful talk.
  - Sex apart from marriage restricts freedom.

➤ Unhealthy sexuality comes because of the sex-saturated culture in which we live and because of Internal pressures that include:
  - Curiosity.
  - Uncontrolled fantasy.
  - The search for identity and self-esteem.
  - The search for intimacy and closeness.
  - Escape from the pressures of life.
  - Distorted thinking.
  - Satan's activities and temptations.

➤ Sex apart from marriage can influence people emotionally, spiritually, physically, or in terms of their interpersonal relationships.

➤ In counseling,
  ▪ Look first at your own sexuality, attitudes, areas of temptation, and other sexual issues.
  ▪ Listen with sensitivity.
  ▪ Try to determine what the counselee thinks about sex.
  ▪ Consider how your goals and the counselee's may be different.
  ▪ Give help with practical issues, including self-control.
  ▪ Help counselees find forgiveness and restoration.
  ▪ Give accurate information.
  ▪ Sometimes, consider the need for referral.

➤ To prevent unhealthy and unbiblical sex apart from marriage,
  ▪ Provide accurate sex education.
  ▪ Help people with practical issues that deal with self-control. The two most common issues are sexual intercourse apart from marriage and masturbation.
  ▪ Help people find realistic alternatives to harmful sex apart from marriage.

➤ When the Bible is in conflict with social values or scientific data, the biblical teaching always takes precedence in setting standards and moral behavior.

20

Sex Within Marriage*

Roberto and Joanne had been married for twelve years when they came to the counselor. They were devoted parents to their three children, ages nine, seven, and three; committed Christians; active church members; both successful in their careers; but increasingly isolated from each other at home. Joanne had made the appointment, and at the last minute Roberto decided to come, but he was not enthusiastic about seeing a counselor and complained from the beginning.

The counselor had heard similar stories from other couples. In the early days of their marriage, they were infatuated with each other, both showing their love in affectionate ways, freely giving to one another, and participating in frequent, passionate lovemaking. Roberto felt appreciated by his wife and pleased that he could perform as a sex partner. Joanne felt her husband's care and affection and concluded that her efforts to please Roberto sexually stimulated greater sexual ecstasy in their lovemaking.

This changed after their first child was born. Joanne found that the demands of motherhood and her work away from home left her feeling tired most of the time. When she finally dropped into bed at the end of her busy days, she was more interested in sleep than in sex. Roberto felt replaced by the baby that they had created together, and the young father no longer felt important or wanted. Instead of responding with enthusiasm to Roberto's sexual overtures, Joanne complained about his insensitivity, selfishness, and lack of appreciation for all the work she was doing.

Perhaps it was not surprising that the couple began to drift apart. Roberto started spending more time with his friends and his work. Whenever he was home, he complained about Joanne's busyness or housekeeping, and often their evenings ended with arguments, unlike earlier in the marriage, when the evenings would have concluded with enthusiastic sex. One night, Joanne woke up and found her husband masturbating while he watched a sexually explicit video. She flew into a rage, but he defended himself by shouting that self-stimulation was his way to keep from getting involved sexually with one of the women at work who was more attentive to him than his own wife was.

Next day, when their emotions had calmed, Joanne announced that she was going to see a counselor to ask if there was any hope for the marriage. At first Roberto refused to go with her, but he changed his mind when he began to think of his wife talking about their sexual secrets before some "dispassionate shrink."

If you were the counselor, how would you have helped Roberto and Joanne?[1] Perhaps there still are people who believe that sex and sex problems are topics for physicians to discuss with patients, but not issues for Christian counselors, especially pastors, to consider with their counselees. This viewpoint isn't held by

* I am very grateful to Christopher McCluskey for reading and giving a helpful critique of this chapter.

many who are actively involved in counseling. Issues of sex often arise in counseling, and they cannot be ignored, especially when they are an integral part of marriage conflicts, as was the case with Roberto and Joanne. God created sex when he made the world and created human beings. Sex was part of his plan, something beautiful to be enjoyed by the human race, but something that has been marred and disfigured by the Fall. Helping people deal with sexual problems is an important and significant responsibility for any Christian counselor.

Sometimes, the sex problems come first and produce marital discord. More often, it seems, marital conflict or a drifting apart comes first. This generates so much anger, disappointment, resentment, fear, or tension that mutually satisfying sex no longer occurs. Regardless of which comes first, sex problems or marriage problems, it is clear that sex and marriage are so closely interwoven that problems in one area invariably influence the other. This chapter will focus primarily on sex; marital problems will be discussed in chapter 29.

The Bible and Sex Within Marriage

Some of the early church fathers viewed genital sexuality as only acceptable within marriage and only for procreation. Erotic passion was to be spurned at all costs, and abstinence even within marriage was assumed to be the superior mode of life. Happily, from the perspective of Christians today, these attitudes began to change over the centuries, and by the time of the Reformation, both Catholics and Protestants were more positive about sexuality. Luther was especially frank in his writing about this topic.[2] Certainly, the Bible never treated sex as a taboo subject. Almost every biblical book says something about sex, and some of the descriptions, especially in Song of Solomon, are explicit and even sexually arousing. From these biblical passages we can make a number of conclusions about sexuality, including the following.

1. *God Created Us as Sexual Creatures and Declared That Sex Is Good.* When he created human beings, he made us male and female and declared that his creation was good. He instructed the first husband and wife to "be fruitful and increase in number"—instructions that clearly involved nakedness and sexual intercourse.[3] This was not considered shameful or, at best, was tolerated by God. Sex, in contrast, is evidence of God's goodness, something for which we can express praise and gratitude.

2. *Genital Sexuality Has Three Purposes: Procreation, Union, and Pleasure.* The first birth in the Bible is described as a result of sexual intercourse plus "the help of the Lord."[4] Obviously, sex is involved in the conception of children and in the divine command to multiply. It also appears to be a fundamental way by which a husband and wife become united as "one flesh." Theologians have debated whether intercourse immediately unites a couple into one flesh and whether a couple can have a one-flesh relationship without sexual intercourse. Perhaps most would agree, however, that genital sex in marriage is a basic and important way for a couple to express commitment to the one-flesh relationship.[5]

Is sex also intended for pleasure? Undoubtedly, the clearest answer comes from the Song of Solomon. In vivid poetic language, this little book describes the pleasures of physical sex between married lovers. The descriptions are explicit but never offensive.[6] The same is true of Proverbs. "Rejoice in the wife of your youth. . . . Let her breasts satisfy you always. May you always be captivated by her love."[7]

In the New Testament, we read that a husband and wife are depriving one another of sexual intimacy when they refuse to give physical pleasure and satisfaction to each other. The only exception to this is when a married couple agrees to abstain from sex temporarily and for the purpose of retreating spiritually for a special time of prayer [8]

3. *Sexual Intercourse Is for Marriage.* In our society, promiscuity is common, and some see sex as little more than flesh rubbing against flesh for the purpose of achieving erotic experiences. This is not true for everybody, of course, but for many people warmth, concern, love, trust, and especially commitment are all relegated to a position that is of secondary importance to the sensations that come from foreplay and orgasm. This chapter draws on research of writers who study sex between unmarried partners, but the emphasis here is on sex between *marriage* partners who have committed themselves to each other in a marriage relationship. When the Bible speaks approvingly about sex, it refers to intercourse between married couples. Quoting Genesis, Jesus spoke with favor about the permanence and "one flesh" nature of marriage. Paul noted that marriage (not intercourse outside of marriage) is the desirable answer for a person who is struggling with sexual self-control. When marriage occurs, the husband and wife are to give their bodies freely to each other and not to hold back sexually.[9]

4. *Sexual Immorality Is Condemned Strongly.* King David was doing nothing original when he had sex with Bathsheba while her husband was away and then tried to hide what they had done. Psalms 32 and 51 are among several that describe the anguish that followed, including the grief that came when the child of this union died. When God commanded us to abstain from sexual immorality, this was not because the Creator wanted to take away our fun. It was because he wants to protect us from the misery that comes when we give in to lustful passions and accept the self-centered sexual values of people who neither know nor respect God's Word.[10] The Bible portrays adultery as something that is attractive but ultimately foolish and destructive.[11]

In contrast, the biblical view of sex within marriage is affirmed enthusiastically. Couples are free to engage in sex as often as they want and can use a variety of sexual techniques. This does not give couples freedom to use methods that in any way would not be honoring to God. Using constraints, sadistic methods, practices that make one person feel uncomfortable, or drugs or alcohol to enhance feelings, for example, is outside the realm of sexuality as God intended it to be. When the gift of sex is misused or abused, it ceases to be excellent. Instead, it leads to problems, difficulties, and regrets that arise later, if not immediately.

The Causes of Sexual Problems Within Marriage

Most people probably approach marriage with enthusiasm and look forward to the sexual freedom that will follow. Many of these people are disappointed when they discover, sometimes on the honeymoon, that sex within marriage is not as consistently exciting or pleasurable as they had eagerly anticipated. There can be a variety of causes for this disappointment.

1. *Misinformation About Sex.* Despite the modern openness about sex and widespread beliefs that we are highly informed about the subject, counselors often are amazed at the ignorance and lack of accurate knowledge that characterize many

couples. Sex researcher William Masters wrote that "the greatest cause of sexual problems is misinformation, misconception, and taboo."[12] In most other areas we are taught knowledge systematically, but sex education is left to be gathered randomly from a variety of sources, including adolescent joking, television programs, sexually explicit movies, and other media (magazines or novels), and sometimes from the often controversial sex education courses in schools. Is it surprising that so many people are left with confusion, misinformation, unrealistic expectations, inhibitions about asking questions, distorted fantasies, the effects of various erotic experiments, and a failure to realize that males and females are sexually aroused in different ways? Sexual instincts and urges are inborn, but a knowledge of love-making must be learned. When the learning is inadequate or accompanied by painful and other abusive experiences, subsequent sexual adjustment problems often arise.

2. *Cultural Values and Attitudes.* The society in which one grows up and in which one lives often molds sexual attitudes and behavior. In past decades, sex was not discussed openly, media depictions of sex were limited, and marital fidelity was the expected norm. Some people considered sex to be dirty, a taboo subject that polite society never mentioned, something that interested men but was of little concern to women, who were assumed (at least by men) to be passive and lacking in sexual interest or arousal. When immoral sexual behaviors became known, there was community outrage and shame, although some of the loudest critics may secretly have wished that they could experiment in similar ways. Overall, the cultural attitudes and high moral standards probably contributed to the relatively low frequency of intercourse apart from marriage, but they also must have created misunderstanding and sexual frustration, even in married couples.

Then things began to change. Sex became a subject that could be discussed more openly. Old taboos began to break down, sexual intercourse outside of marriage became more accepted, and the media—especially television, movies, and popular magazines—began the long, continuing, and subtle process of challenging traditional views of marital fidelity and sexual responsibility. Perhaps the openness reached its peak in the sexual revolution that followed publication of Alfred Kinsey's 1948 book *Sexual Behavior in the Human Male*. It was not until the 1980s that many of Kinsey's research methods and conclusions were found to be deeply flawed, but his profound influence already had made a major impact. This influence continued in the twenty-first century with the production of a widely viewed film about Kinsey's life and morals.[13] Openness about sex and the growing availability of sexually explicit visual images, including pornography, have combined to create a greater public awareness about the joys of sex. This, in turn, has elevated our expectations about sexual enjoyment, made us less tolerant of sexual problems in own lives and marriages, given greater cultural sanction to extramarital sex, and led to a belief that sexual awareness, fulfillment, and ecstatic genital experiences are the signs of healthy adult maleness and femaleness.

Cultural expectations like these can generate anxiety and feelings of insecurity in people whose sexual experiences are different. It would be naive to assume that there is guilt, misery, or regret in all who engage in sex apart from marriage. Many live according to the cultural standards and experience no apparent ill effects. However, there are many others, including young people, whose sexual urges are especially intense and difficult to control, who yield to temptation but who are afraid of getting caught, pressured to experience orgasm as quickly as possible, and plagued by guilt shortly thereafter. Sexual fulfillment is diminished when intercourse is hurried, primarily self-centered, or lacking in relaxed tenderness. People in such situations feel cheated and disappointed. Often there are shame, self-criticism, and the loneliness that many thought sex would take away.

Early experiences like these can have adverse effects on marriage later. When initial expectations have not been met in marriage, or when marital faithfulness has not been maintained, sexually experienced people may feel less willing to work at solving sexual problems and more inclined to seek satisfaction elsewhere in a society that sanctions promiscuity. Later, sexual problems, such as premature ejaculation or impotency, can be related as much to ingrained psychological and social attitudes as to physiological malfunctioning. Changes in cultural values, the explosion of often distorted sexual information in the media, changing sexual expectations, earlier unfulfilling sexual experiences, and previously learned attitudes all can contribute to sexual problems within marriage.

3. *Pornography.* Alex is a counselor who started viewing pornography when he was working to help a sexually addicted counselee. At first Alex justified his late-night viewing as a way to understand the world of his client, but the more often he watched, the more he came to enjoy the experience. Like many other men, Alex was experiencing the feeling of potency and the temporary relief from stress that came when he masturbated while watching pornographic pictures. The experience was pleasurable, quick, and free of the need to expend relational energy in satisfying his wife. Needless to add, this man's pornographic experiences were interfering with the sexual intimacy of his marriage.[14] Although the influence of pornography and the prevalence of addiction are most common in men, the problem exists as well in women.[15] Pornography contributes to sexual problems in marriage both in men and women.

4. *Busy Lifestyles and Stress.* Think about the sexual frustrations in the marriage of Roberto and Joanne. What led to their problems? The coming of a baby had added stress to their already busy lives, and the frequency of their lovemaking faded as the pressures of life and the need for sleep became more prominent. When work, the demands of parenting, church activities, and other pressures combine to create anxiety, or push us into time-starved lifestyles,[16] interest in sexual intercourse declines—in part because of physical reasons. In men, for example, prolonged stress sharply decreases the level of testosterone, the primary male hormone. Distracted by the problems and pressures of life and lacking both energy and sexual drive, many men would rather sleep or watch the late show than make love to their wives. In both husbands and wives, when busyness and stress levels go up, interest and involvement in sexual activity tend to go down.

Mutually pleasurable sexual intercourse takes physical and mental energy. It also takes a relaxed, unhurried attitude that is not greatly concerned about time. When a young couple is first married, often they can sleep late on weekends because they have no children to demand their attention, to interrupt their lovemaking, or to interfere with sexual spontaneity. These couples often have a great deal of vigor and natural energy. As they grow older, the husband and wife may have an undiminished desire for sex, but, as we have seen, they also have less energy, more responsibilities and demands on their time, increased mental or physical fatigue, and a need for more sleep. Growing children demand attention, and their presence often forces couples to reduce the frequency and spontaneity of sexual intercourse. When they are able to get alone in bed, the attitude is to "hurry so we can get some sleep," or to "keep very quiet so the kids won't wake up." It requires almost no sophistication for us to realize that common concerns like this can interfere with relaxed sexuality and can create sexual tensions within the marriage.

5. *Boredom.* After a couple has been married for a while, they get accustomed to each other. They run out of novel ways to have sex, foreplay becomes shorter, and coitus becomes routine. After several years, the sexual activities that once were so exciting have become monotonous. Partners spend little time stimulating each other sexually, and sometimes the husband and wife become less interested in their appearance. Sex under such circumstances is not very fulfilling, to say the least, and the stage has been set for an extramarital experience with someone who appears to be more exciting, attractive, and novel than one's mate.

Some couples cope with their boredom by fantasy, including the viewing of pornography. During the act of intercourse, one or both may fantasize about previous, desired, or exotic sexual involvements. As we have seen in an earlier chapter, fantasies are common and not necessarily wrong. Sometimes, they add variety to sex and increase its pleasure. But they also can be guilt-inducing and harmful for Christians who are seeking to avoid lustful thinking. In addition, fantasies can hinder intimacy if one can reach orgasm only by thinking of some person other than one's spouse.

6. *Physical Causes.* Sometimes physical restrictions like surgery, endocrine disturbances, obesity, diabetes, or injuries prevent sexual behavior. At other times health concerns may cause people to be afraid of intercourse. In one research study, for example, it was found that 80 percent of heart attack patients were afraid to resume sexual activity after their illness, and 42 percent of the men had difficulties attaining and maintaining an erection.[17] When physiological influences prevent intercourse or create sexual problems, psychological tensions often come as well, and a vicious circle develops: the physiological problem creates psychological tension that, in turn, hinders physical functioning. In some cases physiological malfunctioning (real or imagined) is used as an excuse for abstaining or for one's sexual difficulties.

Perhaps the most common physical hindrance to sexual fulfillment is the use of drugs, including alcohol. Since alcohol relaxes people, minimizes anxiety, and makes them less inhibited, some couples drink before intercourse. In quantity, however, alcohol dulls sensations. It is one of the principal causes of impotence in males. The impotence then creates anxiety and a fear that one is sexually inadequate. These anxieties hinder further attempts at intercourse, especially if the man has a few more drinks to relax before trying again.

7. *Psychological Blocks.* Sexual intercourse should be a relaxed expression of love and intimacy, but this can be blocked if psychological barriers interfere. Many of these have been implied in the previous paragraphs: sex is hindered by unrealistic expectations, stress, pressured lifestyles, fear of discovery, or anxiety lest intercourse aggravate existing physical conditions. Other potential blocks include the following:

- Conflict between the husband and wife. Relaxed expressions of love and intimacy cannot coexist with bitterness, perpetual conflict, and continuing anger. It is not true that sex is the best way to deal with misunderstanding, disagreements, anger, jealousy, or a distrust of one's mate.

- Personal problems and insecurities in the husband. Domineering men, males who feel guilty about compulsive masturbation or other sexual behavior apart from marriage, men who have a driven need to perform well in bed, and those who lack tenderness, patience, or kindness can all have sexual problems in their marriages.

- Personal problems in the wife. These might include fears about pain during intercourse, the idea that sex is dirty, guilt about past sexual behavior, fear of pregnancy, dissatisfaction with the husband, or feelings of inferiority, insecurity, or embarrassment. Some women have grown tired of sex or disinterested and agree to intercourse only to please their sometimes insensitive husbands, hoping that the experience will be over quickly.

- Doubts about one's masculinity or femininity. What does it mean to be masculine or feminine? There is confusion over this issue, both in the church, where there are different viewpoints, and in the society, where traditional male and female roles are breaking down. In bed, however, the roles are clear. It is the male penis that enters the female vagina. If a couple, especially the male, cannot perform in bed, this is a great threat to his self-esteem and feelings of sexual adequacy. Even when male impotency has clear physical reasons, the inability to get an erection is, for many, a psychological trauma. For women, a common sexual problem is the inability to have an orgasm, even when there is a strong desire to do so. This can be a threat to one's self-concept as a woman. Hysterectomies also can be difficult for women because they know they no longer can bear children. For some this leads to the feeling that a part of their femininity is gone. When problems in the genital area raise doubts about one's maleness or femaleness, this hinders further sexual functioning. More doubts often follow, and another vicious cycle begins.

- Sexual fears. These are of various types and include the fear of pregnancy that we already have mentioned, fear that sex will be painful, fear of not being able to perform adequately, fear of being compared with previous sexual partners, fear that one's sexual advances will be rejected, fear that the penis is too small or too large, fear of losing self-control, or fear of intimacy. Each of these can be sexually inhibiting, since fear and love (including sexual love) tend to be mutually exclusive. When you have one—fear or love—you don't have much of the other.[18]

- Differences in sexual preferences. Sometimes there are differences in the frequency with which a husband and wife want intercourse (one may want it more frequently than the other), differences in the preferred time for intercourse, and differences in opinion concerning what is appropriate for a couple (one may want oral-genital contact, for example, but the other person does not; one likes to try a variety of positions or locations for sex, but the other does not). These differences may seem minor, but they can create serious blocks to sexual satisfaction.

- Guilt. This is one of the most common psychological blocks. Guilt over past sexual behavior, present extramarital activities, homosexual tendencies, masturbation, or recurring fantasies can create sexual problems in marriage. When a person gets sexual satisfaction apart from marriage, sex with one's spouse is likely to be less satisfying.

- Marital power conflicts. Sex can be a powerful weapon in marriage. Withholding sex or demanding it can be ways by which some couples assert their authority, get revenge, or obtain favors or decisions from a partner. Sometimes, this is discussed openly. More often, withholding of sex is a passive way to react. "I'm too tired for sex" or "I don't feel well" may at times be ways of saying, "I'm going to get even with you by withholding sex."

- Sexual dysfunctions. The most common of these are summarized in Table 20–1. All are conditions that prevent couples from performing sexually. Each of these dysfunctions has a physical basis, but there also may be psychological causes. Most often, these are treated by physicians or counselors with specialized training in sex therapy.[19] For the nonspecialist, it can be helpful to recognize these disorders and reassure counselees that they are not rarities and that they can be treated successfully.

- Miscellaneous causes. Other blocks to sexual fulfillment may include persisting depression, a lack of privacy, the belief that sex in some way undermines spirituality, or distractions that come from worry about one's career or family finances. A poor self-concept can also undermine sexual intimacy. In describing her reluctance to have intercourse, one women wrote, "I'm so flat chested that I feel sexless." Others gave equally revealing reasons for avoiding sex: "I'm so fat, I can't enjoy myself," "I can't stand his breath," "He seems so selfish in his love-making that I feel used," "My wife ridicules my ability to make love. . . . I am somewhat clumsy," "I just can't forgive him for the affair he had." Clearly, sexual problems can have a variety of causes and can have a profound influence on both individuals and marriages.

Psychological blocks to sex often lead to vicious cycles similar to those mentioned earlier in the chapter. The psychological blocks to sexual fulfillment usually come first. Because of these fears and attitudes, sex is not satisfying. The realization that intercourse is not satisfying then intensifies the fears and creates even stronger psychological blocks. This makes sexual fulfillment even more unlikely. In time, it becomes difficult to distinguish the causes from the effects.

The Effects of Sexual Problems Within Marriage

When sexual problems appear, some couples simply "give up" and don't try to resolve their difficulties. They may fear discussing the frustrations or believe that things will never get better. Others develop headaches, abdominal pain, fatigue, emotional distress, or other symptoms that hide the sexual problem and can provide an excuse for abstinence. When there is no sex, this can be very difficult for a spouse who wants sexual fulfillment.

In addition to the avoidance of intercourse, sexual difficulties in marriage can have several other major effects:

1. *Lowered Self-Esteem.* Self-esteem and sexual capability often go together, especially in men. If intercourse is not mutually satisfying, the husband and wife both may have doubts about their sexual competence—doubts that sometimes

are made worse by the joking of one's mate. If a man cannot maintain an erection or arouse his wife, for example, he is likely to experience a loss of confidence about his sexual and manly capabilities. If his wife jokes about the fact that he may be losing his virility, this strikes an even greater blow to his self-esteem, and his ability to perform sexually is hindered further.

2. *Selection of Substitute Activities.* When sex within marriage is not satisfying, husbands and wives often turn to substitute activities. These include masturbation, viewing pornography, sexually explicit novels, increased fantasies that become a second-best substitute for the real thing, or extramarital sex. Affairs are

---

Table 20–1

Common Sexual Dysfunctions

Orgasmic Dysfunction
Sometimes known as frigidity, this is a condition in which the female is unable or unwilling to experience full sexual pleasure, including orgasm.

Vaginismus
This is an involuntary contracting of the muscles surrounding the vagina so that the entrance closes tightly when penetration is attempted.

Erectile Dysfunction
Also known as impotence, this is the inability of a male to achieve or to maintain an erection.

Premature Ejaculation
This involves the ejaculation of semen, with a resulting loss of erection, immediately before, just at, or shortly after insertion of the penis into the vagina.

Delayed Ejaculation
The opposite of premature ejaculation, this occurs when the penis remains erect, but ejaculation does not occur.

Dyspareunia
This is intercourse that is painful.

Inhibited Sexual Desire
This is a disorder in which the appetite for sexual intercourse is inhibited. It occurs in both men and women and appears as though the sex desire is totally blocked.

Unconsummated Marriages
This involves the inability of a couple to have intercourse, even though they come together sexually, know what to do, have been trying, but they have been unable to get the penis into the vagina.

Sexual Aversion Disorders
Here a person has a persistent avoidance of all sexual contact, including an aversion to genital contact with one's mate.

more likely when there are sexual problems within marriage, but instead of the hoped-for fulfillment, affairs can lead to guilt, concerns about secrecy, and further marital, sexual, and personal frustration.

3. *Deteriorating Relationships.* Sexual problems can create anger, resentment, interpersonal tension, impatience, and communication breakdowns. It would be overly simplistic to conclude that sexual problems lead to divorce, but it is accurate to conclude that sexual tensions, coupled with other marital pressures, contribute to marriage breakups. It is difficult to have a really good marriage when there are sexual dissatisfactions and incompatibilities.

4. *Increased Motivation.* Some couples (fewer than we might wish) face their sexual problems with a new determination to make sex better. Open to suggestions, determined not to blame each other, and willing to work on the problems, these couples invariably see improvement both in their sexual relationships and in their marriages. These are the people with whom counselors most like to work.

Counseling and Sexual Problems Within Marriage

It is not easy for people to talk about the intimate details of their sexual lives. Many don't know what terms to use to describe their behavior or the sexual parts of their bodies. They may experience discomfort in reporting unacceptable behavior, exposing secrets, sharing problems, describing past sexual experiences, including sexual abuse, or talking about their sexual fantasies. Imagine how these discomforts are accentuated if the counselor feels uncomfortable as well. Even though the Bible talks openly about sex, counselors can be anxious and embarrassed talking about sex with counselees. Some Christian counselors feel that sexual counseling is spiritually inappropriate, especially for a pastor, because it violates the counselee's privacy or might stimulate the counselor's own sexuality in an unhealthy way.

To hide this insecurity, some counselors try to ignore the subject and avoid any talk about sex. Others use tactics, sometimes unconsciously, that steer the discussion away from sexual issues. A comment like, "I suspect you don't have any sexual problems, do you?" is likely to get a no answer, freeing the counselor to move to more comfortable topics. Other counselors talk of sex in aloof intellectual or theological terms that keep the conversation emotionally detached and vague. These are counselors who have the strange ability to turn conversations about sex into something obtuse and dull. Some counselors announce that sexual problems are all psychological and quickly move to some supposed "real problem" that permits everyone to avoid talking about the sexual symptoms. Some ask a lot of specific questions that may even titillate the counselor but give no help to the counselees. Then there are counselors who enjoy the opportunity to talk to people about their sexuality, apparently deriving personal stimulation and sexual enjoyment when they have the freedom to probe into the sex lives of their counselees.

If you are among those who are willing to counsel people in the area of sex, try to keep aware of the subtle sexual implications that sometimes occur in this type of counseling. When issues of sex are discussed openly and in detail, both the counselor and the counselee can be aroused erotically. At times this is complicated by sexual curiosity on the part of the counselor, seductive behavior in the counselee, or feelings of sexual attraction that sometimes are mutual. The counselor constantly must be alert to these issues. In no case will the counseling be effective if there is erotic involvement with a counselee. Acting on one's sexual impulses in counseling is both bad morals and bad therapy.

Before you continue, please skim back over the previous two paragraphs. Do you see yourself in any of these descriptions? Some of what you read are avoidance tactics that allow counselors to steer clear of uncomfortable topics that may need to be considered. The previous paragraph cites some of the danger signals that are warnings for you to be careful. The counselor must maintain an interpersonal distance from counselees who are seductive or sexually arousing. If you continue to feel attraction for a counselee, it can be wise and helpful to discuss this with another counselor. Never discuss this with a counselee, especially if the counselee appears to be seductive. It always is better to process your feelings with a supervisor or other experienced counselor. Ask yourself if the counselee's behavior can tell you anything about the ways in which he or she relates to his or her spouse or to others apart from marriage.

To really help counselees with their problems, you need to refrain from using avoidance tactics and must take special care to avoid being trapped by the dangers. If you prefer not to talk about sexual issues or know that you should not be talking about them, it is quite acceptable (and probably wise) to refer counselees to another counselor. If, instead, you choose to continue counseling, the following guidelines can be helpful.

1. *Listen with Acceptance and Understanding.* Imagine where your counseling would go if you showed shock and condemnation when your counselees first started talking about their sexual experiences. Your counselees would back off and, fearing more rejection, might not even have the courage to raise the problems with which they are struggling. From the beginning, therefore, it is important that counselors show warmth and an understanding, uncritical attitude. This frees people to talk about their sexual problems and failures, even if they feel embarrassed, ashamed, guilty, and anxious. Gently encourage the individual or couple to talk openly, compliment them for doing so, and, if you think this would help, tell them that it is common to have difficulty in talking about sexual issues. Counselees are more likely to discuss their problems openly when they see that the counselor is relaxed, accepting, not awkward or embarrassed, and wanting to understand and help.

As you discuss sexual issues, remember that one reason for the awkwardness and embarrassment may be the counselee's difficulty in finding words to describe his or her genitals and sexual activities. Your counselee may prefer pet terms or even slang that is not easy to express to a counselor, especially to one who is a Christian.[20] As a counselor, you should be accepting of such language but in general try to use correct terminology (for example, penis, vagina, intercourse, masturbation), making sure that the counselee knows what you are talking about. Recognize that there will be times when you may have to use terms that are more familiar to the counselee. For example, technically it is correct to ask, "Do you have problems with premature ejaculation?" but it may be clearer to ask, "Do you come on too fast?"

2. *Gather Information.* Whatever the problem, it is easier to help when you understand the nature of what concerns the counselee. The following are some of the questions that you may want to have answered as you seek to uncover the causes and think of possible approaches to resolving the problem. Sometimes,

counselees are helped solely by discussing these issues as a response to your questioning.

- What are the sexual problems the couple is having? Encourage them to be specific and honest with as much detail as they think is important to give. Sometimes, you may have to ask for more information, but be sure this is for the benefit of the couple and not to satisfy your own curiosity.
- What do they expect from their sexual relationship? In what ways have they been disappointed?
- How do they feel about issues such as oral-genital sex, mutual masturbation, frequency of sex, or using a variety of sexual positions and locations?
- Who usually initiates sexual activities and how is this done?
- How does the couple communicate about sex? Is some of the communication nonverbal?
- Where and how did they first learn about sex? Ponder first if this is a helpful question.
- What do they think might be causing their present sexual problems? Encourage each of them to give an answer.
- Are there other issues in their lives that might be hindering their sexuality? Are there things like teenagers who interfere with privacy because they are up when the parents want to have sex, physical illnesses that prevent sex, or conflicting work schedules?
- Apart from sex, how does the couple get along with each other?

Before counseling the couple, review the cases of sexual problems that are listed earlier in this chapter. Keep these in mind as you explore issues that might be creating problems for your counselees. If possible, counsel with both the husband and wife together, even though this may not always be possible. Watch to see if the couple answers in the same way. Does one partner condemn, dominate, or put down the other? Periodic private interviews with each may add additional information.

As you gather information, you might form hunches about the causes of the problems. Further questioning in these suspected problem areas can provide additional information and help to confirm or disprove your guesses. At an appropriate time later, you can share your hypotheses with the counselees.

The DEC-R (pronounced "deck-are") model for counseling people with sexual concerns is a four-step process designed especially for people who have little education or experience in dealing with sexual issues, and who can easily be intimidated when clients need to deal with sexual aspects of life and relationships. Designed by Dr. Douglas Roseneau, one of the Christian pioneers in helping people deal with human sexuality, the model involves:

- **Dialogue,** wherein the counselor encourages people to talk about their sexual issues and asks questions like "What is the problem as you see it?" "How long has the problem been present?" "Describe a typical sexual experience for you," "What health issues may complicate this sexual problem?" and "What is your sexual past?"
- **Education,** in which the counselor answers questions, tries to change sexual attitudes, disputes stereotypes, and builds needed skills.

- **Coaching,** [21] which involves guiding people to a resolution of their problems. This may include giving people self-help exercises and other assignments to help them build skills.
- **Referral,** which is helping people get professional treatment that the counselor is not qualified to give.

The DEC-R model is a summary of the counseling principles discussed in this section of the book.[22]

3. *Recommend a Physical Examination.* Many, perhaps most, sexual problems arise from psychological causes, but you should not overlook the possibility of physiological malfunctioning. For this reason, urge couples with sexual problems to get a physical examination. If physical problems are found, the counselor can work with the physician in helping the counselees.

4. *Give Accurate Information.* Information does not always solve sexual problems, but many times counselees have misinformation and myths about sex that the counselor can correct. The giving of information might include the following:

- Answering questions with facts. This rests on the sometimes debatable assumption that counselees know what to ask or how to answer the questions. If you do not have the answers, promise to find them and pass on the requested information in the next counseling session.
- Explaining details of physiology and effective techniques of foreplay or intercourse. This information can be very helpful, providing you do not give too much at one time so that the counselees forget what they learned. Often you can supplement this information with printed materials.
- Instructing couples in sexual exercises that can be done at home. Premature ejaculation, for example, can be treated with a very high degree of success when couples are taught and encouraged to practice "the squeeze technique," in which the woman manipulates the male penis in a way that permits control of ejaculations. A description of these techniques is beyond the scope of this book, but detailed information is available to counselors.[23]
- Describing details of the cycle of sexual arousal in males and females. Many individuals do not realize that men and women get aroused in different ways and that men are aroused and can reach orgasm more quickly than women.
- Disputing common myths and stereotypes about sex that a couple might have. These myths could include the ideas that sex will solve other marital problems, that if you wait until marriage you automatically will have a great sex life, or that great sex comes naturally if you are in love.
- Recommending tapes or giving couples helpful books or articles to read at home and discuss later.[24]
- Providing information about the biblical teaching on sex and sexual fulfillment. This information can be practical and of special value to Christians.

Whenever you give information, allow time for counselees to ask questions, to get clarification, and to discuss practical ways in which the information can be used to improve sexual functioning.

5. *Deal with Specific Problems.* Often the counselor must go beyond providing factual information and help counselees deal with specific problems. The origins

of these problems should be uncovered, if possible, and strategies should be worked out so counselees can take practical steps to resolve the problems with the counselor's guidance and encouragement. At times, counselees will have to face previous sexual sins and learn to experience the liberation of knowing that sins are forgiven when we confess to our loving Savior. There may need to be discussions of practical steps that must be taken to ensure that a recurrence of the sins can be prevented. When marital conflict is apparent, counselors must be careful not to take sides, but to apply the principles discussed in chapter 29 on marriage counseling. When couples deal with their marriage problems, sexual relations often improve.

None of this should hide the fact that for many counselees the sexual problems are more specific and often more serious. Consider, for example, the disorders listed in table 20–1, or problems of sexual addiction, the impact of sexual abuse, including rape and other trauma, the sexual struggles of people with disabilities, sexually transmitted diseases, the one woman in three who apparently has difficulty in feeling sexual arousal, problems with self-control, the person who struggles with a homosexual orientation, or the fear that some people have about showing their bodies, even to their spouses.[25] It is best that counselors who have specialized training as sex counselors handle these types of issues. If you do not have training in this area, listen carefully to your counselees, make whatever suggestions you can, and then try to find a qualified physician or sex therapist to whom you can make a referral.[26]

6. *Stimulate Forgiveness.* Sometimes sexual problems occur or persist because one (or both) of the spouses engages in some kind of behavior that hurts the other. Perhaps the most obvious example is the involvement of one of the spouses in an extramarital affair. When people have been hurt, they can hold grudges or withhold sex, sometimes as a way to get even or as an expression of the emotional pain they are suffering. Sex is not likely to be satisfying if the offending spouse shows no sign of remorse or the other spouse shows no inclination to forgive. We know that God can and does forgive, but this knowledge is not very helpful if the counselee does not know about the healing power of God's forgiveness or if he or she refuses to forgive or to accept forgiveness.

One effective approach for working with unforgiving or unforgiven couples is to arrange a forgiveness session that may last for several hours. Before the session each person should describe his or her emotional hindrances to forgiveness—why it is difficult to forgive or to offer forgiveness. Then the couple meets with the counselor and begins by describing the offensive behavior—what it was, how it began, what happened. At some point the counselor will share the biblical perspectives on forgiveness and remind the victim that forgiveness means that the resentment and need for retribution is gone, even though the pain is likely to persist. Eventually, the perpetrator asks the spouse for forgiveness, the spouse accepts the apology if he or she is willing, and the couple creates a ceremony—like buying rings, burying a significant object, or renewing marriage vows—to signify their new relationship. Later the counselor can follow up to ensure that resentment and criticism do not creep back into the relationship.[27]

7. *Be Alert to the Need for Referral.* Sexual counseling and the treatment of sexual dysfunction are parts of a highly skilled specialty for which some professionals have unique training. A referral is recommended when counselees do not respond to your counseling, when there continue to be sexual problems and dis-

satisfactions, when medical issues are involved, when the counselees' problems are beyond your area of expertise, when a counselee is consistently seductive, or when it appears that prolonged sexual therapy is necessary. Help your counselees see that referral is no more than recognition of the need for more specialized treatment.

In making referrals, be very cautious about encouraging a couple to see a secular sex counselor. Many of these specialists can be helpful, but they have values that are inconsistent with Christian principles; many promote behaviors that feel good but that may not be honoring to God. The following paragraph discusses this further.

Preventing Sexual Problems Within Marriage

Wherever you live, attitudes toward sex are changing. Intercourse apart from marriage no longer is considered immoral by many (probably most) people in the society; instead, it is common to follow the premise that we are entitled to the full satisfaction of our appetites and that we are helpless before the lusts of the flesh. From this follows the assumption that it is impossible, foolish, and wrong to expect us to resist temptation and to abstain sexually. Surrounded by people with this attitude, sometimes in our own churches, how can we teach people to view sex as a monogamous relationship that is both fulfilling and consistent with biblical morality, providing it is confined to the marriage relationship?

1. *Sex Education.* Since misinformation is at the basis of many sexual problems, it would appear that giving accurate information can do much to prevent sexual difficulties. This information can be in five areas: (1) what the Bible teaches about sex; (2) basic facts about male and female anatomy and physiological reactions; (3) information about techniques of intercourse; (4) skills for maintaining abstinence and avoiding vulnerable situations; and (5) teaching healthy sexual attitudes.

Ideally, parents should give this information to their children in the home, presented naturally and in stages, long before marriage is ever contemplated.[28] We know, however, that many people never receive any sex education at home. Sometimes, the schools do a competent job in educating young people, depending on the moral values of the curriculum or teachers. In the church, presentations from the pulpit can help instill healthy and biblical perspectives on human sexuality. In addition, the church can encourage and instruct parents in giving sex education, as well as provide this information directly to young people through youth meetings, retreats, and small group discussions. To prevent misunderstanding and criticism, church-based sex education is done best when there is prior parental approval and support.

2. *Moral Guidance.* Sex education often focuses on physiology and facts about sexuality, but this is not enough. Many people struggle with choices about what is right and wrong, and too often they find little help in the church. How do people make decisions about birth control, artificial insemination, in vitro fertilization, or decisions concerning sexually oriented films and plays? And what is okay for a married couple to do sexually in terms of lovemaking techniques?[29] It is easy for theological discussions of these issues to be ignored or to remain in classrooms and scholarly books but never get down to helping people in their bedrooms. Ethics, including sexual ethics, need to be made practical and discussed in churches before rather than after immoral behavior occurs.

3. *Premarital Counseling.* There is no doubt that couples who are looking forward to marriage also are thinking about their sexual relationship. When sexual issues are discussed as part of premarital counseling, there can be clearer understanding of physiology or lovemaking techniques, more realistic expectations about sex in marriage, and less likelihood of sexual problems, especially at the beginning of marriage. When a good counseling relationship has been established before the wedding, couples are more inclined to return for help if problems arise after the marriage begins. This is especially true if premarital counselors encourage postmarital checkups. When sexual problems or frustrations are discussed early, before they become complicated, then serious difficulties are less likely to develop.[30]

4. *Improving Communication.* If people cannot communicate in general, it is not likely that they will be able to communicate about sex. Teaching people, especially couples, to communicate is one way to prevent sexual problems. Encourage husbands and wives to share their feelings and attitudes about sex. Males do not know automatically how to stimulate a female, and neither do all females know how to arouse a man sexually. The husband and wife can tell each other what is stimulating as well as what each person prefers to avoid. This communication should be honest, gentle, and nonverbal as well as verbal. Taking the hand of one's mate and showing him or her how to stimulate can be an excellent communication technique. When a couple is encouraged to communicate like this, many subsequent sexual problems will be prevented.

How does a counselor encourage such communication without eavesdropping on the intimate details of a couple's sexual life? Many years ago a pastor in my neighborhood used to encourage couples to undress and stimulate each other in his office while the counselor coached them from behind a curtain. This unorthodox method soon became known to other counselors, most of whom considered the pastor's approach to be unethical and more inclined to feed the counselor's own sexual fantasies than to help the couples. The counselor's job is to guide couples in how they can communicate better about sex and then urge them to practice their learning after the counseling session and when they are alone.

5. *Encouraging Effort and Cleanliness.* Good sex, like good marriage, requires time, effort, and a willingness to work at making things better. If sex is to be satisfying and if serious sexual problems are to be prevented, a couple always must be alert to ways in which they can build a better relationship. This may involve reading about sex and trying new positions. It also involves an attitude that says, "I will try to keep myself as attractive as possible, as clean, and at least as concerned about my mate as I was when we were first married."

Married people who get lax about personal hygiene, weight control, and physical appearance find that sex is less satisfying as they grow older. A young woman who once enjoyed sex with her clean-shaven, freshly bathed husband is not going to enjoy sex more if her middle-aged husband is sloppy in appearance, not inclined to shower before sex, and unwilling to shave on weekends. Cleanliness and a determination to improve sex are both preventive measures.

6. *Marriage Seminars and Enrichment Programs.* Over the years, a host of marriage enrichment programs have been developed for the purpose of improving marriage (including sex within marriage) and preventing marital and sexual problems. Before recommending any of these to a couple, try to discover the moral and theological perspectives of the program designers and speakers. Get

information from the seminar advertisements or from previous participants to help you determine if the event is worth the time and money to attend. Busy people can get tired of weekend seminars and workshops if their format never changes, if they are boring or irrelevant, or if the participants are expected to sit passively and listen while speakers talk and the musicians perform. These can be entertaining events that arouse enthusiasm, but try to determine if they make lasting changes in marriages.[31] Sometimes, they do make changes but frequently they do not. At times counselors and church leaders prefer to design their own programs. These can be very helpful, but they too need to be evaluated regarding their ultimate impact.

Conclusions About Sex Within Marriage

Sexual fulfillment, God's plan for married people, also teaches about intimacy and closeness to him. There is a parallel between letting go sexually, as in orgasmic release, and in accepting one's complete dependence upon God.[32] Genital union is an experience of euphoria, ecstasy, and intense union that can be a foretaste of heaven. There is a spiritual component of the sexual experience when couples are able to bring their sexuality before God and ask for an awareness of his presence as they come together.

Helping people deal with sexual problems in marriage need not be a distraction from spirituality. The help can come without advocating self-centered, narcissistic, hedonistic pleasure. Instead, sexual counseling involves helping a husband and wife relate more effectively to each other, experience the marital closeness that God intended, and be free of sexual hang-ups so they can reach out more effectively to love God and serve others.

KEY POINTS FOR BUSY COUNSELORS

➤ Sometimes, the sex problems come first and produce marital discord. More often, it seems, marital conflict or a drifting apart comes first, and this generates so much anger, disappointment, resentment, fear, or tension that mutually satisfying sex no longer occurs.

➤ The Bible teaches that:
  ▪ God created us as sexual creatures and declared that sex is good.
  ▪ Genital sexuality has three purposes: procreation, union, and pleasure.
  ▪ Sexual intercourse is intended for marriage.
  ▪ Sexual immorality is condemned.

➤ Common causes of sexual problems within marriage include:
  ▪ Misinformation about sex.
  ▪ Harmful cultural values and attitudes.

- The impact of pornography.
- Busy lifestyles and stress.
- Boredom.
- Illness and other physical causes.
- Psychological blocks.

➤ Psychological blocks to sexual intimacy include:
- Conflict between the husband and wife.
- Personal problems and insecurities in the husband.
- Personal problems in the wife.
- Doubts about one's masculinity or femininity.
- Sexual fears.
- Differences in sexual preferences.
- Guilt.
- Marital power conflicts.
- Sexual dysfunction.

➤ Sexual difficulties in marriage can lead to
- Lowered self-esteem.
- Involvement with alternative sexual activities, including masturbation, pornography, fantasy novels, or extramarital affairs.
- Deteriorating relationships between the husband and wife.
- A renewed determination in some couples to make sex better.

➤ In counseling couples who have sexual problems within marriage, the counselor should keep aware of his or her own sexuality and the temptation to be aroused by the sexual talk and activities of our counselees.

➤ To counsel individuals or couples having sex problems within marriage
- Listen with acceptance and understanding.
- Gather accurate information.
- Consider recommending a physical examination in some cases.
- Give accurate information and sex education.
- Deal with specific sexual problems.
- Encourage couples to forgive and to accept forgiveness.
- Consider making referrals to qualified sex therapists.

➤ The prevention of sexual problems within marriage comes through:
- Sex education that sometimes comes long before marriage.
- Moral guidance.
- Discussions about sex as part of premarital counseling.
- Improving communication in the marriage.
- Urging couples toward increased cleanliness and efforts to keep working to improve their relationship.
- Encouraging attendance at sexual or marriage enrichment seminars.

➤ There is a spiritual component to the sexual experience when couples are able to bring their sexuality before God and ask for an awareness of his presence as they come together.

21

Homosexuality*

How does it feel to be homosexual and struggling? Several years ago one of my students volunteered to give me an answer. Times have changed, and I have lost contact with the man who wrote the following, but the experiences he described still apply to many people today:

"I never decided to be more attracted to men than to women. If I did have the chance to choose, I certainly would not have chosen to be the kind of person all other kids considered to be a freak. I felt totally helpless when my sexual urges were toward boys and not girls. I had fantasies about men all the time. . . . I masturbated almost every day, sometimes more than once a day. Every time I thought about other boys rather then girls. When I tried to think of girls while masturbating, it didn't work.

"I dealt with this discovery alone. I never told anyone about my 'sexual identity.' I was so afraid of rejection. I remember rejection in seventh grade when all the other kids called me 'fag' or 'queer.' No one even knew about me at that time. I couldn't bear to think how they would react if they really did know. All through high school and most of college I kept my secret—and my pain—to myself.

"When I got to college, I fell in love with another guy. He was not homosexual, and I had to keep my secret from him. We were roommates for three years, and he never knew about me until just before graduation. What was hard for me in this situation, aside from the terrible hurt that he could not love me back, was the realization that it was more than my sex drive that was gay. I felt like I was perverted to the depths of my being.

"I had been a Christian since I was seven years old and had asked God to take away my homosexuality many times. He never did. It became hard to reconcile the fact that Scripture says homosexuality is wrong with my strong sexual and emotional attraction to men. It was at this time that I began to experiment a bit with the gay scene in the city. I went to gay bookstores and made phone calls to the gay hot line. There was so much promise of gratification and fulfillment in these places. I began to lead a double life. I was leading Bible studies back on campus and very much involved in campus ministry, but every once in a while, I would go downtown to the bookstore. I always felt guilty and dirty when I left, but that did not stop me from going the next time. The promise of fulfillment was so strong!

"I finally told someone about my struggles. She was very understanding and did not reject me. After some time I was even able to tell my roommate. This did not stop me from going to bookstores right away, but it was the first step in the healing process. I couldn't handle this alone any longer.

"Since then, God has put some wonderful people in my life who have helped me to have the courage not to fall into temptation. Some of these friends also struggle with homosexual temptation, but we are trusting in Christ's victory over sin to give us power over the sin of homosexuality. It took some people who were compassionate and caring to hear my struggles and help me understand them. I do not know when or if my temptation to engage in homosexual acts will go away, but I am no longer burdened by the belief that I am hopeless and that there is no power over these temptations. My identity is in Christ not in my temptations."

* I am deeply grateful to Dr. Mark Yarhouse for his helpful and detailed insights in the preparation of this chapter.

W hen the second edition of this book was published, a number of reviews appeared, many of which were positive and complimentary. The major criticisms tended to revolve around the chapter on homosexuality. Many of the reviewers had strong opinions about homosexuality, and they tended to evaluate what I had written based on how closely my writing aligned with their beliefs. I am not surprised at this. It is probable that most of us respond in similar ways when we feel strongly about some issue. With the possible exception of abortion, homosexuality may be the most controversial issue to be discussed in this book. Some will like what appears in the next few pages, some will not, and some may disagree strongly. In the chapter I will seek to show respect for different viewpoints, maintain a gracious spirit, evaluate the conflicting research as well as I can, give guidelines for compassionate and sensitive counseling, and be true to the biblical teaching about homosexuality as I understand it. And when the book is published, I anticipate learning again from readers as I have in the past.

Broadly defined, homosexuality is an erotic attraction to persons of one's own sex. Although homosexuality includes sexual thoughts, feelings, fantasies, and overt sexual acts with same-sex partners, the term usually is not applied to preadolescents, to individuals (usually young people) whose curiosity leads to brief experimental erotic involvement with a person of the same sex, or to people in prisons or other isolated same-sex environments who temporarily engage in homosexual behavior because opposite-sex partners are not available.

It is important to recognize that there are great differences among those who feel a sexual attraction to others of the same gender. Psychological researcher Mark Yarhouse suggests that there is a three-tier approach to understanding and counseling.[1] The first tier includes all those who have a *same-sex attraction*. This is the largest and most inclusive group. It includes people who keep their same-sex attraction hidden as well as those who are openly gay in their sexual behavior and self-identity. Many people who have same-sex attractions move away from these as they grow older and clearer about their sexual identity and lasting preferences. The second tier is smaller, involving people whose same-sex attraction persists over time. These are people with a *homosexual orientation*. They know that they are most attracted to people of the same sex and feel that they would be most fulfilled sexually with same-sex experiences, but many people with a homosexual orientation never let others know of this consistent same-sex preference and never engage in any homosexual act with another human being. These are people whose lives show that a homosexual orientation does not necessarily demand that there be a homosexual behavioral response.[2]

The third tier, *gay identity*, refers to people who are open in saying that "I am gay." This self-identification tends to emerge in early adulthood when, more often than within the other two tiers, people are likely to refer to themselves as gay or lesbian and engage in homosexual acts. A homosexual *act* is any behavior that involves engaging, at least occasionally, in sexually stimulating actions with another person of the same sex.

At all these levels or tiers, there are both males (usually called gays) and females (called lesbians). They are of all ages, come from all occupations and socioeconomic levels, possess a variety of interests, and may or may not be active church members. Like those whose sexual attraction is primarily or exclusively toward the opposite gender, people with a same-sex attraction may or may not be successful in their careers and esteemed members of their professions. Although some may "cruise" in and out of gay bars looking for sexual partners (despite the increasing impact of AIDS), many more are respected and often married members of the community who are not always thinking about sex any more than heterosexuals think only about sex. Despite some common beliefs to the contrary, there are no typical homosexual mannerisms or personality types. Some are open about their sexual preferences; others keep their sexuality well hidden. While many are lonely and insecure, it cannot be assumed that people at any of the tier levels are mentally disturbed, socially incompetent, more lonely than heterosexuals, or perpetually "unhappy gays."[3] In fact, we cannot even assume that humans can be divided into two groups—homosexual and heterosexual. The Kinsey researchers suggested a scale with seven points in which zero represents a person who is exclusively heterosexual, three is midpoint, and six represents a person with exclusively homosexual tendencies and actions. Subsequent researchers, including those who are critical of Kinsey's methods or conclusions, nevertheless have agreed with the Kinsey team that few people are at the zero or six positions on the scale.

Over the years, homosexuality appears to have been viewed in different ways. Although it was prevalent among Greek, Roman, and other earlier cultures, much of this may have been homosexual activity associated with religious rituals, initiation rites, or sex between soldiers or others who were in same-sex environments but who did not necessarily have lifelong sexual attraction to others of the same gender. In later centuries, homosexuality often was viewed as something sinful, abnormal, perverted, and illegal. It was ignored by most heterosexuals (including church members), treated by psychiatrists who viewed it as a sexual deviation or diagnosable disorder,[4] and kept under cover—in the closet—by people who wanted to keep their homosexual tendencies from becoming known.

There may be debate about when things began to change, but certainly the writings of sex researcher Alfred Kinsey over sixty years ago did much to bring homosexuality to greater public awareness. A few years later a government-sponsored report on homosexuality rocked Britain, and before long homosexuality had become a topic of government and media debate on both sides of the Atlantic. *Gay* and *lesbian** began to be used as activist terms (in the 1950s and 1970s, respectively) to express affirmation and to replace more negative terms.[5] It became widely accepted that there were scientific data to show that 10 percent of the world's population was homosexual.[6] In 1993 one scientific article even boosted this figure and stated that lesbians and gay men compose "10 to 15 percent of the general population,"[7] but not even the Kinsey researchers gave that high a figure.

In their 1948 book, Kinsey and his colleagues estimated that 4 percent of the American population was homosexual and that 37 percent of the male population had participated in at least one homosexual act. They added that about 10 percent of white males "more or less" were exclusively homosexual during at least a three-year period between the ages of 16 and 55.[8] Later researchers criticized the Kinsey research for its use of biased samples. For example, they built some of their conclusions on interviews with sex offenders who had been impris-

---

* Throughout this chapter the words *gay* and *lesbian* are used to refer to males and females, respectively. The term *homosexual*, and sometimes the word *gay* are used to refer to persons of both sexes.

oned for crimes of rape and sodomy. A large number of men were found to be exclusively homosexual, but these men had been imprisoned in an environment where no women were present. In spite of this research bias, however, the 10 percent figure has persisted, even though more credible studies suggest that the percentage is much lower. Probably, about 2 to 3 percent of the population could be considered homosexual, although some research suggests that an even smaller percentage of males consider themselves to be exclusively homosexual.[9] These numbers have remained constant, suggesting that the emergence of the gay rights movement and the passage of gay rights laws have not enticed more people into homosexuality.[10]

As homosexuality became more visible, large numbers of homosexual persons who previously were silent about their sexual orientation came forward to declare their same-sex preferences, to form powerful gay organizations, and to demand a stop to government, cultural, religious, and media discrimination. The American Psychiatric Association voted to drop homosexuality from its manual of mental disorders, concluding that homosexuality is a disorder only when it is subjectively disturbing to an individual. The psychological organizations followed and so did politicians, who became partners in advocating gay rights, inclined to condemn people who might disagree.

Homosexuality was thrust into even greater public awareness with the outbreak of the AIDS epidemic. Discussions about homosexuality soon invaded every part of society: the military, politics, government, the courts, schools, sports, science, professional societies, the entertainment world, business, industry, media, and the church. Heated debate over the ordination of homosexuals continues in several denominations, gay churches have been established, gay marriage is staunchly debated even as it inches toward greater public acceptability and legal status, and an influential organization of evangelical homosexuals continues to grow as it has since 1974.[11]

Perhaps there still are some Christians who try to ignore homosexuality. More common are those who make ill-informed and insensitive comments about people who experience same-sex attraction. At the other end of the spectrum are those who want to make Christian homosexuality a legitimate, God-created lifelong sexual orientation and way of life. Regardless of their perspectives on homosexuality, it appears that many Christians now are willing to show love as Jesus would, without demanding that gay and lesbian people "must change their sexual orientation in order to become eligible for our love"[12] in the church. In the midst of all this debate, however, many believers are not sure what they think.

This uncertainty is easy to understand. Homosexuality is not easily defined, its causes are still debated, there are many myths about the characteristics of homosexual people, and there is controversy about whether one's sexual orientation can change. All of this is complicated by widespread fear within the society and often within the church. Many people seem afraid of the growing political influence of gays and lesbians. Rarely mentioned is the fear in many people, including some of the critics, that same-sex desires or attractions might be found within themselves. These fears even have a name, *homophobia*, the fear of homosexuals or homosexuality.

Theologian Richard J. Foster has noted that the issue of homosexuality has wounded many people. "Those who are clearly homosexual in their orientation often feel misunderstood, stereotyped, abused, and rejected," he wrote. "Those who believe that homosexuality is a clear affront to biblical norms feel betrayed by denominations that want to legislate homosexuality into church life." In addition are those who "agonize over their own sexual identity, those who feel torn by conflicting sexual urges and wonder if perhaps they are latent homosexuals. Perhaps this group suffers the most. They are cast into a sea of ambiguity because the church has given an uncertain sound. On their right, they hear shrill denunciations of homosexuality, and though they appreciate the concern for biblical fidelity, they have been offended by the brash, uninformed, pharisaical tone of the pronouncements. From their left, they hear enthusiastic acceptance of homosexuality, and though they appreciate the compassionate concern for the oppressed, they are astonished at the way the Bible is maneuvered to fit a more accommodating posture." Foster adds that all who are "caught in the cultural and ecclesiastical chaos over homosexuality need our compassion and understanding."[13]

If we are to support individuals who experience same-sex attraction, we first must rid ourselves of the harmful stereotypes and misconceptions that so often are imposed on a group of people who, usually through no choice of their own, find themselves attracted to others of the same sex.

The Bible and Homosexuality

In an attempt to clarify the biblical teachings about homosexuality, numerous biblical scholars and other Christian writers have written books and articles that sometimes reach conflicting conclusions.[14] Could it be that many authors, biblical experts, researchers, political activists, professional counselors, and others start with an opinion about homosexuality and then do research or interpret Scripture in ways that support their positions?[15] Often, this is an unconscious bias, but it can be true even for people who try to be open minded. It is not surprising, then, that some have used Scripture to support sweeping condemnation of homosexuals or of the gay rights movement, while others use the same Scripture verses to explain away the sinful implications of homosexuality and conclude that it is a condition that comes from God.[16]

Most theologians would agree that God's intention for healthy human sexuality is heterosexuality. This can be argued from the design of male and female genitals and from the creation account where Adam and Eve were commanded to come together for procreation. The Bible says little about homosexuality and probably nothing about the long-term homosexual orientation and same-sex commitments that have become common today. The term is mentioned only seven times, and in each case the reference is relatively brief.[17] In these passages, homosexuality is never approved or condoned, but neither is it singled out as being worse than other sins.

In contrast, actions that are promiscuous, violent, harmful to others, or against the laws of God are sinful and strongly condemned. Some of the biblical criticisms of homosexuality appear to be of this type. There are writers who suggest, for example, that in Romans 1:26–27, Paul is describing pagan, same-sex religious rites that were perverse and that sometimes involved frenzied public castrations or homosexual activities. That might explain Paul's strong condemnation of this kind of behavior, but there is no mention of idolatrous homosexuality in the text. In general, this passage condemns people who worship something other than

God. When they turn away from God or don't care about his guidelines for living, people participate in all kinds of sinful situations, including idolatrous or selfish homosexual actions.

What about people who do care about God? What about a same-sex couple that makes a loving commitment to each other and determines to live together in a long-term relationship? Since committed gay relationships apparently were not seen in Bible times and were never addressed by biblical writers, can we conclude that these partnerships are divinely approved or that they are wrong? It is weak to argue that something is approved or disapproved by God just because it is not mentioned or not condemned in Scripture. Internet pornography is never mentioned in the Bible either, but this does not make it right. However, in every Bible passage that mentions homosexuality, it is mentioned negatively. It seems likely, therefore, that erotic homosexual acts are wrong regardless of whether or not the participants are committed to one another.

Whether or not this is true, how do we evaluate homosexual thoughts and feelings? What can be said to persons who have sexual fantasies and impulses that are primarily homosexual but are kept hidden and never lead to overt homosexual acts? What can be concluded about people, including Christians, who appear to live normal lives, who are faithfully committed to heterosexual marriages, but who are bothered by persisting same-sex attractions that might sometime "slip out" and become apparent to others?

To have same-sex attractions, feelings, and desires is nowhere condemned in Scripture, but when one dwells on such thoughts and continually engages in sexual fantasy—homosexual or heterosexual—then thoughts become lust, and lust clearly is sin. The Christian can expect to be tempted, even as Jesus was tempted,[18] but the Bible gives a message of hope. The Scriptures show that we can avoid dwelling on lustful thoughts or giving in to sinful temptations of any kind, including homosexual temptations.[19]

The Causes of Homosexuality

Despite probably thousands of scientific studies, one conclusion seems clear: *There is no clearly identified single cause of homosexuality.* The research tends to fall into two broad categories. The psychological/environmental causes focus on the role of early relationships and past experiences in causing homosexuality. The biological/genetic causes look for chemical, hormonal, or other physical influences that could indicate a built-in predisposition to be homosexual. Both viewpoints are supported by research.[20] In addition, there are those who combine the two categories into one and others who add a third broad category of spiritual causes. All of this can complicate our efforts to find the causes of same-sex attractions, identity, and erotic behavior.

For much of the twentieth century, the emphasis was on early experiences as a cause of homosexuality, but as we approached and moved into the twenty-first century, more research attention has shifted to possible neurological, genetic, and biological causes. At least three influences have led to this shift. First has been the failure of psychological theories and research to explain homosexuality completely. Second, as scientific methods have become more precise and sophisticated, there has been more interest in discovering what these new techniques may uncover. Third, and probably most important, is the influence of powerful gay and lesbian activist groups that work toward freedom from discrimination and that disagree with people who propose moral or environmental causes of homosexuality. Some of these activists are highly involved in promoting their agendas with politicians, professional counselors, and media representatives. If convincing evidence can be found for in-born, biological causes of homosexuality, then the activist agenda is supported, moral or biblical arguments against the sinfulness of homosexuality are weakened, and there would be no reason to consider homosexuality as anything other than normal. From this it would follow that changing one's in-born sexual orientation is as impossible as changing one's racial features.

Even as the research and the debates continue, almost everybody agrees that homosexuality is not something that people choose deliberately. At some time every person comes to realize that he or she is sexually attracted primarily to males or to females. If a person's primary attraction is to others of the same sex, the question of how this happened is likely to arise. In the absence of clear answers, we must be content to draw on several possibilities.

1. *Biological Theories.* One review of research on the physical causes of homosexuality concluded that biological influences "are correlated with homosexuality and may contribute to its development." But since the research data still are "incomplete, controversial, and subject to alternative interpretations . . . an understanding of any causal relationship between biological factors and sexual orientation is still primarily speculative."[21] The writers of these words are careful to avoid any sweeping statements about the biological causes of homosexuality because, at least for now, there are no conclusive research results to demonstrate that homosexual orientation has a biological cause.

There are studies that present intriguing conclusions, however. Some researchers have focused on ways in which hormones in the mother may affect sexual orientation prior to the child's birth or bring changes in brain structure that differ between homosexual and heterosexual individuals. When women are distressed during pregnancy, their hormone levels change, and some have concluded that this change can influence sexual orientation. Also relevant are the many studies that seek to find a genetic cause of homosexuality. Often, these studies compare homosexual orientation in twins. If identical twins both develop homosexual orientation, this suggests genetic causes, but as critics note, twins often have similar environments, and this may be the cause. In their book reviewing scientific research and homosexuality, psychologists Stanton L. Jones and Mark A. Yarhouse have concluded that the best recent study of genetic causation suggests that genetics may *not* be a significant explanation for the causes of homosexuality.[22]

What does this mean for the counselor and his or her counselees? There is a growing body of evidence to suggest a possible biological link to homosexuality, but at present this evidence is not strong, and the research methodology is not always exemplary. It is of interest to note that today research methods are being scrutinized as carefully as the research results. This careful observation of methodology has come about because the design of research often reflects the researcher's bias. This can increase the likelihood of biased results. All of this suggests that while researchers continue their work, counselors should recognize that there is some evidence for biological causes, but it also is important to look for psychological, environmental, and moral causes of homosexuality. Sadly, once again the evidence is not conclusive.

2. *Parent-Child Relationships.* Psychoanalytic theories have given some of the most complete and widely accepted views about the origin of homosexuality.[23] Based on Freud's view that homosexuality is produced by arrested sexual development, psychoanalytic writers have concluded that homosexual males usually are raised in families with a weak, passive, often-absent, ineffective father and/or a domineering mother. This mother subtly teaches her son to be passive and dedicated to her. He has no strong male example to follow and eventually discovers that he is less competent than his peers in relating to girls. As a result, the son loses confidence in his masculinity and dreads the thought of intimacy with women. Daughters in such families perceive their fathers as being unfriendly and rejecting, so the girls have little opportunity to relate to men. They relate better to women.

Even though it is less prominent than it was earlier, this has been a dominant theory to explain the origins of homosexuality. Critics have noted, however, that many of these conclusions have come from interviews with people who have sought counseling, especially psychoanalysis. This is not a representative group of homosexuals, most of whom do not seek counseling. Also the theory has been based largely on what adult homosexual males can remember about their childhood experiences. What they remember may not be what actually happened, and there is no way to verify what really occurred. It should be added that psychoanalytic theories often focus on male homosexuality, but the conclusions do not necessarily apply to females.

More systematic research has yielded mixed support for the psychoanalytic viewpoint.[24] One interesting study in Canada compared male Catholic seminary students who identified themselves as having a homosexual orientation with students who were heterosexual. When compared with their heterosexual classmates, the homosexual seminarians scored significantly lower on level of intimacy with their fathers.[25]

A thought-provoking, and perhaps more believable variation, of this view was suggested by a Christian writer named Elizabeth R. Moberly. Her research suggests that homosexuality does not come from relationship problems with the opposite-sex parent. It comes because of a defect in relating to the same-sex parent. In normal development, needs "for love from, dependency on, and identification with, the parent of the same sex are met through the child's attachment to the parent" of the same sex. If this relationship is lacking or disrupted, the young person unconsciously attempts to restore the attachment. The person who becomes homosexual has a need to make up for "earlier deficits in the parent-child relationship. The persisting need for love from the same sex stems from . . . the earlier unmet need for love from the parent of the same sex."[26] One way to repair this deficit, to fulfill unmet needs, and to successfully treat homosexuals is to "build a healthy nonsexual relationship with a member of the same sex."[27] According to this view, homosexuals are helped best by caring, same-sex, heterosexual counselors who help their counselees focus on same-sex relational needs.

While many homosexuals do experience disruptions in parent-child relationships, others do not. Children in the same family do not all become homosexual, even though there may be similar parent-child relationships. There can be different explanations for this. Each parent has a unique relationship with each child. Favoritism and performance-based love can intensity the lack of love that one child senses, even though another child in the same family has no doubt about being loved. The uncertain role of parent-child relationships has led some counselors to seek other early-experience explanations for homosexuality.

3. *Other Family Relationships and Experiences.* Different writers have proposed that homosexuality results when:

- Mothers distrust or fear women and teach this to their sons.
- Mothers distrust or fear men and teach this to their daughters.
- A son is surrounded by too many females (mothers, sisters, aunts), but he has limited contact with adult males, so he learns to think and act like a girl.
- Parents who wanted a daughter but got a son subtly raise the boy to think and act like a girl. A similar situation arises when parents wanted a son but got a daughter. In both cases the child has great confusion about sexual identity and orientation.
- A son is rejected or ignored by the father and hence feels inadequate as a male and unsure how males relate to females.
- A daughter is rejected by the mother and hence feels inadequate as a female—so she can't relate well to males.
- One or both parents have a negative view of sex, so the child gets a distorted view of sex and then struggles with his or her own sexual identity and adjustment.
- A mother or father is so overindulgent that the child is overly attached to the parent, unable to break away, and convinced that no mate could ever compare with the opposite-sex parent.

Perhaps a list like this could continue for several pages, but enough has been stated to show that the roots of homosexuality can be complex and often are embedded in the family setting. Sometimes, that family contributes both psychological and biological influences on sexual orientation. There is some evidence, for example, that a small percentage of gay men develop their homosexual orientation as a result of being the youngest or almost youngest child in a family with older brothers. Is this the result of some genetic influence, or have the younger brothers learned something from their older siblings that accounts for a same-sex orientation?[28]

4. *Other Early Experiences.* If you do a computer search of the causes of homosexuality, you will find a host of other explanations, many stemming from early experiences.

- Some people have had traumatic sexual experiences that have had a later impact on their sexuality.
- For various reasons, some people are afraid of the opposite sex. Lasting fears may arise from lack of frequent contact with opposite-sex persons, rejection by those of the opposite sex, or embarrassing experiences with someone of the opposite sex.
- Sometimes, a child or young adolescent has trouble relating to same-sex peers or feels inadequate and different. Perhaps a young boy is embarrassed because he is teased in the locker room about his small penis, or he lacks athletic abilities that the others possess. In some cases children feel so inadequate or uncomfortable with their sexual identity that they want to be members of the opposite sex.

None of these seems strong enough to lead people to a primary homosexual orientation. But what about people who grow up or live in same-sex environments? Do boys' and girls' schools, seminaries and monasteries, prisons, armies, and similar settings encourage or facilitate the likelihood of homosexual attractions, behavior, or relationships? Possibly. National surveys and comparisons of homosexual prevalence rates in urban, suburban, and rural settings has verified that the environment can elicit same-sex attraction and behavior.[29]

In any society, a child learns what it means to be male or female. If there is no opportunity to learn culturally accepted male or female roles, or if the society (like ours) has vaguely defined roles, then the child's behavior and attitudes can become confused. Children can reach adulthood not knowing what to expect or how to react to the opposite sex. For a few, it may be more comfortable to retreat into homosexuality, especially if these young people already have begun to sense same-sex preferences in themselves.

At this point, you are not alone if you have concluded that from scientific and clinical perspectives, we really don't know and maybe can't know why some people experience same-sex attraction while others do not.[30]

5. *Willful Choice.* Some popular books have suggested that homosexuality results from a deliberate choice. This view is common among those who conclude that homosexuality is a choice that can be abandoned by an act of will and voluntarily purged from one's life. This view of homosexuality as a willful choice is not held by experienced professionals, including Christian professional counselors, and the view is not accepted by many people who have a homosexual orientation. Sexual attraction to the members of one's own sex rarely, if ever, comes as a willful and conscious decision. As they grow toward adulthood, some people begin to realize that they are attracted primarily to people of the same sex through no deliberate choice of their own. This realization can be so disturbing that many individuals try to hide it even from themselves. Often, these people conclude that they must have been born with a genetic predisposition to homosexuality, even though, as we have seen, at present this conclusion is not supported by research.

Both homosexual and heterosexual tendencies appear to be acquired before one realizes what is taking place. These feelings of attraction are not wrong. Regardless of whether one has a same-sex or opposite-sex attraction, there is a need for love and approval, but how a person acts on these sexual attractions is not always socially or biblically appropriate.

Whenever a person experiences pleasure from sexual activities with someone of the same or opposite sex, the sexual activities become more appealing the next time. It doesn't matter how the behavior got started. More important is whether the sexual activities continue. For many young people, a passing sexual encounter, even with a same-sex person, isn't especially satisfying, so it is unlikely to be repeated. But for people whose backgrounds and tendencies make them vulnerable, one sexual experience can lead to another and a vicious cycle begins. Homosexual acts (including masturbation stimulated by homosexual fantasies) increase homosexual tendencies that, in turn, lead to more homosexual acts. Of course, a similar cycle can begin when persons with heterosexual tendencies choose to engage in sexual activities with persons of the opposite sex. According to the Bible, this heterosexual cycle isn't wrong within marriage, but outside of marriage such physical involvement is sinful.

The Effects of Homosexuality

People who promote gay rights and those who oppose gay rights can both be strong in proclaiming their contrasting and deeply held positions. Both may use sweeping statements that can be expressions of emotion more than fact. Despite widespread promiscuity in the gay community, it appears that most homosexual individuals are neither extremist nor sex crazed, and many same-sex couples are able to live together in mutually supportive relationships for a prolonged period of time. Often, these are the couples who lead the ongoing movement to make gay marriage legal.[31] Even so, none of this should hide the fact that many people with homosexual tendencies are depressed, anxious, and unhappy.[32] Their same-sex attraction can permeate or influence various areas of their lives whether they acknowledge their same sex attractions or keep them hidden.[33] Of course, sexual orientation affects all individuals in unique ways, but homosexuality influences five areas especially: one's lifestyle, emotional stability, self-concept, interpersonal relationships, and family ties.

1. *Lifestyle Effects.* Media reports sometimes give disturbing pictures of gay communities and homosexual lifestyles. Periodically, reports surface to describe schoolteachers, youth leaders, or even religious leaders who sexually molest young boys or girls and lure them into homosexual acts. Others have described gay bars where both men and women rendezvous with other homosexuals looking for mutual acceptance, friendships, and sex. Stories such as these undoubtedly describe only a minority of homosexuals, but the rumors and reports about gay and lesbian behavior have aroused fear and revulsion in the minds of many people, including church members.

Counselors should remember that there is no typical homosexual lifestyle. It is inaccurate, insensitive, and unkind to conclude that most homosexuals are bar-hoppers, activists who march in gay pride parades, child molesters, effeminate (in males—masculine in lesbians), or constantly preoccupied with sex. When we hold stereotypes like these, especially if we do not know any homosexuals, we are inclined to push away gay and lesbian people, denying them the love and acceptance that should be found in the church community. As we have seen, most people with a same-sex orientation are law-abiding, accepted members of the community. They may keep their sexual orientation hidden, but it is probable that in your church, circle of friends, place where you work, or college where you study, more people that you realize experience same-sex attractions.

These same-sex attractions can influence people and their lifestyles in different ways. Those who keep their preferences hidden sometimes live with a quiet and persisting fear that the homosexual orientation might surface inadvertently and lead to the loss of friends, rejection from fellow Christians, and subtle discrimination at work, church, school, or elsewhere. Many struggle alone, afraid to tell even a close trusted friend about their tendencies, deprived of the support and prayers of other human beings who could show understanding and Christian love. It is not difficult to understand why many people eventually give up the secrecy, come out of the closet, and let others know of their sexual orientation.

2. *Emotional Instability.* For many years, mental-health professionals viewed homosexuality as evidence of deviance or mental illness. Then, as we have seen, organizations of mental-health professionals declared that homosexuality was not

a pathological condition, a sexual variant, or evidence of mental illness. With limited support for their conclusions, apart from personal preference or the impact of political pressure, most mental-health professionals decided that gay or lesbian people did not need to be changed or treated unless they requested help in adjusting to their homosexuality.

Despite these assertions, there are studies showing that people who identify themselves as gay, lesbian, or bisexual have increased risks of major depression, generalized anxiety disorder, conduct disorder, substance abuse or dependence, suicidal thought, and suicide attempts.[34] Following a broad review of the research, one writer concluded that in all of these studies researchers found at least some evidence for more psychopathology in lesbian, gay, and bisexual individuals when they were compared with heterosexual respondents.[35] Studies have shown, too, that same-sex couples and individuals with a homosexual orientation are more likely than others to seek counseling for their psychological distress.[36]

Is this psychopathology in some way caused by the homosexuality? The vast majority of scholars would say that the symptoms of distress are not part of the sexual orientation per se. Rather, the symptoms come because there is so much stress in gay and lesbian people produced by heterosexuals who are critical, disapproving, and discriminating. Some research shows that homosexual people perceive that they are the objects of discrimination, but how do we know that this assumed discrimination actually occurs? After reviewing many of these studies, psychologist Jon Ebert concluded that "scholars have been extremely premature in their conclusion that psychological distress is developed from social stigmatization. At best, we can conclude that the individuals who are in same-sex relationships perceive and interpret their distress as being due to stigmatization from their sexual orientation."[37]

Whatever the source, it is clear that homosexual people often struggle with psychological issues that can be alleviated with help from counselors.

3. *Self-Concert Effects.* With the recent openness about homosexuality, some gays have concluded not only that "gay is good," but that to be gay is to be superior to others. More prevalent may be the inner insecurity and lower self-esteem that come to anyone who is different from the majority. Guilt over homosexual tendencies or actions, loneliness, fear that one's homosexuality might be detected, concerns about rejection, a sense of hopelessness, and anger have all been seen in homosexuals. Others struggle with issues of identity and questions about their place in society. While the activities of the gay-lesbian movement seek to bolster the self-worth and public acceptability of homosexuals, there are individuals who struggle with their same-sex attraction but who do not feel any kinship with the gay activists. Some, but not all, gay or lesbian people visit gay bars and nightclubs in an attempt to find love and support from understanding people who can bolster individual self-confidence and salve the inner pain.

4. *Relationship Effects.* How does the person with a homosexual orientation relate to other people? The answer may depend on whether the homosexuality is kept hidden or is known to others. When an individual struggles alone, there can be an attitude of constant vigilance and reluctance to get close to others, lest the hidden tendencies slip out and become obvious. Married people who keep their homosexuality hidden (at times even from their mates) may discover that their sexual preferences, fantasies, or fears of misunderstanding and rejection can put a

strain on their marriages. In contrast, those who are open about their homosexuality may succeed in building lasting supportive relationships with others of the same sex, but others never form these relationships, or find that they can be temporary and unfulfilling.

Ideally, the church should be a place where there is love and acceptance, but fear of homosexuality (homophobia) often abounds in church settings. One of my former students read an earlier draft of this chapter and wrote that he feels accepted by other people when they assume he is heterosexual, but he senses that a barrier goes up if others discover that he struggles with homosexuality. "I want to be accepted as a fellow Christian who is like others in the church, except that I struggle with homosexuality," he wrote. "Sometimes, I wonder if the only place where a person like me can really feel accepted is in heretical gay churches instead of in the true church of Jesus Christ." When gay or lesbian people struggle alone, there can be discouragement, guilt, a stifling of spiritual growth, and sometimes a highly visible decision to come out of the closet along with a flight to one of the gay churches that openly accept and even encourage homosexuality.

Then there is one's relationship with God. Many Christians fail to distinguish between homosexual behavior (including lust), which is sin, and homosexual tendencies and desires, which in themselves are not sinful. Failure to recognize this distinction can lead to perpetual self-condemnation, struggles to squelch same-sex attractions, and alienation from God, who understands, forgives sinful behavior, and enables us to live pure and Christ-honoring lives.

5. *Family Effects.* Homosexuals who have children from a previous heterosexual marriage, and those who adopt children, often find that gay parenting has unique challenges and criticisms. Within the society, there may be concern that when gay or lesbian parents raise children, (1) the children will grow up gay if raised by a homosexual parent, (2) the children might be molested sexually if raised in a gay home environment, or (3) the children will be stigmatized by their peers if the parental sexual orientation becomes known. No evidence exists to support the first two of these fears, and only minor data supports the third.[38] Children of gay parents lack the example that comes from having both a male and female parent in the home, but the same is true of children who grow up in single-parent families when the parent is heterosexual.

For many people who openly identify themselves as homosexuals, relating to children is far easier than relating to their own parents. Many parents are crushed when they learn that a child is homosexual, and fears are greater as parents consider the prevalence of AIDS among gays. Confused, guilt ridden, and fearful, parents sometimes feel shunned by their friends and uncertain how to react to their gay children and their homosexual friends or partners. Adult gay children, in turn, may feel sad and guilty because of the pain their homosexuality has inflicted on their parents. All of this can create tension in the home.[39]

Counseling and Homosexuality

The place to begin counseling is with your own attitudes. If you are afraid of gay, lesbian, or bisexual people; make jokes about them; condemn them; uncritically accept stereotypes about them; or are unfamiliar with the complexity of homosexuality and its causes, then it will be more difficult for you to understand and help individuals who experience same-sex attraction. Jesus loved sinners and those who were tempted to sin. We who seek to follow in his steps have a model for relating to people regardless of their attitudes, activities, or presumably their sexual preferences. If we sense no inner compassion for overt homosexuals or for people with homosexual tendencies, then we must ask God to give us the compassion and the sensitivity that we lack. We must examine our own attitudes toward gay and lesbian people, seek to understand the diversity of homosexuality, and avoid counseling homosexually oriented people so long as our negative attitudes persist or we are unwilling to change.

At some point, most counselors will see people who struggle with homosexual issues. These issues include struggles with one's homosexual orientation and temptations, estrangements from one's family, loneliness and inability to find or to trust others who can give support, struggles with self-esteem, anti-gay attitudes or harassment, mental-health concerns, or grappling with the issue of whether to be honest with others about one's homoerotic tendencies.[40] Counselors can feel overwhelmed by these issues, especially if there has been little prior contact with homosexual people or if the counselor harbors biases and myths. The gay movement and almost all professional publications insist that there can be no change in homosexual orientation and that attempts to bring change are unethical as well as impossible.[41] For Christian counselors, however, perhaps the major request from counselees is their desire for help in making a change.

Change is never easy for homosexuals and their counselors. The counselee drop-out rate is high, and enthusiastic reports from ex-gay ministries may be overly optimistic, built more on case histories and testimonies than on solid research. At the conclusion of their detailed review of the research on change, two highly respected Christian counselors concluded that they did not "share the optimistic and seemingly universal generalization of some conservative Christians who seem to imply that anyone with any motivation can change, if change is taken to mean complete alteration of sexual orientation to replace homosexual with heterosexual erotic orientation."[42] Part of the debate concerns what we mean by change. Earlier we mentioned the Kinsey seven-point scale, where zero represents complete heterosexuality and six indicates complete homosexuality. Perhaps there are few if any people at these two extremes. If change means movement of one or more points toward the heterosexual end of the scale, then change appears to be very possible. Stanton Jones and Mark Yarhouse, who are quoted above, add that "change of homosexual orientation may well be impossible for some by any natural means. Yet the position that homosexuality is unchangeable seems questionable in light of reports of successful change," including the findings of several respected counselor-researchers.[43]

Change from homosexual tendencies and behavior is more likely when the following are present. The more that are present, the greater may be the likelihood for change. It must be stated, however, that even if all of these conditions are met, some people may not change. We still do not know, for sure, which predictors in this area are most reliable. It seems likely however, that change may be more likely when:

- The counselee honestly faces his or her homosexuality.
- The counselee has a strong desire to change.

- There has been limited or no involvement in homosexual practices.
- The person is not deeply involved in homosexual attachment to others.
- The counselee is willing to break contact with homosexual companions who tempt the counselee into homosexual behavior.
- The counselee determines to avoid gay Internet sites, gay pornography, or other stimulants toward homosexual activity.
- Gender identity issues are not a concern (i.e., there is no inner struggle over whether the person is really a male or a female).
- There is a willingness to avoid drugs and alcohol, since these leave one more vulnerable to temptation.
- The counselee experiences acceptance and love apart from homosexual friends and contacts.
- The counselee is able to build a close nonsexual intimate relationship with the counselor or other same-sex person.
- There is an overall religious commitment and positive mental health.[44]
- The counselee has a desire to avoid sin and to commit his or her life and problems to the Lordship of Jesus Christ.

With these issues in mind, the counselor can help in the following ways.

1. *Determine What the Counselee Needs and Wants.* When someone comes for help, what does he or she want—elimination of all homosexual tendencies, help in stopping gay or lesbian behavior, sanction for continuing homosexual activity, knowledge of the biblical teaching on homosexuality, help in relating better to a same-sex lover, or something else? Some counselees really do not know what they want, and as you talk together, it becomes clear that the real problem is not what they first stated. Sometimes, the counselee has no real desire or motivation to be different but comes at the urging of a parent, youth leader, or spouse who is hoping for change. Do not assume that you know what the person wants until you ask and discuss the counselee's answers. When the counselee's goals are at odds with the counselor's values or beliefs about what counseling can accomplish, these differences must be discussed, and in some cases a referral will be the best alternative.

2. *Instill Realistic Hope.* It is not easy to counsel individuals who experience same-sex attraction. While homosexual actions can be stopped and completely forgiven by God, homosexual tendencies are much more difficult to eradicate. Sometimes, a person will not change to a heterosexual orientation, but he or she can be helped to live a victorious, meaningful life free of homosexual behavior.

A number of ministries exist to help homosexual men and women change their sexual orientation. Often, these ministries produce helpful books and impressive case histories of change, but it is rare for these groups to permit careful studies of their effectiveness. Outside observers have noted that in many cases change fails to occur, and people who thought they had changed later returned to their prior homosexual behavior.[45] One researcher tried to find solid evidence for change but was only able to locate eleven published research reports.[46] While success rates varied, there were cases where change from homosexual to heterosexual orientation did occur, especially in people who have strong religious beliefs. With these uncertainties, how do counselors respond to people who request change? From the beginning. it helps to give counselees a realistic picture of what they are facing.

- There is evidence that change is possible and that some homosexually oriented people have shifted and become primarily heterosexual.
- It also is clear that for many people the desired change does not occur despite their best efforts, desires, prayers, and determination.
- For some people there may be partial change.
- Regardless of sexual orientation, control of sexual behavior is possible. People who struggle with same-sex orientation can choose not to be sexually active and can live fulfilling, celibate lives.
- Even though one's sexual orientation is not deliberately chosen nor easily changed, there still are ethical choices that one can make.[47]
- Although this rarely is mentioned in professional publications, it seems clear that many people with homosexual tendencies, nevertheless, are able to form lasting marital relationships and have fulfilling sex with their opposite-sex spouses.

Even though change is difficult, there is cause for hope, especially when the person sincerely wants to change, but you may have to keep reminding your counselees (and yourself) of this possibility. Sinful homosexual actions can be stopped with the help of God; innate homosexual predispositions may be changed, but if that doesn't happen, the sexual orientation can be lived with and life still can be fulfilling.

3. *Share Knowledge*. Counselees may believe some of the greatest myths about homosexuality. As counseling progresses, be alert to these myths and look for opportunities to challenge the misconceptions and to replace them with accurate information about homosexuality and about human sexuality in general. It can be encouraging for the counselee to know, for example, that people with homosexual feelings are not all incompetent, mentally ill, perverted, rejected by God, or unable to function effectively in society. At some time you probably will share the biblical statements about homosexuality, especially the three-tier distinction—same-sex attraction, homosexual tendencies, gay identity—and how all of this differs from homosexual acts.

4. *Show Love and Acceptance of the Person*. In a courageous and insightful chapel address, one of my former seminary students talked about his homosexual tendencies and his ministry among the gay community.

Come to one of the dozens and dozens of gay bars in Chicago with me tonight and at 3 a.m. I will show you some of the nicest people in the world who are crying out to be loved—hundreds and hundreds of them—and where are we who know of the love of Christ? Surely, the search for love often takes on twisted and sinful expressions, but the hunger, the heart's cry, the vacuum seeking to be filled with the love of God is there, and it is the same as yours and mine. Christian friends need to be there; not tract-wielding preachers, but listening compassionate friends. . . .

More than anything else, a person who struggles with gayness, Christian or non-Christian, has a desperate need for love. He or she has been hurt by pathogenic family patterns, twisted environmental influences, or basically the sin that affects each of us. More than being a victimizer, the gay person has been a victim of sin. He has been hurt and usually has suffered greatly for his orientation, which he did not inherit or choose, but rather learned long before the age of accountability. Often, as a last resort in falling into gay sex, the person has sought love, which becomes eros defiled. So why does he or she need a Christian friend? Because we have Christ in us, and we know the love of Christ—the redeeming, sanctifying, healing power of God's incarnate love. Our whole world has a desperate need to see this love of Christ, to feel it, to touch it, to experience it personally, and we are his instruments.[48]

According to this speaker, actively gay and lesbian people can benefit greatly from the experience of connecting with caring people of both sexes without the necessity of sexual involvement. Being with a sensitive body of believers can give this support and connection. In turn, churches and individual Christians should be more willing to connect with homosexual people, engage in dialogue with them, and show acceptance and understanding. I once visited a thriving emergent church that met in a building that was next door to a gay bar. The neighbors got to know one another, and a number of the bar patrons came to church one morning when the pastor was talking about homosexuality. He did not dilute his biblical message, and they did not necessarily agree with his conclusions, but the neighbors showed respect for one another, despite their disagreements, and friendships developed. To break with one's gay friendships or homosexual behavior can be threatening and involves a genuine grief process as one pulls away from people who have been supportive and accepting. If there is no supportive community of believers willing to accept the homosexual, then there can be an easy retreat back into the old lifestyle.

The experience of a close, nonsexual relationship with a counselor of the same sex is the basis of Moberly's approach to helping homosexuals. When there is acceptance and love from another same-sex human being, healing is most likely to come especially if the relationship is supported by prayer.[49]

5. *Encourage Behavior Change.* Even when there is love and acceptance, change will not come to the person who continues his or her sexual involvement with other homosexual persons. If this involvement has continued for a long time, it may be especially difficult to stop. After a deliberate decision to change, the counselee may experience relapses and at times may resist the idea that change is desirable. Such resistance should be discussed in a straightforward, patient, kind, and firm manner.

One way to help change behavior is to avoid people, publications, and situations that are sexually arousing. This may lead to loneliness and a change in lifestyle that the counseling can address. Remind the counselee that Christ forgives[50] and that the Holy Spirit always is present to help us resist temptation and forsake sinful behavior. All of this will be easier if there are other human beings to give ongoing encouragement and human contact.

At some point there also can be value in discussing the counselee's whole lifestyle. Sex is a part of life, but so are worship, work, family, recreation, time management, recreation, exercise, and rest. One does not find fulfillment in life solely through sexual satisfaction, and neither do problems all disappear if counseling considers only sex. Unless the counselee finds satisfaction and personal feelings of identity in nonsexual parts of life—such as in his or her relationship with Christ, church involvement, work, or recreational activities—there will be a tendency to slip back into homosexual relationships when the pressures build. A more balanced life is a common-sense remedy, especially for the many minor and fleeting homosexual feelings and actions.

6. *Recognize That Counseling May Be Complex and Time Consuming.* Homosexuality is a complicated issue, often deeply ingrained and difficult to treat, especially by a counselor who has limited training or experience in working with this group of people. Progress is never a straight line between the two points of where you and the counselee begin to where you want to be. As with all counseling, there will be ups and downs in working with homosexual people.[51] These might include:

- Fear of failure, especially when the inevitable relapses or setbacks appear. Counselees need reassurance at such times so they know this is common and to be expected.
- Fear of success that comes to people who don't know how to live more fulfilling lives, so they will pull back.
- Wanting to abandon the efforts to change and go back to the familiar. Often this comes because the familiar is more comfortable, and change is hard, even though it might be desired.
- Anxiety because of temptation that lures counselees back into their old behaviors. This is where support from others and accountability are important.
- Plateaus that discourage because there seems to be no progress for a while. This is common.
- The appearance of new problems. Often, when one problem gets better, another suddenly appears. Assure counselees that these can be dealt with.
- The emergence of new emotions. This can be frightening for some counselees. Encourage counselees to be aware of the emotions, to consider why they might be there and to face them honestly.

None of this is meant to discourage you. Instead, it should alert you to the complexity of your task and show that in some cases, referral to another, perhaps more experienced, counselor may be the best way to help.

At the risk of oversimplification, I will mention only three of the many approaches to counseling homosexuals.

(a) The Psychoanalytic Approaches. Long, expensive, and in-depth, this approach aims at helping the homosexual gain insight into the causes of his or her orientation. The traditional approach assumes that a homosexual orientation comes because the same-sex parent has failed to bond with the child and to teach appropriate behaviors and independence. Sometimes, the opposite-sex parent has had excessive impact. In treatment, a same-sex therapist makes up for the inadequate same-sex parenting and models appropriate behaviors and perceptions. After almost a century of psychoanalytic theory, there still is debate about whether homosexuals are really helped by this approach. Even if it could be shown that they are helped, it is unrealistic to think that most counselees could afford the numerous sessions of individual counseling that would be required for psychoanalytic treatment.[52]

One of the most controversial psychoanalytically based approaches is reparative therapy, perhaps stated most clearly by psychologist Joseph Nicolosi.[53] He believes that homosexuality is a developmental problem that almost always arises from problems in family relationships, especially between father and son. As a result, the boy does not develop male gender identity, so he becomes homosexual. Treatment involves individual and group therapy that deals with father issues, self-acceptance, clarification about what it means to be male, and nonsexual intimacy with other males, including the counselor. This acquisition of masculine identity is viewed as a lifelong process. The American Psychological Association and American Psychiatric Association have both condemned this approach as being nonscientific, proclaiming that change in sexual orientation is impossible. Nevertheless, some evidence suggests that reparative therapy may bring change in sexual orientation.[54]

(b) The Behavioristic Approaches. Based on principles of conditioning and learning, these approaches try to help counselees unlearn their preferences for the same sex and relearn a heterosexual orientation. More common, at least in the professional publications, is the use of cognitive-behavioral techniques to help people deal with the depression and other problems associated with their sexual orientation and to cope with their sexual minority status. Unlike psychoanalysis, little or no emphasis is placed on consideration of the family interactions or developmental abnormalities that may have caused homosexuality. The emphasis is more on changing behavior and reducing anxiety, but they may do little to alter homosexual tendencies. At present there is little evidence about the extent to which such changes in behavior are permanent.[55]

(c) Christian Healing Ministries. There a number of groups and organizations that exist to shepherd people in the church who deal with same-sex attractions.[56] For example, Exodus International is a respected umbrella organization for over one hundred religiously oriented support groups that seek to help people change their sexual orientations. Many groups advertise in newspapers and give case histories of people who have changed. These anecdotal reports attract attention, but professional counselors discount them because it is possible to find case histories for almost any kind of behavior change. More rigorous studies have been done, however, and there is evidence that change does occur, but the results are inconclusive. Some of these groups are criticized because they work from an either-or perspective (a person is either homosexual or heterosexual), which ignores variations of intensity in homosexual orientation or same-sex attraction.

Preventing Homosexuality

How homosexuality is prevented and whether it can be prevented depends in large measure on how homosexuality is defined and what we believe about its causes and treatment. This chapter builds on the conclusion that at present there is more evidence for the view that homosexuality is a learned condition that is affected mildly, if at all, by genetic, chemical, neurological, or other biological influences. If this is true, then homosexuality can be prevented by providing learning experiences that stimulate heterosexuality. Of course, this does not mean that we give lectures or reading assignments and expect that these will prevent homosexuality. The learning must start in the home even before the child knows how to read.

1. *Building Healthy Home Environments.* Since homosexuality often appears to arise from undesirable parent-child relationships, the family is where prevention must begin. No healthy parent, especially those with a satisfying marriage, turns to a son or daughter for sexual experiences or permits other adults or older siblings to engage in traumatic or homoerotic acts with younger children. No father rejects or ignores his children if he has a satisfying marriage, a career that does not dominate his time, and the feeling that he is secure in his masculinity and adequate as a male. Perhaps children are less likely to become homosexual if there has been a warm, emotional relationship, especially with both parents.

All of this suggests that the church is contributing to the prevention of homosexuality when it stimulates healthy family patterns in which the father and mother maintain clearly differentiated roles, the children are respected and disciplined, and the parents have a mutually satisfying relationship. None of this is meant to suggest that stable homes guarantee that homosexuality will never develop. Homosexuality is complex, and simplistic solutions do not apply, but good home environments do stimulate healthy sexual attitudes in the family members.

2. *Giving Accurate Information About Homosexuality.* It is sad to observe the condemnation and horror with which so many Christians still react to homosexuality. If they grow up in such an environment, young people learn to fear homosexuals and to suppress any same-sex attractions within themselves. As a result, these people cannot get understanding and help from parents, youth leaders, or others in the church. In time, there may be a drift toward homosexual groups who are understanding, accepting, and loving. By its condemning attitude, therefore, the church sometimes pushes people into situations in which overt homosexual behavior is encouraged.

The alternative is for churches to teach what the Bible says about sexual control, love, friendship, and sexuality, including homosexuality. Church leaders should demonstrate an attitude of compassion and encouragement rather than one of repulsion and condemnation. Stereotypes about homosexuality (some of which are taught in popular Christian books about gays) should be exposed for what they are: untruths that alienate people, perpetuate ignorance, stimulate fear, push homosexuals away from Christian fellowship, and serve mainly to boost the critic's own sense of self-righteous superiority. All of this implies that issues like homosexuality should be discussed in the church instead of being denied.

Since overt homosexuality can become a habit in response to environmental stimulation, the church should emphasize the importance of sexual self-control. This comes through prayer, meditation on the Scriptures, avoidance of sexually arousing situations or people, deliberate decisions to avoid sinful actions, and the habit of being accountable to an understanding friend or counselor.

3. *Promoting Moral Standards for Healthy Sexuality.* Several organizations exist to assist churches and homosexuals to understand homosexuality and to encourage monogamous homosexual partnerships among Christians. The motives of these groups may be compassionate and even committed to Christian principles, but Stanton Jones has pointed out some of the weaknesses in their literature and promotional materials.

Jones and Yarhouse add that the church can no more guarantee healing to homosexuals than it can guarantee partners for single heterosexuals who long for marriage. But for homosexuals and heterosexuals, the divine standards are the same: sexual faithfulness within in heterosexual marriage or celibacy outside of marriage.[57]

4. *Developing Healthy Self-Concepts.* As we have seen, some observers have argued that many males are open to homosexuality when they have low self-concepts. When they fail in masculine activities—including athletics, love, and careers—males can feel dejected, inadequate, or unmasculine. As a result, they look for safe relationships where they do not have to act like males or prove their maleness. Contacts with homosexual friends may provide this acceptance that other parts of the society do not give. Perhaps something similar happens with women. In contrast, churches and homes can help individuals build realistic and positive self-concepts that are not dependent on acting in ways that require stereotypical masculine or feminine behaviors.

Conclusions About Homosexuality

Even though you might disagree with some of the preceding paragraphs, please remember that this chapter has attempted to summarize what is known about homosexuality, to point to some issues of controversy, and to cut through the emotional rhetoric so we can understand and help those homosexually inclined persons who seek our counsel.

It is impossible to estimate how many people, including Christians, struggle with same-sex attractions and temptations to engage in homosexual acts. Afraid of rejection or of being misunderstood, these people are reluctant to admit their tendencies. Often, they struggle alone, grappling with guilt or self-condemnation, and seeking to find rationalizations that might explain or pardon their sexual thoughts or actions. People like this can be helped, and the church can be a safe place where they can find the help they need. For the sensitive counselor who tries to understand, counseling with gay and lesbian people is not much different from other types of counseling. It involves applying the power of the Gospel to transform lives within a counseling setting.

At this time in history, there is widespread interest in homosexuals and openness about homosexuality. Never before, perhaps, has there been such an opportunity for church members and Christian counselors to make an impact on people who live with same-sex attraction and homosexual orientation.

KEY POINTS FOR BUSY COUNSELORS

➤ Homosexuality is not new, but it has gained greater prominence with the Kinsey research, the AIDS epidemic, and the emergence of the activist gay-lesbian movement.

➤ A homosexual *act* is any behavior that involves engaging, at least occasionally, in sexually stimulating actions with another person of the same sex. In contrast, a homosexual *orientation* involves feeling a sexual attraction toward members of the same sex. Many people with a homosexual orientation never engage in any homosexual act with another human being. Some of these people develop a gay identity that shapes much of their lives, attitudes, and actions.

➤ Homosexuality is only mentioned seven times in the Bible. Every time it is mentioned negatively, usually in the context of sinful actions. It would seem that the concept of homosexual partnerships with committed same-sex people is not mentioned in the Bible because it was not present in biblical times.

➤ Most Christians would agree that a homosexual orientation is not wrong but that homosexual acts are sinful. Biblically sanctioned genital sex is to be limited to that within heterosexual marriage.

➤ Despite thousands of scientific studies, there is no clearly identified single cause of homosexuality. Theories, most backed by some research, attribute homosexuality to:
  - Biological, genetic, neurological, or other physical influences.
  - Unhealthy parent-child relationships, including homes where an absent or distant father and a strong mother combine to stimulate homosexuality in boys.
  - Unhealthy relationships with parents of the same or opposite sex.
  - Other youthful experiences, including traumatic sex or erotic experiences with older same-sex people.

➤ It is generally agreed that homosexuality is not a willful choice.

➤ The effects of homosexuality can include:
  - Lifestyle effects.
  - Emotional instability.
  - Self-concept effects.
  - Problems with relationships.
  - Strained relationships with family members.

➤ Counselors should begin by evaluating their own attitudes. Homophobic counselors are not effective counselors.

➤ There is debate and no clear-cut evidence about whether a person can change from a homosexual to a heterosexual orientation. There are clear examples of people who have changed and of others who have not changed.

➤ In counseling homosexuals, consider the following:
- Determine the counselee's needs and goals.
- Instill realistic hope.
- Share accurate knowledge.
- Show love and acceptance of the person.
- Encourage behavior change.
- Recognize that counseling may be complex and time consuming.

➤ Prevention can include:
- Building healthy home environments.
- Giving accurate information about homosexuality.
- Promoting moral standards for healthy sexuality.
- Developing healthy self-concepts.

➤ Christian counselors and churches can have a significant impact in helping homosexual people.

22

Abuse and Neglect

In her work as a counselor, Janice had helped many women in the struggle to recover from abuse. She had reassured many of them with the message that what they had experienced was not their fault. She had reminded them that they had control over how they would respond. She had talked with them about their anger, their feelings of devastation, their memories of terror, their questions about why it had happened.

Then it happened to her.

Leaving her office after a day of counseling, Janice stepped into the hall and suddenly was grabbed from behind. "It took a few moments for me to realize what was happening," she wrote later. "I felt panic rising, and an impulse to fight back, but somehow I knew that to keep the situation from spinning out of control, I had to maintain control over myself."

Janice was forced to the floor. The man sat on her, unrolled duck tape, and wrapped it around her head, sealing her eyes shut. He demanded her jewelry and purse. When she heard him unzipping his pants, Janice realized that he intended more than robbery. He stripped her then stuck his erect penis into her mouth. When he saw that the tape over her eyes was coming loose he threw a coat over her head and proceeded to rape her.

Then he ran.

Janice crawled to an alarm on the wall, alerted the police, and waited while they hurried to her aid. During those minutes alone, Janice remembered thinking that this experience could change her life forever. Then one phrase started running through her mind: "He can't take what I don't give him." He could take her jewelry and force himself on her sexually, but he could not take the things that mattered most—like her self-esteem, her supportive family, her memories, and her determination to recover. The revulsion, panic, and anger did not flood over her until she was back in her office with the police and with her husband, who had rushed to the scene.

Ten years after this dreadful experience, Janice was courageous enough to write about her experience in a magazine for counselors. Following the attack she had learned to control the fear, to handle the anger without denying it, to grapple with the emotional, psychological, and physical trauma of having been violated. Her theories about trauma recovery had been put to the test. "When the theoretical becomes actual," she wrote, "the world becomes a different, far more threatening place."[1]

Like Janice in the days before her attack, we who are counselors can read about abuse and neglect, can reach some understanding about how it impacts people, and can do the best we can to be effective counselors. A few who read these words will understand better because they have been victims, but even if we have never experienced abuse, we still can connect well with people like Janice and be helpful. Violence and abuse, especially in the home, appear to be increasing all over the world. Only now are we beginning to comprehend the widespread prevalence of a problem that has been with us for centuries. Media attention, public outcries, and stories about victims have riveted people's attention on sexual violence, the worldwide sexual exploitation of children and women, mate beating in the home, child neglect and abuse, clergy and youth leaders who molest young boys and girls, and mistreatment of the elderly, often by their own adult children. Various observers and a host of professional counselors and researchers have confirmed that these problems of abuse and neglect not only are getting more attention; they are getting worse.[2]

Abuse is difficult to define, perhaps because the term covers so many types of physical and psychological maltreatment. Visit the Internet and type in "child abuse," or "sexual abuse," and you will discover literally millions of information sites and research articles. Many give definitions similar to the following:

- *Child abuse* involves physical or mental injury, neglect, sexual exploitation, or any other mistreatment of young people who are under the age of eighteen. These acts are committed by a person or persons who are satisfying their own lusts or other desires by exploiting vulnerable young people. This includes parents, older siblings, babysitters, teachers, or day-care providers.
- *Mate abuse* (sometimes called spouse abuse or marital abuse) most often involves the husband as the abuser and the wife as the victim, although husband abuse is relatively common. Mate abuse involves the attempt to control or coerce one's spouse physically or emotionally through deliberate assault, threats of violence, forced involvement in sexual acts, and/or emotional mistreatment, including ridicule, demeaning comments, neglect, and constant criticism.
- *Elder abuse* is the maltreatment of older people and includes rough handling, beating, negligence, verbal condemnation, ridicule, withholding food or medication, financial exploitation, sexual mistreatment, and ignoring the person's needs for comfort and human contact.
- *Sexual abuse* may overlap with any of the above. According to the National Clearing House on Child Abuse and Neglect Information, sexual abuse of children is "inappropriate adolescent or adult sexual behavior with a child. It includes fondling a child's genitals, making the child fondle the adult's genitals, intercourse, incest, rape, sodomy, exhibitionism, sexual exploitation, or exposure to pornography."[3] Sexual abuse with adults includes rape or other forced sexual acts, sexual exploitation of counselees by their counselors, or other forms of sexual assault.
- *Emotional abuse* includes both verbal and nonverbal actions that reject, ridicule, criticize, or in other ways demean another human being. This is in direct contradiction to the old children's nursery rhyme that "Sticks and stones may break my bones, but words will never hurt me." Words and neglect can cause serious harm.
- *Neglect* is the lack of adequate care-giving. Most often this is experienced by children, by the elderly, or by handicapped or physically ill people who are unable to care for themselves and who are not given adequate nutrition, supervision, medical care, hygiene, education, or interaction with other human beings. The perpetrators most often are family members, but neglect also happens in nursing homes, treatment facilities, prisons, or similar institutions.

- *Spiritual abuse* involves the exploitation of people in churches or in other religious bodies by leaders who most often are authoritarian, controlling, image conscious, and intolerant of criticism. While leaders may take sexual advantage of some in their flock, more often the leaders make excessive demands for their followers' allegiance, time, money, devotion, and rigidly prescribed behaviors. Often these demands are justified by theological arguments, and those who disagree are in danger of condemnation, ridicule, greater control, or ejection from the community of their fellow believers and friends. Spiritually abused people may not be harmed physically, but they feel confused, used, afraid, disillusioned with spiritual authorities, even unable to trust in God.[4]
- *Other abuse* could include the harassment of neighbors by juveniles, the physical and emotional exploitation of employees by their employers or fellow workers, and most other behavior where one human being deliberately inflicts physical and emotional pain in an effort to harm a helpless and unwilling victim.[5]

Technically, abuse most often refers to exploitation by people who are relatives, care-givers, or close associates of the victims; abuse by strangers is considered assault and handled solely by police and criminal courts. But the trauma to victims can be intense regardless of the perpetrator's identity. Many victims are reluctant to report abuse, especially when the abuser is a family member. Children, the elderly, or detainees who are abused in prison settings often are unable to report abuse. Some, like very young children, are not even aware that the pain they experience is abuse. Others, like many rape victims, are embarrassed to report their experiences, and some say nothing because they fear reprisals or other harm if the rapist is identified or apprehended.

We appear to be living in the midst of an epidemic of abusive behavior. Even though much of it may go unreported, the figures that do get tabulated are both staggering and growing. They vary from country to country, and because they change so rapidly, anything that might be included here could quickly be outdated. There was a time when believers dismissed all of this as something that rarely occurs in Christian circles. No longer can we maintain such naiveté. Christians are not immune to abuse, some of which even arises within the church. Abuse is a problem that Christian counselors are likely to encounter with increasing frequency as people who are abuse victims become more willing to talk about their traumatic experiences.

The Bible and Abuse

In large measure, the Bible is a book about violence. Biblical history abounds in accounts of murder, military battles, retribution, and martyrdom, all culminating in the torturous crucifixion of Christ. Often the violence resulted from the sinful acts of disobedient people whose lives were corrupt in the sight of God.[6] But violence also came as the result of wars that God had sanctioned in order to punish the wicked and administer justice. When discipline and reprimand are mentioned in Proverbs,[7] the purpose is to bring correction and to prevent foolish actions or running wild.[8] Discipline is intended as an expression of love, correction, and guidance.[9]

Nowhere does the Bible sanction, overlook, or approve of child, mate, elder, sexual, or other forms of abuse. Genesis 34 describes the rape of Dinah, one of Jacob's daughters. When her brothers learned about this, they took revenge on the rapist and his whole family. Jacob appeared to stand by, less concerned about his daughter and more worried about what all of this would do to his safety. This parental passivity brought an angry retort from Jacob's sons, who proclaimed their outrage about a stranger treating their sister like a prostitute.[10]

Despite the scenes of violence in the Bible, nonviolence is sanctioned, especially in the New Testament. Jesus condemned not only murder, but the harboring of angry thoughts toward another person.[11] "Stop judging others," he said in the Sermon on the Mount, or we will be judged in similar ways for our own faults and weaknesses.[12] In Colossians, husbands are told to love their wives and never to treat them harshly.[13] Fathers are instructed to avoid aggravating their children, lest they become discouraged and quit trying.[14] Employers are instructed to be "just and fair" to their employees.[15] No room is allowed for employee abuse or harassment. Elsewhere, believers are told to "get rid of all bitterness, rage, anger, harsh words, and slander, as well as all kinds of malicious behavior."[16] Instead, we are to "be kind to each other, tenderhearted, forgiving one another, just as God through Christ has forgiven you."[17] Among believers there is to be "no sexual immorality, impurity, or greed among you. Such sins have no place among God's people. Obscene stories, foolish talk, and coarse jokes—these are not for you. Instead let there be thanksgiving to God."[18] In 1 Timothy and James, we read about the importance of treating elderly relatives and other seniors with care and respect. There is no place for elder abuse among believers.[19] All of these describe divine ideals. They show that God is opposed to abuse. His people must be equally opposed.

Does any of this have relevance for the victims of abuse? Jesus told us to love our enemies and pray for our persecutors. "Don't resist an evil person," he said. "If you are slapped on the right cheek, turn the other, too." We are instructed to forgive those who sin against us, and to not be anxious about anything.[20] These instructions have led some pastors or other Christian counselors to advise victims to submit passively to repeated beatings, harassment, and other abuse.

Janice, the woman whose story we told at the beginning of this chapter, is an orthodox Jew, but as part of her recovery she applied many of these teachings of Jesus. Surely, the Lord is not instructing us to abandon self-defense or to stand by passively while somebody is raped or while children or elderly parents are abused by family members. The words of Jesus are ideals, but they are not presented as impossibilities. To avoid retaliation, to forsake bitterness, or to offer forgiveness are steps to healing, but it takes time for a victim or a victim's family to reach this point. In time, and with the help of God and support from others, including a counselor, people can forgive their abusers, pray for their enemies, and trust God for inner peace in the midst of difficult life situations. This does not prevent victims and their families and counselors from taking action to bring justice within the legal system, to prevent further abuse, to protect victims from additional harm, and ultimately to bring about the nonabusive ideals that the Scriptures clearly teach.

The Causes of Abuse

At some time while I was writing the preceding paragraphs, a disturbed sixteen-year-old in Minnesota shot his grandfather and the older man's female companion, then went to the local high school and began firing. Within minutes he had killed a teacher, a security guard, five students, and himself. The newspapers called it murder, the latest incident of school violence committed by an emotionally distraught young man who had planned his actions for weeks and even had discussed his intentions with friends. People in the community where this happened buried their dead and struggled with the question of "Why?"

The same question arises whenever one human being hurts another. Why would anyone abuse another, physically or psychologically? The most basic answer is human sinfulness, but this does not explain why some people act in sinful abusive ways while most others do not. Once again, we are confronted with behavior that has no simple or single cause. The rapist who attacked Janice doubtless had reasons that differed significantly from the teenager who shot his classmates in Minnesota. The middle-aged daughter who neglects and mistreats her elderly mother differs from the father who takes sexual advantage of his little girl. As we list some causes of abuse in the following paragraphs, remember that for each of your counseling cases, all, part, or none of the following may apply. Every situation will have its own unique causes.

Before we look at these causes, it is important to dispel one misconception that victims and their families frequently believe. It is *not* correct to assume that victims of abuse usually ask for it by giving subtle hints to indicate that they would like to be mistreated. It is cruel and inaccurate to conclude, for example, that rape victims somehow really want to be raped and that they could prevent this personal sexual attack if they really wanted to escape. On rare occasions, victims may subtly invite the attacker's assaults, but this is unusual and certainly not the norm. Rape is a violent attack on a woman or man[21] in which sex is used as a weapon. For most victims it is a humiliating and often a life-changing experience. Rape victims, like all other recipients of abuse, do not encourage it to happen, and neither do they secretly enjoy the experience. Giving this reassurance to the abuse victims can be one of the first and most helpful ways to begin counseling.

What causes abuse to occur? The following are among the numerous, complex, and overlapping reasons that counselors have discovered.

1. *Environmental Stress.* Introductory psychology textbooks often describe the frustration-aggression theory. This is the view that whenever people get really frustrated, a common reaction is to respond to these feelings by verbally or physically lashing out at some other person or object. The frustrated driver who leans on the car horn to get other motorists moving or the aggravated tennis player who throws his racket on the ground are examples.

It is easy for parents to get frustrated with crying, whining children and to wish there was some way to silence them. It can be very frustrating to have older relatives who are getting more and more dependent and unable to care for themselves, especially if these older people are chronic complainers. If financial or work pressures begin to build, it is easy to direct frustrations toward family members, especially if these family members are weak, unable to help, or powerless to defend themselves. Sometimes, even trivial stresses can trigger abuse, such as the crying child who interrupts parental activities or the frustration of cleaning up after a messy feeding or soiling. Frustrations like these may lead to a verbal or physical reaction, but in themselves these rarely lead to ongoing or intense abuse. How, then, does one get from reacting to frustrations to ongoing abuse?

It is widely recognized that abuse often occurs in three phases. First is the tension-building stage, where frustrations and stresses increase and coping techniques become less and less effective. There may be periodic abuse at this stage, but often it is explained with rationalizations, such as "it was a tough day at work," or "it should not have happened, but it could have been worse." As time passes, however, the incidents often get more frequent and perhaps more aggressive. In the second stage, the violence erupts. Sometimes, it comes without warning and may not even have a major cause. Like steam building in an enclosed container of boiling water, there is an explosion that is loud and unpredictable, often the result of built-up tension that bursts forth in violence. In some cases this is reported to authorities or to relatives, but often the victim is either too young or too embarrassed to understand and talk about it. If the victim is an adult, he or she may decide to let it pass, fearing that talking about it might trigger more violence. Stage three follows. This is a stage of remorse in the abuser, profuse apology, great feelings of regret and shame, with promises never to let it happen again. Sometimes, the abuser floods the victim with gifts, affection, and attempts to give a somewhat reasonable explanation about why it happened. This is a time when the victim feels hope and may believe that the abuse will never happen again. Life returns to normal, but then the tensions build again until the cycle repeats itself.

A buildup of stress in the life of the abuser is never an excuse for violence, even if the victim creates the stress. Nevertheless, the stress buildup may explain why some people are abusive. This also may explain, in part, why abusers do not always limit their attacks to one family member. When stress builds, the abuser may attack the spouse but also may direct the violence toward children or other family members. One investigation of in-home violence and abuse found that 58 percent of the males who abused their children at home also abused their adult female partner. Half of in-home males who were physically violent to children also sexually abused them. In 86 percent of homes with partner violence, the children were also physically assaulted. Whether or not the cause is stress, apparently ongoing abuse permeates entire families.[22]

2. *Learned Abuse.* Children who are abused or who observe violence in their parents often become abusers themselves in later life.[23] An older study of elder abuse found that one in four hundred children who were reared nonviolently attack their parents in later life, compared to one in twelve who were abused by their parents.[24] Another report showed that children who are neglected never learn how to care for others, so they grow up to become neglectors of their own children.[25]

3. *Personality Influences.* Abusers often are insecure, impulsive, threatened, or people with low self-concepts. Some wife beaters feel jealous, possessive, or intimidated by their wives, so the husband tries to boost his own feelings of inadequacy by being tough and dominant in the presence of the wife. Some child batterers feel inadequate as parents, so they attempt to manage their offspring with violence. Other parents have a low tolerance for the normal hyperactive behavior of their children, so violence becomes a way to gain control.[26] Convicted rapists

often are angry men who release pent-up feelings of rage and bolster their feel-ings of sexual inadequacy by attacking women, using sex as a weapon. Some-times, there are ongoing power struggles between the abuser and the victim, leading to more abuse. In his book on family violence and abuse, psychologist Grant L. Martin adds that many men abuse because they have an inability to handle their anger, are emotionally dependent, or act out because they cannot express their anger or other emotions in more appropriate ways. Many of these men have low self-esteem, lack assertiveness, have rigid beliefs about the roles of males or of parents, or lose control because of their alcohol or drug dependency.[27] Sometimes, people simply are overwhelmed by family responsibilities.

When an elderly lady died of starvation, the community was outraged. Then a newspaper reporter described the helpless feelings of her son. The mother had been confused, incontinent, blind, helpless, and uncooperative. She refused to eat and sometimes would take food from her mouth and hide it in her pockets. The son had a job, had no help in caring for his mother, and knew nothing about community social services that could have given assistance. He never abused his mother verbally or violently. He abused her by neglect because he simply did not know how to cope.[28]

4. *Cultural Issues.* In accounting for abuse, what is the role of television, sexu-ally violent movies, pornographic materials, and news reports about abuse? We live in a world where violence is condemned but, at the same time, permitted on our television sets, viewed in our theatres, graphically taught in our video games,[29] and modeled by our governments in their aggressive actions against other nations. Martin writes that "the reluctance of our police to intervene in cases of domestic violence, clergy who encourage the abused woman to be sub-missive to the husband, and mental-health workers who blame women for vio-lence all contribute to the perpetuation of violent relationships."[30] Violence and abuse thrive and grow in violent and abusive cultures.

Abuse also thrives in cultures or families where social attitudes sanction vio-lence or harassment. This includes places where women are assumed to be infe-rior, children are demeaned, or members of minority groups are assumed to be of lesser value than the majority. For example, domestic violence is likely to be more common in homes where the husband thinks women are inferior and that men are to keep their wives submissive. Sometimes, church leaders communicate this message and encourage violence, most often unintentionally, when they preach about biblical submission.

Whatever its source, the violent nature of the culture is a reflection of the vio-lent nature of human beings. Jeremiah wrote about the deceitfulness and desper-ately wicked hearts of human beings.[31] Jesus pointed to the same core problems. "It is the thought-life that defiles you. For from within, out of the person's heart, come evil thoughts, sexual immorality, theft, murder, adultery, greed, wicked-ness, deceit, eagerness for lustful pleasure, envy, slander, pride, and foolishness. All these vile things come from within; they are what defile you and make you unacceptable to God."[32]

All of this points to the complexity and difficulty of trying to pinpoint causes of abuse. Unlike some other problems, however, in counseling the victims of abuse, there may be less interest in why it happened and more of a need to consider ways to help people recover from the effects of abuse.

The Effects of Abuse

What does abuse do to people? In part, the answer depends on the age, personality, gender, type of abuse, and past experiences of the victim. Journalist Philip Yancey once attended an international conference of forty-five Christian groups involved in working with women who seek to escape from their lives of prostitution.[33] An estimated twenty-five million people work as prostitutes worldwide, and some estimate that at least half of those are children, both male and female. When Yancey asked what percentage would like to get out of the business he was told "all of them." Many work as virtual slaves in brothels, especially in Asia and Western Europe, and their lives reflect loneliness, shame, depression, hopelessness, and addictions to drugs and alcohol.

Abuse can affect people in a variety of ways. When compared with people who have not been abused, incest victims are more inclined to distrust others and have low self-esteem, conflicts over sexual identity, feelings of guilt or shame, isolation, and loneliness. When they are courageous enough to tell what is going on, other family members often disbelieve them, the abuser denies what has been happening, and sometimes the abuse is worse the next time when the victim and abuser are alone.[34] Incest and other forms of sexual abuse can lead to what counselors sometimes call a post-sexual-abuse-syndrome, characterized by anxiety, sleep disturbances, anger, sexual dysfunction, substance addiction, fear, and low self-esteem. Many abuse experiences lead to problems later in life, especially if the abuse occurred when the victims were young.[35] Often there are chronic anxiety, difficulties in forming stable relationships, depression, and problems with self-esteem and with sex. Abused teenagers can have difficulty adjusting later in life, and they have a higher than normal tendency to engage in delinquent behavior. As we might expect, abused wives feel afraid, angry, depressed, lacking in self-esteem, and often helpless. Rape victims are more likely than other women to suffer from anxiety, depression, sexual difficulties, family tensions, impaired work and social adjustment, withdrawal from others, self-condemnation, apathy, and inertia.[36] Victims of elder abuse often feel confused and helpless, but most don't complain or report the abuse even if they are able to do so. The fear of being abandoned, placed in an institution, not believed, socially isolated, or further abused can lead many to suffer in silence and sometimes even to find reasons to excuse the abusive actions of their adult children.

At the risk of oversimplification, these diverse effects of abuse could be grouped into four general categories. Abuse influences the victim's feelings, thinking, actions, and spirituality.[37]

1. *Feelings.* Victims often feel angry, afraid, ashamed, guilty, embarrassed, confused, and worthless. Many victims report feeling violated, dirty, vulnerable, and afraid to trust others. Depression is common, and sometimes victims experience self-pity and fear of getting close to others. When they become parents, some victims of abuse may be afraid that they will lose control of their own emotions and hurt their own children. It is common for victims to wonder if they did something bad or wrong so that they deserved or subtly invited the abuse.

2. *Thinking.* People who have been abused often have low self-concepts and think of themselves as being worthless, unattractive, incompetent, inadequate, dependent, or unwanted by others. Sadly, when people think this way, they often act in accordance with their thinking and become what they feared. Often victims

have low morale and impaired concentration. Abused children, battered wives, and mistreated old people sometimes blame themselves for the treatment they receive and think that they must deserve to be abused. Frequently, there is a willingness to take more abuse without resisting because the victim feels so helpless and afraid of the consequences if the abuse is reported.

3. *Actions.* Abuse can lead victims to develop antisocial behavior, learning disabilities, interpersonal tensions, inefficiency at work, and sometimes a tendency to become violent and abusive themselves. Addictions to drugs, alcohol, food, or sex are common, and some victims are afraid to venture outside, especially if they were abused away from home. Many of these behaviors are self-destructive, but they also can be ways to avoid anxiety. It is not unusual for people to have sexual problems or an aversion to sex, especially if they have been abused sexually. One study of almost three thousand people who had been abused as children showed that both male and female victims had higher rates of childhood and adult mental disorders, personality disorders, anxiety disorders, and psychiatric treatment than comparison groups that had not been abused.[38] Many, however, go on with life as best they can, but they recognize that because of the abuse, life will "always be different" than it might have been if the abuse had not occurred.

4. *Spirituality.* Where is God in all of this? For some victims there is theological confusion and questioning. Why, they wonder, would God allow this to happen? Could any good possibly come from such a painful experience? Why did God not answer prayer and prevent or stop the abuse? Many are angry at God, and this may be directed toward the Christian counselor. Often there are struggles with doubt, the seeming inability to forgive, or questions about whether they can ever hope again or trust God to protect them.

Try to keep two cautions in mind as you reflect on these effects of abuse. First, most of these indicators are not limited to abuse victims. Anxiety, interpersonal tensions, or spiritual questioning, for example, can characterize a number of psychological problems. If you see these in a counselee, please do not assume that their presence somehow proves that abuse has occurred. Second, realize that some victims appear to be unusually resilient and may not show many, if any, effects of the past or ongoing trauma.[39] In contrast to what counselors have believed for many years, recent research shows that neglect, rather than abuse, may cause the greater damage to victims. Many victims suffer the most painful experience of their lives, but after a brief period of grieving, they return to normal functioning and never lapse into serious depression or other symptoms. Janice discovered, for example, that her religion, her network of supportive friends and family, and even the positive experiences she had with the police all helped her to return to her normal activities. She found, as well, that the mundane repetition of necessary tasks, like doing the laundry or buying groceries, anchored her back into the world and her family.[40]

In considering the effects of abuse, try to remember that the victim is not the only one who suffers. Family members, boyfriends, mates of rape victims, and close friends may all react with anger, confusion, prejudice, and feelings of helplessness, revulsion, and embarrassment. Husbands of rape victims sometimes feel personally violated because of what has happened to their wives. In turn, this can lead to marital tension, depression, and further stress on the victim.

Finally, we should not forget the abuser. Often these people feel deep and lasting remorse, especially after their abusive behavior becomes public knowledge. Many are frightened, guilt-ridden, confused, or angry, but they find little support or sympathy from others. Few attempt to understand abusers, often because there is anger about the harm they have caused. Forgiveness is rare, and counselors seem reluctant to realize that many abusers need help as much as their victims.

Counseling and Abuse

It can be difficult to counsel the victims of abuse and neglect as well as the perpetrators. Compassionate counselors, even those with long experience, can be shocked and repulsed when they observe the physical and psychological pain that human beings inflict on others, sometimes repeatedly. When abuse concerns children or the elderly, counselors can have difficulty knowing if they should believe the reports they hear. At other times we may suspect abuse but wonder what to do if the counselee denies it. The majority of abused children do not reveal their experiences during childhood, and when they do admit abuse, it is common for them to later deny that it really happened.[41] Men, including male ministers and other counselors, often find that female counselees are too ashamed or embarrassed to talk with a man about abusive sexual experiences and would prefer to talk with a woman counselor. Some evidence suggests that it is counselors who are more reluctant to talk. Often they avoid asking counselees if they have been abused, despite evidence that past abuse can lead to the kinds of adult psychopathology that often are discussed in the counseling room. Some counselors are too uncomfortable to raise the issue of abuse, don't want to disturb their clients psychologically, believe that other issues are more pressing, or fear that suggesting abuse might arouse false memories of abuse that never really happened.[42]

Recovery from abuse can be viewed as a process having overlapping stages. These may vary, depending on the type of abuse.

First, there is an impact stage. This may only last for a few hours or a few days and is characterized by shock, disbelief, anxiety, and fear. Since the victim may be too afraid, embarrassed, or confused to report the abuse, the whole experience is hidden from others, sometimes for years, although its impact spills out in some of the aftereffects that we have considered. When abuse is reported, the victim may feel overwhelmed by the presence of too many professionals or police officers asking questions, sometimes with little sensitivity to the victim's emotional state. Close family members may be the ones who can best help at this stage. Sometimes, pastors or counselors are called and are able to give support, guidance as decisions are made, or help in finding medical care and safety.

A stage of denial often follows. In order to cope with the stress, the victim tries to push aside the trauma of abuse and return to a pre-crisis stage of functioning, as if nothing has happened. At this time victims need to feel secure, organized, and in control. To others, and even to the victims themselves, it may appear that everything has returned to normal, but the impact of the trauma still persists and will need to be dealt with before complete healing occurs. The denial stage may be over within a short time, although it may last for years.

The treatment stage has three parts according to psychologist Diane Langberg, who has worked for most of her professional career to bring healing to sexually abused women.[43] Part one involves helping counselees feel safe, in the presence of a compassionate counselor who reflects Christlike character. This is a period when victims need to talk about their memories, express feelings, struggle with guilt and anger, talk about their anxieties or depression, and feel counselor support. Slowly, there is a merger into part-two goals. These include facing both the past and present, working through one's grief, and resuming some of the daily activities that help the counselee feel a movement back toward normal living. Eventually, you can help the victim to confront the abuser and learn to forgive. Part three involves reestablishing relationships and rebuilding life. This is a time of integration as the individual begins to feel free from being controlled or dominated by the effects of the sexual assault or assaults. These experiences come to be viewed as painful and significant events in the past, but the person has now grown to a higher level of psychological and spiritual maturity, and is able to move on with life.

Perhaps you have detected that the healing process from abuse takes time and cannot be summarized adequately in a few sentences. Effective counseling is not limited to people with special expertise in the treatment of abuse; God can and often does use inexperienced counselors to bring healing. However, many less experienced counselors prefer to refer abuse victims to more seasoned Christian professionals who are able to give specialized help. If you have not had experience in counseling abuse victims, you might be wise to contact a local rape or sexual assault center where experienced helpers can give information and assistance as you work with victims and their families. Many of your counselees can find additional comfort and help by joining support groups where sexual assault victims assist and encourage one another, often under the guidance of a counselor. Others find help through community or church support networks that provide emotional support, understanding, and information.

Although everyone involved needs support, guidance, and help in coping with the stress and emotional reactions to abuse, much of your counseling will depend on the type of abuse and on the counselee's unique experiences.

1. *Helping the Children of Abuse.* Frequently, the outside observer has few or no indications that a child is being abused. There may be no scars and the child can look healthy, but inappropriate behavior such as aggression, altered sleep patterns, or inappropriate sexual behavior may be evident, any of which might suggest that something is wrong. Other indications of abuse or neglect could include the following:

- The child seems to be unduly fearful, especially of parents.
- The child appears to be undernourished or inappropriately fed.
- The child is poorly groomed or not appropriately dressed for the weather.
- The child has injuries or apparent sicknesses that are inappropriately treated in terms of bandages or medications.
- The child is withdrawn and depressed or overactive and aggressive.
- The child seems disinterested, unable to concentrate, inclined to cling to adults other than the parents, or unable to get along with other children.
- The parents are rigid, highly demanding of their children, and inclined to punish harshly.
- The parents have experienced multiple stresses, such as marital discord, divorce, debt, frequent moves, job loss, or other pressures.

Despite the fact that they have been told to be quiet, some children will talk about the abuse. Listen carefully if they give hints about abuse and, if you can, ask them to describe what they mean in more detail. Counselors who work with children sometimes ask their young counselees to draw a picture of what has happened. We know that children have vivid imaginations and sometimes make up stories, but young children do not have the capacity to fantasize about some things that they haven't experienced. As they get older, children and adolescents begin to realize that most people won't believe that an apparently normal adult like one's own father, a respected youth worker, teacher, relative, or community leader could be capable of repeated, unchallenged sexual molestation of a minor. The child who dares to report abuse faces a skeptical and unbelieving audience and risks the possibility of humiliation and punishment as well.

Child abuse, including incest and sexual abuse, is an issue that involves the whole family. The young victim may be the person who suffers most and is noticed first, but other family members need help as well. For this reason, most counselors try to involve the entire family in the counseling process, especially when the abuse occurs within the home. Remember, too, that in most of the places where this book is read, counselors—including pastors, youth workers, and teachers—are legally required to report suspected abuse to the authorities. Failure to do so is a violation of the law.

2. *Helping Victims of Neglect.* Neglect has been called "the most nebulous of abuse allegations."[44] It is difficult to define, hard to detect, and often impossible to prove. Sometimes, it is deliberate, but at other times neglectful parents or other care-givers fail to understand the extent of the neglected person's needs for contact, assistance, stimulation, guidance, or other care. Neglect can involve grown children who have busy lives and rarely bother to contact their aging parents who live alone, or neglect can include career-oriented fathers who assume that their sons and daughters have all they need if they are given sufficient food, housing, or money. These are examples of nonmalicious people who fail to realize what the people in their care really need. Of course, there also are situations in which emotionally deprived or unbalanced care-givers appear unable to give help because of their own inadequacies. The problems may be complicated if the care-givers have a long-term history of self-neglect or if the people under their care resist help. An example is the older person who needs assistance but insists on being independent and rejects all offers of help.

There is no standard procedure for helping people who have been neglected. It is best to involve others in the helping process. This might include the church, social service agencies, medical practitioners, or others. As a counselor, if you suspect that neglect has become abuse, you must report it to local authorities, who, in turn, will take action to intervene.

3. *Helping Adult Victims of Incest and Abuse.* It is not surprising that victims sometimes carry the pain of childhood abuse into adulthood and never share the secret with anyone. Depending on where you live, reports of abuse suggest that 20 percent or more of adult women and a significant but smaller number of males have been sexually victimized as children. It is sobering, then, to ponder how many silent victims of abuse may be in your church or college community, or may pass through your counseling office without mentioning their abusive backgrounds. When abuse is mentioned on the radio or in public talks, the speakers often get hundreds of messages from listeners who have been abused.

If you have any reason to suspect abuse in a counselee, do not hesitate to raise the issue gently. Some counselors do this routinely as part of their intake interviews. Mention that the problem is common, that victims do not deserve the abuse, that they rarely do anything to stimulate it, and that help is available to people who want to get over their feelings of shame and hurt. Often the gentle, caring, nonjudgmental encouragement of a sensitive counselor is all the counselee needs to break a long-guarded secret and finally deal with the bottled-up feelings and questions about abuse. As with most of the issues discussed in this chapter, a variety of hotlines and support groups are available to help people face and move beyond their abusive pasts. A number of churches also have ministries and support groups for victims of incest, abuse, and/or rape.

4. *Helping the Victims of Rape.* Victims respond to rape in various ways, often depending on their past experiences with sexual abuse. The majority show what used to be called rape trauma syndrome (RTS), although this term is used less frequently at present than it was previously.[45] As we have seen, initially there is a period of acute stress immediately following the rape. There may be fear, anger, anxiety, shock, and disbelief, which often are expressed by crying, sobbing, tenseness, nausea, or restlessness, but sometimes are hidden behind a calm, composed exterior. At this point, the victim may be flooded with feelings of terror, concern for her safety, and guilt because she did not struggle more. Some women, even from the beginning, wonder if the myth really is true, which says that women secretly attract rapists.

The counselee probably will be sensitive to someone who will listen, show acceptance, and believe her story.[46] This is especially important if she has faced subtle disbelief and rejection from family, friends, police, or medical personnel. The counselor can encourage the expression of feelings, help the woman find competent medical and legal aid, give support when she does encounter criticism, help her and her friends recognize the myths about rape, encourage the victim to discuss her fears for future safety, and give assurance of continued support as the woman faces difficult situations in the coming weeks.

Two or three weeks after the rape, many women begin to experience nightmares, irrational fears, and restless activity. Often there is a decision to move, change a phone number, stay indoors at night, or spend more time with close friends. In all of this the victim is in the process of reorganizing her life after an experience that for many has been terrifying. These women need support, freedom to express feelings, acceptance, an opportunity to talk with someone who considers them "normal," and guidance as they make decisions. Many will want to discuss the issue of "Why me?" and will need to be reassured of God's continued care, love, and concern. At times these victims may want to talk about things other than the rape, and prefer to get on with routine life activities or to go out for dinner or to a movie. Often, it helps for a counselor to take the initiative in helping or offering to help these women, instead of waiting for the victim to seek more traditional counseling. It also is helpful to counsel with the families and spouses if possible. These people can be very supportive to the victim but, as we have seen, relatives often have feelings of their own that need to be expressed, attitudes that need to be changed, and misconceptions that need to be corrected.

Instead of the process that we have been describing, a second general response to rape is seen in victims with previous physical, psychiatric, or social difficulties. Sometimes, these people develop more intense symptoms, such as depression, psychotic or suicidal behavior, psychosomatic disorders, drug use, excessive drinking, or sexual "acting out" behavior. These women need referral for help that is more in-depth than crisis counseling.

A third major response to rape is a silent reaction. This is seen in women who have not told anyone about the rape, have never talked about their feelings or reactions, and have carried a tremendous psychological burden, sometimes for years. Later in life these women may develop anxiety, fear of men, avoidance of sexual behavior, unexplained fears of being alone or going outside, nightmares, and a loss of self-esteem. If these people are abused again, they often spend more counseling time talking about the pent-up emotions concerning the first rape than about the current situation.

Despite its traumatic effects, the good news is that rape victims usually are able to reorganize their lives and protect themselves from further assault.[47] This is most likely when victims get the medical treatment, psychological help, practical guidance, and spiritual support they need after rape.

Even though the previous paragraphs have focused on the rape of women, there is significant evidence of men being raped, especially in all-male environments, such as jails and prisons. Male inmates fear being raped more than anything else. Many have experienced multiple rapes, exposing them to HIV/AIDS and other sexually transmitted diseases. Although rape is always a violent act, male rape is more focused on dominance and control of other inmates than on sexual satisfaction or release. Prison sexual predators typically are heterosexual, but the trauma on victims is even greater because they interact daily with their abusers and often have limited opportunity to get counseling or legal assistance. Of course, rape of men is not limited to prisons and to the actions of heterosexual males, but wherever it occurs, men tend to be less willing then women to report rape because of the embarrassment and threats to their masculinity.[48]

The violent and sexual victimization of one human being by another is a gross deviation from God's intended plan. Often, rapists are young, married, employed people whose personal or family lives are disturbed, who can't relate successfully to the opposite sex, and who deny that they are a menace to society. In each case, rapists need more than supportive counseling. They need to know God's forgiveness, to experience the power of God to transform lives, and to participate in counseling designed to deal with those underlying issues that led them to initiate the act of rape.

5. *Helping the Victims of Mate Abuse.* Most mate abuse involves the physical and psychological mistreatment of a wife by her husband, but husband abuse does occur and may be increasing. Because of their greater strength, men are better able to inflict injury on their wives, but women often do more physical harm because they tend to attack with something other than their hands.

In both cases the victim often has low self-esteem and, in the case of wife abuse, there may be a distorted belief that the husband's role as head of the home gives him the right to tyrannize his family. Sometimes, the victim is even made to feel that she, rather than the abuser, is the real cause of the problem. In other cases, the abusive mate usually may be loving and willing to provide for the family, except for periodic and often unpredictable explosions of rage and violence.

Once again, most victims are reluctant to report the abuse. There is realistic fear that the abusing mate could explode in more violence if he (or she) discovers that the family aggression has been reported. A woman whose livelihood depends on her abusive husband is reluctant to risk being cut off from food and shelter, especially if this would make her solely responsible for the care of her children. Some Christian women believe (and are told by their pastors) that wives should be submissive to their husbands, even if the husband's behavior is intensely violent and life threatening.

Counselors, therefore, should be alert to nonverbal signs of spouse abuse. These include:[49]

- A history of miscarriages.
- Frequent visits to the emergency room for treatment of illnesses or injuries.
- Signs of ongoing stress, such as headaches, gastrointestinal ailments, vague "not feeling well" complaints, or excessive use of tranquilizers or alcohol.
- Withdrawal and isolation from friends, church, and family.
- Moody, discouraged, unpredictable, or depressive behavior, sometimes accompanied by periodic suicide attempts.
- Frequent absence from work.
- Reports from others, including neighbors or family members, about conflict or disruption in the home.
- References to previous abuse or violence in the home.

If you suspect abuse, do not be reluctant to raise the issue. Pastors often know families better than nonpastoral counselors, and in many communities pastors still are able to make home visits where there are unusual opportunities to make observations and to explore issues with possible victims who might not come for counseling voluntarily. Wherever you counsel, try to learn as much as you can about the home situation and seek to determine the likelihood of future harm or danger. When the abuse has been revealed, most victims need support, the calming effect that comes from a caring counselor, and guidance in making practical decisions. Ultimately, the Christian counselor wants to help the couple maintain and heal the marriage, but when the risk of further violence seems high, it may be wise to help the abused mate and children get away from the danger and withdraw, at least temporarily, to a place of security and safety. This could be the home of a church family, but it also may mean the use of a community emergency shelter for abused spouses and children. When this removal seems best, you would be wise to get the advice and guidance of community resources, such as a lawyer, law enforcement officials, or medical personnel. Once again, it is important to remember that whenever you suspect abuse, you must report it. This is a requirement that is not limited to counselors. Many counselors lack experience in this kind of social intervention, so it is helpful to know what community assistance is available and what legal issues might be involved.[50]

Once the immediate danger is lessened, counseling is likely to focus on issues of guilt, low self-esteem, the biblical position on husband-wife relationships, the difficulty of learning to forgive, and the battered mate's feelings of guilt, anger, discouragement, hopelessness, and worries about coping in the future. Later, the counselor may be involved in helping the husband and wife deal with issues of communication, conflict resolution, sexual adjustment, husband-wife roles, trust, and other issues of marriage counseling.

6. *Helping the Victims of Elder Abuse.* Maurice Chevalier once said that "growing

old isn't so bad when you consider the alternative." For many older people, the alternative—death—would seem to be much better, especially if one's life is bombarded with physical or psychological abuse. This abuse does not come only from younger family members. Sometimes, the elderly are abused by hospital personnel, employees of nursing homes, neighborhood vandals, their own mates, or impatient workers in stores or government offices. Since few older people seek counseling, it is probable that the pastor may be the first to suspect elder abuse.

Whenever an older person talks about mistreatment, the counselor can listen with sympathy and sensitivity. Remember that some older people are unable to think clearly, and their reports of mistreatment may be more imagined than real. It is wise, therefore, to talk with care-givers, including the older person's relatives. Abuse of the elderly is more probable when older people have needs that are great, but the care-givers have limited resources or abilities to meet these needs.

Counseling often will involve support for the older person and help for the family as they learn to cope in ways that are compassionate and nonabusive. This may mean finding individuals or community and church groups who can provide emotional support for both the old person and the family, home nursing care, visitation, transportation, and other more tangible expressions of help. If the old person is in a living situation where abuse continues, he or she may need guidance and practical help in finding other accommodations.

7. *Helping the Abusers.* The victims of abuse are hurting people who often can get help from caring counselors. We have noted, however, that abusers need counseling too, but instead they more often are condemned, ignored, and incarcerated without treatment. As a result, a large number of untreated abusers and sex offenders repeat the violence after their release from prison.

Treating abusers is not easy. At least at the beginning, many abusers deny what they have done, excuse their actions, or try to shift the blame onto the victim or somebody else.[51] Perhaps it is not surprising that recurrences of battering are reduced when abusers are arrested. The reality of fines, imprisonment, and social disgrace makes denial less possible and forces at least the first-time abusers to get serious about counseling.

Counseling abusers can be a long-term process dealing with the counselee's anger, low self-esteem, and lack of self-control. Many lack communication, problem-solving, conflict-resolution, and stress-management skills. Since many victimizers were earlier victims of abuse, it often is important to deal with attitudes and insecurities that have built up over a lifetime. Some abusive counselees have never learned how to express their feelings—especially their feelings of anger—in nonviolent, socially appropriate ways.[52] Some have rigid and domineering attitudes about leadership or the role of the husband or parent. Others are entrenched in erroneous beliefs—such as the myths that victims enjoy the battering, that victims encourage it, or that violence is the macho way to assert authority and demonstrate masculinity. All these attitudes must be challenged and changed if abuse is to stop.[53] This is time-consuming work, best done by experienced and patient counselors.

Although individual counseling can be helpful with abusers, there also is value in group treatment. By meeting with other abusers, the counselee sees people who understand because they have similar problems. As they interact in the group, counselees can learn to express feelings in ways that are nonviolent, feel acceptance and support, and learn how to develop needed communication, stress-management, anger control, and other social skills. Old attitudes can be challenged, sometimes by victims of abuse who are invited to tell what it was like to be abused so abusers can see that victims do not enjoy the experience. Since many abusers lack the social skills needed for responsible community living, group counseling becomes an education in violence-free living and interacting.

Abusers also need to understand forgiveness, including the ability to forgive themselves. They need to see that abuse is a serious sin, but it is not an unpardonable sin. The God who forgives can and will give pardon, help, and guidance to those who sincerely want to rebuild their lives and live in ways that do not hurt others. To be a helper in this rebuilding process can be a demanding but highly fulfilling role for any counselor.

8. *Helping the Counselor.* After many years of working intensively with trauma victims, Diane Langberg writes about the profound impact that comes to counselors who listen to the pain of others. Over time, counselors themselves can begin to experience the symptoms of trauma that their counselees show. Sometimes called secondary or vicarious trauma, this is a mental-health problem for counselors and for medical personnel and others who work with trauma victims.[54] Confronted with so much pain and evil, in time the helpers begin to experience the anxiety, fear, hypervigilance, sleeplessness, nightmares, and anger that their counselees feel. Often they develop growing cynicism, pessimism, and hopelessness. Some even begin to challenge their faith. Trauma counselors can feel isolated, vulnerable to spiritual struggles, and unable to handle the stress. It is not surprising that this leads many trauma workers and counselors to leave their jobs and move to work settings that are less demanding.

How do counselors protect themselves against the long-term harmful influences that come from working with these counselees? Langberg gives five recommendations:[55]

- Know yourself, including how you react to stress, criticism, personal anxieties, and depression. A lack of self-understanding can make the stresses worse.
- Set limits. This includes limiting your exposure to traumatic material, not dwelling on details of your counselee's trauma or sharing this with others, determining how many of these counselees you can handle without wearing yourself down.
- Maintain strong professional connections. This allows you to keep perspective, to share with other counselors or pastors, and to get a broader perspective on your field.
- Maintain a healthy personal life. This includes making time for play, rest, family, friends, and activities that have nothing to do with trauma.
- Develop your spiritual life through worship, study, prayer, and other spiritual disciplines. This involves friendships and other associations with fellow believers.

9. *Some Ethical Issues.* Abuse is not limited to physical violence. Sometimes, other forms of abuse can be equally disruptive. These include verbal battering, sexual harassment, expressions of racism or sexism, discrimination against the elderly (often known as ageism), homophobia (the fear and hatred of homosexuals), hazing on college campuses, economic subjugation, inhumane treatment of

prisoners, or bullying in schools.[56] Sexual harassment, for example, has been compared to tiny drops of water. Each drop may be of minor importance and have a very small effect, but months and years of regular droplets erode even the hardest of substances. It is difficult to intervene in this "droplet" kind of abuse, but whenever a counselor encounters violence of any kind, the counselor is confronted with at least three important ethical issues.

The first concerns what we do when we have *suspicions of abuse*. Do we ignore our suspicions, try to forget them, or investigate further? Counselors are not law enforcement agents, so we are not free to investigate in ways that are open to the police. We are required by law to report suspicions of abuse, but this can have major consequences if we have very limited evidence but make a report nevertheless.

Perhaps the best way to get information is to ask. Some counselors inquire about abuse as part of their first-meeting evaluations with every counselee. Asking is part of the routine initial assessment. This can be done in nonthreatening ways. Instead of asking outright if a person has ever been abused, approach it through general questions about the counselee's childhood. "Tell me about your background." "What was the best thing that happened in your childhood?" "What was the worst thing that happened?" "How was discipline handled?" "Did anything happen that, today, you would view as abuse?" "Did a family member or other person ever hurt you or do anything to you sexually?" Questions like these are less threatening and appear to be a part of getting to know the counselee better. Of course, in most counseling, these kinds of questions will be answered easily without a need to pursue them further.[57]

The second ethical issue concerns *confidentiality*. Effective counselors respect the privacy of their counselees and commit to confidentiality, but what does one do if a counselee has been harmed physically and is in danger of being harmed again? How do we respond when we learn that innocent children are being victimized by abusive parents or other adults? What is the responsibility of a pastor or other counselor if he or she discovers that some innocent party is in danger? Do we break confidentiality to warn the victim? At the beginning of counseling, most professionals inform their counselees in writing that in situations like this, confidentiality will not be maintained.

As we have seen repeatedly, some ethical decisions have been resolved by the government by requiring mandatory reporting if evidence of abuse exists. This has raised concerns among some pastors and professional counselors. If you suspect abuse, for example, report it as the law requires, and then discover that your suspicions were wrong, what will be the consequences? Will the counselor be sued? When the reported abuse incidents cannot be substantiated, this can leave the suspected abusers feeling very angry and emotionally mistreated, especially if the report has become public knowledge in the community or church. Clearly, it is important for every counselor to be familiar with the reporting laws of his or her community or country.

Organizations of professional and pastoral counselors have standards of ethics that emphasize the importance of confidentiality. When counselees threaten to harm themselves or others, however, professional counselors are ethically bound to warn or otherwise protect people (including counselees) who are in danger. Often, of course, the counselee has no intention to harm others despite his or her talk, but when the threat appears to be serious, the counselor has a legal and professional responsibility to give a warning.

It can be helpful to remember that confidentiality is not the same as secrecy. Secrecy is the absolute promise to never reveal information to anyone, regardless of the circumstance. Confidentiality is the promise to hold information in trust and to share it with others only if this is in the best interest of the counselee or sometimes in the interest of society. On occasion the counselor needs to break confidence in order to take action that is likely to prevent violence. This, rather than infringement on anybody's rights, surely is the intent of many professional statements of ethics and mandatory reporting laws.

A third and closely related issue concerns direct counselor *intervention* in a counselee's life. Assume, for example, that you are the pastor of a church who one night discovers a deacon's wife at the door begging for protection from her abusive husband. Most of us would agree that the woman should be taken in and not sent home, but the counselor's responsibility also may extend to getting victims to medical treatment facilities, helping abuse victims—including children and the elderly—get out of an abusive home situation, calling the police, or otherwise getting involved in helping those who cannot help themselves. For the Christian, the act of helping the abused and abusers cannot always be confined to a comfortable counseling office.

Preventing Abuse

What would motivate young people or political activists to walk into a peaceful school setting and begin shooting randomly? It has happened in different parts of the world within recent years, and it always leads to shock, grief, pain, intense fear, and emotional trauma in the lives of teachers, parents, and especially young students. This extreme form of abuse is part of a broader picture of school violence that includes bullying, ridicule, fistfights, and sometimes individual shootings. In response, counselors are working together with community and school officials to develop positive and supportive school environments, to teach social skills, and to assess and treat children who are at risk for violent behavior.[58]

In addition, some counselors and community people have established telephone hotlines to give immediate, twenty-four-hour access for people who are victims of abuse, neglect, or other forms of mistreatment. It is well known that the development of self-help and support groups can be helpful for both victims and abusers.

Churches, especially those that are larger and with more resources, have developed peer support groups, telephone crisis lines, safe shelters for battered women and their children, and education for church attendees. In some communities, smaller churches band together to partner with schools, police departments, and other community agencies to promote educative and preventive programs. The following are additional suggestions.

1. *Education.* Throughout communities, including Christian communities, public education and awareness is good prevention. Several years ago the American Psychological Association developed a program called Adults and Children Together (ACT) Against Violence. It was designed to provide psychologists and other counselors with information about the abuse of children, and with tools to help prevent

violence in children's lives. Working with community agencies, teachers, juvenile justice officials, police officers, and others, counselors got involved in spreading violence prevention information and in teaching skills to adults.[59]

Educational programs for preventing violence and sexual assault on college campuses have existed for a longer period of time and have focused largely on providing information for both women and men. Assault is less frequent when students know how to protect themselves, what to do in case of an attack, where to report violence or suspected abuse, what is myth and what is factual about abuse, or where to get further information. Similar results have been reported with teenagers who live in violent neighborhoods. When they have information about how to handle stress or are given violence managing strategies, the attacks tend to be fewer.[60]

Busy counselors have limited time for prevention, but those who get involved, even minimally, can see the benefits of providing awareness and skills that prevent future violence.

2. *Stimulate Individual and Family Stability.* As we have seen, abuse often occurs in families where there is intense stress, misunderstanding of husband-wife or parent-child roles, or an inability to cope with family or neighborhood pressures. By helping people deal with the demands of child-rearing, marital pressures, or the needs of elderly parents, we can reduce some of the underlying causes that lead to abuse. Even in high-violence neighborhoods, children with close family bonds are less likely to experiment with delinquency. In contrast, violence, fighting, vandalism, and other forms of misbehavior most often come when children have been raised in homes where parents lack effective parenting skills. These may not be violent or unloving parents. Often, they are parents who are overwhelmed by the demands of child-rearing. When these parents get help from counselors, teachers, churches, or seminars, delinquency in their children is much less likely to occur.[61]

3. *Teaching Interpersonal Skills.* The previous paragraphs have mentioned repeatedly that abusers often lack skills in effective communication, handling conflict, dealing with feelings, solving problems, negotiating when there are differences of opinion, managing anger, or coping with stress and crises. Often the best way to prevent abuse is to teach abusers and their victims how to handle life more effectively, especially when stresses arise.[62]

4. *Social Action.* Ultimately, prevention will have to focus on ways to eliminate some of the psychological and social environmental issues that stimulate abuse and battering.

All of this may seem far removed from the work of Christian counselors or from the ministry of the local church. Throughout the Bible, however, there is an emphasis on helping the sojourner, the orphan, the widow, the poor, the helpless, and those who are in need. In today's society, surely no person is more powerless than the victim of abuse. The follower of Jesus Christ has a responsibility to give help and protection to those who, for a variety of reasons, have become abused and abusers.

Conclusions About Abuse

She's an adult now, but when Sharon Bates was nine years old, she recorded a song that became a hit recording. Written in reaction to a news report about child abuse, the lyrics began, "Dear Mr. Jesus, I just had to write to you; something really scared me when I saw it on the news. A story about a little girl beaten black and blue." The song concluded with the words, "Dear Mr. Jesus, please tell me what to do. And please don't tell my daddy, but my mommy hits me too."*

All over the country, radio stations received requests to play the song. After playing it, one New York City radio station began getting three thousand calls a day, many from callers who wanted to share their own experiences with abuse. Some stations followed the song with the telephone numbers for child abuse hot-lines, and many of these counseling facilities suddenly were swamped with calls. When Sharon Bates was flooded with requests for personal appearances, her Christian parents humbly concluded that all of this came from God. They decided that much of the money generated by Sharon's unexpected stardom should be donated to child-abuse charities.

"You can go on with child-abuse announcements all you want," suggested the program director of a Chicago radio station, "but this song causes an emotion in you that you really are not prepared for. People call to say thank you for playing the record. And that's never happened before."

This chapter began with the story of a counselor named Janice who was raped in the hallway outside her office. Sometime later her attacker was caught and brought to trial. When she entered the courtroom to give her testimony, the man was in chains, guarded by two armed deputies, but Janice felt a flood of emotions as she looked her attacker in the face. After his conviction and as part of his sentencing, Janice was allowed to deliver a Victim's Impact Statement. It was not a "Dear Mr. Jesus" song, but a letter that she read the courtroom. In part, Janice wrote:

> I don't wish you harm in prison. Even in prison . . . I hope you reflect upon what kind of person you are and what you have done, and decide, in whatever way is possible in prison, to better yourself and contribute to others. . . . Though you robbed me of possessions, safety, and peace of mind, I would not let you take away what I value most. I would not allow this trauma to keep me from focusing on what is most important to me. I still have the love of my family and friends, the values and customs we share, the joys and sorrows of our lives together, and the richness of our relationships. I am grateful to God that you could not harm any of these.[63]

The abuse and family violence that were prominent when Sharon Bates sang her song and when Janice read her letter still bring horror to many lives. They are big issues for many victims and their families and, in some ways, for many perpetrators. They are issues that no church or Christian counselor can ignore—least of all, people like us who have been alerted to the pressing needs of those who are the victims and the perpetrators of abuse.

* Lyrics to "Dear Mr. Jesus" reprinted by permission, all rights reserved, words and music by Richard Klender, © 1985 Klenco, Inc. (Klenco Music Group).

KEY POINTS FOR BUSY COUNSELORS

➤ Abuse is difficult to define, perhaps because the term covers so many forms of physical and psychological maltreatment. Abuse includes neglect as well as child, mate, elder, sexual, emotional and spiritual mistreatment, and exploitation and neglect of one individual by another.

➤ The Bible speaks honestly about violence, but abuse is never condoned. Especially in the New Testament, nonviolence is stressed and retribution is prohibited. This does not prevent victims and their families and counselors from taking action to bring justice within the legal system, to prevent further abuse, to protect victims from additional harm, and ultimately to bring about the nonabusive ideals that Scripture teaches.

➤ There is no concise list of the causes of abuse, but the following can contribute to abusive actions:
  - Environmental stress.
  - Past learning that teaches people to abuse.
  - The perpetrator's personality.
  - Cultural influences, such as violent television or movies and the general cultural acceptance of violence.

➤ Abuse can impact people in a variety of ways. Most of the symptoms of abuse can be summarized under the headings of emotional responses (feelings), influences on thinking, changes in action, and spiritual influences.

➤ Counseling often undergoes several states. These include:
  - Helping people deal with the traumatic impact of the abuse.
  - Walking with counselees through a stage of denial.
  - A healing stage that involves talking about memories and ongoing emotions, facing the reality of what has happened, forgiving the perpetrator, and being helped to pick up the responsibilities of daily living and moving forward with life.

➤ There are general principles for counseling, but often there are unique interventions with people who:
  - Are children who have been victims of child abuse.
  - Have been neglected.
  - Are adult victims of incest and abuse.
  - Are victims of rape or attempted rape.
  - Have been victimized by their marital partners.
  - Have experienced elder abuse.
  - Are the perpetrators of abuse.
  - Are counselors of the abused and their abusers.

- ➤ There are unique ethical issues involved in dealing with these people.
- ➤ Abuse prevention involves:
  - Education to help people understand abuse and learn how to protect themselves against it.
  - Strengthening family ties and building stronger families.
  - Teaching interpersonal skills.
  - Taking social action to counteract abuse.
- ➤ No Christian counselor can ignore the prevalence of abuse and neglect or can overlook the need for counseling and preventive efforts.

PART FIVE

Identity Issues

23

Inferiority and Self-Esteem

Jason is the captain of his school basketball team. Affirmed by his coach, popular among his classmates, genuinely liked by his teammates, and cheered by the crowds at his school games, Jason is an outstanding basketball player. Everybody agrees.

Except Jason.

Sometimes, he wonders why he never feels good enough. His friends tell him to be less hard on himself. Jason will admit that he has good athletic ability, and he knows, in his heart, that he is better than anybody else on the team. But he sets such high standards for himself that he never is satisfied, no matter how well he plays. After the games he thinks about the baskets that he missed rather than the shots he scored. He constantly compares himself with players on other teams who are better, and he doubts that he is good enough to pursue his dream of a career in professional sports.

Jason grew up in a stable family, but his dad never came to the games. His mother believed that pride is the greatest sin, and she often told her children that people who think good things about themselves are "just showing off" and pretending to be "big shots." Only recently has Jason begun to realize that his mother has deep insecurities of her own—insecurities that she passes on in a desire to help her children develop humility. Instead, Jason and his siblings have been molded to feel deeply inferior and inadequate no matter what they do. Some have given up, accepted their inferiority, and may never change. Jason wants to succeed, but in his own eyes his accomplishments are never good enough, regardless of the affirmation and applause that come from others.

There are many people like Jason. They feel inferior, inadequate, insecure. A century ago, William James, the early American psychologist, wrote that mental anguish often follows when people believe they are insignificant and unworthy. On the other side of the Atlantic, Austrian psychiatrist Alfred Adler concluded that every person has feelings of inferiority. Sometimes, these feelings push people toward healthy actions and achievements, but inferiority feelings also can be so overwhelming that they cause us to withdraw from others and to develop what Adler called an "inferiority complex." Because of inferiority feelings, we compare ourselves to others, and this leaves us feeling even more inadequate and inferior. Adler believed that the way to escape this inferiority trap is to stop making comparisons and to give up the natural human striving for superiority. In later years, others proposed that people overcome their feelings of inferiority by developing a positive and healthy self-esteem.

The word *self-esteem* appears frequently in our language along with related terms such as *self-image* and *self-concept*.[1] Self-image and self-concept refer to the mental pictures we have of ourselves. The pictures usually include a listing of character traits, strengths, weaknesses, abilities, and physical features. Self-esteem means something slightly different. This term refers to the evaluation that an individual makes about his or her worth, competence, and significance. Whereas self-image and self-concept involve a self-description, self-esteem involves a self-evaluation.

These terms overlap, and often they are preceded by adjectives such as *good, bad, positive,* or *negative.* People who have good self-concepts, for example, tend to describe themselves using desirable words—like *competent, confident, understanding,* or *patient.* People who have a positive self-esteem evaluate themselves as being worthwhile and capable. Low self-esteem is the opposite. It involves negative opinions about oneself, beliefs that one is incompetent, unworthy, and inferior to others. All these self-perceptions are carried around in our minds, and often they change as the result of our experiences or the opinions we hear from others. Sometimes, however, they become deeply ingrained and stubbornly maintained in spite of contrary evidence. Almost always they influence how we think, act, feel, plan for the future, and present ourselves to others.

The importance of a good self-image and positive self-esteem has become almost universally accepted by mental-health professionals, at least in the United States and Canada. Many approaches to counseling in the mid-twentieth century focused on the goal of helping counselees improve their self-concepts. In his book *Reality Therapy,* for example, William Glasser wrote about the need to help people feel that they are worthwhile to themselves and to others.[2] Carl Rogers, who probably was the most influential of the self-esteem psychologists, wrote about the importance of self-worth and unconditional positive regard. Humanistic theorists taught about the need for people to believe in themselves, to care for themselves, and to gain self-esteem. In all of this, the underlying message seemed to be that "everyone has a problem with a deep-rooted sense of inferiority," and that everyone needs a more positive self-concept.[3] These ideas became prominent in schools that emphasized children's self esteem, in business, on television, and even in the church. In one of his earlier books, popular pastor Robert Schuller called self-esteem "the greatest need facing the human race today," our "universal hope," and the basis for a "new reformation" that would carry us forward from the Protestant Reformation of Luther and Calvin.[4]

This focus on overcoming inferiority and building self-esteem led to a heated debate among many Christians. Today, much of the fury has subsided, but the debate still continues in some places. Well-known Christian counselor Jay Adams became a strong critic of terms like *self-esteem, self-love,* and *self-image.* He used words like *paganism* and *a plague* to describe the self-esteem movement, and has argued that Scripture focuses on human sinfulness and self-denial rather than on self-worth or self-affirmation. The Bible is not intended to "make us satisfied with ourselves as we are, but to *destroy* any satisfaction that may exist," Adams wrote. "You must treat yourself like a criminal, and put self to death every day."[5] Though far removed from the Adams camp, psychologist Paul Vitz has taken a similar view in a book that criticizes our modern overemphasis on the self and calls psychology a new religion that is based on worship of the self.[6]

Writing from a rich background of clinical experience, counselor David Carlson takes a different approach. Carlson realizes how many people are devastated by a poor self-image, but in his view the solution is not to give a pep talk designed to boost the self-image. Instead, people need to be helped to find a biblical kind of self-esteem.

Self-love, as I understand the concept biblically and psychologically, includes the following: (1) accepting myself as a child of God who is lovable, valuable, capable; (2) being willing to give up considering myself the center of the world; (3) recognizing my need of God's forgiveness and redemption. Christian self-esteem results from translating "I am the greatest, wisest, strongest, best" to "I am what I am, a person made in God's image, a sinner redeemed by God's grace, and a significant part in the body of Christ."[7]

As Christian counselors, we are likely to encounter many people who feel inferior and have a poor self-esteem, although the problem may not be as prevalent as some earlier writers have suggested. Because of the debates and confusion about self-esteem, it is crucial that we understand and share the biblical teaching about human worth. It is then that we can be most effective in helping people overcome their feelings of inferiority. It is then, too, that we can develop understanding and self-perceptions based on the truths of Scripture.

The Bible and Self-Esteem

The notion of self-esteem, as we think of it today, was not a part of the cultural world in which the Bible was written.[8] The words we have been using, like *self-love, self-image,* or *self-concept* are psychological terms that were never used in biblical times or by biblical writers. However, the Bible does teach about human nature and about God's creation of human beings, and from this we can reach conclusions about inferiority and self-esteem.

1. *The Biblical Teaching About Human Worth.* The Bible constantly affirms that human beings are valuable in God's sight. We were created in God's image with intellectual abilities, the capacity to communicate, the freedom to make choices, a knowledge of right and wrong, and the responsibility to administer and rule over the rest of creation.[9] Since we were created in God's image, we possess great value and significance—not because of what we think about ourselves or what we have made of ourselves but because of how we were made by God. Even after the Fall, we are described as "a little lower than God" (and lower than angels) but crowned with "glory and honor."[10] Because he loves us, God sent his own Son to pay for our sins and to make possible our redemption and renewed communion with God the Father.[11] He has sent angels to guard us, the Holy Spirit to guide us, and the Scriptures to teach us. We are the salt of the earth and the light of the world. Individuals who trust in God will spend eternity with him in a place prepared for us in heaven.[12] The Bible is full of evidence that shows our eternal value in the sight of God.

2. *The Biblical Teaching About Human Sin.* The Bible teaches that because of Adam's disobedience, sin entered the world. As a result, all people are sinners who have become alienated from God and condemned because of their sinful natures and actions.[13] Sin is rebellion against God. It represents a doubting of God's truthfulness and a challenge to his perfect will. Sin leads to interpersonal conflict, attempts at self-justification, a tendency to blame others for our weaknesses, psychosomatic problems, verbal and physical aggression, tension, and a lack of respect for God.[14] All of this influences the way we feel about ourselves, often producing guilt and undoubtedly lowering our self-esteem.

Even in our fallen state, however, God still loves and values us. He hates the sin but loves the sinner. He knows that we are ungodly and helpless, but this does not mean that we are unredeemable and worthless. Indeed, because of his love and mercy, he sent his son to die so that we could be redeemed, made righteous, and brought back into his family as fully forgiven sons and daughters.[15]

Sin breaks one's relationship with God, but sin does not negate the fact that in God's sight we human beings are still at the apex of divine creation, and of immense worth and value.

3. *The Biblical Teaching About Pride and Humility.* Some Christians who believe in the concept of human sinfulness have argued that self-esteem is a form of pride. Since pride is greatly abhorred by God,[16] these believers assume that self-condemnation and inferiority are attitudes that keep us humble. From this perspective, inferiority and low self-esteem are not the cause of most human problems, as some psychologists believe. Instead, inferiority feelings are more good than bad because they keep us from pride.

Pride is an exaggerated, often arrogant, unreasonably high opinion of oneself in relation to others. It involves taking a superior attitude that disregards the concerns, opinions, and desires of other people. In essence, it is an attempt to claim for oneself the glory that rightly belongs to God. Although Scripture condemns it, Western thinking and much of modern psychology see less difficulty with pride than with inferiority and low self-esteem.[17]

Even as pride tends to be ignored in psychological writings, humility also has been of little interest. The emerging field of positive psychology recently has demonstrated a fresh interest in the value of humility,[18] but over the years, psychological writers have tended to view humility as a religious concept that has little psychological relevance. In dictionaries, humility tends to be equated to inferiority and defined as an attitude of low opinion of one's importance or value.

This is very different from the New Testament picture where humility is viewed as an accurate self-appraisal, a freedom from inflated self-importance, and a healthy interest in the needs of others. The humble person accepts his or her imperfections, sins, and failures, but also acknowledges the gifts, abilities, and achievements that have come from God. Humility is not a self-negation or the rejection of our God-given strengths and abilities. Humility involves a grateful dependence on God and a realistic appraisal of both strengths and weaknesses.

Two New Testament passages present the clearest biblical perspective on humility. Both point to the humility of Christ. In Matthew 11:29, Jesus describes himself as being humble and gentle. He was aware of his dependence on God the Father, he showed a servant mentality as he stooped to wash the disciples' feet, but he never expressed inferiority, self-debasement, or low self-esteem. In Philippians 2:1–11, we read about Jesus taking on the form of a servant and humbling himself in obedience to God. Here we see humility alongside a positive self-esteem but with no hint of arrogant pride. The apostle Paul was deeply aware of his sinful past and continuing imperfections, but he also recognized that he had been redeemed and greatly used by God. His was a realistic self-image. It was characterized not by pride, but by a humble evaluation of what God had done and was doing through him. Self-esteem, a realistic self-appraisal, and humility go together.

4. *The Biblical Teaching About Self-Love.* The Bible assumes that we will love ourselves.[19] This conclusion is difficult for some Christians to accept because they

equate self-love with an attitude of superiority, stubborn self-will, or self-centered pride. Self-love, however, is not an erotic, neurotic, or ecstatic self-adoration. Self-love means to see ourselves as sinners who have been saved by grace—people who are created, valued and loved by God, gifted members of the body of Christ (if we are Christians), and bearers of the divine image. We can love ourselves because God loves us, his Spirit lives within us, and we can gratefully accept the abilities and opportunities that God has given. This biblical view of self-love must become the basis of self-esteem.

Undoubtedly, some of the disagreement about self-esteem comes because basic terms are defined differently. For example, self-worth must not be considered the same as self-worship, self-love is not the same as selfishness or self-centeredness, and self-affirmation is different from self-conceit. We can be aware of ourselves without being absorbed in ourselves. Self-denial is not the same as self-denigration, putting off the sinful nature is not the same as putting yourself down, humility is different from humiliation, and being unworthy is not the same as being worthless.[20] The Christian can have positive self-esteem, not because of human works and human nature, but because of God's grace and divine redemption.

The Causes of Inferiority and Low Self-Esteem

There can be numerous causes for low self-esteem and feelings of inferiority.

For example, self-esteem often is low in people with physical deficits such as handicaps, unattractive features, or obesity.[21] Poor children show more evidences of inferiority than those who grow up in better home situations.[22] Members of minority groups often are made to feel inferior due to racism that degrades people because of their skin color or ethnicity and "systematically denies access or privilege to one racial group while perpetrating access or privilege to members of another racial group."[23] Even the country or culture where one lives can have an impact on self-esteem. Unlike many Eastern or Middle Eastern countries, Western societies focus on individual achievement, independence, autonomy, self-sufficiency, and competition. In these countries, people find their identity less in their families or groups and more in their personal accomplishments and successes. When success does not come, feelings of inadequacy and inferiority often appear instead. To a large extend, therefore, inferiority and low self-esteem are stimulated more by some cultures than by others.[24] In some countries the whole population seems to view themselves as being inferior to the people of other, often more-developed countries. This can lead both to feelings of inferiority in the citizens and often to anger at the perceived inequities. Additional reasons for inferiority and low-self-esteem in your counselees could include the following.

1. *Faulty Theological Beliefs.* As we have seen, any of us will feel inferior if we conclude that all humans are worthless, that sin makes us of no significance to God, and that the way to be humble is to condemn ourselves and even deny the gifts and abilities that the Lord God has given to each of his children. All of these views are held by sincere people, many of whom assume, incorrectly, that self-esteem is wrong or that feelings of inferiority should typify committed Christians.[25]

In talking to his disciples, Jesus said, "If anyone wants to be my follower, you must put aside your selfish ambition, shoulder your cross, and follow me. If you try to keep your life for yourself, you will lose it. But if you give up your life for me, you will find true life."[26] Committed Christians do not live self-centered, self-gratifying, self-affirming lives. Instead, we are to abandon selfish personal ambition so we can serve Christ sacrificially.[27] It does not follow, however, that the person who denies selfish ambition or the drive for personal gratification also must deny his or her God-given gifts and abilities. Believers have been forgiven, adopted into God's family, and endowed with special gifts and responsibilities that enable us to serve Christ and the church more effectively.[28] When we deny the existence of these gifts or strengths and revel in our inferiority, we are engaging in self-deception rather than self-denial.

2. *Sin and Guilt.* When God created human beings, he gave us a standard of right and wrong, guidelines for living in accordance with his universal principles. When we violate these principles, we are guilty, and as a result we feel remorse, shame, and disappointment in ourselves. This contributes to our feelings of inferiority and undermines self-esteem, especially if we never experience forgiveness.

3. *Parent-Child Relationships.* Counselors generally agree that the basis for a child's self-esteem is formed during his or her early years. Most parents are inconsistent in their child-rearing and feelings about their children. Even the most patient parent explodes in criticism at times or withholds acceptance and warmth. Children rarely, if ever, are damaged by such minor parental fluctuations, but more lasting feelings of inferiority come when parents:

- Criticize, shame, reject, and scold repeatedly.
- Frequently remind their children that they are not as good as their siblings or other children.
- Express the expectation that the child probably will fail and not amount to anything significant.
- Ridicule, neglect, or ignore their children and their activities or accomplishments.
- Set unrealistic standards and goals.
- Punish repeatedly and harshly.
- Indicate that from the parental perspective, the child is stupid, inadequate, a bad athlete, or in other ways incompetent.
- Imply that children are a nuisance.
- Avoid cuddling, hugging, affectionate touching, or other expressions of love.
- Overprotect or dominate children so they are more likely to fail when forced to be on their own.
- Constantly yell at the kids, giving the message that what they do is always wrong.

These rarely are deliberate attempts to create inferiority in children. More often they are child-rearing practices that emerge, become established ways to control children, and have the effect of destroying the child's feelings of value. At times probably every counselor hears some variation of this sentence, "My mother (or father) told me all the time that I was no good, and I just came to believe it. Now it is hard to change."

4. *Experiences of Defeat or Failure.* In a society that values success and accomplishments, it is difficult to accept failure, rejection, and criticism. A person who has failed to reach some important goal or who has been belittled can conclude that he or she is of no value: "Look at what people think of me" is the prevailing

thought. "Look how I mess things up." This is accentuated in cultures that value people based on what they accomplish rather than on who they are. When this is the prevailing view, people who don't succeed are made to feel worthless. If their peers, siblings, or colleagues succeed, jealousy can appear, and this further contributes to low self-esteem.[29]

I saw this during my years as a seminary professor. Classmates would graduate on the same day and go forth to start their ministries. Several years later, some of these people would be pastors of growing churches, while others had churches that appeared to be struggling and showed no evidence of effectiveness or growth. Had I chosen to ask, all these pastors would have agreed that God is sovereign and that he chooses to bless some with growing ministries but not others.[30] They also would have agreed that from a purely human perspective, some of them were successful, whereas others, perhaps equally dedicated, were not successful. As I write these words I can think of several former students and pastor friends who have struggled. Some have left the ministry in discouragement. They may have squelched feelings of jealousy as they have watched their more prominent classmates, but in their hearts these disappointed leaders feel like failures, inferior, wounded, and with lowered self-esteem.[31] This is a picture that applies far beyond the ministry and into the lives of counselors and to many of the people who come for counseling.

Sometimes, failure does not come because we tried and failed, but because others expect us to fail. In situations like this, people may be motivated to try harder and prove that the nay-sayers are wrong. Others conclude that since they are not expected to succeed, there is no purpose in trying. With this attitude, nothing is ventured, so nothing is gained. Failure is assured, and self-esteem erodes further.

5. *Unrealistic Expectations.* As they grow up, most people develop expectations for the future and ideals that they would like to attain. When these expectations and ideals are unrealistically high, failure is more likely and feelings of inferiority can follow.

6. *Faulty Thinking.* Sometimes, we assume that high achievers and successful people rarely have doubts about their abilities and competency, but this is not necessarily true. Many high achievers reach their goals but feel insecure in their positions of success. Some may wonder if they really are as competent as others assume. Few high achievers ever measure up to their own standards of excellence. Some even wonder if their successes came because of chance rather than as a result of personal competence. A young man who became an outstanding quarterback told a reporter, "I first got to throw the ball because the coach was frustrated. We were losing so badly that he decided he had nothing to lose by choosing me." Another student confessed, "I only got into graduate school because the dean knew my dad." Even though others may view them as being bright and talented, many of these people feel like imposters. They have successful careers, but they also have inferiority feelings because of the way they think about themselves.[32]

Psychologists sometimes write about self-talk. This is the conversation that goes on in our minds most of the time. It is conversation that allows us to think through issues, plan for the future, and guide our behavior. Some of the ideas that run through our minds are assumptions that we have learned to accept and that undermine self-esteem. Here are examples.

- I must meet other people's standards and expectations if I am to be accepted and loved.
- Whenever I fail to reach my goals and expectations (or the expectations of others), I should feel pressured, ashamed, or a failure.[33]
- If I don't succeed as an athlete, hostess, businessperson, or parent (or whatever other role is important), then I am inadequate.
- I should do what (some significant person or group) expects me to do.
- I've got to win. Failure is unacceptable.
- I'm a phony. I'm not nearly as good as other people think I am.

Some counselors have described these as the lies we believe.[34] They are statements that we rehearse in our minds, even though they may have little or no basis in reality. They are thoughts that can set us up for failure, feelings of inferiority, and low self-esteem. If it is not to control us, thinking like this must be challenged, perhaps by a friend or counselor, or counteracted with more realistic self-talk. Where is the solid evidence to support the erroneous conclusions we hold about ourselves?

7. *Community Influences and Myths.* Every society has values that are emphasized by the mass media and demonstrated in homes, schools, governments, businesses, and social settings. In many cultures, for example, it is widely assumed that a person's worth depends on one's intelligence, physical attractiveness, education, money, powers, and achievements. People sometimes are encouraged to manipulate circumstances and one another to attain and retain these symbols of success. Many people believe that possessing these symbols will increase one's self-esteem, that their loss or non-attainment increases one's sense of inferiority. This is a cultural myth that can lead to lowered self-esteem when the status symbols are not attained, when they are attained and found to be meaningless, or when they are acquired and then lost.

The Effects of Inferiority and Low Self-Esteem

All of us have heard inspiring stories of people who faced handicaps or other great obstacles and then, with unflinching determination, rose to overcome the deficiencies. Whenever he ran for public office, Abraham Lincoln lost the election, but he persisted until he was elected president of the United States. Another president, Theodore Roosevelt, was a nearsighted and sickly child who learned boxing and horseback riding in order to toughen himself. Winston Churchill failed at school but became a great statesman and communicator. As the twenty-first century began, a cancer survivor named Lance Armstrong won the grueling Tour de France repeatedly. Examples like these have led some observers to conclude that many people succeed not only despite their weaknesses and feelings of inferiority but because of them. For these people, difficult life experiences become a prod that pushes them to overcome inferiorities that hold others back.

Less admirable, perhaps, but more common are those who try to hide their inferior feelings and boost sagging self-esteem by acquiring the trappings of power or success. We may see this in insecure men who act tough, people from poor environments who go into debt so they can buy impressive cars or wear flashy clothes, or uneducated people who use big words in an effort to impress others and try to cover their sense of inferiority by showy overreactions. Perhaps the French playwright Molière had something similar in mind when he wrote *Le Bourgeouis Gentilhomme* about an ordinary man who decided to act as though he were a sophisticated gentleman.

There are other ways to react. Researchers have shown, for example, that people with feelings of inferiority may:

- Feel isolated and unlovable.
- Tend to withdraw from other people.
- Feel too weak to overcome their deficiencies, lacking in the drive or motivation to defend themselves.
- Be angry at others or at themselves, but be afraid of angering others or attracting attention.
- Have difficulty getting along with others.
- Be submissive, dependent, and so sensitive that their feelings are hurt easily.
- Have lower curiosity or creativity.
- Be less inclined to disclose themselves to others.
- Have difficulty getting along with others.
- Be jealous or critical of others.
- Have difficulty getting along with others.
- Be characterized by self-criticism, self-hatred, self-rejection, or depression.
- Be driven to gain power, superiority, or control over others.
- Not be able to accept compliments or expressions of love.
- Be poor listeners, poor losers, or both.

In their work as Christian counselors, Beverly and Tom Rodgers once worked with a highly esteemed surgeon who took a different approach in dealing with his feelings of inferiority. Peter had graduated from medical school with honors and had become renowned for his professional competence and dedication to his work and patients. When his alcoholic father died, however, Peter became very anxious, started having panic attacks, and was unable to work. The counselors learned that as a child the doctor had been severely abused and had grown up feeling wounded and worthless. Over the years, all his effort to succeed as a surgeon was an attempt to build his self-esteem and convince himself that he was worth at least something. Peter hadn't shown any of the symptoms in the above list. Instead, he brilliantly succeeded in overcoming his felt deficiencies and hiding his insecurities from others and, in many ways, from himself.[35]

All of this shows that low self-esteem can influence people in a variety of ways. Everybody feels inferior at times, but when the inferiority feelings are intense or long lasting, virtually all human actions, feelings, attitudes, thoughts, and values are affected.

Counseling People with Inferiority Feelings and Low Self-Esteem

Feelings of inferiority and low self-esteem build up over many years, so it is realistic to expect that change will come slowly.[36] Counselors can help in a variety of ways.

1. *Give Genuine Support, Acceptance, and Approval.* People who feel inferior have a tendency to respond negatively to expressions of approval or affirmation that

are perceived to be unrealistic, abrupt, or not genuine. If a counselor is too enthusiastic in giving praise or approval, counselees don't believe what they are hearing and at times may even decide to avoid the counselor. There are people who feel comfortable with their low self-concepts and do not always want to change. Thoughts that they are incompetent allow people like this to remain in a comfort zone that may not always be pleasant but that gives them excuses for not doing anything different. People with low self-esteem are not moved by a back-slapping attitude that says, "Buck up, you really are a significant person." It is more helpful to give continuing support, gentle encouragement, and mild but sincere approval for achievements that clearly can be evaluated as good.

2. *Share the Biblical Perspective on Self-Esteem.* Counseling will not be very successful if the counselee has heard or is convinced that inferiority is the same as humility or that a healthy self-esteem is equivalent to sinful pride. Christians must be helped to see the biblical teachings about human worth and self-esteem. They must be shown that self-condemnation is both destructive and wrong in the sight of God, who has redeemed us and given us a new nature. It may take a long time before ideas such as these will be accepted, but their acceptance is important, especially for believers who want to overcome feelings of inferiority.

3. *Seek to Develop Understanding and a Realistic Self-Evaluation.* Counselors recognize the value of insight in helping people search out the sources of their attitudes and learn ways to think and behave differently. Without guidance from a more objective observer, however, introspection can lead an insecure person to become more self-condemning as he or she focuses on the negative and overlooks significant facts about life that are positive. Encourage counselees to look at past experiences that may have shaped the person's thinking. Look for events that were affirming as well as condemning. Remind the counselee—often if necessary—that we need not be prisoners of the past. As we understand the past roots of behavior and thinking, we are better able to rise above these and change.

Often, it helps counselees if they can list their good traits, strengths, and assets, as well as weaknesses, inabilities, and less desirable characteristics. As the list is developed, preferably on paper, ask "What is the objective evidence (in the form of past experiences or other people's opinions, for example) that each item on the list—both positive and negative—should be there?" Remember to emphasize the counselee's strong points, special talents, or gifts and consider how each of these can be put to better use. The positive psychology movement that began in earnest at the start of this century is accumulating an impressive body of evidence to show that people function better at work, at home, and in life when they build on their strengths rather than dwelling on their weaknesses.[37] Too often, people focus so much on their weaknesses that they inhibit or deny their God-given talents and abilities.

At times, you probably will notice that some people are reluctant to acknowledge their strengths, lest they appear proud or too self-centered. For some the sharing of one's inferiorities and incompetencies also can be a subtle, often unconscious manipulation of others. When a person talks about how he or she is a failure and of no value, other people feel some pressure to deny this evaluation and give assurances that the self-condemning person is, indeed, a person of worth. This kind of praise and affirmation is neither spontaneous nor really affirming. As a result, the inferiority feelings persist.

At other times, people are reluctant to admit their strengths because they prefer to stay engrossed in their assumed inferiorities. If they admit that they have strong points, the pressure is on to develop and use these positive traits and take responsibility for their actions. That takes effort, and there is a new realization that failure is possible. For persons with a poor self-concept, the risk may seem too great. It is safer to wallow in one's inferiorities, so counselors need to gently but firmly encourage their counselees into new ways of behaving.

4. *Change Unhealthy Self-Talk.* People with low self-concepts often dwell on their inferiorities and focus their minds on self-defeating thoughts; irrational self-evaluations, thinking about their weaknesses; and on what have been called "destructive mental scripts." These are expectations of failure that often come true. When people expect to fail, often they do fail.

Some people talk openly about their incompetencies. This may be a self-protective way of announcing, "I am so incompetent that you should not expect much from me." If something is attempted and failure follows, then nobody is surprised. Sadly, when people talk enough about their inferiorities, others believe what they are hearing and the speaker's self-esteem slides lower.

Some people say nothing to others about their inferior feelings, but they keep telling themselves that they are worthless. Nobody sees these inner messages, so the self-talk is never challenged. Even so, counselees can be helped to replace the negative thoughts with thinking that is more positive. It can help if people stop dwelling on weaknesses and focus on their God-given strengths. All Christians can benefit if they apply the words of Philippians 4:8: "Fix your thoughts on what is true and honorable and right. Think about things that are pure and lovely and admirable. Think about things that are excellent and worthy of praise." In addition, urge counselees to find a few caring and supportive friends who are willing to give realistic affirmation and frequent reminders that thinking and self-talk should focus on what God has given and not on selfish ego-building. It is helpful for all of us to remember that God made each of us wonderfully complex human beings, evidence of marvelous divine workmanship.[38]

Enrico Caruso was a great Italian tenor who used self-talk whenever he was unsure of himself before a performance. When facing a demanding role, sometimes a little voice inside of his head seemed to say, "You can't do it, Enrico! You can't do it!" Caruso told his friends that he seemed to have two inner personalities, the Little Me and the Big Me. The Little Me told him that he couldn't do it. The Big Me had a different message and told him that he could do it. This Big Me voice was positive and filled with confidence.

Sometimes before a concert, Caruso would be seen backstage muttering to himself, "Get out, Little Me! Get out, Little Me!" Then Big Me would take over, and the singer would walk confidently on stage, lifted by his little self-talk experience.[39] Perhaps Caruso had never read Philippians 4:13, but this has a Big Me kind of self-talk message: "I can do everything with the help of Christ who gives me the strength I need." We succeed because of the ways in which God has equipped us and gives us strength.

5. *Stimulate the Forming and Pursuit of Realistic Goals.* There can be two kinds of goals—long-range and short-term. Long-range goals are often major (like getting a college degree, buying a house, earning a promotion, or even reading to the end of this long book). Short-term goals are more immediate and more easily attained (like completing this chapter, passing a test, finishing a do-it-yourself project, or introducing yourself to a new neighbor). Long-range goals can seem overpower-

ing and unattainable, so the person who feels inferior declines to tackle them. Counselees may be reminded, however, that long-range goals can be broken down into short-term projects. As each short-term goal is reached, we experience a sense of accomplishment and edge slightly toward our long-term aspirations.

Encourage counselees to write down their long-range goals and priorities. Then show them how to break these down into much smaller, attainable goals. As the smaller goals are reached, the individual can experience a feeling of success, with a resulting boost in self-image. There even may be value in rewarding oneself whenever a goal is reached.

In all of this, the counselor can help counselees set realistic goals that are likely to be achieved, give encouragement as the counselee attempts new activities, help the counselee evaluate what went wrong when there is failure, encourage the person to try again, and, when necessary, point out that periodic failure is not proof of one's innate inferiority.[40] There may be times when counseling involves encouraging a counselee to attend school or enroll in a training program that will make goals more attainable and failure less likely.

Counselors and their counselees can remember that no human being is completely alone. God gives strength and guidance to those who seek his help. He directs individuals in the development and attainment of goals and priorities. He helps people get more realistic and healthy self-perceptions that are consistent with biblical teaching. He also helps them develop new skills.

6. *Stimulate New Ways of Thinking.* Thoughts about inferiority and low self-esteem live in the mind. It follows, then, that one way to help counselees is to help them change their thinking. How can this be done?

- Urge counselees to avoid dwelling on the negative, to resist the natural tendency to think hypercritical thoughts, to refuse to make critical and bitter comments. When a person has been hurt by a business partner or treated unfairly by a former spouse, it is easy to think negative thoughts and to make critical comments. Many times these resentful and angry thoughts or comments have no impact on the person who caused the problem, but the bitterness comes back to hurt the one who is bitter and filled with negative thinking. It can be helpful when a counselor or accountability partner can hold the bitter person accountable for his or her negative thinking and talking. When these persist, they alienate others, arouse more anger in the critic, and further undermine the critical person's self-esteem. Bitterness can grow and corrupt many people by its poison.[41]
- Encourage counselees to give frequent encouragement, compliments, and respect to others. Respecting and affirming people whom God has created helps people respect themselves.
- Help counselees avoid behaviors that reinforce negative thinking and that, in turn, can lower self-esteem. Negative behaviors include treating other people as objects to be manipulated, dwelling on past experiences that have been painful, refusing to forgive or to make peace when relationships are strained.
- Point out behaviors in the counselee that show his or her low self-esteem, discuss these actions, and consider how they can be changed. When people act more confidently, in time they often feel more confident.
- Teach counselees to deal with sin in their lives. It is impossible to feel good

about ourselves when we deliberately disobey God's principles for our lives. Sin can lead to guilt, self-condemnation, depression, and a loss of self-esteem. Counselees must be helped, therefore, to face their sin, to confess it to God and sometimes to one or two others, to forsake it, and to remember that God forgives and forgets.[42]

■ Encourage people to forgive. The inability to forgive, especially the inability to forgive oneself, can undermine self-esteem. It is important to remember that vengeance and the administration of justice are God's responsibilities, not ours.[43] At times, all of us must ask him to help us forgive, to give up our grudges, and to really accept the fact that wrongs and injustice can be committed to God, who will both forgive those who are sorry and bring justice to unrepentant wrongdoers. At times, the counselor's greatest contribution to a counselee's self-esteem may be to help him or her accept forgiveness and learn to forgive.

■ Meditate regularly on God's Word. He loves us and communicates with us through the Bible. This book can help individuals keep a realistic perspective when there is a tendency, instead, to slip into thoughts of one's own inferiorities and incompetence.

7. *Encourage Group Support and Social Interaction.* Finding acceptance in a group of people can do much to stimulate self-esteem and help an individual feel worthwhile. Group counseling often is a helpful way to build self-esteem, providing the group members are supportive, wanting to help, and not inclined to use the group as a vehicle for criticizing other people and tearing them down. Active involvement in a church or other religious group can also boost self-esteem.

Preventing Inferiority and Low Self-Esteem

Ideally, the local church is a body of believers with a commitment to worship and world evangelism, along with a determination to teach, care for, build up, and do good deeds for one another. All of this should be free from the power struggles, manipulation, and status-seeking that characterize so much of our society. Of course, none of us is perfect, so most churches fall short of this ideal. Even so, the Christian community can have a powerful influence in changing self-concepts and preventing individual feelings of inferiority. This can come through teaching, support-giving, and parental guidance.

1. *Prevention Through Teaching.* We have seen that many people with low self-esteem have been taught that spiritual people should constantly put themselves down and feel inferior, even as insignificant as worms. Some are taught that God is either a harsh judge who is waiting to pounce on our misdeeds so he can condemn us, or a being who delights in squelching our personalities and taking the fun out of life. Harmful and distorted views like these need to be challenged and replaced with the biblical teachings on human worth, forgiveness, pride, and the importance of loving and valuing ourselves because of God's love and how he has made us.

A person's self-concept cannot depend on human goals and achievements alone. Each person's sense of belonging, worth, and competence comes because we are loved and held up by the sovereign, almighty God who teaches us about sin and divine forgiveness, endows us with unique abilities and gifts, makes us into new creatures, and gives the true reason to have a healthy self-esteem because we have been redeemed by Christ.[44]

Within the church, Christians should learn that we can love ourselves because God loves us and has made us his children. We can acknowledge and accept our abilities, gifts, and achievements because they come from God and with his permission. We can experience the forgiveness of sins because God forgives unconditionally. Furthermore, believers can praise God for what he is doing in and through our lives. There is no institution that comes near to the church in being able to educate people toward a more realistic self-concept.

2. *Prevention Through Christian Community.* Self-esteem is strengthened when people feel accepted and valued by others. Often this acceptance is found in the church, where there is care and support, especially in times of need. One feature of the emergent churches is their deliberate attempts to provide community for believers and nonbelievers alike, without smothering or overwhelming newcomers or reluctant participants. The church also can help people acquire new practical skills and values that avoid the materialism and trappings of success that are so common in society. We can learn to love one another as brothers and sisters, each of whom has important gifts and contributions to make to the body of Christ.[45] In part, this is idealistic. People's dress, bearing, and speech can reveal their social status, and the variety of cars in some parking lots shows that the congregation is divided economically. Nevertheless, since God is unimpressed with these status symbols, we should attempt to keep them from influencing our interpersonal relationships and values within the body of Christ.

3. *Prevention Through Parental Guidance.* Many self problems begin in the home, and it is there that the problems can be effectively prevented. Younger children need plenty of physical contact and spontaneous expressions of affirmation and pleasure, including times for play. Older children need encouragement, consistent discipline, praise, and time spent in communication. Parents with high self-esteem and expressions of affirmation toward one another are more likely to have children with high self-esteem. It is important, then, to help mothers and fathers overcome their inferiorities and build more positive self-concepts.

Conclusions About Inferiority and Self-Esteem

Jennifer Cochran is a psychologist who found that there were two major sources of self-esteem in the college students she studied. One group built their self-esteem on external sources, such as how well they did academically or the approval that came from others. Even though these people had good self-esteem, they also reported more stress, anger, academic problems, relationship conflicts, drug and alcohol use, and symptoms of eating disorders. The other group also had good self-esteem, but they based their self-worth on internal sources, such as being a virtuous person or adhering to moral standards. These people had higher grades, less stress, and were less likely to use alcohol and drugs or to develop eating disorders. Cochran's research team concluded that the best source of self-esteem, and the better mental health, came when people had goals and beliefs that were bigger than themselves, such as what they might be able to create or contribute to others.[46]

Maybe this sounds technical and of little interest to Christian counselors, but the research has relevance for anybody who is interested in self-esteem. When people try to impress others to build self-esteem, there can be other problems in life. But when the focus is on caring, meeting the needs of other people, developing projects, or doing things for people other than ourselves, then not only is self-esteem strong, but there are fewer other problems. The Christian believes that human worth comes from the love, words, and actions of God. We find our greatest value in knowing him, serving him, and loving others. How sad that many Christians have misunderstood biblical teaching so that feelings of inferiority have built up in themselves and in others. In contrast, it is encouraging to realize that the church and church-related counselors can play a vital role in the understanding, counseling, and prevention of low self-esteem and inferiority problems.

KEY POINTS FOR BUSY COUNSELORS

➤ Many people feel inferior, inadequate, and insecure.

➤ The words *self-image* and *self-concept* and *self-esteem* are common, but they have slightly different meanings. Whereas self-image and self-concept involve a self-description of the mental pictures we have of ourselves, self-esteem involves an evaluation of our own worth and value.

➤ From a biblical perspective,
  - Human beings are created in God's image and are valuable in his sight.
  - All people are sinners who have become alienated from God and condemned because of their sinful natures and actions. Even in our fallen state, God loves us, sent his son Jesus Christ to redeem us, and restores all who confess their sin and put their faith in Jesus.
  - Pride is an unreasonably high opinion of oneself based on one's innate nature and human accomplishments.
  - Humility is an accurate self-appraisal in which the person accepts his or her sins but acknowledges the gifts, abilities, and achievements that have come from God.
  - Humility is not self-negation or the rejection of our God-given strengths and abilities. Humility involves a grateful dependence on God and a realistic appraisal of both strengths and weaknesses.

➤ Inferiority and low self-esteem can have a variety of causes, including
  - Faulty theological beliefs.
  - Unconfessed sin and guilt.
  - Childhood experiences that have taught inferiority.
  - Experiences of defeat or failure.
  - Unrealistic self-expectations.
  - Self-defeating thoughts (self-talk) or comments to others.

➤ There can be different reactions to inferiority feelings and low self-esteem, most of which are designed to hide or make up for the assumed inferiorities.

> To counsel people with low self-esteem:
  - Give them genuine support, acceptance, affirmation and approval.
  - Give them accurate biblical teaching about self-esteem.
  - Seek to develop self-understanding and a realistic self-evaluation.
  - Change unhealthy self-talk.
  - Stimulate the forming and pursuit of realistic goals.
  - Stimulate new ways of thinking.
  - Encourage group support and social interaction.

> The prevention of unhealthy self-perceptions and low self-esteem can come through teaching, Christian community, and parental guidance.

> There is research evidence to support the conclusion that a strong self-concept and positive self-esteem are associated with good mental health.

24

Physical Illness

It was part of a routine physical examination. The doctor recommended a stress test, which would involve walking on a treadmill while a small medical team monitored my heart and blood pressure. I had done this before. I knew the routine. I was in good health and great physical condition. I had no symptoms of anything amiss, so I left my office, went to the hospital for the test, and expected to walk away with a clean bill of health.

That didn't happen. A few minutes into the stress test, the doctor announced that they were stopping the treadmill. I protested. I had lots of energy. I knew I could keep walking. I wasn't out of breath. Then they told me they had to stop because I had "a problem." Shortly after I got home, my doctor called and urged me to make an appointment with a cardiologist as soon possible. Three days later they wheeled me into a surgical room for a relatively routine procedure known as an angiogram, in which they could look at my arteries and, if necessary, clear out some of the blockage that the doctors suspected. They did an angioplasty, and because that was not completely successful, the doctors arranged for me to have open heart surgery to celebrate my birthday a few days later.

On the morning of the operation, I remember lying on a gurney, talking to my family when somebody entered the room to stick me with a needle. Four or more hours later, I opened my eyes in a different room, looking at the doctor standing by my bed in his light blue surgical clothes, telling me that they had done a quadruple bi-pass, that everything was fine, and that my heart was now in good shape. There were tubes draining fluids from my body, and I could see the clear bag of liquid that was slowly putting nutrients into my system.

I had never been in the hospital before. Apart from colds and occasional bouts with the flu, I had never been sick. I have visited people in hospital beds, but soon people were visiting me. I had sent people cards and flowers, but now other people were sending them to me. I had urged others to listen to their doctors and take time to heal, but now people were telling that to me. I determined that I would rebound quickly, but then I discovered that my energy was gone. The next day I needed help on both sides to walk a few steps from the bed to the chair. In the weeks that followed, I learned what it was like being in recovery, slowing down to rethink the direction of my life, putting aside my work for a while, taking the time to listen to what God might be saying, without being pressured by the incessant activities of my hyperactive life.

I had completed about one-third of my revision of this book when the surgery interrupted. Today I am doing very well—pretty much recovered completely, thanks to God and to the support and care of my family and close friends, and because of the prayers of many people. Maybe the following pages will sound more authentic than they might have sounded otherwise because I now know a little more about physical illness than I did before. I can use myself as the case story to open this chapter because this is something that I've experienced. I've been there.

Everybody knows that the human body is a remarkable collection of diverse chemicals, billions of cells, hundreds of muscles, miles of blood vessels, and a variety of organs. Amazingly, they all work together without being plugged in to any power source, enabling the body to grow, heal itself, fight disease, adapt to temperature changes, react to environmental stimulation, and survive a host of physical abuses. This includes the activities of skilled surgical teams who can cut into the chest, take out a heart, sew in some new arteries, and tuck it all back in behind the ribs. Centuries ago, the psalmist praised God for making us "so wonderfully complex."[1] And the more we learn about the amazing human body, the more we can stand in awe both of our physical complexity and of the Creator who made us.

Of course, the body does not last forever, at least in this world. Sometimes, it is injured beyond repair. It can break down, and even when the body is cared for carefully, eventually its parts wear out. We don't think much about this when we are healthy. When there are no physical problems, we take the body for granted. Colds and periodic bouts with the flu are annoying but usually only temporary interruptions to the activities of life. When sickness is more serious, painful, or long-lasting, however, we are forced to recognize our own limitations. Physical suffering vividly confronts us with the stark reality that each of us inhabits a body that is destined to die. Since most of us try to avoid thoughts of illness and sometimes even ignore symptoms, it becomes more difficult to tolerate or accept sickness when it does come. Sickness inhibits our activities, slows us down, makes life more difficult, and often seems to have no meaning or purpose. If the illness persists, we start to ask hard, largely unanswerable questions like "Why me?" or "Why is this happening now?" Often, the sickness is accompanied by anger, discouragement, loneliness, hopelessness, bitterness, and confusion. Counseling the physically sick and their families can be a major challenge for Christian counselors. An entire specialty within psychology is committed to the study and application of psychological principles to health care and to people who are physically sick.[2]

The Bible and Physical Illness

Sickness is mentioned often in the Bible. The physical illnesses of Miriam, Naaman, Nebuchadnezzar, David's newborn child, Job, Lazarus, Epaphroditus,[3] and a variety of others are described with clarity in both the Old and New Testaments. When Jesus came to earth in person, his concern for the sick was so important that almost one-fifth of the Gospels is devoted to the topic of healing.[4] The disciples were instructed to carry on this healing ministry,[5] and the book of Acts records how the early church cared for those with physical illnesses.

This biblical emphasis on physical illness points to several conclusions that may be helpful for Christian counselors.

1. *Sickness Is a Part of Living.* Even though some people are healthier than others, there are few of us who go through life without experiencing at least an occasional illness. The Bible does not state this specifically, but it seems likely that sickness entered the human race as a result of the Fall. Since that time, people have known what it is like to be unhealthy. The Bible is not a scientific book; it makes no attempt to diagnose, categorize, or systematically list the symptoms of mental and physical illness or deformity, but it does mention symptoms in passing. It refers directly or indirectly to boils, dysentery, epilepsy, fever, hemorrhaging, indigestion, infirmity, inflammations, insanity, leprosy, palsy, speech impediments, blindness, deafness, inability to talk, and a number of other physi-

cal conditions. It is implied that each of these can lead to psychological as well as physical distress, and there is an underlying assumption that sickness is an expected part of living in this world.

2. *Care, Compassion, and Healing Are Important for Christians.* By his words and actions, Jesus taught that while sickness is common, it also is undesirable. He spent much of his time healing the sick,[6] he encouraged others to do likewise, and he emphasized the importance of compassionate caring for those who were needy and unhealthy. Even to give someone a drink of water was considered praiseworthy, and Jesus indicated that helping a sick person was the same as ministering to Jesus himself.[7] Elsewhere, believers are instructed to pray for the sick and to help them in practical ways.[8] Clearly, the Bible teaches that Christians have a responsibility to care for those who are not well.

3. *Sickness, Sin, and Faith Are Not Necessarily Related.* When Job lost his family, possessions, and health, a trio of well-meaning but ineffective comforters argued that all these problems resulted from the victim's sin. Job was reluctant to believe this, and later it was confirmed that sickness does not always come as a result of individual sin—a conclusion that Jesus clearly taught in John 9.[9] All sickness comes ultimately because of the Fall. There is no doubt that physical illness and personal sin sometimes *are* related, but we cannot conclude that individual cases of sickness necessarily result from the sick person's sin.[10]

This becomes clearer as we examine the healing miracles of the New Testament. Sometimes, people improved because they personally believed that Christ would heal. The woman who had been hemorrhaging for twelve years is a good example.[11] There were other times, however, when a person other than the patient had faith and a healing occurred. At different times, several parents came to Jesus, asked about healing for their children, and saw them healed.[12] In the Garden of Gethsemane, a servant's ear was healed, even though no person apparently had faith except Jesus. In contrast, Paul was a man who had great faith in Christ's ability to heal, but the apostle had an ongoing "thorn" in his flesh that never left.[13] Still others had no faith and no healing.[14] From these examples it surely is clear that to be sick is not necessarily a sin or indicative of a lack of faith.[15]

The Bible gives no support to those Christians who proclaim that sick people are always out of God's will or lacking in faith. God has never promised to heal all of our diseases in this life, and it is both incorrect and cruel to teach that instant and lasting health always will come to those whose faith is strong.

4. *Sickness Raises Difficult and Crucial Questions About Suffering.* In his classic little volume on pain, C. S. Lewis summarized two basic questions that face anyone who suffers.[16] These questions often arise in counseling: If God is good, why does he permit suffering? If he is all-powerful, why doesn't he stop suffering? Entire volumes have been written to grapple with these questions,[17] but it seems probable that our finite human minds will never completely comprehend the reasons for suffering.

For most of us, pain and suffering do not make any sense. We do what we can to reduce pain in ourselves or others, and we pray for the pain to go away. The Bible lifts the veil of confusion slightly when it teaches that suffering keeps us humble, refines our faith, conforms us to Christ's image, teaches us about God, and produces patience, maturity, perseverance, and character. Suffering also teaches us to be more compassionate and caring.[18]

I once had a friend whose seminary career was interrupted by a diagnosis of terminal cancer. To the surprise of his physicians and the gratitude of those who prayed, my friend recovered and eventually became chaplain of a large hospital, where he counseled with suffering patients and their families every day. In time he became head of an organization of chaplains. My friend's own suffering enabled him to better understand and counsel with others who suffered. Then he died at a relatively young age. None of us knows why God worked like this in his life.[19] Sometimes, suffering seems to have a clear purpose; often it does not. But counselors are called to give help to those whose pain we cannot know and have never felt.

5. *Serious Illness Can Raise Difficult Issues About the Right to Die.* For reasons that are not clearly understood, some people seem to reach a time when they let go of life and die, even though they have not been sick. Most of us have seen this in elderly people who lose the will to live and their bodies shut down. For these individuals, it seems, a healthy cardiovascular system is less important than their conclusion that life is no longer worth living, so they die.

More common, however, are the examples of people who develop such severe, painful, debilitating, and lingering illnesses that they want to die, even though they continue to live. Sometimes, these people beg to die and urge their doctors and relatives to withdraw all support systems, including food. These increasing requests for what is known as assisted suicide, and the willing compliance of some compassionate relatives and medical personnel, have thrown the legal and medical professions into great debate. It is a debate that some Christians try to ignore and that some theologians find frustrating because they find no unequivocal guidance in Scripture. The problem is complicated by confusing laws and calls for more countries to follow the example of those nations that allow the giving of medications that hasten death.

Shortly before this chapter was written, every newspaper in the country carried daily stories about the last days both of Pope John Paul II and of a previously unknown woman named Terri Schiavo. The pope was unusually popular among people of all faiths. He carried his terminal illnesses with dignity, suffered graciously, died while the world watched in admiration, and was mourned by millions. In contrast, Schiavo was a brain-damaged woman kept alive by a feeding tube and by highly publicized court battles between her husband and her parents. "What makes a life worth living?" one newspaper columnist wrote. "Is life strictly one's own, to be terminated when pride or convenience dictates, or is it a gift from God, to be endured to the bitter end?" It was called a clash of worldviews that dominated the media, was debated in the United States Congress and at the White House, made its way to the Supreme Court, and occupied the attention of theologians, students, and ordinary people across the nation. After Terri Schiavo's feeding tube was removed from her body, she died in the midst of great controversy and publicity, even though her name may be forgotten by the time these words are published.

The Christian counselor needs to grapple with issues such as these. Christians believe that all of life comes from God and is taken from us as he wills. Euthanasia—a word that the current debate tends to shun—is more controversial but opposed by most people who value human life. Surely, there can be no biblical support for an attitude that hastens death because the patient wants to die, that condones starving someone to death because he or she is difficult to care for, or that withholds health care from someone who is comatose or brain-dead. But do we use every technical and medical means available to keep someone alive and maybe in pain, people who in past years would have died of natural causes? These questions have no simple answers, but Christian counselors need to be aware of these and related health-care issues that arise in times of serious physical illness. They are issues that come to counselors, especially from the families of severely ill patients.

The Causes of Sickness and Related Problems

Every illness goes through several stages.[20] The first of these, the *incubation stage*, starts and finishes before the patient even knows that the disease is present. Of course, there can be a variety of causes, including human contact with viruses and disease-carrying plants or animals, diet deficiencies, lack of exercise or good body care, injury, hereditary defects, the ingestion of harmful substances (like drugs or poisons), the wearing out or degeneration of body organs, or contact with extreme heat or cold—to name some of the most obvious. The *symptomatic stage* appears when there are changes in the body that indicate a physical problem. These body changes indicate the nature of the disease and become the first clues that the medical professional uses to make a diagnosis. The *resolution stage* depends on the body's ability to heal itself and on interventions such as surgery or medication that are designed to return the body to its normal functioning. This is followed by the *recovery stage* that replenishes the body's ability to resume normal activities and to fight diseases on its own in the future.

Sickness involves much more than physical malfunctioning and recovery. Any illness can bring a variety of psychological and spiritual reactions that concern physicians, family members, and nonmedical professionals such as counselors. Many of these psychological-spiritual influences, including the following, can complicate or accentuate the physical illness and may delay or prevent recovery.

1. *Stress and Helplessness.* It is not easy to be sick, especially when routines are disrupted, when a person does not know what is wrong with his or her body, when there is uncertainty about when or whether recovery will occur, and when one is in an unfamiliar environment such as a hospital. When people are sick enough to seek medical attention, they must submit themselves to the care of strangers, some of whom may be overly busy and distracted, or more aloof and scientific than they are compassionate and sensitive.[21]

The stress of illness often leaves people feeling helpless and out of control, especially when the illness is serious or when hospitalization is involved. It can be very threatening and disruptive to experience even a temporary loss of one's physical strength, intellectual alertness, bowel or bladder control, speech, control of limbs, or ability to regulate one's emotions. All of this is made more difficult if these losses come while we are on semipublic display in a hospital room, sometimes surrounded by strangers and knowing that we may be interrupted at any time by the unexpected arrival of visitors.

Many of us grow up learning that human beings are capable, independent, and masters of our own destinies. An illness shatters these beliefs, at least temporarily and sometimes quickly. An accident or stroke can leave a previously mobile individual unable to move. Normally strong and active people suddenly may feel weak and in need of constant care and help. The patient is expected to comply with doctor's orders and is told what medications to take and when to take them. It can be awkward and embarrassing when a physically ill person is expected to undress—or be undressed—in the presence of strangers, and to submit passively to a variety of diagnostic and treatment procedures, even if this means exposing private body parts for others to view and touch. In hospitals people are told when to go to sleep, when to wake up, when and what to eat. Day or night hospital personnel may appear at the door armed with needles and instructions to take blood or to give injections. Sometimes, the patient even needs help in going to the bathroom.

Probably, most care-givers want to treat patients with respect and dignity, but this can be forgotten, especially by busy medical personnel who are used to the insensitive ways in which patients sometimes are treated. When people are sick enough to need ongoing medical treatment, they must put their lives and bodies into the hands of strangers with whom they have no personal ties and whose competence they may not be able to judge. It can be frightening, embarrassing, and threatening to have these strangers manipulating, viewing, drugging, operating on, or even removing parts of one's body.

At times like these, patients need closeness to the people they love, but sickness often separates them from supportive and caring friends and from customary routines. If the sickness or injury leaves one physically deformed, forced to slow down, or passively dependent on others, the person may fear that loved ones will no longer show love or respect. Sometimes, there is a desire to have visitors who show that they care, mixed with the hope that "nobody will come and see me looking like this."

2. *Guilt and Self-Criticism.* Sickness or accidents may lead people to think that their suffering is punishment for previous sins or failures. As we have seen, this was the view of Job's counselors, and it has been accepted by people ever since. When a person lies in bed for long hours wondering "Why?" or "Why me?" there can be overwhelming feelings of guilt or self-condemnation, especially if there is no recovery or there are no people with whom these issues can be shared and discussed.

3. *Fear and Depression.* It is not difficult to think of reasons why a person might be afraid or depressed during a time of sickness. The reasons might include fear of pain or further complications, worry about a coming surgical medical procedure, confusion about the nature of one's illness and prognosis for recovery, uncertainty about the future, or even worry about what one might say when under the influence of an anesthetic. At times, there is anger at oneself, at the illness, at one's doctors, at others (including family members, ministry visitors, or a counselor), or at God. Chapter 8 showed how anger often leads to depression. With some illnesses these feelings may be accentuated by physically produced chemical changes that alter one's mood.

It is well known that there are wide individual differences in how people react to their illnesses and the accompanying feelings. Without denying the nature of their illnesses, some people are able to have a cheerful attitude throughout and even see humor in their difficult circumstances. When former U.S. President Ronald Reagan was shot by an attempted assassin, he joked on the way into the operating room and expressed the hope that the physicians were all Republicans. Medical personnel have long known that a positive attitude in the patient can both hasten and facilitate recovery. In contrast, recovery is slowed and sometimes the patient becomes more susceptible to further illness when he or she is depressed, struggling with helplessness, self-critical, embarrassed, excessively frustrated, scared, or hypercritical and angry at doctors and other care-givers. When the counselor is aware of these issues, he or she is better able to understand and help patients and their families.

4. *The Experience of Pain.* There are great individual differences in how people experience pain, in how they respond to it, and in the intensity and duration of pain. Pain that is intense and brief—such as that experienced in the dentist's chair—is different from the gnawing, never-ending pain of some cancer patients. Pain that is understood and known to be short-term—like an occasional headache—is handled differently from pain that is long lasting or undiagnosed.

Acute pain refers to discomfort that is of limited duration. In contrast, chronic pain persists, often for months or years. Like back pain, arthritis, or ongoing headaches, chronic pain may subside temporarily, but it is never far from awareness. It occurs in hospital patients, but it occurs, as well, in people who are trying to live their lives and go about their normal activities while they are impacted by pain. One respected report estimates that in the United States almost half the population lives with some kind of chronic condition.[22] This accounts for 75 percent of the health-care costs. It is not surprising that persisting pain often leads to depression, isolation, and feelings of hopelessness. The problem may be accentuated by physicians, mental-health professionals, or pastors, who are uncomfortable in the presence of people with pain and untrained in pain management, so they back away from patients whose pain persists.[23]

Psychological researchers have teamed up with medical and other specialists to study pain and pain management, but the task is difficult. People show differences in their awareness and tolerance of pain, and there is evidence that these psychological responses largely are unrelated to the physiological measures. Some people report feeling very little pain, even though physiological measures indicate that the pain should be severe; in turn, there can be extreme discomfort but few physiological indicators that pain exists. Many years ago a researcher found that soldiers injured in battle complained less of pain (some with serious wounds reported no pain at all) and required less pain medication than civilians who experienced similar injuries. The difference appeared to be in how they perceived the injury. The civilians were annoyed because of their unwanted injuries, but the soldiers were relieved to still be alive and safe.[24] Also, some people may feel pain but be reluctant to complain, fearing that others will perceive them as being weak or querulous.

Why do some people feel little pain even with a major illness, while others feel great pain even when there is no discernible organic disease? Why do some deny their pain and pretend that it doesn't exist, while others almost seem to enjoy the suffering and use it for their own advantage, like getting out of work or other responsibilities? While differences like these may have some biological explanations, many of the individual differences in pain tolerance result from a person's attitudes about pain, cultural and family backgrounds, past experiences with pain, personal values, and religious beliefs. Some people, for example, stoically believe that pain is a sign of weakness or that it should be accepted and endured as something permitted by God. Others discover that the degree of pain depends on one's level of anxiety. When people are anxious about pain, this can intensify both the illness and the pain that is felt.[25] These factors have led pain management specialists to assume that psychological issues are of such importance that they always must be considered when pain is an issue.[26]

These differences are not necessarily good or bad. A high ability to tolerate pain, for example, is no more a sign of strength—or weakness—than is a low level of tolerance. It is important, however, that counselors recognize and accept these differences. They influence a sick person's emotions, reactions, prognosis for recovery, and response to counseling.

5. *Family Influences.* When a person is sick or in pain, his or her family is affected, and the family's reactions then can influence the patient either positively or negatively. Changes in family routines as the result of an illness or disability, financial hardships, difficulties in scheduling hospital or doctor visits, and the loss of opportunity for sex between a husband and wife can all create tension that sometimes leads to fatigue, irritability, and worry. Visits from family members are supposed to make the patient feel better, but sometimes these contacts create more tension and worsen the illness.

In attempting to reassure one another and prevent worry, the patient and family sometimes refuse to discuss their real fears or feelings with one another. As a result, each suffers alone, fearing the worst but pretending that all is well and that recovery is on the way. This well-intentioned deception is a game that everybody plays but almost nobody admits or feels comfortable discussing.

In reflecting on the illness and death of his mother, Henri Nouwen once wrote a letter to his father in Holland and expressed feelings that we often see in our counselees. "Isn't it true that it is much harder to say deep things to each other than to write them?" Nouwen observed. "I am quite familiar with my own inclination, and that of others, to avoid, deny, or suppress the painful side of life, a tendency that always leads to physical, mental, or spiritual disaster."[27] If the illness is terminal, subsequent grief becomes much harder because family members missed the golden opportunity to discuss their intimate feelings together before the loved one died.

None of this is intended to paint a bleak picture of physical illness or chronic pain. Some families never have the problems we have mentioned. But they appear frequently in other cases and sometimes are noticed by a counselor, even though they are not seen by the patient or the family members. Once again you may observe how fears, anxieties, and threats can affect the course of treatment, influence everyone's attitudes toward the illness, and have a bearing on the speed or likelihood of recovery.

The Effects of Physical Illness

It can be difficult to separate the effects of sickness from the causes. Pain, feelings of helplessness, emotions, and family reactions to an illness can all be as much the effects of sickness as they are causes of additional physical and adjustment problems. Reactions to the sickness, such as guilt, anger, or depression, can complicate the illness and cause it to get worse. This can lead to more guilt, anger, or depression, so a vicious cycle develops.

Because they focus on helping people who have problems, counselors are more likely to see the negative effects of an illness, but they fail to notice the more positive benefits. One study of 345 male heart attack victims showed that when men grumbled about their illnesses and blamed others (citing problems with the family, for example, or stress at work), there was a much greater likelihood of morbid thinking and another heart attack. Things were much different in men who could see some benefits in their heart attacks. These people often reviewed or changed their life values and religious views, worked to improve interpersonal relationships, made an effort to reduce stress, and took better care of their bodies. As a result, there were "fewer reinfarctions and lower morbidity."[28] The effects of an illness need not always be negative.

In many cases, however, the effects of an illness are more negative than positive. The following reactions are among those that are seen often and may have to be dealt with by a sensitive counselor.

1. *Denial.* Since sickness is so unwelcome, there is a tendency to deny its seriousness and sometimes its presence. At times, probably most people have noticed symptoms that could indicate something seriously wrong, but the symptoms are dismissed as being of no relevance. After suffering a heart attack, a man in his forties described how he had experienced periodic chest pain for several years, but every time he had dismissed it as heartburn. Denial of a physical problem may be more difficult if a serious illness has been diagnosed, but even some of these patients persist in denying the reality of their illnesses. The reality of the illness is explained away with comments such as, "I'm sure the doctor is overreacting. This can't be true. Probably the diagnosis is wrong. Surely God already is healing me."

2. *Defensiveness.* Readers of introductory psychology textbooks often learn about defense mechanisms. These are ways of thinking that enable us to deny reality and pretend that a frustration or conflict is of little importance. This thinking is very common. It is used automatically, usually without prior deliberation, and often without our even being aware that it is taking place. Its purpose is to protect us from anxiety.

A number of defense mechanisms have been identified, and many are seen in sick people and their families.

- *Rationalization* is the tendency to make excuses ("They've probably misinterpreted the test results." "I was tired when they took the tests, so they probably are invalid.")
- *Projection* lets people blame their feelings of anger, fear, or helplessness on someone else ("My problem is with the doctor who is trying to make me look sick so he can get more money from my insurance company." "My wife keeps cooking spicy foods, and this is the major problem.")
- *Reaction formation* is the tendency to display, in excess, the opposite of what one feels ("Look at how well I am and how much I'm improving day by day." "Have you noticed how the color is coming back into my face?")
- *Magical thinking* lets us pretend ("The doctor keeps reading those medical journals, and I just know they will find a new cure before long.")
- *Repression* is an unconscious forgetting of things that we don't want to remember.
- *Suppression* is a more deliberate forgetting. Like repression, this also is used to push unpleasant reality out of conscious awareness.

These kinds of thinking can be helpful if they give people time to gather strength and acquire the knowledge needed to cope more realistically with their illnesses. When the defenses and denial persist, the patient or family member is being unrealistic and may be rudely awakened later when reality hits.

3. *Withdrawal.* When people are sick, they can benefit from the support, help, and love that come from others. For some people this is not easy. They feel threatened by their dependence on others, unwilling to appear weak, and afraid of being misunderstood. As a result they withdraw, sometimes announcing that they are fine on their own, or sliding into self-pity and loneliness when the caregivers agree to go away.

4. *Depression and Anxiety.* These emotions are common with any serious illness, but some of the most interesting research findings have come from studies of depression and anxiety in cardiac patients. For example, one study of almost nine hundred heart attack patients found that those who were depressed were three times more likely to die in the year following their heart attack than nondepressed patients, regardless of how severe the initial heart disease had been.[29] Not surprising was the finding in another study that depressed heart patients who felt they did not get enough support from family and friends had the highest death rates. Depressed patients who reported the most support had the same death rates as nondepressed patients.[30] A major study by researchers in Montreal compared over 15,000 heart attack patients with an equal number of non-patients in 52 countries. There were differences between the groups in issues, such as smoking rates, amount of exercise, high blood pressure, and other physical measures, but significant differences also were found in levels of depression, anxiety, stress, and other emotional variables.[31] It is increasingly apparent that psychological and behavioral issues play a huge role in the development of physical illness and in recovery. It is not surprising, therefore, that counselors and other mental-health professionals are becoming increasingly involved in the treatment of cardiac and other types of patients.[32]

5. *Resistance and Anger.* Some patients come out fighting. Since it isn't easy to fight disease, especially when so much is out of the patients' control, they direct their anger to doctors, nurses, family members, pastors, or others, including counselors. Criticism, complaining, noisy protests, and demands for relief often characterize these patients and create frustration in their own lives and in the lives of others. Often, this resistance has its basis in anger over one's condition and anxiety over what the future holds. Sadly, this anger can trigger further physical problems and sometimes leads to sudden death.

6. *Manipulation.* Some people go through life trying to manipulate others by subtle or more obvious control tactics. When these people become ill, it is not surprising that they use the sickness to control others or to get attention and sympathy.

7. *Malingering and Hypochondriasis.* Sickness can bring benefits such as attention and sympathy from others, a reason to do nothing, freedom from responsibility, and socially sanctioned permission to stay home from work and to get up late. Some people enjoy the benefits of being sick, and as a result they never get better, or they experience a series of physical symptoms for which there is no organic basis and little relief.

Malingering is a deliberate fabrication or exaggeration of physical or psychological symptoms in order to receive some kind of benefit from remaining a patient. Sometimes, malingering is brief (such as the student who pretends to be sick so he or she can stay home from school and avoid a big test). At other times, it may be more long-lasting (as with the workman who fakes an injury in order to get workman's compensation). Suspicion of malingering often angers doctors and family members, but there is no really effective way to prove that the "patient" is malingering, and physicians sometimes fear lawsuits if they fail to treat a supposed malingerer who really does have an illness or injury.

Hypochondriasis also is an assumed illness, but there is no conscious effort to appear sick. Hypochondriacs tend to be preoccupied with disease or illness, so they look for physical symptoms and assume that even the most minor physical changes are indicators of sickness. When doctors can't find anything that is wrong, these people get angry and sometimes look for a new doctor. "I don't know what's wrong with the medical profession," a cartoon character complained. "I've been to twenty-three doctors this year, and everybody tells me there's nothing wrong with me." Even though they believe that their illnesses are real, these people are using their symptoms to get attention, relationships, feelings of importance, or guidance from authority figures. Sickness becomes a way of life for these individuals. They may not like their persisting symptoms and visits to doctors, but for these people being sick is easier than living life without any physical complaints.

8. *Hope.* Even when the medical news is not encouraging, some patients and their families still respond with hope.[33] In her well-known book, *On Death and Dying*, psychiatrist Elisabeth Kübler-Ross reported that whenever a patient stops expressing hope, death often follows soon.[34] Even seriously ill people who have realistic views of their condition find that hope sustains and encourages them, especially in difficult times. Medical and nonmedical counselors have found that patients get along better when there is at least a glimmer of hope. This does not mean that doctors and others must lie about the patient's condition. It means, writes Kübler-Ross, that "we share with them the hope that something unforeseen may happen, that they may have a remission, that they may live longer than expected."[35] For the Christian there is even greater hope in the knowledge that the loving sovereign God of the universe is concerned about us both now and for eternity.

Counseling and Physical Illness

Jesus never set up an office in the temple, waiting for people to come for counseling. Instead he went to where the people were, to their homes, to the streets, to places where he most likely would find those who were sick, anxious, confused, handicapped, and needy. He never limited his services to those who made appointments with him or to people with prestige, money, and status. Instead, he counseled the outcasts, the sinners, the despised tax collectors, the pompous religious leaders.

In counseling the sick, often it will be necessary to go to them. As you move away from the office, remember the basic principles that apply to all counseling: the importance of counselor warmth, empathy, and genuineness; the value of listening patiently and gently encouraging sick people or their families to talk about their fears, anxieties, anger, future, or the illness itself; the need for confidentiality; and the importance of showing acceptance, understanding, and compassion—without being gushy or condescending. In contrast to those who are physically healthy, sick people often are more sensitive to these counselor characteristics.

Every illness is unique, but based on his experiences as a physician, Dr. Gregg Albers has suggested that there are phases of sickness that most patients and their families go through. These are illustrated in Figure 24–1. The reaction phase appears near the beginning of an illness when physical symptoms become worse. Often, there are emotional reactions, such as the anxiety, anger, depression, denial, and resistance we have already discussed. Eventually, the patient reaches the phase when he or she begins to accept the reality and severity of the illness. There is a logical acceptance of the need for treatment, an emotional acceptance that the disease is serious, and often a recognition that this may have long-term and spiritual implications. It is then that a reversal often begins. The patient gets treatment, support from others, a recognition that some things are getting better, and a slow growth back to recovery. This is like a return from the valley. Sometimes, this involves a return to normal functioning, but in some cases full recovery does not occur and the person lives with some disability (represented by Y on the diagram). In other cases, people grow beyond their illnesses and have more healthy lives or attitudes as a result.

Even as people with illness go through these stages, their family members go through them as well, although at any given time the family and the patient may be at a different phase. For example, the patient may get to the acceptance phase before the family members, or the family members may get there first. It should

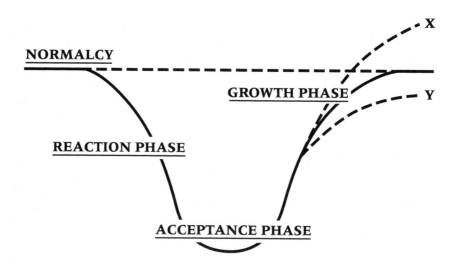

Figure 24–1. The Phases of Illness.* During the descending period or reaction phase, physical and emotional decline occur until the patient reaches the low ebb of the acceptance phase. Then there is a reversal into a phase of growth as physical health and spiritual strength increase. Recovery occurs when the patient returns to normal physical activity and emotional stability. The dotted line "X" suggests that the patient can recover and improve beyond his or her usual capabilities. The dotted line "Y" represents a patient who has some disability and cannot return to normal functioning.

*Adapted with permission from Gregg R. Albers, *Counseling the Sick and Terminally Ill* (Dallas, TX: Word, 1989), 26.

be remembered, too, that often there will be relapses or setbacks, so the progression of the illness is not as smooth as the illustration may imply. Whatever the stage of the illness, try to keep the following principles in mind as you counsel with patients and their families.

1. *Be Aware of Your Own Attitudes and Needs.* When a person is found to have a serious or terminal illness, even doctors, nurses, clergymen, friends, and family members sometimes tend to withdraw and leave the patient to face the problem alone. It has been found that some of the best counseling in these situations is done by men or women who clean the patient rooms or deliver the meals. These people are regular visitors, who can be cheerful and, depending on their schedules, willing to both listen and talk.

This sad observation points to the fact that most of us don't like to face sickness, especially serious illness, so we avoid people who are ill. Perhaps we are threatened because these people remind us that we all are susceptible to illness. Maybe we are uncomfortable because we don't know what to say, are not sure how to react to the patient's anger and discouragement, or feel incapable of dealing with difficult questions such as "Why me?" or "Do you think I'm going to die?" The sight of severely injured persons, perhaps with physical deformities or tubes and machines attached to their bodies, can create discomfort in the counselor and sometimes involuntary reactions of shock that the patient is quick to detect.

For some counselors, working with people who are sick and their families is no problem. If the counselor has been sick or hospitalized in the past, he or she may have greater understanding of patients now. This does not always happen, however, and some of us never become accustomed to hospitals or sickness. If this is so, the counselor should take time—perhaps right now before you read further—to ponder the reasons for this discomfort in the presence of sick people. An understanding of our own attitudes toward sickness and physically ill people can help us become more effective as counselors. Central to all of this is the issue of prayer and spiritual preparation for counseling. Since Christians are instructed to care for one another,[36] we can ask our compassionate God to give us the ability and sensitivity to be compassionate in turn.

2. *Learn and Apply Guidelines for Visiting the Sick.* The Bible calls us to help those who cannot help themselves, including the sick and orphans.[37] Traditionally, the pastor visits those who are sick and infirmed, reading Scripture, bringing comfort and encouragement, listening patiently, and praying. Sadly, in the fast-paced world where we live today, these visits often have become rushed and superficial. As a result, "both the patient and the pastor may be more anxious because of the brevity of the visit than relieved by the kindness intended."[38]

For most counselors, it is easier to counsel people in the familiar surroundings of our offices. Of course, this is not always possible with sick people because of their physical limitations. As a result, the counselor goes to the patient. When the church is involved, this visitation is a role that different members of the congregation should take; this role should not be limited to the pastoral staff. In visiting and counseling the physically ill, there are generally accepted guidelines that the counselor should know and remember. These are summarized in Table 24–1.

3. *Be Sensitive to Unique Boundary Issues Relating to Counseling Outside the Office.* When he walked on earth, Jesus healed people wherever he encountered them, but sometimes he went to homes. Home visits have been part of Christian ministry ever since, often following guidelines similar to those in Table 24–1.

Table 24–1

Guidelines for Visiting and Counseling the Sick

For All Patients

- Visit frequently if possible, but be sensitive to the patient's physical condition so that visits are not too long but also not too rushed.
- Let the patient take the lead in shaking hands or other physical contact.
- Stand or sit where you can be seen easily—the side of the bed is more suitable than the foot of the bed.
- Give the patient freedom to talk and listen carefully and attentively.
- Use your resources as a Christian: prayer, Scripture, encouraging comments, etc. Be sensitive to the surroundings. Whether you should pray audibly should be determined by the Holy Spirit and the situation—the patient, his or her spiritual background, the people present, etc. Suggest prayer rather than asking if the patient wants it. In any case, keep it short.
- Take the appropriate precautions against contagious disease.
- Consider leaving devotional or other materials that the patient might be able to read later.
- Evaluate each visit to determine how visits and counseling could improve in the future.

For Patients at Home

- Call before visiting to make sure this is a convenient time.
- Try to take another person with you or visit at a time when another person is in the home, if possible.
- Try to call at a time when there can be time for private discussion.
- Review and abide by the boundaries issues discussed in the text of this chapter.

For Hospital Patients

- Upon arrival, check at the reception desk, introduce yourself, and make sure that a visit at this time is acceptable.
- Do not enter a room that has a closed door or a "no visitors" sign.
- Try to call when there are not a lot of other visitors present.

Do:

- Be friendly and cheerful.
- Be reassuring and comforting.
- Help the patient relax.
- Recognize that anxieties, discouragement, guilt, frustrations, and uncertainties may be present.
- Give reassurance of divine love and care.
- Answer questions as best you can and be willing to discuss the patient's concerns or those of his family.
- Get the patient's permission before you share anything, such as prayer requests, with the church congregation or others.

- Be sensitive to the needs of concerned family members.
- Promise to pray for the patient during the illness, and then act on this promise.

Don't:

- Speak in an unnatural tone of voice.
- Talk about your own past illnesses or hospital experiences.
- Force the patient to talk. Your silent presence can often be very meaningful and reassuring.
- Assume that the patient is unaware of your conversation with family members just because the patient is asleep or in a coma.
- Promise that God will heal them. Sometimes, in his wisdom, God permits illness to persist.
- Visit when you are sick.
- Visit when you are in a rush.
- Talk loudly.
- Sit, lean on, or jar the bed.
- Visit during mealtimes.
- Whisper to family members or to medical personnel within sight of the patient.
- Share information about the diagnosis or about anything else that might be considered confidential.
- Question the patient about the details of the illness.
- Tell the family how to decide when presented with medical options (but help them talk it through and decide together).
- Criticize the hospital, the treatment, or the medical personnel.
- Spread detailed information about the patient when you complete your visit.

For psychologists and other professional counselors, the guidelines for home visits are different. When a counselor and counselee meet in an office, there is the expectation that the two of them will have a focused discussion on a problem issue, without distractions or a lot of informal discussion. When the counselor visits a home, however, the counselee often views this as a social visit, with refreshments, interaction with family members, and conversation that has little relevance to the specific problem. One psychologist visited the home of a counselee who had a large and rambunctious dog who enjoyed jumping on the counselor and barking, much to the delight of the counselee, who proceeded to tell stories about the dog and question the counselor about his interest in animals. All of this distracted from the counseling, especially when the conversation was interrupted by telephone calls and the presence of family members who periodically wandered in and out of the room.

The best way to prevent this is to set some guidelines prior to the visit. Explain that this is not a social visit. It is a counseling session in the home (or hospital room) that is similar to what might occur in the counselor's office. Indicate that the focus of the visit is on the counselee's concerns and that privacy and confidentiality are important. Some counselors prepare a simple page of guidelines to clarify what is expected, and these are mentioned whenever the conversation tends to veer away from a counseling relationship. Of course, the counselor can learn from observing how the counselee interacts with others in the home, but for best results, a professional relationship should be maintained even when the counseling occurs away from the counselor's office.[39]

4. *Deal with the Specific Feelings and Concerns of the Sick Person.* When calling on somebody who is sick, it is important to be sensitive to the patient's physical condition, but this does not mean that sensitive topics are to be avoided. Common mistakes include:

- Avoiding sensitive topics on the assumption that the physically ill person cannot handle emotional issues.
- Radiating excessive cheerfulness and optimism, hoping that a cheerful attitude will drive away worries.
- Talking about anything except the sick patient, perhaps because the visitor is uncomfortable and feels better directing attention elsewhere.
- Asking a lot of questions about the patient's physical condition or dwelling on the negative aspects of the illness so that the visit turns into morbid "isn't-it-terrible" introspection.
- Talking enthusiastically and optimistically about miracles or healing while the realities of the present sickness are ignored.

Effective counselors avoid extremes like these. Recognize that patients sometimes want to discuss their feelings and concerns, while at other times they prefer to talk about something else. As with all other types of counseling, you have to earn the right to be a helper. Sometimes, you will raise a sensitive issue and get a cold or evasive response, clearly indicating that the person does not want to share certain personal issues with you. At times like this, nothing is gained by pushing the person to talk. It is better to show your continued interest, be available, respect the individual's privacy, and be sensitive to the following issues that you or the patient may choose to bring up later.

(a) Fear. Does the physically ill person or some family member experience any of the fears described earlier in this chapter? Are there additional fears that he or she may be willing to talk about? Many people are reluctant to admit their fears. They need to feel that it is safe to express their emotions, that the counselor is a safe person with whom they can share, and that the fears will not be dismissed as being unimportant. Many fears are not based on real facts. They come because people do not know what to expect, or they make assumptions that may not be valid. When counselors or medical personnel listen with an understanding attitude and give accurate information and realistic reassurance, fears often subside. The Christian counselor can pray with the patient or the family, asking God to bring an inner sense of peace even in the midst of uncertainty and physical disability. Philippians 4:6 and 7 can be helpful to read and discuss.

(b) Discouragement. An old hymn proclaims that Christians should "never be discouraged" if we "take it to the Lord in prayer." This correctly teaches that discouraging situations are a reason for prayer and for recognizing "what a friend we have in Jesus," but as we noted in an earlier chapter, the hymn also has reinforced the questionable conclusion that discouragement is wrong. Sometimes, people are unwilling to admit their discouragements and don't want to talk about the things that make them discouraged. Here again, the counselor can show that it is understandable and acceptable to be discouraged at times. Counselees can be helped to understand and do what they can to deal realistically with the sources of the discouragement.

(c) Anger. Most of the feelings that come with an illness can affect the patient's condition, even when he or she does not recognize that the emotion is present. For example, anger is not always expressed in obvious ways. Withdrawal from others, criticisms of one's family or the hospital staff, demands for attention or special treatment, whining and constant complaining, depression, refusal to pray or to talk about God, and persistent dwelling on the questions about why all of this is happening can all be veiled evidences of anger against God, oneself, and others. Anger cannot be resolved when it is suppressed or denied. Instead, it can simmer like a pan of water on a stove, until it boils over and burns people who are nearby. After asking for divine help, the counselor can encourage the counselee to face the anger honestly, admit that it is present, talk about it, confess it to God and to others who have been hurt, and ask for divine help so that the anger can be controlled and not allowed to control the patient and put the body under more pressure.

(d) Self-Pity. When a person is sick, forced to slow down, and often alone, there is more time to think about present circumstances. Often the mind drifts to thoughts of what is bad about the illness or about life in general. This can lead to more of the fears, discouragement, and anger that we have already considered. For some people the slide into self-pity soon follows.

Self-pity and brooding may be pleasant for a while. These attitudes may elicit sympathy from others or feelings of self-righteous indignation about the unfairness of life. If this attitude persists, however, the person can become bitter,[40] and others are driven away, unwilling to listen to the complaining.

When a person is entangled in self-pity, point this out gently. The patient may respond with anger or denial, but the counselor must be accepting and understanding, yet firm. Help the counselee think about the positive as well as the negative things in life. Can anything good come from this illness? Can there be a more realistic view of the present situation? Encourage the counselee to pray, confessing bitterness and asking for divine forgiveness, direction, and a fresh perspective on the current situation. It may be helpful to ponder what one can do to make the best of the illness. Talk about the possibility that the best solution for the present may be rest, which gives the body time to experience physical rejuvenation, reevaluation of one's life, and time spent in communication with God.

(e) Guilt or Bitterness. The psalms confirm what counselors often observe: physical illness can come from inner feelings of guilt or from persisting bitterness.[41] When David confessed his sin and experienced forgiveness, his guilt faded and his physical illness disappeared. Research has shown that the experience of forgiveness can promote health and reduce health risks.[42] Even if guilt is not at the core of an illness, it can make an illness worse and hinder the recovery process.

(f) Difficult Questions. Although they may not always say what they are thinking, many sick people struggle with questions, such as: "Why am I experiencing this?"; "Why is this happening to me and not to somebody else?"; "What will happen to me and my family if I don't get better?"; "Do these doctors really know what they are doing?"; "Does the staff in this hospital really look after old people like me, or do they ignore us and conclude there isn't much hope for recovery in patients who are elderly?"; "While I have this serious illness, what do I do about my sexual desires and frustrations?"

Counselors and family members often think about questions like these but are reluctant to raise or discuss them with the person who is sick. These are not questions that need to be brought up frequently unless the patient keeps raising them. If the counselee never mentions issues like these, however, the counselor should raise them—preferably when there is time for discussion without interruption. Of course, these questions are not always answered easily. As we have seen, the Bible gives some answers, but it also teaches that God's ways often are beyond the capacity of our human ability to understand.[43]

Also difficult to understand and talk about is the issue of death. Billy Graham once wrote about a "conspiracy of silence" that leads most people—medical personnel included—to avoid even mentioning the possibility of death, lest this destroy the patient's morale or raise topics that are too uncomfortable to discuss.[44] Some physicians and others hide the fact that a patient may be dying, and when the end nears, the patient may be ignored by family or friends. There may be an effort to engulf the patient in a forced cheerfulness that prevents an honest discussion of death and avoids consideration of how the family will cope with its loss or where the patient will spend eternity.

Sometimes, a family member may ask you if a patient should be told the truth about a serious or terminal diagnosis. Probably it is true that most terminally ill patients sense when death is approaching even before they are told. A frank, honest, and caring discussion of the patient's condition and prognosis does much to retain trust and confidence in the medical team. When this is accompanied or followed by unhurried talking about the situation, the counselee can feel free to discuss his or her feelings, be helped to put practical and financial affairs in order, resolve interpersonal tensions, say good-bye to loved ones, and ensure that there is a peace with God.

5. *Help People Deal with Pain.* No one knows with certainty how many people suffer from chronic pain associated with arthritis, migraine headaches, back problems, and various physical illnesses. In the United States it is estimated that about 20 percent of the population has physical, sensory, psychiatric, or mental disabilities that interfere with daily living. Many of these people, more than 50 million, experience pain that never goes away completely. It is pain that these people must learn to accept and live with for the rest of their lives.[45] For most of these patients, treatment involves the use of pain medications often accompanied by surgery, but significant research is accumulating to show that pain has a strong psychological component. The psychological treatment of pain can be very effective, even without medical interventions.[46]

It is known, for example, that anxiety can stimulate pain and interfere with the body's coping mechanisms. Depression and chronic pain have a cyclical relationship in which the increase in one can lead to the increase in the other. Excessive thinking about one's health and physical condition can increase the body's sensitivity to pain, and that, in turn, increases the awareness and concern about one's health. Add this to the evidence that only 50 percent of pain patients take prescribed medication as directed, and it is easy to understand why teams of specialists treating pain increasingly include psychologists and counselors.[47] Biofeedback, relaxation, meditation, cognitive-behavioral counseling, and other psychologically based interventions are used with increasing frequency and effectiveness in helping people control and sometimes eliminate their pain by changing their attitudes, perceptions, and behavior.[48] Christian counselors will not be surprised to learn, in addition, that long-term studies of people who are religious or spiritually committed have increased chances for living longer, handling pain better, and recovering more quickly from surgery.[49]

6. *Teach People to Cope with the Illness and Its Stresses*. Journal articles sometimes express ideas in very formal ways. For example, coping has been defined as "a psychological strategy mobilized to decrease, modify, or diffuse the impact of stress-generation life events." Simply stated, coping is a way to reduce stress. To help sick people cope, counselors can use any of the following methods.

- Help people explore the meaning of their illness or disability. This involves encouraging people to express their feelings about being medically limited or impaired. It encourages people to struggle with their questions about the meaning of the pain. When they are aware of their feelings or struggles and open about them, people with illnesses are less controlled by their emotions.
- Provide counselees with relevant medical information. This can include facts about the illness, the counselee's present medical status, the prognosis for recovery, and the likely impairments that will persist. This information reduces anxiety, denial, and the sense of being out of control.
- Help patients develop and maintain supportive family and group experiences. Sometimes, this may involve getting people into groups with others who share a similar physical condition or disability. These groups can give additional coping skills, role models, and opportunities for dealing with both frustrations and possibilities for the future.
- Teach people how to function in the community, even though the pain or the disability might persist. Sometimes, this involves life-management skills, vocational direction, and dealing with social stigma.[50]
- Encourage decision making. Some physically ill people engage in melancholy brooding, give up trying to live fulfilling lives, or withdraw from activities that they are capable of doing. These behaviors and attitudes can make matters worse, hinder recovery, and leave the person feeling miserable. The counselor can challenge these perspectives gently, help people develop more balanced perspectives on the present, and guide them as they make realistic decisions about the future. Some patients will be faced with permanent limitations and handicaps, but counselors can show that life can still be lived fully with the mental abilities, opportunities, and physical capacities that remain.

7. *Instill Hope*. The Christian recognizes that serious illness and even death are not the end of meaningful living. Hope is at the basis of our Christian faith. It is more than the wish that God will perform a miracle. It is the confidence that God, who is living and sovereign, also controls all things and can be expected to bring to pass that which ultimately is best.[51] Often, that means recovery; sometimes, it means long years of suffering or incapacity; eventually, it means passing through death and, for the believer, into eternal life with Christ. Anger, frustration, uncertainty, stress, times of denial, and disappointment almost always are

present with serious illness, but these can be countered by the hope that we have as Christians—not a hope in some emotionally based fantasy of what might happen—but a hope that is based solidly on the Bible's teachings about God and his creation.

8. *Help the Family and Staff.* When an individual has a problem, the family almost always is affected. This is especially true when a family member is ill, since most of the issues that concern patients also concern their families. In addition, home routines tend to be disrupted, finances may be strained, and at times there is the struggle of facing and coping with an approaching death. Therefore, families, as well as patients, can benefit from counseling. In turn, this can help the patient cope with the illness more effectively.

Counselors also can help patients indirectly by working with those who give treatment. Patients and families keep passing through the hospital doors, but the staff remains, constantly coming into contact with new patients but often having limited contact with the people who have left and recovered. Many staff people are overworked, underpaid, frequently criticized, and emotionally drained by their ongoing contact with pain or sadness and by sometimes impatient, distraught, or critical patients and family members. Some health-care professionals entered their fields with a desire to bring hope and healing, but they discover too late that their work is less involved with the art of healing and caring, and more concerned with the administration of sophisticated procedures and complicated tests. As a result, many health-care professionals feel that the healing touch of the care-giver has been replaced by the administration of medications or the use of sterile stainless steel objects. Add to this the shortage of professional care-givers, the resulting overwork, the disillusionment among care-givers, and the struggles that many face in trying to balance their personal and professional lives. It is not difficult to understand why burnout is common and why doctors, among others, have higher than average rates of suicide, alcoholism, drug abuse, divorce, and dropout from their professions.

Hospital personnel may not request the counselors' help, especially if the counselors are infrequent visitors to the hospital, unlike chaplains or others who are there frequently. Even so, counselors should be alert to what may be the pressing but unexpressed needs of staff people who could benefit from counseling. Sometimes, it is best to start by giving casual, sensitive, supportive encouragement that helps staff people deal with their emotions and unanswered questions. Often, when a counselor shows concern on the ward, this leads to later more in-depth counseling elsewhere.

9. *Help the Malingerer and Hypochondriac.* For some people the sickness goes on despite medical treatment. It rarely helps to ignore the symptoms or to confront the patient by stating that the illness has an emotional basis. Medical treatment doesn't help much either. Someone has stated that no medication will cure a psychologically based illness, and no surgery will cut it out. The illness ultimately must be treated at its cause—the underlying anxiety and inability to cope with a symptom-free life.

Nonmedical counselors first must ensure that the illnesses are, in fact, nonorganic. This only can be determined by a physician and, as we have seen, sometimes even doctors have difficulty in deciding if a reported illness really has no biological basis. If the medical report finds no apparent physical basis for the symptoms, the counselor can proceed along the lines suggested in chapter 9 on anxiety. Although the symptoms may have no organic basis, they nevertheless are very real to the counselee. The counselor should show an understanding of the discomfort but attempt, in addition, to discover and help the counselee deal with underlying anxieties. Also, try to determine what needs are being met by the symptoms. These might include the needs to be noticed, to control others, to get attention, and to be dependent. The counselor's goal is to help the person to learn how to meet these needs in healthier ways.

Prevention and Physical Illness

The diagnosis of a chronic physical illness can lead to "many rapid and stressful life changes that in turn generate considerable emotional distress."[52] Anxiety, depression, and family conflict are among the emotional distresses that often appear following the onset of a serious illness. Although family members or pastoral counselors may see the emotional reactions in a patient, these may be overlooked by medical personnel who are focused on treating the physical illness. When the emotional responses to the disease are ignored, however, these psychological influences can reduce the patient's ability to improve, make the physical condition worse, and increase the risk for death. Some patients, "driven by their emotional distress and accompanying symptoms, may become frequent visitors to physicians' offices, experience unnecessary hospital admissions, or find themselves subjected to invasive medical procedures that later prove costly and unnecessary."[53] Sometimes, a medical professional will recommend that the patient get counseling to deal with the emotional issues, but this well-intentioned suggestion can make matters worse if the patient then concludes that he or she now has psychological problems as well as a physical illness.

Medical crisis counseling (MCC) is a short-term approach that focuses on helping patients and their families deal with their illnesses and concerns about the future. It encourages their active cooperation with the medical treatment team, teaches self-coping skills, and gives social support. The patient is helped to recognize that this psychological help is not a signal that he or she is mentally ill; it is a part of treatment that helps with adjustment to the illness and that can contribute to recovery.[54]

The medical profession, associations dealing with specific illnesses, and the media give considerable attention to ways in which disease and injury can be prevented or avoided. Counselors and church bodies also can help with the prevention of illness-related problems.

1. *Encourage People to Face Their Concerns and Discuss Their Attitudes Toward Sickness and Death.* Since these can be difficult issues to face, many healthy people avoid them. As a result, the realities of sickness and death hit with greater impact when we are forced to face them. This trauma could be lessened if those who are healthy would maintain contact with people who are sick and suffering. Often, these people need help and support, but they tend to be ignored by healthy people who may feel uncomfortable in the presence of those who are sick.

The realities of facing an illness also might be handled better if each of us could give prior deliberate thought to our own possible sickness, death, and funeral preferences. When these issues can be discussed openly with family members while everyone is well, later decisions are easier. This kind of discussion need not be morbid or imply wishful thinking. It is an acknowledgment of the mortality that we all have on this earth. It is a way to prepare for the future and to open lines of communication before crises arise.

It is of even greater importance to discuss emotions when an illness is diagnosed. Fear, anger, guilt, confusion, concern about the family, thoughts about death, and other concerns should be raised and discussed realistically. The sooner this is done, the better; otherwise the concerns can fester and complicate both the illness and the recovery process. One of my friends is in his thirties, limited by a physical illness, living life to the fullest as best he can, but with his funeral planned in case the illness should lead to an unexpected early death. On the night before my open heart surgery, my wife and I had an honest talk about what might happen if I did not survive, and we talked about who would be asked to conduct the funeral service. Counselors can encourage this kind of healthy sharing. This, in turn, can prevent more intense emotional or physical problems later.

2. *Help People See Meaning in Sickness and Suffering.* When I was a graduate student, I had the privilege of meeting Victor Frankl. His book *Man's Search for Meaning* has sold over nine million copies and was required reading for students in my early days as a college professor.[55] Frankl was incarcerated in a Nazi prison camp during World War II, and he watched as some people gave up the fight to live, while others were able to see purpose in their suffering and found meaning in living, even amidst the horrors of Auschwitz.

To be arrested and incarcerated because of one's ethnic background or beliefs seems like a different kind of suffering from the painful and weary experience of living with a debilitating chronic illness. Often, we see persistent pain and sickness as harmful and bad, but this is not necessarily so. Physical illness can bring us face-to-face with our own limitations, give us a clearer perspective on life and eternity, and teach us more fully about the love and forgiveness of God. Illness is often what people need to slow them down so they can get better—if not physically, then at least emotionally and spiritually. When a counselee can see sickness in this more meaningful light, it sometimes is easier to live with questions that are unanswered and perhaps unanswerable from a human perspective, questions about why people get sick, stay sick, and suffer.

3. *Give People Information.* Many years ago researchers discovered that surgical patients recover faster and experience less pain when they are told before treatment what to expect during and after the surgery.[56] When the patient and family know what is coming, the discomfort and anxiety can be handled much more effectively.

4. *Strengthen People's Christian Commitment.* Any person who has faced a medical crisis or who has been sick for a long period of time knows the comfort that can come through Christian music, prayer, meditation on the Bible, worship, the knowledge that others are praying, and the supportive presence of family and close friends. These spiritual resources can prepare us for the crises of life and can bring us through these difficult times. The Bible never teaches that believers are exempt from suffering or illness, but neither does it say that we need to bear these burdens alone.[57] When we are in the habit of bearing each other's burdens and casting our burdens on God in prayer, then we are better prepared for facing illness, uncomfortable medical procedures, and death when they come. The physical and psychological pain will remain, but underneath is the assurance that God cares and is in control.

Conclusions About Physical Illness

Prior to World War II, a Swiss physician named Paul Tournier first proposed a concept that he termed the "medicine of the whole person." Widely accepted today, the medicine of the whole person was a new idea when Tournier suggested that whenever a person is sick, his or her whole being is affected—the physical, psychological, and spiritual. Jesus demonstrated this concern for whole persons when he ministered to spiritual needs, but he also had a deep and practical concern about individual suffering, social conditions, mental struggles, and physical illness. We who are his followers must have a similar compassionate concern for whole persons. To divorce the physical, psychological, social, and spiritual parts of a person from each other is both unbiblical and impossible. To recognize the importance of all these enables us to counsel more effectively in working with the physically ill and their families.

KEY POINTS FOR BUSY COUNSELORS

➤ Counseling the physically sick and their families can be a major challenge for Christian counselors. The entire field of health psychology deals with the psychological implications of physical illness.

➤ The Bible mentions sickness frequently. Among its conclusions are the following:
- Sickness is a part of living: at times everybody gets sick.
- Care, compassion, and healing are important for Christians.
- Sickness, sin, and faith are not necessarily related.
- Sickness raises important questions about suffering.
- Serious illness can raise difficult ethical questions about the right to die.

➤ The psychological and spiritual implications of sickness are caused by:
- Stress and helplessness.
- Guilt and self-criticism.
- Fear and depression.
- The experience of pain.
- Family influences.

➤ Illness leads to different reactions that can be of concern to counselors. These reactions include:
- Denial.
- Defensiveness.
- Withdrawal.
- Depression and anxiety.
- Resistance and anger.
- Manipulation of others.

- Malingering or hypochondriasis.
- Hope.

➤ To counsel the physically ill and their families,
  - Be aware of your own attitudes and needs.
  - Learn and apply appropriate guidelines for visiting the sick.
  - Be sensitive to unique boundary issues.
  - Deal with the specific feelings and concerns of the patient.
  - Help people deal with pain.
  - Teach people to cope with their stresses.
  - Instill hope.
  - Help the patient's family and the treatment staff.
  - Help the malingerer and the hypochondriac.

➤ Counselors cannot always prevent the illness, but they can prevent illnesses from getting worse and they can take action to hasten recovery. These preventive activities include:
  - Encouraging people to face their concerns and to discuss their attitudes toward the sickness and death.
  - Helping people see meaning in sickness and suffering.
  - Giving accurate information.
  - Strengthening the patient's Christian commitment.

➤ To separate the physical, psychological, social, and spiritual parts of a person is both impossible and unbiblical. To recognize the importance of all these enables counselors to work more effectively with the physically ill and their families.

25

Grief

Before they lost their husbands, Mildred and Helen lived in the same neighborhood, attended the same church, and had been friends for many years. The husbands died at about the same time, but the circumstances of their deaths were very different.

Mildred's husband had cancer. The illness was discovered about a year before his death, but despite surgery and the best medical treatment available, his condition deteriorated as the months passed. Mildred devoted herself to caring for the man to whom she had been married for more than forty years. When he was hospitalized, she visited him every day. When he was at home, she cared for him tenderly, even when she was exhausted from taking care of his every need. With reluctance and only at the urging of her children and doctor, Mildred finally agreed to let her husband return to the hospital, where he spent the last days of his life.

During the year of this illness, the couple talked openly and often about death, heaven, and their life together. They had long discussions about the things they regretted and the pleasant experiences they had shared. It was difficult, but they forced themselves to talk about the coming funeral and how Mildred would cope as a widow.

Helen and her husband had no time for similar conversations. During a vacation trip within weeks of his planned retirement, Helen's husband collapsed in a restaurant and was dead on arrival at the local hospital. A massive heart attack had taken his life and jolted Helen into unexpected widowhood.

From the beginning it was clear to their friends that these two Christian women were handling their grief differently. Mildred talked freely about her husband and admitted her loneliness and "empty heart." Slowly, she resumed her activities at church, even though she didn't feel like participating at first. She determined to keep involved in the lives and activities of her grandchildren, and eventually moved into a facility for senior citizens, where she could be independent but surrounded by friends and opportunities for activity. It took time, but as the months passed, Mildred began to pick up the activities of her life again. Today, she spends much of her time "helping the old people," even though she herself is well into her eighties.

Helen withdrew from people after her husband died. She stopped seeing her friends, appeared to lose interest in the grandchildren that previously had been so important in her life, and spent most days sitting in front of a television set, feeling depressed and engulfed in self-pity. After years of closeness with her husband, Helen concluded that life was no longer worth living and that she never would be happy again. Despite the urgings of her children and her doctor, Helen rarely ate healthy or regular meals. Soon her health began to deteriorate, and two years after her widowhood began, Helen's heart stopped one night while she slept. "She died of a broken heart," her friends and children said to one another at the wake. She also died without any joy, without saying good-bye, and without seeing her grandchildren grow up.

Mildred and Helen were two good friends who mourned in different ways and whose lives went in very different directions in the later years.

At some time almost all of us see loved ones die and experience the pain of grief. "When death separates us from someone we love there is a time when we think no one has suffered as we have," wrote Billy Graham.[1] Perhaps no two people grieve in the same way, and the methods of handling grief are unique and personal, but the pain of grieving is universal.

Grief has gripped people since the beginning of human existence, so it is not surprising that counselors have studied bereavement carefully. In 1917, for example, Freud published a detailed psychological study of grief.[2] Almost thirty years later Erich Lindemann, a Harvard professor, wrote a highly acclaimed paper based on his interviews with grieving relatives.[3] Soon books and articles began to appear, including the one that probably is most famous, *On Death and Dying*, written by a previously unknown psychiatrist named Elisabeth Kübler-Ross.[4] Probably more than any other publication, this book stimulated development of a whole new body of literature and a field of study known as *thanatology*—the branch of knowledge that deals with dying, death, and bereavement.

Grief is a normal response to the loss of any significant person, object, or opportunity. It is an experience of deprivation and anxiety that can show itself in one's behavior, emotions, thinking, physiology, interpersonal relationships, and spirituality. Grief is not limited to the loss of a loved one through death. Any loss can bring grief, including divorce, retirement from a job, amputation of a limb, the departure of a child to college or a pastor to some other church, moving from a friendly neighborhood (or watching a good neighbor move), losing a home or other valued possession, the death of a pet or plant, loss of a contest or athletic game, health failures, or even the loss of one's youthful appearance, confidence, or enthusiasm. Sometimes, desirable and long-anticipated events—like the move to a better job or graduation from college—can bring grief (mixed with happiness) because valuable memories or relationships are being lost and left behind. Doubts about one's faith, the waning of spiritual vitality, or disillusionment about the actions of a trusted religious leader can all lead to sadness and emptiness that indicate grief. In summary, whenever a part of life is lost or taken away, there can be grief.

Even though grief can have a variety of causes, most often it is associated with the loss of a loved one or other meaningful person who has died. This grieving is never easy. We may try to soften the trauma by dressing up the corpse, surrounding the body with flowers or soft lights, and using words like "passed away" or "departed" instead of "died," but we cannot make death into something beautiful.[5] Christians take comfort in the peace that comes from God and in the certainty of the resurrection, but these do not remove the emptiness and pain of being forced to let go of someone we love. When any of us encounters death, we face an irreversible, unalterable situation that cannot be changed. Even though "death is swallowed up in victory,"[6] the loss of a loved one can be devastating, and grief can be overwhelming. Eventually everybody dies,[7] but in the meantime most of us will grieve at least periodically. Grieving gives counselors a difficult but rewarding challenge—to help people deal with death and bereavement.

The Bible and Grief

Death and grieving are mentioned often in the Bible. In the Old Testament, for example, we read about Jacob mourning over the loss of Joseph and refusing to be comforted, David grieving over the anticipated loss of his infant son and the death in battle of his grown sons Amnon and Absalom, and Jeremiah lamenting the death of King Josiah.[8] Especially moving is David's grief when he learns that his closest friend, Jonathan, had died in battle.[9] The Psalms tell us of God's presence and comfort as we "walk through the valley of death,"[10] and we learn that the Word of God encourages those who weep with grief.[11] Isaiah introduces us to the Messiah, "a man of sorrows and acquainted with bitterest grief," who knew the pain of being rejected by those whose sins he came to bear.[12]

In the New Testament, the many passages on death and grief might be grouped into two categories. Each deals with the influence of Jesus Christ.

1. *Christ Has Changed the Meaning of Grieving.* Some people have no belief in an afterlife. For them, there is no hope for the future, and death is the end of a relationship forever. Surveys have shown, however, that most people believe in an afterlife, even those who have no religious beliefs. These people find hope in the midst of their grief.

The Christian perspective is built on New Testament passages that give us reason to hope, even in times of sorrow.[13] Paul's first letter to the Thessalonians states that "since we believe that Jesus died and was raised to life again, we also believe that when Jesus comes, God will bring back with Jesus all the Christians who have died."[14] We can comfort and encourage each other with these words,[15] convinced that in the future "when the trumpet sounds, the Christians who have died will be raised with transformed bodies. . . . For our perishable earthly bodies must be transformed into heavenly bodies that will never die . . . then the Scriptures will come true: Death is swallowed up in victory."[16]

For the Christian, death is not the end of existence; it is the beginning of life eternal. The one who believes in Christ knows that Christians always will be with the Lord. Physical death will still be present as long as the devil is allowed to have the power of death, but because of the crucifixion and resurrection, Christ has defeated death and promised that the one who lives and believes in Christ will never die.[17]

This knowledge is comforting, but it does not eliminate the intense pain of grief and the need for solace. In a discussion of death, Paul encouraged his readers to take courage and not lose heart, since the believer who is absent from the body is present with the Lord.[18] Christians are encouraged to be strong and steady, always enthusiastic about the Lord's work, "knowing that nothing we do for the Lord is ever useless"[19] as we look forward with confidence to the certainty of the resurrection.

2. *Christ Has Demonstrated the Importance of Grieving.* Early in his ministry, Jesus preached his Sermon on the Mount and spoke about grieving. "God blesses those who mourn, for they will be comforted," he said.[20] When Lazarus died, Jesus was deeply moved. He accepted, without comment, the apparent anger that came from Mary, Lazarus's sister, and he wept with the mourners. Jesus knew that Lazarus was about to be raised from the dead, but the Lord still grieved.[21] He also withdrew by himself (perhaps to grieve) when he learned that John the Baptist had been executed.[22] In the Garden of Gethsemane, Jesus was "crushed with grief,"[23] perhaps with anticipatory mourning, more intense but similar to that experienced by David as he watched his infant son die.[24]

Even for the Christian who believes in an afterlife, grief is normal, healthy, and intensely felt. It also can be pathological and unhealthy. As we will see, this difference is of special concern to any Christian counselor.

The Causes of Grief

For five months following the attack on the World Trade Center in New York, a group met weekly with two counselors. They came from different ethnic backgrounds, had different levels of education, were of different ages, and were at different stages in their lives. Some were survivors, others were family members of the victims, and a few were rescue workers. They had little in common except that all were grieving, and that was enough to pull them together. There was no set agenda for their meetings, and the conversations often were wide-ranging. Near the beginning they discussed the utter incomprehensibility of what had happened, and at different times they shared their pain, longing, emptiness, experiences on that fateful day, and concerns about whether life would ever again be normal. At different times they all wondered if their grieving was normal, and they struggled to resume their activities, such as going to work or preparing for Christmas. "When I walk down the street, I feel people know what has happened to me," one lady said. "They know because of the vacant look in my eyes."[25]

Why did this group meet together voluntarily? They were helping one another come to terms with their losses, and although nobody thought this way, they were moving through tasks like the following that most grieving people face.[26]

- Accepting that the loss has taken place and that it is real and permanent.
- Experiencing and expressing the emotions and deep thoughts that are associated with loss. This includes reliving special moments from the past, recalling warm memories, and expressing sadness, loneliness, acute sorrow, and sometimes anger, which may be directed at the deceased person, at somebody else, or at God.
- Untangling oneself from the ties that bind the person to the deceased or to whatever else has been lost. This involves letting go, saying good-bye, and slowly adjusting to an environment and lifestyle in which the deceased person or lost object is missing permanently. It does not mean that the deceased person is forgotten. A reevaluation of the relationship and continuing emotional bonds persist, but the grieving person moves on with the realization that from this point life will be different because an important person has gone.
- Reinvesting one's energy into forming new relationships, pursuing new projects, setting new goals, and cultivating fresh dreams or aspirations. This stage often seems to be the most difficult because people feel guilty and insecure about reinvesting their energies into new things. This also can be difficult because grieving people often feel depleted and drained of the energy that may be needed to keep moving.

Nobody can say how long the mourning process will last. It may take only a few weeks of a few months, depending on what or who was lost and on the nature of the relationship. Adjustment to the death of a spouse is likely to take longer (some suggest that three to four years is typical) than the loss of a friend or sibling who lives many miles away. The sudden death of a child who commits suicide will be harder, in most cases, than the loss of an elderly parent whose health has been failing.[27] Even then, life is never like it was before the loss occurred.

Some writers and counselors have tried to identify specific stages of grieving, but today it generally is agreed that there is no orderly succession through which all grieving will pass. Normal grief usually includes intense sorrow, pain, loneliness, anger, depression, physical symptoms, and changes in interpersonal relationships. Often there is denial, fantasy, restlessness, disorganization, inefficiency, irritability, a desire to talk considerably about the deceased, an unconscious adoption of the lost person's mannerisms, and a feeling that life no longer has meaning. Some writers suggest that grieving involves "meaning reconstruction."[28] This is a fancy way to say that the death of a loved one forever alters the meaning of life so that grieving involves a reevaluation of the bereaved person's life purpose. Even though the mourner may never recover completely from the loss, most people eventually return to a measure of productivity and a restoration of mental and physical well-being. Grief counselors sometimes refer to this process of normal grief as "uncomplicated mourning."

In contrast are the people whose grief is abnormal, pathological, and complicated. This is grief that is intensified, delayed, prolonged, denied, or otherwise deviating from the more common expressions of sorrow. This is grief that keeps the mourner in bondage to the deceased person and prevents one from coping and moving on with life. Often, there are no symptoms unique to unhealthy grief. Instead, the behavior seen in normal grieving appears with greater intensity and longer duration. There may be deep feelings of dejection, lack of interest in the outside world, a diminished capacity to love, withdrawal, and greatly lowered self-esteem. For some there is busy hyperactivity, a persistent giving-up attitude of helplessness and hopelessness, intense guilt, extreme social withdrawal or moodiness, impulsivity, antisocial behavior, excessive drinking, and veiled threats of self-destruction (sometimes followed by serious attempts at suicide). Some people show a strong self-condemnation, especially if they feel responsibility for the death. This can be seen in car drivers who survived a crash in which somebody was killed.

Counselors now prefer to group all these symptoms into what is known as *complicated grief*. Terms like *pathological, neurotic,* or *unhealthy* grieving are rarely used, so throughout the remainder of this chapter we will replace these older terms with references to grief that is complicated. Impacting perhaps 15 percent of people who have lost a loved one, this condition includes many of the characteristics described in the above paragraph and includes changes in all personal relationships, an ongoing sense of meaninglessness, a prolonged yearning or searching for the deceased person, and a sense that one's core beliefs have been ruptured.[29] Very different is *delayed grief,* in which a person shows none of the expected symptoms of grieving. This may indicate denial, anger, or guilt that allows the person to go on as if nothing has happened until the reality of the loss hits at a later time. Although this kind of grief is thought to be relatively common, some researchers question its existence.[30]

Why is some grief normal while other grief is complicated? There is no simple explanation, but several influences seem to determine how one will react to a loss.

1. *Prior Anticipation.* Grieving may be more difficult when a loss is unexpected, untimely (when a person dies at the prime of life, for example), or sudden and traumatic (involving violence or an accident.)

Anticipatory mourning (which is a term used increasingly in place of the older words *anticipatory grief*) involves grief that is brought on by the slow dying of a loved one. Often, the period of anticipation and prior preparation can make the grief process smoother, especially if the deceased person and the survivors had opportunity to absorb the reality of what is happening; express their feelings, including sorrow; and complete "unfinished business," such as expressing love or asking forgiveness, making plans for the future, and saying good-bye. When there is time for this kind of discussion, the survivors often feel less guilt, self-condemnation, or regret after the death occurs. This does not always lead to an easier grieving process later, however. Sometimes, the more intense intimacy that builds during the anticipatory period makes the loss seem greater when it does occur. If the death does not occur when it was expected, there can be ambivalence in the survivors, who vacillate between wanting it to be over and dreading the inevitable.[31]

2. *Type of Loss.* Each type of loss brings its own kind of suffering and reaction.

The death of a revered and respected leader can bring grief to thousands of people, especially if the leader symbolized the hopes and expectations of those who mourn. This mass grieving differs from the grief experienced by a close relative of someone who dies.

In adult life, the death of a parent is the most common type of bereavement and the loss that is handled best, especially if the parent is older.[32] The death of a sibling may bring a personal threat and involve a there-but-for-the-grace-of-God-go-I feeling that can make the mourning more poignant and difficult, especially if the sibling was young. Loss of a wife or husband is likely to be much more difficult. The joys, challenges, and burdens of life that previously were shared now must be borne alone, and that can be very stressful. Often, this involves learning to live alone, with loneliness, anxiety, and the need to make decisions or do routine tasks (like paying bills, cooking meals, or taking out the trash) that previously were shared. Even more difficult is the loss of a child. Parents often feel guilty, angry, depressed, self-condemning, and incompetent because they failed to protect the child from death, even when there may have been nothing they could have done. There can be a sense of injustice because we don't expect children to die before their parents, especially young children. Often, there is a widespread outpouring of grief and condolences to the family, probably because so many of the mourners are able to understand how the loss of their own children could have a devastating impact. For many couples a child's death may weaken a marriage. If the marriage has been under stress for other reasons, the loss of a child may be more than the marriage can bear. This is not to deny that for some couples the child's death may draw them together, so that they help each other and the surviving children cope.[33]

It is not surprising that grief is greater, the closer the relationship between the griever and the deceased. Grief also is more intense and more likely to become complicated (unhealthy) if the griever was very dependent on the deceased. In addition, if the relationship involved both love and strong negative feelings, then the survivor is left with guilt and anger in addition to the sadness. All of this makes grieving harder.[34]

3. *Beliefs.* Out of a desire to help others (and often in a sometimes unconscious attempt to help themselves), many grieving people have written books about their own sorrows and struggles with grief and readjustment. Often, these writings describe the turmoil and deep pain involved in grieving, but many also point

to the sustaining power of religious beliefs. There may be periods of doubt, confusion, and even anger with God, but in time the healing power of one's faith becomes evident. After describing her intense sorrow after the loss of two children, Nancy Guthrie described how submission to God is much harder on some days than on others. She wrote about her beliefs but then added, "That is what I believe. It is not necessarily how I feel."[35] For many grieving people, religion gives support, meaning, and hope for the future. Christians believe, in addition, that the Holy Spirit who lives in each believer gives supernatural comfort and peace in times of mourning. This can be true even for those who previously drifted away from their faith or who claimed to be agnostic. Many have found the solace that comes from belief in God and involvement in the community of believers.

There is abundant evidence, therefore, that religious beliefs can help patients and families cope with terminal illness, soften the initial pain of death in survivors, help people deal with their losses, and facilitate the grieving process.[36] When a grieving person has no religious beliefs or refuses to consider the claims of Christ, there is no reason for hope. As a result, the pain can be greater, the grieving can be more difficult, and presumably there is greater potential for complicated grief.

4. *Background and Personality.* One indication of how grief will be handled in the future is how the mourner reacted to separations and losses in the past. If previous separations were difficult and problem producing, and if change has always been difficult or resisted, then present grieving may be more difficult as well. Handling grief also may be hard for people who are insecure, dependent, unable to control or express feelings, prone to depression or anxiety, or living under stress. Grievers differ in the way they grieve because they differ in the ways they handle stress, face the realities of loss, maintain close contact with others who could give support, view life after death, are able to be flexible, or have skills for coping with crises. Grieving always is difficult, but it clearly hits some people harder than others.

5. *Social and Cultural Environments.* Perhaps all cultures have socially sanctioned ways of meeting needs at the time of bereavement. These social mores are built around both religious beliefs or practices and the racial or ethnic backgrounds of the grievers. In multicultural cities like Toronto, Singapore, or Chicago, for example, people in the Chinese or Islamic neighborhoods express their grief in ways that differ from the customs of people from Jewish, Latin, African, or European backgrounds. Cultural and religious groups also differ in the extent to which they allow, discourage, or encourage the overt expression of sorrow. There are different practices concerning the wake and the social behavior that is expected of visiting friends and relatives. Even funerals differ, although it appears that in almost every culture the funeral offers group support to the bereaved, opportunity to express religious beliefs and rituals, and visual confrontation with the dead body.

In spite of these social, cultural, and religious variations, there also are commonly held values. In American, Canadian, Australian, British, and other Western societies, for example, there has tended to be an intolerance of prolonged grieving. These countries value efficiency and pragmatism, so death often is seen as an inconvenience, embarrassment, or interruption. Emotional expressions are not encouraged, and grief is viewed as something that, while inevitable, should end as quickly as possible. Despite the efforts of hospice providers and other groups that are committed to helping people die with dignity away from sterile hospital environments, many people end life far from their homes or families. In a world where mobility and interdependence are increasingly valued, family members travel frequently, live with greater ease in different parts of the world, have fewer close contacts with others, and more easily can deny or ignore the reality of death. This can make the loss more traumatic for close relatives of the deceased, and there are fewer intimate people nearby who can give continual in-depth support. Instead, we have encouraged ourselves and one another to deny death and to respond to the bereavement of others with little more than cards, cut flowers, casseroles, or maybe a quick visit. Of course, this description is not true of everyone, and neither does it apply to all communities, but surely many of us will recognize that our modern social attitudes toward death greatly influence how mourners are able to experience, express, and work through the grieving process. This has significance for counselors who cannot ignore these cultural issues when they counsel.

6. *Other Issues.* As we have seen, closeness to the deceased, suddenness of death, and the age of the dead person are only some of the issues that impact the grieving process. Grieving may also be prolonged and more difficult when:

- The death is considered exceptionally untimely, such as the death of a successful adult in the prime of life and at the beginning of a promising career.
- The mode of death is considered incomprehensible, senseless, or tragic, such as a murder, suicide, serious accident, or terrorist attack.
- There was such extreme dependency on the lost person that the mourner feels immobilized and has had little basis for building self-confidence, personal identity, or meaning in life.
- The mourner's work environment, family, or other environmental circumstances disallow or disapprove of any expression of grief.
- The dead person extracted a promise from the survivor that he or she would never grieve, be sad, remarry, or move.
- The survivor feels a sense of guilt because he or she participated in the event that caused the death (for example, the leader who organized and was leading a mountain climbing weekend in which one of the participants fell and was killed).
- The grieving is short-circuited by well-meaning friends, family members, co-workers, or fellow Christians who make comments, such as: "Shouldn't you be over this by now?" or "The funeral was several weeks ago, so don't you think it is time to get on with your life?"
- There is a premature jumping back into normal activities without allowing time to acknowledge and assimilate the loss.
- The grieving person believes, contrary to biblical teaching and the example of Jesus,[37] that Christians should so rejoice that they never grieve. This is the sincere but harmful view that grieving is a sign of spiritual immaturity or lack of trust in God.

The Effects of Grief

It was a terrible and unusual accident when a tree branch fell on to the playground of an elementary school and killed a nine-year-old boy who was playing with his friends. For at least six months after the tragedy, the boy's mother appeared to be in a daze. She was aware of her son's death, of course, but she had trouble with concentration and memory. Her counselor realized that the mother needed to let the reality sink in before she could begin to express her deepest feelings and begin to rebuild her life. Later the counselor wrote: "I had to keep reminding myself that I can't take away her pain, but I can sit with her, honor her feelings, and accompany her on her journey without rushing her along."[38]

Grieving often begins with a period of shock, numbness, denial, intense crying, and sometimes a period of dazed disbelief, such as the nine-year-old's mother faced. Then the grieving process tends to move into a prolonged period of sorrow, restlessness, apathy, memories of the past, loneliness, and sleep disturbances. Only later is there a slow waning of the grief symptoms and a resumption of normal life activities.

Despite trends like these, most counselors resist attempts to identify specific stages of grieving. Probably, you can be more helpful if you know some of the common effects of grieving. Even these don't always appear, and they cannot be put into any standard order of appearance.

1. *Physical Effects*. Bereavement can be bad for your health because grief can put stress on the body at a time when people are least able to resist the onslaught of illness. Grief interferes with the body's immune system so that viruses and other disease-causing organisms are more difficult to resist, especially during the first six months of mourning.[39] The death rate increases significantly during the first years of widowhood when there are marked increases in congestive heart failure, high blood pressure, strokes, and cancer. In addition, stress can lead to exhaustion, weakness, headaches, shortness of breath, indigestion, loss of appetite, and difficulties in sleeping. Many years ago a study of 95,647 widowed people in Scandinavia found that the death rate during the first five years was 6.5 percent higher than expected by the statistical tables. The suicide rate was 242 percent higher than expected, and the rate of traffic deaths was 153 percent higher.[40] Findings like these have led to the conclusion that "the many stresses associated with profound loss can have a serious, and even lethal, impact on a sizable minority of bereaved persons."[41]

2. *Emotional and Cognitive Effects*. It comes as no surprise to find that grief also affects both how a person feels and how he or she thinks. As we have seen, depression is common following the death of a loved one, and often there are feelings of inner emptiness, guilt, anger, irritability, withdrawal from others, forgetfulness, dreams about the deceased, declining interest in sex, nightmares, errors in judgment, and feelings of loneliness. For many there is a loss of energy, disorganization of routines, and a realization that even the most simple activities that once were automatic now require the expending of considerable energy. At a time when the grieving person feels least able to handle extra pressure, there usually is an increase in things that have to be done, including the submission of claims for insurance, consolidating and changing names on bank accounts, paying extra bills connected with funeral and hospital expenses, meeting with lawyers concerning the deceased person's will, changing names on legal documents, such as the mortgage or car title, informing government agencies and providers of pensions, and even handling daily hassles like the tap that starts leaking or the lawn that needs to be mowed. All of this can create a lot of frustration and put addi-

tional stress on the grieving person. It is not surprising that anxiety and panic attacks are common during the bereavement period.

In writing about the loss of his wife, C. S. Lewis observed that symptoms of grief come in waves, and rarely are all present at the same time.[42] As the months pass they tend to fade, but sometimes they come back with renewed intensity when they are least expected. For example, in the presence of outstanding reminders of the loss (such as later visits to the hospital where the person died), many of the old grief feelings and reactions sweep over the person with new intensity. In addition, almost all survivors experience anniversary reactions. The first Christmas, Easter, birthday, or wedding anniversary after the loss can be difficult emotionally, as can the anniversaries of the death. These anniversary reactions may continue for years. Sometimes, when people are not free to mourn immediately after the death, a full grief reaction will be triggered by a later anniversary or other reminder of the loss.

3. *Social Effects.* The death of a loved one is a major social disruption. When a spouse dies, the surviving mate must learn to relate to others as a single adult. Old friends may not know how to relate to the survivor, and a widower may feel awkward to be the only unaccompanied person at a gathering of couples with whom he and his wife used to associate. Relationships between the survivor's spouse and the dead person's family may show new and unexpected tension, particularly if the survivor starts dating. The parents of a younger woman who has died may feel threatened and even angry when their son-in-law remarries and the grandchildren start talking about their "new mom." In all of this, family members find new demands on their time and must adapt to new roles.

To avoid some of these social tensions, grieving people often withdraw from others, get busy so they won't have to face their anxieties, or start traveling. In themselves, none of these is harmful, but each can become a way to escape and deny the reality of one's new, unfamiliar, and uncomfortable social status.

4. *Spiritual Effects.* The death of a loved one or any other significant loss can be like a concrete roadblock that drops into the path of life and forces an abrupt stop. Sometimes, people can detour around the obstacle and move forward again with relative ease, especially if the loss was of minor significance. More often, however, there is a forced reevaluation of one's life, goals, values, and beliefs.

In times like these, many people turn to their religious resources and leaders for support and meaning. Times spent in prayer, meditation, Bible reading, and devotional books[43] can be very comforting, as can the presence of caring Christian friends who come alongside and bring their presence and love along with the flowers or other expressions of compassion and sympathy. Even as some people find God in the midst of loss and grieving, others turn away and abandon long-held beliefs and religious practices because these seem to offer little help. "Many grief stricken people do indeed find comfort in spiritual or religious traditions," wrote one counselor, but others "find spiritual traditions hollow and devoid of meaning."[44] Part of the difference, no doubt, is in the nature of the spiritual tradition. Even when the grieving person has faith built on the solid Christian foundation that most readers of this book would accept as true, it is common for even dedicated believers to question their beliefs in times of loss. Often, they struggle with disturbing questions about why God permitted the loss to occur and about his nature and sovereignty. Questions like these have no easy answers, and even if they did, the grieving person does not need intellectual answers, at least in the beginning. A more helpful response from others is not to argue but to listen, to be present, and to ask for God's peace and healing.

When there has been intense loss, it can take many months to dismantle that concrete block in the road or get around it. The grieving person may not always see this, but the presence and peace of God, often shown in the behavior of caring Christian friends, can significantly influence the bereaved person and bring healing.

5. *Unhealthy Effects.* Complicated grief reactions occur whenever grief is denied, ignored, delayed, or never ending, so there is ongoing fear, helplessness, withdrawal, and other evidences of psychological unhealthiness. This most often occurs when the death or other loss was sudden, unexpected, or traumatic; the mourner has been excessively dependent on the deceased; there was an ambivalent relationship (love mixed with hatred or dislike) between the survivor and the lost one; or there was unfinished business between the mourner and the deceased (such as siblings who had not talked for years, family conflicts that had never been resolved, confessions that hadn't been made, or love that had never been expressed). Complicated grief also can appear when the survivor faces new or difficult challenges, such as making important business decisions alone or being left with the responsibility of raising children without a partner.

When grief is complicated, the survivor may show several of the following behaviors, few or none of which appeared before the loss occurred. Be alert for grieving persons who show:

- Unwillingness to talk about the deceased person or other loss, often accompanied by intense sadness whenever the dead person's name or other situation is mentioned.
- A tendency to speak of the deceased person in the present tense (saying, for example, "He doesn't like what I am doing").
- Open or subtle threats of self-destruction.
- Persisting and deep depression, often accompanied by guilt and low self-esteem or a lack in self-confidence.
- Withdrawal and refusal to interact with others.
- Increased or excessive drinking or substance abuse.
- Persisting illnesses that appear to be psychosomatic.
- Excessive hostility, moodiness, guilt, impulsivity, or antisocial behavior.
- Refusal to change the dead person's room or dispose of his or her clothing and other objects.
- Resistance to all offers of counseling.
- Intense busyness and unusual hyperactivity.
- Stoic refusal to show emotion or to appear affected by the loss—this often indicates denial or avoidance of grief.
- A happy, almost euphoric attitude, sometimes explained as "rejoicing in the Lord."

It is widely agreed that the most intense grieving will be completed within a year or two. If the evidences of grief continue longer, especially if some of the above symptoms are present, this is a strong clue that there is complicated (pathological) grief.

6. *Grief Without Death.* Most of the preceding paragraphs have focused on grieving following the death of a loved one, but throughout we have noted that there

can be similar reactions following other losses. Consider, for example, the grieving and sense of loss that can come to people who must leave their participation in a much-loved area of sports. This may be seen in the young person who has worked literally every day for years to achieve athletic competence, only to experience an injury. "Life is absurd," one of these people cried out. "Just when I began to put it all together, I pull this muscle. I'm so depressed. . . . Why me? Why now? I'll never be able to get to this place again. I'm so afraid I'll never recover. Is there any doctor who can help me get going? The stress is unbearable, to say nothing of the physical pain itself. It's just not fair. I feel like dying. A terrible loss."[45] In addition to the powerful impact of athletic injuries, research also shows the strong effects of performance slumps, or forced retirement from competition.[46] Many athletes show all the characteristics that we have listed, including reevaluations of their life purposes, goals, and spiritual beliefs. For many people these stressful grieving experiences are no less intense than grief that follows a death.

Other examples, some of which may be especially difficult, include loss of:

- Physical health, including loss that comes through illness, or the onset of a disability.
- Security. The onset of neighborhood violence, political upheaval, or terrorist dangers can all lead to symptoms of lost security.
- Opportunity. This can include the experiences of people who have striven to get into a special school but do not get accepted, people who are passed over for an important promotion, or authors who have labored for years to write a book that no publisher wants to print.
- A close relationship, including dissolution of business partnerships, the breakup of a couple that has dated for a long time, conflict in a family, divorce, or the loss of intimacy that occurs when a husband or wife has an affair. Other relationship losses that were mentioned earlier include a move from close neighbors, separation from a church where there were close friendships, graduations that put an end to contact and camaraderie with fellow students, or moving to a different place of employment.
- One's home, possessions, status, job, or career. Often, this includes the loss of one's identity, especially in people whose identities are tied to their positions or careers.[47]

Counseling and Grief

C. Everett Koop gained national recognition when he was the United States Surgeon General, serving as the country's chief medical officer when the AIDS epidemic began. Before then, Dr. Koop was known as a highly regarded pediatric surgeon whose work frequently brought him into contact with dying children and grieving parents. One day the famous physician learned that his own son had died as he was climbing in the mountains of New Hampshire. In a moving and inspiring portrayal of their grief, young David Koop's parents wrote about their sadness and the faith that had sustained them throughout life. "Our family life never will be the same," they wrote, "but we are trusting in the Lord to help us accept the empty place in our family circle and to keep us constantly aware that David is in heaven—which is far better for him." Like the hundreds of parents whom he had counseled, Koop and his wife found a permanent void in their lives after David's death. "In an effort to be comforting, so many Christians glibly say, 'God will fill the void,'" they wrote. "Instead, we found that the void is really never filled, but God does make the void bearable."[48]

In their grieving, the Koop family discovered what some well-meaning counselors have failed to realize: the grieving are not looking for pat responses from people who come to talk. Instead, grief-filled people need understanding, reassurance, and contact with sensitive individuals who care enough to listen.

1. *Counseling and Normal Grief.* Most grieving people get through the difficult, long process of healing with no special help and often without counseling. The most widely available sources of help are family members, friends, clergy, and physicians. These people can help in several ways.

- Encourage discussions about death or other losses before they occur. When dying persons and their families are free to express their feelings and discuss their loss before it happens, the anticipatory mourning may make grieving more familiar and perhaps a little easier after the loss occurs.
- Be present and available. "There is a sort of invisible blanket between the world and me," C. S. Lewis[49] wrote after his wife died, but even though he did not want to talk with others, he knew that the presence of other people could be important, even if they were talking to one another. As a counselor, try to be available after the funeral. If the mourner is a special friend, phone periodically to touch base, and be alert to giving support or expressing concern on holidays and anniversaries.
- Make it known that expressing emotions is good and acceptable, even when the loss does not involve the death of a loved one, but do not pressure the grieving person to show feelings.
- Do not be surprised when there are times of crying, frustrations, or withdrawal, but make it known that you are available and accepting nevertheless.
- Be a careful listener. Recognize that grieving people need, at their own time, to talk about issues, such as the feelings and thoughts that are being experienced, the details of the loss and funeral, reminiscences of past contacts with the deceased, the ultimate reasons for death ("Why did God allow this now?"), and thoughts about the future. Guilt, anger, confusion, and despair will all be expressed at times and need to be heard by the helper rather than condemned, squelched, explained away, or dismissed with a glib religious cliché.
- Don't push. The best counselor listens and responds when the counselee wants to discuss issues related to the loss, but also is willing to back off if the griever wants to talk about something else or wants to withdraw. In these ways the counselor communicates a sensitivity to the fluctuating needs and feelings of the grieving person.
- Help the grieving person make decisions, but gently try to discourage the making of major decisions (such as the sale of a house or a move to another part of the country) at least until a few months have passed.
- Gently challenge irrational conclusions ("I killed him because I was driving when we had the accident."), then give the grieving person opportunity to respond and discuss the issue.

- Determine if the person needs practical help, such as meal preparation or baby-sitting. Then try to provide what is needed.
- Do not discourage grieving rituals. These include participation in a wake, funeral, memorial service, or other religious rituals that can make death more real, demonstrate the support of friends, encourage expression of feelings, and stimulate the work of mourning.
- Be alert to people who may be forgotten in the grieving process. A deceased person's spouse or children are likely to get most of the counselor's attention, but remember that grandchildren, friends from work, neighbors, fellow worshipers, and others can benefit from the care-giving that comes from sensitive counselors.[50] When a single person dies, remember that there often are fiancés (or fiancées), close friends, or others who grieve along with the family. This group might include the partner of a gay or lesbian person. Whether or not you approve of these relationships, remember that the grieving partner also needs support and often benefits from grief counseling.
- Do not ignore the grieving that may come to people who are experiencing the loss of a job, possession, opportunity, pet, or close relationship with somebody who is still alive. These people often are reluctant to show their grief, lest they be ridiculed or their grief be dismissed as of little importance. If a loss is important to the griever, it is important to the counselor as well.
- Pray for the bereaved and comfort them with words of Scripture without preaching or using religious clichés as a means for stifling the expression of grief.

In all of this, remember that the counselor's goal is to support the mourner and not to build unhealthy dependency, stimulate denial, or encourage the avoidance of reality. In time the support of family and the care of friends will help the bereaved persons work through the grief and resume normal activities once again.[51]

2. *Counseling and Complicated Grief.* Most often, friends and pastors help people through the normal process of grieving. Counselors are more likely to be involved with survivors who show complicated grief reactions. At the beginning, these people may resist help, but if they are not rushed, many will begin to cooperate with the counselor. There are several ways in which counselors can help.[52]

- Try to determine if there are risk factors that would make healing more difficult. Most of these have been mentioned in the preceding pages. Was the loss especially traumatic or sudden, for example, or do you see any of the unhealthy effects of grief that have been described? Better assessments can help the counselor understand behaviors and attitudes that need to be changed.
- Encourage the expression of feelings and attitudes. As you listen, try to avoid the exhortations and insensitive quoting of Bible verses that may have come previously from friends. None of these are wrong, and Scripture certainly can be very comforting, but grieving people tend to prefer the presence of a caring listener rather than a counselor who talks a lot

using clichés and routine phrases. If you see that the bereaved person is disturbed by the duration or high intensity of grief, anger, guilt, or other feelings, encourage discussion of these issues. If these are not extreme, give reassurance that they are a natural and expected part of the grieving process.

- Suggest to counselees that they keep a grief journal in which they record their emotions and reactions. When mourners get into the habit of expressing their pain, loneliness, despair, or anger on paper, they deal with these emotions better. Later, they can reread earlier entries in the journal and see how much progress they have made.

- Help counselees understand the grief process. The goal is not to give long explanations of what typically happens as people grieve. Instead, let people know some of what frequently transpires so they can understand that their grieving is not abnormal or pathological. Some people may find it helpful to read books that can be discussed later. Often, it can be helpful to put a counselee into contact with others who can give support and realistic perspectives. Widows, for example, often can benefit from contact with other widows who are further along in the grief process. This conversation can be helpful to the new widow and to the one who has been widowed longer. [53]

- Try to discover how people dealt with loss in the past and encourage counselees to return to these or similar methods again. Sometimes, people who have enjoyed gardening, music, art, or a favorite hobby discover that these can be ways to channel emotions away from oneself and onto something unrelated to grief. When spring arrived following the death of her husband, one widow struggled with the issue of whether to grow summer flowers once again, as she had done in the past. She lacked the motivation to do this because she felt drained of energy and was sad because her husband would not be around to enjoy the garden. Encouraged by her children, however, she went back to working in her garden, determined to grow flowers in memory of her husband, and later concluded that growing and tending to the flowers had been a very therapeutic activity.

- Invite the person to discuss the past. What were the high points or low points in the counselee's relationship with the person who died? If the counselee has lost an opportunity, what was good and bad about the dream that now is gone? The counselor can promote this discussion by gentle encouragement and by showing interest in what is being shared. Sometimes, this process is facilitated by looking, with the counselee, at photographs, treasured possessions of the past, or things that were valued by the deceased person.

- Remember that stories can be therapeutic. Encourage the counselee to tell stories about the past and, later in the process, stories about what would be ideal for the future now that the loss has occurred.

- Encourage the person to reach out. This may not come at the beginning of grief, but often the act of reaching out to others can turn attention away from oneself and give new reason for living and hope for others.

- Encourage talk about the future. After there has been time to talk about emotions, gently challenge irrational thoughts or plans that appear to be unrealistic or made in haste. Look for opportunities to encourage discussion of practical issues, such as raising children, meeting financial needs, or dealing with loneliness and sexual frustrations. Remember that the goal is to help counselees avoid denial, deal instead with the reality of the loss, and begin to explore ways in which they can reengage with life in a new way. This is not done by denying memories of the person, objects, or opportunity that now are gone. The reengagement fully remembers what has been lost but ponders what now can be done in the next phase of life.

3. *Counseling When Children Die.* As we have emphasized, each type of grief is unique, in part because some losses are felt more intensely than others. One of the most difficult grieving experiences is the loss of a child, regardless of the child's age. Fatal accidents involving children, the loss of a child through Sudden Infant Death Syndrome (SIDS),[54] or the terminal illness of a child can create a grief that appears beyond endurance. Parents of children who are stillborn or lost through miscarriages often grieve with almost equal intensity. Even when children are weak or malformed before death, it is difficult for parents to accept the reality of death after a life that was so short. While the loss of an only child may seem worse than others, most parents would argue that the loss of a child is intensely painful whether or not there are siblings.[55] Guilt, self-condemnation, anger, despondency, and unanswered questions abound.

Often the grief leads to tension, parental conflict, and miscommunication in the home. For example, the wife may feel that her husband doesn't care as much about the death because he doesn't cry as much as she does. The husband, in turn, may be hiding his true feelings because he does not want to upset his wife. The counselor should be aware that the breakup rate for grieving parents is high. Part of counseling, therefore, should focus on the marriage and on how the couple's relationship is surviving through the grieving process.

As with other forms of grief, those who have lost children must be helped to express feelings, accept the loss, and learn to readjust. Often, this help comes from neighbors and friends, from church members, and from the support of other parents who have experienced similar losses. Whereas the losses may be felt most intensively by parents of young children or teenagers, even older parents whose children are grown experience special loss, largely because most people assume that children are expected to outlive their parents.

4. *Counseling Children Who Grieve.* In the midst of their grieving, relatives sometimes try to protect children from the realities and sadness of death, especially the death of a parent. It should be remembered, however, that children also have a need to grieve and to understand as best they can.

To adequately grasp the reality of death, children must be able to distinguish between themselves and others, between living and nonliving, between thought and reality, and between past, present, and future. Whether or not the child has this understanding, he or she must be helped to comprehend the finality of death, to express emotion, and to ask questions. It is important to reassure children, repeatedly and by actions, that they are loved and will be cared for. Children often interpret death, especially the death of a parent, as a form of rejection. When a sibling dies there may be guilt, confusion, fear of isolation, and anxiety about whether "I might be next." Children are sensitive to any signs of adult insecurity and need to know that they will not be forsaken. Sometimes, they misbehave to test the limits, looking for reassurance that everything is still under control. Many child psychologists and other experts agree that, with the possible exception of the very young, children should be present at the wake and/or funeral, since young people need the emotional support and opportunity to accept the reality of the loss, just as adults have these needs.[56] It also can be helpful to find one of the illustrated books on death or loss that are written specifically for children.[57]

5. *Controversies.* Loss and grieving affect almost everyone, so it is not surprising that this topic has been studied intensively for many years. Some of these studies have led to conclusions that tend to be controversial.

(a) The Effectiveness of Grief Work. Although most counselors would disagree, some researchers have concluded that it makes no difference whether a survivor goes through what has come to be known as grief work (expressing feelings about a loved one's death, writing about one's emotions, or telling others about the anxieties or somatic complaints that have come with the grieving).[58] Time is the best healer for bereavement, according to these studies, not the work of counselors. This is true regardless of the type of loss. Findings like this give hope for people who never get or accept help during times of grieving, but there also is evidence to support the opposite position that grief work does help.

(b) Bonding with People Who Have Died. Instead of encouraging people to let go of a deceased relative, some counselors suggest that it is better to encourage counselees to build a continuing bond with the person who has died. This can be accomplished through remembering good times of the past, thinking of the dead person on a continual basis, imaging the person's reactions to current life situations or problems, writing a letter to the dead person, or continuing to talk to the deceased.[59] These practices would appear to be beneficial, providing that the grieving person does not withdraw into a realm of denial or unreality. More controversial is the suggestion that survivors seek to make contact with the deceased through mediums or other means. This clearly is condemned in the Bible, although it was done. At one time King Saul banned all the mediums and psychics from the land, but then, when he was worried about the outcome of a battle, he disguised himself, went to a medium, and asked her to arouse Samuel.[60] By this time, however, the Lord had left Saul and he died shortly thereafter.

(c) Healing Memories. Although it appears to be less prominent at present, some Christian counselors have stressed the benefits of helping people "heal" memories from the past. At times, grief cannot be overcome because the counselee has unresolved and deeply buried guilt, anger, hurt, or attachments to the deceased person that no longer can be discussed with the person who has died. Healing of memories is an approach based on prayer in which the counselor and counselee join together and seek the Holy Spirit's guidance as they remember (and sometimes relive) memories or attitudes from the past. Then they seek divine forgiveness and healing.

Some have criticized the Freudian overtones of this approach, and a number of extreme healing-of-memories books have advocated methods that could be harmful. There are more responsible writers and practitioners in the field, however,[61] and their work has demonstrated how the power of Christ can help people deal with grief and other painful issues from the past.

Preventing Complicated Grief

In itself, grief cannot and should not be prevented. When survivors show little or no grief, this may indicate that the grieving process is being denied or avoided, although it is important to remember, once again, that there are individual differences in the ways in which people move through the grieving process.

1. *Before the Loss*. It is not easy to discuss death or other loss, especially when everybody is healthy, but the best prevention begins long before a loss occurs.

(a) Developing Healthy Attitudes at Home. When parents are open and honest about death, children learn that this is an issue to be faced honestly and discussed openly. Misunderstandings can be prevented, and this is a natural time to answer questions. Probably, none of us can prepare adequately for a loss, but an open attitude in a marriage and in a home facilitates communication and makes later discussions more natural.

(b) Clarifying Family Relationships. Grief can be complicated when there is anger, guilt, jealousy, bitterness, competitiveness, unforgiveness, or other issues that never were resolved before the death. To prevent complications later, families or close friends should learn to express their feelings and frustrations on a regular basis, forgive one another and accept forgiveness, express love and appreciation, and develop healthy interdependence that avoids manipulation or immature dependency relationships. For some couples or families, these are goals that they cannot reach without the help of a counselor.

Many people have regrets when they reach a time of grieving. They regret the things they did not say, the questions they did not ask, the love they did not express, or the emotions they did not reveal before the loved one died. This later regret can be prevented if things that need to be said are said before a death or other loss occurs.

(c) Keeping Active. People who are involved in a variety of recreational, worship, work, or other activities find that they have fulfilling involvements that help soften the pain when losses occur, including the loss of a loved one or the loss of good health. Usually, active people also have an established network of friends who frequently are there to give support and help in times of need.

(d) Stimulating Mental Health. Well-adjusted people who have learned how to handle more minor crises successfully usually handle major losses with success as well. These people are not afraid to express emotions freely, face frustrations openly, and admit and discuss their struggles or problems honestly.

(e) Anticipating Loss. It is difficult to talk about end-of-life issues, such as what we would like our families to do if we ever are terminally ill and only can be kept alive by machines, how we want our possessions to be distributed, whether we would like to donate our organs for scientific study or to keep others alive, what we would like for funeral arrangements, whether we prefer burial or cremation, and our hopes for survivors after we are gone, including how they would get along financially. It is no easier talking about the desires of a spouse, parent, or friend, even when that person is in good health. Later, when death does occur, the grieving survivors are spared additional pain if the initial decisions about the funeral have already been made with the deceased person's prior help. In contrast, there are difficult situations like the daughter or other adult child who wonders what to do as a parent fades physically but appears to be denying any discussion about her impending death.

Within recent years hospice has grown as a movement committed to enhancing the quality of life for the terminally ill, helping these patients and their families prepare for death. A major objective is to make it possible for patients to die at home in familiar surroundings and with loved ones nearby. Since this is not always possible, hospice volunteers and medical personnel try to create homelike settings within the confines of a hospital or other treatment facility, sometimes in a specially designed patient room. When trained volunteers, pastors and other Christian caregivers, medical personnel, and professional counselors all work together, family members can be helped to make a smoother transition from terminal illness to death and into the initial months of bereavement.

Hospice provides a specialized form of anticipatory mourning. Instead of denying the reality of the terminal illness, the patients and their families talk about the imminent death and are free to be honest about their sadness. As a result, the subsequent grieving is less likely to be complicated. Such honesty is also important in talking with children who are dying.

(f) Theological Understanding. All of the above is stronger when people understand life-after-death issues and experience the comfort that comes from Christ long before the end arrives. The Bible says a great deal about death, the meaning of life, the reality and promise of eternal life for believers, the reality of hell, and the pain of mourning. These biblical truths can be comforting, especially if they are taught and understood before the grieving process begins.

2. *At the Time of the Loss.* The hours and days following a death or other loss can have a strong influence on how grief is handled.

(a) Communicating the News. It is difficult to announce a death or other major loss, especially if the loss was sudden or unexpected. For this reason, medical personnel, police officers, and others often carry out this task quickly and explicitly (sometimes that means abruptly). Much better is to communicate the news gently and preferably in a location that is private enough to permit the free expression of emotion. Give the survivor time to respond, ask questions, and be surrounded by two or three friends who can provide continuing initial support.

(b) Giving Support. Grief is easier and less likely to develop complications if there are people who can give support and help in making decisions. Pastors and chaplains often give the initial care to the bereaved, but the Christian leader's task is much easier and more effective if other Christians give additional support on an ongoing basis.

(c) Planning the Funeral. In a fast-changing world, long-established funeral customs have been discarded or changed to fit changing lifestyles. These changes are not necessarily bad, but it should be remembered that funeral rituals do serve such useful functions as helping survivors accept the reality of death, receive the support of friends, get practical help during the time of readjustment, and experience the peace and presence of God. Funerals should develop a balance between a realistic acknowledgment of grief and a rejoicing over the fact that believers who are absent from the body are present with the Lord. A carefully planned, worshipful funeral service can facilitate the grieving process and help prevent complicated grief.

(d) Using Medications. In an effort to sedate the grief-stricken, caring physicians sometimes give sedatives and other prescribed medications to survivors at the time of major loss. Although there may be nothing wrong with this as a temporary measure, there is a danger that chemicals can dull the pain and inhibit the grief process. In general, therefore, the use of medications does not contribute to the long-term prevention of complicated grief.

3. *After the Loss.* The continuing presence of supportive care-givers, including pastoral counselors, can help the griever during the months following the loss. It is during this time that the counseling procedures described in this chapter can help counselees adjust without developing complicated grief.

4. *Death and the Church.* It is well known that care for the dying and their families, preparation for a death, help with grieving, and the prevention of complicated grief among survivors very often comes within the context of caring church or other religious communities. Help for the whole congregation can come through pastoral care and counseling when these are needed, the preaching of periodic messages on the subject of death and related topics, small groups of classes that give education about death and about heaven, encouraging church members to read a book or two about bereavement, and encouraging believers to pray and care for the spiritual, emotional, and practical needs of the grieving. Be alert to events in the community or church body, such as a disaster or the passing of a respected leader, because these give opportunities to raise issues about death in a congregation. When death and dying are talked about in the church, these topics are more likely to be talked about in the home.

5. *Death and the Grief Counselor.* Should a grief counselor ever cry? What about a doctor or nurse who has treated the patient and been helpful to the family? It can be difficult for any of us to be in the presence of death and grieving, and there will be times when we cannot and probably should not hold back the tears. Family members and counselees can be helped by such expressions of counselor empathy, unless the care-giver loses control so that he or she no longer gives the appearance of being able to help.

Bereavement in other people or families can remind counselors and other care-givers of their own past losses, of bereavements that are still to come, or of the inevitability of one's own death. Care-givers can deal with their own needs and prevent burnout if they follow several guidelines.

- Do not try to help more people than you can handle at one time. It may take time and experience to determine one's own limit. This is difficult for pastors because they have no control over the number of terminal illnesses or deaths that may occur in the congregation at any given time.
- Give yourself permission to grieve. Admit your sadness after someone dies, and try not to feel guilty if you do not grieve in the same way or with the same intensity after each death. This diversity is normal for all care-givers, including grief counselors.
- Surround yourself with people who can give support and help. Care-givers are reluctant to ask for help, but we all need the support and help that comes from others and from God.
- Get away. Everybody needs time for rest, worship, play, pleasant times for interaction with other people, and reflection. Without this, care-givers of any kind can burn out quickly.

Conclusions About Grief

Grief is a universal experience. Few escape it, some are trapped by it, and those who come through it often feel that they have had a painful refining experience. Grief is not something that we seek or grasp eagerly. Sometimes, it comes without warning, is received reluctantly, and only can be conquered when it is faced honestly with divine help and with the support of other human beings. It is a pain that God often uses to mature us and to make us more equipped for the Master's use.

Walter Trobisch was a godly man whose writings were used to help millions of readers in the 1970s and 1980s. One clear October morning he died of heart failure in his little home in the foothills of the Austrian Alps. "My whole world stopped the day he died," his wife wrote.

> I can now recognize . . . grief similar to what John Steinbeck describes: "After seeming cut off and alone, you will be able to pick up a thread and draw a string and then a rope leading back to life again." After a close partnership and marriage of twenty-seven years, learning to walk alone again was no easy task. . . . It took me many years to learn that no man on this earth can satisfy the deepest longings of a woman's heart. Only one can do that. He is also the only one who can help me live with that deep hole, that deep pain in my heart. . . . The pain is still there. He hasn't filled it up yet, but he has made a bridge over it. I can live with it now and I can stand on this bridge and reach out to others.[62]

Counselors know that helping a person through the grieving process is no easy task. But God uses people like you and me to help people like Ingrid Trobisch grow through this experience and learn again to reach out to others.

KEY POINTS FOR BUSY COUNSELORS

➤ Grief is a normal response to the loss of any significant person, object, or opportunity. It is an experience of deprivation and anxiety that can show itself in one's behavior, emotions, thinking, physiology, interpersonal relationships, and spirituality.

➤ Grief is mentioned often in the Bible. It is seen in the lives of many Bible personalities. The New Testament shows us that:
  ▪ Christ has changed the meaning of grieving.
  ▪ Christ has demonstrated the importance of grieving.

➤ Normal grief differs from person to person.
  ▪ Usually it involves intense sorrow, pain, loneliness, anger, depression, physical symptoms, and changes in interpersonal relationships.

- Sometimes, there is denial, fantasy, restlessness, disorganization, inefficiency, irritability, and a desire to talk considerably about the deceased.
- It is common for grieving people to feel that life no longer has meaning.

➤ *Complicated grief* refers to grief that appears to be unhealthy or not normal. Complicated grief does not always have unique symptoms. Instead, normal grieving appears for a longer duration and with greater intensity. Complicated grief may include:

- Deep feelings of dejection, lack of interest in the outside world, a diminished capacity to love, withdrawal, and greatly lowered self-esteem.
- Busy hyperactivity, a persistent attitude of helplessness and hopelessness, and intense guilt.
- At its most intense, extreme withdrawal, moodiness, impulsivity, antisocial behavior, excessive drinking, and thoughts of suicide.

➤ To predict how one might react to a loss, consider that grieving might be more difficult if:

- The loss was not anticipated.
- The loss was traumatic, unexpected, or violent, as in accidents, homicide, suicide, or the death of young people.
- The mourner lacks religious beliefs and resources.
- The person's background and personality suggest that flexibility is unlikely.
- The mourner's cultural, ethnic, or social group discourages healthy grieving.

➤ Grieving can lead to:

- Physical reactions, including increased susceptibility to illness.
- Emotional and cognitive effects.
- Social disruption.
- Spiritual responses either positive or negative.
- Evidences of unusual behavior.

➤ Remember that feelings of loss and grieving are not limited to sorrow over the death of a loved one. Grieving can follow the loss of health, a valued possession, a close relationship, a promising career, or one's home, possessions, status, job, career, or reason for hope.

➤ Effective counseling involves coming alongside the grieving person to offer your presence, support, encouragement, sensitivity, willingness to listen, help in making decisions, and spiritual comfort.

➤ Counseling will be unique when there is complicated grief, loss of a child, or an effort to help children grieve.

➤ Healthy grieving can be facilitated, and complicated grief can more likely be avoided if counselors are aware of how they can intervene before the loss, at the time of the loss, and after the loss.

➤ The church provides one of the most effective means for helping people grieve.

➤ In all of this, remember that counselors grieve too and should make efforts to prevent burnout and take care of themselves.

➤ Grief is a universal experience. Few escape it, some are trapped by it, and those who come through it (the majority) often feel that they have had a painful refining experience. God often uses these experiences, frequently working through counselors and church leaders, to bring maturity to believers and to make them more equipped for serving Christ and their fellow human beings.

26

Singleness

Most of his boyhood friends probably were married by the time he started his career. He was still single. He had friends of both sexes, but no wife or children. He relaxed and had meals in the homes of other people, but he had no home of his own. He knew what it was like to care for an aging parent, but he never knew the joys or challenges of being a parent himself. He knew where he was going and had his career mapped out, but there was no helpmeet with whom he could share life. He knew what it was like to be considered a misfit, a threat to other people, somebody who was different. Perhaps there were people who thought he was still single because he had some kind of a problem. Maybe they thought he was scared of intimacy, unwilling to make a commitment, or secretly gay. He was a healthy young man with all the hormones, sexual urges, and temptations that human beings experience, but he never had a wife with whom he could be sexually intimate. He knew how to laugh, how to hold his own in debates, how to play with little kids, but there were times when he cried, and sometimes he felt very lonely and alone.[1]

Usually, we don't think of him this way, but Jesus was a single adult.

When Jesus lived on this earth, there may not have been many single adults in the villages he visited. Fast-forward to the twenty-first century, and the number of unmarried adult men and women is astronomical—and their ranks are swelling rapidly. In the United States, for example, about 40 percent of the adult population is single. In part, this is because people are marrying later in many countries, the divorce rate remains high or is increasing, attitudes toward relationships are changing so that singleness is more accepted, and better health care means that widows and widowers live longer. The single population includes parents without partners; millions of widows; members of celibate religious communities, including priests and nuns; the majority of college students; most homosexuals; separated people who are still married but living apart from their mates; those who have chosen not to marry; and others whose lives are spent waiting for the day when they will walk to the altar. In addition, there probably are millions of husbands and wives whose marriages have grown busy, cold, or distant. The spouses coexist under the same roof and maybe share the same bed, but they live isolated lives that, in practice, could be classified as single.

Sometimes, singleness is seen as a swinging, no-strings-attached, carefree lifestyle, but for most single people nothing could be further from the truth. In societies where people walk in pairs, those who are alone seem like misfits. They may be welcomed to social gatherings where almost everyone is married, but people without partners can feel out of place, even in their own families. Sometimes plagued by loneliness, insecurity, or low self-esteem, many singles face frequent reminders that they are out of step with society. Singles tend to pay higher taxes and may have difficulty getting credit, insurance, mortgage loans, job promotions, or even decent seating in a restaurant.

It is not surprising that an entire industry has developed that caters to the needs and desires of the singles boom. Internet dating and mate-finding programs are popular, widely advertised, and sometimes very successful, especially those that use personality profiles and computer searches to link mutually compatible people.[2] There is a growing housing market focused on singles, coaching and counseling services exist for the unmarried, exercise equipment and fitness clubs often market their products and services to singles, supermarkets stock specifically packaged foods that come in single servings, and a plethora of singles vacation packages are available, including cruises. The Christian publishing industry has dozens, maybe hundreds, of singles books rolling off the presses, many written by singles and some produced by older, married counselors. One even gives this unique guarantee to his readers: be dating in six months or your money back.[3] Most of these books focus on dating, relationships, loneliness, or finding a soul mate, but there is a shift to a new emphasis on living a fulfilled life whether or not one is married.[4]

For those who want to get married, meeting other singles can also be a problem. Contacts in singles bars or night spots can be fleeting and destructive. Christians are more likely to turn to an Internet dating service or to the church. Although attitudes are changing, many singles still find that they are unwelcome or at best tolerated by church members who don't know how to relate to singles, don't always want them around, and sometimes blatantly reject unmarried people—especially if they are divorced. None of this should hide the fact that many singles live meaningful, productive lives, as Jesus did. Many others find it difficult to be single, however, and even those who function well can benefit at times from Christian counseling.

The Bible and Singleness

Adam was the first person to experience singleness, but this didn't last long. God declared that it was "not good for the man to be alone. I will make a companion who will help him."[5] The result was creation of the woman, and Adam became the first married man. Clearly, marriage was God's intention for the human race. He expected that a man and woman would unite together for companionship, sexual fulfillment, perpetuation of the human race, and partnership in their use and control of the environment.

Even at the beginning, surely God knew that a happy blissful marriage would not be everyone's experience. The tendency for men to die earlier than women and the influence of wars that often reduce the male population both would ensure that there never would be enough men for all the women in the world. Further, in this imperfect and sinful world, there are those who fear intimacy with the opposite sex, find it difficult to make commitments, have marriages that break up, or never enter a heterosexual marriage in the first place because of their homosexuality. In addition, some people lose their spouses in death, and for a variety of reasons, others choose not to marry.

These people are not necessarily unhealthy or unnatural because they are single. Some people, for example, prefer to remain single because they have no desire to marry. Others choose to remain single so they can devote themselves more fully to God's work.[6] For many believers the single state is a special gift that God bestows on selected people, including some who are not at all enthusiastic about being recipients of the gift.

Paul elaborated on this in detail in 1 Corinthians 7, where he discussed sex, presented a high view of marriage, but also considered singleness. Marriage and singleness are both gifts from God, we are told.[7] Noting that he himself was unmarried, the apostle wrote very positively about the single lifestyle. Marriage is fine, he said, but singleness is even better.[8]

> I am trying to spare you the extra problems that come with marriage. . . . An unmarried man can spend his time doing the Lord's work and thinking how to please him. But a married man can't do that so well. He has to think about his earthly responsibilities and how to please his wife. His interests are divided. In the same way a woman who is no longer married or has never been married can be more devoted to the Lord in body and in spirit, while the married woman must be concerned about her earthly responsibilities and how to please her husband. I am saying this for your benefit, not to place restrictions on you. I want you to do whatever will help you to serve the Lord best, with as few distractions as possible.[9]

Here Paul elevates the single life as a way of living in which the individual can give undivided devotion to Christ, free of the greater responsibilities and financial pressures that often come with marriage. But how many Christian singles, even deeply committed believers, really view life like this? Maybe it was fine for Paul and for some super-spiritual single people today to view their unmarried state as a way to "serve the Lord best, with as few distractions as possible." It seems more likely, however, that many single believers put greater emphasis on wondering why they have not found a life partner, struggling at times to fit into society, praying and looking for a mate, grappling with feelings of inadequacy, or resisting pressures from parents who are critical of their unmarried adult children. Others may be active in building their lives and careers apart from having a mate. These people are not flying aimlessly, going in circles until they are able to land into a marriage. They have decided to move on with their lives, but even for them, singleness is not easy. For many, unmarried life brings a number of problems.

The Causes of Singleness Problems

What is there about singleness that can lead to problems? To answer, let us look at five major groups of single people. Each has a somewhat unique set of challenges and needs relating to their being unmarried.[10]

1. *Some Have Not Yet Found a Mate or Have Decided to Postpone Marriage Temporarily.* It is well known that in recent years there has been a growing trend for people to postpone marriage. In the latest U.S. Census, for example, the median age for marriage had increased from 23.2 to 26.7 for men and from 20.8 to 25 for women, compared to the previous generation.[11] Many younger people want to travel, get established in their careers, or otherwise experience the freedoms of

adulthood before taking on the responsibilities of marriage. Unlike their parents when they were getting started, many singles today conclude that getting married later is preferable because it gives them more time to decide what they want in their lives and in a spouse. In addition, changing social attitudes have led many, including Christians,[12] to conclude that sex apart from marriage is natural and acceptable, so there is no need get married before engaging in sexual intercourse. The apostle Paul wrote that people who cannot control themselves should marry,[13] but most people in our society do not accept that kind of teaching, concluding instead that people who cannot or don't have a desire to control themselves should give in to their urges and have sexual intercourse outside of marriage. In time, many of these people will marry, but often they have little motivation to hasten the process "until the right one comes along."

Students—some of whom may be reading these words—individuals whose work involves travel, those getting started in the business world or preparing for a professional career, and many others have every intention of getting married but have no problem with waiting a few years. These singles face many of the problems and challenges that concern all unmarried people, but there is no rush to find a mate, no panic over the prospects of being single, and no assumption that life is on hold until they get married. These people have chosen to postpone marriage and perhaps even to "kiss dating good-bye"[14] for a while. They have a healthy outlook, and they are not often seen in counselors' offices with a concern about still being single. For them, singleness is not seen as a tragedy that has come as the result of unwanted circumstances. Instead, singleness is viewed as a choice that can be changed later.

Others are unmarried and more concerned about their singleness. They live with a waiting mentality that says, "I can't make any plans on my own, and I shouldn't make any major decisions because these might have to change if I get married to somebody whose ideas and goals are different." Such an attitude may be reinforced by well-meaning but sometimes insensitive friends or relatives who imply that life isn't complete until one has a mate. This is an attitude that can immobilize single people so that they are always looking for the appearance of a possible mate, living in the future and waiting for that time when marriage will make life complete. For these people every date is seen as a potential opportunity for marriage. Their dating partners sense this and back away quickly. This eager attitude also leads some people to "jump" at the first opportunity for marriage—and discover later that they have landed in marital chaos. "I would rather be single and wish I was married," said one of my students, "than to be married and wish I was still single."

2. *Some Choose to Stay Single.* Early in life, some people make the deliberate decision to remain single, but for others this decision is more of a gradual awareness and acceptance of the fact that marriage is unlikely. Of course there are good reasons for choosing to remain single. These include a conviction that singleness is God's calling, a shortage of eligible marriage partners, a desire for continuing freedom, or commitment to a career that involves living in circumstances where finding a partner is unlikely or commitment to a marriage is impractical. Others may conclude that singleness is preferable because they have had bad experiences with marriage, have watched their friends go through painful divorces, are committed to careers that demand long hours and freedom to move, feel shy and self-conscious with the opposite sex, or are afraid of intimacy. Regardless of the

reasons, increasing numbers of people appear to be content to stay single, and in many countries this is becoming more acceptable for both men and women.

Some onlookers, including church members and probably a lot of mothers, have difficulty understanding why any person would prefer to be remain single. The belief still persists that people who remain single must have problems; they must be gay, are afraid to leave home, or have some quirk or more severe problem that prevents them from finding a mate. These opinions are rarely stated overtly, but they can pressure a single person to enter into a relationship that is not wanted and for which the individual may feel unsuited. Even without such pressures, people who are single by choice or circumstances may wonder if the conclusions of others might be true. These people may think, "Perhaps I *am* gay, afraid, too choosy, or a social misfit." Possibilities like this are best considered honestly and evaluated realistically. Otherwise, they can fester and quietly bother the unmarried person for years.

3. *Some Have Had Marriages Break Up.* If a marriage has been unhappy for a long time, its ending may bring at least a temporary sense of relief. Even so, to be single again following a separation or divorce is not easy. Many experience loneliness, struggles in adjusting to the transition from marriage back to singleness, and feelings of failure along with bitterness. Often, the person experiences difficulties with self-image as the formerly married person struggles with questions such as "Where do I fit now?" or "Who am I?" All of this can be made worse by criticism or social ostracism that comes from others, including family members, friends, unforgiving church members, or insensitive co-workers. People who have lost a mate through death usually feel the sympathy and support of friends or relatives, but this kind of compassionate caring rarely comes to those whose marriages have ended through separation or divorce.

4. *Some Have Lost a Mate.* The chapter on grief discussed the pain, loneliness, and great sense of loss that comes to those who have lost a mate. Perhaps only those who have had similar experiences really can understand. As we have seen, when a death occurs, relatives and friends reach out to offer support and comfort, but the grief persists long after the funeral is over and the friends have gone back to their regular routines. The loneliness does not leave. There is continuing sadness, emptiness, and the pressures of learning to live alone, making decisions that previously were shared, and thinking of oneself as single again. All of this may be especially difficult for those who are older.

5. *Some Have Other Reasons for Singleness.* Overlapping with the above categories are situations that reduce the likelihood of marriage. These include:

- Chronic illness and disabilities, both physical and mental, that reduce the person's potential for marriage and could interfere with the development of a fulfilling relationship with someone of the opposite sex.
- Unrealistic views about what members of the opposite sex are like.
- Immaturity, including an inability to give and an unwillingness to accept responsibility or to make commitments.
- A belief that cohabitation is better than marriage, despite the accumulation of evidence showing that cohabitation can have a number of traps and adverse effects on subsequent marriage.
- Homosexuality, real or imagined, that sometimes motivates people to spend life alone or in same-sex relationships.

The Effects of Singleness

Singleness is not a disease or a condition that needs help from counselors. Just as some husbands and wives have marriage problems while others do not, so some singles have singleness-related problems that do not concern others. When I have asked participants at singles conferences to list their greatest sources of stress and frustration, often the lists have nothing to do with their singleness. Like married adults, singles also have problems coping with job stress, handling finances, getting along with difficult people, managing time, controlling weight, making career decisions, and finding direction in life. Still, some issues are especially common among singles, and these are the topics that most often arise in counseling sessions.

1. *Problems with Loneliness.* There are times when all of us feel lonely, but this may be a greater problem for single people, especially those who live alone or singles who have experienced a marriage breakup. "It's hard to create things to do when you're alone," one person wrote in a seminar for singles. "My major stress is loneliness and the feeling that somehow I might never be able to cultivate an intimate relationship." "I lack fulfilling companionship," commented another. "It's lonely to come home to an empty apartment and have nobody there with whom I can share joys, hurts, or events of the day." Another person said it differently: "The pressures in my life are greater because I don't have a shoulder to cry on, somebody to laugh with, or even someone to say, 'I understand. It's okay.'"

John R. W. Stott is known around the world as an outstanding preacher and writer.[15] He never married, and when asked about the challenges of being single, he responded that the first problem was "the tendency to personal loneliness. Any single person knows more about loneliness than somebody who is sharing his life with a wife and family. This has meant that I have needed to cultivate friendships and force myself to spend time in the company of others." Perhaps related to being alone is another difficulty that Stott identified. "Singleness limits one's ministry in terms of acceptance. There are some people who distrust one's ministry because they feel you don't understand their problems if you're not married."[16]

2. *Problems of Self-Esteem.* If other people distrust your work or ministry and don't think you can understand their problems, it is easy to wonder if they may be right. Soon you begin to question your own competence or value. The same is true if you know that others think something is wrong with you because you're still single, don't accept you fully, dismiss your opinions, or don't want to date you or have you as a marriage partner.

Several participants in a singles seminar wrote that they fear rejection so much that they lack the courage to reach out to others. "I have a terrible lack of self-worth since I failed at my marriage," one woman wrote. "Is there something wrong with me? I'm afraid others won't accept me." Few comments were sadder than those of the person who wrote: "It is hard for me to feel that anyone would want to talk to me about anything other than work. Whenever I have tried to reach out to make friends, I have realized how much I am hurting. After a while, it hurts too much to try anymore."

A once-popular song proclaimed, "You're nobody 'til somebody loves you." Its concluding line, "So find yourself somebody to love," reflected a philosophy that still guides many singles into transient relationships, often sexual in nature, that frequently end in further rejection and even lower self-esteem. Single or married, when people try to bolster their sagging self-worth through attention-getting behavior, unrealistic decisions, or ill-advised dating or marriage, the result often is failure, self-criticism, self-pity, discouragement, and further feelings of low self-esteem.

3. *Problems with Identity and Direction.* Even though singleness may be more accepted today than it was in previous generations, the fact remains that most adults do get married. This can leave the single person wondering why he or she was left behind. Many wonder how or where they fit into a culture of couples. This is of special concern for the single person who is unhappy with the present, has no direction for the future, and is waiting to build the rest of life on a hoped-for relationship with somebody else. Surely, it is neither healthy nor wise to go through some of the best years in life drifting along and hoping to find personal identity and life purpose in a marriage that might never occur. It is much better when each person, single or married, works at finding his or her strengths and abilities, determining God-given purposes in life, developing spiritual gifts, pursuing education, and building relationships with a variety of people. Feelings of lonely aimlessness and lack of identity are likely to remain in the person who is self-absorbed or waiting inactively for a hoped-for marriage that, it is assumed, finally will give a purpose-driven life.

"My biggest stress is that I don't know where I'm going—even at my age," wrote one single lady on her fifty-first birthday. "I want God to direct me totally in every aspect of my life, but I have just resigned from my job and I plan to start all over." Lack of direction and problems of identity concern people of every age—regardless of marital status.

4. *Problems with Sex.* When God created male and female, he made us with hormones. He made sex a part of human experience and planned that men and women, within marriage, would enjoy each other's companionship and bodies.

But what does the single person do with these God-given sexual urges? "Why can't I just have sex and have it now?" one seminar participant wrote. Others expressed similar concerns. "I'm having trouble waiting," "I have a lot of sexual frustration but no sexual outlet." "It's especially hard for me to adjust to being celibate when all my life I had planned on getting married."

As sexual standards have changed and sex apart from marriage has become more common, it seems likely that more and more people are simply giving in. Some engage in sexual relationships in an attempt to find instant intimacy, to feel loved, to bolster self-esteem, to experience feelings of sexual potency, sometimes to express their anger and frustration, or maybe just to enjoy the experience. Lauren Winner was a single woman when she emerged as an articulate defender of sexual chastity and a perceptive guide for single people who struggle with their sexuality.[17] She was determined to be abstinent, but she was honest enough to acknowledge that this was not always so. "My own history with chastity is nothing to be proud of," she wrote. "I knew, dimly, that Christianity doesn't look kindly on premarital sex, but I couldn't have told you much about where Christian teachings about sex came from. It would not have been too difficult, of course, to get more clarity on the sexual issue. But I didn't do that for one principal reason: I wanted, should the opportunity arise, the option of having sex."[18]

Undoubtedly, most singles, including Christians, fantasize and masturbate at least periodically. These behaviors may be followed by regret and guilt that can complicate but do not solve the problem of sex for singles.

5. *Problems with Emotion.* Whenever people have problems that cannot be solved to their satisfaction, there is a tendency to get angry. It happens to all of us. Sometimes, this hostility is directed toward God, "fate," other people, or even ourselves. It is a short step from anger to a persisting bitterness, which can corrupt like poison.[19] For some singles this bitterness persists as an angry response to the question, "Why is it that I'm not married?" In addition to the anger, some singles also have guilt over their thoughts, attitudes, words, or actions.

Then there are periodic fears: fear of being alone as one grows older, fear that singleness is evidence of God's displeasure, fear of making unwise decisions, since there is nobody with whom to discuss plans. Seminar participants listed some others: fear of adding weight that would make one less attractive to the opposite sex, fear of never having intimate friends, and even fear "of getting so used to being single that I will start to like it and retreat from others."

Again it is emphasized that these emotions, while common, are not limited to singles, and neither are they characteristic of all or even a majority of unmarried people.

6. *Miscellaneous Problems.* Some early research suggests that singles, especially single men, may be more unhappy, less satisfied with their lives, more prone to mental illness, and generally less well adjusted than their married counterparts. Involvement with a church apparently does not eliminate such differences.[20] Undoubtedly, differences like these may be due to the unique stresses that some singles face. It is not easy to be a single parent, for example, making decisions about raising children and always having to be available without the help and support of a partner.[21] Some single adults feel the pressure of living at home and trying to get along with parents who persist in treating their unmarried adult offspring like children or teenagers. Others feel pressure from married people who become matchmakers, who criticize or envy the single lifestyle, or who at times are threatened and unsure how to act in the presence of a single adult, especially a single person of the opposite sex or one who is divorced. Some singles struggle—often alone—with the pain of broken engagements, desired relationships that never developed, or the worry that one's "perfectionistic attitudes" or "high standards" may ensure that marriage never occurs. Older singles face the difficulties of trying to build a social life when there are constrictions caused by loss of friends or failing health. Then there are the previously mentioned problems of social prejudice that make it difficult for singles to get housing, insurance, credit, or job promotions.

Counseling Singles

Sometimes, single people appear to be happy in their unmarried state, fulfilled, and well adjusted, but behind this glamorization of being single there may be hidden self-doubt, self-blame for failed relationships, and a lack of self-confidence. Singles who come for counseling often bring cultural attitudes that one experienced counselor begins to challenge from the beginning. "Over and over again . . . I revisit four separate 'pillars of wisdom' that support the fabric of [my] therapeutic work" with singles, writes Karen Gail Lewis.[22]

- Blame: The counselor challenges the common automatic assumption that the counselee is to blame for being single. The truth is that counselees often are not to blame, but they come to believe this and spend a lot of time trying to uncover what they have done wrong and how they can fix it.

- Ambivalence. The counselee needs to be reminded that it is common to swing back and forth between discouragement about the stigma of singleness and enthusiasm about the glamour and benefits of being single.
- Origins. Many counselees assume that present problems all come from childhood or intimacy issues. For example, women seem "socially conditioned to take responsibility for making relationships work, so they say, *'I'm too fat, I've had a horrible childhood, I'm afraid of intimacy—that's why I'm still single.'* "[23] Remind counselees that this is not necessarily true. There can be many reasons for singleness, and often they do not indicate some kind of psychological pathology.
- Depression. Many singles who say they are depressed about being single often need to hear that instead it may be that they are responding to the uncertainty of whether they will marry and may be carrying the family's grief about the singleness.

Often, it is very therapeutic for counselees to realize that they are not necessarily to blame for their singleness, it is okay to have fluctuating emotions, the problems don't all come from childhood where they can't be solved, and the depression is more likely to result from lack of hope or closure. It also can be helpful to assist counselees as they deal with loneliness, anger, guilt, interpersonal relations, self-esteem, sex apart from marriage, or homosexuality, to name a few. These are all discussed in other chapters of this book. In addition, the counselor might focus on the following:

1. *Being Aware of Your Own Attitudes Toward Single People.* No counselor is likely to be effective if he or she has a negative attitude toward singles, thinks that they are in some way inferior, or feels either envy or threat in the presence of single people. Singles, as we have seen, often feel like misfits in the church. Many feel unwanted, tolerated at best, or sometimes the objects of subtle prejudice and not-so-subtle pressures. Remember that it is *not* true that most single adults are excessively lonely, frantically looking for a mate, bad credit risks, social misfits, afraid of intimacy or responsibility, spiritually immature, constantly angry, or wallowing in self-pity. Each single, like every married person, is a unique human being with individual strengths and needs. Some have a lot of problems because of their singleness; the majority do not.

2. *Help Unmarried People with Acceptance of Their Singleness.* Unmarried counselees can benefit from the supportive acceptance and the patient listening of a counselor who will hear their stories and understand their struggles without condemning. When a single counselee experiences this kind of acceptance, probably he or she will be more open to facing the frustrations of singleness honestly. There may be more willingness to seriously consider the biblical teaching that for some people the single life is God's special calling. Counselees can be helped to see that to be single is not necessarily to be second best and that being unmarried is not a one-way ticket to a life of misery and incompleteness. In your counseling, be realistic enough to acknowledge that loneliness and single-living frustrations are likely to persist, but you also may want to remind counselees that the single individual also avoids some of the equally frustrating problems that are faced by married couples. As you discuss these issues, be sure to give the counselee ample

time to express his or her feelings and ideas. Remember, we don't solve problems *for* people; we solve problems *with* them.

3. *Guide Interpersonal Relationships.* Since the single person has no mate, he or she must be helped to build intimate relationships apart from marriage. Sometimes, this can be difficult because a subtle pressure can creep in and hinder the relationship. The people involved begin to wonder, "Is this the one?" "Could this be 'that special relationship'?" What if I say or do something to hurt the friendship?" When there is a fear or unwillingness to discuss such thinking openly, both people get uncomfortable, conversation gets difficult, and one person—usually the man—backs away. To avoid this, encourage the couple to acknowledge the insecurities openly, clarify each other's intentions honestly, and agree to forget about a more in-depth relationship at least temporarily while they get to know each other better and continue with their nonromantic friendship.

For Christians, this can be helped by an attitude that consistently places the relationship in God's hands and is willing to have him lead, even if it means that couples go their separate ways. The counselor also can help people recognize the differences between friendship and romantic love. Friendship is a relationship in which two people enjoy each other's company, and have a mutual acceptance, respect, willingness to assist one another, and freedom to share experiences and feelings. Friends are comfortable in each other's presence, they understand each other, and there is mutual trust. Friends care for each other and often care about the same issues. They may be on similar vocational, spiritual, personal, or other life journeys. The closest friends are what C. S. Lewis called "kindred souls," who often have similar values, interests, and passions.[24] Like David and Jonathan, friends can love each other, but it is a nonerotic love that rarely is discussed. In contrast, the relationship and the love each person has for the other are discussed more often in romantic partnerships. While romantic love has many of the same features as friendship, the relationship is more characterized by mutual fascination, a strong desire for sexual and other physical intimacy, and such exclusiveness that the love relationship takes precedence over all others. Clearly, it is possible to have good friendships without romantic love. Presumably, the best marriages are those that have both.[25]

Some counselees also may need help in meeting new friends. Singles bars or health clubs may not be the best places to make these contacts. Even those who look in the church may find that some congregations (especially those that are small) don't have many single adults. As we have noted, there are church members (and even some pastors) who are reluctant to have singles in the congregation. These same people may be annoyed when an unmarried person leaves the church and begins attending a Christian singles group that meets elsewhere.

This resistance can be broken down by singles who establish roots in their communities. This could involve getting active in neighborhood activities, volunteering for responsibilities in the church, showing a sincere interest in others of all ages (rather than talking mostly about one's own concerns or sticking only with other single people), and remembering that it is best to develop a variety of friendships, if possible, rather than searching for a "best friend."

4. *Help Singles Deal with Their Sexuality.* Christian counselors can play a significant role in coming alongside singles to help them deal with painful past sexual experiences, set and maintain sexual boundaries, and meet the needs for intimacy apart from sexual intercourse.[26]

Among the many books for singles, few are as honest as one titled *Real Sex: The Naked Truth About Chastity*. The author, Lauren F. Winner (who was mentioned a few pages back in this chapter), shows convincingly that "our usual methods for helping people cope with sexuality are not working. Repeating biblical teachings about sex is simply not enough. Urging self-discipline isn't enough. Reminding people of the psychological cost of premarital sex or infidelity is not enough. What we need is something larger and deeper: a clear vision of what chastity ultimately is and the most important context in which it is practiced."[27] Winner writes that chastity is a spiritual discipline. It is something we do, like prayer, fasting, tithing, or pulling away for times of solitude. These practices may be individual activities, but they are done in community, alongside others in the body of Christ. The spiritual disciplines do not get us into heaven or obliterate all temptations, but practicing the disciplines aligns one's feelings, desires, and habits with the will of God.[28]

5. *Stimulate Realistic Life Planning*. In addition to facing problems and dealing with them honestly, it is psychologically healthy for people to make plans for the future. Certainly, it is not wrong for single people to hope for marriage or to recognize that marriage is a possibility for the future, but it is not healthy to build our whole lives around events that are largely uncertain. It is better to live fully in the present even as we keep aware of possibilities for the future. For singles, this involves facing the fact that marriage (or remarriage) may or may not be a possibility. It includes the consideration and development of one's abilities and gifts, a prayerful pondering of God's will for the present and the future, the formulating of long-range and short-term goals, and movement into a plan of action that will make these goals attainable.

The counselor can help with these deliberations, guiding counselees in their thinking and encouraging realism. At times singles will need help with practical issues, such as finding a job, balancing a budget, or managing a household. This may be a special need for young adults who are just getting started, parents without partners, or people who recently have lost a mate. In all of this, the goals of counseling are first to help people accept and deal with their problems, then give guidance as they learn to be both single and satisfied.

Unmarried counselors might ponder the unique impact that their own singleness could have on their single counselees. When she wrote her book about sexuality, Lauren Winner probably had a greater impact on her unmarried readers because at the time she was single and struggling to maintain her own sexual purity. Earlier we mentioned John R. W. Stott, the well-known Bible scholar who has discussed both the difficulties and the benefits of serving in a pastoral role, even though he was never married. It is interesting to ponder how many single seminary students and graduates have been encouraged by Stott's example, and have persisted in finding places of service, despite the tendency in many churches to shy away from hiring pastors who are not married. Like other singles who are successful in their careers or professions, unmarried Christian counselors and pastoral leaders can be significant mentors and models for others in their lifestyles and life planning.

6. *Working with Single Parents*. There are three ways in which single-parent families can form: there is divorce or separation, one of the parents dies, or an unmarried person adopts or bears a child. In some countries, including the United States, single-parent families are increasingly common. This is because divorce is

more common and because single parents are adopting children, especially foreign-born children, at an increasing rate.[29]

Abundant evidence points to the conclusion that the stresses of being a parent are especially intense among single mothers. The majority of these women work and have inadequate incomes, low standards of living (because they can't afford anything better), and excessive demands on their time. It is difficult to be patient when one is tired, worried about paying bills, and struggling to raise children alone. It is not surprising that when compared with their single counterparts, single parents are much more likely to be depressed, impatient, stressed, inclined to get angry, insensitive to their children, and abusive.[30] The strain is lessened when other people are available to give support and encouragement, but many single parents feel a lack of social support.[31] They are starved for social involvement and find it difficult to keep in contact with friends or family. Life for these people is too busy, and according to one report, single mothers are four times more likely than married mothers to seek mental-health services.[32]

All of this may paint an overly negative portrait of single parenting. Many, probably most, single parents are hard working, dedicated to their children, and concerned about their welfare. Life may be difficult and stressful at times, but for many single parents the rewards of parenting are great and relationships with their children are good. This is especially true when single parents have supportive friends, caring church contacts, and opportunities both to express their frustrations on occasion and to get outside perspectives and practical guidance from friends or a counselor. In addition, single parents can be reminded that their children also may struggle with having only one parent. These young people need understanding, love, contact with adults of both sexes, and opportunity to have some involvement with two-parent families that can give a broader perspective on adult and family life. Then there should be honest, open, genuine, loving communication within the home. When the missing parent has died or is gone because of a divorce, he or she should be described realistically—not torn down in criticism but also not lifted up onto a pedestal.

All these suggestions apply equally to the parent in the home and to the other parent who has visiting rights. The children can be appreciated and enjoyed by both parents, but the visiting parent especially should try to avoid overpermissiveness or overindulgence. Help parents who live apart from their children to see that giving lavish gifts or experiences deny reality, create further tension or unrealistic expectations, and often are unhealthy attempts to buy affection or to create contrast between the two parents. These behaviors may be sincere efforts by one parent to express love for the children. Often, however, the giving reflects parental frustration or bitterness and can be harmful to the children, who become unwilling pawns in a mother-father struggle.

The counselor can help single parents find supportive relationships. For some, this support comes from the single person's family of origin who gives encouragement, security, connection, and a sense of worth. Other single parents connect with neighbors or people at work who can give social interaction and informal support. Some single parents find it helpful to be in contact with other parents who can engage in parent-to-parent support and encouragement. If you make these informal linkups between married couples and single parents, try to find couples who are not threatened by close contact with single parents. Then, of course, there is help that comes from church.

Several times we have noted that there still are church leaders who don't want divorced people or single parents in the church because of problems that might result. It is true that churches and Christian counselors sometimes attract singles who are afraid to build relationships, complainers, or inclined to use the church to find a mate, free baby-sitting, or temporary bed partners. Working with singles in the church, especially single parents, can take a lot of time, and success is not always guaranteed. But single people, including parents without partners, can add a great deal to churches, and it is helpful to remember that the issues they may face are not confined to singles. Helping people always involves time and risk, but the rewards can be great—for the counselee, the counselor, the church, and the kingdom of Christ.

7. *Help People Wait.* Counselors tend to want change and progress, so they are not always enthusiastic about helping people wait. Waiting is not easy, especially in this era of speed, high technology, efficiency, and impatience with inconvenience. When things are not happening quickly, there can be a tendency to make quick decisions and take independent action. But the Christian has volunteered to be under the Lordship of Christ, who is in no hurry and often makes us wait for our own good. This does not imply that we are expected to sit in one spot and do nothing. Single or married, Christians determine to do what God wants, acting in accordance with his will so far as this can be determined now. We trust that God's plans for us will become apparent, in his timing.

Some singles may live life as a waiting game, assuming that if they have enough faith or patience and please God enough, he will give them the desires of their hearts in the form of a perfect husband or wife. But God does not conform to that kind of thinking. Single counselees, like people who are married, must be encouraged to trust God's goodness, to wait on him daily, and to seek his help in accepting his best for each of our lives.

Preventing Problems of Singleness

Following a conference for singles, one of the participants wrote a note to the speaker. "Single or married, we all live in the same world. We are all part of a family, whether present or removed, and shouldn't we have common interests and concerns? Singles as well as married couples can be very narrow in their perspectives—all wrapped up in their own concerns and with little interest in the world around them. The single person should have a greater incentive to aggressively reach out and take part in all of life. We singles tend to be too timid! Whether you are married or single is incidental; the point is you can control the quality of your life. For the Christian this should have special meaning."

Somebody has suggested that it's a terrible waste of a life to never accept one's singleness, to resent it, and to spend life waiting for somebody to come along. A lot of people don't like being single and wish things were different. There is nothing wrong with this attitude. But a lot of these same people jump into their careers, live life to the fullest, build friendships, and sometimes have significant ministries without waiting for somebody else to fulfill them. How can counselors stimulate this positive attitude that prevents singles problems?

1. *Encourage Singles to Make Decisions and to Be Active.* Singleness problems are less likely when unmarried people are helped to be honest about their struggles, to trust God for their present and future needs, to reach out to others in a spirit of

giving and friendship, to evaluate their life goals periodically, to work toward the fulfillment of these goals, and to develop a balanced life that combines worship, work, play, rest, and periods of both socializing and solitude. Married or single, when people are active and involved in meaningful activities, there is less time or reason to dwell on problems.

2. *Build Stable Marriages and Healthy Families.* Some singles are reluctant or afraid to marry because they have watched their married friends struggle with tensions in the relationship and sometimes have the marriages collapse. Others live difficult lives as divorced people or single parents because their own marriages have ended in disaster, and there is a hesitation about trying again. Some may be like the businessman friend of mine who watched his parent's marriage end in divorce and who sees his sister struggle to keep stability and raise the children in a marriage where the husband is abusive. Whenever he talks about marriage, my friend's comments are negative, often in the form of biting comments about controlling wives. He is one of many people who have distorted, unhealthy, nonbiblical, and negative views of marriage. In contrast, counselors and other Christians can model healthy marriages and talk about marriage in a positive way. Teaching about marriage and the family may be an indirect and often effective way to prevent problems that singles and married people both face.

This teaching can occur in the counselor's office, but it can have a broader impact when it is taught in community seminars and in the church. To reduce the increasing incidence of divorce among believers, to cut down the number of unfulfilling and status-quo marriages, and to help singles get a more balanced perspective on family relationships, individual counselors and churches can:

- Restate their commitments to the family and to the institution of marriage.
- Give strong, clear, biblical teaching and preaching on marriage, the family, and singleness.
- Encourage fathers to be more active in parenting and couples to be more involved in marriage building.
- Discourage thinking that creates unrealistic ideals about marriage and the family, or that encourages child-centered marriages.
- Make premarital counseling a priority when people do choose to marry, including people who have been married previously.
- Teach communication and conflict resolution skills.
- Encourage singles to participate in singles seminars or group activities, but urge them as well to be involved in workshops, training sessions, spiritual retreats, and activities that are broader than a focus on singleness or families.

3. *Work to Change Church Attitudes.* Something is wrong with a church that sees single adults as misfits, has no place in the body for unmarried people, lacks programs to meet the needs of singles, and shows no understanding (or desire to understand) their struggles—especially if the single person is divorced.

Pastors and other leaders can set the tone for changing unhealthy attitudes toward singles. Married persons can be encouraged to welcome singles into the church and into their homes. It may be helpful to remind people that Jesus and Paul were single. They might not be welcome in some churches today, and certainly they would be unacceptable to many pulpit committees who maintain a prejudice against single pastors.

Recently, the church that I attend acknowledged that the people were gathering on Mother's Day and made an effort to affirm the mothers who were present. All of this was introduced, however, with some very sensitive comments about the women in the congregation who were not mothers, who maybe would like to be mothers but struggle with the pain of infertility, who were alone because their children were far away and not present to celebrate, or who maybe hoped someday to be mothers but were not married. These people were made to feel very much a part of the Mother's Day celebration without being forgotten, or in any way demeaned because they did not have children. Surely, there is a place in the church for Mother's Day and Father's Day celebrations, for sweetheart banquets, couples groups, and family-related church programs, providing these do not overlook, marginalize, or demean singles. Undoubtedly, most organizers of these activities have no intention of excluding the unmarried; more often there is insensitivity and a nonawareness of the singles in the congregation.

Christian counselors, church leaders, and members of the congregation should all remember that single people are significant and equal members of the body of Christ. Unmarried adults should have full acceptance in the church community.

4. *Stimulate Ministries to Singles*. While single adults should be integrated into the mainstream of the church, there also can be programs to meet their unique needs. Singles groups in the church (or groups combining singles from several smaller churches) are most helpful when they reach out to newcomers, avoid an emphasis on matchmaking or dating, provide for and at times involve the children of singles in social gatherings, are sensitive to the personal and spiritual needs of group members, and are led by mature, sensitive, preferably unmarried leaders. Don't forget that singles have different needs and interests. An eighty-seven-year-old widow and a twenty-two-year-old college student are both single, but the similarity stops about there. They mostly have different needs, perspectives, and hopes. Since most churches are small, it is not easy or even wise to have programs for everybody. Still, Christians need to think creatively about ways to minister to one another, including singles, whether or not we have detailed programs. When there are teaching, worship, social interaction, and opportunities for service, many singles are willing to come together. Often, this kind of interaction and outreach has potential for preventing many singles problems and providing ways for handling existing problems before they get worse.

Conclusions About Singleness

Everybody expects that counseling books will focus on problems, and this chapter is no exception. Millions of adults in the world are single—never married and formerly married—and many will remain that way. These people struggle with the same issues and face most of the same problems that married persons encounter, but, in addition, there are unique challenges in being single. These problems must be understood and faced honestly by single people and by their counselors.

To be single, however, is not to be second class or second best. Despite the disadvantages and disappointments, there are advantages to being single, and counselors must not forget these. Singles have every potential for developing full, meaningful, Christ-centered lifestyles. Individual counselors and the church can make this possibility a reality.

KEY POINTS FOR BUSY COUNSELORS

➤ In recent years there has been a significant increase in the numbers of unmarried people. These never married and previously married people can and do have fulfilling lives, but many also experience the pressures of living as singles in a couples-oriented culture that puts high value on marriage.

➤ Marriage was instituted by God, but there is nothing in Scripture to demean singleness. In contrast, the Bible teaches that some people are called by God to a single life. In 1 Corinthians 7, marriage is affirmed, but singleness is elevated to a state that may even be preferable.

➤ There are five major groups of single people. Each has a unique set of challenges and problems that may be brought to a counselor.
  - Some have not yet found a mate or have decided to postpone marriage temporarily.
  - Some choose to stay single.
  - Some have had marriages break up.
  - Some have lost a mate.
  - Some have other reasons for their singleness, including chronic illness or disabilities that make marriage difficult, unrealistic perspectives that lead to an avoidance of marriage, or homosexuality.

➤ Single people may struggle with any of the following problems, most of which also can be problems for married people:
  - Loneliness.
  - Self-esteem issues.
  - Problems with identity and direction.
  - Sexuality.
  - Emotional issues, including anger and fear.
  - Other issues, including pressure from matchmakers, difficulties in living alone, or frustration in finding a desired mate.

➤ In counseling singles:
  - Be aware of how your own attitudes may impact your counseling with singles.
  - Help counselees accept their singleness.
  - Guide interpersonal relationships.
  - Help counselees deal with their sexuality.
  - Stimulate realistic life planning.

- Give help to single parents.
- Help people wait.

> Singleness need not be a problem-filled state. To prevent problems:
  - Encourage singles to make decisions and to be active.
  - Work to build healthy marriages and stable families that can model good marriage relationships and break down distorted views of marriage.
  - Work to change the church's attitudes toward singleness.
  - Develop good singles ministries in churches and communities.

> Being single is not the same as being second class or second best. Despite the advantages and disappointments, there are advantages to being single, and counselors must not forget these. Singles have every potential for developing full, meaningful, Christ-centered lifestyles. Individual counselors and the church can make this possibility a reality.

27

Choosing a Marriage Partner

I've never met Heather and David. Their story appeared in a magazine after they'd been married for seven years.

Their relationship began in college where they met, dated for a few years, and decided to get married following graduation. After getting engaged, however, they agreed to put a hold on their marriage plans until Heather could get started in graduate studies. Shortly thereafter she left for Louisiana, and David stayed behind in Pennsylvania. Neither was surprised when the distance and time apart put a strain on their relationship. Heather started dating another man in graduate school and began to question whether she should marry David or even get married at all. "It was largely a spiritual crisis about wanting to do my own thing and control my own life," she stated later. David had his own crisis when he learned what his prospective bride was thinking, and before long he too began to have second thoughts about the marriage.

In the end they went ahead with the wedding, after being counseled by a pastor, but even as they made the final wedding preparations, they wondered if they were doing the right thing. Now that seven years have passed, do they consider themselves to be soul mates? "I'm not sure what the term 'soul mate' means," David said. "Before marriage you don't really know if it's 'the one,' and afterward, you're in the marriage relationship, so you have to live in the commitment—that person is 'the one,'" whether you like it or not.

For couples like Heather and David, marriage is a lifelong commitment. Their vacillation before the ceremony was not unusual. For most people, finding a potential life partner (or soul mate) can be a challenge, and even when two people are engaged it is common to wonder if they really are making the right choice.[1]

As they were filming a documentary titled *Wandering Towards the Altar*, two University of Chicago professors asked an undergraduate class what they thought would be the most important decisions of their lives. One by one the students talked about what careers they would pursue and where they might go to attend graduate school. Everybody was surprised when one young man said that for him the most important decision would be choosing the woman who would be his wife and the mother of his children. His classmates could not understand why he would waste his time thinking about marriage instead of planning his career. As they watched all of this, the professors were alarmed at the emphasis on careers and the fact that so few of these young people had given any serious thought to marriage. The students believed that careers could be exciting and fulfilling, while marriage was likely to be limiting. They saw marriage as a way to satisfy their emotional and sexual needs, but they argued that "if you settle down too early you'll probably miss out on the real opportunities of young adulthood, such as traveling, meeting new people, or living and working in exciting places."[2]

In a changing world it is not surprising that perspectives on marriage are changing as well. Attitudes toward marriage differ from country to country and from one generation to another. It is well documented, for example, that the average age for getting married is older now than it was a generation ago. According to one sociologist, over 30 percent of Americans who will marry still have not done so when they reach age 35.[3] For many of these people, careers and other activities have become of greater importance; marriage will come when it can be fit in. Often marriage no longer is considered sacred or permanent. Living together apart from marriage, entering marriages casually, and dissolving marriages freely are all accepted without question or hesitation. In the minds of many single people, the careful choice of a life partner and the commitment to live with one's chosen mate "for better or for worse until death" has been replaced with a self-centered attitude that sees marriage as little more than a convenient living arrangement that always can be terminated if love grows cold.

In contrast, most Christians still acknowledge the permanence of marriage, at least in theory, if not in practice. Divorce, while common in Christian circles, is not encouraged, and single people take the choice of a mate seriously. Some religious groups teach that "God has one special person" for each of us and that it is important "not to miss God's best for your life." This attitude creates great anxiety in unmarried people who never are told how to be sure if a choice is right, but who fear they might be missing God's blessing if their choice is wrong. The problem is complicated when parents or church friends claim that they "are led to believe" that one person is the divinely chosen mate, but the single young person does not agree.

In their efforts to choose a mate wisely, many unmarried people seek input from a friend, older couple, or pastor. Some might even talk this over with a professionally trained counselor. Books on counseling tend to overlook this subject,[4] but helping another person in the wise choice of a life partner can be one of the counselor's most fulfilling tasks.

The Bible and Mate Selection

The Bible makes many positive statements about marriage, but it says little about mate selection. Jesus gave his sanction to marriage, and so did Paul, but neither discussed how a marriage partner should be chosen.

This silence may reflect the fact that in biblical times choosing a mate was not a responsibility for the couple as it is for many people today. Consider, for example, the choice of a wife for Isaac. His father sent a servant on a long journey to find a suitable candidate. The servant sought divine guidance in this process, and God gave a sign from heaven that Rebekah was the right one. Her parents were consulted, and they asked the girl if she was willing to leave her family (perhaps forever) and travel to marry a man whom she had never met. Nobody ever talked about love or dating. Everybody assumed that the Lord was guiding in this choice, but personality, compatibility, sexual attraction, love, or the bride and groom's preferences were not part of the decision-making process.[5] With Jacob the situation was different. He was away from his parents when he fell in love, so the groom went directly to Rachel's father, although not to the bride.[6]

Both Isaac and Jacob married later in life, but apparently many people in Bible times married young—sometimes as early as age twelve or thirteen. The parents usually made the decision, just as they still do in parts of the world today, but the young person could make his or her wishes known and sometimes even refused to go along with the parental choice. After a marriage had been arranged, there often was a period of unbreakable betrothal or engagement, followed by a ceremony of marriage. Unlike Mary and Joseph, who were in this engagement stage when Mary became pregnant,[7] it appears that sometimes the groom didn't even see the bride's face until they were in bed together after the wedding. Even the thought of such a prospect can send shivers of anxiety up and down the spines of many contemporary single people—no doubt including some who might be reading these words.

Do we have biblical guidelines for choosing a mate today? Perhaps, there really is only one: believers are to marry only other believers. The Christian should not marry a non-Christian. "Don't team up with those who are unbelievers. How can goodness be a partner with wickedness? How can light live with darkness?" we read in Paul's second letter to the Corinthians. "How can a believer be a partner with an unbeliever?"[8] This is a warning that the Christian and non-Christian cannot partner in a union of harmony either as business partners or as marriage partners. A similar idea is emphasized in 1 Corinthians[9] and specifically applied to marriage when Paul states that the unmarried woman is free to marry whomever she wishes but only if the marriage is acceptable to the Lord, which would imply that she must marry a fellow believer.[10]

What about divine guidance? Just as Abraham's servant expected and experienced divine leading in selecting a wife for Isaac, perhaps most Christians would agree that we still can expect God's leading in mate selection. Several biblical passages teach that believers can expect divine leading, even though this may not come in dramatic or seemingly miraculous ways.[11] Christians are divided over the issue of whether God has only one choice for a person who is seeking a life partner. It is difficult to find biblical support for the idea that in all of the universe, God has only one person for each of us, that the identity of this person will be revealed in time, and that life will be miserable if you marry someone else. Clearly 1 Corinthians 7 teaches that marriage and singleness are both acceptable to God, and the choice of a mate is governed only by the requirement that Christians must marry Christians. Beyond that, it would appear that a Christian is free to choose a marriage partner based on his or her own careful thinking and the thoughtful input of sensitive other people, including parents or a Christian counselor.

Causes of Good and Poor Mate Selection

Choosing a marriage partner can be a difficult experience, especially in societies where the choice mostly depends on the couple. Often young, inexperienced, and blinded by infatuation and sexual attraction, it is easy for many people to make choices that later prove to be unwise. As a result, their marriages are miserable, and so are their lives and the lives of any children that may be conceived. Knowing this, some people are afraid, unwilling, or at least reluctant to take the risks of choosing a mate and building a marriage.

For most unmarried people in the world, this is not a problem. They are like a young international student at University of Kentucky who was twenty-four when his parents called from India. They told their son, Yogesh Shukla, that they had selected a wife for him and wanted him to return home for the wedding. As a dutiful son who would not think of displeasing his parents, the young man packed his bags and went home, where he married a young woman named Sarita whom he had never met. Today, the couple is happily together in a marriage that was arranged carefully by their parents. One report suggests that as many as 96 percent of the marriages in India and three out of every five marriages worldwide are arranged.[12] The procedures for arranging a marriage vary from one religion to another and differ from place to place, depending on the norms of the culture or subculture. The matchmaking process usually is thorough, detailed, and well established. Today, more than in generations past, the prospective husband and wife often are involved in the selection, and they even may have the freedom to veto the parental choice. After the wedding, some arranged marriages become abusive and filled with great unhappiness, although many arranged marriages work out very well. For people like Yogesh and Sarita, there always was the expectation that they would never have to worry about picking a spouse because they knew that their parents would handle that for them. For them, as for many others, genuine love has developed. Their role as a married couple is to get along as well as they can. "Whether people marry for love or fall in love after marriage, they should always try to work it out," Sarita said. "At the end of the day, you just want someone to talk to, share your day with. Someone to live for."

In contrast to marriages that are arranged by parents, choosing a mate based on desire and building a marriage on love are relatively recent concepts even in the Western world.[13] Many of the early Catholic and Reformation Protestant church leaders were skeptical about the single person's right to freely choose a mate. There was a general view that parents should have the major role in mate selection, and very often marriage was not about love or happiness—it was about a political or economic arrangement between two families. More than any others, the twentieth century liberalized attitudes toward marriage and marriage selection. Probably, most of us would agree that it is best to let individuals and couples make their own choices, but this can lead to considerable anxiety. To help people choose wisely and lessen the risk of making a mistake, counselors might consider five important questions.

1. *Why Do People Choose a Marriage Partner?* Despite the prevalence of arranged marriages in other parts of the world, in Western cultures most people get married because they are in love. But *love* can be a confusing and ambiguous word. To fall in love is to feel an exhilarating, exciting closeness and intimacy with another human being. But this emotional high cannot and does not last by itself forever. For deep love to persist and grow, there must be a giving, other-centered relationship similar to that described in 1 Corinthians 13. It may be that for most people, deep and secure love comes after marriage rather than before. (That has been the experience of both Heather and David in North America and Yogesh and Sarita from India.) To *be* in love, therefore, is to experience a state of emotional exhilaration; to *grow* in love is to involve oneself deliberately in acts of giving and caring. A feeling of being in love is not in itself a solid basis for marriage (and neither is the fact that "we don't love each other anymore" a basis for divorce). The biblical marriages, like marriage in many countries today, were based on issues other than feelings, and even in our society it is probable that people really marry for reasons other than love.

These reasons may be diverse, but often they center on the idea of needs. One theory of mate selection, for example, claims that opposites attract and that single people are drawn to potential partners who can meet their needs by supplementing their areas of weakness. Initially, of course, loving relationships form between people who are alike in many social and cultural ways, but at a deeper level it may be that a dominant person is attracted to someone who is less dominant or an introvert may choose a person who is extroverted.

More accepted is the broader view that marriage meets mutual needs for companionship, security, support, intimacy, friendship, and sexual fulfillment. In addition, some marry because of premarital pregnancy, social pressure from friends or parents, the desire to escape from an unhappy home environment, a fear that one will be left alone, a "rebound" reaction to the breakup of a prior engagement, or a compulsion to rescue some unfortunate single person. Each of these reasons for marriage meets some need, although none in itself can be the basis for a mature and stable relationship.

No doubt you have noticed that some of these reasons for selecting a mate are immature and self-centered; others are more rational and may result from mutual deliberation and respect. In all of this it is wise to remember that people marry, ultimately, because God created us male and female, instituted marriage for companionship, mutual support, and sexual expression, and declared in his Word that marriage is honorable.[14] This must not be forgotten as we help people struggle through the choice of a marriage partner.

2. *Why Do Some People Not Choose a Marriage Partner?* The same God who created marriage apparently did not expect that everyone would find a mate. Jesus never had a wife, and an unmarried apostle Paul wrote that singleness should be considered a superior state, since the unmarried person can be free to "serve the Lord best, with as few distractions as possible."[15] Some people remain single, therefore, because they believe that this is the will and calling of God for their lives.

There are other and probably more common reasons why some people do not marry. First, there is the failure to meet eligible partners. Since there are more women than men, it follows that there are not enough potential husbands to go around. In addition, most people want a mate who has similar interests or education, but many people who desire marriage may not be able to find such compatible prospects. Consider, for example, the believer who wants a Christian mate but who lives in an area where there are few eligible Christians present. The desire for marriage may be strong, but the prospects are not.

Second, some people fail to take advantage of the opportunities that are present. Busy with education, career building, travel, or other activities, these people decide to postpone marriage, but eventually the number of prospects declines. Others have high expectations but keep waiting for someone better and discover too late that they have passed by some excellent opportunities for marriage.

Nobody likes to mention this, perhaps, but people in a third category stay single because they are unattractive to those of the opposite sex. Other things being equal, people who are looking for a mate prefer to find somebody who is physically attractive. Probably more often, psychological characteristics drive others away. Single people who are excessively timid, afraid of the opposite sex, too aggressive or loud, insensitive, socially inappropriate in their dress and mannerisms, or self-centered often cannot relate well in dating. The individual who is overly aggressive or appears too eager to get married very often scares off and drives away potential mates. In contrast, some single people are reluctant to get involved with anyone who is so passive that he or she gives the impression of not being interested in pursuing the relationship.

There are a number of research studies on mate selection, some of which view the process as an exercise in self-marketing. They may not think this way, but in many ways individuals looking for a mate present themselves and their attributes in as positive a light as possible, and they seek to find the best partner they can get for what they have to offer in return. It is not surprising that people who place dating advertisements in newspapers and magazines are presenting themselves in a positive light and indicating what they are looking for in a dating relationship or prospective mate. One research team reviewed a number of these advertisements and found that men most often market their financial and occupational resources, while women still tend to describe their physical attractiveness and appealing body shape.[16] The personal advertisements also reflect cultural differences. Whereas Americans value independence and individualism, Chinese singles emphasize their commitment to family and society.[17] Another study compared "mate preferences" over a fifty-year period and found that both men and women mentioned their interest in mutual attractiveness, and both (but especially men) also were interested in good financial prospects. Unlike their parents, contemporary men are less interested in whether a potential mate has domestic skills.[18] When one group of college students posted information about themselves on an Internet mate-selection site, 40 percent later admitted to researchers that they lied online in an effort to look better.[19] It seems probable that self-descriptions in newspaper and magazine advertisements are distorted as well. All of this suggests that self-marketing is big in mate selection and that some may still be single because they are marketing themselves poorly.

Fourth, there is a failure of some people to achieve emotional independence, and this reduces their prospects for marriage. An unusually strong dependence upon one's parents or guilt over leaving a parent can cause one to remain single. This can be a commendable choice when responsible people make the deliberate but often difficult choice to remain single because of the duty to care for needy family members. Of course, sometimes even this can be an excuse to keep from taking the risks of entering a marriage and building intimacy.

A fifth reason for choosing singleness is the decision of some people to find intimacy apart from traditional marriage. This might involve cohabitating couples, people involved in homosexual relationships, or individuals joining a commune or religious community where there is nonsexual intimacy.

Finally, there are those people who simply do not want to marry. This group includes homosexuals, those who have been hurt in previous relationships, and people who are afraid of the opposite sex, scared of intimacy, and/or unwilling to risk losing their independence. It would be naive and disrespectful to conclude, however, that there is some hidden reason buried deep in the mind of every person who decides to remain single. Large numbers of mature, well-adjusted people prefer to remain single in spite of social pressures that might push them toward marriage.

3. *Where Do People Find Mates?* Several decades of research have confirmed that most people select mates from people who are of a similar age, education, social class, economic or income level, religion, race, and place of residence. This is changing as travel and cross-cultural communication both get easier. People often cross racial, religious, and other barriers, and many are able to build successful

marriages despite their different backgrounds. But crossovers can bring pressure that makes marital adjustment more difficult. Within recent years, for example, increasing numbers of women have been marrying younger men. Often, these are good relationships except for the issue of children. Older women tend to be involved in careers and are less willing to have children; their husbands, in contrast, are more inclined to want families. This can create tension.

In looking for a mate, therefore, most people try to find someone who is of similar background and social-religious-educational level. Within this broad category the choice is narrowed by one's personal standards, parental approval or disapproval, and by the single person's mental image of an ideal mate. Since few people can measure up to these great expectations, there often must be a relaxing of one's standards, a willingness to accept the less desirable characteristics in a potential mate, or a decision to remain single in hopes that the ideal person will eventually come along.

Guided by a mental image of what they might be looking for, many unmarried people go about their daily activities with at least some alertness to the single people who might be seen, met, or befriended at school, work, church, social, and athletic gatherings, conferences, or in the neighborhood. Sometimes, a couple will meet as casual friends or work associates, and a more personal relationship begins to build later. In addition to this more casual way of meeting prospective mates, the Internet has given rise to online mate-selection services. One of the best was developed by a Christian clinical psychologist who designed a highly sophisticated relationship-personality profile with 436 questions built around 29 categories, including self-concept, emotional energy, sexual passion, personality traits, communication style, spirituality, beliefs, values, and family background. Participants take the questionnaire and then, in exchange for a fee, are matched to others with whom there is the highest level of compatibility.[20] Promoters of these services often proclaim their effectiveness enthusiastically, but researchers aren't so convinced. Preliminary investigations question the scientific validity of some of the questionnaires, there is concern about people lying when they complete the match-making questionnaires, and to date there are no published studies on the stability of the marriages that result from Internet matches.[21]

4. *Why Do Some People Choose Unwisely?* Choosing a mate is one of life's most important decisions. It involves emotions and passions, but it also needs to involve our brains, lest we make foolish choices that we will regret later. Social pressures, the influence of parents and friends, sexual urges, or strong desires to get married are among the influences that edge people into unhealthy relationships. In addition, almost everybody brings expectations to their marriages, and these may face abrupt challenges when reality appears. Sometimes, single people look for a mate solely on the basis of what they can receive from marriage, but when married partners expect to receive without giving, they are headed for disappointment. The lopsided desire to receive, without giving, is a mark of immaturity that is rarely seen in more stable marriages where needs are met as each spouse gives to the other.

With a few minutes' reflection, most of us could list reasons why people make unwise marital choices. Future tensions almost always will arise if somebody chooses a marriage partner primarily to escape a difficult home situation, prove that one is an adult, rebel against parents or a former partner, escape the stigma of being single, get an in-house sexual partner, bolster self-esteem, improve social status, or find somebody "to take care of me." Other circumstances that signal potential problems include wide age differences, recent mental illness in one or both individuals, evidence of financial irresponsibility and instability, substance abuse in one or both of the partners, differing religious beliefs, wide cultural or obvious racial differences, or participants who have never dated anyone other than the intended mate. Good marriages can occur despite obstacles like these, but when several are present or when a couple appears to have unhealthy motives for choosing a mate, the choice is likely to be regretted later.

5. *Why Do Some People Choose Wisely?* Despite all of the potential for failure, many people make wise choices of a marriage partner. There can be several reasons for this.

(a) Similar Religious Convictions. In Western cultures, most people first get to know their future mates through dating. Since one never knows when a dating relationship may lead to marriage, it is wise for unmarried Christian persons to limit their dating to other believers. Christians who choose wisely often pray about mate selection, at first alone and later as a couple. This principle may be of less interest to people for whom religious beliefs or spirituality are not important, but even here, it would seem that couples are more likely to be compatible if they share similar beliefs and values.

(b) Similar Backgrounds and Complementary Needs. We have seen that marriage selection is best when the man and woman are similar in things such as age, interests, values, socioeconomic level, and education. In addition, it is helpful if the couple can meet each other's needs. Try, however, to distinguish between complementary and contradictory needs. Complementary needs fit so well together that a relationship is smooth and compromise is rarely needed. Contradictory needs clash and require frequent resolution. If both people enjoy social contacts but one person is outgoing and the other is a little shy, this can be complementary. In contrast, if one person loves parties and the other prefers to remain at home, these contradictory needs make conflict more likely.

(c) Emotional Resonance. Single people sometimes wonder how they will know when "the right one comes along." It isn't helpful to give the common answer "You'll just know," but some relationships do feel harmonious and right. To use another cliché, in good relationships there is good chemistry between the couple. With other relationships, the "spark" isn't there. To choose a mate on the basis of such feelings alone would surely be unwise, but to ignore one's feelings or to overlook the fact that there are no feelings of attraction also would be a mistake.

(d) Compatible Personalities. Counselors sometimes write about the importance of a potential husband and wife having compatible personalities. Sometimes called "marriageability traits," these characteristics might include:

- An ability to work through problems and to persist until there is some resolution.
- Flexibility.
- Similar spiritual interests.
- Common beliefs and values.
- A willingness to share intimate thoughts and feelings.
- Emotional stability.

- Good communication skills.
- Appreciation for each other.
- A good sense of humor.
- The ability to give and receive love.
- Comfort in expressing emotions.

A survey of seven hundred twenty-year-olds found that most were looking for people who had warmth, kindness, openness, a good sense of humor, physical attractiveness, good social status, positive personality traits, and what the researchers termed "expressivity."[22] Another research team reported that the physical attractiveness of the woman in the relationship was more important than personality in predicting good marital interactions.[23] Other research found that "people are happiest in their relationships when they believe they have found a kindred spirit, someone who understands them and shares their experiences." In time, if it becomes apparent that the similarities are not as common as they once thought, partners in good relationships tend to downplay the differences and see positive characteristics in their partners that may not be evident to other people.[24] This may give a hint to the well-known tendency for people in love to see idealized traits in each other. Apparently, this self-deception and idealization of a partner can last into marriage and even increase marital stability.

Whether or not this happens, it is good to remember that nobody can meet all of the ideal marriage traits that we assume to be of importance. For mate selection, a feeling of love or a strong urge to get married cannot be the sole basis for making a wise choice. The outside perspective and guidance of a friend or counselor can be helpful and important if one is to attain subsequent marital stability and happiness.

Effects of Good and Poor Mate Selection

Good choices do not always lead to good marriages, but careful selection of a partner does give a solid foundation on which to build a husband-wife relationship. Marriage involves effort, risk, and times of difficulty and disappointment. These never are easy experiences, but it is more pleasant and motivating to work in partnership with a compatible teammate in life than with someone who apparently was the wrong choice.

Many people, however, make choices that, in retrospect, seem to have been unwise, but the couple determines nevertheless to build the best relationship possible considering the circumstances. This is what Sarita and Yogesh Shukla were prepared to do had their parents not been so successful in arranging the marriage. People who determine to make their marriages succeed discover that loving actions often create loving feelings. In time, relatively good marriages can result.

In contrast, other people never recover from poor mate selection. Unhappiness and conflict characterize the marriage, and the relationship is dissolved emotionally if not legally through separation and divorce. Counseling people in the selection of a marriage partner has the goal of preventing such unhappy endings to marriage.

Counseling and Mate Selection

If you are married there is a good possibility that you had premarital counseling, but it is less probable that any counselor helped you select your mate. When people fall in love, they tend to overlook the faults in each other, ignore danger signals, and dismiss the counsel of more objective persons. Few are likely to come for counsel until after a potential mate has been chosen, and most do not even come then. The counselor's help is most likely to come through informal talks with young people before they fall in love, through devotionals and other public speaking to singles groups, through aside discussions with counselees who have come to get help for other problems, or through counseling with the never-married and formerly married who come for help in evaluating the wisdom of their mate choices. There are several goals for this counseling, goals that apply equally to young unmarried persons and to older individuals, including widows and divorced persons who would like to get married or married again.

1. *Encouraging Spiritual Evaluation.* Since the Bible is so clear in its teaching that believers should marry only believers, this must be emphasized repeatedly. Even when they believe this, people often look for excuses to justify their dating of non-Christians. Some indicate that the couple is merely friends with no plans to get serious or that the dating relationship could open opportunities for the Christian to lead his or her friend to Christ. Although Christians sometimes do lead potential mates to Christ, the reverse is true as well and perhaps more likely—non-believers cause Christians to stumble spiritually or to lose spiritual vitality. This needs to be stated clearly at some time in counseling: dating nonbelievers is risky and best avoided.

When a potential marriage partner is being considered, encourage the counselee to ask questions, such as the following, and suggest that the answers be discussed with the counselor.

- Is my potential mate a believer? How do I know this?
- Does his or her life show evidence of the fruits of the Spirit (Galatians 5:22, 23)?
- Have my partner and I ever discussed our spiritual lives, struggles, and goals?
- Have we ever prayed together? If not, why not?
- Do we agree on a church, on our basic standard of living, hoped-for lifestyle, views about right and wrong, and our perspectives about a Christian home?

2. *Giving Reassurance.* At times a counselor might be approached by some who are concerned because they have not found a mate and fear that they never will get married. Often, these counselees wonder if something is wrong with them, or they may think that God has let them down by not allowing them to get married.

Encourage these people to admit and express their feelings, including feelings of anger and frustration. Often, these counselees know that God cares for all of us and wants the best for his children, but in coming for help their goal is to find a mate rather than to hear about the possible benefits of singleness. As you observe and talk with these counselees, try to determine if they are overly eager, timid, insensitive, domineering, self-focused, or inclined to show other traits that might be driving away members of the opposite sex. Is a counselee's life so bound up in the desire to marry that little else seems to matter? Some people live in the future, missing the present while their energies and attentions are focused on how life will be better when they earn more money, graduate from college, get a better job, or get married. In the meantime, while they wait, their lives are empty, nonproductive, on hold, and sometimes pretty dull. People like this should be encouraged to live life to the fullest now. If they do find a mate, this will be great. If no marriage partner appears, then life still can be worthwhile and fulfilling.

Once you get into this kind of thinking, counselees are more likely to be open to reminders that despite its disappointments, the single life can be fulfilling and even a special calling. With this in mind, is the counselee willing to remain single? If not, why not? And in the meantime, how will he or she live?

3. *Giving Guidance in Mate Selection.* In many ways counseling is a specialized form of education. Certainly, this is true when you are asked to give practical guidance to people who are looking for prospective partners. This guidance involves at least two issues: finding places where there are other single people and learning how to relate.

It is obvious that one does not find a mate by sitting at home watching television and waiting for God's gift of marriage to arrive at the door. Surfing the web of Internet mate-selection services is better, although there must be live conversation and eventually face-to-face contact if the Internet is to deliver on finding someone. Ultimately, to meet potential marriage partners, one must go to where they are. For some, this means singles bars, but for many people, including believers, this is not considered a suitable place to find a mate. More desirable places to meet are churches, colleges, evening or weekend courses, vacation trips, sports events, Christian single adult groups, and conferences. If one goes to these places primarily to find a marriage partner, however, this becomes apparent to everyone. Nothing drives people away like a single person's overanxious desire to latch on to somebody who appears to be eligible. It is better to get involved in groups that have interesting and pleasant people with similar interests, knowing that participating can be enjoyable whether or not potential marriage partners are involved.

Some counselees may need to be reminded that they should look neat and attractive, learn how to ask questions and be at ease interacting with others, and try to be good listeners who are interested in other people. It is important for people to be themselves rather than pretending to be something they are not. Gently, the counselor can point out failings in these areas and, if necessary, do some role playing in which the counselor and counselee pretend to be strangers so they can practice relating to each other. People with good social skills are more attractive to others.

4. *Evaluating Motives, Ideals, and Maturity.* Why does the counselee want to find a mate (or why does he or she not want to marry)? The counselee's answers to these questions may not be what the counselor expects. It is helpful to determine, sometimes by raising tentative questions, if there are unhealthy reasons for wanting or not wanting marriage. Some may want marriage because of social and family pressures, the desire to escape an unpleasant home situation, the

need to prove that one is an adult, a determination to show that one is not lesbian or gay, or the feeling that marriage is now or never. If the person has chosen to remain single, recognize that there may be valid reasons for this decision, but try to determine, as well, if there also might be unhealthy or unsuspected reasons. Is there a fear of marriage or of sexual intimacy? Is the person rebelling against something, including traditional forms of marriage or social pressure? Is he or she trying to prove something? Ask the counselee to discuss these attitudes. Talk together about their implications and the possible reasons for their presence. If there is a desire for change, discuss how this might be done. Try to focus attention on specific issues and talk about how the counselee could take action to change.

At some time it may be good to ask a counselee to describe his or her "ideal mate." Then discuss this expectation. Is it unrealistic? Is it causing the counselee to overlook or reject potentially good marriage partners who do not fit the ideal? Can parts of the ideal be changed without lessening his or her moral standards?

As these issues are discussed, try to assess the counselee's level of maturity. Immature single people make immature marriage partners, and this can lead to problems in dating, marriage, and parenting. The spiritually maturing Christian shows a desire to be like Christ, accompanied by some evidence of the fruits of the Spirit in his or her life.[25] Much more difficult is finding a useful definition of psychological or emotional maturity. The list of traits that characterize mature adults appears to be endless, and the definitions are so diverse that the word *maturity* becomes almost meaningless. Even so, we all know when we see it, and we have little difficulty identifying behaviors that are immature. To complicate matters, it is hard to instill maturity into people who don't have it.

In counseling it may be best to look for immature behaviors and discuss these over time with counselees. For example, it is widely agreed that mature people

- act appropriately for their age, without trying to look older or younger,
- assume responsibility for their actions,
- are willing to postpone immediate gratification so that greater satisfaction can be attained later,
- are able to make choices and live with the consequences of their decisions,
- respect other people who may have opinions and beliefs that differ from their own,
- can look at themselves and their problems objectively, and
- have a realistic and essentially positive self-image.

In areas like these, where does the person succeed, and where does he or she fail? How could these traits and attitudes be developed? The more of these that are present, the greater the likelihood of successful mate selection and marital stability.

5. *Helping People Break Relationships.* In the process of dating and building a relationship, it is common for a couple to discover that their friendship is not going to lead to marriage. Sometimes, they reach this conclusion together and decide to go their separate ways, but often one person decides that separation is best. How does one break the news graciously? Consider sharing the following

helpful guidelines, written by younger people who have been through broken relationships themselves, and who work for a magazine that is read mostly by Christian singles in their twenties:[26]

- Realize that initiating a breakup takes courage. Almost nobody enjoys breaking bad news to another person or confronting painful reality.
- Start with a hint that a breakup may be coming. Instead of abruptly announcing that the relationship is over, express your dissatisfactions: that there appear to be tensions that were not there before, that you are beginning to question whether this could be a lasting relationship, something is bothering you about the relationship, etc.
- When you are ready to break up, be straightforward and decisive. Consider this advice: "Don't put off breaking up if you know it's inevitable. For both your sake and the other person's, do it sooner rather than later. Do it in person—and in private. Breaking up over the phone or worse, via e-mail, is cowardly, impersonal, and insulting. And breaking up in a public setting to avoid a scene may prevent your partner from expressing emotions that may come back to haunt you later."[27]
- Offer concrete reasons for the breakup without laying the blame on the other person. Blaming the other person brings denials and defensiveness.
- Avoid clichés such as "It's not you, it's me," "It just seems best," or worse: "God told me to end the relationship." The latter uses a spiritual statement to avoid dealing with the issues and implies that the other person has missed hearing from God.
- Try to allow time for the other person to express how he or she feels.
- If you have made a firm decision, don't waver or give the other person reason for hope. This means not vacillating, reconsidering, leaving the door open in case something changes, or ending the breakup meeting with physical expressions of affection.
- Don't agree that "We can still be friends." This keeps unrealistic hope alive. It is best to make a clean break.
- Resist the urge to keep in contact, making regular phone calls "just to say hi," or sending frequent email messages.

In addition to helping counselees initiate a breakup, there also will be times when a counselor may be involved in helping the person who has been in a dating relationship or engagement that the other person has terminated. At the beginning, remind these counselees that they are about to go through a painful grieving process that will take time to get over. Encourage the expression of emotion: alone, through journaling, and in sharing with a caring friend or two. After some time for initial grieving, suggest that the person begin to pick up life again by getting involved in activities that do not involve the former relationship partner. Urge the counselee to avoid contact with the other person, such as calling or looking for opportunities to see him or her. Point out the dangers of self-talk and mental reflection that can keep hope alive, stimulate bitterness or self-pity, or rehearse what might have been done to keep the relationship alive. In all of this, encourage the person to pray constantly, knowing that God understands and heals broken hearts. Then discuss what the counselee has learned from the situation. "Mistakes and wrong choices are constructive when they provide knowledge and guidance for the inevitable *next time*."[28]

6. *Encouraging Patience*. In all of this, encourage counselees to be patient, to pray regularly about a marriage partner, to trust in God's leading and timing, and to be alert for opportunities to meet potential mates. Pray for and with your counselees, asking for patience, for purity and protection for both the counselee and his or her potential mate, and for the willingness to accept singleness joyfully if this is God's plan.

Preventing Poor Mate Selection

In the selection of a marriage partner, it may be that the best protection against mistakes is to be forewarned. This chapter is written for counselors, but portions of what appears in the preceding pages could be presented to single people privately or to singles groups, church youth groups, classes, or weekend conferences. If you present this type of material, be sure that there is opportunity for people to discuss what they hear, to ask questions, and to ponder how—in practical ways—this learning can be applied to their own lives.

It is best to present and discuss these principles early in a person's life rather than later. As we have noted, facts about mate selection tend to lose significance and influence after one has fallen in love. If facts and warnings can be given *before* emotional bonds are allowed to develop, it seems more likely that error will be avoided and potentially harmful involvements may be resisted. Most parents, pastors, and other counselors know how difficult it can be to talk about possible dangers of a relationship after the participants are emotionally involved. When all of this is understood and practiced, the counselee will have made much progress toward the prevention of poor mate selection.

With some counselees, prevention will start long before a prospective mate appears. Immature or self-centered people, for example, can often profit from individual or group counseling that helps them cope more effectively with life in general. This can remove some of the unhealthy attitudes and behaviors that may lead to unwise selection of a marriage partner.

Conclusions About Mate Selection

Eric Fromm was a famous psychoanalytic writer who described mate selection as an exercise in bargaining.

> Our whole culture is based on an appetite for buying, on the idea of a mutually favorable exchange. Modern man's [or woman's] happiness consists in the thrill of looking at the shop windows, and in buying all that he can afford to buy, either for cash or on installments. He (or she) looks at people in a similar way. For the man an attractive girl—and for the woman an attractive man—are the prizes they are after. "Attractive" usually means a nice package of qualities which are popular and sought after on the personality market. What specifically makes a person attractive depends on the fashion of the time, physically as well as mentally.... At any rate, the sense of falling in love develops usually only with regard to such human commodities as are within reach of one's own possibilities for exchange. I am out for a bargain, the object should be desirable from

the standpoint of its social value, and at the same time should want me, considering my overt and hidden assets and potentialities. Two persons thus fall in love when they feel they have found the best object available on the market, considering the limitations of their own exchange values.[29]

This is a blunt humanistic analysis, but it contains an element of truth.[30] "Striking a marriage bargain" may be more overt in cultures where dowries and bride prices are part of a deal, but wherever we live, it seems true that mate selection includes some type of exchanges.

The Christian recognizes that marriage involves much more. It is the joining of two individuals so that they become one and yet remain unique but interlocking personalities. It seems unlikely that within this world there is only one, perfect, God-ordained person for each of us, but it surely *is* true that God can and often does lead individuals to marriage partners who will meet their needs and with whom they can blend their lives. Often he leads through counselors who are willing to give guidance as single people make the choice of a mate.

KEY POINTS FOR BUSY COUNSELORS

➤ With soaring divorce rates and broken families now common, the possibility of choosing the wrong person creates anxiety among many who are contemplating marriage.

➤ The Bible says very little about mate selection, possibly because in biblical times and in many parts of the word today, selection has not been viewed as a free choice made by the potential marriage partners.

➤ Choosing a marriage partner can be a difficult experience, especially in societies where the choice mostly depends on the couple. Often young, inexperienced, and blinded by infatuation and sexual attraction, it is easy for many people to make choices that later prove to be unwise.

➤ To help people choose wisely and lessen the likelihood of making a mistake, counselors should give careful thought to the following questions:
  ▪ Why do people choose a marriage partner?
  ▪ Why do some people choose to remain single?
  ▪ Where do people find a mate?
  ▪ Why do some people choose unwisely?
  ▪ Why do some people choose wisely? (In part, wise choices involve choosing people with similar religious convictions, similar backgrounds, complementary needs, emotional resonance, and compatible personalities.)

➤ Marriage involves effort, risk, and times of difficulty and disappointment. Good choices do not always lead to good marriages, but careful selection of a partner does give a solid foundation on which to build a husband-wife relationship.

> In counseling people who are concerned about mate selection:
>   - Encourage spiritual evaluation. The Bible is clear that believers in Christ should not marry unbelievers.
>   - Give counselees reassurance.
>   - Guide people in the mate-finding process. This includes direction in where to meet unmarried people and how to relate.
>   - Evaluate and, if needed, help people change their motives, ideals, and degree of maturity.
>   - Guide people who are in a relationship and want to break up.
>   - Help those who have been in a relationship that the other person has terminated.
>   - Encourage patience.

> Poor or unwise selection can be prevented if the above principles can be taught to individuals or small groups in advance of the development of any relationships.

PART SIX

Family Issues

28

Premarital Counseling

They called her the runaway bride. Her story dominated the news for several days, and her disap-pearance sparked a massive search by family, friends, neighbors, strangers who had never met her, and more than one hundred police officers who worked round the clock trying to solve the mystery of why she had vanished and where she had gone. Hundreds prayed for her safe return, asking God to protect her from danger and criminal harm.

Jennifer was thirty-two at the time, less than a week before her wedding.[1] It was expected to be a magnificent celebration, costing an estimated $50,000. Following an elaborate ceremony in the local Baptist church, there was to have been a lavish reception for six hundred guests. The details had been worked out, the bridal showers had been held, the wedding party had been selected, the invitations had been sent, most plans had been made, but nobody could find the bride.

A few days later, hundreds of miles from home, she called the police to report that she had been kidnapped by a man and woman in their forties who were driving a blue van. Through sobs she told the dispatcher they had held her at gunpoint, but when police and FBI officials began asking ques-tions, Jennifer confessed that her story was a fake. Apparently, overwhelmed by the wedding plans, she cut her hair to avoid recognition and fled across the country on a Greyhound bus.

Back home, there were mixed feelings when people heard the news. Her friends and family were greatly relieved. Her fiancé said he still planned to marry her, that the wedding was only postponed. The police were understanding but contemplating whether she could be charged for the thousands of dollars they had spent in their search. Some people were annoyed or puzzled. Others were amused. News reporters dubbed her the runaway bride and concluded that her cross-country flight was a much-publicized case of pre-wedding jitters and cold feet. The authorities had a different view. They charged her with violating the law by reporting a crime that had not occurred and by causing large amounts of taxpayer money to be spent in the search to find her after she was reported missing.

After returning home, Jennifer checked into a residential treatment center, where she was seeing a therapist to help her deal with the public ridicule and trying to understand why she had run from her own wedding. A judge levied a heavy fine, but Jennifer also was talking with a producer who wanted to tell her story in a movie.

M any years before Jennifer ran away, psychologist Carl Rogers gave a sober-ing perspective on marriage. His words remain relevant today. "If 50–75 percent of Ford or General Motors cars completely fell apart within the early part of their lifetimes as automobiles," the public outcry would be overwhelming, and drastic steps would be taken to correct the situation.[2] But this happens to many marriages and hardly anyone raises a complaint. Divorce is frequent, fewer than half of the marriages that persist can be considered successful, and often couples seem unable or unwilling to do anything to make things better.

Perhaps this is because so few people demand or seem to expect much from marriage. Next time you are near a newsstand, look at the front pages of the tabloids or celebrity magazines. Don't be surprised if more than half the headlines concern television personalities, movie stars, or other well-known people who are cheating on one another, exchanging mates, or engaging in high-profile sexual escapades and marital breakups. This is news about celebrities, and hardly anybody is surprised or alarmed. In many places a marriage permit is easier to obtain than a driver's license, and there is no required waiting period between the time when a couple decides to get married and when they tie the knot. It is more difficult to get into a Rotary or Kiwanis club than to get into a marriage—and service clubs like these expect more of their members. A prospective bride and groom may come together for all the wrong reasons: to escape from a difficult home situation, to add excitement to their lives, to hide a pregnancy, to escape from loneliness, to get married like all their friends, to get ahead financially, or some equally fleeting motive that launches their marriage on a foundation that often is too flimsy to survive the pressures, challenges, and storms of daily living. Despite the effectiveness of premarital programs, estimates suggest that only 30 percent of couples use these services, and of those who do, most get their premarital counseling from clergy in religious settings.[3]

Even in the church we tend to leave premarital counseling (perhaps "preceremonial" counseling is a more accurate term) to the pastor, while the relatives and church members are content to remain smiling spectators. They come to the wedding, bring their gifts and cards, attend the showers, and have cake at the reception—all the time hoping that the marriage will last and that somebody has been guiding the couple in preparing for this crucially important step in life. The same dedicated church members who encourage prayer meetings before selecting a pastor or launching a new program for community outreach are less likely to think about praying for couples who are beginning a Christian marriage that they hope will last for a lifetime.

Premarital counseling and prayer may be downplayed, but many families are committed to hiring a wedding manager to help plan and coordinate all the details of the big day. I don't know if Jennifer, the runaway bride, had a wedding manager for the lavish event that was planned, and neither do I know if she and her fiancé had been counseled prior to their planned marriage. Based on the newspaper reports, we might guess that they had both a manager and a premarital counselor. Even so, the upcoming wedding and maybe the prospect of marriage caused Jennifer to panic and run. Her story was sensational, but she is not alone in having premarital jitters. Perhaps most engaged couples can understand, including those who are older. About the time of Jennifer's bus ride, I got a letter from a widower friend who is over sixty and was planning to get married again. In describing his coming wedding, he wrote "even though I've been there before, I am frankly scared witless!"

Unlike most of the topics in this book, premarital counseling is primarily preventive. It comes before problems arise rather than after. It focuses on education and giving information. It is less concerned about healing wounds that exist than about building a union that will survive future pressures. Since few people are enthusiastic about preventive counseling (most assume that problems happen to others but never will happen to them), there is a tendency to resist and sometimes to resent this help. Counselors can become disillusioned with premarital counseling, and many wonder if it is worth the effort. One experienced counselor concluded that premarital counseling was futile because most of the couples in his church approached the counseling with "amused tolerance." So in that church, the prospective brides and grooms must promise only to seek a competent marriage counselor at the first sign of problems.

When a couple resists premarital counseling, however, it seems unlikely that they would seek counseling at the first sign of marital difficulty. Wisely, therefore, many churches and religious leaders insist on premarital counseling before they will consent to perform a church wedding. The benefits of this counseling have been acknowledged later by many grateful and happily married couples. Perhaps there are others who never think back to their premarital counseling, but who nevertheless experience marital fulfillment that, in part, is due to the guidance that came formally or informally before the wedding.

The Bible and Premarital Counseling

Did Mary and Joseph get premarital counseling? Probably not. If they acted according to the custom of the time, a written contract of engagement was signed under oath, and then the bride went home to learn the duties of a good wife and mother. If she was unfaithful during that time, the husband-to-be could have her stoned to death, or he could give her a statement of divorce (even before their marriage). When Joseph learned that Mary was pregnant, he decided to divorce her quietly, but he changed his mind when an angel appeared and announced that Mary had been impregnated without sexual intercourse and was to be the mother of the Messiah.[4] We are not told what Mary and Joseph learned about marriage during this period of engagement, and neither does the Bible give any direction about how people should prepare for marriage today.

In all of Scripture the closest we come to premarital counseling is Paul's advice in 1 Corinthians 7. He encourages people to remain single, but acknowledges that it is better to marry than to burn with lust.[5] He warns that marriage will bring challenges and pressures, and he notes that it is difficult for married people to serve the Lord wholeheartedly because part of their focus is on pleasing each other.[6] Elsewhere in the New Testament, we read what an ideal marriage should be like, what roles the husband and wife should fulfill, and how they should function as parents.[7] Beyond this, however, there are no clear biblical examples or specific instructions for premarital guidance.

Reasons for Premarital Guidance

Assume that you are a researcher wanting to prove that premarital counseling works. How would you do your research? Probably, most people who do premarital counseling believe in its effectiveness, but proving this can be very difficult. A good (or bad) marriage may occur for a number of reasons, but it is hard to design research to prove that premarital counseling is one of those reasons. Psychologist Scott Stanley has written about the lack of research, but his experiences lead him to believe that premarital counseling and other education can be effective, in part, because this

- can slow couples down so they spend more time in deliberation,
- sends the message that marriage matters,

- teaches couples where they can go for help if they need it later, and
- can provide certain kinds of training, including relationship enhancement or communication skills that can lower the risks for later marital distress or divorce.[8]

At least seven contemporary influences can contribute to unhealthy marriages. In one individual or couple we may not see all seven. Eventually, however, they all are likely to be seen by counselors who work with different couples or individuals. Premarital guidance, including counseling, can help people deal with these when they arise.

1. *Unrealistic Expectations That Can Lead to Disillusionment.* When they approach marriage, perhaps most people assume that they have unique relationships. Most think it is unlikely that their marriage would be destroyed by the pressures that lead others to the divorce court. Perhaps there are Christians who assume—incorrectly it would seem[9]—that their marriages will be more blissful and have a higher likelihood of survival than the marriages of nonbelievers.

Writing in a magazine for young single people, one author identified four unrealistic expectations that should be examined more closely and rejected. "Here's what marriage isn't," he wrote:

- A cure for loneliness. Even when they have relatively good relationships, husbands and wives can be lonely, lacking intimacy.
- An escape from boredom. "Getting married in order to generate a little excitement in your life is a terrible motivation. Why? Because once the merry-go-round stops—once the novelty wears out—you'll immediately start looking for the next ride."
- A rowdy sex romp. Sex is "the ultimate bonding activity for a couple to share," but it's not the only activity, and after the first year or so, the excitement and motivation both wane.
- An easy transition. On the contrary, the transition from single to married life can be a major challenge in coping, even when the relationship is good.[10]

Even though the failure rate for marriage is well known, many people apparently do not realize that meaningful marriages grow slowly and only with commitment and effort. Often there is impatience, insensitivity, self-centered attitudes, inadequate skill in relating, and great disappointment and disillusionment when the expectations for marriage are not met quickly.

Premarital counseling lets couples express, discuss, and realistically modify their assumptions about what lies ahead. Conflicting expectations between the man and the woman can be seen and hopefully be resolved. With the counselor's help, the couple can learn that dreams and expectations for a good marriage only become reality when there is mutual giving and consistent effort. Learning like this comes slowly, but it can help couples anticipate and sometimes avoid the disillusionment that clouds the anticipated brightness in many marriages.

2. *Personal Immaturity That Can Lead to Insensitivity.* On a cold January morning, I was walking past the local high school when I saw a male teenager walking toward me, carrying a baby-sized doll. "I know what course you are taking in that high school," I joked as we met and stopped for a brief conversation. Everybody knows that it is easier and more pleasurable to get pregnant than to take care of a

25.4

child, but to impress this on young people, some schools offer courses in which the students are required to pretend that they have a child for several weeks. The "child," in the form of a doll like the one being carried by that teenager I met, has to be changed, has an inner mechanism that makes crying sounds even late at night, and can't be left by itself or put on a shelf for the evening. The young man I spoke with described how he and his classmates had learned a lot about the realities and responsibilities of parenting because of their class. Before we parted, I pointed out—with a smile—that in real life he would need to have more clothes on his "baby" than the diaper, which was all the doll was wearing in the brisk Chicago winter weather.

High schools can offer courses to teach people what married life or parenting will be like, but courses cannot teach everything. People who are irresponsible before marriage tend to be irresponsible after the wedding. While they are dating and thinking enthusiastically about the future, differences tend to be overlooked. If one or both of the participants are self-centered, hypercritical, impatient, competitive, or insensitive, these immature traits may not be noticed, but they will put a strain on marital stability later.

When the couple settles in to daily routines after the honeymoon, each person's attitudes, mannerisms, and sometimes troublesome characteristics begin to surface. If these can be discussed, understood, and in some way resolved or accepted, then the marriage builds and grows. When the differences are ignored, denied, or allowed to become the basis of arguments and criticism, the marriage begins to weaken.

Immature people tend to be self-centered. At different times these individuals may be manipulating (overtly or in a more subtle way), exploiting, or competing with their mates, all in an attempt to satisfy their own needs. These tactics put strain on the marriage, but the partners often are insensitive both to each other and to the ways in which their self-centered behaviors are destroying the relationship. Premarital counseling should seek to uncover and discuss the self-centered tendencies that can put pressure on a marriage. The couple can be taught how to resolve differences and helped to develop the communication skills, sensitivity, and willingness to accept and meet each other's needs. If these skills are not learned before marriage, they can be the basis of more serious conflicts later.

3. *Changing Roles That Can Lead to Confusion.* There was a time when the roles of husband and wife were defined clearly and accepted widely throughout the community. In many places this still is true, but things are changing. Even within the church there is debate over the meaning of Bible passages such as Ephesians 5:21–33, which concerns the roles of husband and wife. This change and debate is not necessarily bad, but it can lead to later problems. Confusion and conflict may follow when a man and woman each come to marriage with unclear roles and vague expectations about their own and each other's responsibilities. Differences like these often come from what we observed in each of our families when we were growing up. Examples are not difficult to imagine. Assume that a young man grew up in a home where the woman did all the domestic chores, but his future wife is from a family where the parents shared household responsibilities. When the couple gets married and there are dishes to be washed or a house to be cleaned, the differing assumptions about roles can lead to tension unless the couple has learned to communicate about their expectations honestly, nondefensively, and in giving and loving ways.

25.5

Premarital counseling provides opportunity for a couple to begin this type of communication. Together they can learn to discuss their different role expectations and decide on areas of responsibility. Failure to do this can lead to confusion and conflict that can be avoided if the husband and wife operate in ways that assist each other, regardless of their customs or family traditions.

Role clarification must not ignore biblical teaching. According to the Scriptures, both the Christian husband and the Christian wife must be filled with the Spirit— daily confessing sin, giving thanks, and praying for the Holy Spirit to control each of their lives.[11] There also must be an attitude of mutual submission to each other, but the more stringent requirements are laid on the husband. He must love his wife unselfishly, discipline his children fairly, and lead the family wisely. The wife, in turn, is instructed to submit to her husband and respect him.[12] In no way does this give a man the right to harm, dominate, ignore, or be insensitive to his wife or children. And in no way does this imply that women are inferior. The husband and wife are equally valuable and equally important in the building of a good marriage, but they do have different responsibilities. These broadly defined scriptural roles for husbands and wives cannot be changed or ignored in order to accommodate cultural trends. Nevertheless, there is considerable room for variation as individual couples decide on their specific duties and behaviors, providing these decisions are considered within the broad guidelines outlined in the Bible.

4. *Alternative Forms of Marriage That Can Lead to Uncertainty.* What is a traditional family? Toward the end of the twentieth century, this became a major question in American politics as different Christian groups and political parties proclaimed their commitment to family traditions and traditional family values but tended to have different ideas of what traditional families looked like. For many years the traditional family was thought to consist of a male husband who was the primary provider, legally married to one female, his wife, who in turn bore and was the primary care-giver for one or more children that were fathered by the husband. As the culture changed, this definition changed, and some historians were quick to point out that the so-called traditional family in the United States and Canada was not really traditional because it was not much more than a hundred years old. When I typed "traditional family" into a computer search engine, I got forty-two million hits showing that in different cultures, historical eras, political groups, and sociology textbooks there were different perspectives on traditional families.[13]

Many of the current alternatives to traditional marriage and the traditional family can be consistent with biblical teaching. These include marriages in which both husband and wife work to build careers or contribute to the family income, marriages in which the couple decides to have no children, single-parent families where one partner in a marriage or former marriage raises the children alone, or blended families where a husband and wife, each of whom was previously married, come together with their children and form a new marriage and family group. Other alternatives, like trial marriage or gay marriage, are viewed by most Christians as being unbiblical, harmful, and not to be condoned.

All of this can leave some couples confused and uncertain. Can they find alternatives to traditional marriage that might be healthy and supported biblically? Is a lifetime commitment to a monogamous marriage realistic in the twenty-first century? Is it wise for a couple to live together in cohabitation before marriage as a way of testing whether the marriage would last? The counselor may have no problem in answering questions like these, but many couples need to think them

25.4

through carefully, in light of the Scriptures, and with the guidance of a counselor who is patient, gentle, and not inclined to lecture.

This guidance may be very helpful if it is introduced to groups or individuals long before they have chosen a prospective life partner. One team of researchers studied attitudes among teenagers concerning marriage, sexual behavior, and alternative living arrangements.[14] The majority viewed marriage as a lifelong commitment, viewed divorce negatively, and demonstrated a growing acceptance of premarital counseling and other forms of marriage and family-life education. Only one-third expressed positive attitudes toward premarital sex, but the majority indicated that they would engage in sexual intercourse before marriage or already had done so. And about half expressed approval of cohabitation, in which a couple lives together with full sexual involvement, even though they are not married. In this, their thinking is consistent with unmarried people around the world,[15] but increasing research indicates that couples who live together before marriage tend to have poorer subsequent marriages than those who do not.[16]

When they live together, a couple learns that they can have sex and companionship without committing to marriage with its financial responsibilities and risks of divorce. If a cohabitation arrangement goes sour, one or both of the partners can just leave, without a lot of hassle, even though there may be a lot of pain. Many couples report that they move in with each other because of the financial, convenience, and housing benefits rather than viewing this as a trial to evaluate their compatibility for marriage.[17] Even so, based on the National Survey of Families and Households, there is evidence that cohabiters who later marry are 50 percent more likely to divorce than people who did not live together.[18] It appears that the experience of living together leads to lower levels of overall commitment and lower levels of happiness. As the percentage of those who have cohabited before getting married has soared, a greater percentage of those marriages are failing.[19]

5. *Loosening Sexual Standards That Can Lead to Immorality.* Sex before marriage is not new, and neither is it rare, even among Christians. What is newer is the increasing approval and acceptance of premarital sex, the widespread involvement of so many people in sex apart from marriage, and the flood of arguments that are used, often in a casual way, to justify sexual behavior that is condemned in Scripture.[20]

Because of these attitudes, dating for many has become a time for exploring each other's bodies and genitals, more than each other's interests, beliefs, values, goals, minds, feelings, and expectations. Love is reduced to sex, and there is a de-emphasis on respect, responsibility, understanding, care, and developing interpersonal relationships with people other than one's partner. What is assumed to be increasing sexual freedom in reality involves increasing bondage to the demands of one's physiological drives. By ignoring divine standards that free us for maximum life fulfillment, many have cast away their freedom and settled for a biological enslavement. To many these words will seem archaic and best buried in the past, but despite current moral standards, even among Christians, the Bible still refers to widespread sexuality as immorality. As a part of premarital counseling, issues like these should be discussed honestly, faced realistically and compassionately, and examined biblically.

6. *Previous Experiences That Can Lead to Overconfidence.* Books on premarital counseling tend to assume that most couples are young, inexperienced, and

about to enter their first marriage. Of course this is not always true. Many prospective brides and grooms have been married previously. Some have had unhappy past experiences and now hope for something better. Others have lost a much-loved mate and are hoping that the new marriage will restore some of the lost happiness. Older widows and widowers at times resist the cautions of their adult children and assume that older couples "know all about marriage" because of their long years of experience. The resistance may be even greater if the counselor who gives caution is considerably younger than the engaged couple.

Not all previously married couples resist, however. Many recognize the need for new adjustments and appreciate the help that can come from a sensitive counselor. Even as the counselor shows respect for the value of past experiences, he or she can challenge unrealistic attitudes or expectations, help the couple see potential problems that even experienced people might miss, and give guidance to resolve issues that may have been unresolved in the previous marriages. Perhaps nothing can create chaos in a new marriage like overconfidence because of past marital experiences. Counseling before a second or third marriage will be different, but it can be as important and helpful as counseling for those who have never married.

7. *Circumstances That Can Signal High Risks for a Marriage.* In a book like this, written for Christian counselors, you might expect to read how marriages are better and divorces are fewer in places where large numbers of people go to church and are active as Christians. Sadly, that conclusion is wrong. If you live in the United States, you know that the southeast part of the country is a region widely known as the Bible Belt. States like Alabama, Tennessee, Arkansas, and Oklahoma form "the conservative heartland" where core values prevail, church attendance is high, evangelical Christianity is very prevalent, and yet divorce rates are higher than any place else in the country. Together, church and political leaders in these locations are trying to discover why marriages are so unstable in the Bible Belt and how they can be strengthened. One result of this investigation has been the growing acceptance of pre-engagement and premarital counseling for couples who are thinking about marriage, church and community programs that teach about relationships, and workshops with titles like "To Marry or Not to Marry," even for people who have no potential mate in sight. Churches are making premarital counseling a prerequisite for a church wedding, and in some states—including Florida, Arizona, and even Minnesota in the north—legislators are offering financial incentives for couples who attend counseling or premarital education classes before they marry.[21]

Much of this comes because so many couples bring high-risk circumstances to their engagements and new marriages. Some of these red-flag dangers have been mentioned in earlier chapters: a pregnant bride; one or both participants on the rebound from a previous marriage or engagement; serious involvement with alcohol or other drugs; a history of abuse or other violence, emotional problems, mental instability, serious mental, or physical handicaps; no financial security; contrasting cultural backgrounds or religious beliefs; wide gaps in education or age differences; knowing each other for a very short time—to list some of the most common. Couples may not see that these are obstacles to a good marriage, and for some these differences can and will be overcome. But counselors and leaders of marriage education courses need to urge caution and thorough discussion of issues such as these before the couple moves ahead with marriage. In this way a lot of potential misery may be avoided.

Two researchers with an interest in marriage preparation studied a sample of 964 college students who came from homes where the parental marriages were not stable and the students themselves were likely to be at high risk for instability in their own future marriages. Overall, these students had high motivation to participate in marriage preparation, including premarital counseling, but they also had less optimism about how their own future marriages might turn out, and this, in turn, decreased their motivation to stay with the premarital programs. When they did stay, most did not want to get premarital guidance from clergy or churches, although there was more willingness to stay with religious counselors who had struggled with tensions in their own marriages and had overcome their problems.[22] If single people have grown up in the midst of marital strife at home and are pessimistic about their own chances for marital success later, or if they view marriage as a temporary relationship that lasts "until divorce do us part," then there is less commitment to counseling and less willingness to persist in dealing with marital pressure when difficult times arise. This challenges the premarital counselor to help couples build stable attitudes and behaviors that will undergird new marriages and help them endure.

The Effects of Premarital Counseling

Many books, articles, seminars, and premarital counselors tend to overlook the important question of whether this premarital preparation really improves marriages, reduces the incidence of family disintegration, and prevents divorce. Married individuals often report that their premarital counseling was beneficial, but we cannot reach solid conclusions based on personal testimonies or self-report surveys. Some couples are unhappy in spite of their premarital counseling, and others have good marriages, even though they never had premarital guidance. To some extent the lack of scientific data may reflect the previously mentioned difficulties of trying to measure and precisely evaluate something as vague as effectiveness of premarital counseling.

One of the best and most helpful reports has come from a research group that did a "comprehensive, meta-analytic review and critical evaluation" of existing research on the effectiveness of premarital prevention programs. Results revealed that the average person who participated in a premarital prevention program was significantly better afterward than 79 percent of people who did not participate. These findings, from highly regarded research teams, concluded that "premarital prevention programs are generally effective in producing immediate and short-term gains in interpersonal skills and overall relationship quality." In addition, it was found that marriage quality is significantly better in people who experienced the premarital programs than in couples who did not have the experience. The researchers were quick to add that these are short-term results that cannot answer the question of whether premarital preparation has long-lasting effects.[23] Some evidence suggests that the long-term effects do persist, however, especially in men who are taught better communication skills.[24] In the meantime, researchers continue their work, and counselors continue as well, based on the reports of people who believe they have been helped. In all of this there is general agreement that premarital guidance is most effective with couples whose adjust-

25.9

ment is relatively good and who are motivated to learn from the programs that they go through.

Why do premarital counseling and other forms of preparation have an impact? During counseling, couples may be confronted with problem areas that might not have been noticed previously. Such knowledge can lead these couples to pause, to work on their problem issues, to get further counseling, or even to delay marriage until the difficulties are resolved. Even if the research support never is conclusive, the Christian counselor has a responsibility, before God, to help couples live fulfilled and God-pleasing lives. When people find fulfillment in their marriages and families, they are better able to serve God effectively and to raise and nurture children in Christ-honoring ways.

True premarital counseling is something much broader than a few precerimonial meetings with a pastor. When viewed in its broader context, premarital counseling is a part of Christian discipleship. Perhaps this broader education for marriage has not been studied empirically, but it has been mandated biblically.

Premarital Counseling

As we have seen, couples often approach premarital counseling or other marriage preparation programs with mixed feelings. While many recognize its potential value, there also is the feeling that "our love is so unique that we don't need this—especially now when we are so busy." Others may come with trepidation and defensiveness, afraid that the counselor will suggest that the marriage is unwise. Counselors should be alert to these attitudes so they can be discussed and the couple can have their uncertainties addressed. It also is important for counselors to know some of the reasons why people resist and what might be done to counter these resistances. Also, it is helpful to know what people would like from premarital education and counseling. Researchers have found the following answers:

- Couples are more strongly likely to participate if they have a positive overall attitude toward counseling and if counseling has been recommended to them, presumably by somebody they respect.[25]
- There is more openness to counseling if it focuses on issues that people want to discuss. High on the list are improved communication and problem-solving skills.[26]
- The characteristics of the counselor-leader are important to some couples.[27]
- Couples shy away from counseling if they know that past secrets and relationship issues will have to be shared. This leads to increased fears that the current relationship will be undermined by that information.[28]

One research team sent questionnaires to almost 1,000 couples who had been married between one and five years. Each couple was asked to look at a list of problems and indicate which of these was most problematic to newly married people. Here is the list in order of priority: balancing job and family, deciding on the frequency of sexual relations, handling issues revolving around finances, resolving differing expectations about household tasks, improving skills in communication and conflict resolution, settling on the time spent with parents, and dealing with the issue of time spent alone as a couple.[29] These issues should be at the basis of premarital education.

25 √10

1. *The Purposes of Premarital Counseling*. There are different approaches to pre-marital counseling, but most seek to help individuals, couples, and groups of cou-ples to prepare for and build happy, fulfilling, Christ-honoring, and successful marriages. Each of the following goals might be explored with couples, but the alert counselor will realize that no two counseling situations are the same, so some of these may require more attention than others.

(a) Teaching About Marriage. Few are likely to come for this reason, but there are counselees who need a fresh focus on the importance of marriage. It is critical to the fulfillment and future of the participants, but it also is important for their children, extended families, and communities. Teaching about marriage may help some couples realize the destructive power of divorce and the need to take mar-riage seriously as a relationship that needs to be nurtured and built.

The Bible makes a number of statements about marriage and emphasizes its importance. The family is modeled after the relationship that Christ had with his church, and although no two marriages are alike (since each individual and each couple is unique), every marriage should reflect the influence of Christ in the home. Sometimes, a couple will have little interest or knowledge of spiritual mat-ters, but the Christian counselor must gently raise such issues. Scriptural passages such as 1 Corinthians 13, Ephesians 5:21–6:4, Colossians 3:16–21, 1 Corinthians 7, and 1 Peter 3:1–7 should be read, discussed, understood, and applied to the couple's relationship.

(b) Assessing Marital Readiness. The realities of marriage sometimes cause people to grow up quickly, but it is better if there is a strong element of psycho-logical and spiritual maturity prior to the wedding. Most of us could agree with the counselor who concluded that no marriage will survive the pressures of life and the stresses of our age unless the bride and groom both have an element of maturity. This includes the ability to put aside immediate gratification in order to receive a greater benefit in the future, an ability to share and compromise, con-cern for each other's welfare, and the ability to face problems honestly and to work at finding realistic solutions. Equally important is the couple's commitment to each other and to making the marriage successful. The counselor can look for evidences of these behaviors as the conversation continues.

It also can be helpful to look for answers to several questions. Why does the couple really want to get married? What do they expect from marriage, and how realistic are these expectations? How similar are their backgrounds in terms of education, place of residence, religious beliefs, age, race or socioeconomic level? Have they discussed their views of the husband and wife roles in marriage? In discussions of these and other issues, the counselor can watch for signs of imma-turity, rigidity, tension, lack of commitment, and communication breakdown.

With the counselor's encouragement, couples should consider their own and each other's strong and weak points, values, prejudices, beliefs, attitudes about the husband and wife roles in marriage, and expectations or plans for the future. During the engagement period, there often is a tendency to camouflage injured feelings and hide differences of opinion in order to keep the relationship running smoothly. These differences need to be acknowledged and discussed so the coun-selees learn to better understand themselves and each other.

To aid with the evaluation, some couples find it helpful to read books together or work through one of the premarital counseling manuals that are designed to prepare individuals for marriage. These books can be discussed together and with

25.11

the counselor.[30] In addition, many counselors have found it helpful to recommend psychological tests to help in the self-evaluation process. There are hundreds of these tests, but some are not very reliable or valid, and many are difficult to get, especially if you are not a licensed professional counselor. At times, tests are misinterpreted by people (including counselors) who may not be familiar with what the test is designed to show.

Table 28–1 is a short list of tests that most often are used by premarital counselors.[31] Each of these has been used by hundreds of thousands of couples, and each has been evaluated scientifically. If you recommend any of these tests, be sure to allow sufficient time to discuss results with the prospective bride and groom after they take the tests. This prevents misinterpretation and often leads to issues that are more important to the counseling than what the test results show.

(c) Exploring Possible Problem Areas. Even when a couple has a great relationship, there will be adjustment problems when two people of different gender and family backgrounds come together to share life intimately. How will the couple handle finances, different values, in-law pressures and expectations, differing interests, conflicts that might arise over choice of friends, preferences about recreation, vocational demands, political differences, and variations in spiritual beliefs or maturity? Then there is the issue of sex. Are there fears, unhealthy attitudes, or different expectations for the honeymoon? Of course, some of these issues will be more important than others, but it is best if the couple can discuss these potential problem areas, even though all the discussions need not be in the counselor's presence.

Despite their feelings of enthusiasm, most couples approach marriage with at least some anxiety. They may not be stressed enough to become runaway brides, or grooms, but there are likely to be concerns about details of the ceremony or honeymoon. Frequently, there are concerns about whether the marriage will turn out okay, or whether it will become like the problem-plagued marriages of their friends or parents. In premarital counseling, couples can be encouraged to talk about their anxieties and inhibitions. By discussing their fears and insecurities together, they can relieve some of the anxiety and learn how to deal with potentially threatening situations.

There are three helpful approaches that can reduce stress before and during the early months of marriage.

First, the counselor can provide information. It is easy to assume that people know more than they do. A pastor's son may know less about spiritual things than you expect. A nurse may know little about family planning. A banker's son may have no idea about how to set up a budget or handle the financial aspects of marriage. Despite the free discussion of sex in our society, premarital counselors often discover that young people (and some who are older) know little about the basics of human sexuality, even if they have been sexually active. In counseling, therefore, watch for knowledge gaps. If it appears that a couple needs information, this can be provided through the counselor's instruction, the distribution of books or pamphlets,[32] or putting counselees into contact with competent professionals, such as a trusted family physician, a financial planner, or a person who can give accurate and helpful information.

Second, the counselor can stimulate mentoring by a more experienced couple. Good rapport between the couples is one of the most important requirements for successful mentoring. Learning occurs more easily, and potential problems can be

25.12

Table 28–1

Useful Inventories for Premarital Counseling

The following are perhaps the most frequently utilized assessment tools that counselors have used to help assess the strengths, weaknesses, and special characteristics that individuals or couples would bring to a marriage. It should not be assumed that these are the best or the only valid tools. An Internet search for "premarital inventories" will reveal a number of others. In most cases the man and woman take the inventory separately and then discuss their results together, preferably with the help of a counselor.

For more information on each of these, please go to the web site. Each of the following is appropriate for Christian counselees, regardless of theology. While the Taylor-Johnson Temperament Analysis is strictly secular, each of the others has roots in different Christian traditions.

Taylor-Johnson Temperament Analysis—*www.tjta.com* is a 180–item questionnaire designed to help individuals and couples develop awareness of personality characteristics that could influence their relationships with others, including prospective life partners. The test measures several traits, including dominant-submissive, hostile-tolerant, and self-disciplined-tolerant. The test is not limited for use with couples before marriage, but it often is used in premarital counseling.

Prepare-Enrich—*www.prepare-enrich.com* is a series of five 125–item inventories that have been developed over a twenty-five-year period and taken by over 1.5 million couples. The tests uncover relationship issues that couples are likely to face. Unlike some other inventories, this one must be administered by a specially trained counselor. Many pastors and other Christian counselors have found it helpful to get this training. Prepare-Enrich has offices around the world, and the inventories are available in languages other than English.

FOCCUS—*www.foccusinc.com* is a short name for Facilitating Open Couple Communication, Understanding & Study. FOCCUS is described as "an internationally used inventory designed to provide engaged couples and those working with them a personalized profile of what is needed in their marriage preparation process. It is both a starting place for couple discussion and a map of what issues need time and attention, affirmation or problem-solving." The inventory has 156 items and different options for scoring and is suitable for use with couples of groups or couples.

RELATE—*www.relate-institute.org* offers relationship evaluations that deal with personality characteristics, similarities, and differences in a couple, insights into the role of family environment, and suggestions for improving relationships—all summarized in a twenty-page report with "easy-to-apply graphs and summaries that showcase your responses and your partner's responses so you can quickly identify trouble areas and topics for further discussion."

discussed more openly when the couples enjoy being together and are able to communicate freely. Various programs have been developed and tested to guide the more experienced couples in their mentoring.[33] While these can be very helpful, they are not necessary if the mentoring couple is sensitive to the needs of the protégé couple, and open about their own marriage.

Third, the counselor can help to stimulate effective communication skills. It is widely known that failure to communicate is one of the most fundamental problems in troubled marriages. Before they marry, couples must be shown the value of spontaneous, honest, sensitive communication. As they are encouraged to discuss their feelings, expectations, differences, attitudes, and personal hurts, they can learn to communicate about significant issues, listen carefully as they try to understand each other, and talk through problems without putting down each other or hiding what they truly feel.

As you counsel, watch for and point out behaviors that could hinder communication. There could be problems, for example, if one person does most of the talking while the other remains silent and seemingly passive, if one shares feelings but the other talks on a more cognitive level, or if one responds spontaneously and openly but the other seems guarded and more cautious or introverted.

(d) Planning the Wedding. The counselor, especially the pastoral counselor, may play a major role in the wedding by performing the ceremony. Premarital counseling can be a time for (1) making sure that all legal requirements are met (such as obtaining a license and getting blood tests), (2) going over details of the service, and (3) urging the participants to put limits on the expenses and planned activities for the wedding. There may be limited success with the latter goal, since families in our culture often use weddings to impress others with their social status and financial success. As a result, families go into huge debt that takes years to pay off. It is important to help people recognize that for Christians a wedding can be a service of praise and witness to the couple's mutual commitment to Christ. Too often this message gets lost in the midst of expensive flower arrangements, dresses, photography costs, limousines, numerous attendants, lengthy guest lists, and expensive meals and refreshments. Based on media reports, there is evidence that all of this commotion was one of the major reasons that Jennifer, the runaway bride, ran away.

2. *The Format for Premarital Counseling.* Obviously, a counselor cannot accomplish all these purposes in one meeting together. Most premarital counselors are likely to recommend at least five or six one-hour sessions prior to the wedding. This can be demanding both for the counselor and for the couple, but the usefulness of premarital guidance is lessened if time pressures and everybody's busyness combine to convince the counselees that a briefer period of premarital counseling would suffice. Religious couples most often expect to get their premarital counseling from a pastor, but this can put tremendous pressure on church leaders, who already have multiple responsibilities and multiple weddings to perform. Sometimes, engaged couples will be combined into groups that are more informative than interactive, but this classroom type of atmosphere misses many of the personal issues that need to be discussed openly and freely in private by the couple.

Each counselor should think through his or her own format for premarital counseling. Try to start several months prior to the planned wedding date and be

25.14

adaptable. Nothing is more likely to kill healthy premarital counseling than a rigid format that requires everyone to conform to the counselor's prearranged course. Some couples will need more time; others will need less. If several marriages are being planned, you may want to begin by meeting once or twice with each couple alone, and then see several couples together for group premarital counseling. One researcher asked 170 engaged couples what they would prefer for premarital counseling. They wanted at least some one-to-one counseling from a minister, but they were also very open to weekend retreats, small-group discussions, classes, and a workbook.[34] The following is only one of several formats that you could use.[35] Whatever approach you take, try to keep flexible. For example, you may need fewer than six sessions, or more, and discussion of the wedding ceremony may need to be brought up earlier in the process than in the last session.

Session one. This is a time for building rapport and getting comfortable with the premarital counseling process. Encourage the couple to talk about themselves, their backgrounds, families, interests, and hopes. Listen carefully at first and resist the tendency to begin dealing with problem areas. Ask why they want to get married and listen to their expectations about marriage.

Discuss the premarital counseling. What would they like to accomplish? Share your perspectives and policies about this kind of counseling—its purposes and goals, its benefits, its length, and how you would like to proceed. If you plan to give readings, tests, or other recommended assignments, talk about these, their purpose, and the importance of getting these done. Some counselors will give one or two inventories in the first session, or you might ask counselees to complete these at home and bring them back at the next session.

Ask about spiritual interests and the relationship that each has with Jesus Christ. Are they both believers? Does Christ have a central place in their relationship? What are they doing alone and together to build their Christian lives? Do they pray together? At the beginning, try to avoid asking in ways that might lead your counselees to get defensive if they have little or no spiritual dimension in their lives.

Session two. Discuss the biblical view of marriage: its origins (Genesis 2:18–24); its purposes (such as companionship, sexual union, child-rearing, or a reflection of God's relationship with the church); its permanence (Matthew 19:3–9). Look at the major biblical passages that deal with marriage and discuss how these apply to the counselees. Be practical and specific. Do not let this become a lecture, but include the counselees, getting their observations, questions, and discomforts. If you have given tests, try to get these scored as soon as you can so they can be discussed.

Sessions three and four. This is a time to consider the practical issues of day-to-day living. Try to deal with the issues that concern your counselees. These might include some of the following.

- What do they expect to experience as a married couple that single life would not provide?
- In what ways are they different from each other? How are they the same? How can they live with these differences? (The test results may help with this discussion.)
- What are the parents' attitudes toward the marriage?

- How do the man and woman each anticipate dealing with in-laws after marriage? Do they see some good and bad things about the in-laws? Do they agree on these? Where will the couple spend Christmas? That last question can lead to a lot of yuletide tension if it is not resolved before holidays get closer.
- Do they like each other's friends? Does either have friendships that might cause problems for the other? If so, how will they deal with these disagreements? And how will they form friendships after marriage?
- What do they like to do for recreation, hobbies, or vacations?
- What are their plans for where they will live? How did they make that decision? How will they make decisions about furniture and decorating their new home?
- Do they have a budget that will work? How will they decide on major purchases? Who will buy what? What are their attitudes toward credit cards? Have their past spending habits, including use of credit cards, shown potentially troublesome attitudes toward money and possessions?
- What are their attitudes toward children? Are they agreed on whether to have children, or on how many they want and when?

Many couples have discussed issues like these before meeting with a counselor, but the counselor may point out things that have been overlooked. Often the discussions may take more then two sessions, but remember that the talk can continue apart from the counseling, and any questions or major differences can then be considered in later counseling sessions.

At some time in the process you need to talk about principles for good communication. Encourage couples to practice these as they talk. If you notice communication breakdowns in your counseling sessions, point these out and talk about how these can be corrected. Ask yourself if the couple can listen and express their feelings or ideas honestly and without being angry or critical. Communication is an art that may be learned best through the discussion of sensitive and important issues. A counselor can facilitate this process.

Session five. Discuss the meaning of love (see 1 Corinthians 13:4–8) and its relationship to sex. What questions and concerns do they have about sex? If they are slow in asking questions, you might raise issues such as the following.

- What are the differences in how men and women reach orgasm, how does the timing differ, and how can they stimulate each other to fulfilling sex?
- What methods of contraception will they use, and how will these be purchased?
- What are different methods or positions for sexual intercourse?
- What fears or insecurities do they have?

The counselor who discusses these issues must be well informed, comfortable in discussing sex, and knowledgeable about where to get more help if necessary. A physician, for example, may be more helpful than a nonmedical counselor in dealing with specific sexual questions. Even when they are well informed, some counselors may choose to have sexual issues discussed by some other counselor. This decision may come, for example, because the counselor feels uncomfortable talking so freely abut sex or because the counselees would rather talk to somebody else. For many people, this kind of discussion with one's pastor-counselor feels awkward and too personal. Perhaps most counselees would prefer to have detailed discussions of sexual intimacies with someone who does not have the pastoral role.

Counselors who do decide to discuss sex with their counselees may find that the couple either may be more naive or more experienced than expected. In this part of premarital counseling, it can be helpful to find out where they are in their sexual experience with each other. At times the counselor may have to ask potentially embarrassing personal questions, so it is important that everybody feels comfortable with this before moving forward. One other caution is that the counselor should only ask questions and discuss issues that are genuinely helpful for the future marriage and not primarily questions that satisfy the counselor's own curiosity or sexual interests.

Session six. This involves discussion of the wedding ceremony, the legal requirements, the nature of the reception and its costs, and plans for the honeymoon. If you have not already done so, emphasize to the couple that it can be helpful to have additional sessions two or three months after the wedding so everybody can assess how things are going, including the problems and joys of their young marriage. Make a note in your appointment book to call the couple when it is time to meet after the wedding.

3. *Variations in Premarital Counseling.* Many people are anxious about counselors and reluctant to seek counseling help. Premarital counseling provides a relatively nonthreatening experience in which problems and issues are discussed and counselees get exposure to the counseling process. Hopefully, this experience will make it easier for individuals or couples to seek counseling if they feel that can be beneficial in the future.

In all of this, it is important to remember that premarital counseling must not become a rigid procedure. Some couples are older, are more mature, have been married previously, have read books or attended seminars on marriage, are personally sensitive to others, and are spiritually alert. These men and women may need a different number of sessions and may be concerned with different issues than those that interest a young couple in their early twenties. Some couples will show clearly that they are ready for marriage and that their choice of a marriage partner is good. With others, counseling may show that the proposed marriage is a poor risk. Some will resist this conclusion, but others may agree that it is wise to delay the marriage or break the engagement. Counselees need support, encouragement, and guidance as they make these kinds of difficult decisions.

Differences like these call for different approaches to counseling before marriage. At times you may want to encourage couples to read and discuss books, listen to tapes, attend seminars, or meet together with other couples who are addressed by a physician, financial planner, or other resource person. Sometimes, engaged couples are encouraged to attend marriage enrichment programs that are designed for married people but have been found to be beneficial for engaged people who learn to avoid future marital distress.[36] Looking over the different premarital programs, Christian psychologist Everett Worthington, Jr., concluded that they all are effective to the extent that they (1) have clear goals; (2) last at least six to twelve weeks; (3) emphasize communication, conflict management, and problem-solving focused on the issues that couples consider to be most important; and (4) include information, interaction between the partners, and

25.17

discussion. Giving information in time-limited sessions may be effective, but there is no research to support this method. Similarly, a focus on the couple's family of origin has not been demonstrated to be effective.[37]

Prevention of Marital Problems

All of the issues discussed in the previous chapters have been presented in the form of problems that we can try to understand, resolve through counseling, and prevent. Unlike the others, this chapter is different because its whole emphasis is on prevention. Premarital counseling seeks to prevent marital problems and personal conflicts that could make life miserable, difficult, unfulfilled, and unproductive after marriage. All of this assumes that good marriages start before the wedding.

Good marriages also start long before the preceremonial counseling that we have been discussing in this chapter. By watching movies or television, many people—including young people—get a distorted, unrealistic, and nonbiblical view of marriage that can lead to problems later in life. By observing parents and other older adults, including other parents, young people learn what to expect in marriage, what they want in their own marriages, and what they do not want. From this it would seem wise to start premarital education with children. Informal discussions with flower girls and ring bearers can provide a good opportunity for teaching, especially when we remember that weddings often make a great impact on children. Sunday School classes, children's camps, or youth meetings can be opportunities for impressing young minds with healthy attitudes and biblical truths teaching about marriage.

One writer has looked carefully at all types of community-based marriage preparation programs and suggested practical ways to build healthy marriages through outreach to teenagers.[38] His focus is on ways in which churches and other faith communities can more effectively build attitudes and skills into teenagers that, in turn, will lead to healthier dating and stronger marriages. To my knowledge, at this point there are no credible research studies to evaluate the effectiveness of these programs, but suggestions such as the following are worth applying.

- Help parents become better models of healthy relationships and train them how to teach, coach, and encourage their teenagers so they can relate to peers in healthy ways.
- Integrate the teaching of interpersonal skills and the value of commitment into existing programs, including religious education, youth clubs, camps, or intergenerational events.
- Sponsor workshops on relationship skills, including dating, conflict resolution, sex, and dealing with peer pressure. Be sure the speakers and musicians are able to connect with their youthful audiences.
- Teach older kids and young adults how to mentor and coach those who are younger in issues relating to dating, relationships, and marriage.
- Reach out to at-risk teens. "Youth at higher risk for relationship violence, sexually transmitted diseases, or pregnancy have a greater need for positive values, accurate information, credible role models, and consistent support. Emerging evidence suggests that faith-based organizations can

significantly impact" and reduce juvenile crime, substance abuse, and teen sexual at-risk behaviors.[39]

■ Build support across all levels of the community, involving schools, businesses, government, civic organizations, and faith communities other than one's own.

Some youth leaders would suggest that the late high-school years are too late to begin this kind of instruction because attitudes are formed and crystallized much earlier. One of my daughters works with inner-city teenagers who most often come from poor families where there have been poor parental role models and neighborhoods that are characterized by violence, substance abuse, gang activity, teenage pregnancies, and interpersonal conflict. After teaching abstinence in the schools and working with an evangelistic organization, my daughter concluded that in addition to a relationship with Christ, these young people have a desperate need for learning interpersonal skills. It's a slow process, but my daughter Jan and her associates are making progress in teaching young people about marriage and family relationships that are unlike anything they have seen before. Programs like this around the world have a high potential for reducing and, hopefully, preventing future marital and family conflict.

Wherever we live, the whole church should be involved in similar educational initiatives. Guided by the pastor's example, church leaders and parents can correct popular misconceptions about marriage and build a realistic and biblical view of the family long before marriage becomes a possibility. Family conferences, Bible studies, meetings of youth groups, discussions in adult singles groups, sermons, viewing films and video tapes, and encouraging the reading of good books or articles are common ways to instill healthy attitudes toward marriage. High-school students may have little interest in housing, finances within marriages, or in-law relationships, but they are interested in sex, male-female roles, home life, and ways in which they can evaluate themselves as potential mates. College students should be encouraged to take a course in marriage and family, although it is wise to recognize that some professors and textbooks fail to take biblical values into account. In the church, discussions of dating can point out that each date is a learning experience that can help unmarried people learn to respect, communicate with, and relate to the opposite sex.

The building of better marriages and families is a lifelong process. It begins in the home, continues in the church and society, is emphasized in premarital counseling, and must be practiced daily as a man and woman build their relationship together.

Conclusions About Premarital Counseling

Les and Leslie Parrott are counselors who have devoted much of their adult lives to helping others, including engaged couples, build better relationships. Many years ago, Les and I traveled together on a speaking trip throughout Asia, so I can easily picture an experience that he and Leslie had during a stop-over to change planes in Japan. Sitting across from them was Robert McNamara, Secretary of Defense, who worked in the Johnson, Kennedy, and Nixon administrations, the one man more responsible than any others for getting the United States involved in the Vietnam War.

25.19

Les "felt compelled to talk to him," so for the next half hour they chatted together. Mr. McNamara was on a tour promoting his controversial book, *In Retrospect*, in which he confesses to the mistake of getting his country involved in a war that could never be won. In the context of their conversation, Les asked this famous man why he wrote such a self-incriminating book. He didn't hesitate in giving his answer. "I wanted this generation to learn from my mistakes," he said.[40]

In many ways, premarital counseling is the work of teaching this generation to learn from our mistakes. Counselors usually are busy people. They have a demanding and difficult job, helping people get untangled from problem situations and teaching them how to function more effectively. Surrounded by so many cries for help, it is easy for the counselor to ignore or casually dismiss those who do not have pressing problems. As a result, prevention is overlooked and new problems continue to develop—problems that must be handled later.

Apparently, the first mention of premarital counseling was in 1928.[41] Since that time counselors have shown increasing interest in prevention. In no area is preventive counseling and education more possible, more accepted by the society, and more important than in the area of preparation for marriage. In no counseling area is the church more experienced and more respected even among nonbelievers. Christian counselors have a responsibility to show that premarital counseling really works, and to demonstrate how it can be done. This involves helping people anticipate difficulties in marriage and family living, teaching skills in how to communicate and resolve problems effectively, and showing them how to build marriages that are lived in accordance with God's plan as revealed in the Bible.

KEY POINTS FOR BUSY COUNSELORS

➤ Unlike most of the topics in this book, premarital counseling is primarily preventive. It comes before problems arise rather than after. It focuses on education and giving information. It is less concerned about healing wounds that exist than about building a union that will survive future pressures. Even so, many people are so busy planning their weddings that they have limited motivation for premarital education, including counseling.

➤ The Bible teaches about marriage in several places, but there are no biblical examples of premarital counseling as we know it today.

➤ It is difficult to do credible research on the effectiveness of premarital education, but it would appear that premarital counseling is valuable in that it:
  ▪ Slows couples down so they can spend time thinking about their marriage.
  ▪ Sends the message that marriage matters.
  ▪ Teaches couples where they can go for counseling if they need it later.

- Provides training in issues like communications skills, problem-solving, and conflict resolution so the risk of later marital distress or divorce is lessened.

➤ The premarital counselor seeks to counter any combination of the following seven influences that can contribute to unhealthy marriages:
  1. Unrealistic expectations that can lead to disillusionment.
  2. Personal immaturity that can lead to insensitivity.
  3. Changing roles in marriage that can lead to confusion.
  4. Commonly accepted alternative forms of marriage that can lead to uncertainty.
  5. Loosening sexual standards that can lead to immorality.
  6. Previous experiences with marriage that can lead to overconfidence.
  7. Circumstances that can signal high risks for a marriage.

➤ Premarital counseling can force people to consider potential risks and learn to take action to prevent the possible harm from occurring.

➤ Couples are most likely to participate in premarital education if they:
  - Have a positive overall view of counseling.
  - Have had the counseling recommended by somebody they respect.
  - Know that the counseling will focus on issues they want to discuss.
  - Respect the counselor and his or her expertise or experiences.
  - Are not afraid that they will be forced to reveal embarrassing secrets about past relationships.

➤ The purposes of premarital counseling include:
  - Teaching about marriage.
  - Assessing readiness for marriage.
  - Exploring possible problem areas.
  - Planning the wedding.

➤ Premarital counseling can take several forms. The chapter outlines one format that has six sessions. The chapter also gives alternative approaches to fit the unique characteristics of different couples.

➤ Premarital counseling seeks to prevent marital problems and personal conflicts that could make life difficult, unfulfilled, and unproductive after marriage. All of this assumes that good marriages start before the wedding. The best premarital education begins before people are engaged or even before they are adults.

➤ Premarital counseling helps a couple entering marriage learn from the mistakes of others, avoid those mistakes, and have a better marriage as a result.

25,21

29

Marriage Issues

Geoff and Marilyn had been married for eighteen years before they entered the counselor's office. Both in their early forties, they spent their time-pressured days caring for three school-aged children and working in highly demanding jobs. Geoff was an investment consultant, fiercely committed to making his business successful, often working late into the evenings and on weekends. Marilyn taught fourth grade and did it so well that she earned the outstanding teacher award at her school. Both were stressed by their demanding lifestyles and quick to blame the other for their unraveling marriage.

"She's always angry and complaining," Geoff declared as soon as they sat down.

"I can't trust you to say a single positive thing about me or the kids," Marilyn shot back in disgust. "I'm the only one who works to make this family important."

Soon Marilyn was launching into a list of her husband's failures, and he was defending himself aggressively. A tsunami of mutual bitterness, distrust, and disappointment flooded the room until Marilyn suddenly stopped, looked directly at the counselor, and declared, "Either this helps or it's over."

Married life for Geoff and Marilyn had not always been like this. At the time of their wedding, they were like most others who walk down the aisle—deeply in love, brimming with happiness, looking forward to a successful marriage and a great life together. But like so many other marriages, all over the world, theirs had slowly disintegrated. Some counselors might ask couples what it was like at the beginning and try to uncover the reasons that brought the change. This can be helpful, but the counselor that Geoff and Marilyn saw took a different approach. He pointed out that many couples look at marriage as a way for each to get their individual needs met, but he suggested that, in addition, they might pretend that their marriage was a third party, a flesh-and-blood person as real as Geoff and Marilyn, a person that they had been responsible for over the years. Then he asked each to describe what that person looked like.

"I see this gaunt, frightened individual, like the survivors of concentration camps you see in films," Geoff began. "The eyes keep looking at me, pleading with me to do something." Marilyn envisioned a little girl with stringy blond hair, a dirty face, raggedy clothes, and tears running down her cheeks. The counselor asked if they would be willing to care for the lost, needy individual that they had pictured, an individual that, in fact, was their long-neglected relationship. Both agreed, despite some hesitations and resistance to what they might have to do.

In the months that followed, the counselor helped Geoff and Marilyn learn to communicate without blaming and name calling, rebuild trust and respect that had been lost, deal with conflicts that had been tearing them apart, and help the gaunt, emaciated creature—their marriage—survive and get better. In time the couple began to see what the counselor called "a wonderful irony" that by making personal sacrifices for the sake of their relationship, they each were enabled to further their own emotional and spiritual growth. Slowly the marriage got better, the couple became more giving, and they worked on the assumption that whenever either could do something for the good of the other, the relationship got better. That formerly gaunt creature, or scruffy little girl, that was their marriage, got healthier.[1]

T here is no evidence that Geoff and Marilyn had a Christian marriage counselor or a Christian marriage, but they had learned what thousands of others have learned: marriages often disintegrate, but marriage counseling can reverse this process. That is good news because it is well known that marriage is not a very stable institution—at least in the Western world. The divorce rate remains high, and many who stay together have marriages that either seethe with conflict, like the marriage of Geoff and Marilyn, or that limp along in a relationship that is tolerable but not especially happy.

Before we begin our look at troubled marriages and ways in which counselors can help, it is important that we pause to note this positive fact: many marriages *are* happy and healthy. The reasons for this are not always clear even to those who have been married for many years. Researchers have not helped. Most scientific studies have dealt with marital conflict, and although there are numerous seminars and popular self-help book on keeping marriages strong, researchers have tended to ignore the study of healthy relationships.[2] Many years ago, *Psychology Today* magazine surveyed three hundred couples who had been married for at least fifteen years and described themselves as "happily married." The respondents agreed that important issues were "having a generally positive attitude toward one's spouse" and viewing the partner as one's best friend. Almost as important was a belief in the importance of commitment. In essence, the couples said, "I am married to someone who cares about me, who is concerned for my well-being, who gives as much or more than he or she gets, who is open and trustworthy, and who is not mired down in a somber, bleak outlook on life." Marriage was viewed as something people should stick with and work to develop, in spite of difficult times. In addition, happily married people agreed about their aims and goals in life, had a desire to make the marriages succeed, and were able to laugh a lot. To the researchers' surprise, fewer than 10 percent of the happily married people mentioned good sexual relations as an important ingredient for good marriages.[3]

These conclusions are more than twenty years old and limited to the responses of people in only one part of the world. As the years have passed, marital commitment seems to have become less common, unhappiness appears to be the norm, and many see divorce as a convenient and increasingly accessible fire escape should marital conflicts get too hot to handle. Marriage breakups among high-profile couples, especially publicity-seeking movie stars, distract from the importance of the commitment that is necessary if marriage is to endure and thrive. "Irreconcilable differences" become reasons for marriage breakups, and no-fault divorce allows marriage to be terminated quickly and legally when one or both of the spouses simply lose the desire to stay together. Marriage, the permanent union created by God, is treated more and more as a temporary arrangement of convenience.

These cultural attitudes, coupled with the stresses that put pressure on modern marriages, often create problems that come to the counselor's attention. It is not easy to help couples resolve marital conflict and build better marriages, but an estimated 80 percent of counselors in private practice see couples who are having marital problems.[4] The percentage of pastors counseling couples probably is higher. Despite the difficulties of this work, however, helping troubled marriages can be one of the most rewarding of all counseling experiences.

The Bible ands Marital Problems

Marriage is one of the first topics that the Bible discusses.[5] It is mentioned throughout the pages of Scripture and considered in depth in the New Testament. The purposes of marriage, the roles of husband and wife, the importance of sex, and the responsibilities of parents are all discussed, sometimes more than once.[6] Marriage failure is mentioned in the Old Testament law and treated in more detail by Jesus and Paul in their discussions of divorce.[7]

Even though it discusses marriage in various places, the Bible says almost nothing about the ways to help troubled marriages. Finding a mate is described as a good thing, a treasure,[8] and believers are encouraged to enjoy interpersonal and sexual relationships with their spouses.[9] In contrast, the book of Proverbs picturesquely decries the difficulties of living with a nagging, complaining marriage partner. Sharing a house with such a person is as annoying as "the constant dripping on a rainy day." Trying to stop the complaints is "like trying to stop the wind or hold something with greased hands."[10] Imagine the difficulties of trying to do marriage counseling when the wife, husband, or both are like this. Although the Bible describes some good marriages, there is evidence that Lot, Abraham, Jacob, Job, Samson, David, and a number of others had marital tensions at least periodically.[11] These are acknowledged honestly, but marital problems, per se, are not analyzed.

It should be remembered that marital conflict often is a symptom of something deeper, such as selfishness, lack of love, unwillingness to forgive, anger, bitterness, communication problems, anxiety, sexual mistreatment, substance abuse, feelings of inferiority, sin, and a deliberate rejection of God's will. Each of these can cause tension in the home, each can be influenced by husband-wife conflict, and each *is* discussed in the Bible. Thus, while the Scriptures deal with marital conflict only indirectly and in passing, the issues underlying many marriage problems are considered in detail. Many of these topics also are discussed elsewhere in this book.

The Causes of Marital Problems

In Genesis 2:24, we read that in marriage a man "leaves his father and mother and is joined to his wife, and the two are united into one." Over the centuries maybe millions of sermons have been built around this verse, focusing on three verbs. The man *leaves,* the couple *is joined,* and the two *become one.* These could be viewed as the three purposes of marriage.

Leaving involves a departure from parents and implies a public and legal union of husband and wife into a marriage. When the couple has made this public commitment, they have a greater reason to give themselves to building a committed relationship. *Being joined* is from a Hebrew word that means "to stick or glue together." Like two pieces of paper that are glued together, the couple cannot be pulled apart without one or both being torn. When a couple is dedicated to loving, drawing together, and remaining faithful to each other, the bond is strong and more likely to last.

Becoming one involves sex, but it goes beyond the physical. It means that two people share their dreams, hopes, fears, material possessions, thinking, feelings, joys, difficulties, successes, and failures. It does not mean that the two personalities are squelched, obliterated, or so merged that each person's uniqueness is gone. These distinctive personalities and traits persist, but they are developed in partnership with those of one's mate to make a complete relationship.

None of this is common or popular thinking today. Several years ago an informal magazine survey found that people wanted happiness and the opportunity to realize their potential, build careers, and have fulfilled lives. When these self-focused goals were not being reached, many considered divorce as an alternative. Perhaps this still is true. In their book *When Bad Things Happen to Good Marriages*,[12] Christian counselors Les and Leslie Parrott note that even though most marriages have good beginnings, sooner or later everyone "bumps into some bad things." Building on the Parrotts' analysis, the following paragraphs divide the many causes of marital problems into three broad categories.

1. *Some Things Surprise Couples*. This may be most true for people who marry without knowing each other well, but surprises even come to couples who have dated or been engaged for a long time prior to the wedding.

Surprise One: Unfulfilled Expectations. As we mentioned in an earlier chapter, conflicting and unfulfilled expectations can appear early in a marriage. Both the husband and the wife have learned about marriage from their parents and maybe from watching their friends. Usually, each new spouse has developed routines and ways of doing things that are brought to the marriage and may come into sharp conflict with the new partner's lifestyle. The surprises can be complex or as simple as the wife who expected to cuddle in her husband's arms as they would drift off to sleep every night and the husband's habit of watching the late show on television and falling asleep on the couch during the commercials. Sometimes, couples have different expectations about how they will celebrate birthdays, spend their weekends or their money, or fulfill different duties at home. When variations like these are ignored, frustrations build and problems become more difficult to handle.

Surprise Two: Disappointing Sex. Perhaps every couple brings some sexual fears and uncertainties into marriage, even those who are sexually experienced. Couples also bring hopes and expectations that their sex life will be exciting and consistently satisfying. Then they hit some of the sexual difficulties that we discussed in chapter 20. A lack of accurate knowledge, the inability to perform adequately, inhibiting attitudes about sex, differences in sex drive, insufficient opportunities for privacy, or unrealistic expectations are among the surprises that can arise. Impatience, frigidity, impotence, or the discovery of the partner's past sexual experiences also hinder the intimacy that was anticipated, and this, in turn, can create more tension and hinder smooth sexual functioning. Add the busyness of lifestyles, insensitivity in one or both of the partners, or the appearance of nonsexual marital conflicts, and there are more surprising interferences with sexual functioning. When these problems are not resolved, marriages almost always suffer.

Surprise Three: Faulty Communication. In the professional journals, this probably is the most commonly mentioned cause of marital discord. When they are dating and getting to know each other, couples have little difficulty communicating, but things can change when two people are living together and trying to blend their lives. Sometimes, the problems come because, to their surprise, the couple discovers that either or both of them have never learned to communicate clearly and efficiently.

At its core, communication involves the sending and receiving of messages. Messages are sent verbally (with words) and nonverbally (with gestures, tone of voice, facial expressions, words on a paper, images on a computer screen, actions, gifts, or even periods of silence). When the verbal and the nonverbal contradict, a double message is sent. This leads to confusion and communication breakdown.

As an example, consider the woman who says verbally, "I don't mind if you go on the business trip," but whose slumping posture, resigned tone of voice, and depression-like lack of enthusiasm says, "I *really* don't want you to go." In contrast, a wife gets a confused double message when her husband says "I love you and like spending time with you," but never is home, never takes his wife out to dinner, or never does anything to show his love and appreciation. In good communication the message sent verbally is consistent with the message sent nonverbally.

Good communication also demands that the message sent is the same as the message that the other person receives. Assume, for example, that a man buys his wife a new dishwasher because he loves her. The wife, however, does not believe she is loved because her husband never says the words "I love you." She wonders if the dishwasher has come because the husband feels guilty about something. Clearly, there is miscommunication here because the message being sent (love expressed by the gift of a dishwasher) is not the message that is being received.

All of this is complicated by the ways in which a couple interacts. Research has shown convincingly that the content of communication is less important than how the messages are conveyed. The happiest couples, those who communicate effectively, know the value of the relationship and avoid harsh or negative comments. In contrast, the unhappy couples don't respect each other. They are "really nasty with each other, and they struggle to find positive things to say about each other or the relationship." These are the people whose marriages are most likely to collapse. Counselors can spot this within minutes, even before the husband and wife say much about the issues that divide them.[13]

Most of us would agree that occasional miscommunication between spouses is inevitable and should come as no surprise. When miscommunication is more common than clear communication, the marriage can develop serious problems because poor communication tends to breed more of the same. In considering this, try to remember that good communication is learned. Even when it has not been good or a couple is surprised to discover their communication difficulties, everybody can learn to communicate better. One example is Geoff and Marilyn, whose story started this chapter.

Surprise Four: Unhealthy Relationships. Getting close to another person is risky. We open ourselves to criticism and possible rejection when we let another person know us intimately, become aware of our insecurities, or see our weaknesses. Since most of us have learned the value of fending for ourselves, it is not easy to trust another person—even when that other person is a marriage partner.

Unhealthy relationships in marriage tend to take one of two directions: the husband and wife either drift apart or merge together. In their extremes, neither of these is healthy, and in most cases neither was anticipated. When they *drift apart*, the couple stops sharing confidences, developing life goals together, or being vulnerable. The process is so slow that it isn't noticed at first. Each begins to look at life independently of the other, and different goals and hopes begin to appear. There is an increasing tendency to be defensive, to criticize, and to put down each other or to engage in subtle manipulation. As defensive and self-centered attitudes develop, these create tension and push the husband and wife further apart.

In contrast, some couples so integrate their lives and personalities that they *merge together* into a relationship that is engulfing. Both partners lose their identities and may even feel trapped. In some cases, one person so overpowers the other that the dominated spouse feels overwhelmed, suppressed, and defeated. When there are marital problems, neither the husband nor the wife is able to step back, look at their individual needs, and evaluate how one's own faults may be contributing to the tension. In time, there may be a verbal or physically violent reaction as both partners try to tear away from the confinement of such a stifling relationship. Sometimes, the enmeshing of personalities develops because sincere believers want to become "united into one," as the Bible teaches. However, there is a failure to recognize that oneness does not mean a suffocating or squelching of each other's God-given gifts, personalities, and individualities. When a husband and wife respect each other's uniqueness and seek to move forward in partnership, these relationship surprises are less likely to appear.

Surprise Five: Unwise Choices. In many ways, the course of life and the strength of relationships are both shaped by the choices we make. Unwise choices can sink careers and crumble marriages. Before reading further, you might take a minute to reflect on how past choices shaped the direction of your life, in good ways and bad. Then consider the implications of choices like these:[14]

- A husband or wife chooses to put some large charges on a credit card but keep this choice secret from his or her spouse.
- A husband knows that working late every night is interfering with his marriage and family life, but he decides to keep doing this in order to advance his career.
- One of the spouses chooses to get involved romantically with another person and chooses, as well, to keep this a secret.
- A wife chooses to tell her mother or best friend things about her marriage when she knows that this would infuriate her husband.
- Somebody chooses to persist in a bad health habit despite numerous warnings that this can be harmful.
- A couple chooses to avoid discussion of a difficult problem, hoping that it will disappear or resolve itself if it is ignored.

Sometimes, choices are made on the spur of the moment, without much deliberation. Consider the driver who chooses to change lanes on a busy freeway and has a serious accident as a result. At other times, decisions are made deliberately after a lot of reflection and prayer. In either case, the results might be surprising, and they are likely to persist long after the decision has been made. Counselors can help couples evaluate past choices, adapt to bad choices, and learn how to make better choices in the future. In many ways, good marriage and good parenting are both about making good choices.

Surprise Six: Secrets. Every married person brings secrets into the relationship. The secrets may be personal: ("I am afraid of intimacy," "I struggle with homosexual urges"), rooted in the present, or rooted in the past ("My father abused me"). Most often the secrets are about ourselves, but they can be about our mates ("I know that my spouse had an affair that he or she has never mentioned") or about some other person ("I know that the best man in our wedding struggles with alcoholism"). Some of these secrets can be put on a shelf and forgotten, especially if revealing them would cause damage to the relationship. But other secrets are best discovered, revealed, or confessed. Sometimes, the revelation of secrets is painful, but revealing secrets can be very helpful in building relationships.

At times a spouse notices things that his or her partner wants to keep hidden or may not even recognize. My wife sees things in me that I don't even see in myself, including negative traits in my life or unhealthy ways of relating to other people. If she points them out gently, I learn from her observations and become a better husband, father, and person as a result. For many couples, however, weaknesses and other secrets are raised in insensitive ways so that the secrets bring problems rather than growth.

2. *Some Things Undermine Couples*. When two people marry, each comes with perhaps two or more decades of past experiences, secrets, and ways of looking at life. Each has perspectives that are not shared by the other, and sometimes, even when there is a sincere desire for compromise or synthesis, couples still have difficulty resolving their differences. The problems are more complicated if either or both of the partners have an unwillingness to change, an insensitivity to the other person's viewpoints, or a refusal to acknowledge the differences. These can be issues that quietly sneak up on a marriage and undermine relationships often before anybody sees what is happening. The issues include the following.

Issue One: Busyness. Several years ago I wrote a book titled *Breathless: Transform Your Time-Starved Days into a Life Well Lived*.[15] The book did not sell very well, maybe because people were too busy to buy it or to read it. At the time, I wondered why I wrote it, because, if anything, my lifestyle was breathless, and hyperactivity—including my busyness in writing that book—was interfering with my marriage. Busyness is a common problem that doesn't need elaboration or documentation because it is so well understood. When lives get too busy, marriages and other relationships suffer. We struggle to manage our time, our careers, our families, or our calendars, but despite our best intentions, we can lose our spouses in the rush. The tyranny of busyness is likely to come up at some time in most marriage counseling.

Grouchiness and irritability often sweep into a marriage on the heels of busyness. Busy people tend to be tired and impatient people. Pressured by time-starved days and by too many things that need to be done, husbands and wives can be in a perpetual hurry, impulsive, and sometimes exhausted. Sex gets pushed aside, and so does time to pause, to communicate, and to be still for a few minutes with one's spouse or with God.

Issue Two: Role Confusion. We live at a time when traditional male-female roles have undergone major revision. In years gone by and in some countries today, the roles of the husband and the wife were well-defined and accepted by almost everybody. This is not true anymore, and as a result, there can be confusion or conflict over what it means to be a husband or wife. Society gives little guidance because opinions are so diversified and changing so rapidly.

The Bible is more explicit,[16] but Christians differ in their interpretations of the scriptural passages that outline husband-wife roles. As a result, there is disagreement, accompanied at times by both competition and feelings of threat. Often, this tension centers on the nature and extent of the wife's work or career goals.

Issue Three: Inflexibility. Several times we have mentioned that when a man and woman marry, each brings a unique personality to the marriage. Sometimes, these personality differences complement each other and blend into a mutually compatible relationship. Often, marriages take on personalities of their own, each of which can have strengths and weak points. There can be difficulties, however, if one or both of the partners are rigid, unwilling to give or strongly resistant to change.

When a couple first marries, there usually is a time of excitement, enthusiasm, and idealism. As the partners grow older, the months turn into years, careers develop, and children arrive and grow up, the marriage must change and mature if it is to stay healthy. When couples are too busy or too rigid to work at building and enriching their relationships, problems are likely to develop.

Issue Four: Religion. The Bible warns of problems when a believer and an unbeliever try to blend together in marriage.[17] Counselors often observe tensions when a husband and wife differ from each other in their denominational preferences, degree of commitment to spiritual things, interest in religion, or expectations about the religious education of children. Sometimes, these differences create tension in other areas, such as choice of friends, views about ethics, whether and to whom charitable donations will be given, or how to spend time on the weekends. Religion can be a binding, strengthening force in a marriage, but when a husband and wife have different viewpoints, religion also can be a disruptive focus for marital tension.

Issue Five: Value Differences. How should we spend our time and money? What are our goals? These questions concern values—the issues that are really important in life. When a couple has similar values, the marriage is often healthy and growing. When values are in conflict, the relationship may be one of tension, power struggles, and mutual criticism. Value conflicts are at the heart of many marital problems. They sneak up, undermine stability, and sometimes appear when they are least expected.

For example, consider how value alternatives like the following could create potential for conflict.

- "Credit cards should never be used," versus, "Credit cards can be used on occasion to make a major purchase or to get us over a financial crisis."
- "Divorce is never right," versus, "Sometimes, divorce is the best solution to difficult marital problems."
- "We should never miss church on Sunday," versus, "Sometimes, it is okay to skip worship services."
- "Succeeding in one's career is of major importance in life," versus, "Building a family is more important than building a career."
- "Abortion is always wrong because it is murder," versus, "In some circumstances and with some people abortion is okay."
- "Children should be taught spiritual beliefs and values," versus, "Children should be given the freedom to find their own beliefs."

Views like these tend to be at the core of one's being. Many are held firmly and influence how we act or relate to other people. In addition, values sometimes become the basis for intense conflict, especially if cherished beliefs are challenged by one's mate.

Issue Six: Conflicting Needs. For more than a century, psychologists have debated about the existence and nature of human needs. Most agree that we each need food, rest, air, and freedom from pain, but there also are psychological needs, such as the need for love, security, and contact with others. In addition, it seems that most people have unique personal needs, including the need to dominate, to control, to possess, to achieve, or to help and rescue others. If one spouse has a need to dominate while the other wants to be controlled and guided, then there may be compatibility. But if both husband and wife have a need to dominate, this creates potential for conflict. If both are devoted to career building, there can be conflict, especially in discordant situations where, for example, each spouse wants to accept a career advancement that will involve a family move, but the other spouse resists.

Issue Seven: Personality Differences. Marriage is a bringing together of two personalities that aren't likely to be totally compatible. Sometimes, for example, an outgoing, gregarious person marries someone who is more reticent and shy, or a person who is frugal and careful with money finds a spouse who is more inclined to spend freely. In relationships like these, the traits in the one person complement what the other lacks. Problems are more likely when the differences sneak up on a couple and cause undermining conflict. When one spouse is open (freely sharing about needs, temptations, attitudes, and feelings) but the other spouse tends to hold things in, these differences can create communication problems and value differences. In one long-term study of several hundred marriages, researchers found that unhealthy traits frequently led to marital instability, distress, and eventual divorce. Often, these traits were noticed but ignored at the time of the engagement. Later, when they could not be put aside, they surfaced and led to misery in the years that followed.[18]

Issue Eight: Money and Debt. Consider these questions: How are the family finances going to be earned? Who controls the money? Who pays the bills? How is the family money going to be spent? What things are really needed, and which are merely desirable? Is a budget necessary? How much should be given to the church or to other charities? What happens when there is a shortage of money? How do we handle debt?

Answers to questions like these reflect one's financial values and attitudes. When a husband and wife have different answers to these kinds of questions, there is potential for conflict. Once again, it is difficult to determine whether financial tensions cause other problems or whether the reverse is more accurate. It is true, however, that a harmonious financial relationship is essential if there is to be a harmonious marriage.

Issue Nine: Boredom. As the years go by, husbands and wives settle into routines, get accustomed to each other, and sometimes slip into self-absorption, self-satisfaction, or self-pity, each of which can drain any remaining excitement from a marriage and allow boredom to undermine the relationship and take away the luster that once existed. When marriage is dull and routine, couples sometimes begin to look elsewhere for variety and challenge. This, in turn, creates further marital tension.

Issue Ten: A Weakening Emotional Bond. The emotional bond between a husband and wife has been called the "golden thread that holds partners together."[19] Over time, the bond can weaken, sometimes because of the differences that the preceding paragraphs have discussed. Growing research suggests that marriages are more likely to survive and thrive when there is forgiveness, hope, determination to overcome differences, and a commitment to keep the husband-wife bond strong. As we will see, this has significant implications for marriage counseling.[20]

3. *Some Things Jolt Couples.* During the day that I was writing the earlier paragraphs of this chapter, somebody sent me an email to announce that a mutual friend had lost his adult son to suicide. That evening I opened a message from a counselor friend who was asking for prayer for his wife who had been diagnosed with a serious form of cancer. A few days earlier I had talked at length with a thirty-four-year-old friend who, within the course of one week, had received his Ph.D. and had been diagnosed with a very rare form of brain cancer that the physicians do not know how to treat. As part of our discussion, we talked about how his family is reacting.

At times, every marriage experiences jolts. An unexpected medical crisis, a sudden death, a discovered infidelity, a natural disaster, a deep disappointment, a financial or career collapse—these are among the crises that can throw a family into turmoil and severely shake the stability of even the best of marriages.

Sometimes, the jolts are like the aftershocks of an earthquake. They keep reappearing and stirring up more anxiety and tension. These stresses, which may come from other people or from stressful situations, can test the ability of counselors to give consistent help and guidance. They might include:

- In-laws who criticize or otherwise make persistent demands on a couple.
- Children whose needs and constant demands can interfere with the depth and frequency of husband-wife contacts, and sometimes drive a wedge between the spouses.
- Friends, including opposite-sex friends, who make time demands on the couple and sometimes lead one or both of the spouses into infidelity.
- Infertility that leads to ups and downs of hope and disappointment as the desired pregnancies never materialize.[21]
- Vocational and career demands that put pressure on the husband and/or wife, create fatigue, and take time from the marriage.
- Financial reverses that put pressure on the family budget and lead to worry and sometimes disagreements about spending patterns.

In many ways the counselor's goal is to help couples stay together and thrive when life pulls them apart. At different times, every marriage has its unique set of forces pulling it apart. The best counselors seek to understand these forces and assist couples as they deal with the surprises, jolts, and issues that sneak up and undermine their marriages. Perhaps no counseling work is more difficult. None is more fulfilling.

The Effects of Marital Problems

It can be difficult to separate the effects of marital distress from the causes. For example, sexual and financial difficulties can cause marital tension, but marital tension can also lead to problems in bed or in balancing the checkbook. Although there is a circular relationship between cause and effect, the counselor also can observe several specific effects of marital tension.

1. *Confusion, Despair, and Hopelessness.* Caught in the middle of conflict and watching one's marriage disintegrate, the husband and/or wife often feels overwhelmed and confused about what to do next. Sometimes, there are frantic, frequently futile, attempts to make amends. Sometimes, there is despair and a resigned attitude that says, "Things will never get better, so why try?"

Nearly every marriage goes through periods when the couple's original hope and enthusiasm for their relationship both fade, at least temporarily. When this happens, hope is replaced by sadness, hurt, and anger. More mature or experienced couples realize that the spark often can return to their marriage, but sometimes the partners feel hopeless, and hopeless feelings are contagious. One goal of counseling, therefore, must be the cultivation and recovery of hope.

2. *More Conflict.* Many people have grown up in homes where conflict was always handled in the same way—with more yelling, criticism, name calling, and conflict. Like a gasoline fire fueled with more gasoline, the inferno gets worse. Sometimes, this cycle of conflict as a response to conflict occurs in the counselor's office. The counselor has the challenge of pouring the waters of calmness onto this blaze and helping couples learn to communicate more effectively and with less volatility.

3. *Withdrawal.* It is impossible to estimate the number of people who are legally married, living together, and sometimes sleeping in the same bed, but who are emotionally and psychologically divorced. The husband and wife may even engage in similar activities, go places together, and sit alongside each other in church, but there is little warmth, concern, communication, intimacy or love. At the core, in marriages like this the spouses have stopped being friends. Like those who respond to their frustrations with yelling and name calling, people who withdraw often have learned early in life that this is the safest way to deal with stress. By withdrawing emotionally from each other, the partners avoid the pain of their disintegrating marriage and social stigma of divorce. Tensions remain, but there are few battles, and the marriage persists as an uneasy truce that may extend for a lifetime.

4. *Desertion.* This is the most extreme form of withdrawal. When the marital and family pressures get too intense, some people simply leave. It is difficult to compile statistics on the incidence of desertion, but there is evidence that thousands of mates desert their spouses and families each year and leave hurt feelings, confusion, anger, uncertainty, financial pressures, and one-parent families behind. Depending on where one lives, the courts can decree that a deserting spouse must return or meet family financial obligations, but these people are difficult to find, and many ignore the court orders. Since most deserters are from lower-class families, the deserted mate often cannot afford the costs of bringing legal action against the spouse who has left. As a result, children are raised by one parent, usually a hard-working mother, and grow to adulthood without ever knowing the parent who left.

5. *Separation or Divorce.* Divorce might be viewed as the legal termination of a once promising, hope-filled, and satisfying relationship that has been coming apart socially, spiritually, and emotionally. Even though it is common, divorce is never a happy solution to marital problems. Apparently as common among Christian couples as among nonbelievers, divorce is used too often and too quickly as a way to escape marital difficulties. Even so, there are times when divorce may seem to be the most feasible alternative to a problem-plagued marriage.[22]

Counseling and Marital Problems

Counseling one person can be a difficult task. Counseling a husband and wife together (which is how most marriage counseling is done) can be even more difficult. To be effective it requires special skill and alertness in the counselor. Frequently, one or both of the spouses come with skepticism about the value of counseling, and sometimes there is an attitude of resistance or hostility. William Doherty, one of the most respected marriage counselors in the world today, recently wrote that counseling with couples "may be the hardest form of therapy." He adds that "most therapists aren't very good at it" and points out that the process is "unnerving" due to the fact that marriage counseling often begins with the threat that the couple will split up if the counselor's interventions are unsuccessful.[23] This is the kind of work that demands a lot of prayer and reliance on the guidance of the Holy Spirit. Before starting (and frequently thereafter) counselors should look at themselves to clarify some of their own attitudes, possible prejudices, motivations, and vulnerabilities.

1. *Be Alert to Yourself.* What is your attitude toward marital problems? Are you critical of those who have marital difficulties, inclined to condemn, prone to take sides, annoyed because these problems take so much time from your schedule, afraid that marital counseling might arouse anxieties about your own marriage? Do you hold strong views (prejudices) about marriage that might interfere with your objectivity—views such as the conviction that men need to be dominant or that women should give up their careers to care for their families? Are you nervous, lest your counseling be a failure?

Periodically, counselors need to remind themselves that their reputations never rest on the outcome of a few cases. Probably, there are thousands of books and articles on marriage counseling, but no one person can master all the techniques. Every counselor is unique, and every couple is unique. The helper's challenge is to be available to the couple, as technically skilled as possible, and sincerely willing to allow the Holy Spirit to work through the counselor as an instrument of healing. Your help will be most effective if you can commit the counseling to God and then try to provide an atmosphere where constructive discussion is possible. In addition, the counselor tries to understand both sides of the situation from the perspectives of the people involved.

Intimate discussions about marriage can arouse sexual and other feelings in the counselor—feelings that must be admitted to oneself and handled, perhaps with the help of a friend or other counselor. In contrast, some counselees may cast you into a role that you may neither recognize nor want. A woman, for example, might see her male counselor as "a kind, understanding man—so different from my insensitive uncaring husband." The husband, in turn, may think of the male counselor as a threat to the marriage and one who really doesn't understand the wife. In situations like these, try not to react in accordance with your feelings, and be careful not to let the counselee's expectations influence your behavior so that you overreact or become the kind of person that the counselee expected. When counselors have colleagues with whom they can discuss issues like these, the dangers are greatly reduced, and the counseling is more likely to be effective.

2. *Be Alert to Special Issues.* Perhaps because marriage counseling is so needed and so challenging, a host of seminars, workshops, degree programs, and books

have appeared over the past few decades, all designed to help marriage counselors do their jobs better.[24] Some of these approaches are built around influential therapists with names like Jay Haley, Salvador Minuchin, Cloé Madanes, and Virginia Satir.[25] Others are built around a body of techniques or theoretical positions. The early approaches tended to be like individual psychotherapy, trying to uncover and heal conflicts that existed within each husband, wife, or other person in the family. In the 1970s, something called *systems theory* emerged with its view that problems are between people rather than buried within. According to these therapists, in marriage counseling the couple or their whole family becomes the unit that needs to be treated. If one person changes for better or for worse, everybody else in the system changes as well. If the husband gets sick or becomes alcoholic, everybody in the family unit is affected. If a new baby enters the family or a new daughter-in-law becomes part of the family, everybody is impacted and needs to make adjustments. From this perspective, counseling is most effective if the marital unit or the whole family is treated as a unit, instead of focusing on individuals.[26]

Systems theory has become the basis of family therapy and of many approaches to marriage counseling. All of this history has raised procedural questions that marriage counselors need to consider, but that may not be present in other forms of counseling.

(a) Should the Couple Be Seen Alone or Together? Many counselors would answer "both." Sometimes, after an initial joint session, counselors will see the husband and wife separately for a few minutes or a few sessions. Often, this gives new information and different perspectives on the problem. At times, you will find that each spouse has a different opinion about what the major problem is and who is primarily responsible. Sometimes, you will discover that one of the partners wants counseling and the other does not. In some cases you will discover that one or both of the spouses have problems that will benefit from individual counseling. Marriage, however, is a relationship, and marital problems involve conflicts between two people. If these can be observed and discussed together (sometimes with the children or other family members present), progress may be greater and faster. Whether you see the couple separately or together, be careful to strive for impartiality. Taking sides can often hinder your counseling effectiveness.

(b) Should There Be Time Limits for Counseling? Near the end of the twentieth century, brief strategic therapy emerged as an approach to counseling that could be effective in bringing change within a shorter time period than the more traditional approaches. Sometimes, "a couple may need to change as fast as possible in order to avoid irreparable damage to the marriage," Gary Oliver and his colleagues wrote in their book on brief therapy. "With its emphasis on beginning change in the first session, a solution-based, brief approach can begin to help a couple immediately. The initial interventions help couples to identify what has worked in the past and focus on finding ways to repeat the successful actions. This has the possibility of getting change going right away."[27] Christian psychologist Everett L. Worthington, Jr. proposes a brief-therapy approach as a way to bring hope back into marriage.[28] In an earlier work he suggested three stages of counseling: assessment, intervention, and termination.[29] At the beginning, Worthington asks the couple to agree to three sessions for assessment and evaluation of their difficulties. After that, the couple and the counselor decide whether they should continue. If they continue, the counselor suggests that eight to sixteen sessions should be sufficient to complete the counseling intervention stage, followed by termination. This is not a rigid approach; sometimes, the counseling stops after a few sessions, and at times it goes longer.

(c) Should the Counselor Work Alone or Alongside Another Counselor? Sometimes, a man and woman, often a husband and wife, can work together as a counseling team.[30] This lets the couple have a male and female perspective and the co-counselors can model good communication and interpersonal relationships. This also avoids the fear in some couples that the counselor may tend to side with the spouse of the same gender. The dual counselor arrangement can be time-consuming, however, and can put pressure on the counselors, especially if they are married and subject to some of the same stresses that face the counselees. Nevertheless, mature couples who work together smoothly often are able to counsel other couples with special effectiveness.

3. *Try to Determine Why Each Couple Comes for Counseling.* When a couple comes for counseling, probably your first question is why they are there. That is not always an easy question to answer. Sometimes, the husband and wife may give different answers to the question of why they have come. Very often the stated problems may not be the real issues that are creating tension in their marriage. Those real issues may not emerge until later. On occasions the real reasons may be hidden deliberately. For example, the couple may talk about their financial difficulties, but the real purpose for coming is to show their friends that counseling won't work so the couple can justify the divorce that one or both of them really want. Often, the stated reason for coming is vague (for example, "We're not getting along," or "We're arguing a lot"). To complicate all of this, there is evidence that counselors tend to jump to their own conclusions about why couples come. These conclusions may reflect the counselor's theoretical position, theology, or prejudices but have no bearing on the couple's reasons for seeking help.

What are the reasons that bring most people for marriage counseling? A research team decided to study this systematically.[31] They looked carefully at 147 couples seeking marital therapy and found that when they were asked, the most commonly reported reasons for seeking help were problems with communication and a lack of emotional affection. When individual couples were surveyed, however, the research team discovered that most often the husband and wife gave different reasons for coming. The researchers concluded that "asking about the reasons for seeking therapy generally does not provide the same information" as responses to a questionnaire.

This is not intended to discourage you as a counselor, but to remind us all of the difficulty of getting to the real problems that couples face. Often, it helps to ask for specific examples of tension between the couple. Because husbands and wives so often bring different perspectives, each needs to be heard, sometimes privately one at a time. Whether they are seen separately or together, gently probe for more details and try to raise questions that will give more information and a clearer understanding of the problems. By asking the husband and wife to describe specific incidents of conflict, the counselor is enabled to understand not only the sources of dissension but also the accompanying feelings of rejection, anger, hurt, frustration, and fractured self-esteem.

Ultimately, all of this is intended to help the couple and the counselor assess the marriage and determine what is broken and needs to be fixed. Problems will

CHRISTIAN COUNSELING

vary considerably, of course, and here, as in all counseling, the stated problem may not be the only or the major source of difficulty. Often, there are concerns about loss of intimacy, communication breakdowns, frequent conflict, sex, money, husband-wife roles, religion, physical abuse, drinking, conflicting values, and a variety of similar issues. Counselees can be asked how they feel about each problem, how they have tried to solve the problems in the past, what has worked, and what has not.

In making your assessment, two issues are of great importance. First, try to discover where the couple is spiritually. Are they both believers? Are they growing spiritually, or has religion become what William James once called "a dull habit"? The Christian counselor is likely to use different terminology and take a more overtly Christian approach when it is clear that the husband and wife are believers. Second, be careful not to spend all of your initial time in discussing the problems. When they come for counseling, a couple already feels defeated and well aware of the pain and conflict in their marriage. If the whole session is spent in a listing of problems, the counselees may feel so discouraged that they are reluctant to return for the next session. Even as you gather information, remember that among the main purposes of the early sessions are to start the process of change and to give hope.

4. *Partner with the Couple in Setting Counseling Goals.* The counselor, the husband, and the wife each approach marriage counseling with expectations and goals. These goals may be vague or clearly defined. Some will be realistic; others will not. Some counselees will come with high expectations and a determination to work at healing the troubled marriage; others may have little hope or motivation to change. Some may come with positive expectations about the value of counseling, but others—most often husbands—may be more skeptical. When goals are clear, realistic, and accepted by everyone, marriage counseling starts with a high potential for success. When the goals are vague or in conflict (e.g., the husband wants a smooth separation, but the wife wants a reconciliation), then counseling will be more difficult.

(a) Recognize and Formulate Your Goals as the Counselor. It is unlikely, probably impossible, that any counselor can approach marriage counseling with complete neutrality. A few paragraphs back we discussed the counselor's values and beliefs about marriage. These are likely to make their appearance when we work with counselees to formulate goals. Most of us have values and goals (some of which we may not have thought about clearly) that give direction to our counseling. These goals may include:

- Instilling and maintaining hope.
- Keeping the husband and wife together.
- Identifying and understanding the specific issues that are creating the marital problems.
- Teaching the couple how to communicate constructively.
- Teaching problem-solving and decision-making skills.
- Helping the counselees understand the counseling relationship.
- Helping them express their frustrations, disappointments, and desires for the future.
- Teaching the couple how to build a marriage based on biblical principles.
- Helping them see what their marriage could be like and helping them turn

the vision into reality through the encouragement, guidance, and prayers of the counselor.

What are your goals for marriage counseling in general or for the different couples that you counsel? When these are recognized clearly, counseling can be more effective, the counselor knows where he or she is going, and it is easier to concentrate on helping the counselees reach their goals.

(b) Determine Counselees' Goals. When the counselor, husband, and wife have similar goals, the counseling is easiest. Very often there are discrepancies, but this does not mean that hope is gone. Before moving forward it is important that everybody involved has clarity in terms of what each hopes to achieve through the counseling. Helpful questions include:

- How would you like your marriage to be different?
- What would you like to get out of counseling?
- What do you think your spouse would like to accomplish through counseling?
- What are things you long for in your marriage?
- How do you think these could be attainted?
- What have you tried that has not worked in the past?
- What has worked?
- What might prevent these from working again?

(c) Try to Set Mutually Acceptable Goals. Many people have vague and distant goals (such as "We want to have a happy Christian marriage"), but reaching these is more likely when they can be broken down into smaller goals that are more specific, more attainable, and more immediate. Some counselors work on a contract approach, in which the husband and wife each agree to change behavior in some specific way during the times between counseling sessions.[32] He, for example, agrees to take out the garbage nightly; she agrees to let him read the paper alone before dinner. When a couple sets attainable goals like these with the counselor's help, there is increased motivation to attain the goals, and the couple can learn about communication and problem-solving in the process. As goals are reached, the couple is encouraged because they see specific progress.

What do you do when there is disagreement about goals? Suppose, for example, that counselees want help in attaining goals that the counselor considers unrealistic or immoral. If a wife complains that her husband has been unfaithful, but the husband wants the freedom to have "occasional sexual contacts during business trips," the Christian counselor is faced with a goal conflict. The counselor realizes the benefits of not taking sides when a couple disagrees, but in this case the husband wants permission to continue behavior that clearly is sin, according to the Bible. In a noncondemning but honest way, these differences in goals and values must be discussed. The counselor's purpose is not to manipulate people or force them to change, but neither should people be helped to act in ways that the counselor considers morally wrong, psychologically harmful, or detrimental to the marriage. Despite differences, usually there are at least some goals that everyone accepts, and it is possible to start there. Sometimes, as counseling continues and as goals are clarified, the differences are not as divergent as they first appeared. If counselor-counselee goal conflicts persist, even after continued discussion, or if the husband and wife continue to have conflicting goals, then withdrawal from the counseling and referral to another counselor may be undesirable but still the best options.

(d) Reaching the Goals. Each marriage is unique, and every marital problem is in some ways different from all others. It is not possible, therefore, to give a step-by-step recipe for successful marriage counseling. As we have seen, a great number of marriage counseling techniques have been proposed, but most of these are intended to help counselors focus on what we might call the three Ps of counseling: the persons, the problems, and the processes.

5. *Focus on Persons*. The previously mentioned research on building a strong emotional bond in marriage shows that counseling involves more than solving practical problems, such as improving communication, changing annoying personal habits, or resolving sexual problems.[33] Couples that have strong marriages often find that there is an emotional bond that persists, keeps the relationship strong, and is able to remain firm even when disagreements arise. When this bond is weak, couples may analyze their problems carefully and reach mutually agreeable conclusions but then discover that tensions still persist. This is because of what some counselors call *the fallacy of the reasonable solution*. It is the view that reasonable solutions don't always bring peace even when these solutions are accepted by reasonable people. Tension persists because many problems are more emotional than rational. Logic and rational analysis fail to help because emotional, personality, or past-experience issues get in the way and prevent people from taking action to reach practical conclusions.[34]

The counselor must seek to understand persons, with their feelings and frustrations, even as counselors understand problems. Sometimes, helpers are so intent on solving problems and finding how-to-do-it answers that they become insensitive to the pain and personalities of the people with whom they are working. The basic counselor qualities of empathy, genuineness, and warmth are crucial in marriage counseling. On occasion, counselees may feel that nobody takes the time and energy to listen, to understand, and to show genuine care. When, in contrast, they see that the counselor is listening to the couple as persons, progress already has been made toward solving the problems and dissolving difficulties.

6. *Focus on Problems*. Once you have built rapport and shown that you care for the counselees as people, there is greater freedom to focus on the problem issues. As you listen and ask information-gathering questions, try to be supportive and slowly move the counseling toward tentative solutions. Guide in the consideration of attitude change, behavior changes, confession, forgiveness, or reexamination of perceptions. Discuss alternative courses of action for the future, encourage and teach counselees how to try out these solutions, and take time to evaluate what works and what does not.

7. *Focus on Processes*. When they come for counseling, most people focus on *content* issues: the husband feels criticized all the time, the wife is depressed, the couple can't agree how to handle a rebellious teenager. Even as they recognize the importance of dealing with issues like these, professional counselors are equally or more inclined to focus on what they call *process* issues.

According to the dictionary, a process refers to the changes or continuous actions that are taking place during a period of time. In counseling, the word *process* often is used to describe the continuous ways in which people relate to each other or interact with the counselor during the counseling sessions.

Carefully watch the couple as they interact with you and with each other in counseling. Listen to their descriptions of how they relate to others. Try to point out how the couple is relating,[35] and then talk about and practice ways in which they could relate better. Are there other ways of relating that could be practiced between sessions? Be sure to discuss all of this when the couple returns.

If a couple came to you and reported disagreements about finances, it would be helpful to learn *what* each spouse is thinking (that is content), as well as to learn *how* they talk about their financial differences (that is process). If they can learn new ways to talk and interact, they often can apply this learning to resolve the content differences. During counseling, therefore, ask yourself questions such as the following.

- How does the couple communicate?
- How do they interact in public and in private?
- How do they handle disagreements?
- How do they interact when each perceives a problem in a different way?
- Do they criticize each other?
- Do they attack each other's integrity or use put-downs and subtle (or not so subtle) criticisms?
- Do they build up each other?
- Does one person dominate the other?
- Does one or both of the partners withdraw when there are disagreements?

Fuller Seminary professor Cameron Lee gives a clear illustration of all this when he describes a fictional couple that he named Jamie and Eric. They married with high hopes and enjoyed being together, but as the months passed there were increasing disagreements about a number of content issues. Their first real argument was a bitter disappointment to them both, but soon the verbal conflicts became more frequent and reached the point where there would be a flare-up at the slightest provocation. Jamie accused Eric of being unfeeling and selfish; he accused her of being a controlling nag. Both felt wounded and victimized, but nothing changed because each believed that the other had the responsibility to change first. Teaching this couple how to deal with the specific content issues that divide them probably would not have helped much, according to the counselor. Instead, Jamie and Eric would need to change their attitudes, perceptions of themselves and each other, and the process of assigning blame, feeling victimized, and willfully insulting or hurting each other.

Where would Jamie and Eric begin? Because of their history of conflict, they would need to make a commitment to avoid hurting each other and, instead, agree not to say or do the things that devalue the other. As Christians, they could be reminded about how God views them, loves them despite their flaws, and forgives. Each would need to esteem the other. This requires that Jamie and Eric would commit to changing themselves and to stop trying to change each other. "Christian humility in marriage entails giving up my self-righteous 'you change first' stance" and, instead, involves changing for the benefit of the other. Julie and Eric needed to learn a new process for relating, even more than they needed to deal with the issues that divided them. Counselors can help people like this couple to learn what all married couples need, "to esteem our spouses when we see them as God does—as flawed people like ourselves who are nevertheless the objects of God's incomprehensible grace."[36]

8. *Be Aware of Common Mistakes That Can Be Avoided.* Every counselor makes mistakes, but some of these can be avoided if we are warned about them in advance.[37]

Mistake Number One: Lack of Structure. When a couple enters the office and exchanges attacks and counterattacks, the counselor can lose control, and the session becomes a repetition of the wars they have in their home. It is good to set some guidelines, sooner or later. These might include asking each person not to interrupt the other or to talk about issues without name calling or attacking the spouse's character. When both agree, the counselor can intervene when the rule is violated.

Mistake Number Two: No Plan for Change. Some counselors like to let couples come up with their own solutions, but the nature of marital conflict is that the husband and wife have not been able to do that. Suggestions and guidance from the counselor keep the process moving without endless repetition of failures.

Mistake Number Three: Giving Up Too Quickly. This often comes because the counselor feels overwhelmed, so he or she wants to withdraw or encourage the couple to separate. This can be avoided if the counselor takes time to assess the marriage and the process of interaction early in the counseling. Ask God to give hope to you as a counselor and show you ways that the couple can improve. Discuss this, as well, with other counselors who can give you a clearer perspective.

Mistake Number Four: Assuming All Couples Are Equal. Remember that each couple is unique. What works with one may not work with another.

Mistake Number Five: Abandoning One's Values About Marriage. In the face of a couple in conflict, it is easy for a counselor to forget his or her beliefs and values about marriage and move too quickly to recommend separation. If a counselor really believes in the sanctity and permanence of marriage, it seems likely that he or she will do whatever possible to save and improve the marriages that come for counseling.

Eventually, as you move toward termination, you may want to help counselees review what they have learned. Encourage them to launch out more and more on their own. Remind them that marriage counseling, like all other Christian counseling, is intended to help people grow personally, interpersonally, and spiritually. As counselors, our greatest successes come when couples learn to build marriages that are yielded to Jesus Christ, based on biblical principles, characterized by a commitment to each other, and growing as the husband and wife are helped to work at skillful communication, goal attainment, and conflict resolution.

Preventing Marital Problems

Wherever you live or whatever church you attend, it is probable that you are not far from people having marriage problems. The rates vary from place to place, but around the world marital tensions are common, family violence appears to be frequent (even when it is hidden from people outside the home), and divorce rates are high. Three out of four couples that file for divorce never see a counselor, and the people who do wait an average of six years after the beginning of serious marital problems before they go to a counselor.[38] Very often these couples are surrounded by resources and trained helpers who are willing and available to help. Seminars, weekend workshops, marriage enrichment programs, books, and articles about marriage are abundant. Within recent years, there has been a dramatic increase in the number of undergraduate and graduate-level marriage and family counseling courses and degree programs. Seminaries have developed courses in family-life education, and churches are becoming aware of the need for more teaching about marriage and family issues, including the unique needs of step-families and single-parent families. Others have noted that crisis intervention often provides opportunities to work with couples and families, helping them both to deal with the present problems and to avoid long-term destructive patterns of problem-solving. A perusal of the chapter titles in this book will point to a number of problem areas that could create or worsen existing marital difficulties. Dealing with these problems as they arise and working to prevent them can keep these issues from becoming a cause for marriage tensions.

Research investigations of marital failure and stability have added their own suggestions for prevention. For example, researcher John Gottman and his associates at University of Washington have discovered a number of significant conclusions that can help in counseling and prevention. Some of these are summarized in Table 29–1.[39]

In addition, there are specific preventive actions that may be taken by counselors, pastors, professors, and leaders of clinics, churches, or parachurch organizations.

1. *Teach Biblical Principles About Marriage.* Christians believe that God, who created both male and female and who initiated marriage, also has given guidelines for marriage in the pages of Scripture. These guidelines need to be taught clearly at home and church, and modeled consistently by Christian leaders. We live in a society that propagates nonbiblical values about sex and marriage, so the biblical teachings about sex and the meaning of love need to be reinforced frequently. This might include reminding congregations and other groups that the whole community, church, and country can be strengthened when there are people who know how to be loyal to one another and are able to commit to building the common good.

2. *Stress the Importance of Marriage, Marriage Enrichment, and Marital Commitment.* Because life for most people consists of innumerable demands, commitments, and responsibilities, it is easy to shunt one's marriage to a lesser order of priority. Work, church, community responsibilities, and other activities take precedence over time spent with one's spouse and family. This is a special problem for people like pastors or business leaders who deal with crises or who are called repeatedly to make important decisions. When a mother calls, distraught because she has caught her son with drugs, does the pastor skip his daughter's soccer game to meet immediately with the parishioner, or does he go to the game and agree to see the caller later? Does a professional woman skip dinner with her husband to work late on company business? Is a counselor who promotes a marriage enrichment program likely to be convincing if he or she has never attended the event and has no plans to go? It is easy to assume that "I can deal with my own marriage later," but this can become a way of life that erodes marital or family stability. Building a marriage takes time, effort, and commitment if it is to grow and

Table 29–1

Selected Research That Guides Prevention of Marital Conflict

- **Research:** Within three or four minutes, it is possible to predict which new-lywed couples will divorce. The clues are found in the ways in which they communicate. Couples who divorce early in their marriages "are openly contesting and fighting each other. There is an attack and defend mode with escalating conflict," says researcher John Gottman. These couples display more negative emotions, words, and gestures and fewer positive ones. **Implications for Prevention:** Help couples avoid negative comments and see what is positive in their relationship.[40]

- **Research:** Unlike younger couples who fight, couples who divorce in midlife avoid one another. They sit in restaurants without talking to each other. They are passive, distant, often bored, not inclined to raise or discuss differences, not showing much laughter, love or interest in the other. **Implications for Prevention:** Divorce can be prevented when counselors help these couples reconnect, stop blaming each other, get more involved with one another, and build new visions.[41]

- **Research:** The happiest couples value each other, say positive things about each other, and are not out to put down the other. **Implications for Prevention:** Seek to build these kinds of interactions.[42]

- **Research:** Divorce was more likely when spouses were critical of their partners, disillusioned about the marriage, believed the challenges of the marriage were outside their personal control, and assumed that their struggles against hard times would weaken rather than strengthen their marriages. **Implications for Prevention:** Help couples change their perceptions about each other, about their marriages, and about their ability to do something to make things better.[43]

- **Research:** Arrival of the first child can put pressure on a marriage and increase the likelihood of marital problems and divorce in 67 percent of the couples studied. "What predicted the stable or increasing marital satisfaction of mothers were the husband's expression of fondness toward her, the husband's high awareness for her and their relationship, and her awareness for her husband and their relationship. In contrast, what predicted the decline in marital satisfaction of mothers were the husband's negativity toward his wife, the husband's disappointment in the marriage, or the husband or wife having described their lives as chaotic." **Implications for Prevention:** Warn couples that this happens, help each be aware of what the spouse is experiencing, try to respond in positive rather than critical ways, and approach problems as something a couple can control and get through together.[44]

- **Research:** Marriages are stronger when the husband and wife have a strong emotional bond. The emotional bond is strongest when there is a willingness to forgive, when the couple knows how to communicate, and when they have conflict resolution stills. **Implications for Prevention:** Encourage forgiveness and teach better communication and conflict-resolution skills.[45]

develop. This needs to be emphasized in churches and elsewhere. Even more, it needs to be modeled by counselors and church leaders. If you are in a position to do so, encourage people to make marriage a high-priority item. Marriage enrichment seminars can help and so can discussion groups, the reading of helpful books, videotapes that discuss marriage, and biblical sermons dealing with marriage. Try to stimulate couples to do things together and for each other. Help them establish priorities, work toward mutual goals, and think of ways to bring variety and fun into their marriages. Some research has shown that marriage enrichment and education programs are most effective when couples who attend a workshop go to a counselor for periodic booster sessions as part of a follow-up relapse prevention program.[46]

3. *Teach Using the Wedding as a Teaching Tool.* For many years counselors and clergy focused on marriage education and gave little attention to the wedding. Some counselors are discovering, however, that the wedding matters and can have significance beyond the details of flowers and bridesmaids. Working with couples who are planning the wedding can be an effective way to help them deal with their new in-laws, handle conflict and different opinions, deal with money issues, and begin working together as a unit focused on a common issue. When the bride or groom has differences of opinion with future in-laws, for example, it is best to let each person intervene with his or her own parents because "relationships with in-laws aren't strong enough in the early years to withstand serious conflict."[47]

4. *Teach Principles of Communication and Conflict Resolution.* Married people are not the only members of the congregation or community who need help in learning how to communicate and deal with conflict. When there is gossip, backbiting, insensitivity, and stubbornness, there also will be tension and conflict. By teaching Christians how to get along with one another, we help them build better relationships within the family and without. Married people, for example, should be shown the importance of listening, self-disclosure, mutual acceptance, and understanding. Of special importance, perhaps, is teaching couples and others how to forgive.[48] Empathy, warmth, and genuineness do not need to be limited to counseling sessions. Everybody benefits when these attributes can be learned and practiced in marriage and throughout the church.

5. *Encourage Counseling When Needed.* Like individuals, couples often are reluctant to seek counseling. For some this may be embarrassing and seen as an admission of failure. Many couples with problems feel isolated, lacking support, and not even sure where to reach out. This is especially true of leaders who have marital difficulties. In contrast, it can be emphasized from the pulpit, in premarital counseling sessions, and elsewhere that going for counseling can be a sign of strength. There needs to be guidance in helping people know where to get help and how. When couples do come for counseling (most do not), they can be reminded at times that future difficulties can be stopped from getting worse if counseling is sought early—not after the problems have grown progressively worse.

Conclusions About Marriage Problems

As you reach the end of a chapter like this, it would not be surprising if you are overwhelmed with all of the facts, research data, and suggestions for helping couples to deal with their marriage tensions. As the author of this book, I can feel somewhat overpowered as well. There are so many competent people working to understand and improve marriages, to help counselors, and to do research studies that enable all of us to make marriages better. Despite it all, married couples still struggle, argue, separate, and divorce. Many don't realize how their difficulties as a couple can impact their health, their children, their relationships with other people, and their spirituality. Perhaps there is no topic in this book that is as massive and as difficult to understand as the issue of helping people with their marriage struggles.

Even so, God uses imperfect people like you and me to make a difference in other people's marriages. That is both sobering and cause for thanksgiving. We know that marriage is the most intimate of all human relationships. When this relationship is good and growing, it provides one of life's greatest satisfactions. When it is unstable or monotonous, it can be a source of great frustration and misery. God surely wants marriages to be good—a model of the beautiful relationship between Christ and his church.[49] The Christian counselor can help couples meet this biblical ideal, especially when he or she understands biblical teaching, knows counseling techniques, and is motivated to see marriages get better.

KEY POINTS FOR BUSY COUNSELORS

➤ This is a chapter about marital problems and counseling, but it important to remember that many marriages *are* happy and healthy, and they stay that way.

➤ Marriage, sex, parenting, marital problems, and divorce all are mentioned in the Bible, but whereas the Scriptures give many guidelines for personal behavior and relationships, there are few, if any, instructions that are addressed specifically to helping troubled marriages get rejuvenated.

➤ Almost all marriages begin with high expectations, but problems can come from many sources that might be grouped into three categories: some things come as surprises, some things sneak up on couples gradually and undermine the marriage, and some things jolt relationships.

➤ *Surprises* that create marriage problems include:
   - Unfulfilled expectations.
   - Disappointing sex.
   - Faulty communications.
   - Unhealthy relationships.
   - Unwise choices.
   - Secrets.

➤ *Undermining influences that sneak up on a couple and harm a marriage include:*
   - Busyness.
   - Role confusion.
   - Inflexibility.

- Religion.
- Value differences.
- Conflicting needs.
- Personality differences.
- Debt and money issues.
- Boredom.
- A weakening emotional bond.

➤ *Jolts* to marriage may include unexpected medical crises, a sudden death, a discovered infidelity, a natural disaster, a deep disappointment, a financial or career collapse, or any other crisis that can throw a family into turmoil and severely shake the stability of even the best of marriages.

➤ It is difficult to separate the causes of marital problems from the effects, but effects include:

- Confusion, despair, and hopelessness.
- More conflict.
- Withdrawal, desertion, separation, and sometimes divorce.

➤ In counseling couples:

- First take a close look at yourself and your attitudes and biases.
- Be alert to special issues that relate to couples counseling.
- Try to determine why the couple has come for counseling.
- Partner with the couple in setting goals.
- Focus on persons.
- Focus on problems.
- Focus on processes.
- Be aware of common mistakes; then avoid them.

➤ To prevent marriage problems:

- Teach biblical principles about marriage.
- Stress the importance of marriage, marriage enrichment, and commitment to marriage.
- Use the wedding as a teaching tool.
- Teach principles of communication and conflict resolution.
- Encourage the use of counselors.

➤ Perhaps there is no topic in this book that is as massive and as difficult to understand as the issue of helping people with their marriage struggles. Perhaps there is no type of counseling that can be more fulfilling.

30

Pregnancy Issues

Mr. and Mrs. A. have been married for almost twenty-five years. From the beginning of their marriage, they wanted to have children, and they rejoiced every time Mrs. A. got pregnant. For some reason, however, her body rejected every pregnancy. Six or seven times they went through the pain of a miscarriage shortly after discovering that they had conceived a child. Eventually, they accepted the reality that they would never have children of their own, so they started the long and frustrating process of adoption. At times these parents may wonder what it would have been like to have biological children of their own, but today they are grateful for the children that were adopted as babies and for the solid, loving relationships they have with their teenagers.

Mr. and Mrs. B. have also tried repeatedly to get pregnant, but for them the pregnancies never occurred. They live near one of the best infertility clinics in the world, have been through a variety of tests, have consulted with outstanding doctors and followed their recommendations, but still there has been no pregnancy. As devout Christians they have prayed for children, like Hannah in the Old Testament, but they remain childless. Now the adoption agency says that they are too old to adopt, so they face the reality that there may never be children in their home to call their own.

Mr. and Mrs. C. had a different problem near the beginning of their marriage. Getting pregnant was not a problem, but when their daughter was born, her little body had a number of deformities and physical malfunctions. Despite the best medical treatment, she died after a few days. On a day when the young parents had been expecting to welcome a newcomer to the baby's room that they had decorated so carefully, they were standing instead at a graveside with their friends and family, clinging to each other as they watched a tiny casket being lowered into the ground.

Mr. and Mrs. D. were in their forties when they discovered that another child was on the way. Parents of three healthy children, this couple assumed that they were past the stage of changing diapers and starting over to raise another child. Slowly, they grew to accept the reality of their unexpected pregnancy, and today they find great joy in their surprise child, but adjusting to the pregnancy and the new baby were extremely difficult in the beginning. Today the other three are gone and have children of their own, while Mr. and Mrs. D. continue to guide their teenage son through the high-school years on his way to adulthood.

The details have been changed, but these couples all represent people that I know. In all except one of the examples, I have had several couples in mind as I have written each of the above paragraphs.

Nobody knows how many people struggle with issues surrounding pregnancy. It is impossible to determine how many couples try in vain to bear children but are unable to do so even after repeated attempts. Others conceive a child but have their pregnancies end in miscarriages, most bringing devastating disappointment and loss. Crises come to other couples when a child is born with physical or mental disabilities that will prevent normal growth and development. Then there are both married and unmarried people who have unwanted pregnancies. These couples include those who had no desire for children at all, who had planned to start families later, or who had wanted to stop childbearing because their families already were big enough. Few issues arouse more controversy than debates about the abortion of unwanted children, what to do about teenage pregnancy, or how to give accurate sex education or abstinence education so young people will not get pregnant. Each of these issues may come up in counseling; each is in some way related to pregnancy. Many of these pregnancy-related issues lead to shock, frustration, anxiety, anger, embarrassment, discouragement, and/or confusion, which is brought to the counselor's office.

The Bible and Pregnancy Issues

The Old Testament story of Hannah concerns a godly woman who was married to a caring man named Elkanah, but the couple had no children. Year after year they went to the temple to worship God, and Hannah would spend time in prayer, asking for a child. "O LORD Almighty," she prayed one year, "if you will look down upon my sorrow and answer my prayer and give me a son, then I will give him back to you. He will be yours for his entire lifetime."[1] In a time when childlessness was seen as an indication of God's displeasure, Hannah described herself as a woman who was "very sad" and "praying out of great anguish and sorrow" because of her infertility.[2] Elkanah tried to be comforting, but his wife remained downhearted and sometimes too sad to eat. We can only guess at the depth of her joy when she conceived and gave birth to Samuel.

The Bible does not give a lot of direct teaching about pregnancy issues, although we can learn from stories like that of Hannah. Several conclusions are clear.

1. *Children Are Valuable and Gifts from God.* Consider these words from Psalm 127:

> Children are a gift from the LORD;
>   they are a reward from him.
> Children born to a young man
>   are like sharp arrows in a warrior's hands.
> Happy is the man whose quiver is full of them![3]

2. *Childlessness Is Cause for Sadness.* Hannah was not the only woman who grieved because she was barren. Sarah, Rebekah, Rachel, Elizabeth, and others felt disgrace, distress, and shame when they were unable to bear children. In contrast, one of the biblical hymns of praise describes how God "gives the barren woman a home, so that she becomes a happy mother. Praise the LORD!"[4] Today few parents consider childlessness a sign of God's displeasure, but infertility can bring sadness, even as children can make our lives happy and give us reason to praise God.

3. *Pregnancy Apart from Marriage Is Wrong.* King David's brief sexual affair with Bathsheba is well known. When David realized that Bathsheba was pregnant, he tried to hide the evidence that he was the father, even resorting to murder. The months that followed were probably the lowest point in David's life. The baby became "deathly ill," and for a week David prayed fervently without food or sleep until the child died. He struggled with intense guilt, and although he received

God's forgiveness, the king lost his kingdom and lived for the rest of his life with constant threats to his family and eventually from his own family members. David's secret sin was revealed, exposing him to public disgrace "openly in the sight of all Israel."[5]

Very different are the events surrounding Mary's pregnancy. We hear about them every Christmas. Because Joseph, her intended husband, was a just man, he "decided to break the engagement quietly, so as not to disgrace her publicly."[6] He changed his mind only after an angel appeared and explained that Mary's pregnancy was unique among all others before or since because the child within her had been conceived by the Holy Spirit. Throughout its pages the Bible condemns immorality,[7] including rape and sexual intercourse with a variety of partners.[8]

4. *Human Life Begins Long Before Birth.* Much of the debate surrounding abortion concerns the issue of when the merger between an egg and a sperm becomes a person. Some of the debate is accompanied by interesting inconsistencies. If a pregnancy is aborted at, say, twenty-five weeks after conception, the fetus is assumed to be "tissue" that can be thrown away. If a pregnant woman delivers prematurely at the same twenty-five-week point in the pregnancy, every medical effort is made to keep the "premature baby" alive so he or she can survive and mature.

The Bible does not tell us when we start to be humans, but it seems clear that the developing fetus already is human in God's eyes. When he was called to serve the Lord, Jeremiah heard some strange words: "I knew you before I formed you in your mother's womb. Before you were born I set you apart and appointed you as my spokesman to the world."[9] Apparently, God considered Jeremiah to be a person long before he was born.

Other Bible passages would support this conclusion. The psalmist wrote that he was "born a sinner—yes, even from the moment my mother conceived me."[10] Psalm 139:13–16 praises God who "made all the delicate, inner parts of my body and knit me together in my mother's womb," seeing every part of the development process and laying out every part of the life that would follow. The fetus was not considered to be merely some impersonal biological organism. Human life was assumed to start before birth. If that is true, then life must start at some time during the gestation (prenatal development). It is difficult to argue that it starts at some time other than conception.[11]

5. *Pregnancy Is Not Always a Cause for Rejoicing.* Jacob and Rachel had one of the most touching love stories in the Bible. For seven years Jacob worked for his future father-in-law in return for Rachel, but "his love for her was so strong that it seemed to him but a few days."[12] Finally, the wedding day approached, and Jacob waited expectantly. Imagine the shock that followed when the couple finally were alone, the bride's veil was removed, and Jacob found himself in bed with Leah instead.

"It is not our custom to marry off a younger daughter ahead of the firstborn," Jacob was told when he protested to his father-in-law. To get Rachel, the young man had to work for another seven years. Then when he finally got the wife for whom he had waited so long, she was barren. Eventually, she gave birth to Jacob's favorite son, Joseph, but when she got pregnant a second time, Rachel died in childbirth.[13] It was not a happy time.

Pregnancies are not always happy occasions, and neither is there rejoicing when a couple wants to have a baby but cannot. Because of the physical implications, medical consultation always will be a part of pregnancy issues. But often there also is a need for counseling from a sensitive Christian counselor.

The Causes of Pregnancy Problems

Pregnancy problems can be divided into two broad categories. The first concerns those people who want to have a child but who cannot do so. The most common causes are infertility and the loss of a pregnancy through miscarriage or through the death of a child within a few weeks of birth. The second major category of people with pregnancy issues concerns those who have a pregnancy but did not want to have a child.[14]

At the most basic level, all pregnancy problems have a physical cause. Infertility, for example, has been defined as an inability to conceive after a couple has had at least one year of attempted conception, when intercourse has been timed midcycle, and when no methods of contraception have been used. The condition affects about 10 percent of the population and influences couples of all ages, although older couples have higher rates than those who are younger. In about one third of the cases, the major cause is with the male, who has low sperm production or blockages in the sperm delivery system. Among the causes in women, ovulation may not occur normally, blockage may prevent the sperm from reaching the egg, or the body may produce antibodies that kill the sperm or abort the fertilized egg. Infertility strikes about 10 to 15 percent of married couples, and the rate has been increasing partly because many people now choose to postpone childbearing until after thirty when fertility tends to be declining. Some evidence suggests that the presence of pesticides, cigarette smoke, or different types of chemicals in the air or in the body can all contribute to infertility problems. Most infertility problems can be diagnosed accurately, and many are treated successfully.

When a woman does get pregnant, she has about a 20 percent change of having a miscarriage—the spontaneous abortion of the fetus. Most often this occurs early in the pregnancy; if it happens beyond the fifth month of pregnancy, it is termed a stillbirth. This is nature's way of saying that something is abnormal about the pregnancy. In time, most women who miscarry will get pregnant again and carry the baby to full term, but some women have repeated miscarriages. Like couples who are infertile, these people remain childless.

In contrast, unwanted pregnancies occur when contraceptives were not used or were ineffective. It is then that many people are confronted with the practical question of whether to have an abortion. For some this becomes a time when couples are forced to decide whether their stated opinions about abortion will be reflected in their actions.

Like all physical conditions, each of these pregnancy issues has a strong psychological impact that can complicate life further. Often, both the man and the woman feel inadequate, guilty, deeply disappointed, or angry at each other, at themselves, or at God. Whereas mental-health professionals sometimes assume that women bear the greatest pain from infertility or repeated miscarriages, there is growing evidence that men also feel like failures and struggle from low self-esteem, shame, or internal questioning about their manhood. Some couples experience a breakdown in communication or commitment to the marriage, mood disorders, or sexual dysfunction.[15]

Infertility tends to impact men and women in different ways. Women, for example, can feel lonely, cut off from leisure activities, and socially isolated if most of their friends are raising children.[16] Men may be more inclined to turn toward activities that substitute for parenting, even while they and their wives keep trying to have a child. One major study followed a group of three hundred married men whose wives could not get pregnant.[17] Many of these men turned to activities, such as developing a hobby, making home improvements, or focusing more on their careers. About one quarter of the men devoted their attention to other people's children—spending time with nieces or nephews, coaching base-ball players, or leading a church youth program. These men and their wives had relatively few lasting marriage or personal problems, and many of them later were able to adopt. In contrast, a minority of the men (roughly 12 percent) focused attention on themselves—lifting weights, body building, or pursuing other macho activities that could increase their feelings of masculinity. These men were the most poorly adjusted. Many had marital problems, and over half got divorces by the time they reached midlife. With both husband and wife, the infer-tility created depression, marital tension, anger, anxiety, and spiritual struggles.

From this it must not be assumed that all childless couples have physical, psy-chological, or even infertility problems. Some people make a logical, prayerful, carefully considered decision to have no children, at least for the present. Both husband and wife may feel called to serve God in special careers, for example. They may decide that their work or ministry might be hindered by the presence of children, or might, in turn, interfere with the healthy development of children. In other cases, the decision not to have children may reflect insecurity, fear of intimacy, a desire to avoid responsibility, fear of sex, or some other internal or interpersonal conflict.

The inability to have a child when one is wanted invariably is disappointing, even though the cause is physical and often temporary. The ways in which people respond can influence their personal mental health, happiness in middle age, the stability of a marriage, and whether they eventually are able to bear children, adopt, or choose to remain childless.

Psychological issues like these also accompany unwanted pregnancies. In addi-tion to the anger, frustration, regret, confusion, anxiety, fear, and depression, there may be an increase in the use of drugs or alcohol. Often there is conflict between partners or with parents about whether to have an abortion. These might be considered effects of the pregnancy, but they also are causes of further conflict and tension. The problem is worse when a pregnant woman or couple feels little support from others. Parents, church people, and sexual partners some-times show little care or concern, especially to unwed mothers. In addition, the emotional issues that swirl around the topic of abortion can leave pregnant women and their partners feeling both confused and pressured to make immedi-ate, life-changing decisions. After they make those decisions, whatever they decide, there can be criticism and rejection from those who disagree.

The Effects of Pregnancy Problems

Childlessness and unwanted pregnancies arouse similar emotional reactions, but the effects also differ depending on the circumstances.

1. *Childlessness.* Whenever a couple suspects an infertility problem, their disap-

pointment is buoyed by hope. Often, they consult with various infertility specialists and eventually a pregnancy occurs. If this does not happen, even after repeated attempts to get pregnant, or if there is medical confirmation that the husband or wife is unable to contribute to a pregnancy, there comes a period of surprise and shocked disbelief. This may be followed by the anger, grief, and lowered self-esteem that we described earlier. Some couples withdraw from friends, who might ask questions or joke about "when you two learn how to get pregnant." For some, it can be painful to be around children, and it is not unusual for couples to avoid Christmas celebrations or other family gatherings because it is too difficult to see delighted nieces and nephews showing their excitement or playing together. In time, these kinds of reactions may be replaced by denial and a reluctance to admit the problem, followed finally by acceptance and a decision to find alternative sources of satisfaction. These might include a greater devotion to work, the decision to adopt or become foster parents, or involvement with other people's children through community, church, or family activities.

Already, we have seen that when infertility is discovered, women especially feel guilty and inadequate. Many experience family and social pressure to bear children, and there can be a sense of failure or a feeling of sexual incompetence when pregnancy does not occur. Not surprising is the constant concern and focus on the problem, which is often accompanied by story swapping with other infertile couples.

In a world that is growing in sensitivity to other cultures, counselors should remember that childlessness is perceived and handled differently in various subcultures or in different parts of the world. In Western countries, childlessness tends to be followed with thoughts of new technologies and how these might be utilized to stimulate a pregnancy.[18] In poorer countries or neighborhoods, these advanced medical options are less available, and women must accept the fact that they will not have children. In many places childless women are treated badly, especially by in-laws. Infertile men also live a difficult life, but the problems are more easily concealed. Depending on the community and its morals, men who are able to produce sperm can gain prestige by impregnating someone other than their wives, but of course this puts more pressure on the women who cannot conceive.[19] In the Old Testament, women like Sarah, Rachel, and Hannah must have experienced special inner turmoil because they knew that their husbands had impregnated other women.[20]

One study of four hundred infertile couples found that most were caught in a "hope-despair cycle." At the start of each month, there is hope that "this time it might be different," followed by increasing pressure, anxiety, and despair when pregnancy does not occur.[21] This creates tension that can disrupt marital stability, influence bodily cycles, and delay conception even further.

The hope-despair cycle also is seen in couples who are childless because of repeated miscarriage. Each time the woman gets pregnant, there is hope that this time the baby will be carried to full term. When the miscarriage (or stillbirth) occurs, hopes are dashed again, and the couple has a fresh experience of disappointment and grief. Often, there are attempts to assign blame for the loss, frequently there are great feelings of helplessness, and almost always there is a need to work through the grief with supportive friends or relatives. Sometimes, however, family members and others feel uncomfortable talking about these issues, and the couple is left to cope largely on their own.

The grieving problems are complicated by the fact that outsiders may be compassionate, but to them the baby was never real. Society often views the prenatal or early childhood loss as insignificant, leaving the parents feeling very alone and misunderstood.[22] From the couple's perspective, however, the baby had a distinct personality, maybe had already been given a name, and was very much alive. Unlike other forms of grief, there is loss of a person who can never be known. Along with the child, there is loss of promise, expectation, hope for the future, and perhaps even standing in one's family or culture. For parents the loss is much more real and traumatic than it is for most others. Parents sometimes feel that the world is going by—as though their child and their role as parents were not lost, but never existed.[23] The counselor should not minimize the intensity of the loss or respond with an upbeat focus on the future or the possibilities of other pregnancies.

Counselors at fertility clinics have noted that many couples are reluctant, even ashamed, to admit their infertility or problems with repeated miscarriages. Some tend to feel that childlessness is an indication of inadequacy as a male or female. Many feel uncomfortable discussing sex, even with a medical counselor. Others may resist a genital examination by physicians, and some may fear that they will be told, "It's all psychological, so go home, relax, and try again to get pregnant."

The counselor should be aware of this reluctance to talk about infertility. If a married couple remains childless after several years of marriage, you may wish to gently raise the issue, but try not to fall into the pressuring attitude of well-meaning relatives or friends. If the couple does not wish to talk about their childlessness, assure them of your availability to talk at any future time and, unless there is evidence of more serious implications from the childlessness, do not press the issue further.

2. *Unplanned and Unwanted Pregnancies.* Psychologist Everett L. Worthington, Jr., divides unplanned pregnancies into two broad categories: those that come too early and others that are too late. The too early pregnancies include teenage pregnancy, pregnancies in unmarried couples who sleep together, pregnancies that occur immediately before or after a wedding and thus disrupt plans to start families later, or back-to-back children (pregnancies that occur too closely together). The too late pregnancies include those that come after a planned family is complete, accidental unexpected pregnancies, and pregnancies that occur in midlife. Each affects people somewhat differently.[24]

Consider, for example, the struggles faced by an unwed mother. Sexual intercourse apart from marriage is becoming widely accepted, even among Christian young people, but this does not make it right. As we have seen, the Bible condemns intercourse apart from marriage, and, depending on where one lives, illegitimate pregnancies still are disapproved socially. Of course the male, whose sperm impregnates the woman, is as much a part of the problem as the unwed mother, but the father's identity sometimes is unknown even to the woman. Males can hide their involvement, and since they do not show physical evidence of the pregnancy, sometimes the father disappears, leaving the unmarried mother (and sometimes her family) to face the problem alone. In contrast, in some communities or parts of the world, men (especially those who are younger) take pride in their ability to cause a pregnancy because this is seen as evidence of their virility. Even so, many of these males still fail to take responsibility for the child that is created, so the mother is left to cope without the father's help or support.

Especially in places where out-of-marriage pregnancies are disapproved, unmarried mothers often try to keep the pregnancy hidden for as long as possible. Anxiety, fear of parental reaction, concern about social judgment, guilt, self-condemnation, and sometimes anger all serve to keep the unwed mother preoccupied and away from sources of help, support, and prenatal care.

When an unwanted pregnancy is confirmed, often there can be shock, anger, condemnation of others or of oneself, fear, panic, disappointment, or confusion, especially if the pregnancy involves teenagers. When an unwanted pregnancy is confirmed, individuals or couples are not likely to run first to a counselor, not even to a pastoral counselor, but when counselors do get involved, they may see all of the above emotions brought into the office. Despite the counselor's personal feelings about the pregnancy, the emphasis should not be on moral exhortations, theological discussions, or intellectual debates about why the girl became pregnant. These might be dealt with later, but initially the counselee needs help in coping with the crisis and making decisions about the immediate and long-range future. Very often this leads to discussions about abortion.

3. *Abortion.* In January of 1973, the United States Supreme Court granted women the absolute right to abortion on demand during the first six months of pregnancy, and an almost unqualified right to abortion (for "health reasons," with "health" including psychological, physical, social, and economic well-being) during the final three months. Suddenly, abortion ceased to be a crime and became a right. It ceased to be a privilege of the affluent and became available to all, sometimes subsidized by taxpayer dollars. The resulting shouts of approval and cries of disapproval have continued to the present and have been heard and echoed around the world. In the meantime, the number of legal abortions has increased drastically.

As we noted earlier, much of the debate about abortion centers on the question of when human life begins. The Supreme Court concluded that it did not need "to resolve the difficult question of when life begins." Since "those trained in the respective disciplines of medicine, philosophy, and theology are unable to arrive at any consensus, the judiciary, at this point in the development of man's knowledge, is not in a position to speculate as to the answer."[25] The justices may or may not have been wise to avoid this issue, but it is of crucial importance. If life begins at birth, then abortion is not terminating a human being's existence. If human life begins earlier, especially at the time of conception, then abortion is legalized murder.[26] Earlier we noted the irony of a legal code that makes it a crime to destroy a baby (or fetus) born prematurely, but makes it legally acceptable to destroy another child of identical age who had not yet been born. The same doctors who spend anxious hours and thousands of dollars fighting to save the life of a baby born prematurely will, with hardly a thought, arrange for the death of a same age but unborn child through abortion. The same law that stresses civil rights denies these rights to the unborn.

The Christian counselor must grapple with these issues, preferably before he or she counsels people concerning abortion. There is little or no convincing biblical, theological, physiological, medical, or other evidence to support the view that human life really begins at some specific time during the nine months between conception and birth. Abortion clearly is wrong in the opinion of those who believe that life starts when the male sperm and female egg unite at conception. It is not merely a medical procedure, legal issue, or counseling problem. It is a violation of the commandment, "You shall not kill."

Perhaps most Christian counselors would agree with these conclusions, but others would not. The issue is complicated by other ethical concerns, such as the rightness or wrongness of abortion when the fetus is deformed, the pregnancy results from rape, or the mother's life and health clearly are in danger if the pregnancy continues.

Today, abortion is relatively (although not always) safe, common, easy to obtain (depending on where one lives), and widely accepted as one way to solve the pregnancy problem efficiently, quietly, and quickly. This does not hide the debate surrounding the question of how the woman—and indirectly the man—is affected by abortion. Case histories, some very moving and traumatic, are cited both by those who counsel with women following abortions and others who have reviewed psychological, medical, social, and other evidence that supports the harm that abortion does to both women and their husbands or other male partners.[27] In contrast, a body of research and the writings of many pro-abortion advocates suggest that abortions may not be psychologically harmful.[28]

It is well known that the results of scientific experiments often reflect the prior beliefs of the researchers, who, unconsciously, may influence the data to support their positions. Could the debate and the supporting data over postabortion trauma reflect some of this bias? One recent study, claiming to be scientific, concluded that legal abortion "entails little physical or mental health risk," but that "current abortion politics include efforts to make abortion a more threatening, stressful, and stigmatized experience and to create a postabortion syndrome." The researchers then examined "how antiabortion activists spread myths and misinformation aimed at women's appraisal processes."[29] This kind of reporting disguised as scientific evidence occurs on both sides of the debate, stimulates anger, reflects blatant bias, and does little to clarify the issues. More helpful are those who recognize that many women do come through abortions without harm, but who know, as well, that postabortion problems come to a sizeable subgroup that would seem to involve at least 30 percent of women.[30] These studies may not agree that a postabortion syndrome exists, but there is agreement that a significant number of women—and a surprising number of their male partners—feel guilt, grief, shame, feelings of detachment, depression, emotional aloofness, and inner psychological pain following an abortion.[31]

"The aftermath of abortion is not simply a little guilt or sadness or a wondering about the moral implications of one's actions," wrote one counselor in response to an earlier edition of this book. "It generally goes far beyond that and involves deep grieving, self-destructive actions, broken relationships, sexual dysfunction, low self-esteem, increase in self-abuse, child abuse, suicide, alcoholism, and drug involvement . . . and a crying out to a God they fear can never forgive them for 'murdering' (their word) their own children." These reactions, seen in a counseling center, would not seem to be true for all women who have abortions, but the fact that so many do experience postabortion trauma suggests that the risk of a severe psychological reaction is high.

This discussion of abortion should not hide the fact that many couples with unwanted pregnancies carry their babies to full term and either raise them or allow their children to be adopted. The fates of these children depend on the attitudes of the parents, especially the mothers, and on the environments where the children are raised. As we might expect, unstable mothers or those who resent their unwanted children tend to have poorly adjusted children.[32] In contrast, when mothers accept their unplanned children and raise them in loving homes, or when the children of unplanned pregnancies are placed in caring adoptive homes, the young people can be happy and normal.

4. *Perinatal Loss.* This is a term used to describe the death of a fetus or newborn child after the twentieth week of the pregnancy until a month or two after the birth. This has been called a "uniquely devastating and shocking" form of bereavement because parents who were anticipating great joy in the coming of a new child suddenly must shift and grapple with death, mourning, loss, and funeral issues that were not anticipated. When a child is stillborn or lost shortly after birth, there can be intense grief, depression, anxiety, a higher risk for later post-traumatic stress disorder (PTSD), physical or mental illness, and often marital tensions. Frequently, each spouse handles the grief in his or her own way, but there may be communication breakdowns because the feelings of loss are so overwhelming and difficult to express. Sometimes, each partner tries to protect the other, so they stop talking and sharing more painful thoughts and feelings. Often, the couple feels isolated and not understood.[33] Many of the same feelings are present when there is a miscarriage, the loss of a child earlier in the pregnancy.[34]

Although this is not a loss through death, when children are born with physical or mental deformities and continue to live, the parents may struggle with frustration, anger, discouragement, guilt, and sadness because many of their hopes for the child's future have died, even though the infant is alive and may be well physically.

Sudden Infant Death Syndrome (SIDS) is another cause of intense grief in parents of very young children. Although these infant deaths rarely occur before the child is one month old (and rarely after the first birthday—the peak is between two and four months), they come without warning, have no clearly identified cause, and bring many of the same reactions that follow other childhood loss. In addition to the grief, parents sometimes are subjected to police interrogation because child abuse and neglect is so common in the society. Often, family members experience self-blame and sometimes suspicion from relatives, even though nothing could have been done to prevent the death. Counselors can help SIDS parents refrain from blaming themselves and concluding that the death was the result of poor child-care practices that led to the baby's death. Siblings, who often resent the coming of a new brother or sister, frequently respond to the death with intense inner guilt, which they are afraid or unable to share.

Once again, tension and misunderstanding between parents can be high following SIDS. Sometimes, a wife will feel that her husband doesn't care because he doesn't cry much. He, in turn, may stifle the tears because he doesn't want to upset his wife. This type of misunderstanding puts tremendous strain on the relationship and illustrates the communication breakdowns that can occur as parents grieve.[35]

Counseling and Pregnancy Problems

If you skim back over this chapter, you will be reminded of the many references to grief, sorrow, anxiety, anger, depression, confusion, guilt, communication breakdown, and husband-wife tension. These are common in most pregnancy problems, and many will make their way into counseling sessions. In addition, there can be struggles as couples wonder why they are childless, what they can do about infertility or unplanned pregnancies, whether abortion is an alternative, or the reasons for miscarriage, stillbirth, infant death, or the birth of deformed children. Often, these parents bring theological questions about the power and will of God or moral choices about what they should do next. Many of the standard counseling methods are used with parents and family members who face pregnancy issues, but there are unique approaches as well.

1. *Childlessness.* Only a few years ago, it was logical to assume that most couples wanted to have children and that childless couples probably had some physical or psychological problem that prevented childbearing. Today, of course, this is no longer a valid assumption. For a variety of reasons, many couples decide to delay or avoid starting a family, so the counselor or others cannot assume that childlessness is a problem.

When it is a problem, couples may choose to hide their distress, sometimes in an effort to turn aside prying comments from people curious to discover why the marriage has produced no offspring. At other times the wife, husband, or both will show visible signs of sadness or aloofness at family-centered gatherings. If you suspect some concerns about childlessness, ask yourself if this is something that you ought to raise as opposed to it being raised by some other person. Stated bluntly, sometimes couples struggle with issues that are none of your business. On the other hand, if it seems appropriate for you to raise the issue, do so with simple, nonthreatening questions, such as, "How are things going at home these days?" or "Do you ever miss having kids around the house?" Be alert to casual comments that tell you to back off or that invite further questions or exploration of the childlessness issue.

When you are involved in helping a childless couple, the following are guidelines that you may want to remember.

- Since childlessness may have several causes, including the choice to remain childless, do not assume that you know why there are no children. As you talk together, raise the question about the reason for the childlessness.
- When there is a desire for children but an inability for the wife to get pregnant, make sure that they are seeing a competent physician. Often the medical practitioner will refer the couple to a specialist in infertility issues.
- Do not condemn, probe into areas of sexual intimacy that need not be discussed, assume that all couples should have children, or joke about this issue that is not a laughing matter for most involuntarily childless couples.
- Be open to a focus on the theological issues involved. These include the erroneous idea that God is punishing a couple by preventing pregnancy or that he doesn't care. There is no scriptural basis for either view. Couples should be helped to discuss these concerns, including the questions of "Why?" or "Why us?"
- Guide discussion of alternate routes to pregnancy and the associated ethical considerations. When they are unable to initiate or maintain a pregnancy, couples sometimes begin to wonder about alternatives, such as artificial insemination of the husband's sperm into the woman, artificial

insemination of sperm from a donor other than the husband, in vitro fertilization,[36] or the controversial issue of surrogate motherhood. Most counselors will not have the technical knowledge to discuss these procedures adequately, but it is helpful to note some of the emotional and moral issues that accompany these actions. For example, most couples probably would not object to the husband's sperm being inserted into the wife, but is it moral to have sperm from another man injected? If this is done and results in a successful pregnancy, how does the couple, especially the male who could not produce the needed sperm, feel about giving birth to a baby that is from another man? If the father feels guilt and failure, he has a reminder of this every day in the child who is growing up in the home. Should the artificial insemination later be revealed to the child? What if he or she wants to meet the "real" father? Clearly, these are complex moral, physical, and psychological issues.[37]

- Help the couple find alternatives to bearing children. Guide as they realistically discuss adoption, become foster parents, or adapt to life without children. Discuss meaningful activities that can give purpose to life apart from children.

- Do not forget that many couples will need consistent encouragement and emotional support. The issues listed above are more than intellectual concerns. Each has a lot of feelings involved, and these must be recognized by the counselor and not squelched. The need for support may be of special importance during the down times of the hope-despair cycle, or whenever a new medical or other procedure has been tried and found to fail. Some of this support can come from the local church, but many couples have found help in support groups where there is mutual encouragement, sharing of information, learning about options, and expression of feelings with other individuals or couples who understand. Sometimes these groups can sensitize the church to issues of infertility, and often there is prayer and spiritual growth. National organizations for infertile couples can be found on the Internet,[38] can provide information, and often can help groups get started. Some Christian couples choose to form their own support groups, perhaps drawn from one or several local churches.

Following medical diagnosis and treatment, many of those who are involuntarily childless eventually are able to have children. Those who cannot bear children naturally often are able to have families through adoption. Of those who stay childless, some will continue to grieve or even live with anger and bitterness. Most, however, will learn to accept their childless state and make healthy adjustments—sometimes as the result of a counselor's perspective and help.

2. *Unplanned and Unwanted Pregnancies.* It is obvious that the forty-five-year-old married woman who unexpectedly gets pregnant clearly has needs and challenges that differ from those of a seventeen-year-old unmarried teenager. These differences must not be forgotten, but some similarities apply to almost all people with unplanned pregnancies.

First, there may be initial fears and insecurities. It is realistic to assume that the new baby will bring inconvenience, extra costs, life and family disruption, and sometimes the threat of disease, such as the retardation that is more common when mothers are older. It is not helpful to discourage these concerns or expressions of emotion or to dismiss them as being of minimal or temporary importance. It is much more helpful to show unruffled acceptance and understanding. Remember that a loving, wise, forgiving God will guide as we counsel during what, for many, is a life-altering crisis experience.

At times the initial fears are expressed through a strong resistance to counseling and even anger directed toward those who try to help. As an example, the unmarried young woman may resist because she has been brought or sent for counseling against her will, she may never have learned to trust people (especially men—which presents a challenge for male counselors), or she may expect the counselor to be a condemning, unforgiving authority figure. Unwed fathers may have their own kinds of insecurities and resistances.

During the initial session, try to give calm reassurance that you will help, but avoid gushy or pious clichés. Attempt to find out what kind of help is needed and what the counselee(s) and the family members see as their immediate steps for action. Even though you should encourage a physical examination for the mother, try to discourage quick decisions, such as a rush to the abortion clinic or crisis pregnancy center or an immediate decision to get married. It is best to wait even for a day or two until the original emotions have been expressed and there has been time to adjust to the initial shock. For most, however, it can be helpful to discover as quickly as possible whether the woman really is pregnant. In all of this remember that prayer can have a calming, helpful, and reassuring effect.

Second, often you can help with practical decisions. Major questions include "How do I respond to this pregnancy?" "Who needs to know now, and how do I tell these people?" "How do I handle the reactions of others to the news?" "What changes do I need to make and how soon?" Some conclude that abortion is the best and most logical choice. Others decide to keep the baby and begin to make life adjustments. For unmarried couples, this may involve plans to marry, although hasty marriages have a higher likelihood of failing. A marriage immediately after conception can be successful if the couple shows some evidence of maturity and if they have had a good and growing relationship prior to the pregnancy.

Some unmarried mothers decide to remain single and bear the child to the time of birth. Some find maternity homes, while others go to live with distant relatives or foster parents. In an increasing number of cases, the unmarried mothers stay at home, where they continue with work or schooling and openly bear the child. Each of these alternatives should be discussed along with the issue of the baby's future. As subjects like these are considered, there also can be discussion about whether to keep the baby or make him or her available for adoption.

Regardless of whether the pregnant woman is single or married, practical issues impact a group that is broader than the counselor and counselee. Family members have opinions, but, even more, they may have legal and financial stakes in the pregnancy. Underage mothers are responsible to their parents. Married women and their husbands are equally involved in decision making. If a couple is unmarried, regardless of their age, the father also has a responsibility for the mother's and baby's immediate and long-range futures. When Bathsheba discovered her pregnancy, her high-profile husband was actively involved in making decisions, some of which were very unwise and resulted in the whole situation becoming much worse. In modern times it is possible to draw on the advice and expertise of others in the community, including physicians, social agencies, adoption centers, lawyers, and sometimes school officials. Do not make the assumption that the fathers are willing to leave the child's future in the hands of the mother or her family. Increasingly, unmarried fathers, like those who are married to the mother, want to be actively involved in making decisions about the future of the child.

Third, often there may be need for continued counseling. Among the unmarried, after the initial decisions have been made, either or both of the parents may experience continuing guilt, shame, anger, insecurity, a lowered self-image, or similar emotional struggles. Married couples may have difficulties adjusting to the new child, and there also may be anger or self-criticism for not taking more care to prevent a pregnancy. The issues of concern will differ from situation to situation, but the counselor can help, especially if he or she has been accepting, non-condemning, and helpful from the beginning. Early in counseling you might want to suggest that further sessions could be helpful—if not before the baby's birth, then shortly thereafter.[39]

The mother may need someone with whom she can share the details of child-bearing or the grief that comes if the baby is given up for adoption. Ideally, family members are the best people to give this kind of support, but sometimes this is not forthcoming. When a child is conceived apart from marriage, for example, the young mother's parents may be unwilling or unable to listen compassionately or discuss anything concerning the new grandchild. The counselor can be available to the entire family to help with discussion of feelings, moral questions, and plans for the future. If the child is stillborn or deformed, this can create additional guilt, grief, and confusion—all of which should be talked through.

Regardless of the parents' circumstances, unwanted pregnancies can be traumatic experiences, even in this age of sexual laxity and moral decline. The Christian counselor can use this experience to demonstrate and point people toward the love, compassion, and forgiveness that are found in Jesus Christ. He cared for little children even when they were rejected and pushed aside by others.[40] Sometimes, married couples can be helped to rethink their views on raising another child or on contraception in the future. Unmarried parents can be helped to reach new conclusions about responsibility and moral choice. In the church, believers can be encouraged to show compassion, acceptance, and forgiveness, instead of gossip, criticism, and rejection. In these ways, the pain of unwanted pregnancies can be turned into a learning and personal growth experience that can help individuals and couples live more Christ-honoring lives in the future.

3. *Abortion.* Thirty years have passed since about 2,000 church leaders gathered for a major congress on the family. As program director at this conference I was to oversee preparation of an Affirmation on the Family that would be distributed following our meeting. After many hours, a highly focused team prepared statements on marriage, parenting, childhood, divorce, sexuality, and other family issues. Shortly before this statement was to be released to the press and distributed at a ceremony with some celebrities present, I was informed that a strong disagreement had arisen over the wording in our paragraph statement on abortion. Overall, we probably spent more time working on this short abortion statement than on any other parts of the document, but the Christians who were present at that conference held some very strong and conflicting opinions on this subject. The controversy over abortion continues today, with strong opinions and

intense feelings on both sides of the debate, both within the church and with-out.[41] Certainly, there are stubborn, irrational, and angry people on both sides, but the debates over abortion are much more reflections of deep values that are held by dedicated people who have differing core beliefs about this significant topic.

Every Christian counselor needs to think through this issue *before* a counselee appears raising questions about abortion. In general, the psychological and professional counseling literature maintains that abortion has few risks and that keeping the baby may create greater problems than terminating a pregnancy. This conclusion is contested by those who work every day with women who bear the pain and trauma of the abortion experience.

When a woman talks with you about abortion, initially it is best to let her discuss feelings and alternatives openly while you serve as a supportive, caring, and understanding counselor. If the father is available and willing, he should be involved in the counseling as well. It may be helpful to discuss how abortions are performed, and questions should be referred to a competent physician, preferably a gynecologist or other expert. Alternatives to abortion (such as adoption or keeping the child) should be discussed, and you may want to enlist the help of an experienced crisis pregnancy counselor.[42] It is difficult for counselors to hide their own views about abortion, and probably they shouldn't. Ultimately, however, the woman must decide what to do, before God. The counselor is there to help.

What do you do if the woman decides to get an abortion, but you, the counselor, believe this is morally wrong? It has been suggested that the counselor can either help the woman find competent medical care or graciously withdraw from counseling and refer her to a counselor who is not opposed to abortion. Is this really a wise course of action for the counselor who believes that abortion is sin? Nobody would suggest that a drug-abuse counselor should send a strong-willed drug abuser to another counselor who is neutral on the issue or to someone who believes that drug abuse should be a free choice because it allows the drug user to control his own body. If the counselor believes that abortion is as self-destructive and as sinful as drug abuse, then we owe it to the woman, to her family, to the unborn child, and to God to demonstrate our caring concern while we lovingly urge that abortion be avoided.[43] When clear sin is involved, Christian counseling cannot be neutral.

After abortion, many counselees can profit from individual or group counseling that focuses on issues such as feelings about the surgery, guilt, forgiveness, attitudes toward sex, contraception, the meaning of femininity, and biblical teachings about life, death, and sex. The goal here is not to condemn or to instill guilt. Instead, you should try to help the counselee experience God's cleansing and forgiveness, express feelings, work through the grief process that often follows abortion, reevaluate the meaning of sexuality, consider the biblical teachings about sex and life before birth, and help counselees grow beyond the abortion. Help them move into a future where they can begin or continue serving God and others as true disciples of Jesus Christ.[44]

4. *Prenatal Loss*. The loss of a child, either before or shortly after birth, is no less a grief experience than the death of an adult. Sometimes, couples are expected to "get over it quickly," and caring but insensitive friends may urge them to get pregnant again as soon as possible.

Instead, the couple needs support and sensitive grief counseling. Encourage the parents to agree to an autopsy. This lets them understand what happened and helps to relieve some of the guilt. Funerals and memorial services can be important, especially since these can bring comfort from others and an increasing awareness of God's presence in this time of crisis.

After the death of a newborn child, many medical facilities are active in giving psychological help even while the mother is still in the hospital. Specialists in the study of perinatal loss have noted, however, that there are great differences between one couple and another. These researchers have concluded that "in our view, it is important that all health-care professionals who interact with mothers or parents who have suffered a perinatal loss do so in a supportive, empathic, patient, and respectful manner. Care providers should be accepting and validating of the individual's experience, provide accurate information, inquire about each individual's needs, empower each person to decide the kind of help he or she wants, and assist in problem solving."[45] At some time it also can be helpful to explore the reasons for the loss, including the possible roles of parents, other people, or God.[46] There are no easy answers to these questions, but even their consideration can be helpful to grieving couples, especially to those who struggle with the role that God may have played in the baby's loss.

Preventing Pregnancy Problems

Some conclusions about prevention are self-evident and may seem simplistic. To prevent infertility, a couple needs expert medical diagnosis and treatment, sometimes accompanied by counseling. Good prenatal care and medical intervention can help prevent many (but not all) miscarriages, stillbirths, birth defects, and infant deaths. To prevent premarital pregnancies, young people need sex-education that includes moral guidelines and practical help in learning and applying abstinence and self-control. To prevent unwanted pregnancies, couples may need information or reminders about effective contraception, healthy sexuality, or sometimes medical procedures like a vasectomy. To prevent abortion, there needs to be better education about abortion procedures, postabortion trauma and grief, and alternative ways to cope with an unwanted pregnancy. If prevention is to be effective, each of these general suggestions must be adapted to individuals.

In addition there can be prevention that focuses on sex, support, and suffering.

1. *Sex.* This has caused intense pleasure and incredible misery since the beginning of the human race. One poignant Old Testament drama concerns a young man named Amnon, David's son, who was so much in love that others noted his haggard look. Through a series of shrewd moves, including deception, Amnon was able to get alone with the woman for whom he had so much attraction, and when she resisted his sexual advances, he raped her. "Then suddenly Amnon's love turned to hate, and he hated her even more than he had loved her. 'Get out of here!' he snarled at her."[47] The young man's intense sexual urges had led to forced intercourse, followed by regret, injustice, family problems, and death.

Out-of-control sexual urges always have led to regrettable consequences. Some cultures are less tolerant of the blatant sexuality that we in the West find paraded before us on television; in various forms of entertainment, including movies; and in advertising, business, education, and sometimes religious circles. Even in cultures where sexuality is more discretely hidden, Internet sexuality breaks through to reach anybody who wants it. None of us should find it surprising that with all of this stimulation, many people fall into sexual sin, followed by personal regret and increasing numbers of unwanted pregnancies—many of which end in abortion.

This must be countered by realistic and sensitive sex education that includes accurate information, clear teaching about biblical morality, and practical guidance to help people maintain self-control. The focus of this education may be on the young, but older people, including people who are married, parents, and even senior citizens, could benefit from clearer understanding of healthy sexuality—as opposed to the more popular self-centered sexuality.

2. *Support.* When he created the human race, God declared that "it is not good for the man to be alone," so Adam was given a partner. From that time until the present, human beings have looked to one another for love, support, help, and encouragement.[48] Even so, many people try to handle life's problems alone. A few take pride in their rugged individualism and shun offers of help when this might be useful. For many, there may be an insecurity or reluctance to get close to other human beings; for some there may be nobody with whom to relate. Whatever the cause, individuals are likely to have more difficulty when they try to handle problems and stresses without God and the support of other people.

Most communities and many churches have support groups, including groups for infertile couples, for parents whose children have died or been born with a biological disability, for women who suffer from postabortion syndrome, or for parents coping with difficult young children. These groups can give the encouragement, reassurance, useful information, and love that enable participants to cope better with present stress and equip them to avoid future problems. When a church provides some of this support, stresses are reduced and future problems can be anticipated and prevented.

3. *Suffering.* Professional counselors say very little about suffering, except to suggest ways in which suffering can be escaped or avoided. Nobody likes to suffer, and most health-care providers and counselors, including Christian counselors, endeavor to help people cope with and grow beyond their suffering. Suffering is not always bad, however. Sometimes, it is unavoidable, and often it appears to be a prerequisite for personal and spiritual growth. Eventually, most counselors will see this in the lives of friends or family members who suffer and touch many lives as a result.[49] Jewish psychiatrist Viktor Frankl saw this when he lived as a prisoner in a Nazi concentration camp and later built his whole theory of counseling around the value of suffering.[50] When people complain about their suffering, see no meaning in their pain, or develop attitudes of bitterness, there is misery that may have a psychological as well as a physical basis.

Few experiences are more painful than the loss of a child near the time of birth. Parents, or those who plan some day to be parents, have no real understanding of the silent suffering that many couples feel because of their inability to bear children. Pregnancy-crisis counselors, as we have seen, often describe the suffering that comes to some women following the abortion of an unwanted child. Each of these experiences can glibly be passed off by insensitive relatives and church members. Still, the victims of pregnancy problems often retain the pain, holding their frustrations and feelings within and wondering why they take so long to recover. When Christians can be helped to understand the meaning and value of suffering, continuing spiritual and psychological problems often can be prevented.

Conclusions About Pregnancy Issues

Books, book chapters, and articles can teach us about pregnancy issues, but most of us learn most when we see the struggles in our own lives or in the lives of people we know. Several years ago one of my students and his wife discovered that they were expecting their first child. The joy of this news turned to sorrow when the couple learned that the baby would be born without a brain.

When they decided against abortion, their doctor dropped them as patients, and they had difficulty finding another physician. The wife carried the baby for nine months and followed all the principles of good prenatal care. Periodically, they would express the hope that God would heal and that the baby would be normal, but when the child was born, she was formed perfectly from the eyes down, but there was no brain. The couple took turns holding their little girl. They gave her a name, cried until there were no more tears, and then made arrangements for her funeral.

When the mother recovered physically, the couple determined to have another pregnancy, but soon they learned that probably they were infertile. Their experiences taught them about the hope-despair cycle, and before I lost track of them they were in the midst of the long process of adoption. I never heard if they ever became parents of a healthy child or children. They experienced deep sadness and inner turmoil, but this never curtailed their spiritual growth, forced them to withdraw from others, or led to psychological problems. I would not be surprised if many people have been encouraged personally and spiritually by the example of this couple. The husband was training to be a counselor. Perhaps he and his wife have been able to help others who have experienced pregnancy problems but have grown nevertheless.

KEY POINTS FOR BUSY COUNSELORS

➤ There are no accurate statistics to indicate how many people struggle with pregnancy-related issues. These include infertility, unexpected or unwanted pregnancies, and the loss of a child before or shortly after birth.

➤ The Bible values children, includes several examples of couples who were unable to have children, and records the experiences of David and Bathsheba, and of Mary and Joseph, who were not anticipating their pregnancies. Despite these examples, there is little practical advice in Scripture about how to deal with pregnancy-related issues.

- ➤ Pregnancy problems fall into two broad categories:
  - Pregnancies and childbirth that are wanted but do not occur.
  - Pregnancies that occur but are not wanted or expected.

- ➤ Each of these categories is likely to bring emotional reactions, including shock, depression, anger, disappointment, anxiety, and disruption of one's plans and goals.

- ➤ When a couple does not have children, the causes can involve:
  - Infertility, wherein the woman does not become or remain pregnant.
  - The spontaneous abortion of a fetus. This is known as a miscarriage if it occurs early in the pregnancy or a stillbirth if it occurs later.
  - The deliberate decision of the couple to not have children.

- ➤ Unwanted childlessness or pregnancies arouse similar emotional reactions, but the effects also differ depending on the circumstances:
  - Infertility can bring emotional reactions in both the woman and man, guilt, feelings of sexual inadequacy, and failure. Often the couple feels isolated and misunderstood. In some cultures they are ashamed at being childless.
  - Miscarriage or stillbirths bring grief, often accompanied by hope that it will be different if another pregnancy occurs. It is common for couples to feel isolated because outsiders fail to appreciate the depth of their grief.

- ➤ When an unwanted pregnancy occurs, the mother or couple may need help in dealing with the emotions, in coping with the crisis, and in making decisions about the immediate and long-range future.

- ➤ Every counselor must decide his or her perspective about abortion. There is evidence both that many women appear to have no lasting effects of abortion and that many do experience postabortion emotional reactions. Regardless, it is important to determine whether abortion is the taking of life. Part of the answer concerns answers to the question of whether life begins at conception. Most Christians would appear to take this view and conclude, as a result, that abortion is morally wrong.

- ➤ When a child is stillborn or lost shortly after birth, there can be intense grief, depression, anxiety, a higher risk for later post-traumatic stress disorder (PTSD), physical or mental illness, and often marital tensions.

- ➤ In counseling pregnancy issues:
  - Do not assume you know why a couple is childless.
  - Be sure that couples are getting medical guidance for their pregnancy problems.
  - Avoid questions that are not your business or that only satisfy your curiosity.
  - Be willing to discuss theological issues, including the "Why" question.
  - Discuss practical steps that can be taken, including adoption.
  - Give ongoing emotional support and encouragement.
  - Remember that a loving, wise, forgiving God will guide as we counsel during what, for many, is a life-altering crisis experience.

- ➤ In addition to education and medical treatment, the prevention of pregnancy problems includes clearer perspectives on sex, support, and suffering.

31

Family Issues

Mary Pipher is an outstanding family counselor—one of the best in the business. Through her books and her therapy she has helped a lot of families and fellow counselors, but even the best therapists sometimes fail. Mary Pipher described the Correys as her most spectacular failure.

"From the moment I met the Correys in my waiting room, I was baffled about why they were together," Pipher wrote. "Frank was tall, good looking, and suave; Donna dowdy and sullen. They were both in their midforties, although Frank looked younger than that and Donna older. She barely bothered to greet me, and stared resentfully at Frank. As soon as we were seated, Frank jumped in to complain about Donna's spending. He was clearly used to being in charge, confident and eager to explain their situation. And Donna was used to being passive and angry."[1]

As the family story unfolded, both agreed that Donna was a big spender who ran up large credit card bills but had little to show for her extravagance. Frank blamed the spending on Donna's depression and low self-esteem; Donna pointed out that Frank was a very successful businessman, had lots of money, and could easily afford to pay the credit card bills. Pipher sized up the situation, made a few suggestions for change, and ended the first session. When they returned, and in subsequent sessions, the Correys had either ignored the counselor's suggestions or done them grudgingly and then complained. They liked meeting with the counselor, but it was clear that nobody was changing and none of the counselor's interventions was working.

Piper's "exasperation and confusion peaked during one session in which, as Frank itemized her wasteful spending, Donna actually fell asleep. After I woke her, I asked Frank how he felt about Donna's sleeping. He insisted that he did not mind that much. After all, Donna was tired. At this point I almost jumped out of my office window." The counselor appreciated Frank's hard work, but she did not understand him and struggled with his lack of cooperation. She wondered how she could work with Donna, whose personality and values were so different from those of the counselor. As Piper "worked harder and harder to fix this couple, they seemed to become more locked into their original problem behaviors." Finally, the counselor fired them and suggested that they find another counselor. "There was Frank, not as unhappy at being fired as I would have hoped. And Donna, smiling for the first time since we had met. As she left the office, she said almost kindly, 'Don't be too hard on yourself. We are nutty and we're hard nuts to crack.'"

In the months that followed, Piper thought a lot about this couple and wondered what she had done wrong. "A wise counselor once told me that our first task in any therapeutic encounter is to find something to respect in our clients. Without respect it's impossible to help anyone." Piper had forgotten this. She had no respect for Donna and sensed that the couple knew this. "Being a therapist is intellectually taxing, emotionally draining work, and respect is what fuels the process," Piper concluded. "Without it, the work is mechanical, for us and our clients."

Sooner or later, every counselor is asked to help people deal with family problems. Sometimes, the families may be like the Correys, people that you can't respect or understand but who radiate both unhappiness and a seeming unwillingness to change. Others may be distressed couples who struggle to get along, individual family members being abused in their homes, or little kids who wear sad expressions and live in the midst of family turmoil, shouting, and criticism. "Polls and research reports confirm that many people today are scared, fearful about their safety, worried about their families, and lacking in hope for the future. Almost every day the newspapers and television reporters tell us about crime, abuse, uncontrolled sexuality, militant groups that push their perverted values, teenage pregnancies, poverty-stricken families, single-parent frustrations, poor schools, neglected children, and kids that kill other kids. In our homes—including the homes of Christians—there is conflict, tension, insensitivity, communication breakdown, and probably more abuse than we dare admit. We face endless demands that rob us of our time, pull us apart, and disrupt our hopes for family unity and stability. A host of forces shake our homes and cause our families to crumble, but three are of major impact: catastrophic change, persistent pressure, and pervasive pessimism."[2]

These words are relevant today, even though they were written over a decade ago near the beginning of a major book on the family. At the time, preparations were under way for a large family conference, and as one of the planners, I suggested that somebody should write a pre-conference book that would give an overview and update on the status of the family. It was a spontaneous idea, so when the planning group suggested that I should write this book my answer was a clear and unequivocal no. Only after several months did I change my mind, reluctantly. It was a daunting challenge to comprehend the current state of the family and to recommend how families could be strengthened. The task is no less challenging now.

One day, in the early stages of my work on that family book, I was telling my wife about all the family problems my research was uncovering. I had read that Harvard psychiatrist Robert Coles once told a group of professional family therapists how he had come to see the family as "a means by which people pull together, learn from one another, gain mutual strength, and sometimes collectively fail, but still nevertheless persist." I knew that was true, but my work was finding something very different—families torn apart by turmoil, conflict, distrust, and instability. Back at my computer I decided to turn aside from the problems, temporarily, and write a list of some truths about the family that were positive and that might be helpful for counselors and families to ponder. The list appears in Table 31–1.[3]

In recent years, family counseling has become an increasingly complex and diversified specialty within the counseling field. There are a number of well-developed theories of family therapy, perhaps several hundred widely used family intervention techniques, and various counseling goals.[4] At the core of this diversity, however, there is general agreement that family counseling exists to improve the functioning of dysfunctional as well as more normal families, to teach families how to cope with their stresses, and to build healthy family relationships.

The Bible and Family Problems

The biblical writers were not hesitant to mention family tensions. The first family of the Bible, that of Adam and Eve, was shaken by murder when Cain killed his brother. Years later, Abraham had family problems when his wife, Sarai, had con-

Table 31–1

Truths for Our Families*

1. Despite all the change and turmoil that disrupt family life, God is still aware of what is going on and is still in control.
2. If most people had to do it over, they would marry the same spouse they have now.
3. Divorce rates are high, but most marriages stay intact.
4. While some women (and men) experience at least one domestic-violence incident during a given year, most do not.
5. The majority of families are not seriously dysfunctional and in need of recovery.
6. No family is perfect and without problems and periodic crises.
7. All parents make mistakes, but most kids survive very well, even without therapy or twelve-step programs.
8. When families and marriages have problems, counselors often can help.
9. It may be difficult, but it is possible to have good marriages, healthy families, and stable kids even when we live in bad environments or in a chaotic, immoral, God-rejecting society.
10. We can raise kids successfully even if we don't have all the answers.
11. We can raise kids successfully even if we haven't read parenting and marriage books and even if we aren't perfect.
12. Even good parents sometimes have rebellious kids.
13. Even bad parents sometimes have healthy, adjusted kids.
14. When things are not going well in the family, this does not mean that all is hopeless.
15. We won't understand everything that happens to us.
16. God cares about each of our families.

* Adapted from Gary R. Collins, *Family Shock: Keeping Families Strong in the Midst of Earth-shaking Change* (Wheaton, IL: Tyndale House, 1995), 85.

tinuing conflict with a servant named Hagar, who had borne a son that Abraham had fathered, at Sarai's suggestion. Elsewhere the Old Testament describes twin brothers named Jacob and Esau, whose lifelong conflict was complicated when their mother, Rebekah, sided with Jacob in the dispute. When he had a family of his own, Jacob mourned because he was led to believe that his favorite son, Joseph, had been killed by wild animals. In fact Joseph had been rejected by his jealous brothers and sold into Egyptian slavery. Many years later, David had a wife who "looked at him with contempt," children who were at odds with each other, several deaths in his immediate family, the need to flee from his own son Absolom, and the actions of another son, Adonijah, who grabbed the throne from his elderly father, perhaps in part because "King David, had never disciplined him at any time."[5] Subsequent rulers had similar problems; 1 and 2 Kings, for example, give a history of numerous royal families in which murder and family conflict were common.

Especially poignant is the Old Testament account of Eli, the high priest who raised young Samuel. Eli was a faithful servant of the Lord, but he failed as a father, perhaps because he was more involved in his ministry than in his duties as a parent. Eli's sons were self-centered men who had little respect for spiritual things and engaged openly in sexual immorality.[6] Their father was rebuked by God and ultimately died because he failed to do anything about the behavior of his irresponsible children.

Despite family conflicts such as these, the Bible says little about how families should function.[7] In the New Testament, for example, Paul never mentions the family in six of his letters, and neither are families mentioned in Hebrews, James,[8] the three epistles of John, Jude, or Revelation. In Colossians, the family is mentioned in only four verses out of ninety-five, and the statements are succinct: "You wives must submit to your husbands as is fitting for those who belong to the Lord. And you husbands must love your wives and never treat them harshly.... Fathers, don't aggravate your children. If you do, they will become discouraged and quit trying."[9] A parallel passage in Ephesians is only a little longer,[10] and in the other epistles family issues are mentioned only briefly.[11]

Even though the references are sparse and brief, the biblical teaching on the family appears to support several conclusions. For example, the father is called to be head of the home; his responsibilities include loving his wife in a way that demonstrates Christ's love for his children.[12] It is sad that some men have taken this to mean that they are to dominate their families with insensitivity and authoritarian control that appears to be far from Christlike. Instead, the home is to be a place where there is to be mutual submission and commitment between the husband and wife. In turn, the parents—especially the fathers—are responsible to instruct and discipline their children in ways that God would approve, ways that teach obedience without making the children angry, bitter, or discouraged.[13]

Why doesn't the Bible say more about family issues and ways to solve problems in the home? Earlier, we mentioned the conclusion of Gene A. Getz, who is a well-respected pastor and Christian educator. He suggests that what was written to the church also applies to individual families. "Most of the New Testament, then, can be applied directly to individual family units. We *do* have a guidebook for the family unit! The Church simply becomes an umbrella concept that includes the home. The family is really the *Church in miniature*. True, on occasions the New Testament writers zero in on special needs that are uniquely related to family living. But in the most part, what was written to believers as a whole applies directly to Christian living in the smaller context of the home."[14]

This leads to the conclusion that biblical teachings about interpersonal relations, love, forgiveness, conflict resolution, self-denial, personal integrity, caring, the teaching of biblical principles, maturity, and spiritual growth all must be applied to the family. Perhaps it is valid to conclude that "the whole of the New Testament, and particularly the New Testament correspondence, serves as a guideline for family living."[15]

The Causes of Family Problems

Every family is unique. This impacts how they cope with problems and how they can be helped. For example, there are several influences that mold every family and create family distinctives. These influences include:[16]

- Events, experiences, stresses and *influences from the past*. These might include the death of a parent, the presence of an alcoholic family member, or the disruption caused by war or a tsunami. Past influences can impact family members for decades.
- Events and *influences from the present*. Consider how families are affected when the main breadwinner loses a job, the family moves to another part of the country, or a family member gets married. Each of these can guide how the family drama develops. Notice that the present and past influences can be negative or positive: the good can shape the family as much as the bad.
- The *worldviews* of family members. Worldviews are the assumptions we make about the universe, God, human beings, right and wrong, or similar core values. If a family believes that God exists and is in control, for example, that family might handle stress differently from a family or family members who assume that God does not exist. Sometimes, the family members have different and conflicting worldviews. A teenager, for example, may have views at odds with the parents.
- *Expectations for the future*. To understand families and make them better we cannot ignore how people view the future and what they expect. It is sad that many people go through life without hope for the future. When there is hope, however, there often is more determination to make things better even in the midst of difficulties.
- The *impact of decisions*. The health of families often depends on the decisions that family members make. Robert Coles once wrote about a father who was extremely disappointed when his only son was born with Down's Syndrome. At first the father was angry, heartbroken, and depressed. Later he decided to follow a counselor's suggestion to volunteer on weekends in a home for older children who needed special education. The decision to get involved did not remove the family disappointment about their son, but the man began to see how he could make a significant impact. One decision changed a father, impacted his family, and had an influence on a lot of kids. Think how families are shaped by the decision to move overseas on a missionary assignment or to invite an older relative to move in so better care-giving can be available.
- The impact of *family stages*. Every family matures and grows just as each individual grows. A couple with two preschool children is very different from the same couple when they have two children in college.
- *Racial and cultural distinctives* can put some families at odds with their neighbors. Some minority families are unable to adjust to the communities where they live. Other families may have children who have perspectives that differ from their immigrant parents.
- *The place of God*. For some families he has no place, and this impacts how families deal with stress. Other families believe in God but may have theological views that can create more stress and guilt. Regardless of what they believe, every family is under the hand of God who is sovereign despite the ways in which he is viewed by family members.

When they come for counseling, family members often need help with a crisis that they can't handle. Usually, one or two family members will appear because they are having problems communicating, handling their finances, dealing with difficult children, or struggling with an emotional issue.[17] When stresses like these interrupt lives, interfere with work, and disrupt families, the crises begin to build and slowly get worse.

We have seen that family stresses have existed since the beginning of the human race, but they began to get systematic study in the 1930s, when families were struggling with intense financial pressures brought on by the Depression. Later, during World War II, families struggled with the stresses of separation, losses, and reunion. This led one writer to propose the *ABC=X Model of Family Stress*, where A refers to a stressful event or situation, B is the family's resources, and C is the way family members view the situation. Together these three influences determine the severity of the crisis X. According to this view, family counseling involves helping people reduce the stress (A), learn better coping skills (B), and/or learn to see the situation from a new or different perspective (C).[18]

1. *Family Stresses.* The stresses faced by an individual or a family are not always bad. The arrival of a new baby or the move to a new home can be positive. It may be best, therefore, to think of stresses as life challenges. These are any events or circumstances, positive or negative, that require the family to change. When there are a lot of changes all coming together, the stress level is higher.

Some family challenges are family-specific. They might include surgery that temporarily incapacitates a mother or the disruption that comes when a basement floods or a fire destroys part of the house. These occur within the family, although they may arouse concern and offers of help from neighbors or extended family members. Other challenges and problems come from outside the home. Already, we have mentioned work pressures that create chaos in some homes and out-of-control lifestyles that keep everybody running. Television has stifled communication in many homes, replaced togetherness, and presented programs that paint a generally negative view of the family. There may be unexpected job losses or other forced transitions, economic trends that put some families under tremendous financial pressure, or wars that involve the sudden removal of a family member who is flown to a dangerous combat zone. In addition, there might be the discovery of AIDS in a family member, the decision of one family member (most often the father) to desert the family, the emergence of domestic violence, one family member's use of drugs or alcohol, or the interference of in-laws or others who can disrupt family stability. One task of the counselor, then, is to identify the forces that have shaped the family and to understand some of the major stresses.

2. *Family Resources, Strengths, and Skills.* Along with the stresses, every family brings a truckload of skills, strengths, weaknesses, patterns of relating, expectations, past successes or failures, and other experiences that may hinder or help the road to recovery. There may be attitudes and behaviors in family members that impede flexibility and hinder the chances for recovery. Some families have trouble coping because they lack the knowledge, skills, and flexibility to make changes. The effective counselor has the challenge of watching the family, trying to spot issues that are entangling the family members, and making suggestions for change.[19]

(a) The Issue of Communication Styles. Some families communicate well, but in other homes it may be common for family members to hide their feelings or to express them in ways that ignite conflict. These people do not know how to share their feelings or express themselves clearly. Some families have taboo topics that they never talk about—topics such as money, sex, conflict, spiritual issues, or feelings. Other family members never laugh when they are at home, rarely say what they really think, fail to listen, or never communicate without yelling or the use of sarcasm and other destructive forms of communication. Some family members give double messages: their words say one thing, but their actions say something different. It is difficult for a family to cope with a crisis if the family members lack the skills to communicate effectively.

(b) The Issue of Intimacy. Sometimes, family members are afraid to get close to one another. They don't spend time together, may not trust or respect one another, rarely share problems, and have difficulty handling crises because they have never learned to work together closely. When families are not close, problem-solving is harder.

(c) The Issue of Rules. Probably every social group has some rules about what is and is not acceptable. Most often these rules are unwritten, and many are never mentioned, but people learn to abide by them, nevertheless. I see these in the church that I attend, the fitness club where I work out, and the neighborhood where I live. Certainly, these are true in families. Sometimes, families have almost no rules, and this can be confusing, especially to the children. Other families have rigid rules that stifle the growth of individual family members. Religious families, families that are attempting to advance socially, families that have at least one prominent member, military families, and some minority-group families have all been identified as often having tight rules that can prevent flexibility, exclude outside sources of help, and hinder coping in times of stress. To help families, especially families that are different from yours, try to determine the rules.

(d) The Issue of Family or Personal History. Often these are family secrets that no family member is supposed to reveal, or issues that "our family doesn't talk about." Sometimes, family members keep secrets from each other—such as an illegitimate pregnancy, a mentally disabled child who was given up for adoption, a previous marriage and divorce, an affair that is over but not forgotten, or an arrest that is kept well hidden. This deception keeps some family members always on guard and others suspicious about what they suspect but don't know. Sometimes, the family members all know about family secrets, but they keep these hidden because of the family honor. All of this can hinder honest coping in times of crisis when honesty is important if readjustment is to be successful.

(e) The Issue of Personal and Family Goals. These can be the vocational, economic, social, or other goals that some family members set for themselves or for other family members. One Christian pastor decided that all three of his sons would enter the ministry. When one of the sons rebelled openly against this goal and another resisted passively, the father repeatedly expressed his disappointment and reacted with outbursts of anger and intensified pressure for his sons to conform to his wishes. It can be healthy to have family goals and ambitions, but when these are held rigidly or when one family member sets the goals for another, there can be trouble—especially when things don't turn out as expected. Life rarely proceeds smoothly, and families that can't readjust their goals often have problems.

(f) The Issue of Values. These are beliefs and ways of thinking that often are accepted by everybody in the family until one or more of the family members begins to think otherwise. "Everybody in our family goes to college," "Women in our family never work outside the home," "Nobody in our family ever drinks," "Everybody in our family is Presbyterian" can be examples of strongly held values that some, often younger, family members may challenge. When families aren't willing or able to adapt to changes, conflict often follows.

(g) The Issue of Commitment. It is difficult to build family togetherness and to deal with problems when one or more members of the family have no desire or time to be involved. Some career-motivated people work for companies that expect 100 percent commitment from their employees. The job requires a willingness to work long and hard for the company "family." Employees often have little energy or desire to build rapport at home or to deal with evolving problems.

When family problems arise, the minimally committed family members may resist getting involved. Family counselors, in turn, struggle with the ethical issues of trying to force unwilling family members to participate in problem-solving. Often, a minimally committed or overly busy family member can be persuaded to come for at least one session, and at times this can be a means of securing a longer-term commitment. At times, however, the counselor will have to work with the willing family members, realizing that coping will be more difficult when some members of the family are too busy or unmotivated to be involved.

(h) The Issue of Role Clarity. Each family assigns roles to its members.[20] Some of these roles involve activities—like who takes out the garbage, writes the checks, cooks the meals, or takes the kids to the dentist. Other roles are emotional; some family members become encouragers, jokers, problem solvers, or etiquette advisors. Usually, these roles evolve at the beginning of a marriage, often based on what the husband and the wife saw in their own homes. Sometimes, however, there are conflicts over who does what. These conflicts are especially acute when roles are held rigidly or when there is role confusion.

To this list, we might add two technical words, *triangulation* and *detouring*. These refer to behavior that often appears in discussions about family relationships. A triangle is a group of three people in which two exclude the third. For example, a mother and daughter may form a coalition against the father or against the daughter's husband. One of the parents may enlist a child as an ally in struggles with the other parent. Sometimes, a husband and his mistress are aligned against the wife. Triangulated families rarely (if ever) function smoothly.

Detouring is another word for *scapegoating*. By criticizing a rebellious son, a daughter who refuses to eat, or a school teacher whom they call incompetent, parents are kept too busy aligning against their common object of scorn to argue with each other. More basic and potentially destructive problems, like a marriage conflict, are ignored or pushed aside so the couple can unite to fight a different battle. It appears that these kinds of detours often appear in church families. By fighting sin, or getting involved in church politics, family members temporarily view themselves as championing a righteous cause and are able to avoid the pain of dealing with serious problems within their own homes.

All these issues can contribute to family stress, but all are areas where counseling can add strength to the family. Families, for example, can learn to communicate better, to develop intimacy, to face and evaluate the rules of family history or conflicting goals that may be creating problems. In addition, families can be reminded of their strengths, including their religious beliefs, their education, their financial resources, or their commitment to each other. In the midst of crises, it is easy to focus on the negative while we fail to notice that there are good features in most families that can help to build stability and prevent disintegration.

3. *Family Perceptions*. This is the C part of the ABC=X equation. Over time, families develop shared assumptions or perceptions about what their family is like and how they differ from other families. When there is stress, some families perceive themselves as being capable of handling the problem and making changes, while other families see themselves as being vulnerable and unable to rise to the new challenges. These differences arise from the different perceptions families have of themselves. Consider the differences of families who think "We are the Smiths and Smiths are overcomers," in contrast to a family that thinks "We are the poorest family on the block, and our family doesn't have the ability to cope with problems." When we understand how families perceive themselves, we can understand families better and know better how to intervene and help them.[21]

All over the world, perceptions of the family are changing. We see it in the language. Books and articles on sexuality tend to use words like *couples* or *partners* instead of referring to husbands and wives. *Marriage* no longer is a term restricted to the lifelong union of one man and one woman. Even the word *families* has taken on a variety of meanings. The family could include (1) the more traditional, two-generation family with one woman married for a lifetime to the same man, who works together with his spouse to raise their biological or adopted children, (2) extended three- and four-generation families, (3) families with foster children, some of whom come and go, (4) single-parent families headed by either the mother or the father, (5) gay or lesbian couples with or without children, (6) remarried-stepfamilies that sometimes are known as blended families, or (7) groups of several people living together with no legal ties to each other but who have strong mutual commitments.[22] Many of these families are trying to raise children who are shunted back and forth from one family unit to another, never feeling settled and never knowing where they fit.[23] Sometimes, there are parent-child role reversals, where the young person adopts parental behaviors (such as caretaking, supporting, or nurturing) and the parent seeks to please the children or gain their approval. There can be parent-child coalitions in which each parent sides with one or two children against the other parent and his or her family allies. Other family units have a parent-child overinvolvement, where parents become enmeshed in their children's multiple activities, schoolwork, and lifestyles.

Then there are family temptations like those that are summarized in Table 31–2. These are not deliberate efforts to break up families, but like all temptations, they are subtle influences that put any of us on the slippery slope of neglecting the families that God has given us. It hardly is surprising that some family members, including young children, are confused about their roles and immobilized when a crisis creates pressure and nobody knows what to do. This is when families suffer and counselors are called to help.

The Effects of Family Problems

At the beginning of this century, an expert on family therapy wrote an article that described eighteen major "trends, problems, and dilemmas" facing families around the world. Some of the items on the list are not surprising. These include the changing nature of male-female relationships, rising divorce rates and their

---

Table 31–2

Temptations Families Face*

1. The temptation to let life's rush swallow us up.

2. The temptation to be an absentee father.

3. The temptation to wonder—is being a mom worth the trouble?

4. The temptation to miscommunicate: jumping to conclusions that may not be valid.

5. The temptation to ignore differences between men and women.

6. The temptation to neglect speaking the truth in love.

7. The temptation to drift apart and lose family closeness.

8. The temptation to misunderstand family leadership.

9. The temptation to blur boundaries between family members.

10. The temptation to be an inactive "couch potato" family.

11. The temptation to forget to love.

12. The temptation to forget to discipline.

13. The temptation to give up on God.

* Adapted from Tom L. Eisenman, *Temptations Families Face: Breaking Patterns That Keep Us Apart* (Downers Grove, IL: InterVarsity, 1996).

---

implications, the increasing magnitude of addictions and their impact on families, the worldwide increase in domestic violence, the continuing quest to find effective child-rearing practices, and the galloping spread of HIV and AIDS-related illnesses and deaths. Others on the list, including the following, may not come to mind so quickly, but each of these can have a significant effect at least on some families:

- A greater longing for spirituality and a coherent belief system.
- The proliferation of wars, starvation, persecution, and other natural disasters.
- The escalation of crime and violence.
- The stealing of people: child snatching and adult kidnapping that may be the work of disgruntled family members or strangers seeking to pull victims into prostitution and tyranny.
- The increase in homeless and "throwaway children."
- Huge waves of immigration that lead to more cultural pluralism and often to more prejudice.
- The advent of cyberspace and new media influences that can portray violence and family instability, inculcate values, and facilitate potentially harmful contact with strangers.[24]

As a counselor or pastor, you are not likely to see all these influences, but they will appear at different times to impact the people with whom you counsel. These and other family problems can influence people in a variety of ways. As you might expect, despair, frustration, sadness, anger, anxiety, confusion, and feelings of helplessness are often mentioned in family counseling sessions. Family violence or verbal abuse may reflect frustration over family problems, and sometimes more than one family member will withdraw physically or try to escape from problems with the help of alcohol or other drugs. Sexual immorality, adjustment difficulties, negativism, delinquency, academic problems, depression, psychological withdrawal, communication breakdowns, declines in work efficiency, career indecision, and even incest have all been observed as outgrowths of family tensions.

Sometimes, family problems are kept well hidden from outsiders. Only within the privacy of the home is there evidence of family pressure. In addition to the communication breakdowns that have been mentioned earlier, members of dysfunctional families may avoid or ignore one another, physically or sexually abuse family members, attempt to manipulate or control one another, blame each other for the family problems, or hurt one another verbally with critical, judgmental, sarcastic, or put-down comments. Often, there is a lack of trust, feelings of low self-esteem, noncooperation, bickering, and sometimes placating—handling each other "with kid gloves" in an attempt to maintain peace within the volatile home situation.[25]

In an environment like this, spiritual growth is possible but difficult. It is not easy to be a maturing Christian when one's home life is filled with conflict and destructive interpersonal behaviors and attitudes.

Counseling and Family Problems

Counselors focus on the negative. That is our job. People come with stories of misery and conflict, and our goal is to help. When we hear one story of family stress after another, it is easy to look for the negative and to miss the bright side of family life.

Certainly, the divorce rate is high, but many marriages stay intact. Whereas far too many women and children experience violence or sexual abuse in their homes, the majority do not. Many people are raised in highly dysfunctional families, but the majority do not need recovery programs to overcome the impact of bad family backgrounds. Despite high rates of teenage pregnancy, and the large numbers of latchkey kids who come home every day to empty houses, smaller families have given many children more intimate contact with their parents, educational opportunities are better, and many women have been able to combine careers and parenthood successfully.

At times, however, even the best families have problems, and some may come for counseling. Family counselors can use one or more of several theoretical approaches to help families, some of which are summarized in Table 31–3. Selecting the approach to use can be a challenging task, depending in part on the issues that are impacting each family and the counselor's level of training. Most of these approaches are used by specialists with high levels of training in family therapy. How, then, does the nonspecialist help families to function better?

One useful approach is the *Levels of Family Involvement* (LFI) model that origi-

Table 31–3

Some Approaches to Marriage and Family Counseling

Classical: This is the traditional psychoanalytic approach. One family member who is viewed as the patient enters long-term counseling with the therapist who uses therapeutic methods to treat individual problems. As the individual improves, it is assumed that the marriage and family will be affected positively.

Collaborative: In this approach a husband and wife, or two or more other family members, are seen individually by different counselors. These counselors may confer periodically, comparing notes and sharing information that can be mutually beneficial.

Concurrent: Here different family members are seen separately but by the same counselor. This gives one counselor the perspective of different family members, but some critics have wondered about favoritism or the counselor's ability to remain neutral and refrain from taking sides, even unconsciously. A variation of this is consecutive counseling in which one spouse or other family member is seen for counseling, and then, following termination, another family member is seen.

Conjoint: Here the family is seen together. The counselor assumes that the family operates as a social system. Counseling teaches everyone in the system to act differently, so there is greater understanding, better communication, and less harmful behavior.

Cognitive-Behavioral: These are learning approaches to counseling. Problems are defined in terms of behavior that one or more family members would like to see terminated, decreased, increased, modified, or developed. In counseling, harmful behaviors are unlearned, and new skills and behaviors are learned. Brief solution-focused therapies might be fit into this category.

Crisis: Here the counselor assumes that whole families will come for help in dealing with a crisis that impacts them all. Usually, the family is seen together and helped in several ways, including:

- Giving immediate practical guidance and support as needed.
- Defining the problem as a family need rather than as an individual problem, even though one family member may be showing the major symptoms.
- Focusing on the present rather than analyzing the past.
- Reducing family tensions by psychological and sometimes pharmacological means.
- Helping to deal with the crisis-producing stress: this also teaches families how to solve problems.
- Identifying sources of referral where families can be helped with more specialized assistance.

Conflict Resolution: Working with whole families, the counselor attempts to teach conflict resolving and problem-solving skills that might be practiced in the counseling session or at home. Sometimes, there is an attempt to change the entire family structure by assigning new tasks, teaching new roles, changing rules, or teaching new communication skills.

Contract: Perhaps used less now than it was used in the past, in this approach married couples or family members are helped to make and keep family agreements in which there are agreed-upon *performances* or behaviors that lead either to special *privileges* (as rewards for something accomplished) or to *punishment*. This is a form of behavior-change therapy in which all participants agree on the behavior to be changed, and everybody agrees on the consequences to follow if there is change or no change.

Combined: This is a combination of two or more of the above, which may be difficult to apply in practice.

nated with psychologist William J. Doherty and has been helpful to counselors, including physicians and pastors, who work with families but who lack in-depth training and experience in family therapy.[26] The LFI has five levels, each of which describes how counselors may address the families with whom they are working. Each level builds on the ones that have come before. The most appropriate level to use with any family depends on the specifics of the situation and the counselor's level of training.

Level 1—Institutional Orientation. This does not involve any counseling. The focus is on providing family services that primarily benefit an institution such as a church, business, school, or community. Examples include providing child care so parents can attend worship services or attend a community meeting.

Level 2—Information and Advice. Here the focus is on providing knowledge, information, or advice. It may involve teaching a class on parenting or communication skills, recommending useful books, or giving advice about a child-rearing problem. A teacher may guide parents who want to help a child get better grades, or a youth leader may interact with teenagers about spiritual growth.

Level 3—Feelings and Support. This involves giving support, encouragement, and guidance to families that are dealing with stress. The counselor at this level needs to have good listening skills, an awareness of individual and family reactions to stress, the ability to encourage openness and the expression of feelings, and knowledge of stress management techniques and ways to help others solve problems. Ideally, the counselor at this level would have an awareness of his or her own feelings about family stress and an ability to show compassion without becoming engulfed in the situation emotionally. In addition, the counselor should have the sensitivity and ability to tailor recommendations to the unique needs, concerns, and feelings of family members. Examples at this level might include guiding parents after a daughter has run away from home, or helping a couple decide whether an elderly relative would be better in an assisted care facility.

It is at levels 2 and 3 that the counselor may want to involve others in the helping process. This might include members of a church congregation (depending on the problem) or other family members. Although many families are scattered geographically or split by disagreements and tension, the extended family (which includes grandparents, aunts, uncles, and cousins), nevertheless, can provide help in a variety of ways. Often, it no longer works this way, but ideally the family can provide help as it:

- Teaches values and guides in the development of religious beliefs and ethical standards.
- Teaches principles of self-control, including control of sexual impulses or addictive responses to interactive technology.
- Provides a place where individuals get feedback about their behavior.
- Teaches basic skills, including human relations and conflict resolution skills.
- Gives guidance in solving problems.
- Provides information about the world and about outside sources of help.
- Mediates disputes.
- Gives practical assistance when needs arise.
- Is a haven for rest, recuperation, and recreation.
- Gives people an identity and a place to feel accepted.
- Controls behavior when it gets out of line.
- Helps individuals master emotions such as anxiety, depression, guilt, doubt, or feelings of helplessness.
- Gives support during crises and through the much longer periods involved in adjusting to loss and separation.[27]

As families change and face new influences, family members often support, help, guide, and encourage one another, although this becomes increasingly difficult as family members scatter and have limited contact. Even in scattered or dysfunctional families, however, family members tend to hold up one another in times of change and crisis.

Frequently, the traditional helping roles of family members are taken over by neighbors, friends, co-workers, and fellow church members. This network of relatives and friends becomes the support system that backs up people in need and gives acceptance, guidance, encouragement during times of crises or change, tangible assistance (like assistance with meals or household chores), help with willpower or self-control, and a reason to hope. It generally is agreed that people who have well-developed support systems tend to have less mental and physical illness and are better able to cope with stress. This kind of support can reduce the need for more in-depth counseling and can back up the counselor's work at any of the five LFI levels.

Although many people think of the family as their major support system, at times whole families need support. Often, this support comes from individuals and other families in the community, and often the help comes from the church. Working together, families in the church can help other families and individuals meet crises and cope with the realities of life. As adjuncts to Christian counseling, including family counseling, supportive families within the church and community are without parallel.

Level 4—Brief Focused Interventions. This type of counseling does not involve changing the whole way a family interacts. Instead, the focus is more on helping them find solutions to specific problems, such as the inability of parents and teenagers to agree on limitations, the need to develop better conflict resolution skills, or the best ways to deal with a family member's growing use of alcohol. Brief, solution-focused therapies have become increasingly popular, as have the techniques of coaching. Usually, the counselor and counselees focus on specific problems, have specified goals, and develop plans to reach these goals, and then the counselor guides as the plans are applied. At this level the counselor needs to be skilled in asking questions, understanding family dynamics, working with counselees to develop and apply problem-solving techniques, working with family members for a short period of time to change specific behaviors, and knowing how to make referrals if more serious problems become evident.

Level 5—Family Therapy. This is a more long-term and in-depth form of counseling that most often is done by counselors with special expertise and backgrounds in family therapy. Often, these are families that have long-term dissension, dysfunctional ways of interacting, resistance to change, and sometimes ongoing crises. There may be high levels of emotion in the counseling sessions, significant interpersonal tension, and long periods with little evidence of progress. Any of the approaches listed in Table 31–3 may be used, depending on the counselor's training or theoretical perspective and the problem that the family brings to counseling.

As we have seen earlier, many family counselors assume that no problem ever exists in isolation. If an individual family member is having problems, this may indicate as much or more about the counselee's family attitudes and communication as it does about the counselee. The person who comes for counseling, then, may be a symptom bearer whose highly visible problems really signal that something is amiss in the family. Treating the counselee will not help much if he or she continues to live in an unhealthy family. Indeed, if the counselee starts to change behavior and improve, this could create confusion and even chaos in a family's ways of operating. The family confusion, in turn, could create more problems for the counselee.

As an example, consider a three-person family with an alcoholic father. As long as the father is drinking, the mother and child may have a clear purpose—to protect and provide for themselves and to work at changing the alcoholic's drinking behavior. Let us assume, however, that the alcoholic goes for treatment, stops drinking, and determines to assume his role as head of the family. Suddenly, the child, but especially the mother, may feel that there is less purpose for living. As a result, she may get depressed, so the father and child team up to care for the mother. I watched this seesaw take place in a neighborhood family that I once knew. Whenever the husband was drinking, the wife would complain, but otherwise she would be fine. When he would stop drinking, sooner or later she would get depressed and become so hard to live with that he would start drinking again. It appeared that her depression would drive him to drink. I have wondered what happened to the child who grew up in this perpetually unstable home. Clearly, the entire family could have benefited from help. That is the goal of the systems approach to counseling—to help families replace old behavior with new and better ways to cope.

While the individual counselee may be seen alone, family therapists more often prefer that family members come together for counseling as a unit. Over fifty years have passed since counselors began this practice of seeing couples or whole families in treatment, and hundreds of research studies have attempted to evaluate these approaches. When a team from the American Association of Marriage and Family Therapists (AAMFT) did a comprehensive review of these research studies, the results were impressive. It was clear that "couples and family therapy is as effective as, and in many problem areas more effective than, individual therapy. But in marked contrast with the older vision of family therapies, most of the current approaches freely mix individual, couple, family, and group-session formats. Confrontation in these therapies is rare," according to the AAMFT report.[28] The emphasis is on nurturing alliances with family members. The focus is on bringing change over time rather than using single, more abrupt interventions. In terms of distressed marriages, the only therapies that were found to be effective for relationship difficulties were those involving conjoint couples treatment in which the husband and wife are counseled together.

In the family counseling approaches, the counselor watches the family interact, points out their characteristic ways of relating, mediates their disputes, and teaches them more effective ways to communicate and relate to one another. The family members learn how to listen, to express their thoughts and feelings, to be flexible, to understand one another, to deal more effectively with conflict, and to develop a greater sense of mutual awareness and support. Occasionally, a family will discover that something simple, like initiating family celebrations, can help to reduce tension and stimulate family togetherness. Sometimes, as they work together, family members come up with problem solutions of their own—solutions that they can try out and discuss in later counseling sessions. In many respects, therefore, family counseling is a specialized form of group counseling in which all the group members are related to one another.

As with other forms of counseling, family approaches work best if there is at least minimal direction. One highly experienced therapist suggests a seven-step process.[29]

Step 1: Responding to an Emergency. Families most often want counseling in response to a crisis or emergency. The counselor's first task is to give reassurance and express a willingness to help. Sometimes, you can make immediate suggestions that enable the family to hang on until there is time to meet for an appointment. That initial appointment should come soon, and there will be times when you decide to meet with the family immediately. Even in this time of crisis, however, try not to take over or allow family members to become dependent on you. Your job is to give direction without taking control.

Step 2: Finding a Family Focus. Often, the family concludes that one member is the source of the problems. Everybody encourages you to work with that problem person, and they may be surprised when you suggest that the whole family should be involved in counseling. Sometimes, you may have to start with the problem person and slowly pull in the other family members.

"I see whoever comes," writes family therapist Frank Pittman. If somebody is important but absent, the counselor might even call or write a note to explain why the whole family should be seen together. Children are not always encouraged to be present, since they can be disruptive or distracting. "The group to be assembled is not based on biology or proximity or fault, but on power. Whoever has the power to sanction or prohibit change must be included."[30]

Step 3: Defining the Crisis. As you listen to family members describe the problem, try to find answers to several questions. What brought on this crisis? Why did it happen now? When was the last time there was peace in the family before the crisis? Has something like this ever happened before?

It may take several sessions before you begin to make sense of the situation. Sometimes, you will have to keep probing until you get a clear picture of the family problems and their ways of interacting. You may have to admit repeatedly that you don't understand. Keep asking for more details until things do make sense to you. You may want to have private consultations with different family members based on the assumption that one or two people in the family, including children or grandparents, may be able to give a clearer picture of what is going on.

Step 4: Calming Everyone Down. This may have to come early in the counseling. Before the family can work together to improve the situation, it may be necessary to give reassurance, to model calmness (even if you do not feel calm), and to instill hope. At some time you may want to share some of your initial conclusions about what is creating problems in the family.

Step 5: Suggesting Change. This involves making suggestions and gently guiding as people decide what changes should be attempted. You may want to help the family negotiate some contracts—behaviors that each family member will agree to do after the counseling session. You may spend time discussing communication or pointing out how the family members miscommunicate when they are together. There may need to be a reconsideration of family rules, roles, unrealistic expectations, limits, or better ways to get along with one another. Parents may need help in learning to be more assertive. The problem family member may need guidance in changing behavior, and the family may need help in adjusting to this change. The family members may need help in learning to relate to one another in ways that are consistent with biblical principles. All this will take time for discussion and the practice of new behaviors both within the counseling room and between sessions.

Step 6: Dealing with Resistance to Change. After you begin making suggestions, you quickly discover who cooperates and who resists change. Often, the person who most resists is not the previously identified problem family member. Sometimes, one or more people will get critical, try to withdraw from counseling, or attempt (perhaps unconsciously) to manipulate other family members so that change is prevented. At times you may need to point out how triangulation and detouring are hindering the counseling progress. At this point you have moved from the stress that created the crisis and are dealing with some of the family's cherished and long-established ways of relating. Here the counselor needs skill in keeping people motivated to change even when they feel threatened, guilty, angry, or impatient.

Step 7: Termination. The crisis that brought the family to counseling is likely to disappear in a short time. Your task as a counselor is to help the family cope with the immediate situation and learn how to relate in better ways. This will equip them for relating to one another and learning how to handle crises in the future. When you or they feel that no further progress is being made, it is time to terminate the counseling. In doing so, try to leave the door open so family members can return for further help if they choose to do so at a later time.

You may agree that this Level 5 type of family therapy is not for the faint-hearted, the impatient, or the inexperienced. Counseling like this can be fulfilling, but it is difficult and demanding work that can be easy to read about but difficult to put into practice.

Preventing Family Problems

Books on parenting, improving marriage, or building stronger families appear to roll off the presses in great numbers. No doubt the reason for the popularity of these books is because they sell. Many people want to know how to better nurture families and how to avoid the problems that destroy marriages and cause families to collapse. Some of these books have common sense advice, many have inspiring stories, and most offer hope.[31] Sometimes, these books list characteristics that can be developed to make healthy families. Communicate and listen, says one writer.[32] Encourage family commitment, be flexible, and show respect even when you disagree, suggests a former president of the American Family Therapy Academy.[33] The secrets of a healthy family, says another, is to express a lot of appreciation, spend time together, develop a high degree of spiritual commitment, and deal with crises in ways that help children learn and grow.[34]

One counselor was asked by the vice president of Wal-Mart to tell employees how they could get ahead at work without losing their families. Along with his wife, the counselor, Paul Faulkner, located a group of thirty families headed by parents that were known to be successful in their careers and in their families. The Faulkners visited these people in their homes, observed them on several occasions over a four-year period, and concluded that the parents had a strong commitment to Christian principles, were seen as models by their children, taught their kids how to give, were able to leave their work at the office, did not focus much on making or retaining money, sometimes brought their children to work, demonstrated a remarkable ability to overcome difficulties and tragedies, and had a refreshing sense of humor. Talking about humor in their family, the wife of one corporate executive said that "on a scale of one to ten, humor is a fifteen!"[35]

Professional writers more often give direct guidelines for preventing family problems. My former teaching colleague, Charles Sell, has written about the usefulness of church-sponsored seminars and family-life conferences; teaching about the family in Sunday School classes and sermons; training couples in marriage enrichment and parenting skills; stimulating family devotions; encouraging regular family nights, especially in homes where there are young children; initiating programs of family camping; or developing family clusters in which several families meet together periodically to encourage each other and share their concerns and problems.[36]

Since most of these programs are centered in the local church, non-attenders are likely to miss good opportunities for training and family enrichment that come through local congregations. Is it possible that radio or television programs and more popular books or articles are the major types of preventive help that some people will get?

The Christian counselor must learn to be creative in helping to prevent family problems. In addition to church-based prevention programs, it may be wise to work with schools, parent-teacher organizations, community service clubs (like Rotary or Kiwanis), government agencies, the media, or established family ministries. Secular agencies may have values and views on the family that differ from those of Christians, but it is possible to communicate and work with other groups, even to deal openly with spiritual issues, providing we show respect for different viewpoints. Whatever one's spiritual perspective, however, there also is the barrier of trying to interest people in prevention. You are most likely to have receptive audiences if you can talk in interesting, practical, and nonthreatening ways about parenting, day-to-day family issues, or building stronger families. Unless we can move away from church buildings and penetrate communities with guidelines for family living, we are likely to see a continuation of the problems that disrupt families and bring many people for family counseling.

Conclusions About Family Problems

Some families have problems or unique experiences that only are shared by a few others. Among families that have unique needs and stresses are military families, families of professional counselors, ministers, famous people, professional athletes, alcoholics, incarcerated prisoners, and families of people with AIDS. Blended families, homeless families, missionary families, multicultural families, and families of the terminally ill or mentally ill are among the others who have unique features. Probably, you can think of others that might be added to the list. Each of these may require special understanding and counseling expertise in addition to the guidelines presented in this chapter.

No one counselor can be familiar with all of these groups. Each of us can listen, however, and each of can learn from families even as we work with them. The counselor's goal is to be available, willing to be used by God to touch lives, and sensitive to the Holy Spirit's guidance as he or she seeks to bring healing into the families who need help.

In spite of our best efforts, however, some families break up, and marriages end in divorce. This is the topic to which we turn in the next chapter.

KEY POINTS FOR BUSY COUNSELORS

➤ Families have a lot of problems, but it is helpful to remember that most families are not dysfunctional; most struggle, but ultimately they get along very well.

➤ The Bible gives several detailed examples of dysfunctional families—most often the families of respected spiritual leaders. In contrast, there are only a few scriptural guidelines for building healthy families. This may be because the biblical teachings on the church and on Christian living apply equally well to families, so special family-building directions may not be necessary.

➤ Several influences mold every family and create family distinctives. These can also contribute to family problems. The major influences include:

- Events, experiences, stresses, and influences from the past.
- Events and influences from the present.
- The worldviews of family members.
- Family expectations for the future.
- The impact of past decisions.
- The impact of family stages.
- Cultural and racial distinctives.
- The influence of God in the family.

➤ Some counselors find it helpful to use the *ABC=X Model of Family Stress,* where A refers to a stressful event or situation, B is the family's resources, and C is the way family members view the situation. Together these three influences determine the severity of the crisis X.

➤ According the ABC=X model, family counseling involves helping people:
  ■ Reduce the stress (A).
  ■ Learn better coping skills, including the reduction of harmful behaviors and the development of new behaviors and resources (B).
  ■ See their situation from a new or different perspective (C).

➤ The effective counselor has the challenge of watching the family, trying to spot issues that are entangling the family members, and making suggestions for change. Look for these issues that might cause problems or need to be changed:
  ■ Communication styles.
  ■ The family's ways of handling intimacy.
  ■ Family rules.
  ■ The family's personal history.
  ■ Personal and family goals.
  ■ Family and individual values.
  ■ The degree of commitment to the family
  ■ Each family member's roles in the family.

➤ In counseling, the Levels of Family Involvement (LFI) model can be helpful. This has five levels:
  ■ Level 1: This involves helping institutions function better because family members are cared for. No counseling is involved at this level.
  ■ Level 2: Giving information and advice
  ■ Level 3: Helping people express feelings and giving support.
  ■ Level 4: Brief, focused, strategic counseling intervention.
  ■ Level 5: More detailed family therapy.

➤ There are various approaches to family therapy. Here is one seven-stage model:
  ■ Respond to the presenting emergency.
  ■ Deal with the family focus person but get everyone involved.
  ■ Deal with the current crisis.
  ■ Calm everyone down.
  ■ Suggest some changes.
  ■ Deal with resistance to change.
  ■ Terminate the counseling.

➤ The prevention of family problems can come through the counseling, the church, or community involvement.

➤ As you counsel, remember that some family groups have unique needs and problems. These include immigrant families, military families, and families with a substance abuser or a family member who has an incurable illness.

➤ Here is one important truth about families: God cares about each of our families.

32

Divorce and Remarriage

It's an interesting group, nothing like the father, mother, and two children that sometimes adorn the covers of books on the family. When they got married, Larry and Jennifer were both single parents. Eight months after Larry's wife died in an accident, he married Jennifer, who had divorced her abusive and alcoholic husband three years previously. Larry had two daughters, ages ten and thirteen; Jennifer had come to her new marriage with a seven-year-old daughter and a son who was nine.

When they came to the counselor's office, Larry and Jennifer were ready to quit. Each told the same story: "We both have tried to make it work. We really love each other, but our kids haven't been able to accept us as being together. We thought things would improve, but they keep getting worse. We don't know what to do but agree that the marriage was a mistake and that we need to end the relationship as soon as we can."

Since the day of the marriage, the children had not blended well into their new extended family. There had been temper tantrums, disrespect, academic failure, complaining, and several episodes when one or more of the kids had run away. The home was described as being very confusing, filled with a lot of fear, anger, and a none-too-subtle struggle for power. Larry was afraid of losing his daughters, who didn't like their new mother. Jennifer had a tone of desperation in her voice when she expressed anguish about the possibility of failing at marriage again.

Like other blended families, this one had a cast of other people who impacted the home in various ways. Larry's former in-laws disapproved of his new marriage. Jennifer's former husband undermined his children's confidence in Larry. Both sets of parents, Larry's and Jennifer's, had their own opinions and interactions with the new family. There were so many people involved that the counselor decided to team up with another counselor in hopes that together they could understand and intervene in the complex of marital and family relationships. Different forms of family counseling were used to make sure that everybody was heard and involved. For Larry and Jennifer, counseling focused on helping them sort out the confusing family patterns, relate better to the different children, and learn how to stand together against efforts within their family and without to sabotage their marriage and to bring down the new family.

Larry and Jennifer are not unusual. They represent a family that reflects the complexities and the difficulties of building relationships after both divorce and remarriage.[1]

Six divorced women, all Christians, were having breakfast one morning when their conversation turned to Cindy. They all knew her. They knew she was planning to get a divorce, and they knew, as well, that she was not willing to hear anything that might convince her otherwise. Frustrated with Cindy's determination to leave her husband, the six friends began to compile a list of the things they wish they had known before their own divorces, and the things they so desperately wanted to tell Cindy before she made her final decision. Here is the list.[2]

- Your life will change more than you realize. Even when the ex-spouses cooperate, routines and lifestyles change, the children are deeply impacted, and it is likely that there will be a need to make major adjustments, especially if there is a remarriage.
- Your life won't be more carefree. One of the women at the breakfast talked about "those seemingly hidden emotional wounds that can pop up when we least expect." Another described the unique features of dating a man who had been divorced. "Because of our pasts, we have several barriers in our current relationship—one of which is the fear of trusting and loving again."
- You will trade one set of problems for another. Even the most amiable breakups can bring big challenges and deep wounds. Dividing the family assets is one example. Another concerns the emotional impact of the divorce on the couple, their children, their parents and other relatives, their friends, and the people at church. Remarriage may be anticipated enthusiastically, but that too brings challenges, especially if the remarriage involves blending two groups of children.
- Feelings can be deceiving. Sadly, in the midst of marital tension too many people make decisions based on emotions and regret their actions later.

Cindy never listened to her friends. She went ahead with her divorce and probably discovered what most divorced people learn: divorce is never easy. Cindy's friends knew that she was not making a casual decision to end her marriage—few people do. They also knew, from their own experiences, that divorce can be one of the most agonizing choices that any couple makes. One of Cindy's friends wrote that they "understood the anger, panic, abandonment, and feelings of being trapped that lead many people to divorce. Be we also experienced the other side of being single again. We'd seen the lives of our children changed forever. Years later, we continue to live with the ongoing pain and complications of a destroyed marriage."[3]

Even when a couple agrees to terminate their marriage, it hurts to separate. Guilt, anger, resentment, fear, and disappointment often dominate the divorced person's thinking, and frequently there is loneliness, confusion, lowered self-esteem, insecurity, a sense of rejection, and the haunting concern about who was at fault. When children are involved, the pain can be even greater as sensitive parents watch innocent young people suffer because their families have been torn apart. Somebody has suggested that no one wins in a divorce. All lose—the couple, their children, their parents and the community at large.

From this we must not conclude that all divorce is destructive or that the remarriage of divorced persons always leads to misery and more marital problems. Many divorced or remarried people would say that their lives after divorce are better than they were in the midst of the previous unhappy marriages. Millions of people, including Christians, have come to accept the reality of infidelity and divorce as ways of life for many in modern society. Divorce may be seen as a welcome route to freedom or a convenient escape hatch from the difficulties of marriage. This does not deny the fact, however, that for the majority, divorce brings pain and significant turmoil. "When I conduct coping with divorce seminars," said the minister of counseling at a large church, "the people don't just sit there and listen. Many of them cry!"

The Bible and Divorce

No marriage—no matter how good—is immune to bad things. We all suffer private problems and sometimes public pitfalls:

- Sexual unfulfillment that quietly hardens our hearts,
- Financial debt that shrouds us in shame,
- Hope deferred by the anguish of infertility,
- Communication meltdowns that tempt us to quit trying,
- Ugly addictions that drive us into secret lives,
- Personal pain from an abusive past that keeps us from loving in the present.
- The list could go on and on. The bad things that interfere with a good marriage are countless.[4]

Counselors Les and Leslie Parrott, who wrote these words, add that "there is nothing in the world worse than a bad marriage, and at the same time nothing better than a good one."[5] Bad marriages have led many people to divorce with the hope that they will find someone or something that is better. Christian counselors see this often. They also see the turmoil of unhappy marriages and the pain of divorce. Many are like the pastor friend who called when I was writing the previous section. He is planning a forthcoming sermon and wants to give a clear and accurate statement about the biblical teaching on divorce and remarriage. But he has a church filled with people who have been divorced, some more than once, and he wants to be sensitive to where they are, without stirring up guilt and more pain about their past choices. He does not want to reinterpret or dismiss biblical teachings in an effort to make divorce and remarriage seem easier and more acceptable theologically. He is a compassionate pastor who wants to minister to his people, but he knows that ignoring or de-emphasizing biblical teaching is neither compassionate nor helpful. What is true of this pastor is true of all Christian counselors. If we are to be effective in helping people, we must have a clear understanding of the scriptural statements about divorce and remarriage.

This would be easier if biblical scholars were united in their conclusions, but sincere and competent Christian writers disagree. In part, this is because the Bible passages often deal with specific situations that can be difficult to interpret and apply today. Most of the biblically based viewpoints tend to fall into one of four categories, each of which has strong advocates.[6] First are those who conclude that marriage is for life, that divorce is never permitted on biblical grounds, and that remarriage of a divorced person always is adultery. Second, some conclude that there are legitimate biblical grounds for divorce and remarriage, including desertion and adultery, wherein one person has been left by a spouse who has had sexual intercourse outside of the marriage and has no desire to reconcile. Third is the view that some circumstances arise in marriage that defy solution. Divorce then becomes necessary for the sake of the mental, emotional, or physical health of one of the spouses or their children. This view is based less on specific biblical teaching and more on general biblical principles of compassion and sensitivity. Fourth is a view held mostly by Roman Catholic writers, that a church court can annul a marriage and thus pave the way for remarriage.

1. *The Teachings of the Old Testament.* From the beginning, the Bible presents

marriage as a permanent, intimate union between a man and a woman.[7] This is God's unchanging ideal, but since the Fall, human beings have lived on a less than ideal level. The Bible recognizes this, and so in Deuteronomy 24:1–4 there are brief guidelines that govern the practice of divorce—a practice that is tolerated but never commanded or divinely encouraged.

According to the Old Testament, divorce was to be legal (with a written document), permanent, and permissible only when "uncleanness" was involved. Regrettably, the meaning of "uncleanness" has become a subject for debate. Some have maintained that it includes any inappropriate behavior; others have restricted the term and argued that uncleanness refers only to sexual infidelity. Jesus seems to have agreed with this second view.[8]

2. *The Teachings of Jesus.* In the New Testament, Jesus reaffirmed the permanent nature of marriage, pointed out that divine permission for divorce was given only because of human sinfulness (and not because it was God's ideal), stated that sexual immorality was the only legitimate cause for divorce, and taught that the one who divorces a sexually faithful spouse and marries another commits adultery (and causes the new mate also to commit adultery).[9]

There has been some debate about the meaning of "unless she [or he] has been unfaithful" in Matthew 5:32 and 19:9. The Greek word for unfaithfulness is *porneia*, which refers to all sexual intercourse apart from marriage. This behavior violates the one-flesh concept that is so basic to biblical marriage. Even when unfaithfulness is involved, however, divorce is not commanded; it merely is permitted. Forgiveness and reconciliation still are preferable to divorce. Nevertheless, if divorce does occur under these circumstances, it is the opinion of many evangelical biblical scholars that the innocent party is free to remarry.[10]

3. *The Teachings of Paul.* In responding to a question from the Corinthians, the apostle echoes Christ's teaching and then adds a second permissible cause for divorce: desertion by an unbelieving mate.[11] This same passage deals with religious incompatibility—when a believer and an unbeliever are married. These theologically mixed marriages are not to be ended in divorce (except when the unbeliever deserts), even though the differences in religious beliefs may create tension in the home. By staying married, the believing mate sanctifies the marriage, Paul writes, and in time the nonbelieving mate may be brought to Christ.

4. *Teachings on Remarriage.* Along with the controversies about the biblical teaching on divorce, there is equally strong debate and disagreement about the biblical views of remarriage. At the time of Christ, controversy in the Jewish community centered on the causes of divorce. Many never questioned the right to remarry once divorce occurred. In contrast, the focus of contemporary evangelical Christians has centered more on the question of remarriage.

Bible-believing scholars generally agree that God intended marriage to be a permanent and exclusive union between a man and woman who find their sexual fulfillment within marriage. Divorce is nowhere commanded in Scripture, and neither is it encouraged. God hates divorce[12] but he does permit it, first when one's mate is guilty of sexual immorality and unwilling to repent and live faithfully with the marriage partner,[13] and second, when one of the mates is an unbeliever who willfully and permanently deserts the believing partner. Does this give the divorced person the right to remarry with God's approval?

Matthew 5:32 and Matthew 19:9 appear to indicate that where the mate has been sexually unfaithful (*porneia*) and divorce occurs, the faithful partner has the right to remarry because the immorality has dissolved the marriage. In 1 Corinthians 7:15, where the unbelieving partner leaves and initiates a divorce, the believer is set free to marry if he or she so chooses. Not all biblical scholars would agree with this interpretation, and none of this addresses the question of whether remarriage is wise, even if it is permitted. Paul urged the unmarried (this could include the formerly married) to remain single.[14]

5. *Related Issues.* Some major issues about divorce are not addressed in the Bible or are not specifically related to divorce, even though they concern Christian counselors, pastors, and divorcing or divorced couples who want to live in accordance with God's principles.

First, the Bible says nothing about the divorce of two nonbelievers. Clearly, this is undesirable, since it violates God's one flesh ideal and often involves adultery, a behavior that always is sinful regardless of a person's beliefs. Nevertheless, there are no specific divine guidelines for non-Christian divorce. Many would agree that an individual who was married and divorced prior to salvation is free to remarry after becoming a Christian.

Second, we must emphasize the importance of forgiveness, even though this is not tied specifically to divorce in the biblical passages. Although God hates divorce and forbids adultery,[15] these are not unpardonable sins. God forgives those who confess and repent, and he expects his followers to do the same.[16] It is wrong (and surely sinful) for Christians to treat the divorced as if they are tainted people, forbidden to serve in the church or take any leadership positions.[17] Whenever sin is forgiven, we are to stop dwelling on the past and instead must focus our attention on living in ways that are pure and free from further sin.[18]

David R. Miller is a Christian counselor who respects the difficulties of finding clear biblical teachings, especially about remarriage. Realistically, however, he concludes that divorced people do and will remarry, regardless of what their religious leaders think. Divorce and remarriage are a fact of life, among both Christians and nonbelievers. This leaves Christian counselors and church leaders with a choice. Either we consider these divorced and remarried people to be second-class Christians and exclude them from full participation in the church, or we accept them as part of the body of Christ, welcome them into the church, counsel them as best we can, and help them make decisions and live lives in accordance with biblical guidelines.[19]

Third, all of this appears to overlook those marriages where there is no infidelity or desertion, but where homes are filled with violence, physical and mental abuse, deviant forms of sexual behavior (including forced incest), foul language, failure to provide for a family's physical needs, alcoholism, a refusal to let other family members worship, or other destructive influences. Emotional and physical harm, along with the fear and mental anguish that they create, can make home a hell rather than a haven. Some mates try to defend themselves and their children, believing that to stay in a marriage and home where there is violence is better than trying to survive and raise children alone in a hostile world. Often, however, there comes a time when the victim either responds with violence in return or decides to separate from the marriage. Is divorce justified in these circumstances?

Here the Scriptures appear to be silent. Some might encourage the victims of abuse to stay in their difficult circumstances and to suffer in silence, hoping that this behavior might lead to the mate's conversion or change.[20] However, submitting meekly to physical and mental attack seems to be neither wise nor healthy. The abuser is psychologically and spiritually unhealthy. In addition, he or she is sinning. While such behavior must be forgiven, it cannot be condoned by a mate who passively stands by, says nothing, and lets various family members, including children, get hurt. Legally, the mate who allows this to continue could be in violation of the law and seen as an accomplice to child abuse, even though he or she resists it and tries to stop it. Common sense, love for one's family members, and regard for one's personal safety would all indicate that such victims need to get out. The church and the Christian counselor surely have no alternative but to support such a decision and to assist victims in finding a place of safety.

In itself, abuse does not appear to be a stated biblical justification for divorce, even though many divorces occur because of this. Sometimes, as a result of separation, the recalcitrant, hard-hearted person comes to the place of repentance and determination to reconcile. Whether or not this happens, in many cases at least temporary separation may be necessary for the physical, psychological, and spiritual well-being of the abused mate and family members. This is one of those many cases where problems arise that are not addressed specifically in Scripture but where Christians seek to act in accordance with our God-given wisdom, Christian compassion, and general biblical guidelines.

The Causes of Divorce

There is no one cause of divorce. This will not surprise counselors. Every marriage is different, and each divorce is precipitated by a unique combination of causes and circumstances. In previous chapters we have considered some of the causes of marital problems.[21] When these problems are not resolved, divorce is more likely. In addition, the following influences sometimes motivate one or both of the spouses to take action that will dissolve their marriage. We begin with the two generally accepted biblically sanctioned reasons for divorce.

1. *Sexual Unfaithfulness.* One experienced counselor has called infidelity the most common disruptive force in families, the most devastating, and the most universally accepted justification for divorce.[22] Although both of the partners may contribute to the adultery in some way, usually one is involved in the actual offense.[23] This only may be a one-time, spur-of-the-moment occurrence, but this can have a huge impact on families, even when the infidelity is confessed and discussed together by the couple. Whereas the offender may experience regret or guilt, the innocent partner feels betrayed, rejected, hurt, and sometimes self-condemning because he or she was not able to satisfy the wayward mate. It becomes more difficult to believe that one's spouse can be trusted in the future, and often there is anger, threat, and lowered self-esteem. We have seen that unfaithfulness is a legitimate biblical reason for divorce, but, under such circumstances, forgiveness and reconciliation are preferred when possible. Separation and divorce may be an easy and fast way to deal with an immediate problem, but ultimately this can be even more painful than staying together and trying to heal the marriage and bring restoration. The believer knows that all things are possible with God, even the restoring and growth of a marital relationship that has been ruptured by infidelity.[24]

2. *Desertion.* To the words of Moses and Jesus, Paul added desertion as a second legitimate reason for divorce. When an unbelieving partner leaves, the believer is

free to divorce. Suppose, however, that a believer forsakes the marriage. Does that justify divorce? The New Testament word for "depart" (*koridzetai*) is used thirteen times, and in no case does it imply divorce. The word means "to depart or separate." If the departed spouse, Christian or non-Christian, has been involved in sexual immorality or if the departure is so prolonged that there is little prospect of reconciliation, then perhaps an informal divorce has taken place whether it was sought or legally sanctioned. Probably, there is no value in denying that the marriage has, in fact, been dissolved.

3. *Escalating Conflict.* Following a whirlwind romance, one couple married within a month and soon began having problems. He enjoyed sailing; boats made her seasick. She liked to socialize with other couples; he wanted her company alone. He liked to have sex in the morning; she preferred evenings. Their relationship had genuine good times with laughter and happiness, but as the months passed there were more arguments, disagreements, and misunderstandings until they ended their marriage in divorce. This was a couple who married without really knowing each other. When they were faced with the reality of living together, they discovered that there were more differences than similarities. They each knew the value of working to improve the relationship, but with so little in common, conflicts became more prevalent and the couple lost hope.

While there is no biblical basis for separations such as this, many couples reach the point of being fed up with their unrewarding, seemingly incompatible, and frequently conflict-dominated relationships. As divorce has become more accepted and easy to get, there has been an increase in people who get divorces after ten, twenty, or more years of marriage. Some of these couples may be willing to put up with their dysfunctional relationship until the children are older, but then the conflict-ridden marriages are ended. These people may have begun their marriages with the belief that conflict would be minimal. Instead, they discovered what the famous family therapist Salvador Minuchen believed: conflict is an integral part of married life. Conflict is not the problem so much as the inability of couples to handle and resolve their differences.

4. *Social and Cultural Acceptance.* When a society is more accepting of divorce and remarriage, it is easier for a couple to abandon their marriage and go their separate ways. In many parts of the world, legal barriers to divorce have been lowered, the media have become more supportive of infidelity, the church has become more permissive, and many people have become less inclined to accept the sanctity and permanence of marriage. In addition, the women's liberation movement and some segments of academia (including university psychology and counseling departments) have become more verbal in their support of divorce. Entertainment, political, athletic, and other celebrities appear to be more open about their infidelities, often seeming to publicize their affairs as ways to draw attention to themselves and to boost their careers. While family values and commitment to marriage have come back into fashion, especially in some political circles, many people show by their actions that career advancement and personal fulfillment are such major goals in life that everything else—including a commitment to marriage—takes a lower priority. These social attitudes combine to make divorce a more viable option when marital tensions arise. Marriage termination is even easier when a couple is surrounded by friends who no longer disapprove of divorce or who have gone through divorces themselves without apparent ill effects. This is an attitude that says if others are doing it, why not us?

5. *Personal Immaturity*. Sometimes, divorce is caused by immaturity in one or both of the partners. Immaturity is difficult to define, but surely it includes an unwillingness to make and keep commitments, a disinclination to assume responsibility, a tendency to dominate, an insensitivity to the needs or interests of other people, and a self-centered view of life that insists upon the fulfillment of one's own wishes and rights. Attitudes like these stimulate conflict and work against attempts both to resolve difficulties and to avoid divorce.

Long-married couples know that marriage is a giving relationship. It involves a determination to encourage each other and a willingness to make the relationship work no matter what comes along. For many couples with strong marriages, divorce has never been an option. Their good relationships are built on dedication, persistence, sensitivity, communication skills, and a willingness to forgive. These marks of maturity are traits that some people never develop, and for this reason, their marriages frequently are unstable.

6. *Persisting Stresses*. When it is strong enough or when it lasts long enough, almost any stress can put so much pressure on a marriage that the couple may drift apart and/or begin thinking about divorce. Ongoing physical or psychological abuse, continuing financial pressures, boredom, alcoholism or other substance abuse in at least one of the partners, or the rigidities and resentments that can build up over the years have all led to divorce, especially when the spouses have seen their parents' marriages end, sometimes for similar reasons. When the marriages of friends or family members have broken up, there is less resistance to keeping one's own marriage together when stresses build.

Washing over all these reasons is the shift away from biblical values and the widespread rejection of absolute truth. The Old Testament book of Judges ends with a sobering statement. In those days there was no king, "so the people did whatever seemed right in their own eyes."[25] As a result, there were no commonly accepted values, no basis for authority, and nothing to stop the culture from sliding into moral chaos. Some might say this is where we are today. Others would take a less extreme view, acknowledge that God is protecting us from the end results of our rejection of him, but acknowledge that the moral and ethical shifts do not bode well for the future of marriage or of society. In a book on counseling and divorce, David Thompson says it in a more colorful way: "Where prior generations may have faced a road paved smooth with absolute values, the frost of relativism has caused that road to buckle and become filled with potholes for today's travelers," and marriages.[26]

The Effects of Divorce

More than thirty years ago, a writer named Jessie Bernard published an influential book titled *The Future of Marriage*.[27] Building on limited research and questionable data, the author wrote that a woman would have to be "slightly mentally ill," if she could "be happy in a relationship which imposes so many impediments on her, as traditional marriage does."[28] When she wrote her book, Bernard was among those who believed that lifelong commitment to monogamous marriage was a confining idea. Both adults and children would be happier, more fulfilled, and better adjusted, according to this thinking, if people gave themselves greater freedom to engage in sexuality apart from marriage and to come and go as they would like. According to these people, marriage was out; cohabitation and casual sex were in.

This conclusion was "just plain wrong," according to a report that appeared early in the twenty-first century.[29] Sifting through hundreds of research articles and building on their own empirical investigations, two scholars demonstrated the ways in which a committed, monogamous marriage is good for people, emotionally, physically, sexually, and economically. Other studies reached similar conclusions[30] and were supported by significant research that showed the long-term, harmful effects of divorce. In one landmark study, for example, researchers followed over one hundred children from divorced homes for twenty-five years.[31] The results were startling. Contrary to popular belief that the children would bounce back after the initial pain of the split, the majority suffered well into adulthood. When they came from divorced families, children grew into adults who were more insecure, lacking in confidence, and deeply concerned about their own marriages and ability to be parents. These adult children from divorced homes knew that a marriage breakup can thoroughly disrupt one's life, routines, feelings of self-worth, and sense of security. Like others who have been through divorce, the family members learned that divorce can affect people physically, psychologically, and spiritually long after the divorce. Often, it leads to emotional upheaval, irrational decisions, and interpersonal tensions. It affects the two people involved and their children, but its influence can extend as well to parents, other family members, fellow employees, friends, neighbors, people in the church, and even grandchildren who might be born later.[32]

Of course, each divorce is unique, and people do not all respond in the same ways. Although there is plenty of evidence to show the devastating effects of divorce, there also is evidence pointing to the ability of many people to get through it and to restore some semblance of normality into their lives. For example, high-conflict marriages adversely impact children, whether or not the couple stays together. In contrast, children adjust better if the parents are able to communicate without a lot of turmoil and if both commit to the well-being of their children.[33]

Some writers have attempted to divide the divorce process into stages, but none of these has strong research backing, probably because divorces are all so unique that they cannot all be fit into the same predictive pattern. Nevertheless, there are some common patterns. In most cases, one spouse is ahead of the other in deciding to end the marriage. When the issue is mentioned openly, the spouse who hears the news often feels helpless and devastated. The person who initiates the separation tends to have more power, since he or she has initial control. This can lead the other partner to try, unconsciously, to equalize the power, sometimes in overaggressive behavior, efforts to find allies within the family or without, or even in the development of psychological symptoms. Although this pattern appears in many marriage breakups, it may apply in similar ways when an individual breaks away from home, leaves a long-term employment situation, terminates a business partnership, quits college, or decides to change roommates or churches.

During this time people often begin to withdraw emotionally before they mention their thinking to anybody or before they separate physically. In a marriage, one spouse—sometimes termed the initiator—realizes that the relationship is going down and begins to wonder, privately at first, if the marriage might be over. Usually, without much conscious awareness, the initiator begins to withdraw his or her emotional investment from the relationship. There is a gradual gathering of information: could I make it on my own, how would the kids or my spouse respond, would I be lonely, could I find someone else, what would divorce do to my career, to my relationship with Christ? Unhappiness may be communicated in subtle ways during this period, but there is no mention of separation because the initiator is still pondering the idea and doesn't want to arouse suspicions, arguments, or possible retaliation. When the initiator raises the issue of a breakup, he or she has had time to think about the separation and find some secure niches and sources of support elsewhere.[34]

Sometimes, the couple comes for counseling at this time, but often one or both of the spouses has made the decision that counseling won't work and that the marriage is over. One or both of the partners may express the need for help in reconciliation, but secretly they want the counseling to fail, since this gives a greater rationale for continuing on the path to separation. All of this can leave scars in the form of depression, anger, anxiety, low self-esteem, feelings of failure, guilt, or self-doubt, especially in the partner who wants the marriage to continue.

Eventually, there comes a time when the couple must negotiate legal details of the separation, including how their possessions will be divided. The husband and wife may become adversaries, each trying to work out the best deal for themselves with the help of their legal advisors. This can be a period of tension, insecurity, anger, and sometimes a lot of expense. Each of the partners may admit to some fault in the marriage breakup, but more often there is blame and criticism of the mate.

Death in a family starts a period of mourning when friends, relatives, and others come together to give support and solace. Divorce in a family also involves a period of mourning, but often the friends and relatives scatter, sometimes torn apart by their confusion, anger, and uncertainty about how to respond. This can leave the separating partners feeling alone and abandoned. Even when the divorce is wanted, there can be sadness over the loss of a relationship that once was happy and fulfilling, along with difficulties in picking up the demands of life and learning to live without a mate. In time, most people begin to face the reality of their new status in life; set time aside for reflection and maybe for meditation, reading, and prayer; get involved with new friends; deliberately resist the tendencies to blame themselves or others; fight self-pity; and seek God's guidance in making realistic plans for the future. The pain is likely to last, and feelings of loss will persist, but often it is through the help of counselors that people are best able to adjust and move forward.

In counseling people during this time, counselors may observe the emotional, behavioral, social, physical, and spiritual effects of divorce. Most likely they also will see the effects of divorce on children.

1. *Emotional Effects.* As we have seen, divorce can be accompanied by an almost endless range of emotions, including anxiety, guilt, fear, sadness, depression (sometimes accompanied by thoughts of suicide), anger, bitterness, and frustration. Since divorce involves the loss of a love and the death of a relationship, it is valid to see this as a grief experience with all of the emotions that grieving involves. Unlike grief over a physical death, however, this is more psychological. It involves the tearing away and the death of a part of oneself. Like all grief reactions, the pain and sense of sadness seem greater at Christmas, holidays, anniversaries, and other special times of the year.

2. *Behavioral Effects.* Divorce affects how one feels, but it also influences what

one does. Routine activities have to continue, but preparing meals, paying bills, cleaning house, solving problems, and doing routine activities are now done without the help of a partner. If there are children, the divorced person must adjust to becoming a single parent, either living apart from the children or with the children present in a one-parent family. Often, the divorced parent must cope with the behavioral, academic (school work), and emotional effects of the divorce on the children.[35] Preoccupied with issues like these, one's work often suffers. Quality and quantity of output may decline, efficiency can drop, and relationships with work colleagues may suffer.

3. *Social Effects.* When a marriage breaks up, there is a ripple effect that extends to others, including:

- Family members in addition to the children, including parents and other relatives whose reactions may range from shock, rejection, rage, and fear to support and encouragement.
- Allies, such as personal friends, lawyers, some fellow church members or co-workers, and supportive relatives who encourage but sometimes complicate the situation with their unsolicited advice and opinions.
- Critics (some of whom may be in one's church or family) who reject, condemn, blame, and sometimes treat the divorced person judgmentally.
- Married friends who may feel threatened and many who are not sure how to react in the presence of the newly divorced person.
- Other single people, including many who may be understanding, some who are critical, and a few who could be potential dating partners or would like to make themselves available for a future relationship.

Divorced people often experience loneliness, insecurity, confusion about whether they should date or remarry, and concerns about identity or self-confidence. People who have been married for a long time feel awkward dating again. Most struggle with the issues of sex and self-control. In a minority of cases, the divorced person reacts to people as he or she has done in the past, remarries into a similar situation, repeats the same mistakes, and experiences another divorce. More often the difficulties of a disastrous first marriage are avoided in a subsequent marriage, but different problems develop, so that about 60 percent of second marriages fail.[36] Since at first they did not succeed, many people have initial fears of trying again.

4. *Physical Effects.* Divorce can be bad for one's health. It is well documented that stress affects the immune system and leaves the body with a reduced ability to fight off infections and disease. While this chapter was being written, *The Wall Street Journal* reported a study of 8,652 divorced and widowed people between ages 51 and 61. The longer they had been without their partners, "the higher the likelihood of heart or lung disease, cancer, high blood pressure, diabetes, stroke, and difficulties with mobility, such as walking or climbing stairs." Another study of 127,545 adults by the U.S. National Center for Health Statistics showed that divorced people reported more smoking, physical inactivity, and heavy drinking than married individuals, all of which can contribute to greater health problems.[37]

When they go through a divorce and adjust afterward, most people experience periods of indecision, confusion, or vacillation, all of which can put stress on the body that, in turn, increases the likelihood of disease.[38] In addition, sometimes there is a hyper-alertness, as if the person is waiting anxiously for something else to go wrong. The body, of course, cannot maintain a continuing state of tension and vigilance, so stress-produced illness often follows.

5. *Spiritual Effects.* How does all of this affect the Christian's spiritual life? As with any crisis, divorce can pull some people closer to Christ for strength and guidance. Others may get angry at God and spiritually rebellious, especially if there is rejection and criticism from the church. More common, perhaps, is the tendency to withdraw spiritually or drift away from God and from spiritual interests or activities. Worship becomes less important, personal times of prayer and Bible study become less frequent, and in the midst of all the other pressures, there is a gradual drifting away or letting go of spiritual interests and activities.

6. *Effects on the Children.* It will come as no surprise for you to read that divorce influences children in a variety of ways, depending in part on the child's age. Almost always, however, there is anger, a sense of loss and abandonment, fear about the future, a tendency to blame oneself accompanied by guilt, resentment at parents, and delays in maturity. In addition, there can be academic and relationship problems in school, regression to more childish behavior, such as bed-wetting or a return to thumb-sucking, and various forms of acting out and rebellion. One researcher interviewed 70 people, ages 18 to 35, and sent a survey to another 1500 young adults, all of whom had grown up in homes where the parents had divorced. The research confirmed that even though most children of divorce grow into successful and stable adults, the majority report that they were affected adversely by the parental divorce. These young adults had painful memories from their childhood years and often felt that they were living "between two distinct worlds," in which they had to act in different ways in their efforts to please both parents.[39] "Many adults with very successful lives still carry the residual trauma of their parents' breakup," according to one researcher from Johns Hopkins University.[40]

Clearly, children are the casualties of divorce. The separation may bring a relief from in-house arguing, abuse, and other turmoil, but there also are major changes in living conditions, concerns about the parents' capacity to parent, and often a need to take sides with the inner turmoil that this decision creates. All these childhood experiences can put pressure on the parents to do what they can to help the children. Often, one of the counselor's greatest roles is to help divorcing and divorced parents with this challenge.

Counseling and Divorce

A core purpose of Christian marriage counseling is to keep marriages together by helping couples develop smoother, more fulfilling, Christ-centered marital relationships. This type of counseling can be difficult, but it also can be very fulfilling, especially when the counselor is successful and marriages improve.

It is more difficult to work with couples who have decided to separate and who have no mutual desire for reconciliation. Even so, these people need counseling, and that is the purpose of Christian divorce counseling. It attempts to help an individual or couple separate from a marriage (a) in a way that is consistent with biblical teachings, (b) with a minimum of pain or destruction to themselves or to others, including their children, and (c) with a maximum of growth and new learning.

1. *Clarifying the Counselor's Own Attitudes.* Divorce counseling is rarely easy. Before beginning, ask yourself if you resist helping people who are divorcing, strongly oppose divorce, tend to be critical of divorced people, are likely to be angry with the individual or couple who comes for divorce counseling, or would be determined to keep them together regardless of their wishes. It might be difficult to see this in yourself, but if you have attitudes or values that will hinder your effectiveness, it seems unlikely that you will be able to listen carefully, understand without condemning, or be able to resist the pressures or your own inclination to take sides. It may be that you are like the lawyers or judges who withdraw from cases in which they are likely to be too personally or emotionally involved. Some very competent counselors would be wise to avoid this kind of work.

It can be helpful to take time for personal reflection on your attitudes toward divorce, divorced persons, and people who are going through divorce. In good conscience, can you help people face a divorce that is acceptable biblically? What if the proposed divorce has no biblical justification? Would you be able to forgive, support, and help even those who clearly are in the wrong? (If you abandon them, where will they get straightforward honest answers and compassionate help?) As a follower of Jesus Christ, what is your responsibility to people who are frustrated, confused, angry, and despondent because of marital breakdown? No one can answer these questions for you. Before God, and preferably with the help of a friend or another counselor, each counselor must consider difficult personal questions like those listed above before getting enmeshed in the demanding, sometimes heart-rending work of divorce counseling.

2. *Determining Goals.* One of the counselor's first and most difficult goals is to gain trust and to convince each of the divorcing partners of the counselor's neutrality.[41] Especially at the beginning, each spouse may be determined to present his or her position to the counselor, discredit the other partner's position, and try to enlist the counselor as an ally. It takes a while to show one's neutrality (especially if the counselor knows that he or she does not really feel neutral) and to get the participants working on goals that they both can accept. Ideally, the counselor may hope that the couple will abandon the divorce proceedings, reconcile, and replace their conflict-filled marriage with a new Christ-honoring relationship with each other. What is ideal, however, often is not very likely, especially if the couple has no such desires. In some cases it may be more realistic to strive for a logical, respectful, mutually agreeable resolution of problems, but in divorce counseling, couples often have no desire to be logical. I once read about a couple who fought so vociferously in the counseling sessions that the counselor had difficulty restraining them. "There is something you don't understand about divorce," the wife explained in the midst of one of these conflicts. "You are trying to be logical, but divorce is neither a civilized nor logical matter."[42]

As we will see in a later chapter, there may be some biological basis for the wife's statement. When intense emotion is involved, as is true in vehement conflict or trauma, a part of the brain is at work that does not involve the cognitive, reasoning facilities. Not all divorce counseling involves people like this couple, however, and for many it is possible to use logic or thinking to arrive at goals that may include the following:

- Encouraging couples to calm down from vindictive or self-centered hostile ways of relating. This may involve the counselor's modeling calmness and encouraging counselees to speak more slowly and without raising their voices or interrupting. This may seem like a small issue, but it is a huge step toward dealing with issues.

- Getting the agreement of both husband and wife to work together on the marriage at least for a specified period of time.
- Helping counselees evaluate their marital situation realistically, including consideration of the prospects for avoiding divorce.
- Discovering and discussing the counselees' expectations and desires for counseling, and evaluating whether these are (a) feasible, (b) consistent with the counselor's own moral and ethical standards, and (c) goals that the counselor can, without hesitation, help the counselees achieve. (Counselors are likely to have reduced effectiveness if they try to help counselees reach goals that the counselor cannot embrace or endorse.)
- Discussing biblical teachings on divorce and remarriage, and helping counselees make application of these teachings to their own marital situation.
- Helping couples admit, confess (to God and to each other), and change attitudes and actions that are sinful or harmful to the marriage relationship.
- Assisting those who need help in finding competent financial or legal assistance.
- Helping counselees reach mutually acceptable agreements concerning such practical issues as the division of property, alimony, or child custody and support.
- Guiding as couples formulate and perhaps practice ways for explaining the situation to children. Sometimes, this may involve including children in some counseling sessions.
- Teaching ways to avoid belittling, blaming, and criticizing each other, especially in the presence of children.
- Helping the spouses understand the effects of divorce on children (including grown children) and encouraging counselees not to use children in manipulative ways either to force children into taking sides or to get messages to the ex-spouse.
- Helping the couple (sometimes together, but more often separately) to cope with the emotions of divorce, including feelings of failure and rejection.
- Guiding in the adjustment to the post-divorce single life.
- Encouraging counselees in their spiritual growth and in their involvement with other people, including church people and Christian divorce recovery groups, where there is support, encouragement, friendship, and spiritual nourishment.

Unlike couples who come for marriage and family counseling, divorcing people may be less willing to come together or even separately, especially if they have made a firm decision to separate. Try to emphasize that some mutual sessions could be helpful, especially when the couple needs to make decisions about life after the divorce. Some counselees will prefer to leave those negotiations to their attorneys, but the counselor can offer to be present when these negotiations take place. Be available to help even if only one of the spouses comes for counseling.

3. *Working on Emotional, Identity, and Other Practical Issues.* For most people, divorce is a crisis, so counselors can give the support, guidance, and practical help that people in crises need.[43] In addition, a number of practical issues may arise. Often, these will come from the counselee, but at times the counselor may want to bring up issues such as effective ways to handle emotions and thinking, deal with conflict, or find a new identity.

(a) Handling Emotions. It is difficult to make an emotional separation, even from a relationship that no longer is intimate. It is possible for divorcing people to grieve over the loss of the relationship even if they do not feel grief over separating from a person whom they may have grown to dislike. As we have noted, anger, anxiety, frustration, depression, and a host of other feelings flood the divorced or divorcing counselee, sometimes when they are least expected. Often, there are conflicting feelings. Relief at being free, for example, may occur along with deep feelings of loneliness or rejection.

Most counselees will find it helpful to admit and express their emotions, but counselors can try to encourage movement beyond this emotional expression stage. Several guidelines may help with this growth. Encourage counselees to:

- Admit and express emotions honestly as they arise.
- Ask God to help them resist hatred, resentment, and bitterness. In a poignant farewell address to his staff on a day when they all must have felt angry and disappointed, Richard Nixon made a powerful statement: "Those who hate don't win until you hate them back—and that will destroy you." No matter how much one has been hurt, nothing is gained by revenge.
- Forgive, with God's help, and pray for those who have created pain and disappointment.

(b) Avoiding Harmful Thinking. When people are able to change their thinking, often this leads to changed feelings. The feelings that come with divorce often follow thinking of people who are facing changes in their lives. Counselees can be encouraged to accept what may not be changeable (in this case divorce), and then learn to resist dwelling on thoughts that can arouse painful feelings. One divorce counselor has called these the emotional traps of the past.[44] They include the following, which are not limited to divorcing couples but can apply to other problem situations as well:

- Making sweeping generalizations about oneself or others. These generalizations may have little or no basis in fact, but they can pull people down. Examples might include: "I am completely incompetent as a parent," or "My former spouse wants to get even with everybody."
- Developing and anticipating unrealistic expectations.
- Living out self-fulfilling prophecies. For example, a person may conclude that "from now on my life will be miserable." This attitude, in turn, can make life miserable.
- Always being defensive and expecting the worst. This can lead to behavior that alienates people and brings the worst.
- Wallowing in one's problems, talking about them incessantly, and always focusing on the negative.

- Blaming others persistently, especially one's mate.
- Rushing to new jobs, new locations, or new churches in an attempt to start fresh but without careful prior thought to the wisdom of the new moves.
- Living through others, such as finding satisfaction only in one's children or in the achievements of others.
- Assuming that life only can be meaningful again when there is another marriage.

(c) Guiding Mediation. Until recently, divorcing couples almost always turned to lawyers or accountants for help in resolving such practical issues as child custody, division of property, alimony, or tax preparation. By the end of the twentieth century, however, divorce mediation had become a fast-growing profession among counselors and others who understand legal issues relating to separation or divorce but who may not be lawyers.[45]

Mediation is a cooperative approach to conflict resolution that seeks to avoid the combative, adversarial approach. It is a system based on the needs of the parties and on their abilities to support themselves, let go of the past, and move on with their lives. Perhaps all counselors are likely to be involved in some mediation, but this is an area that requires special training if one is to do it well. Counselors who lack this training would be wise to find some competent and impartial person who is qualified to mediate successfully.

Even when a trained, nonlegal mediator is involved, couples often will want to consult with legal advisors. Encourage counselees to select attorneys carefully, to hire someone who specializes in divorces, and to avoid do-it-yourself divorce. It is best to select and work with competent Christian lawyers, if these are available. Such men and women are more likely to have an appreciation for the sanctity of marriage and be less inclined to stimulate hostility between the separating spouses.

(d) Finding New Identity. Divorce plunges the formerly married person into singleness again. The individual is alone now, often a parent without a partner, and labeled with new title: *divorced.* This can bring insecurities and the need to readjust. The newly divorced sometimes dwell in the past and wonder how they will fare in the future. Will they be accepted? How will they relate to married friends?

It helps if these people can discuss their insecurities and talk about life once again as a single person. Some may need help with self-esteem, learning to accept themselves as God accepts them. Others may need to be put in contact with other same-gender people who have gone through a divorce and can give fresh perspectives. Remind counselees that it isn't easy to change our identities, and it takes time to shift in the ways we think about ourselves.

4. *Building and Redefining Relationships.* Divorce impacts relationships in a number of ways. Often, the divorced person finds new friends and builds new relationships, but he or she also must redefine relationships with the former spouse, the children, old friends and relatives, or people in the church, among others.

(a) The Former Spouse. When a couple has shared the same bed, goals, joys, trials, and hopes, it is difficult to separate, to become the brunt of the ex-spouse's anger, to deal with one's own feelings of anger or rejection, to be comfortable in talking to or about one's former partner, and to avoid showing excessive curiosity about the former mate's present life. It can be stressful for divorced people who struggle with loneliness and daily hardships to hear reports or to watch a former mate remarry and appear to be happy. Getting along with one's ex-mate requires patience and understanding on both sides, especially at the beginning when feelings are strong. Later, as time passes and new relationships are formed, the emotional entanglement may subside, but this may take many months, during which regular talks with a counselor or understanding friend can be helpful. In most cases it may be best if the counselee can make a clean break with the former mate. Seeing an ex-mate reminds one of the past that has gone, arouses feelings that appeared to be subsiding, and can delay healing and the beginning of a new life. It is difficult to make a clear break, however, if the two ex-partners live in the same community or are committed to sharing child-rearing responsibilities.

(b) The Children. How do children really feel about the divorce of their parents? To find out, the British Broadcasting Corporation gave video cameras to twenty-one British children and invited them to record their feelings. All of the divorced parents gave their permission. One of the children was named Ben Gedye.

> Ben was seven years old when his parents separated, ten years old when he talked to his camera over a three-month period. Repeatedly, he expressed his love for both of his parents but talked about his concern that he might make them more unhappy. He didn't want to go away to boarding school but made that decision himself because he thought that if he was away at school he would not hurt either of them.
>
> "All we ever do is go back and forth, back and forth," Ben said glumly to the camera, with sorrowful eyes peering out from behind oversize glasses. In his hand he turned a toy cube over and over and said, "It's like we are a toy for them to play with, that we have to share."
>
> Ben talked about the traumas of his life, his jealousies and insecurities, his father's new wife who "stole my daddy." He talked about the conflicts with his new stepbrother, who is a good athlete, in contrast to Ben, who is not.
>
> The parents and the new stepmother have all tried to cooperate, and all share a concern for Ben and his sister. When the documentary was shown, Ben had reached age thirteen. "One of the things I learned from making the film was that things . . . change," he said, in reflecting on his experience. "I've learned that life moves on, and you can't dwell on sad things."[46]

Watching their parents go through a divorce can be painful for children, especially during the first twelve to eighteen months following the separation. Often confused, afraid, and insecure, these young people may hold their emotions inside and rarely have the opportunity, like Ben, to share them even to a video camera. Instead, the feelings and frustrations may be expressed in truancy, fighting with siblings, competing with half brothers or sisters, running away (for Ben it was escape to a boarding school), nightmares, sickness, regression to more childish behavior, or school problems (academic difficulties and frequent absences). The problems can be greater when the child does not get along with the custodial parent, when contact with the other parent is significantly reduced, or when parents disagree about how children should be co-parented.[47] While many parents genuinely want what is best for their offspring, sometimes children become unwilling weapons used by the husband and wife to attack and manipulate each other. Children may become like prisoners of war pulled from one camp to the other and subjected to brainwashing. At first these children are hurt and uncertain about their futures. In time they become angry and resentful of being used.

Even when they determine to get along and do whatever they can to help their children, the separating parents also can have difficulties. The parent who is given custody of the children often feels overwhelmed with the responsibility to care for the children alone and to meet their needs at a time when everyone is vulnerable emotionally. The other parent may feel guilty, lonely, sad, or angry because of the separation, but sometimes happy to be relieved of the child-rearing responsibilities.

How do divorcing and divorced parents relate to their children? There can be no rules that apply to all, of course, but there are guidelines that parents could find helpful. These can be shared and discussed with counselees.

- Remember that the children are not adults. Do not expect them to be your confidants or to take on adult roles that they cannot handle.
- Be the parent you are (without trying to be a buddy, big brother, or big sister).
- Do not force the children into playing the role of the parent who is not present.
- Be honest with your children, but also be aware of how much information they can handle.
- Do whatever you can to be sensitive to their feelings.
- Do not criticize your former spouse in front of the children—even if you have good reason to criticize.
- Resist any temptations to make your children undercover agents who report on the other parent's current activities.
- Recognize that the children of divorce need both a mother and a father. Don't deny them this right, if at all possible.
- If the children live with the other parent, don't shower them with good times and gifts before sending them back to the realities of daily living. Children need to see and spend time with the departed parent in a real life setting.
- Be open with the children about your dating life and social interests. At the same time, be alert to their feelings. In time, Ben Gedye learned to get along with his new stepmother, in large measure because both parents and the father's new wife all worked to help him adjust.
- Help the children keep alive their good memories of the past marriage.
- Work out a child-care and management arrangement with your ex-spouse. If necessary, seek a mediator who can help the former partners agree on ways that lead to the best growth and development of the children.
- If possible, try not to disrupt the many areas in your children's lives that offer them safety and security.
- If your child does not resume normal development and growth within a year or eighteen months of the divorce, consider consulting a counselor or school psychologist.[48]

It should not be assumed that divorce affects only younger children. Some couples live together in misery and sometimes in conflict, avoiding divorce until the children are grown and have left home. We can admire the dedication of these parents and their concern for the children, but many fail to realize that adult children also can be hurt deeply by a parental divorce.[49] And there is evidence that children who live in homes marked by conflict also are affected negatively by the tensions.[50]

(c) Other Adults. Some friends may be supportive at the time of divorce, but others are critical, unsure how to help, threatened by the divorced person's new status, uncertain about what to say, or inclined to withdraw. Parents of the divorced couple often are confused, angry, hurt, disappointed, and not certain how to act, especially if there are grandchildren in the custody of the former son-in-law or daughter-in-law. Often, the divorced person doesn't know how to relate to the couples with whom the husband and wife formerly had a relationship. The counselor can encourage talk about these issues and can give support and guidance as former relationships are redefined and as new relationships are formed.

(d) The People at Church. The local congregation should be a place where people find support, caring, and love. Too often, however, church members are inclined to show criticism, subtle rejection, and sometimes avoidance of anyone who is divorced or divorcing. Sometimes, the church people are deeply disappointed, sad, and not sure how they should relate to divorced people in their midst. Some are distressed over the theological implications of divorce, especially if it is followed by another marriage. When confronted with these attitudes, counselors can assist in two ways: by helping church members understand, accept, and (if necessary) forgive the divorced people in their midst, and by helping counselees face and cope with church rejection. If the counselor also is a pastor or other church leader, he or she can lead the way by modeling Christlike attitudes toward divorced people.

5. *Helping Divorced People Rebuild Their Lives.* The divorced person cannot live in the past or worry excessively about the future. Bills must be paid, work must be done, life must go on. The counselee can be helped to identify and learn from past mistakes, make immediate decisions about such practical issues as housing and finances, reestablish life priorities, set realistic goals for the future, and move ahead to accomplish God's purpose for his or her life.

Sooner or later many divorced people begin thinking about whether they should start dating and moving toward another marriage. The Christian must determine whether remarriage is permitted biblically, although many believers seem to pass over this consideration. Christian counselors will differ in their views on this issue, but at some time the possibility of remarriage should be discussed with counselees.

In the meantime, divorced people may resist the need to start dating again, "like teenagers." Some fear that they never will find a new spouse, and it is common to wonder if there will be a repeat of earlier mistakes. At times there are fears about how the children would react to another marriage, especially if the potential new mate also has children that would all be part of a blended family.

The counselor can help with these fears. Discourage people from marrying too quickly, and if you feel comfortable doing so, help them choose another mate cautiously and wisely. Before marrying again, divorced persons could be encouraged to ponder what they learned from the past failed marriage and how mistakes can be avoided in the future. Premarital counseling should be considered essential. This will be different from counseling with never-married couples who have not had the experiences of the formerly married. Table 32–1 gives some considerations for couples anticipating a new marriage.[51]

If children are involved, it may be helpful to discuss some of the problems

Table 32–1

Some Issues and Questions for Couples Facing Remarriage

- Give some reasons why you are ready to remarry.
- List some reason why you are not yet ready to remarry.
- What is the evidence that you have moved beyond your previous marriage? What issues from the past are in danger of impacting your new marriage?
- Who have you not forgiven from your previous relationship?
- What traits and strong points do you bring to a new marriage? (This is a look at self-concept.)
- What is there about you—your attitudes, personality, and weaknesses—that could bring potential problems to your new marriage and your new spouse?
- What are your top ten needs, and how will these be met in your marriage?
- What are the top ten needs of your intended spouse, and how can you meet these needs?
- Who are the people in your life that could undermine your marriage, and how can you overcome their influence?
- In addition to the above, if you remarry, what are the major problems or obstacles that you are likely to face? In what specific ways will you get over these?
- Who will be impacted by the new marriage, and how will they be affected?
- What is your relationship with God, and how does this align with the spirituality of your intended spouse?
- What is the evidence that your intended marriage is consistent with biblical principles?
- If you get married and have difficulties, how will you resolve conflict, and where will you go for counseling help if you sense the need for this?

found in blended families.[52] In the BBC documentary, Ben Gedye talked about adjusting when his father married a woman with a son who was Ben's age. Both boys felt pushed out, jealous of the other, and struggled with the adjustment of rooming together. Other issues for blended families can include: fears that the new marriage will fall apart like the ones that came before, disagreements over finances (previously divorced people sometimes want to keep their money separate from each other), problems arising from the husband and wife having different authority over different children, the possibility of unequal financial realities for children in the same household, children's attempts to divide the newly married couple in hopes of breaking up the marriage, parental jealousy of children's allegiances, increased danger of sexual involvement with the new spouse's children, and unclear relationships with grandparents. Not surprising, especially at the start of a new marriage, there is closer bonding between each child and his or her biological parent than between the child and the new stepparent. This can create further tension, especially in times of stress. We should emphasize, however, that many blended families work well from the beginning. The problems that might arise do not make successful remarriage impossible, but it is helpful to know that blended families encounter unique difficulties as they try to combine old loyalties with new ties.[53]

In all of this, remind yourself and your counselees that God wants the best for his children. He forgives those who confess and guides those who want his leading. Divorced persons and their counselors are not left alone to fend for themselves. The Holy Spirit is the constant guide and companion of committed divorced believers and their Christian counselors.

Preventing Divorce

The most obvious way to prevent divorce is to build stronger marriages—marriages based on scriptural principles and characterized by love, commitment, and open communication. Marriage enrichment programs are one way to accomplish this. It is widely agreed that these seminars build better marriages and steer people away from divorce, but at present there does not appear to be a lot of solid empirical research to back up this conclusion. One problem is that people whose marriages could most benefit from the enrichment programs often are the ones who are least likely to attend. Prevention of divorce becomes more difficult as the couple becomes more firmly committed to their decision to separate. Perhaps a key element in divorce prevention is to instill hope. There are several ways in which this can be done.

1. *Counseling.* When they come for counseling, many couples have abandoned most hope. Point out to them that they care enough about the marriage to give counseling a try, which indicates that there must be at least a glimmer of hope. Before a couple decides to separate, they have a responsibility before God, to themselves, and to their families to do whatever is possible to bring renewal to the marriage and avoid divorce. This assumes a calm and reasoned approach to marriage problems, but often this is lacking. Nevertheless, if a husband and wife both agree to work at resolving conflicts and building a better relationship, there is a good possibility that divorce can be prevented. One of the counselor's main challenges may be getting the couple to this point of commitment.

2. *Self-Examination.* With or without counseling, each spouse can be encouraged to ask, "What am I doing (or failing to do) that contributes to the problems in my marriage?" Are there constant criticisms, unrealistic expectations, attitudes of bitterness, refusals to forgive, evidences of unwillingness to work at building the marriage, or equally harmful attitudes and behaviors that contribute to the marital tension? Has there been marital infidelity, lying, or other destroyers of trust? Jesus instructed his followers to look at (and presumably to remove) the faults in themselves before criticizing others.[54] Most people have blind spots and do not see themselves clearly, but God can enlighten understanding, often through the observations of a counselor or the insights of another person who is close. Even when they have insight into their own attitudes and harmful actions, it is difficult for individuals or couples to change without divine help and the supportive guidance of a counselor.

3. *Reconciliation.* It is rare, but some couples file for divorce and then try to reconcile. Most often reconciliation comes only after hours of realistic, often draining, discussion of the problems involved. Surely, however, reconciliation is the desire of a God who is willing to help and who never wants divorce.

At different times we have noted that the divorce rate among Christians, at least in the United States, appears to be no different from divorce among nonbelievers. This sobering conclusion does not undermine the fact that only God can mend and bind a broken marriage. Separately and together, couples who want to prevent separation must seek divine wisdom, strength, and guidance as they work to keep their spiritual lives growing and their motivation consistent while they make changes that will rebuild their relationships. Daily Scripture reading, a commitment to worship, and personal times of prayer are powerful forces that open couples to the healing power of God.

This brings us to the influence of the church. Believers are instructed to bear one another's burdens, care for one another, and pray for each other. For Christians, prayer, compassion, caring, and support are not optional. These are commanded by God. To prevent divorce in their midst, believers should be instructed to pray for married couples, even when their marriages are healthy. Effective prayer and compassionate caring can accomplish much, including healing,[55] and perhaps even the healing of unhealthy marriages.

Conclusions About Divorce

Recently a friend went to take the exam to get his license as a psychologist. The exam was open only to people who had completed rigorous training, and my friend had studied for weeks to prepare for the big test. A few weeks later he got the results and learned that he had failed. The news came as no surprise. In the state where he lives, the licensing exam is difficult and few people pass, at least on the first try. So now my friend is studying again, preparing to take the exam the next time it is offered. When he finally passes, as he will, his license will be evidence that he is competent to counsel and charge for his services.[56]

Almost every license is granted on the basis of competence. A driver's license proves that the recipient has passed a test and knows how to drive. A license to practice medicine means that the doctor has mastered a body of knowledge about the body's functioning and has acquired the necessary skills to diagnose and treat diseases. In contrast, almost anybody can get a marriage license, and it has nothing to do with one's competence to be a husband or wife. Schools teach driver's education, but they rarely give courses in marriage competence, and church family life programs sometimes are no better. Perhaps it is not surprising that so many marriages break down and disintegrate into divorce.

Building a good and lasting marriage is rarely easy. It is romantic and idealistic for a couple to think that their love is strong enough to resist problems, but stable marriages more often build on persisting commitment, knowledge, sensitivity, interpersonal skills, and a willingness to live in accordance with biblical teaching. The Christian counselor, like others in the local congregation, can help to ensure that good marriages are built, cared for, and repaired when there are signs of breakdown. Backed by prayer and the support of others, marriages can grow, broken relationships can be restored, and divorce can be prevented. When divorce occurs, despite the counselor's best efforts, the separated couple can be helped to deal with the separation and rebuild their lives. This, too, is a part of Christian marriage counseling.

KEY POINTS FOR BUSY COUNSELORS

➤ For most people, divorce brings pain and turmoil, even when divorce was wanted.

➤ From the beginning, the Bible presents marriage as a permanent, intimate union between a husband and wife.

➤ Divorce is nowhere commanded in Scripture, and neither is it encouraged. God hates divorce but he does permit it, first when one's mate is guilty of sexual immorality and unwilling to repent and live faithfully with the marriage partner, and second, when one of the mates is an unbeliever who willfully and permanently deserts the believing partner.

➤ Christians disagree about whether the Bible permits remarriage of divorced persons. Matthew 5:32 and Matthew 19:9 appear to indicate that when the mate has been sexually unfaithful and divorce occurs, the faithful partner has the right to remarry because the immorality has dissolved the marriage.

➤ There is no single cause of divorce. Among the common causes are:
  ▪ Sexual infidelity.
  ▪ Desertion by one of the mates.
  ▪ Escalating conflict.
  ▪ Greater cultural acceptance of divorce, making separation easier.
  ▪ Personal immaturity.
  ▪ Persisting stress.

➤ Divorce impacts people in different ways, but counselors often see:
  ▪ Emotional effects, including anxiety, guilt, fear, sadness, depression, anger, bitterness, and frustration.
  ▪ Behavioral effects that include declining work productivity and difficulties in completing routine tasks.
  ▪ Social effects, including changing relationships with family, friends, work colleagues, and fellow church members.
  ▪ Physical effects, including increased illness and declining health.
  ▪ Spiritual effects, in which some people draw closer to Christ but others drift away.
  ▪ Harmful effects on the children, even when the divorcing couple tries to make the separation smooth for the children, and even when the offspring are adults.

➤ Christian counseling with divorced and divorcing people seeks to help the individual or couple separate from a marriage:
  ▪ In a way that is consistent with biblical teachings.
  ▪ With a minimum of pain or destruction to themselves and others.
  ▪ With a maximum of growth and new learning.

➤ In working with divorced and divorcing people, counselors seek to:
  ▪ First be clear on their own attitudes toward divorce.
  ▪ Help counselees determine counseling goals.
  ▪ Work on emotional, identity, and other practical issues.
  ▪ Build and redefine relationships with the former spouse, extended family, the couple's children, and others.
  ▪ Help divorced people rebuild their lives.

➤ The most obvious way to prevent divorce is to build stronger marriages—marriages based on scriptural principles and characterized by love, commitment, and open communication. Marriage enrichment programs are one way to accomplish this, but so are counseling, self-examination, and efforts to replace divorce proceedings with reconciliation.

➤ Ultimately, it is God alone who brings separating couples back together.

➤ Counseling people who are considering separation, divorcing, or approaching remarriage can be difficult work, but it can make a huge difference in the lives of the family members who are involved.

PART SEVEN

Control Issues

33

Mental Disorders

Andy Behrman is in his mid-forties, married, a father, living in Los Angeles, where he works as a successful writer and public speaker. That's a big change from where he was less than fifteen years ago when his life fell apart.

During the years when he was growing up, Andy's family never suspected that anything was wrong, although he always felt "different." His mother and sister were very driven, still are, and his father was "somewhat obsessive-compulsive," but apart from Andy's mood swings and compulsive need to wash his hands repeatedly, he was assumed to be a normal kid. Eventually he got through college and became a successful public relations consultant, all the while hiding the out-of-control mood swings that pulled him into depression and then into emotional states that were "full of excitement, color, noise, speed," with nights "fueled by drugs, anonymous sex, aimless travel, and midnight pastrami binges."

According to his web site, Andy "slept only three hours a night. Sometimes, he didn't go to bed for days. He was a public relations agent, an art dealer, a hustler, and a forger who made millions. He would fly from Zurich to the Bahamas, then back again to balance out the hot and cold. He spent his money on wild shopping sprees all around the globe, buying up clothing, paintings, and extravagant gifts for friends. He gave complete strangers spontaneous gifts of thousands of dollars from the cash he kept in his freezer. He was moving at breakneck speed—fueling his behavior with drugs and alcohol."

At some time, when this was all starting, Andy saw the first in a parade of psychiatrists. "I only went to those doctors when I was in my down periods, feeling terrible," he said later. "I didn't go when I was feeling elated or manic. My lows were filled with rage, anger, and irritability. I was dysfunctional and agitated, really miserable with life, and desperately trying to get back to where I had been the day before," when he had soared with excitement and an overload of sensory stimulation. At his most psychotic period, he imagined himself chewing on sidewalks and swallowing sunlight. In the midst of an emotional high, he was drawn into an art counterfeiting scheme, "the most exciting proposition I'd heard in years." Andy soared with exhilaration until he was arrested and sentenced to prison. "I thought I wouldn't make it to my next birthday," he told a reporter. "I saw eight psychiatrists before I got my diagnosis." Bipolar disorder. All together, over his twenty years of undiagnosed, out-of-control bipolar disorder, Andy took thirty-seven different medications prescribed by his doctors and had nineteen electroconvulsive shock treatments.

Finally stabilized by medications, Andy wrote Electroboy: A Memoir of Mania. *It's an honest look at his life, a book that one reviewer called funny, always honest, raunchy, and likely to be distasteful to some readers. At last report it was being adapted as a motion picture—the story of a man who experienced a severe emotional disorder and recovered to tell about it.*[1]

I n my early days as a professor, undergraduate students would enroll in my Introduction to Psychology class, where they would learn about scientific methods, emotion, principles of learning, theories of personality, and other topics that I tried to make interesting and relevant. But none of this captured student interest as did the classes on abnormal psychology. The students were eager to learn why some people, including college-age young people, would develop symptoms of mental illness. They showed interest in the different types of pathology and how treatment by counselors and other mental-health professionals could bring improvement—and sometimes failed. Occasionally, the whole class would visit a local mental hospital and spend a weekend interacting with the patients and staff, learning firsthand about the struggles of people who were mentally ill.

Mental disorders were recognized as far back as the sixth century B.C. Egyptian documents make references to senile dementia, melancholia, and hysteria. Early philosophers like Hippocrates and Plato proposed causes for psychopathology, and in the centuries that followed, a variety of fascinating but sometimes torturous treatments was proposed for relieving the symptoms and dealing with people assumed to be lunatics, demon possessed, or out of their minds. This began to change with the emergence of effective treatment methods, including the development and widespread use of psychopharmacological drugs. Even so, the interest in psychopathology continues, especially when school teachers, employers, neighbors, pastors, or others find that somebody they know struggles with mental illness.

What Is Mental Illness? There is no answer that everyone would accept, but in general this term describes a broad variety of symptoms that could fall into several overlapping categories. First, there usually is some sort of *distress,* which could include anxiety, depression, anger, or other suffering that is emotional or psychological more than it is physical. *Deviance* indicates that the person thinks or acts in ways that most people in the society would consider to be unusual or socially inappropriate. *Disability* and *dysfunction* both refer to the fact that the person with a mental disorder may be unable to attain his or her goals, have difficulty handling the day-to-day routines of living, or not be able to hold a job or a clear conversation. People with phobias, personality disorders, or deep depression would be examples.

The distress, deviance, or disability may be mild and minimally bothersome, but these also can be more disruptive and sometimes of severe intensity. In mild disorders the symptoms are hardly noticed. The person functions well in all areas, is interested and involved in a wide range of activities, gets along well with others, is generally satisfied with life, and has no major worries or problems in life, although all may not be well. The person with a bipolar (manic-depressive) disorder, for example, may have minor mood swings but be able to function normally with medication that makes needed chemical changes in the brain. At the other extreme are those whose thinking may be distorted, whose communication may be faulty, whose contact with reality is impaired, who have difficulty getting along with others, who often cannot function in society, and who may be in persistent danger of self-harm or of harming others.[2] Andy Behrman was able to hold a job and hide some of his impulsive behavior, but he and his closest friends knew that his life was out of control.

What some will call mental illness, insanity, or nervous breakdown, professional counselors are more likely to call psychopathology, emotional disturbance, or mental disorder. The latter term is used by the American Psychiatric Association in its classification manual, and this is the term that will be used most often in this chapter.

Mental disorders are not all the same. Several hundred, perhaps thousands, of disorders have been identified and classified into different categories. Perhaps it is not surprising that with all the different types of disorders, the classifications have differed as well. One of the most widely used is the medically oriented classification in the *Diagnostic and Statistical Manual* (DSM) of the American Psychiatric Association. As this classification is revised periodically, often because of intense lobbying by special interest groups,[3] the manual gets a new edition identified by a Roman numeral, such as DSM-IV. This publication classifies and categorizes disorders into five domains of information known as axes. For our purposes, Axis I is the most relevant because it contains the major mental disorders that counselors are likely to encounter. These can be categorized according to their symptoms and severity of impairment. Schizophrenia, for example, is a disorder that can be mild, moderate, or severe in intensity. It has a variety of causes and can be divided into several types, each of which has its own list of symptoms—only some of which may be present in any one person.

It is beyond the scope of this book for us to describe even the major mental disorders, but Table 33–1 gives an overview based on the DSM-IV classification.[4] Although counselors may not be familiar with all of the disorders, it is important to be aware of the major symptoms of psychopathology, the major causes of mental disorders, and some of the ways in which mental patients and their families can be helped.[5]

The Bible and Mental Disorders

The Bible says little about mental disorders and does not use the language of psychopathology. It does give us insights into human nature, shows us our human condition before God, gives some understanding of human suffering, and offers hope. In his letter to the Romans, Paul described how sin entered the human race, ruled over all people, and gave us deprived minds to do what we should not do. As a result, our "minds became dark and confused. . . . Instead of worshiping the glorious, ever-living God," humans worshiped idols.[6] Some were made out of wood or stone; today the idols have names like materialism, success, or power.

In the Bible, sin refers both to specific acts of sin and to a state of sinfulness that have left the human race in a condition of brokenness and helplessness. Sin's effect can be seen everywhere—in our moral standards, criminal actions, interpersonal conflicts, and undoubtedly in our symptoms of psychopathology. The message of the Gospel is that God does not leave us to flounder in the consequences of sin. Along with the brokenness, we can have hope because God had compassion on us and sent his Son Jesus Christ to redeem us. He gives us the gift of eternal life after we die, and periods of fulfilled life while we are here on earth.[7] In both the Old and New Testaments, we see God as a compassionate shepherd who knows that his human flock can be harassed and helpless but who cares for us with compassion and gentleness.[8] Church leaders and other elders are exhorted to be shepherds of God's flock that is under their care.[9] Throughout its history the church has had the privilege of caring for the weak and helpless. The mentally ill have not always been treated with understanding and dignity, but

Table 33–1

Major Mental Disorders

(Groups of Conditions in DSM-IV)

1. Disorders usually first diagnosed in infancy, childhood, or adolescence:
   - Mental retardation
   - Learning disorders (including reading disorders)
   - Motor skills disorder
   - Communication disorder (including stuttering and language disorders)
   - Pervasive developmental disorders (including autistic disorder and Asperger's disorder)
   - Attention-deficit and disruptive behavior disorders
   - Feeding and eating disorders of infancy or early childhood
   - Tic disorders
   - Elimination disorders (including enuresis and encopresis)
   - Other disorders of infancy, childhood, or adolescence
2. Delirium, dementia, and amnesic and other cognitive disorders:
   - Delirium
   - Dementia
   - Amnesic disorders
   - Other cognitive disorders
3. Mental disorders due to general medical condition not elsewhere classified
4. Substance-related disorders:
   - Alcohol-related disorders
   - Amphetamine-related disorders
   - Caffeine-related disorders (including caffeine intoxication, caffeine-induced anxiety disorder, and caffeine-induced sleep disorder)
   - Cannabis-related disorders
   - Cocaine-related disorders
   - Hallucinogen-related disorders
   - Inhalant-related disorders
   - Nicotine-related disorders
   - Opioid-related disorders
   - Phencyclidine-related disorders
   - Sedative, hypnotic, and other related disorders
5. Schizophrenia and other psychotic disorders

6. Mood disorders:
  - Depressive disorders
  - Bipolar disorders

7. Anxiety disorders (including panic disorders, phobias, post-traumatic stress disorder, acute stress disorder, and generalized anxiety disorder

8. Somatoform disorders (including pain disorders and hypochondriasis)

9. Factitious disorders (disorders in which physical or psychological symptoms are feigned)

10. Dissociative disorders (including amnesia and multiple personality disorder)

11. Sexual and gender disorders:
  - Sexual dysfunctions (including disorders of sexual desire, arousal, or sexual functioning)
  - Paraphilias (including exhibitionism, pedophilia, sexual masochism, sadism, fetishism, or voyeurism)
  - Gender identity disorders

12. Eating disorders (including anorexia nervosa and bulimia nervosa)

13. Sleep disorders

14. Impulse-control disorders (including kleptomania, pathological gambling, and pyromania)

15. Personality disorders

16. Other conditions (including medication-induced disorders, malingering, relational problems, academic problems, occupational problems, religious or spiritual problems, bereavement, phase-in-life problems, acculturation problems, and noncompliance to treatment)

---

overall the church has been at the forefront of pastoral care for those with physical, psychological, and spiritual needs.

Even though there are no biblical classifications of mental disorders and little is said about treatment, it is clear that psychopathology was recognized and perhaps common. King David once pretended to be insane. His behavior was feigned, but it gives a brief insight into some of the symptoms of psychopathology that were recognized in Old Testament times. David "pretended to be insane, scratching on doors and drooling down his beard," so that his enemy considered him to be a madman.[10]

Many years later, King Nebuchadnezzar of Babylon had a dream followed by a voice that sounded forth and came down from heaven:

O King Nebuchadnezzar, this message is for you! You are no longer ruler of this kingdom. You will be driven from human society. You will live in the fields with the wild animals, and you will eat grass like a cow . . . until you learn that the Most High rules over the kingdoms of the world, and gives them to anyone he chooses.

That very same hour the prophecy was fulfilled, and Nebuchadnezzar was driven from human society. He ate grass like a cow, and he was drenched with the dew of heaven. He lived this way until his hair was as long as eagle's feathers and his nails were like birds' claws.

After this time had passed, I, Nebuchadnezzar, looked up to heaven. "My sanity returned, and I praised and worshiped the Most High and honored the one who lives forever."[11]

In the New Testament, Festus (the local Roman leader) interrupted Paul's presentation of the Gospel and shouted, "Paul, you are insane. Too much study has made you crazy!"[12] The word translated "insane" in one version of the Bible is given different English words elsewhere. The King James Bible, for example, used the term "lunatic" rather than "insane," but some more modern translations refer to seizures or epilepsy.

Like modern medicine, most contemporary people would view epilepsy as a physiological brain disorder that sometimes leads to seizures but should not be equated with insanity. (In modern usage, insanity is a legal term used to describe people who are considered not guilty of criminal actions "by reason of insanity." At the time of their crimes, these people are assumed to have had an inability to fully grasp the meaning of their actions.) Most Christian counselors would agree that physical illness, epilepsy, mental disorders, and demon possession are terms that refer to different conditions, even though many of the symptoms are similar.[13]

The Bible makes reference to many of the emotions that form the basis of mental disorders, including anxiety, anger, discord, jealousy, envy, lust, dissension, selfish ambition, impatience, lack of self-control, idolatry, orgies, marital infidelity, gluttony, drunkenness, strife, lying, violence, and a host of others. There also are biblical examples of suicide, including the deaths of Saul, who fell on his sword, and Judas, who hanged himself.[14]

Despite these biblical references, it does not follow that mental disorders always involve or come from deliberate sin in the afflicted person's life. A few are like David, who took on some characteristics of abnormality for his own purposes. More people are like Nebuchadnezzar, whose psychopathology resulted from a deliberate refusal to obey God. Others are like Job. He was a morally upright, God-fearing man whose physical and emotional problems resulted from causes other than personal sin. Ultimately, all physical and mental disorders are caused by sin, which entered the world centuries ago. Scripture is clear in its teaching that all of us are sinners, but that does not mean that psychopathology necessarily results from deliberate personal sinful actions in the person with a mental disorder. What, then, are the causes?

The Causes of Mental Disorders

Depending on where you live or on when you read these words, the prevalence of mental disorders could be high. The rates vary from place to place, and often there are age differences. When compared with older adults, for example, people under forty-five have about twice the incidence of mental disorders.[15] Children and adolescents seem to be especially vulnerable.[16] Overall, mental disorders are equally divided between men and women, but there are gender differences in the types of problems. Women suffer more often from depression and phobias; men have more problems with drug and alcohol abuse or with antisocial personalities. In addition, men are more reluctant to admit that they have a problem and more resistant to getting help.

Following the September 11 terrorist attacks on the United States, counselors noticed an increase in depression among men, but many refused to admit their symptoms or the need for help. To counter this stigma and to increase awareness of male depression, the National Institute of Mental Health launched a major media campaign with the message *Real Men. Real Depression.* Posters, billboards, magazine ads, television advertising, and signs were hung in high-traffic areas such as airports to raise awareness of depression in men and convey the message that mental illness is not a personal failing, sign of weakness, or evidence of femininity. The campaign targeted men who resist mental-health services.[17]

Whatever the disorders may be, it is clear that they differ from person to person and can have unique symptoms and causes. If we were to visit the psychiatric ward of a hospital, we might find two patients with similar diagnoses but different life histories leading to their hospitalization. Just as a heart attack and appendicitis have different causes, so do the various mental disorders. Despite these differences, all mental disorders arise from a combination of present stresses and past predisposing influences.

1. *Present Stress.* There are at least four categories of stresses that contribute to the development of mental disorders: biological, psychological, social, and spiritual. Biological stresses include disease, the influence of drugs, toxins, or pollutants in the air, brain damage, or physical deprivations, such as a lack of nutrients or insufficient sleep. The person who gets overly tired is more likely to be impatient and depressed. The same is true if a person comes down with a serious illness that is likely to be long-lasting and debilitating.

Psychological stresses include frustrations, feelings of insecurity, inner conflicts, fears, or even the pressure to get things done when we have too much to do. Disappointments also create stress. Think of the athlete who trains for months and then fails to win the long-awaited game or contest. Sometimes, students feel the same sense of loss when they don't pass an exam, or an employee does not get promoted. In a world that values success and achievement, it can be stressful for any of us to face failure, especially those people who set high standards for themselves or feel added pressure from teachers, employers, or family members.

Social stresses are easy to see. When there is economic uncertainty, widespread unemployment, political instability, or threat from terrorist attacks, it can be very difficult for some people to handle the tension and uncertainties. The physical environment also can have an effect. Prolonged periods of heat, darkness, crowding, noise, or other stressful circumstances can make coping more difficult and increase the likelihood of mental disorders. Although there is no evidence that he experienced any mental problems, Paul encountered a number of social stresses of the type that could be difficult for others to handle. He wrote, "I have lived with weariness and pain and sleepless nights. Often I have been hungry and thirsty and have gone without food. Often I have shivered with cold, without enough clothing to keep me warm. Then, besides all this, I have the daily burden of how the churches are getting along."[18]

Paul knew about spiritual stresses as well, and he warned about some of them in Ephesians 6. We humans are subject to the "strategies and tricks of the Devil" who aligns with "evil rulers and authorities of the unseen world," and "wicked spirits in the heavenly realms" that put us under pressure.[19]

2. *Predisposing Influences.* It is well known that the same stresses can impact people differently. When a tornado or hurricane blows through a community and destroys rows of houses, everybody loses their possessions, but the same loss that leaves one person depressed and immobilized may stimulate another to acts of compassion and determination to overcome the loss and to rebuild.

Like present stress, the predisposing background influences can be of several types. Biological predispositions include the effects of heredity, physical health, congenital defects, or other physical influences. Severe depression, for example, may be stimulated by stress, but the condition is worse in some people because their bodies are not able to respond adequately. Psychological predispositions include the effects of early family disharmony, childhood losses, parental neglect or abuse, faulty learning, previous rejection, or an upbringing that was so demanding and rigid that the person always felt like a failure and carried this attitude into adulthood. Research on personality disorders has shown the influence of both genetics and upbringing. Symptoms in adults can be worse when there has been a history of childhood trauma or neglect.[20] When Vietnam veterans diagnosed with post-traumatic stress disorders (PTSD) were compared with veterans who did not show any evidence of the disorder, the PTSD veterans reported more time in combat, more friends killed, greater involvement in killing others, closer relationships with those who died, more combat injuries, and more negative experiences at home after discharge. Many of these veterans had favorable preservice attitudes toward the war, but their traumatic experiences in Vietnam, followed by a lack of support when they came home, combined to create anxiety, depression, and other evidences of abnormality long after the war had ended.[21]

Mental disorders also can depend on sociological predispositions. These include one's social class, place of residence, marital status, socioeconomic level, religious affiliation, or membership in a minority group. When compared to the wealthy, for example, poor people tend to have higher rates of psychopathology. The poor have less control over their circumstances, and because of their lack of resources, they must wait for treatment until their problems get severe. People with more money or access to insurance payments get counseling earlier and are less likely than the poor to be hospitalized or listed in the statistics about those who have mental disorders. The neighborhood where one lives also can have an impact on the prevalence and availability of treatment for mental disorders. An entire specialty of rural psychology has developed to better understand and treat people who live outside of cities. The stresses differ between rural and urban areas, and so does the availability of help.[22]

Spiritual predisposing factors could include the person's past experiences with such harmful predisposing issues as abusive church experiences, involvements with satanic rituals, or a history of blatantly sinful behaviors that have left their scars even in believers who have been forgiven by God.

3. *Locus of Control.* The influence of these present stresses and prior predisposing issues can depend on how much control the person feels he or she has over the circumstances and directions of life. In the 1960s, psychologist Julian Rotter introduced a concept that he called *locus of control.* It quickly became one of the core ideas in psychology. According to this theory, which has an impressive

amount of research support, people can have internal or external locus of control. Internal locus of control characterizes people who believe that what happens in life depends largely on their own decisions and actions. In contrast, people with external locus of control assume that the events in one's life depend on other people, on circumstances, or even on luck or chance.[23]

This idea has been evaluated in a number of research studies concerning health and illness.[24] In general, people who have an internal locus of control tend to be healthier and recover more efficiently from surgery and other illness. People who believe that they can control what happens are more likely to follow doctor's orders, stick with diets, recover faster, and even live longer. More often they tend to be optimistic, probably because in life they have learned to be optimistic. People who don't feel they can control the events of their lives (that is, they have external locus of control) tend to give up trying. They feel more helpless, and as a result, they are more likely to be depressed and sometimes pessimistic. This, in turn, has a negative influence on their health.

Clearly all of this has relevance to mental health. Based on the finding that locus of control is largely learned, psychologist Martin Seligman proposed the ideas of learned helplessness and learned optimism.[25] People who have learned to feel helpless tend to be more depressed and have poorer mental health. In contrast, when people begin to see that they can control their lives, they develop a sense of optimism, and their mental health is better. Over the years this theory has been hotly debated, but it also has become more sophisticated. And this core element remains: the impact of present stress and past influences is tempered according to how much a person feels that he or she is in control of life.

The secular researchers who study locus of control do not spend much time thinking about God, but Christian counselors have wondered if the locus of control idea encourages people to take over control and let go of God. Not so, concluded researchers a few years ago.[26] Strong believers in God may have similarities to people with strong internal locus of control. These Christians believe that the future is positive because God answers our prayer and he honors our faith in submitting difficult situations to his guidance. Like everybody, else these believers can be overwhelmed by stress and past influences, but a sense that things are under control can help to prevent mental disorders and the harmful impact of stress-inducing influences.

4. *Sin and Responsibility.* A number of Christian counselors hold the view that mental disorders result mostly from personal sin in the life of the person with the disorder. Counseling, therefore, involves urging people to confess their sins and change behavior. This viewpoint fails to appreciate both the complexity of mental disorders and the deeply penetrating influence of sin. It is possible to view sin from at least two perspectives: conscious deliberate sins that individuals commit knowingly, and the innate sinfulness that is part of human nature. These might be seen as two types of sin. In a similar way, responsibility can be viewed from two perspectives: either the person is responsible, or somebody else is responsible. This can be shown in a simple diagram (see Figure 33–1).[27]

The causes of mental disorders can be found in all four quadrants, and treatment will consider all four as well.

(a) Quadrant I. Here the person has problems because of something sinful (or foolish) that he or she may have done deliberately and consciously. Responsibility for both the problem and the treatment rests largely with the individual. Encour-

Responsibility for Pathology.

		Oneself	Others
Type	Specific, often Deliberate Conscious Sins	I	II
of			
Sin	Inner Sinful Human Nature	III	IV

Figure 33–1.

aging the counselee to confess, change behavior, learn new skills, and get help in preventing a recurrence are among the most appropriate counseling strategies.

(b) Quadrant II. This involves sinful or other harmful behavior that originates with someone different from the counselee. A person with great feelings of inferiority and low self-esteem, for example, may have developed these attitudes because of the constant sinful put-down criticisms that came from a teacher, parent, or hypercritical spouse. Adult children of alcoholics often suffer because of the drinking excesses of one or both parents. The woman who suffers the consequences of rape may have been an innocent victim, in the wrong place and at the wrong time. Counseling may involve helping individuals forgive, change perceptions, and learn to let go of the long-standing hurts, bitterness, and painful memories.

(c) Quadrant III. This presents a more complicated picture. Some people develop mental disorders not because of specific sins, but because they are pulled down by deeply felt fears, insecurities, immaturities, ignorance, past traumas, inherited physical influences, harmful attitudes, or other aspects of the personality that come because we live in a fallen world and are all deeply affected by sin. The Pharisees in the time of Jesus were models of righteous proper outward behavior, but inside they were full of greed, self-indulgence, hypocrisy, wickedness, and probably a lot of confusion and self-deception.[28] Help for these people could come only with increased insight and understanding, confession, and willingness to let God work to cleanse, change, and bring maturity to the inner life. This is a process that might take a lot of time and more in-depth treatment. Even Jesus did not get very far in bringing change in these people.

(d) Quadrant IV. Many personal problems come because we live in a world where sin permeates the culture—where there is conflict, stress, poverty, inequality, war, disease, and widespread injustice. Until Christ returns to bring perfect justice and an end to sin, these pathological conditions will persist to create both social havoc and sometimes personal mental disorders. Ultimately, the battle will never be won completely prior to the return of Christ. He defeated sin on the cross, but the devil still has some freedom to prowl around like a roaring lion looking for victims to devour.[29] In the meantime, Christians are responsible to resist social injustice, work for peace, and strive to create a better world. Counselors seek to change circumstances that give rise to pathology, teach people how to cope with stress, and help counselees overcome the persisting effects of painful past experiences.

Mental disorders rarely rise from only one of these four quadrants. Most often the influences come from several quadrants. When Andy Behrman agreed to get involved in the counterfeiting scheme that led to his imprisonment, where would we put the problem? Certainly, he made a decision for which he was responsible (Quadrant I), but other people lured him into the scheme (Quadrant II), and it appears that he did what he did because he lives in a sinful world where there is disease, including the biological malfunctioning in Andy's brain that made him a victim of bipolar disorder.

Mainstream psychiatry, psychology, and the other mental-health professions have tended to ignore the role of sin as a cause of mental disorders, or dismiss sin as being an archaic concept that has no place in twenty-first-century thinking. Even within their own ranks, the mental-health professions have been challenged to consider sin seriously, but overall these challenges have not been taken seriously.[30] Whether or not it is acknowledged in the professions, sin is a crucial reality both in Christian theology and in any lasting effort to understand and deal with mental disorders.[31]

In addition to the role of sin in psychopathology, we also need to see the importance of perception. We cannot begin to understand the causes of another person's behavior until we have tried to see the world from his or her point of view. What seems illogical and foolish from the viewpoint of an outside observer may be much more rational and clearly understood when we see the situation from the perspective of the person who acts. We will see this later in the chapter when we look at suicide. It seems so senseless from the perspective of onlookers, but it may be perfectly logical to the distressed person intent on ending his or her life. Near the end of the book this will come up again when we raise the issue of why terrorists and suicide bombers do what they do.

The Effects of Mental Disorders

"Mental illness is a major social problem that consumes millions of tax dollars; costs billions in lost wages, absenteeism, inefficiency, criminal behavior and expensive treatment; characterizes half or more of the homeless who wander the streets; brings continual misery to the millions of people who are in the clutches of mental disorders; and causes incredible stress on families—many of whom fail to understand or know how to help their distraught relatives." That sentence was included in an earlier edition of this book, and it still applies.

At the beginning of the twenty-first century, the United States government issued the first ever Surgeon General's report on mental health.[32] Based on a review of over 3,000 scientific articles and consultations with numerous mental-health providers, the report sought to demonstrate that mental health is fundamental to all health, and that "mental disorders are real health conditions that have an immense impact on individuals and families throughout the nation and the world." The report pointed to impressive evidence, showing that mental-health treatments are effective and that a range of treatments exists for most mental disorders.

Despite these positive statements, there still is a widespread stigma against admitting that one has a mental disorder, and many people who could benefit from treatment do not get it.[33] This was a major finding of President Bush's New Freedom Commission on Mental Health,[34] which sought to deal with the stigma and focused on the idea that mental disorders are real illnesses from which people can recover.[35]

Since the time of that report, a national survey of mental illness and treatment found that many people suffer for many years before they are courageous enough to get treatment or discover where effective treatment is available. According to *USA Today*, "About one in four adults have the symptoms of at least one mental illness every year, and nearly half suffer disorders during their lifetimes, according to a study of 9,282 people published in the *Archives of General Psychiatry*.... Most people with disorders—about four out of five—have mild to moderate mental illness. Overall, 6 percent have disorders that seriously impair their daily lives.... Half of all mental illness begins by age 14, and three-fourths of adults have their symptoms by 24. Only about a third get effective care, and the most serious disorders begin at a young age, often going undetected and worsening for a decade or longer."[36]

However, counselors are most impacted by individual counselees who come for help, by how these people are affected by their mental problems, and by how their families suffer or struggle to cope.

1. *The Effects on Individuals.* John Nash was both brilliant and eccentric when he arrived at Princeton University, where he soon could be seen shuffling around the campus wearing purple sneakers and writing numerology treatises on the blackboards. Described as a "flamboyant mathematical wizard" who sometimes had discussions with Albert Einstein, among others, Nash developed his work in game theory before he was thirty, never realizing that when he was in his fifties, that work would be making a significant impact in economics worldwide. When the Nobel committee wanted to award a prize for game theory, Nash's name came up repeatedly, but he kept being turned down for one basic reason: at age thirty John Nash had descended into his own world of paranoid schizophrenia.

Maybe his university classmates and professors were not surprised. Nash had good looks, a devoted wife, and a son who gave early evidence of becoming a mathematical genius like his father, but overshadowing all of this, John Nash was a tortured, intense, driven, and isolated individual. For decades his mental disorder left him unable to work or to think creatively and rationally. A long line of psychiatrists had tried to help him. He was given antipsychotic drugs and underwent a half dozen involuntary hospitalizations. Then, after decades of torment, he recovered spontaneously. In 1994 he was awarded the Nobel Prize in economics, but perhaps greater fame came from another source when an economist-journalist named Sylvia Nasar wrote a carefully researched and moving biography about Nash's life. The book was titled *A Beautiful Mind*.[37] It became a best seller and later was turned into a major motion picture that won several Academy Awards.

Like all people with mental disorders, John Nash is unique. No two people show identical effects, but there are several commonly seen symptoms, sometimes known as the clinical manifestations of mental disorders. Some are biological, but nonmedical counselors more often notice psychologically unusual emotion, sensation, perception, thinking, and behavior. Once again it is worth noting that the following characteristics can be highly disruptive in the lives of some people but mild and barely noticeable in others.

(a) Emotion. Intense anxiety, depression, anger, guilt, and other painful emotions are so common that counselors often refer to mental disorders as affective or emotional disorders. These emotions can differ in a variety of ways. *Emotional variability* refers to sometimes unpredictable emotional ups and downs. Some people are up all the time, showing euphoria that others would consider unrealistic. In contrast are those who are emotionally down and perpetually depressed. In others there is a swing between euphoria and depression. This emotional variability is characteristic of the bipolar disorders that used to be called manic-depressive disorders. Andy Behrman was given that diagnosis, but today, like millions of others, he is able to live a normal and fulfilling life with his mood swings controlled by medications that correct chemical malfunctioning in his brain. Different from the swings in emotion is *flat affect*, the tendency of some people to remain emotionless, perhaps because they neither feel nor can express feelings. *Inappropriate affect* describes emotional reactions that are unusual, often appearing without any appropriate cause. Examples might include giggling in response to a sad story, crying uncontrollably when there is no cause for sadness, or exploding in anger when there is no apparent reason to do so.

(b) Sensation and Perception. It is difficult to function well if we fail to receive and respond appropriately to stimulation from the world around us. Some mental patients have *enhanced sensitivity*. Their hearing may be especially acute, colors may be brighter, or sometimes the person is unable to relax or concentrate because he or she feels overwhelmed by the flood of data that seems to be bombarding the senses. In contrast, others experience *blunted sensitivity*, including a reduced ability to feel pain, see clearly, or hear well. At times, these people have difficulty sorting out and synthesizing sensations. Some schizophrenics have difficulty watching television, for example, because they can't watch the screen and listen at the same time.[38]

Perhaps more common is *distorted sensitivity*, in which the person misinterprets stimuli and misperceives the world. Delusions (false ideas believed by the individual but not by anybody else), hallucinations (perceptions that a person experiences even though there is no external stimulation), and illusions (misinterpreting sensations) are all seen in some people with mental disorders. Often these are held with strong conviction, and the person's perception doesn't change when presented with evidence to the contrary. Families experience great frustration when they try to convince a disturbed relative that his or her delusions of persecution are without foundation or that the voices heard are not real.

(c) Thinking. Some mental-health professionals suggest that thought disorders are the most obvious indications of mental illness. Often, for example, there is *faulty thought content*, in which the person does not think clearly, logically, or consistently.[39] Apparently, this was one of John Nash's symptoms, along with his paranoia that led to a number of misperceptions.

At times, some faulty thinking may be true of everybody; we reach conclusions that aren't completely rational or realistic. Individuals who suffer from phobias may have unfounded fears of heights, enclosed spaces, or thunderstorms. But the phobic person knows that these thoughts are irrational, even though they may be difficult to ignore or resist.[40] The person with a mental disorder, in contrast, may not recognize that his or her thinking does not make sense, so there is no willingness or ability to change in response to arguments or evidence.

A different kind of thinking concerns *faulty thought progression*. This may include rambling disconnected thoughts, easily interrupted thinking, obsessive thinking, or an inability to think abstractly. In addition, some people appear to be confused, uncertain who or where they are, unable to appreciate the consequences of their behavior, unable to remember, or easily distracted. All these can show that the person is out of contact with reality.

(d) Behavior. It is not surprising that the person with faulty sensation, perception, emotions, and thinking is also likely to act in ways that are odd or socially inappropriate. This is so common that mental disorders are frequently known as behavior disorders. Ritualistic compulsive activity, hyperactivity, withdrawal, childlike behavior, lack of self-control, religious or political fanaticism, and other unusual behaviors can indicate that something is wrong.

Some people, especially young children and the severely disturbed, are not sure how to express their inner turmoil in words. As a result, they try to communicate behaviorally, sometimes acting out the confused feelings and ideas that are inside. The good counselor tries to understand what the behavioral messages may mean.

2. *Effects on Families.* Most people are able to think logically, experience emotion appropriately, and cope with life's stresses more or less effectively. But when another person lacks these abilities, especially a person in one's family, communication and interaction become extremely difficult. Everybody realizes that young children will be immature and act inappropriately, but most adults accept this because we know that young people are learning and that they will mature as they get older. When the immaturity and inappropriate behavior are seen in one's spouse, parents, or grown children, it is much more difficult for family members to be patient, understanding, and able to communicate or to cope.[41]

Unlike the mental patients, who frequently get professional help, families are often left alone to face the uncertainty, confusion, mental stigma, financial pressures, guilt, self-blame, changes in family responsibilities, and tensions that may follow a relative who has a mental disorder. This can be complicated by the fact that mental disorders run in families, and sometimes the family care-givers struggle, in some form, with psychological disorders that are similar to those of the family member who needs the care. Since mental disorders influence so many people, the counselor's work rarely is limited to the mental patients themselves. At times, counseling must extend to families and to others who are affected. This may present a special challenge to pastors and other church-related Christian counselors who often know both the person with the mental disorder and the family members.

Relatives differ in their efforts to cope, but some move through a series of overlapping phases.[42] First, the family tries to ignore or explain away the family member's unusual or deviant behavior. Then comes the first shock of recognition when something happens that is too bizarre or disruptive to be ignored. Next, there may be a period of withdrawal and reevaluation as the family hopes that things will somehow get better. When this fails to happen, the family starts looking for causes and tries to get treatment. Eventually, their optimism collapses, sometimes accompanied by acceptance and the recognition that they may have to give support while they also set limits. With difficulty, family members mourn the loss of the hopes and dreams they had for the afflicted family member. If no improvement comes, the family tries to pick up the pieces and learns to adjust to living with a mentally disabled family member.

Numerous books have been written to help the families of mental patients cope.[43] In addition to describing the nature of mental disorders and effects on the family, these books often give practical suggestions that counselors might share with relatives of counselees with mental disorders.[44] Suggestions for families include the following:

- Accept the reality of the mental illness and the likelihood that families may be impacted for a long time.
- Recognize that a period of adjustment is likely, but that families can and do cope effectively. One study found that family members of people with mental disorders were characterized by *hanging on, being stable*, or *doing well* in coping. Once they got used to their new routines, the majority reported that they were consistently being stable or doing well. Only a minority were just hanging on.[45]
- With the help of a mental-health professional or other counselor, learn to set realistic expectations, firmly but kindly.
- Recognize that grief is a common characteristic of family members, especially when the person with the mental disorder is a child. Allow yourself to grieve, preferably with the help of somebody outside the home. Family members who don't recognize or deal with grief set themselves up for problems in their own lives.[46]
- Try to find a support group of people from other families who care for a relative with a mental disorder. This gives encouragement and a clearer perspective on what is required of the care-giver.
- Find ways to get consistent breaks, including rest and rejuvenation.
- Remember that the family is not the only influence that can make a difference. There are others who can give help. Don't assume all the responsibility for change or recovery.
- Learn to tolerate or overlook behaviors that may seem strange but are neither dangerous nor harmful.
- Recognize "we do the best we can, even though that is not perfect."
- Let go of what cannot be changed; focus on what is possible.
- Learn to set and maintain limits, even when the family member resists.
- Care enough to not let a loved one do anything that will be harmful to themselves or to others.
- Recognize that there will be times when the relative feels burdened by the mental patient's anxiety, worrying, sense of hopelessness, and lack of interest in social activities.
- Remember that care-givers who do not take care of themselves eventually burn out. This is a nice statement to read in a book, but putting the self-care into practice can be very difficult unless some outside person helps the family monitor what they are feeling and how they are coping.

Counseling and Mental Disorders

Imagine what it must have been like at least a couple of centuries ago, but even in some parts of the world today, to live in a community or to share a house with somebody who suffered from a severe mental disorder. There were no convincing explanations for the bizarre, self-destructive, or even aggressive behaviors of these "lunatics," and there were not effective methods for controlling their actions or helping them find relief from their inner torment. The popular treatments were cruel—sometimes people were whipped, starved, chained, seared with hot irons, dunked into freezing water. For most of these, there were explanations, including the belief that these people were possessed with demons that might leave if the body was tortured and made inhabitable. Sometimes, they would drill holes into the person's head (there were no anesthetics) so that the tormenting spirits could get out. Clergy were among those who approved of these methods, sometimes along with exorcisms and other approaches that were ineffective, especially in treating disorders that had a strong physiological basis. It is not widely known that clergy and groups of Christians also were among those who opposed cruel treatment of mentally disordered people and often took the lead in providing compassionate care-giving.[47] Not until the early 1800s were more humane treatment methods more widely proposed and used, first in France and Britain, then in America.

Early American psychiatry used what was termed "moral treatment," an approach characterized by kindness, self-respect, patience, and meaningful relationships. The counselor treated patients as respected human beings, as if they were mentally well. Counseling consisted of resocialization through approaches that today might be called recreational, physical, occupational, industrial, musical, and physical therapies. Moral treatment appears to have been a high point in the history of mental disorders, but it was a movement that got lost in the Industrial Revolution that followed.[48]

1. *Helping People with Mental Disorders.* Because of advances in treatment techniques, most mental disorders are treated today by professionals, but the principles of moral treatment still can be helpful. The community, and especially the church, can provide the ongoing support, warmth, acceptance, caring, and contact with reality that busy professionals often have limited time to give. At times, the pastor or other church leader can help the person with a mental disorder get effective treatment, and frequently the church becomes the greatest source of support for the mentally ill person's family.

Mental disorders are complex, so it is not surprising that treatment can be a complex process as well, best accomplished by professionals working together in teams. Usually, the process begins with a complete physical and psychological examination, followed by a combination of treatments that could be grouped into four broad categories.

Physical treatments include various medical interventions, dietary changes, and sometimes surgery or the use of a few controversial procedures, such as electroconvulsive shock therapy, computer-based brain technologies,[49] or brain imaging.[50] Undoubtedly, the administration of drugs is most effective and the most often used physical-biological approach. The widespread use of these medications has revolutionized treatment, virtually eliminated the cruel methods that once were so common, and brought great relief to millions of patients and their families. Most often these medications are administered and their use is supervised by psychiatrists and other people with medical training, but drug use is not as problem free as we might expect. Some people forget or refuse to take the medication, or they decide to take the pills only when they feel the need. This can have a disruptive effect on the treatment and make the original problems worse. Then there are other challenges.

The decision about which medication(s) to use seems to be as much an art as it is a science. Drug effectiveness and side effects vary considerably from person to person and across time. There is no perfect drug for the problems of psychosis, providing active benefits without risks. Responsible clinicians assert that the process is almost always a quest for . . . just enough medication to control troublesome symptoms but not enough to cause side effects. It can take weeks, even months, to find the right drug and dosage combination—an often long and arduous process for afflicted individuals (and their loved ones). . . . With a condition like schizophrenia, where much denial and avoidance are involved, this can be an especially daunting challenge.[51]

Sometimes, more drugs are added to control the side effects of other drugs, and the process keeps getting more and more complicated. Despite these dangers, it doubtless is true that to treat serious mental disorders without psychopharmacological intervention is "simply irresponsible."[52] No attempt will be made in these pages to classify or describe the different medications. They change frequently, continually are replaced by better drugs, and have different names in different countries. Any listing here would be outdated quickly.[53]

Psychotherapeutic treatments include various types of psychotherapy that tend to focus on emotional-psychological issues. It is difficult for seriously disturbed people to focus on traumatic events from the past that may have contributed to their present difficulties, but the use of drugs often calms these counselees, reduces their anxiety, and enables them to focus. Walking through the past or through the present life stresses, accompanied by a caring, insightful, sometimes challenging counselor, can be very helpful. In addition, cognitive and behavior therapies have been shown to be very useful, and there is value in teaching social skills and counseling with whole families involved so conflicts can be resolved, toxic relationships can be healed, and there can be greater understanding and support.[54] These therapeutic methods are best used by counselors with special training and expertise in working with severely disturbed people.

Community strategies may not focus specifically on the person with the mental disorder but may involve working with community groups to change conditions that can lead to breakdowns or may involve efforts to provide the community care that people with mental disorders and their families need. One place to begin is with the many support groups that are available in many communities and larger churches. Andy Behrman's story first appeared in a book but later was described in a magazine for people with bipolar disorder. These publications for people with mental disorders and their families may not have a distinctively Christian emphasis, but they can give encouraging and useful information, especially after recovery. Counselors can play a significant role in helping counselees and their families select high-quality publications and community resources.[55]

Spiritual interventions tend to be ignored by mental-health professionals, but they are very important to people who believe in God and in his power to help and to heal.[56] Many people rely on their religious beliefs to regain control of their lives and to find hope. Some evidence suggests that people with severe mental disorders who have a strong religious faith and who attend religious services are not merely passive recipients of spiritual support.[57] These people have a greater belief that their problems can be controlled and cured, so they feel more empowered and are more likely to cooperate with professional care-givers in adhering to the various treatment methods. In addition, there can be considerable support from fellow believers who accept the person with a mental disorder, pray together, and reinforce the idea that there is hope.

2. *Helping Families.* We have emphasized that life can be very difficult for those who must live with someone who is deeply depressed, suicidal, inclined to be violent, or seriously disabled mentally. Family members often are the primary care-givers for the mentally ill, but this consumes time, energy, and emotional stamina, and sometimes eats up the family's financial resources. Activities and interests that once were pleasant and daily routines that used to be habitual or uninterrupted may be changed forcibly. Individual lifestyles and goals may be altered. Family togetherness is so often disrupted that a conscious effort is required if the family is to retain a sense of unity. Many have difficulty keeping sensitive both to the needs of the person with the disability and to the needs and goals of the other family members. How can these families be helped?

(a) Support. In addition to the Internet, support groups for families often can be found through community mental-health clinics, government and community agencies, private practice counselors, or churches. Counselors can help family members find groups of other family members who understand and can give guidance and encouragement. The groups help participants deal with the anger, guilt, self-blame, and stigma that are so common. Often the people in these groups help one another learn how to manage and live with relatives who may show bizarre attitudes, aggressive and other antisocial actions, unkempt appearance, poor hygiene, social withdrawal, self-destructive tendencies, and sometimes perpetual and unrealistic demands. When a mental patient comes home following a period of hospitalization, the family may need special support throughout the initial period of readjustment.

This kind of help should come from the church, and often it does, although many church members have little or no understanding of mental disorders, fail to comprehend the pressures that families face, feel awkward around people with mental disorders or their families, and tend to withdraw. This presents a challenge for local bodies of believers to be at the center of supportive care for those with mentally incapacitated family members.

(b) Education. Until a mental disorder strikes, most family members have no understanding of psychopathology. Education, therefore, becomes important in helping family members understand the nature and treatment of mental illness, but it also helps in learning how to cope with the disturbed person, how to give care, and how to keep their own lives from being swallowed up by the distressed family member. Being a care-giver can be difficult, and it is crucially important that family members learn how to cope successfully and how to find ways to get away for periodic breaks.

(c) Counseling. Sometimes, support and education are not enough. Family members need more specialized help in coping with their own feelings of futility, guilt, worry, and insecurity. Since the strain can be so overwhelming, family members may themselves begin to show symptoms of emotional disturbance. This can lead to relapse in the mentally ill person, especially when family members are critical, hostile, or impatient.

In contrast, individual counseling with family members or family counseling can lower tension, give encouragement, promote tolerance, allow the expression of emotions, deal with conflicts in the home, and teach family members how to care for the patient. In one study of schizophrenics, family meetings in the first year following hospitalization reduced relapse sixfold. These meetings were most effective when they were held in the home rather than at a clinic or counselor's office.[58] Meetings like these give opportunity for families to see their strengths, to ask questions, to learn about community resources, to clarify goals, to acknowledge their limitations, and to learn practical ways to get away for a break without feeling guilty or shirking family responsibilities.

3. *Counseling and Suicide.* Sometimes, the pressures of life get too intense, and individuals decide to take their own lives. Most have thought about the idea for weeks or months before. Their suicidal acts are rarely sudden, impulsive, or random, although sometimes there are tragic teenage suicide epidemics where the attention that comes following one suicide leads other teenagers to try something similar.

Why do some people turn to acts of self-destruction, including many who would not be considered to have mental disorders? There can be a variety of reasons.

- To escape from loneliness, hopelessness, depression, academic or work difficulties, financial pressures, or conflicts with other people.
- To punish survivors who are likely to feel hurt and guilty.
- To gain attention.
- To manipulate others (often this can best be accomplished by the threat of suicide).
- To join a loved one who has died.
- To escape from some difficult situation.
- To punish oneself for something that has created guilt.
- To prevent oneself from becoming a burden on others.
- To avoid the suffering and other effects of some dread disease.

Some of the reasons on this list are not very logical. There is no guarantee, for example, that suicide will enable the victim to join a deceased loved one. Gaining attention isn't very satisfying if the person is not present to enjoy the public reaction.

When people try to kill themselves, however, their thinking at the time usually is not logical. When we function normally, we perceive the world accurately, tend to think logically, and have a healthy sense of reality. In times of crisis, however, thinking may be clouded by anxiety, hopelessness, and maladaptive self-defeating behavior. Even those occasional "Russian roulette" types of suicide are not logical, although we might be able to understand the victim's thinking. Young people like to flirt with danger, and because death seems so remote and unlikely, many might play with partially loaded guns or high-speed automobile races because of the excitement.

In the chapter on depression,[59] I listed some of the clues that are seen in people who contemplate suicide. Often these people are overwhelmed by feelings of hopelessness, and many see no further options for dealing with their problems. Suicide may seem like the best way to escape a situation of intense suffering, and some people are so relieved when they finally decide on this solution that they are able to mask their plans with smiles and expressions of false cheer. More often, however, the subtle pre-suicide clues indicate a cry for help.

When a counselee gives indications of suicidal thinking, ask gently if this is being considered. Sometimes, counselees are relieved to have the issue out in the open where it can be discussed. In assessing risk, try to determine if the person has considered a method, has chosen a means that is likely to be lethal (guns are more lethal than swallowing aspirin), has tried suicide before, or has a history of severe problems or mental disorders. All of these increase the likelihood of suicide.

Try to assess what brought the counselee to this point of crisis. What solutions were attempted and failed in dealing with this and similar crises in the past? What could be tried in the future? As you talk with the counselee, challenge romantic ideas about death. Teenagers, for example, sometimes think friends will grieve forever and talk about the victim's wonderful and tragic qualities. Point out that this might not happen, that others will go on with their lives, and that suicide is a permanent solution to what might be a temporary and solvable problem. Try to show respect for the person, don't shame or belittle, avoid arguments if possible, and let the individual know that you care. In all of this, remember the importance of prayer, asking God to give you wisdom and sensitivity.

It is common to find that a counselor's care and interest can defuse the suicide idea, at least temporarily, but if the individual persists in his or her determination, try to contact the family physician, a close relative, a suicide prevention center, or a counselor who has special training in dealing with suicidal emergencies.

What do you do if all of your efforts fail and the person commits suicide? Often counselors and families feel guilt, anger, and self-condemnation because the suicide was not prevented. At times, the counselor may be involved in helping survivors, many of whom show grief mixed with remorse, anger, and other emotions. Sometimes, the suicide is rarely mentioned by relatives, friends, or church members who want to express condolences to the family but aren't sure if they should mention the cause of death. Like any other problem, the pain of suicide is best discussed honestly and compassionately, without attempts to avoid the pain that survivors feel.

For counselors and friends of the person who has died, suicide is a painful and deeply distressing experience. Taking a life, including one's own life, is sin, but it is not the unpardonable sin. Close friends, family members, and even counselors may criticize themselves for not preventing the loved one's death, but ultimately the responsibility for suicide rests with the victim who was unable or unwilling to cope with the pressures of life. Christian counselors and those who worship alongside us in church need to show compassion and sensitivity in the aftermath of suicide. And we must take care not to glamorize the suicide, lest this give reason for others to follow the victim's example.

Preventing Mental Disorders

George Albee was a psychologist who was a critic of individual psychotherapy and a strong advocate of various ways in which mental disorders can be prevented. Some time ago he wrote a concise discussion of prevention that is worth repeating:

> Most of the great plagues that have afflicted humankind through the centuries have been eliminated by effective primary prevention—working with large

groups of people not yet affected by a disease to eliminate sources of infection or contagion and to build up resistance to the disease....

In the case of mental disorders, the key elements are not bacteria, viruses or other noxious organic agents but a high level of current or past stress that may be engendered by many things, including serious marital problems; involuntary unemployment; sexual confusion and guilt; or a childhood history of serious neglect, physical abuse, sexual exploitation and lack of affection.

To lessen the incidence of mental disorders through prevention, we must reduce problems in three areas—organic factors, stress and exploitation of various kinds—and increase resources in three others—coping skills, self-esteem and support groups.[60]

Albee gave examples:

- To reduce organic problems, we can improve nutrition during pregnancy and reduce toxins, such as lead in the environment.
- To reduce stress we need to help people with stress management, and help them get better employment, health care, and housing for the poor and elderly.
- To stop exploitation we need to do whatever is needed to prevent the abuse of children, and the mistreatment of women, minorities, immigrant workers, and others.
- We improve coping skills by teaching people money management, stress management, and basic living skills.
- Self-esteem is increased through "fairer press portrayals of the aged, handicapped, women, and minorities."
- Support groups include developing self-help programs, caring church groups, and community or government organizations that provide health-care, Meals on Wheels, and similar services.

This is a creative proposal that Albee promoted for much of his life.[61] It involves intervention at all levels of society, but it is beyond the capabilities, resources, and time available to most counselors or to most churches. Even as he advocated "prevention through social change," Albee concluded that this is "a faint but persistent hope."[62]

No one person, counseling agency, community, or church can do everything, but each of us can carve out some area of need and work to prevent problems from getting worse. Some will work in drug prevention programs or suicide prevention centers. Others will concentrate on marriage enrichment, pre-retirement counseling, or divorce recovery. Some will stimulate development of support groups that help the survivors of suicide, parents of handicapped children, unmarried pregnant teenagers, children of alcoholics, or others who could develop more severe emotional disorders. For many of us, the best prevention will involve working one to one with people afflicted with mental disorders and their families, helping them cope with current struggles so that more complex problems are prevented. A few will be like Andy Behrman, who has become an advocate for the mentally ill. Others who read these words already may have sensed God's call to work with special groups of people, such as abused children or poor kids in violent neighborhoods, to help them function better and thus avoid future problems.

The church has a significant role to play in this effort. Jesus demonstrated compassion, caring, and social concern, even as he preached the Gospel and called people to repentance. Can we, too, find ways to fulfill the Great Commission while we also care for the needy, including the mentally disabled and those who are especially susceptible to mental illness? The church has an impressive history of compassionate involvement in these areas.

Conclusions About Mental Disorders

In the middle of the twentieth century, the federal government in the United States and mental-health experts embarked on an ambitious program to phase out large mental hospitals and move the mentally disabled into more humane and convenient community treatment centers. I was a student at the time and remember the enthusiasm that everybody felt as we anticipated the positive outcomes of this creative and widely applauded idea. How could we have known that it would fail? The hospitals were depopulated, and the deplorable back wards of psychiatric institutions disappeared, but there were insufficient housing, transitional care, and job training that could integrate former hospital patients into society. Increasing numbers of mental patients spilled into the streets, and a new class of needy people was created—the homeless mentally ill. We still are trying to find ways to correct a well-intentioned program that went sour.[63]

There is cause for hope, however. Despite the prevalence of mental disorders and limited treatment facilities, people do get better. Even people with severe mental disorders can see their symptoms disappear and their functioning restored. The journey is not always easy, and the setbacks may come more often than we would like, but there has been great progress in treatment of mental disorders, and new developments keep appearing.

Jesus once predicted that the poor would always be with us, and perhaps the same could be said for people with mental disorders. Just as the Gospel can reach the poor (as well as the rich), so the Word of God and the comforting help from God's people can bring solace and guidance both to the mentally disabled and to those who are healthier. The late Pope John Paul II spoke about this on several occasions. During a general audience in 2001, he urged people not to be indifferent to brothers and sisters with mental illness, and stated that the church "looks with respect and affection on those who suffer from this affliction and urges the entire human family to accept them, giving special care to the poorest and most abandoned." Two years later, in an address to an international conference on depression, the pope encouraged mental-health workers to help people suffering with severe depression to "perceive the tenderness of God, integrate them into a community of faith and life where they feel accepted, understood, supported, in a word, worthy to love and be loved."[64] Helping people with mental disorders and their families is one of the greatest and most important challenges for the Christian counselor.

KEY POINTS FOR BUSY COUNSELORS

➤ There is no clear definition of mental disorders. These are conditions that can show a broad variety of symptoms that include distress, deviance, and disability or dysfunction.

➤ The distress, deviance, or disability may be mild and minimally bothersome, but these also can be more disruptive and sometimes of intense severity.

➤ The Bible says little about mental disorders and does not use the language of psychopathology. It does give us examples of mental disorders, has insights into human nature, shows us our human condition before God, gives some understanding of human suffering, and offers hope.

➤ Mental disorders come from a combination of influences, including present stress and predisposing circumstances. In both cases these can be biological, psychological, social-environmental, and spiritual. Also significant are whether the person feels that he or she has control over life circumstances and the role of sin.

➤ Mental disorders can be seen in psychologically unusual emotion, sensation, perceptions, thinking, and behavior. These aberrations can be highly disruptive in the lives of some people but barely noticeable in others.

➤ Often the mentally ill person's family also suffers disruption and difficulty in adjusting.

➤ Effective counseling for mental disorders includes:
  ■ Helping the person with the disorder through physical interventions (most often this involves medications), counseling, help in changing social conditions, and spiritual care-giving.
  ■ Giving families support, education, and counseling.

➤ Suicide and threats of suicide sometimes are a part of serious mental disorders, but often suicide is seen in people who are not seriously disordered.

➤ It is important for counselors to know the symptoms of potential suicide, how to intervene to prevent suicide, and the importance of helping family members when a suicide occurs.

➤ The church can play a significant role in helping people with mental disorders and their families.

34

Alcohol-Related Problems*

Loren hasn't had a drink for twenty-five years. He's been tempted many times, and more often than he wants to admit, he has come close to falling. He avoids restaurant foods like rum cake that have alcoholic ingredients because he's afraid that these might pull him down. After all these years, Loren still calls himself a drunk.

He is quick to state the reasons for his ongoing sobriety. "God pulled me back, with the help of a loving wife and the competent people in a clinic for alcoholics," he says. "But I know that if I ever take another drink—ever again, I'll be back where I was before."

Maybe you are familiar with Loren's story. I told it once before.[1] He attended church every week as a child. The whole family went together. Sometimes, the pastor gave emotional sermons about drunkenness, but most people in the congregation self-righteously and naively assumed that alcoholics were outside the church and rarely in contact with Christians. Nobody in the congregation ever admitted to drinking, and alcohol was never seen in Loren's home.

In those days, teenage drinking was much rarer than it is today, but Loren discovered that things were different when he got to college. There, almost everybody drank and drank a lot, including the Christians. Loren quickly discovered that a drink or two would help him feel better, especially when he was under pressure. He would drink more at parties on weekends and increasingly engaged in binge drinking. Once he was arrested for drunken driving, but he managed to hide this from his parents and convinced himself that his increasing use of alcohol was typical student behavior, an opportunity for him to live it up a little and be one of the boys before settling down.

After graduation, Loren got married and jumped enthusiastically into his new job at a stock broker's office. The work was challenging and sometimes stressful, but the future looked bright. Loren enjoyed the opportunity to have lunch with his clients, but some co-workers noticed that he drank more than anybody else and often didn't think too clearly when he got back to work. Often, he later would stop at a bar to unwind on the way home from work, and sometimes he would still be there at one or two in the morning. He looked somewhat scornfully at others who couldn't control their drinking, and he denied emphatically that he had a problem with alcohol.

Loren's wife tried to help. Sometimes, she found liquor hidden in the house; it was poured down the sink. When her husband was too drunk to go to work, she called the boss to explain that Loren was not feeling well. When his parents had a fortieth anniversary celebration, she went to the dinner alone and apologized because her husband was so caught up in his work, when in reality he was drunk. In the evenings, when the kids would ask questions about their father, she brushed them aside and tried to get the children into bed and asleep before Loren would stagger in through the door.

One night he caused a serious accident on the way home from work. A little boy was badly hurt, and Loren found himself in trouble with the law, with his employer, and—at last—with his own conscience. No longer could he pretend that he didn't have a drinking problem. His career was gone,

* I am grateful to Keith Bjorke for reading this chapter and giving helpful feedback and suggestions.

his family was deeply hurt, his spiritual life was in shambles, his health was declining, and the judge left him only two choices: go to jail or enter a rehabilitation program.

He chose the latter and now is glad he did. "If I hadn't stopped drinking and allowed somebody to help me," he admits freely, "I would have been dead a long time ago."

I don't know if Paddy Green's Tavern still exists. Probably not. It was a rundown building on a corner about two blocks from the house where I spent my early childhood. In those days before air conditioning and television, people sat on their front porches on warm summer nights, seeking relief from the heat and talking with the neighbors. Almost every night, but especially on the weekends, we would see men staggering home from Paddy Greens, sometimes falling and not getting up until morning. We who were kids laughed at the drunks, but we stayed away from them because they scared us, especially when they were men that we knew.

There are no taverns or inebriated pedestrians on the streets of the suburban neighborhood where I live today, but those early images still remain in my brain. They are alongside the memories of people I have known who abused alcohol, undermining their own lives and deeply impacting their families. Almost everybody who reads these words has been affected in some way by alcohol abuse. It is a major social, health, economic, and moral problem. It disrupts families, ruins careers, destroys brains and bodies, tears apart friendships, and leads to untold human misery.

Statistics on alcohol abuse vary from year to year and from place to place. In some Middle Eastern Muslim communities, alcohol use is almost nonexistent; in parts of Europe or Latin America almost everybody drinks. Most drinkers use moderation, but some become heavy drinkers, whose dependence on alcohol leads to a variety of problems. In the United States, alcohol misuse is assumed to be involved in at least half of all fatal traffic accidents, about one-fifth of all injuries in the home, 56 percent of fights that lead to hospital treatment, plus large numbers of fire deaths, drownings, arrests, murders, child abuse, and other violence in the home.[2] According to the National Institute on Alcohol Abuse and Alcoholism, about 7.4 percent of the U.S. population (approximately 14 million people) meets the diagnostic criteria for alcohol abuse or alcoholism, more than one-half of American adults have a close family member who has or has had problems with alcohol, and about one in four children younger than eighteen years old is exposed to alcohol abuse or alcohol dependence in the family.[3] A national survey on alcoholism, taken in 2000, confirmed that alcohol abuse is found at all socioeconomic levels and in all age groups, although the rates differ from one group to another. Alcoholism is common among both men and women. It cripples individuals outside of the church as well as those who are inside, including Evangelicals. It is a major killer, ranking third after heart disease and cancer. From an economic standpoint, the abuse of alcohol costs the economy billions of dollars annually in reduced productivity, absenteeism, property damage, treatment costs, and premature deaths.[4] Especially troubling are the findings that both binge and heavy drinking are most common in young adults aged eighteen to twenty-five.

Researchers and counselors often divide substance-related disorders (including alcohol misuse) into several broad categories.

- *Intoxication* refers to "clinically significant maladaptive behavioral changes," which include "inappropriate sexual or aggressive behavior, mood changes, impaired judgment, impaired social or occupational functioning," that may be accompanied by "slurred speech, incoordination, unsteady gait," and sometimes coma.[5] Depending on the social setting, if this behavior is relatively rare, it may be tolerated by others and not viewed as problematic.

- *Dependence* on alcohol (or some other substance) is what normally is called alcoholism. Common symptoms include a strong need or compulsion to drink, an inability to limit one's drinking on any given occasion, and withdrawal symptoms, including nausea, sweating, shakiness, and anxiety after a heavy period of drinking. Over time, the drinker develops a greater tolerance for alcohol and needs to consume greater amounts in order to get high. Alcoholics have been described as people in the grip of a powerful craving or uncontrollable need for alcohol that overrides their ability to stop drinking. This need can be as strong as the need for food or water.[6] Most often, people who are dependent on a substance are the ones who have withdrawal symptoms when they stop using the alcohol or other drug.

- *Abuse* does not include a craving for alcohol, loss of control over the drinking, or physical dependence on the substance. Instead, abuse involves the development of problems that come from frequent drinking. These problems might include failure to fulfill major work or home responsibilities, problems with relationships, or having recurring legal problems, such as driving under the influence of alcohol or arrests for disorderly conduct, including fighting. When he or she is sober, the person understands how the drinking is causing problems, but the drinking continues nevertheless.

- *Substance-induced disorders* include a wide variety of mental conditions that are brought on by the use of alcohol or other harmful drugs. These are organic conditions, wherein the brain or some other part of the body is not functioning normally because of the excessive and continued use of a substance, such as alcohol. Examples include liver disorders, substance-induced psychotic disorder, substance-induced anxiety, and substance-induced dementia.

Wouldn't it be better to forget this complex terminology and use more common terms such as alcoholism or drug addiction? These words are simpler, but over the years they have come to be used so commonly that they fail to express the seriousness of a physiological condition over which an individual may have decreasing control. The majority of counselors and health-care professionals regard alcoholism or other addiction as a chronic, progressive disease in which the dependence on alcohol or other potentially destructive substance increasingly interferes with one's physical and mental health, intellectual capabilities, interpersonal relationships, and ability to function economically and in one's daily activities. Although people may differ in their symptoms and in the speed with which the condition develops, all show physical symptoms, psychological difficulties (including an obsessive craving for the drug), and behavioral problems that disrupt one's social or work life.

This concept of alcoholism and drug dependence as disease fails to use the word *sin*. Is alcoholism always a sickness or is it a sin? The question is not confined to Christians. Physicians and medical insurance companies accept alcoholism as a disease because it is predictable, progressive, physiologically debilitating, and treatable. By calling alcoholism a disease, individuals are less likely to be condemned and more likely to get treatment, which insurance companies will finance. The disease concept also has the potential to relieve the alcoholic of personal responsibility and guilt. At his perjury trial, a former government official argued that he was not guilty of illegal acts because he was suffering from the disease of alcoholism when he broke the law.

Others have challenged the disease concept.[7] Certainly, it is true that some people are physiologically more prone to become alcoholics, but at some time every drinker makes the decision to take a first drink, and at least at the beginning, each person can decide whether to stop or continue. Alcoholism is a progressive addiction that engulfs its victim psychologically and physically, but alcoholism also is a moral condition for which the drinker is at least partially responsible. It is both simplistic and extreme to conclude that alcoholism is *only* a disease or *only* a black-and-white case of sin.

In the pages that follow, we will assume that alcoholism and other substance dependence are both sickness and sin. Both are involved in the development of addiction; both must be considered in treatment. In the remainder of this chapter, the focus will be on the impact of alcohol. The abuse and dependencies on other substances, habits, and addictions will be considered in chapter 35.

The Bible and Alcohol-Related Problems

The Bible does not appear to teach abstinence, but it does teach temperance. In Psalm 104, wine is included among the blessings from God and described as something that makes people glad. In his first miracle, Jesus made wine from water, wine apparently was taken at the Last Supper, and it appears that Jesus himself drank wine.[8] Paul showed no hesitation in urging Timothy to drink a little wine to help his stomach problems and frequent illnesses.[9] Some Bible scholars have questioned the strength of the wine in first-century Palestine, but we know that it was strong enough to produce drunkenness. At the wedding in Cana where Jesus turned water into wine, the headwaiter implied that people drank so freely that at the end of the celebration they were less able to tell good wine from bad.[10] Whether the wine was strong or diluted, the drinker had a responsibility to control his or her input.

Throughout the Bible, excessive drinking is condemned. "Whoever is led astray by drink cannot be wise," the writer of Proverbs warns. "Wine produces mockers; liquor leads to brawls."[11] "Do not carouse with drunkards and gluttons, for they are on their way to poverty."[12] Paul gave a similar warning when he wrote to the Ephesians.[13] Most powerful of all the biblical passages is the description of alcohol abuse in Proverbs 23:29–35.

Who has anguish? Who has sorrow? Who is always fighting? Who is always complaining? Who has unnecessary bruises? Who has bloodshot eyes? It is the one who spends long hours in taverns, trying out new drinks. Don't let the sparkle and smooth taste of wine deceive you. For in the end it bites like a poisonous serpent; it stings like a viper. You will see hallucinations, and you will say crazy things. You will stagger like a sailor tossed at sea, clinging to a swaying mast. And you will say, "They hit me, but I didn't feel it. I didn't even know when they beat me up. When will I wake up so I can have another drink?"

Even as the Bible warns against drunkenness and teaches moderation in drinking, it also considers abstinence favorably. John the Baptist was a special messenger from God who did not drink wine.[14] When men or women took the Nazarite vow, "setting themselves apart to the Lord in a special way," they agreed to "give up wine and other alcoholic drinks." They did not drink vinegar made from wine, other fermented drinks, or anything that came from the grapevine.[15]

Whereas most Christians today would conclude that moderation is good, many believe that abstinence is better, especially in view of the clear dangers inherent in drinking. Alcohol is a mind-altering drug that, for some, can become psychologically and physically addicting. While its moderate use is not condemned or forbidden by Scripture, drinking may fall into the category of an act that is permissible but not beneficial.[16] It is wise to avoid or at least be cautious of any practice or questionable behavior such as drinking alcoholic beverages that can harm the body, numb sensation, dull the mind, make one more susceptible to immorality and other sin, cause harm to other human beings, or make another believer stumble and fall.[17] Sometimes, believers must chose to use self-restraint because this will be for the good and growth of the Body of Christ, the church.

What if another person begins drinking heavily, often becomes intoxicated, develops a dependence on alcohol, or is a substance abuser? Spirit-led Christians, including counselors, have a responsibility to restore people who fall into sinful patterns of behavior that harm themselves or others. When people are physically controlled by dependence on alcoholism or some other substance, getting free by themselves is difficult and involves more than willpower and determination. In a spirit of gentleness, humility, and compassion, the people-helper patiently seeks to "do good," by giving the needed physical help, confronting the fallen one with his or her responsibilities, and trusting that at the proper time, there will be restoration if we do not give up.[18]

The Causes of Alcohol-Related Problems

In 1959 a leader in the field of alcohol research and treatment wrote that almost everyone has an opinion on the causes of alcoholism, but the opinions differed widely. Forty years later another expert admitted that in spite of significant research in the field, there were still major differences of opinion about why people become alcoholics.[19] These differences come because alcohol intoxication, abuse, and dependence are complex behaviors with diverse causes. Most researchers and counselors would agree that there is a combination of influences that make some people especially prone to problems with alcohol.

1. *Biological and Heredity Influences.* Alcoholics Anonymous defines alcoholism as "a progressive illness, which can never be cured" and which "represents a combination of physical sensitivity to alcohol, plus a mental obsession with drinking which . . . cannot be broken by willpower alone."[20] Decades of biological and genetic research support the idea that some people inherit a high vulnerability to alcoholism. When compared to the children of nonalcoholics, the sons and daughters of alcoholic parents are much more likely to become alcoholics when

they grow up. This is true, even when the children of alcoholics are adopted at birth and raised without knowledge of the real parents' alcoholism. In contrast, children of nonalcoholics show no greater than average evidence of alcoholism, even when they are raised by an alcoholic parent.[21]

Despite huge amounts of money spent on sophisticated research with both humans and animals, there still is a lack of clarity on the exact role of biology and heredity in causing alcoholism. Genetic research, for example, has identified a gene (D2) that appears to moderate the type and/or course of alcohol addiction. Research does not substantiate that the D2 gene causes alcoholism; however, it does appear to moderate the course of alcoholism, and there is evidence that it is more common in alcoholics than in the general population. A different kind of research study compared the influence of alcohol on two groups of males in their teens and early twenties. The groups were matched carefully in terms of age, race, religion, education, habits of drinking, and other characteristics, but one group had alcoholic fathers, while the other did not. When these young men were given alcoholic drinks, they responded differently. Even though everyone had identical blood alcohol levels, the children of alcoholics felt less intoxicated and performed better on intellectual and motor tests. This confirms other research that people who become alcoholics initially have greater tolerance for alcohol and less awareness of its impact. As a result, they are less likely to adjust their alcoholic intake and more likely to become addicted.[22]

2. *Home and Family Influences*. Alcoholism seems to run in families. As we have seen, problems with alcohol are more prevalent in people who have grown up in homes where a parent has had problems with alcohol. Genetics or other biological influences may account for some of this, of course, but the family dynamics may be of equal or greater influence. Attempts to study past and present home influences are difficult because what family members report about their homes may not be what really happened in their homes in previous years or what continues to occur at present.

(a) The Family's Role in *Causing* Alcohol-Related Problems. Several years ago a doctoral student named Sandra Wilson asked if I would serve on her faculty committee. She wanted to do research on how children are impacted when they grow up in homes where one or both parents are alcoholic. In the months that followed (and later while she worked on a book that I urged her to write), Sandy introduced me to the fears, guilt, confusion, pain, and challenges faced by children of alcoholics.[23] Eventually, they join a group known as adult children of alcoholics (ACOAs), many of whom go through life carrying the emotional scars of their early years in an alcoholic family. These people have more serious physical problems as adults than those who were raised in nonalcoholic homes,[24] and many of the ACOA people become alcohol dependent or alcohol abusers themselves.

Often, these people are insecure, self-condemning, and afraid of intimacy. Children in alcoholic families learn three rules for survival: don't talk, don't trust, don't feel. When these young people become adults, they continue to have problems with trust, dependency, self-control, identification, and expression of feelings. Compared to young adults from nonalcoholic families, people in the ACOA group report higher levels of anxiety, a greater avoidance of romantic relationships, and a general fearfulness of forming attachments with other adults.[25] Some become depressed, some develop eating disorders, and many live in constant fear of becoming alcoholic like their parents.[26] Despite these fears, many children of alcoholics do slip into the clutches of alcoholism.

As we have seen, genetic and other biological influences may help in leading to this fall, but the home environment and parental attitudes are also important. When parents don't care if the children drink or if there is no concern about the dangers of alcohol, then misuse is more likely to follow. If parents are neglectful or excessively punitive, the children may withdraw or rebel, and drinking problems can follow. In one study of a thousand adult children of alcoholics, 78.2 percent said they had been highly affected by growing up in an alcoholic home; 11.1 percent said they had been moderately affected.[27]

(b) The Family's Role in *Maintaining* Alcohol-Related Problems. When somebody develops serious problems with alcohol, his or her family is greatly impacted. These family members often suffer and would like to see the problem treated successfully, but strange as it may seem, these same family members often act in ways that keep the problem going. How does that work?

Only a few alcoholics live on skid row. Most live at home with their families, and many continue to hold their jobs. As the intoxication becomes more frequent or the alcohol abuse or dependence gets worse, each person in the household is affected. At the beginning, the family members try to deny the reality of the situation. Many times it becomes a huge and disruptive issue that affects and worries everybody, even though it might never be mentioned. Each family member is both protective and critical of the drinker, but each also tries to hold the family together with as little additional strain as possible. There may be attempts to control or stop the family member's drinking, such as hiding any alcohol found in the home or pouring it down the toilet. At some time there may be an effort to understand and eliminate the causes. Often, there is an effort to hide the drinking behavior from friends or from the community, to make excuses for not attending family gatherings or social events. When the problem drinking cannot be hidden or denied any longer, the drinker is repeatedly urged to quit.

Sometimes, the family members slip into survival roles. These are sincere and sometimes unconscious efforts to keep the family together and to prevent it from buckling under the stress. The *enabler role*, for example, is taken by the person, usually the spouse, who seeks to take responsibility for meeting the family needs. Loren's wife is a good example, but even as the enabler tries to keep things running smoothly, there can be feelings of anger, depression, and resentment stirring below the surface. The *family hero*, usually the oldest child, tries to make things better for the family, often takes responsibility for the younger siblings, and may fill in as the nondrinking parent's confidant and helper. The *scapegoat* acts out the family stresses, gets into trouble, and often distracts attention from the drinking problem. According to the family systems theory that we discussed in chapters 29 and 31, most often the scapegoat is the problem person who is brought for counseling, even though the real source of family problems is some other person. In contrast, the *mascot* or *clown* tries to inject humor into a painful situation, while the *lost child* covers up his or her feelings and tries to be the one person whom the family does not have to worry about. Sometimes, the lost child stays away from home as much as possible and often turns to other adults and families for support and closeness. All of this reflects the pain and pathos that infiltrate and characterize the alcoholic's whole family.

Roles like these keep the family going, but they also support the alcoholic in his or her addiction. As long as the family seems to be getting along, there is less motivation to change. The family, therefore, is caught in a trap where winning is impossible. If they adjust to the addiction, the problem is perpetuated, and the pain goes on. If the family doesn't adjust, everybody is hurt, and the pain still continues. Many counselors agree that treatment will be delayed and improvement will be prevented as long as family members perpetuate the problem by denying its reality, hiding it from others, and protecting the drinker from facing the consequences of his or her irresponsible and self-centered behavior. Most families of alcoholics eventually discover that the situation is not helped when there is overprotection of the drinker or continued acceptance of the problem drinker's rationalizations, promises to change, and excuses. The sooner everyone faces the reality of the situation, the better.

We should add that it is not only the family that perpetuates the addiction problem. The problem persists when employers, the drinker's friends, or others overlook the problem and try to ignore its existence. Society as a whole also perpetuates the problem when people fail to admit the seriousness of addiction, laugh at inebriation, tolerate drunken driving, excuse crimes committed under the influence of alcohol, use terms like "happy hour" or "Christmas cheer" to describe alcohol use, permit the free advertising of alcoholic beverages without warnings about its dangers, and portray alcohol use as an effective way to relax and cope with stress. Church leaders add to the problem when they ignore the fact that problems with alcohol hide within most large congregations, or when they fail to provide sensitive help for individuals and families who struggle with drinking problems or other addictions.

3. *Social-Cultural Influences.* If a culture or subcultural group has clear guidelines about the use of alcohol or other drugs, abuse is less likely. Among Jews, for example, young people generally are permitted to drink, but drunkenness is condemned and the rate of alcoholism is low. Sometimes, this changes as Jewish young people move away from their religious roots. Attitudes toward drinking in Russia or Italy appear to differ from those in Jordan or Malaysia, and this has an affect on the ways in which alcohol is used and abused. In contrast, in the United States and Australia, there is a greater tolerance of drunkenness. Teenage and college drinking is winked at as a sign of growing up, and inebriation becomes a topic for television and cocktail hour jokes. Since getting high or binge drinking are the "in" things to do, and since peer pressure is so strong, conditions are more ripe for alcohol abuse.

Conditions are also ripe among people of low socioeconomic status or those who live in geographical areas with widespread and persisting poverty, hopelessness, or lack of meaning in their lives. Alcoholism also is greater among families who struggle with insufficient income, violence and discord in the home, inadequate housing, chronic hunger, and poor health. This may account for high rates of alcoholism in depressed urban neighborhoods, in localities where unemployment is high, in some immigrant groups, or in communities where there are rapid changes that require major adjustments. People drink in part to escape their pressures. Of course, it is difficult to determine whether the poverty and misery lead people to drink, or the excessive drinking and community acceptance of alcohol abuse lead to more poverty and misery.

Religious differences also have an influence on drinking patterns. Some researchers have found that drinking is more accepted and thus more common in some denominational groups, whereas others, such as fundamentalist Christians, tend to frown on drinking altogether. Even this depends on the culture, however. Religious groups may differ markedly in the United States or Canada, but differences may be less noticeable in Chile or France, where moderate alcohol consumption is accepted in almost all religious groups.

In their highly acclaimed book on alcoholism, Anderson Spickard and Barbara R. Thompson conclude that groups with high rates of alcoholism and groups with low rates are not separated by biological or racial differences.[28] The two most important factors are attitudes toward public drunkenness and whether drinking takes place outside of meals. In countries and groups that drink only at meals and do not tolerate public drunkenness, there are lower rates of alcohol abuse. In view of findings like these, perhaps it is not surprising that alcoholism is a major problem in America, especially among young people.

4. *Psychological and Stress-Related Influences*. If we ask people why they abuse or are dependent on alcohol, few are likely to mention their heredity, family background, or cultural group as the main causes. More often abusers will mention how the alcohol or another substance will help them deal with stress, reduce tension, or meet psychological needs. Drinking, taking drugs, or engaging in other addictive behavior can help abusers reduce anxiety or depression, calm (or increase) aggressive or sexual drives, create a sense of euphoria or well-being, escape reality, satisfy curiosity, defy authority, reduce inhibitions, gain peer approval, or get spiritual insights.[29] At least in the beginning, it feels good, so they do it.

Personality characteristics also play a role. Addictive behaviors and substance abuse may be more likely to develop in people who are impetuous and inclined to act more on impulse than on reflection. Other traits associated with abuse and alcohol dependence are emotional immaturity, limited ability to tolerate tension or frustration, low capacity to endure painful or unpleasant feelings, and excessive dependency.[30] Of course, some of these traits may be the result of the addiction instead of or in addition to the cause.

Also psychological are the ways in which alcohol problems emerge as developmental issues. The best way to explain this is to give the example of how a hypothetical teenage male might become addicted.[31] Let's name him Jake. Like most people his age, Jake likes some things about himself and dislikes others. At times he experiences anxiety, fears, guilt, disappointment, and insecurity, but these are mixed with periodic feelings of enthusiasm and hope about the future. Even if there are tensions at home, he is likely to be accustomed to comfort and the immediate meeting of his needs and desires. The advertising messages that bombard his senses will teach him about acquiring possessions, enjoying pleasures, and experiencing endless possibilities. Because of this comfortable childhood, adolescent stresses may hit with special intensity.

His parents may not think about this, but in addition to his first family of adults at home and in school, Jake has what one writer has called a second family consisting of his peer group and the pop culture.[32] In this highly influential peer-pop culture, fun and comfort are paramount. Sex is at the core, along with easily available drugs and alcohol, which may start being used in the sixth or seventh grade. Influenced by his peers and impacted by the thousands of television commercials and attractive beer advertisements that he has seen during his life, Jake may experience pressure from his friends, a desire to see what it is like to drink and get drunk, identification with a group or hero who drinks, or a belief that use of alcohol will prove his manhood and cause more stimulating sex. He might even view the use of alcohol as a way to get even with his parents.

When Jake starts to drink he may feel a sense of euphoria, despite the periodic hangovers. Drinking may make him feel tranquil, less nervous, more adequate, and socially at ease. His problems or stresses seem less severe, and the world looks rosy. If the drinking continues, there may be periodic regrets or remorse during times of sobriety, but the alcohol use persists because the mood change is so pleasant and the danger seems so minimal. By the time Jake is into his twenties, drinking has become a habit. He does a lot of binge drinking with his friends in college, and by the time he reaches thirty, his use of alcohol may have become an integrated part of his lifestyle. Maybe without giving it much thought, he has become addicted both physically and psychologically. Unlike earlier times, his body needs larger and larger quantities of alcohol to create new euphoria and to relieve anxiety. If the alcohol is withdrawn, sickness results. Only more alcohol can take away the symptoms, and sometimes there are severe withdrawal symptoms, including delirium tremens, disorientation, hallucinations, or seizures.

Unless Jake gets help in stopping, by the time he reaches middle age, getting and consuming alcohol has become so important that his personal life, family, social, and business life all suffer. The person who began drinking as a way of relaxation, connecting with friends, and stress management has now become totally dependent on alcohol. As this dependence has built, the need for the alcoholic drug has increased, self-control has lessened, work has suffered, and so have Jake's health, psychological stability, and social relationships. The alcohol has become increasingly important until it is the core around which life is organized. It may be the cause of Jake's problems, but he also may see alcohol as the solution—a magic but tragic potion that dulls the stresses of life. Someday he might agree with the members of Alcoholics Anonymous, who believe that no cure will come until Jakes reaches bottom, admitting that he is powerless over alcohol and unable to manage life without the help of a power that is greater than himself.

5. *Spiritual Influences.* Surely, nobody starts out to be dependent on alcohol. Circumstances, genetics, family background, continuing stress, social pressure, and innocent choices can lead almost anyone into addiction.[33] This route to alcohol abuse is smoother when human beings lack spiritual or religious convictions and moral values.

Many people grow up in homes where there is a spiritual void. There are no religious beliefs or clearly defined spiritually based values. Even though it is known that teenagers who attend religious services regularly are less likely to get involved with drinking or drug use, some parents never encourage or model religious devotion or attendance at worship services. In contemporary cultures where affluence is of great importance, it is more common to worship the gods of materialism, personal pleasure, popularity, and career success. When these prove elusive or when they fail to satisfy, individuals sense their lack of values, increasing stress, and feelings of emptiness, so they try to hide the hollowness by turning to drugs and alcohol.

It could be argued that human beings have an inner need for a real and growing relationship with God. When this craving is denied, unrecognized, or unfulfilled, there is a search for something else that will fill the vacuum. This is stated clearly in the Bible. "Be careful how you live.... Don't act thoughtlessly.... Don't be drunk with wine, because that will ruin your life. Instead, let the Holy Spirit fill and control you. Then you will sing psalms and hymns and spiritual songs among yourselves, making music to the Lord in your hearts. And you will always give thanks for everything to God the Father in the name of our Lord Jesus Christ."[34] Here in a few words is a warning, an implied cause, and an answer to alcohol abuse.

Despite the validity of physical, cultural, psychological, and spiritual causes of alcohol-related disorders, we must never forget the role of sin. The heavy use of alcohol can lead to a variety of social, medical, interpersonal, family, criminal, spiritual, and psychiatric problems. Even if alcohol abusers are addicted and unable to engage in self-control, Christians assume that early in the process, problem drinkers made decisions to submit their minds and bodies to substances that are known to destroy and that could have been avoided. The clear success of so-called faith-based approaches to treatment, such as Teen Challenge or the Salvations Army's rehabilitation centers, reminds us of the role of sin as a cause of alcoholism, and the place of forgiveness, redemption, and the Holy Spirit's power as important parts of the cure.

The Effects of Alcohol-Related Problems

The excessive use of alcohol does not affect everyone in the same way. Some people become charming and loquacious after a few drinks; others become nasty and aggressive. Some hide their alcoholic intake well, but others show almost immediate behavior changes. Even with these differences, however, developing alcohol abusers show many similar physical and behavioral effects of the addiction.

1. *Physical Effects.* Whenever alcohol or any other chemical substance is taken into the body, there will be a physiological reaction. The nature of this reaction depends on the age and physical condition of the person, his or her medical history, the type of drug taken, the amount, and the frequency with which it is used.

Alcohol is a toxin (poison) that affects most body cells. If taken rapidly and without food, the alcohol content of the blood rises, the brain's functioning is impaired temporarily, and the drinker's balance, motor skills, thinking, and emotional responses are influenced. If alcohol is taken consistently and in large amounts, almost every body organ will be affected either directly or indirectly, and severe physical damage can result. For example, in about one-third of all heavy drinkers, the liver cells are destroyed, and the organ is no longer able to process the nutrients in food. This liver disease, cirrhosis, usually is painless until the damage is too advanced to be treated successfully.

Heavy alcohol use also can bring permanent damage to the brain and central nervous system, lead to numerous gastrointestinal diseases, put extra pressure on the heart so that strokes or heart attacks are more likely, impede the manufacture of red and white blood cells, increase the risk of cancer, inhibit the activities of the immune system (this is known by the tongue twisting term *alcohol-related immune system suppression*), lead to impotence, and cause potentially serious risk to a developing fetus through a condition known at fetal alcohol syndrome.[35] Because of these physical aspects of alcohol abuse, medical intervention is a crucial part of treatment.

2. *Psychological-Social Effects.* How can a person tell if he or she has a drinking

problem? One of the most widely used tests includes only four questions and sometimes is known as CAGE:

C—Have you ever felt you should **cut down** on your drinking?
A—Have people **annoyed** you by criticizing your drinking?
G—Have you ever felt bad or **guilty** about your drinking?
E—Have you ever had a drink first thing in the morning (as an **eye opener**) to steady your nerves or get rid of a hangover?

As a quick guide, counselors can ask these same questions. The greater the number of *yes* answers, the more likely a problem exists or is developing. Even if there were all *no* answers, alcohol abuse still might be a problem if the person encounters drinking-related problems with his or her job, relationships, health, or the law.

Since alcohol abuse is so common, most people are familiar with its obvious psychological effects: dulled thinking, inappropriate behavior and emotional responses, self-neglect, withdrawal, and loss of social inhibitions. As the condition worsens, psychological defenses become more noticeable, including rationalizations (making excuses for one's drinking or alcohol-induced behavior), repression (a spontaneous forgetting of shameful and painful memories), projection (blaming others for one's drinking and unacceptable thoughts, feelings, or actions) and, perhaps most common of all, denial that a problem exists. Later, life is built around getting enough of the alcohol; all else is of secondary importance.

It should be added that alcohol dependence also can lead to high rates of interpersonal violence, physical and sexual abuse, risky sexual behavior, and suicide.[36] Often, alcohol-related problems accompany other psychological abnormalities, including depression, high rates of anxiety, problems with impulse control, persisting anger, and more severe disorientation or other mental illness. The drinking problem may help cause these disorders, or the disorders may lead to the drinking. Regardless of which comes first, when the two go together there are increased problems for the substance abuser and his or her associates.

3. *Family Effects.* Some of the family effects of alcohol abuse were mentioned earlier. Families, at first, try to protect, control, and blame the drinker. Then the family members take over the excessive drinker's responsibilities, all the while living with tension, fear, insecurity, and shame. Often, there is embarrassment that leads the family to withdraw from others. As a result, there may be shame, loneliness, and social isolation. In view of the fact that families so often are impacted, it is not surprising that the best treatments also involve family members.

4. *Spiritual Effects.* Although some groups claim that drug use leads to new spiritual experiences,[37] Christians believe that it is very difficult to grow spiritually when one is dependent on and controlled by a drug. Many who abuse or are dependent on alcohol know this, but they feel powerless to stop the drinking. As a result there is greater guilt, shame, and alienation from God. The alcohol becomes an idol of worship—the thing that matters most. This can have adverse spiritual influences on the family, although some families appear to draw closer to God during their time of crisis. Churches can intervene and be helpful with alcoholic families, but too often these people are shunned or pushed away. Sometimes, this is because pastors and church leaders simply don't know what to do

when there is an alcohol abuser and abuser's family in the church. At other times, the church leaders may not be willing to believe or admit that there might be problem drinkers in their congregations.

Counseling and Alcohol-Related Problems

Matt is middle aged, intelligent, likeable, and successful in his career. He also is drunk more days than not. When he came for counseling, he had been attending Alcoholics Anonymous (AA) meetings for several weeks and had not had a drink for about a month, but he had been this route before. Matt had gone through some of the best alcohol treatment programs in the country. He knew all the methods that counselors used. He knew, as well, that the latest counselor probably would be no more successful than the ones who had come before. The more programs one has been through, the less likely that the latest approach will work.[38]

Before we consider what might work with Matt or other alcohol-dependent counselees, it can be useful to know some things that do not help. These include criticism, shaming, coaxing, making the person promise to stop, threats, hiding or destroying the alcohol, urging the use of greater willpower, preaching, quoting Bible verses, or instilling guilt. Families and friends try many or all of these, but they almost never work.

What does work in helping people with alcohol-related problems? Probably thousands of researchers have sought to answer this question and, as a result, several basic treatments are now known to be effective. These are summarized in Table 34–1. There is no one approach that is effective with everybody, but some combination of these will work with most people.

These approaches that work have several common ingredients, according to researchers.[39] They all:

- Avoid confrontation. In every effective approach, there is a good therapeutic alliance among the people involved. No approaches were found to work if they involved criticism and confrontation. All the effective methods demonstrated mutual goal setting, support, and working together.
- Focus on understanding the influences that encourage and reinforce alcohol use or abuse. These influences include people, social situations, ways of thinking, lifestyles, or anything else that can lead the problem drinker to have another drink. The goal is to help people with alcohol-related problems to deal effectively with these tempting influences and people, make behavior changes, and find ways to increase their motivation and ability to stay sober.
- Teach specific skills, including how to build relationships, cope with stress, and stay away from situations that could stimulate drinking. Skills are learned by listening to the experience of others, learning what to do and what to avoid, reading, and receiving advice and feedback. The best skills learning comes from sponsors or other recovering alcoholics rather than from counselors.
- Promote active coping and goal setting. This might include going for a specific period of time without a drink, working toward vocational objectives, or building specific relationships.

Table 34–1

Alcohol Dependence:
Empirically Demonstrated Treatments That Are Effective*

1. Teaching Coping and Social Skills
The goal is to help people manage life and relationships without alcohol. This includes teaching social skills, life-management skills, self-control, how to spot and avoid events that trigger drinking, and how to avoid relapse.

2. Enhancing Motivation
This may use brief strategic counseling methods. Ask open-ended questions, listen, show empathy, encourage responsibility to change, set goals and ways to achieve them, hold the person accountable, discuss costs of drinking behavior. This is shown to be "among the treatments with the strongest evidence" for effectiveness.

3. Environmental and Relationship-Based Treatment
These involve (a) changing the environment and (b) stimulating social support. Includes vocational counseling; relationship counseling; and teaching ways to refuse drinks, how to build family communication and better family relationships, problem-solving skills, and ways to build friendships that do not involve drinking. Could also include involvement with church, community groups, fitness clubs, and other healthy groups.

4. Use of Drugs (Psycho-Pharmacological Treatments)
These are drugs that alter the way the brain reacts to alcohol. The most common
are *disulfiram, naltrexone,* and *acamprosate.* Of course, these only can be prescribed by health-care professionals who are licensed to write prescriptions and monitor treatment.

5. Twelve-Step Programs
These include Alcoholics Anonymous and other programs that are modeled on the same primary focus of moving progressively through the steps to recovery. Usually involves belief in a "Higher Power," acceptance and surrender, receiving support and guidance, attending meetings, sometimes use of slogans.

* This chart has been developed from Jennifer P. Read, Christopher W. Kahler, and John F. Stevenson, "Bridging the Gap Between Alcoholism Treatment Research and Practice: Identifying What Works and Why," *Professional Psychology: Research and Practice* 32 (June 2001): 227–238.

- Focus on socioenvironmental issues. This big word means that the programs proven to be most effective all help people change their environments and find networks of people who will give social support and encouragement. This is where AA is so strong. Social support is critical if there is to be ongoing abstinence.

In line with these guidelines, there are ways in which people with alcohol-use problems can be helped.

1. *Get the Alcoholic Abuser to Admit the Need for Help.* This can be difficult because many alcohol abusers or alcohol-dependent people deny that they have a problem. Sometimes, they don't have accurate information about what constitutes a serious alcohol problem, they may deny the evidence because they don't want to face it, or their alcohol-related behaviors may be hidden by the actions of well-meaning family members who cover for the drinker when he or she does something irresponsible. It now has been demonstrated that treatment is likely to be ineffective if the drinker does not admit the problem or agree to cooperate in treatment.

How can the alcohol abuser get the message that he or she needs help and must agree to get involved? The members of Alcoholics Anonymous believe that the drinker needs to hit bottom in some way. Only then is the person willing to admit that he or she is powerless to control alcohol and unable to manage life without help. Regrettably, some people die or damage themselves irreparably before they hit bottom. Counselors need to consider other ways to help the alcoholic accept the need for treatment before it's too late.

Many problem drinkers first come to the counselor's attention because of some problem that appears to have nothing to do with alcohol. A couple may ask for marriage counseling, for example, because they are having a problem with one of the children. At first the counselor fails to suspect that one of the well-dressed, seemingly relaxed counselees really is an alcohol abuser. For example, the husband may be a successful business executive who anesthetizes himself with alcohol after work every evening while his family goes about the business of life without his involvement.

Even when you suspect alcohol abuse, the counselee often will deny that this is a problem. He or she may agree to complete one of the several alcoholism screening tests that can be found on the Internet, read about alcoholism on the Internet, or complete a simple questionnaire like the one in Figure 34–1. This is not a scientific screening test, and there is no score. Instead, it is a guide that could be used in an interview to help the counselor and counselee assess drinking problems that might be evidence of an alcohol problem.

Since developing alcoholism is characterized by denial that a problem exists, it can help to point out the evidence in a firm, factual, and nonjudgmental way. Family members can give specific examples. Focus on specifics ("Last night at 11 PM you fell, knocked over, and broke the lamp) rather than vague generalities ("You're drinking too much!"). Some counselors suggest that the message is best conveyed nonverbally. If the alcohol user collapses on the living room floor, for example, leave the person there rather than helping him or her into bed. If something was broken or knocked over, don't pick it up. This makes it more difficult for the drinker to deny later that he or she passed out or damaged something in the house.

A Drinker's Checklist

Check all that apply. Within the past six weeks how often have you:

___ Had a drink alone or in secret?

___ Had a drink as soon as you got up in the morning?

___ Felt the need for a drink?

___ Not been able to remember a conversation or appointment while you were drinking?

___ Had difficulty doing your work because of your drinking?

___ Had a hangover?

___ Started drinking and been unable to stop?

___ Been worried that alcohol might not be available when you want it?

___ Hidden alcohol in your house or office so you can be sure it would be available?

___ Gulped drinks, ordered doubles, or become intoxicated intentionally because this makes you feel good.

___ Had legal, driving, financial, or employment problems because of your drinking?

___ Experienced shaking, hallucinations, seizures, or passing out as a result of your drinking?

___ Said or done something while you were drinking that you regretted later?

___ Been annoyed because somebody had made a comment about your drinking?

___ Had another person insist on driving you home after you had been drinking?

Figure 34–1. A Drinker's Checklist.

Most people with alcohol problems have high anxiety and low self-esteem. Try to be careful not to criticize or condemn in a way that arouses anxiety or seems threatening. Convey acceptance of the person but not of the behavior. Listen to the person, but recognize that problem drinkers and other substance abusers tend to be manipulative and specialists in evoking sympathy. The counselor must resist the tendency to give advice, preach, or act like a parent. Instead, show a noncondescending, firm, sensitive attitude to imply that responsibility for recovery must remain with the drinker. In all of this remember that the best counselors are gentle but not soft-hearted in their mannerisms.

2. *Stop the Drinking.* Earlier we mentioned a long-time drinker named Matt. His counselor has three essential ingredients that he requires of every counselee.[40]

- There must be total abstinence from all mood-altering chemicals, not just the alcohol. If this is not done, other drugs can be substituted for the alcohol, and relapse is more likely.

- Significant others must be told about the counseling. If others know, the counselee is more likely to stay with the program because they can now hold the counselee responsible for his or her actions.
- There must be regular contact with other recovering alcoholics. This usually involves participation with AA, but it also can involve church, therapy groups, or other kinds of supportive gatherings.

Matt's counselor believes that these three behaviors give a foundation for recovery. If they are not there, failure is more likely.

Matt agreed. He already had stopped drinking when he came for help, and he was involved with an AA group. Many people, like Matt, can stop drinking on their own, at least for a while, but others may need the help of a physician. This is because in some cases the withdrawal symptoms (including tremors, nausea, sweating, weakness, anxiety, depression, and sometimes delirium) may be severe.

3. *Help the Counselee Get Support.* People who abuse alcohol or other substances often are lonely, immature people who are being asked by their counselors to change a lifestyle that is well entrenched and to give up a substance that they depend on and value. You cannot accomplish this in one or two hours of individual counseling each week. Many substance abusers are best helped within the confines of rehabilitation centers where help is available on a round-the-clock basis. Often assistance comes through group counseling where recovering alcoholics can help each other face the stresses of life, interact with people, find encouragement and understanding, get accountability, and learn to live without alcohol or other chemicals.

The most effective, most utilized, and most studied of these supportive approaches is Alcoholics Anonymous and related groups (like Al-Anon for spouses of people with drinking problems and Alateen for their children).[41] The groups meet in cities and towns all over the world. They are free of charge, are listed in the phone book, and are perhaps the most effective means for helping alcoholics and their families. They are not specifically Christian, but these groups use principles that, in general, are consistent with biblical teaching: acceptance of reality; faith in God (known as a Higher Being): commitment of one's life to divine care; honesty with God, self, and others; desire and readiness to change one's way of life; prayer; making amends; and sharing with others.

Much of the supportive help that AA gives could be provided by the church from members of the congregation who are understanding, familiar with the facts about addiction, and available to give encouragement and practical assistance. In many congregations this would not work because the church members are critical, condemning, or unwilling to help. Other believers are sympathetic, but their support may be limited because they are unfamiliar with the facts of alcoholism or unable to empathize with the struggles of alcoholics and their families. The drinkers, themselves, may have difficulty relating to church people, preferring instead to meet with other recovering alcoholics whose understanding is more experiential and who may still be struggling. Some churches have developed programs for recovering alcoholics that are based on the AA model but are more openly Christian. If these are not available in your area, you may consider encouraging your counselees to get involved both in AA and in the broader, more diversified fellowship of a local church. There is some evidence that AA members often are likely to get involved in community or church activities because they see this as a way of giving back to the community what the community has given to them.[42]

4. *Help with Stress Management and Coping Skills*. Problem drinkers often deal with stress by escaping through the use of alcohol and other chemicals. Counseling must show that there are better ways to deal with the pressures of life. To do this, the counselee must learn that he or she can trust the counselor, who, in turn, must be patient and dependable. Stress in general and ways to cope can be discussed. An additional and perhaps better approach is to take each stressful situation as it arises and help the counselee learn how it can be handled effectively. This will include considerations of interpersonal relations and how to get along with others apart from a reliance on alcohol.

One day Matt's counselor said, "We need to know what works and what doesn't in your attempts to deal with drinking. What has worked for you?'

"Going to meetings," Matt replied, "being honest with my friends in the recovery program, and being honest with my wife."

"Okay, and what hasn't worked?"[43]

The question led to some of Matt's ways of handling stress and how drinking helped him be like any normal guy who could relax and have fun like everybody else. This led to discussions of the fact that he wasn't a normal guy if he could not stop himself from drinking, especially during times of stress.

5. *Encourage Self-Understanding and Changes in Lifestyle*. It did not take long for the counselor to learn the reason for Matt's previous treatment failures and subsequent relapses. "Each time, Matt had decided, albeit unconsciously, that alcoholism was preferable to something frightening beneath the surface of his conscious mind that threatened to break through into full, terrible awareness."[44] With the counselor's encouragement, Matt talked about his parents and how his father had taught him to avoid emotion at all cost. A lot of Matt's insecurities and fears were kept hidden by the use of alcohol to help him feel good. Christmas was especially difficult because Matt had always been disappointed, and the reminders of his past Christmas mornings had led to heavy drinking almost every year in late December.

When a trusting relationship has been established, it can be helpful to look into the root causes of the alcohol abuse. These discussions can lead to insight, but insight is of limited value unless it is accompanied by practical, specific plans for changed behavior. Sometimes, these plans may involve vocational counseling, help with self-esteem, a consideration of spiritual issues, or marital counseling. I am not sure if that happened with Matt, but he and his counselor might have talked about how spiritual matters and help from his wife could help him get through future Christmas seasons with joy and without alcohol.

There also is the issue of lifestyle. After the drinking has stopped, how will life be different? A person's style of life depends on making decisions concerning what will or will not be done now and in the future. As the counselor and counselee consider life planning, it can help to be sensitive to the unique needs of certain groups such as female alcoholics, older alcoholics, or teenagers. And in all of this, remember that decision making will involve both the counselee and the family.

6. *Counsel the Family*. Alcoholism is a family problem. When a family member seriously misuses alcohol, the whole family must receive support, understanding, and help. Sometimes, it is better to give factual information that better enables

the family to understand the addiction. With some families the counselor must show how they might be contributing to the addiction problem or how their protection of the drinker might be prolonging the condition. When the drinker refuses to admit the problem or to come for help, family members may need a counselor's guidance and encouragement to confront the alcoholic relative with specific evidences of his or her alcohol-induced behavior.

As the alcohol abuse or dependence develops, family members often need understanding, encouragement, and practical guidance to help them live and get along as best they can despite the difficult circumstances. Responsibilities for running the household may have to be shifted as the problem drinker becomes less and less capable of being involved. When sobriety returns, everything has to shift again as the family readjusts and learns to accept the recovering alcoholic as a responsible member of the household. When relapses occur, as they often do, roles and responsibilities have to shift again. All of this can be demanding (1) because of the inconvenience and difficulty of making constant changes, (2) because the family looks to previous relapses and fears that any present dry spells will be temporary, and (3) because family members have grown accustomed to functioning smoothly in their roles of living with a problem drinker. Family change is risky for the family, important for the counselee, and accomplished best when there is encouragement from the counselor or outside support group.

7. *Help Counselees and Families Cope with Relapses.* Relapses are common among alcoholics. If these are never anticipated or if they are followed by blame and condemnation from others, then the problem drinker is inclined to give up and conclude that the battle against the bottle can never be won. Matt's counselor knew that the likelihood of relapses goes up immediately after success in treatment, when defenses are down and the counselee is feeling good about the progress. At times like this, the drinker tends to be less careful about avoiding high-risk situations. For Matt the first of his two relapses came as Christmas approached. Feeling more confident in his ability to handle the holidays, Matt took a drink at a party and quickly slid. Talking about it later, he felt shame, self-condemnation, and a sense of failure.

"Disappointed?" the counselor asked. Matt went silent, alone with his thoughts. Then he began to sob uncontrollably. Every December he had felt brokenhearted at his inability to remain sober. This time the Christmas drinking experience actually moved his treatment forward. Matt finally was able to let go of his long-held belief that emotion must never be expressed. He began to work with his counselor again and made significant progress until he became overconfident again. "This isn't uncommon when recovery has been sustained for several months, or years," Matt's counselor wrote later. "The lesson to be learned is how essential it is [for the counselee] to know that an attitude of caution—respect for the power of addiction—must be established and maintained indefinitely."[45]

It is not easy to work with chemically dependent people or their beleaguered families.[46] The counselor can expect failures, and after a relapse he or she must help counselees pick up and keep working on the problem. Recently, I received an email message from a complete stranger who identified himself as a Christian. He wrote, "I have problems with alcohol abuse and serious mood swings. I just can't break the pattern that when major change or stress comes into my life I choose the wrong answer, alcohol, and then I spiral down into an elevated depression or anxiety. Can you please offer insights and godly hope?"[47]

This is the common experience of an individual encountering stress and then reverting to drinking, followed by discouragement and the awareness of another failure. Some research suggests that stress, anxiety, and depression are the primary motives for the use of drugs, including alcohol.[48] Preventing relapses is a major challenge for counselors, but a key to helpful intervention is to understand the causes of relapse and how these can be overcome. Here are causes, all of which are supported by significant research,[49] some of which will sound similar to what we have discussed earlier.

- Know about the relapse process and the likelihood of relapses. When people are surprised by relapses, they are more devastated by them. When there is an awareness that relapses are common and that people can get past them, then there is greater ability to get sober again and continue moving forward.
- Avoid high-risk situations. These are places and contacts with certain people in which an individual's attempt to refrain from a particular behavior is threatened.
- Learn better coping skills. If stress leads to drinking, the counselee needs additional help in dealing with stress. When the stress builds, there need to be supportive people and stress management skills that can reduce the pressure and, in addition, the likelihood of taking another drink.
- Be aware of overconfidence. Counselors call this "self-efficacy," in which the person feels capable of beating the problem. This is a good predictor of ultimate success, but there also is a danger of relapse if the person begins to think that he or she can handle things without further help or accountability.
- Beware of craving. This is the thought, even fleeting, that the alcohol will make things better for a while. When the substance is readily available, the craving can be greater. The subjective experience of craving can put a person on the slippery slope downward.
- Develop a good support system. Research shows that some supporters are better than others.[50] The ones that help the most and do the most to prevent relapses are caring people who strongly encourage the drinker's determination to avoid alcohol, who are available when needed (especially at times of temptation), and who do whatever they can to reduce any pressure to use alcohol or other harmful substance. Sadly, when the abuse continues, friends or relatives who do not abuse substances tend to be alienated, so they withdraw. In turn, the abuser drinks more because there is nobody to help him or her do otherwise.

8. *Recognize and Utilize the Spiritual Dimensions in Counseling.* Perhaps you noticed that Table 34–1 described the empirically demonstrated treatments that are effective, but God was not mentioned. Apart from the AA "Higher Power," there was no indication that spiritual, specifically Christian, approaches to treatment even exist. This is because professional books and articles about alcoholism almost never mention or evaluate the role of Christian treatment approaches, including rescue missions, in helping to free people from alcohol abuse and dependence.[51] It is true, perhaps, that despite their presence worldwide, rescue missions and groups like Teen Challenge may reach a relatively small number of problem

drinkers, but often their approaches are very effective. Rescue mission leaders (who frequently are recovered alcoholics) are a rarely tapped but potentially useful source of information, support, and encouragement for the counselor of alcoholics. If the counselee is to find new meaning and purpose in life, he or she must come to see that true and lasting fulfillment is found only in Jesus Christ.

The counselor must depend on the Holy Spirit's guidance to determine when and how to raise spiritual issues in counseling and whether to present the Gospel. Counselees are most responsive to the Gospel when they recognize that they have a need that can be met only by Christ. Alcoholics are masters at manipulating other people, so the counselor must be careful not to fall into the same pattern, attempting to manipulate individuals into the kingdom. That's not the way it works. The counselee should be presented with the facts of the Gospel (presumably during times when he or she is sober enough to understand). Then urge, but do not coerce, the person into making a decision to commit his or her life to Christ. There are many examples of persons converted to Christ, freed from their alcoholism, and permanently changed through the presentation of evangelistic messages.

From this it should not be assumed that believers never have drinking problems. Certainly they do, and many find that the power of alcohol presents a lifelong struggle, even for people who are strong believers. In all of the work with alcoholic people and their families, prayer is of central importance. Through the intercession of believers and the availability of concerned human helpers, God works to support and restore those who are controlled by alcohol or other chemical substances. He also helps to prevent alcoholism in others.

Preventing Alcohol-Related Problems

Problems with alcohol probably are as old as the human race. We read about this early in the Bible. We see it even more in this media age in which popular magazines, occasional television documentaries, and a seemingly endless progression of scientific papers increase our understanding of the causes, characteristics, and treatment approaches for alcohol abuse and dependence. It is strange, then, that there seems to be so little understanding of the ways in which we can prevent alcohol-related problems. Even so, the prevention of drinking disorders has become a major concern for leaders in government, business, education, the military, and the church. Parent groups, service clubs, schools, health-care and counseling professionals, media people, and a number of others recognize the importance of vigorous, long-term efforts aimed at changing public attitudes toward alcohol and other drugs. The National Council on Alcoholism, the federal Department of Education, the National Institute of Alcohol Abuse and Alcoholism, and similar agencies in countries all over the world have been joined, surprisingly perhaps, by the alcohol industry, which has helped initiate TIPS (Training for Intervention Procedures by Servers of Alcohol), a program designed to educate bartenders, waitresses, and others who serve drinks.[52] Despite these efforts, we still know more about causes and treatment than about prevention. Even so, several preventive guidelines are likely to be helpful.

1. *Stimulate Healthy Home Lives.* Like most of the other issues discussed in this book, the prevention of alcoholism and other drug abuse begins in the home. When children are respected, loved, disciplined, and raised by sensitive, con-

cerned, stable parents, there is greater opportunity for healthy maturing and less likelihood of chemical dependence. When emotional needs are met in the home, when children are helped to cope with stress, and when they are taught a clear set of values, there is a greater sense of security and self-esteem, accompanied by a greater ability to handle the problems of life without drugs.

Also important is the example of parents. When parents drink regularly, children learn to do the same, especially when the parents do nothing to discourage their children's drinking behavior. In contrast, when parents rigidly prohibit and vehemently condemn the use of alcohol, children often react by experimenting with alcohol, especially when their peers do the same. More effective is an open attitude about alcohol, a recognition of its dangers, an encouragement of moderation if not abstinence, and an example of parents who enjoy life without having to rely on alcohol to meet their problems or to enjoy fellowship with others.

It is well known that many homes do not fit this description. Children of alcoholics, for example, often live in families where there is inconsistent or inadequate parenting, frequently accompanied by denial of the reality and influence of alcohol abuse. As we have seen, many of these children feel confused, angry, guilty, afraid, unloved, and ill-equipped to face the demands of adult life. Some have no models of healthy adulthood, but they are greatly impacted by their alcohol-drinking peers. As a result, there is a good possibility that many of these young people also could become alcohol abusers. If this is to be avoided, the children of alcoholics need special encouragement and guidance from caring adults outside the home.

2. *Instill a Healthy Religious Faith.* For many years it was assumed that people with a strong faith and commitment to church were less likely than others to develop alcohol- and other substance-abuse problems. A review of more recent studies indicates that this still is true.[53] From these findings it does not follow that faith in God or attendance at church prevents alcohol abuse, but when compared to their nonreligious peers, a commitment to religion and spirituality lowers the risk of drinking problems developing, especially among younger people. The preventive influence is even stronger if the parents and family also contribute to the development of a nonalcoholic lifestyle.

3. *Provide Community, Media, and School-Based Education on Alcoholism and Alcohol Abuse.* It is true that those who never take a drink will never become alcoholics. However, emotional pleas for abstinence rarely convince or influence people who are pressured by peers or curiosity about the effects of alcohol. Neither is it helpful to ignore the subject of alcoholism on the assumption that discussion will arouse experimentation. When alcohol abuse and dependency are considered in a frank, open discussion, this weakens the temptation to dabble with a dangerous drug, even when that drug is presented on television and elsewhere in society as a jovial and harmless way to relax.

To be effective, preventive education (for prevention of alcohol-related problems but also for prevention of the drug abuse that is discussed in the next chapter) should:

- Begin early, since alcoholics often start their long decline in the teenage years and often sooner.
- Present accurate facts concerning the nature and effects of alcohol.
- Avoid emotional appeals that involve scare tactics and dramatic pictures

but have little factual information. One exception may be the personal stories of pop culture or athletic heroes who can tell their stories and connect effectively with younger audiences.

- Clearly discuss the biblical teachings about wine and drunkenness.
- Teach refusal skills. This involves discussing and practicing how one can say no in an environment where one's peers may all be drinking
- Encourage people to make a decision—to drink or not to drink—instead of drifting into the habit.
- Encourage abstinence as the best and most effective means of prevention.
- Describe the warning signs that indicate developing addiction (see Figure 34–1).
- Alert people to the availability, place, and nature of help for those with developing drinking problems. At the same time, note that going for help is a sign of strength, not weakness.

4. *Teach People How to Cope with Life*. If we can assume that alcoholism and other misuse of drugs often reflect a failure in coping, then one approach to prevention is teaching people to openly face, discuss, and deal with the stress-related problems of life. It has been said that the key to prevention is to reduce exposure to stress when this can be done and to teach healthy skills for dealing with the pressures of life.

Conclusions About Alcohol-Related Problems.

Near the end of their counseling time together, Matt's counselor gave him two pieces of advice. "First, remember that isolation will kill you. Second, always err toward caution." Shortly thereafter, Matt and his counselor went their separate ways. Recently, they met again to celebrate Matt's fourteenth year of sobriety. "He's firmly in recovery from his alcoholism and relapse syndrome," the counselor wrote, "but I know he takes neither for granted."[54] There is no evidence that Matt or his counselor ever drew on the spiritual resources that would have facilitated the healing.

Why should any counselor, especially those who are pastors, get involved in the difficult process of helping an individual or family get over an alcohol-related problem? Theologian Reinhold Neibuhr once wrote that it is "no easy task to deal realistically with the moral confusion of our day, either in the pulpit or the pew and avoid the appearance, and possibly the actual peril, of cynicism."[55] Helping people face the reality and dangers of alcoholism can seem like an exercise in frustration and futility. One academic administrator described alcohol abuse as a blend of emotion, tragedy, personalities, complexity, desire, and lack of control. Add the competition between different community and governmental agencies, the heavy advertising of the alcohol industry, and the sometimes conflicting conclusions of researchers and other specialists, and we can understand why some describe the battle against alcoholism as an experience of taking two steps backward for every three steps forward.[56]

But inactivity and cynicism will accomplish nothing. Each community, each church, and each counselor must consider ways by which we can help people avoid or escape from the sickness and sin of alcoholism. The Christian counselor can be a leader in helping alcohol abusers and their families overcome the alcohol-related problems and live their lives in obedience and submission to Jesus Christ. Only then is this difficult problem truly and effectively resolved.

KEY POINTS FOR BUSY COUNSELORS

➤ The abuse of alcohol is a common problem that involves people of all ages, socioeconomic levels and ethnic groups.

➤ Alcohol-related disorders can be divided into several categories: intoxication, alcohol dependence, alcohol abuse, and alcohol-induced disorders.

➤ Mental-health professions universally consider alcoholism to be a progressive physical and psychological disorder; Christians and other religious people recognize that alcohol misuse also is the result of sinful behavior and often leads to sinful results. This chapter assumes that alcoholism and other substance dependence are both sickness and sin.

➤ The Bible does not appear to teach abstinence, but it does teach temperance. The dangers of excessive alcohol use are clearly stated, and Christians are urged strongly to stay away from alcohol, especially if drinking adversely influences another person, causing him or her to stumble.

➤ Alcohol-related problems are complex and can have a variety of causes. These include:
  - Biological and hereditary influences.
  - Home and family influences.
  - Social-cultural influences.
  - Psychological influences and stress.
  - Spiritual influences.

➤ Alcohol can impact people in various ways, but in every case there are:
  - Physical effects that can come to all parts of the body because alcohol is a poison.
  - Psychological social effects.
  - Family effects.
  - Spiritual effects.

➤ In counseling:
  - Get the alcohol abuser to agree and to admit that he or she needs help.
  - Stop the drinking.
  - Help the counselee get support.
  - Help with stress management and coping skills.
  - Encourage self-understanding and changes in lifestyle.

- Counsel the family.
- Help counselees cope with relapses.
- Recognize and utilize the spiritual dimensions in counseling.

➤ **Several interventions can prevent the development of alcohol-related problems.**

- Stimulate healthy home lives.
- Instill a healthy religious faith.
- Provide community, media, and school-based education on alcohol and alcohol abuse.
- Teach people how to cope with life, apart from alcohol.

➤ **The Christian counselor can be a leader in helping alcohol abusers and their families overcome the alcohol-related problems and live their lives in obedience and submission to Jesus Christ.**

35

Addictions

Bryan—that's his real name—was a workaholic. He rarely took vacations, and whenever he did, work took up most of his time. He worked every evening and on weekends. He worked on all the public holidays, including Christmas. On the day of his father's funeral, he was in his office for much of the day working on a project so insignificant that he can't remember now what it was.

Unlike alcoholics or substance abusers who hide their addictions, Bryan took pride in his work. He got regular promotions and bonuses. He was affirmed by his employer and admired by colleagues who were in awe of his productivity and accomplishments. He regularly missed family gatherings and social events because of the pressure of his work, frequently skipped lunch so he could stay at his desk, but was annoyed whenever somebody close to him would comment on his work obsession.

Members of Alcoholics Anonymous often speak of hitting bottom when the alcohol stops working, family members walk out, long-ignored physical problems make it impossible to continue, and the drinker knows that he or she has to get help. Something like this happened to Bryan. His career was going well, but his family fell apart and so did his body. "I was thirty-eight," he wrote later. "I was recovering from surgery for stress-related gastrointestinal problems. My life was crumbling under my feet, and there was nothing I could do about it. I lost weight. I couldn't eat.... I was a chain-smoking, caffeine-drinking work junkie, dogged by self-doubt." He started getting annoyed with people, and once he angrily confronted a college librarian, demanding to know the name of the irresponsible person who had checked out a book and kept it overdue for three months. "She gave me the name," he wrote later. It was "my own. Work had been the one thing that I had always done well, and now even that was failing me. Yet, I couldn't stop working."

Bryan got counseling, eventually wrote a book about workaholism, and today he counsels others who are addicted to their work. A lot of the people who come to his office are business executives, driven people climbing the corporate ladder, success-oriented individuals who are consumed by their work and flooded with emptiness when they have to stop, however briefly. Does it surprise you that even more of the people Bryan sees in his practice are other counselors, including pastors? Like drug addicts and other substance abusers, they are sacrificing their families, their bodies, and their futures on the altar of a compulsive, driven addiction to work.[1]

S everal years ago I attended a meeting of seminary professors where one of the speakers was a young pastor of a large and quickly growing church. In a question-and-answer period that followed the pastor's talk, somebody asked a question that brought a surprising answer. "Based on your pastoral experience, what do you think is the most important course for us to give our seminary students?" The pastor didn't hesitate in giving an answer. "Require a course on addictions," he said. "That is one of the major problems facing people today." As far as I know, the course was never added to the seminary curriculum, but probably it is needed now more than it was when the pastor made his recommendation.

There was a time when *addictions* primarily referred to a dependency on drugs, such as heroin or cocaine, but the word now has a much broader meaning. The list of addictions has grown and so have the definitions. Everybody knows about addictions to alcohol or drugs, but we often talk about addictions to television, Internet games, shopping, spending, pornography, sex, eating, sports, nicotine, or even chocolate. Some people seem addicted to exercise, politics, or highly arousing church services. While most people hide their addictions, people addicted to care-giving, to church activities, or to work wear their addictions as a badge of honor so the whole world will be aware of their devotion.

An addiction is any thinking or behavior that is habitual, repetitious, and very difficult or impossible to control regardless of the consequences. Usually, the addiction brings short-term pleasure, but there are long-term consequences in terms of one's health, relationships, psychological well-being, and spirituality. If there is no harm to the individual or to others, technically there is no addiction. In most cases, however, addictions are progressive conditions that slowly exert more and more power and control. With many addictions, the control is both psychological and physical. The addicted person may agree that the condition is harmful, but stopping seems to be impossible. Since the addictions meets psychological and/or physical needs, stopping may not even be attempted or seen as a realistic or desirable option. As a result, even after difficult detoxification, the substance abuser often returns to the needle, or the alcoholic returns to the bottle. Even after repeated medical warnings, the smoker may continue to puff on two packs a day, or the obese person continues to overeat and shun exercise. The workaholic continues the self-driving lifestyle and refuses to slow down, even after a near fatal heart attack. It's "been studied over and over and over again," according to the dean of the medical school at Johns Hopkins University. Of the 600,000 people in the United States who have heart bypasses every year, 90 percent do not change their eating habits, get more exercise, or calm their driven lifestyles, even though slowing down would prolong their lives and avoid future heart problems."[2] Perhaps it is not surprising that addictions have become a major health hazard worldwide and have been called "the greatest threat to our nation's health."[3]

In this chapter we will focus attention on two broad categories of addiction: substance-related disorders (which involve the abuse of any drug, medication, or toxin) and addictive behaviors (such as workaholism, out-of control use of the Internet, or unrestrained sex).

The Bible and Addiction

The Bible condemns drunkenness, alcohol abuse, uncontrolled lust, and gluttony, but it makes no specific references to drug abuse, eating disorders, workaholism, or most other addictions that concern us today. We might wonder how those biblical writers would respond if they returned to earth and saw how so many of us are held in the grip of powers like the Internet, video games, or uncontrolled purpose-driven lifestyles? Before they died, the biblical writers were inspired by the Holy Spirit to give us principles for living, including the following that could apply to any addictions that might be present now or arise in the future.

1. *Don't Be Mastered by Anything.*[4] It is possible to become enslaved even by actions or substances that are permissible and not bad in themselves. For example, food and drink are not innately bad, but they can control us and be abused.

In addition, people can be mastered by sexual immorality, greed, idolatry, alcohol, and other influences that gain control.

2. *Obey the Law.* The Bible instructs us to be law-abiding citizens.[5] It is wrong, therefore, to buy, sell, condone, possess, or use any drug or other substance that is illegal where one lives. Violence, driving under the influence of alcohol, or possessing and viewing pornographic images of children are all wrong, even when they do not lead to addiction.

3. *Do Not Assume That Drugs or Other Addictions Resolve Problems or Reduce Tensions.* When pressures build in life, some people use alcohol or other drugs to dull the stress and give a feeling of euphoria or a sense that all is well. Others get involved in work, hobbies, or recreational pursuits that distract from their worries. Temporarily, these behaviors may help a person avoid responsible stress management, but ultimately the stresses cry for attention themselves and the developing addictions no longer provide relief. Instead, the addictions create additional pressures. People may try to escape from their problems through drugs, work, sexual fantasy, hyperactivity, compulsive eating, or other addictive behavior, but all of this fails to acknowledge the scriptural directive to bring our burdens to Christ,[6] with whom we can face issues squarely and deal with them directly.

4. *Recognize That Resistance to Temptation Is Possible.* Despite the many forces that pull us into addictive and other harmful behaviors, God can and will enable us to resist.[7]

5. *Keep the Body Pure.* The Holy Spirit dwells in the body of every Christian, and for this reason we must do whatever we can to keep our bodies free of pollutants—including drugs, excessive amounts of food, lustful thoughts, and immoral sexual behavior. Every human body was made by God, and the Christian body belongs to him both because of divine creation and because of divine redemption. Scripture and common sense tell us, therefore, that we should take care of ourselves so that we can glorify God with our bodies.[8]

6. *Don't Expect to Come to God Through Drugs.* Many years ago a seminary professor wrote a controversial book arguing that psychedelic drugs can offer a superior route to discovering truth and bringing us into a meaningful religious experience.[9] This conclusion denies the fact that we come to God only by way of Jesus Christ,[10] and that we are to come with clear minds[11] rather than brains that are drugged by addictive substances.

7. *Practice Temperance, Self-Discipline, and Self-Control.* These characteristics are prominent in the list of qualifications for Christian leaders,[12] but they apply to those who are not leaders as well.[13] All believers are expected to say no to ungodliness and worldly passions, and "should live in this evil world with self-control, right conduct, and devotion to God."[14] Self-indulgence and selfish ambition are condemned;[15] self-control is commanded[16] and listed as one of the fruits of the Spirit.[17] Gluttony (which could involve addiction to eating), greed (which might involve addiction to possessions and material things), and lust (which could lead to sexual addiction) are all warned against and condemned.[18]

8. *Don't Engage in Any Behavior That Might Lead Another to Stumble.* It is well known that peer pressures are powerful lures that pull people, especially young people, into subsequent addictions. This can happen at any age. Paul warns the believers in Corinth to avoid any behavior, including eating or drinking, that may cause another believer to stumble. A Christian might drink a glass of wine, for

example, and feel no discomfort about doing so, but if this causes somebody else to violate his or her conscience, then the drinker should abstain. "It might not be a matter of conscience for you, but it is for the other person." Eating, drinking, or whatever else we do should be done in ways that bring glory to God.[19]

9. *Don't Get Drunk*. Drunkenness is clearly and explicitly condemned in Scripture and called a sin.[20] It could be argued that this clear prohibition against alcohol abuse could be the basis of a general principle that should guide our response to all potentially harmful substances and addictive behaviors. We should not be in submission to any chemical substance or behavior that can control us so that we cannot be free.

10. *Be Filled with the Spirit*. Ephesians 5:18 instructs us to avoid drunkenness but to be filled instead with the Holy Spirit. A life controlled by the Spirit is presented in the Bible as superior to any alternative, including a life filled with chemical or other addictions.

The Causes of Addiction

Dale Ryan has spent his professional life helping people get free of addiction. Founder of the National Association of Christians in Recovery, he believes that the reasons for addiction are both inside and outside the person who is addicted. According to Ryan, to raise an addict it takes:

- Expensive marketing campaigns from the manufacturers of alcoholic drinks, cigarettes, and other potentially addictive substances.
- Abusive adults: young people who have been abused physically and sexually are more likely to abuse substances earlier, more often, and in greater quantities.
- Social support from peers who use addictive substances and introduce others to potentially harmful drugs.
- Churches that fail to reach younger people. People who do attend services report less drinking, smoking, drug use, and binge drinking when compared to those who do not go to church.
- Physicians who are negligent about discussing abuse with their younger patients.
- Troubled families where alcohol is abused, drugs are used, or relationships are strained.[21]

There is nothing new about the problem of addiction, and neither is this limited culturally. Throughout recorded history and in countries all over the world, a percentage of every population has had serious problems with substance abuse and other types of addiction. Earlier we listed some of the causes of alcoholism: biological and hereditary influences; pressures in the home and the example of parents' environmental influences, including peer pressures and cultural-ethnic mores; persistent stress; spiritual influences; and circumstances that keep the addiction alive and growing once it gets started. All these influences can lead, as well, to nonalcoholic substance abuse and other addictive behaviors. In addition, substance abuse (which involves harmful use of chemicals or toxic substances) and behavior addictions (which concern potentially destructive actions) can each have unique causes of their own.

1. *Causes of Substance-Related Disorders.* All addictive chemicals have one thing in common: they change moods. Some mood changes are very potent and highly addictive; others are much less powerful. It has been suggested that drugs can be placed on a scale ranging from those with the highest potential for addiction to those with lowest potential.[22] This is shown in Table 35–1. Almost any person can become psychologically and/or physically dependent on drugs if that person is exposed to a high dosage for a long enough period of time. With a drug like heroin the time may be short, and the effects are both fast and very dangerous; with caffeine the time is longer and the effects are much less influential.

There are four major categories of substances.

- **Depressants** reduce arousal by decreasing activity in the central nervous system. Alcohol, the most commonly used depressant, impairs motor coordination and judgments. Sedatives, including barbiturates, have a calming effect, such as relaxing muscles, reducing inhibitions, lowering anxiety, and helping people sleep. Some of these are over-the-counter drugs, but more are distributed by prescription and subsequently abused.
- **Stimulants** increase central nervous system activity. Of course, caffeine is the most frequently used stimulant. Trendy coffee bars and well-stocked soda machines in offices and schools encourage people to partake. Chocolate bars, tea, certain types of ice cream, and warm cups of hot chocolate add to the almost universal intake of caffeine that starts with children, often persists into adulthood, and can lead to dependence and headaches as a common symptom of withdrawal.[23] More harmful and more addictive are nicotine (which can impact smokers but also nonsmokers who inhale second-hand smoke), cocaine (which is highly addictive and can lead to powerful states of euphoria and increased alertness), and amphetamines, including speed and some physician-prescribed drugs for weight loss, sleep disorders, and other physical problems. Methamphetamine (meth) is a

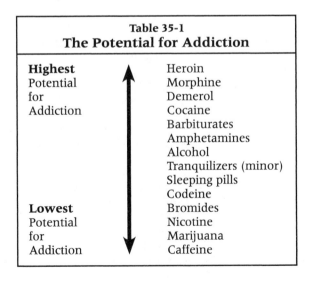

Table 35-1		
The Potential for Addiction		
Highest		Heroin
Potential		Morphine
for		Demerol
Addiction		Cocaine
		Barbiturates
		Amphetamines
		Alcohol
		Tranquilizers (minor)
		Sleeping pills
		Codeine
Lowest		Bromides
Potential		Nicotine
for		Marijuana
Addiction		Caffeine

synthetic stimulant, easily produced, highly addictive, and frequently abused. The drug gives a feeling of euphoria, invincibility, and energy that can keep users going for days without food or rest, but in addition to addiction, the end result of repeated use can be serious cardiovascular and other physical problems.[24]

- **Opiates** include heroin, morphine, and codeine. These drugs dull pain and produce euphoria and relaxation. They are highly addictive, are often overused, and can lead to serious physical problems and withdrawal symptoms.

- **Hallucinogens** heighten sensory awareness and produce hallucinations, delusions, and impaired memory. Marijuana and LSD are the best known of these drugs.[25]

Sometimes, these drugs are combined, and while the experience of using them can be intensely euphoric, the physical dangers are high. MDMA, better known as *ecstasy,* is an example. Combining both stimulant and hallucinogenic properties, this is one of the so-called *club drugs.* These are produced illegally in clandestine labs and often used among young people in bars, dance clubs, campus gatherings, and all-night dance parties known as raves. Used to produce feelings of well-being, high energy, stimulation, sensory distortions, and intoxicating high experiences, ecstasy is widely regarded as a safe drug. In fact, increasing evidence indicates that the drug can be very dangerous. For example, some research shows that MDMA can damage the brain, increase heart rate and blood pressure to potentially dangerous levels, and even lead to cardiovascular failure.[26] In addition, there can be confusion, depression, persistent anxiety, and potentially harmful aggressive and violent behavior. [27]

Other drugs could be added to this list. They include prescription medications that become addictive or inhalants that are sniffed, including glue, gasoline, or various paint products. Within recent years there have been widespread criticisms of drug companies that spend millions of dollars promoting their drugs with manipulative advertising campaigns that communicate the message that the solution to most problems is to be found in taking some kind of pill. One of the worst byproducts of this has been called the development of a Generation Rx: an alarming number of children and their parents who are being given drugs to solve a variety of problems and, in the process, are learning what might be termed "the myth of the magic pill."[28]

There can be many causes for these addictions, but most often the principal influences come from other people, including one's family, peers, or social groups.

(a) Parental and Other Adult Examples. Because they grow up in a culture of pill takers, most children become well acquainted with medicines that take away pain and make one feel better. Teenagers watch parents consume aspirin, cold tablets, sleeping medications, and a host of other drugs. Millions of people relax with coffee, a cigarette, or a drink before dinner, and when problems arise, tranquilizers are available to calm our troubled nerves. Is it surprising that young people follow this adult example and, in turn, perpetuate the idea that drugs are the first line of defense against physical and psychological pain?

Few people would assume that drugs in themselves are bad. Their medicinal value is well known, deeply appreciated when pain is intense, and even accepted by biblical writers.[29] Most people would see no harm in the occasional use of mild stimulants, pain relievers, or relaxants. But even mild drugs can become addicting, sometimes as a result of parental example. If parents take a pill or a drink to calm down in times of stress, it is not surprising that their children do the same. If the drug effects the children the same way it calms the parents, then use of the substance becomes reinforcing, and it is likely to be used again, perhaps with increasing frequency and in greater quantities.

Many substance abusers come from homes where drugs are not misused, but this does not deny the importance of parental example. A high percentage of teenage and adult substance abusers (especially those who use hard, highly addictive drugs) have grown up in homes where addiction and family instability are common.[30]

(b) Peer and Other Social Influences. When they are surrounded by drugs and drug use, why do some people abuse substances while others do not? Several theories have been put forward to answer this question.

Moral theories assume that addictions are evidence of character defects or sinful choices. In general, advocates of these views do not accept the conclusion that addictions have a biological basis. One web site boldly states that the moral viewpoint "is no longer widely considered to have any therapeutic value," but some competent and committed Christians would disagree.[31]

Disease-genetic theories maintain that otherwise healthy people experiment with a drug (perhaps in response to curiosity or peer pressure) and get hooked physically, so that substance abuse becomes a disease that needs medical treatment. Even these theories assume, however, that there are behaviors that lead to the dependencies, so both the causes and the treatment need to involve some element of behavior change. There is wide acceptance of the idea that some people are genetically predisposed to become substance abusers, but, as with alcohol addiction, it is difficult to separate inherited causes from the influence of the abuser's family and environment.

Gateway theories suggest that use of one drug opens the gate to use of substances that are more harmful and addictive. A young person, for example, may start with cigarettes, beer, or alcopops—the sweet tasting, fruit-flavored drinks that come in colorful packages and hide the taste of alcohol—and then move to more addictive substances. A problem with this theory is its failure to say why some make this progression and others do not.

Social theories conclude that race, age, socioeconomic status, the neighborhood where one lives, educational level, peer influences, and similar issues can combine to determine if one takes drugs, what drugs are likely to be used, how the habit is supported financially, and whether the drug use will continue. In North America, for example, gambling addictions soared in the last two decades of the twentieth century in parallel to the growth and influence of the gaming industry.

Psychological theories look within the abuser to see if personality traits, psychological stresses, inner conflicts, hidden fears, or individual needs contribute to substance abuse or the development of other addictions. Many substance users do have inner tensions and frustrations. Some look for experiences, including drug experiences, that will bring excitement, stimulation, intoxication, and feelings of freedom from the worries and problems of life. Once again, however, it still is not clear why some distressed people turn to drugs but many others do not.

Peer cluster theory assumes that peers are the major influences leading to substance abuse. Friends, acquaintances, and siblings often provide the drugs and teach the young person how to use them. In some cases adult gatherings (older peer clusters) also use alcohol and other substances that can lead to addictive behavior.

Blended theory is the view that there are multiple causes of substance abuse and psychological addictions. This assumes that for each individual, the reasons for dependency probably draw from a combination of the above theories. Each of these must be kept in mind as the counselor tries to understand and help the substance abuser.

2. *Causes of Addictive Behaviors.* Alcoholism and substance abuse probably are the most common addictions, but many struggle with addictive behaviors that do not involve chemical substances. Most of these addictions have no obvious physical cause. Instead, they are behaviors that gain increasing prominence in a person's life and slowly become more and more difficult to control. We began this chapter with the story of a counselor who was addicted to his work. He would go on vacation and promise that this would be a time away from work. Inside his suitcase, however, a cell phone, laptop computer, and work-related papers were hidden between the folds of his underwear, the way an alcoholic might try to conceal a bottle. Whenever there was opportunity, he would find some excuse to get away and hurry to a hidden place where he could check his email messages and do a little work. Others have addictions to pornography (which also is hidden), Internet games, sex, compulsive shopping, incessant television, or collecting things, such as rare books or baseball cards. Positive addictions are an additional group of compulsive behaviors that might include continual care-giving,[32] involvement with sports, cycling, hobbies, or other activities that many people view as admirable. In moderation these can bring pleasure and have a positive impact, but they also can be harmful if the behavior becomes compulsive and controlling. Perhaps most gyms or fitness clubs have a few members who seem to exercise all the time, to the ultimate detriment of their bodies. Space does not permit me to discuss these various behavioral addictions in detail, but I will give a little more attention to three that are common.

(a) Gambling Addiction. Several years ago, at a casino in Las Vegas, the winner of the World Series of Poker was asked what he planned to do with all the money. "Gamble it and lose it," he replied without hesitation. This man had no shame in admitting that he was addicted to gambling. Like all compulsive gamblers, he was unwilling and perhaps unable to resist the urge to gamble, even if this might lead to heavy debt, loss of work, family problems, and personal stress. Often, gamblers are arrested for embezzlement, forgery, income tax evasion, or other illegal activities that are providing funds to pay gambling debts and feed the addiction.

Why do they do it? There is no widely accepted cause. Frequently, gamblers are intelligent people who thrive on danger, excitement, and uncertainty. Television and radio advertisements for casinos sometimes give fast-paced portrayals of the thrills and exhilaration that come to casino patrons. These messages picture the possibilities of big winnings, but they fail to mention the losses that are common. Quietly and quickly at the end, these advertisements give a number to call if a person has a gambling problem. There is no talk about the depression, anxiety, and stress that often accompany compulsive gambling. Organizations like Gamblers Anonymous can be successful in helping the people who stay with their GA groups, but most drop out and return to their gambling.

(b) Adrenaline Addiction. Introductory psychology books almost always describe the body's reactions to stress. Whenever we are faced with danger or the need to act quickly, the adrenal glands suddenly produce a group of stress hormones that are pumped through the system, leading to greater alertness and readiness to move or to defend ourselves. This adrenaline shot can prepare us for action, but it also can be exciting and stimulating. It is like a drug injection, except the body itself produces the potentially addictive substance. If the stress continues, so does the adrenaline production and the high energy activities that follow. When the stress situation passes, the adrenaline production slows down before returning to normal.

For many people in these high-energy times, the return to normal never occurs. The adrenaline is always pumping as we go about our highly charged days, dealing with challenges, hurrying from place to place, pushing to produce, working to be successful. We learn to thrive on hyperactivity and enjoy the adrenaline rush. Most workaholics are adrenaline driven, but so are pastors who receive acclaim for their selfless commitment to working all the time in ministry,[33] or mothers who push their children into a variety of activities and, in doing this, teach their kids to be adrenaline driven as well. The excessive and continual experience of adrenaline arousal eventually becomes addicting.

Psychologist Archibald Hart has pioneered in the understanding and treatment of adrenaline addiction.[34] He notes that the clearest sign that one is addicted comes when a person is forced to slow down or decides to take a vacation. Like the substance abuser who has withdrawal symptoms, the adrenaline addict has symptoms similar to those listed in Table 35–2. Even though many people thrive on their many activities and adrenaline surges, the body eventually resists. Ulcers, headaches, gastric distress, anxiety attacks, respiratory problems, sleep disturbances, and heart disease are symptoms of the often self-induced stress and hyperactivity that lead to adrenaline addiction. If pushed consistently by pro-

---

Table 35–2

Signs of Adrenaline Withdrawal

- A strong compulsion to get back into doing something.
- Obsessive concerns about what still needs to be done.
- Vague feelings of guilt when one is idle.
- A mild to moderate feeling of depression. This is known as post-adrenaline depression.
- Restlessness, pacing, finger drumming, or other evidences of impatience and fidgeting.
- Feelings of irritability, impatience, and aggressiveness.
- A strong urge for caffeine (which is an adrenaline stimulant).

Adapted from Archibald D. Hart, "Addicted to Adrenaline," *Christian Counseling Today* 10, no. 2 (2002): 32.

longed stimulation, the adrenal glands eventually shut down to rejuvenate. The result can be a state of adrenaline fatigue sometimes known as hypoadrenia.[35]

Although there are differences from culture to culture and from one community to another, it is common for people in developed countries to value driven lifestyles and the adrenaline addiction that the hyperactivity produces. These are people who are driven to accomplish a lot but feel pressured by limited time and who often are willing to push themselves to the point of collapse. Some churches even encourage this and affirm people who are busy doing the Lord's work all the time. When bodies begin to break down, however, questions begin to arise about coping with the addiction and making changes. Unlike some of the more destructive substance-abuse disorders, there are easier ways to help people (or ourselves) deal with the addiction to adrenaline.[36]

(c) Religious Addiction. Even nonreligious people recognize the widespread personal and spiritual benefits that can come to people who have strong religious beliefs. Like most good things, however, religion can be abused, exploited to manipulate or hurt others, and used in ways that satisfy an individual's unhealthy or pathological needs. Religion is toxic when it is used to avoid commitments, get out of responsibilities, control others, hide from reality, or boost self-esteem. This kind of toxic faith has been defined as "a destructive and dangerous relationship with a religion that allows the religion, not the relationship with God, to control a person's life."[37]

Religious addicts are people who have become controlled by religion or religious activities. Sometimes, these are church members, dominated by the persuasive and guilt-inducing powers of a manipulative and narcissistic leader. Others might be termed churchaholics, people obsessed with a compulsive need to do more and more through church work. These people find satisfaction and affirmation in the work they do. Sometimes, they retreat from reality by immersing themselves in church work to the exclusions of almost everything else.[38] Many religious addicts apparently go to church regularly to get an emotional fix that keeps them high until the next service. Highly emotional and frenzied church services stimulate this addiction more than some of the duller church experiences that seem to be more sleep inducing than emotion arousing. These kinds of toxic faith and religious addictions often show rigidity in their adherents, narrow-mindedness, unwillingness to associate with or learn from others, self-justification, and magical thinking. Unlike some other addictions, the addiction to religion often covers more severe psychological conditions that are not being addressed in healthy ways.

The Effects of Addiction

Nobody starts out to be a substance abuser, and most people who develop addictions never expected that this would happen. Initially, the person is induced to try a new experience through the combined influence of family, personal heroes, peer group, cultural environment, curiosity, or psychological needs. Depending on the substance or on the individual, people are impacted in different ways. Often a person will try the drug or new experience once or twice but never get hooked. In other cases the initial experimentation leads to small steps that follow a downward progression that can involve behavior change, physical deterioration, family stresses, financial problems, career destruction, and increasing psychological disintegration. At the most basic level, there are four steps downward:[39]

- *Experimentation* is where the process begins. The most common substances at this level are alcohol and marijuana, although any substance or experience can be a temptation for experimentation. Inhaling household substances such as shoe polish or paint thinner is the most prevalent form of abuse among young children.[40] For those who are older, experimentation tends to begin in social contexts, such as weekend parties. For many people, the experience does not lead to anything further.
- *Occasional use* is the next step down. The user is still experimenting. He or she feels "I can take it or leave it," and often new substances are tried. Over time, the substance or potentially addictive behavior, such as gambling, is used more often. At this time people can lose control, but usually they are able to recover. It is at this stage, however, that use may be more common and slowly become more and more frequent.
- *Regular use* often means that the substance or behavior develops into a daily occurrence. The abuser denies that he or she has a problem, but the addiction is never far away. Other issues such as school or job performance, health, relationships, or other things of value tend to be pushed aside as the addiction gets stronger.
- *Full-blown addiction* involves getting, keeping, and experiencing the addiction as often as possible. In time the person's brain and body begin to change, and often, greater and greater quantities and frequency of the drug or other experience are needed to produce the high that initially came with small amounts.

Depending on the addiction and on the individual, some people are able to withdraw from their addictions with little or no help, but most need professional guidance. It is well known that psychological and physical withdrawal symptoms can be very disruptive, but the effects of withdrawal depend on the addiction. It is easier to withdraw from caffeine than from nicotine; easier to quit smoking cigarettes than to stop using cocaine.

As we have seen, addictions affect both the victim and his or her family. Families can be destroyed by an addict's behavior. Something similar could be said about society. It is well known that substance abuse and crime often go together, causing pain to the victims and great detriment to local communities and to whole countries. On the national level, addictions of all types contribute to the loss of billions of dollars through absenteeism, declining work efficiency, failing health, and the high cost of treatment programs. Even more pathetic are the shattered lives strewn in the paths that follow progressive addictions. Spiritual emptiness, broken bodies, destroyed relationships, ruined careers, dulled brains, deep feelings of grief, and persisting guilt are among the costs of addictions.

Sometimes, even counselors get discouraged. "I have to limit my work with addicts," one counselor said. "The emotional drain of treating them can be almost more than I can handle."

Counseling and Addiction

There was a time when counselors and neuroscientists each took their own approaches to treatment and ignored the need for different professional groups that could pool their resources and work together. Christian counselors brought their own approaches to treatment and argued that God alone would bring change without the input of psychologists and physicians. These lines of separation between professions still exist, but they are fading.[41] Addictions can be complex combinations of social, psychological, biological, and spiritual influences. For this reason, family counseling, individual and group approaches, behavior therapy (to help people change and control behavior), medical treatment, spiritual interventions, and the support of friends and fellow believers can combine to bring better help than each approach might be able to give on its own. The broader help enables individuals to withdraw from addictive substances and behaviors, get treatment for the physical effects of the addiction, and restore family and other relationships. All of this takes large amounts of time, energy, and commitment from others. It also involves costs, and because of the expense, most substance abusers are not getting treatment.[42] Of those who do get help, many addicted people escape from their addictions, but the failure rate is high and relapse is common.

Some of the treatment fails because counselors, who are highly motivated, often are lacking in proper training and experience. If you are a Christian counselor who lacks training or expertise in working with substance abusers and people with other addictions, try to find a professionally trained counselor and/or physician with whom you can work in helping the addict and his or her family. Recognize that the spiritual leader is not a junior member of the treatment team, especially when he or she can bring the backing of a congregation of people willing to support the addict, but also the treatment team and the person's family.

1. *Counseling Substance Abusers.* Chapter 34 outlined principles for counseling people with severe drinking problems. Most of those principles apply to substance abusers as well, but they will not be repeated here.

It is well known that the treatment of substance abusers can be challenging, but it would be wrong to conclude that these people are unmotivated to change, not responsive to treatment, or always difficult to manage.[43] Treatment may be difficult, but it can be successful, most often when there are several approaches used together. These may include medical care, both individual and group counseling, drug education, support and guidance for the family, inpatient therapy in a rehabilitation facility, aftercare services such as halfway houses or outpatient clinics, and efforts to help the abuser live without drugs. With any one person, these may not all be used, but in various combinations these can be effective.

Where is the Christian perspective in all of this? Some of the most effective programs are build on biblical principles and bring a Christian perspective to treatment. Christian counselors, especially those who are not specialists in this kind of work, often work with medical, rehabilitation, and other professionals to bring support and perspectives that are uniquely Christian. For example, psychologist Mark Yarhouse and his co-authors believe that there are four ongoing themes to consider when offering support to a person who is undergoing treatment for substance abuse: motivation, acceptance, commitment, and support.[44]

The Christian counselor, in partnership with the church, can provide these four elements consistently, both to the substance abuser and to his or her family.

- *Motivation* involves helping people stay with their rehabilitation, even when they feel like giving up or when there are relapses. Motivation is strengthened when the abuser in treatment gets feedback from others about what they see happening. There can be great value in knowing that others are praying and are concerned. Motivation also can be made stronger when family members or friends honestly share how they are being impacted by the substance abuser's actions. This is not meant to instill guilt; it is process of showing love and consistent encouragement.
- *Acceptance* can be expressed in several ways, including the sustained presence of people who care. Abandoning an addiction involves determination and courage. This rarely happens apart from sustained and supportive relationships from others.
- *Commitment building* may involve helping the person admit that he or she cannot control the substance abuse and cannot get free of addictive behaviors without help from others, self-examination, and dependence on God. Often the abuser's family can benefit from the encouragement that comes from others who walk with the family while the treatment continues.
- *Support* does not end when the treatment is over. Eventually, professional treatment will come to an end. Sometimes, because of costs or other influences, the treatment ends before it should. It is here that the sustained and consistent support from others, especially from others in the Christian community, can help people through difficult times. Often, the temptations to go back to the old substances will seem overwhelming and irresistible, apart from the presence of people who can be there to give encouragement and support.

2. *Counseling and Behavioral Addictions.* Compulsive gambling or shopping, procrastination, workaholism, religious addiction, and other failures at self-control sometimes have a physical basis that could benefit from medical treatment. Attention deficit disorders, for example, result from naturally occurring chemical imbalances or neurological malfunctioning that make it difficult for some people to concentrate or control behavior despite their best efforts and intentions. Medications can restore some of the imbalances and help individuals keep more focused.

More often, however, addictive behavior and lack of control (in contrast to alcoholism and the abuse of other chemicals) have roots that are psychological, social, or spiritual. An old hymn urges Christians to "yield not to temptation, for yielding is sin. Each victory will help you some other to win." Every time we yield, it is easier to give in at the next opportunity. This is true whether the behavior is sinful (like gambling) or more psychological.

As an example, consider addictions to pornography, the viewing of erotic sexual images on the Internet. Unlike mature expressions of love within marriage, viewing pornography (like sexual perversions in general) does not require an intimate relationship with another human being. This erotic thinking, with or without stimulating pictures, usually is done alone, although Internet connections with others can be involved. The ongoing fascination with pornography, most often accompanied by fantasies and self-stimulation, is a highly arousing form of mental adultery. Frequently, it is characteristic of individuals who are unable or unwilling to establish intimate nonsexual relationships with persons of the opposite sex. Sometimes, the pornography addict has been hurt in the past, is afraid of the opposite sex, or fears his or her ability to perform sexually. In some cases, the fantasies occur in the minds of happily married individuals who are too busy for sex with their spouses. Others may be bored with a lifetime of the same old sexual activities. As a result, the individual engages in mental self-stimulation, pondering erotic behavior that never would be attempted or possible in real life. Generally, it is agreed that the developers of Internet pornography almost always develop their images to appeal to men and especially to adolescent boys who have high levels of sexual curiosity. When the erotica is in the mind or on the computer screen, nobody else knows about it, and the fantasies grow without much restriction.[45]

Like all behavior addictions, erotic thinking and the increasing use of Internet pornography grow because some need is not being met in a more effective, healthy, less compulsive way. The need for communication and close contact with other human beings, for example, may have been replaced with fantasy.[46] This fantasy is pleasant and not considered harmful (at least in the beginning), so the individual doesn't try to stop. In time the lustful thoughts and or use of pornography become increasingly frequent, there is greater withdrawal from others, and the person seems unable to abandon what has become a progressively compulsive habit.

What can be done to help people get out of the trap of behavioral addictions? It is well known that alcoholics and other substance abusers rarely can stop by an act of will. When the temptations return or the biological needs are strong enough, the drinking or drug use begins again. It may seem logical to assume that behavioral addictions might be easier to control because the biological influences are less, but these addictions also can be difficult to control.

Part of the reason for this lies with the concept of *habituation*. Think of a situation in which a person or an animal is exposed to a stimulus that leads to a response. A loud noise leads to a startle reaction. If that noise is repeated several times, however, the sound may become annoying, but the startle reaction does not recur. To get another startle reaction, there has to be a stronger and more unusual sound or other stimulus. In this example, the body has habituated or become accustomed to the original noise. Soon it will become accustomed to repeated exposure to the second noise.

Apply this to the abuse of a drug. The first time a young person takes a substance, even in a small amount, the effect can be powerful. There may be euphoria and even intoxication. Before long, however, that original dose makes no difference, and the person needs more of the same drug to get the original effect. If he or she wants an even greater effect, more has to be taken. Eventually, large quantities are needed for the euphoric effect. In addition, as more of the drug is ingested, the body gets used to the substance and needs it just to maintain the equilibrium that originally came without the drug. This also works with medications. The one pill that originally took away pain ceases to bring a response after a time, and increasing amounts of the original drug are needed to take away the pain. In time, the body also needs some of the painkiller to function efficiently. Eventually, through the process of conditioning, the mere thought of the drug or

sighting of the pill can trigger a biological craving that only can be met by ingestion of the substance.

Now let us return to behavior addictions. An Internet image that might have
been stimulating sexually at the beginning no longer stimulates after a while, and
more explicit pornography is needed to achieve the same arousal. After a period
of time, the thought of pornography or even the sight of a computer screen can
trigger an intense urge to look. At a simpler level, some people become conditioned to check repeatedly for new email messages. The process may be a result of
psychological conditioning as much as a physical reaction, but these urges are
extremely difficult to resist, and the addictive behavior is hard to stop. (Maybe
that describes you; sometimes it is a danger for me when I am writing, perhaps a
little bored by my own book, and tempted to get lured away by checking to see if
there are new entries in my email inbox). An outsider may think it is ridiculous
for a person to say he or she needs to shop, to play video games, to look at
pornography, or to gamble, or even to keep checking for email messages, but to
the addicted person this behavior is highly controlling, and the lure can be almost
irresistible.

Even so, the effects of habituation can be reduced if the person can be weaned
away from the addictive substance or behavior. In addition, many of the behavioral addictions will yield to a repeated four-part solution that involves determination, replacement, need fulfillment, and lifestyle management.

(a) Determination. Addictive behavior will persist unless the individual determines to change. This is unlikely to be a one-time-only decision. Addictive
behaviors are pleasurable, and relapse is common, even after repeated decisions
to quit. Despite these failures, the counselee must be motivated to change, or
there will be little progress. Like substance abusers, behavior addicts are most
likely to stick with any change program when people are available to offer
encouragement and accountability.

(b) Replacement. Cognitive-behavioral counselors have suggested several ways
to find replacements for compulsive behavior and persisting thoughts. *Thought stopping* seems like a gimmick, but it works for many people. Whenever an unwanted
thought comes to awareness, the individual thinks STOP or even says this out loud
if nobody else is around. *Thought switching* follows. As soon as the undesired thinking is interrupted, the person quickly focuses attention on something else. Sometimes, this is accompanied by *success rehearsal,* in which the person imagines that he
or she will be successful, instead of thinking about failure.

It may be that the Bible gives similar guidelines. We are instructed to get rid of
"the sinful, earthly things lurking within you. Have nothing to do with sexual sin,
impurity, lust, and shameful desires. Don't be greedy for the good things of life,
for that is idolatry . . . get rid of anger, rage, malicious behavior, slander, and dirty
language."[47] When these things are allowed to persist in the mind, they can stimulate overt behavior.[48] It is not difficult to stop and throw out unhealthy thoughts
or behaviors, but it is hard to keep them from returning unless we bring in
replacement thinking and actions. After we have stripped off our old evil nature
and wicked deeds, in its place we are to clothe ourselves "with a brand-new
nature that is continually being renewed" as we learn more and more about
Christ.[49] Lustful thoughts can be replaced with other thinking that is healthy and
Christ honoring. Some Christian counselors suggest that whenever unhealthy
thoughts appear they should be replaced by mentally reciting a Bible verse.[50]

Of course, none of this is likely to work if the counselee stays in the presence of people or stimuli that cause a return of the addictive behavior. Gamblers can not go to gambling casinos, people addicted to pornography can not keep pornographic materials that they can view, workaholics can not smuggle work away with them on vacations. This advice can be difficult to implement. The person who is addicted to Internet pornography or to work may not be able to stay away from the computer because computers are so much a part of our lives and are needed for so many things. Even a simple technique like moving the computer screen can help, however. If the computer is in a more prominent part of the house or if the screen can be viewed from the door of a room, there is less temptation to go online to addictive sites. That even extends to the compulsive checking of email messages.

(c) Need Fulfillment. We have seen that addictions often arise because some need is not being met in more healthy ways. Counseling can help the counselee ponder what needs are being met by the addiction, and how these needs can be met in other ways. The compulsive television watcher, for example, may need contact with other human beings but has a fear of intimacy or lacks interpersonal skills. Counseling could help the individual relate to people in ways that are fulfilling and less threatening. If television has become the only way to relax, perhaps other less addictive hobbies can be developed. The compulsive eater may snack whenever there is boredom or a stress buildup. This person needs help in learning more effective methods for managing stress.

(d) Lifestyle Management. Lifestyle changes may be the starting point for healing many behavior addictions, especially the addiction to adrenaline. Humans need time for relaxation, restoration, and recovery, but often this is ignored. Archibald Hart notes that many people, especially workaholics, "abuse our bodies for six days—then spend the seventh in religious activities that are as adrenaline demanding as what we do during the other six days!"[51]

Lifestyle management may involve making physical changes, including regular sleep or physical exercise, that can slow down the body, burn excess adrenaline, develop new habits, and move the counselee away from dependence on the addictive behaviors. Hart adds that it can help to reorder one's values and "make sure that your priorities, goals, commitments, and friendships are what you really want. Stop trying to please others or keep up with them," he adds, especially for people who are addicted to adrenaline. Help counselees learn to relax without their addictions and rearrange their priorities. Recognize that this cannot be hurried and is much more effective when the Holy Spirit is working to change an individual's life. Some of this may sound simplistic, but the treatment of behavior addictions often involves slow and steady guidance as the counselee is helped to move away from the behavior that has become so valued and needed.

Preventing Substance Abuse and Behavior Addictions

Nobody knows how often professional athletes take steroids and other substances to enhance their performances. It is illegal, of course, and there are consistent efforts to test for the presence of skill-enhancing drugs. Sometimes, this drug use is very difficult to detect, so the substances continue to be used, giving some people unfair advantage over their competitors. All of this has led to repeated calls for mandatory drug testing, not only in the locker rooms of athletes but in other places as well. If an airline pilot or train operator uses alcohol or other substances, this can put many innocent lives in danger. If someone in the military uses drugs that might impair clear reasoning, this could have serious implications. Urinalysis is not always the most accurate way to detect illicit drug use, but in recent years there has been a decrease in those who complain that the mandatory testing for drugs is wrong or an invasion of privacy.

Even when drug testing is used, there is little evidence that this prevents substance abuse. It might deter some people whose jobs or careers would be in jeopardy if drug use was discovered, but for most people, addictions continue and the problem keeps growing. There is a lot of talk about prevention and a lot of research, but overall there do not seem to be many clear guidelines for preventing abuse and addiction. In the preceding chapter on alcoholism, we listed several preventive guidelines: stimulating stable homes, instilling healthy religious faith, teaching people how to cope with life, and providing community, media, and school-based education relating to abuse and addiction. Each of these, along with the suggestions that follow, can apply to the addictive behaviors that are discussed in this chapter.

1. *Teach Refusal Skills.* Several years ago the words *"just say no"* became the basis of a national drug prevention program. The three-word slogan was creative and easily remembered, but it failed to acknowledge that some people want to "just say no" but are unable to do so because they don't know how. Swayed by peer pressure, inner conflicts, environmental stress, poor adult modeling, or family attitudes and tensions, many people need more than a good slogan if they are to resist the pleasures and temptations that lead them into substance abuse and behavioral addictions.

Nevertheless, the "just say no" prevention campaign has served some useful purposes. Parents, teachers, church leaders, and others in the society need to be aware of the signs of addiction. Educational programs like the "just say no" advertisements helped to increase this awareness so that sensitive adults are more able to spot problems and intervene early, before developing addictions get worse. In addition, when young people or other potential addicts are encouraged to say no, this helps increase the motivation to avoid or to stop addictive thoughts and actions.

2. *Skill Learning.* In their homes, schools, and churches, individuals should be taught how to resist peer pressures and harmful social attitudes. We don't learn to resist by pretending that problems don't exist. Instead, young people (and some who are older) need to think about peer pressures before they arise and ponder how these and other unhealthy influences are best avoided. Thirty years ago I was involved in a small way with a very successful program for the prevention of teenage substance abuse that built on the assumption that people will avoid drugs when they learn skills that enable them to cope with life's pressures—without leaning on addictive substances or behaviors.

Addictive problems should be less likely when potential abusers are informed about addiction, feel loved and accepted without undue pressure to succeed, are given opportunities to find fulfilling activities without the need to rely on addictive behaviors, and have a healthy and supportive home life where parents or other family members are free of substance abuse or other addictive behaviors. All of this can help people cope with life and find fulfillment without addiction.

In educating young people and teaching living skills, the teachers may be as important as what is taught. A fifty-year-old schoolteacher may have the facts to be taught, but if that teacher rarely uses the computer and has never tasted any drug stronger than coffee, he or she is not a very credible instructor for teaching hormone-endowed thirteen-years-olds to avoid pot or Internet pornography—even if that teacher is sincere, informed, and dedicated. Sometimes, the best teachers are heroes, local sports stars, and others who are admired and able to connect well with their audiences.

3. *Meeting Needs.* Several times we have stated that addictive behaviors often arise because needs are not being met in more healthy ways. This may include needs for excitement and periodic adrenaline surges, especially among the young. Substance abuse and other addictions are less common and less needed when people feel accepted, secure, loved, and capable and are living fulfilling lives. By stimulating maturity we weaken the need for addictions.

4. *Building Religious Faith.* The research that we considered in the chapter on alcoholism applies as well to other addictions. When people have strong religious faith and regularly attend religious services, they are less likely to develop addictions.[52]

Conclusions About Addictions

We began this chapter with a look at one man's addiction to work. He is past that now, but he knows that overwork is like so many other addictions: "a way that vulnerable human beings seek, for understandable reasons, a sanctuary from the uncertainties and vulnerabilities of their present lives."[53] Addictions can be highly destructive forces, but for some people they are roots to ecstasy and euphoria or escapes from the drudgeries or the pressures of their lives. Behind many of the problems that we see in our counseling rooms, there are addictions to overwork, overdrinking, or overcontrol by some force or forces that are carefully hidden and increasingly difficult to abandon. You may not be an addictions counselor, dealing with recovering alcoholics or people trying to get off meth or cocaine, but addictions may lurk behind many of the issues that counselees bring to your attention.

Nobody knows how many people are held in the grips of addictions. Some get help and are freed from their addictive cycles. Many do not. Some of these addicted people may sit next to us in church or at work, struggling to control addictions that are still hidden. Helping people cope with addictive behavior is one of the major and most important challenges facing Christian counselors and the church. That pastor we mentioned earlier is right: addictions probably should be a required course for all seminary students and certainly for counselors and counseling students as well.

KEY POINTS FOR BUSY COUNSELORS

➤ An addiction is any thinking or behavior that is habitual, repetitious, and very difficult or impossible to control regardless of the consequences. Usually, the addiction brings short-term pleasure, but there are long-term consequences in terms of one's health, relationships, psychological well-being, and spirituality.

➤ The Bible condemns drunkenness, alcohol abuse, uncontrolled lust, and gluttony, but it makes no specific references to most of the addictions that concern us today. Nevertheless, there are biblical principles that can apply to addictions that might be present now or arise later.

➤ When a chemical interferes with a person's productivity, tranquility, efficiency, or well-being, and when a person is made aware that this is happening but still persists in using the chemical, then that person is addicted, at least psychologically. If one gets physically ill when the drug is withdrawn, then there is physical dependence as well.

➤ There can be many causes for the abuse of substances, but most often the principal influence is other people, including one's family, peers, or social groups. To determine causes, counselors can look into these three areas.

➤ Behavior-based addictions have no obvious physical cause. Instead, they are behaviors that gain increasing prominence in a person's life and slowly become more and more influential and difficult to control. Examples include addiction to gambling, to one's own adrenaline, and to religion, all of which can be fueled by continuing surges of adrenaline.

➤ At the most basic level, there are four steps that lead to dependence on a substance or an addiction to some behavior: experimentation, occasional use, regular use, and full-blown addiction.

➤ Spiritual emptiness, broken bodies, destroyed relationships, ruined careers, dulled brains, deep feelings of grief, and persisting guilt are among the costs of addictions.

➤ Treatment may be difficult, but it can be successful most often when there are several approaches used together. These may include medical care, both individual and group counseling, drug education, support and guidance for the family, inpatient therapy in a rehabilitation facility, aftercare services such as halfway houses or outpatient clinics, and efforts to help the abuser live without drugs.

- In helping abusers, Christian counselors can bring unique help through four themes:
  - Motivation involves helping people to stay with their rehabilitation, even when they feel like giving up or when there are relapses.
  - Acceptance can be expressed in several ways, including the sustained presence of people who care.
  - Commitment building may involve helping the person admit that he or she cannot control the substance abuse and cannot get free without help from others, self-examination, and dependence on God.
  - Support involves sustained and consistent support from others, especially from others in the Christian community who can help people through difficult times, including times when there is strong temptation to return to the drug, alcohol, or other substance.

- In helping people with behavior addictions or lack of control, such as compulsive gamblers or people addicted to work, recognize that these most often have roots that are psychological, social, or spiritual. Behavior addictions, including erotic thinking and the increasing use of Internet pornography, grow because some need is not being met in a more effective, healthy, and less compulsive way.

- Many of the behavioral addictions will yield to a repeated four-part solution involving determination, replacement, need fulfillment, and lifestyle management.
  - Determination: Addictive behavior will persist unless the individual determines to change. Counselors can help with this.
  - Replacement: This involves finding replacements for compulsive behavior and persisting thoughts.
  - Need fulfillment: Counseling can help the counselee ponder what needs are being met by the addiction and how these needs can be met in other ways.
  - Lifestyle management: Humans need time for relaxation, restoration, and recovery, but often this is ignored. Note that changes like this cannot be rushed.

- To prevent substance abuse and behavior addictions:
  - Teach refusal skills so people know how to say no to opportunities to use the substance or engage in the potentially harmful behavior.
  - Teach skills for living so people can cope with life without having to escape through the abuse of substances of other unhealthy behaviors.
  - Teach ways to meet needs. Substance abuse and other addictions are less common and less needed when people feel accepted, secure, loved, capable, and living fulfilling lives. By stimulating maturity, we weaken the need for addictive substances and behaviors.
  - Encourage individuals to get involved in church and religious services.

- Nobody knows how many people are held in the grips of addictions. Helping people cope with addictive behavior is one of the major and most important challenges facing Christian counselors and the church.

36

Financial Counseling

Louis and Stephanie are active in their church, popular with their friends, and proud of their two young children. When they got married five years ago, they both were working at well-paying jobs and had big dreams for the future. After living for a year in a small apartment, they took out a big loan, bought a recently constructed house, filled it with new furniture, and surrounded it with professional landscaping. With their two incomes they were able to pay the bills, but there was nothing left over for emergencies or for savings.

Then Louis lost his job. There was nothing wrong with his work or his commitment as an employee, but Louis was one of many who were let go when his company merged with another. For three months the young couple struggled financially, and when Louis finally got another job, his salary was lower than before. The financial problems escalated when the baby arrived. Stephanie kept working because they needed her income, but there were the additional costs of child care, doctor's visits, and the increasing needs of their growing family.

They refinanced the house to get lower monthly payments, even though they paid higher interest. Credit cards were used to pay for clothes, household maintenance, medicines, and sometimes groceries. Soon they were paying only the minimum on their credit card bills, and eventually they hit their credit limit and could not charge anything more. Louis took a part-time job to raise money, but this put more pressure on Stephanie. The couple who loved each other and had always related well found that they were increasingly irritable and impatient with each other. Their lives were dominated by worry, fatigue, and uncertainty about how they could get out of the financial quagmire that was pulling them deeper and deeper into debt.

Louis and Stephanie are fictional, but their story is real. Change a few of the details, and most of us have seen financial struggles like this, perhaps even in ourselves. People overspend, overborrow, fail to anticipate financial crises such as the loss of a job, and go deeper and deeper into debt. Some find themselves in the offices of trained financial advisors; others turn to pastors and other counselors. Some might come to you.

Books on counseling almost never mention money. The Bible warns that the love of money is at the root of all kinds of evil.[1] Counselors often see that abuse and mismanagement of money are at the root of all kinds of human problems. Even so, money problems rarely are discussed in professional counseling journals, despite the fact that individual tension, marital and family conflict, interpersonal strife, anger, frustration, anxiety, worry, suicide, driving ambition, and a host of other issues at times are related directly or indirectly to the pursuit and management of money.

In itself, money is not the problem. We need money to buy, sell, and meet our individual needs. Problems come because of our individual and cultural *attitudes* toward money and our *inefficiencies* in handling finances wisely. The Christian counselor discovers this frequently. Sometimes, finances are listed as the basic problem; more often financial struggles are presented as a part of some broader problem, such as anxiety, work stress, struggles with identity, marital conflict, or adjusting to retirement. Whether or not a counselor does financial counseling, counselee concerns about money often surface in counseling.

The Bible and Finances

Sometimes, counselors and others are reluctant to talk about money, but the Bible has no similar hesitations. Scriptural statements about possessions, riches, money, and the management of finances can be summarized in the form of several basic principles.

1. *Money and Possessions Are Given by God and, in Themselves, Are Not Innately Bad.* God supplies all our needs, expects us to trust him for our finances, and has shown that we need not be anxious or worried about having enough.[2] There are people who squander their money through mismanagement, and others who confuse their real needs with their desired extras. Even so, in terms of basics, such as food and clothing, God provides. Sometimes, his provisions are in great abundance, but at other times, he chooses to provide only the barest necessities.

Within recent years, significant controversy has surrounded a theological view most often known as the health-and-wealth gospel. This theology, which has "shaped the faith of millions," maintains that God consistently rewards faithful living and generous giving with affluence and abundance.[3] It is the view that people who give generously have a guarantee that they will receive a lot; it is the message that the more one gives, the more one gets. Critics have noted that this view has the appearance of a magical formula, which is not supported in the Bible. It tends to be taught by Christian leaders and others who are appealing for gifts of money and base their appeals on the idea that this giving will produce significant material benefits. Certainly, money given generously to those in need does lead to a storing up of treasure for the giver, but this treasure appears to be something for the future and not necessarily bounty here on earth.[4] For reasons known only to God, sometimes he permits hunger and financial hardship, even among his faithful followers who give without holding back. He loves faithful givers but does not promise that giving will be followed by affluence in terms of material possessions. He does promise to supply our needs, even though he doesn't always give what we want or think we need.[5]

2. *Money and Possessions Must Be Viewed Realistically.* In a well-known parable, Jesus described a man whose life had been spent in the accumulation of wealth. Then the man died. He was unprepared to meet God and was forced to leave his precious possessions to somebody else. Jesus called this man a fool.[6] He was rich in worldly wealth but poor in his relationship with God.

Things have not changed in the twenty-first century. Many people still live lives dominated by the love of money and the pursuit of affluence. The Bible does not condemn riches. Some of the greatest leaders in biblical times were very wealthy, but they were not consumed by the desire to get more or to cling to what they had. According to the Scriptures, money is temporary.[7] Certainly it can bring pleasure, comfort, and satisfaction, but ultimately it does not satisfy or bring lasting happiness and stability.[8] Perhaps this is one reason why we are warned to keep our lives free from the love of money and be content with what we have.[9] If riches increase, we are not to set our hearts on them.[10] Even though money in itself if not condemned in Scripture, love of money and dependence on riches clearly are wrong.

3. *Money and Possessions Can Be Harmful.* The rich young ruler came to Jesus with a theological question but walked away grieving when he heard the answer: give to the poor.[11]

Apparently, a love for money prevented his spiritual growth. At another time Jesus taught that we cannot love both God and money. Eventually, we will come to the point of loving the one and detesting the other.[12] We can gain the whole world and keep everything but lose our souls.[13]

This does not have to happen, of course. Some people handle riches very well, without pride or hoarding, but this can be difficult. Wealth may distract us from God, and a desire for things can lead to pride and disobedience.[14] Nowhere is this stated more clearly than in 1 Timothy 6:6–10, where the dangers of loving money are contrasted with an emphasis on godliness and a warning about the dangers of craving money and longing to be rich.

> True religion with contentment is great wealth. After all, we didn't bring anything with us when we came into the world, and we certainly cannot carry anything with us when we die. So if we have enough food and clothing, let us be content. But people who long to be rich fall into temptation and are trapped by many foolish and harmful desires that plunge them into ruin and destruction. For the love of money is at the root of all kinds of evil. And some people, craving money, have wandered from the faith and pierced themselves with many sorrows.

The Bible also shows that greed and the overemphasis of money can lead to interpersonal tension. A man once came to Jesus complaining about a family squabble, and the Lord blamed the problem on greed. Then he warned that even when we have abundance, real life consists of more than possessions.[15]

4. *Money and Possessions Should Be Managed Wisely.* In the parable of the talents, Jesus warns about the mismanagement of our resources and ends with the unfaithful servant losing what he had been given and being alienated from his friends.[16] The parable suggests that:

- God entrusts resources to his servants.
- Some people are given more and some are given less.
- God expects us to manage what we have been given with the goal of making wise investments.
- God condemns laziness and mismanagement of resources.
- Each of us is accountable to God to manage what we have been given.
- God's' work can be advanced or hindered by the ways in which we plan and manage what we have been given.[17]

Resources that are managed wisely should be:

- Gained honestly. Trying to make money quickly and dishonestly is condemned in the Old Testament book written by Solomon, the wisest and richest man in the Bible.[18]

- Invested carefully. Returning to the parable of the talents, we are reminded that the wise servants managed their resources wisely, making good investments, and did not hoard or mismanage what they had.[19]
- Spent realistically. This means keeping out of debt whenever possible. The Bible never mentions credit cards, since these are modern inventions. Since credit cards put us into debt, however, it seems unlikely that they would have been sanctioned by biblical writers. We are instructed to pay off all our debts, including what we owe to the government in taxes and other charges.[20] Perhaps it is necessary to borrow at times, but when we do, we become slaves to others, and this can lead to various personal and interpersonal problems.[21]
- Shared joyfully. God loves cheerful givers, and throughout the Bible there is emphasis on giving to God, to the poor, and to one another.[22] Sometimes, this giving is followed by receipt of material wealth and/or spiritual blessing,[23] but, as we have seen, this doesn't always happen. It goes beyond biblical teaching to assume that "when we give, we also get." Believers should give joyfully in gratitude to God but without expecting or demanding immediate monetary or material returns.

Since the Bible speaks often about money and money management, these are issues that must concern every Christian as well. They are issues that cannot be ignored because they come up repeatedly in counseling.

The Causes of Financial Problems

Many people live from payday to payday, financially flush at certain times of the month but flat broke at other times. Others manage to get along without great hardship, but saving seems impossible, and there barely is enough to meet family needs. Some might argue that the pressures come because there are too many expenses but too little income. Financial difficulties appear at all socioeconomic levels, however. For the wealthy, financial problems involve greater amounts of money, but the root causes are similar to those faced by less prosperous people.

1. *A Culture of Consumerism.* Americans and Canadians live in cultures that are steeped in consumerism. Every day, most of us are subjected to endless advertising, creatively developed by marketing experts intent on selling us their products. At the time of this writing, the advertising industry was spending more than $15 billion every year on advertisements targeted to children and adolescents. The figures are much higher for advertising focused on adults.

On the surface, these advertising messages describe products and try to motivate consumers into buying more. At a deeper level, the messages communicate that buying and possessing things bring happiness, pleasure, better relationships with others, independence, status, greater life satisfaction, and fulfillment. Individuals, families, and companies are lured into debt by promises of easy credit, no-interest payments, and buy-now-pay-later financing. The prospects of immediate gratification, greater convenience, and happier lifestyles can overpower any sense of caution and lead people to make financial decisions that they regret later. "Preapproved" credit card offers roll through the mail, come to us on the Internet, and target increasingly younger consumers.

What has been called a *Consumer Culture* is not limited to Canada and the United States.[24] These two countries are mentioned because the consumerism mind-set appears to be most prevalent in the West, and it is here that almost everybody is impacted. Sadly, this is a mentality that is becoming worldwide. Consumer debt may be less in some other countries, but Visa, Master Card, and persuasive advertising are worldwide—or will be soon.[25] Advertising, consumption, materialism, and the capitalistic economic system are pervading cultures and impacting our homes, workplaces, universities, entertainment industries, churches, and counseling offices. Understanding "the struggle for a good life in a materialistic world" is crucial to understanding human life and human problems in this contemporary age. The consumer culture and its values provide the background against which we understand people's spending patterns and financial decisions."[26]

2. *Distorted Values.* The way one handles money can be a good indicator of one's values. Each of us spends money or wants to spend it on the things we consider important, but often these are the things that put us into debt. To understand the causes of debt and other financial problems, counselors should be aware of values that can be harmful.

(a) Materialism. This involves a devotion to material things. It is an attitude that leads people to pursue money, possessions, pleasure, and the good things of life, whether or not they can be afforded. It can be seen in an impatient unwillingness to wait until there is money to buy what one wants. Sometimes, it leads to overindulgence, overcharging, and overspending on luxuries and marks of status that are nice to have but may not really be needed. Money and the accumulation of possessions can have a seductive power that gives a false sense of security, freedom, control, and influence. It overlooks the statement of Jesus that none of us should be greedy for what we don't have, since "real life is not measured by how much we own."[27]

Some of the great biblical leaders had considerable wealth. Abraham, Job, Solomon, and a number of other Old Testament kings are examples. These people never gave evidence of pursuing riches in a selfish pursuit of materialistic values. They accepted their wealth with thanksgiving and as God-given, even as they determined to know and serve him better. Many wealthy people today have similar attitudes toward their possessions.

More common, it seems, is an attitude that finds reasons for the accumulation of things. The roots of this thinking may be planted in the societies where we live, but internally there are rationalizations to justify spending. Many of us think, for example, that "as long as it doesn't hurt us or control us, surely it is all right to have the best." Some might conclude that if they have more, then more will be available to give to missions or the poor. This kind of reasoning can be legitimate, but often it is a less than conscious veil to hide our materialism, even from ourselves. We can criticize the materialistic and excessive cravings of others but never realize that our own purchases may be for selfish, greedy, or other unhealthy motives. Perhaps the rich young ruler had a similar attitude, but Jesus told him to give his possessions to the poor. It has been said often that the best way to free oneself from materialistic control is to be willing to give away what one has.

(b) Covetousness and Greed. These words imply a desire for more, even if others are made poorer as a result. A writer who claimed to be Christian once wrote a book titled *How to Have More in a Have-Not World*. This get-more attitude is entrenched in our modern ways of thinking, even though it is condemned in Scripture, where there is deep concern for the poor and strong criticism of greed.[28] This greed can cause a variety of problems, including unmanageable debt, family arguments, and national inflation. In Western countries we don't worship idols of wood and stone, but many people, Christians included, seem to worship money and material things.

(c) A Desire to Get Rich Quickly. Perhaps people always have been impressed with the idea that one can earn a lot of money quickly and with little effort. The Scriptures warn against these get-rich-quick schemes,[29] but the itch for more entices some people to invest hard-earned funds into programs that, more often than not, fail to deliver what they promise. In some people, this desire to get rich fast leads to pathological problems with gambling.[30]

(d) Pride and Resentment. The church at Laodicea took the proud attitude that it was rich and in need of nothing.[31] Attitudes like this still exist in some wealthy and successful people who fail to realize that they are poor, needy, wretched, and miserable if they ignore God, rely on their wealth for security and happiness, or fail to admit that possessions and successes come as a divine gift. How different was the attitude of David when he gave his wealth to be used in the building of the temple. In his prayer before the people he said, "O LORD our God, even these materials that we have gathered to build a Temple to honor your holy name come from you! It all belongs to you! Riches and honor come from you alone, for you rule over everything."[32]

In contrast to people who have possessions, there are the resentful poor who are angry at God because of their lack of wealth and envious of those who have more. Values like these suggest that some financial problems may be caused less by the possession or lack of material things and more by the attitudes that we have toward money and possessions.

3. *Unwise Financial Decisions.* There are many ways to waste the money we can't afford to lose. Sometimes, the waste comes because of unwise financial decisions that include the following.

(a) Impulse Buying. This needs no explanation. It involves seeing and buying something because it is in front of us and we want it, but it is a purchase that is made without thinking much about quality, prices, whether the purchase really is needed, or whether we can truly afford it. Often, displays of merchandise are set up to encourage impulse buying. These include the attractively arranged products that everybody must pass before they check out at the supermarket, the merchandise in tourist shops that are not available in other places, the "once-in-a-lifetime" deals that we learn about from telemarketers and media advertisements, or products designed and placed to get the attention of children who are with their parents or grandparents. It is a good policy to resist making purchases in situations like these.

(b) Carelessness. Without the limiting influence of a budget, some people spend money carelessly and then are surprised when the wallet is empty or the bank account is overdrawn.

At times, perhaps all of us dream of being rescued by someone who will pay our bills. When people win lotteries or inherit large sums of money, however, the wealth often is gone within a short time, and there is little to show for the windfall. Apparently, many who are careless with small sums of money are careless, as well, with large amounts.

(c) Speculation. There is an old adage that many people ignore. It says that if you can't afford to lose it, don't speculate with your money, no matter how bright the prospects. The Bible warns against speculation,[33] and so does common sense, but many people ignore these warnings and lose their money in attempts to get rich quickly. It is sad that the people who can least afford it are the people who buy lottery tickets every week, hoping to win the jackpot.

(d) Cosigning. This involves signing a statement to say that you promise to pay if someone else fails to remove a debt. Often cosigning is done for worthy motives (to help a friend get a loan, for example), but when the friend cannot or does not pay, the cosigner is left with the debt, and the friendship often disintegrates. Little wonder that the wise and wealthy Solomon, writing under divine guidance, warned against cosigning.[34]

(e) Neglect. Financial problems are common when people neglect their finances, let bills go unpaid, and never balance checkbooks. Sometimes, this is the result of laziness, but more often, perhaps, the neglect occurs because people either get busy with more interesting things or are so overwhelmed with financial issues that they keep avoiding what they need to do. Sometimes, government and other social programs inadvertently encourage this neglect. When help is available for deserving people, the lazy and undeserving also come for money. They see this as their entitlement and, in turn, are encouraged not to work. This creates a financial strain for everyone and can jeopardize the continued existence of genuinely needed programs. Closely aligned with this neglect of finances is the neglect of property. When people fail to take care of property, there can be faster deterioration, costlier repairs, and further decline in one's financial situation.

(f) Wasted Time. To a large extent we decide how to spend our time, including our time at work. For salaried employees this is less of a financial issue, but for the self-employed or for people who are paid according to productivity, time equals money. When a person is disorganized, undisciplined, or inclined to waste time, there is a resulting loss of income.

(g) Buying on Credit. As we have seen, buying on time is one of the prime characteristics of the consumer culture and a major cause of financial problems. It is easy to fall into the credit card trap. First, the buyer purchases something with the intent to pay for it when the bill arrives at the end of the month. In the meantime, the buyer sees something else that he or she wants when a sale comes along. One or two additional purchases are made on the assumption that the payments can be spread over a couple of months. If the minimum payment on the bill is minor, it is easy to rationalize that an additional purchase will only raise the payment by a few dollars, so more debt goes on the credit card.

This is a process of slow financial self-strangulation. Using a credit card may not seem like spending money, so there is temptation to buy more than might be purchased otherwise. As a result, impulse buying is encouraged, and eventually the credit card balances expand. In the meantime, the finance charges accrue and, in effect, add to the cost of each item. For millions of people, credit card buying becomes a license to spend money that they don't have and can't spare for goods that they do not need.

All of this leads to increased debt that is costly financially and binding psychologically. Caught in the credit card trap, it is hard to get out. The stresses are greater when people are forced to use a limited salary to pay a high price for something that was purchased with borrowed funds but now has been used, broken, or discarded already. As the credit card pressure builds, many family arguments and personal tensions build as well. Undoubtedly, it is true that credit cards in our pockets can be like time bombs with the potential to shatter peace, happiness, and mental stability.

4. *Lack of a Budget.* A budget is another term for a spending plan. When a plan exists and is followed, there are controls on spending, less impulse buying, and fewer debts. When there is no financial plan, there is no control on spending. What we spend begins to exceed what we earn, and this leads either to a deficit at month's end, or a turning to credit cards (or home equity loans or interest-only mortgages) to make ends meet.

5. *Lack of Giving.* Hoarding is wrong, and the person who refuses to give hardly can expect to receive God's blessing and financial guidance.[35] Believers are to give in three areas: to God, to other believers, and to the poor.[36] We can assume that givers have no guarantees of receiving abundant material blessings in return, but we also know that the believer who fails to follow the biblical directives on giving is courting financial problems.

The Effects of Financial Problems

Previous paragraphs have identified several of the results that come with financial stress. These include:

- Worry about money or how to pay the bills. Some surveys and estimates suggest that as much as 70 percent of all worries concern money.
- Family and marital problems that arise or increase because of financial pressures, arguments over spending priorities, conflicts about inheritances, or similar money issues.
- Guilt, envy, jealousy, resentment, or pride—each of which is sinful and each of which can be stimulated or accentuated by financial issues and distorted values.
- Emotional emptiness and unhappiness that come to those whose main interest in life is the acquisition and accumulation of riches.
- Spiritual decline or dullness that often follows when there are wrong attitudes about possessions, too many concerns about money, or violations of biblical principles for handling finances.

Friendships also can be affected. Tensions between friends may build when one has a sudden increase in money. More often friendships disintegrate because a person becomes greedy, envious, embarrassed by debts, or intent on making loans from others. These are good ways to lose friends.

At times, financial problems put most of us under stress, which can bring physical illness, anxiety, discouragement, interpersonal tension, and inefficiency as a result. For some people, there also can be uncontrolled, irresponsible spending, especially if riches increase suddenly. For others there may be bankruptcy, with the resulting family pressures and psychological trauma. Clearly, money and possessions, either too much or too little, can stimulate a number of the problems that people bring to a counselor.

Counseling and Financial Problems

Helpful books on money management appear with some frequency.[37] Counselors can review these and then loan or recommend them to counselees, who often are able to solve their financial problems without additional help. Others will benefit from counseling that may focus on one or more of the following issues.

1. *Help the Counselee Acknowledge the Problem and Determine to Solve It.* Every counselor knows that it is difficult, if not impossible, to counsel successfully with a person who won't admit that a problem exists. It is equally difficult to help someone who claims "things have always been this way and never will be different."

People who appear to be avoiding problems nevertheless may worry about them. Sometimes, people are jolted from their lethargy when some valuable possession is repossessed or when a creditor sues for payment. More often, people can be helped to get involved when a counselor acknowledges that the problems seem unsolvable but is able to offer both help and hope. Gently urge the potential counselees to face the reality of their situations and give encouragement when this is done. Point out that God supplies our needs and that it *is* possible to get out of debt and to manage money efficiently. Try to emphasize that the solution to financial problems depends less on the state of the economy than on the way individuals and families handle their financial attitudes and resources. When counselees begin to experience hope, this may not eliminate worry, but it gives people courage to look again at their financial problems and, with the counselor's help, to work at finding solutions.

Even with this encouragement, the realistic counselor knows that for some people there is little hope because they don't want to change or are unwilling to work on financial problems. People like this may have to experience financial disaster before they are motivated to work on the problem. For some the motivation may never come.

2. *With the Counselee, Seek Divine Guidance.* In the midst of crises, it is easy to be so distracted by circumstances that we take our eyes off God. Counselees should be reminded that God has abundant riches and knows our needs.[38] He has instructed us to cast our burdens and anxieties on him,[39] and surely this includes financial burdens. If someone asks for divine help and expects it, then God will meet the person's need. He also will help us to be content in any circumstances, including our current financial state.

All of this implies that prayer should be an important starting point in financial planning. Counselors can pray with the counselee, asking God to lead as the practical details of financial planning are discussed. Then encourage the counselee and his or her family to pray together about this as they work together on their money problems.

3. *Teach Biblical Principles of Finance.* People with financial problems are in a hurry to get some relief. Rarely are they interested in sermons or in philosophical talks about finances, but they need to understand, nevertheless, that there are biblical guidelines for managing money. These principles, some of which are summarized in Table 36–1, must guide the Christian counselor and should be shared explicitly at various times as the counseling continues.

Table 36–1

Biblical Principles of Finances

- *God Owns Everything.* We are stewards of God's possessions. What he has entrusted us to manage is what he has loaned us (Psalm 50:12, 15; 24:1; Matthew 25:14–30; Luke 12:42–48; 19:8).
- *Stealing Is Wrong.* Since God owns everything, to steal from another is also to steal from God. Stealing includes cheating on income tax, taking supplies that rightfully belong to an employer, and gaining money in other unethical ways (Exodus 20:15; Leviticus 19:11; Deuteronomy 5:19; Mark 12:17; Luke 16:10–12; Ephesians 4:28).
- *Coveting Is Wrong.* To covet is to want something that we see others enjoying. It implies dissatisfaction with the possessions and opportunities that God has given. God can help us to be content with what we have. Coveting also can involve clinging to our own possessions so that we are excessively distraught when something is lost, broken, or stolen (Exodus 20:17; Deuteronomy 5:21).
- *The Relentless Pursuit of Riches Is Dangerous.* This can lead to evil and foolish actions, spiritual problems, and harmful values, including pride and wasted time (1 Timothy 6:9–10, 17–18; Proverbs 23:4–5).
- *Giving Is Right.* It is an expression of our love and gratitude to God. It is pleasing to God. He expects us to give when we have very little to spare, to give consistently and proportionately, and to give generously—both to God and to those in need (Mark 12:41–44; John 12:1–10; 1 Corinthians 16:2; 2 Corinthians 8:1–8; 9:6–8; Proverbs 3:9–10).
- *Money Management Is Right.* This is illustrated in the parable of the talents. Jesus criticized the poor manager. God expects us to be good stewards of what he has given (Matthew 25:14–29; Genesis 1:28).

4. *Help Counselees Develop and Follow a Financial Plan.* It is very difficult to control finances if there is no blueprint for money management. A financial plan involves several elements that can be discussed in counseling. Some of the following steps can be initiated in the counseling session, completed by the counselees at home, and discussed in later sessions.

(a) Get the Facts. This involves making a list on paper of one's assets and liabilities. Completing Figure 36–1 is one way that this might be done. Getting an accurate picture of the current financial situation can be an important first step in solving financial problems. When net worth is increasing every year, the person is moving ahead financially. When the net worth is decreasing, the person is declining financially.

(b) Establish Goals. What are the counselee's financial hopes and plans? Begin with some general goals—like getting out of debt, being able to provide for the family, doing what we can to advance the cause of Christ, saving for the education of children and for retirement, having enough money to travel, or owning a home.

Getting the Facts: Assets and Liabilities

Assets (What We Own)

Savings	$ _____
Checking Accounts	_____
Value of Car	_____
Value of House	_____
Resale Value of Furnishings	_____
Cash Value of Insurance	_____
Other Assets	_____

Total   _____

Liabilities (What We Owe)

Unpaid Balance on Car	$ _____
Home Loan (Mortgage)	_____
Other Debts (List)	_____

Total   _____

Net Worth (Difference between
Assets and Liabilities) $ _____

Date   _____

Figure 36–1. Getting the Facts: Assets and Liabilities.

When these general goals have been written down, it is good to be more specific in listing long-range and short-term goals. What specifically does the counselee hope to have achieved in ten years, five years, and one year from now? Help counselees be realistic in terms of their educational level, present income, and debts. A man who has a debt that is greater than his annual income cannot realistically expect that all debts will be gone within a year, but he can set a goal to have a portion gone within the next twelve months.

In setting goals remember that these should fit within scriptural guidelines about finances. Help counselees be honest and fair in all financial dealings, including the payment of taxes. Encourage people to avoid selfish indulgence, to show a financial concern for others, and to avoid borrowing, except, perhaps, for major purchases such as a home or car, and, on occasion, for bill consolidation. Emphasize that financial goals are best set after seeking God's guidance through prayer and study of the Bible.

(c) Set Priorities. Few people can meet all their financial goals immediately, so there must be decisions about what can be done now and what must wait until later. Tithing, paying off debts, and eliminating the misuse of credit cards must be high on the priority list.

One financial counselor has suggested that we need to distinguish among needs, wants, and desires.[40] *Needs* are the purchases necessary to provide food, housing, clothing, medical care, transportation, and other basics. *Wants* involve choices about quality: whether to get a used or a new car, or whether to eat hamburger or steak. *Desires* are choices for spending surplus funds after other expenses are met. A good used car would meet the need, a new car might be wanted, a fancy sport's car might be desired. In establishing a financial plan and getting out of debt, needs must be met first; wants and desires can be met later. Each expenditure should be evaluated in terms of these categories. In setting priorities, remember once again that time management often has a bearing on finances. In many occupations, to waste time is to reduce income.

(d) Develop a Budget. A budget is a spending plan that enables us to manage and effectively control the expenditures of money. Budgets involve keeping records that help determine where the money is going. Of course, it is not easy to develop and stay within the guidelines of a budget. Some who claim they cannot keep a budget really don't want to make the effort to control their money carefully or to record where the money is going. Most people get along fine without budgeting, but one result of not having a budget may be wasting money on impulse purchases and other unwise spending more than on spending according to one's priorities.

One plan for saving and spending has been called the 10–70–20 plan for budgeting. As shown in the following diagram, each dollar is divided into five parts. A minimum of 10 percent of one's total income goes to God in tithe, and a second portion goes to the government in taxes and to fixed expenses. The remaining portion is working income, and this is divided in three ways. Ten percent of this is saved, 70 percent is for living expenses, and 20 percent goes to pay past debts. When the debts are gone, the 20 percent can be used for making purchases on a cash basis.

Figure 36–2 gives a sample budget worksheet that counselees could use (with modifications for individual differences). This worksheet assumes the 10–70–20 plan and each month allows counselees to plan and evaluate how successful they have been in keeping within the budget.

Help counselees remember that budgets are tools to help manage spending and not straitjackets to bind spenders. If a budget is unrealistic or if one's financial status changes, then the budget should be altered accordingly. This should be done with care, however, and not in an attempt to cover up or justify reckless spending and deviations from the budget plan.

The 10-70-20 Plan for Budgeting

		Working Income		
10% of Gross Tithe	Taxes and Fixed Expenses	10% Savings	70% Living Expenses	20% Debts
1	2	3	4	5

5. *As a Counselor, Keep Track of Your Own Financial Affairs.* Everyone has heard sad stories about marriage counselors whose own marriages have ended in divorce, psychiatrists whose depression has led them to commit suicide, or preachers who condemn sin, then fall into sin themselves. No counselor is perfect or problem free, but it is difficult to be an effective counselor if one's own life is not in order. The banker who goes bankrupt is not likely to be an effective financial counselor.

Before you encourage others to save, tithe, budget, or follow a financial program similar to the 10–70–20 plan, it is good to pause and ask about the management of your own resources. In addition to the embarrassment, your counseling effectiveness is likely to be undercut if you have to say "no" when a counselee asks if you are following your own advice.

6. *Ponder This: Is Financial Guidance Really Counseling?* Counselors who are accustomed to more in-depth and psychologically based problems may feel that financial planning is beyond the scope of Christian counseling and beyond the competence of most counselors. Many counselors may wish to refer their counselees to a banker, accountant, or other trained financial planner. Before making recommendations, it is important to investigate the qualifications of those who offer this kind of service. Some who advertise themselves as financial counselors may lack training or competence. Others may be concerned about getting investment money from their clients and earning a financial advisor's fee on these funds, but have much less interest in helping people cope with their financial problems, get out of debt, and establish a more secure financial future. Like in every other field, there are some professional financial planners who are unethical, but the vast majority have a sincere desire to help and build a group of satisfied clients. Competent financial planners often have the names of present or prior clients who have agreed to give recommendations to anyone who wants to know more about the financial advisor's abilities.

Helping people manage their money and possessions can be one of the most rewarding and visibly successful aspects of Christian counseling. When there is a resolution of financial difficulties, this often has a positive effect on a variety of other counseling problems.

Preventing Financial Problems

Most of the problems discussed in this book only apply to some people. Not everyone becomes alcoholic, deeply depressed, or struggles with marriage problems. But everyone handles money, most of us have financial problems at least periodically, and the Christian counselor will face people who need help in handling their material possessions better. How can the counselor contribute to the prevention of these problems?

1. *Teach Biblical Values Concerning Finances.* This can be part of individual counseling sessions, but it also comes in group meetings (including youth meetings and Sunday classes), special seminars, and sermons. Despite the fact that Jesus talked openly and often about money, some Christian leaders are reluctant to teach about this publicly. This reluctance is understandable because of the perception (which may or may not be valid) that churches are too much focused on getting money from the people who attend or that church leaders put people under pressure to make donations. It is important that we move beyond this concern

and sensitively deal with issues that are biblical and could prevent financial problems for people in the future. In teaching about financial issues:

- Point to the many biblical passages that deal with money and possessions.
- Encourage people to thank God for what they have, instead of making comparisons with others and lamenting their lacks and needs.
- Emphasize the importance of saving and joyful giving.

2. *Teach Practical Guidelines for Managing Money.* This involves showing people how to budget (including tithing and saving), encouraging them to do so, and urging them to share their experiences with other believers. It can be exciting and encouraging for believers to see how God blesses and meets needs when his guidelines are followed.

Most Christian counselors will not be experts in insurance, banking procedures, the preparation of a will, or the best ways to save and invest money. Nevertheless, the counselor can stress the importance of each of these issues and point Christians either to books or to people who can give practical advice. Within the body of Christ, there often are persons with business and financial expertise. These people can be invited to meet with individuals or groups to help with financial planning. This involves members of the body sharing their knowledge and gifts to build up and encourage others.

3. *Help People See and Avoid the Dangers of Buying on Credit.* In the 1920s the American automobile industry popularized installment buying. At the time it was a new form of making purchases that involved buying now and paying later. Credit cards came later, but over the years people in the United States learned to "finance the American dream" and acquire material possessions by delayed payments. In time we became what one writer has called a "credit card nation" that pays with plastic.[41] It was not long before other countries followed the American example, and today making purchases on credit begins with teenagers and extends to the elderly.[42]

Financial advisors sometimes urge their clients to cut up their credit cards so they are never used. Sadly, the credit card companies are aggressive in promoting new cards, and there are places where the possession of a major credit card becomes a necessary means for identification. It can help to show people the dangers of buying on credit, but increasing evidence shows that scare tactics rarely work in getting people to change habits. It is better to emphasize the benefits of living within one's means, resisting advertising to the extent that this is possible, and helping Christians see the biblical prohibitions against going into debt. Increasingly, there are calls to limit the advertising that is geared to young people, who are too young to know that commercial messages are biased and designed to be persuasive, and too easily lured into a materialist mentality that eventually urges people to buy now and pay later. Parents who use credit cards freely teach their children to do the same.

4. *Protect Children from Advertising.* This may seem a long way from Christian counseling and from preventing financial problems, but several professional organizations are urging that advertisements geared to children should be limited. In the United States advertising begins in the schools, where textbooks and other products sometimes carry advertiser's messages. The problem is made

Budget

Month of _____

Gross Income (before taxes) $_____*

Item	A Amount Allocated	B Amount Spent	C Difference (+ or −)
1. *Tithe* (10%)	$	$	$
2. *Fixed Expenses*			
Taxes			
Social Security			
Professional Dues			
Other			
Total	$	$	$
Total Tithe and Fixed Expenses	$ _____ **		
Working Income—Deduct Total Tithe and Fixed Expenses (**) from Gross Income (*)	$	$	
3. *Savings* (10% of Working Income)	$	$	$
4. *Living Expenses* (70% of Working Income)			
Mortgage or Rent			
Heat/Electricity			
Telephone			
Water/Sewage/Garbage			
Gasoline			
Car Repairs			
Insurance			
Medical			
Food/Household			
Clothing			
Home Expenditures			
Gifts			
Vacation			
Buffer			
Other			
Total	$	$	$
5. *Debts* (20% of Working Income)			
Total	$	$	$

6. *Summary of Allocations*
   Gross Income (from * above) $ _____
   Total Allocated (Total of 5 boxes in column A) $ _____
   Difference (Balance or Amount Short) $ _____

7. *Summary of Amount Spent*
   Gross Income (from * above) $ _____
   Total Allocated (Total of 5 boxes in column B) $ _____
   Difference (Balance or Amount Short) $ _____

Figure 36–2. Budget.

worse by television advertising designed for children and adolescents, "enhanced by technology, honed by child psychologists, and brought to us by billions of dollars."[43] Despite the support for restricting advertisements geared to children, this is a political issue that is likely to take a long time to implement. In the mean time, Christian counselors and church leaders can help parents see the benefits of limiting their children's exposure to advertising that comes into the home.[44]

5. *Emphasize Finances in Premarital Counseling.* When people get married, they usually enter an entirely new financial picture. Two incomes and ways of handling money often merge into one, and there is potential for conflict over finances and money management. As they approach marriage, a couple sometimes needs reminders to look at their resources through the eyes of reality. What are their attitudes toward money, finances, saving, tithing, credit cards, or budgeting?

What debts are they bringing to marriage, and how will these be paid? Do the bride and groom have different spending patterns? Does one spend lavishly, while the other tends to be frugal? What are their attitudes toward material possessions, or having a home or car that matches what other couples have? By raising financial questions and giving guidance as couples discuss them, premarital counselors can prevent future conflicts over issues of money and possessions.

6. *Raise the Issue of Finances Whenever There Is a Crisis or Life Change.* Major changes in life—starting college, changing jobs, moving, retirement, prolonged sickness, death in the family—can each bring financial struggles. If these financial issues can be raised early and discussed informally, problems can often be faced and resolved before they become major difficulties.

Conclusions About Handling Finances

In writing to Timothy, the apostle Paul had some advice about finances: "Tell those who are rich in this world not to be proud and not to trust in their money, which will soon be gone. But their trust should be in the living God, who richly gives us all we need for our enjoyment. Tell them to use their money to do good. They should be rich in good works and should give generously to those in need, always being ready to share with others what God has given."[45]

In many ways these words summarize the biblical teaching about finances. In contrast, Satan has used financial pressures to enslave people, push them into accepting self-centered values, plunge them into debt. and cause both worry and a turning away from God and from divine principles of money management. Helping individuals and families to get out of debt and into financial freedom can be a satisfying experience in counseling. For the counselor, this can be a practical way to help people live more in accordance with God's guidelines for our lives, including the wise handling of our possessions.

KEY POINTS FOR BUSY COUNSELORS

➤ Books on counseling almost never mention money, but the Bible speaks of finances and possessions often, and money issues can be a significant part of various issues that are brought to counselors.

➤ According to the Bible:
- Money and possessions are given by God and, in themselves, are not innately bad.
- Money and possessions must be viewed realistically.
- Money and possessions have potential to be harmful.
- Money and possessions should be managed wisely.

➤ Financial difficulties can arise because of:
- The culture of consumerism where many of us live.
- Distorted values, including materialism, greed, a desire to get rich quickly, pride, and resentment because of what others possess.
- Unwise financial decisions, including impulse buying, careless misuse of resources, speculating, cosigning, neglect of financial obligations, neglect of property so that there are added costs for repairs, wasted time in those for whom time is money, and buying on credit.
- Lack of a budget.
- A neglect of giving.

➤ Christian counselors may not feel that they have expertise in advising people concerning their finances, but there are basics that can be shared.
- Help counselees acknowledge the problems and determine to solve them.
- In partnership with the counselee, seek divine guidance.
- Teach biblical principles of finance.
- Help counselees develop and follow a financial plan.
- As a counselor, keep track of your own financial affairs.
- Determine whether financial guidance is part of your work as a counselor.

➤ To prevent problems with handling finances:
- Teach biblical principles concerning finances.
- Teach practical guidelines for handling money.
- Help people see and avoid the dangers of buying on credit.
- Seek to protect children from advertising.
- Emphasize finances in premarital counseling.
- Raise the issue of finances whenever there is a crisis or life change.

37

Vocational Counseling

Ron was not the typical person who might come for career counseling. He was successful in his work as a project manager in the information technology field. His clients and employees both liked him, and his reputation was outstanding. Ron was known for his expertise, attention to detail, and strong focus on making customers happy. At the age of forty-one, he had developed a successful career and was earning a good income. There was only one problem: Ron hated his job and the field in which he was working. He dreaded Mondays when he had to go back to work, and he was having increasing difficulty getting up in the morning and facing another day in a job that he loathed.

Ron's father had worked in a factory and expected that Ron and his brother would do the same. The parents had always paid their bills, but finances were tight and there was little hope that things would get better. Ron and his brother both went to college, but the brother dropped out, spent some time in the military, and then moved from job to job, never able to find a satisfying career. Ron determined to be different. He got his college degree and entered a field that was likely to provide a good income even if it did not provide job fulfillment and satisfaction. Like his brother, Ron also had changed companies several times, most often when he feared that the current company might be moving into financial difficulties. That is when Ron would look for something that appeared to be more stable financially. Then he would move.

His counselor noted that Ron had never stopped to think about what he really wanted to do. "Having spent a childhood doing what his demanding mother wanted and expected, he'd developed a well-calibrated radar for the needs of others, and that had endeared him to clients. Further, after watching his mother struggle to make ends meet, his primary object had been to keep himself financially secure, so he'd simply followed the money." Each of the moves had been successful until he began to struggle with depression and finally began to face the fact that he didn't like the work that he was doing.[1]

There was a time when choosing a career was a once-in-a-lifetime event that usually occurred in late adolescent or early adulthood. While they were growing up, children might have had fantasies about becoming firefighters, teachers, or doctors, but in reality the choices were limited. Most entered lifetime careers in fields that differed little from the vocations of their parents or grandparents. In countries where higher education became increasingly available, probably most students and their parents assumed that the primary purpose of education was to prepare students for successful careers and for making wise vocational choices. Teachers or school counselors might make suggestions about careers, but Christian counselors, including pastors, might not have considered vocational guidance to be a part of their work.

Today, counselors are more involved in helping people make vocational choices. These decisions are crucially important, frequently difficult, and rarely once-in-a-lifetime events. The decisions are *important* because career choices largely determine one's income, standard of living, status in the community, social contacts, emotional health, feelings of self-worth, use of time, general satisfaction with life, and spiritual well-being. Career choices frequently are *difficult* because of the many available careers, the staggering array of jobs, the continual changes in the economy and job market (consider the rise and fall of the dot com industry in the 1990s or the outsourcing of American jobs to other countries), the great potential for making mistakes, and the misery that can come when people get into the wrong type of work. Vocational choices are *rarely once-in-a-lifetime events* because the job market changes so quickly and unpredictably, people change as a result of their experiences or training, and work conditions change as companies merge, positions are eliminated, and work environments are recast into something new. Vocational counseling still involves guidance for young people pondering their work futures, but in addition help may be sought when:

- A person, like Ron, is successful in his or her career but hates the work, wants to change, and has no idea how to do this or where to turn.
- A worker's skills become outdated or are no longer needed.
- A job position is eliminated or transferred to another company or part of the world.
- A business fails or a major company closes, leaving the workers without employment or skills to compete in the changing job market.
- An employee is reassigned overseas and has no idea how to work in a country other than his or her own.
- A worker is fired or laid off.
- Work stress makes the employment situation intolerable. This stress might include unpleasant work colleagues, incessant arguments at the workplace, or job boredom.
- A person needs help in transitioning to retirement.

For the Christian, including the Christian counselor, all of these are influenced by the belief that one's vocational choices should be in accordance with God's will.

The Bible, Work, and Vocational Counseling

The Bible does not address the topic of vocational counseling as we know it, but there are many scriptural references to work. From the beginning it appears that God intended that human beings would work. When he created Adam and put him in the garden, we know that this first human being communicated with God, slept, and became a husband, but it also appears that he worked. He was expected to take care of the garden,[2] and was given the job of naming all living creatures. After the Fall, work ceased to be a pleasant activity and became more of a burden. Along with his wife, Adam was "banished" from the Garden of Eden and sent to work the ground, struggling to scratch a living from it and spending his life sweating to produce food.[3]

Throughout the Bible other examples of work appear frequently. Cain, the first child of Adam and Eve, cultivated the soil while his brother Abel took care of flocks. For at least part of his life, Noah was a shipbuilder who later turned to farming. Abraham was a wealthy livestock owner, and David was a shepherd who later changed careers and became a king. Other occupational groups mentioned in Scripture include prophets, priests, tentmakers, hunters, political leaders, craftsmen, musicians, bricklayers, salespersons, homemakers, carpenters, fishermen, and more.

Although work always appears to have been a part of God's plan for the human race, work often has been difficult, and sometimes it has been abused. Pharaoh greatly abused the people of Israel who were his slaves. The Bible mentions the special burden on employees of the rich who hoarded their wealth and exploited their underpaid workers.[4] For centuries some people have made their work an idol, driving themselves in the vain effort to acquire wealth and accumulate achievements.[5] Others have poured their skills and efforts into work and anxious striving, only to wonder if all of their efforts were useless and without meaning.[6]

For the Christian, work is to be done as service to Christ. Not only can work bring glory to God, but it also enables us to help others and to gain both respect and independence.[7] Stated concisely, work enables us to meet our needs. If we want to eat, most of us have to work.[8] In doing our jobs, we seek to please our employers, but our primary role is to work hard and cheerfully at whatever we do, as though we are "working for the Lord rather than for people."[9] We are serving Christ even when we work for a non-Christian employer.

Does work exist to bring fulfillment, meet our needs, give us pleasure, or bring success and happiness? These commonly accepted ideas are not necessarily wrong, but they are not taught in Scripture. There are several clear biblical conclusions about work and vocational choices.

1. *Work Is Honorable; Laziness Is Condemned.* The early church was instructed to give suitable wages and honor, especially to those whose work involved preaching and teaching.[10] The wife of noble character is pictured as one who works diligently and is praised as a result.[11] In a psalm of praise to God for the work of creation, we read that "people go off to their work; they labor until the evening shadows fall again,"[12] apparently with the approval of God. In contrast, wise King Solomon warned repeatedly of the poverty and foolishness that would come to those who were lazy.[13]

2. *Work Is to Be Interspersed with Rest.* The Bible approves of diligence and quality in work, but it gives no sanction to a person who is a slave to work or the workaholic who never rests or takes a vacation. God rested after creating the world, and in the Ten Commandments he instructed human beings to rest one day out of every seven. Many modern believers do not regard one day as being any more special than another,[14] so they work all the time. Instead, we have a biblical precedent to follow the example of Jesus and the spiritual leaders in Judeo-Christian history who set aside one day each week for worship, rest, and relaxation.

3. *Work Is to Be of High Quality.* Employees and other workers have a responsibility to work honestly, diligently, and well,[15] not merely to please others, but to honor Christ. The pursuit of excellence is a worthy goal; dishonest and shoddy workmanship are clearly unbiblical.[16] Employers are to be fair and just, recognizing that they too have a master in heaven.[17] Each of us must develop and show good stewardship of the talents and aptitudes that God has given.[18]

4. *Work Is Unique and for the Common Good.* Like modern vocational counselors

who emphasize the differences in human interests and abilities, the Bible points out that we each have unique capabilities and responsibilities. Some of this must have reflected innate abilities, but the influence of training probably was of equal importance. During King Solomon's reign and again during the time of Ezra, skilled craftsmen and woodworkers built the temple and taught others to be skilled as well. At the temple dedications and at the celebration after the wall was rebuilt under the leadership of Nehemiah, there were singers and other skilled musicians who used their abilities to lead the people and to bring praise to God.

When a person becomes a Christian, he or she is given one or more special spiritual gifts. These are to be developed, used for the common good, and applied to the building up of other believers in the body of Christ.[19] Some people work more diligently and more faithfully than others, but since our abilities and spiritual gifts come from God, it is he who allows some to become visibly successful while others do not.[20] Because of this, the Christian has no reason for self-centered boasting about his or her accomplishments.[21]

5. *Work and Vocational Choice Are Guided by God.* Some people in the Bible had their life work selected by God before birth. Isaiah, David, Jeremiah, John the Baptist, and Jesus are the clearest examples.[22] Could it be that God still chooses men and women, even before they were born, to accomplish special tasks for him?

Many Christians would agree that God calls at least some people to special ministries and places of service. But there is disagreement about whether he has one (and only one) specific career calling for each of his children. From a counseling perspective, perhaps this is not of special importance. We know that God directs those who acknowledge him and seek his ways,[23] and we can be sure that he gives wisdom to those who ask.[24] When facing vocational decisions, each person can assume that his or her unfolding vocational future is in God's hands and guided by his Holy Spirit, but we know, as well, that we have the responsibility for discerning our own abilities, strengths, or interests, developing the talents and abilities that God has given, and seeking the information we need to make wise vocational choices.

The Christian vocational counselor uses a variety of techniques to help people choose or change careers. In going about this work, the counselor seeks God's guidance and assumes that he will lead both counselor and counselee as they make their vocational decisions.

Causes of Good and Poor Vocational Decisions.

The world of work is changing, even for people who live in remote areas or underdeveloped countries.

- Technology has made it possible for many people to work anywhere, at any time, and to be in immediate contact with people in any part of the world.
- The information age has changed the way we do work and the work we do. This is the effect of instant two-way communication across the globe, huge databases, video conferencing, and easy access to the latest research, world news, or stock-market figures.
- Minorities, older people, and women are becoming larger parts of the

workforce, and their jobs, influence, and vocational opportunities are changing.

- Many less popular or routine jobs are being outsourced to other locations, including other countries where costs may be lower.
- Large numbers of people have multiple careers and sometimes pursue two or three careers at the same time. The old idea of staying with the same job and the same company throughout a career is a way of working that no longer exists in many places. Consider the impact of downsizing, company closings, the fact that many positions become obsolete every year, and the constant appearance of new careers. The world of work changes constantly.
- With the ease of travel and communication between countries and parts of any one country, people are freer to move, go to better jobs, and uproot their families.
- While all of this change is taking place, unskilled and poorly educated workers are increasingly left behind and unable to find productive and financially rewarding work.
- Greater numbers of people are choosing to work at home and independently in their own businesses. This has led one writer to describe the Unites States as a "free agent nation" of independent workers who are transforming the way we live and work.[25] In the years ahead, this independence is likely to characterize workers in many other nations.

Before these changes, counselors proposed a number of theories to explain career choice and guide vocational counselors.[26] These older theories and others that are newer have given sophisticated and helpful guidelines to counselors, but the core of vocational guidance still appears to consist of three parts: help counselees learn about themselves, help them learn about vocations, and guide as they match their talents to the most desirable career. Sometimes, the match is good, appropriate training and job openings are available, and the counselee is able to find a useful and satisfying career or new place in the workforce. More often, perhaps, the process is difficult. High status, high prestige, and high-paying jobs are relatively scarce, but they are sought by numerous people. Many of the more attractive or desired careers require intellectual abilities, unique aptitudes, specialized training, and sometimes personal contacts that few people possess. Because of high demand, intense competition, and limited opportunities, many people are disappointed in their career choices and forced to settle for less desirable alternatives.

Often, this is seen most clearly in poorer communities or neighborhoods where young people feel trapped because they see no way out. Kenyon is an example. He wanted to be a doctor, but he did not have good enough grades, so he decided, instead, to be a professional athlete. In Kenyon's neighborhood, almost everybody agrees that the two best ways out of poverty are to become an athlete or to be an entertainer. Month after month, Kenyon practiced as a basketball player, hoping that his athletic skills would attract the attention of some college recruiter who might offer him a scholarship if he would try out for the school team. It never happened, so Kenyon gave up, worked at menial jobs that were far below his capabilities, spent a little time in jail for selling drugs, and eventually settled into the same poverty and discouraging work that has characterized everybody else in his family.

There are many people like Kenyon, men or women who never have the opportunity to plan careers. In need of work, these people skim the "help-wanted" advertisements and slip into jobs that provide a paycheck and some security but are neither satisfying nor personally fulfilling. Some people stay in jobs like these for their entire lives. Most often they are dissatisfied, unhappy, and in the wrong kind of work. Some get laid off or shift from one position to another, none of which they enjoy or do well.

Even people who enjoy their work often make changes as they go through life. Sometimes, this is involuntary, as companies shut down or downsizing leads to the elimination of jobs. At other times, people are like Ron, who was described earlier. He was successful wherever he worked but hated what he was doing and determined to make a vocational shift. Some estimates suggest that ten years from now as many as half of the working population will be in jobs that do not exist today. Depending on where one lives, young people who are entering the workforce can be expected to change jobs and careers during their working lives. Clearly, vocational guidance must be an ongoing process that involves everyone—not just professional counselors. With or without such guidance, people make vocational decisions that are based on a number of influences.

1. *Family and Social Influences.* Teachers, friends, relatives, and especially parents often expect their children to made career decisions early. At a time when they are immature, idealistic, inexperienced, and struggling with the problems of late adolescence, young people have the added responsibility of choosing from an almost unlimited number of career possibilities. Later in life, if one quits or is forced to leave a job, there is financial and social pressure to find other work as quickly as possible. All of this prevents careful planning and encourages vocational choices that can lead to disappointment and frustration.

Some families exert great pressure on career choices. JG came from a long line of pastors. Among others, his father, grandfather, and two of his great-grandfathers had been clergymen, but when JG announced that he wanted to go into business, he encountered significant opposition. The family would have helped with seminary tuition, but they refused to give any financial support when the young man went to business school. JG was not opposed to the ministry, but his career counselor and his own careful thinking had led him to conclude that a career in the business world would be better for him and might even give opportunities to serve Christ that he might have missed otherwise. Even so, resisting the family pressure was an act of courage and determination.

2. *Personality Influences.* An individual's personality affects both the selection of a vocation and the success or satisfaction that is experienced within one's career. John Holland developed a theory of vocational choice that was built on the assumption that most people can be categorized into six general vocational personality types:

- Realistic is the word to describe people who prefer tangible, practical, skill-based activities that involve physical strength and coordination. Mechanics, farmers, and surveyors fit with this description.
- Investigative personalities are methodical, intellectual, curious, scientific, and able to think critically. These are people who enjoy mathematics or scientific investigation.
- Artistic people are creative, artistic, and aesthetically oriented. These are people who like music, art, acting, and literature.

- Social personalities are sensitive and interested in people, best fulfilled when they are socializing, helping, training, and developing others.
- Enterprising is the word used to describe aggressive, energetic, self-confident, persuasive problem solvers. These people do well as entrepreneurs, politicians, or church planters.
- Conventional people are those who like routine, schedules, and activities that are orderly, systematic, and maybe even inflexible.[27] Look for accountants or financial planners in this group.

People rarely fit into rigid categories like these, so Holland suggests that most people have one dominant personality type, which usually emerges between the ages of eighteen and thirty, plus one or two other types that are of lesser importance. According to the theory, these individual differences have a bearing on vocational choice and degree of career satisfaction and success.

According to the same theory, jobs also can be divided into the same six categories. If investigative type people enter investigative work (such as scientific research), or if social people enter social occupations, such as teaching, medicine, or counseling, there will be a high degree of vocational satisfaction. In contrast, if a socially inclined person gets into a realistic type of job, or if an enterprising person enters a conventional occupation, such as accounting or being an office manager, there is certain to be frustration and unhappiness. This may have accounted for the dissatisfaction that was in Ron, whose story began this chapter. He was managing an office and contacting customers when he really wanted to develop a home-design business that would tap into the artistic part of his personality.

3. *Strengths.* Some people appear to be fully engaged in their work. They are committed, productive, and fulfilled, with low absenteeism and low rates of turnover. These highly engaged people are enthusiastic, energized, successful, and intentional about caring for themselves and their work. This is not true of minimally engaged people.[28] They come to work and do their jobs, but the enthusiasm and commitment are not there. What makes the difference? Why are some people fully engaged and others are not? It appears that the answer depends on the extent to which one's strengths are being used. People who use their strengths at work, church, or elsewhere are more likely to be engaged than people whose strengths are not being used.

The Gallup organization interviewed over two million people from around the world and was able to identify thirty-four key human strengths, including adaptability, ability to connect with others, empathy, a special ability to anticipate the future, and the restorative strength that involves solving problems.[29] Put people in careers (or in churches, organizations, or other settings) where they can use their strengths, and these people are productive and positive. From this, a whole business theory developed based on the conclusion that people should be encouraged to develop and use their special talents and strengths rather than trying to overcome their weaknesses. According to the Gallup researchers, strengths-based organizations thrive because they have employees and managers who have discovered and are using their strengths. Some researchers have proposed, as well, that strong churches tend to be strength-based churches where church members serve in ways that are in accordance with their God-given talents and strengths.[30]

There are tests to help people discover their strengths, but by the time they reach adulthood, most people already know what they do well. If they don't know, they can look back over their lives to see what has been successful and ful-filling, what God seems to have blessed, and what one's closest friends describe as one's core strengths. When strengths are ignored in choosing a vocation, the cho-sen work ultimately is not fulfilling, performance is substandard, and there is not a lot of engagement on the job.

4. *Interests.* These are close to the concept of strengths. The field of vocational counseling often assumes that people will do best in those activities and occupa-tions that interest them most. If a job is boring, it isn't likely to bring much per-sonal fulfillment or sense of satisfaction, even if the salary is high.[31]

We have already implied some of the reasons why a person might choose a vocation for which he or she has no interest. Sometimes, in their need and desire to find employment, people take whatever job is available whether or not they find it interesting. Often these people expect to change positions later, but fre-quently, because of insufficient training or lack of opportunities, they do not or cannot change. Others take a boring job because of the salary or fringe benefits, but since many of these workers have little interest in their work, they look for fulfillment and satisfaction in leisure-time activities—including sports, social clubs, church work, watching television, or other activities.

5. *Aptitudes or Abilities.* When a new pastor arrived to take up his duties at a small church, he called in the associate pastor and gave him a welcome assign-ment. "I know you have been here for a long time," the new pastor began. "I know, too, that you have served the people well, but I have a request. Please take the next week and write a job description for yourself. Forget for the present what the church needs, and write what would make this a perfect job for you." The new pastor was wise enough to know that he would have the loyalty and greatest contribution from his staff if they were doing what they liked to do, what they felt they could do best, and what aligned with their aptitudes and abilities.

Technically, there is a difference between an aptitude and an ability. Aptitude refers to the innate potential that one has for learning something in the future. Ability refers to skills that one already possesses as a result of learning from the past. A student may have an *aptitude* (good potential and capacity) for learning to play a musical instrument, but it is only after years of study and practice that he or she may demonstrate great *ability* (skill and knowledge) as a musician.

Careers are most satisfying when one's aptitudes and abilities relate to one's work. It has been estimated, however, that a large percent of working people are underemployed, which means that they are working below their capacity and ability levels.[32] This is especially difficult for people who are gifted and unusually talented but forced to work in occupations where their greatest skills and capabil-ities are not needed and rarely get used. People who are looking for work often assume that underemployment is better than unemployment. As a result, some spend their whole working lives feeling underemployed, unhappy, unfulfilled, and dissatisfied.

6. *Values.* In another one of my books, I wrote that values are difficult to define and hard to identify. They are the foundational beliefs that anchor our lives, the things that matter to us the most.[33] These are characteristics that are at the core of a person's being; they are traits like honesty, integrity, respect for others, fairness, or being genuine. For some people, basic values might include helping others, being creative, doing work with excellence, or having the greatest possible impact for Christ. When I asked a group of MBA students to identify their values, one

hand shot up, and the student announced "I want to make a lot of money. Nothing is more important to me." That was his core value.

Many people have no awareness of their values, but even without awareness, values are reflected in our daily lives and emerge with special clarity in times of stress, crisis, or important decision making. When an employee lies to a customer or to the boss, takes money from the company, or does sloppy work, that person's values are showing. In the same way, when a person refuses to cheat, distort sales reports, or take steroids to gain an unfair advantage in an athletic event, that is a reflection of values as well. Many people have left jobs, even prestigious or well-paying jobs, because they realized that staying would force them to violate their values at work.

Values can be important in career choice and career satisfaction or dissatisfaction. The worker who values honesty, for example, works best for an employer who also is honest. The same worker likely will be intensely frustrated if he or she is employed by a company where dishonesty and shoddy business deals are common.

7. *Roadblocks.* Throughout this book one message has popped up repeatedly, even though it may never have been stated in this way. *Problems develop and often persist because we have circumstances, other people, attitudes, worldviews, beliefs, ways of thinking, or other roadblocks that get in the way and stop us from moving forward.* A lot of counseling involves helping people who are stuck to get unstuck. Many people choose vocations because they feel pushed by others, pressured to get a job, or motivated by some inner belief or expectation. We began this chapter with Ron's story. He hated his job, but he had moved into the information technology field because it offered the potential for financial security, in contrast to the financial struggles of his parents. He grew up trying to please his demanding mother, so he selected a field where he could work with clients to please them. Ron's growing-up experiences, values, and attitudes toward other people had put him in a job that was leading to increasing frustration.

There are other roadblocks that impede good career choice and vocational success. These may be a belief that there are no options for where one is at the present. Ron held this view. Sometimes, there is incomplete or inaccurate information about an available job, or the information may be there, but the job-seeker fails to investigate carefully. Sometimes, there are hasty and ill-informed vocational decisions that later are regretted. There can be unrealistic self-assessments about what one really can do, unrealistic expectations about what a job might offer, an immobilizing fear of making the wrong vocational choice (which may disappoint a parent), or an unwillingness to take risks. Sometimes, there is equipotentiality. This is a big word that describes a big choice, in which there are several good alternatives available, but since no one stands out above the others, the individual makes no decision—like the proverbial horse that starves to death because it can't decide between the oats and the grain that are available. In the meantime, job-seekers watch opportunities slowly disappear. All of these roadblocks can keep people from making good vocational choices. Certainly, the roadblocks can be important topics to discuss in counseling.

For some people with vocational problems the roadblocks are more circumstantial than psychological. The problems of making wise vocational choices can be complicated when one is exceptionally gifted, middle aged or older, or part of a two-career marriage, where a person's career development may depend somewhat on the career of his or her mate. Women can face unique challenges, especially if they want to be involved in careers that are dominated by males. Because there are fewer opportunities, people in rural areas can have greater difficulty finding employment than people in urban areas. Battered women or women who are forced back into the workplace by difficult circumstances may face special difficulties when they encounter new life and career decisions. Add to this the special challenges of career choice for released prisoners, recovering alcoholics, former mental patients, the physically disabled, or other special needs groups, and we begin to see the unique roadblocks that many people face in making career choices, finding work, and developing career decision-making skills.

8. *Divine Leading.* Most Christians believe that God guides in the lives of his children. Some people want and seek this guidance; others do not. When an individual seeks divine leading in career decisions, he or she can rest in the confidence that God is guiding, but this guidance is not always easy to detect. In addition, there is the issue of God's call. In the Bible we see clear evidence of God calling people into certain ministries. One of the clearest examples is the voice of God that spoke to Moses from the burning bush in the desert. Dramatic calls are rare, however, and some Christians even question whether God still calls people today the way he did in the past.[34] Christian counselors Les and Leslie Parrott struggle with this issue in their book on career counseling and conclude that there are at least four steps in determining a call from God:

- Recognition of a need. This is one aspect of a call, but the recognition of a need is not the same as a call to go in response to the need.
- A strong desire to meet a need. This may take time to appear, and it may come through inner promptings and/or from the urging of other people.
- Ability to help fill the need. God does not call people on the basis of talents, but often he does call people who have enthusiasm and a willingness to use the gifts and strengths that they have to meet the need that they see.
- A growing impression that this is one's life work, at least for now. "If the call is of God there will be a persistent and deepening conviction of the need and of your desire to fill the need, and an increase in your consecrated abilities to help meet the need."[35]

It is true, of course, that most people make vocational decisions without the sense of a call. And even when there is a sense of God's leading, not everyone chooses to follow. Jonah, for example, knew the experience of both ignoring and following divine leading. When God instructed him to go to Nineveh and to preach against it, Jonah hurried off someplace else, and the results were almost fatal. When the call came again, Jonah obeyed and went as he was instructed, and the results were more satisfying. Instead of rejoicing, however, Jonah was displeased, angry, and apparently depressed.[36] His obedience had been less than enthusiastic, and he was not happy in his work. Contrast this with the apostle Paul. His work involved many hardships, but he ended life with a feeling of vocational satisfaction.[37]

It is probable that no one influence alone contributes to good or poor vocational choice. The changing world of work, social and family influences, personality traits, individual strengths and interests, aptitudes, abilities, values, road-blocks, circumstances, and sensitivity to God's leading all combine with job avail-ability and training opportunities to influence the nature and direction of an individual's career. Because this issue can be so difficult and complex, many choose unwisely or drift into a vocation that is not satisfying. When this happens, all of life is affected. Because a person's career decisions and direction can have such a major impact, vocational counseling can be one of the most important and all-encompassing challenges for a Christian counselor.

The Effects of Good and Poor Vocational Choice

We can learn a lot about other people by asking about their work. A person's vocation often gives an accurate picture of his or her education, social status, and economic level. A person's type of work largely determines his or her income level. In turn, this can influence a person's lifestyle, place of residence, choice of friends, leisure activities, feelings of self-worth, and general satisfaction with life. People who like their work often are happy with life in general. When a person is not happy at work, this unhappiness can permeate all of life.

Should people expect to be happy at work? Earlier we noted that this is not a biblical concept, although there is nothing in the Bible to suggest the alternative, that work should be dull and unfulfilling. In much of the world today, people appear to believe that they are entitled to happiness on the job, that the ups and downs of the workplace should not occur. This is unrealistic. Even when a person is in the right vocation and enjoys his or her work, there will be times of frustra-tion and unhappiness. That is the nature of work, especially for people who work in large organizations. Even so, work and life are both likely to be better when there is a good fit between one's work and one's strengths, interests, and person-ality.[38]

This is not the way it is for many people, including many who come for coun-seling. For forty or more years of their lives, they go to work, day after day, and spend long hours in miserable or boring circumstances. Happiness at work, fulfill-ment, service, accomplishments, and productivity are far from their minds and from reality. For some, frustration and unhappiness come near the start of their careers, but often discontent surfaces after several years. Some people hate their work, even though they are doing well. They move up the corporate or profes-sional ladders, only to conclude that they are bored, burned out, tired of the stress, and wanting a new challenge. Many wonder if they would be better suited, more satisfied, more successful or productive, and a lot happier if they were in some other occupation. People who feel euphoric on Friday afternoons and depressed on Sunday nights probably aren't happy in their careers, but for many, thoughts of change go no further than restless dreaming. A few are willing to accept any new job that comes along. But most people lack the considerable courage and often the education that would enable them to take a fresh look at their careers, to set new goals, and even to uproot themselves or their families and change vocational direction. It is easier, less risky, and more secure to accept the current situation and make the best of it.

Ron tried that until he couldn't ignore his depression and frustration any longer. He joined a lot of others who have decided to change and who have con-sulted a counselor for help. More often, it seems that people counsel themselves or talk things over with their friends or families, or sometimes getting help from one of the life-planning self-help books.[39]

As he neared the end of his life, Paul wondered about the direction of his future. He knew that execution was a possibility, but he was willing to "live by believing and not by seeing." Whatever might happen, or wherever he might live or work, he determined to make it his life goal to please Christ all the time.[40] When contemporary Christians have a similar goal, we can be more content on the job and better able to handle the complexities of living. When we are committed to serving Christ in our vocations, our work becomes an opportunity for pleasing God, building relationships, and reaching out to touch the lives of others.

Counseling and Vocational Choices

Within the counseling profession, vocational counseling has become a specialty with a variety of theoretical approaches, unique methods, and career counseling textbooks.[41] Most of these approaches have the goal of helping people find fulfilling careers that match their capabilities and enable them to succeed. We have seen that this career guidance can occur at any time in life. It includes guiding young career seekers, helping adults of any age make vocational changes, assisting senior citizens who still want to work, or counseling with people who have special vocational needs. In most cases, the vocational counselor teaches people to make ongoing evaluations of themselves and their work, exposes people to information about careers (including the need and availability of training), and provides special support and guidance when job choices or changes are being made.

Before we look at vocational counseling in more detail, it may help to get a picture of how Ron was helped to find new directions. There is no evidence that Ron or his counselor were Christians, so God was not brought into the counseling, but their process can be instructive, nevertheless.

Counseling Ron. Ron's counselor, whose name was Karen, makes an assumption that at some level, every counselee knows exactly what he or she wants to do in terms of a vocation. Maybe this is a desire from childhood that has been pushed out of awareness or a life purpose from God who knows each of us intimately and may have a plan for every life.[42] In her counseling, Karen listens closely to see if she can pick up that inner desire that sometimes can seem so elusive.

As with all her clients, Karen began by asking Ron to talk about his life. This is the kind of life history that vocational counselors may skip because it does not seem relevant, but Karen believes that the life history is very important. She described the process with Ron in this way: "I asked him about learning disabilities, his physical and mental health, medications, experience with therapy, recent losses, religious/spiritual affiliation, hobbies, even substance use and experience with trauma. The intake gives me considerable data and makes clear to the client that I consider all of these issues relevant to the career process. This is critical, because otherwise, the client may omit relevant information, thinking that it isn't appropriate to career work."[43] From all of this Karen learned about Ron's family, their expectations, their work history, and their attitudes toward Ron.

Next, the counselor and counselee talked about the story of Ron's career, from his earliest childhood fantasies about what he wanted to be when he grew up, to his vocational history, where he worked and why he left. At a later time, Karen asked Ron to spend time between sessions, listing all his jobs and telling what he liked or disliked about each one, being as specific as possible. From this they began to see themes in his life and could spot his values, attitudes, and strengths. It soon became clear that Ron had always chosen jobs that would guarantee a good salary, unlike the home where he grew up. Never had he asked himself the question "What would I really like to do?"

Following one of the sessions, Ron was given an assignment that Karen calls "nine lives." She asked Ron to pretend that he had nine lives and that he would have to work in each of those lives in jobs that he really enjoyed. His goal was to identify the jobs. There were some rules for completing this assignment. First, Ron would assume that each of the jobs would provide the money required to provide for his needs. Second, he would assume that his friends and family would view each job as worthwhile and prestigious, regardless of what it was. Third, he was expected to pick at least nine jobs. He could choose more but not less.

When he returned, Ron handed over the list, but he stated that many of the jobs were silly and not at all realistic. "That's common," Karen replied, and then they started looking for themes that were there and for things that were not there. You may remember that Ron worked in an office for a large information technology company, but his list of nine jobs had several entrepreneurial ideas, such as building his own business or working from his home. There also were visual themes. Ron had landscape designer, architect, and artist on his list. Not one of the jobs was in an office, and few involved working in a large corporation. When Karen asked him to dream out loud about the kind of business he would like to have, Ron showed an enthusiasm that she had not seen as he described the prospects of building his own company.

Without prompting, Ron began to get information about some of the jobs on his list. As he wandered the Internet he discovered similar positions and learned about their requirements and the nature of the work. Eventually, he contacted some people in these fields and began to form a vision of what he wanted—a vision that Karen believes was hidden within her client but that he had never noticed. Ron was getting in touch with his strengths, values, interests, and the other issues that are important in vocational guidance. As the vision clarified, so did some of the risks, probable family resistances, and obstacles that Ron would have to overcome. These were discussed with the counselor, and eventually Ron moved from his current career and launched his business in the home-design area. Recently, he called Karen to say that he was doing well and planning to open another branch of his growing company.

This is only one case. It is not a model for all or even for most career counseling, but it illustrates a process that might be adapted for other vocational counseling situations. Although each counselee is different, effective vocational counselors should get knowledge of the counselee (the way Karen got to know Ron), have some knowledge of the world of work, and demonstrate an ability to guide those who are making specific decisions. All of this must be within the confines of seeking the will of God. We will consider each of these in the following paragraphs along with some observations about special career-counseling situations.

1. *Knowing the Counselee.* Most vocational counselors begin with an interview that gathers personal and employment information, including the counselee's

past work experiences, successes, frustrations, interests, goals, and dreams. Many would extend the interview to get more general and family information about the counselee, since this all can relate to selecting a vocation that could influence a life direction for many years. Often, this is followed by the use of psychological tests that can give concise information both to help counselees increase self-awareness and to point to broad vocational areas that could be worth exploring. There are a variety of assessment tools, although some are available only to professional counselors. Some of these can be taken on the Internet (usually for a fee) and supplemented with tests that can be acquired more easily. Assessment tools include:

- Mental ability tests that are designed to measure general intelligence, specific intelligence such as emotional or musical intelligence, abstract reasoning, mathematical capability, and verbal abilities.
- Personality assessment tools that identify a variety of personality traits (Examples include the California Psychological Inventory, Edwards Personal Preference Schedule, and Myers-Briggs Type Indicator).
- Interest tests that are designed to measure not only expressed interests but also whether the counselee's general interests are the same as those of successful people in specific occupational groups.[44] (Among the tests in this group are the Strong Interest Inventory and the Kuder Occupational Interest Survey.)
- Aptitude tests that can measure one's potential for learning in areas such as music, art, or college in general. The Scholastic Aptitude Test (SAT) is the best known. The Graduate Record Exam (GRE) is taken by people wanting to enter graduate school in areas such as psychology and engineering, whereas tests such as the Graduate Management Admission Test (GMAT) evaluates the potential for succeeding in business school or MBA programs.
- Strengths tests, a newer addition to the testing arena, are designed to help people discover their key strengths. These tests build on the assumption that people are most engaged in their work and most successful and fulfilled when they work in accordance with their areas of strength.[45]
- Other tests include achievement tests that measure skills and the amount of material that a counselee has learned in a special area, and tests designed to measure areas as diverse as creativity, musical capabilities, flexibility, or potential for learning foreign languages. One example is the Medical College Admission Test (MCAT) for people who want to enter medical school. The test assesses problem-solving skills, critical thinking, and writing skills, in addition to the test-taker's knowledge of scientific concepts and principles that relate to the field of medicine. Christians also might be interested in taking one of the spiritual gifts inventories, although these do not tend to be as well designed and researched as more established psychological tests.

The use and interpretation of tests usually require special training, which some counselors may not possess and may not find useful to obtain. It can be helpful, therefore, to refer counselees for testing at various testing sites, including psychological clinics, university counseling centers, private employment agencies, or vocational guidance centers. The Internet is an excellent source of information about tests and places where they can be taken. This is especially helpful for people who live and work in areas where testing centers are rare or nonexistent. In places where centers do exist, most will have computer-based testing capabilities that often allow a test to be taken and, depending on the test, sometimes scored and interpreted on a computer printout, all while the test-taker is in the office. Before this testing is recommended, be sure to check the costs, since these may vary greatly from place to place and from one test to another. Also, ponder or discuss with the counselee whether testing is even needed, and if so, which are the most helpful tests to take. Sometimes, tests don't tell the person much that is new, and tests rarely take the marketplace into account. As a result, the test-taker is left with information about interests or personality, but information that may not be very practical in helping people make realistic career decisions, especially if a counselee is interested in new or possibly innovative vocational areas.[46]

Even without test results, the counselor can get useful data from counselees themselves, information that can be supplemented and confirmed through observation and consultation with people who know the counselee. Through interviews it is possible to get an accurate indication of the counselee's general mental ability, educational level and potential for further training, specific skills and abilities, personality traits, mental and physical health, personal appearance, interests (including those that are stated and some that are shown by the person's freely chosen leisure-time activities), level of spiritual commitment or maturity, spiritual gifts, and (for older counselees) dependability and efficiency as an employee. Of course, the counselor's observations may not always be accurate, but these observations can be discussed with each counselee and often modified as the vocational counseling process continues.

2. *Knowing the World of Work.* Years ago, somebody suggested that vocational counselors often live in a dream world with little understanding of the realities of life on the job. A counselee with musical talent and interests, for example, may show good qualifications to be a performer but may not realize the difficulties of trying to make a living in a field that is highly competitive, filled with qualified people, demanding in terms of travel and scheduling, and not profitable except for a very few. Vocational counselors need to have some understanding of the job market, especially in societies like ours, where the world of work is changing so rapidly.

Unless you are a specialist in vocational guidance, it is unlikely that you can keep abreast of the thousands of available and ever-changing job opportunities. Nevertheless, a Christian counselor can help by showing people where to get information and by suggesting ways by which such information can be used. Notice that information gathering is the counselee's responsibility. The counselor makes suggestions and guides in the process.

Public and college libraries often keep vocational information on file in the form of books, brochures, catalogs, and government publications.[47] Professional organizations, unions, businesses, and insurance companies frequently publish vocational information that is available for free or at a nominal cost. In addition, the yellow pages of a telephone book can put you in touch with local persons in specific vocations. Such persons may know where to write for further information, may be willing to give vocational information themselves, or may be able to arrange on-site visits for seriously interested career-seekers. And when a person wants information about church-related vocations or about the field of counseling, the best source of relevant information may be you.

Much of the needed information can be obtained from printed information and Internet sources, but if a counselee is able to meet with somebody in a specific field of work, suggest that questions be carefully thought out prior to the meeting. People are busy in their work, and often there are limitations to the time available for information-giving interviews. Whatever the source of information, when a counselee locates a source of information and is looking into one or more specific career possibilities, several questions can be asked, including the following.

- What is the nature of this work? What do people in this field do?
- What personal qualifications are needed in terms of skills, strengths, abilities, interests, experience, or physical requirements?
- What training is required, where is it available, how long does it take, and what does it cost?
- Can anyone enter the occupation, or are there educational, age, gender, religious, or other restrictions? The law may decree that there must be equal opportunities and no restrictions, but the realities of the job may dictate otherwise.
- What are the working conditions?
- What are the approximate starting and potential salaries, including fringe benefits?
- How will the work influence one's personal life in terms of need for travel, overtime, weekend work, or geographical moves?
- Will the work require the compromising of one's ethical principles or religious beliefs?
- What is the potential for the future in terms of available openings, opportunities for advancement, whether the career field will continue to exist, or preparing people for moves to other satisfying work?
- How could this work fit with the Christian's desire to serve Christ and to utilize one's God-given abilities and gifts?

None of this should overlook the fact that God appears to lead some people, but not all, into positions of full-time Christian ministry. It should not be assumed, however, that the committed missionary or pastor is more spiritual or more within God's will than the committed scientist, gardener, or salesperson who also is faithful in following the Holy Spirit's leading.

3. *Guiding Vocational Decisions*. Vocational counselors often are called guidance counselors. This is a good term because their role is to guide counselees as they gather information about themselves and the world of work, then make decisions based on personal reflection and further consultation with friends, family, and others. The counselor's job is not to tell the counselee which specific vocation he or she should enter, and nobody should expect that counseling will reveal the perfect job for each counselee. Instead, counseling will narrow the list of career opportunities down to a few categories of potentially satisfying and realistically feasible kinds of work. The final choice or choices will depend on a number of variables, including the changing world of work, the availability of job positions, the counselee's sense of divine leading, and the counselee's skills, capabilities,

experience, education, strengths, and other influences.

Armed with all of this information and input, how do individuals make vocational decisions? There is no formula, of course, but the best vocational decisions emerge from times of evaluation and reflection. Dreams and visions for the future are not always feasible or attainable, but it can be good for each of us to set aside some time to ponder what we would really like doing vocationally. Many people have no alternative but to take whatever work they can get, but when there are no visions about what might be possible, there can be no vocational direction but only drifting. Counselees should be encouraged to evaluate their abilities and place in life, and ponder what might be possible vocationally. It may help to get a notebook to write down one's interests, strengths, gifts, abilities, areas of experience or expertise, life goals, and vocational objectives. Suggest that counselees take a page to list dreams—things that would be ideal vocationally. This process may take time, and the lists may need to be revised and modified as the self-understanding and reflection process continues. Sometimes, a mate or parent can help with this process, and the exercise can be discussed with the counselor, who may give encouragement but also point out, gently, that some goals probably are not realistic.

Thinking about oneself and one's future can be helpful, but it also is important for counselees to learn how to gather information about potential job or career possibilities. In time, it can be helpful to list possibilities along with the positive and negative aspects of each alternative. Eventually, the counselee should make a decision to pursue at least one alternative. This may be difficult for some counselees because decisions involve commitments and commitments involve the risk of error or failure. It can be helpful to point out that the initial choice is not absolutely final and that slow movement usually is better than no movement. Counselees then can be encouraged to act on the decision by getting more information and training if this is needed or by seeking and trying out a job. Sooner or later, and perhaps periodically, one's vocation will need to be reevaluated and the process may need to be repeated. This is illustrated in Figure 37–1.

For each counselee, vocational guidance is likely to focus on one or more of the following activities.

- Vocational *vision casting*: helping people with the previously described process of anticipating what might be possible vocationally. Even when the dreams are not very feasible, this process can help people think about what alternatives might be possible and worth investigating.
- Vocational *exploration*: evaluating the current job market and helping people find what possibilities currently exist.
- Vocational *selection and placement*: getting information about job possibilities, helping people find positions, and sometimes helping potential employers find employees.
- Vocational *career preparation*: involving evaluation of the positive and negative aspects of an intended job or vocation, and perhaps getting into a training program.
- Vocational *adjustment:* assisting people who have found a desirable career but are having difficulty adjusting. Consider, for example, the missionary who believes he or she is called to the mission field, but has trouble adapting. Sometimes, crisis counseling, helping to resolve interpersonal conflicts,

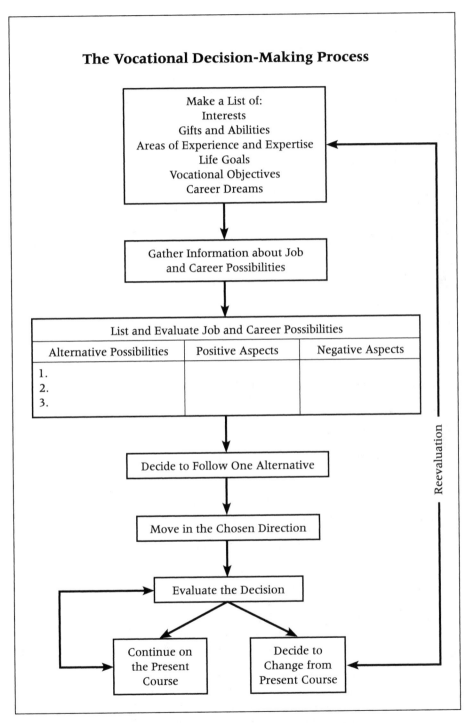

Figure 37–1. The Vocational Decision-Making Process.

or dealing with loneliness or anxiety may be among the ways of assisting these counselees as they adjust to new work situations. Culturally sensitive counselors can be tremendously useful in helping missionaries or other overseas workers make cross-cultural adjustments.[48]

- Vocational or *career change,* including discussion and guidance before, during, and after a forced or voluntary change.

4. *Knowing God's Will.* Thirty years ago a Christian magazine published the story of a man with advanced academic degrees who could not find a suitable job and was employed, instead, as a tool salesman in a neighborhood hardware store. In writing about his disappointments, the man admitted that he had been "holding a grudge against God for withholding . . . the gift of appropriate employment." The writer tried to understand the reasons for his frustrating job situation but concluded that "wish as I might, I was not able to find a portion of Scripture that absolutely guaranteed God would give me employment which allowed the extensive use of my talents."[49]

I don't know where that man is today. Maybe he will read this and write to give me an update. His frustrations sound familiar, however, because I know several people like him. They once dreamed of fulfilling careers, as we suggested earlier. In reality, they have ended up far from the ideal that they imagined when they were younger. How do we counsel people like this? How do we give them vocational guidance? How do we help them determine and accept God's perfect will for their lives?

Perhaps most Christians have their own ideas about how to discern God's will for their lives. Even so, for people who assume that God leads, as I do, there appear to be only a few principles, all of which can be applied to our counselees and to ourselves.

(a) To know God's will we must *want it.* When they say they want God's leading, do counselees *really* want this, or are they seeking, instead, to get a divine rubber stamp of approval for some previously devised plan? Most often, for God to guide, the believer must have a prior willingness to obey. There are exceptions, of course. God led Jonah, even though he had no interest in listening or in following the divine direction. Sometimes, unbelievers were led by God without knowing that he was working in their lives.[50] As a general rule, however, God most often appears to lead people who are willing to be led. When a counselee does not want divine leading, it would be helpful to discuss the reasons for this, to confront the person with his or her reluctance to let God lead, and pray for a change of attitude.

(b) To know God's will we must *expect it.* God has promised to show us his way when we are willing to trust him completely, when we attempt to live holy lives, and when we keep our minds focused on God-pleasing thoughts.[51] He does not play a game of hide and seek, deliberately trying to confuse his followers. He has promised to lead. This must be shared with counselees.

(c) To know God's will we must *seek it.* There are no pat formulas that automatically indicate God's will, and rarely does he lead in dramatic, miraculous ways with voices from heaven, burning bushes, or angelic appearances. Throughout the centuries he has led most often through the Holy Bible and the Holy Spirit.

The Scriptures do not tell us what vocational choice to make or where to go to school for training, but the Bible does give broad guidelines within which choices can be made. The Holy Spirit never leads in ways that are inconsistent with biblical teaching. To know God's will, we need to know the Scriptures and seek to be sensitive to the Holy Spirit's influence and inner leading.

From this it does not follow that counselees should refuse to use their God-given brains. Psychological testing, job analyses, evaluation of the job market and of one's own uniqueness, the completion of application forms, discussions with friends or others who know the job-seeker well, consulting with counselors, and prayers for guidance can all help counselees find God's will as they make career decisions. Trusting that God will lead, they move forward confidently, making the wisest decisions possible in light of the available evidence and opportunities.

(d) To know God's will we must *relax about it*. It is easy for any of us to get flustered or worried. What if the counselee makes a mistake and goes in the wrong career direction? What if he or she cannot find a suitable vocation or job but becomes like that frustrated tool salesman with the graduate degrees? Counselees must be reminded that everyone makes mistakes, but God forgives, restores, and helps us get back on track. Like Jonah who tried to go his own way and Peter who denied Christ, individuals today can know that God restores those who come back to him asking for further guidance. This is true, as well, for people who genuinely want to be led but can't seem to find direction. They are not looking for restoration because they never turned from God in the first place. They may feel frustrated, like Job, but they know that God still leads.

Counselees and their counselors can both profit from the reminder that God, in his wisdom and timing, allows us to be where he wants. He expects us to serve diligently, wherever and whatever the circumstances.[52] When there is anger or anxiety (both of which are common), believers should admit these feelings, perhaps discuss them with a friend or counselor, bring them to God in prayer, and ask that they be removed. In this way counselees can be helped, like Paul, to be content whatever the circumstances.[53]

5. *Vocational Counseling and Special Situations*. How does one do vocational counseling with people who are mentally disabled, psychologically unstable, physically handicapped, terminally ill, minimally educated, lacking in basic social skills, or unable to speak the language of the counselor or of the community where they live? People such as these are rarely mentioned in vocational counseling literature, but all could benefit from meaningful, satisfying work that is within their capabilities. If the Christian counselor is unable to give the needed help, the best help may be to make a referral to a government agency or private counseling facility where there are specially trained vocational counselors who can give the needed guidance.

There are other situations, however, that might involve special circumstances where nonspecialists can give effective vocational guidance. The following are examples.

(a) Vocational Guidance When a Workplace Shuts Down. Twelve thousand employees got the news together: their company would be closing its local facility, and all the workers would lose their jobs within a few months of the announcement. This is a real situation, but it was more than a vocational counseling issue.[54] All those employees were faced with the need to find new jobs in a community where the economy would be deeply impacted and most people would be looking for work. Outside consultants predicted (accurately it turned out) that probably 97 percent of the employees eventually would readjust, but a small percentage would collapse under the intense stress if they were not helped. Since this was a community problem, it needed community solutions. The company that was closing and the community began working together. Local politicians became active in attracting new businesses to the area. Churches and community agencies worked together to help people deal with the stress. Social workers and other counselors trained lay care-givers as Transition Life Advisors (TLAs), and a community spirit arose with the attitude that "we are in this together and we will get through this together." In situations like this, vocational counselors may need to get out of their offices, connect with other care-givers, and use their skills to help meet community crises.

(b) Vocational Guidance When Individuals Are Laid Off. When individuals lose their work or are dismissed from a job, the stress can be intense, especially if the counselee has held the job for a number of years. Often there is grieving, anger, lessened self-esteem, feelings of failure and despair, and frantic searches for work. There can be tensions in the family, including pressures on children who sometimes feel powerless and maybe even feel responsible for the job loss.[55] Stresses like these are not limited to people who are laid off or fired from work. When a company moves to a different location and invites the employees to move, when the employee gets a promotion and moves to a different department in the company away from his or her friends, or when a new opportunity arises, there can be joy mixed with sadness, enthusiasm about the future mingled with reluctance to leave what is secure. In situations such as these, people often need support, encouragement, and guidance in addition to more traditional vocational counseling.

(c) Vocational Guidance When People Get Old. Many people reach retirement age and leave the workforce only to discover that they want to return to work. In addition to its many benefits, retirement can bring boredom, a loss of life purpose, unanticipated financial restrictions, the loss of a meaningful social network, and self-concept problems for people who feel useless when they are not working. Most of the principles outlined in this chapter can apply to this special (and growing) group of people, but many find decreases both in their energy and in the availability of meaningful jobs for older workers. Counselors, however, often find great fulfillment in helping older workers find vocational direction or career opportunities that may be especially enjoyable after years spent in boring or undesirable work.[56]

(d) Vocational Guidance When Counselees Are in Minority Groups. Obed is a Muslim. His family is from the Middle East, but for many years they have lived peacefully and alongside their neighbors in their mostly white, suburban community in North America. They pay their taxes and pay their bills. Like their neighbors, they abhor the terrorist activities of some extremists, and so does everybody else who worships in the mosque where they attend. Obed has a college degree, but he can't find a good vocational direction because of prejudice and fear of terrorists in his community.

Obed is not alone. There are thousands of others, maybe hundreds of thousands of minority workers who cannot build fulfilling and maximally useful careers but must go through life underemployed because of prejudice. In addition to the principles outlined in the preceding pages, these people often need special support, information about vocational opportunities that do exist, hope in the midst of discouragement, and sometimes help in handling stress, including the suspicion, rejection, and criticism that come from people in the community.

(e) Vocational Guidance When Workers Are Highly Stressed. An earlier chapter discussed road rage—the behavior of drivers who express anger at other drivers—often as an irrational expression of stress. Desk rage is a newer concept that describes stress and stress reactions in the workplace.[57] The causes are varied and include boredom in the workplace, anxiety, lack of control over working conditions or work projects, overcrowded conditions, excessive noise, the pressures that lead to burnout, unreasonable deadlines, and the criticisms, disrespect, or irrational demands that come from co-workers or employers. According to one report, 65 percent of American workers report stress in their workplaces at least periodically. The numbers may be different in other countries. One in five workers has quit a job because of stress at work.[58] Among the people who stay, stress at work can lead to anger outbursts, verbal and sometimes physical abuse (including a surprisingly large number of assaults and murders), high rates of absenteeism, and a variety of physical illnesses, such as back pain or intense headaches.[59] All of this involves counselors doing more than vocational guidance. Counselors help people deal with stress or interpersonal conflicts at work because this can have an large effect on work satisfaction and productivity.

(f) Other Crises. The list of unique work-related problems could go on. Some people experience career crashes, in which their businesses go bankrupt, they are overwhelmed by the stress and abruptly move to something simpler, a competitor forces them to shut down, or they are involved in a field that suddenly ceases to function—like the thriving dot-com companies that were so prominent in the 1990s.[60] Others face a crisis when they are passed over for a promotion, burn out on a job, are transferred to a foreign country (when they would prefer to stay home), or are squeezed out of a partnership. These experiences may be traumatic, but often they can be opportunities for people to reevaluate their lives and careers and find new vocational opportunities that are better than what they lost. Even as I was writing this chapter, a friend impulsively quit his frustrating job and now is unemployed. When we met for coffee, we talked about the ways in which this could be an opportunity for him to find something that is better than the frustrating job he left.

All of this points to one clear conclusion. Vocational counseling is a diverse field. It has plenty of opportunities and challenges for Christian counselors who want to make an impact.

Prevention and Vocational Counseling

In many ways, all of vocational counseling is about prevention. When people are helped to find the right vocational fit, counselors are helping to prevent the problems that can arise when there are bad vocational choices. When they find what is good, people prevent themselves from having to face what is not good.

Almost always, prevention is a specialized form of education. In classrooms, counselors' offices, small groups, weekend retreats, church gatherings, community seminars, and sermons, people can be taught and encouraged to apply some of the material presented in this chapter. This career education should be directed to people of all ages and could include consideration of:

- Biblical teachings about work.
- The causes of good and poor vocational choices.
- How to find God's guidance.
- How to get information about vocations and the world of work.
- How to know oneself better, including a knowledge of where to take psychological tests or spiritual gift inventories.
- Service opportunities in various areas of ministry. This kind of information giving is done frequently in missionary conferences, where the needs are presented and people are recruited to consider missionary service.

This educational process can emphasize that vocational choice is not a once-in-a-lifetime decision, at least in the modern world. Most adults (including home-makers and others who are not included in the more traditional definition of the workforce) struggle at times with career dissatisfaction, and this should be acknowledged. Encourage people to be open to further training and to evaluating their priorities, life goals, and job satisfactions periodically, perhaps guided by Figure 37–1. Point out that as one gets older, it becomes increasingly more difficult and risky to change vocations. Nevertheless, when people want change there are things that can be done. These include changing employers or careers (the most risky alternative), changing jobs within the same company or vocational area, learning how to more effectively handle or control work stress, and/or changing one's attitude toward work. Even if little can be done to change the job situation, it is possible to stay with the present job (trusting that God either wants this and/or will bring a change in time), to do one's best for the Lord,[61] and to look for greater satisfaction and service opportunities in avocational, leisure activities, including meaningful church or community service.

In all of this, remember that helping others can occur in various forms, including what leaders and counselors model in their own lives. When a church helps people discover their strengths and spiritual gifts and enables them to serve in places where these gifts are utilized, the church members show greater involvement and engagement in their Christian service. When a company president, pastor, counselor, or other leader focuses on his or her strengths or makes periodic career evaluations, this is a model for others to do the same. Sometimes, the best models make the best teachers.

Conclusions About Vocational Counseling

For most of recorded history, it appears that people chose a career and stayed with it all of their lives. Sometimes, the choice was forced upon them, and the work involved survival with nobody thinking about job fulfillment. It is different in most places today, where there are many vocational opportunities and frequent job changes, beginning with the often unrealistic and glamorous choices of children and ending with new opportunities in the retirement years. All the way through this process, vocational counselors can be helpful.

Regardless of how often they are made, vocational choices are among the most crucial decisions in life. To help people make these decisions wisely can be among the most rewarding parts of the Christian counselor's own work.

KEY POINTS FOR BUSY COUNSELORS

➤ Today, counselors often are involved in helping people make vocational choices. These decisions are crucially important, frequently difficult, and rarely once-in-a-lifetime events.

➤ The Bible does not talk about vocational counseling, but it does say a lot about work. There are several clear biblical conclusions about work and vocational choice.
  ■ Work is honorable; laziness is condemned.
  ■ Work is to be interspersed with rest.
  ■ Work is to be of high quality.
  ■ Work is unique and for the common good.
  ■ Work and vocational choice are guided by God.

➤ The world of work is changing, and this has a significant impact on how counselors help people vocationally.

➤ People make vocational decisions based on a number of influences that include:
  ■ Family and social influences.
  ■ Personality influences.
  ■ Strengths.
  ■ Interests.
  ■ Aptitudes and abilities.
  ■ Values.
  ■ Roadblocks that prevent movement forward.
  ■ Divine leading.

➤ When we are committed to serving Christ in our vocations, our work becomes an opportunity for pleasing God, building relationships, and reaching out to touch the lives of others.

➤ In most cases, the vocational counselor teaches people to make ongoing evaluations of themselves and their work, exposes people to information about careers (including the need and availability of training), and provides special support and guidance when job choices or changes are being made.

➤ For each counselee, vocational guidance is likely to focus on one or more of the following activities (not all with the same person):
  ■ Vision casting, helping people think what might be possible.
  ■ Vocation exploration, evaluating the current job market.
  ■ Selection of a vocation and moving into it.
  ■ Career preparation, which involves evaluation a vocation and perhaps getting the needed training.

- Vocational adjustment for people who have found a vocation but are having trouble fitting in and doing it well.
- Vocational change that involves helping people find something new.

➤ To find God's will for their lives and vocations, people must want it, expect it, seek it, and relax in the belief that God will lead, even though we may not like the ultimate goal.

➤ The vocational counselor must be alert to special counseling situations, including the counseling needs of people whose jobs have terminated, members of minority groups, the elderly, people who work in stressful jobs, and others who are looking for vocational guidance.

➤ Depending on where one lives, young people who are entering the workforce can be expected to change jobs and careers during their working lives. Clearly, vocational guidance must be an ongoing process that involves everyone—not just professional counselors.

➤ Vocational counseling is a diverse field. It has plenty of opportunities and challenges for Christian counselors to want to make an impact.

PART EIGHT

Concluding Issues

38

Crises

Marissa hardly noticed as the fire trucks rushed past the supermarket parking lot where she was loading groceries into her car. She was thinking about other things as she drove home, but everything changed when she saw that the fire trucks were on her street and smoke was pouring from the upper windows of her home. Marissa pulled over, jumped out of the car, and ran to the scene. Her two teenagers were watching as they stood in the cold, their shoulders draped with blankets from the neighbors. Marissa's son had first discovered the fire, rushed his sister out of the house, and had the presence of mind to grab a cell phone and dial 911 to call the fire department.

Today, the family is resettled in their refurbished house, but the fire disrupted their lives for months. Most of their possessions were lost. The drapes, wallboard, carpet, furniture, and all of their clothes had to be replaced. While the insurance adjusters did their work and the house was being repaired, Marissa's family lived in a hotel, learning to adjust to cramped quarters and disrupted lifestyles.

Leonard's crisis was different. Driving home from a church meeting, he was hit by a driver who lost control and veered into the passenger side of Leonard's van. His injuries were minor, but his wife was in critical condition when the paramedics lifted her into the ambulance. For days she lay in the hospital, immobilized by injuries that had broken numerous bones in her body, injured some of her internal organs, and left her with agonizing pain. While Leonard watched, engulfed in guilt and turmoil, his wife pleaded to be taken off life-support machines so she could die in peace and be free of the discomfort. Months after she died, Leonard still carries the guilt along with his grief. He had been driving the car. He felt responsible for his wife's death. He still carries the burden of blame that even he knows is irrational.

Marissa and Leonard are real people who are alive today. They represent the millions of people in the world today who struggle with crises or the aftermath of crisis events in their lives. Some of these are likely to seek counseling. Perhaps they will come to you.

The world changed while this book was being written. Probably it will change more before you read these words, and in all likelihood it will be changing even as you read. During the months that I was working on the preceding chapters, little kids died of hunger in Africa, people were slaughtered by mercenaries in remote parts of Asia and Latin America, soldiers and civilians were blown up or maimed as the result of terrorist attacks in the Middle East, huge walls of water and other rampages of nature surged from the oceans and swept entire communities out to sea, and innocent young girls and boys were sold into prostitution to satisfy the lusts of self-indulgent tourists. Newspapers rarely mention most of the people who suffer through experiences like these, but for each person involved, those events are personal crises. So, too, are the accidents, heart attacks, unexpected surgeries, disappointments, and losses that people face every day, often with no prior preparation and sometimes without much sympathy or help from others.

Briefly defined, a crisis is a turning point that usually cannot be avoided. Crises may be expected or unexpected, real or imagined, actual (like the death of a loved one) or potential (like the prospect that a loved one will die soon). Most often they arrive quickly, and then they're gone, leaving their devastation behind. Sometimes, they crash into our lives like giant breakers smashing against the rocks—again and again, slowly wearing us down.

It often has been stated that the Chinese word for *crisis* involves two characters. One means danger; the other means opportunity. Crises are filled with *danger* because they disrupt life and threaten to overwhelm the people who are affected. As we grow toward adulthood, each of us develops a repertoire of problem-solving techniques that enable us to deal with life's ups and downs. When emergencies or unexpected problems appear, we exert extra effort to cope. As a result, most people meet the insecurities and challenges of life successfully.

There are times, however, when unusually severe or demanding situations arise. There might be a loss of someone or something significant, a sudden need to take over new responsibilities, or the appearance of threatening people or events. Because the new situation is so unique and intense, one's customary ways of handling stress and solving problems no longer are effective. This can lead to confusion and bewilderment, feelings of helplessness, and often increased anxiety, anger, discouragement, sorrow, or guilt. This turmoil may be temporary, but sometimes it persists for several weeks or even years.

Along with the dangers, however, crises also present people with the *opportunity* to change, grow, and develop better ways of coping. Since people in crisis often feel confused and helpless, they tend to be more open to receiving outside help, including the help that comes from rescue workers, from counselors, and from God. Others try to ignore and evade the crisis, even when help is available. These people go about their daily activities in a state of denial, withdraw into irrational fantasies, give up in despair, or respond in socially unacceptable ways that might include violence. Then there are those who react in healthier ways. They evaluate the situation to see if there can be creative, socially acceptable, reality-based problem-solving techniques that can help in the present crisis and add to the person's capacity to deal effectively with difficulties that might come in the future.

When doctors talk of a medical crisis, they refer to a crucial time when there is a change, either toward improvement and recovery or toward decline and death. To experience any kind of crisis is to face a turning point that brings either growth and maturation or deterioration and continuing immaturity. The Christian counselor is in a vital position to influence which direction the crisis resolution will take. Most often this counseling puts the counselor into contact with one or a few people who are dealing with an issue that is of greatest significance to the counselees but of little concern to anyone else.

In contrast, some crises impact whole communities, entire countries, and sometimes the entire world. On December 8, 1941, President Franklin Roosevelt addressed the United States Congress in what has become known as his "Day of Infamy" speech. The European and British Commonwealth nations had been at war for more than a year, but then Pearl Harbor was attacked on what Roosevelt called "a date that will live in infamy." At that point the United States entered the

Second World War, and millions of Americans felt the angst and crisis that had been rocking the stability of Great Britain and so many other nations, especially in Europe. Sixty years later, on September 11, 2001, there was another day of infamy. For decades people around the world had been experiencing terrorist attacks, but nothing grabbed world attention like the events in New York and elsewhere on that sunny September morning. Another U.S. President declared war, this time a war on terror, and as in 1941, millions more people came face to face with fear, anxiety, and uncertainty that they had not faced on the day before.

No discussion of crises is complete without a consideration of broader issues such as trauma, the impact of natural disasters, the fear of terrorism, the pervasive influence of violence, and the stress of national and political crises on children, relief workers, refugees, the military, and missionaries. We cannot talk about psychological counseling or pastoral care without acknowledging the incredibly powerful discoveries of neurobiologists and the increasingly apparent role of the brain's complex functioning. In considering crises, we must look at post-traumatic stress disorder and the neurophysiology that most of this book has ignored. All of this opens our thinking to whole new ways of helping people and to revolutionary ways of crisis management.

Most of the present chapter will keep the focus on individual crisis management, the kind of work we often do with one or two people or with a family. We will keep the emphasis on the psychological and the spiritual. Then in chapter 39 we will broaden our discussion to look at the physiology as well as the psychology of terrorism, trauma, violence, and national disasters that now turn so many of our days into days of infamy.

The Bible and Crisis Types

Much of the Bible deals with crises. Adam, Eve, Cain, Noah, Abraham, Isaac, Joseph, Moses, Samson, Jepthah, Saul, David, Elijah, Daniel, and numerous other people faced crises that the Old Testament describes in detail. Jesus faced crises (especially at the time of the crucifixion), and so did the disciples, Paul, and many early believers. Several of the Epistles were written to help individuals or churches meet crises, and Hebrews 11 summarizes both crises that had happy endings and those that resulted in torture, suffering, and death.

Contemporary writers have identified three types of crisis, each of which has both modern and biblical examples. We will add a fourth.

1. *Accidental or situational crises* occur when there is a sudden threat, disruptive event, or unexpected loss. Examples include the death of a loved one, the discovery of a serious illness, the experience of rape or other violence, social disturbances such as war or economic depression, the loss of one's job or savings, pregnancy apart from marriage, or a sudden loss of respect and status. All are situational stresses that can affect both individuals and their families.

Some of these crises solidify a family, and the relatives pull together to overcome the obstacles and make things better. Often, these crises originate outside the family and involve events such as a natural disaster, a serious house fire, or racial prejudice. When stress is internal—such as a suicide attempt, infidelity, child abuse, or alcoholism—the crisis is more disruptive and inclined to tear the family apart. Even more disruptive are the crises that come in sequence, one following quickly on the heels of another. For some people, the crisis that brings them to counseling is the one that comes as the most recent in a series of stressful changes and losses.

This was Job's experience. Within a short period of time, this religious man lost his family, wealth, health, and status. His marriage appears to have been strained, and his critics soon learned about Job's anger and inner turmoil. He was confused about why a caring God would let so many bad things happen to a good person. Asaph, the writer of Psalm 73, had some of the same struggles.

2. *Developmental crises* happen in the course of normal human development. Leaving home and going away to college, adjusting to marriage and then to parenthood, handling criticism, facing retirement, adjusting to declining health, or adapting to the deaths of one's friends can all be crises that demand new approaches to coping and problem solving despite the fact that most can be anticipated. Abraham and Sarah, for example, coped with moving when their destination was unknown. They faced criticism, many years of childlessness, family stress, and the command of God that young Isaac should be sacrificed. We might wonder how an elderly couple like Zacharias and Elizabeth handled a son as unique as John the Baptist, or how Mary and Joseph were able to raise their unusual and brilliant son Jesus. It seems likely that these were developmental crises—turning points that demanded adjustment and prolonged periods of wise decision making that also led to increased growth.

3. *Existential crises* overlap with the other two. These are situations that all of us face when we encounter disturbing truths, often about ourselves:

> My life has no direction.
> I didn't get the long-anticipated promotion.
> I'm now a widow—single again.
> My marriage has ended in divorce.
> My illness is incurable.
> I have nothing to believe in.
> I have been rejected by my own son.
> My house and possessions are all gone in the fire.
> I've been rejected because of my skin color.
> I'm too old to reach my life goals.

Realizations like these take time and effort to assimilate. They are changes in self-perception that can be denied temporarily, but in time they must be faced realistically if life is to go on and be fulfilling.

After a great spiritual victory, Elijah was chased by Jezebel and ran to the wilderness, where he concluded that his life was a failure. Jonah had similar thoughts as he debated with God. In the midst of his struggles, Job must have wondered what would happen to him now that he had lost everything, including support from people who might have been his friends. Did the disciples also wonder about their uncertain future in the hours following the crucifixion? David created his own crisis when he got Bathsheba pregnant and then tried to cover this up by arranging for the death of Bathsheba's husband, Uriah.

4. *National or community crises* extend beyond individuals to involve large groups of people. When a tornado or earthquake destroys much of a community, an office building is destroyed by a terrorist, or a country is attacked by an outside force, the crisis impacts large numbers of people. Perhaps there is some comfort in

the knowledge that everybody is impacted by the crisis. On the other hand, the pervasive nature of the crisis makes it more difficult because even counselors face the same insecurities and concerns as their counselees.

There are many biblical examples of this kind of crisis, especially represented by the repeated attacks on God's people by foreign armies. Most familiar, perhaps, is the attack on Jerusalem from the armies of Babylon that destroyed the city and took almost everybody captive. Psalm 137 is a song of lament that describes the distress of the whole nation.

> Beside the rivers of Babylon, we sat and wept as we thought of Jerusalem....
> How can we sing the songs of the Lord while in a foreign land?[1]

When people ask about the reasons for their crises, it can be difficult and often impossible for counselors to give definitive answers. Even though the Bible speaks about all types of crises, it does not give clear and complete reasons to explain why crises occur. We know that disobedience led to many of the attacks on Israel,[2] and foolish decisions led to crises in the lives of people like David. But Job never did learn about the debate between God and Satan that led to his crises, and there are some crises, like the death of a young person, that we cannot comprehend or explain. We may agree that every event has a divine purpose and ultimately is under God's control. We know that crises can be learning experiences that mold character, teach us about God and his resources, and stimulate growth. But the ultimate reasons for specific life crises may never be known, at least while we live on this earth. In the meantime, we can help counselees cope and grow through their crises using counseling methods that can apply to them all.

The Effects of Crises

Like all stressful events, crises bring immediate physiological reactions, including the well-known symptoms of rapid breathing, faster heartbeats, higher vigilance, and the increased adrenaline output that makes fighting or fleeing easier. This increased state of arousal can last for days or even weeks. If it persists, eventually it wears down the body and can bring more serious physical and emotional symptoms. This presents relief workers with special challenges as they work long hours with little sleep, sometimes feverishly helping others until they collapse themselves.[3]

In addition to the physical symptoms, people in crises almost always feel a sense of loss and lack of control. The loss of a loved one or of one's home or possessions can be devastating, but also difficult can be the loss of a job, self-esteem, confidence, security, or familiar circumstances that may have changed forever. Trauma researcher Bessel van der Kolk has described how the sense of powerlessness following a crisis also can make the crisis worse. After a major hurricane had ravaged Puerto Rico, van der Kolk traveled to the area. "I arrived in the middle of this devastation, and what I saw were lots and lots of people working with each other, actively putting their lives back together—carrying lumber, rebuilding houses and shops, cleaning up, repairing things."

When government officials arrived on the scene, the people were told to stop their activity until "assorted bureaucracies" could assess the damage, organize financial aid, and find ways to give people loans. Everything came to a halt, van der Kolk wrote later.

People were suddenly forced to sit still in the middle of their disaster and do nothing. Very quickly, an enormous amount of violence broke out—rioting, looting, assault. All this energy mobilized by the disaster, which had gone into a flurry of rebuilding and recovery, now was turned on to everybody else. I saw very vividly how important it is for people to overcome their sense of helplessness after a trauma by actively doing something. Preventing people from moving when something terrible happens, that's one of the things that makes a trauma a trauma.[4]

Feeling a lack of power and control makes a crisis worse, especially if there is no way to escape, fight, or have some kind of impact on making things better. At some time during or after the crisis, there also is likely to be fear, including fear of the unknown, fear of death or abandonment, worry about finances, or fear that one might not be able to recover. Sometimes, people are afraid of what might happen next, or they fear that another crisis is on the way. Following the terrorist attacks in New York, one counselor wrote about how he developed the habit of waking up every morning, and before doing anything else, he would turn on the television news to find out if "the world is still there," if the new day would begin as normal or be another day of national crisis.[5]

It is well known that people also respond to crises by seeking answers, especially in their religious beliefs. When a huge tsunami swept ashore in several countries of Asia on the day after Christmas in 2004, some local psychologists asked that the Western mental-health professionals not come rushing in to help. Apparently, the people were finding hope in their various religions, caring for children that had been separated from parents, and working together as best they could. They needed food, water, and supplies more than they needed secular counseling from well-meaning foreigners who did not understand the ways in which the people interpreted their circumstances according to their culture and their views about God.

Crisis Intervention

Crisis intervention is a way of providing immediate, temporary, emotional first aid to victims of psychological and physical trauma. The intervener must react skillfully and quickly to deal with behavior that is often disorganized, confused, and potentially harmful. Since they frequently appear suddenly and are of limited duration, crises are best treated as soon as possible after they occur. There are several counseling goals:

- To help the person cope effectively with the immediate crisis situation and return to his or her pre-crisis level of functioning, whether or not that level was ideal.[6]
- To decrease the anxiety, apprehension, and other insecurities that may persist during the crisis and after it passes.
- To teach crisis-management techniques so the person is better prepared to anticipate and deal with future crises.
- To consider biblical teachings about crises so the person learns from the crisis and grows as a result.

Crisis counselors should not expect to treat every person (or group of people, including families) in the same way. Scan the research on crisis intervention, and you will discover that the nature of the crisis in some ways determines your approach. The crises of losing one's home in a tornado, losing a teenage daughter through suicide, or facing the results of a severe automobile accident are likely to be different.[7] In addition, there are individual differences in flexibility, customary ways of coping, ability to learn new adjustment techniques, physical and psychological strengths, or levels of emotional and spiritual maturity. Some people tend to be optimistic and able to see humor even in the midst of crises; others are pessimistic and easily overwhelmed. Some are excessively dependent, while others take pride in their independence. Some counselees are able to discuss the crisis and understand its implications. Others are too distraught to think clearly or make rational decisions.

Even with these differences, the counselor can intervene in several ways during times of crisis. Think of the following as a checklist for giving psychological first aid in times of mental-health emergencies.

1. *Make Contact*. People in crises don't always come to a counselor for help. Probably it is more common for counselors and other care-givers to go to others and show our warmth, understanding, and genuine interest.[8] Listen carefully so you can understand the counselee's concerns and point of view before making suggestions for action. Often, the presence of another human being who listens and understands is what a person in crisis needs most. If he or she slips into daydreaming, fantasy, withdrawal, or deep thought, try to bring the discussion back to reality.

Eye contact can reassure the counselee and so can touching. Even when there are no words, touching and other forms of physical contact can communicate care, reassurance, hope, and comfort. Remember, however, that some cultures and subcultures have strong taboos against direct eye contact and against touch. Hugging is a normal form of greeting in many cultures, but in others even a handshake is limited to members of the same sex. Until recently, physical contact was discouraged in counseling, lest counselees misinterpret its meaning and view touch as having sexual overtones that the counselor never intended. Even so, perhaps most of us would agree with the counselor who suggested that "to refrain from any touch whatsoever because of risks of patient arousal or misinterpretation may be an unnecessary overreaction."[9]

Depending, then, on the culture, for most people touch can be comforting, therapeutic, and encouraging. As a counselor, you should realize the value and risks of physical contact, then decide whether your touch could be misinterpreted and whether it might help the counselee. As we have suggested earlier, it also is helpful to ask yourself about your reasons for touching or hugging. Is this more likely to meet your affiliation and sexual needs rather than the needs of the counselee? Even though touching can be an excellent way to make contact and give support, for any individual (including you), it should be guided by this general rule: if in doubt—don't!

2. *Reduce Anxiety*. The counselor's calm, relaxed manner can help reduce anxiety in the counselee, especially when this calmness is accompanied by reassurance. Listen patiently and attentively as the counselee describes the situation. Encourage talk about the insecurities and other feelings that always accompany a

crisis. Try to provide reassuring facts ("There *are* ways to deal with this problem"), state your approval when something is done well ("I think that was a good decision—it shows you are on the right track"), gently suggest other interpretations if the counselee's point of view appears to be overly pessimistic or distorted ("Maybe I could suggest another way of looking at this situation"), and, when possible, offer a prediction about what will happen ("I know it's tough, but I think you can handle this"). Try to answer questions honestly, but without raising the counselee's anxiety level unnecessarily. If a person is seriously injured, for example, you could say, "I don't know the extent of your injuries yet, but you are in the care of good medical people. They are checking out everything, and you can be sure they will do whatever is needed to help you." This is an honest, reassuring statement that doesn't increase anxiety or raise false hopes.

Often, there is value in removing the counselee from a stressful situation, at least temporarily. It may help, for example, to take an anxious relative away from the hustle of emergency room activities and into a quiet side room or down the hall for a cup of coffee. (Be sure to let the emergency room receptionist know where you have gone in case you are needed.) Sometimes, you may want to encourage counselees to take deep breaths, to go for brief walks, or to consciously tighten and then relax muscles. The calming effect of Bible verses such as 1 Corinthians 10:13 can also be helpful. Each of these anxiety-reduction methods can be overused, causing the counselee to feel trapped or smothered, but each can reduce the effects of stress and make it easier to deal constructively with the crisis issues.

3. *Focus on Issues.* In times of crisis, it is easy to be overwhelmed by what appears to be a mass of confusing facts, potential problems, and decisions that need to be made. As a somewhat objective outsider, you are in a good position to help the counselee decide what specific issues must be faced first and what immediate problems need to be solved. Try to focus on the present situation rather than discussing the past or pondering what might happen in the future.

At times, especially near the beginning, you may have to make decisions for the counselee. "Let's go and see another doctor," or "You need to get on a plane and go there tomorrow morning" are directive remarks that counselees sometimes need. Often, this lets the crisis victim feel that something definite is being done to help. Be very careful not to be manipulative, however. Always listen to the counselee's observations, and try to avoid taking actions that the counselee is capable of taking or that you could regret later.

4. *Evaluate Resources.* The counselor's willingness to help is one important resource for the counselee in crisis, but there are others. Some counselees feel security in having one counselor walk alongside them, but there also can be value in finding other people and resources that together can make the crisis care-giving process more effective.[10]

(a) Spiritual Resources. The Christian counselor must never lose sight of the indwelling presence and guidance of the Holy Spirit, along with the comforting words and promises of Scripture. These can be sources of great strength and direction during crises. Some counselors use Scripture as a hammer to push or manipulate counselees into doing what the counselor thinks should be done. This is neither helpful nor ethical. Instead, words from the Bible should be presented as truth, along with the expectation that the Holy Spirit will use them as he desires in the life of the counselee.

(b) Personal Resources. Counselees sometimes become overly dependent during times of crisis. For a while this reliance on others may be necessary and a stabilizing force, but it is good to emphasize the counselee's inner strengths early in the counseling process. Most people have intellectual abilities, skills, past experiences, helpful attitudes, or motives that can help them grow through the crisis. Ask the counselee to list these resources and get input from others who know the counselee well. Point out some of these yourself, making sure that you are being realistic. Remember that a simple listing of the counselee's strengths and reminders of past success in coping can be both reassuring and helpful.

(c) Interpersonal Resources. Often the person in crisis already has a network that may need to be activated, although frequently the network activates itself spontaneously. Family members, friends, business associates, fellow church members, and people in the community often help eagerly when they are made aware of the need. People can be asked to pray, give money, or provide other practical assistance during the time of crisis. If you don't know all the significant others in the counselee's life, ask who should be contacted.

Sometimes, counselees won't want to contact anyone. It can be difficult for some people to accept help even when they know that social support has great therapeutic value. If the counselee doesn't want to bother others, try to point out the importance of mutual dependency and the satisfaction that comes to friends when they are able to help. Be sensitive to the fact that some people are embarrassed about the attention that comes with their crisis. They feel threatened by the implication that they could use assistance, and sometimes even angered by the counselor's attempt to involve others who can help. It is important to discuss all of this with the counselee, who, whenever possible, should be encouraged to seek help from others without the counselor's assistance. If a support network does not exist, try to guide the counselee in developing one. In crisis management, few influences can match the benefit that come from other people who care, are concerned, and want to help.

Despite its great value, sometimes outside support will be less helpful than you might expect. When there is too much dependency on others, counselees may develop a "do nothing" attitude that keeps them from growing. This is most likely when family members become overly involved in their attempts to be helpful. Try to encourage care-givers to be supportive but not stifling.[11]

(d) Pastoral Resources. This overlaps with all of the above, but it is worth noting that the unique contribution of pastors is noted often, even in secular discussions of crisis intervention.[12] Pastoral crisis intervention is more than crisis intervention services performed by people with spiritual or religious training. The pastor brings his or her counseling expertise, integrated with pastoral care, spiritual interventions, a belief system that can bring meaning in the midst of chaos, and the supportive resources of communities of believers. Too often, the pastoral community is ignored by mental-health professionals and other crisis counselors, even though pastors are an invaluable resource that can bring reduction in human distress, "whether or not the distress concerns a significant loss, a crisis of meaning, a crisis of faith, or a more concrete and objective infringement" on the person's normal functioning.[13]

(e) Additional Resources. Every community has legal, medical, psychological, financial, educational, and other sources of help that are available in times of crisis. Sometimes. the counselee needs money, a place to live temporarily, somebody who can watch young children, precooked meals, or other tangible sources of help. The counselor can help counselees find these resources. Local churches often rise to the occasion in crisis situations, and sometimes resources can be found within the body of believers.

5. *Plan Intervention.* After evaluating the problem and considering available resources, decide on a course of action that moves beyond the crisis. Together the counselor and counselee can look at the available facts and list alternative courses of action. How realistic is each one of these? Which should be done first, second, and subsequently?

Some counselees will have difficulty making these decisions. The counselor's goal is not to put more pressure on people who already are under pressure. The purpose is not to force people to make decisions that are too difficult for them to make, but neither should counselees be encouraged to be dependent while they let somebody else solve their problems. Gently, but firmly, the counselor can help the counselee make plans and, if necessary, think of better alternatives when an early plan is unsuccessful.

6. *Encourage Action.* It is possible for people to decide on some course of action but then be uncertain how to get started or afraid to move ahead with the plan. Taking action always involves risk. There is the possibility of failure and later regret, especially if the action involves major life changes, such as moving or changing jobs. The counselor may need to encourage counselees in their actions. Help them evaluate progress and, if necessary, modify plans for taking further action.

It may be helpful to keep the following checklist in mind:

- Listen and learn about the problem.
- List alternatives for action—preferably on paper.
- Decide with the counselee on a course of action.
- Discuss the practical details of how this action can be taken.
- Encourage the counselee and hold him or her accountable as action is taken.
- Evaluate the results of the action.
- Based on the evaluation, continue on the chosen course or repeat the above steps.[14]

In some situations, the crisis never will be resolved completely, even by taking action. When someone loses a loved one in death, discovers the existence of an incurable disease, or fails to attain an important promotion, then the crisis may bring permanent change. In crises like these, the counselee must be helped to face the situation honestly, acknowledge and express feelings, readjust his or her lifestyle, realistically plan for the future (perhaps using the checklist listed above), and rest in the knowledge that God, in his sovereignty, knows and cares about our pain. In all crises, but especially in times of permanent change, it helps if people are surrounded by sincere, concerned, supportive, praying friends who are available to assist whenever and however they are needed.

7. *Instill Hope.* In all counseling, improvement is more likely if counselees can be given a sense of realistic hope about the future. Hope brings relief from suffer-

ing because it is based on a belief that things will get better. Hope helps us avoid despair and releases energy to meet the crisis situation.

The Christian counselor can instill hope by using one or more of the following. First, we can share scriptural truths that give reassurance that is based on the unchanging nature and Word of God. This is an approach that instills hope by stimulating faith in God. It is an approach that helps most when the counselor is familiar with Scripture and growing in his or her own relationship with God. Second, counselees can be helped to examine their self-defeating logic and self-talk. Ideas like "I'll never get better" or "Nothing can be worse than this" may enter the counselee's thinking in times of crisis and block progress. Ideas like these should be challenged gently. Ask where is the evidence for the conclusion that the person will never get better? What could be evidence for a more hopeful outcome? Third, counselors can get the counselee moving and taking some action. Even minimal activity gives the feeling that something is being done and that the counselee is not helpless—like those victims of Hurricane Hugo who were forced to sit and do nothing. Taking action can arouse hope, especially if the activity accomplishes something that clearly is worthwhile.

8. *Follow-up*. Crisis counseling usually is brief. Depending on the severity of the crisis, after one or a few sessions the counselee may return to the routines of life and may not come for counseling again. The counselor may wonder if anything was learned. Will the next crisis be handled more effectively? Is the person able to get along satisfactorily now that that the major crisis has passed? These issues should concern the counselor, who can follow up with a phone call or visit. Often, it is helpful to make contact on anniversaries. Sometimes, people experience a flood of old feelings and insecurities on the birthday of a loved one who has died, on the one-month or one-year anniversary of the start of the crisis, or when a divorced person is alone on a public holiday when families often get together. Even when counseling is no longer needed, follow-up interest like this can be encouraging and reminds the counselee that somebody still cares and has not forgotten.

9. *Referral*. In crisis counseling there will be times when the intervention procedures fail to work effectively, despite the best efforts of the counselor. It is then that referral may be the best option for helping. This has been discussed at different times in earlier chapters, so here I will only restate the truth that no counselor, however competent, is able to help everybody. At times, referral may be the best way to get the most competent help for a counselee in crisis, especially if the person needs the special guidance and expertise that another helper is better able to provide.

Most of the discussion in this chapter has assumed that the counselor is helping one person or a group of several people, such as a family, deal with a crisis. Many of the principles apply equally well when some crisis affects a larger group. If an earthquake shakes an entire region or a rampaging river overflows and fills streets and homes with water, the crisis could impact thousands of people, including counselors. Initially, the victims scramble to help one another, sometimes with acts of bravery and compassion, but the impact is especially powerful because, at least at the beginning, there are no outside resources or people to give help. When electricity fails, phones stop working, communication is disrupted, water stops flowing through the taps, and family members are cut off from each other, the crisis is more intense and disruptive, especially if people are wounded and unable to get medical help. These crises normally are called disasters. Like individual crises, disasters tend to come without warning, and most people face them unprepared. We will discuss these large-scale crises with more detail in the next chapter.

Preventing Crises

As we have seen, some crises are predictable, while others come unexpectedly. It is easier to make prior preparations for the first of these, but even when a disruptive event seems inevitable, many people do nothing to prepare. To protect themselves from worry, some people carry on with life as usual in a way that denies the reality of what might be coming. Others convince themselves that the crisis probably will not occur, but that even if it does, it will not be as bad as predicted and that "we will not be affected as much as others," so nothing is done to prepare. Then there are people who agree that the crisis is coming, but they have no idea what to do, so they do nothing. These people may have no idea that help is available, that there are actions they can take to prevent crisis, or that crisis prevention information is available on the Internet or through community and government agencies. Personality differences also play a role. Some people react with fear or panic when a crisis appears to be imminent, while others decide to take a chance, ride it out, and hope nothing happens. In part, these differences may reflect past experience. A family that lost everything in a previous hurricane is likely to take precautions as another storm approaches, unlike other families that have never experienced a violent storm, so they ignore the warnings.

There are several ways in which counselors may help to prevent crises.

- Help counselees and others see what might be coming. A counselor might see evidence of a developing marriage breakup, for example, before a couple is aware of what is happening. It can help to give warnings, especially when these are supported by evidence and when the warnings lead to actions that prevent serious crisis reactions.
- At times, people need to develop skills such as communication, interpersonal, stress management, self-control, and money management skills. When these are in place and being used, problems can be avoided or their impact can be reduced.
- People can be helped to manage environmental stress and take actions to prevent burnout, exhaustion, uncontrolled debt, or excessive worry. In some cases, people may need help in making physical moves. Examples include assisting people to evacuate their homes as a storm approaches or to move to safe places when an abusive relative threatens danger.
- Often, information helps. When potentially destructive weather is approaching, the media usually give constant updates and suggestions for taking protective action.
- As with all crisis situations, social support and spiritual resources enable people to anticipate what might be coming, and this often softens the trauma when it arrives.
- Counselors and relief workers can take opportunities to get education in crisis prevention and management. Like fire drills in public schools, com-

munities sometimes stage emergency preparedness seminars and work-shops to help key people prepare for what they might do in an emergency.

- Practical steps for minimizing stress can be developed and taught. These may include developing emergency evacuation plans that everybody understands, stocking up on supplies, developing familiarity with safety procedures, and having preestablished plans for communicating and making contact with family members should a major disaster occur. Some of this falls under the umbrella of what has been called stress inoculation training (SIT), which includes teaching people how they can evaluate their circumstances, learn and rehearse new skills, and have prior experiences with stressful situations so everyone is ready when the real crisis occurs.

Sometimes, people also need to accept the fact that prevention is wise and not evidence of weakness or a lack of faith. Men especially need to accept the fact that making preparations does not reflect negatively on their masculinity. Following the attacks on New York, an advertising campaign informed people that post-traumatic stress would be common and that getting help would not be unusual, and neither would it be evidence of weakness. Another campaign emphasized that real men have depression like everybody else and that counseling is a wise and healthy way to respond. According to one counselor, "We have to tell these guys that you're not weak or feminine if you admit to needing help, and that you can become a better man if you're willing to take a look at your emotions and your feelings." With these educational endeavors, the population was being given permission to get help that would prevent problems and crisis reactions later.[15]

Resilience

People have faced crises for centuries, and it is probable that friends, relatives, and spiritual advisors came alongside to help then as they do today. All of this crisis intervention has taught us a lot about the nature of crises and effective ways to help, but one concept seems to have been overlooked, at least until recently. While anguish, anxiety, and even post-traumatic stress appear to be common and the focus of our interventions, none of these is as widespread as *resilience*. This is the human capacity to cope effectively, adapt, maintain equilibrium, and even thrive in times of crises and other major life stresses.

An increasing body of research shows that there are three main features that characterize resilience and that appear to help people adapt in times of crises, disasters, and other stress.[16]

- *Personal characteristics* include a positive outlook, good problem-solving skills, the perception that one is competent, optimism, good intellectual functioning, positive self-worth, good self-regulation and self-control skills, optimistic expectations for the future, and self-efficacy, which is the conviction that one can cope successfully with stressful events.
- *Family environment* means that the resilient children and adults have warm and nurturant families, structured and stable homes, and have experienced good parenting and a sound relationship with a primary care-giver.
- *Broader contextual variables* include positive support outside the family, good role models in the present or past, feeling like one is part of a community,

and links with extended family and support networks outside the home. It also can be helpful for an individual to sense that there are good leaders in the community to help guide people through the crises and disasters.

Resilience is not an innate characteristic that some people have and others lack, according to the "Road to Resilience" education program of the American Psychological Association.[17] Instead, resilience is viewed as a mental muscle that everybody possesses and that everybody can strengthen by exercise (although that may be difficult for people who don't have the three features that are listed above). The goal of resilience building is to help young people deal with day-to-day worries and have a means for dealing with crises and major traumatic events. Children are taught to build and practice their resilience by having a friend and being a friend, taking charge of their own behavior as best they can, setting new goals and making plans to reach them, looking at the bright side in situations, and believing in themselves. Initial research is showing that adults and especially children can be taught behaviors that can make a practical difference when crises happen.

Closely connected with resilience is research in *post-traumatic growth* (PTG).[18] People with resilience adjust to crises and trauma despite the adversity. PTG comes after the crisis and is seen both in people who have shown resilience and those who have not. PTG involves change for the better, which most often is seen in adults, who show an increased ability to cope with life as a result of having survived the crisis. Following the terrorist attacks in New York, there was a marked change, at least temporarily, as people became calmer, friendlier, more considerate, and less frenetic in their pace. PTG is likely to become a more familiar concept in the future, but for counselors, perhaps it is enough to know that many people suffer through crises but come out as stronger and better people as a result. This is consistent with practical observation and biblical teaching about the benefits of suffering. Crises are painful when they occur, but the aftermath can be positive.[19]

Ongoing Crises

Most often we view crises as short-term events that come into our lives and then fade. Some people, however, live and work in situations where the crises never go away. Melika, for example, is a relief worker who lives surrounded by distress and by refugees who are in constant crisis.

It has been five weeks since I last had a decent night's sleep. Three to four hours a night is all that is possible. The refugees just keep coming, even in the night when the roads outside the camp are in the hands of the rebels. They come crying, cradling their dead and dying children, dragging their exhausted parents or aunts or brothers. Some have lost limbs to the arrogant drunkenness of the jungle children. Most of the women and girls have been raped, many more than once. The air is thick with dust or mud, sometimes both at the same time. My sleeping bag is now in tatters, but it hardly matters. I don't spend much time there. I'm not thinking straight right now. It's hard to remember which day this is. I do know there are not enough medical supplies for the numbers already here, let alone those I hear entering the camp today. My stomach, my back, and my legs ache. At times I wonder if I have malaria or something worse.... Tracy told me yesterday I was . . . suffering too much from stress. Ha! What did she expect? A picnic? OK, let's go, another day in paradise.[20]

The people who wait for help in that refugee camp and relief workers like Melika are not the only ones who live with continual stress and crises.[21] The groups include people as diverse as political prisoners who live in fear of being tortured by their captors,[22] missionaries who serve in dangerous environments,[23] sexually exploited children and adults who live with ongoing sexual abuse,[24] military personnel whose lives are steeped in the continual unpredictability of life-threatening insurgency attacks,[25] children—some estimates suggest there are at least 300,000 in more than eighty countries—who have been forced into armed conflict and submission as sexually exploited "soldier wives,"[26] the civilian populations of war zones, perhaps millions of forgotten people who barely survive in refugee camps,[27] and those who live in the gang-infested urban neighborhoods of the world's largest cities.[28] The numbers swell if we add people who work every day in highly stressful jobs or children who wake up every morning afraid to go to school.

Space does not permit us to discuss the diverse needs of groups like this, and neither can we outline ways to adapt our counseling methodologies to bring genuine assistance. Western methods, developed by mental-health professionals in developed countries, can be difficult or impossible to apply in the middle of a coup, earthquake, or refugee camp. How do we adapt our approaches to diverse populations? Some of the most interesting and helpful adaptation has been done by humanitarian workers associated with the worldwide network of World Vision International. In addition to their research on ways to help victims of ongoing crises, World Vision has shown a strong dedication to assisting their employees and volunteers who labor in conditions of intense ongoing stress. These workers know and practice the mental-health principles of getting regular exercise, taking periods for rest and relaxation (that is hardest to put into practice), recognizing signs of burnout and taking actions to prevent this, and finding times for meditation, prayer, and worship. Of greatest significance, however, are the developing of strong relationships with others and participation in teams of care-givers who can share and work together, with mutual support and encouragement. Also important is the quality of leadership that guides these workers. The best leaders are competent in their work, nonauthoritarian, and marked by "strong consultative leadership styles" that stimulate group cohesion and ownership in the work. These conclusions about humanitarian relief workers apply equally well to counselors who work in their own communities with populations of people that cope with ongoing crises.

Conclusions About Crises

Most of this book is about understanding different kinds of stress and about helping people deal with stress-inducing threat, change, relationships, and other problems that can be overwhelming and the cause of what some counselors prefer to call *distress*. Perhaps crises are the most distressing experiences of all. Everybody encounters crises on occasion, but some people face them consistently, and a few even seem to thrive on the challenges that crises present.

In the midst of crisis situations, some human beings come forth as heroes. They may not be noticed or given bravery medals, but these people emerge in stressful times, often without thinking about what they are doing, and take major risks to serve or rescue others.[29] Despite the possibility of dying or suffering serious physical and other consequences, these people are able to keep their fears under control and act in focused ways to accomplish goals that they innately view as being worthy. Some heroes rescue people from burning buildings or swirling rivers, but others courageously protect people from persecution (like the ten Boom family protected Jews when Holland was occupied by Nazi armies), care for the dying and helpless (like Mother Teresa), or risk their safety and reputations to fight for some political cause (like Martin Luther King, Jr., who fought to eliminate segregation in America).

Some have questioned the motives of these people, wondering if they are moved more by challenge, change, or excitement rather than by concern for others. Whatever their motives, heroes make an impact. Their numbers are swelled by thousands of counselors who work laboriously and often selflessly to help ordinary people struggle through crises. Some of these counselor-heroes will read these words. You may be among their numbers. These people may get no affirmation here on earth, but God is aware of their sacrifices and their commitments. Someday many will hear from God himself: "Well done, good and faithful servants."

KEY POINTS FOR BUSY COUNSELORS

➤ A crisis is a turning point that usually cannot be avoided. A crisis may be expected or unexpected, real or imagined, actual or a possibility. Most arrive quickly, and then they're gone, leaving their devastation behind.

➤ There are at least four types of crisis, all of which are mentioned in the Bible

- *Accidental or situational crises* occur when there is a sudden threat, disruptive event, or unexpected loss.
- *Developmental crises* happen in the course of normal human development and include events like cross-country moves, retirement, or the death of a relative.
- *Existential crises* are struggles that occur when people are forced to face disturbing questions about themselves such as "Who am I?" or "What is my life purpose now?"
- *National or community crises* extend beyond individuals to involve large groups of people. Examples include the crises of tornadoes or earthquakes.

➤ In times of crisis, people often experience physical symptoms, confusion, a sense of loss, powerlessness, and a lack of control.

➤ Crisis intervention has these goals:
- To help the person cope effectively with the immediate crisis situation and return to his or her pre-crisis level of functioning.
- To decrease the anxiety, apprehension, and other insecurities.
- To teach crisis-management techniques so the person is better prepared to anticipate and deal with future crises.
- To consider biblical teachings about crises so the person learns from the crisis and grows as a result.

➤ There are several ways in which the counselor can intervene in times of crisis.
- Make contact.
- Reduce anxiety.
- Focus on issues.
- Evaluate resources.
- Plan intervention with the counselee.
- Encourage action.
- Instill hope.
- Follow up.
- Make referrals.

➤ There are ways in which crises can be prevented from occurring or from getting worse when they do occur.

➤ Some people are resilient in times of crisis. There is evidence that resilience can be taught.

➤ Ongoing crises are those that continue for weeks, mostly in the lives of people who are involved with others who also experience the crisis environment.

➤ In times of crisis some people emerge as heroes, but they may not always be noticed and affirmed for their acts of heroism.

39

Trauma, Terror, and Terrorism*

Sampop and Ruchet are two boys from the same village in Thailand's Phang Nga province. Sampop was at the beach selling souvenirs to tourists on that sunny Sunday morning in December. Ruchet was home, and their older brother was out in the family fishing boat. When the tsunami swept ashore, Sampop ran and then watched as the giant wave swallowed countless people from the spot where he had been standing just minutes before. Ruchet rushed from his house and watched as the sea rose quickly and flipped their brother's boat upside down. The brother waved before he went under and disappeared, never to be seen again. The two boys talked about their experiences and drew pictures for their counselors at a children's camp a few weeks after the disaster. Will the memories ever be forgotten?[1]

At a different time and place, a young person who wanted to remain anonymous wrote about living in a kibbutz during a time of war. "The evening that war was declared I remember going into the dining room for supper and standing in the queue behind Uzi, who was one of my best friends. I didn't feel like eating. Next day as I was preparing for work, unexpectedly in the lavatory I found myself weeping. I let the tears stream down as I thought of all my friends who would be leaving the kibbutz that morning, some never to return. It seemed a terrible despairing day. I dried my face and went into work. From that night I stopped sleeping and was alternatively hyperactive or depressed. I knew that I wasn't well, but there didn't seem much I could do about it. I continued in my depressed state to work fairly normally but became increasingly manic during the sleepless night hours, and this increased my weariness during the day. I was clinging to my work to keep me sane, but I was thinking crazy thoughts while I was doing it. I was suddenly deeply ashamed of being Christian. When I think back to my Israeli breakdown, the two emotions I remember most vividly are shame and loneliness. Shame because I wasn't as tough as the Israelis and was causing them worry and concern during a traumatic event."[2]

Dean is a veteran who served in the Middle East and traveled in convoys that often came under attack. He describes the experience of seeing a friend get hit in the head so that his skull was blown away. "You didn't know who the enemy was," Dean told a counselor as part of his treatment for post-traumatic stress disorder. "You don't know who is shooting at you." Dean described how a broken leg had kept him away from the front lines, in a tent where he struggled with anxiety and guilt for not being with his comrades. Since returning home, he has been plagued with frequent nightmares, panic attacks, and depression. The good news is that he's getting help.[3]

T he world changed dramatically on September 11, 2001. For many years and in many parts of the world, terrorism, guerrilla warfare, and mercenary

* I am grateful to Dr. Baris Konur and to Dr. Jon Ebert for reading and helpfully critiquing portions of this chapter.

activity had impacted millions of people and held them in the grip of poverty, hunger, and fear, but, sadly, most of us in the Western world had paid little attention. Then, on a bright and peaceful autumn morning, two hijacked passenger jets were flown into the World Trade Towers, another plane crashed into the Pentagon in Washington, and the controls of a fourth were wrestled from the hijackers and the plane crashed into a Pennsylvania field, far from its intended political target. Before that morning, Westerners had been killed by terrorists overseas, and everybody assumed that a major attack on some Western country, most likely the United States, was a distinct possibility. But the September 11 attacks shook the world and launched what the President of the United States called a war on terrorism. It is a war that would not be won easily, if at all. And as terrorism has continued, so have fear and terror taken their place in the minds of previously secure people.

Terrorism has no universally accepted definition. What one person may define as a terrorist, somebody else may describe as a freedom fighter. Broadly viewed, however, terrorism is "(a) the use of force or violence (b) by individuals or groups (c) that is directed toward civilian populations (d) and intended to instill fear (e) as a means of coercing individuals or groups to change their political or social positions."[4] Terrorism is deliberate, designed to frighten, often highly visible, and intended to turn people against their leaders or against beliefs that the terrorists find objectionable.[5] The people who use terrorism are known as terrorists. To accomplish their goals these terrorists specialize in creating terror with the intention of changing and controlling attitudes and behavior.

Terror is a state of intense fear. Small children are terrified by the dark, and some adults feel terror when they are expected to give a speech or go to the dentist. Unlike parents, dentists, and others who try to reduce fear, terrorists want to create an aroused state of fear in individuals, but especially in whole populations. Counselors are not the only ones who have seen this fear in people following terrorist attacks and threats.

It is obvious, of course, that terror is much broader than the emotions that follow terrorist attacks. Military invasions create terror, and so do political upheavals, floods, cyclones, tornadoes, earthquakes, forest fires, or other disasters. There are children who experienced the December tsunami in Asia that today are afraid to go anywhere near the beaches where they played on the sand in earlier years. Relief workers who have faced political insurgents or military people like Dean who have served in highly dangerous combat zones often continue to struggle with memories of their experiences and ongoing flashbacks that resurrect their fear. Survivors of political torture carry their fears and trauma for a lifetime.[6] Clearly, terror can come from a variety of sources and can have long-lasting psychological and other repercussions.

One other term needs clarification before we continue. *Trauma* can refer to any kind of intense stress, physical or psychological, that disrupts a person's stability. Trauma can come in a diversity of forms, including a strong physical blow to the body, severe injury sustained in an automobile accident or athletic injury, one-time rape or sustained sexual and emotional abuse, or emotionally arousing encounters that do not hurt the body but lead to overwhelming psychological stress. Usually, trauma is highly disturbing, makes a deep impact, shatters one's sense of trust, and can leave people feeling immobilized. When hurricane flood waters engulfed one community, a reporter found a woman standing in the wreckage of her house, surrounded by water, holding a baby and gazing off in to space, traumatized by the overwhelming nature of what had demolished so much of her world.

Unlike past generations of counselors, we live and counsel in times that are being shaped by terrorism—a world that is populated by millions of terror-impacted people and surrounded by everyday reminders of the long-lasting effects of terror and trauma.

The Bible and Terror

The Bible does not address the issues of terrorism, terror, trauma, or disasters in ways that we know these terms today. Terror is mentioned a number of times in the Old Testament, but a concordance revealed just one reference to terrorists, only a few references to disasters (all related to prophecies about the future),[7] and no use of the word *trauma*. Even though the modern terms are not used, however, there are examples of what we mean by these words today.

The events that occurred in the Garden of Eden led to the first human experience of trauma. Like an undercover terrorist, Satan destroyed the sense of confidence and security in Adam and Eve. Fear was introduced into the human race, and fear has shaped attitudes and behavior ever since.

When David went to visit his soldier brothers, most of the army appeared to be terrorized by the giant Goliath. On various occasions throughout their history, the people of Jerusalem were filled with fear and terror when they knew that powerful armies were advancing. The ten plagues that swept over Pharaoh's Egypt must have been disasters that led to significant trauma, and terror surely swept through the people on the ground during the early days of the flood that Noah and his family rode out in the ark. The final book in the New Testament, Revelation, describes numerous frightening events along with the stress and terror that will overwhelm whole populations of people.

As counselors work with victims of trauma and terror, biblical references to fear, hope, peace, and God's sovereignty will have relevance. These will be mentioned periodically in the pages that follow.

The Causes of Terrorism and Terror

Why do people participate in terrorist activities, including those acts that take the terrorist's own life? Who are these people, and what are they trying to accomplish? Questions like these are of interest to all of us, even though they may have limited bearing on the counselor's work.

On the morning of September 11, an airport camera in Dulles airport recorded the actions of two young men in business attire as they passed through security and then walked away to board an airplane that they would commandeer and fly into the Pentagon. There was nothing in the appearance or actions of these people to hint what they were planning. According to a psychologist who has analyzed biographical data from more than four hundred members of terrorist groups, most suicide bombers are not brain-washed youth, indoctrinated into religious zealotry at an early age.[8] They are not disenfranchised or poor, with little hope and nothing to lose by their terrorist activities. Most are married, in their late twenties, upper middle class, educated, and building careers. They look like regular people and, in many respects, this is what they are. Before leaving their home countries and moving to places like Britain, France, or the United States, these individuals were not particularly religious, and they never were in any kind of trouble. While living in foreign lands, many of them met fellow expatriates, built friendships, gravitated to mosques that were associated with militant groups, and eventually acquired the beliefs of their friends.

A lot of these people—they are not all Muslims—are attracted to Western values, affluent lifestyles, and social freedoms. At the same time, they are distressed when they realize that Western influences are sweeping away the national identities and alliances of people in their homelands, undermining values that have existed for centuries, and keeping whole countries enslaved by conditions of poverty, racism, oppression, and the politics of powerful Western nations—especially the United States. An "us-versus-them" mentality emerges, and for some, terrorist acts are seen as the only viable way to bring change. Variations of this thinking motivate members of rightist groups (like neo-Nazis), nationalist separatist groups in countries such as Indonesia or Spain, religious extremist groups, state-supported groups (such as police or military regimes), fundamentalist groups (such as al-Qaeda), and even single-issue groups, including some anti-abortion or environmentalist groups that use violent tactics.[9] All these people are convinced that their actions are justified; all create terror and sometimes are the reason for the fear and trauma in those who come for counseling.

The Psychological Effects of Terrorism, Terror, and Trauma

Probably, thousands of research studies have attempted to get a clearer picture of the psychological symptoms that come in the wake of disasters, accidents, terrorism attacks, or other traumatic events.[10] Shortly after the September 11 events, one trauma expert wrote that "personal security is going to be shaken and everybody's perspective on human life is likely to be shifted.... Nobody is going to feel safe."[11] The initial research, especially in areas near to the disaster, confirmed that there were widespread anxiety, worries about safety, depression, anger, nervousness, hypervigilance, and even distrust. For some people, this developed into post-traumatic stress disorder (PTSD) with its more debilitating symptoms.

Perhaps it is surprising that these psychological symptoms do not seem to have been as prevalent or as long lasting as many counselors predicted. Six months to a year after the U.S. terrorist attacks, most of the symptoms had disappeared, especially those that occurred in people who lived far away from the disaster scene. Inner-city children did not show long-term increases in post-traumatic psychological symptoms, perhaps because many of them cope every day with crime and violence, so there may have been some kind of stress inoculation.[12] Wherever they live, when people hear a fire alarm or other indication of an emergency, generally there is no panic, strangers communicate and try to help others, and many wait before evacuating a building or danger zone because they want to get more information about whether the warning signals real danger or is a false alarm.[13]

When disaster happens some people respond with resilience. Often, they feel that doing something, anything, can lessen the shock and sense of helplessness.

So these resilient people take action, pick up their lives as best they can, and keep going. One psychologist studied survivors in the Sri Lankan civil war and discovered that most were resistant to the psychological distress and determined to bounce back by integrating the trauma into the formation of new identities.[14] When a Thai psychologist found people wandering around, unsure what to do and where to go after the tsunami disaster, he began pairing people together, linking those who seemed to be doing well with those who were struggling. He never thought about therapy at that early time, but urged people to get back into their familiar environments. In the safety of their homes or communities and in contact with their family and friends, most people eventually returned to normal.[15]

Several months ago a friend in the Middle East mentioned in an email message that a restaurant near his home had been destroyed by a suicide bomber who blew up herself along with a number of the restaurant patrons. The next day my friend wrote to say that there were barricades around the restaurant, but that the street was open and traffic was moving by as usual. A few weeks later I visited my friend, who showed me the restaurant, repaired, open for business, and filled with diners. "When you live in the midst of terror, you keep alert, but you go on with your life," my friend stated somewhat nonchalantly. "We can't let terrorists or threats of violence immobilize us." Nobody in that community was denying the dangers and threats of terrorism, but these people were refusing to let the dangers shut down their activities, destroy their resilience, or weaken their determination to keep living as normally as possible.

None of this is intended to suggest that terrorism and trauma have no impact. All traumatic events create stress, whether these events are ongoing crises and problems or one-time occurrences like a serious accident. Despite widespread resiliency, many people responded with significant distress when terrorism came to America. No longer was the Western world a last place of safety. Even people who picked up and kept going knew that there would have to be a new sense of vigilance and a new definition of what is normal. Responses to terrorism or other intense stress largely depend on each person's personality, strengths, past experiences, support network, closeness to the disaster or trauma, and/or ability to have control over circumstances.

How one reacts also depends on how the stress is perceived. If an event is viewed as being dangerous, physically harmful, or otherwise threatening and disruptive, there is likely to be a stress or anxiety reaction even if the perceived threat is not real. Following the Asian tsunamis of 2004, the media reported that many people were afraid to go back to the beaches after the seas had returned to normal. There was no longer a tsunami danger, but the environment stirred anxiety, nevertheless. Most counselors also have seen the reverse of this when some people deny that a genuine threat is dangerous and go about their activities with no apparent concerns or efforts to take precautions.

The immediate effects of a trauma or other stress-inducing event are well known. They include physiological changes in the body—such as more rapid heart beat and breathing, increased muscle tension, and more adrenaline pumping through the system—along with emotional responses, such as fear, uncertainty, anger, or confusion. Sometimes, other reactions appear, such as headaches, nausea, vomiting, fainting, impulsivity, or the appearance of the well-known psychological defense mechanisms. These symptoms may last for a few minutes, hours, or days, but most fade with the passage of time as people are able to assess their circumstances.

In some people, a condition known as *acute stress disorder* (ASD) appears shortly after a traumatic or terrifying event. Usually, the normal stress reactions are present, but, in addition, there may be a sense of detachment, a reduced awareness of one's surrounding so that the person appears to be dazed, a feeling that "this is unreal," and often an inability to remember details of the trauma that has just occurred. The person may be emotionally unresponsive, confused, anxious, and resistant to contact with anybody or anything that would bring reminders of the trauma. ASD usually only lasts for a few days or weeks, but during this time there can be poor concentration, sleep problems, exaggerated startle responses, irritability, and sometimes unwanted memories or reminders of the traumatic event that appear in dreams or in flashbacks. When the trauma that causes this is of greater intensity or longer in duration, ASD is more common. It also is stronger and more likely to appear in people who have had previous stressful experiences, including abuse or violence. It is not surprising to find that stress reactions like these also tend to be more prevalent in people like firefighters, ambulance drivers, or emergency workers who have frequent contact with traumatic situations.[16]

Stress can be reduced by getting people out of the trauma areas, providing an environment of safety, giving reassurance, and allowing victims to describe what happened. It helps, as well, to teach people how to cope with anxiety, reassess their own vulnerability, find the comfort that comes through spiritual healing, and get back into routines and places of stability. The story has been told often about teachers in New York City grade schools who, immediately after the towers were hit, calmly told their five- and six-year-old students to join hands and follow their teachers as they all walked many blocks to safety, to secure places, where the kids were reassured and cared for while they waited to reconnect with their parents. In contrast, following the Hurricane Katrina disaster, almost the entire city of New Orleans was evacuated, and some people were taken hundreds or thousands of miles from home. "Everybody here has been nice," one man told a reporter from a shelter in Utah, "but I don't know where my stuff is, I don't have a job, and I'm farther away from home than I ever have been in my life." Experiences like this make adjustment harder.

The way people respond to stress has been compared to the ways in which they respond to a death. After a loved one dies, it is natural to be overwhelmed, but over time the feeling fades. The loss is likely to leave permanent changes, but eventually the grieving person is able to go back to a more or less normal day-to-day existence. Something similar happens after a terrorist attack, violent crime, industrial accident, or other trauma. It is natural to react physically and psychologically and to have the characteristics described here. Only in some people do symptoms occur that suggest a more serious, post-traumatic stress disorder. These characteristics are more likely to appear in those who have been traumatized previously or were depressed or highly anxious before the stressful event occurred.

Post-traumatic stress disorder (PTSD) often is an outgrowth of the acute stress reaction. The characteristics have been recognized for centuries, but only recently has PTSD been accepted as an established disorder.[17] There are three categories of symptoms.[18] First, the person has the experience of recurring thoughts about the event. These memories come unexpectedly, sometimes in dreams or flashbacks that leave the person feeling as though the events were happening again. Some people are confused about the difference between the memory of the trauma and the actual trauma. The second group of symptoms involves avoidance of people, places, things, or anything else that could bring a memory of the event. People may do anything to push these memories out of their awareness. This avoidance is not always conscious or deliberate. After she had been raped by a white man, an African American woman experienced anxiety and withdrew whenever a white man approached, even though there was no danger. Feelings of anxiety came flooding back whenever a white man entered the room because that was similar to what the rapist had done before his violent act. In addition to avoiding anything that might arouse memories, there also may be lifestyle changes, a refusal to talk about the trauma, or an unwillingness to take part in any activities that might re-arouse anxiety or fresh reminders of what happened. Third is what counselors know as hyperarousal. Here there is sleeplessness, poor concentration, frequent startle reactions, and a high alertness to ways of protecting oneself and one's loved ones. Since these characteristics persist, sometimes for years if they are not treated, they can have a big impact on one's work, relationships, lifestyle, and quality of life.

As PTSD has become better known and more prevalent, there has been more research on the disorder and more suggestions about the ways in which it can be treated.[19] There also have been suggestions that PTSD may be less common than media reports might suggest. Whatever its prevalence, this is a condition that is likely to become more common as terrorism continues. Most often, counseling should begin soon after the trauma, although it seems best to help people to first get reestablished into their homes, families, and work environments because this brings a sense of stability. Most counselors suggest at least three goals for helping. First, provide a safe environment where the person can talk when he or she is ready. Second, encourage at least some discussion of the trauma, done in the presence of an individual or a group that is understanding and accepting. Then, third, the person needs help with specific behaviors, such as learning new coping styles, dealing with self-destructive behavior or attitudes, and finding ways to deal more effectively with the memories. This also may include giving encouragement, instilling hope, and helping people realize that struggles like theirs can be common.

The good news is that excessive and long-lasting stress reactions are not the norm for most people who experience terrorism or trauma. It is important, as well, to recognize that increasingly effective treatment procedures are emerging and Christian counselors are able to help. The help is likely to be more effective when counselors take the time and perhaps get some extra training to familiarize themselves in more detail with the nature of trauma and with the most effective ways to do trauma counseling.[20] Trauma management has become a major specialty with increasing research backing and the ongoing development of more effective intervention techniques. In addition to an understanding of trauma and the effects of terrorism, effective counselors also need a basic understanding of neurophysiology and how this can impact counseling with the victims of trauma and terrorism.

The Neurobiological Effects of Terrorism, Terror, and Trauma

Psychiatrist Daniel Siegal has a wonderful way of teaching people about the brain. Put your thumb in the palm of your hand and then fold your four fingers down from the top so that they face you. That, says Siegal, gives you a remarkably accurate model of the brain. Of course, the brain is far more complex, with its ten to twenty billion interconnected neurons, but its size is about the same as a clenched fist, and by pointing to the fingernails, the hidden thumb, the wrist, and even the line that goes up the center of your palm (that line represents the brain stem at the base of the brain), we can have a good lesson in brain physiology for neurological novices.[21]

Siegal and other neuroscientists sometimes divide the brain into three major areas. The first of these is the *brain stem*, the lowest part of the brain. It comes out of the spinal cord and passes information from sense organs into the brain. It also monitors what gets to the brain and regulates states of wakefulness and sleep.

The *limbic system* (that's where the thumb is in the first illustration) is the part of the brain that controls emotion and helps with the formation of memories. Three parts of the limbic system are especially important for understanding human responses to terror: the hippocampus, the amygdala, and the hypothalamus. These are not as hard to understand as the big names might suggest. First, the *hippocampus* is in the business of taking sensations and ideas that are in your mind at the present moment (that is, short-term memory) and converting these into sensations, ideas, and memories that you will remember for a long time (long-term memory). If the hippocampus is damaged later in life, the long-term memories that have been stored in the brain will still be there, but the person cannot build new memories. These just fade away. Something similar happens in times of intense stress. The hippocampus shuts down, so the short-term memories don't become long-term memories that last.

Part two of our limbic system is called the *amygdala*. This word refers to two almond-shaped collections of neurons that are right at the center of the brain. (Remember that the brain is divided into a left side and a right side, so most of what is on one side of the brain is duplicated on the other side.) The amygdala has been called "one of the important appraisal centers in the brain that evaluate the meaning of incoming stimuli."[22] In animals there is anger when the amygdala is stimulated, but when the amygdala is removed, there is indifference and no reaction to stimuli that normally would produce anger, fear, sexual arousal, or other emotions. The amygdala, then, is an early-warning system that can arouse the body emotionally and physically even before the person recognizes consciously what might be happening.

Third in our look at the limbic system is the *hypothalamus*. This is a small part of the brain, but one of the busiest. It gets information from various sources about blood pressure, skin temperature, how full the stomach is, what is coming in through hearing, smell, and the optic nerves, and whether there are toxins in the system. Along with all of this information, the hypothalamus has power. In different ways it regulates such diverse things as pulse rate, blood pressure, breathing, hunger, thirst, digestion, response to pain, sexual satisfaction, anger, aggressive behavior, the working of the nervous system, and the pumping of hormones into the blood stream to prepare the body to fight or flee.

In addition to the brain stem and the limbic system, the third major brain area is the *cerebral cortex*. This region sits at the top of the brain and spills over a bit to the sides. This is the part of the brain where we think, reason, remember, get sensory information, and have awareness. In humans there are numerous folds in the cortex with ridges and groves—making this the groovy part of the brain.

As most people are aware, the two hemispheres or sides of the brain work together, but the left and right cortex have some different specialties. The left hemisphere is the logical-mathematical-language-focused side of the brain. This is the part that deals with words, symbols, letters, details, analysis, calculations, and scientific concepts. The right brain is more dominant for visual imagery, emotion, art, music appreciation, spatial abilities, and creative imagination.

This brief digression into brain physiology is not a deviation from our interest in counseling. Instead, an awareness of brain functioning has tremendous implications for counseling people following terrorism or trauma. When the terrorists attack or some other trauma is experienced, the body goes into a high state of emergency. When the stimuli begin to arrive from the sensory nerves and through the brain stem, the limbic system "tells" the hippocampus to stop its normal functioning and to go into emergency mode, getting the body ready to flee or to fight. Like firefighters or police officers who leave whatever they are doing, turn on the sirens, and go out to face the emergency, the amygdala sounds the alarm. Immediately, the hippocampus stops what it was doing and sends out neurohormones, including adrenaline, that get the heart beating faster, cause the muscles to tense and get ready for action, and accelerate the breathing in order to supply more oxygen to the body. At the same time, the horrible memories and sensations that come to the amygdala remain there, stuck in what is largely a nonverbal, unconscious part of the brain. The memories never get passed on to the frontal lobes of the cerebral cortex, the location of reasoning, thinking, and understanding. This is because the limbic system is so busy with emergency action that it fails to push the incoming information up to the cortex, where it can be stored as long-term memory and processed logically.

After the trauma or terrorist attack has passed, some people have difficulty picking up and continuing with their lives. They cannot remember details of the traumatic event, because the memories never got to the cortex. Victims of trauma can't walk away and forget the trauma because those memories are lodged in the limbic area of the brain, where they continue to stimulate stress reactions, flashbacks of short-term memories, nightmares, or continuing anxiety. PTSD appears to be about normal body reaction to stress except that the process of getting information to the cortex has been interrupted. Passing that information to the cortex is the job of the hippocampus, but that has been shut down by the ever-pumping stress hormones. As a result, the amygdala never gets the word from the cortex that the danger has passed, so the alarm keeps sounding. PTSD is a condition wherein the full process of dealing with the trauma has been interrupted and prevented from completing its course.[24] When trauma victims or terror-impacted people come for counseling, the talk therapy that counselors normally use may not work and, as we will see, could even make matters worse. Talk involves use of the cortex and dealing with memories that are stored there, but as our walk

Table 39-1

The Three Logics of the Brain

Each area of the brain has its own "logical" ways of directing thought, feeling, and behavior, according to Patricia Berne and Louis Savary.[23] Mostly the areas work together, but sometimes they don't. The three major parts of the brain produce three types of brain logic.

KINESTHETIC LOGIC

Kinesthetic Logic comes from the brain stem. It "doesn't consider ideas, concepts, symbols, images, emotions, or plans." Instead, kinesthetic logic relies on immediate sensations such as smell, taste, or touch that come from outer stimulation. Decisions at this level are made in accordance with whether the stimuli or sensations bring pleasure or pain. This is primitive logic, and it is never-ending. The brain stem is at work even when our minds are busy or when we sleep. At times kinesthetic logic may overrule every other kind of logic in the brain.

LIMBIC LOGIC

Limbic Logic is concerned with safety and survival rather than with pain or pleasure. Whereas kinesthetic logic processes sensory stimuli, limbic logic grasps images and emotions, puts them together, and sometimes combines images and emotions in the environment with those that reside in the brain.

LINEAR LOGIC

Linear Logic takes place in the cerebral cortex of the brain, most often in the left hemisphere of the cortex where concepts, ideas, sentences, plans, ideas, reasoning, and rational thinking operate.

"Whenever you have an experience, each area of your brain assesses it differently: Your brain stem, with its kinesthetic logic" asks if the experience will be pleasurable or painful. Depending on the answer, the experience is either approached or avoided. The limbic system asks if the experience will be life-enhancing or life-threatening. If everything seems okay, the body goes forward with the experience. If there is threat, the body is immobilized to resist or run. The cortex, with its linear logic, is able to ask questions, evaluate the experience, calculate reasonable responses, and initiate action to change.

All three logical symptoms are present from early in life, but they seem to develop in the above order. The child responds first to feelings—that's kinesthetic logic—and only later learns to deal with limbic logic. Linear logic comes last and results from education, personal experiences, and other types of learning. In times of trauma, all three are in operation, but sometimes certain parts of the cortex slow down and the other logics take over.

through the brain has shown, the problem-causing traumatic memories are lodged in a part of the brain that cannot be accessed by talk, at least not initially or easily.[25] There have to be other approaches.

Counseling Following Terrorism, Terror, and Trauma

The growing understanding of brain physiology along with the surging influence of terrorism and the terror together are leading to new waves of research, treatment innovations, and reevaluation of past approaches to therapy. Along with this have come a host of new publications, seminars, and workshops to describe the implications of all this new knowledge.[26] This presents us with the challenge of summarizing and grasping what is likely to persist and be of ongoing practical value for counselors. Here are conclusions that are likely to last.

1. *Avoid the Rush to Debrief.* Debriefing (sometimes called critical incident stress debriefing or CISD) is the process of encouraging trauma-impacted counselees to talk about their experiences and to freely express their feelings. This is based on the core counseling belief that it is better to express emotions than to bottle them up. Increasing evidence says that this is not true for everybody. Sometimes, the debriefing actually can be harmful, something similar to letting a snake out of a cage and then not knowing how to catch the slithering serpent to bring it back under control.[27] Perhaps few researchers would agree that "psychological debriefing is a waste of time,"[28] but overall, there appears to be almost no empirical support for the belief that psychological debriefings reduce stress after trauma or prevent post-traumatic stress disorder.[29] In highly anxious counselees, the move to debriefing can even lead to greater anxiety.

None of this is meant to suggest that there should be no talk about the traumatic events. Often, this can be helpful, providing that it takes place after the counselee has calmed down and the body has had time to complete its work of processing the information into the cortex. There is some evidence that people, including those diagnosed with PTSD, can be helped even if they never talk about the main traumas.[30] When and if the traumatic experiences are discussed, the counselor should not press for more information but, instead, should let counselees say as much or as little as they want and in their own timing.

2. *Provide a Place of Safety, Trust, and Reassurance.* Immediately following a traumatic event, the person is likely to feel highly anxious and confused. Often, there is a mixture of emotions along with a sense of unreality, worry about what might happen next, and a concern that things will never be normal again. Some counselees, such as people who have been sexually abused or exploited, feel a deep sense of shame and embarrassment. They wonder if they really caused the trauma and can be overwhelmed with a sense of helplessness. They need reassurance, acceptance, and the counselor's affirmation that coming for counseling is healthy and not a sign of weakness. Whatever the trauma, in times like this, the person needs a place of refuge, including the presence of a calm person or persons who can give reassurance, understanding, and hope.

When a lady named Paula entered the counseling room, she literally was shaking with both rage and fear because of a traumatic event in her life. The counselor resisted the urge to ask Paula to talk about what was making her so agitated but focused instead on the agitation. In a peaceful setting, Paula was encouraged to breathe deeply, to talk about how her body was reacting, and to cry without embarrassment. At one point Paula was asked if she felt the counselor was too close, and when she answered yes, the counselor moved her chair back and saw Paula relax even more. In all of this the counselor was modeling calmness and showing understanding. Paula's body was calming down, and the stress hormones stopped pumping so ferociously through her body. Nobody could see this, but as Paula relaxed, her hippocampus got back to work, and Paula's brain was better able to process the trauma.

3. *Give Information and Coping Strategies.* This is not as simplistic as it may sound. Daniel Seigel discovered that many of his patients were helped when he gave them a brief description of what was going on in their brains. He told them how their bodies react to stress and, in so doing, helped to reassure them that they were not crazy. One greatly relieved patient, a victim of flashbacks and intrusive images that had made her life miserable, stated that her post-traumatic stress problems were "just that the bad things that happened to me got fragmented in my mind and were never put together into my regular memory by my hippowhatsis."[31]

Counselees also can benefit from learning and applying stress management techniques, such as deep breathing or imaging peaceful scenes, so that they are enabled to calm down when stress builds. Try to help them anchor their lives in routines and relationships that can provide stability and support. Discourage the use of substances that could lead to abuse and an eventual worsening of the problems.[32] Emphasize the person's religious beliefs. These can bring peace and reassurance.

4. *Use Cognitive-Behavioral Techniques.* These are methods, some highly complex, that enable people to get better control of their thinking and actions. There is evidence that these can be very effective in helping people deal with the aftermath of trauma and terrorism.[33]

The methods include teaching people self-control methods, relaxation techniques, and life skills, as well as communication and time-management skills. In addition, counselees can be taught to look for the evidence that their fears are justified (most often the evidence isn't there), identify when they might be overestimating the possibilities of something bad happening, or basing their actions on feelings instead of on facts. Sometimes, counselees are encouraged to keep journals so their thoughts and feelings can be written down, and to get regular exercise, since this stimulates chemicals into the bloodstream that can have a positive influence.

5. *Use Whole-Brain Techniques.* There are a variety of techniques that could help get the different parts of the brain working together following a traumatic event. For want of a better label, we might call these whole-brain techniques. They could include:

- Telling stories. Once again, the insights of Daniel Seigel are helpful. "Coherent stories are an integration of the left hemisphere's drive to tell a logical story and the right brain's ability to grasp emotionally the mental processes of the people in those events," Seigel notes.[34] When people are asked to tell the stories of their lives, they need to engage in planning, using language coherently, interacting with other people, dealing with emotions and memory. Telling a story about one's life "reflects a fundamental capacity for the brain to integrate memory, knowledge, and feeling." When people are asked to tell a story about the future that they imagine, they learn to make something whole and hopeful out of the sometimes chaotic feelings of pain, anxiety, anger, and confusion. This gets the whole brain involved.

- Multisensory interventions. When people experience trauma, the memories are trapped in lower parts of the brain. Those memories have not reached and been stored in the frontal lobes of the cerebral cortex, so it is difficult to speak and think about the trauma. The amygdala, hippocampus, hypothalamus, and brain stem are only marginally affected by thinking, so people cannot talk and process their trauma from the top down. They need to work from the bottom up, and many neuroscientists agree that this bottom-up processing only comes through nonverbal, multisensory therapies. For many years the so-called expressive therapies—music therapy, art therapy, dance therapy, using sand trays, poetry, drama, or novel writing—were on the fringes of respectability.[35] Even now there appears to be little research to link expressive therapies to the psychophysiology of trauma relief, but there are anecdotal accounts to support the impact of what some have termed the body therapies.

- EMDR and other neurologically based therapy techniques. These are the most controversial of the whole-brain therapies, but they can provide remarkable results for some people, although not for all.[36] Eye movement desensitization and reprocessing (EMDR), for example, is a complex therapeutic approach that involves, among other things, eye movements that focus attention on an external stimulus even while the person focuses thinking on internal distressing material. As the eyes move from side to side, there is activation of both the left and right hemispheres of the brain, which, in turn helps people resolve problems caused by a lack of communication between the right and left brain.[37] Other approaches, including Thought Field Therapy (TFT), appear to link lower and upper parts of the brain. Like most newer and somewhat unorthodox approaches, each of these neurologically based therapies has intense critics and enthusiastic advocates. Time and research will determine whether they are effective techniques, but in the meantime, they continue to be used by counselors who have special training in these techniques.

6. *Instill Hope.* Psychologist Michael Wessells has worked with children and adults in refugee camps and war zones. He has concluded that a loss of hope is one of the greatest effects on people in these difficult environments. Hopelessness has been seen, as well, among people who live in gang-infested neighborhoods and communities impacted by terrorism. Often, there is a loss of basic resources in these environments—adequate health care, water, food, and shelter may be missing. It is common for family stability to have been disrupted, especially if a family member has disappeared or died. Having witnessed horrible acts of violence, some people, including children, begin to think that violence is normal,

and they view themselves as helpless victims. It is not surprising, then, that hopelessness is common, especially among the young. "Once young people feel hopeless, they really do give up," according to Wessells. "They don't take the steps that might build a constructive future." Surely, this is because they don't see any possibility for a constructive future.[38]

Often, the counselor does not see much hope either. The Christ-follower never is without hope, but it can be difficult to see the bright side and stimulate others to think in similar ways. Even so, instilling hope and believing that things can be better is an effective way to help trauma-impacted people.

7. *Stimulate Community-Based Interventions.* Western psychology, psychiatry, and other forms of counseling tend to be clinical, individualized approaches that mostly involve one-to-one interventions in which a counselor uses talk to help a counselee solve problems. Often, the counselor and counselee do not know each other before they meet for formal "therapy" or "treatment," and it is rare to involve family members, communities, or religious healers. These Western therapies have been studied extensively, and many have been elevated to research-based *empirically supported treatments* that are assumed to be effective and often are—at least in the Western environments where they have been developed and evaluated by Western scientific methods.[39]

Western approaches have a number of limitations, even when they are used in Western settings. Most often these methods are used with individuals; they focus on emotions, insights, or behavior changes; they deal with problems apart from the counselee's support network; and they often ignore the traumatized person's spiritual or religious beliefs. This tendency to focus on emotional needs may lead counselors to overlook economic, social, cultural, spiritual, or practical issues—like the need for housing and employment. When tangible needs remain unmet, adjustment is harder and it is difficult for counselees to concentrate on what the counselor is saying and trying to accomplish.

Community-based assistance does not involve bringing counselors in to do therapy with trauma- or terror-impacted people. Instead, counselors and other helpers do what they can to mobilize community resources, encourage people to get engaged together in their own recovery efforts, and help them find essentials such as a place to live and access to funds. Some mental-health professionals conclude that empowering communities becomes a major goal for post-traumatic intervention. This community empowerment has three core goals among others: to rebuild schools, reunite families, and resettle children.[40] Community approaches like these recognize that following a disaster or during times of ongoing fear and crisis, communities do not consist of individuals living in isolated bubbles. Every community has churches, synagogues or mosques, youth groups, senior citizen clubs, PTA groups, and others that can be mobilized to go beyond their initial purposes for existence and, instead, bring encouragement, support, healing, and help to one another and to their communities. Often, the best forms of help come when victims of crises work together for a common cause. Following the terrorist attacks in New York City, one counselor who also was the parent of a grade-school child mobilized other parents and encouraged everybody to work together to help in cleaning up the school so the kids could get back to their classes. That is community assistance. It does not replace the need for counseling, but it is a huge supplement to what counselors might do with individuals.[41]

8. *Recognize Group Differences.* When the terrorists attacked Manhattan, did immigrants respond differently from native New Yorkers? Whenever explosions rock resort areas like the terrorist attacks in Bali, do tourists respond differently from the residents? Might the people displaced and sent to refugee camps because of civil strife in Africa be different from people displaced from their homes and businesses by cyclones, tsunamis, or earthquakes? Despite the use of standard methods, isn't the counseling of psychologically wounded military personnel likely to be different from counseling trauma-impacted missionaries.[42] These questions point to the sometimes overlooked fact that some groups may be more vulnerable than others. Children separated from their parents, disabled people in war zones, torture victims, and people exposed to violence in prison or camp settings are among those who may have more difficulty recovering from their traumas. In the midst of other helping activities, the sensitive counselor must never forget the unique circumstances of each victim of trauma. To be effective, counselors must learn as much as they can about the nature of the trauma or the setting where the trauma or terror occurred. The more we can understand our counselees and their unique situations, the more effective our help will be.

Of special importance are the beliefs of victims and their perceptions about healers. Some people resist and fail to profit from even competent counseling. Sometimes, these victims of trauma put more confidence in pastors or local healers than in counselors, believe that talking to strangers won't help, or have theological beliefs that give support and encouragement during difficult times. Never underestimate the healing power of personal beliefs and trusted healers.

9. *Be Cautious in Cross-Cultural Intervention.* Consistent with the previous discussion, there has been debate over the impact of international relief organizations. Without doubt, culturally sensitive and experienced groups like World Vision, the Red Cross, or Salvation Army are enormously helpful to the victims of disasters, terrorist attacks, or other national crises. In contrast, some groups rush in with good intentions but with faulty perceptions and harmful interventions. Following the 2004 tsunami that killed as many as 300,000 people in Asia and left hundreds of thousands homeless, an American psychiatrist estimated that 50 to 90 percent of the people would experience PTSD or depression and need antidepressant drugs (that an American pharmaceutical company was willing to supply for a cost). The World Health Organization (WHO) disagreed. Based on many years of experience with similar tragedies, WHO estimated that no more than 5 to 10 percent of the people would have tsunami-induced mood or anxiety disorders. Local mental-health workers decried the Western tendency to assume that the reactions to the tsunami would be medical. Instead, the international community was asked to help the local people come together to build homes, provide mutual support, open schools, and maintain rituals, such as mourning the dead and applying their own cultural and religious explanations for the floods. One psychologist from Nepal expressed concern that the outside aid groups could "take away the people's resilience, their meaning, and impose the PTSD model which is new and medical for them." Too often, he added, many disaster mental-health programs have little understanding about local culture and have given little thought to how follow-up services would be maintained.[43]

In no way is this meant to be critical of compassionate counselors who go to trauma zones at their own expense, often eager and willing to help. All of us who travel cross-culturally hoping to give help need to work in collaboration with established relief organizations or community leaders to help people figure out what to do to get their lives back on track rather than coming in to give psychotherapy.

Preventing Harmful Responses to Trauma, Terror, and Terrorism

It can be difficult to prevent criminal violence, terrorist attacks, accidents, or similar traumatic events. In part, this is because some of these traumatic situations are not premeditated, some are planned and carried out in secrecy before they occur, most are unpredictable, and events such as disasters are unstoppable even if we see them coming. Governments, international organizations, professional societies, community action groups, and others can work to change conditions so that terrorism and trauma are less likely, but even a war on terrorism can do little to prevent the actions of people intent on doing harm in support of a cause.

Despite the difficulties, there are preventive actions that groups of people, including counselors, can take, in addition to the powerful impact of prayer. What follows are some, but certainly not all of the ways in which adverse trauma reactions can be prevented.

1. *Education*. College and community classes on the nature of terrorism and the impact of trauma can prepare people for action should subsequent traumatic events occur. Organizations like the Red Cross or counseling associations sometimes offer training to help people learn how to be useful in times of disaster or other crises. With the greater threat of terrorism attacks, a number of cities have staged mock disaster drills to help relief workers understand and practice the most effective strategies should evacuation or relief efforts be necessary. Ideally, every counselor or counseling student should have some understanding of effective trauma-management skills.

2. *Stress Inoculation and Stress Management*. These are specialized forms of education. Stress-inoculation training is intended to teach people how to cope by learning and practicing stress-management skills. This might involve helping people learn how to reduce anxiety, work within high-stress occupations, avoid burnout, cope with life transitions, or take precautions to avoid crimes of violence. On a less psychological level, it also can be useful to prepare evacuation plans, teach employees what to do if a company is destroyed and people are cut off from one another, or agree within families how to make contact in the event of an emergency that could separate family members. Surely, churches should have similar emergency plans and rapid-response teams to prepare for potential emergencies.

3. *Focus on Children*. Children tend to be resilient, but they too can be impacted by trauma and fear-inducing events in their environments. To prevent unhealthy coping, parents and teachers can be encouraged to give realistic reassurance, answer questions honestly, teach children about the source of terrorism and other dangers, increase their capabilities for avoiding potentially dangerous situations and people, limit television viewing—especially repeated news coverage of carnage following disasters and terrorist attacks—keep things as normal as possible, and model calmness.[44] Scared adults tend to create scared children, so parents

and others sometimes can help their children by taking care of their own anxieties.

4. *Focus on God.* In dangerous times it is natural for anybody to be anxious, but the God of all comfort can help human beings—even scared human beings—experience calm. This comes through association with other believers and supportive family members, but it also involves focusing on the nature of God, giving thanks even in the midst of trauma, and praying consistently[45] for peace and guidance in the face of danger, disaster, and trauma.

Conclusions About Trauma, Terror, and Terrorism

This chapter began with the story of Sampop and Ruchet, two boys from Thailand who watched as the tsunami washed over their community. A few weeks after tragedy, they joined forty-two other kids at a camp in the mountains of northern Thailand, where they met a Yugoslavian trauma therapist named Nila Kapor-Stanulovic. Nobody pressed the children to talk about their experiences, but they were asked to draw pictures and then describe them to the other campers. Most drew pictures of water swallowing up cars, trees, boats, houses, and people. As the week went by, the children played games, expressed themselves in a variety of verbal and nonverbal ways, and broke into groups that each wrote and performed a puppet show. By the end of the week, the children that had arrived with a hesitant and sometimes withdrawn demeanor were laughing, playing, and expressing lots of energy.

Will this week of trauma management bring permanent change? If other camps are an indication, the answer is yes. Terror, natural disasters, trauma, and other intense stress can be highly disruptive, but in time the resilient human body can recover and go on. The memories will never be forgotten, but slowly the victims of trauma will grow beyond their horrifying experiences and live productive lives. Wherever they live, Christian counselors can have a role in this kind of rewarding recovery process.

KEY POINTS FOR BUSY COUNSELORS

➤ Unlike past generations of counselors, we live and counsel in times that are being shaped by terrorism, terror, trauma, and the fear of uncertain danger.

➤ The Bible says little about these terms in the way we use them today, but within its pages we can find helpful words about fear, anxiety, peace, and hope.

➤ The causes of terrorism are complex. Often, people in countries that have little in the way of freedom or affluence perceive the gap between the Western nations and poor countries. Trapped in their frustrating conditions, many see no alternative except to express their frustration and perhaps try to bring some equity by attacking and destroying those who have more.

➤ Terrorism is intended to instill fear, and frequently it succeeds, even as it also destroys. Terrorism often is justified by extreme religious beliefs and by fanatical leaders, including religious leaders.

➤ Terrorism, terror, and trauma can bring a number of stress reactions, including acute stress disorder and post-traumatic stress disorder. In both cases, the first step toward treating these conditions is to meet with the counselee in a place of safety and trust.

➤ All terrorism, terror, and trauma, including accidents and disasters, bring stress, but resilience and natural recovery are far more common than the stress disorders.

➤ It is important to understand the basic neurobiological reactions to stress because they help us understand how the stress-impacted person reacts and can best be helped.

➤ The following counseling approaches are suggested:
  - Avoid the natural tendency to encourage debriefing.
  - Provide a place of safety where the counselee can meet with a person who is calm and can be trusted.
  - Give information and coping strategies.
  - Use cognitive behavioral techniques to help with stress control.
  - Use whole-brain techniques, especially telling stories and perhaps expressive (body) therapies.
  - Instill hope.
  - Stimulate community-based interventions, including methods for empowering communities.

- Recognize group differences. Some groups are more vulnerable than others.
- Be cautious of cross-cultural interventions.

➤ Methods for preventing unhealthy responses to terrorism and trauma consider education, teach stress inoculation and stress management, focus on helping children, and focus on the help that comes from God.

➤ Counselors can help people who live in fear of terrorism or need help to recover from the actions of terrorists, from trauma, and from other intense stresses.

40

Other Issues

Miriam Poser was ten years old when her family first discovered that she was anorexic. Struggling with low self-esteem, even at this early age, Miriam concluded that she was overweight, that the extra weight was responsible for all her problems, and that the solution was to slim down. Without telling anybody about her decision, Miriam decided to reduce the amount she ate.

When her parents noticed the weight loss and took her to the doctor, Miriam was diagnosed with anorexia nervosa and admitted to a hospital where she was required to eat until she reached her normal weight.

"I shed the pounds just as fast as I could after being released," Miriam wrote later. "Every therapy session failed because I wanted to lose weight at all costs, and I saw no reason for not losing weight. At one stage, I was so underweight that I became depressed and didn't have a reason for living." When Miriam tried to kill herself, she was readmitted to the hospital, but this time she was on a psychiatric ward, where she remained for six months.

Throughout all of this, the parents had not been told about anorexia nervosa. They knew nothing about how families could work together to help their daughters—and sometimes their sons—deal with the disorder. As Miriam received physical care and other treatments, however, the whole family came for counseling. Eventually, they joined a group with other families that had anorexic children.

"We learned how to deal with everyday problems in the family," Miriam wrote. "Meeting with other families with anorectic daughters meant a lot to me, because I could make new friends with people who had gone through the same thing, had similar problems, and thought, acted, and felt like I did. Multifamily therapy was a very important part of my road to health and where I am today."[1]

Before work began on the revised edition of this book, a questionnaire was sent to several hundred counselors asking for suggestions about topics to be included.

Depression, anxiety, guilt, and marriage problems were among those most often suggested, but there were other topics on those lists, including the struggles that people like Miriam have with eating disorders. This chapter deals with some of the less frequently encountered counseling issues that make their way into the counseling room. No one counselor can deal effectively with all these problems, but at times we have no alternative except to do the best we can with the skills and knowledge that we've got.

The counselor's work can be complicated when several problems are combined in one person. The man or woman who struggles with marriage difficulties also may be depressed, anxious, and struggling to make ends meet financially. The couple who comes for help in handling a rebellious child may feel trapped between generations, worried both about the child and about elderly parents with a host of problems of their own. The man who seeks help with vocational decisions also may struggle with interpersonal conflicts, discouragement, low self-esteem, and an emerging drinking problem.

Sometimes, the presenting problems are influenced by unique circumstances. Even if you have no prejudice, you may need extra understanding to counsel with people who are not of your race, ethnic background, sexual orientation, or socioeconomic level. What if their values or religious beliefs differ from yours? In your heart, you may want to treat all people equally, but your work cannot ignore the unique challenges that come in working with people who are physically disabled, mentally handicapped, unable to speak your language freely, or tied to a relative who needs constant care. Counseling in a private practice is likely to differ from counseling that occurs in a church, a prison, a military community, or a psychiatric hospital. In all these situations, the basic counseling principles may be the same, but they need to be adapted to each individual and to each unique setting.

To make these adaptations, counselors need to be flexible. It also helps to be aware of less common issues, such as those that will be presented in the following pages. These are not listed in any special order of importance, but each may be encountered at some time in your counseling work.

Counseling People with Physical Disabilities

How would you counsel with someone who has impaired hearing? Communication could be difficult, especially if the counselee uses sign language and you do not. The presence of an interpreter could help, but this interferes with confidentiality and may inhibit the counselee from sharing concerns that are intimate or embarrassing. Lip reading and visual communication may be more important than in other types of counseling, but could this hinder your counseling style or maybe invalidate some of your assessment procedures? People who are hearing-impaired often have problems with depression, loneliness, relationships, or self-concepts, and these are difficult to discuss if communication is blocked by faulty hearing.[2] Some people encounter prejudice or misunderstanding, even from sensitive counselors. When hearing is impaired, it is easy to wonder what others are saying and sometimes reach unfounded conclusions that an insensitive counselor might label paranoid.[3]

Hearing impairment is one example of a *disability*. The word refers to any mental, physical, or emotional condition (defect or impairment) that can hinder a person's ability to function normally. The disabilities may range from minor impairments that may not be noticed by others to limitations that are severely inhibiting. Disabilities can be temporary (such as the loss of mobility following surgery) or permanent. They result from congenital impairment, injury at birth or during childhood, or from the loss of some capacity later in life. There is increasing evidence that environmental toxicants lead to a variety of developmental, physical, cognitive, learning, and behavioral disabilities. These toxic substances include lead poisoning, pesticides, pollutants in the air, and the use of drugs or alcohol.[4]

For many years disability was viewed as an all-or-nothing condition: either the person had a disability or did not. The emphasis was on deficits and what the person could not do. Today, within the culture and many professions, it is more common to recognize that although there are things that a disabled person *cannot* do, there are many that he or she *can* do. There is a move away from the old view of people with disabilities as an incapacitated subsection of the population that has defects and a need for special treatment. Instead, it is more realistic to see disabled people as a minority like African Americans, Muslims, or immigrants, most of whom are part of their communities, living independent lives, attending classes, holding jobs and building careers, paying their taxes like everybody else, and having active social and family lives. This puts a greater emphasis on the strengths of people with disabilities rather than a focus on their limitations.[5] Medical treatment is designed to assist the disabled person as much as possible in the physical area, and the rehabilitation task is to help the individual live with the disability and reach maximum effectiveness.[6]

1. *Helping Families.* It can be very difficult for parents to learn that their child has a disability. Parental guilt, rejection of the disabled person, overprotection, criticism of physicians or schools, impatience with other family members, unrealistic expectations, feelings of embarrassment, and anger with God are all common. Many families with a disabled child show increased levels of anxiety and depression, lowered self-concepts and self-esteem, feelings of frustration, and decreased marital and personal satisfaction.[7]

These families need understanding, support, and sometimes practical assistance (such as help with child care or household chores) as they cope with their unique stresses. They need help in learning to live fulfilling lives with a disabled person present. This is extremely important because families that feel out of control and engulfed by the needs of the disabled person are families that experience the greatest difficulty adjusting and living meaningful lives. In contrast, when parents can be optimistic, focused on family togetherness and cooperation, there is lower overall stress.[8] The presence of a disabled sibling can limit the freedom of brothers and sisters who can become "disabled by association" if they feel restricted and unable to thrive normally.[9] Counselors can help all family members learn to cope. Part of the help may come from putting the family in contact with other families of disabled children or adults. Mutual-aid groups and Internet connections also give support, encouragement, and practical guidance as families cope together.

Sometimes, the parent is the family member who has the disability. Disabled parents often face interference from others and discouragement because of their limitations and lack of outside support. Counselors often can give the encouragement and guidance to help these people be effective parents.[10]

2. *Helping People with Disabilities.* Children who are born with disabilities learn to accept these as they adjust to life. If the disability comes later, the adjustment tends to be much more difficult. "I've lost the ability to walk," said one man whose injury in a car accident had left him paralyzed from the waist down. "I can't control my bowels or bladder. I can't have sex like I did before. I can't ride my motorcycle or play football. I've lost a lot of my freedom." Whenever there is a loss of mobility, sight, a limb, or control over some part of the body, a grief reaction often follows. There can be shock, denial, anger, sometimes unrealistic hope, and often depression. People wonder why this happened to them, and sometimes they expect that God will bring a miraculous healing. If this does not occur, there can be despair, thoughts of suicide, sadness about being a burden to others, and a sense of hopelessness about the future.

How does one escape from this emotional trap? The process will take time, but often it comes as the disabled person is helped to express feelings and to consider possibilities for living as fulfilling a life as possible. Sometimes, this involves learning to live with physical limitations, overcoming transportation barriers, building a positive self-concept, finding a suitable vocation, learning to cope with society's stereotypes, and developing a willingness to accept help with those things that no longer can be done without assistance.[11]

In helping people function despite their limitations, the counselor will not always work in the traditional one-to-one relationship. Helping often involves aligning with physical therapists, educators, physicians, and other specialists. The counselor's work may involve cooperation with the counselee's friends or work colleagues, and sometimes counseling involves the whole family.

It also may involve looking at your own attitudes. If you jump to invalid conclusions about the physically disabled, are uncomfortable in working with counselees who have disabilities, or have biases about their supposed characteristics or attitudes, then you are not likely to be effective in counseling. Regardless of your attitudes, if you are willing to learn from your counselees with disabilities, your whole counseling work is likely to be enriched. We also can learn from other counselors who are disabled. Their numbers are small, and some have disabilities that could impact their counseling work adversely, but there is no reason why many people with disabilities should not enter the counseling field and make a contribution like other counselors.[12]

Jesus was very much concerned about disabled people—the lame, blind, deaf, epileptic, and deformed. He accepted them completely and met their needs. The Christian counselor must do likewise. Counseling may require creative approaches, forsaking some favorite techniques and working within a network of other helpers. This can be rewarding work, especially if one sees the disabled person growing in skills, psychological stability, and spiritual maturity.

Counseling People with Intellectual Disabilities

Jean Vanier was born in Canada, the son of former Canadian Governor General Georges Vanier. After moving overseas, the younger man was shocked to discover that in the small European town where he lived, mentally retarded people were institutionalized along with people who had mental disorders.[13] One day, Vanier invited two of the mentally disabled men to come and live with him. There was no intention of doing anything beyond this, but others heard of Jean Vanier's actions, came to see what he was doing, and left to start homes elsewhere. The result has been the worldwide expansion of L'Arche (a French word that means the ark). These are residential group homes for mentally disabled people who learn to live together and care for one another, often with the help of local professionals, including counselors. The growth of the movement may have been helped when the well-known counselor-priest Henri Nouwen left an active and productive teaching career at Harvard and moved to live in the L'Arche community in Toronto.[14]

In an earlier chapter[15] we noted that mental disabilities most often become evident before age eighteen, persist indefinitely, and seriously hinder both the ability to learn and the capacity to live independently or to function in a way that is appropriate for one's age. Sometimes, the cause is genetic, but mental disabilities also may result from brain damage or childhood disease. Probably, the best known form of mental disability is Down Syndrome, often recognizable by the facial features of the people affected. The extent of one's mental limitations and the ability to function independently differ significantly from person to person, but many organizations are devoted to helping these people and their families live fulfilling lives, despite their disabilities.[16] While mental disabilities most often appear to have a physical basis, some physically normal children grow up with limitations because they have not had sufficient sensory or intellectual stimulation.[17]

Mental disabilities in childhood differ from disabilities that may develop later in life. Chemically induced disorders, diseases such as brain cancer or Alzheimer's, brain tumors or head injuries, arteriosclerosis, strokes, AIDS, excessive drinking, use of certain drugs, cardiovascular disorders, and even faulty nutrition can all interfere with clear thinking. Many of these mental disorders and limitations are permanent, but some are reversible.

Depending on the degree of impairment, mentally disabled people often can be taught at least some self-management skills. Many are able to find simple but satisfying careers and can live with a measure of independence, sometimes within communities like those of L'Arche. These people profit from counseling if they can avoid overdependency and are able to comprehend what the counselor is saying. Medications often help, and in some cases medical treatment can greatly reduce the mental disability.

Parents, spouses, and other family members respond to mental disabilities in many of the same ways they respond to physical limitations. Often, there is guilt, anger, depression, embarrassment, financial strain, and difficulties in coping. Most often the family must learn to live with the mentally disabled person, making adjustments and learning to accept care-giving responsibilities just as they would with aging or chronically ill relatives. These family care-givers often need support and practical guidance to help them cope.

Counseling People with Eating Disorders

Peter Paul Reubens was a Flemish painter who lived in the early seventeenth century and, like his contemporaries, painted beautiful women who were consistently plump. Apparently, these women were not worried about keeping slim or shedding pounds. How different we are in the twenty-first century, at least in parts of the West and especially among Americans who have been called the fattest people in the world.[18] We might also be the most diet conscious, with millions on diets, thinking about going on diets, or concerned because they are putting weight back on following a diet. Probably hundreds of diet programs, including some that have a Christian basis, are embraced enthusiastically, tried with varying degrees of faithfulness, and most often found to be useless in reducing weight long term.[19] According to one writer, "If 'cure' from obesity is defined as reduction to ideal weight and maintenance of that weight for five years, a person is more likely to recover from most forms of cancer than from obesity."[20]

Eating disorders have a variety of causes.[21] These include the availability of inexpensive and good-tasting food served in large portions; unhealthy eating habits, such as snacking on low-cost calorie-laden foots and soft drinks; sedentary lifestyles that involve as little exercise as possible and hours seated in front of computer or television screens; or more frequent eating in restaurants where the portions tend to be larger than at home and the food less nutritious.[22] There is increasing evidence that many eating disorders, including obesity, begin in childhood, often with the food industry's promotion of unhealthy fast foods and the willing compliance of parents.[23] In addition, high levels of stress lead not only to increased eating but to eating of high-carbohydrate and high-fat foods that have been shown to reduce the brain's chronic stress response system.[24] Clearly, eating disorders have psychological, environmental, relational, spiritual, and physical implications. The rates differ from country to country,[25] but in the United States alone, the government estimates that about 65 percent of the population is obese or overweight.[26] We would be good models for a Peter Paul Reubens painting, but large numbers of people are more concerned about shedding pounds and losing weight. People with anorexic or bulimic disorders have an unhealthy concern about their weight and weight loss.

In counseling people with eating issues, it is important that counselors work in partnership with medical professionals because of the physical implications of eating disorders. Nonmedical counselors are not qualified to treat people physically, and our counseling is likely to be more effective when we have at least a minimal understanding of the physiological aspects of the three most often encountered eating disorders: obesity, anorexia nervosa, and bulimia.

1. *Obesity.* There are formulae to determine if a person is overweight or obese, but one physician has suggested that the best test is the "the eyeball test."[27] If a person looks fat, the person is fat.

For many people there are significant psychological implications to being overweight. The culture tends to joke about overweight people, shuns them, and sometimes shows prejudice against them. This, along with the obese person's own perceptions, can lead to discouragement, negative views of one's body or one's work, and self-criticism.[28] Discrimination may be hardest on overweight children and adolescents. When compared with other children, these overweight youngsters have fewer friends, have lower self-concepts, get more teasing, experience more bias from others, feel more dissatisfied about their bodies, and are more likely to consider suicide.[29]

(a) Causes of Obesity. Extra weight comes from eating more calories than are burned up for energy. We already have identified some of the diverse reasons for this, but most can be grouped into physical causes and psychological-social causes.

Physiological causes have two types. External influences are issues over which eaters have control, including what they eat, how much they eat, and how much exercise they get. In contrast, the internal influences are largely beyond one's control and include genetic variables, fat cell size, or various biological conditions that lead to overweight.

Psychological causes center around habits and other learned behavior. Gregarious people who like to eat and drink when they get together tend to add weight. Some cultures or ethnic groups encourage this more than others. Perhaps most of us recognize the role of stress on weight loss or gain. Sometimes, stress leads to a declining of appetite, but at other times people eat more when they are under stress, feeling sorry for themselves, angry, anxious, guilty, depressed, or bored. During withdrawal from smoking, people tend to crave and eat more carbohydrates, and many have developed habits of eating whenever they watch television. Children who are told to clean their plates can develop life-long habits of eating everything in front of them whether or not they feel hungry. Add to this the tendency for children to eat unhealthy foods, often in response to advertising appeals on television, and we begin to see reasons for the current growth of child-hood obesity, which can lead to a number of health problems. There even is evidence that the cities where we live play a role in obesity. If you live in a place where you can walk to stores and other places, you probably weigh less than people in high-sprawl areas where it is more common to travel by car or public transportation.[30] All of this suggests that overeating can result from a variety of learned and emotional influences.

(b) Counseling Overweight and Obese People. The basics of weight loss are simple: reduce the intake of calories below what the body uses. To reach this goal, hundreds of diets have been developed. They appear in books, pamphlets, magazines, and weight-loss centers that give inspiration, encouragement, behavior modification, and sometimes pre-prepared meals and dietary supplements. Hospitals, counselors, and other professionals are all involved in helping people lose weight.

These weight-control programs often succeed temporarily, but when the lost weight comes back, as it usually does, losing again gets harder. This is not very encouraging, but many would agree with the physician who called obesity "a chronic condition, resistant to treatment, and prone to relapse."

In part, fighting obesity is difficult because the body resists weight loss and fights diets. If the caloric intake is too restrictive, the body (a) lowers metabolism so that fewer calories are needed to maintain weight, (b) becomes more inactive in an effort to maintain body weight, (c) develops weight-loss plateaus, and (d) causes the person to think more about food so consumption is harder to resist whenever food is available.[31] The condition is not hopeless, however. Continuing research is showing the effectiveness of efforts to control obesity.[32] Effective weight loss is likely to be more successful when:

- Counselees learn principles of sound nutrition and are helped to put these into practice. Too often diets are viewed as something temporary that will help with weight loss and can be abandoned as soon as the desired weight is reached. Some counselors would suggest that the word *diet* never should be used because of the implications that better eating is a temporary measure. Sound nutrition must be a lifetime activity if weight loss is to remain permanent. The best time to begin the education is in the home, with children.
- People are helped to understand the physiological and psychological aspects of weight loss, since understanding leads to better compliance with nutrition programs and helps reduce depression and guilt.
- A regular program of exercise is begun and maintained.
- There is a program of encouragement and support, including prayer support or group counseling that can reward the counselee as weight loss goals are met, can help group members deal with setbacks, and can offer encouragement to keep moving forward.
- There is a program of reinforcement to reward the counselee as weight-loss goals are met.
- Counselees are taught self-monitoring—carefully watching and recording

calorie and fat intake, exercise programs, and target goals. Several studies have found that about a quarter of weight-control success is attributable to consistent self-monitoring.[33]

- Psychological issues that may contribute to excess eating, including stress and lifestyle issues, are changed, often through counseling.

- In some cases, and with the involvement of qualified medical personnel, the overweight person is treated with appetite-suppressant medication or with surgery. This is successful in about four-fifths of the patients, especially when combined with changes in diet, stress management, and exercise.[34]

Most weight-loss programs are self-imposed and self-terminated. Success is likely to be better if the weight loss is supervised by a physician, nutritionist, or competent weight-loss specialist. This is true especially when there are likely to be medical complications, if the counselee is not in good health, or if one must lose a lot of weight.

2. *Anorexia Nervosa and Bulimia.* Technically, these two conditions are different, but there are so many similarities that they will be discussed together. Anorexia, the morbid fear of gaining weight and becoming fat, has been known for many years, but the disorder did not leap into prominence until the 1980s. Appearing most often in adolescent females, the anorexic person often concludes that she is overweight, so she goes on a diet and may exercise excessively in order to burn calories. As a result, there can be dangerous weight loss, sometimes hastened by induced vomiting and abuse of laxatives. Other characteristics include hyperactivity, an inaccurate perception of one's own body as being fat despite considerable evidence to the contrary, and physical illness, including menstrual irregularities, eventual chemical deficiencies, weakening of the heart, and sometimes death.

Closely related to anorexia, bulimia also involves an intense focus on food and a strong fear of getting fat. Instead of dieting, however, there are recurring episodes of rapidly eating (gorging or binging may be more accurate words) large quantities of food, followed either by self-induced vomiting and misuse of laxatives or diuretics (this is the purging type of bulimia) or getting rid of the food through fasting, excessive exercise, or other means that are less likely to involve self-induced vomiting (this is the nonpurging type). In both types of bulimia, there can be fluctuating weight and serious health problems as a result.[35]

(a) Characteristics and Causes of Anorexia Nervosa and Bulimia. Dr. Raymond E. Vath is a Christian psychiatrist and leading expert on eating disorders. In a book published several years ago, he concluded that in greater or lesser degrees, all of his patients show eight common characteristics.[36] These traits, which are summarized in Table 40–1, give a description of what these patients are like, but the list also sheds light on the causes of anorexia nervosa and bulimia.

Many of these young people come from communities and especially from homes where standards are high, attractiveness (including a slim figure) is greatly valued, overweight people are viewed negatively, weight is assumed to be under voluntary control, dieting is praised, achievement is prized, the parents often are successful, and there is expectation that the children will be successful as well. Perhaps it is not surprising that eating disorders are more common among professions that emphasize trimness (dancers, figure skaters, models, gymnasts, or actresses, for example) and in places, such as college dorms, where there is com-

Table 40–1

Anorexia Nervosa and Bulimia Common Characteristics*

- *Perfectionism* involves unreasonable standards of perfectionism for oneself, often arising from family expectations or from involvement with careers that demand high standards for performance or body proportions.

- *Low Self-Esteem* often comes because the individual cannot meet the excessive standards and, as a result, feels like a failure, worthless, and unlovable.

- *Sexual Identity Confusion* involves uncertainty concerning what it means to be a mature woman (or man). Often these people have poor sexual adjustment, and sometimes there is a history of promiscuity.

- *Depression* results when people cannot reach their high ideals. The inability to achieve the body build of an aerobics instructor can leave some people feeling defeated, ashamed, and depressed. This is especially true if eating disorders have led to depression in family members.

- *Deception* is a way to hide one's failures and devious eating patterns. This includes eating in private, sometimes stealing food or laxatives, or induced vomiting that is kept secret and often denied.

- *Power struggles* come when the family discovers the illness and tries to force changes in eating patterns. This could involve use of threats, criticisms, or punishment. This, in turn, is met with resistance and further deception.

- *Interdependency* involves both the family and the person with the eating disorder. Parents, for example, may have high standards for their children and sometimes resist the normal process of separation. As a result, the children remain exceptionally dependent on the parents for affirmation and feelings of self-acceptance.

- *Physiological problems* result from the eating disorders but also can be a part of the cause. Women are genetically programmed to have a higher proportion of body fat than men. Different metabolic rates influence the efficiency with which calories are burned. These physical facts can create problems for people who live in a culture that greatly values thinness.

*Adapted from Raymond E. Vath *Counseling Those with Eating Disorders* (Waco, TX: Word, 1986).

petition and emphasis on dating. Many people who become anorexic or bulimic exert unusual effort to reach the high standards that they have seen in their families and set for themselves.

Many women, not only those with anorexia or bulimia, may be confused about the relative importance of professional success and personal beauty. The messages that come from parents, teachers, and the media are confusing: work hard at school but be sure to be popular and pretty; be a professional but show that you are feminine; be assertive and show confidence but don't appear too strong. Fascination with physical fitness and the desire to look trim and healthy can focus attention on one's body and create confusion about how this relates to purpose in life. While this appears to apply mostly to women, similar sex-role confusion also occurs in men, along with an increasing emphasis on physical fitness and appearance. Might this lead to an increase in eating disorders among males?

(b) Counseling People with Anorexia Nervosa and Bulimia. Eating disorders are complex conditions that often resist treatment and rarely respond to the interventions of inexperienced counselors, even when their intentions are good. Most writers suggest a multi-method approach that may include some or all of the following.

Medical Treatment. Eating disorders can do serious harm to the body, and eventually the physical changes can be life threatening. It is crucial, therefore, that there be competent medical intervention at the core of the treatment. Many people with eating disorders do not see or accept the physical seriousness of the illness. Some will resist treatment or refuse to cooperate with physicians. It can help if these patients are enabled to understand the physical implications of their disorders and be convinced that treatment will remove bothersome symptoms, such as insomnia, fatigue, depression, and problems with self-concept.

Counseling and Behavior Change. The counselee needs to get control of the unhealthy eating behaviors, including the binge-purge cycles. Start by encouraging the counselee to keep a record of eating and binging behavior. Include information concerning what and how much is eaten. Where did the eating take place, when, and what emotions were experienced at the time?

Based on this foundation data, the counselee and counselor together can work out rules for behavior control. These might include eating only at planned mealtimes, eating in the same location, and agreeing on the quantities that will be eaten. Sometimes, counselees are encouraged to spend some time in prayer or relaxation before eating, since this can reduce anxious, tension-filled eating. It helps, as well, if counselees agree to resist all-or-nothing thinking—that is the idea that "since I blew it by eating this one chocolate, I might as well go ahead, finish the whole box, and start the diet over tomorrow."

These methods are designed to help the counselee control eating. They all assume that the counselee wants to change, but this may not always be a valid assumption. Sometimes, people are caught in the belief that to be slim is to be better, more admired, and accepted. When eating disorders stem from unhealthy attitudes or beliefs like this, the counseling must focus on education and attitude change. Counselees may need to consider their beliefs that thin is beautiful, that physical attractiveness is all important, or that perfectionism is desirable and attainable. Others may want to change, but ongoing stresses, pressures, or habits lead to a loss of control over eating. When these stresses can be identified, counseling can help people learn to cope with tensions and resist circumstances, people, or situations that might trigger unhealthy eating. Often counselees will need help with problems of sexual identity, parental relationships (including overdependency), depression, feelings of failure, or low self-esteem. Disordered eating is not likely to change until there is a removal of the personal problems and conflicts that lead to the disorder.[37]

Family and Group Counseling. Since eating disorders often begin with family attitudes and interactions, it is logical to involve the whole family in the treatment. Most families are not familiar with anorexia or other eating disorders, and without intending any harm, family members often make matters worse. Counseling and other forms of treatment tend to be more effective, and relapse is less likely when the whole family is involved in learning about the illness and making changes within the family.[38]

In addition to family counseling, some counselors advocate a group approach, in which people with eating disorders, and sometimes their families, can work on issues of self-esteem, interpersonal relations, unhealthy attitudes toward weight or eating, or other shared issues. This appears to have been helpful to Miriam, whose story began this chapter.

Spiritual Counseling. It would be simplistic to assume that people with eating disorders will be able to change their behavior and resume normal healthy eating patterns solely in response to the hearing of a Bible verse, a challenge from a spiritual leader, or the reading of a self-help book. Insensitive confrontations rarely change behavior, especially behavior that is longstanding. It can help, however, to show compassion and support for people with eating disorders and their families, to give encouragement as efforts are made to change, and to help people reevaluate their assumptions about thinness and success. Often, counselees need to learn biblically consistent ways to deal with parent-child relationships, sexuality, self-esteem, responsibility, worry, guilt, and similar issues. Christian psychiatrist Raymond Vath points out that treatment may involve dealing with a counselee's unhealthy attitudes toward perfectionism, self-esteem, or sexual identity. Sometimes, the counselee is dealing with depression, power struggles with parents or others, and dependency issues.[39] All of these reflect problems at a deeper level, where a part of the cause and resolution of the problem is spiritual.

Counseling People with AIDS

AIDS was called a rare condition when the first cases were discovered in 1979, but it quickly came to be regarded as an epidemic, a worldwide crisis, and "one of the most challenging social issues of our time."[40] AIDS—Acquired Immunodeficiency Syndrome—is an infectious disease that is caused by a virus (known as HIV or Human Immunodeficiency Virus) that impacts a person's immune system, leaving it with a reduced ability to fight other diseases and infections. When the immune system is damaged, the person with AIDS (sometimes abbreviated PWA) is unable to resist infections that people with healthy immune systems usually will be able to fight.[41]

HIV is transmitted when blood, semen, vaginal fluid, or sometimes breast milk is exchanged between a person who is HIV-infected and a person who is not. Most often the virus is transmitted in three ways: sexual contact (penis-vagina, penis-rectum, mouth-rectum, mouth-penis, and mouth-vagina), use of unsterilized needles or syringes that are contaminated with blood that contains the virus (most often this involves needle sharing by users of illicit drugs, but occasionally a medical person is accidentally pricked by a dirty needle), or through heredity (a mother with the AIDS virus in her bloodstream can pass this to her unborn child). The disease also can be transmitted by blood transfusions, but this rarely happens, at least in advanced societies, because collected blood is always HIV tested.

The disease is unpredictable and differs from person to person. Some show no symptoms when the virus is first acquired, while others show flulike symptoms that disappear quickly. An average of ten years then passes before more obvious symptoms begin to appear in the form of frequent infections, fever, muscle aches and pains, pneumonia, rare forms of cancer, and other diseases. The person with AIDS does not have an immune system that can protect the body against these diseases, and it is one of these illnesses, more than AIDS itself, which leads to death.[42]

Of course, individuals who remain abstinent or couples who maintain mutually faithful monogamous relationships (in which they have sexual intercourse only with each other) will not receive the AIDS-producing virus through sexual transmission. There is much less protection for people who use condoms and sterile needles but who continue to have sexual experiences with a variety of partners or who use illegal intravenous drugs. Many people fail to take precautions even when they have accurate information or devices such as condoms that offer some protection. Swayed by their sexual passions or the throes of an addiction, few people stop to think about preventing the spread of disease. As a result, the virus keeps being transmitted, and the AIDS epidemic continues to take hundreds of thousands of lives, especially in Africa, Asia, and Latin America.[43] The good news is that research is progressing to discover the sources of the HIV, the course of AIDS, ways in which the disease can be detected earlier, and effective treatment procedures that can be developed and used. In addition, preventive programs are more prevalent, alerting people to the dangers of AIDS and the importance of avoiding sexual experiences that can lead to HIV infection.[44]

1. *The Psychological-Spiritual Implications of HIV/AIDS.* It is not surprising that people are distressed when they learn that their bodies have contracted HIV. Since this is an incurable, ultimately fatal disease, there often is anxiety accompanied by depression, anger, confusion, and intense feelings of hopelessness and helplessness. Fears are intensified by media reports or contacts with friends who have died or are dying from AIDS-related illnesses. Thoughts of suicide are common, especially in the early stages of the disease; the suicide rate is higher among AIDS victims than among a comparable group of people who are not infected. These psychological reactions to the disease change as the disease progresses. When the symptoms become more apparent and the body clearly is having difficulty fighting infections and other illnesses, the AIDS patient senses the approach of death with all the fears, denial, and struggles that accompany the later stages of terminal illness.

Throughout all of this, and unlike other seriously ill individuals, people with AIDS have additional psychological stresses. Often there is guilt over past sexual behavior, promiscuity, or drug use. It hurts to watch one's parents, other relatives, or friends suffer emotionally, both because of the illness and because they now know about the patient's past lifestyle and sexual behavior. Because of widespread fear and misinformation about the disease, people with AIDS often are avoided or rejected by others, including medical personnel, church members, and counselors. Sadly, the Christian community has not always responded with sensitivity and compassion to people infected with HIV/AIDS.

At times, all of us ignore God's guidelines for living, and sometimes the consequences are devastating. The vast majority of people with HIV/AIDS have ignored God's principles for sexuality and are experiencing the self-induced harm that often follows. AIDS is the natural result of sexual activities that the Bible would describe as sinful, but regardless of our actions, when we confess our sins, he forgives and cleanses us from all wrong.[45] Sadly, some Christians have declared that the AIDS epidemic is evidence of judgment from God and in so doing have cut themselves off from ministering to AIDS patients and their friends. Attitudes of care, compassion, understanding, support, and love must extend to the AIDS patients and to their families, many of whom also suffer embarrassment, rejection, ostracism, and great emotional pain. If Jesus walked our streets today, it seems unlikely that he would condemn people with AIDS and turn away from their suffering.

2. *Counseling Implications.* Dr. Gregg Albers is a sensitive and caring Christian physician who has produced a helpful book about counseling people with AIDS.[46] Writing from the perspective of a medical practitioner who has met with many AIDS patients both in the United States and overseas, Albers notes that counseling will depend, in part, on the changing stages of the illness. People who want to be tested to determine if they have contracted an HIV infection often bring fear, guilt, worry, and depression into the counseling room. If the test is negative and no indication of HIV is detected, there can be talk of past sexual behavior and how life can be different in the future. If the test indicates that a counselee does have the virus that leads to AIDS, there can be counseling about who to tell and how to live a fulfilling life, especially when the disease is not exerting great influence during the early years. Different topics will occupy the counselor and counselee as the influence of the disease becomes more apparent and the body is less able to resist other illnesses.

Whatever the stage of the disease, AIDS counselors have identified several therapeutic issues that commonly surface in counseling the PWA.[47] First, there are the feelings that we have mentioned: anxiety, anger, fear, denial, and hopelessness. It is extremely difficult for a young person to face death and to accept the realities of the illness.

Second, often there is a sense of isolation and alienation. The PWA needs social support but tends instead to withdraw. The physical isolation required by medical treatment sometimes intensifies this sense of being alone, and many counselees feel that their families, friends, and neighbors do not want to have any contact. Withdrawal leads to loneliness, more depression, and sometimes even to more withdrawal.

Third, there can be a drop in self-esteem, especially if the PWA feels guilt concerning the sexual behavior or illicit drug use that may have led to the disease.

Fourth, some people jump to conclusions that are based more on rumor and misinformation than on fact. The news that one has been infected by the AIDS virus can lead some people to conclude that life is now over, that there never can be fulfillment or meaning in life, that God never will forgive, that the PWA will be rejected by everyone, or that it never again will be possible to live independently.

For some, of course, there will be immediate and severe limitations, but for many people these conclusions simply are not true.

Fifth, there is the issue of the family. It is not easy for a PWA to tell the family, relate to parents, and deal with the flood of emotions that often come to family members when they learn about the HIV or AIDS diagnosis.

How do we help these counselees? A starting place is to look at one's own attitudes toward AIDS. From a distance we can pray for people with AIDS and know how to counsel them if they come to our offices, but most won't come to us; we have to go to them. This may mean working in communities where we might feel uncomfortable, with people whose values differ from ours, coming alongside other community agencies that might not share our theology, working sometimes as volunteers rather than as counselors. This is work that can be emotionally draining and very stressful. In dealing with people who have AIDS, whether they are in your community, church, or classrooms, the counselor is likely to be ineffective if he or she is afraid of HIV/AIDS. Effectiveness also will be limited if a counselor is unwilling to be face-to-face with pain or death, uninformed about AIDS, uncomfortable about discussing sexual matters, including homosexuality and sexual deviations, judgmental and nonforgiving, or afraid to get emotionally involved with a PWA and his or her family.

For the counselor who does get involved, several counseling goals might be kept in mind.

- Encourage the PWA and the family members to express and openly discuss their fears and other emotions.
- Be aware of misperceptions and make every effort to give accurate information or to show the counselee how to get this information.
- Help the PWA focus on the future. This may involve discussions about dying and death, divine forgiveness, salvation, saying good-bye, and other aspects of grief work. For many, especially those who are in the earlier stages of the disease, planning for the future involves finding as satisfying and fulfilling a vocation and lifestyle as possible before the disease takes control.
- Encourage involvement with other people. Social contact reduces the sense of isolation and alienation that people with AIDS often feel. Many counselors encourage group counseling for people with AIDS. Groups can be safe havens where there can be support, mutual understanding, and sharing of both feelings and effective coping strategies.
- Keep informed of the counselee's medical status. The counselor helps most when he or she works in close cooperation with medical personnel. Remember that each person is unique; each has a repertoire of coping skills and responds to medical and other crises in unique ways.
- Remind the counselee about prevention. Try to help them find sexual fulfillment in a way that is consistent with good health practices and biblical morality.
- Help counselees deal with prejudice and misinformation about AIDS, some of which comes from church people.
- Make consistent use of your spiritual resources. This includes prayer, reading the Scriptures, sharing the good news of God's forgiveness and salvation, coming alongside the counselee in his or her development of spiritual

disciplines, and pointing to helpful literature. All of these can reduce anxiety, instill hope, and help the counselee cope.

If you work with HIV/AIDS patients, find a friend with whom you can talk over your feelings, frustrations, and disappointments. It can be frustrating and deeply draining to work with people who are facing death and dying. As you grow more attached to your counselees, you want to see them improve, but it is important to go through your own grief as the disease takes its toll. Remember, you are there to watch, to support, and to care. God can help us handle emotional pressures like this. The help comes in response to prayer and time alone, but it also comes through other counselors or friends who can give support, understanding, and guidance.

Counseling People in Special Groups

Wherever you are in your counseling career, ten or fifteen years from now you may be surprised to discover that you have become a specialist, working with a unique group of people that you know very little about today. I know one very compassionate and competent Christian counselor who is a leading expert in working with battered and abused women. My friend did not start out to work with this group, but as she worked successfully with a few, her reputation spread and others came to seek her assistance. In an earlier chapter we mentioned counselor/author Mary Pipher, who looked around her Midwestern community and discovered a number of refugees from other countries, struggling to adjust to their new surroundings. Dr. Piper became an expert in working with these people and wrote a moving book about her experiences.[48] Other counselors have become specialists in working with burned-out pastors and their spouses, missionaries who are under stress, retired people, gay or lesbian counselees, cancer survivors, leaders of companies or organizations, people with AIDS, Hollywood movie stars,[49] or members of minority groups, to name a few.

Some counselors make a deliberate decision to focus their training and counseling on a specific group, but for other counselors—perhaps the majority—the specializations emerge as a surprise. Each of us might ask ourselves questions like these: What kinds of counselees come to me most often? What kinds of people do I seem best able to help? What groups do I most enjoy working with? Might God be leading me to work with a special group of people? For some of us, perhaps pastors especially, the needs are likely to be diverse. For others, specialties may or may not emerge.

The next few paragraphs discuss several of these specialty groups. The people in these groups can experience any of the problems discussed in earlier chapters, but each of these groups is characterized by unique needs that have a bearing on how you counsel.

1. *Counseling Women with Premenstrual Syndrome.* Insensitive people (usually males) may joke about it, and some physicians continue to dismiss it as being mostly psychological, but there is solid evidence that premenstrual syndrome (usually abbreviated PMS) is a real, biologically based condition that brings monthly misery to millions of women. Estimates about its prevalence tend to vary. Probably, the majority of women between the ages of fourteen and fifty don't have PMS at all, and others have mild symptoms that are minimally disrup-

tive. However, for an estimated 30 percent of women between twenty-five and thirty-five the days prior to menstruation can be severely debilitating and miserable both physically and emotionally.[50] The wide range of symptoms may include any combination of mood swings, headaches, sinus problems, anxiety, dizziness, crying spells, forgetfulness, irritability, clumsiness, feelings of worthlessness or incompetence, craving for certain foods, abdominal bloating and cramping, panic, depression, poor judgment, and difficulties in coping. Some women get short-tempered and impatient; others have difficulty focusing on their work. A woman's PMS can lead males to be impatient, frustrated, and confused, but telling one's wife to snap out of it doesn't help. Instead, this is likely to create more tension and make matters worse.

PMS is an organically based disorder that lasts from two to fourteen days prior to the menstrual period and usually disappears once the period begins. Despite its prevalence, there is no accepted diagnostic test, specific cause, or treatment. There is evidence of a genetic component to the disorder, and it appears to be more common in women who have a history of depression, are anxious or under stress, or have limited control over the events of their lives.[51] Most women with PMS handle it on their own with over-the-counter medications. Even though it is a medical condition, apparently few women seek the help of a physician, and probably fewer go to a counselor unless the symptoms are especially disruptive and extend to the woman's relationships and ability to function psychologically during the PMS period.

The counselor can encourage women to communicate about their symptoms and feelings. By listening to their wives, many husbands get a better understanding of PMS and its effects. PMS can be viewed as an organically based recurring condition that is able to make life miserable for both the sufferer and her family. This is one of many physical conditions that can have an important influence on the other issues that people may bring to counseling.

2. *Counseling Prisoners and Their Families.* As a teenager, Marcus Baird never would have predicted that he would spend his adult life as a prison chaplain in Chicago. He grew up in a southern state and learned about prisons as a young prison inmate. When he was released, Marcus may have known that the majority of former prisoners soon get back with their old friends, don't have the skills to function without engaging in illegal activities, drift once more into crime, and soon find themselves behind bars again. Instead, Marcus got help, went to college, and now serves as a friend, spiritual mentor, teacher, and counselor who has a significant ministry among young inmates who would like to get free of lifestyles that prevent them from functioning on the outside.

Few of us who live and work outside of prisons have any accurate awareness of the stresses that prisoners often face. Offenders frequently have adjustment, self-esteem, and relationship problems before they ever are arrested. Many have had unusually high levels of life stress before their incarceration, and the stresses of prison may increase anxiety, depression, and stress-related psychological and physical problems. Some inmates have great difficulty adjusting to their restrictive environments and coping with the reality that this will be their home for a period of time, or possibly for the rest of their lives.[52] In addition to those who enter prison with preexisting mental-health problems, the environment can produce despair, low self-worth, high levels of anxiety, increased anger, and more serious mental problems.[53] In addition, lack of acceptance, sexual harassment, and threats of violence may be accompanied by worries about one's family or future. Some estimates suggest that half or more of all prisoners exhibit diagnosable psychological disorders.

Counseling prisoners involves unique approaches that do not apply elsewhere. The counselor must get permission to have access to the prisoner, privacy may be harder to find, and confidentiality may be more difficult to maintain (especially if the counselor learns about impending violence or disruption that could be prevented if it is reported). Counselors need to recognize that each prison culture is unique and that outsiders need to understand something about the environment before doing counseling. Techniques and counseling goals will have to be adapted to the needs of the individual prisoner, and counselors will have to examine their own biases, prejudices, and fears before they attempt this kind of work. In addition, inmates who could benefit from counseling often tend to resist help. Some distrust counselors because of past counseling experiences.[54] Others see mental-health services as "only for crazy people" or fear that anything expressed in confidence will be used against them. Sometimes, inmates view counseling as a sign of weakness and are afraid of ridicule from other prisoners. These are all obstacles that the counselor must overcome.

Prison counselors are often specialists who work for the prison system and perform multiple roles, including assessment, treatment, training, consultation, research, and education. Others, like Chaplain Baird, his fellow chaplains, and numerous dedicated volunteers, are in the prisons as chaplains and chaplain helpers, who have many opportunities for counseling, spiritual ministry, and teaching inmates about life and how to function effectively both within the prison system and outside following their release.[55]

Counselors within the community are likely to have greater contact with the families of prisoners, with former prisoners, with offenders who are on parole or awaiting trial, sometimes with police officers (who often encounter stress and burnout in their work), or with the victims of crime. Special needs exist among the children of incarcerated parents. Often, their environments are not very stable, and they lack consistent care-givers.[56] All these people are under stress, but at least among the adults there is freedom to control some of their own circumstances and to plan for the future. Once again, understanding each of the counselee's unique circumstances is important if counseling is to be effective.

3. *Counseling Military People.* For civilians, working with men and women in the military is a form of cross-cultural counseling. Even though the counselor and counselee share the same citizenship and may have grown up in the same community, life in the military differs from civilian living.

As a group, military personnel and their families may be unusually healthy. There is a camaraderie among military families, a willingness to help one another, and a sense of shared experiences. Despite reports of frequent substance abuse, poverty, and marital conflict among lower-ranking personnel, harshness and insensitivity among some leaders, and pressures on military children, many people function well in military environments. This is especially true for people who like structure.

The stresses, however, also can be great. Frequent moves, long separations from family, continual competition for promotions, interpersonal tensions, assignments to remote duty or dangerous areas, uncertainty about the future, lack of control over one's life and circumstances, never-ending sensitivity to rank and protocol, high expectations that the whole family will conform to military norms, and the continual need for combat readiness can all take their toll on a person's mental health. Especially in times of unusual stress, including combat, mental disorders are common and become the major medical reason why people leave the military.[57] Long deployments away from home, especially first-time deployments, tend to produce high levels of mental distress, as do military operations that involve constant uncertainty and fear of attack like that encountered in places where terrorists are the main enemy.[58] Unlike civilian occupations, the military retires people at a younger age, and this can create unusual stress for long-time military men or women who are nervous about their abilities to function on the outside. It should be noted that the majority of troops show resilience from the stresses of war and adjust without help or without showing evidence of post-traumatic stress.[59] Even so, some military people respond with family violence, incest, sexual promiscuity, and high rates of alcoholism and other forms of substance abuse.

The military is concerned about personal problems, so opportunities are provided for counseling. Presumably, the governments in many countries have something similar to the U.S. family service centers that provide legal and financial counseling, relocation assistance, parenting courses, help with stress management, and sometimes building community connections. Professional counselors also are available, but many service people are reluctant to seek counseling because this goes on the record and could hinder future promotions. Some military people like to appear tough and insensitive to personal needs, so counseling tends to be discouraged, even though this is never mentioned. Chaplains bear much of the counseling load and do so effectively. A visit to the chaplain is not recorded on anybody's record, so this is a safer way to get help. Seldom mentioned is the fact that chaplains also have needs and face many of the same stresses that combat forces encounter. As a result, some chaplains tend to burn out as they try to help others with their problems and stresses.

Civilians, including church leaders and Christian counselors, often are involved in counseling service personnel and military families. Christian servicemen's centers, staffed by civilians or people who formerly were in the military, exist worldwide to encourage, provide Christian fellowship, and counsel with service personnel.[60] In times when large numbers of military people are deployed far from home, civilian counselors can be of help to family members, including parents, who are left behind but deeply concerned about safety and the welfare of their family members in the military. Counselors who live near military facilities have a special opportunity to help service personnel and their families. Like all good counseling, the essence of working effectively with military people is to be sensitive to their stresses and willing to understand the uniqueness of military living.

4. *Counseling the Poor.* It is well known that Jesus showed great compassion for the poor, but there is evidence that counselors do not share this concern. Most counseling techniques and theories have been developed among educated people. Counseling research, training, and innovation have tended to come from college and university settings, far from people who are poor and uneducated. Private-practice counseling caters to those who can pay, and even pastoral counseling has developed through seminaries and professors who work with educated students and church members who tend to be more affluent. None of this denies that among counselors there is widespread compassion and genuine concern for the poor, but often we don't have contact with poor people. They rarely come to

our offices, and if they did, many might find counselor attitudes about the poor that get in the way of effective counseling.

Laura Smith is a psychologist who left a private practice to work with poor people and families. Dr. Smith soon realized that as a psychologist she had been trained in "the culture of Whiteness and class privilege." She wrote that "outside that culture, I initially felt unanchored and a bit directionless, as my new clients did not seem to be playing by the rules that I was used to." Her new counselees were friendly but a little cautious about counseling. They needed time to size up the new counselor and get to know her informally before they made counseling appointments or talked about their problems. "It quickly became apparent that I would need to be flexible, culturally competent, and innovative all day, every day," she concluded.[61] She also learned that some of her previously unnoticed biases were wrong.

It is easy to assume, for example, that poor people live in circumstances that appear to be hopeless and have little hope as a result. "Dragged down by emotional and family devastation, educational failures, criminal convictions, and the domestic violence that so often pervades poor families,"[62] it is natural to assume that all families lose or are losing hope, meaning, and purpose. That is not true, according to Smith's research. Many poor people are able to maintain hope, show resilience, and see possibilities and positive signs in the midst of their difficult circumstances. These people, especially, can profit from counseling.

Another false assumption is the idea that poor people are so overwhelmed by their day-to-day problems that they have no energy or interest left for dealing with counseling issues. It is true that counseling can be difficult if counselees have nothing to eat, no place to live, or no assurances of their safety. These people need practical help, but they also want to talk about their loneliness, depression, anxiety, and concerns for the future. Many are surprised that counselors are willing both to give tangible assistance and to listen to their emotional needs and offer help.

Counseling with the poor is a form of cross-cultural counseling for most of us who read this book. As with all counseling involving people who are not like us, counselors need to build relationships with their counselees, get to know about their lives and their circumstances, and offer counseling services without condescending attitudes or biases, and without abandoning the skills and methods that we use effectively with more affluent counselees.

5. *Counseling Athletes.* People with little interest in athletics may be surprised to learn about the growing influence of a field known as sport psychology. Among their other activities, sport psychologists help people set or achieve goals and help athletes keep focused, avoid distractions, deal with stress, prevent burnout, build self-confidence, keep motivated, and develop peak performance. Many professional sports teams hire sport psychologists to help with performance enhancement, provide counseling, instill confidence, teach relaxation techniques, consult with coaches, help build team cohesion, and provide whatever other psychological help might be needed to enable athletes to perform with maximum effectiveness.[63] In addition to these practical services, some psychologists and other counselors do research to understand the psychology of sports.[64]

Counselors may experience one of their most fulfilling roles in helping athletes who have been sidelined by injuries or athletic failures. In growing up, many young people place all their hopes in becoming successful as a professional athlete. When these people experience career-ending injuries, fail to reach their athletic goals, or are denied opportunities to advance in their dream careers, the loss and disappointment can be overwhelming, leading to a variety of psychological symptoms. The effective sport counselor does not make light of these disappointments but sensitively helps counselees deal with the grief and disappointment and guide them toward alternative goals. Counseling with athletes is most likely to be effective if the counselor understands something about the different sports cultures and expectations.

Bitterness and the Question of Why

Bitterness is an attitude of anger and resentment over what appears to be a justified grievance. The bitter person often is intent on getting revenge, but instead, he or she often gets ulcers, a hypercritical attitude, and rejection from others who don't enjoy being around bitter people. The writer of Hebrews warns against letting bitterness take root because this can "cause trouble and defile many."[65] Most often the person who suffers most from bitterness is the one who clings to a bitter mind-set and looks for opportunities to get even.

Bitterness may be directed toward another person or toward God. Unlike anger, which can appear and then disappear quickly, bitterness tends to persist, sometimes for a lifetime. The bitter person often looks for opportunities to get even but rarely shows any willingness to forgive. Over time the bitter person can sink further and further into a self-created swamp of negativism, hypercriticism, resentment, and sometimes self-pity. In times of difficulty, calamity, or injustice, perhaps the most natural questions to ask are:

- "Why?"
- "Why did this happen?"
- "Why did it happen now?"
- "Why didn't things turn out like I expected?"
- "Why do bad things happen to good people?"
- "Why do some people seem to get away with sinful actions without getting caught or stopped?"
- "Why have I experienced the pain or loss that has come into my life? Why have my prayers not been answered?
- "Where is God when it hurts?"[66]

For centuries, people have struggled with questions like these, and the answers, at best, are incomplete. Even the psalmist wondered if God had forgotten his people who tried to live good lives, while arrogant nonbelievers appeared to have prosperity, health, callous attitudes of self-centered pride, and freedom from the burdens that most of us face. The writer of Psalm 73 acknowledged that he had become bitter as he watched all of this, but when he went into God's sanctuary, he was reminded that in time there would be fair and perfect justice. In the meantime, we suffer, our counselees ask us why, and we can't give very satisfying answers.[67]

In part, we suffer because we belong to a fallen human race. God never promises that good Christians won't ever be murdered or killed in wars, that drunken drivers won't run into our children, that bad storms won't destroy the property of believers, or that missionaries in some primitive country will never get a doctor's injection from a needle contaminated by the AIDS virus. As long as we live in a fallen world, we sometimes will suffer from its fallen condition.

Sometimes, pain will come because of our own actions. It is easy for any of us to be careless, irresponsible, unthinking, or negligent in caring for our bodies, our loved ones, or the things we own. When we experience the consequences, guilt and anger often flood our minds, sometimes with the why questions, and bitterness toward God.

Whether or not we feel personally responsible, suffering apparently comes to help us grow and mature—even when we don't want to grow. For Christians, problems refine our faith, make us more Christlike, teach us about God, and produce perseverance and character.[68] Suffering also enables us to understand and care more effectively for others.[69]

Does suffering also result from sin? All suffering results ultimately from the Fall of humanity into sin, and it seems likely that some of our present problems come because of the sufferer's specific sin. It must be emphasized, however, that the Bible explicitly refutes the idea that specific sin automatically brings resultant suffering.[70] People in need often conclude that "God must be punishing me," but such a conclusion is, at best based on shaky theological evidence.

From the human perspective, a lot of what happens to people in this life is not fair, and we cannot know for certain why people suffer. We do know, however, that bitterness and an attitude of revenge do not make things better. We know, too, that God is compassionate, all-wise, all-knowing, absolutely just, and ever present even when we are like Job and don't understand the reasons. It is not wrong to struggle with *why* questions. Christian counselors should expect to be involved in helping counselees grapple with these issues, even though we know that the ultimate answers are not likely to be found in intellectual debate. Peace is more likely to come from a willingness of the counselee and counselor to acknowledge that the sovereign, compassionate God of the universe is aware of our problems. He is in control, and he gives us reason for hope. He enables us to get free of the bitterness quagmire, to be able to forgive, and to live with the assurance that God knows why things happen as they do and what is coming in the future. Ultimately, only that really matters.

KEY POINTS FOR BUSY COUNSELORS

➤ This chapter deals with issues that are not discussed in detail elsewhere in the book and with circumstances that might influence the ways in which counselors deal with more common problems.

In *helping people with physical disabilities,*

■ Try to focus on the counselee's strengths and abilities rather than focusing on what he or she cannot do.

- Recognize that families need understanding, support, and sometimes practical assistance as they cope with their unique stresses. They need help in learning to live fulfilling lives with a disabled person present.
- Encourage counselees with disabilities to express feelings but also to find ways for living as fulfilling a life as possible.

➤ In *helping people with intellectual disabilities,*

- Help them deal with frustrations and, depending on the degree of impairment, teach self-management skills.
- Recognize that parents and other family members have needs that parallel families of people with physical disabilities.

➤ In *helping people with eating disorders,* make every effort to understand the nature and causes of the disorders. Then, in partnership with medical personnel, focus on the specific psychological and spiritual issues relating to obesity or anorexia and bulimia.

- Help obese people deal with the social rejection, change eating habits, and eliminate the factors such as stress, unhealthy attitudes, or unhealthy lifestyles that can cause and prolong obesity.
- Regarding anorexia and bulimia, try to uncover and help counselees deal with the causes of this condition (see Table 40–1 as a guideline), focusing on helping people change. If possible, involve the family and consider group meetings.

➤ In *helping people with HIV/AIDS,* become as familiar as possible with the nature of the disease. Adapt your counseling to the different stages of the disease. People who first discover their HIV need different counseling than those who are near the end of their lives and facing death.

- Recognize the need for helping people with AIDS and their families deal with the emotional implications of having a terminal illness and one that can have a negative stigma.
- Review and apply the practical guidelines that are presented in the chapter.

➤ In *helping people in special groups,* such as prisoners and their families or people in the military,

- Understand the cultural uniqueness of the group. For example, military families or people in the athletic world often have unique ways of thinking that can impact your counseling.
- In addition to applying general counseling procedures, give encouragement, help in dealing with the causes of the problems, and offer guidance in behavior change.

➤ It is common for people in counseling to struggle with bitterness and questions of why. The counselor can encourage discussion of these issues, try to encourage forgiveness, and help people get a better perspective on the nature, sovereignty, and compassion of God, even when counselees neither see these nor understand how God might be involved with their circumstances.

41

Spiritual Issues

It was the first time I had been to a conference of emergent church leaders. Except for me, they were all in their twenties and thirties, but I was accepted warmly despite the gap between our ages. Apparently, the organizers had invited me to attend because they thought that I would do my best to relate and would be willing to learn.

I did learn—a lot. In many ways, it was a life-changing weekend for me. I saw young people who were committed to Christ, wanting to be faithful followers of Jesus, and willing to devote their lives to reach their generation for Christ whatever it might take. At the same time, I saw people who were frustrated because they couldn't find churches where they felt welcome; they were people who felt like misunderstood misfits in the congregations where some of them had grown up. These young Christians did not care about status, big churches, denominations, well-structured programs, or polished worship services. They were more down to earth, and, in many ways, they seemed close to what the early disciples must have been like when they walked along dusty roads with Jesus.

After the conference we scattered to our homes in different parts of the world, and I lost contact with most of them. Today, some are building churches to reach their own generation, devoting their lives to serving people in need, making an impact in difficult circumstances. Others, including some who returned to their ministries following our conference, have burned out from exhaustion, collapsed spiritually, or been pulled down by their own immorality, marriage failures, or addictions. Despite their young faces and fresh perspectives, these brothers and sisters are not a lot different from older and more established Christian leaders who also began strong but have stumbled and fallen spiritually, morally, and physically.

Probably almost all of us have gone to conferences and come home inspired and more than ever determined to do our work or live our lives with greater effectiveness. Then routines have taken over, and the conferences have faded in memory and influence. Some participants have slid because their youthful enthusiasm, endless opportunities, and constant adrenaline surges have left no room in their lives for quiet times with God, reflection, accountability, or rest. Others have been propelled by their eager passion, but they have zeal without in-depth biblical or theological knowledge. At the conference I attended, some talked about wanting more training, but they had faced rejection and criticism from older Christians and training institutions that were unwilling to accept and nurture young men and women who knew that they could only reach their generation by doing ministry in nontraditional ways. One of the leaders from the conference freely admits that his life and ministry have held together, barely, because an older Christian has come alongside to walk with him, pray with him, stick with him, and give guidance and support through difficult circumstances.

As the oldest person at that emergent conference, a man presumably with more experience and maturity, could I have helped to prevent the spiritual and psychological tragedies that young leaders face? Perhaps experiences and questions like this make a discussion of counseling and spirituality more important than any other chapter in this book. Helping people in their spiritual journeys is what Christian counselors should do best.

Something has been happening in the counseling profession during the past two decades. Throughout most of the twentieth century, mental-health professionals, along with psychologists in general, were not very sympathetic toward religion or spirituality—especially if it was Christian. While there was widespread embracing of multicultural diversity, gender differences, women's issues, and the unique needs of minority groups, spirituality and religion tended to be ignored among secular counselors, or at best acknowledged reluctantly. Graduate schools rarely mentioned spirituality. Professors and practitioners did not attempt to understand religious terminology. Some still talked in their classes about Freud's oft-stated view that religion is harmful and indicative of neurosis.[1] Few counselors had any training in helping people who had spiritual struggles, periodic surveys showed the widespread lack of personal religious faith among secular psychologists, and most appeared to be unfamiliar with the ways religious people think.[2]

How things have changed! Today, graduate school courses on spirituality have become common. The American Psychiatric Association now has included spiritual problems into its *Diagnostic and Statistical Manual.* Professional conference presentations, spirituality workshops, and a host of books published by secular publishing houses all attest to the new interest in spirituality, especially as it relates to counseling.[3] It should be noted that the greater openness to spirituality does not necessarily extend to religion. Many people freely describe themselves as being spiritual, but they would never attend a place of worship because of their distrust or negative views of organized religion. Notice, too, that popular spirituality tends to be individualistic or humanistic and is not necessarily Christian.[4] Christian spirituality is less likely to be dismissed among professional counselors, but it tends to be viewed as one of many forms of spirituality, and not necessarily as a spirituality that is relevant for the twenty-first century. This chapter will be aware of the diverse views of spirituality but will focus on spirituality and religion that is Christian.

It is not easy to help people with spiritual struggles. Sometimes, there are no clear answers to the theological questions that counselees strive to answer. Often, there is confusion about the meaning of the words that tend to be used in discussions of spirituality. Even the word *spirituality* has different meanings. Among Christians, words like *faith, conversion,* or *love* are hard to define, even though these are near the core of the faith. On a more personal level, Christian counselors, as well as their counselees, can feel defeated by sin in their own lives or frustrated because their spiritual growth is so slow. Others are concerned because their lives seem so spiritually dry and without much joy. Most agree that church is important, but the worship services so often are boring, and despite the fact that it claims to be God's Word, the Bible can be dull and irrelevant. Believers pray more out of habit than desire, but their prayers often go unanswered. They want to do good and to love, but their thoughts or actions are not very loving, and their consciences seem insensitive and blunted. Many want their children to grow into godly men and women, but too often, young people leave the church, forsake the faith, and embrace counterfeit spiritualities and values that show no awareness or respect for biblical standards of purity.

This is not what God desires, but they are common experiences, perhaps even in the lives of the counselors or potential counselors who read these words and sense, in their hearts, that they are not spiritually competent to counsel people concerning the issues that will be raised in this chapter. Counseling people with spiritual problems is a challenge at any time, but it is more difficult when the counselor struggles with problems similar to those of the counselees. It has been said that "nobody knows what desperation really is" until he or she has faced another human being who craves help that the counselor cannot give because inside he or she feels "completely empty" and spiritually dry.[5] Unlike most of the previous chapters, this one speaks to the needs of counselors and counselees alike, but while it speaks about problems, it also speaks words of hope and encouragement. Despite the imperfections and struggles that are common to all of us, surely nobody can be more effective in helping with spiritual issues than the helper who bears the title *Christian counselor*.

The Bible and Spiritual Problems

In this age of divergent spiritualities, how do we know God and know about him? Over the centuries, the writings and teachings of religious leaders have enlightened our thinking as well as the experiences of godly men and women who have lived holy lives and walked with God. For many Christians, however, the Bible is viewed as the authoritative Word of God that "never had its origin in the will of man," but came to us instead through people who "spoke from God as they were carried along by the Holy Spirit."[6] No data bank could contain all of God's knowledge, and no human mind could comprehend what he knows,[7] but he has revealed himself in ways that impact us personally and guide our work as counselors.

God's goal is for each believer to mature in Christlikeness, but he knows that none of us will succeed completely, this side of heaven. He wants us to be holy and to follow in Christ's steps, although he knows that nobody will ever do that totally.[8] He wants us to "put on all of God's armor," so that we can "stand firm against all strategies and tricks of the Devil."[9] Since we cannot fight life's battles alone, we are instructed to give our bodies to God so that each is a "living and holy sacrifice—the kind he will accept."[10] We are told in the Bible to stop sinning and to flee from youthful lusts, but God realizes that we are fooling ourselves if we say we have no sin. So we are to confess our sins and to expect forgiveness when we fall.[11] He sets up a high standard for our behavior because he is just and holy, but since no human being can reach God's standards, he has provided a Savior who paid for our sins and failures, all because of his great love and mercy.[12] He has adopted us as his children and requires us to "do what is right, to love mercy, and to walk humbly" with our God.[13] He is merciful and gracious, slow to get angry, full of unfailing love, tender and compassionate, like a father to his children, because he knows that we are weak and only dust so long as we remain in this world.[14] Because of his great love, not only did he send his son to pay for our sins, but he has given us his Holy Spirit, to live within, where he guides, strengthens, and teaches us.[15] We may think that God is far away, at times, but he is ever near, sticking closer than a faithful brother.[16]

The Christian life seeks to be characterized by Christlike worship, character, and service. The first of these three objectives, *worship*, initially involved songs of praise and the offering of sacrifices to atone for sin. Now that Christ has died for our sins, "once for all time," so that he might bring us safely home to God,[17] we are to give our bodies to God and to "let them be a living and holy sacrifice—the kind he will accept." This continual commitment of self to God, along with verbal praise and faithful obedience, is how we worship.

Worship leads to the second objective, which involves the continuing transformation of *character*. We are not to conform to worldly standards. Instead, we are to let God transform us into new people by changing the way we think. This involves disentangling ourselves from sin so we can be holy as he is holy, more like Christ, walking in his steps, and allowing the Holy Spirit to mold us into individuals who are characterized by love, joy, peace, patience, kindness, gentleness, fruitfulness, and self-control.[18]

The Christian must not only be God-centered and self-centered. There also must be *service* to others. We please God when we remember to do good and to share what we have with those who are in need.[19] The biblical view of success radically contradicts that of the world in which we live. "If you want to be great and a leader," Jesus said, in essence, then you must be a servant. We are warned not to compete against one another with envy and selfish ambition, but we are instructed, instead, to do good deeds, to humble ourselves, and to believe that in due time the Lord will lift us up to whatever acclaim we might need.[20] Nowhere in the entire Bible was this seen more clearly than in the life of Joshua. He was given the job of leading a huge group of people who had been led by Moses all of their lives. "Be strong and courageous," God told Joshua repeatedly. "Do not be afraid or discouraged. For the LORD your God is with you wherever you go."[21]

Christlike worship, Christlike character, and Christlike service—these are the goals of the Christian life. In one sense, we press on to reach these goals, like a runner training toward the finish line.[22] In another sense, we grow not by effort, but by yielding ourselves completely to divine control and direction. Throughout the centuries, perhaps thousands of books have dealt with Christian growth, spiritual maturity, and the struggles of believers. The need for spiritual guidance and help with religious struggles is nothing new. Since the time of Christ (and before), believers have grappled with spiritual deadness, periods of stagnation, dark periods in life, and the need for help in Christian growth. It could be argued that the whole Bible is written for such people, teaching us about God, his attributes, and his power to mold believers into instruments that God can use for his purpose, "ready for the Master to use for every good work."[23]

The causes, effects, counseling, and prevention of spiritual problems are all discussed in the Bible. No other subjects are more Bible-based and less illuminated by psychology than the subjects of spiritual growth and solving spiritual problems. The Christian counselor is best equipped to help with such problems, since only the believer has "the mind of Christ," which enables him or her to understand and to help others comprehend and accept the things that come from the Spirit of God."[24]

The Causes of Spiritual Problems

Visit the empty cathedrals of Europe on a Sunday morning or the busy restaurants and shopping malls across America, and it is clear that religion and Sunday worship are far from the minds of most people in many communities. Outward appearances can be deceiving, however. Religion is very much alive and flourishing in countries around the world. Islam is increasing significantly, and Christianity is experiencing significant growth and influence, especially in Africa, Latin

America, and parts of Asia.[25] Add to this the upsurge of involvement with various spiritualities, and it becomes apparent that religion is far from dead. Surveys in the United States continue to show that 90 percent or more of the population claims to believe in God, and as many as 40 percent attend religious services at least once a week. Even psychologists, who as a professional group are not known to be very religious, nevertheless acknowledge the positive role of spiritual practices in helping people cope with the stresses of life.[26]

Statistics change and differ from country to country, but according to one report:

- 95 percent of Americans believe in God, and 92 percent are affiliated with a particular religion.
- Only 40–45 percent of mental-health professionals report a belief in God.
- Only 37 percent of psychiatrists answered yes to the question: "If it were scientifically demonstrated that the use of a spiritual intervention (e.g., prayer) improved patient progress, would you perform that intervention?"
- Teens who attend religious services regularly are less likely to smoke, drink, or use drugs.[27]
- A growing body of scientific evidence shows that people who attend religious services at least once a week enjoy better-than-average health and lower rates of illness, including depression.[28]

Although many people speak positively of religion, it does not follow that these attitudes shape day-to-day behavior. At least in America, our lives are not so much guided by God as by personal feelings and our dreams of success.[29] God, it seems, is tolerated, but only when he can be useful and when he is bland enough to pose no threat or challenge to the more common goals of the good life and good feelings.

In the midst of this environment, a number of deeply committed believers sincerely want to serve God and to grow as Christians, but they struggle with discouragement and a lack of spiritual vitality. These people know that dynamic Christian living is possible, even in a culture that is only superficially religious. They long for a vital Christian spiritual life, even though many are unsure what that means, and most have no idea how to get it. To help these people, we need to understand some causes of spiritual problems that can get in the way of growth.

1. *Where We Are.* For anyone, problems may come because of where they are spiritually. Many people attend services and do good deeds, but they fail to recognize that Christianity, at its core, deals more with one's inner nature than with outer behavior. It is concerned more about what we *are* than with what we *do*. This is stated repeatedly in the Bible, but nowhere with greater clarity than in Ephesians 2.

Prior to conversion we are "dead," doomed by our many sins, controlled by the devil and separated from God, regardless of our religious practices or other deeds. Because of his mercy and love, however, God provided a way to release us from this state of spiritual deadness, forgive us for our sins, raise us to life, and make us his adopted children. This salvation does not come because of our own efforts, but because God gives us salvation as a gift when we completely yield ourselves to him. "God saved you by his special favor when you believed. And you can't take credit for this; it is a gift from God. Salvation is not a reward for the good things we have done, so none of us can boast about it."[30] Nothing in this big book is more important or more significant than the two previous sentences. When we accept God's gift of salvation, he begins to work in our lives, molding us into the kinds of persons he wants us to be. Since he created us and knows us intimately, his plan is best for our lives.

Some people have spiritual struggles because they are not believers; they have never accepted God's free gift of salvation and are trying, in vain, to earn divine favor by their works. Others have committed their lives to Christ, but they have not grown spiritually because they have not known what to do to grow, or they have little real interest in spiritual issues. These people may be long-time Christians who even go to church and serve faithfully in religious activities, but spiritually they still are infants in Christ, not much different and spiritually no more mature than nonbelievers.[31] Still others have turned their backs on Christ and chosen to ignore or reject the religious training that they had in the past. These people may claim to be believers and harbor some guilt over their actions. In time, many will return to their spiritual roots, but at present they are far away from Christ and spiritually dead. All of this points to the conclusion that spiritual problems relate closely to where we are in terms of a relationship with Jesus Christ.

2. *Where We Live.* All of us are impacted by our environments, and there can be no doubt that our spiritual experiences and religious beliefs are shaped by the families where we grew up, the religious values we were taught, the places where we work, and the countries where we live. In some countries, for example, religion is more prominent and promoted. In others there are restrictions, even in countries where governments boast about the religious freedom for their citizens. It is difficult to be overtly Christian in Communist countries, Muslim societies, or Western nations where talk about God or displays of religious symbols are illegal in all public places.

Probably, the home is the most influential shaping force in religious beliefs, especially among children and adolescents. When parents model religious devotion, support the spiritual activities of family members, or encourage their children to be spiritual, the children are impacted, even though later they may choose to leave their religious roots. Research shows that family and peer influences are both significant predictors of the importance of God and religion in the lives of young people.[32] In contrast, the influence is different in homes or peer groups where God is never mentioned or where spirituality and religion are dismissed as irrelevant. Spiritual beliefs, practices, and values are so much grounded in the home that these need to be explored by any counselor who would seek to understand and help people who deal with spiritual issues.

3. *How We Live and Act.* Have you ever considered what most disturbed Jesus during his time on earth? It was not pornography, racism, abortion, violence, political corruption, the misuse of church funds, or the other issues that concern us today. These are important and can cause significant harm, but Jesus reserved his strongest attacks to condemn sin and to fight pious, religious legalism. Both of these, sin and legalism, still cause many spiritual problems.

(a) Sin. Throughout church history, Christians have struggled with three major problems: greed and the abuse of money, lust and the abuse of sex, pride and the abuse of power. More than any others, these behaviors seem to undermine or stifle spiritual growth. The ancient monastic vows of poverty, chastity, and obedience were a direct response to the misuse and abuse of money, sex, and power.[33]

Important as these issues are, however, the biblical meaning of sin involves something more. Sin is any action or attitude that violates or fails to conform to the will of God. We sin by what we think, by what we do or fail to do, and by what we are. Sin is a powerful, pervasive, and penetrating force that can master and enslave us, especially when we fail to repent or admit and confess our faults. Sin is the major cause of spiritual problems, stagnation, and loss of vitality.[34] Facing our sin is a major route to the experience of forgiveness, hope, and joy.

(b) Legalism. When Jesus walked on earth, the Pharisees were religious purists who believed that spiritual maturity came as a result of observing rules. This view has been common in religious circles for centuries and is held today by many people in all subgroups of the Christian church. Often seen in people who sincerely want to please God and live exemplary lives, a legalistic mentality maintains that rules and regulations determine what a good Christian does not do (drink alcohol, for example, watch R-rated movies, dress in certain ways, or shop on Sunday) and what the good Christian does do (such as read the Bible daily, tell somebody about Jesus every week, or attend a specified number of religious services). The psalmist, prophets, Jesus, and Paul all condemned legalistic attitudes such as these.[35] They can lead to sinful pride, and they contradict the very heart of the biblical message. The theme of the Bible is redemption, and we are saved through faith alone.[36]

Does spiritual growth come from following rules? Jesus' condemnation of the Pharisees clearly indicates that the answer is no. True spiritual maturity comes when we walk humbly before God with an attitude of thanksgiving and praise, a deep determination to be obedient, an awareness of our tendencies to sin, and acknowledgment of our need for his continued grace and mercy. This does not mean that we take a passive do-nothing attitude toward our spiritual lives. The Christian must be alert to the devil's schemes to get us off track and must resist him with the Word of God. In addition, spiritual growth is closely related to prayer, meditation on the Bible, involvement with other believers, and a sincere attempt to refrain from sin.

The power and even the desire for holy living must come from God[37] and not from our determination to follow rules that humans have devised. The Scriptures condemn both legalism (the strict keeping of rules) and its twin partners: gnosticism (the belief that spirituality is gained by superior knowledge) and asceticism (the conscious denial of pleasures, experiences, and material things).[38]

4. *What We Think.* It seems that most human problems begin in the mind. Our thinking can lead to self-sufficiency, pride, bitterness, and non-Christian values, each of which can create or accentuate spiritual problems.

(a) Self-Sufficiency. Individual initiative and self-sufficiency are deeply engrained values in many contemporary cultures. Even the church applauds individual success and often advocates possibility thinking that gives little or no thought to the will and power of God. Self-sufficiency, however, is the mark of lukewarm Christianity. It is the absolute antithesis of spiritual maturity. To the people who boast about their self-sufficiency, saying, "I am rich. I have everything I want. I don't need a thing," the Scriptures urge repentance and point out that self-satisfied people really are wretched, miserable, poor, blind, naked, and neither hot nor cold spiritually.[39] Self-sufficiency ultimately leads to spiritual emptiness.

(b) Pride. Is anything in the Bible condemned more often than pride? Similar to self-sufficiency, pride involves a trust in one's own power or resources, and a tendency to derive satisfaction from the contemplation of one's status, capabilities, or accomplishments, especially as these are compared with others who seem to have less. Pride is more easily seen than defined, and more easily detected in others than in ourselves. Pride is self-centered, self-satisfied, and ultimately self-destructive.[40]

(c) Bitterness. On the day that he resigned as President of the United States, Richard Nixon warned his staff against the bitterness that could destroy them. Centuries earlier, the writer of Hebrews warned that bitterness can spring up to cause trouble and corrupt people by its poison.[41] Bitterness can be a powerful and insidious source of spiritual problems.

(d) Distorted Values. What really is important in life? The issue of values has come up several times in earlier chapters. The things people value most tend to be seen in how they spend their money, their time (including spare time), and their mental energies, especially when the mind is free to wander. The value of possessions, money, selfish pleasures, success, and acclaim are among the issues that society and the advertising industry laud as being important. These are not bad in themselves, but each has potential to destroy Christian growth and create spiritual problems.[42] Values like these are subtle in that they can draw us away from God and create a false sense of security.[43]

In contrast to self-sufficiency, pride, bitterness, and distorted values, the spiritually maturing person is transformed mentally and becomes intent on knowing what God wants us to do and how "good and pleasing and perfect his will really is."[44]

5. *What We Lack.* Everyone knows that physical problems and deterioration both come when there is a lack of food, air, rest, and other basic physical necessities. In a similar way, spiritual problems can be caused by a lack of those basic ingredients that are needed for Christian health and growth. The following list is not complete, but it points to nine common spiritual nutrients that might be lacking in the lives of people who seek counseling regarding their spiritual issues.

(a) Lack of Understanding. It might be distressing if we really knew how much spiritual pain and turmoil comes because people lack clear knowledge and understanding of the Bible. For example, consider some of the ideas that are commonly believed but are not taught in the Bible. These include the scripturally unsupported ideas that we are saved by good works, that Christian growth depends entirely on human effort, that God would never understand our doubts or lusts, that personal actions can separate us from God's love, that sometimes he refuses to forgive acts of sin and disobedience even if we confess, that financial or family problems come as God's way of punishing us, that God really doesn't know about or care about our needs and concerns, or that physical illness usually is a sign of God's displeasure and our own lack of faith. Misconceptions like these, some even preached regularly by sincere but misinformed pastors, can create restlessness, uncertainty, spiritual doubt, apathy, and despair.

(b) Lack of Nourishment. Young Christians, like young children, need food to grow, and we all need food to keep alive. Spiritual problems come to people who never spend much time taking in spiritual nourishment in the form of prayer, experiences of worship, instruction from teachers, or Bible reading. For others, there is so much giving out in serving and activity that the giver becomes spiritually depleted and empty. It is a spiritual law, wrote Walter Trobisch, that "the one who gives out much must also take in much," otherwise the one who gives out continually without taking in will run dry.[45] Several years ago the pastor of a large and influential church announced to his congregation that he was taking a sabbatical because he was "running on empty," like a car that had no fuel and was trying to keep going on fumes. There were no moral failures or other problems in this man's life, but he was honest enough to realize that he needed time for rejuvenation if he was to be spiritually healthy and able to lead his congregation faithfully. The people in the church gave him a standing ovation, his church board gave him a leave of absence, and he returned to lead his church after his sabbatical with a healthier balance between what he gives out and what he takes in spiritually.

(c) Lack of Giving. This is the opposite of a lack of nourishment. People who eat too much become fat and, in time, uncomfortable. A similar condition can occur in our spiritual lives. Overfeeding on sermons, Bible studies, devotional reading, Christian radio programs, church activities, and retreats can combine to bring spiritual bloating. Christians are not to be like sponges that soak up and retain everything. Instead, we are called to be vessels, used by God to bring instruction and blessing to others. The essence of Christian love is giving and sharing so we don't grow fat.

(d) Lack of Balance. During his three-year ministry, Jesus lived a balanced life. He ministered, interacted with individuals, rested, spent time in prayer and worship, and relaxed with friends. He had purpose in life, sought God's help in daily living, and took care of himself spiritually, physically, intellectually, and socially. There were seasons in his life when he faced extra pressures or was exceptionally tired, but he never ran himself ragged doing the work of his father.

Many modern people lack this balance. They go all the time, fail to get proper rest or exercise, do not eat a balanced diet, and are so busy—even doing the Lord's work—that their efficiency and spiritual vitality run down. To complicate the issue, in a society that rewards and affirms hyperactivity, many of us wear our excessive busyness as a badge of pride. It is common to have seasons of life when the pressures are great and balance seems like an impossible dream, but overall, a balanced life requires planning, discipline, and frequent reminders that no person in the body of Christ is so important that he or she is indispensable. No person is immune to the spiritual flatness and physical collapse that can follow a lack of balanced living.

(e) Lack of Commitment. Jesus taught that to be a true follower of Christ one must be willing to take up a cross and follow him. This would suggest that genuine Christian growth must be preceded by a commitment to let Jesus Christ be Lord and controller of one's life. Any holding back interferes with spiritual maturing and contributes to lusterless Christianity.

Years ago I read about a Christian leader who watched as hundreds of Christian men and women dealt with the complexities of living. "Some flourished spiritually; others floundered. Some made an impact; others made no mark whatsoever. Some grew in Christ; others dried up spiritually and withered away. Some rejoiced and offered encouragement; others complained and griped. Some deepened and softened; others became more shallow and hardened." What made the difference? There is a one-word answer: Commitment! "Ordinary people who make simple, spiritual commitments under the lordship of Jesus Christ make an extraordinary impact on their world. Education, gifts, and abilities do not make the difference. Commitment does."[46]

(f) Lack of Simplicity. Everybody knows that life is complex, filled with stress, change, difficult relationships, and constant busyness. The widespread focus on success and our materialist drive for possessions both push us toward the greed and covetousness that the Bible clearly condemns.[47] Some spiritual leaders preach that God wants individuals to be rich and that spirituality and material benefits go together. The biblical message is different, with its warnings against hoarding and its emphasis on giving away what we have and caring for the poor.[48] According to Richard Foster, the Old Testament "almost without exception" promised material blessings *for the community* rather than for the individual. "The idea that one could cut off a piece of the consumer pie and go off and enjoy it in isolation was unthinkable."[49]

Lives that are controlled by greed, concern about possessions, and the itch for more are not lives that are growing spiritually. "The love of money is at the root of all kinds of evil," we are warned in the Bible. Some people who crave money "have wandered from the faith" and brought a lot of sorrows into their lives.[50]

(g) Lack of the Holy Spirit's Power. The Holy Spirit lives in the life of every believer, but the Spirit can be stifled and pushed aside.[51] When that happens, spiritual lethargy is certain. In contrast, when the Holy Spirit is in control, our lives develop strength, spiritual understanding, unity with others, love, joy, peace, self-control, and the other spiritual fruits,[52] all of which are designed to bring glory to Christ.

(h) Lack of Spiritual Discipline. Within recent years there has been a significant increase of interest in growth-inducing activities that are known as spiritual disciplines.[53] These are practices, things we can do, that can draw us closer to God and move us toward greater spiritual maturity. Although the listing of disciplines differ, there is a core that most writers acknowledge.[54] They could be divided into three overlapping groups.[55]

- Cognitive disciplines focus on how we think and include meditation, listening, reading the Bible, study, prayer, and discernment.
- Behavioral disciplines are more focused on activity or withdrawal from normal patterns of activity. These disciplines are behaviors and lifestyle patterns that include simple living, frugality, sexual abstinence, fasting, slowing down, observing the Sabbath, periodic solitude, silence, acts of service, sacrifice, and sometimes suffering.
- Interpersonal disciplines deal with relational issues, or are things done in the presence of other people. Here are the disciplines of confession, repentance, forgiveness, submission, humility, corporate worship, singing, involvement in community, participating in the Eucharist (often known as communion or the Lord's Supper), witnessing, and intercession. Often, these disciplines involve service to others in the form of hospitality, healing, encouraging, caring, mentoring, or giving guidance.

The term *discipline* implies that these are practices that most often do not come naturally and that need to be sustained and cultivated. Increasingly, the spiritual disciplines are being incorporated into Christian counseling practice,[56] but often the neglect of the disciplines or inconsistent practice can contribute to spiritual problems or lack of growth.

(i) Lack of Body Life. Even though they may never go to church, all Christians are part of a universal group or "body" that consists of other believers, all of whom are important and gifted, all of whom love Christ (admittedly with differing degrees of commitment), and each of whom should seek to know, love, pray for, help, encourage, challenge, exhort, teach, and minister to others. When Christians attempt to grow on their own, to build their personal empires, or to rise on some ladder of Christian status, they are out of God's will. He has placed us in the body and expects us to grow there, not forsaking mutual involvement with other brothers and sisters.[57]

6. *What We Experience.* Counseling textbooks rarely mention suffering, and when they do, the emphasis is on ways that suffering can be reduced or avoided. Any mention of the good that might come from suffering tends to be dismissed as rationalization or distorted thinking. Christians, in contrast, often believe that personal and spiritual growth can come as a result of suffering,[58] although we still have a responsibility to work diligently to reduce pain and other forms of human misery.

For centuries, Christian writers have struggled to understand the meaning and mystery of suffering. Some claim that any person who has enough faith will be released from the trials that come to the rest of humanity. This is an attractive idea that has no biblical support. Suffering builds patience, strength, and spiritual growth. It is an experience rooted in the human condition. It was the experience of Jesus and, despite its pain, we are told that it should be cause for joy and praise.[59] When we complain about suffering, we undermine one of God's major methods for molding believers.[60]

7. *What We Fight.* Whether or not we consciously recognize this, the Christian is in a battle. Jesus was tempted when he began his ministry and perhaps at other times thereafter. The giants of the faith, both those mentioned in the Bible and others, battled the forces of evil, and the struggle continues today.[61] In this continuing world war, there are no islands of neutrality. We are either fighting the devil or aligned on his side—in attitude if not in activity.

At times the battle is in the intellectual arena where confusion, doubt, nonbiblical thinking, struggles with temptation, and overt heresy are at issue. Sometimes, the battle is physical and involves struggles with disease and injury. Often the conflict centers around psychological discouragement, anger, anxiety, guilt, and other internal conflicts. At times, the battle seems mild, but at other times the attack is more intense. This is true especially when people are tired, not feeling well, or emotionally and mentally drained. Some of the most dangerous battle times follow a spiritually refreshing experience, like a retreat, or come when people have experienced good news or a gratifying success. It is then that we human beings let down our defenses, and Satan's forces move in to take advantage of our spiritual vulnerability. There are many stories of spiritual leaders who have fallen at the height of their success.

As a counselor, have you ever thought that counseling is a form of spiritual battle? Christian counselors help counselees restore relationships, get rid of harmful thinking or destructive emotions, live more joyfully, and overcome the problems of life. All these activities have the effect of undoing the destructive work of the devil and his forces.

Over the centuries Christians have believed that spiritual warfare involves the devious and destructive influence of demons. During his ministry on earth, Jesus encountered the work of demons as they created personal injury, confusion, psychotic-like symptoms, and intense distress in the lives of individuals and their families. In the book of Acts and in the Epistles, we see less emphasis on the demonic, but during the Middle Ages, demon possession and exorcisms were an important part of treatment for deviant or highly unusual behavior.[62] In modern times, even among some Christians, the reality, presence, and destructive power of Satan and his demonic forces have all tended to be ignored or dismissed as bygone superstition.

With his characteristic wisdom and insight, C. S. Lewis began *The Screwtape Letters* with a sobering observation. He wrote that "There are two equal and opposite errors into which our race can fall about the devils. One is to disbelieve in their existence. The other is to believe, and to feel an excessive and unhealthy interest in them. They themselves are equally pleased with both errors."[63] Today, there still are those who disbelieve in the demonic, but increasing numbers of people, especially Christians, seem to be taking "excessive and unhealthy" interest in demons. As a result, many believers are confused and distracted from competent counseling.

It must be remembered that there is a limit to Satan's power and influence. The Bible tells us how to prepare for spiritual battle, warns us against satanic (and demonic) tactics, assures us that the Holy Spirit in us is greater than the devil's forces, and declares that Satan in time will be banished forever.[64] In the meantime, the battle continues, and some people crumble spiritually because they are unprepared and not alert to the dangers.

When we can identify the causes of spiritual and other problems, we often have some direction for our counseling. However, the ways of God are not always comprehensible to the human mind. Sometimes, counselors and their counselees must stand alongside Job, shake our heads in amazement, wonder why, and yield ourselves to the sovereign Lord whose ways are not our ways and whose thoughts are not our thoughts. We who are counselors like to solve problems. It is not easy to accept what God permits, but sometimes that may be our best, most realistic, and only choice.

The Effects of Spiritual Problems

At times, it can be difficult to separate causes from effects. Each of the spiritual issues that we have discussed in the preceding paragraphs can have the effect of creating more spiritual problems. An attitude of pride often leads to more pride. Sin stimulates more sin. Legalism breeds more of the same. Self-sufficiency, distorted values, misunderstandings, selfishness, theological error, and nonbiblical thinking—all are like creeping vines that keep getting larger and better able to squeeze out the vestiges of spiritual life that are struggling to stay alive. How do these influences affect us?

1. *Spiritual Effects.* Following the demise of a prominent television ministry, one of its leaders reflected on what had happened. "A television camera can change a preacher quicker than anything else," he wrote. When this widely viewed television series was at the height of its popularity, "there was no time

taken for prayer or for family because the show had to go on. We were so caught up in God's work that we forgot about God."[65] This is not limited to people in positions of prominence. As I suggested at the beginning of this chapter, even when people are involved in effective Christian activities that hardly get noticed, serious problems can develop if individual spiritual needs are not met or if emerging spiritual problems are left unchecked. There can be a letdown of one's alertness to spiritually destructive forces, a slide into compromising sinful behavior, an increasing tendency to miss worship services or personal devotions, and a decreasing sensitivity to the Holy Spirit's leading or control. The appearance of hypocrisy and phoniness may not be far behind, along with spiritual naiveté, withdrawal from religious activities, hypercritical attitudes, a greater tendency to self-reliance, and increased justification of one's own behavior. The fruit of the Spirit—love, joy, peace, patience, kindness, goodness, faithfulness, gentleness, and self-control—are experienced less and shown to others with decreasing frequency.

Spiritual effects like these may not be evident immediately. Many spiritually dry or dying people are good actors, especially if they know and can use the accepted theological jargon. Even Moses, whose face once shone as it reflected God's glory, kept a veil over his face so the Israelites could not see that the spiritual glory was fading.[66] Many do something similar today. They try to hide their fading spirituality behind a veil of clichés or pious, often hypocritical, actions that others may or may not notice. Real change only comes to those who turn to the Lord, so the veil is taken away and they become genuinely more like Christ.[67]

2. *Physical Effects.* It is well known that psychological tension and conflicts can influence the body physically, but can there also be a spiritually produced sickness and even death?[68] Not all illness comes from sin in the patient's life,[69] but sometimes sin does produce sickness. The good news is that positive spiritual experiences also have the effect of improving health and hastening recovery in people who are sick.[70]

3. *Psychological Effects.* Spiritual struggles and waning spiritual vitality can lead to guilt feelings, self-condemnation, discouragement, lethargy, fear, defensiveness, bitterness, hypercriticism, anger, and distorted values, among other effects.

4. *Social Effects.* Christian unity and togetherness can be a beautiful experience, but Christian conflict can be vicious. In his discussion of spiritual immaturity, the apostle Paul mentioned two issues of special significance: jealousy and strife. When there is spiritual growing, the barriers between people disintegrate;[71] when there are spiritual problems, then unkind criticism, cynicism, and interpersonal tension (jealousy and strife) are among the first and clearest signs of trouble.

5. *Behavioral Effects.* The Christian message is intended to change people, who, in turn, can change their worlds and impact others. Confined to a Roman prison, Paul once wrote about people who were free to preach the Gospel but whose motives were guided by selfish ambition and the desire to stir up trouble.[72] Whatever is happening spiritually within a person will be apparent to others sooner or later. The life of the true disciple reflects Christlike characteristics and seeks to have a part in caring for others and building believers. When Christ is pushed behind human motives or ambitions, there is likely to be insensitivity, distorted values, and evidence of the spiritual deadness inside.

Counseling and Spiritual Problems

With the upsurge of interest in spirituality, we have seen increasing interest as well in related topics, including spiritual direction, spiritual formation, spiritual disciplines, spiritual interventions, spiritual warfare, spiritual journeying, and spiritually sensitive psychotherapy, along with soul care, pastoral care, pastoral counseling, and Christian counseling.[73] To complicate the issue, we have what one whole issue of the *Journal of Psychology and Theology* termed the "tributaries of Christian Spirituality," including the Orthodox, Roman Catholic, Episcopal (Anglican), Reformed, Wesleyan-Holiness, Pentecostal/Charismaticism, and others that might be added, such as the Fundamentalist and mainstream Evangelical traditions.[74] It can be exciting to recognize the robust diversity of these different approaches, but disentangling all of this is beyond the scope of this book. Instead, the following paragraphs will focus on more traditional counseling, with some diversion into the related discipline of spiritual direction.

At the beginning, it may help to remind ourselves that the course of any counseling largely depends on the nature of the counselee's problem. If a person raises theological questions, the counseling will differ from the help given to a defiant and unrepentant individual who is involved in deliberate sin and determined to continue. If a counselee is sincerely concerned about spiritual emptiness in his or her life, the counselor's approach will differ from that taken with someone who is bitter and angry with God. As with every other type of counseling, spiritual caregivers must listen carefully, show acceptance and empathy, and try to determine the nature and causes of the real problem. In every case, counseling people with spiritual issues is likely to involve at least some of the following.

1. *Prayer.* Before, during, and after counseling, the Christian counselor must seek divine guidance. More than any other form of helping, spiritual counseling can involve us in conflict with satanic forces. This is one major reason why Christian counselors need to pray for special strength, wisdom, and direction. At times, counselors may choose to pray directly with the counselee, but it is important to ask counselees for their permission first, since some people could feel awkward and resistant to prayer in a counseling session. It is important, as well, to remember that not all prayer is good. Jesus criticized prayers that were smug or included empty repetition. Prayer can also be an escape from facing reality and responsibility if people want to pray and then do nothing.[75] Regardless, the counselor always should spend at least some time alone in prayer concerning each counselee.

Does prayer have a psychological effect on the people who come for help? The answer appears to be yes. A variety of surveys have shown consistently that about nine out of every ten Americans believe in God, most pray at least on occasion, and over 90 percent believe that he answers. The figures differ from country to country, however, and there are variations depending on how the questions are worded. Even so, a high percentage of Americans believe in God even when he is described as "the all-powerful, all-knowing, perfect Creator of the universe who rules the world today."[76] It is not surprising that a number of research studies show that, unlike most of their secular counselors, many counselees believe in the power of prayer and experience increased psychological well-being and decreased anxiety and other symptoms as a result of praying. Although researchers have difficulty measuring spirituality and defining what they mean by prayer, there is empirical evidence that prayer enhances spirituality and contributes to the effectiveness of psychotherapy.[77]

2. *Modeling.* People imitate and follow people. This was the basis of early social learning theory and is a principle that appears clearly in the New Testament. Jesus was an example for the disciples, Paul instructed the believers to "follow my example, just as I follow Christ's," and Peter urged church leaders to be examples to the flock.[78] Christians, including Christian counselors, are examples of Christian living. The counselor who is not seeking to imitate Christ or to grow as a Christian will not be effective in spiritual counseling, at least in Christian spiritual counseling, because he or she cannot be an effective model. The counselor who wants to be effective in helping those with spiritual problems must recognize that he or she is a model that counselees will follow—and occasionally react against.

3. *Exhorting.* This word often implies urging, insisting, pushing, or pressuring another person to take action or to change. As used in the Bible, however, exhorting tends to have a less demanding tone and is closer to guiding, encouraging, or urging that there be change. Exhortation involves a God-given ability to come alongside to help, to strengthen those who are spiritually weak, to reassure those who are wavering in their faith, to support those who are facing adverse circumstances, and to encourage those who lack assurance or security. At times, the helper will point out sin, challenge the counselee's thinking or conclusions, encourage the counselee to change, guide as decisions are made, and give support as new behavior is tried and evaluated.

4. *Teaching.* Beginning counselors (and some who are more experienced) tend to be advice-givers who tell people what to do. Frequently, this reflects the anxiety of counselors who want to provide immediate answers that ease their own discomforts and relieve the counselee's suffering. There is not a lot of evidence that people change as a result of advice, although advice-givers can delude themselves into thinking that they have given the needed help.

Spiritual growth and counseling can be a slower process of soul care that may involve traveling through times of difficulty and spiritual darkness with the gentle instruction of a wise guide. As a process of guidance and teaching, spiritual counseling includes modeling, giving information, answering questions, stimulating thinking, pointing out errors, and sometimes making suggestions that can be discussed together. The teaching may involve a variety of issues, including one or more of the following.

(a) Knowing and Loving God. Confusion and spiritual problems often come to those who have a distorted or incomplete view of God. To know about the wrath of God without seeing his mercy is to plunge one into fear and guilt. To stress his mercy and love without his holiness and justice can lull people into a false sense of security and a lack of concern about spiritual issues and responsibilities.

God wants us to know him,[79] although this is not something that any human being will accomplish completely, at least in this life. We get to know God better by seeking to understand his Word as revealed in the Bible and as guided by the Holy Spirit, by thinking about his character and thanking him for who he is, by obeying his commands, and finally by participating in worship and service within the church. The better we know him in these ways, the greater the assurance we have in times of stress.

The spiritual counselor does not teach people about God by giving lectures or assigning books to read. More effective for the counselee is seeing God in the counselor's lifestyle, values, conversation, attitudes and, periodic comments about God or about the Bible. We who are counselors cannot teach others to know God unless we, ourselves, are growing in this knowledge and in our own spiritual walk. Helping counselees to know God requires understanding and spiritual depth that will not be perfect, but that far exceeds the teaching of any book on counseling or psychotherapy.

(b) Christian Love. A former president of the American Psychological Association must have astonished many of his colleagues when he wrote that the giving, sacrificial, unconditional Christlike love described in 1 Corinthians 13 is "incomparably the greatest psychotherapeutic agent; something that professional psychiatry cannot of itself create, focus, nor release."[80] Love is the attribute of God that led him to send his Son to earth so that we personally might become acquainted with the Lord of the universe.[81] Counselees need to hear about God's love. Even more, they need to experience and observe this love as it flows from God, through the dedicated counselor (and other Christians), and into the lives of counselees who feel unloved, unaccepted, guilty, confused, and spiritually needy.

(c) Sin and Forgiveness. Unlike many counselors, the Bible never avoids the topic of sin or deemphasizes its prevalence and destructiveness.[82] God hates sin and eventually punishes unrepentant sinners, but he also provided a way out. God's Son, Jesus Christ, came to pay for our sins. When we sin, therefore, we can be forgiven completely. "If we confess our sins to him [Jesus], he is faithful and just to forgive us and to cleanse us from every wrong." People who are skeptical of the Bible's authority may not accept this conclusion, but for those who do, the complete forgiveness of sins can be liberating. God doesn't want sacrifices and penance. He wants confession and a willingness to change. When he hears our confession, he forgives and completely forgets.[83]

The Bible also recognizes the importance of other people in the forgiveness process. We are instructed to confess our sins to one another.[84] This is not to get divine forgiveness because God forgives when we confess to him directly. Nevertheless, confession to others can be therapeutic. Often, it encourages others to forgive in return, and sometimes this forgiveness from God and from other human beings enables counselees to forgive themselves.

The counselor must look for opportunities to share this biblical truth about sin and forgiveness. At times, it will be necessary to confront counselees with their sin and point out the importance of confession, forgiveness, and change. When this is done in a harsh condemning way, the counselor may show a self-righteous superiority, but the counselee is likely to feel intimidated and threatened. Sometimes, Jesus appeared to be harsh in pointing out sin, but more often he was straightforward and quick to show a forgiving and nonjudgmental attitude. Nobody can talk about forgiveness with credibility while he or she refuses to demonstrate it.

As we have seen in earlier chapters, the therapeutic value of forgiveness has become increasingly accepted in psychological circles. To forgive others and to accept forgiveness can have strong benefits, although the psychological perspectives on forgiveness are incomplete because most do not recognize the biblical and theological dimensions.[85]

(d) Holy Spirit Control. Christian counselors must never underestimate the role of the Holy Spirit in counseling. Often he gives counselors discernment and wisdom and supplements our training and experience so that we are more effective in the counseling role. As he works in and through counselors, the Holy Spirit also works in the lives of counselees, bringing healing, identifying sin, teaching about forgiveness, giving guidance, and pointing us to Christ.

In Ephesians 5:18, Christians are commanded to let the Holy Spirit fill and control us. This is a process that involves:

- Self-examination (Acts 20:28; 1 Corinthians 1:28).
- Confession of all known sin (1 John 1:9).
- Complete voluntary submission to God (Romans 6:11–13).
- Asking in prayer for the Holy Spirit's filling (Luke 1:13).
- Believing that we then are filled with the Spirit, and thanking God for this (1 Thessalonians 5:18).

Spirit-filling is not a once-in-a-lifetime event. It is a daily process of breathing out sin through confession and breathing in the fullness of the Holy Spirit. This repeated filling is not always accompanied by emotional highs or ecstatic experiences (although these do come at times), but it does lead to joyful thanksgiving, to mutual submission, and to the development of love, peace, patience, self-control, and the other fruits of the Spirit.[86]

Many of the spiritual problems discussed in this chapter arise and persist because believers attempt to solve problems and grow on their own. It is the Holy Spirit who teaches, strengthens, and empowers counselors and their counselees to overcome the spiritual challenges and other problems of life.

(e) Discipleship. In the Great Commission, Jesus instructed believers to make disciples, a process that involves evangelism and Christian education.[87] At times, the counselor will want to evangelize, sharing the good news of the Gospel, but extreme care must be taken to respect the counselee's purpose in seeking help. It is a violation of counselor ethics to push religious teaching onto counselees who resist such teaching or who want to focus on other issues. The counselor and counselee may discuss the meaning and importance of Bible study, prayer, trust in God, meditation, discipline in our devotional lives, and reaching out to others, but usually this is not the prime purpose for counseling, and insensitive counselors who insist on raising these issues can bring harm to counselees, especially when they might be vulnerable and not ready for the influx of religion. To do this without permission is a breach of ethics that could create legal problems for some counselors, depending on where they live and work.

Even in religious settings, where references to religion are accepted and expected, well-meaning but insensitive counselors may be too hasty in presenting the Gospel or urging counselors to make a commitment to Christ. Wherever they work, Christian counselors might hope to see all of their counselees come to Christ and grow spiritually, but genuine spiritual growth is slow, Holy Spirit directed, and potentially harmful if raised too abruptly, too soon, and too enthusiastically. Seeking the Holy Spirit's leading must be a constant goal for Christian counselors. With his guidance, the effective and sensitive counselor moves gently into discussions of spiritual matters, aware that it is the Holy Spirit who (in his timing and in his ways) convicts people of sin and brings them to repentance and growth as disciples. Those who counsel people on spiritual issues must submit themselves to being divine instruments in this process.

(f) Surrender. Much of our discussion thus far implies that the counselee will surrender his or her life and problems to Christ. Surrender is not a passive waiting for God to take care of everything. It involves an active relinquishing of one's will to God's control. Teaching people to surrender is related closely to other counseling methods; surrender brings additional benefits in dealing with spiritual and other problems.[88]

(g) Balance. Counselees with spiritual problems need to be alerted to the importance of nonspiritual influences, such as eating a balanced diet, getting rest, and taking time for recreation and exercise. Counselees can be helped to develop balanced lifestyles that avoid legalism and self-sufficiency; deal with pride and bitterness; reevaluate values, goals, and priorities; eliminate theological misunderstanding; and are free from the twin problems of spiritual undernourishment and overfeeding.

(h) The Body. As we have emphasized, Christianity is not a do-it-yourself religion. God made us to be social creatures and declared that it is not good for humans to be alone.[89] Christians are pictured as being part of a body, the church. Each of us has specially given abilities and gifts that are to be developed and used to serve and care for one another,[90] and to build up the church so that praise comes to Jesus Christ.[91]

The effectiveness of Christian counseling will be weakened if it exists apart from the support, encouragement, and connection with the body of Christ, the church. Believers are instructed to help one another and to bear one another's burdens. When counselees experience this acceptance and support, they are better able to work with their counselors in handling spiritual and other problems. An earlier chapter mentioned one counselor who expects that all of his counselees will come regularly for counseling, participate in a small group, and attend worship services on a regular basis. This may not work with all counselees, but it is a good means for grounding counseling in the supportive context of a church.

5. *Spiritual Direction.* For Christians in the various Protestant traditions, spiritual direction may seem like something new. Instead, it is an ancient approach to spirituality that appears to have its roots in the monks and nuns who lived in the deserts of Egypt, Syria, and Palestine in the fourth through the seventh centuries. Their practices of spiritual direction were further developed and carried on in the Middle Ages by religious orders such as the Benedictines and Carmelites. Later, spiritual direction became influential in sixteenth-century Spain, and more recently it has been practiced in Catholic, Anglican, and Orthodox traditions. The Protestant interest and involvement in spiritual direction appears to have been more of a twentieth-century development that today is of interest to many believers, including Evangelicals and Christian counselors.

Anything as rich and as complex as spiritual direction cannot be summarized in a few paragraphs. Spiritual direction takes a variety of forms, and there is ongoing discussion about the ways in which it relates to pastoral care, psychotherapy, and other forms of care-giving.[92] This much is commonly accepted: the prime goal of spiritual direction is to facilitate the directee's movement toward a more mature relationship with God. As defined by David Benner, who is an evangelical leader in the movement, *"spiritual direction is a prayer process in which a person seeking help in cultivating a deeper personal relationship with God meets with another for prayer and conversation that is focused on increasing awareness of God in the midst of life experiences and facilitating surrender to God's will."*[93] Unlike counseling, spiritual direction does not exist to solve problems or to reduce symptoms. There is no focus on building a director-directee therapeutic relationship like the bond between counselor and counselee. Instead, the director is more interested in helping the directee get closer to God, even as the director also is getting closer to God and helping another person in the process.

As might be expected, spiritual direction uses a variety of techniques, including various types of prayer, the pursuit of self-knowledge, a willingness to enter into the suffering and pain inherent in personal and spiritual growth, a commitment to detaching from excessive ties to gratification and relationships, and learning to better love one's neighbor.[94] While there is no standardized program to becoming a spiritual director and no licensing requirements, almost all spiritual directors have been directees themselves and are devoted to the ongoing process of getting closer to God. It is valuable for counselors to know what spiritual direction is and to learn more about it, but without personal involvement in the process, counselors are not likely to be competent in bringing spiritual direction into their counseling.

Before leaving this issue, it might be helpful to give brief mention to *spiritual formation*, another concept that is attracting attention among Christian counselors

Psychiatrist Gerald G. May wrote that "spiritual formation is a rather general term referring to all attempts, means, instructions, and disciplines intended towards deepening of faith and furtherance of spiritual growth. It includes educational endeavors as well as the more intimate and in-depth process of spiritual direction."[95] Spiritual formation involves training people in spiritual activities (including the training of seminary students), teaching people how to practice the spiritual disciplines, and allowing the Holy Spirit and the Word of God to shape people spiritually.[96] It can be difficult to know how spiritual formation relates to spiritual direction and how Christian counselors can use either of these to help their counselees.[97]

6. *Spiritual Warfare*. Paraphrasing C. S. Lewis, it would appear that there are two equal and opposite errors into which Christian counselors can fall when they consider the issue of the demonic. One is to assume that all problems have a psychological origin, are best treated psychologically, and do not need deliverance, exorcisms, or confrontations with the devil. The other error is to assume that Satan and his demonic forces are to blame for all problems, that psychological approaches ultimately are powerless, and that exorcisms and rebuking Satan and his forces are the preferred methods (and in some churches considered to be the only methods) of bringing change. Lewis might conclude that demonic forces, themselves, are equally pleased with both extremes.

It is a basic truth of the Christian belief system that followers of Christ are in a spiritual struggle and that each of us should constantly be alert to satanic influences in our own lives and in the lives of our counselees. Ephesians 6 warns that Christians are in a continual fight that is not against people made of flesh and blood, "but against the evil rulers and authorities of the unseen world, against those mighty powers of darkness who rule this world, and against wicked spirits in the heavenly realms."[98] We are never instructed to battle these forces in highly dramatic exorcisms and confrontations with Satan. Instead, we are to "be strong with the Lord's mighty power," to put on "all of God's armor so that you will be able to stand firm against all strategies and tricks of the Devil."[99] When a Christian draws near to God with humility and resists the devil, he will flee,[100] without dramatic confrontations. We are to stand firm against the devil, not trying to resist him with our own strength, but relying instead on Christ's mighty power.

It is important to recognize that satanic-demonic influences can range from temptation, such as that faced by Jesus in Matthew 4:1–11, all the way to total domination, like that shown in the Gadarene demon-possessed men.[101] Temptations can be resisted by a simple prayer, but exorcism is a ritual for dealing with demons that most often is used with people who appear to be highly controlled by the forces of evil. Deliverance is a more simple form of exorcism, used with people who earnestly desire to be freed from apparent demonic influence in some area of their lives. In deliverance, the demonic forces are resisted in the name of Jesus Christ and commanded to leave. In each of these activities—prayer, deliverance, and exorcism—the resulting change is likely to be temporary unless there is a filling with the Holy Spirit and a commitment to practicing spiritual disciplines.

Should the Christian counselor engage in these forms of spiritual warfare? Certainly it is appropriate to pray privately for counselees and sometimes to pray with them. But whether counselors should engage in more overt forms of spiritual warfare, including exorcism, is controversial, in part because it is so difficult to distinguish between psychopathology that has biological or psychological causes and abnormal behavior that is the direct result of demons; between the need for medical treatment or psychotherapy and the need for direct spiritual warfare.[102] Within recent years there seems to have been an increase in occult activity, especially among young people, and there also appears to be new interest and involvement in spiritism, Eastern mysticism, fortune-telling, witchcraft, black magic, demonic-focused video games, and even Satan worship. Many professional counselors and theologians agree that this kind of involvement is dangerous. It can open individuals to control by evil spiritual forces that may sometimes lead to behavior that resembles but often goes beyond the symptoms of psychopathology. These spiritual forces are unmoved by traditional methods of counseling.

On occasion, therefore, the counselor will conclude that counseling is ineffective because of powerful satanic influences within the counselee's life. Be careful that this conclusion is not used as an excuse to cover and explain away either your own incompetence and lack of skill or the counselee's lack of cooperation. If you decide that there could be demonic involvement (preferably after consultation with others who are competent in giving an opinion), then it may be wise to consider exorcism. The methods of exorcism are varied and depend in part on one's theology, but in every case, exorcism involves commanding, in the name of Jesus Christ, that the demonic forces leave the individual and never return. Dealing with the demonic in this way should be done cautiously and reluctantly, only by the spiritually mature,[103] in the presence of other believers, and by those whom the church recognizes as being specially gifted as "discerners of spirits."[104] In moving in this direction, counselors should realize the danger of getting involved with the demonic to such an extent that counselors become experts on demons (more than they are experts on Christ) and so fascinated with the demonic that this dominates their thinking, teaching, counseling, and ministries.

It appears that some enthusiastic but ill-informed people have limited understanding of the causes and treatment of abnormality, attribute all problems to demon involvement, and use exorcisms as a way to avoid the work of counseling or to inadvertently hide their ignorance about human behavior. This can create far more problems than it solves. Counselees can misinterpret comments about Satan, sometimes develop paranoid fears of the demonic, and often have their problems made worse when they hear they are demon possessed. The problems are accentuated when exorcisms fail to bring any change, leaving the counselee to struggle both with the original problem and with the belief that he or she is possessed by demonic forces.

It is important, therefore, that counselors use discretion in mentioning Satan and should be alert to potential counselee misconceptions about the devil. His influence and power should be clearly understood, recognized, and firmly resisted with determination and with the Holy Spirit's power. Most Christian counselees will be able to understand both the devil's influence and the resounding truth that the Holy Spirit who resides in us is greater than the devil who is in the world.[105]

Preventing Spiritual Problems

The Bible is filled with men and women who served God faithfully but who encountered a variety of problems. Some of these came because people slipped into sin, like David, who got involved sexually with a woman who was not his wife. Others, like Jeremiah, Job, John the Baptist, and Jesus himself, lived godly lives, but they were allowed to experience problems despite their exemplary behavior. Jesus told the disciples to expect suffering and difficulties, regardless of their way of life. His life on earth was not easy, and he never promised that his followers would be free of problems. Instead, he said that suffering should be expected, but that it would help us to grow.[106] Paul learned this and reflected on his struggles whenever he was in jail, summarizing the things that he had suffered as a result of his determination to be a faithful follower of Christ.

This all means that believers can expect problems, some of which bring glory to God, but from this it does not follow that we forget about prevention. We know that practicing the spiritual disciplines brings a greater spiritual depth, that lives controlled by the fruit of the Spirit are different and usually better than lives that are self-centered, that people who live in accordance with biblical values ultimately are happier than people like that rich man who hoarded his possessions, tore down his barns, built store houses that were bigger, but then died, leaving it all behind. In-depth spirituality does not come automatically. It has to be nourished and nurtured. Through counseling, but especially through the church, the Christian can be taught how to prevent some of the spiritual problems of life. The preventive measures, surely well known to most Christian leaders, include:

- Committing one's life to Christ and accepting him as Lord and Savior.
- Developing the practice of regular, consistent prayer, Bible study, and other spiritual disciplines.
- Regularly confessing sin and asking for God's forgiveness, guidance, and the power to be obedient.
- Yielding to the Holy Spirit's control and expecting the Holy Spirit's filling.
- Becoming involved actively in a local body of believers where there can be accountability and opportunity for worship in community with others.

- Reaching out to others in evangelism and service.
- Being alert to the devil and his forces, actively resisting these influences with humility and Christ-honoring living.

This is not presented as a complete or simplistic formula to prevent all spiritual problems. Nevertheless, the guidelines presented in this section form the foundation upon which the preventive, discipleship, and mentoring programs must be built.

Conclusions About Spiritual Problems

Unlike some of the other topics that are addressed in this book, the issues relating to spirituality have concerned Christian leaders and care-givers for centuries. Since the Bible speaks so frequently about spiritual issues, some believers have concluded that all our problems are spiritual and that all can be solved through the discovery and application of some biblical principle. We may respect and admire the dedication of many who hold such views, but this is difficult to apply in practice.

Spiritual problems have causes and solutions that most often are described in the Scriptures. The Bible, however, never claims to be a psychiatric diagnostic manual and textbook of counseling procedures any more than it claims to be a medical text. While *all* our problems ultimately result from the fall of the human race, not all human problems are spiritual, in that they involve the counselee's specific relationship with God. Some problems, for example, may be caused by faulty learning, misinformation, early trauma, environmental stress, biological malfunctioning, chemical deficiencies, misperception, errors in decision making, or other issues that may not be discussed by biblical writers. Many times people experience problems that are self-created because of each person's actions or attitudes. In contrast, other problems come from events in the environment or the actions of others that have caused innocent people to suffer through no fault of their own. In all these situations, counseling may involve using techniques derived from the Scripture. More often, the counselor will use methods that are *consistent with the Bible's teachings and values,* but that God has allowed us to discover and develop through social science, medical research, and sometimes common sense.

Christian counseling, then, is deeply concerned with the issues discussed in this chapter, but it goes further. It recognizes that all truth, including psychological truth, comes from God—sometimes through secular psychology and research by a variety of different specialists, including many who are not believers. The Christian evaluates these secular findings carefully and discards that which clearly is inconsistent with the Bible, even though the techniques may work. That which remains is used along with and in submission to biblical teaching. The counselor, so equipped, then seeks to be used by God to touch lives and change them so that people can be helped to live with greater meaning, stability, fulfillment, and spiritual maturity.

KEY POINTS FOR BUSY COUNSELORS

➤ The integration of spirituality into the professional practice of psychology has become a mushrooming area of interest among mental-health professionals. Christian counselors are especially able to help people with spiritual issues.

➤ Counselors need to understand the causes of spiritual problems, especially those relating to Christian spirituality. Causes relate to:
- *Where people are* personally in terms of their relationship with Christ.
- *Where people live.* Some environments, especially home and peer relationships, shape and impact spirituality.
- *How people live and act.* Sinful thoughts and actions, along with legalism, are two crucial issues impacting spiritual problems.
- *What people think.* Probably most human problems begin in the mind. Self-sufficiency, pride, bitterness, and non-Christian values can create and accentuate spiritual problems.
- *What people lack* in terms of:
  - understanding of spiritual issues,
  - spiritual nourishment,
  - giving,
  - balance,
  - commitment,
  - simplicity,
  - Holy Spirit power,
  - spiritual disciplines, and
  - involvement with the church.
- *What people experience*, especially in terms of suffering that leads to growth.
- *What people fight*, in terms of spiritual warfare.

➤ Spiritual problems affect people spiritually, physically, psychologically, socially, and behaviorally, which relates to what they do and how they act.

➤ The course of any counseling largely depends on the nature of the counselee's problem. In counseling for spiritual issues, a selection of the following will be used in each case:
- Prayer. This comes before, during, and after the session, but it may come through silent prayer from the counselor or more focused prayer with the counselor and counselee praying together aloud.
- Modeling. People imitate and follow other people, so the counselor's personal spirituality is a model for counselees.
- Exhorting. As used in the Bible, this involves coming alongside to walk with people in need, strengthening the spiritually weak, and giving reassurance, support, and encouragement. At times the helper will point out

sin, challenge the counselee's thinking or conclusions, encourage the counselee to change, guide as decisions are made, and give support as new behavior is tried and evaluated.

- Teaching. This involves instruction and guidance in basics of healthy spirituality.
- Spiritual Direction and sometimes spiritual formation.
- Spiritual Warfare. This needs to be approached with caution. No counselor or counselee can do battle with demonic forces and succeed apart from the Holy Spirit's guidance and control.

➤ All problems, including spiritual problems, arise because of the fall of the human race into sin. Often counseling involves dealing with personal sin in the counselee's life, but it is simplistic to assume that this is the major approach for all counseling. Christian counselors seek to be growing spiritually in their own lives and using their gifts, training, and spiritual knowledge to help others using a variety of techniques that are consistent with Christian values.

42

Counseling the Counselor

A young man, filled with enthusiasm and idealism, once decided to list the good things in life. His tally was long and impressive. The list included health, love, good looks, talent, riches, fame, influence, along with other less obvious ingredients that would seem to make life complete.

When the inventory was completed, its author proudly showed it to an older friend and spiritual mentor. "I was trying to impress him with my wisdom and the universality of my interests," the young list-maker wrote later, but the older man did not appear to be impressed.

"It's an excellent list," he said after reading it slowly and with care. "However, I think you have omitted the most important ingredient of all. Without it the whole list will be a meaningless and intolerable burden."

As the young man watched, his friend grabbed a pencil and crossed out the entire page. At the bottom he wrote three words: peace of mind.

"This is the gift that God reserves for his special protégés, he said. "Many have beauty, talent, wealth, and even fame. But most people wait, often in vain and sometimes through their whole lives, hoping to know a deep sense of inner peace."[1]

When he talked to the disciples before the crucifixion, Jesus gave no indication that his followers should expect wealth, beauty, economic security, or acclaim. He never promised freedom from suffering, persecution, sickness, discouragement, vocational uncertainty, or financial strain—but he did promise peace. "I am leaving you with a gift—peace of mind and heart," he said. "And the peace I give isn't like the peace the world gives. So don't be troubled or afraid."[2]

Several years later, during one of his times in prison, Paul mentioned his contentment despite the unpleasant circumstances.[3] In a setting that could have stimulated intense anxiety, discouragement, self-pity, and even anger at God, the apostle instead encouraged his fellow believers to rejoice regardless of the circumstances and to experience the peace of God: "Always be full of joy in the Lord. I say it again—rejoice.... Don't worry about anything; instead, pray about everything. Tell God what you need, and thank him for all he has done. If you do this, you will experience God's peace, which is far more wonderful than the human mind can understand. His peace will guard your hearts and minds as you live in Christ Jesus."[4]

Perhaps it is true that nothing in life is more valuable, more sought, and more often missed than God-given peace of mind. Trapped in the turmoil of their confusing conflicts, ongoing stress, and pressing problems, many of our counselees have no inner sense of peace. Even more tragic is that many counselors fare no better.

Christian counseling can have a variety of goals, but at its core is the effort to help people find peace with God, peace with others, and peace with themselves. Sometimes, this peace comes closer when people admit their problems and talk about their feelings, acquire better interpersonal and communication skills, change their attitudes and control harmful thought patterns, get insights into their own actions, and learn how to change their ways of doing things. All of these are ways in which counselors help people to face and cope with the conflicts that block or disrupt peace.

Whether or not we use counseling methods, ultimate peace for the counselee and for the counselor comes from God. It comes to those who cast their anxieties on the Lord, present their requests to God with prayer and thanksgiving, let their minds dwell on thoughts that are pure and Christ-honoring, resist satanic influences, and live in ways that would please Christ.[5] Lasting peace comes from the Holy Spirit, the Comforter, often as we meditate on the Word of God and practice the spiritual disciplines.[6]

The Counselor's Stresses

Christian counselors may understand the causes of problems, the best methods of treatment, and the power of the Holy Spirit in bringing peace to our counselees, but this does not protect us from experiencing many of the same struggles that face our counselees. Counseling can be rewarding and fulfilling work, but it also can be highly stressful. It is not easy to listen to people pour out their stories of depression, disappointment, despair, confusion, and conflict. Along with rescue workers, emergency room personnel, and others who try to help in times of crisis, counselors work under ongoing stress. We work to help people function better, but whenever we are successful, our counselees go off on their own, and they are replaced by more hurting people. After a while, constantly caring for others can hurt the care-givers.[7] Eventually, care-givers need to be cared for themselves.

1. *The Counselor's Work.* At least three influences put stress on counselors. The first of these is the nature of our work. Counseling can be a grueling and demanding calling, according to psychologist John Norcross, who has devoted many years to the study of counselor stress. "A growing body of empirical research attests to the negative toll extracted by a career in psychotherapy. Although each of us experiences distress differently, the literature points to moderate depression, mild anxiety, emotional exhaustion, and disruptive relationships as the common residue of immersing ourselves in the inner worlds of distressed and distressing people."[8] It is well known, in addition, that counselors can experience compassion fatigue, burnout, cynicism, emotional exhaustion, and disillusionment. In part, this depends on each counselor's age, amount of experience, and type of work—some counseling settings are more stressful than others.[9] Research suggests that beginning counselors have some of the greatest stresses because of seven pressures that come to novice practitioners: the ambiguity of the work that they are seeking to do, acute performance anxiety, their fragile self-concepts as practitioners, the ongoing scrutiny of their supervisors and other professionals, emotional boundaries that either are porous or too rigid, inadequate understanding of the therapeutic process, glamorized but unrealistic

expectations about the help they might be able to give, and a lack of respected positive mentors.[10]

One reason for counselor stress is the constant need to be giving. Hour after hour, day after day, we are asked to pour out our insights, sensitivity, compassion, healing skills, and inner energies. We see the needs and feel the pain. We want to bring healing and we long to help. So we give repeatedly, with the noblest of motives, until we run dry or run down from exhaustion. Sometimes overnight, almost without warning, we discover that there is nothing left to give. The Christian counselor, once filled with Christian compassion, finds that he or she is spiritually empty. There are no more inner resources.

While we struggle, needy people keep asking for our help. Like the poor who always will be with us,[11] there always will be those who are hurting psychologically or spiritually, longing for guidance, and searching for peace. Most of us want to help. That may be why we are involved in counseling or have spent many hours working through the pages of a book like this.

Eventually, we realize that no one person can do everything and that nobody can give indefinitely. We know the dangers of trying to go on, but too often we who can challenge others are less able to challenge ourselves.

2. *The Counselor's Attitudes.* An earlier chapter reported an astonishing fact about heart bypass patients. All these men and woman had experienced open heart surgery, and all were told that they would have to change their lifestyles and eating habits if they were to prevent further heart problems. Almost all of them agreed that they needed to change, but when they were contacted two years later, 90 percent had not changed. These people knew that their chances of dying from heart disease were high if they did not change, but they still did not change.[12]

This is not limited to heart patients. Even when they see the evidence of burnout, very few highly successful people make changes in their lives or contact a counselor unless they experience a crisis.[13] Counselors observe their own symptoms of distress but explain this away as one hazard of their profession and conclude that they can get past the stress without making changes.[14] As a result, their effectiveness declines, and they begin to neglect their counselees or use them to meet the counselor's own needs for intimacy, esteem, affirmation, or dominance.[15]

Research suggests that there are three key characteristics or attitudes within well-functioning counselors: self-awareness, self-regulation, and self-balance.[16] Counselors who have *self-awareness* about their own functioning are much more effective in their counseling work. It is possible for counselors to monitor their own behavior, but often it is better to get the consistent input from another person. For example, one counselor looks to his wife to help monitor his functioning. When his wife notices that he is "looking haggard, working longer hours, or traveling too often," he takes her observations seriously and slows down.

The slowing down is a part of *self-regulation*. For each person this will be different, but it may include more actively managing one's lifestyle, energy, relationships, stress levels, or workload. For some counselors, self-regulation means taking active steps to reduce stress, perhaps by seeing fewer counselees for a while, or taking more time off. Sometimes, self-regulation only comes with the help of another counselor who can help reduce anxiety, insecurity, anger, or excessive pressure. It is not enough to be aware of one's own problems; the effective counselor does something about them.

This brings us to *balance*, something that is difficult for any of us who are care-givers. Balance involves taking time to attend to core needs of physical activity, exercise,[17] rest, mental stimulation—not too little but not too much—worship, work, and play. It is easy for counselors to focus on the problems of strangers but ignore the stresses and strains in their own marriages, families, or close relationships. Sometimes, counselors get so involved with counselee needs that they become emotionally depleted and have no physical or mental energy to care for themselves or their families.

In an insightful article, one counselor described his previous habit of listening intensely to people at the office but ignoring the needs of his family when he got home after a busy day. One night after work his wife, Linda, looked him directly in the eyes and said, "You make your living from giving people your full attention. Then you come home and make me feel like I'm a buzzing fly you'd like to swat. Do I have to pay you to get you to listen to me the way you listen to your clients?" For Linda's counselor husband, this was a startling statement that led to a major shift in his behavior. The counselor realized that he had slipped into the habit of giving all his energies to counselees and then would come home radiating with the message that he had no more to give because "I already gave at the office."[18]

3. *The Counselor's Isolation.* Counseling can be lonely work. We sit in a room by ourselves, listening to people with problems and trying to help, sometimes going for several hours without seeing another human being apart from our counselees. Often, counselors work on the front lines of emergencies or medical crises, helping with special needs, trying to help when situations are difficult. Even as they work with others, counselors can feel a myriad of emotional problems themselves—helplessness, confusion about what to do, stress, loneliness, compassion fatigue, feelings of hopelessness when they are trying to give hope, unexpressed desires to escape if only for a few hours, but pressure to remain and keep giving encouragement and help.[19] Is it surprising that care-givers sometimes carry their burdens alone?

Glenn Wagner is a former pastor who courageously told his story of "walking alone" on a journey into depression. His comments about pastors could apply to other counselors as well:

> I felt trapped and alone because the church wasn't able to care for me. I unconsciously felt that I had to keep my struggle to myself. If I were to open up and share my struggle, I feared that I would be rejected by our church leaders and labeled as weak, incompetent, and unspiritual.... I also feared what would happen if the congregation heard of my struggle.... Would they take me seriously as I tried to lead them when I was broken myself? These are thoughts that paralyzed me as I dealt with my depression, and I felt I had no choice other than to walk through my depression alone—which, of course, was a disaster. [20]

How interesting that counselors, who should know better, are reluctant to face or admit their stresses. Instead, perhaps all of us feel at times that we can handle the stresses by ourselves, and bear our burdens alone, lest others perceive us as being weak or incompetent care-givers.

The Counselor's Self-Care

Robert was a good counselor. He knew it. His counselees knew it. "I'm doing well, my practice is pretty full," he told a colleague over lunch. Then he shook his head and whispered what was difficult for him to admit, "But I don't think I want to do it anymore." He had tried to keep the secret hidden for a long time. Now in his early forties, he had spent years getting his training and license as a marriage and family counselor, but his work had ceased to be challenging. He felt stressed, lacking in energy, and emotionally drained. As he talked he also admitted that he felt like a failure—even though he really knew his work was effective in helping people. He wondered if he had made the wrong career choice, confessed that his whole life revolved around helping counselees, and admitted that he had no time or energy for himself or for his family.

Robert didn't quit. With the help of his friend, Robert backed off from his full schedule for a while, reevaluated where he wanted to be, took up some other interests that he had wanted to pursue, and was able to get more balance into his life. To my knowledge, Robert has no spiritual resources in his life, but he was able to avoid burnout by taking some steps toward self-care that can be useful for all counselors.[21] Table 42–1 lists some of the steps that Robert took, along with some others that counselors have found to be helpful.

The Counselor's Supporters

Those of us who work with people often want to get away from people at the end of a busy day. Retreat, of course, is healthy, but sometimes we make the mistake of retreating from those who are willing and able to help refurbish our supply of resources. Family members, close friends, colleagues, and fellow believers are among those who can be helpful, especially if they allow us to be ourselves without having to do off-the-job informal counseling. Some professionals take the time to teach or do research, not necessarily because this is profitable financially, but because there is stimulation and refreshment from interacting with students or other people who are not counselees.

1. *Family.* Many years ago I worked with a colleague who was so busy with his private practice as a marriage counselor that he never was home. His wife handled the family responsibilities, including care for the children, while the husband worked longer and longer hours. Eventually, his family fell apart. He got a divorce and married one of his counselees. I don't know if he got immersed in his practiced and started the same pattern again.

This story is not unusual. Counselors can get so busy that their families suffer and the counselor loses his or her greatest source of strength. Sometimes, of course, counselors have marriage problems or have difficulties with their children, but the healthy response is to get some help and healing. In contrast, one counselor wrote about protecting time for his wife and his family. He wrote about the need to protect his energy for his family. "The time I value most is the time with my family. That part of my life is the most hectic (so many activities for them), but the most rewarding."[22] Effective counselors are careful to keep time and energy for their marriages and families. In turn, the family often gives the replenishment that all counselors need.

Table 42–1

Counselor Self-Care Suggestions

1. **Start a journal.** This can be an informal collection of notations, feelings, observations, experiences, and dreams. Date each entry but don't be rigid about making an entry every day or keeping every entry of the same length. Use the journal as a personal self-conversation. This can help you process feelings, think through decisions, deepen self-awareness, and record observations that might be helpful to reread later. Tape in an occasional photo, sermon outline, or quotation that has been helpful.

2. **Reflect on your history.** Take some time to ponder why you entered the counseling field in the first place. What still is satisfying and what no longer is satisfying? Keep a list of your answers. Your journal would be a good place to keep this record.

3. **Reexamine your motives.** What are your motivations for staying in the counseling field? List both the positive motivations (to help people, be an encourager, use your gifts as a helper, for example) and those that are less positive (wanting to prove yourself, control others, be a rescuer, find the affirmation that you do not get elsewhere, etc.). Show the list to somebody who knows you well and can give a response. What should be added? How might your motives be harming your counselees or yourself? Have you ever considered leaving the field? Why or why not? Record the answers in your journal.

4. **Nourish and replenish yourself.** Consider what you do to nourish and replenish yourself. Be specific. Remember that even Jesus took time away to rest and rejuvenate. We get nourished and replenished in unique ways. Can you rely on some combination of hobbies, concerts, solitude, sports, relationships, vacations, exercise, spiritual practices, sex, travel, or other means to replenish yourself? How can you put this into action? When will you start? Who will hold you accountable?

5. **Think about your strengths and values.** What are your strengths, and how are these being used in your work? Remember that if your strengths and spiritual gifts are not being used, you will not be fully engaged in your work. List your core values. If you are not working within the confines of your values, you will be at least somewhat frustrated, unfulfilled, and unproductive. What changes can you make to be working more in line with your strengths and values?

6. **Deal with your energizers and drainers.** What tasks, kinds of counselees, other people, or activities energize you? What activities, events, or

people drain you of energy and enthusiasm? In what specific ways can you increase the energizers and reduce the drainers from your life and work?

7. **Deal with overextending and overwork.** Overextending involves taking on more than you can handle. Do you do this? If so, can you think of reasons why? How can you prevent or reduce this? Ask similar questions about overwork. Overwork often meets a need of some kind—like giving us an adrenaline rush or making us feel important. What need is being met through your overwork? How can this need be met in more healthy ways?

8. **Watch for signs of burnout.** These include emotional withdrawal from counselees and counseling (even though you may still work as a counselor), avoiding intimacy with the significant people in your life, overindulging in escape behaviors like television or pornography, attempting to control everything, sleeplessness, feelings of helplessness and isolation, irritability, using counselees to meet your own needs, blaming others, or compromising ethical guidelines in your counseling. Signs like these suggest the time has come to make some changes before it is too late.

9. **Consider seeking counseling for yourself.** Many counselors resist getting counseling for themselves, but ask yourself or people who know you well if counseling would be helpful for you. If so, see a counselor.

2. *Friends.* Every counselor knows the joy and freedom of having friends who know little about counseling and are not interested in learning. One of my closest friends and confidants is a professional musician, contemporary worship leader, and technical genius who is thirty years younger than me. We talk about numerous things when we get together, but almost never about psychology. Sometimes, we counsel each other informally, but we prefer to think that we are tossing around our concerns, and this works well for both of us. On occasion, we also hold each other accountable.

At times, all of us can benefit from another person who can hold us accountable. Christian spirituality, personal integrity, and mental stability rarely (if ever) survive in isolation. The Scriptures call us to live in contact with others, encouraging and warning one another,[23] even as we hold one another accountable for actions, lifestyles, and morals. The church is strewn with thousands of former Christian leaders, including a large number of counselors, who were accountable to no human being except themselves, and who fell into immoral, illegal, unethical, and foolish actions as a result. "If you think you are standing strong, be careful, for you too, may fall."[24]

In addition to relationships with close friends, most of us have a group of more casual friends and acquaintances who may not share a lot of our interests but who broaden our experiences and keep us fresh. This group includes fellow worshipers, neighbors, former or present students, or people we know at the fitness centers or clubs where we are members. Without people like this, all counselors tend to be more narrow than their colleagues who are better connected.

3. *Mentors.* Finding a mentor and being mentored can be highly satisfying, especially to counselors who are at the beginning of their careers. Mentors serve as models, encouragers, and guides. They can inspire, answer questions, prevent their protégés from burning out, and help with ethical issues. A good mentor is an experienced friend who walks alongside, showing what good counselors do and what they avoid. I have never met a young counselor, leader, professional, or Christian who did not want and sometimes long for a caring and competent mentor.

Mentoring most often involves a relationship in which a more experienced person seeks to develop and walk with another person who is younger and less experienced. Usually, the mentor is older but not always. Whatever their age difference, sometimes the mentor and protégé become friends and colleagues who mentor one another. Most often, mentoring relationships last for months or even years, but sometimes they can be short. On occasion the mentor and protégé become friends for life. One goal of the relationship is for the protégé to be empowered and guided without being pressed into the mentor's image. When both mentor and protégé are Christians, it is best if the mentor has an ongoing relationship with God, emotional transparency, and a sense of humor, along with basic experience and competence as a counselor. Whatever one's age or experience, there can be benefit in finding a mentor and an equal (arguably greater) satisfaction in being a mentor. Involvement in a mentoring relationship is one of the best ways for counselors of any age to keep perspective and thrive in their work.[25]

4. *Colleagues.* Sometimes, the loneliness of being a counselor is made worse because we work in places where there are not other counselors around. This sense of isolation extends to pastors who are in small churches and to professors who teach in colleges or graduate schools, where there are no other psychology or counseling people on the faculty. The lack of professional associates can leave us feeling isolated and cut off from like-minded colleagues with whom we could talk over decisions, share the challenges of our work, and discuss some of the stress and dissatisfaction that all counselors face. Often counselors will find a consultant or supervisor with whom clinical matters and potential professional problems can be discussed. Even when we do have colleagues, sometimes instead of congeniality and support there can be envy, especially if a colleague has greater success, recognition, personal attractiveness, or capabilities. When these are discussed openly and not allowed to get in the way, good connections with other counselors can be fulfilling and very valuable.

5. *Counselors.* It is difficult and humbling for any of us to admit that "I, who am a counselor, need counseling." You may know all the other counselors in your area, and it might be hard to select one with whom you can talk about yourself. Some professionals look for a counselor who is some distance away, but before moving in that direction, it might be helpful to discuss even this decision with a respected colleague or friend who is closer to home. A number of years ago, psychiatrist Louis McBurney wrote a book with the insightful title *Every Pastor Needs a Pastor.*[26] At times, it can be equally true that every counselor needs a counselor.

The Counselor's Spirituality

Perhaps you have read these words: "I have all the time I need to do all that God intends me to do." I can't identify the source of this wise statement, but it frequently reminds me to reevaluate my work and my priorities. Counselors tend to be compassionate people, but sometimes we take on far more than we can handle and forget that God does not expect us to meet all the needs of humanity. Instead, each of us needs to seek the Holy Spirit's guidance in establishing our priorities. This involves using our God-given brains to ponder what we can and cannot do. Often, it also means seeking the wisdom and guidance of other dedicated believers who know us well.

1. *Pulling Back.* Maybe you have heard about the famous cardiologist who was much in demand as a speaker. He traveled all over the country giving lectures on lifestyle and how to avoid heart attacks. One night his weary body gave out, and he collapsed with a heart attack in the middle of his speech.

How easily we give guidance to others but fail to heed our own words of advice. How quickly we spot hypocrisy in the lives of some Christian leaders but fail to notice the double lives of our own. How freely we tell others to rest, to exercise, to avoid overeating or overwork, but despite our best intentions, we don't follow our own stress-reduction programs and then wonder why we collapse.

Henri J. M. Nouwen was a priest, professor, and counselor who wrote books that contained a wealth of insight. In *The Genesee Diary,* Nouwen described his decision to withdraw from a busy schedule of teaching, writing, and counseling and to retreat for a few months to a Trappist monastery. His desire to serve God had become a tiring job. He had become so much a prisoner of people's expectations that he felt weighed down and far removed from the inner freedom and peace of mind about which he had been writing. So Nouwen stepped back.

But stepping back was not easy. "I had succeeded in surrounding myself with so many classes to prepare, lectures to give, articles to finish, people to meet, phone calls to make, and letters to answer, that I had come quite close to believing that I was indispensable." Was there a quiet stream underneath all the busyness of his world, Nouwen wondered? "Is there a still point where my life is anchored and from which I can reach out with hope and courage and confidence?"[27] Nouwen pulled back from his heavy schedule so he could ponder these questions and reestablish a closer communion with God.

In the midst of a busy ministry, Jesus also took time to pull away.[28] At times he prayed on these mini-retreats. Sometimes, he apparently talked to his friends, and perhaps there were times when he simply rested. People were looking for him and many needed healing, but despite the demands he took time for the rejuvenation he needed.

2. *Setting Priorities.* In the midst of one of his brief retreat times, Jesus was found by Simon and his companions. "Everyone is asking for you!" they exclaimed in their eagerness to bring him back to the crowds. The Lord's reply must have been surprising. "We must go on to other towns as well," Jesus said.[29] He was not disinterested in the people who sought him, but he had carefully thought through his priorities. He knew he had come to preach in different locations, and he was willing to say no to some demands for his time and attention so he could say yes to others.

It is not easy to make decisions about priorities. When this involves saying no, we can feel guilty, especially when fellow believers, prospective counselees, Christian leaders, fund-raisers or others make us feel guilty. It is even harder to say no when we are people pleasers who don't like to disappoint others and who are moved by needs that we are trained to meet. Even so, other people can set our agendas and wear us out when we let ourselves be pressured into making commitments that we should turn down, accept deadlines that are unrealistic, or try to be all things to all people.

The alternative is to take time away to set priorities. What does God want you to do? What are you gifted and especially equipped to do? What are you being asked to do or convincing yourself to do that somebody else could do better? What are your core values and key strengths? Could you come up with a concise mission statement for your life—an indication of what you believe God wants you to do with the time you have here on earth? Do you think this might help you set priorities and avoid stress?

Think about a counselor whom we will call Sara. She is a licensed psychologist with a degree in clinical psychology, but she does not like counseling. It bores her, and she does not feel confident in her ability to help people deal with their problems. Everybody knows that Sara is a terrific teacher and engaging seminar leader who is a specialist in stress management. Even though she is single, her church invited her to lead a marriage retreat for couples and then be available to counsel any who wanted to talk between the teaching sessions. How do you think Sara should have responded? Ask a person like Sara to teach college students about stress, and it would be easy for her to say yes. Ask her to lead that retreat, and she will say no immediately, without any guilt or second thoughts, because she has learned to turn down opportunities to do what she does not do well. There are others who can do the retreat better. As you may have guessed, this description of Sara is fictional, designed to illustrate an important conclusion: setting priorities that utilize our strengths and gifts makes it easier to manage our lives and is good stewardship of the time and gifts that have come to us from God.

3. *Drawing on God's Power.* When Jesus trained the twelve disciples and sent them away for on-the-job training, he gave them power so they could speak and heal.[30] The disciples were not to serve in their own strength. They got their power and authority from the Lord himself.

Maybe there is no research evidence to support this conclusion, but it seems that many counselors who call themselves Christian try to find their strength in counseling theories and techniques. Personal prayer, reflection on the Scriptures, solitude, and the other spiritual disciplines may be acknowledged as being important, but they rarely appear in the lives of these counselors. Corporate worship is of minor importance, and there is little time for uninterrupted confession and communication with God. It is not surprising that these care-givers have little to give spiritually, and often their counseling differs little from the approaches of their secular colleagues.

Several years after his sojourn in the Genesee Monastery, Henri Nouwen reflected on the place of prayer in the helper's life. "You cannot consider yourself a witness for God's presence," he wrote,

> when your own life is cluttered with material possessions, your belly is overfull, and your mind crowded with worries about what to do with what you have.... In our utilitarian culture, in which we suffer from a collective compulsion to do

something practical, helpful, or useful, and to make a contribution that can give us a sense of worth, contemplative prayer . . . is not useful or practical but a wasting of time for God. It cuts a hole in our busyness and reminds us and others that it is God and not we who creates and sustains the world. . . .

Once we really know him in prayer then we can live in this world without a need to cling to anyone for self-affirmation, and then we can let the abundance of God's love be the source of all our ministry.[31]

Consistent prayer, daily meditation on the Word of God, and practice of the other spiritual disciplines enable us to know God, to obey him, and to serve him more fully as his servants and counselors. The counselor draws consistently on his or past training and experiences. We use a variety of techniques in our counseling and help people work toward a variety of goals. But if counseling is to be Christian and maximally effective, we need to be servants who are guided and empowered by the Holy Spirit, and strengthened day-by-day with the insights of Scripture and persisting periods of prayer and discipline.

4. *Reevaluating Lifestyles.* The book of James gives a very practical definition of religion. "Pure and lasting religion in the sight of God our Father means that we must care for orphans and widows in their troubles, and refuse to let the world corrupt us.[32] This is a good theme verse for counselors. Our lives are to be characterized by helping others and by keeping our lives holy. Whether or not they are counselors, Christians are responsible for caring actions (helping) and Christlike living (holiness).

Helping is the focus of counselor training programs. Students are trained to be competent in the use of caring skills and counseling techniques. We all learn about boundaries, ethics, and theories. Often there is a focus on warmth, empathy, and genuineness—three basic counselor characteristics. This emphasis on helping and caring behavior is at the core of what counselors do.

Holiness, the importance of keeping ourselves from being contaminated by the world, is the other part of the biblical definition of pure religion. Unlike the emphasis on helping, personal holiness rarely gets the attention of counselors. Even so, "God has called us to be holy, not to live impure lives." Our lifestyles and characteristic behaviors should be exemplary, clean, and upright. This does not mean that we are to withdraw from the world.[33] As long as we deal with the sin and tragedy in the lives of counselors, and as long as we live on this polluted planet, our minds and actions are likely to be affected. On a consistent basis, therefore, we need to confess our sins and to experience God's forgiveness.[34] Ideally, every Christian, counselors included, is to have an attitude of humility and a determination to be obedient. We will never be perfect this side of heaven, but we can live holy lives by thinking and acting in conformity to the moral precepts of the Bible, in contrast to the sinful ways of the world. It is a tall order, but if we are to maximize our Christian counseling effectiveness, we must strive for holiness, keeping control over our own lifestyles, ways of thinking, and speaking. All of this implies that at the core, Christian counselors should be people who genuinely are different.

The Counselor's Relevancy

During their years in college, seminary, or graduate school, students are surrounded by journals and books—sometimes fat books like this one—and usually are well-acquainted with the flood of information available on the Internet. Their professors (at least the good ones) strive to keep abreast of recent and emerging developments in their fields, and these new ideas often find their way into lectures and discussions with students. Then comes that happy day when the seniors graduate. Clutching their diplomas, these people scatter, are absorbed into the job market, and lose contact with their professors and their old alma mater.[35]

Unless we make an effort to prevent this, many of us get involved in our counseling and other work but lose contact with emerging developments in our fields. Some pastors get caught in the challenges of ministry and rarely read.[36] Counselors can get so busy in their therapeutic work that they become oblivious to professional issues, trends, or recent research that could have practical implications for counseling. People whose work takes them to isolated communities or to some countries overseas feel far removed from the mainstream trends in their professions and not always sure how to get updates on the Worldwide Web. To keep relevant and maximally effective, we need to keep abreast of developments in our fields. But how does one do this without wasting time and energy searching for resources that may be difficult to find? There can be several answers.

1. *Conferences and Seminars.* Attendance at a meeting for professional counselors, pastoral counselors, laypeople, or others may consume a large block of time and be expensive, but the formal presentations can be helpful, and often there is great value in the informal interaction with other participants. In looking for a conference, look for the speakers and topics, then go with those that tend to be most relevant for your work. Remember that lectures are not always the best way to learn and that some conferences can be entertaining and inspiring but have no follow-up and little practical relevance for your counseling work after the conference ends.[37]

2. *Publications.* Every year thousands of journal articles are published, numerous teaching tapes and video courses make their appearance, and magazines keep appearing (and sometimes disappearing as they fade from prominence).[38] By far, of course, books are the largest form of publication. Thousands are published every year, most dealing with issues other than counseling, but if we add together all the self-help, counseling, advise-giving, and psychology-psychiatry books, there are more titles on the market than any one person can master. Books may have catchy titles and great promises on their covers, but every reader knows that many of these volumes are poorly researched, not well written, largely impractical, sometimes more sensational than accurate, and not worth buying or reading. It is difficult to plough through the new offerings to find the gems, but the search is not hopeless.

To find good titles, look at the advertisements in magazines or in professional journals that you respect. Skim the book reviews because these can alert you to helpful titles. Make some time in your schedule to browse regularly in bookstores. Even if there are good bookstores in your area, also browse on the Internet. In writing the preceding chapters, I have gone repeatedly to the web sites of the larger Internet booksellers and typed in a topic. This has alerted me to a number of new publications, many of which have online reviews. Sometimes, you then can find the books in a library or bookstore and get the information you want.

As you look at books, remember that covers (including cover descriptions and endorsements) are designed to attract buyers. Even the location of the book in the store can be a part of the marketing plan—the ones near the door often are the ones that booksellers are being paid to push prominently. Remember the old adage that still is true: you can't judge a book by its cover. You can look for the author's qualifications, however. Where did he or she get training, and what are the author's experiences? If the writer is a professor or teacher, what is his or her institutional affiliation? Might that tell you something about the author's perspective? Has the book been endorsed by someone whom you respect? Who is the publisher? Some consistently publish better quality books than others. Many publishers have a theological or other orientation that will be reflected in all of their books. Do you agree with this perspective? By asking other readers and by relying on some of your own experiences, you are likely to find publishers that tend to publish books that are most helpful for your work.

On occasion you will see a book in a library or hear an author interview that may interest you in purchasing a helpful book. Many professionals in the publishing industry agree that word-of-mouth endorsements can be the best advertising. Ask other counselors what they are reading and finding helpful. The books they read may be helpful to you as well.

3. *The Internet and Interactive Technologies.* Even a decade ago, nobody could have imagined the vast strides that have been made in the accumulation, storing, distribution, and interactive response to information. Whatever we need to know about human problems, counseling, or any other topic, we can get information at any time, from almost anyplace in the world, inexpensively, and with minimum effort. Not only can we acquire instant information in words, sounds, and visual images, but we can respond immediately, interact with what we are receiving, and in turn contribute to the changing and growing body of knowledge. Books like the one you are reading can be helpful (I hope you agree), but they would be more valuable if a team of programmers and researchers could keep some books updated continually on the Internet. That can be expensive, but readers can supplement the pages of books or the lectures of professors by searching web sites and blogs, or by interacting with others using the Internet. Three major problems with this are: (1) the lack of time for getting the information we need and sorting it, (2) the difficulty of determining what Internet information is valid and what is not, and (3) the problem of information overload.[39] There are so many web sites and so much information awaiting us in cyberspace that it becomes difficult to extract what we need while we pass over information that may be inaccurate and useless but presented in very attractive formats.

To get dependable information, go to the web sites of trusted organizations like the American Psychological Association, the American Counseling Association, or similar associations in other countries. If you use one of the major search engines and generate a lot of hits, look for government- or university-sponsored sites because these tend to have consistent credibility. Professional groups like those dealing with trauma or attention deficit disorder can yield useful information. Also helpful are professional journals with web sites that may summarize journal articles. Eventually, each Internet searcher finds favorite and trusted sites. Email newsletters also can be helpful. For several years, the author of this book has produced a free weekly newsletter that is short (one page), and deals with counseling and coaching.[40] With all of this information availability it is becoming progressively easier to download or interact with much of this information through old-fashioned desktop computers or a variety of faster, wireless technology and gimmickry.

4. *Other Resources*. The possibilities for keeping up to date professionally are almost endless. For example, consider audio and video disks or tapes, continuing education and other distance learning courses or workshops, public lectures or demonstrations given at local educational institutions or through video broadcasts, and other resources delivered with technology that only now is being introduced. Many counselors also find help by joining a counseling organization such as the Christian Association for Psychological Studies, pastoral counseling organizations, or national organizations of counselors such as the Association of Christian Counsellors in Britain, CPPC in Brazil, or the American Association of Christian Counselors in the United States. Even as these resources provide information, many provide helpful contact with other counselors as well.

Just as the spiritually dry counselor is not very able to help people spiritually, so the professionally outdated and emotionally drained counselor is unlikely to be effective in helping people cope with the various problems of life. The input of information from other people and resources can keep us mentally alert, professionally stimulated, and more effective as counselors.

The Counselor's Legacy

Someone has said that the dictionary is the only place where success comes before work.[41] This is true of almost every area of life, including counseling. In this world, if we want to be successful, we have to work—diligently and consistently.

Many workers can see the benefits of their labors almost immediately, but that isn't true of counselors. The effectiveness and success of our work are measured in changed lives. Sometimes we see these changes; often we do not. Sometimes we are encouraged by our work; frequently we are not. Some professionals are acclaimed and affirmed publicly for their counseling successes; most of us are not. Instead, we work day after day and hope we are making an impact on the lives of others—but we aren't always sure, especially when change is slow. We can work for weeks without seeing any apparent progress, and sometimes our counselees get discouraged (or threatened by the counseling process), so they drop out. Did we help these people in any way? At times, every counselor wonders if he or she is doing anything worthwhile.

One hundred years from now, if the world survives until then, most of us will have been forgotten by everybody, except God. He knows our minds and is acquainted intimately with all our ways. He who is sovereign and omniscient knows our motives, is familiar with our frustrations, forgives our failures, remembers our work, and knows our successes. In the light of eternity, his evaluation of our work is the only one that counts.

When James and John came to Jesus asking for positions of prominence and influence in his kingdom, the Lord taught us all a valuable lesson.[42] In this world, he said, the most prominent people lord it over those who are beneath them and like to have authority. In contrast, the believer lives by a different standard. From God's perspective, the greatest people are those who are servants. In God's kingdom, the dictionary is NOT the only place where humility comes before significance or servanthood comes before success.

Whenever we close the pages of this book and return to our counseling rooms, we are certain to be involved with difficult and sometimes demanding work. As we grow older, hopefully each of us will leave a legacy of lives that have changed, not because of our efforts alone, but because God has allowed us to be his instruments in helping those with whom we counsel.

But the ultimate legacy of any Christian counselor is to be a faithful servant—giving of ourselves to honor God and to serve him as we serve others. There can be no better goal for counselors and no greater mark of counselor success.

KEY POINTS FOR BUSY COUNSELORS

➤ Christian counselors may understand the causes of problems, the best methods of treatment, and the power of the Holy Spirit in bringing peace to our counselees, but this does not protect us from experiencing many of the same struggles that face our counselees.

➤ The main stresses for counselors are:
  - The counselor's work, which can be demanding and stressful.
  - The counselor's attitudes, which can include frustration and burnout but which demand a willingness to build self-awareness, self-regulation, and self-balance into our lives.
  - The counselor's isolation, which can leave us feeling lonely, pressured, cut off from counseling colleagues, and trying to handle our stresses alone.

➤ There are a variety of ways in which counselors can care for themselves. These are summarized in Table 42–1.

➤ Other people can be a great source of support and help for counselors. These people include:
  - Family.
  - Friends.
  - Mentors and protégés.
  - Colleagues.
  - Counselors who can counsel counselors.

➤ Counselors must live God-centered, God-directed lives, not need-centered lives that are built on meeting the needs of other people. Counselors build our own spirituality by:
  - Pulling back, reducing our hectic schedules, taking time for rest and reflection.
  - Setting priorities, building our lives on our values and our developing relationships with Christ.
  - Drawing on God's power as the source of our spiritual growth, strength, and counseling effectiveness.
  - Reevaluating and changing our lifestyles.

➤ Just as the spiritually dry counselor is not very able to help people spiritually, so the professionally outdated and emotionally drained counselor is unlikely to be effective in helping people cope with the various problems of life. The input and information from other people and resources can keep us mentally alert, professionally stimulated, and maximally effective as counselors.

➤ Counselors keep relevant through:
   ▪ Attendance at conferences and seminars.
   ▪ Reading books, journals, and other print publications.
   ▪ Learning from the Internet and interactive technologies.
   ▪ Using other resources, including courses, disks, and audiocassettes; being in professional organizations; or subscribing to newsletters.

➤ It can be very difficult for counselors to evaluate our work. But the ultimate legacy of any Christian counselor is to be a faithful servant—giving of ourselves to honor God and to serve him as we serve others. There can be no better goal for counselors and no greater mark of success.

PART NINE

Future Issues

43

Counseling Waves of the Future

In preparing to write a new book, two Harvard Business School professors did research intended to identify the one hundred greatest American business leaders of the twentieth century.[1] These leaders had different personalities, leadership styles, and fields of business, but they all had made a significant and lasting impact. Many showed vision, perseverance, courage, a hunger for innovation, and a willingness to take risks, but only one characteristic was shared by every person on the list. Each of the business giants had an innate ability to notice the forces that were shaping the times in which they lived. Then, based on what they saw, these leaders were creative enough to think of business ventures that could become successful. Perhaps we could call these people great noticers who had "an acute sensitivity to the social, political, technological, and demographic" influences that would define the eras in which they lived and that could be the basis for successful business enterprises. "Just as the times profoundly influenced these business masters, they, in turn, profoundly influenced their times."[2]

The Bible describes people like this. In the midst of a list of thousands of warriors who were committed to helping David become king, we read about a small group of two hundred descendants of Issachar, one of Jacob's sons. There is no evidence that these were businesspeople, but all of them "understood the temper of the times and knew the best course for Israel to take."[3] They were not fortune-tellers or people with special powers to predict the future; they were careful observers of the times in which they lived. Then, based on what they had seen and what they were observing, they were able to discern the wisest direction for the future.

Over the centuries, thousands of people have made predictions about the future, and most have been wrong.[4] The best predictions appear to have been made by people who carefully looked at the times in which they lived and then made educated assumptions about what could lie ahead.[5] That is the purpose of this final chapter. During the past two or three decades, we have seen changes that could impact counseling significantly and give our field new directions and possibilities. We will look at these trends, but not in an effort to predict the future. Only God can do that. We look at the trends to help us anticipate what might be coming, and to help us find better ways to prepare for counseling people in the years that lie ahead.

Four Perspectives

In a project that lasted for several years, the Gallup research organization surveyed over two million people around the world, hoping to discover their unique talents and assets. Based on these interviews the researchers eventually identified thirty-four core human strengths.[6] One of these they labeled *futuristic*. This strength characterizes people who always seem to be thinking about the future. They have a strong interest in current and future trends and most often are visionaries who have an ability to sense where we might be going. Futuristic people get impatient when they see organizations, churches, professions, or projects being held back by outdated traditions, narrow thinking, or individuals who are afraid to take risks and move ahead. Futuristic people can be idealistic, but they also energize others and can be inspiring leaders who move things forward. If you are one of these futuristic people, your friends know it and so do you.

Most people do not have what the Gallup organization terms "futuristic" as one of their strengths, but all of us have at least one or more of the following overlapping perspectives when we think about the future. We tend to be persisters, predictors, planners, or preparers.

Persisting with what we know and not budging is common among people who dislike change and resist it, especially when there does not appear to be a good reason for doing things differently. When we live in times of terrorism, uncertainty, economic fluctuations, torrents of new information, and spiritual confusion, these persisting people argue that the best course of action in uncertain times is to keep on the course that already has been charted and shown to work.[7] Certainly, jumping in new directions or following the latest fads can make chaotic situations worse and can lead to greater instability.

For Christian counselors there are some things that we should refuse to change, even if we are futuristic visionaries. We persist in our trust in God and our belief in the authority of the Bible. We hold fast to basic Christian doctrines and, for most of us, keep using proven counseling techniques, including the evidence-based techniques that have been shown to work in the past.[8] Probably, most of us would agree that change for the sake of change is not healthy. But neither is rigidity. Sometimes, a persisting refusal to change can leave us entrenched in irrelevance. All of us frequently face the challenge of deciding when to persist and hold on to what should remain the same, and when to let go and move in a different direction.

Predicting the future can be an enjoyable exercise, especially for people who are creative, who enjoy dreaming about possibilities, and who like making good guesses about what is likely to happen. In 1949 novelist George Orwell wrote a captivating and convincing novel about what the world might be like in 1984.[9] Orwell's predictions never came to pass, although one recent Internet survey showed that almost 60 percent of the respondents thought that the novelist's nightmarish vision of the future still was a possibility. Long before 1984, Jesus was asked to make a prediction about when specific events would happen in the future. "No one knows the day or the hour when these things will happen," Jesus said, "not even the angels in heaven or the Son himself. Only the Father knows."[10] Making predictions about the future of counseling can be entertaining and challenging, but the value of this exercise might be questionable unless we carefully look at the past, see trends in the present, and from this foundation make projections about what might come in the future.[11]

Planning is discussed at different places in the Bible. Jesus talked to his disciples about how foolish it would be for a king to go into battle or for a man to start building a tower without prior planning.[12] King Solomon wrote about the value of making plans, but with the input of many counselors who could give advice.[13] Good planning and hard work lead to prosperity,[14] and plans succeed when we let the Lord direct our steps.[15] In contrast, plans made without God's guidance or against his will are likely to fail.[16]

Planning involves drawing on human knowledge and wisdom. We do this best when times are relatively stable and we have some control over our circumstances. God can plan with maximum efficiency because, better than any human being, he understands the times, knows what lies ahead, and has absolute control over the future.[17] In contrast, the effective human planner asks for God's guidance in the planning, seeks the input of others, and prays for God's blessing and continued direction as the plans are carried out. In terms of counseling and its future, it is wise to carefully plan our careers, counseling sessions, conferences, and training programs. This book, like most others, is the result of many hours of careful planning.

Preparing for the future is different from making plans.[18] Good preparation and good planning may both seek to hear God, to obey him, to be guided by him, and to move forward and make changes that are led by him. The planner, however, devises a map for the future and uses this to guide future direction. In contrast, the preparer gets ready and then waits for God to reveal the way. Planning involves human creativity and wisdom; preparation focuses on discernment and faith in God's leading.

John the Baptist was a preparer, getting people ready to meet Jesus whenever he might choose to reveal himself.[19] In the Old Testament, Joshua also was a preparer. When he began his career as a leader, he put his confidence in God and then told the people to get ready, to prepare to see how God would do what none of them had ever seen before.[20] Preparers purify themselves and make themselves available for God to act.

I still remember my excitement when I read the first few paragraphs of Rick Warren's book *The Purpose-Driven Church*:

Southern California is well known for its beaches. . . . Many of our schools offer physical education courses in surfing. If you take a class on surfing you'll be taught everything you need to know about surfing: how to choose the right equipment; how to use it properly; how to recognize a "surfable" wave; how to catch a wave and ride it as long as possible.... But you'll never find a course that teaches you "How to Build a Wave." Surfing is the art of riding waves that God builds. God makes the waves; surfers just ride them . . . when surfers see a good wave, they make the most of it, even if that means surfing in the middle of a storm.... Our job as church leaders, like experienced surfers, is to recognize a wave of God's Spirit and ride it.[21]

When I read this, I got a new perspective on the role of Christian counseling and its future. Of course, the counselor seeks to help people deal with their problems and prevent new problems from developing, but our task can involve something greater. We can seek to discern what God is doing in the world and in people's lives. As Christian counselors, we can prepare ourselves to become aware of whatever waves God is creating. Like surfers, counselors seek to ride the waves that God builds and to help their clients do the same.

How do we prepare ourselves to see these waves? When we consider the future of Christian counseling, how do we see where God is moving or what he is blessing, and then catch those waves? How do we know what God wants us, our counselees, or our field of counseling to become? Like those corporate business leaders and the wise men of Issachar, we carefully observe what is happening around us, we become sensitive to the forces that are shaping the times in which we live, and from this we discern the best courses of action for the future. But there is more. We prepare for the future by anchoring ourselves in basic Christian values and beliefs, taking the time to know God better, listening for his voice, and becoming like the open-minded people of Berea. They listened carefully to messages that might be from God and searched the Scriptures so they could discern what was true.[22]

Where is Christian counseling going, and where might God be working? The following list will change in years to come, and future readers will need to adapt what appears in the remainder of this chapter. Still, from the perspective of the early twenty-first century, there appear to be at least ten waves of change that could be moving us in new directions. They are waves that encourage us to make projections into the future and prepare for what God may be doing. No one counselor can ride all these waves or others that will appear, but depending on one's strengths, interests, calling, and training, the best way to finish this book is to catch a wave or two and go surfing.

Before jumping in, it is good to observe that waves of change differ from the waves that surfers ride. Waves from the ocean come in sequence. One wave moves in, crashes on the beach, and fades away. Then another follows. The waves of change all come at once, and they tend to interact with one another. The changing nature of one wave will influence and, in turn, be influenced by what is happening in all of the others. Maybe this is a challenge for you. Maybe it's confusion. Perhaps, you prefer to persist in what you are doing and let others ride the waves of the future. Whatever your perspective or sense of calling, I hope that some counselors will be encouraged to recognize the waves of God's Spirit and venture forth to lead the way in riding them.

1. The Tsunami of Technology

Sometimes, I joke with my students about the old days when I was in graduate school or beginning my teaching career. "We used quaint devices called *typewriters,*" I tell them. "We handed in *papers* to our professors, instead of submitting our work electronically. We checked spelling in something called *dictionaries* and did our research in *libraries,* looking in books because we had no Internet or web sites. We listened to music on the *radio*—a device that only worked if it was plugged into the wall, we talked on telephones that also needed to be connected to the wall, and we never got distracted with video games because they didn't exist."

Even a few years ago, who could have imagined the technological advances that we take for granted today, and who among us now can fathom what we will accept as normal in only a few years? The explosion of technologies with their multifaceted influence in our lives cannot be considered a mere wave; technology has hit us like a powerful tsunami and with the same characteristics. Like tsunamis, technology has come with unexpected force. It has influenced almost every aspect of our culture, shown its power to destroy community and relationships, and leaves the landscape permanently changed. But unlike tidal waves of water, the digital revolution never lets up, and often it brings positive waves as well as those that demolish much of what has been built in the past.

We'll start with the positive. Because of technology, useful information is available, from anywhere in the world, at any time, and from limitless sources. This positively impacts the way we learn, get information for use in understanding our counselees, do psychological testing, conduct research, and access the research findings of others.[23] Interactive digital capabilities allow all of us to stay at home while we attend or lead conferences, do therapy, get consultation, and conduct seminars that can reduce or prevent problems. The ethics and effectiveness of virtual therapy are still being debated, but there can be no doubt that these approaches make counseling and counselors available to people—especially those in remote communities—who never would have therapeutic help otherwise.[24] For all of us, technology has transformed how we communicate, shop, do business, get medical treatment, use our time, are entertained, keep connected, and impact others.[25]

Technology, especially the Internet, can connect and empower people, but it also can leave people feeling isolated, disconnected from other people, and marginalized.[26] It can be used for great good, to build communities and to disseminate helpful information, but it also can be used to destroy relationships or families[27] and connect terrorists and others who are determined to kill. Cyber-technology "has the potential to transform every economic and social institution, from business to education to health care to government."[28] It represents great potential to some people, but it presents enormous stress[29] and threat to others, especially to those (including governments) that resist open communication and instead prefer repressive, secretive, hierarchical bureaucracies. It is a sad fact that the same technology that can be used to spread useful and uplifting information easily disseminates pornographic and violent images that stimulate destructive sex, ruthless violence, distorted thinking, and Internet pornographic addiction.[30]

Most counselors, especially those who are older, are not highly sophisticated in the skills of technology or knowledge about the powers and dangers of cyberspace. Nevertheless, we cannot ignore this wave that God has allowed to sweep over our world, bringing influences that are both good and bad.[31] We will continue to benefit from high-speed digital ways of connecting with our counselees, colleagues, and others.[32] We will use technology to get updated information through web pages, chat rooms, blogs, search engines, and electronic databases. Increasingly, we will take courses and seminars, get and give consultation, learn about trends in the field, and provide services, including counseling and mental-health education that is accessible, affordable, and adaptable to individual counselees.[33] On a personal level, most of us will continue to utilize technology when we shop, communicate across the miles, report emergencies, pay bills, and worship in creative ways. Innovative counselors will develop more games and video programs to teach mental-health principles and basic Bible knowledge. In addition, technology will help us to see what our clients are learning from cyberspace, know ways to counter virtual sex and Internet-induced violence, and learn ways to protect ourselves from identity theft and other unethical uses of technology.

Like many good things, technology has been hijacked by media and other entrepreneurs who use it to spread harmful values and destructive attitudes. But we can look to the positive side of technology and watch how God uses it for his kingdom. "In this time of crisis and confusion and uncertainty, when the forces of vertigo have knocked us off our feet, a historic opportunity is unfolding," writes Rex Miller. "We can let the dikes bust and surrender as the water rushes over us, or we can embrace the new paradigm along with the best of the old and actively participate in changing the world."[34]

2. The Waves of Globalism

At least until recently, counselors and their neighbors kept focused on their own communities, churches, or work, without giving much thought to the rest of the world. Sometimes, we heard from missionaries who served in faraway places, but overall we had a narrow perspective that centered on ourselves and on our own needs close to home. I used to think that this parochial perspective was distinctively American, but my travels soon convinced me that it is a universal characteristic to concentrate on our own cultures and countries and go about our activities, blithely ignoring the rest of the world.

For centuries God allowed us to remain isolated from one another, with limited awareness of what was happening elsewhere. We developed our own languages, ways of living, values, standards, food preferences, religions, and methods for helping people who had problems. Missionaries, diplomats, colonizers, and occasional anthropologists or businesspeople traveled between cultures, but the rest of us stayed at home, in part because transportation was difficult and expensive. Staying home was more comfortable, and we lacked the media connections that would make us aware of other places.

This inward-looking attitude is changing rapidly. Increasing numbers of international people and members of minority groups are moving into cities and neighborhoods that may not have been multicultural before. People whose parents never ventured far from home are taking overseas vacations and volunteering for short-term mission trips that take them to other countries. News that once came slowly through newspapers and magazines now comes live through television and computers, making us instantly aware of terrorist activity, world hunger, tribal wars, cyclones or hurricanes, tsunamis, and political unrest in various parts of the world, including our own countries. The reverberations from these changes are reaching into every community, home, business, church, and counseling office whether we see this or not.

Several perceptive writers have shown us how walls between cultures and countries are coming down, communication barriers are fading, and events in distant parts of the world are having global repercussions. In a book published a decade ago, historian Samuel Huntington predicted that Western, Arabic, and Eastern civilizations were headed for a major confrontation because of different worldviews and values—especially the clash between Western arrogance, Islamic intolerance, and Sinic [Chinese] assertiveness.[35] More recently, best-selling author Thomas L. Friedman has written about forces that have flattened the walls dividing up the world, and impacted us all. The flatteners, according to Friedman, include the collapse of the Berlin wall; the appearance of the PC-Windows network; the Internet browser; the spontaneous appearance of virtual communities; the outsourcing of work to other countries where costs are cheaper; the globalizing of companies like Wal-Mart, MacDonalds, and Sony; the growth of search engines like Yahoo and Google; and the ability of all of us to communicate in ways that are digital, mobile, personal, and virtual.[36] All of this gives an example of how the waves of change—technology and globalization—have an impact on one another.

How does this globalization change relate to counselors, counselees, and the future of counseling? The answer to this question, like almost everything discussed in this chapter, is changing as I type these words and later as you read them, but this much seems likely:

- Most counselors will learn what many already have discovered: the counseling techniques and theories that work with one group or in one location can be ineffective or even harmful elsewhere.
- Increasingly, communities will be more multicultural; the irrelevant counselors and churches will be those that persist in ignoring these changes.
- Counselor training will be two way. Americans or British counselors won't just teach other counselors in places like Caracas or Kuala Lumpur. The people who have been our students and live in other parts of the world will be teaching us more than they do now, and all of us will be better counselors because of this cross-cultural learning.
- One country's standards for training, ethics, licensing, and other professional issues will influence and be influenced by those in another country.
- Counseling across the miles is likely to increase because of the availability of interactive technology. That same technology will enable counselors to learn from colleagues around the world through international seminars, workshops, and consultation.
- Counselors and other mental-health professionals are likely to be increasingly involved in working with diplomats, business leaders, and others to help diverse groups break down barriers, deal with conflicts, learn to communicate across cultures, heal the ravages of prejudice and war, or resolve what has been called ethnopolitical conflict.[37]

All of this suggests that the flattening of the world will have a major impact on counseling, living, doing business, diplomacy, and missions in the future.[38] I cannot find research support for this conclusion, but it seems that some individuals, including counselors, have an innate sensitivity to international issues and a unique ability to connect with people of other cultures. These are the counselors who relate unusually well with international people in their own communities. These are counselors with international hearts who are likely to ride and impact the globalism wave of the future.

3. The Multi-Waves of Biotechnology

How would you respond if an email message appeared on your computer, claiming to come from the pope, inviting you to give a speech to an important Vatican conference, and offering a private Papal audience for you and your family? Probably, most of us would pass this off as a joke and forget about it. That was the reaction of psychiatrist Daniel Siegel, who changed his mind when a formal letter arrived from the Pontifical Council for the Family, confirming the earlier Internet invitation. Apparently, Pope John Paul II had heard of Seigel's work and wanted his involvement in the Vatican conference.[39]

Seigel is known as an engaging speaker whose insights into what he terms *interpersonal neurobiology* have been bringing the latest findings of brain science into the therapist's consulting room. When Seigal was studying psychiatry in the 1980s, the field was focused on defining emotional and mental problems as purely medical illnesses best treated by drugs. "I hated to see colleagues and trainees seeing patients for half an hour for a meds check, then sending them off until their next appointment three months later," Seigel told an interviewer.[40] Meanwhile, many in the nonmedical professions like psychology and social work were still resisting the increasing evidence that biological influences were as significant or more so than the social-psychological theories that long have been the basis of counseling and other forms of talk therapy.[41]

Like people who stand seaside on a windy day watching wave after wave come crashing ashore, all counselors are being bombarded with new, sometimes exciting surges of biologically based information that is likely to change the way we do counseling. Probably, most counselors are not aware of these changes, and unless we are specialists, most of us cannot begin to comprehend the cascading developments in biotechnology, nanotechnology, bioethics, genetic engineering, and other fields of science. These forces have potential to change our lives for good and to revolutionize counseling, including Christian counseling. These developments also have the potential to be used in destructive ways by unethical or amoral people, but also by well-meaning people who have no thought-out ethical standards or clear values.

I write this book near the end of my professional career. If I could begin again today, I would go into the same profession that has brought fulfillment and fascination during my adult life, but I might take a different focus. I would learn more about the physiological basis of behavior and the ways in which brain chemistry, neurophysiology, and genetics have the potential to change the field of counseling. I might try to get a better understanding of genomics, bioinformatics, biocomputing, nanotechnology, and other fields that I don't comprehend today.[42] If I were more involved in academia or in Christian professional organizations, I would do whatever I could to promote courses and a greater understanding of the biological foundations of behavior. I would catch one of the neurophysiological waves that God is allowing to develop and ride it, for the glory of God and for the good of people like our counseling colleagues and our counselees. I look with admiration and awe on those counselors, many of whom are young, who have chosen to ride one of these ever-changing biotechnology waves. It is a safe prediction that many of these young leaders will shape the counseling profession in fresh new ways.

4. The Waves of Whole-Brain Thinking

It is well known that the human brain is divided into two parts or hemispheres, sometimes called the left brain and the right brain. The two hemispheres work together and share information through a thick band of millions of nerve fibers called the *corpus callosum*. Despite this cooperation, each hemisphere appears to have special capabilities. In chapter 39 we noted that the left hemisphere is the logical-mathematical-language-focused side of the brain. This is the part that deals with words, symbols, letters, details, analysis, calculations, and scientific concepts. In contrast, the right brain is more dominant for visual imagery, graphs, charts, emotion, art, music appreciation, spatial abilities, and creative imagination.

In much of the Western world, left-brain science, economics, technology, logic, and ideas have dominated mental activity for many years. When psychologists designed intelligence tests, they focused on left-brain tasks and so did educators and the developers of talk therapy. In corporations and industries, the left-brain focus enabled companies like General Motors or Mitsubishi to make automobiles that were high in quality, technology, efficiency, and safety. Right-brain issues like design or color were relegated to minimal importance, as reflected in the oft-quoted statement of Henry Ford that people could have any color car they wanted as long as they chose black.

Harvard Professor Howard Gardner was one of the first to challenge the idea that left-brain functioning is the only or major determiner of intelligence. Gardner's research showed that there are multiple intelligences, including the right-brain relational, emotional, musical, and spatial intelligences that are equal in importance to the more left-brain linguistic and logical-mathematical intelligences.[43] The importance of right-brain thinking made its way into businesses like Procter and Gamble, where a vice president for design, innovation, and strategy was hired to help people steeped in finance and research to understand that marketing and sales success are significantly related to how product packaging is designed and how easy it is for the products to be used.[44] The big car companies also have hired experts in design, based on the conclusion that in making purchases, many potential customers are less moved by facts about fuel efficiency, price, or quality but are more influenced by design, color, and whether they like the looks of the car. Apparently, this has been a trend as many large corporations have become less interested in finding potential employees with MBAs and the ability to analyze markets or deal with numbers. Instead, there has been a greater demand for right-brain designers, artists, storytellers, inventors, and big-picture observers.[45]

Journalist Daniel Pink has written an interesting book that documents this movement away from an almost exclusive emphasis on left-brain thinking to more emphasis on the right, conceptualizing side of the brain.[46] This is not a call to emphasize one side of the brain over the other. Instead, Pink's book maintains that at last we have a more balanced emphasis, since both sides of the brain impact fields like education, marketing, service industries, medicine, and counseling.

For many years counselors who work with children have known that young people are not able to express their feelings in words nearly so well as they can communicate through play, drama, drawing pictures, or telling stories. In the age of widespread terrorism, many adults have shown, as well, that they express themselves and deal with their problems through what have been called expressive therapies.[47] Once relegated to the fringes of counseling respectability, these nonverbal therapies that involve music, art, dance, and something called sand tray therapy are becoming more mainstream.[48] Some counselors have reported success in using specially created video games to treat phobias and other anxiety disorders. The games simulate driving, flying, heights, tight spaces, and other fear-inducing situations that game-player/counselees can utilize to help deal with their problems. This is of special interest in the American culture, where more than half of all people over the age of six play computer and video games, and where the video-game business is larger than the whole motion picture industry.[49] Video games and other expressive methods are proving to be more effective than originally thought, especially when the expressive approaches are used in partnership with the more traditional left-brain, talk therapies.[50] To date, most of the research evaluating expressive therapies is in the form of anecdotes and case histories with little that is solid empirical investigation.

Howard Gardner has been more research oriented in his fascinating book on changing minds.[51] Counselors know that if people can change their thinking, then changes in behavior often follow. The logic of an effective speaker or the persuasive comments of a counselor or teacher can change people's thinking and actions. This is change that results from the left-brain focus on ideas, concepts, and theories. There are times, however, when this left-brain emphasis does not bring change. Instead, people are moved to change because of stories, experiences, feelings, pictures, and involvement in activities with other people. That is right-brain activity, which can be equally persuasive or even more influential than the left-brain arguments.

Is this new emphasis on the whole brain really a wave for the future of counseling? Should Christian counselors supplement their talk therapies with more right-brain expressive experiences? It could be argued that long-proven spiritual disciplines such as prayer, solitude, meditation, service, worship, and confession are highly therapeutic practices that involve both right brain and left. Developing the fruits of the Spirit—including love, joy, peace, gentleness, and self-control—also make use of both left and right brain and are important elements to recovery from trauma and anxiety. The waves of whole-brain thinking may not be as big a swell as some of the others we are discussing, but something fresh is happening that may change the nature of the work we do in helping others.

5. The Waves of Postmodernism

Perhaps it was thirty years or more ago when a student walked into my office and began talking about postmodernism, deconstructionism, and other concepts that I had never heard. I did not realize at the time that these were well-entrenched ideas in the culture, but not in my world, in my church, or in the Christian counseling field that occupied so much of my time. It did not take long for me to start learning about the postmodern philosophy that even then had changed so much of education and the ways in which we live, do business, and relate to one another. Before long, I began talking about postmodernism in seminars and my classes, arguing that we need a new type of counseling for the twenty-first century, especially if we are to be effective in reaching people outside the church. Mostly, I was greeted with blank stares and shrugs of disinterest. Like other Christians, I even watched as some of our fellow believers attacked postmodernism, tried to dismiss it as a passing fad, and spoke naively about eradicating it.[52]

Theologian D. A. Carson has shown that many Christians who write and speak about postmodernism have an incomplete and distorted understanding of what postmodernism involves.[53] Even so, the culture, including much of secular psychology and therapy, has embraced many of the basics of postmodernism and moved on, often no longer even using the word *postmodernism* that some Christians still view as something new.[54] If the Christian church and Christian counseling are to remain relevant, we cannot ignore the basic worldviews of our culture. We will need to make changes in our thinking and practices, even as we hold to basic biblical truth.[55] In an age impacted by postmodern concepts, counseling will need to be a more interactive relationship between counselor and counselee, with more emphasis on stories, experiential learning, and modeling from counselors who are genuine, authentic, and trustworthy. In the first chapter of this book, we discussed the impact of postmodernism on Christian counseling, so none of this needs to be repeated here.

Postmodernism has a variety of tenets that are inconsistent with Christian doctrine, but God has allowed this wave to flood over our world. If we ignore it, fail to understand it, or never adapt our counseling to the postmodern mind-set, we ensure our own irrelevance.[56] Whether or not we like or recognize this, in many ways each of us is being swept along and forced to ride the postmodern wave.

6. The Waves of Change in Spirituality

It is no secret that new waves of spirituality have swept over the world during the past three or four decades. Of course, spiritual beliefs have been at the core of cultures since the beginning of time. The Old Testament often mentions the idols, gods, and spiritual practices of diverse societies. Anthropologists have shown us the belief systems of isolated peoples who for centuries have relied on their religious rites to bring solace and a sense of control over their circumstances. The modern world has known about major religions and the denominational diversities within Christianity, Islam, and Judaism.

Much of this awareness faded with the age of enlightenment when religion and spirituality often were dismissed as irrelevant vestiges from less sophisticated times and peoples. Then, in the later decades of the twentieth century, perceptions began to change again. There appeared to be an emerging realization that something was lacking in the intellectualism, humanism, hedonism, materialism, and secularism that so many people had embraced. As we approached a new century, it was becoming clear again that Pascal might have been right when he wrote about a God-shaped vacuum in every heart that we can't fill on our own.[57]

In earlier chapters we noted that psychologists, psychiatrists, and other mental-health professionals have been among the most resistant to spiritual influences in their personal lives or their practices, but this too is changing. Books, seminars, and talks at professional conferences increasingly focus on spirituality.[58] There is not a widespread acceptance of organized religion, especially Christianity, but counselors are recognizing that many of their counselees believe in some kind of god and that these people cannot be helped by counselors who ignore or shun spirituality. No longer is spirituality a taboo topic in counseling, although it seems strange that many in the counseling profession appear to assume that working with spiritual people is fine for any counselor, even those who are not spiritual themselves or have no training in working with religious and spiritual counselees.

With the greater interest in non-Western and divergent spiritualities, there also has been a new interest in alternative therapies and other healing practices. These approaches may involve counselors recommending special diets, exercise, or herbal remedies, but the alternative approaches also include more controversial procedures such as aromatherapy, yoga, tai, hypnotherapy, guided imagery, acupuncture, massage, and therapies that claim to redirect or stimulate life energies or vital forces. Often these practices are used with people who have pain, anxiety, depression, and headaches. The treatments are advertised in counseling magazines and tend to be offered as alternatives to more traditional, technology-based, Western medicine and other approaches. Sometimes, these methods are used by counselors who have limited knowledge or experience in their use, and there is increasing professional concern about the ethics of counselors using at least some of the alternative therapies that have questionable validity.[59]

Many of the current spirituality and alternative therapy approaches have been around for centuries, and there is abundant evidence of their effectiveness. The evidence is mostly anecdotal and not scientific or rigorous, but many who advocate these methods would argue that Western research methods do not have the ability to measure and systematically evaluate every procedure, especially those that are not based in Western left-brain thinking. Christians would agree if they were asked to give scientific documentation to prove the value of prayer, religious retreats, worship, or solitude.

Christian counselors may have discomforts about the widespread interest in non-Christian spirituality or ancient alternative therapies. For those who believe in Satan's existence, some of what passes as spirituality appears to be antibiblical, perhaps even from the devil. We know, however, that sometimes God accomplishes his purposes by using people and movements that oppose him.[60] A few years ago, spirituality was never mentioned in counseling circles or at psychology conventions, but now it is acceptable even to discuss Christian spirituality in professional settings. This popularization of spirituality gives counselors new opportunities to talk about spiritual issues with their counselees. The emergence of spirituality, including that which is anti-Christian, opens new doors of opportunity for Christian counseling.

7. The Waves of Changing Churches

A highly respected Christian psychologist recently wrote an article about megatrends that are affecting the future of Christian counseling.[61] Lay counseling will thrive, the psychologist suggested. The size of churches will increase, so there will be more big congregations with more programs focused on mental-health issues. The majority of people in the Christian community will hold research in low esteem, counseling will be supplemented and sometimes replaced by spiritual direction, and a minority of Christians will continue to resist counseling and maintain that it isn't needed.

Time will show if these predictions are correct. Undoubtedly, some of what the counselor suggests will occur, especially in more traditional churches with older congregations. In chapter 3, however, we took a different approach in our look at counseling and the church. We considered how postmodernism is shaping a younger generation that tends to shun mega-churches. Instead, these people prefer to be part of more intimate but socially active emergent congregations that reflect the postmodern preference for experiential worship and interactive participation. We have noted that many people under forty have tried a variety of non-Christian spiritualities, have had diverse sexual and substance-induced experiences, and have developed skepticism both about traditional religion and about the effectiveness of traditional approaches to counseling.

A host of books, many written by perceptive pastors, are showing that there are waves of change occurring in the church. While many churches are almost empty and appear to be dying, others are thriving, seeking to bring the true message of the Gospel to a generation of spiritually starved people. These people may not always like religion, but they long for an authentic faith that is part of a community where believers live out their beliefs in a culture of change and in a world impacted by postmodernity.[62]

Where does counseling fit into these church waves that seem to differ from one part of the world to another? Just as a creative younger generation of believers and church leaders is riding the waves of change to build new churches, so can a younger generation of counselors move beyond the foundations and approaches of their professor-counselors to mold forms of Christian counseling that will have unforeseen positive impact on new generations.

8. The Waves of Changing Professionalism

These are exciting times and scary times for people who are in the mental-health professions. The times are exciting because there are so many creative career possibilities,[63] emerging methods and research findings, changes in the profession that offer new opportunities,[64] and events in the world that provide challenges for innovative care-givers. The times are scary because there is a lot of uncertainty, and the obstacles to progress can be huge: getting the degrees, fulfilling the training requirements, passing the licensing exams, learning to navigate the profession's changing landscape, finding fulfilling employment, avoiding the ethical problems that can lead to legal problems, and rising to new challenges in the profession. In the United States this includes dealing with the complexities of the public health system, managed care and insurance companies, ever-changing legal issues, competency education, licensing boards, and the role of pharmacology, including prescription privileges for counselors without medical degrees.[65] The journey can differ from one place to another because different countries, states, or provinces have different standards and requirements for professionals.[66] If they are to thrive in environments that are so much in flux, young professionals have a special challenge to be flexible, innovative, and willing to take risks.[67]

New specialties are developing that were not prominent or even in existence a few years ago. These include health psychology,[68] pain management,[69] working with government agencies and elected officials,[70] specializing in rural practice,[71] developing prevention programs,[72] and working with the courts as trial consultants.[73] Dual competence professionals have special opportunities. These include professional counselors who also are pastors, lawyers, researchers, writers, business people, medical practitioners, or licensed teachers. The dual competence opens new doors.

Of greater interest to counselors might be the changes in counseling practice. In the United States, for example, there is evidence that the emerging "integrated health care system" is likely to put counselors into treatment teams along with physicians and other health-care specialists. The result could be "a seismic change coming to the American health-care system," that puts psychotherapy "on the brink of another tectonic shift that could well discredit the majority of approaches therapists use today."[74] An in-depth survey among experienced counselors predicted that: (a) cognitive-behavioral, culture-sensitive, cognitive, and eclectic/integrative theories would increase in use; (b) classical psychoanalysis, solution-focused therapies, and transactional analysis would decline; (c) directive, self-change, and technological interventions—like online therapy, video therapy, and telephone counseling—will continue to increase; (d) there would be greater use of techniques that are brief and inexpensive; (e) methods based on scientific research (evidence-based methods) would be used more; and (f) master's level counselors will have more rigorous training and will need certification to practice.[75] These are speculations, and they only apply to one country, but they are based on emerging trends and point to possible changes in the ways in which we will do our work.

Once again, we ask if these professional issues are waves of change that some of us need to catch and ride. Ponder, as well, which of these many issues we can ignore if we are still to be considered competent to counsel. If you are a mental-health professional, you have possibilities and challenges that other counselors don't have. If God has put you in this position, what is his desire and your role in serving most effectively?

9. The Waves of Nontraditional Education

Every counselor is a teacher. We teach people to live better, cope with stress, apply new skills, know God better, and relate to others. We use words, experiences, stories, the example of our own lives, and a variety of other methods. Sometimes, we teach parents, married couples, teenagers, or victims of abuse or other trauma. Some of us teach classes, seminars, or church congregations. A few of us teach students how to counsel so they learn, in turn, how to teach their counselees how to function better.

Every counselor also is a learner—at least the good counselors are learners. That is why we read books and journal articles, go to conferences, scan the Internet, do research, observe how other counselors work, and sometimes get counseling for ourselves.

For centuries, teaching and learning were relatively simple, compared to the present. When he was teaching the disciples, Jesus used a model that still applies. He taught the disciples by giving them:

- Authority, so they were empowered to learn and teach (Luke 9:1).
- Instruction about what they needed to know (Luke 9:3–4; 10:2–9).
- Warnings about resistance they might encounter (Luke 9:5; 10:10–12).
- Practical on-the-job experience (Luke 9:2; 10:1).
- Feedback and debriefing (Luke 9:10; 10:17–20).
- Encouragement and affirmation about what they had done well (Luke 10:18–20).
- Problems to solve (Luke 9:12–17).
- An example in himself of what he expected of them (Luke 9:11). The disciples had a perfect model and mentor.

In summary, Jesus used words, experiences, warnings, feedback, encouragement, and examples that his followers could see. We do the same when we teach and learn, but the process now is both more efficient and more complex. We tap into data banks, use computers, download content and visual imagery, learn by playing video games, connect instantaneously, and employ digital methods to simulate reality so we can learn skills and deal with potential crises. Even the grade-school student can sit in front of a computer, communicate face-to-face and live with other kids and adults at any place in the world, and see things with a vividness that their parents would never have dreamed possible. We can watch surgeons do detailed operations when the patient and doctor are thousands of miles apart, be in the midst of war zones, or sit in and watch master counselors do their work. No longer do we need to feel trapped in classrooms, lined up in rows, listening to somebody talk and tell us things that we could learn in more interesting ways and with more effectiveness through interactive e-learning, accessible anywhere through the inexpensive wireless hand-held devices that we carry in our back pockets. No longer do we assume that education exists to pass on truckloads of information that students regurgitate on tests, professors use to determine grades, and everybody quickly forgets. It is more important that we all learn to think rather than to recall, and to relate our learning to our lives and counseling work. Can technology enable us to do a better job at thinking and applying what we know?

Digital and other technology is revolutionizing education, including counselor education.[76] Counseling students can take courses, watch experienced counselors, administer psychological tests and get them scored, do practice counseling, receive supervision, utilize all kinds of visual aids, submit learning assignments, meet with professors, and build counseling practices, all because of digital technology. It is true that high-tech learning and service delivery lack something that only seems to come from face-to-face encounter, but education has undergone a revolution and the revolution will continue, only faster. This is a wave of change that we cannot ignore both because of the times in which we live and because counselors are both teachers and learners.

It is probable that most readers of this counseling book are not experts in technology and not committed to developing sophisticated understanding of emerging trends in e-learning. Most will look at the ten waves that this chapter cites and focus their strengths and gifts in areas other than education. But God appears to be at work in this fast-moving field. Like powerful tsunamis, hurricanes, and cyclones, the forces that bear down upon us cannot be ignored by the counselor-learner-teacher. We need especially gifted people who can be pioneers in paving new ways for counselor and theological education.

Bill Gates is a visionary who is known worldwide for his prominent role in launching the Information Age and giving us Microsoft. In one of his books he gives this title to a section of chapters: COMMERCE: THE INTERNET CHANGES EVERYTHING.[77] It is not fanciful to take the same statement and replace the word *commerce* with *learning, counselor education*, or even *counseling*. The Internet changes everything. This is a powerful thought about a powerful wave of change.

10. The Waves of Positive Psychology

In its first issue of the twenty-first century, the *American Psychologist* devoted most pages to an introduction of positive psychology. The lead article was co-authored by Martin Seligman, former APA president and the man who has come to be known both as the father and the founder of positive psychology. Seligman has argued that for more than a century psychology and the other mental-health professions have focused on learning about mental illness, the causes of problems, and effective ways for helping people deal with their adversities. These efforts have led to enormous progress, but the exclusive focus on pathology has resulted in a picture of human beings that lacks "the positive features that make life worth living. Hope, wisdom, creativity, future mindedness, courage, spirituality, responsibility, and perseverance" have been ignored.[78] In contrast to this traditional emphasis on the negative, positive psychology has been proposed as a new focus on the forces that build character strengths and values. These are influences and character traits that can help us thrive and live worthwhile lives, even under conditions of adversity.

As we move into the twenty-first century, positive psychology has become a popular movement, both in North America and around the world. It has been featured on the front covers of the major news magazines, promoted in various international conferences, detailed in a variety of books and research projects, and given rise to the largest annual award in psychology, the Templeton Positive Psychology Prize, established by Sir John Templeton.[79] In an interview, Seligman emphasized that positive psychology "is not remotely intended as a replacement for all of therapy," but instead is proposed as a way of "teaching our clients optimism, gratitude, forgiveness, identifying their signature strengths, and moving them in the direction of recrafting their lives."[80] One of the most interesting early developments has been the development of a book that classifies positive emotions as a contrast to the *Diagnostic and Statistical Manual of Mental Disorders (DSM)* of the American Psychiatric Association.[81] Traditional counseling is built on the "unspoken premise that it is beneficial to talk about one's troubles and to overcome them by confronting them," Seligman writes.[82] Positive psychology is presented as a supplement to therapy that helps people see a better future and build on their strengths instead of focusing on weaknesses.

Positive Psychology is a secular movement that makes no claims to have Christian or spiritual roots. Despite its strong humanistic and postmodern undercurrents, however, positive psychology resonates with much of Christian thinking. Consider forgiveness as an example. Before Positive Psychology, guilt and bitterness often were a focus of counselors, but today there also is a strong awareness of the benefits of genuine gratitude, forgiving, and accepting forgiveness from other people. Depression always will be a major concern for counselors, but the new movement has focused as well on happiness and ways to build optimism.

Positive Psychology's references to kindness, love, self-control, courage, and hope come close to the fruits of the Spirit listed in Galatians 5:22–23. The positive psychologists may study these as constructive human traits, which they are, but Christian counselors deal with many of the same topics, knowing that lasting positive changes come through the power and guidance of the Holy Spirit.

As these words are being written, Positive Psychology appears as a fresh surge among the waves of counseling and psychology. Is God behind this movement, changing thinking in a profession that once was strongly disinterested in the very topics that the Bible discusses and that Positive Psychology promotes? Is this a wave that some Christian counselors should ride—perhaps you?

The Future of Counseling: Where Are the Leaders?

Even people who live far from the sea know that waves don't last very long. Some are big, impressive, and worth riding, and make a major impact when they splash onto the beach; others slip in and slip out hardly noticed. Nobody can be sure if the ten waves will be worth riding or if they will amount to nothing. Other observers on the beach may see different waves of influence, even now, and choose to ride trends that I have overlooked.

Whatever your perspective, perhaps you will agree that the field of Christian counseling needs leaders. We need women and men who are futuristic in their orientation, who see possibilities that others don't see, who have competence in counseling and respect from their peers, who are more intent on building a better future and mentoring younger counselors than in building their own careers or promoting their books and seminars. Like the business giants who were described at the beginning of this chapter, the future shapers of Christian counseling need to be people with an innate ability to notice the forces that are shaping the times in which they live. These leaders need to be creative enough to think of future directions for Christian counselors and courageous enough to carve out new paths and move forward.

People like this are rare. Most don't set out to be leaders; they are chosen by God and astonished when he puts them into leadership positions. These are people like Daniel, Joseph, Esther, Nehemiah, and Mary the mother of Jesus. They may be surprised at their calling and amazed when God blesses them and uses them to change the course of a nation or a profession. These are likely to be younger, deeply committed to Christ, spread across the world, avid learners, individuals who notice what is happening around them, people committed to bringing change even if somebody else gets the credit. Probably, there are counselors and leaders like this in my generation, but I have not seen many. Still, I have great optimism that God will raise up a new generation of counselor leaders who understand the waves that this chapter has mentioned, who can see other emerging influences, and who are willing to become God's instruments in making a difference. For those of us who are older, there can be no greater legacy than to look for these emerging leaders, to encourage them, mentor them, and help them grow to their full potential.

Whatever your role in Christian counseling now and in the future, I leave you with three challenges. *Keep focused on God*, trusting him, worshiping him, maintaining a spirit of obedience to him, keeping connected with a community of fellow believers who are committed to him. *Keep learning*, recognizing that the man or woman who stops learning also stops growing and slides into irrelevance. Then, *keep caring*. Counselors are called to be care-givers, drawing on the strengths, spiritual gifts, training, experiences, and opportunities that God has provided. The best carers make a commitment to take care of themselves and their families and to do what they can to avoid burnout in their work with others. None of us will be perfect counselors because we are not perfect people. But the counselors God uses are those who keep focused on God, keep learning, and keep caring. As God uses you to help others and to impact lives, become all you can be, trusting God to mold you into one of his choice Christian counselors.

KEY POINTS FOR BUSY COUNSELORS

➤ This is not a chapter about predicting the future. It is a chapter about discerning the times, looking for waves of influence that appear to be having an influence on Christian counseling, considering what God might be doing in the world, and suggesting areas in which counselors can prepare for the future.

➤ According to Rick Warren, many concepts currently labeled "innovative" or "'contemporary" are not new ideas at all. Everything seems new if you are ignorant of history.

➤ At least ten waves of change have relevance for the future of Christian counseling:
1. *Technology*, especially the ability to connect digitally, continues to impact people at every level.
2. *Globalism*, along with technology, is flattening walls between cultures and changing communication, commerce, and counseling.
3. *Biotechnology*, in all of its diversity, could be the major force shaping early twenty-first-century life.
4. A *focus on the whole brain*, both left and right hemispheres, has implications for emergence of new therapies.
5. *Postmodernism* continues to shape younger generations and the ways in which they respond to counseling.
6. *Spiritualism* of various kinds is opening doors for Christian counselors.
7. *Churches are changing*, especially those shaped by younger, high-tech Christians who have been shaped by postmodernism.
8. *Professional counseling* is changing in many ways and shaping the direction of how we all do counseling.
9. *Nontraditional education*, technology, and distance learning are shaping counselor education, including lifelong continuing education.

10. *Positive psychology* is a fast-growing movement that has made a major impact, even in its short history.

➤ A future-directed orientation keeps counseling from becoming irrelevant and repetitious.

➤ Christian counseling needs leaders who are competent counselors with a futuristic perspective and a willingness to take risks. Experienced mentors can help these new leaders grow to their maximum potential and become leaders who shape the future of counseling.

Notes

1. The Changes in Counseling

1   In order to respect individual privacy and identity, the case histories in this book are ficti- tious, but often they are built on real situations or on a combination of events from the lives of several people. In some cases I have identified people with initials, like RW, because this book is read internationally and common names differ from country to country. On rare occasions, a case history will use a real name. This is done with the written permission of the person or persons involved and usually because the case seems stronger if the reader knows the real identity of those who are involved.

2   The story of RW is the story of a real person. I have changed some details to protect his privacy. Two months after leaving the rehabilitation program, he was arrested. He is in jail (for the third time) at the time of this writing.

3   Cited by Jeffrey A. Kottler, *Making Change Last* (Philadelphia: Brunner-Routledge, 2001), 41.

4   For an in-depth discussion of change, including self-change, see Howard Gardner, *Changing Minds: The Art and Science of Changing Our Own and Other People's Minds* (Boston, MA: Harvard Business School Press, 2004).

5   Janet Polivy and C. Peter Herman, "If at First You Don't Succeed: False Hopes of Self- Change," *American Psychologist* 57 (September 2002): 684.

6   It would be inaccurate to imply that the False-Hope Syndrome is widely accepted in psy- chology. Following the appearance of the original article by Dr. Polivy and Dr. Herman, the *American Psychologist* 58 (October 2003): 818–824 carried a number of letters from other researchers who challenged the validity of the FHS. I have included it in the book because I have been more impressed by the evidence in favor of the FHS than by the opposing arguments and evidence.

7   Kottler, *Making Changes Last.*

8   Ibid., 139.

9   Ibid., 107.

10 The following four principles for relapse prevention are taken from M. D. Spiegler and D. C. Guevremont, *Contemporary Behavior Therapy* (Pacific Grove, CA: Brooks/Cole, 1998).

11 R. L. Rogers and C. S. McMillan, *Relapse Traps* (New York: Bantam, 1992).

12 Jeffrey A. Kottler, *Travel That Can Change Your Life* (San Francisco: Jossey-Bass, 1977).

13 Ephesians 3:20.

14 Ephesians 3:16.

15 Philippians 3:3; 4:13.

16 Despite the beliefs of some counselors that short-term treatment is ineffective, there is evidence that brief strategic therapies often work very well. In the United States, where many of these therapies have been developed, the catalyst has not only been our busy lifestyles. Insurance companies that once paid for long-term treatment rarely do so any more, so faster approaches have needed to be developed and refined.

17 For a fascinating discussion, see M. Rex Miller, *The Millennium Matrix: Reclaiming the Past, Reframing the Future of the Church* (San Francisco, CA: Jossey-Bass, 2004).

18 John Naisbitt, Nana Naisbitt, and Douglas Philips, *High Tech—High Touch and Our Search for Meaning* (New York: Broadway Books, 1999), 115.

19 Ibid., 115, 117.

20 Ibid., 185.

21 Some of these changes are summarized in Gary R. Collins, *Soul Search: A Spiritual Journey to Authentic Intimacy with God* (Nashville, TN: Thomas Nelson, 1998).

22   See, for example, Robert C. Greer, *Mapping Postmodernism: A Survey of Christian Options* (Downers Grove, IL: InterVarsity, 2003); Stanley J. Grenz, *A Primer on Postmodernism* (Grand Rapids, MI: Eerdmans, 1996); and Leonard Sweet, *Postmodern Pilgrims* (Nashville, TN: Broadman & Holman, 2000). Written for counselors but more philosophical and difficult to read is Del Loewenthal and Robert Snell, *Post-Modernism for Psychotherapists: A Critical Reader* (New York: Brunner-Routledge, 2003).

23   For a discussion of these types of therapies, see Cathy A. Malchiodi, ed., *Expressive Therapies* (New York: Guilford, 2004). The book discusses art, music, dance/movement, drama, poetry, play, sandtray, and other expressive therapies.

2. The Counselor and Counseling

1   William R. Miller and Kathleen A. Jackson, *Practical Psychology for Pastors*, 2nd ed. (Englewood Cliffs, NJ: Prentice-Hall, 1994).

2   C. R. Rogers, G. T. Genlin, D. V. Kiesler, and C. B. Truax, *The Therapeutic Relationship and Its Impact* (Madison: University of Wisconsin Press, 1967).

3   Les Parrott, III, *Counseling and Psychotherapy*, 2nd ed. (Pacific Grove, CA: Brooks/Cole, 2003), 24–35.

4   R. R. Carkhuff, *The Art of Helping in the 21st Century* (New York: HRD Press, 2000), 173.

5   Galatians 5:22–23.

6   Peter F. Wilson and W. Brad Johnson, "Core Virtues for the Practice of Mentoring," *Journal of Psychology and Theology* 29 (Summer 2001): 121–130.

7   For a discussion of the biblical foundations that are the basis for Christian counseling, please see Gary R. Collins, *The Biblical Basis of Christian Counseling* (Colorado Springs, CO: NavPress, 1993).

8   Karen Kersting, "Religion and Spirituality in the Treatment Room," *Monitor on Psychology* 34 (December 2003): 40–42.

9   The evidence presented in this paragraph implies, for example, that adults "are more likely to have harmonious marital relationships and better parenting skills" *because* they attend church and are influenced positively by church attendance. But the reverse also could be true. Perhaps people who have developed harmonious marital relationships and better parenting skills on their own are, in turn, more likely to attend church. Does church attendance lead to better family relationships, or do good family relationships lead people to go to church? We really do not know which is the cause and which is the effect. Either way, however, the evidence is strong that good relationships and church attendance often go together.

10   Cited in Rebecca Clay, "The Secret of the 12 Steps: Researchers Explore Spirituality's Role in Substance Abuse Prevention and Treatment," *Monitor on Psychology* 34 (December 2003): 50–51.

11   Kersting, *Religion and Spirituality*, 41–52.

12   See Mark R. McMinn, *Psychology, Theology, and Spirituality in Christian Counseling* (Wheaton, IL: Tyndale, 1996), for an excellent discussion of when, if, and how to introduce issues like prayer, sin, Scripture, spirituality, confession, or forgiveness into counseling.

13   This is a risky question in light of the fact that many readers of this book are students. It may be that you have no desire to counsel but are reading this book as a course assignment. Even so, this section applies to you because it looks at our motives. This can be helpful for any of us, whatever we are doing.

14   Adapted from Eugene Kennedy and Sara C. Charles, *On Becoming a Counselor: A Basic Guide for Nonprofessional Counselors* (New York: Crossroad/Herder & Herder, 2001).

15   "The Road to Burnout," from APA Help Center, *http://findingthemuse.com/_wsn/page17.html target7* (accessed 1997).

16   Steven Berglas, *Reclaiming the Fire: How Successful People Overcome Burnout* (New York: Random House, 2001).

17   Andrew N. Garman, Patrick W. Corrigan, and Scott Morris, "Staff Burnout and Patient Satisfaction: Evidence of Relationships at the Care Unit Level," *Journal of Occupational Health Psychology* 7 (July 2002): 235–241.

18   See, for example, Ayala Malach Pines, Adital Ben-Ari, Agnes Utasi, and Dale Larson, "A Cross-Cultural Investigation of Social Support and Burnout," *European Psychologist* 7 (December 2002): 256–264.

19   Acts 2:42–47.

20   Summer H. Garte and Mark L. Rosenblum, "Lighting Fires in Burned-out Counselors," *Personnel and Guidance Journal* (November 1978): 158–160.

21   John 14.

22   Matthew 28:20.

23   John 14:16, 26; 15:26; 16:7.

24   Galatians 5:22–23.

25   John 14:16, 26; 16:7–15.

26   Psalm 55:22; 1 Peter 5:7.

27   For a further discussion of the role of the Holy Spirit in counseling, see Edward E. Decker, Jr., "The Holy Spirit in Counseling: A Review of Christian Counseling Journal Articles (1985–1999)," *Journal of Psychology and Christianity* 21 (Spring 2002): 21–28.

3. The Church and Counseling

1   Wayne E. Oates, ed., *An Introduction to Pastoral Counseling* (Nashville: Broadman, 1959), vi.

2   When I wrote previous editions of this book, I spent hundreds of hours going through journals and books, looking for up-to-date information that I could summarize. For this edition, I sit surrounded by books and articles, but I've paid for access to literally thousands of professional articles on every topic in this book. This information overload, with the constantly expanding data bank of Internet resources, makes the research task both more convenient and more overwhelming.

3   Romans 15:1; Galatians 6:2.

4   As an example of the need for helping, notice the number of times that the words or a variation of the words "one another" appear in the New Testament Epistles. We are instructed to build up, accept, admonish, be devoted to, be at peace with, serve, bear the burdens of, be kind to, teach, encourage, confess our faults to, pray for, and love one another (Romans 14:19; 15:7, 14; 12:10, 18; Galatians 5:13; 6:2; Ephesians 4:32; Colossians 3:16; 1 Thessalonians 5:11; James 5:16; 1 John 4:7). While this activity extends beyond counseling, it also includes much of what is involved in the counseling process.

5   Among the influences that have changed my thinking are books by Reggie McNeal, *The Present Future: Six Tough Questions for the Church* (San Francisco, CA: Jossey-Bass, 2003); Milfred Minatrea, *Shaped by God's Heart: The Passion and Practices of Missional Churches* (San Francisco, CA: Jossey-Bass, 2004); and Dan Kimball, *Emerging Worship: Creating Worship Gatherings for New Generations* (Grand Rapids, MI: Zondervan, 2004).

6   In my writing over the years, I rarely have quoted in a later book from one of my earlier books. This is one of those rare exceptions. The quotation is from Gary R. Collins, *How to Be a People Helper* (Wheaton, IL: Tyndale, 1995), 80–81.

7   See Galatians 6:2.

8   1 Peter 2:5.

9   This paragraph is adapted from the cover copy of the David Benner book cited below in footnote 15.

10   In an earlier book, I attempted to summarize some of the secular trends in spirituality and contrast these with the traditional Christian beliefs. See Gary R. Collins, *The Soul Search: A Spiritual Journey to Authentic Intimacy with God* (Nashville: Thomas Nelson, 1998).

11   After the American Psychological Association published a series of articles on spirituality, several readers wrote critical letters, including a former APA president who asked, cynically, if the organization now intended to publish articles on astrology and mental health or produce a monthly column on horoscopes. See "Letters" in *Monitor on Psychology* 35 (February 2004).

12   Among the professional resources, see William R. Miller, ed., *Integrating Spirituality into Treatment: Resources for Practitioners* (Washington, DC: American Psychological Association, 1999); P. Scott Richards and Allen E. Bergin, *A Spiritual Strategy for Counseling and Psychotherapy* (Washington, DC: American Psychological Association, 1997); P. Scott Richards and Allen E. Bergin, eds., *Handbook of Psychotherapy and Religious Diversity* (Washington, DC: American Psychological Association, 2000); P. Scott Richards and Allen E. Bergin, eds., *A Casebook for a Spiritual Strategy in Counseling and Psychotherapy* (Washington, DC: American Psychological Association, 2004); Edward P. Schafranske, *Religion and the Clinical Practice of Psychology* (Washington, DC: American Psychological Association, 1996); and L. Sperry, *Spirituality in Clinical Practice: Incorporating the Spiritual Dimension in Psychotherapy and Counseling* (Philadelphia: Brunner-Rutledge, 2001).

13   W. A. Barry and W. J. Connolly, *The Practice of Spiritual Direction* (New York: Seabury Press, 1982). For a more recent, more detailed practical guide see Gary W. Moon and David G. Benner, eds., *Spiritual Direction and the Care of Souls: A Guide to Christian Approaches and Practices* (Downers Grove, IL: InterVarsity Press, 2004).

14   Barry and Connolly, *Practice of Spiritual Direction*, 8.

15   David G. Benner, *Sacred Companions: The Gift of Spiritual Friendship and Direction* (Downers Grove, IL: InterVarsity Press, 2002).

16   One of the best and most helpful discussions of spiritual direction is a book by David G. Benner, who is both a spiritual director and a clinical psychologist. David G. Benner, *The Gift of Being Yourself: The Sacred Call to Self-Discovery* (Downers Grove, IL: InterVarsity, 2004).

17   Some of the ideas in this paragraph are adapted from Gary W. Moon, "Psychotherapy and Spiritual Direction: Reflections and Cautions on the Integrative Path," *Christian Counseling Today* 11 (2003): 32–38.

18   Erwin Raphael McManus, *An Unstoppable Force: Daring to Become the Church God Had in Mind* (Loveland, CO: Group, 2001).

19   Brian D. McLaren, *The Church on the Other Side: Doing Ministry in the Postmodern Matrix* (Grand Rapids, MI: Zondervan, 2000), 7.

20   McNeal, *Present Future*, 1, 2.

21   Robert E. Webber, *The Younger Evangelicals: Facing the Challenges of the New World* (Grand Rapids, MI: Baker, 2002).

22   See Andy Crouch, "The Emergent Mystique," *Christianity Today* 48 (November 2004): 36–43.

23   For an excellent introduction to the emergent church, written by a pastor who heads a lively emerging congregation, see Dan Kimball, *The Emerging Church: Vintage Christianity for New Generations* (Grand Rapids, MI: Zondervan, 2003). For a controversial but generally helpful critique of the emergent church conversation, see D. A. Carson, *Becoming Conversant with the Emerging Church: Understanding a Movement and Its Implications* (Grand Rapids MI: Zondervan, 2005).

24   Matthew 16:18.

25   See especially Acts 2:42–47; 4:32–35.

26   There is a growing movement toward church-based theological education where, instead of dependence on seminaries and Bible colleges, churches are becoming focused centers of education that involve "cradle-to-grave life development for everyone in the church." The people in these churches have good social interaction, but their focus is broader than the social club.

27   Matthew 28:19–20.

28   Mark R. McMinn and Amy W. Dominguez, "Psychology Collaborating with the Church: Guest Editors' Introduction: Psychology and the Church," *Journal of Psychology and Christianity* 22 (Winter 2003): 291.

29   A special issue of the *Journal of Psychology and Christianity* 22 (Winter 2003) contains a number of insightful articles that give examples of psychology-church collaboration in different settings and internationally.

30   See, for example, M. E. P. Seligman and M. Csikszentmihalyi, "Positive Psychology: An Introduction," *American Psychologist* 55 (2000): 5–14; Lisa G. Aspinwall and Ursula M. Staudinger, eds., *A Psychology of Human Strengths: Fundamental Questions and Future Directions for a Positive Psychology* (2002); Corey L. M. Keyes, ed., *Flourishing: Positive Psychology and the Life Well-Lived* (Washington, DC: American Psychological Association, 2003); C. R. Snyder and Shane J. Lopez, eds., *Handbook of Positive Psychology* (Oxford: Oxford University Press, 2002); Martin E. P. Seligman, *Authentic Happiness: Using the New Positive Psychology to Realize Your Potential for Lasting Fulfillment* (New York: Free Press, 2002).

31   The Center was founded in 1999.

32   Please see *www.churchpsych.org* for more information on the Center for Church-Psychology Collaboration, including a listing of professional articles relating to its work. See also Mark R. McMinn, Katheryn Rhoads Meek, Sally Schwer Canning, and Carlos F. Pozzi, "Training Psychologists to Work with Religious Organizations: The Center for Church-Psychology Collaboration," *Professional Psychology: Research and Practice* 32 (2001): 324–328.

33   According to research summarized several years ago by psychologist Stanton Jones, psychologists appear to be the least religious of all the academic disciplines. Only 33 percent

of clinical psychologists described religious faith as the most important influence in their lives, compared to 72 percent of the American population. See Stanton L. Jones, "A Constructive Relationship for Religion with the Science and Profession of Psychology: Perhaps the Boldest Model Yet," *American Psychologist* 49 (1994): 184–199.

34 This interest in spirituality is seen in the publication of several books by the American Psychological Association. For example, in addition to those cited previously, see Lee Sperry and Edward P. Shafranske, eds., *Spiritually-Oriented Psychotherapy* (Washington, DC: American Psychological Association, 2005), or William R. Miller and Harold D. Delaney, *Judeo-Christian Perspectives on Psychology: Human Nature, Motivation, and Change* (Washington, DC: American Psychological Association, 2005).

35 E. L. Worthington, Jr., T. A. Kurusu, M. E. McCullough, and S. J. Sandage, "Empirical Research on Religion and Psychotherapeutic Processes and Outcomes: A 10-Year Review and Research Prospectus," *Psychological Bulletin* 119 (1996): 448–487.

36 Please see footnote 26. Also, Kathryn M. Benes, Joseph M. Walsh, Mark R. McMinn, Amy W. Dominguez, and Daniel C. Aitkins, "Psychology and the Church: An Exemplar of Psychologist-Clergy Collaboration," *Professional Psychology: Research and Practice* 31 (2000): 515–520; and Laura C. Edwards, Brian R. K. B. Lim, Mark R. McMinn, and Amy W. Dominguez, "Examples of Collaboration Between Psychologists and Clergy," *Professional Psychology: Research and Practice* 30 (1999): 547–551.

4. The Community and Counseling

1 Genesis 6:11.

2 See, for example, Genesis 13:7.

3 For further information see Rod J. K. Wilson, *Counseling and Community: Using Church Relationships to Reinforce Counseling* (Vancouver: Regent College, 2003); Judith A. Lewis, ed., *Community Counseling: Empowerment Strategies for a Diverse Society* (Stamford, CT: Wadsworth, 2002); and James H. Dalton, Maurice J. Elias, and Abraham Wandersman, *Community Psychology: Linking Individuals and Communities* (Stamford, CT: Wadsworth, 2002).

4 This research and Professor Kaplan's experience are summarized by Rebecca A. Clay, "Green Is Good for You," *Monitor on Psychology* 32 (April 2001): 40–42.

5 Numerous books and research articles are adding to our knowledge of how environments impact people and how changing the environment can change attitudes and behavior. For example, see Winifred Gallagher, *The Power of Place* (Big Bear Lake, CA: Perennial, 1994); Rachael Kaplan, Stephen Kaplan, and Robert L. Ryan, *With People in Mind: Design and Management for Everyday Nature* (St. Louis, MO: Island Press, 1998); or Albert Mehrabian, *Public Places and Private Spaces: The Psychology of Work, Play, and Living Environments* (New York: Basic Books, 1980). A computer search of books in this area reveals some books that deal with the interaction of people and places, including books on architecture and city design, but these are mixed with a large number of books that advocate New Age thinking about communion with "mother earth" and other concepts that are foreign to biblical teaching.

6 See the research on noisy environments by Gary W. Evans, cited in Clay, "Green Is Good."

7 See, for example, Leo Sher, "Alcoholism, Seasonal Depression, and Suicidal Behaviour," *Canadian Journal of Psychiatry* 47 (November 2002): 889; and Erin E. Michalak, Clare Wilkinson, Kerenza Hood, Chris Dowrick, and Greg Wilkinson, "Seasonality, Negative Life Events and Social Support in Community Sample," *British Journal of Psychiatry* 182 (May 2003): 434–438.

8 Mark 1:32–35.

9 Ron Taffel, "From Crucible to Community: Renewal in the Midst of Calamity," *Psychotherapy Networker* 25 (November-December 2001): 23–24, 39–40.

10 See, for example, the early work by Benjamin H. Gottlieb, ed., *Social Networks and Social Support* (Beverly Hills, CA: Sage Publications, 1981), 14. Gottlieb and his associates did not include the spiritual dimension in their discussion.

11 One group of researchers studied Evangelical Protestant clergy to discover how they coped with work-related pressures, including the stresses of constantly giving help to others. Most found strength by deliberately balancing the activities in their lives, maintaining healthy social relationships, having a vital spiritual life that included spiritual disciplines, and emphasizing both God's grace and his sense of calling in their lives. See

Kathryn Rhoads Meek, Mark R. McMinn, Craig M. Brower, Todd D. Burnett, Barrett W. McRay, Michael L. Ramey, David W. Swanson, and Dennise D. Villa, "Maintaining Personal Resiliency: Lessons Learned from Evangelical Protestant Clergy," *Journal of Psychology and Theology* 31 (Winter 2003): 339–347.

12 George A. Bonanno, "Loss, Trauma, and Human Resilience: Have We Underestimated the Human Capacity to Thrive After Extremely Aversive Events," *American Psychologist* 59 (January 2004): 20–28.

13 See, for example, Frederic Flach, *Resilience: The Power to Bounce Back When the Going Gets Tough*, rev. ed. (New York: Hatherleigh Press, 2003); and Saul Levine, *Against Terrible Odds: Lessons in Resilience from Our Children* (Boulder, CO: Bull Press, 2001).

14 Mary Pipher, "Healing Wisdom: The Universals of Human Resilience," *Psychotherapy Networker* 26 (January-February 2002): 59–61.

15 Erik K. Laursen and Scott M. Birmingham, "Caring Relationships as a Protective Factor for At-Risk Youth: An Ethnographic Study," *Families in Society* 84 (April-June 2003): 240–246.

16 Bonanno, "Loss, Trauma, and Human Resilience."

17 It should be added that at times professional counselors also do more harm than good.

18 The comparative effectiveness of professional versus nonprofessional helpers was a major topic of concern over twenty years ago. I searched several data banks and was unable to locate more recent articles, perhaps because the following earlier articles so effectively documented the effectiveness of nonprofessionals as helpers. Much of the research is summarized by Joseph A. Durlak, "Comparative Effectiveness of Paraprofessional and Professional Helpers," *Psychological Bulletin* 86 (1979): 80–92. See also John A. Hattie, Christopher F. Sharpley, and H. Jane Rogers, "Comparative Effectiveness of Professional and Paraprofessional Helpers," *Psychological Bulletin* 95 (1984): 534–541; and Michael Gershon, *The Other Helpers: Paraprofessionals and Nonprofessionals in Mental Health* (Lanham, MD: Lexington Books, 1977).

19 The article is a little outdated, but for a fascinating study of the counseling effectiveness and training of bartenders, hairdressers, industrial supervisors, and divorce lawyers, see Emory L. Cowen, "Help Is Where You Find It: Four Informal Helping Groups," *American Psychologist* 37 (April 1982): 385–395.

20 See Hans Toch and J. Douglas Grant, *Police as Problem Solvers: How Frontline Workers Can Promote Organizational and Community Change*, 2nd ed. (Washington, DC: American Psychological Association, 2005). See, also, Hans Toch, *Stress in Policing* (Washington, DC: American Psychological Association, 2002).

21 This has been termed the *helper-therapy principle*. It is the idea that the people who reach out often are the people who are helped the most. The very act of helping others can be therapeutic.

22 For information about Division 46, the Division of Media Psychology of the American Psychological Association, go to *www.apa.org* and search the site for the division information.

23 Some of what follows is drawn from my textbook on Christian coaching. At the time of this writing, it is the only available in-depth introduction to Christian coaching. See Gary R. Collins, *Christian Coaching: Helping People Turn Potential into Reality* (Colorado Springs, CO: NavPress, 2001). Further information about coaching also can be found at my web site, *www.garyrcollins.com*. Click on the coaching icon.

24 The quotation is taken from an experienced church planter, writing anonymously in *Rev! magazine* 7 (January-February 2004): 56, 57.

25 This diagram, and most of what appears in this section, is adapted from the coaching book cited above in footnote 23.

26 John 10:10.

27 Steven Berglas, "The Very Real Dangers of Executive Coaching," *Harvard Business Review* 80 (June 2002): 86–92.

28 Adapted from Judith A. Lewis, *Community Counseling* (Pacific Grove, CA: Brooks/Cole, 1989).

29 Galatians 6:9–10.

5. The Core of Counseling

1 Job 1–2, 32–37.

2 This was discussed further in chapter 3.

3   Allen E. Bergin and Sol L. Garfield, eds., *Handbook of Psychotherapy and Behavior Change* (New York: Wiley, 1993).

4   This research is summarized by Everett L. Worthington, Jr., "Religious Counseling: A Review of Published Empirical Research," *Journal of Counseling and Development* 64 (1986): 421–431. Dr. Worthington is a highly respected Christian research psychologist at Virginia Commonwealth University.

5   Bergin and Garfield, *Handbook of Psychotherapy.*

6   This may be different now, but in 1984 Howard Clinebell found that only about 10 percent of counselees brought problems like these. See Howard Clinebell, *Basic Types of Pastoral Care and Counseling* (Nashville: Abingdon, 1984), 103.

7   John 3:16; 10:10.

8   It should be recognized that some non-Christian counselors will accept our help but reject our Christian message. Jesus must have experienced this with the ten lepers (Luke 17:11–19), only one of whom is described as coming to faith in Christ. But Christian counseling is not dependent on a person coming to faith, nor is it to be withheld from nonbelievers. We are instructed to do good to all people, not only to believers, even though these may get our special attention (Galatians 6:10). It should be added that in most secular counseling settings, the Christian counselor is forbidden to present a Christian message. In these settings, the counselor's beliefs (either Christian or non-Christian) are likely to come out in more indirect ways. Sometimes, the counselee will ask about religion or raise a religious issue, and this frees the counselor to talk about spiritual issues even as he or she respects the fact that the counselee may believe differently. When spiritual or religious talk is forbidden, some Christian counselors feel they no longer can work in such a setting. These are issues that pastors and counselors in Christian counseling settings rarely have to face.

9   Ephesians 2:14.

10 Galatians 5:14.

11 Ephesians 5:21–6:9; Philippians 4:2–3.

12 Carl Jung, *Modern Man in Search of a Soul* (New York: Harcourt, Brace & Co., 1933), 269.

13 In chapter 6 we will discuss the legal requirements that counselors face in every state of the United States, in every province of Canada, and in many parts of the world. For example, these include the legal stipulations that issues such as child molestation or threats of aggression toward others must be reported to local authorities.

14 None of this should distract from the fact that sometimes very effective counseling can occur in hospital rooms, at accident scenes, or in other places that are less than ideal.

15 C. H. Patterson and Suzanne C. Hidore include this idea in the subtitle of their book *Successful Psychotherapy: A Caring, Loving Relationship* (Northvale, NJ: Aronson, 1997). See also Lawrence M. Brammer and Ginger MacDonald, *The Helping Relationship,* 8th ed. (San Diego, CA: Allyn and Bacon, 2002).

16 C. R. Rogers et al., *The Therapeutic Relationship and Its Impact* (Madison: University of Wisconsin Press, 1967).

17 Galatians 5:22–23. See also 1 Corinthians 13.

18 Gordon W. Allport, *The Individual and His Religion* (New York: Macmillan, 1950), 90. More than fifty years after Allport, positive psychology founder Martin Seligman also was an APA president. I took time to peruse some of his writings, and although I was unable to uncover a statement as strong as that of Allport, it is clear that Seligman also holds a strongly positive view of love as a key element in most relationships.

19 Earlier editions of this book titled this section "The Techniques of Counseling." Today, what were described earlier as techniques or methods more commonly are referred to as skills.

20 Perhaps more than anyone else, Gerard Egan has clarified these helping skills and taught thousands of emergent counselors through his books, classes, and training programs. See Gerard Egan, *The Skilled Helper,* 7th ed. (Belmont, CA: Wadsworth, 2001); and Gerard Egan, *Exercises in Helping Skills: A Training Manual to Accompany the Skilled Helper,* 7th ed. (Belmont, CA: Wadsworth, 2001). See also Gerald Corey, *Theory and Practice of Counseling and Psychotherapy,* 6th ed. (Belmont, CA: Wadsworth, 2000).

21 In this paragraph, and throughout this book, readers are encouraged to be aware of cultural differences. In the American culture, for example, eye contact is valued; in other cultures it is considered disrespectful to look directly into the eyes of another person,

especially a person who is older or respected. For this cultural reason, some Asians, Africans, or others will not look directly at the counselor.

22   Some of this research is summarized by William G. Nicoll, "Brief Therapy Strategies and Techniques," in *Interventions and Strategies in Counseling and Psychotherapy*, ed. Richard E. Watts and Jon Carlson (Philadelphia, PA: Taylor & Frances, 1999), 15–30.

23   The best summary for Christian counselors is by David G. Benner, *Strategic Pastoral Counseling: A Short-Term Structured Model* (Grand Rapids, MI: Baker, 2003). Also helpful is Charles Allen Kollar, *Solution-Focused Pastoral Counseling: An Effective Short-Term Approach for Getting People Back on Track* (Grand Rapids, MI: Zondervan, 1997).

24   For a good summary written from a secular perspective, see Willyn Webb, *Solutioning: Solution-Focused Interventions for Counselors* (Philadelphia, PA: Taylor & Francis, 1999).

25   The theophostic approach is an exception to this.

26   For an excellent overview written from a Christian perspective, see Stanton L. Jones and Richard E. Butman, *Modern Psychotherapies: A Comprehensive Christian Appraisal* (Downers Grove, IL: InterVarsity, 1991). See also Les Parrott III, *Counseling and Psychotherapy*, 2nd ed. (Pacific Grove, CA: Thomson/Brooks/Cole, 2003); Raymond J. Corsini and Danny Wedding, *Current Psychotherapies*, 6th ed. (Itasca, IL: Peacock, 2000); and Gerald Corey, *Theory and Practice of Counseling and Psychotherapy*, 6th ed. (Belmont, CA: Wadsworth, 2000).

27   D. Smith, "Trends in Counseling and Psychotherapy," *American Psychologist* 37 (1982): 802–809.

28   See for example, Gerald M. Rosen, "Self-Help Treatment Books and the Commercialization of Psychotherapy," *American Psychologist* 42 (January 1987): 46–51; Gerald M. Rosen, "Remembering the 1978 and 1990 Task Forces on Self-Help Therapies," *Journal of Clinical Psychology* 60 (January 2004): 111–113; and Mark Floyd, Nancy L. McKendree-Smith, and Forrest R. Scogin, "Remembering the 1978 and 1990 Task Forces on Self-Help Therapies: A Response to Gerald Rosen," *Journal of Clinical Psychology* 60 (January 2004): 115–117.

29   An example is a study of people with anxiety disorders: Michelle G. Newman, Thane Erickson, Amy Przeworski, and Ellen Dzus, "Self-Help and Minimal-Contact Therapies for Anxiety Disorders: Is Human Contact Necessary for Therapeutic Efficacy?" *Journal of Clinical Psychology* 59 (March 2003): 251–274.

30   The use of reading as an adjunct to counseling or as a direct means of self-help is termed "bibliotherapy." Many research articles have shown its effectiveness, especially with counselees whose problems are less severe. Examples of these articles include Mark Floyd, "Bibliotherapy as an Adjunct to Psychotherapy for Depression in Older Adults," *Journal of Clinical Psychology* 59 (February 2003): 187–195; and Timothy R. Apodaca and William R. Miller, "A Meta-Analysis of the Effectiveness of Bibliotherapy for Alcohol Problems," *Journal of Clinical Psychology* 59 (March 2003): 289–304.

31   For an excellent discussion of Internet use to supplement counseling, see Edward Zuckerman, "Finding, Evaluating, and Incorporating Internet Self-Help Resources into Psychotherapy Practice," *Journal of Clinical Psychology* 59 (February 2003): 217–225.

32   Marion K, Jacobs, Andrew Christensen, John R. Snibbe, Sharon Dolezal-Wood, Alice Huber, and Alexander Polterok, "A Comparison of Computer-Based Versus Traditional Individual Psychotherapy," *Professional Psychology: Research and Practice* 32 (February 2001): 92. See also Ron Kraus, Jason Zack, and George Stricker, *Online Counseling: A Handbook for Mental Health Professionals* (St. Louis, MO: Elsevier Academic Press, 2004).

33   Jack A. Naglieri, Fritz Drasgow, Mark Schmit, Len Handler, Aurelio Prifitera, Amy Margolis, and Robert Velasquez, "Psychological Testing on the Internet: New Problems, Old Issues," *American Psychologist* 59 (April 2004): 150–162. See also Tom Buchanan, "Online Assessment: Desirable or Dangerous?" *Professional Psychology: Research and Practice* 33 (April 2002): 148–154.

34   *www.supportpath.com* gives a listing of online support groups and chat rooms for several hundred diseases and conditions.

35   Dave Robson and Maggie Robson, "Ethical Issues in Internet Counseling," *Counselling Psychology Quarterly* 13 (September 2000): 249–257; Janice W. Murdoch and Patricia A. Connor-Greene, "Enhancing Therapeutic Impact and Therapeutic Alliance Through Electronic Mail Homework Assignments," *Journal of Psychotherapy Practice & Research* 9 (Fall 2000): 232–237; and J. A. Oravec, "Online Counselling and the Internet: Perspectives for Mental Health Care Supervision and Education," *Journal of Mental Health* (UK) 9 (April 2000): 121–135.

36 Francisco Vincelli, "From Imagination to Virtual Reality: The Future of Clinical Psychology," *CyberPsychology & Behavior* 2 (June 1999): 241–248. Notice the title of the journal.

37 Examples include J. Michael Tyler and Russell A. Sabella, *Using Technology to Improve Counseling Practice: A Primer for the 21st Century* (Washington, DC: American Counseling Association, 2003); Stephen Goss and Kate Anthony, eds., *Technology in Counselling and Psychotherapy: A Practitioner's Guide* (New York: Palgrave Macmillan, 2003); and Hans Toch and J. Douglas Grant, *Virtual Reality Therapy for Anxiety Disorders* (Washington, DC: American Psychological Association, 2005).

38 Issues such as these are discussed in detail in some of the available books on group counseling. These include: Edward E. Jacobs, Robert L. Masson, and Riley L. Harvill, *Group Counseling: Strategies and Skills*, 5th ed. (Belmont, CA: Thomson/Brooks/Cole, 2006); Marianne Schneider Corey and Gerald Corey, *Groups: Process and Practice*, 7th ed. (Belmont, CA: Thomson/Brooks/Cole, 2006); Samuel T. Gladding, *Group Work: A Counseling Specialty*, 4th ed. (Upper Saddle River, NJ: Prentice-Hall, 2002); and Gerald Corey, *Theory and Practice of Group Counseling with Infotrac* (Belmont, CA: Wadsworth, 2003).

6. The Legal, Ethical, and Moral Issues in Christian Counseling

1 Joshua 1:9.

2 Joshua 1:7, 8.

3 Acts 17:11.

4 Acts 17:16, 21.

5 Acts 17:28.

6 Much of the following discussion is adapted from the first chapter of an earlier book. Please see Gary R. Collins, *The Biblical Basis of Christian Counseling for People Helpers* (Colorado Springs, CO: NavPress, 1993).

7 From James W. Sire, *Naming the Elephant: Worldview as a Concept* (Downers Grove, IL: InterVarsity, 2004). The quoted definition is analyzed and altered by Sire as he develops his book.

8 I write from a Christian perspective, most specifically a Protestant evangelical orientation. I view the Bible as the Word of God, given to holy men (and possibly women) as they were moved by the Spirit of God to communicate in a written form that is infallible in its original manuscripts. I believe that "as we know Jesus better, his divine power gives us everything we need for living a godly life" (2 Peter 1:3).

The Bible, in my opinion, gives us guidelines and principles that, when obeyed, help us to grow in wisdom as counselors. The Bible never claims to be a textbook for counseling, and neither does it deal specifically with many of the issues that counselors encounter today. From my perspective, we can learn from psychology, research, experience, discussions, and cognitive deliberations, but these conclusions must not be retained if they contradict Scripture as we understand it to the best of our ability.

Over the years I have learned that I am a futurist with perspectives that often are ahead of the mainstream. Travel in a variety of countries has given me an international perspective and an awareness that the concepts presented in this book may not apply without adaptation elsewhere. I have had many interactions with people whose Christian beliefs and perspectives differ from mine and with others whose worldviews are not even Christian. I may disagree with these people, even as they disagree with me, but I strive to be respectful and learn from them, as Paul respected and learned from the Athenians (Acts 17:16–34). I believe in prayer and in the guidance of the Holy Spirit. I have sought this spiritual guidance in writing this book and pray that it will be helpful to readers and of great practical value, even if you disagree with some aspects of my worldview or theology or perspectives on the church.

Words like these rarely appear in books like this, but readers have a right to know what to expect, especially as we look at worldview and biblical/theological issues. For a fuller view of theology as it relates to counseling, please see *The Biblical Basis of Christian Counseling* (cited in footnote 6). That book is not intended as a definitive Christian theology, but as a summary of Christian beliefs especially as they impact our counseling and our counselees.

9 Adapted from Collins, *The Biblical Basis*, 16–18.

10 "Protecting one's turf" is a cliché that might not be understood by readers in other countries. In the context of legal issues in counseling, the words mean protecting one's property, rights, or area of influence so this is not taken over by another group that is able to persuade lawmakers that the original turf owners should be replaced. In counseling, this struggle over turf often has involved religious counselors and professional counselors, each arguing that the other is not qualified to practice in a given area such as a pastoral setting where mental-health issues arise.

11 Perhaps it is a little outdated, but in my opinion the best book on legal issues for Christian counselors is by George Ohlschlager and Peter Mosgofian, *Law for the Christian Counselor: A Guidebook for Clinicians and Pastors* (Waco, TX: Word, 1992). Unfortunately, the book is no longer in print and available. More recent is a book by Ronald K. Bullis, *Sacred Calling, Secular Accountability: Law and Ethics in Complementary and Spiritual Counseling* (Philadelphia: Brunner-Routledge, 2001). See also Bruce D. Sales, Michael Owens Miller, and Susan Hall, eds., *Laws Affecting Clinical Practice* (Washington, DC: American Psychological Association, 2005). In 2006, the American Psychological Association began publication of a series of books, each titled *Law and Mental Health Professionals,* but with a different edition for each state in the United States.

12 Romans 13 discusses the importance of submitting to government authorities.

13 Christian counselors, especially those who are psychologists, may want to consult Thomas F. Nagy, *Ethics in Plain English: An Illustrative Casebook for Psychologists,* 2nd ed. (Washington, DC: American Psychological Association, 2005).

14 To find a Christian coach check with the Christian Coaches Network at *www.christiancoaches.com.* Unlike counseling, most coaching occurs using the phone or other technical connections, so coaches and their clients do not need to be in the same locality.

15 Philippians 4:8.

16 James 4:7–8.

17 1 Corinthians 10:12. For further discussion of these issues see Randy Alcorn, "Strategies to Keep from Falling," *Leadership* 9 (Winter 1988): 42–47.

18 1 John 1:9.

19 Some of the items on this list are adapted from a book by Peter Mosgofian and George Ohlschlager, *Sexual Misconduct in Counseling and Ministry: Intervention, Healing and Self-Protection* (Waco, TX: Word, 1995). I do not know of any other book on counselor sexuality that is as complete, well researched, and biblical as this book. Unfortunately, this book may be difficult to locate because it is no longer in print.

20 1 Thessalonians 5:22 KJV.

21 1 Corinthians 10:12.

22 Adapted from Mosgofian and Ohlschlager, *Sexual Misconduct,* 262.

23 1 John 4:4.

24 In a discussion of her crush on an attractive client, one therapist wrote "there were no obvious conflicts between Dennis [her husband] and me, but things were flat." As a result, she was more vulnerable as a counselor. She avoided entrapment by discussing her feelings with a consultation group of other counselors. She then told her husband, and, together, they renewed the strength of their relationship. See Mary Jo Barrett, "The Crush: Challenging Our Culture of Avoidance," *Psychotherapy Networked* 26 (March-April 2002): 41, 58.

25 2 Corinthians 2:11; 11:14; 1 Peter 5:8.

26 C. S. Lewis, *The Screwtape Letters* (Glasgow: Collins-Fontana Books, 1942), 9.

7. The Multicultural Issues in Christian Counseling

1 Acts 1:8.

2 Acts 2:7–12.

3 Galatians 3:28.

4 Mary Pipher, *Another Country: Navigating the Emotional Terrain of Our Elders* (New York: Riverhead Books, 1999). The quotation is from the book jacket text.

5 Pipher, quotation attributed to May Sarton.

6 American Psychological Association, "Ethical Principles of Psychologists and Code of Conduct," *American Psychologist* 57 (2002): 1060–1073. See also American Psychological Association, "Guidelines for Providers of Psychological Services to Ethnic, Linguistic, and Culturally Diverse Populations," *American Psychologist* 48 (1993): 45–48.

7 American Psychological Association, "Guidelines on Multicultural Education, Training, Research, Practice and Organizational Change for Psychologists," *American Psychologist* 58 (May 2003): 377–402.

8 The first, third, and fifth of these competencies are suggested by Derald Wing Sue and David Sue, *Counseling the Culturally Diverse: Theory and Practice,* 4th ed. (New York: Wiley, 2003): 18–24. This section is drawn from Nancy Downing Hansen, Fran Pepitone-Arreola-Rockwell, and Anthony Greene, "Multicultural Competence: Criteria and Case Examples," *Professional Psychology: Research and Practice* 31 (December 2000): 652–660; and from Richard B. Stuart, "Twelve Practical Suggestions for Achieving Multicultural Competence," *Professional Psychology: Research and Practice* 35 (February 2004): 3–9.

9 I heard this in a sermon one time. The speaker stated that "we all have been abused and if you disagree, then you are in denial." Following the sermon I made an appointment with the speaker and challenged his conclusion. This was the only time in my life that I have done that. The speaker politely dismissed my perspective and stayed with his stated conclusion. Sadly, he left the ministry a few months later and became a counselor.

10 This view is known as "ethnocentric monoculturalism." The quotation is taken from page 764 in an article by Derald Wing Sue, "Whiteness and Ethnocentric Monoculturalism: Making the 'Invisible' Visible," *American Psychologist* 59 (November 2004): 761–769. Dr. Sue is a leader in the development of multicultural competence among counselors, but his article shows an overall lack of awareness of the bias against religion that characterizes many in the psychological profession, including counselors who proclaim the importance of cultural sensitivity. This bias is documented in detail by Richard E. Redding, "Sociopolitical Diversity in Psychology: The Case for Pluralism," *American Psychologist* 56 (March 2001): 205–215.

11 I asked a friend from another culture to read and critique this chapter. At this point in the chapter he wrote. "If you, the reader, do not have any friends who are of a different culture, ask yourself what this might say about you or about your attitudes to different cultures."

12 The January 2005 issue of *Monitor on Psychology* has a number of articles intended to help white counselors understand and work effectively with Hispanic/Latino counselees.

13 This discussion is drawn from Howard C. Stevenson, "Wrestling with Destiny: The Psychology of Anger and Healing in African American Males," *Journal of Psychology and Christianity* 21 (Winter 2002): 357–364; and from Arthur L. Whaley, "Cultural Mistrust: An Important Psychological Construct for Diagnosis and Treatment of African Americans," *Professional Psychology: Research and Practice* 32 (December 2001): 555–562. See also Donald R. Atkinson, George Morten, and Derald W. Sue, *Counseling American Minorities,* 5th ed. (Boston: McGraw Hill, 1998); and Nicholas A. Vace, Susan B. DeVaney, and Johnston M. Brendel, *Counseling Multicultural and Diverse Populations: Strategies for Practitioners* (New York: Brunner-Routledge, 2004).

14 W. H. Grier and P. M. Cobbs, *Black Rage* (New York: Basic Books, 1968).

15 Vetta L. Sanders Thompson, Anita Balize, and Maysa Akbar, "African-Americans' Perceptions of Psychotherapy and Psychotherapists," *Professional Psychology: Research and Practice* 35 (February 2004): 19–26.

16 The experiment took place between 1932 and 1972 and involved 399 men in the late stages of syphilis. Most of these men were illiterate farm workers from one of the poorest counties of Alabama. On May 16, 1997, U.S. President Bill Clinton apologized to the eight remaining survivors. Clinton said, "The United States government did something that was wrong—deeply, profoundly, morally wrong. It was an outrage to our commitment to integrity and equality for all our citizens . . . clearly racist." For more details see James Jones, *Bad Blood: The Tuskegee Syphilis Experiment* (New York: Free Press, 1993). See also Susan M. Reverby, ed., *Tuskegee's Truths: Rethinking the Tuskegee Syphilis Study* (Chapel Hill: University of North Carolina Press, 2000).

17 Whaley, "Cultural Mistrust," 560.

18 I have been unable to find the origin of the cultural iceberg concept. It is used often in books and articles describing cross-cultural communication and understanding. More information is easily found on the Internet.

19 Do you (or your counselees) have more of an internal or external locus of control? To find out, you can take a locus-of-control questionnaire on the Internet. Go to "search" and type in "locus of control." Several free questionnaires are likely to become available.

20 This is the perspective of a Canadian scientist named James W. Berry, who has published several articles concerning acculturation. He identifies four "modes" of acculturation: *integration, assimilation* (when the immigrant identifies solely with the new culture), *separation* (where only the traditional culture is embraced), and *marginalization,* which involves lack of involvement and rejection of both cultures. For a recent example of Berry's work, see J. W. Berry, "Psychology of Group Relations: Cultural and Social Dimensions," *Aviation, Space, & Environmental Medicine* 75 (July 2004): C52–C57.

21 In the United States, the Spanish-speaking Hispanic/Latino population is growing at a fast rate, but there are relatively few professionally trained Hispanic mental-health counselors. Until there are more Spanish-speaking professionals, Hispanic researchers and counselors are developing methods that can be used by culturally sensitive non-Hispanic counselors to reach this part of the population. Sadie F. Dingfelder, "Closing the Gap for Latino Patients," *Monitor on Psychology* 36 (January 2005): 58–61.

22 As used in these pages, *indigenous* methods are those based in the worldviews, beliefs, and practices of other cultures. *Alternative* methods are practices that are alternatives to traditional medicine. In this book we have not used the term *complementary* approaches, but these are used as adjuncts to conventional medicine or therapy. Christian counselors will find that professional care-givers often consider indigenous methods also to be alternative or complementary methods.

23 Based on research from Harvard Medical School, reported by Kathryn P. White, "Psychology and Complementary and Alternative Medicine," *Professional Psychology: Research and Practice* 31 (December 2001): 671–681.

24 This is from the publisher's description of Jeffrey A. Kottler and Jon Carlson with Bradford Keeney, *American Shaman: An Odyssey of Global Healing Traditions* (New York: Brunner-Rouledge, 2004).

25 Theophostic Ministry is one alternative Christian approach that has been investigated by professional researchers. For example, see David N. Entwistle, "Shedding Light on Theophostic Ministry 1," *Journal of Psychology and Theology* 32 (Spring 2004): 26–34.

26 Fernando Garzon is one Christian psychologist and researcher who has studied Theophostic Ministries (TPM) scientifically. In a personal note to the author of this book, (June 10, 2004) Dr. Garzon wrote, "It's tough to research this area because of so much polarization around TPM. Nobody likes you because you won't blanketly support either position," for or against TPM.

27 One example is the June-July 2003 issue of the *American Psychologist*, which devotes the entire issue to "Prevention That Works for Children and Youth." Articles address community interventions, family-strengthening approaches for the prevention of youth problems, enhancing school-based prevention, and opportunities for preventing problems in health-care settings.

28 See Kennon M. Sheldon and Laura King, "Why Positive Psychology Is Necessary," *American Psychologist* 56 (March 2001): 216–217. This is the first in a series of articles devoted to positive psychology. Research articles and books on positive psychology are now making their appearance.

8. Depression

1 Unlike most of the cases in this book, we are not using fictitious names with this example. Andrea and Russell Yates are real people. I have tried to be accurate and sensitive in this account, determined to show respect and sensitivity for the people involved. Most of the material in this history is adapted from an interview by Leslie Armstrong, "The Andrea Yates Saga—From the Inside Looking Out: An Interview with Russell Yates," *Christian Counseling Today,* 10, no. 4 (2002): 36–42.

2 One estimate suggests that postpartum depression occurs in about 10 percent to 15 percent of all deliveries, except for adolescent mothers, where it appears in about 30 percent of the cases. Usually, it appears within six months but can be treated successfully. In the case of Andrea Yates, it was intensified by her underlying predisposition to psychosis. See Archibald D. Hart, "The Psychopathology of Postpartum Disorders," *Christian Counseling Today* 10, no. 4 (2002): 16–17.

3 This is adapted from a book by Vance Havner, *Though I Walk Through the Valley* (Old Tappan, NJ: Revell, 1974). The book was written following the death of Havner's wife. The title is taken from Psalm 23:4.

4 There is abundant information about depression on the Internet. In addition to the professional sources that I have consulted for this chapter, I have gone to the Internet for updated information. One helpful source is *www.psychologyinfo.com/depression*. This site also contains information about many of the other issues discussed in this book.

5 For more detailed information, see Francis Mark Mondimore, *Bipolar Disorder* (Baltimore:

Johns Hopkins, 1999); also Holiday Rondeau, "Our Lost Children: Bipolar Depression and the Church," *Journal of Psychology and Christianity* 22 (Summer 2003): 123–130.

6   Mood disorders, for example, occupy a very large section of the highly respected, detailed, and frequently consulted book by Harold I. Kaplan and Benjamin J. Sadock, ed., *Comprehensive Textbook of Psychiatry/VI*, 6th ed. (Baltimore, MD: Williams & Wilkins, 1995).

7   Job 3; Numbers 11:10–15; Jonah 4:1–3; Exodus 6:9; Matthew 26:75.

8   1 Kings 19.

9   Matthew 26:37–38.

10 See, for example, Psalms 34:15–17; 103:13–14; Matthew 5:12; 11:28–30; John 14:1; 15:10; Romans 8:28.

11 2 Corinthians 4:8, 9, 17, 18.

12 Romans 15:13.

13 I have chosen not to reveal the sources for these myths. Christian counselors may find interest in an observation by Christian psychiatrist John White. In his book *The Masks of Melancholy* (Downers Grove, IL: InterVarsity, 1982), he cites the case of a man whose depression disappeared permanently once he understood the grace of God. Then he added, "among the thousands of patients I have treated . . . he is the only seriously depressed person whose psychological needs were met by a spiritual understanding. More frequently I see spiritual understanding restored by psychiatric treatment" (p. 201).

14 For a detailed discussion of the causes and treatment of chronic depression, see Jeremy W. Petit and Thomas E. Joiner, *Chronic Depression: Interpersonal Sources, Therapeutic Solutions* (Washington, DC: American Psychological Association, 2006).

15 This is discussed in more detail by Archibald D. Hart, *Unmasking Male Depression* (Nashville, TN: Word, 2001).

16 For example, one research report stated that "Strong evidence supports a genetic basis for many psychiatric illnesses, such as . . . depression." But the author acknowledges that it is unclear how genes, including defective genes, may interact with environmental influences to create the depression. Massoud Stephane, "Genetic and Environmental Interactions in Psychiatric Illnesses," *Journal of Neuropsychiatry & Clinical Neurosciences* 15 (Summer 2003): 386–387.

17 Keith Brodie, Chancellor of Duke University, quoted in "New Hope for the Depressed," *Newsweek* (January 1983): 39–42.

18 Anne Derouin and Terrill Bravender, "Living on the Edge: The Current Phenomenon of Self-Mutilation in Adolescents," *The American Journal of Maternal/Child Nursing* 29 (January-February 2004): 12–18.

19 Jenny K. Yi, Jun-Chih Giseala, and Yuko Kishimoto, "Utilization of Counseling Services by International Students," *Journal of Instructional Psychology* 30 (December 2003): 333–342.

20 Aaron T. Beck, Gary Emery, and Ruth Greenberg, *Anxiety Disorders and Phobias: A Cognitive Perspective* (New York: Basic Books, 1990).

21 Rene Spitz, "Anaclitic Depression," *Psychoanalytic Study of the Child* 2 (1946): 312–342.

22 D. A. Cole and L. P. Rehm, "Family Interaction Patterns and Childhood Depression," *Journal of Abnormal Child Psychology* 14 (1986): 297–314.

23 Jay R. Turner and Donald A. Lloyd, "Stress Burden and the Lifetime Incidence of Psychiatric Disorder in Young Adults: Racial and Ethnic Contrasts," *Archives of General Psychiatry* 61 (May 2004): 481–488.

24 Sidney J. Blatt, *Experiences of Depression: Theoretical, Clinical, and Research Perspectives* (Washington, DC: American Psychological Association, 2004). Dr. Blatt identifies the two types of depression as anaclitic depressing, arising from feelings of loneliness and abandonment, and introjective depression, which comes from feelings of failure and worthlessness.

25 The theory of learned helplessness was suggested originally by psychologist Martin Seligman. See, for example, Christopher Peterson, Steven F. Maier, and Martin E. P. Seligman, *Learned Helplessness: A Theory for the Age of Personal Control* (New York: Oxford University Press, 1995).

26 A. T. Beck, *Cognitive Therapy of Depression* (New York: Wiley, 1980).

27 This diagram is not completely original. It is a variation of similar diagrams that have appeared in other books.

28 1 Kings 18–19.

29 This is discussed by Hart in *Unmasking Male Depression*.

30 E. McGrath, G. P. Keita, B. R. Strickland, and N. F. Russo, eds., *Women and Depression: Risk Factors and Treatment Issues* (Washington, DC: American Psychological Association, 1990).

31 Judith B. Schwartzman and Kathleen D. Glaus, "Depression and Coronary Heart Disease in Women: Implications for Clinical Practice and Research," *Professional Psychology: Research and Practice* 31 (February 2000): 48–57.

32 Hart, *Unmasking Male Depression*. Hart's book includes an entire chapter titled "When Depression Strikes Below the Belt."

33 In my research for this chapter I was surprised to learn that the likelihood of suicide "was predicted better by child sexual abuse (experienced on average 20 years previously) than by a current diagnosis of depression." See John Read, Kirsty Agar, Suzanne Barker-Collo, Emma Davies, and Andrew Moskowitz, "Assessing Suicidality in Adults: Integrating Childhood Trauma as a Major Risk Factor," *Professional Psychology: Research and Practice* 32 (August 2001): 367–372.

34 J. C. Coyne et al., "Living with a Depressed Person," *Journal of Consulting and Clinical Psychology* 55 (1987): 347–352.

35 For example, see Michael Babyak, James A. Blumenthal, Steve Herman, Parinda Khatri, Murali Doraiswamy, Kathleen Moore, W. Edward Craighead, Ten T. Baldewicz, and K. Ranga Krishnan, "Exercise Treatment for Major Depression: Maintenance of Therapeutic Benefit at 10 Months," *Psychosomatic Medicine* 62 (September-October, 2000): 633–638; Peter Salmon, "Effects of Physical Exercise on Anxiety, Depression, and Sensitivity to Stress: A Unifying Theory," *Clinical Psychology Review* 21 (February 2001): 33–61.

36 In parts of the United States and perhaps in other countries, psychologists are now able to get special training and be licensed to prescribe medications for depression and other mental-health issues.

37 Nicole Highet and Peter Drummond, "A Comparative Evaluation of Community Treatments for Postpartum Depression: Implications for Treatment and Management Practices," *Australian & New Zealand Journal of Psychiatry* 38 (April 2004): 212–218.

38 Erin E. Michalak, Clare Wilkinson, Kerenza Hood, Chris Dowrick, and Greg Wilkinson, "Seasonality, Negative Life Events and Social Support in Community Sample," *British Journal of Psychiatry* 182 (May 2003): 434–438.

39 This is how ECT is described in "Electroconvulsive Therapy," *NIH Statement Online* 1985 June 10–12; 5 (11): 1–23.

40 For a more detailed, ten-step approach to counseling those who have experienced loss, see Hart, *Counseling the Depressed*, 133–145.

41 Hebrews 1:3; 13:5; Colossians 1:16–17; John 14:1–4, 26–27.

42 The basics of learned helplessness were introduced by Martin E. P. Seligman (see Peterson, Maier, and Seligman, *Learned Helplessness*). In a different book Seligman wrote about learned optimism, Martin E. P. Seligman, *Learned Optimism* (New York: Knopf, 1991). The impact of optimism on depression is discussed by Christopher Peterson, "The Future of Optimism," *American Psychologist* 55 (January 2000): 44–55.

43 This list is adapted from the pioneering work of Farberow and Shneidman. See N. L. Farberow and E. S. Shneidman, eds., *The Cry for Help* (New York: McGraw-Hill, 1965). More recent is Edwin S. Shneidman, *Comprehending Suicide: Landmarks in 20th Century Suicidology* (Washington, DC: American Psychological Association, 2001); and Edwin S. Shneidman, *Autopsy of a Suicidal Mind* (New York, Oxford University Press, 2004).

44 Philippians 4:11–13, 19.

45 David J. A. Dozois and Keith S. Dobson, *The Prevention of Anxiety and Depression* (Washington, DC: American Psychological Association, 2004); and Esteban A. Cardemil and Jacques P. Barber, "Building a Model for Prevention Practice: Depression as an Example," *Professional Psychology: Research and Practice* 32 (August 2001): 392–401.

46 "What a Friend We Have in Jesus."

47 John 16:33; James 1:2–3, 12.

48 Matthew 26:37–38.

49 S. C. Thompson, "Will It Hurt Less If I Can Control It? A Complex Answer to a Simple Question," *Psychological Bulletin* 90 (1981): 89–101.

50 See, e.g., Psalms 1:1–2; 119:9–16.

51 Philippians 4:8.

52 In part, however, the family or other social group is not always helpful. There is research that social support can be either depression-buffering (and therefore preventive) or depression-maintaining (helping people to persist in their depressions). See Scott A. White, Holly Jackson, Brenda Joy Martin, Kimberley McKay, Jessica Part, and La Cheryl Taylor, "Christians and Depression: Attributions as Mediators of Depression-Buffering Role of Christian Social Support," *Journal of Psychology and Christianity* 22 (Spring 2003): 48–58.

53 Havner, *Though I Walk Through the Valley*, 66–67.

9. Anxiety

1 Philippians 4:6, 7.

2 Ron Taffel, "Confronting the New Anxiety," *Psychotherapy Networker* 27 (November-December 2003): 30–37, 59.

3 Ibid.

4 This was suggested by Charles Spielberger, *Understanding Stress and Anxiety* (New York: Harper & Row, 1979).

5 Sometimes, anxiety and excitement are confused. People think they are excited and move forward with abandon, when, in reality, they are anxious and should proceed with caution. At other times people may be anxious, when, in reality, they are excited and could be free to move forward enthusiastically.

6 Abby J. Fyer, Salvatore Mannuzza, and Jeremy D. Coplan, "Panic Disorders and Agoraphobia," in *Comprehensive Textbook of Psychiatry*, ed. Harold I. Kaplan and Benjamin J. Sadock, vol. 1 (Baltimore: Williams and Wilkins, 1995), 1191–1204.

7 Chapter 39.

8 2 Corinthians 11:27–28.

9 Philippians 2:20. The RSV uses the words "genuinely anxious," the NASB uses the words "genuinely . . . concerned," and the NLT says that Timothy "genuinely cares" about the welfare of the Philippians. I have the impression that more recent translations are less inclined to use the word "anxiety" to describe healthy concern.

10 Matthew 6:25–34.

11 1 Peter 5:7.

12 Philippians 4:6, 7. You will note that the case history that began this chapter refers to a person who failed to experience the promise of this verse. There may be several reasons, including the fact that many anxieties have a physiological basis that respond best to medical treatment. Christians believe, however, that God can and sometimes does overrule medical conditions at his discretion.

13 Matthew 6:33.

14 Philippians 4:6.

15 The quotation is from Dawn Gould Lepore of the Charles Schwab Corporation, source unknown.

16 For a concise discussion of the unconscious from a Christian counselor, see the entry on the unconscious, written by Bruce Narramore and included in *Baker Encyclopedia of Psychology*, ed. David G. Benner and Peter C. Hill, 2nd ed. (Grand Rapids, MI: Baker, 1999), 1236–1237. The Bible does not mention the unconscious, but in Romans 1:18–19 the writer describes people who push truth away from themselves. There is knowledge in their hearts, but it is known instinctively. Does this suggest something similar to the unconscious?

17 1 John 1:9.

18 Richard Simon, "Editorial," *Psychotherapy Networker* 26 (September-October 2002): 2.

19 Archibald D. Hart, *The Anxiety Cure* (Nashville, TN: Word, 1999). Most of the discussion in this section is adapted from Hart's book.

20 Mary Sykes Wylie and Richard Simon, "Discoveries from the Black Box," *Psychotherapy Networker* 26 (September-October 2002): 26–37, 68. For a colorful and popular discussion of the brain and human behavior, see James Shreeve, "Beyond the Brain," *National Geographic* 207 (March 2005): 2–31.

21 Hart, *Anxiety Cure*, 27.

22 Ibid., 25.

23 Technically, this is known as substance-induced anxiety disorder.

24 Deuteronomy 28:65–66, NIV.

25 Archibald D. Hart, *The Hidden Link Between Adrenalin and Stress* (Waco, TX: Word, 1986).

26 Rebecca A. Clay, "Bringing Psychology to Cardiac Care," *Monitor on Psychology* 32 (January 2004): 46–49.

27   Several years ago, in a controversial but widely read book, two Christian writers attacked this "visualization" approach and called it "demonically inspired and unalterably hostile to Christianity." See Dave Hunt and T. A. McMahon, *The Seduction of Christianity* (Eugene, OR: Harvest House, 1985), 140. I agree with those who view this perspective as an over-reaction. At about the same time that Hunt and McMahon published their book, a more balanced perspective appeared, written by respected Christian counselor H. Norman Wright, *Self-Talk, Imagery and Prayer in Counseling* (Waco, TX: Word, 1986).

28   This is not news to Christian counselors, but half a century ago when these words came from the president of the American Psychological Association, the words of Gordon Allport seemed revolutionary. He wrote "Love—incomparably the greatest psychotherapeutic agent—is something that professional psychiatry cannot of itself create, focus, nor release. . . . By contrast . . . the Christian religion . . . offers an interpretation of life and a rule of life based wholly on love." Gordon W. Allport, *The Individual and His Religion* (New York: Macmillan, 1950), 90, 92ff.

29   1 John 4:18.

30   Note Hebrew 13:6.

31   The role of love in anxiety reduction and psychological health is widely recognized by the field of positive psychology. See, for example, Martin E. P. Seligman, *Authentic Happiness* (New York: Free Press, 2002); and Christopher Peterson and Martin E. P. Seligman, *Character Strengths and Virtues: A Handbook and Classification* (New York: Oxford University Press, 2004).

32   See, for example, Margaret Wehrenberg, "10 Best-Ever Anxiety-Management Techniques," *Psychotherapy Networker* 29 (September-October 2005): 46–49, 56.

33   Richard M. Suinn, "The Terrible Twos—Anger and Anxiety: Hazardous to Your Health," *American Psychologist* 56 (January 2001): 27–36. See also Jerry L. Deffenbacher and Richard M Suinn, "Systematic Desensitization and the Reduction of Anxiety," *The Counseling Psychologist* 16 (January 1988): 9–30.

34   Reid Wilson, "Everyday Courage," *Psychotherapy Networker* 24 (September-October 2000): 58–63, 80, 98. See also Graham Campbell, "The Anxious Client Reconsidered," *Psychotherapy Networker* 25 (May-June 2001): 40–45.

35   See Catherine Weber, "The Mood Food Connection: Nutrition and Anxiety," *Christian Counseling Today* 8, no. 4 (2000): 44–50.

36   In most places, only medical professionals are licensed and considered qualified to prescribe medication. More recently, in the United States and perhaps in some other countries, clinical psychologists and other nonphysicians can qualify to prescribe medications legally.

37   Of course, bias or fear of drugs is not the only reason that some people resist medication. On the day that I was writing this section, I got an email message from a friend in Asia asking if I could recommend a counselor in Japan who would be willing to help a man deal with his anxiety and depression but without using medication. The man was a pilot who did not want to take medication lest it impair his flying and the safety of his passengers.

38   Richard Balon, "Developments in Treatment of Anxiety Disorders: Psychotherapy, Pharmacotherapy, and Psychosurgery," *Depression & Anxiety* 19, no. 2 (2004): 63–76.

39   Campbell, "The Anxious Client," 44.

40   Taffel, "Confronting the New Anxiety," 33.

41   This is the theme of the article by Wilson, "Everyday Courage."

42   Everything in these sentences is taken from Jesus' teachings in John 14. See especially verses 1–3, 16–18, 25–28.

43   William Hendrickson, *Philippians* (Grand Rapids, MI: Baker, 1962), 193.

44   James 1:22.

45   David J. A. Dozois and Keith S. Dobson, eds., *The Prevention of Anxiety and Depression* (Washington, DC: American Psychological Association, 2004).

46   Matthew 6:31–35.

10. Anger

1   Most chapters in this book will present case material that is new. The story of Pastor Frank is an exception. It appeared in a prior edition of this book and is repeated here in modified form because of its unusual realism and relevance.

2   Etienne Benson, "Goo, Gaa, Grr: Researchers Are Still Looking for Consensus on How

and When Anger First Appears in Infants," *Monitor on Psychology* 34 (March 2003): 50–51.

3   Tori DeAngelis, "When Anger's a Plus," *Monitor on Psychology* 34 (March 2003): 44–45.

4   James I. Packer, *Knowing God* (Downers Grove, IL: InterVarsity Press, 1973), 136.

5   Mark 3:5.

6   Romans 3:23.

7   Psalm 78:38. See also Daniel 9:9.

8   2 Peter 3:9. See also Psalms 10 and 73, where God's justice against the wicked is withheld temporarily.

9   Romans 1:31.

10   Romans 2:5; 1 Thessalonians 1:10. See also Revelation 6 and following.

11   For example: Ecclesiastes 7:9; Proverbs 16:32; Matthew 5:22; Galatians 5:20; Ephesians 4:26; Colossians 3:8; James 1:19–20.

12   Ephesians 4:20.

13   Psalm 37:8.

14   Romans 12:19; 14:4; Ephesians 4:31; Hebrews 12:15: Matthew 7:1–5.

15   Deuteronomy 32:35.

16   This raises some interesting implications for nations that attack one another and continue the attacks in the name of revenge. And what does this say about governments that support this kind of international revenge?

17   Proverbs 14:29; 15:18; 29:11, 20, 22.

18   James 1:19. See also 1:20; 3:1–14; 4:1–2.

19   This statement is not intended to overlook the fact that abuse can be stimulated by the actions of the abuse victims. The problem is not always one-sided, arising solely from the abuser.

20   Proverbs 14:17, 29; 29:22.

21   Proverbs 22:24–25.

22   Proverbs 11:13; 16:28; 20:19; 26:20; 29:19; 2 Corinthians 12:20.

23   See chapter 8.

24   Proverbs 10:18; 26:24–26.

25   2 Timothy 4:2; Luke 17:3–4.

26   Proverbs 15:28.

27   1 John 1:9; James 5:16; Matthew 6:12; 18:21–22, 33–35.

28   1 Peter 2:23.

29   1 Corinthians 13:4–5; Proverbs 10:12.

30   Proverbs 16:32.

31   Galatians 5:22–23.

32   Suzanne Fremont and Wayne Anderson, "What Client Behaviors Make Counselors Angry? An Exploratory Study," *Journal of Counseling and Development* 65 (October 1986): 67–70.

33   Jonah 4:1.

34   Matthew 2:16–18.

35   Matthew 20:24.

36   Mark 3:5; 10:14.

37   The view is widely accepted that when anger is held within, it eventually expresses itself, often in acts of abuse or other violence. But the overall instinct theory of anger is less popular and has been criticized for its lack of evidence to give it support.

38   From Carol Tavris, *Anger: The Misunderstood Emotion* (New York: Simon & Schuster, 1989).

39   Mark 3:1–5.

40   The role of relationships in producing anger is discussed in an excellent book by Harriet Lerner, *The Dance of Anger: A Woman's Guide to Changing the Patterns of Intimate Relationships* (Quill, 1997).

41   There is increasing research on the differences in how men and women experience and express anger. Melissa Dittmann, "Anger Across the Gender Divide," *Monitor on Psychology* 34 (March 2003): 52–53.

42   Some research suggests that there is a biological basis for linking personality to how something is perceived. Our brains respond to emotional stimuli based on the personality we harbor. According to Stanford University professor John D. Gabrieli, "Depending on personality traits, people's brains seem to amplify some aspects of experience over others. All of the participants (in one study) saw positive and negative scenes, but people's reactions were very different—one group saw the cup as being very full and the other saw it

as very empty." This research is summarized by Siri Carpenter, "Different Dispositions, Different Brains," *Monitor on Psychology* 32 (February 2001): 66–68.

43 See, for example, G. Fong, D. Frost, and S. Stansfeld, "Road Rage: A Psychiatric Phenomenon?" *Social Psychiatry and Psychiatric Epidemiology* 36, no. 6 (2002): 277–286; Tara E. Galovski and Edward B. Blanchard, "Road Rage: A Domain for Psychological Intervention?" *Aggression & Violent Behavior* 9 (March-April 2004): 105–127. For a more complete discussion of road rage, see Tara E. Galovski, Loretta S. Malta, and Edward B. Blanchard, *Road Rage: Assessment and Treatment of the Angry, Aggressive Driver* (Washington, DC: American Psychological Association, 2006).

44 Ronald T. Potter-Efron, "One Size Does Not Fit All: Learning to Recognize the Many Faces of Anger," *Psychotherapy Networker* 28 (May-June 2004): 27–28.

45 Toxic anger and its treatment are discussed in detail by W. Doyle Gentry, *Anger Free: Ten Basic Steps to Managing Your Anger* (New York: Morrow, 1999).

46 See chapter 8 where I discuss how depression often results from anger held within.

47 Ephesians 4:30–31.

48 Howard Kassinove and Raymond Chip Tafrate, *Anger Management: The Complete Treatment Guidebook for Practice* (Atascadero, CA: Impact, 2002).

49 A number of research studies support this conclusion, including Brad J. Bushman, Roy R. Baumeister, and Angela D. Stack, "Catharsis, Aggression, and Persuasive Influence: Self-Fulfilling or Self-Defeating Prophecies?" *Journal of Personality & Social Psychology* 76 (March 1999): 367–376; also Brad J. Bushman, "Does Venting Anger Feed or Extinguish the Flame? Catharsis, Rumination, Distraction, Anger and Aggressive Responding," *Personality & Social Psychology Bulletin* 28 (June 2002): 724–731.

50 Matthew 5:38–44.

51 Raymond Chip Tafrate, Howard Kassinove, and Louis Dundin, "Anger Episodes in High and Low Trait Anger Community Adults," *Journal of Clinical Psychology* 58 (December 2002): 1573–1590.

52 DeAngelis, "When Anger's a Plus," 44.

53 This constant exposure to anger and aggression probably characterizes some extremist Muslim communities and has been well documented in African American males who live in poorer communities. See Howard C. Stevenson, Jr., "Wrestling with Destiny: The Cultural Socialization of Anger and Healing in African American Males," *Journal of Psychology and Christianity* 21 (Winter 2002): 357–364.

54 Patricia Van Velsor and Deborah L. Cox, "Anger as a Vehicle in the Treatment of Women Who Are Sexual Abuse Survivors: Reattributing Responsibility and Assessing Personal Power," *Professional Psychology: Research and Practice* 32 (December 2001): 618–625.

55 See footnote 49 above and Tavris, *Anger*, 120–150.

56 Stevenson, "Wrestling with Destiny."

57 This involves getting to the "core hurts" that so often arouse anger. Steven Stosny, "Cease Fire: Five Steps to Anger Management," *Psychotherapy Networker* 27 (January-February 2003): 21–22.

58 1 John 1:9; James 5:16.

59 People who aren't really sorry can ask God to help them change.

60 1 John 1:9.

61 Matthew 6:14–15.

62 The movie *Anger Management* starred Jack Nicholson and Adam Sandler. It was reviewed by Andy Seiler, "'Anger' Could Be a Raging Hit," *USA Today,* April 10, 2003.

63 Jennifer Daw Holloway, "Advances in Anger Management," *Monitor on Psychology* 34 (March 2003): 54–55.

64 This was first suggested by Milton Layden, *Escaping the Hostility Trap* (Englewood Cliffs, NJ: Prentice-Hall, 1977). Numerous research studies have shown the effectiveness of "cognitive treatment," including self-talk, in dealing with anger. See, for example, Kassinove and Tafrate, *Anger Management*; J. L. Deffenbacher, D. A. Story, R. S. Stark, J. A. Hogg, and A. D. Brandon, "Cognitive-Relaxation and Social Skills Interventions in the Treatment of General Anger," *Journal of Counseling Psychology* 34 (1987): 171–176; S. L. Hazaleus and J. L. Deffenbacher, "Relaxation and Cognitive Treatment of Anger," *Journal of Consulting and Clinical Psychology* 54 (1986): 222–226; and Ronald Siddle, Freda Jones, and Fairuz Awenat, "Group Cognitive Behaviour Therapy for Anger: A Pilot Study," *Behavioural & Cognitive Psychotherapy* 31 (January 2003): 69–83.

65 Philippians 4:8.

66 Philippians 4:4–11.

67 Galatians 5:18–25.

68 This would be consistent with James 1:19–20.

69 Proverbs 22:24–25.

70 S. R. Heyman, "Psychological Problem Patterns Found with Athletes," *Clinical Psychologist* 39 (1986): 68–71.

71 It will come as no surprise to internationally sensitive readers that these differences depend in part on culture. One interesting research project compared Asian and American athletes. Asian athletes tended to be more perfectionistic, more work oriented, more family oriented, less aggressive, and less angry. Conversely, the American athletes appeared to be more aggressive, less work oriented, more inclined to complain about practice, less tied to their families, and less guilty about defeating opponents. See Tom Ferraro, "Aggression Among Athletes: An Asian American Comparison," *Athletic Insight: Online Journal of Sport Psychology* 1 (June 1999): *www.athleticinsight.com/Vol1Iss1/Asian_Aggression.htm.*

72 1 Peter 1:13; Philippians 4:8.

73 Layden, *Escaping the Hostility Trap*, 34.

11. Guilt and Forgiveness

1 For any readers who might wonder, I am still keeping JD's struggles confidential by changing numerous details in his story.

2 Earl D. Wilson, *Counseling and Guilt* (Waco, TX: Word, 1995), 11.

3 G. Begum, *Guilt: Where Religion and Psychology Meet* (Minneapolis, MN: Augsburg, 1970); see also S. Bruce Narramore, "Guilt: Where Theology and Psychology Meet," *Journal of Psychology and Theology* 2 (1974): 18–25.

4 S. Bruce Narramore, "Guilt," in *Baker Encyclopedia of Psychology and Counseling*, ed. David G. Benner and Peter C. Hill, 2nd ed. (Grand Rapids, MI: Baker, 1999), 534–536.

5 See, for example, Becca Cowan Johnson, *Good Guilt, Bad Guilt: And What to Do with Each* (Downers Grove, IL: InterVarsity, 1996).

6 Isaiah 53:6; Romans 3:23.

7 David Yau-Fa Ho, Wai Fu, and S. M. Ng, "Guilt, Shame and Embarrassment: Revelations of Face and Self," *Culture & Psychology* 10 (March 2004): 64–84.

8 In his classic book *Guilt and Grace* (New York: Harper & Row, 1962), Paul Tournier used the terms "true guilt" and "false guilt." Roughly equivalent to appropriate and inappropriate guilt, Tournier's terms, in my opinion, now seem more confusing than helpful, so I have avoided using them in this chapter.

9 Psalms 6, 32, 38, 51, 102, 130, and 143.

10 S. Bruce Narramore, *No Condemnation* (Grand Rapids, MI: Zondervan, 1984).

11 Ibid., 155. Narramore suggests that Protestants rely on 1 John 1:9, while many Catholics abuse the confessional in the same way—to give temporary relief from sin.

12 Matthew 26:75.

13 1 Peter 2:24.

14 1 John 1:9.

15 Matthew 6:14–15. For an excellent and readable discussion of forgiveness see Lewis B. Smedes, *Forgive and Forget* (New York: Harper & Row, 1984).

16 Colossians 3:13; Ephesians 4:32.

17 Matthew 18:25–35.

18 This view of sinless perfection is in contrast to 1 John 1:8–10.

19 Philippians 3:12–16.

20 Tournier, *Guilt and Grace*, 24.

21 Narramore, *No Condemnation*, 30–31.

22 Tournier, *Guilt and Grace*, 15–16, 18.

23 S. Bruce Narramore and J. H. Coe, "Conscience," in Benner and Hill, *Baker Encyclopedia of Psychology and Counseling*, 253–254. According to these authors, "conscience" also has a variety of definitions among counselors and among theologians.

24 Romans 2:15.

25 1 Timothy 4:1–2.

26 1 Corinthians 8:10–12.

27 1 Corinthians 10:25–29.

28 Genesis 2:17; 3:4–5, 22. See also S. Bruce Narramore, "Guilt: Its Universal Hidden Presence," *Journal of Psychology and Theology* 2 (1974): 295–298.

29 Genesis 3:8.

30 1 John 1:8–10.

31 John 16:8.

32 Job 1:9–11; Revelation 12:10.

33 Antjie Krog, *Country of My Skull: Guilt, Sorrow, and the Limits of Forgiveness in the New South Africa* (New York: Random House, 1999).

34 Romans 6:23.

35 Psalm 73.

36 C. W. McLemore, "Defense Mechanisms," in Benner and Hill, *Baker Encyclopedia of Psychology and Counseling*, 319–321.

37 Joel Johnson, "Desire, Guilt and Holiness," *Christian Counselor* 2 (Spring 1987): 6.

38 Julie Fitness, "Shame and Guilt," *Journal of Social & Personal Relationships* 20 (October 2003): 701–702.

39 1 John 1:9.

40 The movie starred Robert De Niro.

41 Occasionally, I have shown film clips from this movie to illustrate forgiveness. I am grateful to my friend Everett Worthington, Jr., for including this story in one of his books on forgiveness and thus reminding me of its relevance for this book as well. Everett L. Worthington, Jr., *Forgiving and Reconciling: Bridges to Wholeness and Hope* (Downers Grove, IL: InterVarsity, 2003), 66–67.

42 O. Hobart Mowrer, *The Crisis in Psychiatry and Religion* (Princeton, NJ: Van Nostrand, 1961), 82. As a young professor, I invited Dr. Mowrer to spend a day on the campus where I was teaching. He taught us all a lot about guilt and forgiveness from a humanistic perspective. He also took me aside at the end of the day and recommended that we not require visiting speakers to work so long and to speak so often without a break. I took his advice and later found myself giving the same advice to people who invited me to speak on their campuses.

43 Karl Menninger, *Whatever Became of Sin?* (New York: Hawthorn, 1973).

44 Michael E. McCullough, Steven J. Sandage, and Everett J. Worthington, Jr., *To Forgive Is Human* (Downers Grove, IL: InterVarsity, 1997); Michael E. McCullough, Kenneth L. Pargament, and C. E. Thoreson, *Forgiveness: Theory, Research, and Practice* (New York: Guilford Press, 2000); and Everett L Worthington, Jr., *Forgiving and Reconciling: Bridges to Wholeness and Hope* (Downers Grove, IL: InterVarsity, 2003). For a collection of helpful research articles on forgiveness, see the work of Christian psychologist and researcher Everett L. Worthington, Jr., especially his edited books, *Dimensions of Forgiveness: Psychological Research and Theological Speculations* (Philadelphia, PA: Templeton Foundation Press, 1998), and *Handbook of Forgiveness* (New York: Brunner-Routledge, 2005).

45 John 8:3–11.

46 1 Corinthians 10:12.

47 Matthew 7:1; Romans 12:19–20.

48 1 Samuel 12:1–14.

49 1 Samuel 16:7; Psalms 103:14; 139:1–4; 1 John 1:8.

50 1 Peter 3:18 NIV.

51 1 John 1:9; James 5:16.

52 Charlotte Van Oyen Witvliet, "Forgiveness and Health: Review and Reflections on a Matter of Faith, Feelings, and Physiology," *Journal of Psychology and Theology* 29 (Fall 2001): 212–224; Kevin S. Seyboki, Peter C. Hill, Joseph K. Neumann, and David S. Chi, "Physiological and Psychological Correlates of Forgiveness," *Journal of Psychology and Christianity* 20 (Spring 2001): 250–259; Garry Cooper, "Forgiving Extramarital Affairs," *Psychotherapy Networker* 26 (May-June 2002): 15; and Fernando Garzon, Julie Richards, Mark Witherspoon, Stacey Garver, Zongjian Wu, Lori Burkett, Heather Reed, and Leroy Hill, "Forgiveness in Community Cultural Contexts: Applications in Therapy and Opportunities for Expanded Professional Roles," *Journal of Psychology and Christianity* 21 (Winter 2002): 349–356.

53 McCullough, Sandage, and Worthington, *To Forgive Is Human*, 15.

54 Ibid.

55 David F. Walker and Richard L. Gorsuch, "Dimensions Underlying Sixteen Models of Forgiveness and Reconciliation," *Journal of Psychology and Theology* 32 (Spring 2004): 12–25.

56 1 John 1:9.

57 Lewis Smedes. *Forgive and Forget: Healing the Hurts We Don't Deserve* (San Francisco: Harper & Row, 1984), 12, 190.

58 F. LeRon Shults and Steven J. Sandage, *The Faces of Forgiveness: Searching for Wholeness and Salvation* (Grand Rapids, MI: Baker, 2003).

59 Everett L. Worthington, Jr., and J. W. Berry, "Can Society Afford Not to Promote Forgiveness and Reconciliation?" in *Promoting Social, Ethnic, and Religious Understanding and Reconciliation*, ed. Robert L. Hampton and Thomas P. Gullotta (Washington, DC: Child Welfare League of America 2004), 159–192.

60 Ephesians 4:32.

12. Loneliness

1 M. G. Davis, "Solitude and Loneliness: An Integrative Model," *Journal of Psychology and Theology* 24 (1996): 3–12.

2 Douglas LaBier, *Modern Madness: The Emotional Fallout of Success* (Reading, MA: Addison-Wesley, 1986).

3 S. A. Cappa, "Loneliness," in *Baker Encyclopedia of Psychology and Counseling*, ed. David G. Benner and Peter C. Hill, 2nd ed. (Grand Rapids, MI: Baker, 1999), 698–699; and A. Storr, *Solitude* (New York: Free Press, 1988).

4 Genesis 2:18.

5 Genesis 1:28.

6 Psalm 25:16.

7 Matthew 27:46.

8 2 Timothy 4:9–12.

9 Matthew 4:1–3.

10 Mark 1:35 is an example.

11 Luke 9:10 and Matthew 26:36–44.

12 For a fascinating discussion of how technology has contributed to our loneliness, see Laura Pappano, *The Connection Gap: Why Americans Feel So Alone* (Piscataway, NJ: Rutgers University Press, 2001).

13 Y. Amichai-Hamburger and E. Ben-Artzi, "Loneliness and Internet Use," *Computers in Human Behavior* 19 (January 2003): 71–80.

14 Janet Morahan-Martin and Phyllis Schumacher, "Loneliness and Social Uses of the Internet," *Computers in Human Behavior* 19 (November 2003): 659–671.

15 Craig W. Ellison, "Loneliness: A Social-Developmental Analysis," *Journal of Psychology and Theology* 6 (Spring 1978): 3–17.

16 Literally thousands of articles have discussed and studied attachment in a variety of human situations. There even is a journal known as *Attachment & Human Development* that publishes articles on this subject. One example of the research is a short article with the long title "The Ties That Bind: Attachment: The Nature of the Bonds Between Humans Are Becoming Accessible to Scientific Investigation," *Nature* 429 (June 2004): 705. The author, Melvin Konner, wrote, "However amorphous attachment may seem . . . , it is one of the most important determinants of human well-being, and we would do well to bring it into scientific focus."

17 Steven R. Asher and Julie A. Paquette, "Loneliness and Peer Relations in Childhood," *Current Directions in Psychological Science* 12 (June 2003): 75–78.

18 Cary L. Cooper and James Campbell Quick, "The Stress and Loneliness of Success," *Counselling Psychology Quarterly* 16 (March 2003): 1–7.

19 Rose Beeson, Sara Horton-Deutsch, Carol Farran, and Marcia Neundorfer, "Loneliness and Depression in Caregivers of Persons with Alzheimer's Disease or Related Disorders," *Issues in Mental Health Nursing* 21 (December 2000): 779–806; and Rose A. Beeson, "Loneliness and Depression in Spousal Caregivers of Those with Alzheimer's Disease Versus Non-Caregiving Spouses," *Archives of Psychiatric Nursing* 17 (June 2003): 135–143.

20 Henri J. M. Nouwen, *Reaching Out: Three Movements of the Spiritual Life* (Garden City, NY: Doubleday, 1966), 15.

21 Hatim A. Omar, "Adolescent Violence as Viewed by High School Students," *International Journal of Adolescent Medicine & Health* 11 (July-December 1999): 153–158.

22 W. A. Sadler, "Cause of Loneliness," *Science Digest* 78 (July 1975): 58–66.

23 John 3:16.

24 1 John 1:9.
25 This is discussed in a book with a revealing title, Richard Lamb, *The Pursuit of God in the Company of Friends* (Downers Grove, IL: InterVarsity, 2003).
26 John 3:16; Romans 8:35–39.
27 Romans 8:14–17.
28 Proverbs 18:23.
29 Romans 8:9; 1 Corinthians 6:19; 1 John 4:13.
30 Romans 8:26–31.
31 If you are serious about considering how the church can be a different kind of community, consider reading the excellent but sometimes disturbing volume by Reggie McNeal, *The Present Future: Six Tough Questions for the Church* (San Francisco: Jossey-Bass, 2003).
32 Brian D. Dufton and Daniel Perlman, "Loneliness and Religiosity: In the World but Not of It," *Journal of Psychology and Theology* 14 (Summer 1986): 135–45.
33 Nouwen, *Reaching Out*, 28–29.
34 Paul Tournier, *Escape from Loneliness* (Philadelphia: Westminster, 1962). The book was first published in French in 1948.
35 This term is taken from the cocoons that caterpillars spin before they change into butterflies. Cocooning refers to the tendency of individuals, married couples, and families to retreat to their homes, close the doors, turn on the air conditioning, and withdraw from the busy world for an evening or a weekend.
36 One interesting research project systematically compared ways in which people ages thirteen to eighty-three coped with loneliness in Canada, Argentina, and Turkey. There were significant differences among the three countries; cultural background clearly affected the strategies used to cope with loneliness. The study was designed in Canada and conducted by a group in Toronto. Is it surprising that the Canadians got the best scores in the coping tests that were administered? The researchers are known to be highly competent, and undoubtedly they were aware of cultural differences in how people respond to research questions. This may have accounted for some of the differences. Even so, the results are significant in showing that we cope with loneliness in differing ways, depending on our cultural backgrounds. Ami Rokach, Hasan Bacanli, and Gina Ramberan, "Coping with Loneliness: A Cross-cultural Comparison," *European Psychologist* 5 (December 2000): 302–311.

13. Childhood
1 A good example is by David Stoop and Jan Stoop, eds., *The Complete Parenting Book: Practical Help from Leading Experts* (Grand Rapids, MI: Revell, 2005). One book has summarized the parenting advice given throughout the twentieth century. According to Ann Hulbert, *Raising America: Experts, Parents, and a Century of Advice About Children* (New York: Alfred A. Knopf, 2003), a lot of the advice is contradictory and raises questions about whether we know what we are doing. If you are a student, required to read this book by one of your teachers, do not assume that the previous sentence gives you an excuse for skipping this chapter.
2 Lloyd H. Rogler, "Historical Generations and Psychology: The Case of the Great Depression and World War II," *American Psychologist* 57 (December 2002): 1013–1023.
3 Psalm 127:3–5; Jeremiah 22:30; Genesis 30:22–23. Rachel, Sarah, Hannah, Michal, and Elizabeth were among the biblical women whose childlessness caused considerable distress.
4 Mark 10:14.
5 Psalm 127:3; Matthew 18:10; Psalm 103:1–3; Titus 2:4; Matthew 18:1–6.
6 Exodus 20:12; Mark 7:10–13; Proverbs 1:8; 4:1; 13:1; 23:22; Ephesians 6:1.
7 Romans 1:30; see also 2 Timothy 3:1–5.
8 Acts 5:29.
9 Titus 2:4; Deuteronomy 6:1–9; Proverbs 22:6; 2 Corinthians 12:14; Colossians 3:21.
10 Gene A. Getz, *The Measure of a Family* (Ventura, CA: Regal, 1976), 83–94.
11 Deuteronomy 6:1–7.
12 Luke 2:52.
13 These and other issues are discussed in detail in Harold I. Kaplan and Benjamin J. Sadock, eds., *Comprehensive Textbook of Psychiatry/VI* (Baltimore, MD: Williams and Wilkins, 1995), chapters 33–37.
14 See, e.g., Deuteronomy 6:1–9; Proverbs 22–26; Psalm 78:1–8.

15 Debbie B. Riley, Geoffrey L. Grief, Debra L. Caplan, and Heather K. MacAulay, "Common Themes and Treatment Approaches in Working with Families of Runaway Youths," *American Journal of Family Life* 32 (March-April 2004): 139–153.

16 Marc H. Bornstein and Linda R. Cote, "Mothers' Parenting Cognitions in Cultures of Origin, Acculturating Cultures, and Cultures of Destination," *Child Development* 75 (January 2004): 221–235; Jennifer M. Bonovitz, "The Immigrant Child," *American Journal of Psychoanalysis* 64 (June 2004): 129–141. For a moving discussion of this issue, read Mary Pipher, *In the Middle of Everywhere* (New York: Harcourt, 2002).

17 Gary Cooper, "How Anxious Parents Create Anxious Kids," *Psychotherapy Networker* 27 (September-October 2003): 16–17. This brief report summarizes research headed by psychologist Janet Woodruff-Borden and reported in the Winter 2002 issue of the *Journal of Clinical Child and Adolescent Psychology*.

18 Gary W. Evans, "The Environment of Childhood Poverty," *American Psychologist* 59 (February-March 2004): 77–92.

19 World Vision has produced some of the best resources for helping these children at risk. For example, see the following, all published in Federal Way, WA, by World Vision, Inc.: Phyllis Kilbourn, ed., *Children in Crisis* (1996); Phyllis Kilbourn, *Street Children* (1997); Phyllis Kilbourn and Marjorie McDermid, eds., *Sexually Exploited Children: Working to Protect and Heal* (1998); Patrick McDonald with Emma Garrow, *Children at Risk: Networks in Action* (2000); Phyllis Kilbourn, ed., *Children Affected by HIV/AIDS: Compassionate Care* (2002).

20 One example is Potter's House in Guatemala City. It began when two single female counselors (including one of my former students) collected blankets and delivered them one Christmas Eve to the people who lived in the city dump. Slowly the outreach grew and now Potter's House is committed to bringing all of these children (they are referred to as "the treasures") and their parents out of the dump and into environments where they can get better education, receive health care, and learn skills that will enable them to be independent instead of scrounging every day in the dump. For more information see *www.pottershouse.org.GT*.

21 William Doherty, "See How They Run: When Did Childhood Turn into a Rat Race?" *Psychotherapy Networker* 27 (September-October 2003): 38–46, 63.

22 One must be careful not to assume that better achievement and adjustment come only because of more meals together. It may be that some other issue, like parental care of discipline, leads both to the better test scores and the more frequent meals together. When two events appear together it cannot be assumed that one causes the other. This does not undermine the finding that overly busy lifestyles appear to have a harmful influence on children.

23 Margaret L. Stuber, "Children's Reaction to Illness, Hospitalization, and Surgery," in Kaplan and Sadock, *Textbook of Psychiatry*, 2455–2469.

24 Joel D. Bregman and James C. Harris, "Mental Retardation," in Kaplan and Sadock, *Textbook of Psychiatry*, 2207–2241. See also Patricia Ainsworth and Pamela C. Baker, *Mental Retardation* (Jackson, MI: University Press of Mississippi, 2004); Joyce Brennfleck Shannon and Joyce S. Shannon, *Mental Retardation Sourcebook* (Auckland, NZ: Omnigraphics, 2000); and Mary Beirne-Smith, Richard F. Ittenbach, and James R. Patton, *Mental Retardation*, 6th ed. (Upper Saddle River, NJ: Prentice-Hall, 2001).

25 L. Eugene Arnold and Peter S. Jensen, "Attention Deficit Disorders," in Kaplan and Sadock, *Textbook of Psychiatry*, 2295–2310. See also Russell A. Barkley, *Taking Charge of ADHD: The Complete, Authoritative Guide for Parents*, rev. ed. (New York: Guilford, 1998); and Russell A. Barkley, *Attention-Deficit Hyperactivity Disorder* (New York: Guilford, 2000).

26 Vincent J. Monastra, *Parenting Children with ADHD: 10 Lessons That Medicine Cannot Teach* (Washington, DC: American Psychological Association, 2004).

27 See, for example, Cheryl Sanders and Gary D. Phye, *Bullying: Implications for the Classroom* (Washington, DC: Academic Press, 2004); Dorothy Espelage, *Bullying in American Schools: A Social-Ecological Perspective on Prevention and Intervention* (Mahwah, NJ: Laurence Erlbaum, 2003); Rebecca S. Griffin and Alan M. Gross, "Childhood Bullying: Current Empirical Findings and Future Directions for Research," *Aggression & Violent Behavior* 9 (July 2004): 379–400; Maurice J. Elias and Joseph E. Zins, "Bullying, Other Forms of Peer Harassment, and Victimization in the Schools: Issues for School Psychology Research and Practice," *Journal of Applied School Psychology* 19 (2003): 1–5; and Pamela Orpinas and Arthur M. Horne, "Bullying Prevention: Creating a Positive School Climate

and Developing Social Competence" (Washington, DC: American Psychological Association, 2006).

28 A. E. Grills and T. H. Ollendick, "Peer Victimization, Global Self-Worth, and Anxiety in Middle School Children," *Journal of Clinical Child and Adolescent Psychology* 31 (2002): 59–68.

29 Tracy Vaillancourt, Shelly Hymel, and Patricia McDougall, "Bullying Is Power: Implications for School-Based Intervention Strategies," *Journal of Applied School Psychology* 19 (2003): 157–176. For in-depth discussion of peer relations of all types, see Janis B. Kupersmidt and Kenneth A. Dodge, eds., *Children's Peer Relations: From Development to Intervention* (Washington, DC: American Psychological Association, 2004).

30 According to a UNICEF report, *The State of the World's Children*, published in 1997, at least 100,000 children in the United States are believed to be involved in commercial sexual exploitation. For more information, see *www.asha.viva.org* and follow the links.

31 E. E. Werner and R. S. Smith, *Vulnerable but Invincible: A Longitudinal Study of Resilient Children and Youth* (New York: McGraw-Hill, 1982), and Meyer D. Glantz and Jeanette L. Johnson, *Resilience and Development: Positive Life Adaptations* (New York: Kluwer Academic Publishers, 1999).

32 Isaiah 1:2.

33 1 Samuel 3:11–13.

34 Olivia N. Velting, Nicole J. Setzer, and Ann Marie Albano, "Update on and Advances and Assessment and Cognitive-Behavioral Treatment of Anxiety Disorders in Children and Adolescents," *Professional Psychology: Research and Practice* 35 (February 2004): 42–54.

35 Benedetto Vitiello and Peter S. Jensen, "Disruptive Behavior Disorders," in Kaplan and Sadock, *Textbook of Psychiatry*, 2311–2319; and John B. Rein, Gerald Patterson, and James J. Snyder, eds., *Antisocial Behaviors in Children and Adolescents* (Washington, DC: American Psychological Association, 2002).

36 Erin B. McClure, Tom Kubiszyn, and Nadine J. Kaslow, "Advances in the Diagnosis and Treatment of Childhood Mood Disorders," *Professional Psychology: Research and Practice* 33 (April 2002): 125–134.

37 Peter Szatmri, "Schizophrenia with Childhood Onset," in Kaplan and Sadock, *Textbook of Psychiatry*, 2393–2398.

38 In the United States, for example, as many as one out of every five people in the United States has a learning disability, and often these children require special education in school. *Twenty-fourth Annual Report to Congress* (Washington, DC: U.S. Department of Education, 2002).

39 For an excellent discussion of play therapy, written by an experienced play therapist and Christian counselor, see Daniel S. Sweeney, *Counseling Children Through the World of Play* (Wheaton, IL: Tyndale House, 1997). See also Tara M. Hall, Heidi Gerard Kaduson, and Charles E. Schaefer, "Fifteen Effective Lay Therapy Techniques," *Professional Psychology: Theory and Practice* 33 (December 2002): 515–522. The most effective play therapists also are aware of cultural and diversity issues that enter children's play. See Kevin O'Connor, "Addressing Diversity Issues in Play Therapy," *Professional Psychology: Research and Practice* 36 (October 2005): 566–573.

40 Edward R. Christophersen and Susan L. Mortweet, *Treatments That Work with Children: Empirically Supported Strategies for Managing Childhood Problems* (Washington, DC: American Psychological Association, 2001).

41 Amy M. Duhig, Vicky Phares, and Robyn W. Birkeland, "Involvement of Fathers in Therapy: A Survey of Clinicians," *Professional Psychology: Research and Practice* 33 (August 2003): 389–395.

42 Debra B. Nevas and Barry A. Farber, "Parents' Attitudes Toward Their Child's Therapist and Therapy," *Professional Psychology: Research and Practice* 32 (April 2001): 165–170.

43 This is family therapy. It will be discussed later in the chapter. The counselor may discover that the parents are so highly conflicted that counseling the children is not likely to be successful until the parents can be helped. See Benjamin D. Garber, "Directed Co-Parenting Intervention: Conducting Child-Centered Interventions in Parallel with Highly Conflicted Co-Parents," *Professional Psychology: Research and Practice* 35 (February 2004): 55–64.

44 Family therapy has become a specialized type of counseling with specialized training. Several books give overviews. For example, see Roger Lowe, *Family Therapy: A Constructive Approach* (London: Sage Publications, 2004); and Irene Goldenberg and Herbert Goldenberg, *Family Therapy: An Overview* (Stamford, CT: Wadsworth, 2003).

45 L. Eugene Arnold, ed., *Helping Parents Help Their Children* (New York: Brunner/Mazel, 1978).

46 There are many books available to help parents raise children effectively. Often these can be recommended to parents or used to educate ourselves. Consider, for example, Edward R. Christophersen and Susan L. Mortweet, *Parenting That Works: Building Skills That Last a Lifetime* (Washingdon, DC: American Psychological Association, 2002); Gary and Carrie Oliver, *Raising Sons and Loving It: Helping Your Boys Become Godly Men* (Grand Rapids, MI: Zondervan, 2000); Annette M. La Greca, Wendy K. Silverman, Eric M. Vernberg, and Michael C. Roberts, *Helping Children Cope with Disasters and Terrorism* (Washington, DC: American Psychological Association, 2002); and James Dobson, *The New Strong-Willed Child* (Carol Stream, IL: Tyndale, 2004).

47 Gene Getz, *Measure of a Family* (Ventura, CA: Regal, 1977), 13.

48 G. C. Gard and K. K. Berry, "Oppositional Children: Taming Tyrants," *Journal of Clinical Child Psychology* 15 (1986): 148–158.

49 Remind parents that some kids never do learn to hang up their clothes—especially if they have a father who doesn't pick up his clothes either. The parent works on this until the child leaves home; then the spouse can take over!

50 Roger P. Weissberg, Karol L. Kumpfer, and Martin E. P. Seligman, "Prevention That Works for Children and Youth," *American Psychologist* 58 (June-July 2003), 425.

51 Karol L. Kumpfer and Rose Alvarado, "Family-Strengthening Approaches for the Prevention of Youth Problem Behaviors," *American Psychologist* 58 (June-July 2003): 457–465.

52 Mark T. Greenberg, Roger P. Weissberg, Mary Utne O'Brian, Joseph E. Zins, Linda Fredericks, Hank Resnik, and Maurice J. Elias, "Enhancing School-Based Prevention and Youth Development Through Coordinated Social, Emotional and Academic Learning, *American Psychologist* 58 (June-July 2003): 466–474.

53 Abraham Wandersman and Paul Florin, "Community Interventions and Effective Prevention," *American Psychologist* 58 (June-July 2003): 441–448.

54 Anna C. Salter, *Predators, Pedophiles, Rapists, and Other Sex Offenders: Who They Are, How They Operate, and How We Can Protect Ourselves and Our Children* (New York: Basic Books, 2003).

55 Suzanne Bennett Johnson and Susan G. Millstein, "Prevention Opportunities in Health Care Settings," *American Psychologist* 58 (June-July 2003): 475–481.

56 There are numerous practical books on this subject. For example, see Robert Wolgemuth, *The Most Important Place on Earth: What a Christian Home Looks Like and How to Build One* (Nashville: Thomas Nelson, 2004).

57 1 Thessalonians 5:11; Hebrews 3:1, 3; 10:25.

14. Adolescence

1 Armand M. Nicholi, Jr., ed., *The Harvard Guide to Modern Psychiatry* (Cambridge, MA: The Belknap Press of Harvard University Press, 1978), 519.

2 In 1904 G. Stanley Hall, one of the pioneers in American psychology and first president of the American Psychological Association, published a massive two-volume study of adolescence. He described the teenage years as a period of "storm and stress," and his work triggered literally thousands of research studies designed to help subsequent generations understand and counsel young people.

3 Joseph Adelson, "Adolescence and the Generalization Gap," *Psychology Today* 12 (February 1979): 33–37. The conclusions that Adelson reached over a quarter century ago probably still apply.

4 S. I. Powers, S. T. Hauser, and L. A. Kilner, "Adolescent Mental Health," *American Psychologist* 44 (1989): 200–208; and G. L. Welton, "Adolescence," in *Baker Encyclopedia of Psychology and Counseling*, ed. David G. Benner and Peter C. Hill, 2nd ed. (Grand Rapids: MI: Baker, 1999), 46–48. It is of interest that one major resource book on adolescent mental-health disorders includes an entire section on "The Positive Perspective on Youth Development." See Dwight L. Evans, Edna B. Foa, Raquel E. Gur, Herbert Hendin, Charles P. O'Brien, Martin E. P. Seligman, and B. Timothy Walsh, *Treating and Preventing Adolescent Mental Health Disorders* (New York: Oxford University Press 2005), 497–527.

5 American and Canadian readers will recognize that these time frames correspond roughly to the middle school, high school, and college years.

6 In preparing this and the following two or three chapters, I have gone several times to research by the Barna group. This will be reflected in later pages. Concerning American teenagers, see George Barna, *Real Teens: A Contemporary Snapshot of Youth Culture* (Ventura, CA: Regal Books, 2001). Please recognize that adolescent cultures vary significantly from country to country and Barna's research does not necessarily apply cross-culturally. In the United States, teenage pregnancies have declined during the past decade, but the numbers are much higher than they were a generation or more ago.

7   From the Barna Research Group web page, *www.barna.org*, October 8, 2001.

8   Ibid. Once again it is important to recognize that these are categories determined by research in the United States, which may not apply to other countries.

9   It is well known that Erikson suggested the term "identity crisis" to describe the major issue facing adolescents. Some observers have suggested that this is not a universal characteristic of youth, and for many it isn't even a crisis. E. H. Erikson, *Identity: Youth and Crisis* (New York: Norton, 1968).

10   Ecclesiastes 11:9–10.

11   Luke 2:52.

12   Notice, for example, that Jesus was obedient to his parents—a trait that is not likely to be common among preadolescents today.

13   The quotation is from 1 Peter 5:6–7. See also Acts 2:17; Proverbs 20:29; 1 John 2:13–14; Titus 2:4–6.

14   This has become a major concern not only to teenagers and their parents, but to political leaders and health-care professionals. See, for example, Dianne Neumark-Sztainer, *I'm, Like, So Fat!: Helping Your Teen Make Healthy Choices About Eating and Exercise in a Weight-Obsessed World* (New York: Guilford, 2005).

15   From the Barna Research Group web page, *www.barna.org*, November 3, 2003. Of course, these figures are likely to change as time passes and do not necessarily apply across cultures.

16   Alison Lutz and Dean Borgman, "Teenage Spirituality and the Internet," *Cultic Studies Review* 1 (2002): 137–150.

17   Lynn Schofield Clark, *From Angels to Aliens: Teenagers, the Media, and the Supernatural* (New York: Oxford University Press, 2003).

18   Erikson, *Identity*, 156.

19   Bill Beausay, *Teenage Boys: Surviving and Enjoying These Extraordinary Years* (Colorado Springs: Waterbrook, 1989), 5–12. For an in-depth study of teenage girls, see Norine G. Johnson, Michael C. Roberts, and Judith Worell, *Beyond Appearance: A New Look at Adolescent Girls* (Washington, DC: American Psychological Association, 2001).

20   An Internet search will lead to numerous specific types of adolescent disorders. For books, see Scott W. Henggeler, Sonja K. Schoenwald, Melisa D. Rowland, and Phillippe B. Cunningham, *Serious Emotional Disturbance in Children and Adolescents* (New York: Guilford, 2002), or Melvin Lewis, *Child and Adolescent Psychiatry: A Comprehensive Textbook*, 3rd ed. (New York: Lippincott Williams & Wilkins, 2002).

21   Edward P. Mulvey and Elizabeth Cauffman, "The Inherent Limits of Predicting School Violence," *American Psychologist* 56 (October 2001): 797–802.

22   Robert B. Pettit, "Sexual Teens, Sexual Media: Investigating Media's Influence on Adolescent Sexuality," *Journal of Social & Personal Relationships* 20 (April 2003): 262–263.

23   "Teenage Pregnancy," *Search Institute Source* 1 (Minneapolis: November 1985): 1, 2.

24   See, for example, Esther Coren, Jane Barlow, and Sarah Stewart-Brown, "The Effectiveness of Individual and Group-based Parenting Programmes in Improving Outcomes for Teenage Mothers and Their Children: A Systematic Review," *Journal of Adolescence* 26 (February 2003): 79–103; and Louise J. Keown, Lianne J. Woodward, and Jeff Field, "Language Development of Pre-School Children Born to Teenage Mothers," *Infant and Child Development* 10 (September 2001): 129–145.

25   Natasha Slesnick, *Our Runaway and Homeless Youth: A Guide to Understanding* (Westport, CT: Praeger, 2004).

26   Sabrina D. Black, "Odds Are, You Know a Teen Who Gambles," *Christian Counseling Today* 8 (2000): 24–27, 73.

27   From the "Youth Suicide Fact Sheet" posted on the web site of the American Association of Suicidology (*www.suicidology.org*), March 19, 2004.

28   For an in-depth consideration of suicide in adolescence, see Alan L. Berman, David A. Jobes, and Morton M. Silverman, *Adolescent Suicide: Assessment and Intervention* (Washington, DC: American Psychological Association, 2006). For guidance in helping families following a successful suicide, see Nadine J. Kaslow and Sari Gilman Aranson,

"Recommendations for Family Interventions Following a Suicide," *Professional Psychology: Research and Practice* 35 (June 2004): 240–247.

29 Ron Taffel, "The Wall of Silence," *Psychotherapy Networker* 25 (May-June 2001): 52–64. The quotation is from page 64.

30 Isaiah 1:2.

31 To help parents understand, you might encourage them to read Beausay, *Teenage Boys*, or Marcel Danesi, *My Son Is an Alien* (Lanham, MD: Rowman and Littlefield, 2003). Written by an anthropologist, this is described by the publisher as an entertaining, informative look at cultural influences on today's youth.

32 Laurence Steinberg and Wendy Steinberg, *Crossing Paths: How Your Child's Adolescence Triggers Your Own Crisis* (New York: Simon & Schuster, 1994). I am grateful to one of my former students, K. Zachary Brittle, for pointing me to the Steinberg book and for alerting me to the concept of parental identity crises when their children reach the teenage years.

33 Hector R. Bird, "Psychiatric Treatments of Adolescents," in *Comprehensive Textbook of Psychiatry/VI*, ed. Harold I. Kaplan and Benjamin J. Sadock (Baltimore, MD: Williams and Wilkins, 1995): 2439–3446.

34 Of course there are many good books about parenting, but one of the most realistic and helpful may be by lawyer Russ Robinson, *Walking the Parenting Tightrope: Raising Kids Without Losing Your Balance* (Grand Rapids: Baker, 2005).

35 For other helpful discussions on understanding and counseling teenagers, see Les Parrott III, *Helping the Struggling Adolescent: A Counseling Guide* (Grand Rapids, MI: Zondervan, 1993); Josh McDowell and Bob Hostetler, *Handbook on Counseling Youth* (Nashville, TN: W Publishing, 1996); and Andrew J. Weaver, John Preston, and Leigh W. Jerome, *Counseling Troubled Teens and Their Families: A Handbook for Pastors and Youth Workers* (Nashville, TN: Abingdon, 1999). More recent are books by Ron Taffel, *Breaking Through to Teens: A New Psychotherapy for the New Adolescence* (New York: Guilford, 2005); Matthew D. Selekman, *Pathways to Change: Brief Therapy with Difficult Adolescents*, 2nd ed. (New York: Guilford, 2005); Euthymia D. Hibbs and Peter S. Jensen, *Psychosocial Treatments for Child and Adolescent Disorders*, 2nd ed. (Washington, DC: American Psychological Association, 2005); and Evans et al., *Treating and Preventing Adolescent Mental Health Disorders*. For a broader perspective, not written from a Christian viewpoint, see Richard M. Lerner and Laurence Steinberg, eds., *Handbook of Adolescent Psychology*, 2nd ed. (New York: Wiley, 2004).

36 Jerome Price and Judith Margerum, "Four Most Common Mistakes Treating Teens," *Psychotherapy Networker* 24 (July-August 2000): 52–55.

37 Adapted from Taffel, "Wall of Silence," 69.

38 The following information is adapted from an article by Jeremy R. Sullivan, Eleazar Ramirez, William A. Rae, Nancy Peña Razo, and Carrie A. George, "Factors Contributing to Breaking Confidentiality with Adolescent Clients: A Survey of Pediatric Psychologists," *Professional Psychology: Research and Practice* 33 (August 2002): 396–401.

39 Karol L. Kumpfer and Rose Alvarado, "Family-Strengthening Approaches for the Prevention of Youth Problem Behaviors," *American Psychologist* 58 (June-July 2003): 457–465.

40 Ibid., 458.

41 It is not always easy to evaluate the effects of educational programs on prevention. There is increasing evidence, however, that prevention programs can be preventive. Some of this research is discussed by Abraham Wandersman and Paul Florin, "Community Interventions and Effective Prevention," *American Psychologist* 58 (June-July 2003): 441–448. Perhaps as a result of prevention efforts, within the past decade or two, in the United States there have been substantial declines in both injury-related deaths and homicide during the teen years. Likewise, teen pregnancy has declined every year since 1991, and weapon carrying has continued to decrease. Encouraging as these trends may be, the United States continues to have the highest teenage pregnancy rate of any country in the industrialized world. Likewise, annual adolescent homicide rates exceed those of the other twenty-three wealthiest countries combined. See Robert W. Blum, "Trends in Adolescent Health: Perspectives from the United States," *International Journal of Adolescent Medicine & Health* 13 (October-December 2001): 287–295.

42 Maureen A. Buckley and Sandra Hundley Zimmermann, *Mentoring Children and Adolescents: A Guide to the Issues* (Westport, CT: Praeger, 2003). Written from a secular perspective, this book presents practical information and up-to-date research on the

effectiveness and limitations of mentoring, types of mentoring programs, and key figures in the mentoring movement.

43   Matthew 28:19–20.

15. Twenties and Thirties

1   Douglas Coupland, *Generation X: Tales for an Accelerated Generation* (New York: St. Mary's, 1991; New York: HarperCollins, 2000).

2   For a good summary of millennials, see Wendy Murray Zoba, *Generation 2K: What Parents and Others Need to Know About the Millennials* (Downers Grove, IL: InterVarsity, 1999).

3   The concept of two distinct phases, emergent and young adulthood, came to my attention after this chapter was written and the book was ready for the publisher. I considered changing the chapter title to "Emerging Adulthood and Young Adulthood," but I decided against this because of suggestions that emergent adulthood may be a luxury of educated and middle- or upper-class people and not something that is universal. See chapter 9 in Jack O. Balswick, Pamela Ebstyne King, and Kevin S. Reimer, *The Reciprocating Self: Human Development in Theological Perspective* (Downers Grove, IL: InterVarsity, 2005). See also J. J. Arnett, "Emerging Adulthood: A Theory of Development from the Late Teens Through the Twenties," *American Psychologist* 55 (2000): 569–580.

4   People in their twenties tend to be dismissed as politically naive and apathetic. It is true that many do not vote, and may be apathetic toward politics, believing that "the federal government is run by an elite group of elderly men with no connection with the real world." But an article in *Relevant* magazine, a cutting-edge Christian publication for people in their twenties, *www.relevantmagazine.com*, suggests that many people in their twenties and thirties are very involved politically. See Michael Reitz, "Behind the Scenes: How Twenty-Somethings Are Running D.C.," *Relevant* 7 (March-April 2004): 34–35.

5   Alexandra Robbins and Abby Wilner, *Quarterlife Crisis: The Unique Challenges of Life in Your Twenties* (New York: Jeremy P. Tarcher/Putnam, 2001). Following publication of the book, it became a national best seller, and the authors appeared to discuss "twenty-something" issues on numerous major television talk shows and were interviewed by prominent newspapers and magazines in the United States, Canada, and England.

6   Daniel J. Levinson et al., *The Seasons of a Man's Life* (New York: Alfred Knopf, 1978); and idem, *The Seasons of a Woman's Life* (New York: Alfred Knopf, 1988).

7   For a perspective on turning thirty, written for people who are in the process of entering their thirties, see Jason Boyette, *Pocket Guide to Adulthood: 29 Things to Know Before You Hit 30* (Orlando, FL: Relevant, 2005). For a summary, see Jason Boyette, "9 Things to Know Before You Turn 30," *Relevant* 17 (November-December 2005): 68–70.

8   Why were there only four baby boom countries? One explanation is that each of these countries was heavily involved in the war effort, but, unlike Japan, most of Europe, and other parts of the world, the four baby boom countries did not have to rebuild cities, buildings, or infrastructure. Instead, in the baby boomer countries people had more children and focused on rebuilding a better life.

9   Landon Y. Jones, *Great Expectations: America and the Baby Boom* (New York: Ballantine Books, 1986).

10   I admit that this is a personal opinion, based largely on my observations of seeker-sensitive churches and my conversations with young adults who prefer a more emergent kind of church experience. This is discussed in chapter 3 of this book and in several excellent books, including Robert E. Webber, *The Younger Evangelicals: Facing the Challenges of the New World* (Grand Rapids: Baker, 2002); and Dan Kimball, *The Emerging Church: Vintage Christianity for New Generations* (Grand Rapids: Zondervan, 2003).

11   Gene A. Getz, *David: God's Man in Faith and Failure* (Ventura, CA: Regal, 1978), 4.

12   2 Samuel 6:16, 20–23.

13   2 Samuel 5:4.

14   Genesis 41:46.

15   1 Timothy 4:12.

16   Titus 2:6–7.

17   Some of the following is adapted from a book that I wrote several years ago to help people adapt to young adulthood. Gary R. Collins, *Getting Started: Direction for the Most Important Decisions of Life* (Old Tappan, NJ: Revell, 1984). The book is no longer in print.

18   Martha Irvine, "The Life and Times of an Online Gamer," Associated Press, December 28, 2004, *http://www.post-gazette.com/pg/04363/433337.stm*.

19   Howard Gardner, *Frames of Mind: The Theory of Multiple Intelligences* (New York: Basic Books, 1993); also Howard Gardner, *Intelligence Reframed: Multiple Intelligences for the 21st Century* (New York: Basic Books, 2000).

20   Daniel Goleman, *Emotional Intelligence: Why It Can Matter More Than IQ* (New York: Bantam, 1995).

21   Adapted from Daniel Goleman, "What Makes a Leader?" *Harvard Business Review,* November-December 1998, 93–102.

22   The counselor might prefer to refer people like this to a good life coach. Also, there is a variety of books on the market to help people manage their lives. One of the best is by Jim Loehr and Tony Schwartz, *The Power of Full Engagement: Managing Energy, Not Time, Is the Key to High Performance and Personal Renewal* (New York: Free Press, 2003), although this may be too advanced for most counselees who need to manage their lives. For a Christian perspective, see Randy Frazee, *Making Room for Life: Trading Chaotic Lifestyles for Connected Relationships* (Grand Rapids, MI: Zondervan, 2003).

23   See chapter 18.

24   Romans 12:18.

25   I tried to summarize and critique some of these new spiritualities (which used to be known as New Age spiritualities) in Gary R. Collins, *The Soul Search: A Spiritual Journey to Authentic Intimacy with God* (Nashville, TN: Oliver-Nelson, 1998).

26   See, for example, the writings of Dallas Willard, Richard Foster, or David Benner. From a Roman Catholic perspective, see the insightful writings of Henri Nouwen. For a good instruction to early spiritual writers, see Richard J. Foster and James Bryan Smith, eds., *Devotional Classics: Selected Readings for Individuals and Groups* (San Francisco, CA: HarperSanFrancisco, 1993).

27   Chapter 3 discusses the emergent church, as does Kimball, *Emerging Church.*

28   Gary W. Moon and David G. Benner, eds., *Spiritual Direction and the Care of Souls: A Guide to Christian Approaches and Practices* (Downers Grove, IL: InterVarsity, 2004). See also David G. Benner, *Sacred Companions: The Gift of Spiritual Friendship and Direction* (Downers Grove, IL: InterVarsity, 2002).

29   This is the definition of autonomy given by Gerard Egan and Michael A. Cowan, *Moving into Adulthood* (Monterey, CA: Brooks/Cole, 1980), 98.

30   Ibid., p. 97.

31   Ibid., p. 141.

32   Erik H. Erikson, *Identity: Youth and Crisis* (New York: Norton, 1968).

33   Gary R. Collins, *Christian Coaching: Helping Others Turn Potential into Reality* (Colorado Springs, CO: NavPress, 2001), 92–93.

34   Erik H. Erikson, *Childhood and Society*, rev. ed. (New York: Norton, 1963).

35   Levinson, *Seasons of a Man's Life*, 91. Levinson and his associates refer to the Dream with an initial capital letter to "identify and emphasize our special use of the word." I have followed their example.

36   Bruce Wilkinson, *The Dream Giver* (Sisters, OR: Multnomah, 2003).

37   J.R. Briggs, "Confessions from a Young Timothy," *Rev!* 6 (July-August 2003): 56.

38   Mentoring for professional counselors, including some of the ethical implications, are discussed in an entire issue of *Journal of Psychology and Christianity* devoted to mentoring (vol. 19, Winter 2000), and by W. Brad Johnson, "The Intentional Mentor: Strategies and Guidelines for the Practice of Mentoring," *Professional Psychology: Research and Practice* 33 (February 2002): 88–96. See also Peter F. Wilson and W. Brad Johnson, "Core Virtues for the Practice of Mentoring," *Journal of Psychology and Theology* 29 (Summer 2001): 121–130. Among the helpful books on mentoring, see W. Brad Johnson and Charles R. Ridley, *Elements of Mentoring* (New York: Palgrave McMillan, 2004). Psychologists Johnson and Ridley are committed Christians, although their book is written for a more secular market. For a more explicitly Christian perspective, see Bobb Biehl, *Mentoring: Confidence in Finding a Mentor and Becoming One* (Nashville, TN: Broadman & Holman, 1996); and Ted W. Engstrom and Ron Jenson, *The Making of a Mentor* (Milton Keynes, UK: Authentic Publishing, 2005).

39   Collins, *Soul Search*, 5, 6.

40   George Gallup, Jr., and Timothy Jones, *The Next American Spirituality: Finding God in the Twenty-First Century* (Colorado Springs, CO: Cook, 2000).

41   Richard Lamb, *The Pursuit of God in the Company of Friends* (Downers Grove, IL: InterVarsity, 2003).

42 Several years ago a young Catholic writer described the spirituality of his generation in Tom Beaudoin, *Virtual Faith: The Irreverent Spiritual Quest of Generation X* (San Francisco: Jossey-Bass, 1998). Two years later, the Gallup research organization documented some of the changes in Gallup and Jones, *Next American Spirituality.* See also Robert Webber, *Ancient-Future Faith: Rethinking Evangelicalism for a Postmodern World* (Grand Rapids, MI: Baker, 1999); Leonard Sweet, *Post-modern Pilgrims: First Century Passion for the 21st Century* (Nashville, TN: Broadman & Holman, 2000); Dan Kimball, *Emerging Worship: Creating Worship Gatherings for New Generations* (Grand Rapids, MI: Zondervan, 2004); and Mildred Minatrea, *Shaped by God's Heart: The Passion and Practices of Missional Churches* (San Francisco, CA: Jossey-Bass, 2004). A more academic study of one emergent church is Gerardo Marti, *A Mosaic of Believers: Diversity and Innovation in a Multiethnic Church* (Bloomington, IN: Indiana University Press, 2001).

43 This is the conclusion of Frederick M. Hudson, *The Adult Years: Mastering the Art of Self-Renewal,* rev. ed. (San Francisco, CA: Jossey-Bass, 1999).

44 Gail Sheehy, *Passages: Predictable Crises of Adult Life* (New York: Dutton, 1976). To make this more contemporary and cross-cultural, I have changed the names of some of Sheehy's categories and added one or two others.

45 Thomas E. Joiner, Jr., Zachary R. Voetz, and M. Donald Rudd, "For Suicidal Young Adults with Comorbid Depressive and Anxiety Disorders, Problem-Solving Treatment May Be Better Than Treatment as Usual," *Professional Psychology: Research and Practice* 32 (June 2001): 278–282.

46 Two unusually successful young adults have published a book to help individuals and teams of people get unstuck. Written primarily for business readers, the book may help some motivated counselees (or their counselors) get unstuck. Keith Yamashita and Sandra Spataro, *Unstuck: A Tool for Yourself, Your Team, and Your World* (New York: Portfolio/Penguin, 2004).

47 Levinson et al., *Seasons of a Man's Life,* 337.

48 C. Farren, J. D. Gray, and B. Kaye, "Mentoring: A Boom to Career Development," *Personnel* 61 (1984): 20–24. This, of course, is an early study of mentoring. In the two decades that have followed this publication, thousands of mentoring studies and books have appeared, and mentoring has become a popular topic. Sadly, it seems that mentoring is more often talked about than done.

49 Warren G. Bennis and Robert J. Thomas, *Geeks and Geezers: How Era, Values, and Defining Moments Shape Leaders* (Boston, MA: Harvard Business School Press, 2002).

16. Forties and Fifties

1 Calvin A. Colarusso, "Adulthood," in *Comprehensive Textbook of Psychiatry/VI,* ed. Harold I. Kaplan and Benjamin J. Sadock (Baltimore, MD: Williams & Wilkins, 1995), 2495, 2506.

2 C. G. Jung, *Psychological Reflections,* ed. Jolande Jacobi (New York: Harper Torchbooks, 1961), 125.

3 Frederic M. Hudson, *The Adult Years: Mastering the Art of Self-Renewal,* rev. ed. (San Francisco, CA: Jossey-Bass, 1999), 158–159.

4 Bob Buford has written about this in *Stuck in Halftime: Reinvesting Your One and Only Life* (Grand Rapids: Zondervan, 2001). See also Buford's books *Halftime: Changing Your Game Plan from Success to Significance* (Grand Rapids, MI: Zondervan, 1997) and *Game Plan* (Grand Rapids: Zondervan, 1999). The books are interesting but tend to be focused on people who have unusual wealth, success, and ability to be independent. See also John Maxwell, *The Journey from Success to Significance* (Nashville, TN: J. Countryman, 2004).

5 At the beginning of the twenty-first century, life expectancy is closer to the mid-seventies, but this figure hides the fact that women live longer than men, that members of some ethnic groups live longer than others, and that life expectancy differs significantly from country to country, depending in part on the quality of medical care and the quality of life. One more recent book has looked at human development, including the middle years, from a theological perspective: Jack O. Balswick, Pamela Ebstyne King, and Kevin S. Reimer, *The Reciprocating Self: Human Development in Theological Perspective* (Downers Grove, IL: InterVarsity, 2005).

6 Jung, *Psychological Reflections,* 121, 123.

7 Colarusso, "Adulthood," 2504. The relative rarity of a midlife crisis in women is discussed by Daniel Levinson, in *Seasons of a Woman's Life* (New York: Knopf, 1996).

8 Martin G. Groder, "Boredom: The Good and the Bad," *Bottom Line Personal* 7 (March 15, 1986): 9–10.

9 See footnote 4.

10 Fern Schumer Chapman, "Executive Guild: Who's Taking Care of the Children," *Fortune* 115 (February 16, 1987): 30–37.

11 Roberta L. Coles, "Elderly Narrative Reflections on the Contradictions in Turkish Village Family Life After Migration of Adult Children," *Journal of Aging Studies* 15 (December 2001): 383–406.

12 Lorraine Dennerstein, E. Dudley, and J. Guthrie, "Empty Nest or Revolving Door? A Prospective Study of Women's Quality of Life in Midlife During the Phase of Children Leaving and Reentering the Home," *Psychological Medicine* 32 (April 2002): 545–550.

13 For an interesting discussion of counseling people when their parents suddenly seem to be older and in need of greater care, see Terry Hargrove, "When You're 64," *Psychotherapy Networker* 29 (July-August 2005): 45–51, 62.

14 There are literally thousands of books on marriage and probably hundreds on marital affairs. You can find them at *www.Amazon.com* or at *www.Christianbook.com*. One of the better books is by Les and Leslie Parrott, *When Bad Things Happen to Good Marriages: How to Stay Together When Life Pulls You Apart* (Grand Rapids, MI: Zondervan, 2001).

15 Jim Conway, *Men in Mid-Life Crisis* (Elgin, IL: David C. Cook, 1978), 124.

16 Ibid., 105.

17 Ibid., 137ff.

18 Helping people get unstuck from their halftime inertia is a major thrust of the work of Bob Buford through his books and seminars. See *Game Plan, Stuck in Halftime*, or *www.Halftime.org*.

19 The quotation and much of this paragraph are adapted from Colarusso, "Adulthood," 2505.

20 The following discussion is adapted from an article by Martin Groder, "The Fine Line Between Courage and Foolhardiness," *Bottom Line Personal* 7 (September 30, 1986): 11–12. The article is old, but the conclusions still apply.

21 Many of the later chapters in this book discuss topics that come up at middle age. See, for example, the chapters on anxiety, marital problems, sex, self-esteem, and vocational counseling.

22 E. Erikson, *Young Man Luther* (New York: Norton, 1962); E. Erikson, *Gandhi's Truth* (New York: Norton, 1969). Some of the material in these paragraphs is adapted from Peter M. Newton and Dorian S. Newton, "Erik H. Erikson," in Kaplan and Sadock, *Textbook of Psychiatry*, 479–486.

23 Mentoring has become popular in the counseling/psychology profession. One practical guide for counselors is by W. B. Johnson and J. M. Huwe, *Getting Mentored in Graduate School* (Washington, DC: American Psychological Association, 2003). See also Melissa Dittman, "Building Mentorships for Success," *GradPSYCH* 3 (January 2005): 40–44. For broader discussions of mentoring, go to Amazon.com where, when I checked, 800 mentoring books were listed. The focus of these books is more about the broader mentoring relationship and less about the benefits for mentors. See, for example, two of the books written by Christian authors: W. Brad Johnson and Charles R. Ridley, *The Elements of Mentoring* (New York: Palgrave/McMillan, 2004); and Robert Tamasy and David A. Stoddard, *The Heart of Mentoring: Ten Proven Principles for Developing People to Their Fullest Potential* (Colorado Springs, CO: NavPress, 2003).

24 Jung, *Psychological Reflections*, 121.

25 Ray Ortlund and Anne Ortlund, *The Best Half of Life* (Ventura, CA: Regal, 1976), 116.

17. The Later Years

1 B. F. Skinner and M. E. Vaughn, *Enjoy Old Age: A Program of Self-Management* (New York: Norton, 1983); and E. H. Erikson, J. M. Erikson, and H. Q. Kivnick, *Vital Involvement in Old Age: The Experience of Old Age in Our Time* (New York: Norton, 1986). The Swiss counselor Paul Tournier was a comparatively young seventy-three when he wrote his book on aging, Paul Tournier, *Learn to Grow Old* (New York: Harper & Row, 1982).

2 Melissa Dittman, "Fighting Ageism," *Monitor on Psychology* 34 (May 2003): 50–52.

3 Sara Honn Qualls, Daniel L. Segal, Suzanne Norman, George Niederehe, and Dolores Gallagher-Thompson, "Psychologists in Practice with Older Adullts: Current Patterns, Sources of Training, and Need for Continuing Education," *Professional Psychology: Research and Practice* 33 (October 2002): 435–442.

4 *Modern Maturity*, the AARP magazine, has the largest circulation of any magazine in the world.

5   Ken Dychtwald, *Age Power: How the 21st Century Will Be Ruled by the New Old* (New York: Jeremy P. Tarcher/Putnam, 1999). See also, Ken Dychtwald and Joe Flower, *The Age Wave: How the Most Important Trend of Our Time Can Change Your Future* (New York: Bantam, 1990).

6   Jamie Chamberlin, "No Desire to Fully Retire," *Monitor on Psychology* 35 (November 2004): 82–83.

7   Job 12:12.

8   Psalm 71:18.

9   Ecclesiastes 12:1.

10   Ecclesiastes 12:13.

11   Leviticus 19:32; Proverbs 16:31; 20:29.

12   Titus 2:2–3.

13   Ephesians 6:3. The last nine words in this quotation are taken from Exodus 20:12 and Deuteronomy 5:16.

14   Pat Moore with Charles Paul Conn, *Disguised* (Waco, TX: Word, 1985), 62.

15   Becca R. Levy, Martin D. Slade, Suzanne R. Kunkel, Stanislav W. Kasl, "Longevity Increases by Positive Self-Perceptions of Aging," *Journal of Personality and Social Psychology* 82 (August 2002): 261–270.

16   Warren G. Bennis and Robert J. Thomas, *Geeks and Geezers: How Era, Values, and Defining Moments Shape Leaders* (Cambridge, MA: Harvard Business School Press, 2002).

17   Margaret Morganroth Gullette, *Aged by Culture* (Chicago: University of Chicago Press, 2004), 3–4.

18   Ibid., 8.

19   According to the National Osteoporosis Foundation (*www.NOF.org*), osteoporosis occurs in both men and women, although women are four times more likely to develop the disease than men.

20   John Monopoli and Frank Vaccaro, "The Relationship of Hypochondriasis Measures to Correlates of Personality in the Elderly," *Clinical Gerontologist* 26 (2003): 123–137; and Paul T. Costa, Jr., and Robert R. McCrae, "Hypochondriasis, Neuroticism, and Aging: When Are Somatic Complaints Unfounded?" *American Psychologist* 40 (January 1985): 19–28.

21   Jean Henry and Warren McNab, "Forever Young: A Health Promotion Focus on Sexuality in Aging," *Gerontology and Geriatrics Education* 23 (2003): 57–74; and K. Ludeman, "The Sexuality of the Older Person: Review of the Literature," *Gerontologist* 21 (1981): 203–208.

22   Barbara Stancil and Payne Pittard, "Sex and the Elderly: No Laughing Matter in Religion," *Journal of Religious Gerontology* 15 (2004): 17–24.

23   Many of these studies are summarized in books on aging, such as James E. Birren and K. Warner Shaeie, eds., *Handbook of the Psychology of Aging*, 5th ed. (St. Louis, MO: Academic Press, 2001); Nancy R. Hooyman and H. Asuman Kiyak, *Social Gerontology: A Multidisciplinary Perspective*, 6th ed. (Allyn & Bacon, 2001); Harold Cox, *Aging Editions 04/05*, 16th ed. (New York: McGraw Hill/Dushkin, 2003); and Sara Honn Qualls and Norman Abeles, *Psychology and the Aging Revolution: How We Adapt to Longer Life* (Washington, DC: American Psychological Association, 2000).

24   Many of the findings on cognition in the elderly have come from the Seattle Longitudinal Study, a long-term evaluation of aging that began in 1956 and is most often associated with the name of K. Warner Schaie. For example, see K. Warner Schaie, Sherry L. Willis, and Grace I. L. Caskie, "The Seattle Longitudinal Study: Relationship Between Personality and Cognition," *Aging, Neuropsychology, & Cognition* 11 (June 2004): 304–324. For another in-depth study of aging and mental abilities, see Douglas Powell and Dean K. Whitla, *Profiles in Cognitive Aging* (Cambridge, MA: Harvard University Press, 1994).

25   Adapted from Joanne M. Schrof, "Brain Power," *U.S. News & World Report* (November 28, 1994).

26   For a concise summary of emotional and psychiatric issues in the later years, see Robert N. Butler, Myrna I. Lewis, and Trey Sunderland, *Aging and Mental Health: Positive Psychological and Biomedical Approaches*, 5th ed. (Boston, MA: Allyn and Bacon, 1997). See also Dan Blazer, *Emotional Problems in Later Life: Intervention Strategies for Professional Caregivers*, 2nd ed. (New York: Springer, 1997).

27   Sometimes, older people need help from their children, but there also is a need for retired people to care for their own increasingly frail parents. For a discussion of this problem and a case history of a retired lady with an elderly mother, see Terry Hargrave, "When You're 64," *Psychotherapy Networker* 29 (July-August 2005): 44–51, 62.

28   Dennis Pelsma and Mary Flanagan, "Human Relations Training for the Elderly," *Journal of Counseling and Development* 65 (September 1986): 52–53.

29   Moore, *Disguised*, 76.

30   Jimmy Carter, *The Virtues of Aging* (New York: Ballantine, 1998), 1, 2.

31   Ibid., 5. Some will not agree, but in my circle of friends, Jimmy Carter is considered "the best ex-president we have ever had." For a fascinating discussion of Carter's initial efforts, in part through the Carter Center in Atlanta, see Douglas Brinkley, *The Unfinished Presidency: Jimmy Carter's Journey Beyond the White House* (New York: Viking, 1998). The dust jacket of the book states "Jimmy Carter left the White House in January 1981, defeated in his bid for reelection and rejected by the American public—but hardly broken." Brinkley notes that "if anything, he was more vigorous at seventy than at forty" (p. xii).

32   Richard J. Leiderer and David A. Shapiro, *Claiming Your Place at the Fire: Living the Second Half of Your Life on Purpose* (San Francisco, CA: Berrett-Koehler, 2004), xiii.

33   Ibid.

34   Ibid., 9.

35   Ibid., 4.

36   These and other obstacles are discussed by Butler et al., *Aging and Mental Health*, 208–212, and by American Psychological Association, "Guidelines for Psychological Practice with Older Adults," *American Psychologist* 59 (May-June 2004): 236–260.

37   Professional counselors, including psychologists, see the need for this kind of training. For recommendations and a survey of counselors and the elderly, see Sara Honn Qualls, Daniel L. Segal, Suzanne Norman, George Niederehe, and Dolores Gallagher-Thompson, "Psychologists in Practice with Older Adults," 435–442.

38   For up-to-date information on Alzheimer's Disease, go to *www.alz.org* or to *www.alzforum.org*.

39   N. L. Mace and P. Rabins, *The 36-Hour Day: A Family Guide to Caring for Persons with Alzheimer's Disease, Related Dementing Illnesses, and Memory Loss in Later Life*, rev. ed. (New York: Warner Books, 2001). AD became better known when former U.S. President Ronald Reagan was diagnosed with the disease. Christian readers may recognize the name of Robertson McQuilkin, who resigned from his post as President of Columbia International University in order to care for his wife, Muriel, who suffered from AD for twenty-five years. See Robertson McQuilkin, "The Gradual Grief of Alzheimer's," *Christianity Today* 48 (February 2004): 64–65.

40   This view is expressed by Nancy K. Schlossberg, *Retire Smart, Retire Happy: Finding Your True Path in Life* (Washington, DC; American Psychological Association, 2004). See also Melissa Dittmann, "A New Face to Retirement," *Monitor on Psychology* 35 (November 2004): 78–79. See also Audrey L. Canaff, "Later Life Career Planning—A New Challenge for Career Counselors," *Journal of Employment Counseling* 34 (June 1997): 85–93.

41   Margery Hutter Silver, "The Significance of Life Review in Old Age," *Journal of Geriatric Psychiatry* 35 (2002): 11–23; Susan Malde, "Guided Autobiography: A Counseling Tool for Older Adults," *Journal of Counseling and Development* 66 (February 1988): 290–293.

42   Juliette Shellman, "'Nobody Ever Asked Me Before': Understanding Life Experiences of African American Elders," *Journal of Transcultural Nursing* 15 (October 2004): 308–316.

43   Hideaki Hanaoka and Hitoshi Okamura, "Study of Effects of Life Review Activities on the Quality of Life in the Elderly: A Randomized Controlled Study," *Psychotherapy & Psychosomatics* 73 (September-October 2004): 302–311; Ellen Davis Jones and Rebecca Beck-Little, "The Use of Reminiscence Therapy for the Treatment of Depression in Rural-Dwelling Older Adults," *Issues in Mental Health Nursing* 23 (April-May 2002): 279–290.

44   Joel Sadavoy and Lawrence Lazarus, "Individual Psychotherapy," in *Comprehensive Textbook of Psychiatry/VI*, ed. Harold I. Kaplan and Benjamin J. Sadock (Baltimore, MD: Williams and Wilkins, 1995), 2593–2597.

45   These issues are discussed further by Bob G. Knight, *Psychotherapy with Older Adults*, 3rd ed. (Beverly Hills, CA: Sage, 2004). See also Bob G. Knight, *Older Adults Psychotherapy Case Studies* (Beverly Hills, CA: Sage, 1992); and Michael Duffy, *Handbook of Counseling and Psychotherapy with Older Adults* (New York: Wiley, 1999).

46   Family counseling is discussed in more detail in chapter 31. See also Andrew J. Weaver,

Linda A. Revilla, and Harold G. Koenig, *Counseling Families Across the Stages of Life: A Handbook for Pastors and Other Helping Professionals* (Nashville, TN: Abingdon Press, 2002).

47 Terry Lynn Gall, "Religious and Spiritual Attributions in Older Adults' Adjustment to Illness," *Journal of Psychology and Christianity* 22 (Fall 2003): 210–222.

48 A. Silver, "Group Psychotherapy with Senile Psychiatric Patients," *Geriatrics* 5 (1950): 147–150.

49 Butler et al., *Aging and Mental Health*, 360–362. See also Ronald W. Toseland, *Group Work with Older Adults* (New York: New York University Press, 1992).

50 Dychtwald, *Age Power*, 8.

51 Some of the following has been suggested by David O. Moberg, *Spirituality and Aging: Spiritual Dimensions of Aging Theory, Research, Practice and Policy* (Binghamton, NY: Haworth Pastoral Press, 2001). See also Melvin A. Kimble and Susan H. McFadden, *Aging, Spirituality and Religion: A Handbook*, vol. 2 (Minneapolis: Fortress, 2003).

52 Liz Carpenter, "The Silver Lining," *The Milwaukee Journal Magazine* (December 15, 1985): 18–21, 46–47.

53 The Dialogues of Plato, vol. 2. *The Republic*, trans. Benjamin Jowett (New York: National Library, n.d.), bk. 1, 329.

18. Conflict and Relationships

1 Psychologist Barry Schwartz addresses this in "Self-Determinism: The Tyranny of Freedom," *American Psychologist* 55 (January 2000): 79–88.

2 Genesis 6:11, 13.

3 Luke 22:24.

4 Acts 5; 6:1; 15:2, 7.

5 Acts 15:36–41; Galatians 2:11–21.

6 2 Corinthians 12:20–21.

7 Proverbs 10:18–19; 12:22; 13:3; 15:1, 28, 31; 16:24, 28; 17:9; 19:22; 24:26; 26:20; 28:23, 25.

8 Matthew 5–7 may take on a new perspective if you read these chapters as a commentary on interpersonal relations.

9 Matthew 18:15–35; 20:20–28; 22:36–40; Luke 12:13–15; 22:24–26.

10 Mark 9:50; 2 Timothy 2:14, 24; Philippians 4:2; 1 Thessalonians 5:13; 1 Corinthians 13:4–8; Ephesians 4:31–32.

11 James 4:1–2.

12 Romans 12:17, 18.

13 Matthew 5:9; Proverbs 12:20; Hebrews 12:14.

14 Isaiah 9:6; Luke 2:14.

15 Matthew 10:34.

16 Ephesians 2:14–17.

17 John 14:27; Philippians 4:7.

18 1 Corinthians 2:14–3:3.

19 1 Corinthians 2:14.

20 Galatians 5:19–21.

21 1 Corinthians 3:1–3.

22 Galatians 5:22–23.

23 Genesis 13:1–9.

24 Acts 6:1–6.

25 Henry Blackaby, *Created to Be God's Friend: Lessons from the Life of Abraham* (Nashville, TN: Nelson, 1999), 89.

26 Revelation 12:9; John 8:44; 2 Corinthians 11:13–15; Job 1:7; Matthew 4:3; 1 Thessalonians 3:5; 1 Peter 5:8.

27 Ephesians 6:10–12; James 4:7; 1 Peter 5:8.

28 Joyce Huggett, *Creative Conflict: How to Confront and Stay Friends* (Downers Grove, IL: InterVarsity, 1984), 14.

29 1 John 4:4; Matthew 25:41; Revelation 20:7–10.

30 Luke 12:13–15.

31 Matthew 7:3–5.

32 Rehoboam tried this approach when he first became king of Israel. This hard line failed and created long-term rebellion and interpersonal tension; see 2 Chronicles 10.

33 Les Parrott III, *High-Maintenance Relationships: How to Handle Impossible People* (Wheaton,

IL: Tyndale, 1996). See also Les Parrott III, *The Control Freak: Coping with Those Around You; Taming the One Within* (Wheaton, IL: Tyndale, 2000). Many of the difficult people types described in this paragraph are described in detail, along with suggestions for coping with each, in Robert M. Bramson, *Coping with Difficult People* (New York: Dell, 1988).

34 Roy J. Eidelson and Judy I. Eidelson, "Dangerous Ideas: Five Beliefs that Propel Groups Toward Conflict," *American Psychologist* 58 (March 2003): 182–192.

35 Proverbs 15:1.

36 The lack of commitment is seen often in couples who are contemplating marriage but are afraid to commit. This is reflected in the humorous title of a book by James D. Barrom, *She Wants a Ring—And I Don't Wanna Change a Thing: How a Man Can Overcome His Fears of Commitment and Marriage* (New York: Perennial Currents/HarperCollins, 2001).

37 C. M. Stocker and L. Youngblade, "Marital Conflict and Parental Hostility: Links with Children's Sibling and Peer Relationships," *Journal of Family Psychology* 13 (1999): 598–609; and Mari L. Clements, "For the Sake of the Children: Effects of Marital Conflict in Intact Families," *Journal of Psychology and Christianity* 23 (Winter 2004): 58–62.

38 Tim Ursiny, *The Coward's Guide to Conflict: Empowering Solutions for Those Who Would Rather Run Than Fight* (Naperville, IL: Sourcebooks, 2003), xvii.

39 1 Corinthians 13:13; 1 John 4:8; John 13:35.

40 Ephesians 6:18.

41 Ephesians 6:19.

42 Ursiny, *Coward's Guide*, 25–34.

43 I have summarized these stages, drawing from Donald C. Palmer, *Managing Conflict Creatively: A Guide for Missionaries and Christian Workers* (Pasadena, CA: William Carey Library, 1990). The stages were proposed by Christian management consultant Norman Shawchuck.

44 Jesus addressed this issue in Matthew 7:3–5.

45 John Ortberg writes about the importance of truth-tellers in our lives who can point out things we often miss seeing in ourselves. See John Ortberg, "The Gift Nobody Wants: Confrontation," *Rev!* 6 (May-June 2003): 44–53.

46 Ephesians 2:14–16; 4:29; 5:1.

47 For a good discussion of position bargaining and its alternatives, see Roger Fisher, William Ury, and Bruce Patton, *Getting to Yes: Negotiating Agreement Without Giving In*, 2nd ed. (New York: Penguin, 1991); and William Ury, *Getting Past No: Negotiating Your Way from Confrontation to Cooperation* (New York: Bantam, 1993).

48 Matthew 15:18–20.

49 This section is built on an older but still relevant article by Laurence Eck, "Blessed Are the Peacemakers: Resolving Business Conflicts, Part 2," *Bookstore Journal* (March 1987): 49–51.

50 Table 18–2 was built from a mimeographed sheet of notes that I found in one of my files. I want to express my gratitude to the anonymous person who did the groundwork for this table and to Scott Thelander who refined and expanded it.

51 For guidelines to mediation and for access to professional Christian mediators, contact *www.peacemaker.net*.

52 Fisher et al., *Getting to Yes*.

53 Books on mediation and negotiation appear with some frequency and can be accessed by an Internet search. Examples include Ken Sande, *Peacemaking for Families* (Wheaton, IL: Tyndale, 2003); Bernard Mayer, *Beyond Neutrality: Confronting the Crisis in Conflict Resolution* (San Francisco, CA: Jossey-Bass, 2004); and Christopher W. Moore, *The Mediation Process: Practical Strategies for Resolving Conflict* (San Francisco, CA: Jossey-Bass, 2003).

54 1 John 4:16–19; John 13:35.

55 2 Corinthians 13:11; Philippians 4:5–6.

56 Romans 12:18.

19. Sex Apart from Marriage

1 Stephen Arterburn, *Every Man's Battle: Winning the War on Sexual Temptation One Victory at a Time* (Colorado Springs, CO: WaterBrook, 2000).

2 Stephen Arterburn and Shannon Ethridge, *Every Woman's Battle: Discovering God's Plan for Sexual and Emotional Fulfillment* (Colorado Springs, CO: WaterBrook, 2003).

3 Tim Stafford, "Great Sex: Reclaiming a Christian Sexual Ethic," *Christianity Today* 31 (October 2, 1987): 25.

4 Walter O. Bockting and Eli Coleman, *Masturbation as a Means of Achieving Sexual Health* (New York: Haworth Press, 2003).

5 U.S. Attorney General, *Final Report of the Attorney General's Commission on Pornography* (New York: Rutledge-Hill Press, 1986). One research report has shown that television ratings of violence and sex tend to entice boys between the ages of eight and eleven to watch the programs that are warned against. See Brad J. Bushman and Joanne Cantor, "Media Ratings for Violence and Sex: Implications for Policymakers and Parents," *American Psychologist* 58 (February 2003): 130–141.

6 Lewis B. Smedes, *Sex for Christians* (Grand Rapids, MI: William B. Eerdmans, 1976), 20.

7 See 1 Corinthians 7.

8 Romans 13:14; 1 Corinthians 7:9.

9 See, for example, Exodus 20:14, 17; Matthew 5:32.

10 Exodus 22:16–19; Leviticus 18; Matthew 5:27; 1 Corinthians 6:9; Hebrews 13:4.

11 Hebrews 11:25.

12 Acts 15:20, 29; 21:25; 1 Corinthians 5:1; 6:13, 18; 2 Corinthians 12:21; Ephesians 5:3.

13 Matthew 5:32; 19:9.

14 1 Corinthians 7:2; 1 Thessalonians 4:3.

15 1 Corinthians 6:16–20.

16 Isaiah 57:3; Jeremiah 3:8–9; Ezekiel 23:43; James 4:4; Revelation 2:20, 23.

17 Exodus 20:14; Leviticus 18:20; Deuteronomy 5:18; 22:22–34; Matthew 5:27–30; John 8:4.

18 1 Corinthians 6:9–10; Galatians 5:19–20; Colossians 3:5.

19 Genesis 1:27–28, 31.

20 Genesis 2:25; 3:9–11.

21 1 Corinthians 6:13, 18.

22 Proverbs 5:1–8; 1 Corinthians 6:9–10; 1 Thessalonians 4:3; Ephesians 5:3–7; Colossians 3:5–6.

23 1 Corinthians 7:9.

24 Rodney L. Bassett, Glenn Mowat, Tara Ferriter, Matthew Perry, Eric Hutchison, John Campbell, and Peter Santiago, "Why Do Christian College Students Abstain from Premarital Sexual Intercourse?" *Journal of Psychology and Christianity* 21 (Summer 2002): 121–132. See also Waylon O. Ward, *Sex Matters: Men Winning the Battle* (McKinney, TX: Allison O'Neil, 2004).

25 Stafford has a good discussion of this issue; see "Great Sex," 33–34. See also Frederica Mattewes-Green, "What to Say at a Naked Party," *Christianity Today* 49 (February 2005): 48–49.

26 Matthew 5:28.

27 According to Stafford, "Great Sex," 43, Luke 22:15 should be translated, literally, "I have lusted [have a strong desire] to eat the Passover with you."

28 Ibid.

29 Ephesians 5:3–4.

30 Luke 2:52; Acts 16:2; 1 Timothy 3:7; 1 Thessalonians 5:22.

31 1 Corinthians 6:12.

32 This appears to be the message of 1 Corinthians 6–7.

33 This distinction was made by Smedes, *Sex for Christians*, 190–200; some of the discussion that follows is drawn from Smedes' analysis.

34 Christopher and Rachel McCluskey, *When Two Become One: Enhancing Sexual Intimacy in Marriage* (Grand Rapids, MI: Revell, 2004), 27.

35 Ibid.

36 Vigen Guroian, "Dorm Brothel: The New Debauchery, and the Colleges That Let It Happen," *Christianity Today* 49 (February 2005): 45–51.

37 Gary H. Strauss and Mark A. Yarhouse, "Human Sexuality in a Sexually Polymorphous World," *Journal of Psychology and Theology* 30 (Spring 2002): 99–100. See also S. A. Rathis, J. S. Nevid, and L. Fichner-Rathus, *Human Sexuality in a World of Diversity* (Boston, MA: Allyn and Bacon, 2002).

38 Matthew 15:18–19.

39 Lonnie Barbach, "Sexual Fantasies," *Bottom Line Personal* 8 (January 15, 1987): 13–14. This is an old report, but as sexuality has become more prevalent in the media, we might assume that these 1987 figures would be at least as accurate in the twenty-first century.

40 Ephesians 6:10–12.

41 2 Corinthians 11:14–15; 1 Peter 5:8.

42 John 12:35–40; 1 Corinthians 2:14.

43 Romans 1:24–28, 32.

44 Stafford, "Great Sex," 27.

45 For guidance see Joyce J. Penner and Clifford L. Penner, *Counseling for Sexual Disorders* (Dallas TX: Word, 1990). The Penners write from a Protestant evangelical perspective. Also helpful is a book by former priest Eugene Kennedy, *Sexual Counseling* (New York: Continuum, 1987).

46 For an excellent discussion of sexuality and sexual misconduct in the counselor and pastor, see Peter Mosgofian and George Ohlschlager, *Sexual Misconduct in Counseling and Ministry: Intervention, Healing, and Self-Protection* (Dallas, TX: Word, 1995). For a secular perspective, see Kenneth S. Pope, Janet L. Sonne, and Jean Holroyd, *Sexual Feelings in Psychotherapy: Explorations for Therapists and Therapists-in-Training* (Washington, DC: American Psychological Association, 1993).

47 Kennedy, *Sexual Counseling*.

48 John 10:10; 3:16.

49 Matthew 6:12–15; Mark 11:25.

50 John 8:11.

51 Among helpful books, see Gale Wheat and Ed Wheat, *Intended for Pleasure: Sex Technique and Sex Fulfillment in Christian Marriage*, 3rd ed. (Grand Rapids, MI: Revell, 1997); McCluskey and McCluskey, *When Two Become One*; Judith K. Balswick and Jack O. Balswick, *Authentic Human Sexuality: An Integrated Approach* (Downers Grove, IL: InterVarsity Press, 2000); and Douglas E. Rosenau, *A Celebration of Sex: A Guide to Enjoying God's Gift of Sexual Intimacy*, rev. ed. (Nashville, TN: Nelson, 2002).

52 For a discussion of spirituality and sexuality, see Chuck M. MacKnee, "Profound Sexual and Spiritual Encounters Among Practicing Christians: A Phenomenological Analysis," *Journal of Psychology and Theology* 30 (Fall 2002): 234–244.

53 One excellent guide is by Stanton L. Jones and Brenda B. Jones, *How and When to Tell Your Kids About Sex: A Lifelong Approach to Shaping Your Child's Sexual Character* (Colorado Springs, CO: NavPress, 1993).

54 This view was argued persuasively by Smedes, *Sex for Christians*, 152–160.

55 These are adapted from an unpublished paper written by several of my former students: Joan Barlett, Marty Hansen, Isolde Anderson, and Jay Terbush. For practical and helpful information on dating, all written from a Christian perspective, see Henry Cloud and John Townsend, *Boundaries in Dating* (Grand Rapids, MI: Zondervan, 2000); Joshua Harris, *I Kissed Dating Goodbye*, updated ed. (Sisters, OR: Multnomah, 2003); and Joshua Harris, *Boy Meets Girl: Say Hello to Courtship* (Sisters, OR: Multnomah, 2000).

56 1 Corinthians 10:13b.

57 Proverbs 5:1–20; Ephesians 4:19–20; Colossians 3:5; 1 Corinthians 6:9–11.

58 1 John 1:9; 1 Corinthians 6:11; for a more detailed discussion of self-control, see Arterburn, *Every Man's Battle;* Arterburn and Ethridge, *Every Woman's Battle; and* Arterburn, Stokey, and Yorkey, *Every Young Man's Battle: Strategies for Victory in the Real World of Sexual Temptation* (New York: Random House, 2002).

59 I have not been able to find any recent studies on this, but in a 1987 survey, 35 percent of *Christianity Today* readers (and 47 percent of pastors) reported that they masturbated at least once a month or more often. The most common estimates are that 90 percent of males masturbate at least on occasion.

60 Some have argued that the sin of Onan, described in Genesis 38, is a form of masturbation because he "spilled his semen on the ground." Even a casual reading of the text indicates, however, that Onan's sin involved disobedience to God by refusing to impregnate the wife of his deceased brother, as was required by the Old Testament law.

61 Philippians 4:8; 1 Corinthians 10:31.

62 I Corinthians 6:12.

63 For a discussion of masturbation published in a magazine for young Christians, see Dave Roberts, "U Can't Touch That: What Does the Bible Really Say About Masturbation?" *Relevant* 7 (March-April 2004): 52–53. See also R. E. Butman, "Masturbation," in *Encyclopedia of Psychology and Counseling*, ed. David G. Benner and Peter C. Hill (Grand Rapids, MI: Baker, 1999), 726–727; and Gary H. Strauss, "Promoting 20/20 Vision: A Q & A Ministry to Undergraduates," *Journal of Psychology and Theology* 30 (Fall 2002): 228–233. In this article, Strauss includes his answer to the college students struggling with masturbation and another question from a married male who wants to know if masturbation is acceptable when his wife is gone. Strauss gives some helpful and insightful guidelines but does not specifically answer the questions that the writers raise.

64 Stafford, "Great Sex," 43–44.
65 Matthew 5:27–28.
66 Strauss, "Promoting 20/20 Vision," 232.
67 I have given more detail in this section of the book than I have given elsewhere. I am aware that many of my readers are students, reading this book as part of a course on counseling. My guess is that many struggle with masturbation and find this topic more personal than most of the other sections of this book. Most of those students will not find their way to the footnotes, but for you who do, know that I have tried to give practical guidelines that can be of help to you as well as to your classmates and to the people that you might counsel.

20. Sex Within Marriage

1 This question will be discussed further later in the chapter.
2 S. L. Jones, "Sexuality," in *Baker Encyclopedia of Psychology and Counseling,* ed. David G. Benner and Peter C. Hill, 2nd ed. (Grand Rapids, MI: Baker, 1999), 1107–1113.
3 Genesis 1:27–28; 2:24–25.
4 Genesis 4:1.
5 Jones discusses this issue, pointing out that the belief that sexual intercourse immediately unites a couple into one flesh (1 Corinthians 6:16) raises questions about the marital status of a person who has had sex with more than one person. Jones writes that "theologians generally conclude that becoming one flesh denotes a process of growth between married persons in which sexual intercourse is a necessary but not sufficient precondition." See Jones, "Sexuality," 1109.
6 See, e.g., Song of Solomon 7:1–10.
7 Proverbs 5:18–19.
8 1 Corinthians 7:2–5.
9 Matthew 19:4–6; 1 Corinthians 7:1–9; 1 Thessalonians 4:1–8.
10 1 Thessalonians 4:1–8; 2 Timothy 2:22.
11 Proverbs 5:1–11, 20, 23; 6:23–33; 7:5–27.
12 Quoted in Eugene Kennedy, *Sexual Counseling* (New York: Continuum, 1987).
13 *Kinsey* is an R-rated movie that appeared in 2004. One review commented that as well as his methods, Kinsey's morals and personality also were "flawed."
14 Louis McBurney, "The Appeal of Porn; Why Men Get Hooked," *Marriage Partnership* 19 (Fall 2002): 54.
15 Marnie C. Ferree, "Female Sexual Addiction: A Hidden Disease," *Christian Counseling Today* 9, no. 4 (2001): 30–33.
16 I once wrote a book about this. Gary R. Collins, *Breathless: Transform Your Time-Starved Days into a Life Well Lived* (Wheaton, IL: Tyndale, 1998). The book is no longer in print.
17 C. B. Dhabuwala, A. Kumar, and J. M. Pierce, "Myocardial Infarction and Its Influence on Male Sexual Function," *Archives of Sexual Behavior* 15 (1986): 499–504.
18 1 John 4:18.
19 For information about the availability of competent sex therapists, and about specialized training in this area, please go to *www.sexualwholeness.com.* This site is developed and maintained by Christians and gives information about the Institute for Sexual Wholeness, the American Board of Christian Sex Therapists (ABCST), and the Christian Association for Sex Educators (CASE). At the time of this writing there are very few Christians who are professionally trained and certified as sex therapists apart from those trained by the Institute for Sexual Wholeness, working in partnership with Psychological Studies Institute in Atlanta.
20 Kevin Leman discusses this in a thought-provoking and humorous chapter that describes the names we give to penises. These words are likely to be different, depending on one's culture and generation. Especially awkward for the counselor might be the experience of having a counselee describe a sexual action or body part, and you do not know what the counselee's term means. There is one way to deal with this: admit that you are not familiar with the term and ask the counselee to try again with other words. See Kevin Leman, *Sex Begins in the Kitchen: Because Love Is an All-Day Affair,* 2nd ed. (Grand Rapids, MI: Revell, 1999).

21 This part of the counseling process should not be confused with the life coaching that was discussed in chapter 4 of this book. Life coaching does not involve training in counseling or psychotherapy and is different from the coaching mentioned here.

22 The DEC-R model is discussed in a chapter by Douglas E. Rosenau, Michael Sytsma, and Debra L. Taylor, "Sexuality and Sexual Therapy: Learning and Practicing the DEC-R Model," in *Competent Christian Counseling*, ed. Timothy Clinton and George Ohlschlager (Colorado Springs, CO: WaterBrook, 2002), 490–515.

23 For example, see Joyce J. Penner and Clifford L. Penner, *Counseling for Sexual Disorders* (Dallas, TX: Word, 1990), and Douglas Rosenau, *The Celebration of Sex*, rev. ed. (Nashville, TN: Nelson, 2002). See also C. McCluskey, *Coaching Couples into Passionate Intimacy* [Videotape] (Edgar Springs, MO: Coaching for Christian Living, 2001). Information also is available on the Internet. For example, I typed in "squeeze technique" and found a concise, factual, and inoffensive description of the procedure.

24 There are many of these resources, some better than others, and new books, tapes, and videos are appearing all the time. Among the better, and more recent, see Christopher and Rachel McCluskey, *When Two Become One*; Louis McBurney and Melissa McBurney, *Real Questions, Real Answers About Sex: The Complete Guide to Intimacy as God Intended* (Grand Rapids, MI: Zondervan, 2005); and Lisa Graham McMinn, *Sexuality and Holy Longing: Embracing Sexual Intimacy in a Broken World* (New York: Wiley, 2004). See also books on sexuality by Archibald D. Hart and by Stephen Arterburn. The McCluskey book has an excellent discussion of the "love-making cycle" that can be helpful information to any married couple.

25 Some of these issues are discussed by Penner and Penner, *Counseling for Sexual Disorders*; Rosenau, *Celebration of Sex*; Diane Mandt Langberg, *Counseling Survivors of Sexual Abuse* (Wheaton, IL: Tyndale, 1997); Debra I. Taylor, "Enhancing Sexual Desire in Women: Why One in Three Married Women Express Difficulty in Feeling Sexual Desire," *Christian Counseling Today* 9, no. 4 (2001): 12–15; Joyce Penner, "Treatment of Sexual Dysfunction in Women," *Christian Counseling Today* 9, no. 4 (2001): 22–20; Diane M. Langberg, "Post-Trauma Sexuality" *Christian Counseling Today* 9, no. 4 (2001): 30–33.

26 Please see footnote 20; also *www.sexualwholeness.com* can give some guidelines for finding qualified sex therapists or getting specialized training for yourself.

27 The forgiveness session was described in an article published in the Winter 2001 issue of the *Journal of Family Psychotherapy*, summarized and reported by Garry Cooper, "Forgiving Extramarital Affairs," *Psychotherapy Networker* 26 (May-June 2002): 15–16. See also the excellent practical article by Mark and Deb Laaser, "Recovering from Infidelity," *Christian Counseling Today* 12, no. 1 (2004): 47–51.

28 There is research evidence pointing to the value of marriage education for teenagers. See Benjamin Silliman, "Building Healthy Marriages Through Early and Extended Outreach with Youth," *Journal of Psychology and Theology* 31 (Fall 2003): 270–282.

29 Writing in *Marriage Partnership* magazine, Louis and Melissa McBurney reported that the editors receive "many, many questions from Christian couples, who want to know what is and is not okay to do sexually." Their article discusses oral-genital sex, use of vibrators, changing sexual positions, and other practices. Bottom line, the writers suggest that most things are acceptable if they do not violate scriptural principles and if both husband and wife are comfortable in using them. See Louis and Melissa McBurney, "Christian Sex Rules: A Guide to What's Allowed in the Bedroom," *Marriage Partnership* 18 (Spring 2001): 34.

30 Premarital issues are discussed in chapter 28.

31 For an evaluation of two marital enrichment programs and references to other evaluation efforts, see Glenice A. Burchard, Mark A. Yarhouse, Everett L. Worthington, Jr., Jack W. Berry, Marcus K. Kilian, and David E. Canter, "A Study of Two Marital Enrichment Programs and Couples' Quality of Life," *Journal of Psychology and Theology* 31 (Fall 2003): 240–252.

32 James R. David and Francis C. Duda, "Christian Perspectives on Treatment of Sexual Dysfunction," *Journal of Psychology and Theology* 5 (Fall 1977): 332–336.

21. Homosexuality

1 Mark A. Yarhouse, "Same-Sex Attraction, Homosexual Orientation, and Gay Identity: A Three-Tier Distinction for Counseling and Pastoral Care," *Journal of Pastoral Care and Counseling* 59 (2005): 201–212.

2   Sometimes, counselors also refer to *latent* homosexuals. These people are sexually attracted to same-sex individuals, but latent homosexuals are unable to admit to themselves that their basic orientation is toward people of the same gender.

3   This is the term used in a book by Tim LaHaye, *The Unhappy Gays* (Wheaton, IL: Tyndale, 1978).

4   Early editions of the *Diagnostic and Statistical Manual* of the American Psychiatric Association included homosexuality as a diagnosable disorder.

5   John Court, "Homosexuality," in *The Complete Book of Everyday Christianity*, ed. Robert Banks and R. Paul Stevens (Downers Grove, IL: InterVarsity, 1997), 501–505.

6   In a debate on homosexuality, Episcopal bishop John Spong stated that "scientific data" seemed to put the "figure of gay and lesbian people *in the world* at about 10% of the population" (italics added). From a debate between the Rev. John Spong and the Rt. Rev. John Howe at Virginia Protestant Episcopal Seminary, February 1992 (audiotape available from Truro Tape Ministries, 10520 Main Street, Fairfax, VA 22030).

7   Kris S. Morgan and Rebecca M. Nerison, "Homosexuality and Psychopolitics: An Historical Overview," *Psychotherapy* 30 (1993): 133.

8   Alfred C. Kinsey, Wardell B. Pomeroy, and Clyde E. Martin, *Sexual Behavior in the Human Male* (Philadelphia: Saunders, 1948), 650–651.

9   Patricia Painton, "The Shrinking Ten Percent," *Time* (April 26, 1993): 27. Some of the differing figures about the incidence of homosexuality come because researchers disagree about how to define and measure homosexuality. One highly regarded study reported that 2 percent of men and 0.9 percent of women in the U.S. population identified themselves as homosexual, and an additional 0.8 percent of men and 0.5 percent of women identified themselves as bisexual. See Edward O. Laumann et al., *The Social Organization of Sexuality* (Chicago, IL: University of Chicago Press, 1994), chapter 8.

10   David G. Myers, "A Levels-of-Explanation View," in *Psychology and Christianity: Four Views*, ed. Eric L. Johnson and Stanton L. Jones (Downers Grove, IL: InterVarsity, 2000), 77.

11   The group, Evangelicals Concerned, has a web site at *www.ecinc.org*.

12   Chad W. Thompson, *Loving Homosexuals as Jesus Would: A Fresh Christian Approach* (Grand Rapids, MI: Brazos Press, 2004).

13   Richard J. Foster, *Money, Sex and Power: The Challenge of the Disciplined Life* (New York: Harper & Row, 1985), 107.

14   The list of books continues to grow. For a listing of Christian books please go to *www.Christianbooks.com* and type in "homosexuality" as a search word.

15   I do not deny that I am in this group. We all are.

16   It is of interest that many of the same biblical passages that are used to condemn homosexuality are dismissed as "clobber passages" by a web site for evangelical homosexuals who take the same passages and give them a completely different interpretation. See *www.ecinc.org*.

17   Genesis 19:1–11; Leviticus 18:22; 20:13; Judges 19:22–25; Romans 1:25–27; 1 Corinthians 6:9; 1 Timothy 1:10. Five other passages refer to homosexuality in the context of male prostitution: Deuteronomy 23:17; 1 Kings 14:24; 15:12; 22:46; 2 Kings 23:7.

18   Hebrews 4:15.

19   1 Corinthians 10:13.

20   In a personal note (October 27, 2005), Mark A. Yarhouse notes that the methodology of this research "is not always exemplary," and "the bias of the researchers can increase the likelihood of biased results."

21   C. Rosenak and H. Looy, "Homosexuality," in *Encyclopedia of Psychology and Counseling*, ed. David G. Benner and Peter C. Hill (Grand Rapids, MI: Baker, 1999). The article is on pages 571–578. The quotation is on page 572.

22   The research summarized in this paragraph is adapted from pages 60–82 in Stanton L. Jones and Mark A. Yarhouse, *Homosexuality: The Use of Scientific Research in the Church's Moral Debate* (Downers Grove, IL: InterVarsity, 2000). In concluding their discussion of biological theories and research, Jones and Yarhouse conclude that "some of the studies cited to support these theories have not been replicated, have been of small sample sizes or have serious methodological flaws. The best recent study . . . suggests that genetics may not be a significant causal factor."

23   For a classic study of the psychoanalytic view of homosexuality, see I. Bieber and Associates, *Homosexuality* (New York: Basic Books, 1962).

24   Rosenak and Looy, "Homosexuality," 574.

25   Ray A. Seutter and Martin Rovers, "Emotionally Absent Fathers: Furthering the Understanding of Homosexuality," *Journal of Psychology and Theology* 32 (Spring 2004): 43–49.

26   Elizabeth R. Moberly, *Homosexuality: A New Christian Ethic* (Cambridge, UK: James Clarke, 1983), 5–6. It is neither fair nor possible to summarize Moberly's insightful theory in a few sentences. Shortly after the appearance of Moberly's book, her theory received some support in a book by Richard Green, *"The Sissy Boy Syndrome" and the Development of Homosexuality* (New Haven, CT: Yale University Press, 1987). Green found that fathers of feminine boys recalled spending less time with their sons during the early years as compared to fathers of masculine boys. It is interesting to note that the mothers of feminine boys also recalled spending less time with their sons as compared to the mothers of masculine boys. This view seems to rest on the invalid assumption that homosexuality and feminine characteristics in males go together.

27   Moberly, *Homosexuality*, 10. See also Elizabeth R. Moberly, "Attachment and Separation: The Implications for Gender Identity and for the Structuralization of the Self: A Theoretical Model for Transsexualism, and Homosexuality," *Psychiatric Journal of the University of Ottawa* 11 (December 1986): 205–209.

28   James M. Cantor, Ray Blanchard, Andrew D. Peterson, and Anthony F. Bogaert, "How Many Gay Men Owe Their Sexual Orientation to Fraternal Birth Order?" *Archives of Sexual Behavior* 31 (February 2002): 63–71. This research found that one gay man in seven (about 14 percent of gay men) appears to owe his sexual orientation to fraternal birth order.

29   Laumann et al., *Social Organization of Sexuality*.

30   Many writers would agree. "At present, researchers have not found any environmental [or biological] factors that consistently predict and possibly cause homosexuality," wrote Rosenak and Looy, "Homosexuality," 574. Jones and Yarhouse agree, *Homosexuality*, 91.

31   Theologian and Bible scholar John R. W. Stott wrote about this long before the gay marriage debates that came with the start of the twenty-first century. See John R. W. Stott, "Homosexual Marriages: Why Same-Sex Partnerships Are Not a Christian Option," *Christianity Today* 29 (November 22, 1985): 21–28. See also Robert Benne and Gerald McDermott, "Thirteen Bad Arguments for Same-Sex Marriage: Why the Rhetoric Doesn't Stand Up Under Scrutiny," *Christianity Today* online (August 26, 2004). For arguments against gay marriage, see Erwin J. Lutzer, *The Truth About Same-Sex Marriage: Six Things You Need to Know About What's Really at Stake* (Chicago, IL: Moody 2004); and Glen T. Stanton and Bill Maier, *Marriage on Trial: The Case Against Same-Sex Marriage and Parenting* (Downers Grove, IL: InterVarsity, 2004). For arguments in favor of gay marriage, see David G. Myers and Letha Dawson Scanzoni, *What God Hath Joined Together?: A Christian Case for Gay Marriage* (San Francisco, CA: HarperSanFrancisco, 2005).

32   Tim LaHaye discusses this in *The Unhappy Gays*. The book has some good conclusions, but these are overshadowed by the author's heavy-handed and insensitive treatment of homosexuals, most of whom need compassion and encouragement rather than criticism. For more scientific support for the unhappiness in homosexuals, see footnote 34.

33   For an in-depth consideration of the influence of same-sex attraction on identity, see Mark A. Yarhouse, "Sexual Identity Development: The Influence of Valuative Frameworks on Identity Synthesis," *Psychotherapy* 38 (2001): 331–341.

34   S. D. Cochran, J. G. Sullivan, V. M. Mays, "Prevalence of Mental Disorders, Psychological Distress, and Mental Services Use Among Lesbian, Gay, and Bisexual Adults in the United States," *Journal of Consulting and Clinical Psychology* 71 (February 2003): 53–61; D. Fergusson, J. Horwood, and A. L. Beautrais, "Is Sexual Orientation Related to Mental Health Problems and Suicidality in Young People?" *Archives of General Psychiatry* 56 (1999): 876-880; S. Gilman, S. D. Cochran, and V. Hughes, "Risk of Psychiatric Disorders Among Individuals Reporting Same-Sex Sexual Partners in the National Comorbidity Survey," *American Journal of Public Health* 6 (2001): 933–939; R. Herrell, J. Goldberg, W. True, V. Ramakrishnan, M. Lyons, S. Eisen, and M. Tsuang, "Sexual Orientation and Suicidality: A Co-twin Control Study in Adult Men," *Archives of General Psychiatry* 56 (1999): 867–874.

35   Susan D. Cochran, "Emerging Issues in Research on Lesbians' and Gay Men's Mental Health: Does Sexual Orientation Really Matter?" *American Psychologist* 11 (2001): 931–941. The quotation is on page 934. This conclusion is at odds with the conclusions of other writers, many of whom based their conclusions on less research than was reviewed by Cochran.

36 Cochran et al., "Prevalence"; Gilman et al., "Risk"; and J. Bradford, C. Ryan, and E. Rothblum, "National Lesbian Care Survey: Implications for Mental Health Care," *Journal of Consulting and Clinical Psychology* 62 (1994): 228–242. See also Tonda L. Hughes, Carrol Smith, and Alice J. Dan, eds., *Mental Health Issues for Sexual Minority Women: Redefining Women's Mental Health* (Binghamton, NY: Haworth Press, 2003).

37 Jon Ebert, "Questioning Psychological Distress in Religiously Mediated Change," PsyD doctoral dissertation, Wheaton (Illinois) College, 2003, p. 22.

38 David Cramer, "Gay Parents and Their Children: A Review of Research and Practical Implications," *Journal of Counseling and Development* 64 (April 1986): 504–507. Cramer describes a study of more that five thousand gay men and women; 28 percent of the women and 13 percent of the men were parents. I have not been able to find any research that is more recent to either refute or confirm these findings. A brief review of the many books on gay parenting and of some of the more recent research articles indicates that the authors write to argue for their viewpoints, making it difficult to find more balanced data. One more recent study concluded that "despite prejudice and discrimination, lesbians and gay men have often succeeded in creating and sustaining family relationships._._._.In general, the picture of lesbian and gay relationships emerging from this body of work is one of positive adjustment, even in the face of stressful conditions." Charlotte J. Patterson, "Family Relationships of Lesbians and Gay Men," *Journal of Marriage and the Family* 62 (November 2000): 1052–1069.

39 Numerous books have appeared to address these issues. From a conservative, evangelical perspective, see Joe Dallas, *When Homosexuality Hits Home: What to Do When a Loved One Says They're Gay* (Eugene, OR: Harvest House, 2004). For a secular, psychologically informed viewpoint, see Ritch C. Savin-Williams, *Mom, Dad, I'm Gay: How Families Negotiate Coming Out* (Washington, DC: American Psychological Association, 2001).

40 Research supporting these conclusions is summarized by Julie A. Murphy, Edna I. Rawlings, and Steven R. Howe, "A Survey of Clinical Psychologists on Treating Lesbian, Gay, and Bisexual Clients," *Professional Psychology: Research and Practice* 33 (April 2002): 183–189.

41 For example, in a recent article on treating people who are distressed by their sexual orientation, the authors note that only "a very small minority of the professional community still contends that same-sex sexual orientation is either immoral and/or an illness and that treatment should be made available for those who seek it." Later, in what appears to be a somewhat acknowledgment, the authors note that "until the scientific debate is settled, we must accept that in some isolated and rare circumstances, conversion therapy might be effective." Jon S. Lasser and Michael C. Gottlieb, "Treating Patients Distressed Regarding Their Sexual Orientation: Clinical and Ethical Alternatives," *Professional Psychology: Research and Practice* 35 (April 2004): 194–200.

42 Jones and Yarhouse, *Homosexuality*, 148. This quotation appears at the end of a chapter that examines research dealing with the question "Can Homosexuality Be Changed?" These two authors have done intensive research in this area and will report their findings in a book that is yet to be completed and titled.

43 Jones and Yarhouse, *Homosexuality*, 148. For an excellent discussion of the topic of counseling and change, written from both a professional psychological and Christian perspective, see Earl D. Wilson, *Counseling and Homosexuality* (Dallas: Word, 1988).

44 One research team studied 140 individuals attempting to change their homosexual orientation due to their religious beliefs. Survey results indicated that from a group of 248 people, 60.8 percent of the males and 71.1 percent of females abstained from any type of physical homosexual contact for more than a year. Of those who were not successful, the majority (88.2 percent) indicated that they still were attempting to change and believed that it was possible to change their sexual orientation. Kim W. Schaeffer, Lynde Nottebaum, Patty Smith, Kara Dech, and Jill Krawczyk, "Religiously-Motivated Sexual Orientation Change: A Follow-up Study," *Journal of Psychology and Theology* 21 (Winter 1999): 329–337.

45 Ariel Shidlo and Michael Schroeder, "Changing Sexual Orientation: A Consumers' Report," *Professional Psychology: Research and Practice* 33 (June 2002): 249–259. These authors interviewed 202 people who had sought change. The majority failed to change their sexual orientation, although most felt counseling had helped in other ways. See also Douglas C. Haldeman, "Gay Rights, Patient Rights: The Implications of Sexual Orientation Conversion Therapy," *Professional Psychology: Theory and Practice* 33 (June 2002):

260–264. For a good critique of Haldeman's arguments against change, see Jones and Yarhouse, *Homosexuality*, 140–145.

46   Warren Throckmorton, "Initial Empirical and Clinical Findings Concerning the Change Process for Ex-Gays," *Professional Psychology: Research and Practice* 33 (June 2002): 242–248.

47   David G. Myers and Malcolm A. Jeeves, *Psychology Through the Eyes of Faith* (New York: Harper & Row, 1987), 111–113.

48   I am grateful to Marty Hansen for allowing me to quote from his chapel address at Trinity Evangelical Divinity School, February 2, 1978. The talk was a long time ago, and I have since lost contact with this former student, but his conclusions still are valid.

49   Moberly, *Homosexuality*. This approach also seems to underlie much of the work of Wilson, *Counseling and Homosexuality*, who clearly has been influenced by Moberly's work.

50   1 John 1:9.

51   The following list is adapted from Wilson, *Counseling and Homosexuality*, 104–112.

52   In writing this paragraph, I looked at some of the recent reports on the psychoanalytic treatment of homosexuals. One article was especially interesting because of its conclusions that surely apply worldwide. Olli Stråström and Jussi Nissinen, "Homosexuality in Finland: The Decline of Psychoanalysis' Illness Model of Homosexuality," *Journal of Gay and Lesbian Psychotherapy* 7 (2003): 75–91. For a readable overview of psychoanalytic treatment methods, see Lack Drescher and Ann D'Ercole, eds., *Psychotherapy with Gay Men and Lesbians: Contemporary Dynamic Approaches* (New York: Haworth, 2003).

53   Joseph Nicolosi, *Reparative Therapy of Male Homosexuality: A New Clinical Approach* (Northvale, NJ: Jason Aronson, 1991).

54   Robert L. Spitzer, "Can Some Gay Men and Lesbians Change Their Sexual Orientation? 200 Participants Reporting a Change from Homosexual to Heterosexual Orientation," *Archives of Sexual Behavior* 32 (October 2003): 403–417.

55   For the counselor who has a serious interest in these therapies, see Christopher R. Martell, Steven A. Safren, and Stacey E. Prince, *Cognitive-Behavioral Therapies with Lesbian, Gay, and Bisexual Clients* (New York: Guilford, 2002).

56   Mark A. Yarhouse, Lori A. Burkett, and Elizabeth M. Kreeft, "Competing Models for Shepherding Those in the Church Who Contend with Same-Sex Attraction," *Journal of Psychology and Christianity* 20 (Spring 2001): 53–65.

57   From an earlier paper, quoted in Jones and Yarhouse, *Homosexuality*, 149–150.

22. Abuse and Neglect

1   This description is adapted from Janice's own published account of her attack, recovery, and therapeutic conclusions. Janice Starkman Goldfein, "Reclaiming the Self: One Woman's Refusal to Allow a Nightmare to Define her Life," *Psychotherapy Networker* 28 (January-February 2004): 46–55.

2   Before starting this chapter, I began searching the professional research literature on abuse and violence. I knew this problem was widespread, but I was amazed by the number and diversity of published studies and by the global nature of the abuse problems.

3   From the web site of the National Clearinghouse on Child Abuse and Neglect, *http://nccanch.acf.hhs.gov*, an agency of the U.S. Department of Health and Human Services, Administration for Children and Families.

4   For more information please go to an Internet search source like Google or Yahoo and type in "spiritual abuse." My search uncovered over two million hits.

5   There are exceptions, depending on the local laws. In many countries the spanking of children is not considered abuse. Incarceration in jails, the "toughening" of military recruits, the rigorous demands of athletic coaches, or medical and dental procedures that inflict pain but are intended to bring healing usually are not considered abusive. The mistreatment of prisoners, however, is abuse regardless of the rationale given by the detaining countries to justify their actions.

6   Genesis 6:11–12, for example, describes a time before the Flood when the earth "had become corrupt in God's sight, and it was filled with violence . . . and depravity everywhere."

7   Proverbs 29:15.

8   Proverbs 22:15; 23:13–14; 29:15, 17–18.

9   Hebrews 12:5–6.

10   Genesis 34:31.

11 Matthew 5:21–23.

12 Matthew 7:1–2.

13 Colossians 3:19.

14 Colossians 3:21.

15 Colossians 4:1.

16 Ephesians 4:31.

17 Ephesians 4:32.

18 Ephesians 5:3–4.

19 1 Timothy 5:1–8, 17; James 1:27.

20 Matthew 5:39, 43; 6:14; Philippians 4:6.

21 We tend to think of rape as an act of violence directed against women, but there is increasing evidence that the rape of men is common, especially in all-male environments, such as prisons.

22 Nancy D. Kellogg and Shirley W. Menard, "Violence Among Family Members of Children and Adolescents Evaluated for Sexual Abuse," *Child Abuse and Neglect* 27 (December 2003): 1367–1376.

23 For example, one study found that 76 percent of abusers had been abused as children. See Linda L. Marshall and Patricia Rose, "Family of Origin Violence and Courtship Abuse," *Journal of Counseling and Development* 66 (May 1988): 414–418.

24 S. K, Steinmetz, "Battered Parents," *Society* 15 (1978): 54–55.

25 Cantwell B. Hendrika, "Psychiatric Implications of Child Neglect," *Harvard Medical School Mental Health Letter* 3 (December 1986): 5–6.

26 Sometimes, the perpetrators of abuse will try to blame the victim. A parent, for example, may complain that the abuse came because a child was out of control. More often, however, the abuse comes from family stress or the inabilities of abusers to control themselves. See B. Murray Law, "Family Circumstances, Not Children's Misbehavior, Spur Abuse," *Monitor on Psychology* 35 (December 2004):15; and J. B. Reid, K. Kavanaugh, and D. V. Baldwin, "Abusive Parents' Perceptions of Child Problem Behaviors: An Example of Parental Bias," *Journal of Abnormal Child Psychology* 15 (1987): 457–466.

27 Grant L. Martin, *Counseling for Family Violence and Abuse* (Waco, TX: Word, 1987).

28 Paul Chance, "Attacking Elderly Abuse," *Psychology Today* 21 (September 1987): 24–25.

29 Steven Johnson's, *Everything Bad Is Good for You: How Today's Popular Culture Is Actually Making Us Smarter* (New York: Riverhead, 2005) is a highly controversial book in which the author argued that video games, even those that are violent "function as a kind of safety valve" that "may have a deterrent effect on violence." This has been soundly refuted. See Editorial, "Deadening the Heart: Killer Video Games Are No 'Safety Valve,'" *Christianity Today* 49 (October 2005): 31.

30 Martin, *Counseling for Family Violence*, 38. I am grateful for Martin's influence on this paragraph and the one that follows.

31 Jeremiah 17:9.

32 Mark 7:21–23.

33 Philip Yancey, "Back from the Brothel," *Christianity Today* 49 (January 2005): 80.

34 L. N. Ferguson, "Incest," in *Encyclopedia of Psychology and Counseling*, ed. David G. Benner and Peter C. Hill (Grand Rapids, MI: Baker, 1999), 613–614.

35 Neville King, Bruce J. Tonge, Paul Mullen, Nicole Myerson, David Heyne, Stephanie Rollings, and Thomas H. Ollendick, "Sexually Abused Children and Post-Traumatic Stress Disorders," *Counselling Quarterly* 13 (December 2000): 365–375. See also, Timothy P. Melchert, "Clarifying the Effects of Parental Substance Abuse, Child Sexual Abuse, and Parental Caregiving on Adult Adjustment," *Professional Psychology: Research and Practice* 31 (February 2000): 64–69.

36 A search of the Internet will uncover a number of rape hotlines and crisis prevention centers. Check, as well, to see if there are rape hotlines and other services in your local community. Most of these sources will give statistics about rape that more or less are in agreement.

37 In her excellent book on sexual abuse, Diane Mandt Langberg refers to what she terms the aftereffects of abuse. She identifies three categories, the emotional, physical, and spiritual aftereffects. Diane Mandt Langberg, *Counseling Survivors of Sexual Abuse* (Wheaton, IL: Tyndale, 1997).

38 Josie Spataro, Paul E. Mullen, Philip M. Burgess, David L. Wells, and Simon A. Moss, "Impact of Child Sexual Abuse on Mental Health: Prospective Study in Males and Females," *British Journal of Psychiatry* 184 (May 2004): 416–421.

39 This argument and the research that supports it are summarized by Malcolm Gladwell, "Getting Over It," *Psychotherapy Networker* 29 (March-April 2005): 51–55.

40 Goldfein, "Reclaiming the Self," 52.

41 Kamala London, Maggie Bruck, Stephen J. Ceci, and Daniel W. Shuman, "Disclosure of Child Sexual Abuse: What Does the Research Tell Us About the Ways That Children Tell?" *Psychology, Public Policy, and Law* 11 (March 2005): 194–226.

42 Megan Young, John Read, Suzanne Barker-Collo, and Rachael Harrison, "Evaluating and Overcoming Barriers to Taking Abuse Histories," *Professional Psychology: Research and Practice* 32 (August 2002): 407–414.

43 Langberg, *Counseling Survivors*. Langberg's book is detailed and practical and consistently reflects Christian values and perspectives. The paragraph that follows is a gross oversimplification of Langberg's work and includes some statements that move beyond her book.

44 Janice H. Carter-Lourensz and Gloria Johnson-Powell, "Physical Abuse, Sexual Abuse, and Neglect of Child," in *Comprehensive Textbook of Psychiatry/VI*, ed. Harold I. Kaplan and Benjamin J. Sadock (Baltimore, MD: Williams and Wilkins, 1995): 2455–2469. The quotation is on page 2459.

45 The term was used by A. W. Burgess and L. L. Holmstrom, "Rape Trauma Syndrome," *American Journal of Psychiatry* 131 (September 1974): 981–986. Apparently, the term continues to be used in legal circles to describe people victimized by rape, but even now some legal experts are questioning its continued usefulness. See Jacquelyne R. Biggers and Chong I. Kim, "Rape Trauma Syndrome: An Examination of Standards that Determine the Admissibility of Expert Witness Testimony," *Journal of Forensic Psychology Practice* 3 (2003): 61–77; and Mila Green McGowan and Jeffrey L. Helms, "The Utility of the Expert Witness in a Rape Case: Reconsidering Rape Trauma Syndrome," *Journal of Forensic Psychology Practice* 3 (2003): 51–60.

46 This section of the chapter is written from the perspective of women who have been raped, but many of the same conclusions apply to male victims.

47 This has been the experience of Janice, whose story appeared at the beginning of the chapter. It is the theme of the article by Gladwell, "Getting Over It," and is the conclusion of an article by George A. Bonanno, "Loss, Trauma, and Human Resilience: Have We Underestimated the Human Capacity to Thrive After Extremely Aversive Events?" *American Psychologist* 59 (January 2004): 20–28.

48 James E. Robertson, "Rape Among Incarcerated Men: Sex, Coercion and STDs," *AIDS Patient Care & STDs* 17 (August 2003): 423–430.

49 These are adapted from Martin, *Counseling for Family Violence*, 51.

50 These issues also are discussed in Martin, *Counseling for Family Violence*. See also Michèle Harway and Marsali Hansen, *Spouse Abuse: Assessing & Treating Battered Women, Batterers, & Their Children*, 2nd ed. (Sarasota, FL: Professional Resource Press, 2004).

51 In searching for books and articles on the treatment of abusers, I was surprised at the relatively small amount of available resources. Martin, *Counseling for Family Violence*, has two excellent chapters on treating abusers (chapters 5 and 8). These are helpful because they discuss treatment from both psychological and Christian perspectives. See also Cloe Madanes. James P. Keim, and Dinah Smelser, *The Violence of Men: New Techniques for Working with Abusive Families: A Therapy of Social Action* (San Francisco, CA: Jossey-Bass 1995). Christopher M. Murphy and Christopher I. Eckhardt, *Treating the Abusive Partner: An Individualized Cognitive-Behavioral Approach* (New York: Guilford, 2005); David J. Livingston, *Healing Violent Men: A Model for Christian Communities* (Minneapolis: Augsburg, 2001); and Catherine Clark Kroeger and Nancy Nason-Clark, *No Place for Abuse: Biblical & Practical Resources to Counteract Domestic Violence* (Downers Grove, IL: InterVarsity, 2002).

52 Anger management is a problem for abusers in all socioeconomic groups. One study of college students found, for example, that psychologically and physically violent male daters consistently had problems managing their anger. Kristen Lundeberg, Sandra M. Stith, Carrie E. Penn, and David B. Ward, "A Comparison of Nonviolent, Psychologically Violent, and Physically Violent Male College Daters," *Journal of Interpersonal Violence* 19 (October 2004): 1191–1200.

53 Some of this is elaborated in an article on the treatment of fathers who abuse: Katreena L. Scott and Claire V. Crooks, "Effecting Change in Maltreating Fathers: Critical Principles for Intervention Planning," *Clinical Psychology: Science and Practice* 11 (Spring 2004): 96–111.

54 Vicarious traumatization was first discussed in detail by Laurie Anne Pearlman and

Karen W. Saaskvitne, *Trauma and the Therapist: Countertransference and Vicarious Traumatization in Psychotherapy with Incest Survivors* (New York: Norton, 1995).

55 Langberg, *Counseling Survivors*, part six of the book.

56 Bullying is not new, but within recent years there has been a new focus of attention on the causes and prevention of bullying. See, for example, Pamela Orpinas and Arthur M. Home, *Bullying Prevention: Creating a Positive School Climate and Developing Social Competence* (Washington, DC: American Psychological Association, 2005).

57 Who to ask about abuse, when to ask, how to ask, and how to respond are discussed in more detail by Young et al., "Overcoming Barriers to Taking Abuse Histories," 412.

58 Garret D. Evans and Jannette Rey, "In the Echos of Gunfire: Practicing Psychologists' Response to School Violence," *Professional Psychology: Research and Practice* 32 (April 2001):157–164; Edward P. Mulvey and Elizabeth Cauffman, "The Inherent Limits or Predicting School Violence," *American Psychologist* 56 (October 2001): 797–802.

59 Karen Kersting, "Spreading the Word on Early Violence Prevention," *Monitor on Psychology* 35 (May 2004): 42–43.

60 Katherine Irwin, "The Violence of Adolescent Life: Experiencing and Managing Everyday Threats," *Youth & Society* 35 (June 2004): 452–479.

61 For an excellent collection of practical articles concerning prevention of violence in the home, see Peter G. Jaffe, Linda L. Baker, and Alison J. Cunningham, eds., *Protecting Children from Domestic Violence: Strategies for Community Intervention* (New York: Guilford, 2004).

62 Perhaps the readers of this book will excuse some parental pride. Our daughter Jan works with disadvantaged African American teenagers in an urban community where violence and substance abuse are especially high. In addition to her evangelistic work with a Christian youth organization, Jan and several colleagues have developed a program to teach high school students basic social and coping skills. The after-school program is based on the premise that these young people need to learn effective living skills that they have not learned or seen modeled in their homes. The program is voluntary, but at the time of this writing, it is continuing to grow significantly as young females and males both seek to get in and to participate, often enthusiastically.

63 Goldfein, "Reclaiming the Self," 55.

23. Inferiority and Self-Esteem

1 At the time of this writing, an Internet search of these words uncovered almost 10 million hits (web sites or articles available online) for *self-esteem*, 31 million for *self-concept*, 35 million for *self-image*, and about 700,000 for *inferiority*. It is interesting to speculate how much this is a reflection of culture. In the American culture there appears to be a lot of interest in issues of self-esteem and self-concept, but more group-oriented cultures may have much less interest in these concepts.

2 William Glasser, *Reality Therapy: A New Approach to Psychiatry* (New York: Perennial, 1989), and idem, *Reality Therapy in Action* (New York: HarperCollins, 2000).

3 The quotation is from page 10 in a book by Terry D. Cooper, *Sin, Pride and Self-Acceptance* (Downers Grove, IL: InterVarsity, 2003).

4 Robert Schuller, *Self-Esteem: The New Reformation* (Nashville, TN: W Pub Group, 1982).

5 Jay E. Adams, *The Biblical View of Self-Esteem, Self-Love, and Self Image* (Eugene, OR: Harvest House, 1986), 79, 106.

6 Paul Vitz, *Psychology as Religion: The Cult of Self-Worship*, 2nd ed. (Grand Rapids, MI: Eerdmans, 1994).

7 David Carlson, *Counseling and Self-Esteem* (Waco, TX: Word, 1988), 12.

8 John C. Ortberg, Jr., "The Goal of Self-Transcendence," *Christian Counseling Today* 9, no. 1 (2001): 22–26.

9 Genesis 1:26–28.

10 Psalm 8:4–5.

11 John 3:16.

12 Psalm 91:11–12; Hebrews 1:14; Luke 12:12; Matthew 5:13–14; John 14:1–3, 26.

13 Romans 3:25; 5:12, 17–19; 6:23a; 7:18.

14 Genesis 3:11–13; Psalm 32:1–5; Romans 3:11–18.

15 John 3:16; Romans 5:1, 8–11, 14–17.

16 Proverbs 16:18; James 4:6; 1 Peter 5:5.

17 This is the view of James R. Beck. I have drawn from Beck's two insightful articles in writing the next three paragraphs. See J. R. Beck, "Humility," in *Encyclopedia of Psychology*

and Counseling, ed. David G. Benner and Peter C. Hill, 2nd ed. (Grand Rapids, MI: Baker, 1999), 591–592; and J. R. Beck, "Pride," in Benner and Hill, *Encyclopedia,* 907–908.

18 John H. Harvey and Brian G. Pauwels, "Modesty, Humility, Character Strength, and Positive Psychology," *Journal of Social and Clinical Psychology* 23 (October 2004): 620–623; and Julie Juola Exline and Anne L. Geyer, "Perceptions of Humility: A Preliminary Study," *Self and Identity* 3 (April-June 2004): 95–114.

19 Matthew 22:39; Ephesians 5:28, 29. Some of the discussion about self-esteem concerns the long-standing theological debate about whether "as yourself" in Matthew 22:39 is a command or a statement of fact. There are arguments on both sides. I tend to agree with Stott that this is "not a command to love ourselves . . . self-love here is a fact." Further discussion concerns whether this fact of self-love is evidence of sin. See J. R. W. Stott, "Am I Supposed to Love Myself or Hate Myself?" *Christianity Today* 28 (April 20, 1984): 26–28.

20 Some of these differences are discussed in detail by Carlson, *Counseling and Self-Esteem,* 25–30.

21 See, for example, Melissa Dittman, "Weighing in on Fat Bias," *Monitor on Psychology* 35 (January 2004): 60–62; and J. Kevin Thompson and Linda Smolak, *Body Image, Eating Disorders, and Obesity in Youth* (Washington, DC: American Psychological Association, 2002). These and other causes of inferiority are discussed briefly by T. L. Brink, "Inferiority Complex," in Benner and Hill, *Encyclopedia,* 620–621.

22 Gary W. Evans, "The Environment of Childhood Poverty," *American Psychologist* 59 (February-March 2004): 77–92.

23 This definition of racism is taken from Charles R. Ridley "Building Self-Esteem in Racially Diverse Populations," *Christian Counseling Today* 9, no. 1 (2001): 46–49.

24 My friend Nagi Abi-Hashem periodically reminds me of the cultural differences between American and Middle Eastern perspectives on psychological and counseling issues. He discusses this further in N. Abi-Hashem, "Self-Esteem," in Benner and Hill, *Encyclopedia,* 1084–1087.

25 A variation of this view is held by Christians who advocate a "self-crucifixion" approach to theology. This assumes that humans are worthless, that our desires, thoughts, and individual abilities should be denied or "crucified," that we should "put our human nature down," and that Christ's thoughts and attitudes should completely engulf our lives. This view seems to be spiritual, but it denies (and therefore squelches) the individual gifts, abilities, personalities, and capacities that come to each of us from God and are intended to be used in his service. The self-crucifixion view fails to realize that Christians have been crucified with Christ (in the past), but nevertheless we now live as new creatures in vital fellowship with him. This does not mean that we are to become robots who reject our abilities and squelch our personalities. Instead, we are to submit these to divine control and trust that God will work through the unique individual differences he has given to each person.

26 Matthew 16:24–25.

27 See, e.g., James 3:13–16.

28 Romans 12:4–8. See also 1 Corinthians 12.

29 M. Dittmann, "Study Links Jealousy with Aggression, Low Self-Esteem," *Monitor on Psychology* 36 (February 2005): 13.

30 Psalm 75:5–7.

31 For a further discussion of pastoral self-esteem see Rujon W. Morrison, "The Pastor's Struggle with Self-Esteem," *Christian Counseling Today* 9, no. 1 (2001): 50–51.

32 This was discussed further by Pauline Rose Clance, *The Impostor Phenomenon: Overcoming the Fear That Haunts Your Success* (Atlanta: Peachtree Publishers, 1985).

33 These first two statements were suggested by S. Bruce Narramore, *You Are Somebody Special* (Grand Rapids, MI: Zondervan, 1974), 29.

34 Chris Thurman, *The Lies We Believe* (Nashville TN: Thomas Nelson, 2003); and William Backus and Marie Chapian, *Telling Yourself the Truth* (Minneapolis, MN: Bethany House, 2000).

35 Beverly and Tom Rodgers, "The Severely Wounded Child," *Christian Counseling Today* 9 (2001): 32–40.

36 This conclusion is not accepted by everyone. In preparing this chapter I found several books that claim to remove inferiority and raise self-esteem in only a few days.

37 See, for example, the entire issue of *American Psychologist* 55 (January 2000); also

Christopher Peterson and Martin L. P. Seligman, eds., *Character Strengths and Virtues* (Washington, DC: American Psychological Association, 2004); and Lisa G. Aspinwall and Ursula M. Staudinger, eds., *A Psychology of Human Strengths* (Washington, DC: American Psychological Association, 2003). An earlier volume, based on a Gallup Organization study of over two million people worldwide, reported how people who focus on strengths function better without being held back by feelings of inferiority or low self-esteem. See Marcus Buckingham and Donald O. Clifton, *Now, Discover Your Strengths* (New York: Free Press, 2001).

38   Psalm 139:14–15.

39   The story about Enrico Caruso is adapted from William J. Petersen and Randy Petersen, *The One Year Book of Psalms* (Wheaton, IL.: Tyndale, 1999), September 10.

40   Some readers will notice that this process is very similar to the coaching that we discussed in chapter 4 and to brief, strategic-focused therapy.

41   Hebrews 12:15.

42   1 John 1:8–9; James 5:16.

43   Romans 12:19.

44   For a practical and widely acclaimed book on building self-esteem and preventing self-esteem problems see Robert S. McGee, *The Search for Significance: Seeing Your True Worth Through God's Eyes* (Nashville, TN: W Publishing Group, 2003).

45   1 Corinthians 12:4–25.

46   M. Dittman, "Self-Esteem That's Based on External Sources Has Mental Health Consequences, Study Says," *Monitor on Psychology* 33 (December 2002): 16. For another example of research showing how self-esteem is associated with positive mental health, and how low self-esteem can be associated with mental disorders, depression, suicidal tendencies, eating disorders, substance abuse, and violence, see Michal Mann, Clemens M. H. Hosman, Herman P. Schaalma, and Nanne K. de Vries, "Self-Esteem in a Broad-Spectrum Approach for Mental Health Promotion," *Health Education Research* 19 (August 2004): 357–372.

24. Physical Illness

1   Psalm 139:14.

2   For example, see Robert G. Frank, Susan H. McDaniel, James H. Bray, and Margaret Heldring, eds., *Primary Care Psychology* (Washington, DC: American Psychological Association, 2004); Robert J. Gatchel and Mark S. Oordt, eds., *Clinical Health Psychology and Primary Care: Practical Advice and Clinical Guidance for Successful Collaboration* (Washington, DC: American Psychological Association, 2003); and a three-volume *Handbook of Clinical Health Psychology* published in 2002 and 2004 by the American Psychological Association.

3   Philippians 2:25–27.

4   This is reported by Morton T. Kelsey, *Healing and Christianity: A Classic Study* (New York: Harper & Row, 1963), 54.

5   Mark 6:7–13; Matthew 10:5–8; Luke 9:1–2, 6.

6   This healing proved both his power over Satan and his Messiahship.

7   Matthew 25:39–40.

8   James 5:14–16.

9   See especially John 9:2–3 and Luke 13:1–5.

10   Matthew 9:2–6; 1 Corinthians 11:29–30.

11   Matthew 9:20–21.

12   Mark 7:24–30; 9:20–27; Matthew 9:18–19, 23–26.

13   2 Corinthians 12:7.

14   Matthew 13:58.

15   I know that some will not agree with my conclusion. For a differing view, see John Wimber and Kevin Springer, *Power Healing* (San Francisco: HarperSanFrancisco, 1991).

16   C. S. Lewis, *The Problem of Pain* (New York: McMillan, 1982).

17   For example, see Philip Yancey, *Where Is God When It Hurts?* (Grand Rapids, MI: Zondervan, 1997); Garry Poole, *How Could God Allow Suffering and Evil? Tough Questions*, rev. ed. (Grand Rapids, MI: Zondervan, 2003); or Gregory A. Boyd, *Is God to Blame?: Beyond Pat Answers to the Problem of Suffering* (Downers Grove, IL: InterVarsity, 2003).

18   2 Corinthians 2:7–10; 1 Peter 1:6–7; Romans 8:28; Hebrews 12:11; Psalm 119:71; James 1:2–4; Romans 5:3–5.

19   Timothy A. Malyon was a long-time friend. He was deeply devoted to Christ, a member of the wedding party when I got married, and a man whose life and death inspired us all. It was an honor to know him. Many who read these words can point to similar people in their own lives. Perhaps we never will understand why God has used or is using their lives in the ways he has.

20 This is adapted from page 34 of a book by Christian physician Gregg R. Albers, *Counseling the Sick and Terminally Ill* (Dallas, TX: Word, 1989). This book is volume 20 in the thirty-volume Resources for Christian Counseling series, under the general editorial direction of Gary R. Collins.

21 It is widely acknowledged that medical personnel (and counselors) often begin their careers with an attitude of compassion and a determination to care, but in time they become distant and aloof, largely to protect themselves from the overwhelming effects of so much pain and suffering. This withdrawal by professionals can be evidence of burnout or unconscious attempts to prevent the symptoms of burnout.

22 *Chronic Conditions: Making the Case for Ongoing Care* (September 2004 Update) is a 68-page report produced by Partnership for Solutions, a national initiative funded by the Robert Wood Johnson Foundation and housed at Johns Hopkins University. The full report is available online, free of charge, at *www.partnershipforsolutions.com*. The report evaluates chronic illness in the United States, but many of the findings can be adapted to other countries.

23 Rebecca A. Clay, "Overcoming Barriers to Pain Relief," *Monitor on Psychology* 33 (April 2002): 58–60.

24 Reported by Troy L. Thomson, "Chronic Pain," in *Comprehensive Textbook of Psychiatry/IV*, ed. Harold I. Kaplan and Benjamin J. Sadock (Baltimore, MD: Williams and Wilkins, 1985), 1212–1215. The study was by a researcher named Beecher, but I was unable to find the original article, even after several Internet searches.

25 For example, see Chris Eccleston, Geert Crombez, Sarah Aldrich, and Cathy Stannard, "Worry and Chronic Pain Patients: A Description and Analysis of Individual Differences," *European Journal of Pain* 5 (2001): 309–318.

26 Vera A. Gonzales, Michael F. Martelli, and Jeff M. Baker, "Psychological Assessment of Persons with Chronic Pain," *NeuroRehabilitation* 14 (2000): 69–83. A special pain management clinic in Minnesota is typical of those that are led by professionals who appreciate the psychological-physiological basis of pain and use psychological methods to treat chronic pain patients. S. Martin, "Embracing the Mind-Body Approach: Mark B. Weisberg Co-owns a Multidisciplinary Clinic Specializing in Pain," *Monitor on Psychology* 33 (April 2002): 69. For more detailed information, see Robert J. Gatchel, *Clinical Essentials of Pain Management* (Washington, DC: American Psychological Association, 2005); Robert J. Gatchel and James N. Weisberg, eds., *Personality Characteristics of Patients with Pain* (Washington, DC: American Psychological Association, 2000); and Dennis C. Turk and Robert J. Gatchel, eds., *Psychological Approaches to Pain Management: A Practitioner's Handbook,* 2nd ed. (New York: Guilford, 2002).

27 Henri J. M. Nouwen, *A Letter of Consolation* (San Francisco, CA: Harper & Row, 1982), 28, 30.

28 G. Affleck et al., "Causal Attribution, Perceived Benefits, and Morbidity After a Heart Attack: An 8-Year Study," *Journal of Consulting and Clinical Psychology* 55 (1987): 29–35.

29 Nancy Frasure-Smith, François Lespérance, Martin Juneau, Mario Talajic, and Martial G. Bourassa, "Gender, Depression, and One-Year Prognosis After Myocardial Infarction," *Psychosomatic Medicine* 61 (January-February 1999): 26–37.

30 Rebecca A. Clay, "Research to the Heart of the Matter," *Monitor on Psychology* 32 (January 2001): 42–45.

31 David S. Sheps, Nancy Frasure-Smith, Kenneth E. Freeland, and Robert M. Carney, "The INTERHEART Study: Intersection Between Behavioral and General Medicine," *Psychosomatic Medicine* 66 (November-December 2004): 797–798. See also Nancy Frasure-Smith and François Lespérance, "Depression and Other Psychological Risks Following Myocardial Infarction," *Archives of General Psychiatry* 60 (June 2003): 627–636; and Nancy Frasure-Smith, François Lespérance, Ginette Gravel, Aline Masson, Martin Juneau, and Martial G. Bourassa, "Long-Term Survival Differences Among Low-Anxious, High-Anxious and Repressive Copers Enrolled in the Montreal Heart Attack Readjustment Trial," *Psychosomatic Medicine* 64 (July-August 2002): 571–579.

32 Rebecca A. Clay, "Bringing Psychology to Cardiac Care," *Monitor on Psychology* 32 (January 2001): 46–49.

33   During the time when this book was in the process of revision, I have been in consistent contact with a thirty-year-old friend who is battling brain cancer. He has struggled with intense pain, painful treatment procedures, and consistently negative medical reports from the doctors, but he has pressed on with an obvious awareness of the seriousness of his illness, and a confidence in God. My friend freely acknowledges that God can heal but that he might not. Hundreds, probably thousands, have been inspired by my friend's example. At different times he and I have talked openly about his feelings, struggles, and faith. My friend is an unusual man who defies many of the stereotypes of how people face terminal illness and the reality of death.

34   Elisabeth Kübler-Ross, *On Death and Dying* (New York: Macmillan, 1969).

35   Ibid., 123.

36   1 Corinthians 12:25–26.

37   Matthew 25:34–40; James 1:27.

38   Albers, *Counseling the Sick*, 177. I am grateful to Albers for his observations about the rushed nature of many visits to the sick.

39   Samuel Knapp and Jeanne M. Slattery, "Professional Boundaries in Nontraditional Settings," *Professional Psychology: Research and Practice* 35 (October 2004): 553–558.

40   Bitterness can lead to other problems; see Hebrews 12:15.

41   Psalms 38:4–8; 32:3–4.

42   Everett L. Worthington, Jr., and M. Scherer, "Forgiveness as an Emotion-Focused Coping Strategy That Can Reduce Health Risks and Promote Health Resilience: Theory, Review and Hypotheses," *Psychology and Health* 10 (2004): 385–405.

43   Romans 11:33.

44   Billy Graham, *Facing Death and the Life After* (Waco, TX: Word, 1987), 51.

45   Hanoch Livneh and Richard F. Antonak. "Psychological Adaptation to Chronic Illness and Disability: A Primer for Counselors," *Journal of Counseling & Development* 83 (Winter 2005): 12–20.

46   Siri Carpenter, "Hope on the Horizon: Behavioral Researchers Are Uncovering Promising New Ways to Treat Chronic Pain," *Monitor on Psychology* 33 (April 2002): 61–66. See also Livneh and Antanak, "Psychological Adaptation," 12–20; and Eric P. Simon and Raymond A. Folen, "The Role of the Psychologist on the Multidisciplinary Pain Management Team," *Professional Psychology: Research and Practice* 32 (April 2001): 125–134.

47   Morgan T. Sammons, "Pharmacological Management of Chronic Pain: I. Fibromyalgia and Neuropathic Pain," *Professional Psychology: Research and Practice* 35 (April 2004): 206–210.

48   Simon and Folen, "Role of the Psychologist." See also Stacey A. Williams, "Easing Migraine Pain," *Monitor on Psychology* 33 (April 2002): 71; and S. Y. Tan, "Cognitive and Cognitive-Behavioral Methods for Pain Control: A Selective Review," *Pain* 12 (1982): 201–228.

49   David B. Larson and Susan S. Larson, "Spirituality's Potential Relevance to Physical and Emotional Health: A Brief Review of Quantitative Research," *Journal of Psychology and Theology* 31 (Spring 2003): 37–51.

50   These first four suggestions are adapted from Livneh and Antonak, "Psychological Adaptation to Chronic Illness," 117.

51   Hebrews 11:1.

52   This is the basis of an excellent article and research report dealing with therapeutic interventions that prevent emotions such as depression or anxiety from making the physical illnesses worse. Gerald P. Koocher, Erin K. Curtiss, Irene S. Pollin, and Krista E. Patton, "Medical Crisis Counseling in a Health Maintenance Organization: Preventive Intervention," *Professional Psychology: Research and Practice* 32 (February 2001): 52–58.

53   Ibid., 52.

54   MCC is summarized by Koocher et al., "Medical Crisis Counseling," and by Irene Pollin and Susan Baird Kanaan, *Medical Crisis Counseling: Short-Term Therapy for Long-Term Illness* (New York: Norton, 1995).

55   Viktor E. Frankl, *Man's Search for Meaning*, rev. ed. (New York: Pocket, 1997).

56   As an example see L. D. Egbert, "Reduction in Post-Operative Pain by Encouragement and Instruction to Patient," *New England Journal of Medicine* 270 (1964): 825; L. M. Wallace, "Psychological Preparation as a Method of Reducing the Stress of Surgery," *Journal of Human Stress* 10 (1984): 62–76; and Patrick Callaghan and Ho Cheung Li, "The Effect of Pre-Operative Psychological Interventions on Post-Operative Outcomes in Chinese

Women Having an Elective Hysterectomy," *British Journal of Health Psychology* 7 (May 2002): 247–252.
57 Galatians 6:2; Psalm 55:22.

25. Grief

1 Billy Graham, *Facing Death and the Life After* (Waco, TX: Word, 1987), 164.
2 Sigmund Freud, "Mourning and Melancholia," in *Collected Papers of Sigmund Freud*, trans. J. Riviere, vol. 4 (London: Hogarth Press, 1953). These papers appeared first in German and were published in English in 1925.
3 Erich Lindemann, "Symptomatology and Management of Acute Grief," *American Journal of Psychiatry* 101 (1944): 144–148.
4 Elisabeth Kübler-Ross, *On Death and Dying* (New York: Macmillan, 1975).
5 It is of passing interest, perhaps, that when Dr. Kübler-Ross died, her friends and family announced this on a web site with these words: "August 24, 2004 Elisabeth shed her earthly cocoon to become a beautiful butterfly."
6 1 Corinthians 15:55; Hosea 13:14.
7 According to Hebrews 9:27, "it is destined that each person dies." The only exceptions are the Old Testament figures Enoch and Elijah and those believers who will be alive when Christ returns. Then, those "who are still alive and remain on earth will be caught up in the clouds to meet the Lord in the air and remain with him forever" (1 Thessalonians 4:17).
8 Genesis 37:34–35; 2 Samuel 12:15–18; 13:37; 18:33; 2 Chronicles 35:25.
9 2 Samuel 1.
10 Psalm 23:4.
11 Psalm 119:28.
12 Isaiah 53:3–4.
13 The two passages are 1 Corinthians 15 and 1 Thessalonians 4.
14 1 Thessalonians 4:14.
15 1 Thessalonians 4:18.
16 1 Corinthians 15:52–54.
17 1 Thessalonians 4:17; Hebrews 2:14–1; 2 Timothy 1:10; John 11:25–26.
18 2 Corinthians 4:14–5:8.
19 1 Corinthians 15:58.
20 Matthew 5:4. Some Bible scholars, including D. A. Carson, *The Sermon on the Mount* (Grand Rapids, MI: Baker, 1978), argue that this statement about mourning is a personal grieving over personal sin and has nothing to do with those who mourn and need comfort because a loved one has died. William Barclay gives the verse an even different interpretation but admits that the verse could be taken literally; see Barclay, *The Gospel of Matthew*, vol. 1 (Philadelphia, PA: Westminster, 1975).
21 John 11.
22 Matthew 14:12–13.
23 Matthew 26:38.
24 2 Samuel 12:15–23.
25 Marcia Sheinberg, "A Community of Grief," *Psychotherapy Networker* 26 (March-April 2002): 50–55.
26 The tasks cited in the text are adapted from Nagi Abi-Hashem, "Grief Therapy," in *Baker Encyclopedia of Psychology and Counseling*, ed. David G. Benner and Peter C. Hill, 2nd ed. (Grand Rapids, MI: Baker, 1999), 521–523; and J. William Worden, *Grief Counseling and Grief Therapy: A Handbook for the Mental Health Professional*, 3rd ed. (New York: Springer, 2001).
27 Each of these situations is discussed in a special section on Death in the Family in a professional journal. See Nadine J. Kaslow and Sari Gilman Aronson, "Recommendations for Family Interventions Following a Suicide," *Professional Psychology: Research and Practice* 35 (June 2004): 240–247; and Norman Abeles, Tara L. Victor, and Lisa Delano-Wood, "The Impact of an Older Adult's Death on the Family," *Professional Psychology: Research and Practice* 35 (June 2004): 234–239.
28 Robert A. Neimeyer, ed., *Meaning Reconstruction and the Experience of Loss* (Washington, DC: American Psychological Association, 2001).
29 Karen Kersting, "A New Approach to Complicated Grief," *Monitor on Psychology* 35 (November 2004): 51–52. See also Robert A. Neimeyer, Holly G. Prigerson, and Betty Davis, "Mourning and Meaning," *American Behavioral Scientist* 46 (2002): 235–251.

30 George A. Bonanno and Stacey Kaltman, "The Varieties of Grief Experience," *Clinical Psychology Review* 21 (July 2001): 705–734.

31 The issue of anticipatory mourning or grief is controversial. See Robert Fulton, "Anticipatory Mourning: A Critique of the Concept," *Mortality* 8 (2003): 342–351; and Theresa A. Rando, ed., *Clinical Dimensions of Anticipatory Mourning: Theory and Practice in Working with the Dying, Their Loved Ones, and Their Caregivers* (Champaign, IL: Research Press, 1999).

32 When the parent is younger, the death is more difficult to handle; see H. Finkelstein, "The Long-Term Effects of Early Parent Death: A Review," *Journal of Clinical Psychology* 44 (1988): 3–9. The different types of mourning associated with different kinds of loss are discussed by Sidney Zisook, "Death, Dying and Bereavement," in *Comprehensive Textbook of Psychiatry/VI*, ed. Harold I. Kaplan and Benjamin J. Sadock (Baltimore, MD: Williams and Wilkins, 1995), 1713–1729.

33 Early in my publishing career, I was honored to know Nancy Guthrie, who worked with one of my publishers. Years later, Nancy and her husband lost two children to a disease known as Zellweiger Syndrome. She describes her experiences in two moving and helpful books: *Holding on to Hope* (Wheaton, IL: Tyndale House, 2002) and *The One Year Book of Hope* (Wheaton, IL: Tyndale House, 2005).

34 J. William Worden, *Grief Counselling and Grief Therapy: A Handbook for the Mental Health Practitioner,* 3rd ed. (Philadelphia, PA: Brunner-Routledge, 2004).

35 Guthrie, *Holding on to Hope.*

36 Kevin J. Flannelly, Andrew J. Weaver, and Karen G. Costa, "A Systematic Review of Religion and Spirituality in Three Palliative Care Journals, 1990–1999," *Journal of Palliative Care* 20 (Spring 2004): 50–56. According to the authors, following their literature review, "Religion is a fundamental coping mechanism for many people when dealing with grave illness. Research in the U.S. and Great Britain on people grieving the death of a family member or close friend found a strong association between their psychological health and their ability to find meaning in their loss through religious beliefs. Other studies have also found religious beliefs to be of considerable help in dealing with grief."

37 John 11:33–36.

38 Ashley Davis Prend, "No Timetable for Grief: Recovery from Loss Has a Pace of Its Own," *Psychotherapy Networker* 26 (September-October 2002): 23–24. Similar conclusions are presented in a detailed textbook on grieving, written by a marriage and family therapist who wrote about grief after her twenty-two-year-old son, training for a triathlon, was struck and killed by an inattentive driver. See Dorothy S. Becvar, *In the Presence of Grief: Helping Family Members Resolve Death, Dying, and Bereavement Issues* (New York: Guilford, 2001).

39 M. Hall and M. Irwin, "Physiological Indices of Functioning in Bereavement," in *Handbook of Bereavement Research*, ed. Margaret S. Stroebe, Robert O. Hansson, Wolfgang Stroebe, and Henk Schur (Washington, DC: American Psychological Association, 2001), 473–491.

40 Jaako Kaprio, Markku Koshenvuo, and Heli Rita, "Mortality After Bereavement: A Prospective Study of 95,647 Widowed Persons," *American Journal of Public Health* 77 (March 1987): 283–287.

41 This was a conclusion of a committee of psychologists who wrote a major paper on the role of psychologists in providing end-of-life care. William E. Haley, Dale G. Larson, Julia Kasl-Godley, Robert A. Neimeyer, and Donna M. Kwilosz, "Roles for Psychologists in End-of-Life Care: Emerging Models of Practice," *Professional Psychology: Research and Practice* 34 (December 2003): 626–633.

42 C. S. Lewis, *A Grief Observed* (New York: Seabury, 1961), 66–67.

43 Many of these are available, including a book of devotions by Lois Mowday Rabey, *Moments for Those Who Have Lost a Loved One* (Colorado Springs, CO: NavPress, 2004).

44 Shannon Hodges, "Book Review of 'In the Presence of Grief: Helping Family Members Resolve Death, Dying, and Bereavement Issues,'" *Journal of Counseling and Development* 83 (Winter 2005): 120–121.

45 G. P. Lynch, "Athletic Injuries and the Practising Sport Psychologist: Practical Guidelines for Assisting Athletes," *The Sport Psychologist* 4 (1988): 161–167.

46 This is summarized by David Lavallee, J. Robert Grove, Sandy Gordon, and Ian W. Ford, "The Experience of Loss in Sport," in *Perspectives on Loss: A Sourcebook*, ed. John H. Harvey (Philadelphia, PA: Brunner/Mazel, 1998): 241–252.

47 Many of the losses in this section are discussed in more detail in Harvey, *Perspectives on Loss.*

48 C. Everett Koop and Elizabeth Koop, *Sometimes Mountains Move* (Wheaton, IL: Tyndale, 1979), 40, 73.

49 C. S. Lewis, *A Grief Observed*, 1.

50 There are many books intended to help counselors do grief counseling with family members and friends of the deceased. One example is by Dorothy S. Becvar, *In the Presence of Grief*.

51 For a more detailed discussion of grief, especially after the loss of a spouse, see Florence W. Kaslow, "Death of One's Partner: The Anticipation and the Reality," *Professional Psychology: Research and Practice* 35 (June 2004): 227–233.

52 Some of these were suggested by the American Psychological Association's Ad Hoc Committee on End-of-Life Issues. See footnote 41, Haley et al. "Roles for Psychologists."

53 Phyllis R. Silverman has been a leader in stimulating widow-to-widow contacts. See her book Phyllis R. Silverman, *Widow to Widow*, 2nd ed. (New York: Brunner-Routledge 2004). A similar book is by Genevieve Davis Ginsburg, *Widow to Widow: Thoughtful, Practical Ideas for Rebuilding Your Life* (New York: Da Capo Press, 2004).

54 SIDS is the leading cause of death among infants who are one month to one year old, but according to one web site, "Despite years of research and numerous studies, SIDS is still unpredictable and unpreventable." A number of web sites give information about SIDS, including ways that parents can reduce the risk.

55 For discussions about the loss of an only child, see Kay Talbot, *What Forever Means After the Death of a Child: Transcending the Trauma, Living with the Loss* (New York: Brunner-Routledge, 2002).

56 A good resource on helping children who grieve is by Nancy Boyd Webb, ed., *Helping Bereaved Children: A Handbook for Practitioners*, 2nd ed. (New York: Guilford, 2002). See also J. William Worden, *Children and Grief: When a Parent Dies* (New York: Guilford, 2001).

57 An Internet search or a bookstore recommendation can be a good place to start in finding these books. Examples are Karyn Henley, *Gram's Song* (Wheaton, IL: Tyndale 2003), which is written from a Christian perspective, and a book produced by a division of the American Psychological Association, Joyce C. Mills, *Gentle Willow: A Story for Children About Dying* (Washington, DC: Magination Press, 2003). See also Michaelene Mundy, *Sad Isn't Bad: A Good-Grief Guidebook for Kids Dealing with Loss* (St. Meinrad, IN: Abbey Press, 1998). Be sure that the selected books are appropriate for the age of the grieving child.

58 Garry Cooper, "'Grief Work' Doesn't Help," *Psychotherapy Networker* 26 (July-August 2002): 18; and Margaret Stroebe, Wolfgang Stroebe, Henk Schut, Emmanuelle Zech, and Jan van den Bout, "Does Disclosure of Emotions Facilitate Recovery from Bereavement? Evidence from Two Prospective Studies," *Journal of Consulting & Clinical Psychology* 70 (February 2002): 169–178.

59 This bonding is proposed by the APA Ad Hoc Committee on End-of-Life Issues. Please see Kersting, "A New Approach to Complicated Grief"; and Haley et al., "Roles for Psychologists." Becvar, *In the Presence of Grief*, describes a "mystical experience" in which she believes that her deceased son was trying to contact her. Although this may be accepted in many cultures, it generally is not accepted by Christians or by helping professionals in Western society.

60 1 Samuel 28.

61 Among the better books in this field are two written by former Asbury Seminary professor and pastor David A. Seamands. See Seamands, *Healing for Damaged Emotions: Recovering from the Memories That Caused Our Pain* (Wheaton, IL: Victor Books, 1981), and idem, *Healing of Memories* (Wheaton, IL: Victor Books, 1985).

62 Ingrid Trobisch, "Let the Deep Pain Hurt," *Partnership* (September/October 1985): 43–45.

26. Singleness

1 Adapted from Bob Vetter and June Vetter, *Jesus Was a Single Adult* (Elgin, IL: David C. Cook, 1978).

2 At the time of this writing, one of the most popular of these in the United States and Canada is *www.eHarmony.com*, founded by psychologist Neil Clark Warren. It has a reported membership base of six million single people who are interested in finding "soul mates." Chapter 27 discusses eHarmony in more detail.

3 Henry Cloud. *How to Get a Date Worth Keeping* (Grand Rapids, IL: Zondervan, 2005).

4 Margaret Feinberg, "Single and Fabulous: Both Attitudes and Books About Singleness Are Shifting," *Christian Retailing* 51 (April 4, 2005): 44–45.

5 Genesis 2:18.

6 Matthew 19:11–12.

7 1 Corinthians 7:7.

8 1 Corinthians 7:1, 2, 8.

9 1 Corinthians 7:28, 32–35.

10 Researcher George Barna makes this point in *Single Focus* (Ventura, CA: Regal Books, 2003). Too often discussions about singles lump all unmarried people together, overlooking the significant diversity within the singles population.

11 This is from the 2000 Census, reported by Feinberg, "Single and Fabulous."

12 According to Lauren F. Winner, "three surveys of single Christians conducted in the 1990s turned up a lot of premarital sex: Approximately one-third of the respondents were virgins—that means, of course, that two-thirds were not." Lauren F. Winner, "Sex in the Body of Christ," *Christianity Today* 49 (May 2005): 28–33.

13 1 Corinthians 7:9.

14 This is the title of a popular book written by a twenty-one-year-old named Joshua Harris. With its emphasis on viewing love, purity, and singleness from God's perspective rather than thinking that love and romance are to be enjoyed "solely for recreation," this book "turned the Christian singles scene upside down," according to one reviewer, and, at the time of this writing, sales of the book were approaching one million copies. Joshua Harris, *I Kissed Dating Goodbye*, updated edition (Sisters, OR: Multnomah, 2003).

15 It was my privilege to attend Stott's church when I was a student living in London.

16 A *HIS* interview with John R. W. Stott, *HIS* 36 (October 1975): 19.

17 Lauren F. Winner, *Real Sex: The Naked Truth About Chastity* (Grand Rapids, MI: Brazos Press, 2005). See also, Winner, "Sex in the Body of Christ."

18 Lauren F. Winner, "Deeper into Chastity," *Christianity Today* 49 (May 2005): 32–33.

19 Hebrews 12:15–16.

20 Norman L. Thiesen and Benedict B. Cooley, "The Psychological Adjustment of the Single Male Adult Compared with Married Males and Single and Married Females Aged 25–34," *Journal of Psychology and Theology* 7 (Fall 1979): 202–211.

21 An Internet search will reveal a number of books devoted to single parenting. These include Gary Richmond, *Successful Single Parenting* (Eugene, OR: Harvest House, 1998); Armin A. Brott, *The Single Father: A Dad's Guide to Parenting Without a Partner* (New York: Abbeville Press, 1999); and Michele Howe, *Going It Alone: Meeting the Challenges of Being a Single Mom* (Peabody, MA: Hendrickson, 1999).

22 Karen Gail Lewis, "The Four Pillars of Wisdom: Helping Singles Counteract Conflicting Cultural Messages," *Psychotherapy Networker* 24 (November-December 2000): 75.

23 Lewis, "Four Pillars of Wisdom," 77.

24 C. S. Lewis, *The Four Loves* (London: Fontana, 1960), 62.

25 One of the best discussions of true friendship that I have read is in a chapter titled "The Ideals of Spiritual Friendship," in David G. Benner, *Sacred Companions: The Gift of Spiritual Friendship and Direction* (Downers Grove, IL: InterVarsity, 2002), 61–84.

26 Sharon Morris, "Singles, Sex, and Celibacy," *Christian Counseling Today* 9, no. 4 (2001): 47–49.

27 Winner, "Sex in the Body of Christ," 30.

28 Ibid., 31.

29 A. D. Compaan, "Single Parents," in *Baker Encyclopedia of Psychology*, ed. David G. Benner and Peter C. Hill, 2nd ed. (Grand Rapids, MI: Baker, 1999), 1125–1127.

30 Support of these conclusions is found in the following articles, selected from a larger database of empirical studies published since 2000: John Cairney, Michael Boyle, David R. Offord, and Yvonne Racine, "Stress, Social Support and Depression in Single and Married Mothers," *Social Psychiatry & Psychiatric Epidemiology* 38 (August 2003): 442–449; S. Targosz, Paul Bebbington, G. Lewis, T. Brugha, R. Jenkins, M. Farrell, and H. Meltzer, "Lone Mothers, Social Exclusion, and Depression," *Psychological Medicine* 33 (May 2003): 715–722; Melanie Lutenbacher, "Relationships Between Psychosocial Factors and Abusive Parenting Attitudes in Low-income Single Mothers," *Nursing Research* 51 (May-June 2002): 158–167; and Sheryl L. Olson, Rosario Ceballo, and Curie Park, "Early Problem Behavior Among Children from Low-Income, Mother-Headed Families: A Multiple Risk Perspective," *Journal of Clinical Child and Adolescent Psychology* 31 (December 2002): 419–430.

31 John Cairney et al., "Stress, Social Support, and Depression," and Olson et al., "Early Problem Behavior."

32 A. D'Ercole, "Single Mothers: Stress, Coping and Social Support," *Journal of Community Psychology* 16 (1988): 41–54.

27. Choosing a Marriage Partner

1 The story of David and Heather is told by Lisa Ann Cockrel, "The Search for a Soul Mate," *Relevant* 5 (November-December 2003): 54–55.

2 Ibid.

3 Ibid. The sociologist is Stephen Nock at the University of Virginia.

4 I confess that I almost did not include the chapter on mate selection in this edition of the book. My reason for thinking this way may be similar to the reason that most counseling books do not discuss this issue: it seems that in comparison to major problem issues such as depression, marriage conflict, or anxiety, a lot fewer people are likely to ask a counselor about choice of a mate. Even so, I still believe that this is a very significant issue, not only for counselors but for single readers of this book. Preventing poor decisions can be a significant way to avoid later problems.

5 Genesis 24.

6 Genesis 29.

7 Matthew 1:18–21.

8 2 Corinthians 6:14–16.

9 1 Corinthians 5:9ff.

10 1 Corinthians 7:39.

11 Psalm 32:8; Proverbs 3:5–6; 16:3, 9.

12 These statistics and the story of Yogeth and Sarita is adapted from Samieh Shalash, "It's All Arranged—60 Percent of World's Marriages Decided in Advance for Couples," from Knight Ridder Newspapers, *http://www.bluegrassmarriages.org/news/shalash_krn_01.html* (accessed June 30, 2006).

13 Stephanie Coontz, "What's Love Got to Do with It? A Brief History of Marriage," *Psychotherapy Networker* 29 (May-June 2005): 56–61, 74.

14 Genesis 1:27; 2:18; 1 Corinthians 7:9; Hebrews 13:4.

15 1 Corinthians 7:35.

16 Elizabeth Jagger, "Marketing Molly and Melville: Dating in a Postmodern, Consumer Society," *Sociology* 35 (February 2001): 39–57.

17 Ranna Parekh and Eugene V. Beresin, "Looking for Love? Take a Cross-Cultural Walk Through the Personals," *Academic Psychiatry* 25 (Winter 2001): 223–233.

18 David M. Buss, Todd K. Shakelford, Lee A. Kirkpatrick, and Randy J. Larsen, "A Half Century of Mate Preferences: The Cultural Evolution of Values," *Journal of Marriage and the Family* 63 (May 2001): 491–503.

19 David Knox, Vivian Daniels, LaKisha Sturdivant, and Marty E. Zusman, "College Student Use of the Internet for Mate Selection," *College Student Journal* 35 (March 2001): 158–160.

20 This is a description of *www.eHarmony.com*, designed by psychologist Neil Clarke Warren. See Dan MacMedan, "eHarmony: Heart and Soul," *USA Today*, May 19, 2005.

21 One study specifically evaluates eHarmony.com and concludes that "online matchmakers' escalating claims that their services derive from scientific methods remain questionable because solid empirical evidence for such claims is rarely offered. Unfortunately, even when available, the quality of such evidence leaves much to be desired due to conceptual as well as technical problems." The claims of effectiveness from eHarmony.com have "serious logical flaws" and "additional shortcomings_._._._related to the involved variables, research design, and sampling biases." James Houran, Rense Lang, Jason P. Rentfrow, and Karin H. Bruckner, "Do Online Matchmaking Tests Work? An Assessment of Preliminary Evidence for a Publicized 'Predictive Model of Marital Success,'" *North American Journal of Psychology* 6 (2004): 507–526. See also Jessica E. Donn and Richard C. Sherman, "Attitudes and Practices Regarding the Formation of Romantic Relationships on the Internet," *CyberPsychology & Behavior* 5 (April 2002): 107–123. For popular books on Internet dating and mate finding, see Andrea Orr, *Meeting, Mating, and Cheating: Sex, Love, and the New World of Online Dating* (New York: Reuters Prentice Hall, 2003); and Evan Marc Katz, *I Can't Believe I'm Buying This Book: A Commonsense Guide to Successful Internet Dating* (Berkeley, CA: Ten Speed Press, 2004).

22 Susan Sprecher and Pamela C. Regan, "Liking Some Things (in Some People) More Than Others: Partner Preferences in Romantic Relationships and Friendships," *Journal of Social and Personal Relationships* 19 (August 2002): 463–481.

23 Diane S. Berry and Katherine M. Miller, "When Boy Meets Girl: Attractiveness and the Five-Factor Model in Opposite-Sex Interactions," *Journal of Research in Personality* 35 (March 2001): 62–77. A study of date selection found, as well, that men placed more importance on a potential date than women did. The women, in turn, favored characteristics associated with financial security. See Christina M. Frederick and Craig S.Morrison, "Date Selection Choices in College Students: Making a Potential Love Connection," *North American Journal of Psychology* 1 (1999): 41–50. What a college student prefers in a date, of course, may not be correlated with what that same student might want in a long-term marriage.

24 Sandra L. Murray, John G. Holmes, Gina Bellavia, Dale W. Griffin, and Dan Dolderman, "Kindred Spirits? The Benefits of Egocentrism in Close Relationships," *Journal of Personality & Social Psychology* 82 (April 2002): 563–581.

25 Galatians 5:22–23.

26 The magazine is *Relevant*. You can learn more from *www.relevantmagazine.com*. Cara Baker, Erika Larson, and Jessica Leopold, "Parting Ways: How to Break Up Graciously," *Relevant* 4 (September-October 2003): 46–47.

27 Ibid., 47.

28 Ibid., italics in the original.

29 Eric Fromm, *The Art of Loving* (New York: Bantam, 1956), 2–3.

30 With some adaptation, Fromm's description probably could be extended to other people-finding situations, such as an individual searching for a job or a church looking for a new pastor.

28. Premarital Counseling

1 The facts in this story are taken from published accounts. The woman's real name is Jennifer, but I have chosen not to use her last name or hometown, even though her real identity was widely known at the time of her disappearance.

2 Carl Rogers, *Becoming Partners: Marriage and Its Alternatives* (New York: Delacorte, 1972), 11.

3 The 30 percent figure is reported by Carlos E. Valiente, Catherine J. Belanger, and Anna U. Estrada, "Helpful and Harmful Expectations of Premarital Interventions," *Journal of Sex and Marital Therapy* 28 (January-February 2002): 71–77. The conclusion that "premarital counseling is performed most often by members of the clergy in various religious settings" comes from Michael D. Bruhn and Rhonda Hill, "Designing a Premarital Counseling Program," *Family Journal: Counseling and Therapy for Couples and Families* 12 (October 2004): 389–391.

4 Matthew 1:18–25.

5 1 Corinthians 7:8, 26–27, 29.

6 1 Corinthians 7:28, 33–34.

7 Ephesians 5:22–6:4; Colossians 3:18–21; 1 Peter 3:1–9.

8 Scott M. Stanley, "Making a Case for Premarital Education," *Family Relations: Interdisciplinary Journal of Applied Family Studies* 50 (July 2001): 272–280.

9 "A 1999 study by the Barna Research Group raised eyebrows when it concluded that divorce rates among conservative Christians were much higher than for other faith groups. And church-attending Christians were much more likely to divorce than atheists and agnostics." This is from an article by Jason Boyette, "What Marriage Isn't: Four Reasons Not to Say 'I Do,'" *Relevant* 12 (January-February 2005): 43–44. The Barna research was conducted in the United States, and the findings, while very sobering, may not be true of other countries or at other time periods.

10 Boyette, "What Marriage Isn't." The quotations are all on page 44.

11 Ephesians 5:18–20.

12 Ephesians 5:21–6:4.

13 Lest there be any question about this, I did not check all forty-two million references, but I saw enough to observe the diversity of thinking both about what constitutes family tradition in different cultures and about the ways in which families are changing. Among the numerous books discussing family changes, the following focuses on changes that have occurred over the past thirty or forty years, including: the popularity of cohabita-

tion and gay marriage, dual-earner couples, the impact of divorce, single-parent families, and the effects of religion, poverty, the Internet, media, technology, and government on changing perspectives on marriage. See "family change," in *Handbook of Contemporary Families: Considering the Past, Contemplating the Future*, ed. Marilyn Coleman and Lawrence H. Ganong (Thousand Oaks, CA: Sage Publications, 2003).

14   Paige D. Martin, Gerald Specter, Don Martin, and Maggie Martin, "Expressed Attitudes of Adolescents Toward Marriage and Family Life," *Adolescence* 38 (Summer 2003): 359–367.

15   For example, see Sharon Sassier, "The Process of Entering into Cohabiting Unions," *Journal of Marriage and Family* 66 (May 2004): 491–505; Patrick Heuveline and Jeffrey M. Timberlake, "The Role of Cohabitation in Family Formation: The United States in Comparative Perspective," *Journal of Marriage and Family* 66 (December 2004): 1214–1230; Céline Le Bourdais and Évelyne Lapierre-Adamcyk, "Changes in Conjugal Life in Canada: Is Cohabitation Progressively Replacing Marriage?" *Journal of Marriage and Family* 66 (November 2004): 929–942; and Judith A. Seltzer, "Cohabitation in the United States and Britain: Demography, Kinship and the Future," *Journal of Marriage and Family* 66 (November 2004): 921–928.

16   A host of studies evaluates the impact of cohabitation, and the findings are by no means conclusive. One study demonstrated, for example, that pre-engagement cohabiters have "more negative interactions, lower interpersonal commitment relationships quality, and lower relationship confidence," but this was not consistent with all cohabiters. See Galena H. Kline et al., "Timing Is Everything: Pre-Engagement Cohabitation and Increased Risk for Poor Marital Outcomes," *Journal of Family Psychology* 18 (June 2004): 311–318. Another study compared cohabitating couples with cohabiters who marry and concluded that "cohabiters who marry report higher levels of happiness as well as lower levels of relationship instability, disagreements, and violent conflict resolution." Susan L. Brown, "Moving from Cohabitation to Marriage: Effects on Relationship Quality," *Social Science Research* 33 (March 2004): 1–19.

17   Sharon Sassler, "The Process of Entering Cohabiting Unions," *Journal of Marriage and Family* 66 (May 2004): 491–505.

18   L. L. Bumpass, J. A. Sweet, and A. Cherlin, *The Role of Cohabitation in Decline Rates of Marriage*, based on a National Survey of Families and Households, NSFH Working Paper No. 5., August, 1989. See also S. L. Brown and A. Booth, "Cohabitation Versus Marriage: A Comparison of Relationship Quality," *Journal of Marriage and the Family* 58 (1996): 668–678.

19   Michael McManus and Harriet McManus, "How to Create an America That Saves Marriages," *Journal of Psychology and Theology* 31 (Fall 2003): 196–207.

20   Ephesians 5:3–5.

21   Adapted from Ellen Barry, "It Must Be Love, but Let's Be Sure," *Los Angeles Times*, May 22, 2005.

22   Stephen F. Duncan and Melissa M. Wood, "Perceptions of Marriage Preparation Among College-Educated Young Adults with Greater Family-Related Risks for Marital Disruption," *Family Journal: Counseling and Therapy for Couples and Families* 11 (October 2003): 342–353.

23   Jason S. Carroll and William J. Doherty, "Evaluating the Effectiveness of Premarital Prevention Programs: A Meta-Analytic Review of Outcome Research," *Family Relations: Interdisciplinary Journal of Applied Family Studies* 52 (April 2003): 105–118.

24   Elizabeth A. Schilling, Donald H. Baucom, Charles K. Burnett, Elizabeth Sandin Allen, and Lynelle Ragland, "Altering the Course of Marriage: The Effect of PREP Communication Skills Acquisition on Couples' Risk of Becoming Maritally Distressed," *Journal of Family Psychology* 17 (March 2003): 41–53.

25   Kieran T. Sullivan, Lauri A. Pasch, Tara Cornelius, and Ellen Cirigliano, "Predicting Participation in Premarital Prevention Programs: The Health Belief Model and Social Norms," *Family Process* 43 (June 2004): 175–193.

26   Two surveys found these to be the major areas of interest: Kieran T. Sullivan and Carmen Anderson, "Recruitment of Engaged Couples for Premarital Counseling: An Empirical Examination of the Importance of Program Characteristics and Topics to Potential Participants," *Family Journal: Counseling and Therapy for Couples and Families* 10 (October 2002): 388–397; and Carlos E. Valiente et al., "Helpful and Harmful Expectations."

27   Sullivan and Anderson, "Recruitment of Engaged Couples."

28   Valiente et al., "Helpful and Harmful Expectations."

29 Gail S. Risch, Lisa A. Riley, and Michael G. Lawler, "Problematic Issues in the Early Years of Marriage: Content for Premarital Education," *Journal of Psychology and Theology* 31 (Fall 2003): 253–269.

30 I am reluctant to list too many of these because new books are being added constantly, and some of the older books go out of print without warning. In addition, there are audio and video programs being developed and produced. Counselors may want to look for books by H. Norman Wright, David and Jan Stoop, or Les and Leslie Parrot. The Parrots have a program built around their book *Saving Your Marriage Before It Starts* (Grand Rapids, MI: Zondervan, 1995). See also the Parrot's *Saving Your Second Marriage Before It Starts* (Grand Rapids, MI: Zondervan, 2001), and *Getting Ready for the Wedding: All You Need to Know Before You Say I Do* (Grand Rapids, MI: Zondervan, 1998). Couples who want to read about sexuality might look for books by Clifford L. Penner and Joyce J. Penner, *Sex 101* (Nashville, TN: W Publishing, 2004), or Christopher and Rachel McCluskey, *When Two Become One: Enhancing Sexual Intimacy in Marriage* (Grand Rapids, MI: Revell, 2004).

31 Jeffry H. Larson, Kenneth Newell, Glade Topham, and Sheldon Nichols, "A Review of Three Comprehensive Premarital Assessment Questionnaires," *Journal of Marital and Family Therapy* 28 (April 2002): 233–239. For a broader, in-depth analysis and summary of a variety of assessment tools, including inventories, for evaluating couples, see Len Sperry, ed., *Assessment of Couples and Families: Contemporary and Cutting-Edge Strategies* (Philadelphia, PA: Brunner-Routledge, 2004).

32 Les and Leslie Parrott, eds., *Getting Ready for the Wedding: All You Need to Know Before You Say I Do* (Grand Rapids, MI: Zondervan, 1998) is an extremely helpful and easy-to-read book that includes a number of helpful questionnaires and plenty of practical suggestions.

33 Two recommended programs are the SYMBIS Approach (Saving Your Marriage Before It Starts) by Les and Leslie Parrott, and the Marriage Savers approach developed by Michael and Harriet McManus (*www.marriagesavers.org*). See Les Parrott III and Leslie Parrott, "The SYMBIS Approach to Marriage Education," *Journal of Psychology and Theology* 31 (Fall 2003): 208–212; and Michal J. McManus and Harriet McManus, "How to Create an America That Saves Marriages," *Journal of Psychology and Theology* 31 (Fall 2003): 196–207. An Internet search of "marriage mentoring" will lead to a number of other helpful articles.

34 L. M. Williams, "Premarital Counseling: A Needs Assessment Among Engaged Individuals," *Contemporary Family Therapy* 14 (1992): 505–518.

35 For more detailed guidance, see Everett L. Worthington, Jr., *Counseling Before Marriage* (Dallas, TX: Word 1990); H. Norman Wright, *The Premarital Counseling Handbook*, reprint edition (Chicago: Moody Press, 1992); H. Norman Wright, *How to Counsel a Couple in Six Sessions or Less* (Ventura, CA: Regal, 2002); and Robert F. Stahmann and William J. Hiebert, *Premarital & Remarital Counseling: The Professional's Handbook*, 3rd ed. (San Francisco, CA: Jossey-Bass, 1997).

36 Glenice A. Burchard, Mark A. Yarhouse, Everett L. Worthington, Jr., Jack W. Berry, Marcus K. Kilian, and David E. Canter, "A Study of Two Marital Enrichment Programs and Couples' Quality of Life," *Journal of Psychology and Theology* 31 (Fall 2003): 240–252.

37 Worthington, *Counseling Before Marriage*, 2. See also J. S. Ripley, E. L. Worthington, Jr., and D. G. Benner, "Premarital Counseling," in *Baker Encyclopedia of Psychology*, ed. David G. Benner and Peter C. Hill, 2nd ed. (Grand Rapids, MI: Baker, 1999), 899–901.

38 Benjamin Silliman, "Building Healthy Marriages Through Early and Extended Outreach with Youth," *Journal of Psychology and Theology* 31 (Fall 2003): 270–282.

39 Ibid., 275.

40 This story is told by Les and Leslie Parrott in *Getting Ready for the Wedding*, 7. The book by Robert S. McNamara is *In Retrospect: The Tragedy and Lessons of Vietnam* (New York: Vintage, 1996).

41 The first mention of premarital counseling was in a 1928 article in *The Journal of Obstetrics and Gynecology*.

29. Marriage Issues

1 The story of Geoff and Marilyn is adapted from Terry Hargrave, "The Ineffable 'Us-ness' of Marriage," *Psychotherapy Networker* 25 (July-August 2001): 55–61.

2 This conclusion is documented by Jennifer S. Ripley, "Introduction: Reflections on the Current Status and Future of Christian Marriage," *Journal of Psychology and Theology* 31

(Fall 2003): 175–178; and by Mark A. Young, "Healthy Relationships: Where's the Research?" *Family Journal: Counseling & Therapy for Couples & Families* 12 (April 2004): 159–162. One recent study tried to determine what built strong marriages and concluded that "for each couple the factors contributing to the longevity of their happy marriage were numerous and unique. While the most commonly mentioned factors included friendship, love, and similar backgrounds or interests, a wide range of responses were elicited." See Leslie L. Bachand and Sandra L. Caron, "Ties That Bind: A Qualitative Study of Happy Long-Term Marriages," *Contemporary Family Therapy: An International Journal* 23 (March 2001): 105–121.

3   Jeanetter Lauer and Robert Lauer, "Marriages Made to Last," *Psychology Today* 19 (June 1985): 22–26.

4   William Doherty, "Bad Couples Therapy," *Psychotherapy Networker* 26 (November-December 2002): 26–33. In the secular counseling literature, couples therapy or couples counseling refers to counseling with any kind of couple, including unmarried, homosexual, or cohabitating couples. As used in the present chapter, couples counseling or couples therapy refers specifically to a married male-female couple.

5   Genesis 2:18–25.

6   For example, see Ephesians 5:21–33; Colossians 3:18–25; 1 Peter 3:1–7; Hebrews 13:4.

7   Deuteronomy 24:1–4; Matthew 5:31–32; 19:3–9; 1 Corinthians 7:10–16. Divorce is discussed in more detail in chapter 32.

8   Proverbs 18:22.

9   Proverbs 5:18; Ecclesiastes 9:9.

10   Proverbs 27:15–16; see also Proverbs 19:13; 21:9.

11   Ravi Zacharias has taken one biblical marriage as a model for his book, *I, Isaac, Take Thee, Rebekah: Moving from Romance to Lasting Love* (Nashville, TN: W Publishing, 2004). For an older, but interesting critique of thirteen biblical marriages, including those of Abraham and Sarah, Jacob and Rachel, Boas and Ruth, Ahab and Jezebel, Hosea and Gomer, Joseph and Mary, and Aquillia and Priscilla, see Richard L. Strauss, *Living in Love: Secrets from Bible Marriages* (Wheaton, IL: Tyndale, 1978).

12   Les and Leslie Parrott, *When Bad Things Happen to Good Marriages* (Grand Rapids, MI: Zondervan, 2001).

13   Much of this research is posted on the web site of the Gottman Institute, *www.gottman.com*. For example, see "First Three Minutes of Discussion About On-going Areas of Marital Conflict Are Predictive of Divorce for Newlyweds," posted September 27, 1999, *http://web.psych.washington.edu/news/story.php?news_id=31*.

14   Adapted from Parrott and Parrott, *When Bad Things Happen*, 43–44.

15   Gary R. Collins, *Breathless: Transform Your Time-Starved Days into a Life Well Lived* (Wheaton, IL: Tyndale, 1998). Despite its limited sales, this is a book that I was proud to have written. It began with a very warm forward written by my friend Les Parrott III. Periodically, when my life gets too busy, I return to what I wrote. The book is no longer in print or available.

16   Ephesians 5:21–33; Colossians 3:18–25; 1 Peter 3:1–7.

17   1 Corinthians 7:12–16; 2 Corinthians 6:14–16.

18   E. L. Kelley and J. J. Conley, "Personality and Compatibility: A Prospective Analysis of Marital Stability and Marital Satisfaction," *Journal of Personality and Social Psychology* 52 (1987): 27–40. For a more recent example of research on personality issues and marriage, see M. Brent Donnellan, Dannelle Larsen-Rife, and Rand D. Conger, "Personality, Family History, and Competence in Early Adult Romantic Relationships," *Journal of Personality and Social Psychology* 88 (March 2005): 562–576.

19   Everett L. Worthington, Jr., Andrea J. Lerner, and Constance B. Sharp, "Repairing the Emotional Bond: Marriage Research from 1977 Through Early 2005," *Journal of Psychology and Christianity* 24 (Fall 2005): 259–262. The quotation is from page 259.

20   Ibid.

21   For an insightful discussion of infertility and its impact on a marriage, see Deborah Derrickson Kossmann, "Barren: Coming to Terms with a Lost Dream," *Psychotherapy Networker* 26 (July-August 2002): 40–45, 58.

22   Please see chapter 32, where divorce and its implications are discussed in more detail.

23   Doherty, "Bad Couples Therapy," 26, 28.

24   Any listing of marriage counseling books is likely to be outdated soon, but examples include: Michele Harway, ed., *Handbook of Couples Therapy* (New York: Wiley, 2004);

Robert P. Rugel, *Treating Marital Stress: Support-Based Approaches* (New York: Haworth, 2003); Alan S. Gurman and Neil S. Jacobson, eds., *Clinical Handbook of Couple Therapy* (New York: Guilford, 2003); and Richard B. Stuart, *Helping Couples Change* (New York: Guilford, 2004). Recommended Christian approaches include DeLoss D. Friesen and Ruby M. Friesen, *Counseling and Marriage* (Dallas, TX: Word, 1989), Everett L. Worthington, Jr., ed., *Christian Marriage Counseling: Eight Approaches to Understanding and Helping Couples with Problems* (Grand Rapids, MI: Baker, 1996); and Worthington's more recent work, *Hope-Focused Marriage Counseling: A Guide for Brief Therapy,* rev. ed. (Downers Grove, IL: InterVarsity, 2005).

25 The most strategic books by these authors are Jay Haley, *Strategies of Psychotherapy;* Salvador Minuchin, *Families of the Slums;* Cloe Madanes, *Strategic Family Therapy;* and Virginia Satir, *Conjoint Family Therapy.* For an interesting summary of the work of Salvador Minuchin, see Mary Sykes Wylie, "Maestro of the Consulting Room," *Psychotherapy Networker* 29 (May-June 2005): 41–50.

26 An excellent history and update of the systems-based, family therapy movement is found in Peter Fraenkel, "Whatever Happened to Family Therapy?" *Psychotherapy Networker* 29 (May-June 2005): 30–39, 70.

27 Gary J. Oliver, Monte Hasz, and Matthew Richburg, *Promoting Change Through Brief Therapy in Christian Counseling* (Wheaton, IL: Tyndale, 1997), 197. In addition to the Oliver, Hasz, and Richburg book, see David G. Benner, *Strategic Pastoral Counseling: A Short-Term Structured Approach,* 2nd ed. (Grand Rapids, MI: Baker, 2003); and Charles Allen Kollar, *Solution-Focused Pastoral Counseling* (Grand Rapids, MI: Zondervan, 1997).

28 Worthington, *Hope-Focused Marriage Counseling.*

29 Everett L. Worthington, Jr., *Marriage Counseling with Christian Couples* (Downers Grove, IL: InterVarsity, 1989).

30 A good example is in the work of Louis and Melissa McBurney, who work together in counseling pastoral couples. The work is described in a book by Louis McBurney, *Counseling Christian Workers* (Waco, TX: Word, 1986).

31 Brian D. Doss, Lorelei E. Simpson, and Andrew Christensen, "Why Do Couples Seek Marital Therapy?" *Professional Psychology: Research and Practice* 35 (December 2004): 608–614.

32 A. D. Campaan, "Marital Contract Therapy," in *Baker Encyclopedia of Psychology*, ed. David G. Benner and Peter C. Hill, 2nd ed. (Grand Rapids, MI: Baker, 1999), 714–715.

33 Worthington et al., "Repairing the Emotional Bond."

34 The fallacy of the reasonable solution is not limited to marital counseling. It applies to a number of situations, including parent-teen conflicts, theological or political discussions, or any kind of interpersonal or racial tensions.

35 Some counselors videotape counseling sessions (with the counselees' prior written permission) and later use the tapes to show counselees how they interact and to teach them how they could interact more effectively.

36 Cameron Lee, "Esteeming Your Spouse," *Christian Counseling Today* 9 (2000): 28–31. The quotations are from page 31.

37 The list in this section is adapted from William Doherty, "Bad Couples Therapy."

38 Doss et al., "Why Do Couples Seek Marital Therapy?"

39 If you have a special interest in marriage counseling, see the excellent best-selling book by John M. Gottman and Nan Silver, *The Seven Principles for Making Marriage Work: A Practical Guide from the Country's Foremost Relationship Expert* (New York: Three Rivers Press, 2000).

40 Sybil Carrère and John Mordechai Gottman, "Predicting Divorce Among Newlyweds from the First Three Minutes of a Marital Conflict Discussion," *Family Process* 38 (Fall 1999): 293–301; Sybil Carrère, Kim T. Buehlman, John M. Gottman, James A. Coan, and Lionel Ruckstuhl, "Predicting Marital Stability and Divorce in Newlywed Couples," *Journal of Family Psychology* 14 (March 2000): 42–58; John Mordechai Gottman and Robert Wayne Levenson, "A Two-Factor Model for Predicting When a Couple Will Divorce: Exploratory Analyses Using 14-Year Longitudinal Data," *Family Process* 41 (Spring 2002): 83–96.

41 Gottman and Levenson, "A Two-Factor Model for Predicting When a Couple Will Divorce."

42 Carrère and Gottman, "Predicting Divorce."

43 From research by K. T. Buehlman and John M. Gottman, reported in J. M. Gottman,

What Predicts Divorce?: The Relationship Between Marital Processes and Marital Outcomes (Hillsdale, NJ: Erlbaum, 1994).

44   Alyson Fearnley Shapiro, John M. Gottman, and Sybil Carrère, "The Baby and the Marriage: Identifying Factors That Buffer Against Decline in Marital Satisfaction After the First Baby Arrives," *Journal of Family Psychology* 14 (March 2000): 59–70.

45   Worthington et al., "Repairing the Emotional Bond."

46   Kim Ryan and John Gottman, "Do Couples Education Programs Help?" *http://www.gottman.com/research/projects/couples/.*

47   Hillary Stout, "Why Weddings Really Do Matter," *The Wall Street Journal*, June 9, 2005.

48   Everett L. Worthington, Jr., "Forgiveness in Marriage: Research Findings and Therapeutic Applications," *Christian Counseling Today* 12 (2004): 60–61. Christian counselor-researcher Worthington has emerged as an expert on forgiveness, forgiveness research, and the role of forgiveness in marriage.

49   Ephesians 5:23–30.

30. Pregnancy Issues

1   1 Samuel 1:11.

2   1 Samuel 1:15–16.

3   Psalm 127:3–5.

4   Psalm 113:9.

5   The account of David's sin with Bathsheba is found in 2 Samuel 12. The quotation is from verse 12.

6   Matthew 1:19.

7   See, for example, Ephesians 5:3–5 and Colossians 3:5.

8   Deuteronomy 22:28; 2 Samuel 13:9–14; 1 Samuel 2:22.

9   Jeremiah 1:5.

10   Psalm 51:5.

11   I fully acknowledge that this is my conclusion and that others, including other committed believers, will disagree.

12   Genesis 29:20.

13   Genesis 35:16–19.

14   Most of the discussion in this chapter will focus on married heterosexual couples or an unmarried male and female who produce a pregnancy. Due in part to space limitations, we will not discuss issues such as the desire of homosexual couples to have a child, ethical issues concerning the implantation of a fertilized egg into the embryo of a surrogate mother, or similar controversial ethical issues relating to pregnancy or adoption.

15   Janet Takefman, "Psychological Factors in Male Factor Infertility," an article posted on the web site of the American Fertility Association (*www.theafa.org*), 2004. For a personal reflection on the adjustment to infertility, see Deborah Derrickson Kossmann, "Barren: Coming to Terms with a Lost Dream," *Psychotherapy Networker* 26 (July-August 2002): 40–45, 58.

16   Diana C. Parry and Kimberly Shinew, "The Constraining Impact of Infertility on Women's Leisure Lifestyles," *Leisure Sciences* 26 (July-September 2004): 295–308. Kimberly J. M. Imeson and A. McMurray, "Couples' Experiences of Infertility: A Phenomenological Study," *Journal of Advanced Nursing* 24 (1996): 1014–1022; J. Jirka, S. Schuett, and M. J. Foxall, "Loneliness and Social Support in Infertile Couples," *Journal of Obstetric, Gynecologic & Neonatal Nursing* 25 (1996): 55–60.

17   John Snarey, "Men Without Children," *Psychology Today* 22 (March 1988): 61–62.

18   Discussions of these alternatives can be found on the Internet. See also, Jane Hayes and Julie Miller, eds., *Inconceivable Conceptions: Psychotherapy, Fertility and the New Reproductive Technologies* (Philadelphia, PA: Brunner-Routledge, 2003).

19   F. van Balen and H. M. W. Boss, "Infertility, Culture, and Psychology in Worldwide Perspective," *Journal of Reproductive and Infant Psychology* 22 (November 2004): 245–247. For other social and psychological effects of infertility, see Kathryn J. Watkins and Tracy D. Baldo, "The Infertility Experience: Biopsychosocial Effects and Suggestions for Counselors," *Journal of Counseling and Development* 82 (Fall 2004): 394–420.

20   Abraham, Sarah's husband, had a child with Hagar; Jacob was able to impregnate Leah but not Rachel; and Hannah's husband Elkanah had children with Peninnah, his other wife, who, in turn, mocked and taunted Hannah and reduced her to tears because she had no children (1 Samuel 1:6–7).

21 This hope-despair continuum was one conclusion of an unpublished study by psychologist Betsy Haarmann reported by Beth Spring, *The Infertile Couple* (Elgin, IL: David C. Cook, 1987), 60–61.

22 J. C. Vance, J. M. Najman, M. J. Thearle, G. Embelton, W. J. Foster, and F. M. Boyle, "Psychological Changes in Parents Eight Months After the Loss of an Infant from Stillbirth, Neonatal Death, or Sudden Infant Death Syndrome: A Longitudinal Study," *Pediatrics* 96 (1995): 933–938.

23 This is the view of Shannon M. Bennett, Brett T. Litz, Barbara Sarnoff Lee, and Shira Maguel, "The Scope and Impact of Perinatal Loss: Current Status and Future Directions," *Professional Psychology: Research and Practice* 36 (April 2005): 180–187. For an older but in-depth and compassionate study of 304 parents who had experienced stillbirth, see J. DeFrain and Leona Martens, *Stillborn: The Invisible Death* (Lexington, MA: Lexington Books, 1986).

24 For in-depth discussion of each of these pregnancies, see Everett L. Worthington, Jr., *Counseling for Unplanned Pregnancy and Infertility* (Waco, TX: Word, 1987).

25 *Roe et al. v. Wade*, 93 S.C. 705 1973, at 730.

26 People on both sides of the abortion debate use emotional language that colors the interpretation of the facts. *Murder* is a good example of a loaded word. Pro-abortion supporters almost never use the term; pro-life people tend to use it more often. Even *pro-choice* and *pro-life* are emotional terms, each designed to present the different sides of the debate with more positive images.

27 Examples include Jennifer O'Neill, *You're Not Alone: Healing Through God's Grace After Abortion* (Deerfield Beach, FL: Faith Communications, 2005); Michael Mannion, *Post-Abortion Aftermath: A Comprehensive Consideration* (Lenham, MD: Sheed and Ward, 1994); Theresa Burke, *Forbidden Grief: The Unspoken Pain of Abortion* (San Francisco, CA: Acorn Books, 2002); and Erika Bachiochi, ed., *The Cost of Choice: Women Evaluate the Impact of Abortion* (San Francisco, CA: Encounter Books, 2004), which is a collection of essays, not necessarily written by Christians, but each presenting evidence that legal abortion has in fact harmed women—socially, medically, psychologically, and culturally.

28 See, for example, A. Kero, U. Högberg, and A. Laloiths, "Wellbeing and Mental Growth—Long-Term Effects of Legal Abortion," *Social Science and Medicine* 58 (June 2004): 2559–2569. These authors conclude that "The study shows that women generally are able to make the complex decision to have an abortion *without suffering any subsequent regret or negative effects*, as ascertained at the 1–year follow-up" (italics added). Somewhat different are the findings of another research group that reported no change in self-esteem following abortion. In fact, there was a reduction in distress in many women following an abortion, although "up to around 30% of women are still experiencing emotional problems after a month. . . . Women due to have an abortion are more anxious and distressed" prior to the abortion, "but in the long term they do no worse psychologically." Even so, anxiety symptoms are common and "there has been increasing understanding of abortion as a potential trauma." This is from Zoë Bradshaw and Pauline Slade, "The Effects of Included Abortion on Emotional Experiences and Relationships: A Critical Review of the Literature," *Clinical Psychology Review* 23 (December 2003): 929–958.

29 Lisa Rubin and Nancy Felipe Russo, "Abortion and Mental Health: What Therapists Need to Know," *Women & Therapy* 27 (2004): 69–90.

30 This figure is reported by Bradshaw and Slade, "The Effects of Included Abortion."

31 Susan Dyer Layer, Cleora Roberts, Kelli Wild, and Jan Walters, "Postabortion Grief: Evaluating the Possible Efficacy of a Spiritual Group Intervention," *Research on Social Work Practice* 14 (September 2004): 344–350; Rosanna F. Hess, "Dimensions of Women's Long-Term Postabortion Experience," *The American Journal of Maternal/Child Nursing* 29 (May-June 2004): 193–198; and Sheila Faure and Helene Loxton, "Anxiety, Depression and Self-Efficacy Levels of Women Undergoing First Trimester Abortion," *South African Journal of Psychology* 33 (March 2003): 28–38. The authors of this latter study found that postabortion trauma appears more common in women who have had pre-abortion depression and other psychological problems. For a study of men's reaction to abortion (most had no negative effects), see A. Kero and Ann Lalos, "Reactions and Reflections of Men, 4 and 12 Months Post-Abortion," *Journal of Psychosomatic Obstetrics & Gynecology* 25 (June 2004): 135–143.

32 Judith E. Belsky, Livia S. Wan, and Gordon W. Douglas, "Abortion," in *Comprehensive Textbook of Psychiatry/IV*, ed. Harold I. Kaplan and Benjamin J. Sadock (Baltimore:

Williams & Wilkins, 1985), 1052–1056. See also Antero Myhrman, Paula Rantakallio, Matti Isohanni, and Peter Jones, "Unwantedness of a Pregnancy and Schizophrenia in a Child," *British Journal of Psychiatry* 169 (November 1996): 637–640. Some research suggests that mothers who did not want to have children were less careful to avoid harmful influences during the pregnancy. This, in turn, impacted the health of the children. Susan Altfeld, Arden Handler, Dee Burton, and Leatrice Berman, "Unwantedness of a Child and Prenatal Health Behaviors," *Women and Health* 26 (1997): 29–43.

33   The conclusions from this paragraph are taken from Shannon Bennett et al., "The Scope and Impact of Perinatal Loss," and from P. M. Hughes and S. Riches, "Psychological Aspects of Perinatal Loss," *Current Opinion in Obstetrics and Gynecology* 15 (2003): 107–111.

34   Cathy Maker and Jane Ogden, "The Miscarriage Experience: More Than Just a Trigger to Psychological Morbidity?" *Psychology and Health* 18 (June 2003): 403–415.

35   D. Needham, "Sudden Infant Death Syndrome," in *Baker Encyclopedia of Psychology*, ed. David G. Benner and Peter C. Hill, 2nd ed. (Grand Rapids, MI: Baker, 1999), 1180–1181. According to the SIDS Network (*www.sids-network.org*), in the United States about 7,000 children die from SIDS every year, about one child every half hour.

36   This is a complicated process in which the wife is given hormones to stimulate production of more than one egg, the eggs are "harvested," then they are mixed in the laboratory with sperm from the husband or donor before being returned to the mother's uterus.

37   They are discussed in a more factual but sensitive way by Takefman, "Psychological Issues in Male Factor Infertility." See also Michelle Buckman, *A Piece of the Sky* (Colorado Springs, CO: Cook Communications, 2005); Kathryn Mackel, *The Surrogate* (Nashville, TN: Thomas Nelson 2004); and Edwin Hui, *At the Beginning of Life: Dilemmas on Theological Bioethics* (Downers Grove, IL: InterVarsity, 2002).

38   Resolve is the National Infertility Association. It is a good place to begin an Internet search. The address is *www.resolve.org.*

39   The stresses associated with various types of pregnancy issues are cited by Pamela A. Geller, "Pregnancy as a Stressful Life Event," *CNS Spectrums* 9 (March 2004): 188–197. Writing in technical language, Geller notes that "Healthcare providers should be sensitive to the distress and anxiety experienced by many women and their families as a consequence of these adverse events [including infertility, unplanned pregnancy, fear of childbirth, and pregnancy loss] and the stressful challenge of any consequential decision-making, as well as stressors in their broader life context that can further exacerbate their distress, and make mental health referrals appropriate."

40   Matthew 19:13–15.

41   The final statement was accepted by most of the parties involved, but some accepted it reluctantly, and a few felt that they could not give their approval. When the conference ended, I think we all agreed to disagree and to respect each other's conclusions. The statement was as follows: "We acknowledge that Christians differ in their views concerning the time when personhood begins, but we agree that God has admonished us to choose life instead of death, and has set penalties for those who would, even accidentally, cause a pregnant woman to be injured in such a way that an unborn child is harmed. We believe that compassion for distressed mothers and families, and concern for unborn children, require us to offer spiritual guidance and material solace consistent with the teachings of God's Word. We urge the Church to influence the social-moral climate in which unintended pregnancies occur. We see no grounds on which Christians who are concerned for all human life and for the well-being of the family can condone the free and easy practice of abortion as it now exists in our society. At the same time, we exhort the Church to show compassion for those who suffer because of the abortion experience (Exodus 21:22; Psalm 8; Psalm 139:13–18; Jeremiah 1:4,5; Luke 1:39–66; 10:30–37)."

42   These can be found through the Internet. As a start, go to *www.pregnancycenters.org* or to *www.crisispregnancy.com.*

43   I am grateful to Gregory Jon Smith of Lutherans for Life who suggested this example in correspondence following the first edition of this book.

44   Some writers who have a secular perspective nevertheless acknowledge the importance of spiritual help in pre-abortion and postabortion counseling. For example, the paper by Susan Dyer Layer et al., "Postabortion Grief," states that more than 80 percent of the people studied "reported their religious beliefs and the spiritual intervention played a

strong to very strong role" in helping with postabortion grief. See also Rosanna F. Hess, "Dimensions of Women's Long-Term Postabortion Experience."

45   Shannon M. Bennett et al., "The Scope and Impact of Perinatal Loss," 184.

46   Lise Jind, "Parents' Adjustment to Late Abortion, Stillbirth or Infant Death: The Role of Causal Attributions," *Scandinavian Journal of Psychology* 44 (September 2003): 383–394.

47   2 Samuel 13:15.

48   Genesis 2:19.

49   Numerous people have written about suffering, including the kinds of suffering that have been the focus of this chapter. One book was written by a colleague on the faculty of a theological graduate school where I taught for many years. See John S. Feinberg, *Where Is God?: A Personal Story of Finding God in Grief and Suffering* (Nashville, TN: Broadman-Holman, 2004).

50   Viktor Frankl, *Man's Search for Meaning* (New York: Pocket Books, 1963). Frankl's approach to counseling, known as logotherapy, is discussed from a Christian perspective by Paul R. Welter, *Counseling and the Search for Meaning* (Waco TX: Word, 1987).

31. Family Issues

1   Mary Pipher, "My Most Spectacular Failure," *Family Therapy Networker* 24 (November-December 2000): 28–31, 63. All quotations are taken from these pages.

2   Gary R. Collins, *Family Shock: Keeping Families Strong in the Midst of Earthshaking Change* (Wheaton, IL: Tyndale House, 1995), 5.

3   Adapted from Collins, *Family Shock*, 85. Shortly after this book appeared in print, the publisher summarized what I had written in this list, prepared a colorful poster of truths on the family, and distributed 2,000 copies free to families and counselors. Apparently, many of these framed posters appear in homes, churches, and counselor waiting rooms. To my knowledge, copies are no longer available. The poster featured the outstanding work of calligrapher Tim Botts, and I continue to be grateful to Tyndale House Publishers for giving me a framed copy of the original.

4   For a good introductory overview of family therapy, see Peter Fraenkel, "Whatever Happened to Family Therapy?" *Psychotherapy Networker* 29 (May-June 2005): 30–39, 70. A book-length history is found in Lynn Hoffman, *Family Therapy: An Intimate History* (New York: Norton, 2001). New books appear frequently, most written for professional therapists. Examples include Howard A. Liddle, Daniel A. Santisteban, Ronald F. Levant, and James H. Bray, eds., *Family Psychology: Science-Based Interventions* (Washington, DC: American Psychological Association, 2002); Susan H. McDonald, Don-David Lusterman, and Carol L. Philpot, eds., *Casebook for Integrating Family Therapy: An Ecosystemic Approach* (Washington, DC: American Psychological Association, 2001); Monica McGoldrick, Joe Giordano, and Nydia Garcia-Preto, *Ethnicity and Family Therapy*, 3rd ed. (New York: Guildord, 2005); Lorna L. Hecker and Joseph L. Wetchler, *An Introduction to Marriage and Family Therapy* (New York: Haworth, 2003); Herbert Goldenberg and Irene Goldenberg, *Family Therapy: An Overview* (Belmont, CA: Wadsworth, 2003); and Thomas L. Sexton, Gerald R. Weeks, and Michael S. Robbins, eds., *Handbook of Family Therapy: The Science and Practice of Working with Families and Couples* (Philadelphia, PA: Brunner-Routledge, 2003).

5   1 Kings 1:5–6.

6   1 Samuel 2.

7   It should be noted, however, that many of the biblical passages that we have cited in this section appear to focus less on family dynamics and more on the ways in which God works through key men and women.

8   There is a brief mention of widows and orphans in James 1:27.

9   Colossians 3:18–21.

10   See Ephesians 5:22–6:4; Ephesians has 16 of 155 verses devoted to the family.

11   In 1 Thessalonians 2:7–12 Paul gives an illustration from the home. First Timothy mentions the care of widows and makes a statement about Timothy's home. In Titus, there is an exhortation to wives and mothers.

12   Ephesians 5:25.

13   Ephesians 6:4. Proverbs 22:6 is one of several Old Testament verses on child-rearing.

14   Gene A. Getz, *Measure of a Family* (Ventura, CA: Regal, 1976), 13.

15   Getz, *Measure of a Family*, 20. I would add that much of the Old Testament can be applied to modern families as well.

16 Adapted from Collins, *Family Shock*, 15–32.

17 Perhaps this is outdated, and probably this would not apply to all countries, but these were the four issues that brought most people to counselors according to a survey conducted several years ago. See George A. Rekers, *Counseling Families* (Waco, TX: Word, 1988).

18 This model originated with Reuben Hill, *Families Under Stress: Adjustment to the Crises of War Separation and Reunion* (New York: Harper, 1949). A reprint edition was published in 1971 by Greenwood Press Reprints. For a fuller description of the model, see M. Stanton, "Family Stress Theory," in *Baker Encyclopedia of Psychology*, ed. David G. Benner and Peter C. Hill, 2nd ed. (Grand Rapids, MI: Baker, 1999), 440–442.

19 Some of the following issues originally appeared in a list of "snag points" proposed by Frank Pittman. According to Pittman, snag points are attitudes and behaviors that entangle families in ways that hinder flexibility and make readjustment more difficult. See Frank S. Pittman III, *Turning Points: Treating Families in Transition and Crisis* (New York: Norton, 1987).

20 Ibid., 22.

21 Stanton, "Family Stress Theory," 441.

22 Florence W. Kaslow, "Families and Family Psychology at the Millennium: Intersecting Crossroads," *American Psychologist* 56 (January 2001): 37–46.

23 Janine Roberts, "One Heart for Three Families: The Complexities of Stepfamily Life Can be Dizzying," *Psychotherapy Networker* 26 (May/June 2002): 96, 95.

24 Kaslow, "Families and Family Psychology." The other influences are the search for identity: balancing I, thou, and we; different family branches relocating to different countries and thus creating a massive uprooting; the adoption of foreign-born children; and the increasing numbers of gay and lesbian individuals and couples who are open about their sexual preferences.

25 Adapted from Patricia A. Boyer and Ronnald J. Jeffrey, *A Guide for the Family Therapist* (New York: Aronson, 1984).

26 W. J. Doherty, "Boundaries Between Parent and Family Education and Family Therapy: The Levels of Family Involvement Model," *Family Relations* 44 (1995): 353–358. See also Dale R. Hawley and Carla Dahl, "Using the Levels of Family Involvement Model with Religious Professionals," *Journal of Psychology and Theology* 28 (Summer 2000): 87–98. In writing the next five paragraphs, I have drawn heavily from the Hawley and Dahl article.

27 This list is adapted from Gerald Caplan, *Support Systems and Community Mental Health* (New York: Behavioral Publications, 1974).

28 Douglas H. Sprenkle, ed., *Effectiveness Research in Marriage and Family Therapy* (Alexandria, VA: AAMFT, 2004). The quotation, from a review of an earlier edition of the book, is written by Jay Lebow, "Family Therapy Scorecard: Research Shows the Family Approach Is Often the Treatment of Choice," *Psychotherapy Networker* 27 (January-February 2003): 73–75.

29 Pittman, *Turning Points*, 34.

30 Ibid.

31 I confess that I have written one or two family books myself, and so has my agent, the amazing man who helps me get my books published. See Robert Wolgemuth, *The Most Important Place on Earth: What a Christian Home Looks Like and How to Build One* (Nashville, TN: Nelson, 2004).

32 This is the first of a list of family traits that was developed from a survey by an author who was quoted widely a few years ago. See Dolores Curran, *Traits of a Healthy Family* (Minneapolis: Winston Press, 1983). Other traits on the list include develop a sense of play and humor, share responsibility, have a sense of right and wrong, have a strong sense of family in which rituals and traditions abound, and admit and seek help with problems.

33 This is from a list of well-proven components of "healthy family functioning," developed by Froma Walsh, ed., *Normal Family Processes*, 2nd ed. (New York: Guilford, 1993), 58–59.

34 This is from an empirically derived list reported by Nick Stinnett and John DeFrain, *Secrets of Strong Families* (Boston MA: Little, Brown, 1985). These writers conclude that strong families are characterized by commitment, mutual appreciation, communication, time together, spiritual commitment, and coping ability.

35 Paul Faulkner, *Achieving Success Without Failing Your Family* (West Monroe, LA: Howard Publishing, 1994).

36   Charles M. Sell, *Family Ministry*, 2nd ed. (Grand Rapids, MI: Zondervan, 1995). See also Diana R. Garland, *Family Ministry: A Comprehensive Guide* (Downers Grove, IL: InterVarsity, 1999).

32. Divorce and Remarriage

1   The story of Larry and Jennifer is adapted from a case presented by David A. Thompson, *Counseling and Divorce* (Dallas: Word, 1989), 65–68. For a different case but with remarkably similar dynamics and problems, see Janine Roberts, "One Heart for Three Families: The Complexities of Stepfamily Life Can Be Dizzying," *Psychotherapy Networker* 26 (May–June 2002): 96, 95

2   The example of the six women meeting at breakfast and the summary of their list is adapted from Georgia Shaffer, "What I Wish I'd Known Before I Got Divorced," *Marriage Partnership* 22 (Summer 2005): 46. The article is located at *http:/www.christianitytoday.com/mp/2005/002/7.46.html.*

3   Ibid.

4   Adapted from Les and Leslie Parrott, *When Bad Things Happen to Good Marriages* (Grand Rapids, MI: Zondervan, 2001), 17.

5   Ibid.

6   These categories were suggested by Cyril J. Barber, "Marriage, Divorce, and Remarriage: A Review of Relevant Religious Literature, 1973–1983," *Journal of Psychology and Theology* 12 (Fall 1984): 170–177. This article is more than twenty years old, but it still would appear to be useful today.

7   Genesis 2:18–25; Matthew 19:5; Mark 10:2–12; 1 Corinthians 7:39.

8   Matthew 5:31–32; 19:3–9.

9   Matthew 19:9; Luke 16:18. Perhaps it needs to be added that forgiveness extends to those who commit adultery; adultery is not the unpardonable sin. Certainly, however, this does deemphasize the sinfulness of adultery.

10   Apparently, this also was the opinion of Martin Luther. According to one team of biblical scholars, "Luther states emphatically that Christ allowed divorce only in the case of adultery and desertion. The Christian who is deserted by an unbelieving partner may marry again as long as the future husband is a Christian. From this he concludes that the innocent party in any divorce case be allowed to marry again. . . . His starting point is that only death can dissolve the marriage tie and leave the partner free to marry again. The act of adultery, however, makes the offender as dead in his relationship both to God and to his partner." From William A. Heth and Gordon J. Wenham, *Jesus and Divorce* (Nashville, TN: Nelson, 1984), 79–80.

11   1 Corinthians 7:15.

12   Malachi 2:16.

13   Matthew 19:9.

14   1 Corinthians 7:8, 32–38.

15   Malachi 2:16; Exodus 20:14; Matthew 5:27–28.

16   1 John 1:9; Matthew 6:14–15.

17   In 1 Timothy 3:2, 12 and elsewhere, we read that the church leader ("overseer") must be "the husband of but one wife." The New Living Translation clarifies this by translating the phrase, "faithful to his wife." Biblical scholars differ in their interpretation of this passage. Most agree that this is not intended to limit leadership positions to married men. Some have argued that remarried men are excluded from leadership, even if their first wives have died and they have remarried. Remarriage under such circumstances is not forbidden elsewhere, and in 1 Timothy 5:14 it is encouraged. Presumably, therefore, a person who remarries after the death of a mate can hold a position of leadership. As we have seen, under some circumstances, divorce and remarriage also appear to be permitted for believers. I agree with those who conclude that "faithful to his wife" means that the leader must be a loyal and faithful Christian husband. Presumably, this includes some believers who have remarried following divorce.

18   Romans 6:1–2; 12:1–2; 13:14; 1 Peter 2:11.

19   David R. Miller, *Counseling Families After Divorce: Wholeness for the Broken Family* (Dallas: Word, 1994), 115–117.

20   1 Corinthians 7:16 sometimes is used to support or to justify this decision.

21   See especially chapters 29 and 31.

22 Frank S. Pittman III, *Turning Points: Treating Families in Transition and Crisis* (New York: Norton, 1987), chap. 7, "Infidelity: The Secret Insanity."

23 Frank Pittman, *Private Lies: Infidelity and the Betrayal of Intimacy* (New York: Norton, 1990).

24 For an excellent Christian perspective on affairs, written by a Christian psychologist, see Henry A. Virkler, *Broken Promises: Understanding, Healing and Preventing Affairs in Christian Marriages* (Dallas: Word, 1992).

25 Judges 21:25.

26 Thompson, *Counseling and Divorce*, 17.

27 Jessie Bernard, *The Future of Marriage* (New Haven, CT: Yale University Press, 1972).

28 The reference to Bernard's book and the quotation are found in Glenn T. Stanton, "The Social Experiment That Failed," *Christianity Today* 45 (February 5, 2001): 73.

29 Linda Wait and Maggie Gallagher, *The Case for Marriage: Why Married People Are Happier, Healthier, and Better Off Financially* (New York: Broadway, 2001).

30 See, for example, Glenn T. Stanton, *Why Marriage Matters: Reasons to Believe in Marriage in a Postmodern Society* (Colorado Springs: NavPress/Piñon, 1997).

31 This is a classic study by Judith S. Wallerstein, Julia M. Lewis, and Sandra Blakeslee, *The Unexpected Legacy of Divorce: A 25 Year Landmark Study* (New York: Hyperion, 2001). For an interview with Judith Wallerstein, see Rob Waters, "The Thirty Years' War: Judith Wallerstein and the Great Divorce Debate," *Psychotherapy Networker* 25 (March-April 2001): 40–50, 52.

32 In the first half of his book, *Counseling Families After Divorce*, David R. Miller gives many examples of children and adults who are impacted by divorce. Even when there is no divorce but children live in the midst of marital conflict, there is an increased risk of numerous psychological and other problems. This is the conclusion of Mari L. Clements, "For the Sake of the Children: Effects of Marital Conflict in Intact Families," *Journal of Psychology and Christianity* 23 (Winter 2004): 58–62.

33 T. Kempton, "Divorce," in *Baker Encyclopedia of Psychology*, ed. David G. Benner and Peter C. Hill, 2nd ed. (Grand Rapids, MI: Baker, 1999), 359–362.

34 This process is described in more detail by Diane Vaughan, *Uncoupling: Turning Points in Intimate Relationships* (New York: Vintage, 1990).

35 Archibald D. Hart, *Helping Children Survive Divorce* (Dallas, TX: Word, 1996).

36 This figure is cited in an excellent and helpful book by Les and Leslie Parrott, *Saving Your Second Marriage Before It Starts: Nine Questions to Ask Before (and After) You Remarry* (Grand Rapids, MI: Zondervan, 2001).

37 This quotation and much of the information in this chapter is adapted from a report written by Sue Shellenberger, "Another Argument for Marriage: How Divorce Can Put Your Health at Risk," *The Wall Street Journal*, June 16, 2005. The article summarizes research on the long-term health effects of divorce, done by Linda Waite from the University of Chicago and Duke University's Mary Elizabeth Hughes. The study of over 8,000 people was conducted by different researchers and presented on June 23, 2005, at a conference of the Coalition for Marriage, Family and Couples Education, a Washington, DC, nonprofit organization. Some readers may question the validity of a newspaper article as a source for the information presented in this small section of the chapter, but the *Wall Street Journal* is one of the most credible of American newspapers, and the article is a compilation of recently reported scientific research findings.

38 Could there be a different explanation for the health problems of divorced people? Researchers Waite and Hughes (see footnote 37) acknowledge that the poorer health of divorced people may have something to do with the health of people before they got married. It is possible that people who are healthier and more robust in the first place will be more likely to form lasting, happy marriages. Less healthy people make less healthy choices, so they are more likely to experience divorce with the resulting health problems. Research exploring this alternative explanation has found mixed results. And whatever the causes, there is significant evidence that divorced people, including many who have remarried, have a greater number of health problems than people who have not divorced.

39 Elizabeth Marquardt, *Between Two Worlds: The Inner Lives of Children of Divorce* (New York: Crown, 2005).

40 Reported by Tamar Lewis in "Poll Says Even Quiet Divorces Affect Children's Paths," *New York Times*, November 5, 2005.

41 Jerome Price, "Custody Wars: Strategies for Handling Postdivorce Conflict," *Psychotherapy Networker* 27 (January-February 2003): 59–65.

42 James L. Framo, "The Friendly Divorce," *Psychology Today* 11 (February 1978): 77. If the couple described by this counselor is experiencing a friendly divorce, it is scary to think what an unfriendly divorce might be like.

43 Please see chapter 38; also Judson J. Swihart and Gerald C. Richardson, *Counseling in Times of Crisis* (Waco, TX: Word, 1987).

44 Mel Krantzler, *Creative Divorce: A New Opportunity for Personal Growth* (New York: M. Evans, 1974), 103–116.

45 There is a lot of information on the Internet if you type in "divorce mediation." Of course, many of the mediators and their viewpoints do not come from a Christian perspective. See also Jay Folberg, Ann L. Milne, and Peter Salem, eds., *Divorce and Family Mediation Models, Techniques and Applications* (New York: Guilford, 2004); Marilyn S. McKnight and Stephen K. Erickson, *Mediating Divorce: A Step-by-Step Manual* (San Francisco: Jossey-Bass, 2002); and Corrine J. A. Beck and Bruce D. Sales, *Family Mediation: Facts, Myths, and Future Prospects* (Washington, DC: American Psychological Association, 2001). For examples of research on the effectiveness of mediation, see Robert E. Emery, David Sbarra, and Tara Grover, "Divorce Mediation: Research and Reflections," *Family Court Review* 43 (January 2005): 22–37; and Joan B. Kelly, "Family Mediation Research: Is There Empirical Support for the Field?" *Conflict Resolution Quarterly* 22 (Fall-Winter 2004): 3–35.

46 "A Child's Eye View of Divorce," *London Telegraph*, July 7, 2005.

47 Victoria Bream and Ann Buchanan, "Distress Among Children Whose Separated or Divorced Parents Cannot Agree on Arrangements for Them," *British Journal of Social Work* 33 (March 2003): 227–238

48 Many of these suggestions are adapted from a book that appeared more than thirty years ago, but the guidelines still appear to be relevant. From Jim Smoke, *Growing Through Divorce* (Eugene, OR: Harvest House, 1976), 60–66.

49 Among the studies of older children of divorce are those by Jerome L. Short, "The Effects of Parental Divorce During Childhood on College Students," *Journal of Divorce and Remarriage* 38 (2002): 143–156; and Sarah Corrie, "Working Therapeutically with Adult Stepchildren: Identifying the Needs of a Neglected Client Group," *Journal of Divorce & Remarriage* 37 (2002): 135–150.

50 Clements, "For the Sake of the Children."

51 Two books are especially recommended for couples facing a second marriage: Les and Leslie Parrott, *Saving Your Second Marriage Before It Starts*; and Thomas Whiteman and Randy Petersen, *Fresh Start: 8 Principles for Starting Over When a Relationship Doesn't Work* (Wheaton, IL: Tyndale, 1997).

52 Bridget Freisthler, Gloria Messick Svare, and Sydney Harrison-Jay, "It Was the Best of Times, It Was the Worst of Times: Young Adult Stepchildren Talk About Growing Up in a Stepfamily," *Journal of Divorce & Remarriage* 38 (2003): 83–102.

53 Emily B. Visher and John S. Visher, *Old Loyalties, New Ties: Therapeutic Strategies with Stepfamilies* (New York: Brunner/Mazel, 1988). See also Elaine Fantle Shimberg, *Blending Families: A Guide for Parents, Stepparents, and Everyone Building a Successful New Family* (New York: Berkley Publishing Group, 1999); David S. Chedekel and Karen O'Connell, *The Blended Family Sourcebook: A Guide to Negotiating Change* (New York: McGraw-Hill, 2002). The following books are known to be written by authors with a Christian perspective: Edward Douglas and Sharon Douglas, *The Blended Family: Achieving Peace and Harmony in the Christian Home* (Franklin, TN: Providence House, 2000); Jim Smoke, *7 Keys to a Healthy Blended Family* (Eugene, OR: Harvest House, 2004); and Terri Clark, *Tying the Family Knot: Meeting the Challenges of a Blended Family* (Nashville, TN: Broadman and Holman, 2004).

54 Matthew 7:3.

55 James 5:16.

56 Shortly after this paragraph was written, my friend took the exam again and passed.

33. Mental Disorders

1 Adapted from Sara Solovitch, "The Shocking Tale of Andy Behrman," *BP Magazine* 1 (Summer 2005): 30–34. You can learn more about Andy Behrman, his life, his book, and the condition of bipolar disorder at *www.electroboy.com*.

2 There a number of excellent Internet sources that provide information on mental illness.

These web sites are in many countries and include *www.nami.com* (for the National Alliance for the Mentally Ill, which is an advocacy group) and *www.nimh.nih.gov*, which will get you to the National Institute for Mental Health.

3 For example, see Mary Sykes Wylie, "The Politics of PTSD: How a Controversial Diagnosis Battled Its Way into DSM," *Psychotherapy Networker* 28 (January-February 2004): 36–38. For a discussion of the issues surrounding classification, see Bruce E. Bonecutter, "Classification of Mental Disorders," in *Baker Encyclopedia of Psychology*, ed. David G. Benner, and Peter C. Hill, 2nd ed. (Grand Rapids, MI: Baker, 1999), 203–207; or Benjamin J. Sadock and Harold I. Kaplan, "Classification of Mental Disorders," in *Comprehensive Textbook of Psychiatry/VI*, ed. Harold Kaplan and Benjamin J. Sadock (Baltimore, MD: Williams and Wilkins, 1995), 671–692.

4 American Psychiatric Association, *Diagnostic and Statistical Manual of Mental Disorders DSM-IV-TR (Text Revision)*(Washington, DC: American Psychiatric Association, 1994).

5 Information about various mental disorders can always be found on the Internet. In addition, major textbooks on abnormal psychology or psychopathology can be helpful. See, for example, James E. Maddux and Barbara A. Winstead, eds., *Psychopathology: Foundations for a Contemporary Understanding* (Mahwah, NJ: Lawrence Erlbaum Associates, 2004); Henry E. Adams and Patricia B. Sutker, *Comprehensive Handbook of Psychopathology*, 3rd ed. (Austin, TX: Plenum US, 2001); Theodore Millon, Paul H. Blaney, and Roger D. Davis, eds., *Oxford Textbook of Psychopathology* (New York: Oxford University Press, 1999); and Jerrold S. Maxmen and Nicholas G. Ward, *Essential Psychopathology and Its Treatment*, 2nd ed. (New York: Norton, 1995).

6 Romans 5:12, 21; 1:21, 28.

7 Romans 3:23–24; 6:23; John 10:10. In this paragraph I have drawn on pages 19 and 20 of Mark A. Yarhouse, Richard E. Butman, and Barrett W. McRay, *Modern Psychopathologies: A Comprehensive Christian Approach* (Downers Grove, IL: InterVarsity, 2005). This is not a textbook of psychopathology so much as a Christian approach to the various forms of psychopathology. It is highly recommended. Although it is not overtly Christian, one psychologist has written a thought-provoking book that is critical of clinical psychology and other forms of counseling because they have tried to make psychopathology and treatment into something experimental, quantitative, coldly scientific, and amoral. I would argue, instead, that the understanding and treatment of mental disorders require "moral engagement" with a moral problem. See Ronald B. Miller, *Facing Human Suffering: Psychology and Psychotherapy as Moral Engagement* (Washington, DC: American Psychological Association, 2004).

8 Matthew 9:36; John 10:11–16; 1 Peter 2:25; Psalm 23.

9 1 Peter 5:2.

10 1 Samuel 21:13.

11 Daniel 4:31–34.

12 Romans 26:24.

13 Demon possession is discussed further in chapter 41.

14 The Bible does not give detailed teaching about suicide; see Thomas D. Kennedy, "Suicide and the Silence of Scripture," *Christianity Today* 31 (March 20, 1987): 22–23.

15 According to psychologist Laura Carstensen from Stanford University, "There's a lot of evidence suggesting that older people are doing very well. Our challenge is to figure out what they're doing and how they're doing it." See Etienne Benson, "Older and Untroubled," *Monitor on Psychology* 34 (June 2003): 24–25.

16 Marsh, "Serious Emotional Disturbance in Children and Adolescents."

17 Karen Kersting, "Men and Depression: Battling Stigma Through Public Education," *Monitor on Psychology* 36 (June 2005): 66–68.

18 2 Corinthians 11:27–28.

19 Ephesians 6:10–12.

20 Charlotte Huff, "Where Personality Goes Awry," *Monitor on Psychology* 35 (March 2004): 42–44.

21 N. Solkoff, P. Gray, and S. Keill, "Which Veterans Develop Posttraumatic Stress Disorders?" *Journal of Clinical Psychology* 42 (1986): 687–698.

22 Etienne Benson, "Beyond 'Urbancentrism,'" *Monitor on Psychology* 34 (June 2003): 54–55.

23 For more information, see H. M. Lefcourt, "Durability and Impact of the Locus of Control Construct," *Psychological Bulletin* 112 (1992): 411–414; and G. L. Welton, "Locus of Control," in *Baker Encyclopedia of Psychology*, ed. David G. Benner and Peter C. Hill, 2nd ed.

(Grand Rapids, MI: Baker, 1999), 695–696.

24   Jan Walker, *Control and the Psychology of Health: Theory, Measurement and Applications* (New York: Open University Press, 2001).

25   Christopher Petersen, Steven F. Maier, and Martin E. P. Seligman, *Learned Helplessness: A Theory for the Age of Personal Control* (New York: Oxford University Press, 1995); and Martin Seligman, *Learned Optimism: How to Change Your Mind and Your Life* (Northampton, MA: Free Press, 1998).

26   G. L. Welton, A. G. Adkins, S. L. Ingle, and W. A. Dixon, "God Control: The Fourth Dimension," *Journal of Psychology and Theology* 24 (Spring 1996): 13.

27   Adapted from Bruce Narramore, "The Concept of Responsibility in Psychopathology and Psychotherapy," *Journal of Psychology and Theology* 13 (Summer 1985): 91–96.

28   Matthew 23:25–38.

29   1 Peter 5:8.

30   Without doubt the two most prominent challenges came from a former president of the American Psychological Association and a very prominent psychiatrist. See O. Hobart Mowrer, "Sin, the Lesser of Two Evils," *American Psychologist* 15 (May 1960): 301–304; and Karl Menninger, *Whatever Became of Sin?* (New York: Hawthorn, 1973).

31   For two excellent discussions of the role of sin and psychopathology, see chapter 4 in Yarhouse et al., *Modern Psychopathologies*; and Mark McMinn, *Why Sin Matters: The Surprising Relationship Between Our Sin and God's Grace* (Wheaton, IL: Tyndale House, 2004).

32   David Satcher, "Mental Health: A Report of the Surgeon General: Executive Summary," *Professional Psychology: Research and Practice* 31 (February 2000): 5–13.

33   For a closer look at stigma and its impact see Patrick W. Corrigan, ed., *On the Stigma of Mental Illness: Practical Strategies for Research and Social Change* (Washington, DC: American Psychological Association, 2005).

34   *www.apa.org/ppo/pcmharticles.html*. Includes the President's New Freedom Commission on Mental Health background information, links, and full-text articles. See also Zak Stambor, "Reforming Mental Health Care," *Monitor on Psychology* 36 (October 2005): 28–29.

35   Conclusions like this go counter to the beliefs of some Christian counselors who maintain that mental disorders result from sin and sinful behaviors. We have tried to show in earlier paragraphs that sin is at the basis of all human problems. Often deliberate sinful actions are involved, but a more complete explanation would suggest that in this fallen world where sin is very prevalent, mental disorders have a number of causes, including deliberate sin, the influence of stress and past precipitating conditions, and the impact of physical malfunctioning.

36   Marilyn Elias, "Mental Illness: Surprising, Disturbing Findings," *USA Today*, June 7, 2005.

37   Sylvia Nasar, *A Beautiful Mind: The Life of Mathematical Genius and Nobel Laureate John Nash* (New York: Simon & Schuster, 2001).

38   See the encouraging report on schizophrenia written by Patrick A. McGuire, "New Hope for People with Schizophrenia," *Monitor on Psychology* 31 (February 2000): 24–28; also Philip D. Harvey, *Schizophrenia in Late Life: Aging Effects on Symptoms and Course of Illness* (Washington, DC: American Psychological Association, 2005).

39   R. Walter Heinrichs, "The Primacy of Cognition in Schizophrenia," *American Psychologist* 60 (April 2005): 229–242. See also Michael Foster Green, *Schizophrenia Revealed: From Neurons to Social Interactions* (New York: Norton, 2003).

40   A series of articles all under the title "Fighting Phobias" appeared in one issue of *Monitor on Psychology*. See, for example, Lea Winerman, "A Virtual Cure," *Monitor on Psychology* 36 (July-August 2005): 87–89.

41   For a discussion of how families contribute to mental disorders and are involved in their treatment, see Jennifer Hudson and Ron Rapee, eds., *Psychopathology and the Family* (San Diego: Elsevier, 2005).

42   Kenneth G. Terkelsen, "The Evolution of Family Responses to Mental Illness Through Time," in *Families of the Mentally Ill: Coping and Adaptation,* ed. Agnes B. Hatfield and Harriet P. Lefley (New York: Guilford, 1987), 151–166.

43   Because these appear frequently, it is wise to look in bookstores or on the Internet to find such books. Families who care for a person with a mental disorder often can recommend the best and latest books to others. One of the better books is by a former First Lady, Rosalynn Carter, and Susan Ma Colant, *Helping Someone with Mental Illness: A Compassionate Guide for Family, Friends, and Caregivers* (New York: Three Rivers Press, 1999). For a very good focus on the families of schizophrenics, see E. Torrey, *Surviving Schizo-*

phrenia: A Manual for Families, Consumers and Providers, 4th ed. (New York: Harper Perennial, 2001).

44 Some suggesting in the following list are adapted from LeRoy Spaniol, "Coping Strategies of Family Caregivers," in Hatfield and Lefley, *Families of the Mentally Ill,* 213–214.

45 Benita Walton-Moss, Linda Gerson, and Linda Rose, "Effects of Mental Illness on Family Quality of Life," *Issues in Mental Health Nursing* 26 (July 2005): 627–642.

46 Julie Godress, Salih Ozgul, Cathy Owen, and Leanne Foley-Evans, "Grief Experiences of Parents Whose Children Suffer from Mental Illness," *Australian and New Zealand Journal of Psychiatry* 39 (January 2005): 88–94.

47 Suzanne M. Phillips, "Free to Speak: Clarifying the Legacy of the Witch Hunts," *Journal of Psychology and Christianity* 21 (Spring 2002): 29–41.

48 J. S. Bockoven, *Moral Psychiatry in American Psychiatry* (New York: Springer, 1963).

49 Katy Butler, "Alice in Neuroland: Can Machines Teach Us to Be More Human?" *Psychotherapy Networker* 29 (September-October 2005): 26–35, 64–65.

50 Mark Sykes Wylie, "Visionary or Voodoo? Daniel Amen's Cruasade Has Some Neuroscientists Up in Arms," *Psychotherapy Networker* 29 (September-October 2005): 36–45, 66, 68.

51 Yarhouse et al., *Modern Psychopathologies,* 265.

52 Ibid.

53 Among the publications that can help, see Sophia F. Dziegielewski, *Psychopharmacology Handbook for the Non-Medically Trained* (New York: Norton, 2006).

54 David G. Kingdon, and Douglas Turkington, *Cognitive Therapy of Schizophrenia* (New York: Guilford, 2005); C. McLemore, *Toxic Relationships and How to Change Them* (San Francisco: Jossey-Bass, 2003); P. Nathan and J. Gorman, *A Guide to Treatments That Work* (New York: Oxford, 1998); and Ruth O. Ralph and Patrick W. Corrigan, *Recovery in Mental Illness: Broadening Our Understanding of Wellness* (Washington, DC: American Psychological Association, 2005). See also Karen Kersting, "Serious Rehabilitation," *Monitor on Psychology* 26 (January 2005): 38–41.

55 For Internet information about support groups that might have community chapters, begin with the National Mental Health Association at *www.nmha.org.*

56 When professionals show a lack of regard for the value of religious resources in helping people with severe mental illness, Christian counselors need to serve and comprehensively treat this population. Research shows that many of these patients report benefits from using their religious resources, but they are not served most effectively by professionals who ignore religious resources. For research with this population of patients, see Greg M. Reger and Steven A. Rogers, "Diagnostic Differences in Religious Coping Among Individuals with Persistent Mental Illness," *Journal of Psychology and Theology* 21 (Winter 2002): 341–348.

57 Natalia Yangarber-Hicks, "Religious Coping Styles and Recovery from Serious Mental Illness," *Journal of Psychology and Theology* 32 (Winter 2004): 305–317.

58 "Care and Treatment of Schizophrenia—Part II," *Harvard Medical School Mental Health Letter* 3 (July 1986): 1–4.

59 Chapter 8. See also, Alan L. Berman, David A. Jobes, and Morton M. Silverman, *Adolescent Suicide: Assessment and Intervention,* 2nd ed. (Washington, DC: American Psychological Association, 2006).

60 George W. Albee, "The Answer Is Prevention," *Psychology Today* 19 (February 1985): 60–64. The quotation is from page 64.

61 George W. Albee, "Call to Revolution in the Prevention of Emotional Disorders," *Ethical Human Psychology and Psychiatry* 7 (Spring 2005): 37–44; and George W. Albee and Justin M. Joffe, "Mental Illness Is NOT an Illness Like Any Other," *Journal of Primary Prevention* 24 (Summer 2004): 419–436.

62 Albee, "The Answer Is Prevention," 64.

63 An Internet search uncovered hundreds of articles that focus on ways of helping the homeless mentally ill. See, for example, Robert Whitaker, *Mad in America: Bad Science, Bad Medicine, and the Enduring Mistreatment of the Mentally Ill* ((New York: Perseus, 2003); Ramin Mojtabai, "Perceived Reasons for Loss of Housing and Continued Homelessness Among Homeless Persons with Mental Illness," *Psychiatric Services* 56 (February 2005): 172–178; and Sanna J. Thompson, David E. Pollio, Karin Eyrich, Emily Bradbury, and Carol S. North, "Successfully Exiting Homelessness: Experiences of Formerly Homeless Mentally Ill Individuals," *Evaluation and Program Planning* 27 (November 2004): 423–431.

For a comparison of public responses to mental disorders over the years, see Ralph Swindle, Jr., Kenneth Heller, Bernice Pescosolido, and Saeko Kikuzawa, "Responses to Nervous Breakdown in America over a 40-Year Period," *American Psychologist* 55 (July 2000): 740–749.

64 Jay Tokasz, "Remembering Pope John Paul II," *BP Magazine* 1 (Summer 2005): 16.

34. Alcohol-Related Problems

1 In the second edition of this book.

2 J. R. Cheydleur, "Alcohol Abuse and Dependence," in *Baker Encyclopedia of Psychology*, ed. David G. Benner and Peter C. Hill, 2nd ed. (Grand Rapids, MI: Baker, 1999), 59–64.

3 U.S. Department of Health and Human Services, National Institute on Alcohol Abuse and Alcoholism, *Journal: Alcohol Research & Health: Highlights From the Tenth Special Report to Congress, Health Risks and Benefits of Alcohol Consumption* 24, no. 1 (Washington, DC: U.S. Government Printing Office, 2000).

4 H. J. Harwood, D. Fountain, and G. Livermore, "Economic Costs of Alcohol Abuse and Alcoholism, in *The Consequences of Alcoholism*, ed. M. Galanter (New York: Plenum, 1998), 307–330.

5 American Psychiatric Association, *Diagnostic and Statistical Manual of Mental Disorders*, 4th ed. (Washington, DC: American Psychiatric Association, 1994), 197.

6 Adapted from an online pamphlet produced by the National Institute on Alcohol Abuse and Alcoholism (NIAAA), updated 2004, and available at *http://www.niaaa.nih.gov/publications/booklet.htm*.

7 For example, see Herbert Fingarette, *Heavy Drinking: The Myth of Alcoholism as a Disease* (Berkeley, CA: University of California Press, 1989); and Jeffrey A. Schaler, *Addiction Is a Choice* (Peru, IL: Open Court Press, 1999).

8 Psalm 104:5; John 2:9; Matthew 11:19; 26:27–29; Luke 7:33–34.

9 1 Timothy 5:23.

10 John 2:10.

11 Proverbs 20:1.

12 Proverbs 23:20–21.

13 Ephesians 5:18.

14 Luke 7:33.

15 Numbers 6:2–4.

16 1 Corinthians 6:12.

17 1 Corinthians 6:12; 8:9–13; Romans 14:21.

18 Galatians 6:1–10.

19 Cited by Cheydleur, "Alcohol Abuse and Dependence," 60.

20 Alcoholics Anonymous, *44 Questions* (New York: AA General Services Conference, 1989), 4.

21 Jerome H. Jaffe, "Substance-Related Disorders: Introduction and Overview," in *Comprehensive Textbook of Psychiatry/VI*, ed. Harold Kaplan and Benjamin J. Sadock (Baltimore, MD: Williams and Wilkins, 1995), 755–775. Jaffe notes that while genetic factors influence both males and females, alcoholism is more likely to develop in men, perhaps because women are less tolerant of alcohol.

22 This research is reported by Marc A. Schuchit, "Why Are Children of Alcoholics at High Risk for Alcoholism?" *Harvard Medical School Letter* 3 (November 1986).

23 The book is by Sandra D. Wilson, *Counseling Adult Children of Alcoholics* (Dallas: Word, 1989); the dissertation is Sandra Wilson, "A Comparison of Evangelical Christian Adult Children of Alcoholics and Nonalcoholics on Selected Personality and Religious Variables" (abstract in *Dissertation Abstracts International*, 1988, B49; University Microfilms No. 88–23876).

24 Kenneth E. Hart, Dorrie L. Fiissel, and Margaret McAleer, "Do Adult Offspring of Alcoholics Suffer from Poor Medical Health? A Three-Group Comparison Controlling for Self-Report Bias," *Canadian Journal of Nursing Research* 35 (March 2003): 52–72.

25 Michelle L. Kelley, Thomas F. Cash, Amesheia R. Grant, Denise L. Miles, and Melanie T. Santos, "Parental Alcoholism: Relationships to Adult Attachment in College Women and Men," *Addictive Behaviors* 29 (November 2004): 1633–1636.

26 In addition to the book by Wilson, *Counseling Adult Children of Alcoholics*, see Janet Woititz, *The Complete ACOA Sourcebook: Adult Children of Alcoholics at Home, at Work and in Love* (Deerfield Beach, FL: HCI, 2002); and Sara Hines Martin, *Healing for Adult Children of Alcoholics* (New York: Bantam, 1989).

27   Robert J. Ackerman, *Same House, Different Homes: Why Adult Children of Alcoholics Are Not All the Same* (Deerfield, FL: HCI, 1987).

28   Anderson Spickard, Jr., and Barbara R. Thompson, *Dying for a Drink: What You and Your Family Should Know About Alcoholism* (Nashville, TN: W Publishing 2005).

29   Mark A. Yarhouse, Richard E. Butman, and Barrett W. McRay, *Modern Psychopathologies: A Comprehensive Christian Appraisal* (Downers Grove, IL: InterVarsity, 2005), 187–189; J. Van Wicklin, "Substance Abuse," in *Christian Perspectives on Social Problems*, ed. C. DeSanto, Z. Lindblade, and M. Poloma (Indianapolis, IN: Wesley, 1992), 379–397.

30   Yarhouse et al., *Modern Psychopathologies.*

31   R. E. Tarter and M. Vanyukov, "Alcoholism: A Developmental Disorder," *Journal of Consulting and Clinical Psychology* 62 (1994): 1096–1107. The hypothetical story is adapted from George A. Mann, *The Dynamics of Addiction* (Minneapolis, MN: Johnson Institute, n.d.).

32   Ron Taffel and Melinda Blau, *The Second Family: Dealing with Peer Power, Pop Culture, the Wall of Silence—and Other Challenges of Raising Today's Teens* (New York: St. Martin's Press, 2002).

33   This is the theme of chapter 1 in Steven Van Cleave, Walter Byrd, and Kathy Revell, *Counseling for Substance Abuse and Addiction* (Waco, TX: Word, 1987).

34   Ephesians 5:15–20.

35   Marc A. Schuckit, "Alcohol Related Disorders," in Kaplan and Sadock, *Comprehensive Textbook of Psychiatry/VI*, 775–791.

36   For a discussion of the suicide potential in alcohol-dependent people, see Drew Canapary, Bruce Bongar, and Karen M. Cleary, "Assessing Risk for Completed Suicide in Patients with Alcohol Dependence: Clinicians' Views of Critical Factors," *Professional Psychology: Research and Practice* 33 (October 2002): 464–469.

37   At this point I have in mind the use of drugs as part of the religious practices of some Native American, First Nation, or similar groups.

38   This is one of the findings of A. McLellan, A. Alterman, D. Metzger, G. Grissom, G. Woody, L. Luborsky, and C. O'Brian, "Similarity of Outcome Predictors Across Opiate, Cocaine and Alcohol Treatments," *Journal of Consulting and Clinical Psychology* 62 (1994): 1141–1158. Matt's case will be mentioned again in this treatment section. It is taken from Thom Rutledge, "The Voices of Addiction: Avoiding Power Struggles in Alcoholism Treatment," *Psychotherapy Networker* 27 (November-December 2003): 71–76.

39   Jennifer P. Read, Christopher W. Kahler, and John F. Stevenson, "Bridging the Gap Between Alcoholism Treatment Research and Practice: Identifying What Works and Why," *Professional Psychology: Research and Practice* 32 (June 2001): 227–238; Tori DeAngelis, "Today's Tried-and-True Treatments: Practitioners Are Relying on Several Psychology-Grounded and Psychology-Tested Substance Abuse Treatments," *Monitor on Psychology* 32 (June 2001): 48–49. See also Avram H. Mack, John E. Franklin, Jr., and Richard J. Frances, *Concise Guide to Treatment of Alcoholism and Addictions*, 2nd ed. (Washington, DC: American Psychological Association, 2001).

40   Rutledge, "The Voices of Addiction," 71.

41   To read more about Alcoholics Anonymous go to an Internet source like Amazon.com and look at the books on AA. See, for example, Alcoholics Anonymous, *Twelve Steps and Twelve Traditions* (Center City, MN: Hazelden 2002). In addition to people who support AA, some people have been critical, even suggesting, for example, that some people stop being addicted to alcohol and become addicted to AA instead. For a more balanced criticism see Ann Wayman, *Powerfully Recovered! A Confirmed 12 Stepper Challenges the Movement*, 2nd ed. (Boca Raton, FL: Universal Publishers, 2001). See also Glenn D. Walters, "Twelve Reasons Why We Need to Find Alternatives to Alcoholics Anonymous," *Addictive Disorders & Their Treatment* 12 (2002): 53–59.

42   Linda Ferris Kurtz and Michael Fisher, "Participation in Community Life by AA and NA Members," *Contemporary Drug Problems* 30 (Winter 2003): 875–904.

43   Rutledge, "The Voices of Addiction," 72.

44   Rutledge, "The Voices of Addiction," 74.

45   Rutledge, "The Voices of Addiction," 75.

46   Robert J. Meyers and Brenda L. Wolfe, *Get Your Loved One Sober: Alternatives to Nagging, Pleading, and Threatening* (Center City, MN: Hazelden, 2003).

47   The email message from this person arrived while I was writing the present paragraph. Normally, I do not allow myself to get distracted with email messages while I am writing, but I checked this one and was amazed that a message had come that was so relevant to what I was writing. I cannot answer messages about personal counseling issues, but in this case I sent the writer a portion of this chapter along with some suggestions about his problem. I never heard from him again—at least not by the time this book went to press.

48 T. B. Baker, M. E. Piper, D. E. McCarthy, M. R. Majeskie, and M. C. Fiore, "Addiction Motivation Reformulated: An Effective Processing Model of Negative Reinforcement," *Psychological Review* 111 (2004): 33–51.

49 Karen Witkiewitz and G. Alan Marlatt, "Relapse Prevention for Alcohol and Drug Problems," *American Psychologist* 59 (May-June 2004): 224–235.

50 Ibid. See also P. L. Dobkin, M. Civita, A. Paraherakis, and K. Gill, "The Role of Functional Social Support in Treatment Retention and Outcomes Among Outpatient Adult Substance Abusers," *Addiction* 97 (2002): 347–356.

51 For information about rescue missions, go to the Internet and type in "rescue missions." *www.agrm.org* is a good place to start, including an introduction to Victorious Anonymous, which is a more openly Christian alternative to Alcoholics Anonymous.

52 I tried to look this up on the Internet and learned more about this and other prevention programs at *www.beerinstitute.org*. It might be debated if this is the best place to learn about prevention.

53 Melissa S. Strawser, Eric A. Storch, Gary R. Geffken, Erin M. Killiany, and Audrey L. Baumeister, "Religious Faith and Substance Problems in Undergraduate College Students: A Replication," *Pastoral Psychology* 53 (November 2004): 183–188; Stelios Stylianou, "The Role of Religiosity in the Opposition to Drug Use," *International Journal of Offender Therapy & Comparative Criminology* 48 (August 2004): 429–448; John M. Wallace, Tony N. Brown, Jerald G. Bachman, and Thomas A. Laveist, "The Influence of Race and Religion on Abstinence from Alcohol, Cigarettes and Marijuana Among Adolescents," *Journal of Studies on Alcohol* 64 (November 2003): 843–848; Alex W. Mason and Michael Windle, "A Longitudinal Study of the Effects of Religiosity on Adolescent Alcohol Use and Alcohol-Related Problems, *Journal of Adolescent Research* 17 (July 2002): 346–363.

54 Rutledge, "The Voices of Addiction," 75.

55 R. Niebuhr, *Leaves from the Notebook of a Tamed Cynic,* cited by Stephen J. Nelson, "Alcohol and Other Drugs: Facing Reality and Cynicism," *Journal of Counseling and Development* 65 (September 1986): 4–5.

56 Nelson, "Alcohol and Other Drugs," 4.

35. Addictions

1 Bryan Robinson tells his story in "Chained to the Desk," *Psychotherapy Networker* 24 (July-August 2000): 26–37. The book is Bryan E. Robinson, *Chained to the Desk: A Guidebook for Workaholics, Their Partners and Children, and the Clinicians Who Treat Them* (New York: New York University Press, 1998).

2 Alan Deutschman, "Making Change," *Fast Company* 94 (May 2005): 52–62.

3 The words in this sentence are taken from the titles of columns in the June 2001 issue of *Monitor on Psychology*.

4 1 Corinthians 6:12.

5 Romans 13:1–5; 1 Peter 2:13–17.

6 1 Peter 5:7; Psalm 55:22.

7 1 Corinthians 10:13.

8 1 Corinthinas 6:19–20; Romans 12:1.

9 Walter Houston Clark, *Chemical Ecstasy: Psychedelic Drugs and Religion* (New York: Sheed and Ward, 1969).

10 John 14:6; 1 Timothy 2:5.

11 This is implied perhaps in Colossians 3:2; 1 Thessalonians 5:4–8; and 1 Peter 1:13. Notice also Deuteronomy 6:4–5. We are to love God with our minds and strength. This is not possible for one who is under the influence of drugs or some other mind-altering substance. Sorcery also is condemned in Scripture (Galatians 5:16–21; Revelation 9:20–21; 18:23; 21:8; 22:15). In Greek the word for sorcery is *pharmakeia*, which refers to one who prepares drugs for religious purposes.

12 1 Timothy 3:2–3; Titus 1:7–8.

13 Titus 2:2–6; 2 Timothy 1:7 is written to Timothy, who clearly was a Christian leader, but self-discipline here appears to be a goal for all believers.

14 Titus 2:12.

15 Matthew 23:25; Philippians 2:3; James 3:14–16; 5:5.

16 1 Thessalonians 5:6, 8; 1 Peter 1:13; 4:7; 5:8.

17 Galatians 5:23.

18 Proverbs 23:1–3; Luke 12:15; 1 Peter 5:2–3; Proverbs 6:25; Colossians 3:3–5; these are only some, but not all, of the many Bible verses that condemn gluttony, greed, and lust.

19 1 Corinthians 10:23, 24, 29–33.

20 Proverbs 20:1; 23:29–31; Isaiah 5:11; Romans 13:13; 1 Corinthians 5:11; 6:10; Galatians 5:21; Ephesians 5:18; 1 Peter 4:3; 1 Thessalonians 5:7–8.

21 Dale Ryan, "It Takes a Village to Raise an Addict," *STEPS* 14 (2004): 3.

22 This is adapted from the writing of George Mann, for many years medical director of a center for understanding and treating chemical addictions. See George A. Mann, *The Dynamics of Addiction* (Center City, MN: Hazeldon/Johnson Institute, 1987).

23 Use of caffeine differs from country to country. An estimated 85 percent of Americans use caffeine consistently, including children. The effects of caffeine, especially on children, is highly debated. See Eileen O'Connor, "A Sip into Dangerous Territory," *Monitor on Psychology* 32 (June 2001): 60–62.

24 "Surging Trend of Methamphetamine Abuse Rocks the American Landscape," *Hazelden Voice* 10 (Winter 2005): 1–2. See also David J. Jefferson, "The Meth Epidemic: America's Most Dangerous Drug," *Newsweek* 146 (August 8, 2005): 40–48.

25 The four categories are adapted from American Psychiatric Association, *Diagnostic and Statistical Manual of Mental Disorders*, 4th ed. (Washington, DC: American Psychiatric Association, 1994); James R. Beck, "Substance-Use Disorders," in *Baker Encyclopedia of Psychology*, ed. David G. Benner and Peter C. Hill, 2nd ed. (Grand Rapids, MI: Baker, 1999), 1178–1180; and Mark A. Yarhouse, Richard E. Butman, and Barrett W. McRay, *Modern Psychopathologies: A Comprehensive Christian Appraisal* (Downers Grove, IL: InterVarsity Press, 2005).

26 Rafael A. Rivas-Vazquez and Lizbhet Delgado, "Clinical and Toxic Effects of MDMA ('Ecstasy')," *Professional Psychology: Research and Practice* 33 (August 2002): 422–425.

27 Darvin W. Smith, "Ecstasy—Club Drugs," *Christian Counseling Today* 10, no. 2 (2002): 34–36.

28 Rob Waters, "Generation Rx," *Psychotherapy Networker* 24 (March-April 2000): 34–43. See also Barry Duncan, Scott Miller, and Jacqueline Sparks, "Exposing the Mythmakers," *Psychotherapy Networker* 24 (March-April 2000): 24–33, 52–53.

29 When Jesus was on the cross, he refused to take the wine that would have dulled the pain as he died for the sins of the world. Elsewhere, however, he spoke approvingly of the Good Samaritan, whose act of compassion included pouring wine on the wounds. It is well known that Timothy was encouraged to use a little wine for his ailing stomach; see Matthew 27:34; Mark 15:23; Luke 10:34; 1 Timothy 5:23.

30 "Addiction is a family affair" according to a whole chapter in Stephen Van Cleave, Walter Byrd, and Kathy Revell, *Counseling for Substance Abuse and Addiction* (Waco, TX: Word, 1987).

31 Among those who are trained counselors but who believe that moral theories still are valid are Edward T. Welch and Gary Steven Shogren, *Addictive Behavior* (Grand Rapids, MI: Baker, 1995).

32 Beverly Rodgers, "Care Addiction," *Christian Counseling Today* 10, no. 2 (2002): 22–24.

33 Danny Han, "The Driven Pastor," *Christian Counseling Today* 10, no. 2 (2002): 40–42.

34 Archibald D. Hart, *The Hidden Link Between Adrenalin and Stress* (Waco, TX: Word, 1986).

35 Hypoadrenia is a deficiency of the functioning of the adrenal glands. For more information see *www.adrenalfatigue.org*. According to this web site, "although up to 80% of Americans suffer some level of adrenal fatigue at some time during their lives, it remains one of the most under-diagnosed illnesses in the U.S."

36 These coping strategies are discussed later in the chapter.

37 Stephen Arterburn and Jack Felton, *Toxic Faith: Understanding and Overcoming Religious Addiction* (Nashville, TN: Oliver-Nelson, 1991), 31. See also Ronald M. Enroth, *Churches That Abuse* (Grand Rapids, MI: Zondervan, 1992).

38 Arterburn and Felton, *Toxic Faith*, 119.

39 Van Cleave et al., *Counseling for Substance Abuse*, 26–29.

40 This is from a report of the National Inhalant Prevention Coalition, cited in *Monitor on Psychology* 32 (June 2001): 11. According to the report, more than 1,000 products widely available in households can be used as inhalants.

41 This is a conclusion from the Director of the U.S. National Institute on Alcohol Abuse and Alcoholism, Enoch Gordis, "An Eye on the Vanishing Line," *Monitor on Psychology* 32 (June 2001): 38.

42 S. Martin, "Most Substance Abusers Aren't Getting Treatment," *Monitor on Psychology* 32 (June 2001): 11.

43 Robert J. Craig, "Multimodal Treatment Package for Substance Abuse Treatment Programs," *Professional Psychology: Research and Practice* 16 (April 1985): 271–285. This is a dated but concise and excellent overview of basic substance-abuse programs. More recent publications include research reports and books that appear with some frequency. These include Dennis M. Donovan and G. Alan Marlatt, eds., *Assessment of Addictive Behaviors* (New York: Guilford, 2005); G. Alan Marlatt and Dennis M. Donovan, eds., *Relapse Prevention: Maintenance Strategies in the Treatment of Addictive Behaviors* (New York: Guilford, 2005); Richard J. Frances, Sheldon I. Miller, and Avram H. Mack, eds., *Clinical Textbook of Addictive Disorders,* 3rd ed. (New York: Guilford, 2005); and Marc Galanter and Herbert D. Kleber, eds., *Textbook of Substance Abuse Treatment* (Arlington, VA: American Psychiatric Publishing, 2004).

44 The following section is adapted from pages 202–204 of a chapter written by Mark Yarhouse in Yarhouse et al., *Modern Psychopathologies.*

45 In writing this paragraph, I went to a professional search engine and reviewed about fifty studies of the Internet and pornography. Of special interest were the many articles that studied the fascination with Internet sex among university students in countries all over the world (perhaps these people were studied because they were so easily available to professor-researchers) and many articles that report research on the ways in which children are both the targets and the subjects of Internet pornography. Often, these images appear unwanted on computer screens and lead to more curious web searching, followed by more serious addiction, frequently accompanied by masturbation. Cybersex addiction occurs at all socioeconomic levels and in all professional groups, including counselors and clergy. See Mark R. Laaser and Louis J. Gregoire, "Pastors and Cybersex Addiction," *Sexual & Relationship Therapy* 18 (August 2003): 395–406.

46 One study supported the conclusion that there are higher than average levels of loneliness in men who are addictive viewers of Internet pornography. See Vincent Cyrus Yoder, Thomas B. Virden III, and Kiram Amin, "Internet Pornography and Loneliness: An Association?" *Sexual Addiction and Compulsivity* 12 (January-March 2005): 19–44.

47 Colossians 3:5, 8.

48 See, for example, J. P. Maxwell, "Anger Rumination: An Antecedent of Athlete Aggression?" *Psychology of Sport & Exercise* 5 (July 2004): 279–289.

49 Colossians 3:9–10.

50 Thought stopping, displacement of unwanted thoughts, how to break habits, and Scriptural references to replace unwanted thoughts are among the issues discussed with clarity and in detail by Richard P. Walters, *Counseling for Problems of Self-Control* (Waco, TX: Word, 1987).

51 Archibald C. Hart, "Addiction to Adrenaline," *Christian Counseling Today* 10, no. 2 (2002): 30–33.

52 Examples of research include work by Melissa S. Strawser, Eric A. Storch, Gary R. Geffken, Erin M. Killiany, and Audrey L. Baumeister, "Religious Faith and Substance Problems in Undergraduate College Students: A Replication," *Pastoral Psychology* 53 (November 2004): 183–188. The article concluded that "findings indicated that religious faith was inversely associated with drug and alcohol problems in both males and females." John M. Wallace, Tony N. Brown, Jerald G. Bachman, and Thomas A. Laveist, "The Influence of Race and Religion on Abstinence from Alcohol, Cigarettes and Marijuana Among Adolescents," *Journal of Studies on Alcohol* 64 (November 2003): 843–848. Among the conclusions: "Although religion is an important protective factor against alcohol and other substance use for both white and black adolescents, highly religious white youth are more likely than highly religious black youth to abstain from alcohol and marijuana use." Michael S. Dunn, "The Relationship Between Religiosity, Employment, and Political Beliefs on Substance Use Among High School Seniors," *Journal of Alcohol & Drug Education* 49 (March 2005): 73–88. Dunn's analysis concluded that males and females who believed religion was very important were less likely to have initiated alcohol use, to be a current user, and to have participated in binge drinking.

53 Robinson, "Chained to the Desk," 36.

36. Financial Counseling

1 1 Timothy 6:10.

2 Philippians 4:19; Mark 6:7–11; Matthew 6:25–34.

3 The quotation is from Bruce Barron, *The Health and Wealth Gospel: What's Going on Today in a Movement That Has Shaped the Faith of Millions* (Downers Grove, IL: InterVarsity, 1987). For other evaluations of this theology and theological movement, see Robert M. Bowman, Jr., *The Word-Faith Controversy: Understanding the Health and Wealth Gospel* (Grand Rapids, MI: Baker, 2001); and Milmon F. Harrison, *Righteous Riches: The Word Of Faith Movement in Contemporary African American Religion* (New York: Oxford University Press, 2005).

4 1 Timothy 6:18–19.

5 Philippians 4:19.

6 Luke 12:16–21; see also Proverbs 28:20.

7 Psalm 49:10–12; Proverbs 23:4–5; 27:24; 1 Timothy 6:7.

8 Ecclesiastes 5:10; Psalm 52:5–7.

9 Hebrews 13:5.

10 Psalm 62:10.

11 Matthew 19:16–24.

12 Matthew 6:24.

13 Mark 8:36.

14 Deuteronomy 8:11–14; Psalm 52:7; Proverbs 30:7–10; see also Luke 16:19ff. and Job 31:24–25, 28.

15 Luke 12:13–15.

16 Matthew 25:14–30. It should be noted that money in this passage is a simile and not the main emphasis; see verse 13.

17 Adapted from Kenneth M. Meyer, *Minister's Guide to Financial Planning* (Grand Rapids, MI: Zondervan, 1987), 17.

18 Proverbs 28:20; 15:27; 10:9; 11:1; 17:23.

19 Matthew 25:14–30; Luke 12:16–21.

20 Romans 13:6–8.

21 Proverbs 22:7; see also Matthew 18:23–25, the parable of the unforgiving slave.

22 2 Corinthians 9:7; 8:14–15; Proverbs 3:9; 19:17; 1 Corinthians 16:2.

23 Proverbs 3:9.

24 This is the title of a book by Tim Kasser and Allen D. Kanner, eds., *Psychology and Consumer Culture: The Struggle for a Good Life in a Materialistic World* (Washington, DC: American Psychological Association, 2004).

25 For an interesting analysis about how Visa and Master Card have radically changed our whole way of handling finances, see Paul Chutkow, *VISA: The Power of an Idea* (New York: Harcourt, 2001).

26 The quotation in this paragraph is the subtitle of the Kasser and Kanner book cited above. Perhaps it is ironic that some of the wording in this paragraph is adapted from advertising copy, written to encourage psychologists to purchase the book.

27 Luke 12:15.

28 Exodus 20:17; Romans 13:9.

29 Proverbs 28:20, 22.

30 Gambling is an addiction that will be discussed in a later chapter, but see Jon E. Grant and Marc N. Potenza, eds., *Pathological Gambling: A Guide to Treatment* (Arlington, VA: American Psychiatric Publishing, 2004); and James P. Welan and Andrew W. Meyers, *Problem and Pathological Gambling* (Ashland, OH: Hogrefe, 2005).

31 Revelation 3:17.

32 1 Chronicles 29:16, 12. Paul expressed similar values in 1 Corinthians 4:7.

33 Proverbs 21:5; Ecclesiastes 5:15–17.

34 Proverbs 11:15; 17:18; 22:26–27.

35 Luke 12:16–21.

36 Giving to God: Proverbs 3:9; Malachi 3:10. Giving to others: Galatians 6:10. Giving to the poor: Luke 3:11; Proverbs 14:21; 19:17.

37 For example, see Larry Burkett, *Debt-Free Living: How to Get Out of Debt and Stay Out* (Chicago: Moody, 2000); Larry Burkett, *Family Budget Workbook: Gaining Control of Your Personal Finances* (Chicago: Northfield, 1993); Larry Burkett, Ron Blue, and Jeremy White, *The Burkett & Blue Definitive Guide to Securing Wealth to Last: Money Essentials for the*

Second Half of Life (Nashville, TN: Broadman and Holman, 2003); Ron Blue and Jeremy White, *Splitting Heirs: Giving Your Money and Things to Your Children Without Ruining Their Lives* (Chicago: Northfield, 2004); and Ron Blue and Jeremy White, *The New Master Your Money: A Step-by-Step Plan for Gaining and Enjoying Financial Freedom* (Chicago: Moody, 2004).

38 Psalm 50:10–12; Matthew 6:25–34.

39 Psalm 55:22; 1 Peter 5:7.

40 Larry Burkett, *Your Finances in Changing Times*, rev. ed. (Chicago: Moody Press, 1993).

41 For interesting analyses of the credit-buying mentality in the United States, and now in other nations as well, see Lendol Calder, *Financing the American Dream: A Cultural History of Consumer Credit* (Princeton, NJ: Princeton University Press, 2001); Robert D. Manning, *Credit Card Nation: The Consequences of America's Addiction to Credit* (New York: Basic Books, 2001); and David S. Evans and Richard Schmalensee, *Paying with Plastic: The Digital Revolution in Buying and Borrowing*, 2nd ed. (Cambridge, MA: MIT Press, 2005).

42 Karen Kersting, "Driving Teen Egos—and Buying—Through Branding," *Monitor on Psychology* 35 (June 2004): 60–61.

43 This is the opinion of Susan Linn of Harvard Medical School, cited in Kersting, "Driving Teen Egos." Linn has discussed this in detail in Susan Linn, *Consuming Kids: Protecting Our Children from the Onslaught of Marketing & Advertising* (New York: Anchor Books, 2005).

44 Melissa Dittman, "Protecting Children from Advertising," *Monitor on Psychology* 35 (June 2004): 58–59.

45 1 Timothy 6:17–18.

37. Vocational Counseling

1 Karen James Chopra, "Finding True North: How to Help Clients Find a Fulfilling Career Path," *Psychotherapy Networker* 29 (May-June 2005): 83–89. Ron's story is adapted from Chopra's article. We will return to Ron again as the chapter progresses.

2 Genesis 2:15.

3 Genesis 3:23, 17–19.

4 James 5:3–5.

5 Ecclesiastes 2:4–11.

6 Ecclesiastes 2:17–23.

7 Ephesians 4:28; 1 Thessalonians 4:11–12.

8 2 Thessalonians 3:10–12.

9 Colossians 3:22–23.

10 1 Timothy 5:17–18.

11 Proverbs 31:10–31.

12 Psalm 104:23.

13 Proverbs 6:6–11; 12:24; 13:41; 18:9; 20:4; 24:30–34; 26:16.

14 Romans 14:5.

15 Ecclesiastes 9:10.

16 Ted W. Engstrom, *The Pursuit of Excellence* (Grand Rapids, MI: Zondervan, 1982).

17 Ephesians 6:5–9; Colossians 3:22–4:1.

18 Matthew 25:14–30; Romans 12:6–8.

19 Romans 12:3–8; 1 Corinthians 12:4–31; Ephesians 4:7–13.

20 Psalm 75:6–7.

21 Romans 12:3; Jeremiah 9:23–24.

22 Isaiah 49:1, 5; Psalm 139:13–16; Jeremiah 1:5; Luke 1:13–17, 30–33.

23 Proverbs 3:5–6; Psalm 32:8.

24 James 1:5; see also Romans 12:1–2.

25 Daniel H. Pink, *Free Agent Nation: How America's New Independent Workers Are Transforming the Way We Live* (New York: Warner, 2001). I read this book shortly after it appeared and recognized that I have been a free agent worker for a number of years. How else can you characterize a writer of counseling and coaching books who does some private practice, teaching, speaking, and writing, all from a home office but connected technologically with people and research databases all over the world?

26 Among the books that summarize career choice theory and practice are those by Samuel H. Osipow and Louise F. Fitzgerald, *Theories of Career Development*, 4th ed. (Boston, MA: Allyn & Bacon, 1995); Jane L. Swanson and Nadya A. Fouad, *Career Theory and Practice: Learning Through Case Studies* (Thousand Oaks, CA: Sage Publications, 1999); Richard S.

Sharf, *Applying Career Development Theory to Counseling*, 3rd ed. (Pacific Grove, CA: Brooks/Cole, 2001); Duane Brown, ed., *Career Choice and Development*, 4th ed. (San Francisco, CA: Jossey-Bass, 2002).

27 John L. Holland, *Making Vocational Choices: A Theory of Vocational Personalities and Work Environments*, 3rd ed. (Lutz, FL: Psychological Assessment Resources, 1997).

28 Jim Loehr and Tony Schwartz, *The Power of Full Engagement: Managing Energy, Not Time, Is the Key to High Performance and Personal Renewal* (New York: Free Press, 2003).

29 Marcus Buckingham and Donald O. Clifton, *Now, Discover Your Strengths* (New York: Free Press, 2001). See also Curt Coffman and Gabriel Gonzalez-Molina, *Follow This Path* (New York: Free Press, 2002). According to the book cover, the conclusions about strength-based work was based on "The Gallup Organization's Study of 10 Million Cuistomers, 3 Million Employees, and 200,000 Managers."

30 Albert L. Winseman, Donald O. Clifton, and Curt Liesbeld, *Living Your Strengths: Discover Your God-Given Talents and Inspire Your Community* (New York: Gallup Press, 2004).

31 This view was advocated most strongly by E. K. Strong, an early pioneer in vocational counseling who designed what still may be the most widely used interest test, the Strong Interest Inventory. Now almost one hundred years old, the Strong has been revised and updated repeatedly. It can be taken online for a fee. See *www.discoveryourpersonality.com*.

32 Richard Nelson Bolles and Mark Bolles, *What Color Is Your Parachute 2006: A Practical Manual for Job-Hunters and Career-Changers* (Berkeley, CA: Ten Speed Press, 2005).

33 Gary R. Collins, *Christian Coaching* (Colorado Springs, CO: NavPress, 2001).

34 Os Guinness is a writer who has no doubt about God's calling people today. See Os Guinness, *The Call: Finding and Fulfilling the Central Purpose of Your Life* (Nashville, TN: W Publishing, 2003). In contrast, Garry Friesen wrote a very controversial book in which he argued convincingly against the notion of a call to ministry. In no place does God require some kind of a mystical call to ministry, according to Friesen. Requiring people to have a call "creates more problems than it purports to solve. Instead, believers should enter full-time Christian service for the reasons and for the qualifications established in the Bible." See Garry Friesen and J. Robin Maxon, *Decision Making and the Will of God*, rev. ed. (Sisters, OR: Multnomah, 2004), 321.

35 Leslie Parrott and Les Parrott, *The Career Counselor: Guidance for Planning Careers and Managing Career Crises* (Dallas, TX: Word, 1995), 43–44.

36 Jonah 1:2; 3:3; 4:1, 3.

37 Philippians 4:10–13; 2 Timothy 4:6–8.

38 Some of these issues are discussed in a brief article by Kerry J. Sulkowicz, in his column titled "The Corporate Shrink," *Fast Company* 91 (February 2005): 36.

39 Undoubtedly, the most popular of these books is the regularly updated classic by Bolles, *What Color Is Your Parachute?* See also Robert Bittner, *Your Perfect Job* (New York: Random House, 2003). The following are written by Christians: Doug Sherman and William Hendricks, *Your Life Matters to God* (Colorado Springs, CO: NavPress, 1987); John Maxwell, *Journey from Success to Significance* (Nashville, TN: Nelson, 2004); and Dennis Bakke, *Joy at Work: A Revolutionary Approach to Fun on the Job* (Lake Mary, FL: Strang, 2005).

40 2 Corinthians 5:7–9.

41 From a Christian perspective, the best of these books is by Leslie and Les Parrott, *The Career Counselor*. Other books, including some that are classics that have been revised several times, include the following, listed in their order of publication: Elizabeth B. Yost and M. Anne Corvishley, *Career Counseling: A Psychological Approach* (San Francisco, CA: Jossey-Bass, 1997); Richard N. Bolles and Howard Figler, *Career Counselor's Handbook* (Berkeley, CA: Ten Speed Press, 1999); Edwin L. Herr, Stanley H. Cramer, and Spencer G. Niles, *Career Guidance and Counseling Through the Lifespan: Systematic Approaches*, 6th ed. (Boston, MA: Allyn & Bacon, 2003); Norman E. Amundson, JoAnn Harris-Bowlsbey, and Spencer G. Niles, *Essential Elements of Career Counseling: Processes and Techniques* (Upper Saddle River, NJ: Prentice-Hall, 2004); Vernon G. Zuncker, *Career Counseling: A Holistic Approach*, 7th ed. (Belmont, CA: Wadsworth, 2005). See also Darrell Anthony Luzzo, *Career Counseling of College Students: An Empirical Guide to Strategies That Work* (Washington, DC: American Psychological Association, 2000).

42 Many Christians turn to Jeremiah 29:11 to support the idea that God has a wonderful plan for each individual life: "'For I know the plans I have for you,' says the LORD, 'They are plans for good and not for disaster, to give you a future and a hope.'" This is taken from a letter addressed to the people of Israel while they were in Babylon. It appears to

be addressed to a nation of people and not a promise for individuals, although there are clear examples of God's plans for individuals, including Jeremiah and John the Baptist.

43 Karen James Chopra, "Finding True North," 84.

44 It may be discovered, for example, that successful men or women in occupation *x* also enjoy reading novels, gardening, and attending rock concerts. If a test-taker gets a high interest score in these same three areas, it is clear that he or she likes the same things that are liked by people in occupation *x*.

45 A free "VIA Signature Strengths Survey" is available at *www.authentichappiness.org*. This strength-finder test is taken online, and the results appear on the screen as soon as the test is completed. In addition, a widely used test is available to purchasers of one of the following books; they each allow purchasers to take one "discover your strengths" survey per book. See Buckingham and Clifton, *Now, Discover Your Strengths*, or Albert L. Winseman, Donald O. Clifton, and Curt Liesveld, *Living Your Strengths: Discover Your God-Given Talents and Inspire Your Community* (New York: Gallup Press, 2004). As the title suggests, the book by Winseman et al. is written from a Christian perspective. At the time of this writing, the VIA Signature Strengths Survey and the test from one of these two books each give a list of core strengths, but the lists do not necessarily overlap. A person's strengths on one test may not be the same as the strengths on the other. Clearly, the tests are measuring something different, or one (or both) of the tests is not very accurate.

46 There is a variety of books that survey psychological tests and describe their nature and use. One example is by Vernon G. Zunker and Debra S. Osborn, *Using Assessment Results for Career Development*, 6th ed. (Belmont, CA: Wadsworth Publishing, 2001).

47 If you live in the United States, for example, see the latest edition of the U.S. Department of Labor *Occupational Outlook Handbook 2006–2007* (Indianapolis, IN: Jist Publishing, 2006), or J. Michael Farr and Laurence Shatkin, eds., *O*NET Dictionary of Occupational Titles: The Definitive Printed Reference of Occupational Information*, 3rd ed. (Indianapolis, IN: Jist Publishing, 2004).

48 For a discussion of the role of vocational counselors in helping business employees adjust to cross-cultural assignments, see Siri Carpenter, "Battling the Overseas Blues," *Monitor on Psychology* (July-August 2001): 48–49.

49 Meredith W. Long, "God's Will and the Job Market," *HIS* 36 (June 1976): 1–4.

50 For example, see God leading King Cyrus (Ezra 1:1) or his leading King Artaxerxes to give Nehemiah permission to build the city wall and even giving him the necessary supplies. At other times, God used pagan kings to go to war and destroy nations, even though these kings were unaware that God was putting the ideas into their minds and enabling them to win their battles.

51 Proverbs 3:5–6; Romans 12:1–2.

52 Colossians 3:2–24.

53 Philippians 4:11.

54 Deborah Smith, "When Workplaces Shut Down," *Monitor on Psychology* 32 (July-August 2001): 50–51. The "company" in this article was Kelly Air Force Base in San Antonio, Texas. At its peak, the facility employed multiple members of the same family, many second- and third-generation workers, and thousands of others. "While the closing was painful, it was also a success story."

55 Emilie Le Beau, "At a Loss. Mom or Dad Out of Work and You're Unsure What to Do? Employ These Techniques," *Chicago Tribune*, March 10, 2004.

56 For a book written by a former president of the American Psychological Association and geared to older people, see Dorothy Cantor, *What Do You Want to Do When You Grow Up? Starting the Next Chapter of Your Life* (New York: Little, Brown, 2002).

57 Jennifer Daw, "Road Rage, Air Rage, and Now 'Desk Rage,'" *Monitor on Psychology* 32 (July-August 2001): 53–53. I confess that desk rage was a new concept to me, so I looked it up on the Internet. I typed in "desk rage," and to my great surprise there were 837,000 references. I chose not to read them all!

58 Jerry Langdon, "Desk Rage Becoming More Common," *USA Today*, January 15, 2001.

59 Kathryn Hewlett, "Can Low Self-Esteem and Self-Blame on the Job Make You Sick?" *Monitor on Psychology* 32 (July-August 2001): 58.

60 Barry Glassner, *Career Crash: America's New Crisis—And Who Survives* (New York: Simon & Schuster, 1994).

61 Ephesians 6:7.

38. Crises

1   Psalm 137:1, 4.

2   For example, see Jeremiah 6:1–3, 16–19.

3   For a healthy discussion of crisis management for relief workers, especially those who are Christians, see John Fawcett, ed., *Stress and Trauma Handbook: Strategies for Flourishing in Demanding Environments* (Monrovia, CA: World Vision, 2003).

4   The quotations are from page 35 of an article by Mary Sykes Wylie, "The Limits of Talk: Bessel van der Kolk Wants to Transform the Treatment of Trauma," *Psychotherapy Networker* 28 (January-February 2004): 30–36, 38.

5   Michael Ventura, "Is the World Still There?" *Psychotherapy Networker* 26 (September-October 2002): 46–49, 56.

6   F. J. White, "Crisis Intervention," in *Baker Encyclopedia of Psychology*, ed. David G. Benner and Peter C. Hill, 2nd ed. (Grand Rapids, MI: Baker, 1999), 293–294.

7   A number of books deal with the complexities of crisis intervention in different settings. For example, see Albert R. Roberts, ed., *Crisis Intervention Handbook: Assessment, Treatment, and Research*, 3rd ed. (New York: Oxford University Press, 2005); Kenneth France, *Crisis Intervention: A Handbook of Immediate Person-to-Person Help*, 4th ed. (Springfield, IL: Charles C. Thomas, 2002); and Laura Barbanel and Robert J. Sternberg, eds., *Psychological Interventions in Times of Crisis* (New York: Springer, 2005).

8   Jan Ligon, "Mobile Crisis Units: Frontline Community Mental Health Services," in Roberts, *Crisis Intervention Handbook*, 602–618.

9   R. H. Rottschafer, "Physical Contact in Therapy," in Benner and Hill, *Baker Encyclopedia of Psychology*, 874.

10 Judson J. Swihart and Gerald C. Richardson, *Counseling in Times of Crisis* (Waco, TX: Word, 1987), 155–161. This is a helpful book, perhaps now difficult to locate, but written as part of a series of thirty counseling books that I edited in the 1980s, under the title Resources for Christian Counseling.

11 For a summary of research evidence showing the value of social support and the dangers of social overinvolvement, see Judith E. Pearson, "The Definition and Measurement of Social Support," *Journal of Counseling and Development* 64 (February 1986): 390–395.

12 See, for example, George S. Everly, Jr., "Pastoral Crisis Intervention in Response to Terrorism," *International Journal of Emergency Mental Health* 5 (Winter 2003): 1–2; and George S. Everly, Jr., "The Role of Pastoral Crisis Intervention in Disasters, Terrorism, Violence, and Other Community Crises," *International Journal of Emergency Mental Health* 2 (Fall 2000): 139–142.

13 George S. Everly, Jr., "'Pastoral Crisis Intervention': Toward a Definition," *International Journal of Emergency Mental Health* 2 (Spring 2000): 69–71.

14 This is very similar to the basic steps that are taken in coaching. For more details, see Gary R. Collins, *Christian Coaching: Helping Others Turn Potential into Reality* (Colorado Springs, CO: NavPress, 2001).

15 Matthew J. Friedman, "Introduction: Every Crisis Is an Opportunity," *CNS Spectrums* 10 (February 2005): 96–98. For a summary of the media campaign to raise awareness of depression among men, see Karen Kersting, "Men and Depression: Battling Stigma Through Public Education," *Monitor on Psychology* 36 (June 2005): 66–68.

16 Richard G. Tedeschi and Ryan P. Kilmer, "Assessing Strengths, Resilience, and Growth to Guide Clinical Interventions," *Professional Psychology: Research and Practice* 36 (June, 2005): 230–237; Mary Karapetian Alvord and Judy Johnson Grados, "Enhancing Resilience in Children: A Proactive Approach," *Professional Psychology: Research and Practice* 36 (June 2005): 238–245; George A. Bonanno, "Loss, Trauma, and Human Resilience: Have We Underestimated the Human Capacity to Thrive After Extremely Aversive Events?" *American Psychologist* 59 (January 2004): 20–28; and S. S. Luthar and D. Cicchetti, "The Construct of Resilience: Implications for Interventions and Social Policies," *Development and Psychopathology* 12 (2000): 857–885.

17 Russ Newman, "APA's Resilience Initiative," *Professional Psychology: Research and Practice* 36 (June 2005): 227–229; and Karen Kersting, "Resilience: The Mental Muscle Everyone Has," *Monitor on Psychology* 36 (April 2005): 332–333.

18 L. G. Calhoun and R. G. Tedeschi, "The Foundations of Post-Traumatic Growth: New Considerations," *Psychological Inquiry* 15 (2004): 93–102; and R. A. Neimeyer, "Fostering Post-Traumatic Growth: A Narrative Elaboration," *Psychological Inquiry* 15 (2004): 53–59.

19 For example see 2 Corinthians 1:3–7; 12:7–10; Philippians 1:12–14.

20 From Fawcett, *Stress and Trauma Handbook,* 14.

21 In addition to the book by Fawcett, *Stress and Trauma Handbook,* see Gladys K. Mwiti and David O. Gatewood, "The Macedonian Call: Christian Mental Health Professionals and International Trauma," *Journal of Psychology and Christianity* 20 (Spring 2001): 276–281.

22 The psychological effects of political torture are described by William Gorman, "Refugee Survivors of Torture: Trauma and Treatment," *Professional Psychology: Research and Practice* 32 (October 2001): 443–451; Uwe Jacobs and Vincent Iacopino, "Torture and Its Consequences: A Challenge to Clinical Neuropsychology," *Professional Psychology: Research and Practice* 32 (October 2001): 458–464. Other articles in that same journal make up a special section of papers on treating the survivors of political torture.

23 Robert W. Bagley, "Trauma and Traumatic Stress Among Missionaries," *Journal of Psychology and Theology* 31 (Summer 2003): 97–112; Heather Davediuk Gingrich, "Stalked by Death: Cross-Cultural Trauma Work with a Tribal Missionary," *Journal of Psychology and Christianity* 21 (Fall 2002): 262–265.

24 Patrick McDonald with Emma Garro, *Children at Risk: Networking in Action* (Monrovia, CA: World Vision, 2000); and Phyllis Kilbourn and Marjorie McDermid, eds., *Sexually Exploited Children: Working to Protect and Heal* (Monrovia, CA: World Vision, 1998).

25 Rob Waters, "The Psychic Costs of War," *Psychotherapy Networker* 29 (March-April 2005): 13–14; Mark Greer, "A New Kind of War," *Monitor on Psychology* 36 (April 2005): 38–41.

26 Deborah Smith, "Children in the Heat of War," *Monitor on Psychology* 32 (September 2001): 29–31.

27 TV producer Leroy Sievers wrote about his experience of living for several days among 50,000 to 100,000 refugees from the Rwanda war. The people were starving, neglected by the international community, and sitting in filthy conditions. One day a nearby volcano erupted, and the lava flowed over most of the community. Who could comprehend how to help people like this who now are gone, but who have been replaced by others in different places but with similar misery? See Leroy Siever, "The Ghosts of Rwanda," reprinted from the *Los Angeles Times Magazine,* in *The Week* 5 (August 12, 2005): 40–41. For discussions of the mental-health needs of refugees, see Kenneth E. Miller and Lisa M. Rasco, eds., *The Mental Health of Refugees: Ecological Approaches to Healing and Adaptations* (Mahwah, NJ: Lawrence Erlbaum, 2004).

28 David Claerbaut, *Urban Ministry in a New Millennium* (Monrovia, CA: World Vision, 2005).

29 Selwyn W. Becker and Alice H. Eagly, "The Heroism of Women and Men," *American Psychologist* 39 (April 2004): 163–178.

39. Trauma, Terror, and Terrorism

1 Zak Stambor, "Helping Children Cope with Disaster," *Monitor on Psychology* 36 (September 2005): 34–35.

2 Anonymous, "Living through the Yom Kippur War," *Israel Journal of Psychiatry & Related Sciences* 39 (2002): 194–197.

3 Dean's story is taken from Rob Waters, "The Psychic Costs of War," *Psychotherapy Networker* 29 (March-April 2005): 15–16.

4 This is the definition proposed by Anthony J. Marsella, "Reflections on International Terrorism: Issues, Concepts, and Directions," in *Understanding Terrorism: Psychological Roots, Consequences, and Interventions,* ed. Fathali M. Moghaddam and Anthony J. Marsella (Washington, DC: American Psychological Association, 2004), 11–47. The quotation is on page 16.

5 C. Carr, *The Lessons of Terror: A History of Warfare Against Civilians, Why It Has Always Failed and Why It Will Fail Again* (New York, Random House, 2002).

6 See, for example, William Gorman, "Refugee Survivors of Torture: Trauma and Treatment," *Professional Psychology: Research and Practice* 32 (October 2001): 443–451; and Orlando P. Tizon, "Dreams and Other Sketches from a Torture Survivor's Notes," *Professional Psychology: Research and Practice* 32 (October 2001): 465–468.

7 One example is in Jeremiah 20:3–4, where a priest named Pashur arrested and whipped the prophet Jeremiah. The next day, when Jeremiah was released, he told Pashur that he would be given a new name that means "The Man Who Lives in Terror," because the Lord would send terror on the priest and his friends at the imminent time when the king of Babylon would invade Jerusalem.

8 The research is by Marc Sageman from the University of Pennsylvania. His work is cited frequently in articles on terrorism. See M. Sageman, *Understanding Terror Networks* (Philadelphia PA: University of Pennsylvania Press, 2004). The material in the present paragraph is taken from an article by Sadie F. Dingfelder, "Fatal Friendships: Social Groups, Rather Than Formal Organizations, Form the Backbone of Today's Most Dangerous Terrorist Organizations," *Monitor on Psychology* 35 (November 2004): 20–21.

9   Marsella, "Reflections on International Terrorism"; and Fathali M. Moghaddam, "The Staircase to Terrorism: A Psychological Exploration," *American Psychologist* 60 (February-March 2005): 161–169. See also Fathali M. Moghaddam, "Cultural Preconditions for Potential Terrorist Groups: Terrorism and Societal Change," in Moghaddam and Marsella, *Understanding Terrorism*, 103–117.

10 For summaries of these findings, see Yael Danieli, Brian Engdahl, and William E. Schlenger, "The Psychosocial Aftermath of Terrorism," in Moghaddam and Marsella, *Understanding Terrorism*, 223–246; Tom Pyszczynski, Sheldon Solomon, and Jeff Greenberg, *In the Wake of 9/11: The Psychology of Terror* (Washington, DC: American Psychological Association, 2003).

11 P. Reaney, July 11, 2004, reported in David B. Henry, Patrick H. Tolan, and Deborah Gorman-Smith, "Have There Been Lasting Effects Associated with the September 11, 2001, Terrorist Attacks Among Inner-City Parents and Children?" *Professional Psychology: Research and Practice* 35 (October 2004): 542–547.

12 Henry et al., "Have There Been Lasting Effects?" Other research articles supporting the fading of symptoms following the September 11 attacks include Kelley L. Callahan, Mark J. Hilsenroth, Tal Yonai, and Charles A. Waehler, "Longitudinal Stress Responses to the 9/11 Terrorist Attacks in a New York Metropolitan College Sample," *Stress, Trauma and Crisis: An International Journal* 8 (January-March 2005): 45–60; and Jennifer Stuber, Sandro Galea, Betty Pfefferbaum, Sharon Vandivere, Kristin Moore, and Gerry Fairbrother, "Behavior Problems in New York City's Children After the September 11, 2001, Terrorist Attacks," *American Journal of Orthopsychiatry* 75 (April 2005): 190–200.

13 Lea Winerman, "Fighting Fire with Psychology," *Monitor on Psychology* 35 (September 2004): 28–30.

14 This is the conclusion of psychologist Gaithri Fernando, whose research is described by M. Dittmann, "The Aftershock: Predicting How Tsunami Survivors Will Respond," *Monitor on Psychology* 36 (March 2005): 38.

15 Melissa Dittman, "After the Wave," *Monitor on Psychology* 36 (March 2005): 36–38.

16 F. C. Craigie, Jr., "Acute Stress Disorder," in *Baker Encyclopedia of Psychology*, ed. David G. Benner and Peter C. Hill, 2nd ed. (Grand Rapids, MI: Baker, 1999), 42. See also Cheryl Regehr, "Bringing the Trauma Home: Spouses of Paramedics," *Journal of Loss & Trauma* 10 (March-April, 2005): 97–114; R. H. Rade, "Acute Versus Chronic Post-Traumatic Stress Disorder," *Integrative Physiological and Behavioral Science* 28 (1993): 46–56; and Richard A. Bryant and Allison G. Harvey, *Acute Stress Disorder: A Handbook of Theory, Assessment, and Treatment* (Washington, DC: American Psychological Association, 2000).

17 Mary Sykes Wylie, "The Politics of PTSD: How a Controversial Diagnosis Battled Its Way into DSM," *Psychotherapy Networker* 28 (January-February 2004): 36–38.

18 Mark H. Pollack, Kathleen T. Brady, Randall D. Marshall, and Rachel Yehuda, "Trauma and Stress: Diagnosis and Treatment," *Journal of Clinical Psychiatry Audiograph Series* 5 (February 2002): 1–19. See also W. Seegobin, "Posttraumatic Stress Disorder," in Benner and Hill, *Baker Encyclopedia of Psychology*, 889–891.

19 See, for example, Sherry A. Falsetti, "Cognitive-Behavioral Therapy in the Treatment of Posttraumatic Stress Disorder," *Primary Psychiatry* 10 (May 2003): 78–83.

20 A good place to start with the extra training might be with the books that have been appearing with increasing frequency. These include the following, none of which is written from a Christian perspective: Robert Scaer, *The Trauma Spectrum: Hidden Wounds and Human Resiliency* (New York: Norton, 2005); Pauline Boss, *Loss, Trauma, and Resilience: Therapeutic Work with Ambiguous Loss* (New York: Norton, 2005); Marion F. Solomon and Daniel J. Siegel, eds., *Healing Trauma: Attachment, Mind, Body, and Brain* (New York: Norton, 2003); Brett T. Litz, *Early Intervention for Trauma and Traumatic Loss* (New York: Guilford, 2003); Robert J. Ursano, Carol S. Fullerton, and Ann E. Norwood, eds., *Terrorism and Disaster: Individual and Community Mental Health Interventions* (New York: Cambridge University Press, 2003); and Pat Ogden, Kekuni Minton, and Clare Pain, *Trauma and the Body: A Sensimotor Approach to Psychotherapy* (New York: Norton, 2006). For Christian perspectives, see John Fawcett, ed., *Stress and Trauma Handbook* (Monrovia, CA: World

Vision, 2003); and H. Norman Wright, *The New Guide to Crisis & Trauma Counseling* (Ventura, CA: Regal Books, 2003).

21 Daniel Siegel, "The Brain in the Palm of Your Hand," *Psychotherapy Networker* 26 (September-October 2002): 32–33.

22 Ibid., 32.

23 Patricia Berne and Louis Savary, "The 3 Logics of the Brain," *Psychotherapy Networker* 28 (September-October 2004): 40–41.

24 Mary Sykes Wylie, "The Limits of Talk: Bessel van der Kolk Wants to Transform the Treatment of Trauma," *Psychotherapy Networker* 28 (January-February 2004): 30–39.

25 See Wylie, "Limits of Talk"; also Mary Sykes Wylie, "Mindsight: Daniel Siegel Offers Therapists a New Vision of the Brain," *Psychotherapy Networker* 28 (September-October 2004): 29–39; Brent Atkinson, "Altered States: Why Insight by Itself Isn't Enough for Lasting Change," *Psychotherapy Networker* 28 (September-October 2004): 43–45, 67; and Mary Sykes Wylie and Richard Simon, "Discoveries from the Black Box: How the Neuroscience Revolution Can Change Your Practice," *Psychotherapy Networker* 26 (September-October 2002): 26–37, 38.

26 For a practical and diverse summary of intervention strategies, see Elspeth Cameron Ritchie, Patricia J. Watson, and Matthew J. Friedman, eds., *Interventions Following Mass Violence and Disasters: Strategies for Mental Health Practitioners* (New York: Guilford, 2006).

27 For arguments against emotional debriefing that comes too soon, see Pollack et al., "Trauma and Stress"; R. A. Mayou, A. Ehlers, and M. Hobbbs, "Psychological Debriefing for Road Traffic Accident Victims: Three Year Follow-up of a Randomised Controlled Trial," *British Journal of Psychiatry* 176 (2000): 589–593; R. K. Pitman, B. Altman, and E. Greenwald, "Psychiatric Complications During Flooding Therapy for Posttraumatic Stress Disorder," *Journal of Clinical Psychiatry* 52 (1999): 13–18; and Grant J. Devilly and Peter Cotton, "Psychological Debriefing and the Workplace: Defining a Concept, Controversies and Guidelines for Intervention," *Australian Psychologist* 38 (July 2003): 144–150.

28 Simon Wessely, Martin Deahl, Mary Cannon, Kwame McKenzie, and Andrew Sims, "Psychological Debriefing Is a Waste of Time," *British Journal of Psychiatry* 183 (July 2003): 12–14.

29 Steve J. Lewis, "Do One-Shot Preventive Interventions for PTSD Work? A Systematic Research Synthesis of Psychological Debriefings," *Aggression and Violent Behavior* 8 (May-June 2003): 329–343; Jan H. Kamphuis and Paul M. G. Emmelkamp, "20 Years of Research into Violence and Trauma: Past and Future Developments," *Journal of Interpersonal Violence* 20 (February 2005): 167–174; Judith L. Herman, "Early Intervention for Trauma and Traumatic Loss," *American Journal of Psychiatry* 162 (May 2005): 1036–1037. In this latter article Herman writes that "rigorous clinical trials suggest that critical incident stress debriefing is ineffective for preventing the development of posttraumatic stress disorder. . . . Most people may neither want not need this sort of professional 'help.'"

30 Carlotta Belaise, Giovanni A. Fava, and Isaac M. Marks, "Alternatives to Debriefing and Modifications to Cognitive Behavior Therapy for Posttraumatic Stress Disorder," *Psychotherapy and Psychosomatics* 74 (June 2005): 212–217.

31 Wylie, "Mindsight," 36.

32 Jessica Cardenas, Kimberly Williams, John P. Wilson, Gianna Fanouraki, and Arvin Singh, "PTSD, Major Depressive Symptoms, and Substance Abuse Following September 11, 2001, in a Midwestern University Population," *International Journal of Emergency Mental Health* 5 (Winter 2003): 15–28. See also Paige Ouimette and Pamela J. Brown, *Trauma and Substance Abuse* (Washington, DC: American Psychological Association, 2003).

33 Falsetti, "Cognitive-Behavioral Therapy"; and Shawn Powell and Dave McCone, "Treatment of Adjustment Disorder with Anxiety: A September 11, 2001, Case With a 1-Year Follow-Up," *Cognitive and Behavioral Practice* 11 (Summer 2004): 331–336. See also Victoria M. Follette and Josef I. Ruzek, eds., *Cognitive-Behavioral Therapies for Trauma* (New York: Guilford, 2006).

34 Quoted in Wylie and Simon, "Discoveries from the Black Box," 37.

35 For a summary of nonverbal therapies, see Cathy A. Malchiodi, ed., *Expressive Therapies* (New York: Guilford, 2005). It is interesting that the physiology of trauma is largely ignored in this book. See also Babette Rothschild, *The Body Remembers: The Psychophysiology of Trauma and Trauma Treatment* (New York: Norton, 2000); and Joseph LeDoux, *The Emotional Brain: The Mysterious Underpinnings of Emotional Life* (New York: Simon and Schuster, 1998).

36 Lee Cartwright, "Expanding Your Tool Kit: A New Technique that Complements EMDR and TFT," *Family Therapy Networker* 24 (September-October 2000): 71–78. See also Francine Shapiro, ed., *EMDR as an Integrative Psychotherapy Approach* (Washington, DC: American Psychological Association, 2002). Shapiro is the founder and main advocate of EMDR.

37 For detailed information on EMDR see the web site of the EMDR Institute, at *www.emdr.com*. An Internet search will uncover other sites dealing with EMDR and with FTF. According to *www.thoughtfield.com*, "Thought Field Therapy™ (TFT) is a safe and effective technique for the elimination of emotional distress. It gives immediate relief for PTSD, addictions, phobias, fears, and anxieties by directly treating the blockage in the energy flow created by a disturbing thought pattern. It virtually eliminates any negative feeling previously associated with a thought." It appears to be more controversial and less supported by research than EMDR.

38 The quotations from Wessells are in Deborah Smith, "Children in the Heat of War," *Monitor on Psychology* 32 (September 2003): 29–31.

39 The evidence-based therapies are still controversial, and many approaches that appear to work have not yet been validated empirically. See John C. Norcross, Larry E. Beutler, and Ronald F. Levant, eds., *Evidence-Based Practices in Mental Health: Debate and Dialogue on the Fundamental Questions* (Washington, DC: American Psychological Association, 2005).

40 D. Smith, "Empowering Communities," *Monitor on Psychology* 32 (September 2001): 31.

41 The counselor who mobilized the school group was Jack Saul, "Surviving Disaster," *Psychotherapy Networker* 28 (November-December 2004): 40–41. See also, Michael G. Wessells, "Terrorism and the Mental Health and Well-Being of Refugees and Displaced People," in Moghaddam and Marsella, *Understanding Terrorism*, 247–263; Ron Taffel, "From Crucible to Community: Renewal in the Midst of Calamity," *Psychotherapy Networker* 25 (November-December 2001): 23–24, 39; and Robert D. Macy, Lenore Behar, Robert Paulson, Jon Delman, Lisa Schmid, and Stephanie F. Smith, "Community Based, Acute Posttraumatic Stress Management: A Description and Evaluation of a Psychosocial-Intervention Continuum," *Harvard Review of Psychiatry* 12 (July-August 2004): 217–228.

42 Robert W. Bagley, "Trauma and Traumatic Stress Among Missionaries," *Journal of Psychology and Theology* 31 (Summer 2003): 97–112.

43 Rob Waters, "After the Deluge: Is Disaster Mental Health Serving Tsunami Survivors?" *Psychotherapy Networker* 29 (May-June 2005): 17–18.

44 Tori DeAngelis, "Helping Kids Cope with a New Threat," *Monitor on Psychology* 33 (April 2002): 33.

45 Philippians 4:6, 7.

40. Other Issues

1 Miriam's story is adapted from two articles, one written by Miriam and one written by her mother. See Miriam Poser, "Anorexia Nervosa—My Story," *Journal of Family Therapy* 27 (May 2005): 142–143; and Maren Poser, "Anorexia Nervosa—A Parent's Perspective," *Journal of Family Therapy* 27 (May 2005): 144–146.

2 Sandhya Limaye, "Exploring the Impact of Hearing Impairment on Self-Concept," *International Journal for the Advancement of Counselling* 26 (December 2004): 369–374.

3 Camilla R. Williams and Norman Ables, "Issues and Implications of Deaf Culture in Therapy," *Professional Psychology: Research and Practice* 35 (December 2004): 643–648. See also Michael A. Harvey, *Psychotherapy with Deaf and Hard-of-Hearing Persons: A Systemic Model* (Mahwah, NJ: Lawrence Erlbaum Associates, 1989); Kristina M. English, *Counseling Children with Hearing Impairments and Their Families* (Boston, MA: Allyn & Bacon, 2001); and Neil S. Glickman and Sanjay Gulalti, eds., *Mental Health Care of Deaf People: A Culturally Affirmative Approach* (Mahwah, NJ: Lawrence Erlbaum, 2003).

4 Susan M. Koger, Ted Schettler, and Bernard Weiss, "Environmental Toxicants and Developmental Disabilities: A Challenge for Psychologists," *American Psychologist* 60 (April 2005): 243–255.

5 This new paradigm for looking at the disabled is discussed by Rhoda Olkin and Constance Pledger, "Can Disability Studies and Psychology Join Hands?" *American Psychologist* 58 (April 2003): 296–304; and Carol J. Gill, Donald G. Kewman, and Ruth W. Brannon, "Transforming Psychological Practice and Society: Policies That Reflect the New Paradigm," *American Psychologist* 58 (April 2003): 305–312.

6 Constance Pledger, "Discourse on Disability and Rehabilitation Issues: Opportunities for Psychology," *American Psychologist* 58 (April 2003): 279–284.

7 One of the best books in this area, written by a Christian counselor, is by Rosemarie S. Cook, *Counseling Families of Children with Disabilities* (Dallas, TX: Word, 1990). See also Milton Seligman, "Handicapped Children and Their Families," *Journal of Counseling and Development* 64 (December 1985): 274–277.

8 Jessica Jones and Jennifer Passey, "Family Adaptation, Coping and Resources: Parents of Children with Developmental Disabilities and Behaviour Problems," *Journal on Developmental Disabilities* 11 (2005): 31–46.

9 Peter Burke, *Brothers and Sisters of Disabled Children* (London: Jessica Kingsley, 2003). See also Don Meyer and David Gallagher, eds., *The Sibling Slam Book: What It's Really Like to Have a Brother or Sister with Special Needs* (Bethesda, MD: Woodbine House, 2005).

10 Nicole Crawford, "Parenting with a Disability: The Last Frontier," *Monitor on Psychology* 34 (May 2003): 68–70.

11 For an in-depth discussion of disabilities, see Donna Falvo, *Medical and Psychosocial Aspects of Chronic Illness and Disability*, 3rd ed. (Sudbury, MA: Jones and Bartlett, 2005). See also Rhoda Olkin, *What Psychotherapists Should Know About Disability* (New York: Guilford, 2001); and Robert G. Frank and Timothy Elliott, *Handbook of Rehabilitation Psychology* (Washington, DC: American Psychological Association, 2000).

12 I was unable to find any references to psychologists or counselors with disabilities, although I have some colleagues who fit that category. Some writers suggest that a major criteria for admission to the counseling field is the ability of the counselor to work without any limitations that would adversely influence the counseling. For example, if the counselor is unable to hear, this could adversely influence counseling. See Wendy K. Enochs and Colleen A. Etzbach, "Impaired Student Counselors: Ethical and Legal Considerations for the Family," *Family Journal: Counseling & Therapy for Couples & Families* 12 (October 2004): 396–400.

13 This section of the chapter distinguishes between mental *disorders*, which are the mental illnesses that we discussed in chapter 33, and mental *disabilities*, which involve a biological condition that results in limited intellectual capacity so that the person functions cognitively in ways that are not appropriate or normal for one's age.

14 You can learn about L'Arche on the Internet. Like many others, I first learned about L'Arche from my reading of Henry Nouwen's books, including, Henri J. M. Nouwen, *Lifesigns: Intimacy, Fecundity, and Ecstasy in Christian Perspective* (Garden City, NY: Doubleday, 1986); Henri J. M. Nouwen, *The Road to Daybreak: A Spiritual Journey* (Garden City, NY: Doubleday, 1988); and Nouwen's moving story about a young, severely retarded man, *Adam: God's Beloved* (Maryknoll, NY: Orbis, 1977).

15 Chapter 13.

16 An Internet search will reveal a number of web sites devoted both to mental retardation and to Down Syndrome.

17 For a detailed discussion of mental disabilities, see Mary Beirne-Smith, James R. Patton, and Shannon H. Kime, *Mental Retardation: An Introduction to Intellectual Disability*, 7th ed. (Upper Saddle River, NJ: Prentice-Hall, 2005).

18 Greg Critser, *Fat Land: How Americans Became the Fattest People in the World* (Boston, MA: Mariner Books, 2004). For an insightful discussion of obesity, see Cathy Newman, "Why Are We So Fat?" *National Geographic* 206 (August 2004): 46–61. The article notes that there now are more overnourished people than undernourished around the nation.

19 For a discussion of Christian diet programs, with their questionable assumption that obesity most often reflects a spiritual problem, see R. Marie Griffith, *Born Again Bodies: Flesh and Spirit in American Christianity* (Berkeley, CA: University of California, 2004).

20 K. D. Brown, "Obesity: Understanding and Treating a Serious, Prevalent, and Refractory Disorder," *Journal of Consulting and Clinical Psychology* 50 (1982): 820–840.

21 Tori DeAngelis, "What's to Blame for the Surge in Super-size Americans?" *Monitor on Psychology* 35 (January 2004): 46–49.

22 Tori DeAngelis, "Family-Size Portions for One," *Monitor on Psychology* 35 (January 2004): 50–51.

23 Marion Nestle, *Food Politics: How the Food Industry Influences Nutrition and Health* (Berkeley, CA: University of California Press, 2003); and Claudine Fox and Carol Joughin, eds., *Childhood\em\Onset Eating Problems—Findings from Research* (London: The Royal College of Psychiatrists, 2002).

24 These conclusions are from research by Mary Dallman and colleagues at the University of California, San Francisco, cited by Tori DeAngelis, "What's to Blame," but first reported in *Proceedings of the National Academy of Sciences* 100 (September 30, 2003), online.

25 According to the web site of the American Obesity Association, obesity has become "a global epidemic."

26 Tori DeAngelis, "What's to Blame."

27 More scientific is the calculation of one's Body Mass Index or BMI. To get your BMI, go to any Internet search engine, like Google or Yahoo and type in BMI. With almost no searching, you will find a formula that lets you calculate your BMI instantly and determine if you are obese, overweight, or within normal range. The obese person has a higher BMI than the overweight person.

28 These issues, along with treatment, are discussed in detail by Kevin Thompson and Linda Smolak, eds., *Body Image, Eating Disorders, and Obesity in Youth: Assessment, Prevention, and Treatment* (Washington, DC: American Psychological Association, 2001); and J. Kevin Thompson, ed., *Body Image, Eating Disorders, and Obesity: An Integrative Guide for Assessment and Treatment* (Washington, DC: American Psychological Association, 1996).

29 T. DeAngelis, "Size-Based Discrimination May Be Hardest on Children," *Monitor on Psychology* 35 (January 2004): 62.

30 M. Dittman, "Walkable Cities Mean Less Obesity," *Monitor on Psychology* 35 (January 2004): 49.

31 This is the conclusion of an author who wrote about twenty-five years ago, but this still applies. See J. Rodin, "Obesity: Why the Losing Battle?" in *Psychological Aspects of Obesity: A Handbook*, ed. B. B. Wolman (New York: Van Nostrand Reinhold, 1982), 30–87.

32 Leigh E. Rich, "Bringing More Effective Tools to the Weight-Loss Table," *Monitor on Psychology* 35 (January 2004): 52–55; Charlotte Hugg, "Teaming Up to Drop Pounds," *Monitor on Psychology* 35 (January 2004): 56–58; Zafra Cooper, Christopher G. Fairburn, and Deborah M. Hawker, *Cognitive-Behavioral Treatment of Obesity* (New York: Guilford, 2004); and Thomas A. Wadden and Albert J. Stunkard, *Handbook of Obesity Treatment* (New York, Guilford, 2004).

33 Rich, "Bringing More Effective Tools."

34 L. E. Rich, "Along with Increased Surgery, a Growing Need for Support, " *Monitor on Psychology* 35 (January 2004): 54.

35 For more detailed information, see K. R. Kracke, "Anorexia Nervosa," in *Baker Encyclopedia of Psychology*, ed. David G. Benner and Peter C. Hill, 2nd ed. (Grand Rapids, MI: Baker, 1999), 84–86; Paul E. Garfinkel, "Eating Disorders," in *Comprehensive Textbook of Psychiatry/VI*, ed. Harold Kaplan and Benjamin J. Sadock (Baltimore, MD.: Williams and Wilkins, 1995), 1361–1371.

36 Raymond E. Vath, *Counseling Those with Eating Disorders* (Waco, TX: Word, 1986).

37 New psychological approaches continue to appear. For example, see Lisa A. Kotler, Gillian S. Boudreau, and Michael J. Devlin, "Emerging Psychotherapies for Eating Disorders," *Journal of Psychiatric Practice* 9 (November 2003): 431–441; and Allan S. Kaplan, "Psychological Treatments for Anorexia Nervosa: A Review of Published Studies and Promising New Directions," *Canadian Journal of Psychiatry* 47 (April 2002): 235–242.

38 M. Sean O'Halloran and Arlene K. Weimer, "Changing Roles: Individual and Family Therapy in the Treatment of Anorexia Nervosa," *Family Journal: Counseling & Therapy for Couples and Families* 13 (April 2005): 181–187; James Lock, Daniel LeGrange, W. Stewart Agras, and Christopher Dare, *Treatment Manual for Anorexia Nervosa: A Family-Based Approach* (New York: Guilford, 2001); and G. F. M. Russell et al., "An Evaluation of Family Therapy in Anorexia Nervosa and Bulimia Nervosa," *Archives of General Psychiatry* 44 (1987): 1047–1056.

39 Vath, *Counseling Those with Eating Disorders*. More than half of the book deals with deeper-level issues such as those listed in this paragraph.

40 This phrase is used in an excellent summary article by Mark A. Yarhouse and Gloria Anderson, "Persons with HIV/AIDS," *Journal of Psychology and Christianity* 21 (Winter 2002): 333–340.

41 The virus also attacks brain cells and can lead to AIDS dementia complex, a slowly progressing disorder that leads to impaired intellectual functioning, slowed motor activity, apathy, concentration difficulties, and reduced ability to solve problems. Sometimes, these symptoms are followed by loss of coordination and mental disorder.

42 Seth C. Kalichman, *Understanding AIDS: Advances in Research and Training* (Washington, DC: American Psychological Association, 1998); and E. M. Butler, "AIDS," in *Baker Encyclopedia of Psychology*, ed. David G. Benner and Peter C. Hill, 2nd ed. (Grand Rapids, MI: Baker, 1999), 58–59.

43 A significant amount of HIV and AIDS information is available on the Internet. This includes the latest statistical figures. See also Tony Barnett and Alan Whiteside, *AIDS in the Twenty-First Century: Disease and Globalization* (New York: Palgrave/Macmillan, 2003); Darrel Ward and Darrell E. Ward, *The Amfar AIDS Handbook: The Complete Guide to Understanding HIV and AIDS* (New York: Norton, 1998); and Greg Behrman, *The Invisible People: How the U.S. Has Slept Through the Global AIDS Pandemic, the Greatest Humanitarian Catastrophe of Our Time* (Northampton, MA: Free Press, 2004).

44 It should be noted that prevention programs are getting better, but they remain difficult to implement. See, for example, Catherine Campbell, *Letting Them Die: Why HIV/AIDS Prevention Programmes Fail* (Bloomington, IN: Indiana University Press, 2003); also Christopher M.. Gordon, Andrew D. Forsyth, Ron Stall, and Laura W. Cheever, "Prevention Interventions with Persons Living with HIV/AIDS: State of the Science and Future Directions," *AIDS Education & Prevention* 17 (February 2005): 6–20.

45 1 John 1:9.

46 Gregg R. Albers, *Counseling and AIDS* (Dallas, TX: Word, 1990).

47 Richard E. Price, Michael M. Omizo, and Victoria L. Mammett, "Counseling Clients with AIDS," *Journal of Counseling and Development* 65 (October 1986): 96–97.

48 Mary Pipher, *In the Middle of Everywhere: The World's Refugees Come to Our Town* (New York: Harcourt, 2002).

49 Dennis Palumbo, "Psychotherapy in LaLa Land: Confessions of a Hollywood Shrink," *Psychotherapy Networker* 29 (July-August 2005): 52–58.

50 Susan R. Johnson, "The Epidemiology of Premenstrual Syndrome," *Primary Psychiatry* 11 (December 2004): 27–32.

51 Mary Kathleen B. Lustyk, Laura Widman, Amy Paschane, and Erika Ecker, "Stress, Quality of Life and Physical Activity in Women with Varying Degrees of Premenstrual Symptomatology," *Women and Health* 39 (2004): 35–44; and T. Land and Andrew Francis, "Premenstrual Symptomatology, Locus of Control, Anxiety and Depression in Women with Normal Menstrual Cycles," *Archives of Women's Mental Health* 6 (2003): 127–138.

52 Nicole Crawford, "Helping Inmates Cope with Prison Life," *Monitor on Psychology* 34 (July-August 2003): 62–63.

53 Etienne Benson, "Rehabilitate or Punish," *Monitor on Psychology* 34 (July-August 2003): 46–47.

54 Robert D. Morgan, Alicia T. Rozycki, and Scott Wilson, "Inmate Perceptions of Mental Health Services," *Professional Psychology: Research and Practice* 35 (August 2004): 389–396.

55 For more information about Chaplain Baird (including his life story) and about the organization that he represents, Good News Jail & Prison Ministry, please go to *www.goodnewsjail.org*. Chaplain Baird works in Illinois at Cook County Prison.

56 Tori DeAngelis, "Punishment of Innocents: Children of Parents Behind Bars," *Monitor on Psychology* 32 (May 2001): 56–59.

57 Charles W. Hoge, Holly E. Toboni, Stephen C. Messer, Nicole Bell, Paul Amoroso, and David T. Orman, "The Occupational Burden of Mental Disorders in the U.S. Military: Psychiatric Hospitalizations, Involuntary Separations, and Disability," *American Journal of Psychiatry* 162 (March 2005): 585–591.

58 Amy B. Adler, Ann H. Huffman, Paul D. Bliese, and Carl Andrew Castro, "The Impact of Deployment Length and Experience on the Well-Being of Male and Female Soldiers," *Journal of Occupational Health Psychology* 10 (April 2005): 121–137; and Susan Jones, "Paying the Price: The Psychiatric Cost of War," *Archives of Psychiatric Nursing* 18 (August 2004): 119–120.

59 Mark Greer, "A New Kind of War," *Monitor on Psychology* 36 (April 2005): 38–41.

60 One of the best examples and most trusted organizations is Cadence International, a network of civilian missionaries and former military personnel who minister to servicemen and women in different parts of the world. See *www.cadence.org*. About thirty or more years ago, I was privileged to work with Cadence, visiting almost all of their centers worldwide to teach basic counseling skills to the early missionaries in the organization. I was impressed with the organization then, and I remain impressed now.

61 Laura Smith, "Psychotherapy, Classism, and the Poor: Conspicuous by Their Absence,"

American Psychologist 60 (October 2005): 687–696. The quotations are from page 693. See also Ana Wong McDonald, "Five Loaves and Two Fish for the Inner-City Poor," *Journal of Psychology and Christianity* 21 (Fall 2002): 253–256.

62   Smith, "Psychotherapy," 692.

63   Frank L. Gardner, "Applied Sport Psychology in Professional Sports: The Team Psychologist," *Professional Psychology: Research and Practice* 32 (February 2001): 34–39. One team of mental-health professionals works with athletes who have developed eating disorders as a result of trying to get in shape for athletic performance. See Roberta Trattner Sherman and Ron A. Thompson, "Athletes and Disordered Eating: Four Major Issues for the Professional Psychologist," *Professional Psychology: Research and Practice* 32 (February 2001): 27–33.

64   One interesting study investigated the role of prayer in athletes, how they used prayer, for what purposes, and when. See Daniel R. Czech, Craig A. Wrisberg, Leslee A. Fisher, Charles L. Thompson, and Gene Hayes, "The Experience of Christian Prayer in Sport: An Existential Phenomenological Investigation," *Journal of Psychology and Christianity* 23 (Winter 2004): 3–11.

65   Hebrews 12:15, NIV.

66   Philip Yancey addresses this question in his book *Where Is God When It Hurts? A Comforting, Healing Guide for Coping with Hard Times* (Grand Rapids, MI: Zondervan, 2001).

67   The psalmist's struggles are recorded in Psalm 73. His bitterness is mentioned in verse 21. In many ways the entire book of Job is about a man who appeared to be attacked unjustly and struggled with the question of why.

68   2 Corinthians 12:7–10; 1 Peter 1:5–7; Romans 8:28; Hebrews 12:11; Psalm 119:71; Romans 5:3–5.

69   2 Corinthians 1:3–7.

70   John 9:1–41; Luke 13:1–5.

41. Spiritual Issues

1   Sigmund Freud's views about religion were expressed succinctly in his book *The Future of an Illusion* (Garden City, NY: Doubleday Anchor Books, 1927); for a fascinating and extremely well-documented critique of Freud's religious position, see Paul C. Vitz, *Sigmund Freud's Christian Unconscious* (New York: Guilford, 1988).

2   For a summary of some of the secular and religious attitudes toward religious counselees that were prevalent in the 1980s and before, see the carefully written and well-documented paper by Christian psychologist Everett L. Worthington, Jr., "Religious Counseling: A Review of Published Empirical Research," *Journal of Counseling and Development* 64 (March 1986): 421–431. A more complete and updated report is by Everett L. Worthington, Jr., T. A. Kurusu, Michael E. McCullough, and Steven J. Sandage, "Empirical Research on Religion and Psychotherapeutic Processes and Outcomes: A 10-Year Review and Research Project," *Psychological Bulletin* 119 (1996): 448–487.

3   The list of books continues to increase. Please note that most of these books are published after 1995 or into the twenty-first century. See the following, for example. Some of the editors and authors are Christian, but none of these books is written specifically for Christian audiences: Edward P. Shafranske, ed., *Religion and the Clinical Practice of Psychology* (Washington, DC: American Psychological Association, 1996); David A. Steere, *Spiritual Presence in Psychotherapy: A Guide for Caregivers* (New York: Brunner/Mazel, 1997); Kenneth I. Pargament, *The Psychology of Religion and Coping: Theory, Research, Practice* (New York: Guilford, 1997); William R. Miller, ed., *Integrating Spirituality into Treatment* (Washington, DC: American Psychological Association, 1999); Matthew B. Schwartz and Kalman J. Kaplan, *Biblical Stories for Psychotherapy and Counseling* (New York: Haworth, 2004); P. Scott Richards and Allen E. Bergin, eds., *Casebook for a Spiritual Strategy in Counseling and Psychotherapy* (Washington, DC: American Psychological Association, 2004); Len Sperry and Edward P. Shafranske, eds., *Spiritually Oriented Psychotherapy* (Washington, DC: American Psychological Association, 2005); and William R. Miller and Harold D. Delaney, eds., *Judeo-Christian Perspectives on Psychology* (Washington, DC: American Psychological Association, 2005).

4   For a summary of contemporary spirituality, see Gary R. Collins, *The Soul Search: A Spiritual Journey to Authentic Intimacy with God* (Nashville, TN: Oliver-Nelson, 1998).

5   Walter Trobisch, *The Complete Works of Walter Trobisch* (Downers Grove, IL: InterVarsity Press, 1987), 696.

6 2 Peter 1:21, NIV.

7 Romans 11:33–34.

8 1 Peter 1:14–16; 2:21.

9 Ephesians 6:11.

10 Romans 12:1.

11 Romans 13:14; 1 Peter 2:11; 1 John 1:8–2:2.

12 Ephesians 2:4–9.

13 Romans 8:15–17; Micah 6:8.

14 Psalm 103:8, 13, 14.

15 John 14:16–17; Luke 12:12; 1 Thessalonians 4:8; 1 Peter 5:10.

16 Matthew 28:20; Proverbs 18:24.

17 1 Peter 3:18.

18 Romans 12:2; Hebrews 12:1; 1 Peter 1:14–16; 2:21–22; Galatians 5:22–23.

19 Hebrews 13:16.

20 Matthew 20:26–27; James 3:13–14; 1 Peter 5, 6.

21 Joshua 1:9.

22 Philippians 3:12–14.

23 2 Timothy 2:21.

24 1 Corinthians 2:14–16.

25 Philip Jenkins, *The Next Christendom: The Coming of Global Christianity* (New York: Oxford, 2002).

26 In addition, a number of professional counselors acknowledge that spiritual practices help mental-health practitioners themselves with their own stresses. See Paul W. Case and Mark R. McMinn, "Spiritual Coping and Well-Functioning Among Psychologists," *Journal of Psychology and Theology* 29 (Spring 2001): 29–40.

27 The above is adapted from a brochure from National Center on Addiction and Substance Abuse at Columbia University, 2005.

28 From Kevin Helliker, "Why Attending Religious Services May Benefit Health," *Wall Street Journal*, May 3, 2005, *http://www.post-gazette.com/pg/05123/498354.stm*.

29 This was a conclusion from a highly acclaimed study of American life by Robert N. Bellah et al., *Habits of the Heart: Individualism and Commitment in American Life* (New York: Harper & Row, 1985), 281. There does not appear to be evidence that the conclusions of these researchers, published more than twenty years ago, have changed in the intervening two decades.

30 Ephesians 2:8, 9.

31 1 Corinthians 3:1–3.

32 Pamela Ebstyne King, James I. Furrow, and Natalie Roth, "The Influence of Families and Peers on Adolescent Religiousness," *Journal of Psychology and Christianity* 21 (Summer 2002): 109–120.

33 This is the conclusion of Richard Foster, *The Challenge of the Disciplined Life: Reflections on Money, Sex, and Power* (San Francisco: HarperSanFrancisco, 1989).

34 Romans 6:13, 16; Psalm 32:3–4. For an in-depth discussion of the role of sin, written by a Christian clinical psychologist, see Mark R. McMinn, *Why Sin Matters: The Surprising Relationship Between Our Sin and God's Grace* (Wheaton, IL: Tyndale 2004).

35 For example, see Psalm 50:8–15; Isaiah 1:11–17; Hosea 6:6; Matthew 23:23, 24; Colossians 2:23; Galatians 3:2; 5:1. For a discussion of legalism written from the perspective of Christians in their twenties, see Cara Davis, "Legalism: What It's Doing to This Generation," *Relevant* 16 (September-October 2005): 64–65.

36 Ephesians 2:8, 9.

37 Philippians 2:12–13.

38 Colossians 2:8, 16–23.

39 Revelation 3:15–19.

40 Proverbs 16:18.

41 Hebrews 12:15.

42 1 Timothy 6:10; Hebrews 13:5; James 4:3, 13; Matthew 20:25–28.

43 1 Timothy 6:10–21.

44 Romans 12:2.

45 Trobisch, *Complete Works*, 697.

46 Jerry White, *The Power of Commitment: How Ordinary People Can Make an Extraordinary Impact on the World*, rev. ed. (Colorado Springs, CO: NavPress, 1997). The quotation is from page 9 of the first edition.

47   For example, see Luke 12:15; Ephesians 5:3; Colossians 3:5; Exodus 20:17.

48   Luke 12:13–21; Matthew 19:16–23.

49   Richard J. Foster, *Freedom of Simplicity* (San Francisco, CA: HarperSanFrancisco, 1998), 20. See also Ronald J. Sider, *Scandal of the Evangelical Conscience: Why Are Christians Living Just Like the Rest of the World?* (Grand Rapids, MI: Baker 2005); and Ronald J. Sider, *Rich Christians in an Age of Hunger* (Nashville, TN: W Publishing, 1997).

50   1 Timothy 6:9–10.

51   1 Corinthians 6:19; 1 Thessalonians 5:19.

52   1 Thessalonians 1:6; Ephesians 1:6; 3:16; 4:3; Galatians 5:22–23; Colossians 1:29; 1 John 2:20–25.

53   Technically, this sentence should state that the new interest in spiritual disciplines is mostly within Protestant circles, especially among Evangelicals. When compared to many Protestants, the disciplines appear to have been more central and widely practiced among Roman Catholic and Orthodox Christians.

54   For practical summaries of the disciplines, see Adele Ahlberg Calhoun, *Spiritual Disciplines Handbook: Practices That Transform Us* (Downers Grove, IL: InterVarsity, 2005); Richard J. Foster, *Celebration of Discipline: The Path to Spiritual Growth* (San Francisco, CA: HarperSan-Francisco, 1988); Siang Yang Tan and Douglas H. Gregg, *Disciplines of the Holy Spirit* (Grand Rapids, MI: Zondervan, 1997); Dallas Willard, *The Spirit of the Disciplines* (San Francisco, CA: HarperSanFrancisco, 1991); Donald S. Whitney, *Spiritual Disciplines for the Christian Life* (Colorado Springs, CO: NavPress, 1991); and John Ortberg, *The Life You've Always Wanted* (Grand Rapids, MI: Zondervan, 2002).

55   Brian E. Eck, "The Exploration of the Therapeutic Use of Spiritual Disciplines in Clinical Practice," *Journal of Psychology and Christianity* 21 (Fall 2002): 266–280.

56   Ibid.

57   Romans 12; 1 Corinthians 12; Ephesians 4; Hebrews 10:24–25. For a useful discussion of these issues, see Richard Lamb, *The Pursuit of God in the Company of Friends* (Downers Grove, IL: InterVarsity 2003).

58   2 Corinthians 1:3–7.

59   James 1:2–5; 2 Corinthians 12:8–10; 1 Peter 3:14, 17–18; 4:1, 12–16.

60   For a thoughtful analysis of suffering, see Philip Yancey, *Where Is God When It Hurts?* (Grand Rapids, MI: Zondervan, 1997). See also Matt and Beth Redman, *Blessed Be Your Name: Worshipping God on the Road Marked with Suffering* (Ventura, CA: Gospel Light, 2005); and John S. Feinberg, *Where Is God? A Personal Story of Finding God in Grief and Suffering* (Nashville, TN: Holman, 2004).

61   Ephesians 6:12.

62   In an earlier chapter, we noted there is little evidence to support the widely held belief, especially in psychological circles, that the exorcisms and sometimes sadistic witch hunts of the Middle Ages most often were the work of Christians and churches. "In actuality," writes Suzanne M. Phillips, "people with mental illness were not believed to be witches, nor were they executed." See Suzanne M. Phillips, "Free to Speak: Clarifying the Legacy of the Witch Hunts," *Journal of Psychology and Christianity* 21 (Spring 2002): 29–41. The quotation is from page 29.

63   C. S. Lewis, *The Screwtape Letters* (London: Collins-Fontana, 1942), 9.

64   Ephesians 6:11–20; 1 Peter 5:8–9; 2 Corinthians 11:14; James 4:7; 1 John 4:3–4; Revelation 12:9; 20:3,10. For a concise overview of demonic influence and psychopathology, please see Henry A. Virkler, "Demonic Influence, Sin, and Psychopathology," in *Baker Encyclopedia of Psychology*, ed. David G. Benner and Peter C. Hill, 2nd ed. (Grand Rapids, MI: Baker, 1999), 326–332.

65   Richard Dortch, "I Made Mistakes," *Christianity Today* 32 (March 18, 1988): 47.

66   2 Corinthians 3:7, 13; a footnote in the New International Version Study Bible notes that "the purpose of the veil was to prevent the Israelites from seeing the fading of the glory."

67   2 Corinthians 3:16–18.

68   1 John 5:16–17.

69   Job in the Old Testament and Lazarus in the New Testament were men whose sicknesses apparently were not the result of personal sin; see Job 2:3 and John 11:4; also John 9:1–5.

70   David B. Larson and Susan S. Larson, "Spirituality's Potential Relevance to Physical and Emotional Health: A Brief Review of Quantitative Research," *Journal of Psychology and Theology* 31 (Spring 2003): 37–51.

71   1 Corinthians 3:3; Ephesians 2:14.

72 Philippians 1:15–17.

73 Some of these issues are discussed in articles by Theresa Clement Tisdale, Carrie E. Doehring, and Veneta Lorraine-Poirier, "Three Voices, One Song: A Psychologist, Spiritual Director, and Pastoral Counselor Share Perspectives on Providing Care," *Journal of Psychology and Theology* 31 (Spring 2003): 52–68; Gary W. Moon, "A Spiritual Journey in Spiritually Sensitive Psychotherapy: An Interview with David G. Benner," *Journal of Psychology and Christianity* 21 (Spring 2002): 64–71; Nicholas C. Howard, Mark R. McMinn, Leslie D. Bissell, Sally R. Faries, and Jeffrey B. Van Meter, "Spiritual Directors and Clinical Psychologists: A Comparison of Mental Health and Spiritual Values," *Journal of Psychology and Theology* 28 (Winter 2000): 308–329; B. J. Zinnbauer and Kenneth I. Pargament, "Working with the Sacred: Four Approaches to Religious and Spiritual Issues in Counseling," *Journal of Counseling and Development* 78 (2000): 162–172; and Eck, "An Exploration of the Therapeutic Use of Spiritual Disciplines."

74 Gary W. Moon and David G. Benner, Special Issue Editors, "Special Issue: Psychotherapy and Spiritual Direction, Part 1," *Journal of Psychology and Theology* 30 (Winter 2002). The same two authors have included and expanded some of the material from this journal into a book, Gary W. Moon and David G. Benner, eds., *Spiritual Direction and the Care of Souls: A Guide to Christian Approaches and Practices* (Downers Grove, IL: InterVarsity, 2004).

75 C. B. Johnson, "Use of Prayer in Counseling," in *Baker Encyclopedia of Psychology*, ed. David G. Benner and Peter C. Hill, 2nd ed. (Grand Rapids, MI: Baker, 1999), 895–896; also Mark M. McMinn "Spiritual and Religious Issues in Psychotherapy," in Benner and Hill, *Baker Encyclopedia*, 1150–1153.

76 To get survey information, begin with *www.barna.org* but recognize that the Barna research concerns mostly American respondents. The quotation in the text is taken from one of the 2005 Barna Group surveys, cited on the web site. Earlier in the chapter we noted that about 90 percent of Americans claim to believe in God. The figure drops to about 70 percent when God is given the more narrow and personal definition that is cited in the text.

77 For example, see John R. Finney and H. Newton Maloney, "An Empirical Study of Contemplative Prayer as an Adjunct to Psychotherapy," *Journal of Psychology and Theology* 13 (Winter 1985): 284–90; Mark H. Butler, Julie A. Stout, and Brandt C. Gardner, "Prayer as a Conflict Resolution Ritual: Clinical Implications of Religious Couples' Report of Relationship Softening, Healing Perspective and Change Responsibility," *American Journal of Family Therapy* 30 (January-February 2002): 19–37.

78 John 13:14–15; 1 Corinthians 11:1; Philippians 3:17; 4:9; 1 Peter 5:3.

79 Jeremiah 9:23–24; Hosea 6:6; John 17:3.

80 Gordon W. Allport, *The Individual and His Religion* (New York: Macmillan, 1950), 90.

81 John 3:16; 1 John 4:7–21.

82 We have noted the more recent book on sin by McMinn, *Why Sin Matters*.

83 Romans 6:23; Matthew 13:41–42; Romans 8:1; 1 Corinthians 15:3; 1 John 1:8–10; Isaiah 43:23–25; Jeremiah 31:34.

84 James 5:16.

85 Perhaps more than anything else, the interest in forgiveness and the upsurge of research on this topic have come because of a few devoted individuals who have done research in a previously unpopular area, because of the rise of positive psychology where forgiveness is viewed positively, and because of the generous financial contribution to forgiveness research that has come at the initiation of Sir John Templeton through the Templeton Foundation.

86 Ephesians 5:18–21; Galatians 5:22–23.

87 Matthew 28:18–20.

88 Ana Wong-McDonald and Richard L. Gorsuch, "Surrender to God: An Additional Coping Style?" *Journal of Psychology and Theology* 28 (Summer 2000): 149–161.

89 Genesis 2:18.

90 1 Corinthians 12:25. Almost sixty references in the New Testament instruct Christians to do things for one another; we are urged, for example, to show concern, pray for, help, encourage, love, strengthen, serve, and bear the burdens of one another.

91 1 Peter 4:10–11.

92 For example, see two entire issues devoted to spiritual direction in the *Journal of Psychology and Theology* 31 (Winter 2002 and Spring 2003). Of special interest are the articles from these two journals, by Theresa Clement Tisdale et al., "Three Voices"; Gary W.

Moon, "Spiritual Direction: Meaning, Purpose, and Implications for Mental Health Professionals" (Winter 2002): 264–278; Lee Sperry, "Integrating Spiritual Direction Functions in the Practice of Psychotherapy" (Spring 2003): 3–31; Siang-Yang Tan, "Integrating Spiritual Direction into Psychotherapy: Ethical Issues and Guidelines" (Spring 2003): 14–23. See also Nicholas C. Howard, Mark R. McMinn, Leslie D. Bissell, Sally R. Faries, and Jeffrey B. VanMeter, "Spiritual Directors and Clinical Psychologists: A Comparison of Mental Health and Spiritual Values," *Journal of Psychology and Theology* 28 (Winter 2000): 308–320.

93 David G. Benner, *Sacred Companions: The Gift of Spiritual Friendship and Direction* (Downers Grove, IL: InterVarsity, 2002), 94. Benner's chapter "Demystifying Spiritual Direction" is the clearest description of the nature and process of spiritual direction that I have read. Another chapter, "The Ideals of Spiritual Friendship," is well worth the price of the book.

94 Nicholas C. Howard et al., "Spiritual Directors," 309.

95 Gerald G. May, *Care of Mind, Care of Spirit: Psychiatric Dimensions of Spiritual Direction* (San Francisco, CA: Harper, 1982), 6.

96 Dallas Willard, "Spiritual Formation in Christ: A Perspective on What It Is and How It Might be Done," *Journal of Psychology and Theology* 28 (Winter 2000): 254–258.

97 Michael W. Mangis, "Spiritual Formation and Christian Psychology: A Response and Application of Willard's Perspective," *Journal of Psychology and Theology* 28 (Winter 2000): 259–262; and James R. Beck, "Self and Soul: Exploring the Boundary Between Psychotherapy and Spiritual Formation," *Journal of Psychology and Theology* 31 (Spring 2003): 24–36. For a helpful summary of spiritual formation, see M. Robert Mulholland, Jr., *Invitation to a Journey: A Road Map for Spiritual Formation* (Downers Grove, IL: InterVarsity, 1993).

98 Ephesians 6:12.

99 Ephesians 6:10–18.

100 James 4:7, 8; 1 Peter 5:8–9.

101 I am grateful to Rodger K. Bufford for reminding me of this distinction. Most of the discussion in the present paragraph is adapted from Rodger K. Bufford, "Exorcism," in *Baker Encyclopedia of Psychology*, ed. David G. Benner and Peter C. Hill, 2nd ed. (Grand Rapids, MI: Baker, 1999), 416–417. The account of the demon-possessed men in the land of the Gadarenes is recorded in Matthew 8:28–34.

102 This is discussed in detail by Rodger K. Bufford, *Counseling and the Demonic* (Waco, TX: Word, 1988). I confess that I am cautious about all the books that appear to help people deal with the demonic. It seems that many authors base their conclusions about demons on what the demons tell them, ignoring the fact that the devil is the father of lies, and anything alleged to come from a demon cannot be trusted. See also Don Basham, *Deliver Us from Evil: A Pastor's Reluctant Encounters with the Powers of Darkness* (Grand Rapids, MI: Baker, 2005).

103 Notice again the qualifications in Ephesians 6:10–18; see also Matthew 17:19–21; Matthew 9:18, 28–29.

104 1 Corinthians 12:10; 1 John 4:1–3.

105 1 John 4:4.

106 Hebrews 12:5–11.

42. Counseling the Counselor

1 This is an old story, perhaps fictional, adapted from Joshua L. Liebman, *Peace of Mind* (New York: Simon & Schuster, 1946).

2 John 14:27.

3 Philippians 4:12.

4 Philippians 4:4–7.

5 1 Peter 5:7–9; James 4:7; Philippians 4:6–9.

6 Galatians 5:22; John 14:26–27.

7 This is the theme of an article by Eric T. Scalise, "When Helping You Is Hurting Me," *Christian Counseling Today* 12 (2002): 52–24.

8 John C. Norcross, "Psychotherapist Self-Care: Practitioner-Tested, Research-Informed Strategies," *Professional Psychology: Research and Practice* 31 (December 2000): 710–713.

9 Jiang Jiang, Xu Yan, and Zhang Shuyue, "Job Burnout of Psychological Counselors," *Chinese Mental Health Journal* 18 (December 2004): 854–856. See also Ellen K. Baker, "Therapist Self-Care Needs Across the Lifespan," chapter 2 in *Caring for Ourselves: A Therapist's*

Guide to Personal and Professional Well-Being (Washington, DC: American Psychological Association, 2003), 25–36; Charles R. Figley, *Treating Compassion Fatigue* (Philadelphia: Taylor & Francis, 2002); and Patricia A. Rupert and David J. Morgan, "Work Setting and Burnout Among Professional Psychologists," *Professional Psychology: Research and Practice,* 36 (October 2005): 544–550.

10   Thomas M. Skovholt and Michael H. Ronnestad, "Struggles of the Novice Counselor and Therapist," *Journal of Career Development* 30 (Fall 2003): 45–58.

11   John 12:8.

12   Alan Deutschman, "Making Change," *Fast Company* 94 (May 2005): 53–62.

13   Steven Berglas, *Reclaiming the Fire: How Successful People Overcome Burnout* (New York: Random House, 2001).

14   Norcross, "Psychotherapist Self-Care," 710.

15   Baker, *Caring for Ourselves,* 14.

16   Ibid., chapter 1.

17   The title of one brief article implied that counselors already know the importance of regular exercise, but they ignore what they know. See E. Packard, "Reminder: Exercise Helps the Therapist Self-Care," *Monitor on Psychology* 36 (November 2005): 20.

18   Leonard Felder, "I Gave at the Office: Too Often, Therapists Leave Their Listening Skills at Work," *Psychotherapy Networker* 29 (September-October 2005): 60–63.

19   Jamie Chamberlin, "Emergency Caregivers Are at Risk When Working with Children," *Monitor on Psychology* 32 (February 2001): 62–63.

20   E. Glenn Wagner, "Walking Alone: One Pastor's Journey into Depression," *Rev!* 8 (May-June 2005): 48–57.

21   Adapted from Dennis Palumbo, "The Burnt-Out Therapist," *Psychotherapy Networker* 24 (September-October 2000): 64–69.

22   Quoted in Baker, *Caring for Ourselves,* 129. For other excellent discussions of the counselor's self-care, see J. D. Guy, *The Personal Life of the Psychotherapist* (New York: Wiley, 1987); and Mary B. Pipher, *Letters to a Young Therapist* (New York: Basic Books, 2003).

23   Hebrews 10:25.

24   1 Corinthians 10:12.

25   For more detailed discussion of counselor-mentors, see W. Brad Johnson, "The Intentional Mentor: Strategies and Guidelines for the Practice of Mentoring," *Professional Psychology: Research and Practice* 33 (February 2002): 88–96; Melissa Dittman, "Building Mentorships for Success," *GradPSYCH* 3 (January 2003): 40–45; W. Brad Johnson and Jennifer M. Huwe, *Getting Mentored in Graduate School* (Washington, DC: American Psychological Association, 2003); and Peter F. Wilson and W. Brad Johnson, "Core Virtues for the Practice of Mentoring," *Journal of Psychology and Theology* 29 (Summer 2001): 121–130. For an insightful article on mentoring in general, see J. R. Briggs, "Confessions from a Young Timothy," *Rev!* 6 (July-August 2003): 55–60.

26   Louis McBurney, *Every Pastor Needs a Pastor* (Waco, TX: Word, 1977).

27   Henri J. M. Nouwen, *The Genesee Diary: Report from a Trappist Monastery* (Garden City, NY: Doubleday-Image, 1976), 13.

28   Mark 1:32–35; Luke 9:10.

29   Mark 1:37–38.

30   Luke 9:1–2.

31   Henri J. M. Nouwen, *Clowning in Rome: Reflections on Solitude, Celibacy, Prayer and Contemplation* (Garden City, NY: Doubleday-Image, 1979), 53–54.

32   James 1:27.

33   John 17:15.

34   1 John 1:8–9.

35   Except for the periodic fund-raising letters that come from the university or college development offices, fund-raisers always seem to have an uncanny ability to find alumni.

36   Many years ago I heard Gordon McDonald say that pastors who burn out almost always have stopped reading and learning.

37   For an interesting discussion of the effectiveness or ineffectiveness of lectures, see Sue Pelletier, "Do Lectures Deliver?" *Meetingsnet.com* (July-August 2004): 26–32.

38   Currently the best professional counseling journals with a Christian perspective are *Journal of Psychology and Theology, Journal of Psychology and Christianity,* and *Marriage and Family: A Christian Journal.* Others undoubtedly will be added in the years following the appearance of this book.

39 For discussions of this issue, see David Shenk, *Data Smog: Surviving the Information Glut,* rev. ed. (San Francisco, CA: HarperSanFrancisco, 1998); and Laura J. Gurak, *Navigating the Internet with Awareness* (New Haven, CT: Yale University Press, 2003).

40 To subscribe, go to *www.garyrcollins.com,* click on the newsletter icon to see this week's edition, and go to "subscribe" at the bottom of the page if you want to subscribe. See this web site also for updates relating to this book.

41 The quotation has been attributed to a journalist named Arthur Brisbane.

42 Matthew 20:20–28.

43. Counseling Waves of the Future

1 The professors were Anthony J. Mayo and Nitin Nohria. Their book is titled *In Their Time: The Greatest Business Leaders of the 20th Century* (Cambridge, MA: Harvard Business School Press, 2005). Here are the top several leaders that Mayo and Nohria identified, listed in order of influence: Samuel M. Walton (Wal-Mart), Walter E. Disney (Walt Disney), William H. Gates III (Microsoft), Henry Ford (Ford Motor Company), John P. Morgan (J. P. Morgan Chase), Alfred P. Sloan, Jr. (General Motors), John F. Welch, Jr. (General Electric), Raymond A. Kroc (McDonalds), followed by William R. Hewlett, David Packer, Andrew S. Grove, Milton S. Hersey, John D. Rockefeller, Sr., and Thomas J. Watson, Jr. The only woman to make the list of the top 100 was Estée Lauder. Notice that this was intended to be a list of American business leaders, so there was no attempt to include non-Americans, many of whom undoubtedly have made greater impact than some of the Americans cited in the book.

2 The two quotations are from Bill Breen, "The Three Ways of Great Leaders," *Fast Company* 98 (September 2005): 50.

3 1 Chronicles 12:32.

4 For a fascinating and humorous look at centuries of predictions that were wrong, see Laura Lee, *Bad Predictions* (Rochester Hills, MI: Elsewhere Press, 2000).

5 Examples include John Naisbitt, *Megatrends: Ten New Directions for Transforming Our Lives* (New York: Warner Press, 1988); John Naisbitt and Patricia Aburdene, *Megatrends 2000: Ten New Directions for the 1990s* (New York: Morrow, 1990); and William Knoke, *Bold New World: The Essential Road Map to the Twenty-First Century* (New York: Kodansha, 1996). At the time of this writing, it is too early to know if the following will be accurate predictors, but they have attracted a lot of attention: Thomas L. Friedman, *The World Is Flat: A Brief History of the Twenty-First Century* (New York: Farrar, Straus and Giroux, 2005); and Patricia Aburdene, *Megatrends 2010: The Rise of Conscious Capitalism* (Charlottesville, VA: Hampton Roads, 2005).

6 Marcus Buckingham and Donald O. Clifton, *Now, Discover Your Strengths* (New York: Free Press, 2001).

7 This is the perspective of a psychologist who is executive director of professional practice for the American Psychological Association. See Russ Newman, "Leading Psychology Forward: Staying the Course in Uncertain Times," *Professional Psychology: Research and Practice* 35 (February 2004): 36–41.

8 John C. Norcross, Larry E. Beutler, and Ronald F. Levant, eds., *Evidence-Based Practices in Mental Health* (Washington, DC: American Psychological Association, 2006). The publisher of this book notes that "few topics in mental health are as important and controversial as evidence-based practices."

9 George Orwell, *1984* (New York: Signet Reissue, 1990).

10 Matthew 24:36.

11 Probably, this is one of the methods that fortune-tellers use. Many of these people may have satanic ties, even without their own awareness, but it seems that fortune-tellers are very perceptive observers of behavior who base their predictions on what they learn about the past and present circumstances and hopes of their clients.

12 Luke 14:28–32.

13 Proverbs 15:22; 20:18.

14 Proverbs 21:5.

15 Proverbs 16:3.

16 Isaiah 30:1–2.

17 God's plans are mentioned frequently in the Bible. They are plans that always develop as stated. See, for example, Ephesians 3:1–6, 9, 11.

18 I am grateful to Rick Wager for helping me see the difference between planning and preparation.

19 John 1:23; Isaiah 40:3.

20 Joshua 3:1–5.

21 Rick Warren, *The Purpose-Driven Church* (Grand Rapids, MI: Zondervan, 1995), 13–14.

22 Acts 17:10–11.

23 The ethical issues and complexities of Internet research and journal access have been discussed in several cover story articles in a recent publication of the American Psychological Association. See, for example, Tori DeAngelis, "Debating Access to Scientific Data," *Monitor on Psychology* 35 (February 2004): 46–51; and Karen Kersting, "When Done Right, Internet Research Yields Rewards," *Monitor on Psychology* 35 (February 2004): 52–53.

24 Marlene M. Maheu, Myron I. Pulier, Frank H. Wilhelm, Joseph P. McMenamin, and Nancy E. Brown-Connolly, *The Mental Health Professional and the New Technologies* (New York: Lawrence Erlbaum, 2004); Ron Kraus, Jason Zack, and George Stricker, *Online Counseling: A Handbook for Mental Health Professionals* (St. Louis, MO: Academic Press, 2004); and Stephen Goss and Kate Anthony, eds., *Technology in Counselling and Psychotherapy* (New York: Palgrave Macmillan, 2003). For examples of Internet interventions, see Robert L. Glueckauf and Timothy U, Ketterson, "Telehealth Interventions for Individuals with Chronic Illness: Research Review and Implications for Practice," *Professional Psychology: Research and Practice* 35 (December 2004): 615–627; and Brett T. Litz, Lawrence Williams, Julie Wang, Richard Bryant, and Charles C. Engel, Jr., "A Therapist-Assisted Internet Self-Help Program for Traumatic Stress," *Professional Psychology: Research and Practice* 35 (December 2004): 628–634.

25 M. Rex Miller, *The Millennium Matrix: Reclaiming the Past, Reframing the Future of the Church* (San Francisco, CA: Jossey-Bass, 2004). This is an excellent, highly recommended introduction to the ongoing digital revolution, especially as it applies to the church.

26 This is the argument in chapter 1 of a book by John Naisbitt and his colleagues that calls for maintaining high touch contact with one another in a high-tech world. See John Naisbitt, Nana Naisbitt, and Douglas Philips, *High Tech—High Touch: Technology and Our Search for Meaning* (New York: Broadway Books, 1999).

27 Peter Fraenkel, "Beeper in the Bedroom: Technology Has Become a Therapeutic Issue," *Psychotherapy Networker* 25 (March-April 2001): 22–29, 64. For the benefits of online therapy, see Michael Freeny, "Better Than Being There," *Psychotherapy Networker* 25 (March-April 2001): 30–39, 70.

28 Rosabeth Moss Kanter, *E-Volve: Succeeding in the Digital Culture of Tomorrow* (Boston, MA: Harvard Business School, 2001), 15. For interesting analyses of technology, the digital revolution, and business, see Bill Gates, *Business @ the Speed of Thought: Using a Digital Nervous System* (New York: Warner Books, 1999); and Patricia B. Seybold, *Customers.com* (New York: Random House, 1998).

29 For an older discussion of some of the stress produced by technology, see Michelle M. Weil and Larry D. Rosen, *Technostress: Coping with Technology @ Work, @ Home, @ Play* (New York: Wiley, 1997).

30 For examples of the destructive potential of Internet pornography and violence, see Patricia Greenfield, "Inadvertent Exposure to Pornography on the Internet: Implications of Peer-to-Peer File Sharing Networks for Child Development and Families," *Journal of Applied Developmental Psychology* 25 (November-December, 2004): 741–750; Brian S. Mustanski, "Sex and the Internet: A Guidebook for Clinicians," *Archives of Sexual Behavior* 33 (October 2004): 516–518; Kimberly J. Mitchell, David Finkelhor, and Janis Wolak, "Victimization of Youths on the Internet," *Journal of Aggression, Maltreatment and Trauma* 8 (2003): 1–39; Al Cooper, *Sex and the Internet: A Guide Book for Clinicians* (Philadelphia, PA: Brunner-Routledge, 2002); and Mark R. Laaser and Louis J. Gregoire, "Pastors and Cybersex Addiction," *Sexual & Relationship Therapy* 18 (August 2003): 395–406.

31 Marlene M. Matheu et al., eds., *The Mental Health Professional and the New Technologies* (Mahwah, NJ: Lawrence Erlbaum, 2004).

32 Marion K. Jacobs, Andrew Christensen, John R. Snibbe, Sharon Dolezal-Wood, Alice Huber, and Alexander Polterok, "A Comparison of Computer-Based Versus Traditional Individual Psychotherapy," *Professional Psychology: Research and Practice* 32 (February 2001): 92.

33 With the emphasis on wireless technology and innovations in technology, it is easy to forget the value of basic technology, including the use of audiotapes and movies. See, for example, Georgios K. Lampropoulos, Nikolaos Kazantzis, and Frank P. Deane, "Psychologists' Use of Motion Pictures in Clinical Practice," *Professional Psychology: Research and Practice* 35 (October 2004): 535–541; and Danny Wedding, Mary Ann Boyd, and Ryan M. Niemiec, *Movies and Mental Illness: Using Films to Understand Psychopathology* (Ashland, OH: Hogrefe, 2005).

34 Miller, *The Millennium Matrix*, 133.

35 Samuel Huntington, *The Clash of Civilizations* (Cambridge, MA: Harvard University Press, 1996), 183. See also Anthony J. Marsella, "Toward a 'Global-Community Psychology': Meeting the Needs of a Changing World," *American Psychologist* 53 (December 1998): 1282–1291.

36 Friedman, *The World Is Flat.*

37 For an extremely interesting discussion of various applications to ethnopolitical psychology, see Daniel Chirot and Martin E. P. Seligman, eds., *Ethnopolitical Warfare: Causes, Consequences, and Possible Solutions* (Washington, DC: American Psychological Association, 2001).

38 This is the theme of a book by Tom Sine, *Mustard Seed Versus McWorld: Reinventing Life and Faith for the Future* (Grand Rapids, MI: Baker, 1999).

39 This story is told (along with a photograph of Seigel and the late Pope John II) by Mary Sykes Wylie, "Mindsight: Dan Seigel Offers Therapists a New Vision of the Brain," *Psychotherapy Networker* 28 (September-October 2004): 28–39. See also Brent Atkinson, "Altered States: Why Insight Itself Isn't Enough for Lasting Change," *Psychotherapy Networker* 28 (September-October 2004): 43–45, 67.

40 Quoted in Wylie "Mindsight," 33.

41 Mary Sykes Wylie, "The Limits of Talk: Bessel van der Kolk Wants to Transform the Treatment of Trauma," *Psychotherapy Networker* 28 (January-February 2004): 30–41, 67.

42 Some of this is discussed by Juan Enriquez in *As the Future Catches You* (New York: Crown Business, 2001).

43 Howard Gardner, *Frames of Mind: The Theory of Multiple Intelligences* (New York: Basic Books, 1983).

44 Jennifer Reingold, "The Interpreter," *Fast Company* 95 (June 2005): 58–61.

45 I am convinced that to understand present and future trends it is important to learn what is happening in the corporate and business world. *Fast Company* magazine often gives me this insight, and the editors have put a lot of emphasis on the importance of design in industry. The June 2004 and June 2005 issues of the magazine carried a number of stories on the power of design, which is driven by the brain's right side.

46 Daniel H. Pink, *A Whole New Mind: Moving from the Information Age to the Conceptual Age* (New York: Riverhead Books, 2005).

47 For a good summary see Cathy A. Malchiodi, ed., *Expressive Therapies* (New York: Guilford, 2005). See also Lisa B. Moschini, *Drawing the Line: Art Therapy with the Difficult Client* (New York: Wiley, 2004); and Charles Schaefer, ed., *Play Therapy with Adults* (New York: Wiley, 2002).

48 Carolyn Zerbe Enns and Makiko Kasai, "Hakoniwa: Japanese Sandplay Therapy," *The Counseling Psychologist* 31 (January 2003): 93–112.

49 Pink, *A Whole New Mind*, 183–186.

50 As one example, see James W. Pennebaker, *Writing to Heal: A Guided Journal for Recovering from Trauma and Emotional Upheaval* (Oakland, CA: New Harbinger, 2004). This is a book on the methods and impact of expressing emotion through journal writing. The author is a researcher and not a therapist. Some research findings suggest that writing about painful experiences can enhance immune response, reduce recovery time, and promote physical, psychological, and relational well-being.

51 Howard Gardner, *Changing Minds: The Art and Science of Changing Our Own and Other People's Minds* (Boston, MA: Harvard Business School Press, 2004).

52 Overall, attitudes have changed since those early days of ignoring or fighting postmodernism. See, for example, Robert C. Greer, *Mapping Postmodernism: A Survey of Christian Options* (Downers Grove, IL: InterVarsity, 2003); Millard J. Erickson, Paul Kjoss Helseth, and Justin Taylor, eds., *Reclaiming the Center: Confronting Evangelical Accommodation in Postmodern Times* (Wheaton, IL: Crossway, 2004); and Carl Raschke, *The Next Reformation: Why Evangelicals Must Embrace Postmodernity* (Grand Rapids, MI: Baker, 2004).

53 D. A. Carson, *Becoming Conversant with the Emerging Church* (Grand Rapids, MI: Zondervan, 2005). See especially chapters 4 and 5.

54 For examples of how postmodernism is shaping secular therapies, see Cameron Lee, "The Postmodern Turn in Family Therapy," *Christian Counseling Today* 9, no. 3 (2001): 16–19; Alan Parry and Robert E. Doan, *Story Re-Visions: Narrative Therapy in the Postmodern World* (New York: Guilford, 1994); Rosemary Segalla, "Random Thoughts on Couple Therapy in a Postmodern World," *Psychoanalytic Inquiry* 24 (2004): 453–467; and Tom Strong, "Innovations in Postmodern Practice: Continuing the Postmodern Therapy Dialogue: An Introduction," *Journal of Systemic Therapies* 23 (Spring 2004): 1–5. For readers who are willing to stretch their minds, see Del Loewenthal and Robert Snell, *Postmodernism for Psychotherapists: A Critical Reader* (New York: Brunner-Routledge, 2003).

55 Archibald D. Hart, "Counseling the Postmodern Mind," *Christian Counseling Today* 9, no. 3 (2001): 44–47. The entire issue of the magazine is devoted to the relevance of postmodernism to Christian counseling. For an interesting article on the use of postmodern interventions with evangelical counselees, see P. Gregg Blanton, "Opening Space for Dialogue Between Postmodern Therapists and Evangelical Couples," *Family Journal: Counseling & Therapy for Couples & Families* 12 (October 2004): 375–382.

56 See Carl Raschke, *The Next Reformation*; and Graham Johnson, *Preaching to a Postmodern World* (Grand Rapids, MI: Baker, 2001).

57 For a detailed look at American spirituality, see George Gallup, Jr., and Timothy Jones, *The Next American Spirituality: Finding God in the Twenty-First Century* (Colorado Springs, CO: Cook, 2000).

58 Examples include P. Scott Richards and Allen E. Bergin, *A Spiritual Strategy for Counseling and Psychotherapy*, 2nd. ed. (Washington, DC: American Psychological Association, 2005); P. Scott Richards and Allen E. Bergin, eds., *Casebook for a Spiritual Strategy in Counseling and Psychotherapy* (Washington, DC: American Psychological Association, 2004); William R. Miller, ed., *Integrating Spirituality into Treatment: Resources for Practitioners* (Washington, DC: American Psychological Association, 1999); Geri Miller, *Incorporating Spirituality in Counseling and Psychotherapy: Theory and Technique* (New York: Wiley, 2002); David A. Steere, *Spiritual Presence in Psychotherapy: A Guide for Caregivers* (Philadelphia, PA: Brunner-Mazel, 1997); and Len Sperry, *Spirituality in Clinical Practice: New Dimensions in Psychotherapy and Counseling* (Philadelphia, PA: Brunner-Routledge, 2001).

59 Becca L. Greub and John R. McNamara, "Alternative Therapies in Psychological Treatment: When Is a Consultation with a Physician Warranted?" *American Psychologist* 31 (February 2000): 58–63; Kathryn P. White, "Psychology and Complementary and Alternative Medicine," *American Psychologist* 31 (December 2000): 671–681; and Tiffany M. Field, "Massage Therapy Effects," *American Psychologist* 53 (December 1998): 1270–1281.

60 We see this throughout the Old Testament, where God used pagan kings and nations to accomplish divine purposes to punish God's people, but also to free them. Examples include God moving the minds of Kings Darias and Cyrus to give the captive people of Israel their freedom to return to Jerusalem.

61 Everett L. Worthington, Jr., "Five Mega-trends Affecting Christian Counseling," *Christian Counseling Connection,* issue 3 (2004): 1, 3, 9.

62 Some of these words are taken from the title of a book by Steve Taylor, *The Out of Bounds Church? Learning to Create a Community of Faith in a Culture of Change* (Grand Rapids, MI: Zondervan, 2005). See also Steve Rabey, *In Search of Authentic Faith: How Emerging Generations Are Transforming the Church* (Colorado Springs, CO: Waterbrook, 2001); Dan Kimball, *The Emerging Church: Vintage Christianity for New Generations* (Grand Rapids, MI: Zondervan, 2003); and Erwin Raphael McManus, *An Unstoppable Force* (Loveland, CO: Group, 2001).

63 In a thought-provoking edition of *GradPSYCH*, the American Psychological Association publication for graduate students, the cover story was titled "Career Creativity: Meet Seven Psychologists Who Blazed Their Own Paths. Discover How you Can Too." The psychologists who developed new nontraditional career paths included Matt Bellace, who has become a comedian-motivational speaker who tries to empower students to choose drug-free lifestyles; Patricia Cowings, who works for the U.S. government space program; Anthony Pinizzotto, who is a priest and forensic psychologist; and Natalie Hamrick, who helps physicians in the anesthesia department at Indiana University write research projects and analyze data. Profiles of these psychologists are published in *GradPSYCH* 3 (September 2005): 36–44.

64 See the six articles on "The Changing Face of Psychology Practice," in *Monitor on Psychology* 36 (February 2005).

65 These issues appear frequently in professional journals. For example, *Professional Psychology: Research and Practice* often will publish a section of articles dealing with issues like competency-education (August 2005), licensing (August 2001), psychopharmocology (December 2000), and prescription privileges (August 2004). Among the articles on managed care, see Lisa M. Sanchez and Samuel M. Turner, "Practicing Psychology in the Era of Managed Care: Implications for Practice and Training," *American Psychologist* 58 (February 2003): 116–129.

66 One big area of ongoing debate is whether nonmedical counselors, specifically clinical psychologists, should be able to prescribe psychological medications. At the time of this writing, some of the American states permit this when there is sufficient prior training, while others do not. The medical professions, especially psychiatry, are in the forefront of those who resist prescription privileges for psychologists.

67 Mark Greer, "Spreading Out What I Do Keeps Things Interesting," *Monitor on Psychology* 36 (February 2005): 62–64.

68 See the special section of articles on "Innovative Interventions in the Practice of Health Psychology," *Professional Psychology: Research and Practice* 32 (April 20001): 115–141; Lynda H. Powell, Leila Shahabi, and Carl E. Thoresen, "Religion and Spirituality: Linkages to Physical Health," *American Psychologist* 58 (January 2003): 36–52; Tori DeAngelis, "A Successful Marriage of Psychology and Public Health," *Monitor on Psychology* 32 (March 2001): 40–41; and Ronald H. Rozensky, Norine G. Johnson, Carol D. Goodheart, and Rodney W. Hammond, eds., *Psychology Builds a Healthy World: Opportunities for Research and Practice* (Washington, DC: American Psychological Association, 2003).

69 Several articles on pain and counselors working in this area appeared in *Monitor on Psychology* 32 (April 2002): 58–73.

70 See the special section on psychologists as legislators in *Professional Psychology: Research and Practice* 33 (June 2002): 277–288.

71 There is a special section that includes several articles on rural practice and training in *Professional Psychology: Research and Practice* 36 (April 2005): 158–179.

72 See, for example, Esteban V. Cardemil and Jacques P. Barber, "Building a Model for Prevention Practice: Depression as an Example," *Professional Psychology: Research and Practice* 32 (August 2001): 392–401.

73 Bryan Myers and Michael P. Arena, "Trial Consultation: A New Direction in Applied Psychology," *Professional Psychology: Research and Practice* 32 (August 200l): 386–391.

74 The quotations are from page 26 of an article by Barry Duncan, "The Future of Psychotherapy," *Psychotherapy Networker* 25 (July-August 2001): 24–33, 52. See also, Charles Kiesler, "The Next Wave of Change for Psychology and Mental Health Services in the Health Care Revolution," *American Psychologist* 55 (2000): 481–487.

75 John C. Norcross, Melissa Hedges, and James O. Prochaska, "The Face of 2010: A Delphi Poll on the Future of Psychotherapy," *Professional Psychology: Research and Practice* 33 (June 2002): 316–322.

76 An Internet search will show you the latest books in distance learning. Here are examples: Michael Simonson, Sharon E. Smaldino, Michael J. Albright, and Susan Zvacek, *Teaching and Learning at a Distance: Foundations of Distance Education*, 3rd ed. (Upper Saddle River, NJ: Prentice-Hall, 2005); Rena M. Palloff and Keith Pratt, *The Virtual Student: A Profile and Guide to Working with Online Learners* (San Francisco, CA: Jossey-Bass, 2003); and Rena M. Palloff and Keith Pratt, *Building Learning Communities in Cyberspace: Effective Strategies for the Online Classroom* (San Francisco, CA: Jossey-Bass, 1999).

77 Gates writes a lot about educational developments in Bill Gates, *Business @ the Speed of Thought*. The quotation is from page 61. See also Marc J. Rosenberg, *e-Learning: Strategies for Delivering Knowledge in the Digital Age* (New York: McGraw-Hill, 2001).

78 Martin E. P. Seligman and Mihaly Csikszentmihalyi, "Positive Psychology: An Introduction," *American Psychologist* 55 (January 2001): 5–15. Five years after this initial article, Seligman and his colleagues published an upbeat progress report on the exploding development of positive psychology: Martin E. P. Seligman, Tracy A. Steen, Nansook Park, and Christopher Peterson, "Positive Psychology Progress: Empirical Validation of Interventions," *American Psychologist* 60 (July-August 2005): 410–421.

79 Among the more pivotal books are C. R. Snyder and Shane J. Lopez, eds., *Handbook of Positive Psychology* (New York: Oxford University Press, 2002); Martin E. P. Seligman,

Authentic Happiness (New York: Free Press, 2002); C. L. M. Keyes and J. Haidt, eds., *Flourishing: Positive Psychology and the Life Well-Lived* (Washington, DC: American Psychological Association, 2003); P. A. Linley and S. Joseph, eds., *Positive Psychology in Practice* (Hoboken, NJ: Wiley, 2004); and S. J. Lopez and C. R. Snyder, eds., *Positive Psychological Assessment: A Handbook of Models and Measures* (Washington, DC: American Psychological Association, 2004).

80   Mary Sykes Wylie, "Why Is This Man Smiling?" [An Interview with Martin Seligman] *Psychotherapy Networker* 27 (January-February 2003): 26–53.

81   Christopher Peterson and Martin E. P. Seligman, *Character Strengths and Virtues: A Handbook of Classification* (Washington, DC: American Psychological Association, 2004).

82   Seligman et al., "Positive Psychology Progress," 420.

Index